HANDBOOK
of
PSYCHOLOGY

Date Due

HANDBOOK
of
PSYCHOLOGY

VOLUME 1
HISTORY OF PSYCHOLOGY

Donald K. Freedheim

Volume Editor

Irving B. Weiner

Editor-in-Chief

WILEY

John Wiley & Sons, Inc.

Library of Congress Cataloging-in-Publication Data:

Handbook of psychology / Irving B. Weiner, editor-in-chief.
  p. cm.
  Includes bibliographical references and indexes.
  Contents: v. 1. History of psychology / edited by Donald K. Freedheim — v. 2. Research methods in psychology / edited by John A. Schinka, Wayne F. Velicer — v. 3. Biological psychology / edited by Michela Gallagher, Randy J. Nelson — v. 4. Experimental psychology / edited by Alice F. Healy, Robert W. Proctor — v. 5. Personality and social psychology / edited by Theodore Millon, Melvin J. Lerner — v. 6. Developmental psychology / edited by Richard M. Lerner, M. Ann Easterbrooks, Jayanthi Mistry — v. 7. Educational psychology / edited by William M. Reynolds, Gloria E. Miller — v. 8. Clinical psychology / edited by George Stricker, Thomas A. Widiger — v. 9. Health psychology / edited by Arthur M. Nezu, Christine Maguth Nezu, Pamela A. Geller — v. 10. Assessment psychology / edited by John R. Graham, Jack A. Naglieri — v. 11. Forensic psychology / edited by Alan M. Goldstein — v. 12. Industrial and organizational psychology / edited by Walter C. Borman, Daniel R. Ilgen, Richard J. Klimoski.
  ISBN 0-471-38320-1 (cloth : alk. paper : v. 1); ISBN 0-471-66664-5 (pbk.) — ISBN 0-471-66675-0 (set : pbk.)
  1. Psychology. I. Weiner, Irving B.

BF121.H1955 2003
150—dc21

2002066380

Editorial Board

This volume is dedicated to Gerda K. Freedheim—my wife, best friend, kindest critic, and invaluable editor.

Handbook of Psychology **Preface**

Psychology at the beginning of the twenty-first century has become a highly diverse field of scientific study and applied technology. Psychologists commonly regard their discipline as the science of behavior, and the American Psychological Association has formally designated 2000 to 2010 as the "Decade of Behavior." The pursuits of behavioral scientists range from the natural sciences to the social sciences and embrace a wide variety of objects of investigation. Some psychologists have more in common with biologists than with most other psychologists, and some have more in common with sociologists than with most of their psychological colleagues. Some psychologists are interested primarily in the behavior of animals, some in the behavior of people, and others in the behavior of organizations. These and other dimensions of difference among psychological scientists are matched by equal if not greater heterogeneity among psychological practitioners, who currently apply a vast array of methods in many different settings to achieve highly varied purposes.

Psychology has been rich in comprehensive encyclopedias and in handbooks devoted to specific topics in the field. However, there has not previously been any single handbook designed to cover the broad scope of psychological science and practice. The present 12-volume *Handbook of Psychology* was conceived to occupy this place in the literature. Leading national and international scholars and practitioners have collaborated to produce 297 authoritative and detailed chapters covering all fundamental facets of the discipline, and the *Handbook* has been organized to capture the breadth and diversity of psychology and to encompass interests and concerns shared by psychologists in all branches of the field.

Two unifying threads run through the science of behavior. The first is a common history rooted in conceptual and empirical approaches to understanding the nature of behavior. The specific histories of all specialty areas in psychology trace their origins to the formulations of the classical philosophers and the methodology of the early experimentalists, and appreciation for the historical evolution of psychology in all of its variations transcends individual identities as being one kind of psychologist or another. Accordingly, Volume 1 in the *Handbook* is devoted to the history of psychology as it emerged in many areas of scientific study and applied technology.

A second unifying thread in psychology is a commitment to the development and utilization of research methods suitable for collecting and analyzing behavioral data. With attention both to specific procedures and their application in particular settings, Volume 2 addresses research methods in psychology.

Volumes 3 through 7 of the *Handbook* present the substantive content of psychological knowledge in five broad areas of study: biological psychology (Volume 3), experimental psychology (Volume 4), personality and social psychology (Volume 5), developmental psychology (Volume 6), and educational psychology (Volume 7). Volumes 8 through 12 address the application of psychological knowledge in five broad areas of professional practice: clinical psychology (Volume 8), health psychology (Volume 9), assessment psychology (Volume 10), forensic psychology (Volume 11), and industrial and organizational psychology (Volume 12). Each of these volumes reviews what is currently known in these areas of study and application and identifies pertinent sources of information in the literature. Each discusses unresolved issues and unanswered questions and proposes future directions in conceptualization, research, and practice. Each of the volumes also reflects the investment of scientific psychologists in practical applications of their findings and the attention of applied psychologists to the scientific basis of their methods.

The *Handbook of Psychology* was prepared for the purpose of educating and informing readers about the present state of psychological knowledge and about anticipated advances in behavioral science research and practice. With this purpose in mind, the individual *Handbook* volumes address the needs and interests of three groups. First, for graduate students in behavioral science, the volumes provide advanced instruction in the basic concepts and methods that define the fields they cover, together with a review of current knowledge, core literature, and likely future developments. Second, in addition to serving as graduate textbooks, the volumes offer professional psychologists an opportunity to read and contemplate the views of distinguished colleagues concerning the central thrusts of research and leading edges of practice in their respective fields. Third, for psychologists seeking to become conversant with fields outside their own specialty and for persons outside of psychology seeking information about psychological matters, the *Handbook* volumes serve as a reference source for expanding their knowledge and directing them to additional sources in the literature.

The preparation of this *Handbook* was made possible by the diligence and scholarly sophistication of the 25 volume editors and co-editors who constituted the Editorial Board. As Editor-in-Chief, I want to thank each of them for the pleasure of their collaboration in this project. I compliment them for having recruited an outstanding cast of contributors to their volumes and then working closely with these authors to achieve chapters that will stand each in their own right as valuable contributions to the literature. I would like finally to express my appreciation to the editorial staff of John Wiley and Sons for the opportunity to share in the development of this project and its pursuit to fruition, most particularly to Jennifer Simon, Senior Editor, and her two assistants, Mary Porterfield and Isabel Pratt. Without Jennifer's vision of the *Handbook* and her keen judgment and unflagging support in producing it, the occasion to write this preface would not have arrived.

IRVING B. WEINER
Tampa, Florida

Volume Preface

Numerous histories of our relatively young field have been published. The Library of Congress lists 44 history of psychology titles, beginning with G. S. Brett in 1912 to Leahey in 2000, an author in this volume. More histories may have been written without the word *history* in the title, but that still means a history every two years. And now we add the 45th.

Writing history is not easy. First, there is too much to record, and the selection process inevitably involves bias. Then there is distortion in hindsight. Any history of the field should be called, "A Partial History . . ." or even "A Slanted History . . . ," but those titles are understandably undesirable. So, as John Popplestone comments in his introduction, we present a partial history of selected topics.

In keeping with the diverse nature of this *Handbook of Psychology,* we have attempted to provide a comprehensive history—at least one that covers a broad spectrum from our wide-ranging fields of study. The first two chapters are general overviews of psychology as a science and as a profession. These are followed by several basic areas that typically are included in a core curriculum in a graduate program. We then cover a number of major professional areas and lastly three areas of special interest.

The chapter on ethnic minorities is notably different from the others in that it consists of vignettes reflecting on historical events, some very personal, that have characterized the field's perception and interaction with minority groups. The chapter on international psychology includes a unique time line of events covering more than three millennia. Several of the other chapters contain events and stories that have not been recorded in other publications.

We hope that the *History* is both interesting and useful—and that the contributions provide an informative launching pad for this very comprehensive *Handbook of Psychology.*

Many people have helped in the process of completing the *History.* First and foremost are the chapter authors, whose contributions have made the volume possible. A number of persons have read and helped edit chapters: Douglas Detterman, James Overholser, Milton Strauss, Diane Tice, Erik Youngstrom, Gerda Freedheim, and Matt Heimback. I also would like to thank a group of editorial advisors who gave advice early on the contributors and organization of the text: David B. Baker, Florence L. Denmark, Wade E. Pickren, Milton E. Strauss, Wayne Viney, and especially Michael Wertheimer for his helpful counsel. Three staff from the Department of Psychology at Case Western Reserve University have been invaluable with their technical help and patience with a fussy editor: Felicia Bruce, Cynthia Hendrick, and Kori Kosek. Elsie Finley, librarian at CWRU, was tenacious in her pursuit of obscure references. The editors, Jennifer Simon and Isabel Pratt from John Wiley & Sons, were always helpful and encouraging, as well as the staff of Publications Development Company. And lastly, a special thanks to the general editor of the *Handbook,* Irving Weiner, for his patience, careful reviewing of drafts, and constant encouragement.

DONALD K. FREEDHEIM

REFERENCES

Brett, G. S. (1912). *A history of psychology.* London: G. Allen.

Leahey, T. H. (2000). *History of psychology: Main currents in psychological thought* (5th ed.). Upper Saddle River, NJ: Prentice-Hall.

Foreword

The *History of Psychology* is the most recent contribution in a long tradition of the presentation of an account of the important historical developments and landmarks in the field of psychology.

In the beginning, when there were only a few psychologists (in 1892 the new American Psychological Association had 31 charter members), there were some who could reasonably be described as possessing the whole, or at least a significant part, of psychology in their consciousness. However, the ability to speak with authority on the whole of the field of psychology is now no longer in the hands of any single person or source. (A vestigial remnant of this tradition of "universal psychological knowledge" is in the expectation that a doctoral student in psychology should be able to take, and pass, a "comprehensive" examination on the whole field of psychology's subject matter and methodology.) And, the tradition of the comprehensive history of the whole field is also still with us in the vast textbooks that now introduce the area to so many undergraduates—some of which have almost a thousand pages!

But we must grant that the task is an impossible one and anyone who attempts to carry it out will face serious problems. Someone smart enough to solve this problem is smart enough not to try. But, if being smart is not enough and we do decide to take on the task, who will be selected to undertake it and how will they be instructed to go about the actual work? What criteria of selection are in play? If your favorite topic is included, is something else that I really like going to be excluded?

Psychology's history, even if confined to the United States since 1879, is so large and so various that it is probably beyond attempts to cover the whole field in any comprehensive manner. Instead, the editor has wisely elected to sample the field so that a description of the part will indicate the possibilities of the whole.

Can we justify the particular sample of psychology that the editor has arranged here? Since there is no objective standard for inclusion or exclusion, we must honor the scholarship and integrity of the editor even if there is a nagging doubt: "How could the volume omit semiotics, or the activity of Raymond Dodge at Yale in 1924?" The solution is to follow the advice of Aristotle who counseled the observer to suspend disbelief . . . and to get with it.

This author is an unindicted co-conspirator in an attempt to list and define the one hundred most important (central) concepts in general psychology. In the *Dictionary of Concepts in General Psychology* (Popplestone & McPherson, 1988), the publisher selected the number 100 (presumably for its commercial utility), but we coauthors were given complete freedom to compile the list and write the definitions. We decided that there was no really satisfactory way to define the 100 core concepts, so we charged ahead on our own using the indices of several introductory textbooks, the topics in annual reviews, similar informal sampling techniques, and our own intense conversations. There comes a time when one must bite the bullet and *just do it,* even though this leaves a wide target for the cheap shot of the reviewer who asks, "By what criteria were these concepts selected?" but does not offer a feasible and useful alternative.

Qualitative and quantitative judgments of relevance or impact, however carefully made and subsequently justified, cannot be utterly free of criticism and appraisal. In the vast extended field of contemporary psychology there will always be differences of opinion about selection and emphasis—often advocated with great enthusiasm.

If psychology is too large and too variable to be totally inclusive, then we have a similar problem in the selection of the observers. There is no one today who would be so bold as to present him- or herself as having a complete grasp of the whole of the field, to be able to present the kind of detailed, thoughtful history that the readers may reasonably expect.

The editor of the *History of Psychology* has found a solution to these problems in the judicious sampling of the content areas and the careful selection of authors to write about them, while also allowing the authors the intellectual freedom to deal with the content as their experience and consideration allow.

History of Psychology is a unique volume. There is nothing quite like it available for the individual scholar or students, and so it fills a rather special and useful niche that would otherwise be vacant. Partly this is done by using a team of experts in the many topic areas into which contemporary psychology may be compartmentalized. And this new account of an old program is broadened by the recognition that modern psychology acknowledges that it is an applied technology as well as an academic, "scientific" discipline, in which the preservation and acquisition of knowledge about the subject matter is an end in itself.

History of Psychology is intended to be graduate-level text or even appropriate at an advanced undergraduate level. It may also serve as a resource for those seeking a historical overview of a number of the scientific and professional areas in the vast field of psychology.

The editor of *History of Psychology* has defined the field by specifying that each chapter can be seen as a distinct, identifiable, quasi-independent area of knowledge or advocacy. Each topic may well have separate societies or interest groups, with newsletters, prizes, officers, journals, and so forth—the usual structures that manage to define the boundaries and content of an area.

This greater summary of the history-of-psychology-in-our-times begins with two chapters that define the current field and its discontents: psychology-as-a-science and psychology-as-a-profession. Then, *in media res* the content of psychology is presented in the early chapters, which echo the classical topics, as in the headings of every introductory textbook. Following are a reflection more of contemporary psychology-as-application than as content areas. There is overlap, of course, since no area of application is without its support in content. In the later chapters, the shift is from application in the public good to the problems of the professional psychologist and international developments. Finally the last chapter on professional organizations is a description of the field of psychology from the inside, as issues of affiliation and identification are described.

It is apparent to the editor and the authors, that the division of pure versus applied, academic versus guild, and so forth break down, and that psychologists work both in an area of investigation and one of application. The selection of topics has been guided by both classical and innovative standards. While the chapters dealing with substantive psychological topics (theoretical and empirical) are familiar selections, it is the two introductory chapters and latter ones that are innovative and reflect the new world of psychology, in contrast to that shown in older histories (Boring, Murphy, etc.) or the whole-of-psychology handbooks.

The selection of authors and their instructions in proceeding with their tasks are also innovative and worth noticing. Several of the authors are universally recognized as noted scientists and have been leaders in their respective fields for years. But a number are young and drawn from the pool of new historians by choice. Many psychologists are unaware that there is a whole cohort of (mostly young) psychologists whose involvement in the history of psychology is not just a hobby or peripheral interest. These people are committed to psychology as their major discipline but are also fully committed to the study and writing of good histories of psychology. The era when history was taught by the oldest or youngest member of the department by default is long past, and now there is a cadre of skilled, sophisticated scholars who are committed to creating a quality history of psychology.

When the authors were selected and had accepted the invitation to contribute, they were given a great deal of freedom to write a history of their topical area in their own manner, organization, and time scheme, but they were all requested that after being given freedom to organize, emphasize, and structure their subject matter they were also requested to adhere to a similar length and style and to serve more recent (twentieth century) content as well as more remote temporal themes.

In other words, the editor asked the authors to be observant of a minimum number of restrictions (designed to make the volume and the reader's task easier) while at the same time allowing the authors the intellectual freedom to deal with their subject matter as they wished. To these ends the authors have striven to present a text which may well serve as a milestone in the continuing quest to document our growing and diverse field of psychology.

JOHN A. POPPLESTONE
Director Emeritus
Archives of the History of American Psychology

REFERENCE

Popplestone, J. A., & McPherson, M. W. (1988). *Dictionary of concepts in general psychology.* New York: Greenwood.

Contents

Handbook of Psychology **Preface**   ix
    Irving B. Weiner

Volume Preface   xi
    Donald K. Freedheim

Foreword   xiii
    John A. Popplestone

Contributors   xvii

1   **PSYCHOLOGY AS A SCIENCE**   1
    Alfred H. Fuchs and Katharine S. Milar

2   **PSYCHOLOGY AS A PROFESSION**   27
    Ludy T. Benjamin Jr., Patrick H. DeLeon, Donald K. Freedheim, and Gary R. VandenBos

3   **BIOLOGICAL PSYCHOLOGY**   47
    Richard F. Thompson and Stuart M. Zola

4   **COMPARATIVE PSYCHOLOGY**   67
    Donald A. Dewsbury

5   **SENSATION AND PERCEPTION**   85
    Stanley Coren

6   **COGNITION AND LEARNING**   109
    Thomas Hardy Leahey

7   **INTELLIGENCE**   135
    Robert J. Sternberg

8   **EMOTION**   157
    George Mandler

9   **PERSONALITY**   177
    Nicole B. Barenbaum and David G. Winter

10   **DEVELOPMENTAL PSYCHOLOGY**   205
    Ross D. Parke and K. Alison Clarke-Stewart

11   **SOCIAL PSYCHOLOGY**   223
    Jill G. Morawski and Betty M. Bayer

12   PSYCHOLOGY OF WOMEN AND GENDER   249
Jeanne Marecek, Ellen B. Kimmel, Mary Crawford, and Rachel T. Hare-Mustin

13   EDUCATIONAL PSYCHOLOGY   269
Claire Ellen Weinstein and Pamela J. Way

14   ASSESSMENT PSYCHOLOGY   279
Irving B. Weiner

15   ABNORMAL PSYCHOLOGY   303
Winifred B. Maher and Brendan A. Maher

16   CLINICAL PSYCHOLOGY   337
Donald K. Routh and John M. Reisman

17   COUNSELING PSYCHOLOGY   357
David B. Baker

18   INDUSTRIAL-ORGANIZATIONAL PSYCHOLOGY   367
Laura L. Koppes

19   FORENSIC PSYCHOLOGY   391
John C. Brigham and J. Thomas Grisso

20   SCHOOL PSYCHOLOGY   413
Thomas K. Fagan

21   COMMUNITY PSYCHOLOGY   431
Bianca D. M. Wilson, Erin Hayes, George J. Greene, James G. Kelly, and Ira Iscoe

22   HEALTH PSYCHOLOGY   451
Cynthia D. Belar, Teresa Mendonca McIntyre, and Joseph D. Matarazzo

23   UNDERGRADUATE EDUCATION   465
Thomas V. McGovern and Charles L. Brewer

24   ETHNIC MINORITIES   483
Adelbert M. Jenkins, George W. Albee, Vera S. Paster, Stanley Sue, David B. Baker, Lillian Comas-Diaz, Antonio E. Puente, Richard M. Suinn, A. Toy Caldwell-Colbert and Velma M. Williams, and Maria P. P. Root

25   INTERNATIONAL PSYCHOLOGY   509
Henry P. David and Joan Buchanan
Chronology of Milestones in International Psychology   517

26   PROFESSIONAL ORGANIZATIONS   535
Wade E. Pickren and Raymond D. Fowler

Author Index   555

Subject Index   580

Contributors

George W. Albee, PhD
Department of Psychology
University of Vermont and the Florida Mental Health Institute
Sarasota, Florida

David B. Baker, PhD
Archives of the History of American Psychology
University of Akron
Akron, Ohio

Nicole B. Barenbaum, PhD
Department of Psychology
University of the South
Sewanee, Tennessee

Betty M. Bayer, PhD
Department of Psychology
Hobart and William Smith Colleges
Geneva, New York

Cynthia D. Belar, PhD
Education Directorate
American Psychological Association
Washington, DC

Ludy T. Benjamin Jr., PhD
Department of Psychology
Texas A & M University
College Station, Texas

Charles L. Brewer, PhD
Department of Psychology
Furman University
Greenville, South Carolina

John C. Brigham, PhD
Department of Psychology
Florida State University
Tallahassee, Florida

Joan Buchanan, BA
Office of International Affairs
American Psychological Association
Washington, DC

A. Toy Caldwell-Colbert, PhD
Office of the Provost and Chief Academic Officer
Howard University
Washington, DC

K. Allison Clarke-Stewart, PhD
Department of Psychology and Social Behavior
University of California at Irvine
Irvine, California

Lillian Comas-Diaz, PhD
Department of Psychiatry and Behavioral Sciences
George Washington University
Washington, DC

Stanley Coren, PhD
Department of Psychology
University of British Columbia
Vancouver, BC, Canada

Mary Crawford, PhD
Department of Psychology
University of Connecticut
Storrs, Connecticut

Henry P. David, PhD
Transnational Family Research Institute
Bethesda, Maryland

Patrick H. DeLeon, JD, PhD
Office of Senator Daniel K. Inouye
Washington, DC

Donald A. Dewsbury, PhD
Department of Psychology
University of Florida
Gainesville, Florida

Thomas K. Fagan, PhD
Department of Psychology
University of Memphis
Memphis, Tennessee

Raymond D. Fowler, PhD
Office of the Chief Executive
American Psychological Association
Washington, DC

Donald K. Freedheim, PhD
Department of Psychology
Case Western Reserve University
Cleveland, Ohio

Alfred H. Fuchs, PhD
Department of Psychology
Bowdoin College
Brunswick, Maine

George J. Greene, MA
Department of Psychology
University of Illinois at Chicago
Chicago, Illinois

J. Thomas Grisso, PhD
Department of Psychiatry
University of Massachusetts Medical Center
Worcester, Massachusetts

Rachel T. Hare-Mustin, PhD
Amherst, Massachusetts

Erin P. Hayes, MA
Department of Psychology at Chicago
University of Illinois
Chicago, Illinois

Ira Iscoe, PhD
Department of Psychology
University of Texas
Austin, Texas

Adelbert M. Jenkins, PhD
Department of Psychology
New York University
New York, New York

James G. Kelly, PhD
Department of Psychology
University of Illinois at Chicago
Chicago, Illinois

Ellen B. Kimmel, PhD
Department of Psychological and Social Foundations
    of Education
University of South Florida
Tampa, Florida

Laura L. Koppes, PhD
Department of Psychology
Eastern Kentucky University
Richmond, Kentucky

Thomas Hardy Leahey, PhD
Department of Psychology
Virginia Commonwealth University
Richmond, Virginia

Brendan A. Maher, PhD
Department of Psychology
Harvard University
Cambridge, Massachusetts

Winifred B. Maher, PhD
Extension Studies
Harvard University
Cambridge, Massachusetts

George Mandler, PhD
Department of Psychology
University of California at San Diego
San Diego, California

Department of Psychology
University College
London, England

Jeanne Marecek, PhD
Department of Psychology
Swarthmore College
Swarthmore, Pennsylvania

Joseph D. Matarazzo, PhD
Department of Behavioral Neuroscience
Oregon Health Sciences University Medical School
Portland, Oregon

Thomas V. McGovern, PhD
Department of Integrative Studies
Arizona State University West
Phoenix, Arizona

Teresa Mendonca McIntyre, PhD
Department of Psychology
Universidade do Minho
Braga, Portugal

Katharine S. Milar, PhD
Department of Psychology
Earlham College
Richmond, Indiana

Jill G. Morawski, PhD
Department of Psychology
Wesleyan University
Middletown, Connecticut

Ross D. Parke, PhD
Department of Psychology and the Center for Family Studies
University of California at Riverside
Riverside, California

Vera S. Paster, PhD
Department of Psychology
City University of New York
New York, New York

Wade E. Pickren, PhD
Office of the Archivist/Historian
American Psychological Association
Washington, DC

John A. Popplestone, PhD
Archives of the History of American Psychology
University of Akron
Akron, Ohio

Antonio E. Puente, PhD
Department of Psychology
University of North Carolina at Wilmington
Wilmington, North Carolina

John M. Reisman, PhD
Department of Psychology
DePaul University
Wilmette, Illinois

Maria P. P. Root, PhD
Seattle, Washington

Donald K. Routh, PhD
Department of Psychology
University of Miami
Coral Gables, Florida

Robert J. Sternberg, PhD
Department of Psychology
Yale University
New Haven, Connecticut

Stanley Sue, PhD
Department of Psychology
University of California at Davis
Davis, California

Richard M. Suinn, PhD
Department of Psychology
Colorado State University
Fort Collins, Colorado

Richard F. Thompson, PhD
Department of Psychology and Biological Sciences
University of Southern California
Los Angeles, California

Gary R. VandenBos, PhD
Office of Communications
American Psychological Association
Washington, DC

Pamela J. Way, PhD
Department of Educational Psychology
University of Texas
Austin, Texas

Irving B. Weiner, PhD
Department of Psychology
University of South Florida
Tampa, Florida

Claire Ellen Weinstein, PhD
Department of Educational Psychology
University of Texas
Austin, Texas

Velma M. Williams, PhD
Counseling Center
Ball State University
Muncie, Indiana

Bianca D. M. Wilson, MA
Department of Psychology
University of Illinois at Chicago
Chicago, Illinois

David G. Winter, PhD
Department of Psychology
University of Michigan
Ann Arbor, Michigan

Stuart M. Zola, PhD
Yerkes Primate Research Center
Department of Psychiatry and Behaviorial Science
Emory University
Atlanta, Georgia

CHAPTER 1

Psychology as a Science

ALFRED H. FUCHS AND KATHARINE S. MILAR

ORIGINS OF SCIENTIFIC PSYCHOLOGY   1
   The Philosophical Context   1
   The Scientific Context   2
PSYCHOLOGY'S FIRST LABORATORY   3
BEYOND THE FIRST LABORATORY: EVOLUTION
   OF THE DISCIPLINE   6
   Psychology in Germany   6
   Psychology in America   6

THE PSYCHOLOGICAL LABORATORY AND THE
   PSYCHOLOGICAL EXPERIMENT   8
   The Rise of Laboratories in America   8
   The Evolution of the Laboratory Experiment   8
   Defining Psychology and Its Methods   9
   The Rise of Cognitive Psychology:
      Mentalism Revisited   19
REFERENCES   20

ORIGINS OF SCIENTIFIC PSYCHOLOGY

Historical accounts of the development of scientific psychology place the origins of the discipline in Germany at about the middle of the nineteenth century. The ferment produced by British and continental philosophies of mind and the advances of research in sensory physiology provided the immediate context for the beginning of the new psychology. The pursuit of knowledge about mind and its processes has a history that is embedded in the history of philosophy. The late-eighteenth-century declaration that a true scientific study of the mind was not possible posed a challenge that was answered in the nineteenth century when the possibility of a scientific study of mind emerged within philosophy by the adoption of the experimental methods employed to study the physiology of the senses. The synergy of these nineteenth-century developments gave impetus to the "new psychology" whose history embodies continued efforts to develop and maintain psychology as a scientific discipline and to extend the methods of science to an ever-widening field of inquiry within the discipline.

The Philosophical Context

Christian Wolff (1679–1754) first popularized the term *psychology* to designate the study of mind. Wolff divided the discipline between empirical and rational psychology. The data of mind that resulted from observing ourselves and others constituted empirical psychology; rational psychology

referred to the interpretation of the data of empirical psychology through the use of reason and logic. These psychologies were characterized as using knowledge acquired through experience (empirical psychology) or using knowledge that the mind possesses independent of experience (rational psychology) (Murray, 1988).

Immanuel Kant (1724–1804) denied the validity of any rational psychology because, he argued, rational mental processes must be activated by mental content derived from experience; therefore, the study of mind must be confined to questions appropriate to an empirical psychology (Leary, 1978). An empirical psychology of mental content could not, Kant contended, become a proper natural science because mental events cannot be quantified (i.e., measured or weighed), and thus its data are neither capable of being described mathematically nor subject to experimental manipulation. Finally, Kant asserted, the method of observing the mind—introspection—distorts the events observed by observing them. However, Kant suggested, psychology might improve its status as an empirical science by adopting the methods of anthropology to observe the activities of human beings in realistic settings. This study (Leary, 1978), supplemented by drawing upon literature, history, and biography as sources of information about the manifestation of mind in human activity, would base psychology upon objective observations of public events and avoid the limitations of an empirical psychology based solely on internal observation of private events.

Responses to Kant were not long in coming. Jakob Friederich Fries (1773–1843) raised the status of introspection

1

by arguing that it was not inherently more problematic than observing external phenomena; if introspection was unreliable, at least it was not any more so than any other kind of observation. At the same time, Johann Friederich Herbart (1776–1841) offered a system of psychology that was both empirical and mathematical. If psychology needed to be mathematical to be a true science, Herbart proposed that numbers could be assigned to mental events of different intensities and a mathematical description of the relationship among them could be formulated. Herbart could assign numbers to describe experiences of different intensities, but he could not actually measure the subjective intensities in accord with an objective standard. Eduard Friederich Beneke (1798–1854) argued that it was premature to apply mathematics to relationships among mental events absent more accurate empirical observations and reliable means of measurement; psychology could hope to become an experimental discipline by testing "empirical results and theoretical hypotheses under controlled conditions and with the systematic variation of variables" (Leary, 1978, p. 119).

Kant's suggestion that psychology should utilize observations of human beings in their social environment, the rescue by Fries of introspection as a method for observing internal events, Herbart's suggestion that psychological phenomena could, in principle, be described mathematically, and Beneke's suggestion that psychological experiments were possible contributed to the inception of scientific psychology. By suggesting that a science of psychology was not possible, Kant stimulated both counterarguments and the search for the means to make psychology a scientific discipline of equal rank with the natural sciences. It remained for others to attempt to establish introspection as a scientific method, to devise the conditions and methods of an experiment in psychology, and to quantify psychological phenomena and formulate theoretical and mathematical descriptions of the relationships among them.

The Scientific Context

The emerging natural sciences of the eighteenth and nineteenth centuries became increasingly specialized as knowledge increased and as opportunities for specialized teaching and research came into being in the German universities (Ben-David, 1971). The study of physiology emerged as a discipline separate from anatomy as the nineteenth century began. Studying intact physiological systems, *in vivo* or *in vitro,* accelerated the understanding of the functional characteristics of those systems and built on the knowledge gained from the study of anatomy via dissection. The methods and subject matter of physiology, especially sensory physiology, helped to provide the scientific basis for psychology.

Sensory Physiology

Johannes Müller (1801–1858), the "Father of Physiology," produced the classic systematic handbook (*Handbuch der Physiologie des Menschen,* 1833–1840) that set forth what was then known about human physiology and offered observations and hypotheses for further research. Among the formulations that Müller provided in the *Handbuch* was the law of specific nerve energies, which stated that the mind is not directly aware of objects as such but can only be aware of the stimulation in the brain conveyed by sensory nerves. The perceived qualities of stimulation depend upon the sense organ stimulated, the nerve that carries the excitation from the sense organ, and the part of the brain that receives the stimulation.

Müller's pupil, Hermann von Helmholtz (1821–1894), extended the law of specific nerve energies by theorizing that qualities of stimuli within a sensory modality are encoded in the same way that they are encoded among modalities. That is, distinguishing red from green, or a low pitch from a high one, depended upon specialized receptors in the eye or ear, distinct nerve connections within the visual or auditory system, and specific locations within the visual or auditory areas of the brain that receive the stimulation. The testing of the theory depended upon an individual's report of the sensory experience ("I see red"), the nature of the stimulus to which the individual responded (a specific wavelength of the energy spectrum), and knowledge of the physiological organization of the sensory systems. Relating the experience to the stimulus was a matter of experimental research that could be carried out with intact human beings; detecting the activity of nerves and the location of the brain to which stimulation was transmitted was possible then only with *in vitro* preparations of animals. Relating subjective, psychological experience to specific external stimulation was one step in suggesting how psychology might become a science.

Psychophysics

Experiments on the sense of touch were carried out by the physiologist E. H. Weber (1795–1878), who distinguished among the feelings of pressure, temperature, and the location of stimulation on the skin. In conducting experiments in which he stimulated his own skin, Weber explored skin sensitivity and demonstrated that "on the tip of the forefinger and lips two fine compass points could be felt as two when they were less than one-twentieth of an inch apart, but if they were nearer they seemed to be one" (Hall, 1901, p. 727). Not only could touch sensitivity be measured at different points on the skin, but relative sensitivity at a single point could also be measured. Placing a standard weight at a given spot on the skin and then asking for a second weight to be judged "heavier" or "lighter" showed that the amount of weight that could be judged heavier or lighter than the standard varied as a proportion of the magnitude of the standard weight. Thus, the minimal detectable difference between two weights was relative to the weights involved; for heavy weights, differences would have to be large, but smaller differences could be detected when the weights involved were light.

G. T. Fechner (1801–1887), a physicist, saw in Weber's results the possibility of relating mental events to physical events; subjective judgments about physical magnitudes could be compared to the actual physical magnitudes. Fechner had believed since his student days "that the phenomena of mind and body run in parallel" (Marshall, 1982, p. 67). His solution to the problem of relating these two aspects of the world was to make "the relative increase of bodily energy the measure of the increase of the corresponding mental intensity" (Adler, 1966, p. xii). Although Fechner conceived of the possibility independently of Weber's results, he came to realize that his speculations about arithmetic and logarithmic relations between physical and subjective magnitudes were in fact demonstrated by Weber's observations (Adler, 1966; Marshall, 1982).

Weber's results showed that sensory judgments of magnitude formed ratios that were sufficiently regular to assume the status of a law. Fechner designated as Weber's law the mathematical equation that stated that the increase in perceived intensity of a stimulus (the "just noticeable difference") was, as Weber had demonstrated, a constant proportion of the intensity of the stimulus to be increased. The regularity in ratios across a wide range of intensities led Fechner to rewrite the law in terms of a logarithmic progression, with the strength of a sensation equal to the logarithm of the intensity of a stimulus multiplied by a constant established experimentally for the sensory system under study (Murray, 1988, pp. 176–185). "Weber's law" now typically refers to the "simple statement that the just noticeable difference in a stimulus bears a constant ratio to the stimulus" (Adler, 1966, p. xiv), while "Fechner's law" typically refers to the logarithmic relationship that Fechner formulated.

Fechner called the new science that he established *psychophysics* and developed laboratory procedures that became part of the laboratory experiments of the new psychology as well as of the physiological research on the special senses. The measurements of the smallest detectable intensity (absolute threshold) and the smallest detectable difference in intensities between stimuli (difference threshold) for the different senses were pursued by the several methods that Fechner had devised for the purpose (see, e.g., Woodworth,

1938). Resolving differences in results obtained for different methods, testing psychophysical laws over a wide range of stimulus intensities, and developing scales of psychological measurement offered significant research challenges for psychological laboratories well into the twentieth century (Stevens, 1951; Woodworth, 1938).

Mental Chronometry

Johannes Müller had speculated in his *Handbuch* that the speed of transmission of a nerve impulse was greater than the speed of light. Helmholtz tested that hypothesis by measuring the time to react ("reaction time") to stimuli applied to motor nerves of different lengths in a frog and found the time to be much slower than the speed of light (Boring, 1950; Hall, 1901). He extended this research to sensory nerves by measuring the time to respond by a human to a touch on the toe and a touch on the thigh and demonstrated that he time to respond was slower for the impulse that had longer to travel. Helmholtz extended the use of time to measure a sensory-motor response to include spoken responses to words, providing a measure of the time necessary to associate words or ideas.

The determination of reaction times to measure the speed of mental processes was investigated by the Dutch physiologist F. C. Donders (1818–1889). Donders began with the time to make a motor response to a stimulus (simple reaction time) and then added more stimuli, each with a different response. By subtracting simple reaction time from the time taken to make the correct response to one of several stimuli, Donders believed that he had measured the time required to make a choice (Boring, 1950; Woodworth, 1938). He then recognized that his experimental procedure required not only that an observer choose a response from among the several responses possible but also that an observer detect which stimulus had been presented from among the several possible stimuli (discrimination reaction time). Using the subtractive method that he devised, Donders estimated the time for a simple reaction, the time taken to discriminate one stimulus from others, and the time taken to choose a response. The possibility of measuring the time required by mental processes appeared to have been realized, and the reaction-time experiment as well as the subtractive procedure became part of the science of psychology (for modern adaptations, see Posner & Raichle, 1994; Sternberg, 1969).

PSYCHOLOGY'S FIRST LABORATORY

The founding of the first laboratory in experimental psychology has generally been credited (but not without some debate; see Green, 2000) to German physician and physiologist Wilhelm Wundt (1832–1920). Wundt received his MD degree from the University of Heidelberg in 1855. The natural sciences had become legitimized as a proper field of study and were allied with medical training in the universities. Research laboratories for scientific investigations were an accepted part of the university structure, and careers in scientific research were made possible (Ben-David, 1971, pp. 123–124). Wundt, trained in physiology as part of his medical education, pursued independent research as a student and chose physiology, not medicine, for his career (Bringmann, Balance, & Evans, 1975). As a lecturer at the University of Heidelberg, Wundt offered courses privately for a fee, conducted research, and became an assistant to Helmholtz. In 1862, he offered his first course in "psychology as a natural science" (Bringmann et al., 1975) at Heidelberg, and in 1873–1874, the first edition of his book, *Grundzüge der physiologischen Psychologie (Principles of Physiological Psychology)* called for the recognition of psychology as a discipline independent of philosophy and physiology (Blumenthal, 1985a; Fancher, 1996; but see Danziger, 1990).

In 1875, at the age of 42, Wundt accepted a position as professor of philosophy at the University of Leipzig, where he established the first experimental research program in psychology. Chairs in science carried more prestige than those in philosophy, but the limited number of chairs available in science at the time made one in philosophy attractive to Wundt (Ben-David & Collins, 1966). Thus, psychology, like other sciences before it, began as part of the curriculum in philosophy; the acceptance of research laboratories as part of the university establishment permitted the founding of a laboratory in conjunction with Wundt's research.

Wundt had been engaged in psychological research for some time. As early as 1857, he constructed an apparatus in his home to measure reaction time and began accumulating a collection of instruments (kymographs, chronoscopes, tachistoscopes, and devices to measure responses) that were eventually employed in his laboratory (Blumenthal, 1985a, p. 29). Upon his arrival at Leipzig, a space in a former university refectory building was assigned to Wundt to permit him to store his apparatus and to conduct demonstrations associated with his lectures. In 1879, Wundt and students Max Friedrich and American G. Stanley Hall began a program of independent research (Boring, 1965; Bringmann, Bringmann, & Ungerer, 1980) that initiated psychology as "the organized and self-conscious activity of a community of investigators" (Danziger, 1990, p. 18). In 1881, the first issue of Wundt's journal, *Philosophische Studien,* appeared featuring Friedrich's dissertation research, and by 1883, the laboratory had acquired the status and budget of a research institute within the university (Boring, 1965; Bringmann et al., 1980; Danziger, 1990).

Experimental psychology as practiced by Wundt and his students at Leipzig employed the methods of physiology to study the contents and processes of individual human consciousness. Among the studies pursued in Wundt's laboratory were psychophysical experiments to analyze and measure sensations, reaction-time experiments to measure the duration of mental processes, and experiments on attention, memory, and the association of ideas (Cattell, 1888). Wundt extended Donders's subtractive procedure to the measurement of other mental processes, including association and judgment. His American student, James McKeen Cattell (1860–1944), elaborated on Donders' method in his research investigations at Leipzig between 1883 and 1886 and measured the speed of verbal associations. In a particularly innovative set of experiments, he varied the number of letters, numbers, words, or sentences a stimulus card contained and exposed the card to observers very briefly (.01 sec) to measure the number of items that could be contained in consciousness at one time; the result was an estimate of the span of attention, or span of apprehension (Ladd, 1888). Early reports of experiments were enthusiastic in detailing the empirical results that the laboratory could provide but that were beyond the reach of the older philosophical psychology. Reports that the time taken to name a short word was .05 seconds less than the time taken to name a letter of the alphabet (Jastrow, 1886), or that the time taken to name colors or pictures was "about twice as long as the corresponding times for recognizing and naming letters or words" (Cattell, 1947b, p. 25), exemplify this fascination with quantifying dimensions of mental processes. Intrigued by the individual differences in performance that he observed, Cattell would later explore the range of individual differences in a program of mental testing at Columbia University (Cattell, 1947c; Wundt, 1974; Fancher, 1996; Sokal, 1987).

In addition to the psychophysical and reaction time measures that he employed, Wundt's physiological psychology made use of reports of conscious experience. He distinguished between *Selbstbeobachtung* (self-observation), the introspection of the philosophers, and *innere Wahrnehmung* (internal perception); the basis of conscious experience. Self-observation, as traditionally employed, could not meet the standard of scientific observation. To make a *scientific* introspection possible required careful control over the stimulus that was to produce the mental event to be observed and as short an interval as possible between the observation of the event and its recall and report. This was to be achieved by the experiment conducted in the laboratory under carefully controlled conditions; *experimentelle. Selbstbeobachtung* was the form of introspection raised to scientific status by experimental procedures (although terminology when translated from the German can be problematic; compare Blumenthal, 1985a, p. 28 and Danziger, 1980, p. 244). In any case, to ensure that this observational procedure could be a rigorous scientific method to assess mental events and did not lapse into the older philosophical reflection, Wundt established rules or guidelines by which introspection might achieve scientific validity: "(1) The observer, if at all possible, must be in a position to determine when the process is to be introduced; (2) He must be in a state of 'strained attention'; (3) The observation must be capable of being repeated several times; (4) The conditions of the experiment must be such as to be capable of variation of the strength and quality of the stimuli" (R. I. Watson & Evans, 1991, p. 280).

By knowing when a process is to be introduced (a stimulus presented), an observer may concentrate (strained attention) on the observation to be made and, to ensure reliability, be able to repeat the process. Varying conditions allowed the observer to identify changes in consciousness as a function of changes in the conditions of the experiment. Replicating conditions enhanced the reliability of the observations to approach those of the observation of external events. These tight restrictions meant, with minor exceptions, that "the introspective reports from his laboratory are very largely limited to judgments of size, intensity, and duration of physical stimuli, supplemented at times by judgments of their simultaneity and succession" (Danziger, 1980, p. 247).

Confidence in the results of introspection depended upon confidence in the skill and experience of the observer who, as the source of the data, was the critical component in psychological experiments. In Wundt's laboratories, the observer possessed psychological authority and expertise. Experimental control over the introspective process was obtained not only by the rules for the conduct of an experiment but also by the use of observers whose habits of attentiveness and quickness of observation and reporting provided reliable data (Danziger, 1980). Published reports of experiments conducted in German and American laboratories identified each of the observers and their level of experience in introspection (e.g., Geissler, 1909; cf. Bazerman, 1987). The experimenter played a secondary role in manipulating the apparatus, presenting stimuli, and recording responses. The division of labor between experimenters and observers, who were colleagues and collaborators, was primarily one of convenience; roles were routinely exchanged, with few exceptions: Wundt, for example, served as an observer in some of the Leipzig experiments but never as experimenter.

However, the published reports of experiments by Oswald Külpe (1862–1915), a former student of Wundt, failed to identify the observers in experiments that used introspection in his laboratory at the University of Würzburg. Külpe's experiments were designed to explore the thought processes involved in making inferences and judgments. The Würzburg method of introspection, "systematic introspection" (Danziger, 1980; 1990) or "systematic introspectionism" (Blumenthal, 1985b, p. 64), was a form of self-reflection that required thinking about a problem to solve and then retrospectively recounting the thought processes that led to its solution. In these experiments, the experimenter would interrupt the observer's introspective report with questions designed to probe the content of consciousness. This procedure, which shifted the power and authority in the experimental situation from the observer to the experimenter, represented a departure from the careful experimental control over introspection exercised in Wundt's laboratory. Wundt vigorously opposed the Würzburg method as unreliable (Blumenthal, 1985a; Leahey, 1981), particularly as it was applied to those higher mental processes that Wundt believed to be beyond the reach of introspection and, indeed, of any laboratory method. Others pointed out that the "demand characteristics" inherent in this interrogation procedure (Müller, 1911; cited in Kusch, 1995) were likely to bias an observer's responses. The status of introspection as a laboratory method would concern psychology well into the twentieth century.

Wundt argued that experimental self-observation could reveal the existence of mental processes such as apperception (an active attentional process that organized perceptions), volition (will or effort), and emotion, but he strongly believed that these higher mental processes could not be studied using the experimental method. The only methods appropriate for the study of these hidden, higher cognitive processes were naturalistic observation and history. Wundt's physiological psychology was one of "outer phenomena," sensation, perceptions, and movement, while his *Völkerpsychologie,"* the study of language, religion, myth, and culture, was one of "inner phenomena" (Leahey, 1981). Wundt's *Völkerpsychologie* encompasses 10 volumes.

Because so many American students studied at Leipzig (Benjamin, Durkin, Link, Vesta, & Acord, 1992), Wundt assumed a position of particular significance in the accounts of the origins of the new psychology. Nevertheless, pioneers in the new discipline at other German universities attracted their share of students from the United States and from other countries. The development of psychology, even in its early stages, was not the work of a single individual. Much of the development of psychology consisted of attempting to study in the laboratory those psychological processes that Wundt had declared beyond the reach of experiment.

BEYOND THE FIRST LABORATORY: EVOLUTION OF THE DISCIPLINE

Psychology in Germany

One of Wundt's contemporaries who believed that higher mental processes could be the object of experimental investigation was Hermann Ebbinghaus (1850–1909). Inspired by the psychophysics of G. T. Fechner and philosopher J. F. Herbart's attempt to apply mathematics to mental representations, Ebbinghaus used precise quantitative methods to investigate memory (Murray, 1976). He served as both the experimenter and the subject of his investigations. In order to have relatively homogeneous material to learn and to reduce the impact of any previous semantic associations, such as occurred in his early experiments in learning and remembering poetry, Ebbinghaus developed the "nonsense syllable," largely pronounceable consonant-vowel-consonant combinations. He created syllable lists of various lengths that he learned and then later relearned after different lengths of time. The percentage of time saved in relearning the lists became known as the "savings method" of memory (Murray, 1976, p. 206; Hoffman, Bringmann, Bamberg, & Klein, 1987). Ebbinghaus found that the amount of time spent in relearning lists was greater for longer lists and for longer retention intervals. The graph of his results became the standard curve of forgetting, still reproduced in textbooks as a classic result. The curve showed that recall of learned lists was perhaps 85% after one hour, approximately 50% after one day, and as little as 15% after about six days. These findings stimulated a long tradition of memory research (e.g., Postman, 1968). After publication of his monograph *Über das Gedächtnis (On Memory)*, Ebbinghaus established laboratories at several universities and attracted some American students, but his time was increasingly devoted to a editing a journal and writing (Fuchs, 1997). Leadership of memory research fell to Georg Elias Müller (1850–1931) at Göttingen University.

Müller, a dedicated experimentalist, invented the memory drum, a mechanical device for presenting one verbal stimulus at a time, used in conjunction with experiments on serial list learning and list retention. The memory drum, modified subsequently by Müller for research in paired associate learning (Haupt, 1998), became a standard piece of laboratory equipment for studies of verbal learning and memory until replaced by the computer. Müller's research reports on his studies of memory extended from 1893 to 1917 and included

"the theoretical contributions of retroactive inhibition, perseveration, and consolidation" (Murray & Bandomir, 2000). Müller initiated what later was termed the interference theory of forgetting, a position that argues that forgetting is a function of the interference among competing memories at the time that a particular memory is being retrieved and not a function of a decay or loss of memory traces (Murray, 1988). The topic was not addressed directly by Ebbinghaus, but the rapid forgetting that his retention curve recorded has been interpreted as offering evidence of the role of interference in memory (Murray, 1988; Underwood, 1957).

Müller's experimental interests were not limited to memory research. He built on the contributions of Fechner, Ewald Hering, and Mary Whiton Calkins in becoming a leader in the development of the methodology of psychophysics, conducting studies on color vision and investigating paired-associate verbal learning (Blumenthal, 1985b; Murray, 1976). His laboratory was well supplied with experimental apparatus (Haupt, 1998) and attracted a number of psychologists to pursue research with him. Müller's laboratory seems to have been especially hospitable to women interested in psychology; among those studying at Göttingen were, for example, Americans Mary Whiton Calkins, Eleanor Gamble, and Lillien Jane Martin. Other laboratories and universities were less open in this regard (Furumoto, 1987; Scarborough & Furumoto, 1987).

Psychology in America

The results of German investigations in sensory physiology and their significance for the philosophy of mind did not go unnoticed by Americans in the period after the Civil War. William James, abroad for his health and to further his medical studies, wrote to a friend: "It seems to me that perhaps the time has come for psychology to begin to be a science— some measurements have already been made in the region lying between the physical changes in the nerves and the appearance of consciousness at (in the shape of sense perceptions) and more may come of it. Helmholtz and a man named Wundt at Heidelberg are working at it" (James, 1920, pp. 118–119).

In antebellum America, the dominant philosophical tradition was derived from England and Scotland, as exemplified in John Locke's *Essay on Human Understanding* and the texts of the Scottish commonsense realists, Thomas Reid, Dugald Stewart, and Thomas Brown (Evans, 1984, Fay, 1939; Fuchs, 2000a, Roback, 1952) with only modest representation of German (Hickok, 1854; Rauch, 1840) and French (Cousine, 1864) philosophy. British philosophy was empirical, gathering information about mind and mental processes from introspective observation, observation of the behavior of others, and observations of individuals recorded in medical treatises, court proceedings, literature, and poetry. The data were classified under general faculties or categories of mind, such as the intellect and the sensibilities (cognitive and conative, emotional, or motivational states) and the many possible subdivisions, such as memory and reasoning, instincts, and desires (Fuchs, 2000a, 2000b). Results from the investigations in psychophysics, sensory physiology, and the early experiments in psychology were incorporated into later textbooks of intellectual and mental philosophy (e.g., Porter, 1868; McCosh, 1886, 1887). Adding the empirical data to the theological concerns for "soul" did not change the traditional philosophical position of these texts. Even a textbook by G. T. Ladd (1842–1921) that represented the new psychology did not escape fully the theological concerns of the "old psychology" (Ladd, 1888; Evans, 1984; E. Mills, 1969).

Americans traveled abroad for advanced education at British and continental universities after the Civil War; painters, writers, and scientists went in large numbers. With the postwar establishment of the new land-grant universities, professional opportunities arose for faculty members, especially in the sciences, for education not yet available in the United States. With the zeal of converts and crusaders, the first generation of North American psychologists returned from their study abroad to stimulate the development of graduate education within established American colleges and universities and the newer land-grant universities (Kohler, 1990). They wrote textbooks to incorporate the results of the continental laboratories, developed courses for undergraduate and graduate students, created laboratories for teaching and research, and founded journals for the publication of research from the newly established laboratories. The laboratories came to be the locus of education in psychology in universities and colleges (Calkins, 1910; Sanford, 1910) and came to symbolize psychology as science, while psychology, lodged within departments of philosophy, became the introductory course required for further study in philosophy (Fuchs, 2000b).

William James and Evolutionary Theory

The essential break with the mental philosophical past was achieved by William James, whose *Principles of Psychology* (James, 1890) represented the first of the modern textbooks (Evans, 1981). James was a transitional figure, with one foot in philosophy and the other in the empiricism of the new science. His text, while still too philosophical for some of his more empirical colleagues (see, e.g., Evans, 1981; Ross, 1972), nevertheless effectively cut the discipline's past ties

to theology. James was attracted to the new psychology by the possibility of using science to pursue philosophical issues more deeply (Croce, 1999) and called for psychology to be a natural science (James, 1892a). He recognized that while psychology was not yet an established science, it constituted the hope of a science (James, 1892b). His textbooks (James, 1890, 1892b) attracted recruits to psychology's banner to attempt to realize that hope.

William James had been appointed an instructor at Harvard in physiology in 1872; like Wundt, James had earned an MD degree and, again like Wundt, had no real interest in practicing medicine. In 1875, he offered a graduate course at Harvard on the "Relations between Psychology and Physiology" and, again like Wundt, had rooms assigned to him to use for experimental demonstrations to augment his teaching. James, however, was never very enthusiastic about laboratory work; he once declared the psychophysics could never have arisen in a country in which the natives could be bored (Boring, 1950). As a text for his course in psychology, James adopted *Principles of Psychology* (1855) by Herbert Spencer (1820–1903). A course featuring discussion of evolutionary theory was a novelty, since the older, pre–Civil War mental philosophy texts ignored evolutionary theory, while textbooks written after the war wrestled uncomfortably and unsuccessfully with integrating evolutionary theory with theological concerns.

The theory of evolution by natural selection proposed by Charles Darwin (1809–1882) had an enormous influence on American psychology. In his book *On the Origin of Species* (1859), Darwin presented evidence to support his theory of evolution and proposed natural selection as the mechanism responsible. To account for the evolution of intelligent behaviors, Darwin appealed to two mechanisms, sexual selection (the evolution of traits that facilitate mating success) and, more tentatively, as a second mechanism, the inheritance of acquired characteristics (Darwin, 1871). Jean-Baptiste de Lamarck (1744–1829) had proposed that learned changes in behavior that occur during an animal's lifetime can be passed down to that individual's offspring through biological inheritance. This view was shared by Herbert Spencer, who, unlike Darwin, viewed the evolutionary process as a linear progression from "lower" to "higher" forms (Spencer, 1855). Spencer coined the phrase "survival of the fittest" to suggest that those individuals who were best adjusted to their environments would survive. Learned behaviors that facilitated this adjustment to the environment would then be passed to subsequent generations. Adjustment was to the individual's survival what adaptation was to the survival of the species (Boakes, 1984; Buxton, 1985a; 1985b). The absence of evidence for Lamarck's theory led to its abandonment, and evolutionary theory was left with natural selection as the only mechanism of evolutionary change. Nevertheless, Spencer's focus on adaptability during an individual's lifetime (learning) and Darwin's emphasis on individual development during childhood, differences among individuals, the relation between structure and function, and the continuity between animals and humans contributed substantially to the expansion of the topics that psychologists pursued in the name of psychological science.

THE PSYCHOLOGICAL LABORATORY AND THE PSYCHOLOGICAL EXPERIMENT

The Rise of Laboratories in America

William James saw in the early results of experiments in psychophysics and sensory physiology the beginning of science in the measurement of phenomena that the mental philosophers could only describe. Like James, G. Stanley Hall (1844–1924) was impressed by the impetus given to the new psychology by the results from experiments on sensory physiology. Hall, while preparing for the ministry, studied theology and philosophy in Germany and found that science was relevant to these pursuits, especially scientific empiricism.

Hall founded the first American laboratory in the new science of psychology at the Johns Hopkins University in 1883. While Hall's laboratory at Johns Hopkins usually is acknowledged as the first psychological laboratory in the United States, the designation was not without other claimants. Debate over credit for the establishment of laboratories provides some measure of the importance, real and symbolic, that psychologists attached to the laboratory and to the experimental research that it was designed to foster (Capshew, 1992).

By 1893, 20 psychological laboratories were operating in the United States, nearly twice as many as in Europe (Nichols, 1893, as cited by Capshew, 1992). By 1904, there were 49 laboratories of psychology in colleges and universities in the United States (Benjamin, 2000; Camfield, 1973). Psychology had become an accepted part of the curriculum, required for the undergraduate degree in 8 universities and represented in 62 institutions by three or more courses (Miner, 1904). Psychologists argued their case for the new science (and for their own professional careers) to the general public and to trustees and governing boards of academic institutions with some success (Leary, 1987). Not only were courses in psychology and laboratories begun, but journals were established, beginning with Hall's *American Journal of Psychology* in 1887, to make public the results of laboratory investigations as well as to provide an outlet for the theoretical and philosophical articles that were part of the young science. The American Psychological Association (1892) provided annual meetings for the reports of investigations and for psychologists to consider ways to advance the profession. Graduate programs in universities produced over one hundred PhDs between 1892 and 1904; between 1898 and 1903, psychology ranked fourth after chemistry, zoology, and physics in the number of PhDs awarded (Camfield, 1973).

The laboratories founded in American colleges and universities served to initiate students into laboratory practices, familiarize them with standard pieces of laboratory apparatus, and introduce them to the subject matter and opportunities for research in scientific psychology. The experiments of the early laboratory reflected the scientific beginnings of the field: Studies of psychophysics, sensory capacities and sensitivity, memory, attention, and voluntary movement (reaction time) were emphasized in manuals written for the laboratory course (e.g., Judd, 1907; Langfeld & Allport, 1916; Sanford, 1897; Seashore, 1909; Titchener, 1901–1905). The topics represented by these laboratory experiments were also those that continued to be a part of the research agenda of psychologists. Increasingly, however, the interests of psychologists extended beyond Wundt's line of demarcation between topics that could properly be pursued through laboratory experiments and those that could not. Much of the development of psychology consisted of expanding the range of psychological processes that were amenable to scientific investigation within and outside the laboratory while continuing to debate the definition of the field and the methods most useful to its development.

The Evolution of the Laboratory Experiment

In the experiments with which psychology began, such as Weber's study of tactual sensitivity, Fechner's research in psychophysics, or Ebbinghaus's study of memory, a single individual served as both experimenter and observer. In subsequent research in psychophysics and memory, the roles of experimenter and observer became separated in order to eliminate, or control for, possible biases that might stem from knowledge of the experiment and the expectations that might influence an observation, such as knowing the intensity of stimulus to be judged quantitatively (Dehue, 1997, 2000). Separating the role of experimenter from that of observer, interpolating "catch-trials" (in which no stimulus was presented), and randomizing the presentation of stimuli became common practices in psychophysical research and were adapted to other psychological experiments (Dehue, 1997). Moreover, as psychological research expanded to include experiments that assessed the responses of children and animals, requiring little or no introspection, authority became increasingly centered in the experimenter and participants became "subjects" rather than "observers."

Data Treatment and Research Design

Early published reports of "even narrowly focused laboratory studies conducted with small samples were capable of generating reams of detailed data; readers of journal reports were sometimes confronted with tables of data that ran on for pages" (Smith, Best, Cylke, & Stubbs, 2000, p. 260). Summary data were presented not only in tables but also in graphic form. Graphs were a common form of data summary in turn-of-the-century scientific reports [the forgetting curve of Ebbinghaus (1885) and the learning curve of Thorndike (1898) were two influential examples of graphic representation]. In addition, graphs helped to pave the way for the later development of correlation and regression analyses (Smith et al., 2000). In attempting to assess the degree of relation between physical and mental characteristics to each other, Francis Galton (1822–1911) used scatter plots in which one set of scores was arranged as a function of another set, such as the height and weight measures of a group of individuals. From such graphic plots evolved the regression line, the steepness of which reflected the degree of relation between two variables, and, in the hands of Karl Pearson (1857–1936), developed into the mathematical technique of correlating variables and measuring the degree of their relationship by the coefficient of correlation (Fancher, 1996). The development of these statistical methods became critical to the assessment of individual differences and the use of tests in psychology.

Other statistical procedures were employed to assess comparisons between different groups of individuals. Galton's research, for example, on the efficacy of prayer asked "whether those who pray attain their objects more frequently than those who do not pray, but who live in all other respects under similar conditions" (Galton, 1872, p. 126, as cited by Dehue, 2000). A control group was employed in educational research to assess the effects of transfer of training (the influence of practice in one task on performance in another), and, despite arguments over whether participants should be assigned to an experimental or control group at random or by matching individuals, the use of control groups in psychological experiments became an integral part of research design (Dehue, 1997).

The comparison of control and experimental group performances led to the use of statistical procedures for testing the significance of any differences that might be obtained.

Inferential statistics was unknown until the twentieth century: Student's "t" test for comparing mean scores from two groups appeared in 1908. Analysis of variance tests were devised in the 1920s (Smith et al., 2000) but did not become a common part of psychological research designs until the 1930s (Rucci & Tweney, 1980).

With the publication of his *Experimental Psychology* (1938), R. S. Woodworth "introduced a clear distinction between experimental and correlational research" (Winston, 1990, p. 391). The critical distinction made between the two kinds of research was that only in experimental work could the cause of behavior be determined by manipulation of an independent variable; the definition "provided one powerful rationale for the animal research of the thirties, forties, and fifties" (Winston, 1990, p. 397) because manipulations of "causal" variables in animal research provided fewer ethical or practical problems than research with humans. The search for causes of behavior and the theoretical models of learning embodied this definition of the psychological experiment as the means of testing hypotheses. This model of the experiment helped to establish prescriptions for the use of t-tests and analyses of variance as the statistical treatments of choice for the results of experiments, while correlational techniques and regression analyses were utilized by those interested in individual differences.

The methodology of research and standards for analyzing and reporting results of experiments in keeping with psychology's status as a science is reflected in the standardization of the reports of experiments and the definition of the experiment. The model for reports of empirical research for publication in journals of the American Psychological Association evolved from a six-and-a-half-page style sheet published in 1929 (Bently et al., 1929) to the 1983 *American Psychological Association Publication Manual* (3rd edition) that contained about 200 pages of rules for preparing a manuscript (Bazerman, 1987) to the current fifth edition of the manual (2001) of 439 pages. Reports initially emphasized either how quantitative experimental results might aid in understanding philosophical problems or simply let complex data speak for themselves (Bazerman, 1987). The emphasis on hypothesis testing and statistical analyses of comparisons between control and experimental group performance that later came to dominate experimental design and instructions to authors preparing manuscripts reflected the success of Woodworth's definition of what constituted an experiment in psychology.

Defining Psychology and Its Methods

Changes in the psychological experiment in apparatus and methods and the shift in roles of observer and experimenter occurred amid debate over the subject matter of psychology and the methods appropriate to it. The growth in the range of subject matter under experimental investigation and in the methods employed in the study of psychology reflected James McKeen Cattell's definition of psychology's subject matter as anything that a psychologist is interested in, as a psychologist (Cattell, 1947a). The experimental psychology that arose in North America resembled the research practices of G. E. Müller more than those of Wilhelm Wundt in the range of topics addressed in the laboratory and the apparatus and methods that were employed. The psychology that evolved in college and university departments of philosophy and, as the century matured, in independent departments of psychology reflected the functional spirit of the mental philosophers and the influence of the theory of evolution.

Mental philosophy had attempted to describe how mind worked, how its cognitive and conative processes operated to produce volitional acts. American psychologists, imbued with the spirit of evolutionary theory, were focused on the utility of mind and consciousness in the adaptation of species and individuals to the environment. This concern with function (what is mind for? what is its function?—presumably, to aid adaptation) was coupled with other aspects of function, namely, how mind works (how does it function?) and on what mind depends (of what is mind a function? how complex must a nervous system be before mind becomes possible?). These implicit and broad concerns for mental function in psychology were made more explicit and embodied in a self-conscious school of psychology by James Rowland Angell (1869–1949) in response to the programmatic statement of E. B. Titchener (1867–1927), who advocated a structural psychology. These schools of thought were but two among general systematic positions that competed for dominance in psychology (Heidbreder, 1933; Murchison, 1926, 1930; Woodworth, 1948).

Structural and Functional Psychologies

Oswald Külpe's method of systematic introspection had a very strong proponent in Edward Bradford Titchener at Cornell University. Titchener had become interested in Wundt's psychology while studying philosophy and physiology at Oxford University. He translated the third edition of Wundt's *Gründzüge* into English and, when he could find no one in England with whom to study the new science, went to Leipzig to complete his doctorate with Wundt in 1892. English universities were unreceptive to the new psychology; Titchener accepted a professorship at Cornell University, where he remained until his death in 1927.

Titchener presented himself as Wundt's representative in North America, but his psychology was not Wundt's voluntarism (Leahey, 1981; Danziger, 1990). Titchener's view of mind was influenced by the English philosophy of John Locke and his heirs that he had studied at Oxford. The British philosophers viewed mind as a recipient of stimulation: Mental content was whatever had entered mind through the senses. The purpose of the study of mind was to understand how complex mental experience and function could arise from combinations of these elements. Laws of association, by which elements combined, played a significant role in understanding how mind grew from sensory elements.

Similarly, mind was, for Titchener, composed of elements that he identified as sensations, images, and affections. Sensation was the primary experience resulting from stimulation of the senses, images were complex representations that carried thought, and feelings were the elements of which emotions were comprised. Through the direct systematic introspection of consciousness under laboratory conditions, Titchener pursued three goals: the reduction of conscious experience to its basic elements, determining how the elements were connected to form complex perceptions, and identifying the underlying physiological processes. The first of these goals provided the primary focus of research at the Cornell laboratory, as the elements were themselves analyzed for their attributes (which, in a later version of the system, became the new elements of consciousness; see Evans, 1972). Pursuit of the other goals was secondary because they depended upon the successful completion of the first.

The subject of psychology, Titchener argued, was the understanding of the human, adult, normal, generalized mind through the use of introspection; only after psychology had completed that task could the nonhuman, child, abnormal, or individual mind be understood. For Titchener, psychology needed to emulate physics, with its pursuit of the analysis of matter into the smaller units of which it was composed. Titchener stood for rigorous experimental pursuit of the elements of mind, pursued for their own sake and not for any potential application. He disparaged "functional psychology" as essentially the "mind in use" approach of the older, discarded philosophical psychology.

An early response to Titchener's postulates for his structural psychology came from John Dewey (1859–1952), chair of the Department of Philosophy, which subsumed psychology and pedagogy, at the University of Chicago. Dewey perceived that the new method of laboratory experiment would free the older barren mental philosophy from the theological and philosophical constraints of its past and open the way for a useful psychology that would help resolve problems of the asylum, the classroom, and other practical affairs (Dewey,

1884). He facilitated the establishment of a laboratory at the University of Michigan before moving to Chicago. In 1896, Dewey argued against reductionist approaches to the study of consciousness and for a functional analysis and understanding of mind (Dewey, 1896). A functional approach to mind was embedded in the nineteenth century mental philosophy taught in American colleges (Fuchs, 2000a) and its development at the University of Chicago was influenced by pre-Chicago Associations among Dewey and others (Raphelson, 1973).

James R. Angell, a graduate of the University of Michigan and a student of psychology there, built on Dewey's approach in his presidential address to the American Psychological Association in 1906 (Angell, 1907), in his successful textbooks (e.g., Angell, 1905), and from his position as Professor of Psychology at the University of Chicago. Functional psychology dealt not with mental elements as its primary focus but with mental operations; the role of consciousness in helping to adapt an organism to its environment involved psychology in a concern for mind and body relationships (Angell, 1907, p. 86). Functionalism was interested in the uses of consciousness and its role in guiding behavior; it was profoundly practical and reformist. Psychology and other social sciences were useful to a variety of educational and social reforms promoted during the progressive era (Fitzpatrick, 1990; Milar, 1999).

Angell's approach to psychology encompassed the broad range of interests and methods that had developed in psychology since 1879 and reflected the influence that evolutionary theory exerted on psychology in the United States. The science of mind was pursued in the laboratory; mind was its subject matter, and many methods were available for its study. Psychophysical experiments, research on the connections between physiology, especially the nervous system, and mental processes, and direct observation of others, including children and animals, provided data that could supplement the results of introspection under laboratory conditions (Angell, 1905). The use of a variety of methods would, in Angell's view, supplement the results of the direct observations of mind that introspection provides. Functional psychology was interested in how mind worked (i.e., how it functioned) and on its functional relation to the physiological substrate (i.e., on what did mind depend) and its purpose (i.e., its use or function) and was less concerned the content of mind.

Mary Whiton Calkins (1863–1930) attempted to reconcile the differences between the structural and functional psychologies by proposing a psychology of the self that possesses both conscious contents and mental functions. Calkins had begun her study of psychology unofficially at

Harvard with William James and Josiah Royce in 1890; Clark University professor Edmund Sanford tutored Calkins privately in experimental psychology. In 1891, Calkins established the first psychological laboratory at a women's college at Wellesley College, one of the first 12 laboratories in the United States (Furumoto, 1980). She developed the paired-associate technique for the study of verbal learning and memory and published papers on her research and on experiments conducted with students in the Wellesley laboratory (Calkins, 1894a, 1894b).

She pursued further study in psychology with Hugo Münsterberg at Harvard, but not as an officially registered student. Münsterberg petitioned Harvard's president to allow Calkins to be admitted as a candidate for the PhD, but his request was refused. In May 1895, after an unauthorized examination, the following communication was forwarded to The Harvard Corporation: "At the examination, held . . . before Professors Palmer, James, Royce, Münsterberg, Harris, and Dr. Santayana it was unanimously voted that Miss Calkins satisfied all the customary requirements for the degree" (cited in Furumoto, 1980, p. 62). Again, the PhD was denied (Harvard refused to grant the doctoral degree to a woman until 1963). In 1902, four women who had completed graduate study at Harvard were offered PhD degrees from Radcliffe College. Radcliffe, established in 1894, offered almost exclusively undergraduate courses; women who completed graduate work did so at Harvard University. Calkins refused the Radcliffe degree, seeing it as a symbol of Harvard's refusal to admit women on an equal footing with men (Scarborough & Furumoto, 1987). In 1905, Mary Whiton Calkins became the first woman elected to the presidency of the American Psychological Association.

By 1905, the functional point of view had become the dominant view in American psychology (Leahey, 1992). For his part, Angell claimed that functionalism could easily contain Calkins's "Self Psychology," "were it not for her extreme scientific conservatism in refusing to allow the self to have a body, save as a kind of conventional biological ornament" (Angell, 1907, p. 82). Calkins, and Titchener, did not reject the pursuit of identifying the physiological substrates of mental content and processes but placed that pursuit at a lower priority to the study of mind more directly. Indeed, Calkins extended the use of introspection to the study of abnormal experiences of the normal self and included the study by comparative means of abnormal individuals (Calkins, 1901, 1919) among the range of topics to be studied in the new psychology.

In these psychologies, introspection continued to serve as a method for the direct examination of conscious experience, but problems arose when introspective reports from different laboratories contradicted each other. Doubts about the capacity of introspection to serve as a scientific method were brought forcefully into focus by the "imageless thought" controversy. Titchener's psychology proposed that images were the carrier of thoughts, and introspective observations carried out in his laboratory supported his position. Oswald Külpe and his colleagues at the University of Würzburg, however, failed to observe images in their studies of thought processes and concluded that thinking was carried out by "imageless thoughts." How could introspection, as a method, reconcile incompatible results when conscious experience was private and not open to public inspection?

Supporters of introspection as the primary method of scientific psychology added more instructions in an attempt to improve the method (English, 1921) while others advocated its more limited use among other psychological methods (Angell, 1905; Dodge, 1912). The question of whether introspective analysis could indeed serve as a scientific method producing reliable data was present at the start of psychology's history as a science. Introspective observations were reliable within limits: A wavelength of light at a given frequency was reported to evoke the same color sensation in all observers of normal vision. The question lay in the capability of introspection to go beyond such limited observations in the search for elements of mind. Meanwhile other research traditions arose.

Child Study

At Clark University, G. Stanley Hall established a graduate program in psychology that attracted students in numbers sufficient to make Clark a leader in psychology after its opening in 1889. In its first decade, 30 of the 54 doctorates in psychology awarded in the period were earned at Clark (White, 1992). In his laboratory of psychology, Hall fostered the experimental methods that he had learned in Germany and appointed E. C. Sanford (1859–1924) to supervise the experimental work. Hall's primary interest lay in developmental psychology; his recapitulation theory of development reflected the nineteenth-century view that the course of development of an individual parallels the stages of human evolution (Richards, 1992). Thus, "every child, from the moment of conception to maturity, recapitulates, . . . every stage of development through which the human race from its lowest animal beginnings has passed" (Hall, 1923, p. 380). Although the theory was later discredited, it served a useful purpose in stimulating research.

In 1891, Hall introduced the use of child-study questionnaires, the "Clark method" (Danziger, 1985, 1990). Questionnaires were designed to investigate "(a) simple automatisms,

instincts, and attitudes, (b) the small child's activities and feelings, (c) control of emotions and will, (d) development of the higher faculties, (e) individual differences, (f) school processes and practices, and (g) church processes and practices" (White, 1992, p. 29). Much of Hall's research on childhood and that of his students culminated in his two-volume *Adolescence* (1904).

Child psychology was not, however, uniquely the property of Hall and his university. James Mark Baldwin's *Mental Development in the Child and the Race* (1895) and its companion volume, *Social and Ethical Interpretations of Mental Development* (1897), were attempts to bring a genetic account of development into the new psychology and "to bridge the gap between the study of social institutions (i.e., sociology) and the study of individual functioning (i.e., psychology)" (Cairns, 1992, p. 17). Baldwin's contributions were fleeting, for many reasons (see Cairns, 1992, p. 22), among which was that his theoretical formulations were out of step with the heavy empirical emphasis prevalent in psychology at the time. Similarly, Hall's influence was limited by the critical attack from those closely tied to laboratory investigations that his questionnaire research was methodologically weak. Nevertheless, Hall and Baldwin made the psychology of child development and the methods appropriate to its study part of the new psychology.

Individual Differences

Although recapitulation theory influenced Hall's approach to child study, the direct influence of evolutionary theory on child study was slight (Charlesworth, 1992). However, the theory of evolution strongly influenced the study of individual differences. For natural selection to serve as the primary mechanism of evolution, variation in species populations was necessary for the selection of traits that were the basis for adaptation and survival within different and changing environments. Francis Galton, a cousin of Darwin, contributed to the history of psychology through his measures of physical and mental characteristics of individuals who visited his Anthropometric Laboratory.

The measures of physical characteristics such as head size, arm length, height and weight, and performance characteristics such as reaction time and sensory acuity, used by Galton and adapted from the tasks of the psychological laboratories, were employed as mental tests of intelligence. Head size, for example was (falsely) assumed to indicate brain size and intellectual capacity, and speed of responses and visual acuity were assumed to indicate adaptability and survival capability. The term *intelligence* came to be used to designate differences among individuals in their capacity for such complex behaviors as reasoning and problem solving rather than to denote differences among species in adapting to the environment, the more common use of the term in the nineteenth century.

James McKeen Cattell, who had studied with Hall at Johns Hopkins before earning his PhD with Wundt, pursued his interest in individual variation, labeled *"ganz Amerikanisch"* by Wundt (Boring, 1950), while in Francis Galton's London laboratory. Cattell returned to establish a laboratory at Columbia University and adapted laboratory tasks familiar to him from both Leipzig and London to identify and measure differences in reaction time, sensory sensitivity, time estimation, and memory span in undergraduate students (Sokal, 1987; Tuddenham, 1962). Like Galton, he theorized that such tasks as reaction time, sensory acuity, memory, and apprehension spans would reveal an individual's intellectual abilities. His attempt to relate scores on these tasks to academic performance demonstrated little relationship between the performance scores on the laboratory tests to academic performance in courses at Columbia (Sokal, 1987) but nevertheless represents an early effort to measure the intelligence of individuals.

Assessing individual differences among human beings did not necessarily result in appropriate conclusions about the consequences of evolution because of the importance of social and cultural factors in determining differences among individuals. For example, Galton's study of sex differences in psychological characteristics reflected social and cultural views of the capabilities and proper roles for women and men rather than differences that could be attributed to evolutionary forces. This bias was common at the time and addressed by the research of one of James R. Angell's graduate students, Helen Bradford Thompson. Her dissertation, completed at the University of Chicago in 1900 and later published as *The Mental Traits of Sex* (1903), was the first systematic, experimental investigation of sex differences in motor ability, sensations, intellect, and affect. Careful, detailed analysis of the results led to her conclusion that "the psychological differences of sex seem to be largely due, not to difference of average capacity, nor to difference in type of mental activity, but to differences in the social influences brought to bear on the developing individual from early infancy to adult years" (p. 182).

Hall, too, had employed evolutionary arguments to bolster stereotyped ideas about the psychological nature and proper roles of men and women. His rather unflattering assessment of women's abilities attracted little argument from American male psychologists of the time (see Diehl, 1986; Shields, 1975) and played a role in denying opportunities for graduate study and professional employment for women (Milar, 2000).

In 1910, Helen Thompson, writing under her married name, Helen Thompson Woolley, reviewed the literature on sex differences and asserted, "There is perhaps no field aspiring to be scientific where flagrant personal bias, logic martyred in the cause of supporting a prejudice, unfounded assertions, and even sentimental rot and drivel, have run riot to such an extent as here" (Woolley, 1910, p. 340). Similar conclusions could have been drawn about comparisons among races begun before the development of evolutionary theory. These comparisons had also served to justify a hierarchy that placed Caucasians in a superior position, and later studies under the aegis of evolutionary theory continued to be carried out and interpreted in terms of long-held cultural biases (see R. Guthrie, 1998).

Influenced by Cattell and Hall's child study movement, Lightner Witmer (1867–1956), attempted to put performance on laboratory tasks to practical use in the new discipline that he labeled "Clinical Psychology" (McReynolds, 1996). The apparatus and methods of the laboratory experiment were successful in assessing differences among individuals but proved to be of little value for Witmer's purposes (McReynolds, 1996). The failure of laboratory tasks for these applied ends led, in the case of intelligence testing, to the refinement and development of tests modeled on those of Alfred Binet and, in Witmer's case, to the search for more suitable methods for assisting individuals. These efforts also led to attempts to identify characteristics of individuals that, like intelligence, were both measurable and offered promise of relevance, such as personality assessment (Allport, 1937), attitude and aptitude measures, and clinical diagnostic tests (Gregory, 1992). For many psychologists, individual differences were a distraction to the understanding of the general principles governing mind, while for others, the understanding of the individual mind was the most interesting task for psychology. The difference in emphasis and the somewhat separate paths of development of the two pursuits within psychology came to be seen as the two disciplines of scientific psychology (Cronbach, 1957).

The Study of Nonhumans: Animal Psychology

Darwin's theory of evolution had raised questions about the adaptive utility of consciousness; the relation of human to animal ancestry had raised issues of whether there are instincts in humans and whether animals exhibited human intellectual capacities and consciousness in adapting to changed or changing environments. Learning capacities and consciousness seemed in turn to depend upon the complexity of the nervous system: "If there is a Comparative Anatomy there is also a Comparative Psychology" (Chadbourne, 1872, p. 22). George

J. Romanes (1848–1894), a devoted younger friend of the aging Darwin, explored these concerns by collecting anecdotes of wild and domestic animals that provided evidence of capacities for reasoning and problem solving analogous to those exhibited by humans. As part of an animal's intelligent adaptation to an environment, he sought evidence of reason, which he defined as the conscious knowledge of the relation of the means to an end. In addition, Romanes described patterns of instinctive responses that occurred without a conscious awareness of the end to which they were adapted (Romanes, 1892).

Romanes' research methods and anthropomorphic conclusions about the capacities of animals were criticized by C. Lloyd Morgan (1852–1936) for relying on unsubstantiated anecdotes and weak analogical reasoning. Morgan emphasized the importance of observation and encouraged parsimony in interpreting observations of animal behavior (Morgan, 1890–1891, 1896). His caution in this regard came to be known as Morgan's Canon: "In no case should an animal's activity be interpreted in terms of higher psychological processes if it could be interpreted in terms of processes standing lower in the scale of psychological evolution" (R. I. Watson & Evans, 1991, p. 329). Morgan provided a necessary methodological corrective to enthusiastic but unscientific fact gathering by emphasizing both care in making observations and caution in interpreting them.

Morgan employed experimental methods and observation in naturalistic settings and hypothesized that animals learned through association of ideas, in accord with the philosophical tradition of associationism (Warren, 1921) that described how the human mind operated (Cumming, 1999; Furumoto & Scarborough, 1987). Although we can know our own consciousness, we can only infer consciousness in others, including animals; for Morgan, the criterion for inferring consciousness in animals is "circumstantial evidence that the animal . . . profits by experience" (Morgan, 1900, p. 42). In this way, Morgan stimulated interest in the study of learning, not only as an adaptation to the environment, but also as the criterion for inferring animal consciousness or mind.

At Clark, research in animal behavior attempted to describe the animal mind and to study the development of the nervous system. The former research was represented by Willard Small's use of the maze to study the mental processes of the white rat involved in learning (Small, 1900, 1901). The latter research was represented by H. H. Donaldson, who attempted to describe the growth of the nervous system in rats and humans (e.g., Donaldson, 1908). One purpose of this research by Donaldson and Small was to relate the complexities of the nervous system between species and between individuals in the same species to differences in behavioral and mental abilities.

Small employed a version of the Hampton Court maze (Munn, 1950) that later gave rise to the many variations (e.g., the T-maze, multiple T-maze, and the straight alley maze) that became standard laboratory equipment for the study of learning and the testing of learning theories of the 1930s through the 1950s. Donaldson and Swiss American psychiatrist Adolf Meyer are credited with helping to establish the albino rat as the dominant laboratory animal in American psychological laboratories for many decades (Logan, 1999).

The work at Clark proceeded in the spirit exemplified by Morgan and by E. L. Thorndike (1874–1949), who, in 1898, had insisted that "experiment must be substituted for observation and the collection of anecdotes" (Thorndike, 1898, p. 1126). Thorndike's dissertation, *Animal Intelligence* (1898), signaled a major shift from a subjective, introspective, anecdotal study of animals to an objective, quantitative experimental approach with an emphasis on learning (Galef, 1998; Stam & Kalmanovitch, 1998). Thorndike's emphasis on controlled observation was welcomed by Morgan, who advanced "the hope that comparative psychology has passed from the anecdote stage to the higher plane of verifiable observation, and that it is rising to the dignity of science" (Morgan, 1898, p. 250).

Thorndike had pursued graduate study at Harvard with an investigation of the behavior of chickens, until the protests of his landlady forced him to move his chicken experiments to the basement of William James's house (Dewsbury, 1998; Thorndike, 1936). Thorndike subsequently took his two "most educated chickens" to study the inheritance of acquired traits at Columbia University with James McKeen Cattell (p. 265). The topic did not prove very fruitful, and Thorndike chose instead to examine the performance of cats and small dogs in puzzle boxes. The choice of puzzle boxes was influenced by the work of Romanes and Morgan, who had described dogs and cats learning to open garden gates through trial and error (Morgan, 1900). Thorndike's boxes were designed to permit observation of animals' attempts to escape from the box to reach food (Burnham, 1972). Various boxes required manipulation of levers, pulling of loops, or combinations of responses to escape (Chance, 1999; Galef, 1998). Thorndike recorded and graphed the time taken to escape from the box as a function of the number of trials. He interpreted the gradual decline of the curve describing the time taken to escape from the box revealed by the graph to mean that learning proceeded gradually, through trial and error.

Responses that resulted in escape from the puzzle box appeared to be selected from random movements, in a manner analogous to the process of evolutionary selection. Thorndike insisted that responses were made directly to the stimulus situation, without the mediation of ideas. The bond between response and situation was strengthened if the response was followed by a satisfying outcome, or weakened if it was followed by an unsatisfactory consequence. This statement constituted Thorndike's "law of effect." He also held that bonds between the situation and response became strengthened through exercise and weakened by disuse: the "law of exercise" (Thorndike, 1913). Thorndike claimed that these two laws, together with the animal's "readiness" to respond in the situation, accounted for most of animal learning (Thorndike, 1913). In his early work in comparative psychology, Thorndike emphasized a discontinuity between animals and humans. By 1911, however, he reversed his position to emphasize instead the universality of the law of effect and other laws of learning (Bruce, 1997).

Although the thrust of Thorndike's laws was to specify regular relations between a situation and the responses that it may come to evoke, without any attempt to assess the content of the mind of the responding animal, comparative psychology did not immediately follow his lead. Concerns for the adaptive value of consciousness in humans and animals continued to be addressed in the early decades of the twentieth century (e.g., Judd, 1910). Identifying the levels of complexity of nervous systems that would justify inferences about the nature of animal consciousness and capacity for intelligent behavior (e.g., Yerkes, 1905) is best exemplified by what has sometimes been called the first textbook in comparative psychology, Margaret Washburn's *The Animal Mind* (1908) (Jaynes, 1968, cited in Furumoto & Scarborough, 1987). Margaret Floy Washburn (1871–1939), the first woman to earn a PhD in psychology and the second woman president of the American Psychological Association (1921), summarized and organized the scattered literature on animal psychology, provided a history of the movement, and offered an extensive discussion of methodology for research with animals (Washburn, 1908; Goodman, 1980). E. B. Titchener's first doctoral student, Washburn had applied to study psychology with James McKeen Cattell at Columbia, but Columbia, like Harvard and the Johns Hopkins University, permitted women to attend classes only unofficially as "hearers." Cattell, however, encouraged her to apply to Cornell, where she completed her degree in 1894. A report of her Cornell dissertation on the effects of visual imagery on tactile sensitivity was one of the few studies published in Wundt's *Philosophische Studien* that had not been completed at Leipzig.

Washburn sought to understand the animal's conscious experience in an approach to comparative psychology characterized as "subjective, inferential and rigorously logical" (Goodman, 1980, p. 75). Washburn was influenced by the research and writing of both Morgan and Thorndike; like

Thorndike, she advocated the use of objective and rigorous experimental procedures, but, like Morgan, she persisted in her view that animals possessed a consciousness that psychology was obliged to define and characterize (Washburn, 1917, 1926, 1936). To carry out its responsibility, psychology needed to adopt objective and rigorous experimental procedures. Despite the growing emphasis on the sufficiency of behavioral data and the emphatic rejection of mind and consciousness as the only legitimate subject matter for a scientific psychology, as Thorndike advocated, Washburn held to her position (Goodman, 1980).

Behaviorism

Animal psychology had drawn attention to the importance of behavior as a clue to mind, but inferences from behavior about animal consciousness were part of the expected interpretations of experimental results. But the focus of study was changing: "There is unquestionably a widespread movement on foot in which interest is centered on the results of conscious process, rather than in the processes themselves. This is peculiarly true in animal psychology; it is only less true in human psychology. In these cases interest [is] in what may for lack of a better term be called 'behavior'; and the analysis of consciousness is primarily justified by the light it throws on behavior, rather than vice versa" (Angell, 1911, p. 47).

The proposal that psychology reject its traditional definition as the science of mind and consciousness and redefine itself as a science of behavior came from John B. Watson (1913). Watson arrived at the University of Chicago in 1900 to begin graduate work following an undergraduate degree in philosophy and psychology from Furman University (Harris, 1999; O'Donnell, 1985). H. H. Donaldson, who had moved to the University of Chicago from Clark University, brought with him his research program that investigated the relation between the development of the nervous system and the behavior of the rat. Animal laboratories were few; in 1909, only about six laboratories were actively engaged in animal research (O'Donnell, 1985). For his dissertation, Watson chose to investigate the neurological correlates of problem solving in the white rat and carried out additional experiments with rats to determine which sensory modalities were necessary for learning a maze by systematically eliminating one modality at a time. He removed the eyes, tympanic membrane, olfactory bulbs, and whiskers and anesthetized the feet of rats and discovered that the animals seemed to use kinesthetic feedback to reach the goal box (Carr & Watson, 1908; Goodwin, 1999; J. B. Watson, 1907). Watson's first report of these experiments at the annual meeting of the APA held in

December 1906 in conjunction with the American Association for the Advancement of Science (AAAS) led to an outcry by antivivisectionists. He was publicly defended by Angell and by then APA president James Mark Baldwin (Dewsbury, 1990).

Watson had become disenchanted with the language of consciousness and mind, with the method of introspection, and was increasingly concerned about the status of animal research in psychology. Writing to fellow comparative psychologist Robert Mearns Yerkes in 1910, Watson expressed his identity problems: "I am a physiologist and I go so far as to say that I would remodel psychology as we now have it (human) and reconstruct our attitude with reference to the whole matter of consciousness. I don't believe the psychologist is studying consciousness any more than we are" (Watson, 1910, cited in J. A. Mills, 1998, p. 60).

In a series of lectures given at Columbia University in December 1912, Watson laid out his discomfort with a psychology of consciousness and proposed a psychology of behavior to take its place: "Psychology as the behaviorist views it . . . is a purely objective experimental branch of natural science. Its theoretical goal is the prediction and control of behavior. Introspection forms no essential part of its methods, nor is the scientific value of its data dependent on the readiness with which they lend themselves to interpretation in terms of consciousness" (Watson, 1913, p. 158). Although this so-called "Behaviorist Manifesto" did not produce a revolution in psychology (Leahey, 1992; Samelson, 1981), it did help to raise the status of animal research and place a greater emphasis on explaining behavior rather than mind, especially in research on animals (Watson, 1914). Watson's notion that the goal of psychology was to predict and control behavior incorporated the vision of psychology as a tool for social control and, therefore, its application to education, industry, and other areas of applied psychology (e.g., Buckley, 1982). Titchener accused Watson of turning psychology into a technology rather than a science (Samelson, 1981). But technology or not, Watson's view of science as requiring reliability of observations, public and repeatable, vitiated introspection as a scientific method. Watson argued that verbal reports to a stimulus, in a psychophysical experiment, such as "I see red," were behavioral in the same way that an animal might be trained to discriminate the color red from other colors (Watson, 1919).

J. B. Watson (1916) proposed that the conditioned motor reflex could be applied to animals and humans and thus form the building block of behavior. Like Titchener, Watson believed that science proceeded by analysis, but instead of the elements of mind, Watson sought the elements of behavior. The conditioned reflex was the elemental unit from which Watson proposed to build a science of behavior.

The study of reflexes has a long history within physiology (Boakes, 1984; Fearing, 1930). The Bell-Magendie law (Boakes, 1984; Goodwin, 1999) distinguished between the sensory and motor nerves at the level of the spinal cord. This distinction set the stage for an understanding of reflex action and stimulated research on the nature and speed of conduction of the nerve impulse that led to the studies of reaction time by Johannes Müller and Hermann von Helmholtz. Russian physiologist Ivan Mikhailovich Sechenov (1829–1905) demonstrated that cerebral processes could affect reflexive action by stimulating certain areas of the brain with salt crystals to decrease the intensity of reflexive movement of a frog's leg (Boakes, 1984; Koshtoyants, 1965). Sechenov (1863–1965) argued that the cause of psychical or psychological events is in the environment; external sensory stimulation produces all acts, conscious and unconscious, through the summation of excitatory and inhibitory activity in the brain. He suggested that a science of psychology based on introspective reports of humans is too complex and too subject to "the deceptive suggestions of the voice of our consciousness. . . . [O]nly physiology holds the key to the scientific analysis of psychical phenomena" (Sechenov, 1973 cited in Leahey, 2001, p. 216; see also, Boakes, 1984).

Ivan Petrovich Pavlov (1849–1936) was able to instantiate Sechenov's theoretical claims (Koshtoyants, 1965). Pavlov's research on the physiology of digestion that earned him the Nobel Prize in 1904 involved a method of "sham feeding" in which a fistula, or tube, in the esophagus prevented food placed in the mouth of the dog from reaching the stomach. A second tube inserted into the stomach was used to collect gastric juices. In the course of these experiments, Pavlov noted that gastric secretions occurred not only in response to food in the mouth but also merely to the sight of food, or of the assistant who usually fed the animal. He called these "psychic secretions." By using a fistula that could collect salivary secretions for the studies on digestion, Pavlov's student Stefan Vul'fson noted that not only did the salivary glands respond differently to different substances placed in the mouth, for example, sand, wet food, dry food, but, unlike other digestive organs, they showed the identical response when the dog was teased by only the sight of the substance (Boakes, 1984; Todes, 1997). Vul'fson and Pavlov used mentalistic terms in describing the reaction of the salivary glands to the sight of food: Dogs "judged," "sorted out," or "chose" their responses (Todes, 1997, p. 950).

Pavlov later changed "psychic reflex," to "conditional reflex," after experiments demonstrated the experimental regularity of what his co-worker Tolochinov referred to as a "reflex at a distance" (Todes, 1997, p. 951). Drawing on Sechenov's early experiments with inhibition of spinal reflexes, the work in Pavlov's laboratory focused on the establishment (conditioning) and removal (extinction) of reflexes to a variety of stimuli and their control by excitatory and inhibitory activity in the brain. Other investigators who explored questions of adaptation of organisms to environments paid more attention to the acquisition of new behavior than to the removal of established behaviors (Boakes, 1984).

J. B. Watson attempted to demonstrate how research on conditioned reflexes could reveal the origins of complex behavior patterns. In his most famous experiment, conducted with graduate student Rosalie Rayner, he conditioned emotional responses in an 11-month-old infant, "Albert B." By striking a steel bar with a hammer, Watson and Rayner were able to elicit crying in the infant; when they subsequently paired presentation of a white rat, to which Albert had shown no fear, with the striking of the bar, Albert showed fear to the rat. They reported successfully conditioning fear of the rat in Albert, and, further, the fear generalized to a rabbit, a dog, a fur coat, and a Santa Claus mask (J. B. Watson & Rayner, 1920; see Harris, 1979). The study was more a dramatic demonstration than a carefully controlled experiment, but nevertheless exemplified Watson's vision for identifying the origins and development of behavior and provided an approach to the study of the growth and development of children (Mateer, 1918).

Gestalt Psychology

A response to the introspective analysis of consciousness advocated by Titchener and the behavioral analysis of J. B. Watson came in the form of an approach to psychology that arose in Germany at about the same time that behaviorism had arisen in the United States. The term *gestalt,* translated as "whole" or "configuration," referred to an organized entity that was different from the sum of its constituent parts. The term was initially introduced by Christian von Ehrenfels, who pointed out that a melody played in two different keys is recognized as such even though the notes in each case are different. He suggested that combinations of elements produced a *"gestaltqualität,"* or whole-quality, that constituted a new element of consciousness. The use of the term by the triumvirate of Max Wertheimer, Kurt Koffka, and Wolfgang Köhler referred not to a new element but to the organized nature of conscious experience. The gestalt psychologists opposed what they perceived to be artificial attempts to reduce experience or behavior to constituent parts and then to synthesize them again into organized wholes, and articulated their views in influential books (e.g., Köhler, 1929).

Gestalt psychology was initiated by observations on apparent movement (Wertheimer, 1912), in which two lights located at some distance apart give rise to the experience of one light moving from one location to the other when the lights go on and off in sequence. The phenomena seemed incapable of explanation by introspective identification of sensory elements. The gestaltists proposed that the introspection appropriate to psychology was a description of experience, a naive introspection that described the experience without any attempt to subject it to analysis. Perceptual phenomena and conscious experience were not the only domains of gestalt theory; Köhler's research on chimpanzees (Köhler, 1926) suggested that learning occurred not through trial and error but by insight that resulted from a perceptual reorganization that produced a new way of seeing the problem to be solved. Neither Thorndike's trial-and-error explanations of learning nor behavioral analysis of organized goal-directed behavior seemed adequate to account for the behavior of the chimpanzees.

The disagreement with the structural approach to mind and the behavioral approach to behavior derived from fundamentally different assumptions about the nature of science. Titchener, and Watson as well, assumed that science proceeded by analysis, by breaking down chemical and material objects into the elements of which they are composed. The elemental analysis that Titchener perceived to be the hallmark of physics was a nineteenth-century model that had given way to analyses in terms of fields in which forces operated to determine organization of particles rather than particles or elements giving rise to organization (e.g., introducing a magnetic force placed among a random pattern of iron filings organizes the filings in terms of the directions of force). Field theory and the laws of organization were proposed to account for many phenomena (e.g., Ellis, 1950), not only of perception and problem solving and learning, but of, for example, social behavior (Asch, 1955), child development (Koffka, 1927), and thinking (Wertheimer, 1959), and served to prompt research designed to test theories in these areas.

Logical Positivism and Operationism

The abandonment of mind as psychology's subject matter, the increased attention to ensuring that scientific standards were met by procedures for gathering and treating data in laboratory and nonlaboratory research, and increased attention to theory building appeared to be signs of scientific maturity in psychology. These characteristics were most closely identified with the neo-behaviorist theories of learning and behavior that were the focus of much of the laboratory psychology from the 1930s to the 1960s. These theories focused on animal subjects and models of learning and behavior; their theoretical language was influenced by a philosophy of science of the period.

Continuing concern for the scientific status of psychology attracted psychologists to an approach to science advocated by Harvard physicist P. W. Bridgman (1927), who made the case for defining unobservable phenomena, such as gravity or hypothesized physical elements such as an electron, in terms of the operations by which their effects on observable events could be measured (Leahey, 2001; Smith, 1986). E. G. Boring's student, S. S. Stevens (1906–1973), at Harvard in psychology, proposed that psychology adopt a strict operationism (Stevens, 1935a, 1935b, 1939). Only terms that could be defined operationally were scientifically meaningful; for all practical purposes, only a behavioral psychology could meet this criterion (Leahey, 2001; J. A. Mills, 1998; Smith, 1986). The emphasis on operational definitions influenced the language of psychology (Mandler & Kessen, 1959) and the theories of behavior that evolved in the context of operationism and its philosophical forebear, logical positivism, an approach that limited science to observable phenomena. For psychology, it meant defining hunger, for example, in terms of such operations as hours of food deprivation, or a measure of blood sugar level, or the amount of time spent eating, each of which is an observable indicator of the unobservable hypothesized motivational condition of hunger. The neo-behaviorists who shaped what is known as the "Golden Age of Learning Theory" from 1930 to 1950 adopted some ideas from logical positivism and operationism, although each of them was to formulate his own vision of behaviorism (J. A. Mills, 1998; Smith, 1986).

The Neo-Behaviorists: Guthrie, Tolman, and Hull

Edwin R. Guthrie (1886–1959), the "most starkly empiricist of all the neo-behaviorists" (J. A. Mills, 1998, p. 79), defined mind as "a mode of behavior, namely, that behavior which changes with use or practice-behavior, in other words, that exhibits learning" (E. R. Guthrie, 1935/1960, p. 3). The ability to learn, as C. Lloyd Morgan had suggested, characterized the possession of mind in living creatures. Guthrie's theory of learning was deceptively simple: Learning occurs through the development of associations between stimuli and responses. These associations are formed by contiguity: "A combination of stimuli which has accompanied a movement will on its recurrence tend to be followed by that movement" (p. 23). He rejected Thorndike's laws of effect and of exercise, claiming instead that the apparently gradual nature of learning was a result of a series of one-trial situations in which movements, small muscle responses, rather than acts were learned in response to stimuli. The role of the consequences of responding,

whether satisfying or annoying, was to change the stimulus situation, not to strengthen some unobservable bond between stimulus and response.

In contrast to E. R. Guthrie's molecular approaches to learning, Edward Chace Tolman (1886–1959) offered a molar theory of the psychology of learning. For E. R. Guthrie and for J. B. Watson, descriptions of learned behavior were confined to descriptions of stimulus events and responses. Tolman, in contrast, proposed a theory that interpreted behavior in terms of "motive, purpose and determining tendency" (Tolman, 1922, p. 53). For Tolman, cognitive events intervened between the antecedent stimuli and their behavioral consequences. Learning and performance were not synonymous (Innis, 1999; Kimble, 1985; Tolman & Honzik, 1930); performance was the observable behavior, while learning was the hypothesized state that accounted for the change in behavior. Tolman described the action of intervening variables on the functional relationship between the independent and dependent variables; that is, between the environmental stimuli and physiological state of the organism on the one side and the overt behavior on the other (Tolman, 1932, p. 2; see also Innis, 1999; Kimble, 1985). The most important intervening variables were cognitions, defined as expectations about the relationship between signs, stimuli, and significates, rewards or goal objects (J. A. Mills, 1998; Smith, 1986). Tolman hypothesized the formation of "cognitive maps" or cognitive representations of the environment in rats learning a maze. These cognitive maps could be empirically demonstrated in maze experiments in which, for example, blocking a previously used route to a goal resulted in rats choosing the next shortest path to the goal (Tolman, Ritchie, & Kalish, 1946).

Clark Hull (1884–1952) proposed a formal logico-deductive theory of behavior: "In science an observed event is said to be explained when the proposition expressing it has been logically derived from a set of definitions and postulates coupled with certain observed conditions antecedent to the event" (Hull, 1943, p. 3). Hull's theoretical treatment of psychology consisted of a set of postulates and corollaries and their mathematical statements to enable quantitative predictions about behavior. Hull's goal was to develop psychology as a natural science by demonstrating that behavioral phenomena obey universal, quantitative laws that can be stated by equations comparable to physical laws, "of the type governing the law of falling bodies" (Hull, 1950, p. 221). Even centuries after Kant, Hull was striving to demonstrate that psychology could indeed become a science that met the same standards as the physical sciences. For example, Hull (1934a, 1934b) proposed that the serial position effect in learning a list of words (the phenomena that errors occur more frequently in learning and in the recall of words from the middle of a serial list) exemplifies the same general law that describes the pattern of errors made by rats learning a complex maze (more errors occur in the center of the maze than at the start and the finish).

Hull's research program was directed toward the discovery of such laws and the formulation of the equations that described them. His theory of behavior formulated theoretical variables in operational terms, defined them by equations, and predicted experimental results. Experiments by Hull, Tolman, and their students were designed to provide crucial tests of predictions from their respective theories. For example, Hull's theory hypothesized that learning occurred through reinforcement, defined in terms of the extent to which reinforcement reduced a motivational drive; Tolman, on the other hand, argued that reinforcement in this sense was unnecessary for learning (Tolman & Honzik, 1930). Resolution of such theoretical issues was difficult; moreover, the precise predictions from Hull's formal theory were frequently not confirmed, and criticism of the theory began to mount from a variety of sources, including Hull's own students (J. A. Mills, 1998). Differences between the theories of Hull and Tolman came to seem less substantive and more a preference for particular terminology and the reification of intervening variables (Kendler, 1952).

The Radical Behaviorism of B. F. Skinner

Burrhus Frederick Skinner (1904–1990) questioned whether theories of learning were necessary in view of what appeared to be fruitless theoretical tests (Skinner, 1950). He argued instead for a purely empirical description of behavior, eschewing any hypothetical or intervening nonobservable variable in his description of behavior, a position that he had established in his first major publication (Skinner, 1938). His manipulation of the contingency between an operant (emitted) behavior and a reinforcer constituted his program of research, carried out in the operant-conditioning chamber more popularly known as a "Skinner Box." With rats and later pigeons as his experimental subjects, Skinner measured cumulative responses over elapsed time as a function of reinforcement schedules (Ferster & Skinner, 1957). Intervening variables, such as drive or motivation, were defined operationally in terms of number of hours of deprivation or percent of free-feeding body weight. The reports of experiments by Skinner and his followers, with few animals but a large number of responses, met with rejection from editors whose definition of an experiment required a research design comparing experimental and control groups with a statistical test of the significance of the difference between them. The result was the establishment of the *Journal for the Experimental*

Analysis of Behavior in 1958 (Krantz, 1972). Skinner's approach to behavior extended to the development and use of language (Skinner, 1957) and to the technology of teaching (Skinner, 1968).

The Rise of Cognitive Psychology: Mentalism Revisited

The experiments engendered by the debates among the different approaches to learning and behavior continued to dominate the literature of experimental psychology at mid-century. However, the traditional methods and research topics of the psychological laboratory also flourished; although the era of the schools had ended, they left a legacy of influence on the research conducted within psychology. Introspection as a source of psychological data lost its primacy with the end of structuralism; introspective reports resumed their more limited role in assessing the quality and/or intensity of sensory experience in psychophysical experiments. Articles reporting on experiments on perception, stimulated in part by gestalt psychology's emphasis upon perceptual organization, continued to appear in psychological journals, together with studies of the higher mental processes of thinking and problem solving (e.g., Wertheimer, 1959). Functional psychology, more of an attitude than a systematic position, characterized American psychology generally and fostered experiments on serial list and paired associate learning and the interference theory of forgetting, continuing the research tradition emanating from the laboratories of Ebbinghaus and G. E. Müller (McGeoch, 1942). Although research on higher mental processes in animals had not been entirely neglected (Dewsbury, 2000), behaviorism left a legacy of animal research that focused on stimulus-response interpretations of the results of maze learning studies, classical conditioning experiments, and, increasingly, of behavior in operant-conditioning chambers. Psychology redefined itself from the science of mind to the science of behavior. References to mind or mental processes were found only infrequently in textbooks and journals.

The molecular, elemental, and mechanistic analyses of behaviorism, emphasizing peripheral sensory-motor relations, were not limited to research on learning. Child psychology, for example, was strongly influenced by studies of the conditioned reflex (e.g., Mateer, 1918) and Watson's admitted premature claim that, given a dozen healthy infants, he could make of them anything he chose (J. B. Watson, 1924). Emphasis on the study of sensory-motor and nervous-system development in young children led to an emphasis on developmental norms that were postulated to follow relatively fixed maturational principles (e.g., Gesell & Ilg, 1946). These principles and norms were challenged by research that combined behavioral and maturational approaches in examining motor development in children (e.g., McGraw, 1935; 1943).

In the decades of the 1950s and 1960s, the language and models that stimulated psychological research began to change. Explanations of behavior derived from experiments on maze learning and classical and operant-conditioning research came under attack from those studying more complex behavior patterns (e.g., Harlow, 1953). Rote learning of serial lists and verbal paired associates were acknowledged to represent only a limited domain of human learning (Melton, 1956). Information theory, developed during World War II as a tool for measuring the capacity of humans as processors and transmitters of information, provided a new measure of human performance and implied capacities for making judgments and choices (Attneave, 1959). Information theory offered fresh interpretations of choice reaction-time experiments (e.g., Hick, 1952) and the limits of human attention and immediate memory (Miller, 1956). Discussions of human capacities to reduce, transmit, or create information renewed interest in cognitive capacities of decision making and problem solving that suggested analogies to the recently developed technology of the computer.

Interest in cognitive development revitalized child psychology in moving from a focus on sensory-motor development to a focus on thinking, the formation of concepts, and the child's understanding of the world. The theories of Jean Piaget (1896–1980) that describe the development of language and cognition in childhood had appeared in the 1920s and 1930s in Europe (e.g., Piaget, 1929) but had an impact in the United States only decades later (Flavell, 1963). Experimental research that explored cognitive and social development in children came to dominate the field of *developmental* psychology, no longer simply *child* psychology but soon to cover the life span. This shift in emphasis in the study of human development paralleled changes in research on adults and on animals.

Psychologists appeared to be less self-consciously concerned with the status of psychology as a science and more concerned with the kind of science psychology was to be. The behavioral view of a largely passive organism whose mechanical behavior was governed by environmental events became an increasingly less satisfactory model. Calls for a humanistic, rather than a mechanistic, science of psychology (Giorgi, 1970; Maslow, 1966) called for a view of human beings as actively engaged with the environment, thinking and deciding rather than simply responding to external events. The results of Pavlovian conditioning experiments began to be interpreted in terms of cognitive events (e.g., Rescorla, 1966) and signaled the increasing willingness to consider the role of

mental processes that determined behavior in both humans and animals. The journals *Cognitive Psychology* (1970) and *Memory and Cognition* (1973) were founded to provide an outlet to the burgeoning research in human memory that was less characteristic of traditional associationistic theories (Warren, 1921; Robinson, 1932/1964) and more influenced by analogies to computers and conceptions of information processing. Topics of the older mentalistic psychology, such as attention, concept formation, and thinking, became more prominent in psychological research. The term *mind,* banished from the psychological lexicon in the heyday of behavioral theories, began to reappear in textbooks and, more significantly, in developing theories of human and animal cognitive capacities. The magnitude of the shift in research agendas and theoretical constructs suggested that psychology had undergone a revolutionary change, while others regarded the shift as part of the normal historical development of the discipline (Leahey, 1992). Nevertheless, these developments in scientific psychology represent the continuing vitality of the discipline as psychologists address traditional problems of mind and behavior in forging the science of psychology. These efforts inform the content of the volumes and chapters that follow and properly belong to contemporary psychology.

REFERENCES

Adler, H. E. (1966). Translator's foreword. In D. H. Howes & E. G. Boring (Eds.), *Gustav Fechner: Elements of psychophysics* (pp. xix–xxvi). New York: Holt.

Allport, G. (1937). *Personality: A psychological interpretation.* New York: Holt.

American Psychological Association. (1983). *Publication manual* (3rd ed.). Washington, D.C.: APA.

American Psychological Association. (2001). *Publication manual* (5th ed.). Washington, D.C.: APA.

Angell, J. R. (1905). *Psychology.* New York: Holt.

Angell, J. R. (1907). The province of functional psychology. *Psychological Review, 14,* 61–91.

Angell, J. R. (1911). Philosophical and psychological usage of the terms mind, consciousness, and soul. *Psychological Bulletin, 8,* 46–47.

Asch, S. E. (1955). Opinions and social pressure. *Scientific American, 193,* 31–35.

Attneave, F. (1959). *Applications of information theory to psychology.* New York: Holt.

Baldwin, J. M. (1895). *Mental developmental in the child and the race: Methods and processes.* New York: Macmillan.

Baldwin, J. M. (1897). *Social and ethical interpretations of mental development: A study in social psychology.* New York: Macmillan.

Bazerman, C. (1987). Codifying the social scientific style: The APA *publication manual* as a behavioristic rhetoric. In J. S. Nelson, A. Megill, & D. N. McCloskey (Eds.), *The rhetoric of the human sciences* (pp. 125–144). Madison: University of Wisconsin Press.

Ben-David, J. (1971). *The scientists role in society.* Englewood Cliffs, NJ: Prentice Hall.

Ben-David, J., & Collins, R. (1966). Social factors in the origins of a new science. *American Sociological Review, 31,* 451–465.

Benjamin, L. T., Jr. (2000). The psychology laboratory at the turn of the century. *American Psychologist, 55,* 318–321.

Benjamin, L. T., Jr., Durkin, M., Link, M., Vestal, M., & Acord, J. (1992). Wundt's American doctoral students. *American Psychologist, 47,* 123–131.

Bently, M., Hodge, F. W., Passano, E. B., Peerenboom, C. A., Warren, H. C., & Washburn, M. W. (1929). Instructions in regard to preparation of manuscript. *Psychological Bulletin, 26,* 57–63.

Blumenthal, A. (1985a). Shaping a tradition: Experimentalism begins. In C. E. Buxton (Ed.), *Points of view in the modern history of psychology* (pp. 51–83). New York: Academic Press.

Blumenthal, A. (1985b). Wilhelm Wundt: Psychology as a propaedeutic science. In C. E. Buxton (Ed.), *Points of view in the modern history of psychology* (pp. 19–50). New York: Academic Press.

Boakes, R. (1984). *From Darwinism to behaviourism: Psychology and the minds of animals.* Cambridge, England: Cambridge University Press.

Boring, E. G. (1950). *A history of experimental psychology* (2nd ed.). New York: Appleton-Century-Crofts.

Boring, E. G. (1965). On the subjectivity of important historical dates: Leipzig, 1879. *Journal of the History of the Behavioral Sciences, 1,* 5–9.

Bridgman, P. W. (1927). *The logic of modern physics.* New York: Macmillan.

Bringmann, W. G., Balance, W. D. G., & Evans, R. (1975). Wilhelm Wundt 1832–1920: A brief biographical sketch. *Journal of the History of the Behavioral Sciences, 11,* 287–297.

Bringmann, W. G., Bringmann, N. J., & Ungerer, G. A. (1980). The establishment of Wundt's laboratory: An archival and documentary study. In W. G. Bringmann & R. D. Tweney (Eds.), *Wundt studies: A centennial collection* (pp. 123–159). Toronto, Ontario, Canada: C. J. Hogrefe.

Bruce, D. (1997). Puzzling over animal intelligence. *Contemporary Psychology, 42,* 879–882.

Buckley, K. W. (1982). The selling of a psychologist: John Broadus Watson and the application of behavioral techniques to advertising. *Journal of the History of the Behavioral Sciences, 18,* 207–221.

Burnham, J. (1972). Thorndike's puzzle boxes. *Journal of the History of the Behavioral Sciences, 8,* 159–167.

Buxton, C. (1985a). American functionalism. In C. Buxton (Ed.), *Points of view in the modern history of psychology* (pp. 113–140). New York: Academic Press.

Buxton, C. (1985b). Early sources and basic conceptions of functionalism. In C. Buxton (Ed.), *Points of view in the modern history of psychology* (pp. 85–111). New York: Academic Press.

Cairns, R. (1992). The making of a developmental science: The contributions and intellectual heritage of James Mark Baldwin. *Developmental Psychology, 28,* 17–24.

Calkins, M. W. (1894a). Association I. *Psychological Review, 1,* 476–483.

Calkins, M. W. (1894b). Wellesley College psychological studies. *Educational Review, 8,* 269–286.

Calkins, M. W. (1901). *Introduction to psychology.* New York: Macmillan.

Calkins, M. W. (1910). The teaching of elementary psychology in colleges supposed to have no laboratory. *Psychological Monographs, 12*(4, Whole No. 51), 41–53.

Calkins, M. W. (1919). *A first book in psychology* (4th rev. ed.). New York: Macmillan.

Camfield, T. (1973). The professionalization of American psychology, 1870–1917. *Journal of the History of the Behavioral Sciences, 9,* 66–75.

Capshew, J. (1992). Psychologists on site. *American Psychologist, 47,* 132–142.

Carr, H., & Watson, J. B. (1908). Orientation in the white rat. *Journal of Comparative Neurology and Psychology, 18,* 27–44.

Cattell, J. M. (1888). The psychological laboratory at Leipsic. *Mind, 13,* 37–51.

Cattell, J. M. (1947a). The conceptions and methods of psychology. In A. T. Poffenberger (Ed.), *James McKeen Cattell: Man of science* (Vol. 2, pp. 197–207). Lancaster, PA: Science Press. (Original work published 1904)

Cattell, J. M. (1947b). On the time required for recognizing and naming letters and words, pictures and colors. In A. T. Poffenberger (Ed.), *James McKeen Cattell: Man of science* (Vol. 1, pp. 13–25). Lancaster, PA: Science Press. (Original work published 1885–1886)

Cattell, J. M. (1947c). Physical and mental measurements of the students of Columbia University. *Psychological Review, 3,* 618–648. In A. T. Poffenberger (Ed.), *James McKeen Cattell: Man of science* (Vol. 1, pp. 305–330). Lancaster, PA: Science Press. (Original work published 1896)

Chadbourne, C. (1872). *Instinct: Its office in the animal kingdom and its relation to the higher powers in man.* New York: Putnam.

Chance, P. (1999). Thorndike's puzzle boxes and the origins of the experimental analysis of behavior. *Journal of the Experimental Analysis of Behavior, 72,* 433–440.

Charlesworth, W. (1992). Darwin and developmental psychology: Past and present. *Developmental Psychology, 28,* 5–16.

Cousine, V. (1864). *Elements of psychology* (4th ed., C. Henry, Trans.). New York: Ivison, Phinney, Blakeman.

Croce, P. J. (1999). Physiology as the antechamber to metaphysics: The young William James's hope for a philosophical psychology. *History of Psychology, 2,* 302–323.

Cronbach, L. (1957). The two disciplines of scientific psychology. *American Psychologist, 12,* 671–684.

Cumming, W. W. (1999). A review of Geraldine Joncich's: The sane positivist: A biography of Edward L. Thorndike. *Journal of the Experimental Analysis of Behavior, 72,* 429–432.

Danziger, K. (1980). The history of introspection reconsidered. *Journal of the History of the Behavioral Sciences, 16,* 241–262.

Danziger, K. (1985). The origins of the psychological experiment as a social institution. *American Psychologist, 40,* 133–140.

Danziger, K. (1990). *Constructing the subject.* Cambridge, England: Cambridge University Press.

Darwin, C. (1859). *On the origin of species.* London: Murray.

Darwin, C. (1871). *The descent of man, and selection in relation to sex* (Vols. 1–2). London: Murray.

Dehue, T. (1997). Deception, efficiency, and random groups. *Isis, 88,* 653–673.

Dehue, T. (2000). From deception trials to control reagents. *American Psychologist, 55,* 264–268.

Dewey, J. (1884). The new psychology. *Andover Review, 2,* 278–289.

Dewey, J. (1896). The reflex arc concept in psychology. *Psychological Review, 3,* 357–370.

Dewsbury, D. A. (1990). Early interactions between animal psychologists and animal activists and the founding of the APA Committee on Precautions in Animal Experimentation. *American Psychologist, 45,* 315–327.

Dewsbury, D. A. (1998). Celebrating E. L. Thorndike and a century after *animal intelligence. American Psychologist, 53,* 1121–1124.

Dewsbury, D. A. (2000). Comparative cognition in the 1930's. *Psychonomic Bulletin and Review, 7,* 267–283.

Diehl, L. A. (1986). The paradox of G. Stanley Hall: Foe of coeducation and educator of women. *American Psychologist, 41,* 868–878.

Dodge, R. (1912). The theory and limitations of introspection. *American Journal of Psychology, 23,* 214–229.

Donaldson, H. H. (1908). Comparison of the albino rat with man with respect to the growth of the brain and of the spinal cord. *Journal of Comparative Neurology and Physiology, 18,* 345–392.

Ebbinghaus, H. (1913). *Über das gedächtnis: Untersuchen zur experimentellen psychologie* [Memory: A contribution to experimental psychology] (H. A. Ruger & H. Bussenius, Trans.). Leipzig, Germany: Duncker & Humblot. (Original work published 1885)

Ellis, W. D. (1950). *A source book of Gestalt psychology.* London: Kegan Paul. (First published 1938)

English, H. B. (1921). In aid of introspection. *American Journal of Psychology, 32,* 404–414.

Evans, R. (1972). E. B. Titchener and his lost system. *Journal of the History of the Behavioral Sciences, 8,* 168–180.

Evans, R. (1981). Introduction: The historical context. In F. Burkhardt & F. Bowers (Eds.), *The works of William James: The principles of psychology* (Vol. 1, pp. xlx–lxviii). Cambridge, MA: Harvard University Press.

Evans, R. (1984). The origins of American academic psychology. In J. Brozek (Ed.), *Explorations in the history of psychology in the United States* (pp. 17–60). Lewisburg, PA: Bucknell University Press.

Fancher, R. (1996). *Pioneers of psychology.* New York: Norton.

Fay, J. W. (1939). *American psychology before William James.* Brunswick, NJ: Rutgers University Press.

Fearing, F. (1930). *Reflex action: A study in the history of physiological psychology.* Baltimore: Williams & Wilkins.

Ferster, C., & Skinner, B. F. (1957). *Schedules of reinforcement.* New York: Appleton-Century-Crofts.

Fitzpatrick, E. (1990). *Endless crusade: Women social scientists and progressive reform.* New York: Oxford University Press.

Flavell, J. (1963). *The developmental psychology of Jean Piaget.* Princeton, NJ: Van Nostrand.

Fuchs, A. (1997). Ebbinghaus's contributions to psychology after 1885. *American Journal of Psychology, 110,* 621–633.

Fuchs, A. (2000a). Contributions of American mental philosophers to psychology in the United States. *History of Psychology, 3,* 3–19.

Fuchs, A. (2000b). Teaching the introductory in psychology circa 1900. *American Psychologist, 55,* 492–495.

Furumoto, L. (1980). Mary Whiton Calkins (1863–1930). *Psychology of Women Quarterly, 5,* 55–68.

Furumoto, L. (1987). On the margins: women and the professionalization of psychology in the United States, 1890–1940. In M. Ash & W. Woodward (Eds.), *Psychology in twentieth century thought and society* (pp. 93–113). Cambridge, England: Cambridge University Press.

Furumoto, L., & Scarborough, E. (1987). Placing women in the history of comparative psychology: Margaret Floy Washburn and Margaret Morse Nice. In E. Tobach (Ed.), *Historical perspectives and the international status of comparative psychology* (pp. 103–117). Hillsdale, N.J: Erlbaum.

Galef, B. G. (1998). Edward Thorndike revolutionary psychologist, ambiguous biologist. *American Psychologist, 53,* 1128–1134.

Geissler, L. (1909). The measurement of attention. *American Journal of Psychology, 20,* 473–529.

Gesell, A., & Ilg, F. (1946). *The child from five to ten.* New York: Harper.

Giorgi, A. (1970). *Psychology as a human science.* New York: Harper & Row.

Goodman, E. S. (1980). Margaret, F. Washburn. (1871–1939): First woman PhD in psychology. *Psychology of Women Quarterly, 5,* 69–80.

Goodwin, C. J. (1999). *A history of modern psychology.* New York: Wiley.

Green, C. (Ed.). (2000). *Institutions of early experimental psychology: Laboratories, courses, journals and associations* [Online]. Retrieved from www.psychclassics.yorku.ca/Special/Institutions/

Gregory, R. J. (1992). *Psychological testing: History, principles, and applications.* Boston: Allyn & Bacon.

Guthrie, E. R. (1960). *The psychology of learning* (Rev. ed.). Gloucester, MA: Peter Smith. (Original work published 1935)

Guthrie, R. (1998). *Even the rat was white* (2nd ed.). Boston: Allyn & Bacon.

Hall, G. S. (1901). The new psychology. *Harper's Monthly Magazine, 103,* 727–732.

Hall, G. S. (1904). *Adolescence: Its psychology and its relations to physiology, anthropology, sociology, sex, crime, religion, and education* (Vols. 1–2). New York: Appleton.

Hall, G. S. (1923). *Life and confessions of a psychologist.* New York: Appleton.

Harlow, H. (1953). Mice, monkeys, men, and motives. *Psychological Review, 60,* 23–32.

Harris, B. (1979). Whatever happened to Little Albert. *American Psychologist, 34,* 151–160.

Harris, B. (1999). John Broadus Watson. In J. A. Garraty & M. C. Carnes (Eds.), *American National Biography* (Vol. 22, pp. 795–797). New York: Oxford University Press.

Haupt, E. (1998). Origins of American psychology in the work of G. E. Müller: Classical psychophysics and serial learning. In R. W. Rieber & K. Salzinger (Eds.), *Psychology: Theoretical-historical perspectives* (pp. 16–75). Washington, DC: American Psychological Association.

Heidbreder, E. (1933). *Seven psychologies.* New York: Century.

Hick, W. E. (1952). On the rate of gain of information. *Quarterly Journal of Experimental Psychology, 4,* 11–26.

Hickok, L. P. (1854). *Empirical psychology.* New York: Ivison & Phinney.

Hoffman, R. R., Bringmann, W. G., Bamberg, M., & Klein, R. (1987). Some historical observations on Ebbinghaus. In D. S. Gorfein & R. R. Hoffman (Eds.), *Memory and learning: The Ebbinghaus centennial conference* (pp. 57–75). Hillsdale, NJ: Erlbaum.

Hull, C. L. (1934a). The concept of the habit-family hierarchy and maze learning: Part I. *Psychological Review, 41,* 33–54.

Hull, C. L. (1934b). The concept of the habit-family hierarchy and maze learning: Part II. *Psychological Review, 41,* 134–152.

Hull, C. L. (1943). *Principles of behavior.* New York: Appleton-Century-Crofts.

Hull, C. L. (1950). A primary social science law. *Scientific Monthly, 71,* 221–228.

Innis, N. K. (1999, August 20–24). *Expectation and hypotheses: E. C. Tolman and animal cognition.* Paper presented at the 107th annual meeting of the American Psychological Association, Boston.

James, W. (1890). *The principles of psychology* (Vols. 1–2). New York: Holt.

James, W. (1892a). A plea for psychology as a "natural science." *Philosophical Review, 1,* 146–153.

James, W. (1892b). *Psychology: The briefer course.* New York: Holt.

James, W. (1920). Letter to Thomas Ward, Nov., 1867. In H. James (Ed.), *The Letters of William James* (Vol. 1, pp. 118–119). Boston: Atlantic Monthly Press.

Jastrow, J. (1886). Experimental psychology in Leipzig. *Science, 8,* 459–462.

Judd, C. H. (1907). *Laboratory manual of psychology* (Vol. 2). New York: Scribner's.

Judd, C. H. (1910). Evolution and consciousness. *Psychological Review, 17,* 77–97.

Kendler, H. (1952). "What is learned?" A theoretical blind alley. *Psychological Review, 59,* 269–277.

Kimble, G. A. (1985). Conditioning and learning. In S. Koch & D. E. Leary (Eds.), *A century of psychology as science* (pp. 284–335). New York: McGraw-Hill.

Koffka, K. (1927). *The growth of the mind.* New York: Harcourt, Brace.

Kohler, R. (1990). The Ph.D. machine. *Isis, 81,* 638–662.

Köhler, W. (1926). *The mentality of apes.* New York: Harcourt, Brace.

Köhler, W. (1929). *Gestalt psychology.* New York: Liveright.

Koshtoyants, K. (1965). I. M. Sechenov (1829–1905). In I. Sechenov (Ed.), *Reflexes of the brain* (pp. 119–139). Cambridge, MA: MIT Press.

Krantz, D. L. (1972). Schools and systems: The mutual isolation of operant and non-operant psychology as a case study. *Journal of the History of the Behavioral Sciences, 8,* 86–102.

Kusch, M. (1995). Recluse, interlocutory, interrogator: Natural and social order in turn-of-the-century psychological research schools. *Isis, 86,* 419–439.

Ladd, G. T. (1888). *Elements of physiological psychology.* New York: Scribner's.

Langfeld, H. S., & Allport, F. H. (1916). An elementary laboratory course in psychology. Boston: Houghton & Mifflin.

Leahey, T. H. (1981). The mistaken mirror: On Wundt's and Titchener's psychologies. *Journal of the History of the Behavioral sciences, 17,* 273–282.

Leahey, T. H. (1992). The mythical revolutions of American psychology. *American Psychologist, 47,* 308–318.

Leahey, T. H. (2001). *A history of modern psychology.* Upper Saddle River, NJ: Prentice Hall.

Leary, D. (1978). The philosophical development of the conception of psychology in Germany, 1780–1850. *Journal of the History of the Behavioral Sciences, 14,* 113–121.

Leary, D. (1987). Telling likely stories: The rhetoric of the new psychology, 1880–1920. *Journal of the History of the Behavioral Sciences, 23,* 315–331.

Logan, C. A. (1999). The altered rationale for the choice of a standard animal in experimental psychology: Henry, H. Donaldson, Adolf Meyer, and "the" albino rat. *History of Psychology, 2,* 3–24.

Mandler, G., & Kessen, W. (1959). *The language of psychology.* New York: Wiley.

Marshall, M. (1982). Physics, metaphysics, and Fechner's psychophysics. In W. R. Woodward & M. G. Ash (Eds.), *The problematic science: Psychology in nineteenth thought* (pp. 65–81). New York: Praeger.

Maslow, A. (1966). *The psychology of science.* New York: Harper & Row.

Mateer, F. (1918). *Child behavior.* Boston: Badger.

McCosh, J. (1886). *Psychology: The cognitive powers.* New York: Scribner's.

McCosh, J. (1887). *Psychology: The motive powers.* New York: Scribner's.

McGeoch, J. (1942). *The psychology of human learning.* New York: Longmans, Green.

McGraw, M. (1935). *Growth: A study of Johnny and Jimmy.* New York: Appleton-Century-Crofts.

McGraw, M. (1943). *The neuromuscular maturation of the human infant.* New York: Columbia University Press.

McReynolds, P. (1996). Lightner Witmer: A centennial tribute. *American Psychologist, 51,* 237–240.

Melton, A. W. (1956). Present accomplishments and future trends in problem-solving and learning theory. *American Psychologist, 11,* 278–281.

Milar, K. S. (1999). A coarse and clumsy tool: Helen Thompson Wooley and the Cincinnati Vocation Bureau. *History of Psychology, 2,* 219–235.

Milar, K. S. (2000). The first generation of women psychologists and the psychology of women. *American Psychologist, 55,* 616–619.

Miller, G. (1956). The magical number seven plus or minus two: Some limits on our capacity for processing information. *Psychological Review, 63,* 81–97.

Mills, E. (1969). *George Trumbull Ladd: Pioneer American psychologist.* Cleveland, OH: Case Western Reserve.

Mills, J. A. (1998). *Control: A history of behavioral psychology.* New York: New York University Press.

Miner, B. (1904). The changing attitude of American universities toward psychology. *Science, 20,* 299–307.

Morgan, C. L. (1898). Animal intelligence: An experimental study. *Nature, 58,* 249–250.

Morgan, C. L. (1890–1891). *Animal life and intelligence.* London: Edward Arnold.

Morgan, C. L. (1896) *Habit and instinct.* London: Edward Arnold.

Morgan, C. L. (1900). *Animal behaviour.* London: Edward Arnold.

Munn, N. (1950). *Handbook of experimental research on the rat.* Boston: Houghton Mifflin.

Murchison, C. (Ed.). (1926). *Psychologies of 1925.* Worcester, MA: Clark University.

Murchison, C. (Ed.). (1930). *Psychologies of 1930.* Worcester, MA: Clark University.

Murray, D. J. (1976). Research on human memory in the nineteenth century. *Canadian Journal of Psychology, 30,* 201–220.

Murray, D. J. (1988). *A history of Western psychology* (2nd ed.). Englewood Cliffs, NJ: Prentice Hall.

Murray, D. J., & Bandomir, C. A. (2000). G. E. Muller (1911, 1913, 1917) on memory. *Psychologie et Histoire, 1,* 208–232.

Nichols, H. (1893). The psychological laboratory at Harvard. *McClures, 1,* 399–409.

O'Donnell, J. M. (1985). *The origins of behaviorism: American psychology 1870–1920.* New York: New York University Press.

Piaget, J. (1929). *The child's conception of the world.* New York: Harcourt Brace.

Porter, N. (1868). *The human intellect.* New York: Scribner.

Posner, M. I., & Raichle, M. E. (1994). *Images of mind.* New York: Scientific American Library.

Postman, L. (1968). Hermann Ebbinghaus. *American Psychologist, 23,* 149–157.

Raphelson, A. (1973). The pre-Chicago association of the early functionalists. *Journal of the History of the Behavioral Sciences, 9,* 115–122.

Rauch, F. (1840). *Psychology, or a view of the human soul, including anthropology.* New York: M. W. Dodd.

Rescorla, R. (1966). Predictability and number of pairings in Pavlovian fear conditioning. *Psychonomic Science, 4,* 383–384.

Richards, R. (1992). *The meaning of evolution.* Chicago: University of Chicago Press.

Roback, A. A. (1952). *History of American psychology.* New York: Library Publishers.

Robinson, E. S. (1964). *Association theory today.* New York: Hafner. (Original work published 1932)

Romanes, G. J. (1892). *Animal intelligence.* New York: Appleton.

Ross, D. (1972). *G. Stanley Hall: The psychologist as prophet.* Chicago: University of Chicago Press.

Rucci, A. J., & Tweney, R. D. (1980). Analysis of variance and the second discipline of scientific psychology: A historical account. *Psychological Bulletin, 87,* 166–184.

Samelson, F. (1981). The struggle for scientific authority: The reception of Watson's behaviorism, 1913–1920. *Journal of the History of the Behavioral Sciences, 17,* 399–425.

Sanford, E. C. (1897). *A course in experimental psychology. Part 1: Sensation and perception.* Boston: D. C. Heath.

Sanford, E. C. (1910). The teaching of elementary psychology in colleges and universities with laboratories. *Psychological Monographs, 12* (4, Whole No. 51), 58–61.

Scarborough, E., & Furumoto, L. (1987). *Untold lives: The first generation of American women psychologists.* New York: Columbia University Press.

Seashore, C. E. (1909). *Elementary experiments in psychology.* New York: Holt.

Sechenov, I. M. (1965). *Reflexes of the brain.* Cambridge, MA: MIT Press. (Original work published 1863)

Shields, S. A. (1975). Functionalism, Darwinism, and the psychology of women: A study in social myth. *American Psychologist, 30,* 739–754.

Skinner, B. F. (1938). *The behavior of organisms.* New York: Appleton-Century-Crofts.

Skinner, B. F. (1950). Are theories of learning necessary? *Psychological Review, 57,* 193–216.

Skinner, B. F. (1957). *Verbal behavior.* New York: Appleton-Century-Crofts.

Skinner, B. F. (1968). *The technology of teaching.* New York: Appleton-Century-Crofts.

Small, W. (1900). An experimental study of the mental processes of the rat. *American Journal of Psychology, 11,* 133–165.

Small, W. (1901). Experimental study of the mental processes of the rat. *American Journal of Psychology, 12,* 206–239.

Smith, L. (1986). *Behaviorism and logical positivism.* Stanford, CA: Stanford University Press.

Smith, L., Best, L., Cylke, V., & Stubbs, D. A. (2000). Psychology without *p* values. *American Psychologist, 55,* 260–263.

Sokal, M. (1987). James McKeen Cattell and mental anthropometry: Nineteenth-century science and reform and the origins of psychological testing. In M. Sokal (Ed.), *Psychological testing and American society 1890–1930* (pp. 21–45). New Brunswick, NJ: Rutgers University Press.

Spencer, H. (1855). *Principles of psychology.* London: Longman, Brown, Green, and Longmans.

Stam, H. J., & Kalmanovitch, T. (1998). E. L. Thorndike and the origins of animal psychology. *American Psychologist, 53,* 1135–1144.

Sternberg, S. (1969). The discovery of processing stages: Extensions of Donders' method. In W. G. Koster (Ed.), *Acta psychologica, 30, attention and performance II* (pp. 276–315). Amsterdam: North Holland.

Stevens, S. S. (1935a). The operational basis of psychology. *American Journal of Psychology, 47,* 323–330.

Stevens, S. S. (1935b). The operational definition of concepts. *Psychological Review, 42,* 517–527.

Stevens, S. S. (1939). Psychology and the science of science. *Psychological Bulletin, 36,* 221–263.

Stevens, S. S. (1951). Mathematics, measurement, and psychophysics. In S. S. Stevens (Ed.), *Handbook of experimental psychology* (pp. 1–49). New York: Wiley.

Thompson, H. B. (1903). *The mental traits of sex.* Chicago: University of Chicago Press.

Thorndike, E. L. (1898). Animal intelligence. *Psychological Review Monograph* (Suppl. 2, Whole No. 8).

Thorndike, E. L. (1913). The laws of learning in animals. In E. L. Thorndike (Ed.), *Educational psychology: The psychology of learning* (Vol. 2, pp. 6–16). New York: Teachers College Press.

Thorndike, E. L. (1936). Edward Lee Thorndike. In C. Murchison (Ed.), *A history of psychology in autobiography* (Vol. 3, pp. 263–270). Worcester, MA: Clark University Press.

Titchener, E. B. (1898). The postulates of a structural psychology. *Philosophical Review, 7,* 449–465.

Titchener, E. B. (1901–1905). Experimental psychology, a manual of laboratory practice. New York: Macmillan.

Todes, D. (1997). From the machine to the ghost within: Pavlov's transition from digestive physiology to conditional reflexes. *American Psychologist, 52,* 947–955.

Tolman, E. C. (1922). A new formula for behaviorism. *Psychological Review, 29,* 44–54.

Tolman, E. C. (1932). *Purposive behavior in animals and men.* New York: Appleton-Century-Crofts.

Tolman, E. C., & Honzik, C. H. (1930). Introduction and removal of reward, and maze performance in rats. *University of California Publications in Psychology, 4,* 257–275.

Tolman, E. C., Ritchie, B. F., & Kalish, D. (1946). Studies in spatial learning. I: Orientation and the short cut. *Journal of Experimental Psychology, 36,* 13–25.

Tuddenham, R. D. (1962). The nature and measurement of intelligence. In L. Postman (Ed.), *Psychology in the making* (pp. 469–525). New York: Knopf.

Underwood, B. J. (1957). Interference and forgetting. *Psychological Review, 64,* 49–60.

Underwood, B. J., & Schulz, R. W. (1960). *Meaningfulness and verbal learning.* Chicago: Lippincott.

Warren, H. C. (1921). *A history of the association psychology.* New York: Scribner's.

Washburn, M. F. (1908). *The animal mind.* New York: Macmillan.

Washburn, M. F. (1917). *The animal mind* (2nd ed.). New York: Macmillan.

Washburn, M. F. (1926). *The animal mind* (3rd ed.). New York: Macmillan.

Washburn, M. F. (1936). *The animal mind* (4th ed.). New York: Macmillan.

Watson, J. B. (1907). Kinaesthetic and organic sensations: Their role in the reactions of the white rat to the maze. Psychological Review Monograph Supplement, 8, no. 2.

Watson, J. B. (1913). Psychology as the behaviorist views it. *Psychological Review, 20,* 158–177.

Watson, J. B. (1914). *Behavior: An introduction to comparative psychology.* New York: Holt.

Watson, J. B. (1916). The place of the conditioned reflex in psychology. *Psychological Review, 23,* 89–116.

Watson, J. B. (1919). *Psychology from the standpoint of a behaviorist*. Philadelphia: Lippincott.

Watson, J. B. (1924). *Behaviorism*. New York: Norton.

Watson, J. B., & Rayner, R. (1920). Conditioned emotional reactions. *Journal of Experimental Psychology, 3,* 1–14.

Watson, R. I., & Evans, R. (1991). *The great psychologists*. New York: Harper-Collins.

Wertheimer, M. (1912). Experimentelle studien über das sehen das Bewegung. (Experimental studies on the perception of movement). *Zeitschrift fur Psychologie, 61,* 161–265.

Wertheimer, M. (1959). *Productive thinking*. New York: Harper.

White, S. (1992). G. Stanley Hall: From philosophy to developmental psychology. *Developmental Psychology, 28,* 25–34.

Winston, A. (1990). Robert Sessions Woodworth and the "Columbia Bible": How the psychological experiment was redefined. *American Journal of Psychology, 103,* 391–401.

Woodworth, R. S. (1938). *Experimental psychology*. New York: Holt.

Woodworth, R. S. (1948). *Contemporary schools of psychology* (Rev. ed.). New York: Ronald.

Woolley, H. T. (1910). A review of recent literature on the psychology of sex. *Psychological Bulletin, 7,* 335–342.

Wundt, W. (1873–1874). Grundzüge derphysiologische psychologie (Principles of physiological psychology). Leipzig: Englemann.

Wundt, W. (1974). Excerpts from publications on the reaction experiment. In S. Diamond (Ed.), *The roots of psychology* (pp. 695–700). New York: Basic Books.

Yerkes, R. M. (1905). Animal psychology and the criteria of the psychic. *Journal of Philosophy, Psychology, and Scientific Methods, 6,* 141–149.

CHAPTER 2

Psychology as a Profession

LUDY T. BENJAMIN JR., PATRICK H. DeLEON, DONALD K. FREEDHEIM, AND GARY R. VANDENBOS

WHAT DEFINES A PROFESSION?   27
PIONEERING APPLICATIONS OF
   PSYCHOLOGICAL SCIENCE   28
THE BEGINNINGS OF THE NEW PROFESSION
   OF PSYCHOLOGY   29
   The Business Psychologist   29
   The Counseling Psychologist   30
   The School Psychologist   31
   The Clinical Psychologist   32
WORLD WAR I AND THE GROWTH OF
   PSYCHOLOGICAL PRACTICE   33
THE 1920s: THE DECADE OF
   POPULAR PSYCHOLOGY   34
STRUGGLES FOR PROFESSIONAL IDENTITY   34
POSTWAR GROWTH OF THE PRACTICE
   OF PSYCHOLOGY   35

Clinical Psychology   35
Counseling Psychology   37
Industrial Psychology   38
School Psychology   38
A "PROFESSIONAL" JOURNAL WITHIN APA   39
ELECTRONIC PUBLISHING INITIATIVES   40
COMMUNITY INVOLVEMENT   40
TWO ASSOCIATIONAL DEVELOPMENTS   41
   The APA Congressional Science Fellowship Program   41
   APAGS   41
THE PRESCRIPTIVE AUTHORITY (RXP-) AGENDA   41
THE TWENTY-FIRST CENTURY   43
REFERENCES   43

There was a profession of psychology long before there was a science of psychology and even before the term "psychologist" came into public use. In early nineteenth-century America (as in centuries before throughout the world), there were practitioners who counseled people about their marriages, advised individuals about possible careers, aided parents in the rearing of their children, advised companies about employee selection, and offered to cure a host of psychological illnesses through myriad treatments. These practitioners worked under various labels, including phrenologist, characterologist, spiritualist, graphologist, mental healer, physiognomist, mind reader, and psychologist.

To "get your head examined" was big business in nineteenth-century America. Phrenologists, often using a system marketed by brothers Lorenzo and Orson Fowler, measured skull shapes. Phrenology clinics worked with businesses for employee selection, with schools for hiring of teachers, with lawyers for evaluating clients, and with individuals for vocational counseling and advice on marital partners. Thus, there were individuals practicing in most of the venues in which psychologists practice today and offering many of the services that are provided today by clinical,

counseling, school, and industrial-organizational psychologists. However, whether such individuals were "psychologists," and whether they represented a "profession" at that point, are different matters.

WHAT DEFINES A PROFESSION?

Originally, there were three professions: law, medicine, and the clergy. These fields of endeavor were distinct from "trades" in that they required highly specialized areas of education, created their own languages—generally not understood by the populace at large—and developed their own sets of practices, ethics, and so forth. As opposed to science, which traditionally published its newfound knowledge, professions kept their knowledge to themselves. For example, the priests of the Mayans knew by their sophisticated astronomy when the eclipses of the sun and moon would be and used their predictive powers to ensure that citizens paid their appropriate taxes.

In time the word *profession* was not used exclusively for the three original fields but for any career requiring higher education, although today one can hear the terms "profession" and "job" as nearly interchangeable. However, the hallmarks of a profession are still commonly understood to be specialized education, exchange of information (e.g., through journals, books, seminars), accepted standards of practice, and governmental certification and/or licensing.

How psychologists achieved the status of professional is discussed in this chapter, as we explore historical developments, organizational efforts, educational criteria, relations with other professions, and brief histories of its major subspecialties. More detailed histories of the specialties can be found in the relevant chapters in the volume. Also, the role of organizations of the profession is presented in the last chapter of the book.

PIONEERING APPLICATIONS OF PSYCHOLOGICAL SCIENCE

When the science of psychology began in America in the last quarter of the nineteenth century, academicians found themselves in competition with practitioners for the label of "psychologist." The academics sought to draw boundaries between their discipline and the many pseudopsychologies. The new psychological scientists "used their battles with spiritualists [and phrenologists and others] to legitimize psychology as a science and create a new role for themselves as guardians of the scientific worldview" (Coon, 1992, p. 143).

Although American psychologists of the late nineteenth century may have been housed within the academy, they were not bent on a pure science that excluded practical problems. Applications to real-world issues emerged in the earliest days of the new laboratories. Not surprisingly, the first applications were in the field of education.

By 1892, the year in which he founded the American Psychological Association (APA), Clark University president G. Stanley Hall (1844–1924) was the recognized leader of the child study movement in America, a national movement that was directed at educational reform. Hall and his colleagues at Clark organized a research effort using schoolteachers, parents, and college educators (including psychologists) to collect data on children, largely through the use of questionnaires, that would lead to a total understanding of the child. With this understanding, teachers could be better trained, school curricula could be better designed, and education could be better suited to individual student needs. Clark University served as a clearinghouse for these studies, accumulating data from more than 190 different questionnaires. Various universities with child study interests (such as Clark, Stanford University, and the Universities of Illinois and Nebraska) held summer programs for schoolteachers, administrators, and educators in normal colleges (i.e., colleges in which teachers were trained) to dispense the new knowledge of the child and to describe the implications of this knowledge for teacher training and school reform (Davidson & Benjamin, 1987).

Although the questionnaires were the principal research tools of child study, various mental tests were also employed. The mental tests were an outgrowth of the anthropometric tests developed by Francis Galton (1822–1911) in England in the 1880s and imported to America by James McKeen Cattell (1860–1944). Cattell actually coined the term "mental test" in an 1890 article in which he described a proposed program of research based on sensory, motor, and cognitive measures (Cattell, 1890; Sokal, 1982b). A few years later he was confident enough in the validity of the measures to suggest that they had value in school settings as "a useful indication of the progress, condition, and aptitudes of the pupil" and further, that these "tests might serve as a means of training and education" (Cattell, 1893, p. 257). By 1895, several American psychology laboratories had adopted a similar mode of testing and were using the tests as diagnostic instruments, principally of intellectual functioning. This was the start of a measurement of individual differences that would define American psychology, particularly applied psychology, throughout the twentieth century.

Another of the pioneers in applied psychology was a University of Pennsylvania professor, Lightner Witmer (1867–1956), who in 1896 opened the first psychology clinic in America, and perhaps in the world. In March of that year, a local schoolteacher brought a 14-year-old boy to see Witmer. The boy had difficulties with spelling, and the teacher reasoned that if psychology was the science of mind, then it ought to be able to solve such problems. Witmer dealt with the boy's problem successfully. By the summer, Witmer was seeing similar cases at the university, which led to the opening of his clinic (Baker, 1988). So enthused was he with this applied success that he gave an address at the annual meeting of the American Psychological Association that December in which he spoke about using psychology to solve learning difficulties in schoolchildren. He urged his colleagues to use their science to "throw light upon the problems that confront humanity" (Witmer, 1897, p. 116).

The clinic grew slowly at first, with Witmer handling much of the caseload himself, mostly schoolchildren presenting with learning and/or behavioral problems. In 1907, he began editing and publishing a new journal, *The Psychological Clinic,* in which he described the cases and the diagnostic and treatment methods used. In the first issue of that journal, Witmer outlined a program of graduate training in a field he designated as "clinical psychology" (Witmer, 1907). Based on the work in his clinic and his promotional efforts on behalf of applying psychology to the remediation of learning and behavioral problems, Witmer has generally been acknowledged as the founder of clinical psychology and school psychology in America (McReynolds, 1997).

In addition to schools and clinics, the new psychology also quickly found its way into the world of business. In the fall of 1895, Harlow Gale (1862–1945), a psychology instructor at the University of Minnesota, began his research on the psychology of advertising. He sent a brief questionnaire to approximately 200 businesses in the Minneapolis–St. Paul area asking them about their advertising practices. He wrote, "It is our aim to find the mental processes which go on in the minds of the customers from the time they see an advertisement until they have purchased the article advertised" (Gale, 1900, p. 39). Gale discovered that the business community may not have been as interested in psychology as he was in their field; only about 20 businesses returned his questionnaire, a return rate of 10%. In the next 5 years, however, a theoretical debate among advertisers about the nature of consumer motivation led the advertising community to make contact with psychology, initially with Walter Dill Scott (1869–1955), who published books on the psychology of advertising in 1903 and 1908. With his work, the field of industrial psychology was born (Benjamin, in press). By 1915, many psychologists were employed full-time in the business field in advertising, sales, and personnel work.

Thus, whereas many of the early academic psychologists appeared content to remain in their laboratories where they used their new scientific techniques to answer age-old questions of mind, others were lured beyond the ivy-covered walls, motivated by a need for money or a curiosity about problems in the world outside of the academy or by a need to demonstrate the value of the new science of psychology through application. It was the work of those pioneers that marked the beginning of the new profession of psychology, a profession that was to be grounded in science.

THE BEGINNINGS OF THE NEW PROFESSION OF PSYCHOLOGY

It is doubtful that psychologists at the end of the nineteenth century envisioned anything like the profession of psychology that would exist in the 1930s much less the profession of today. Yet the earliest of American psychologists, such as William James (1842–1910), G. Stanley Hall, and James McKeen Cattell, clearly recognized the potential contributions of psychology through applied research. It, perhaps,

was only a small step to move from applied research to establish a role for psychologists as consultants employed outside the university.

The beginning of the twentieth century in America was marked by great social upheaval. American cities were growing rapidly and with them the factories that were the home of the new urban labor. Immigrants came to America in even greater numbers, seeking a better life. Child labor laws and compulsory school attendance laws were passed in tandem to prevent abuses of children in the workplace but also to provide an education needed for an urban workforce and to impart the values of American society important to the melting pot of fully acculturated citizens. There were movements for a national reform in education and for the right to vote for women. As manufacturing capacity exceeded demand, businesses looked beyond their regions to a national consumer base. Advertising became more important to create those broader markets. The types of jobs available expanded considerably as America moved from a largely agrarian/rural society to a factory/urban one; consequently, people sought more information about jobs leading to a new focus—arguably a more scientific one—on adjustment.

The changes in America at the turn of the century virtually clamored for an applied social science to solve the problems of the new society. And, there were psychologists both inside and outside of university settings who were ready to tackle those problems. We will next examine some of the early practical applications of psychology in business, in counseling, in education, and in clinical settings.

The Business Psychologist

At the beginning of the twentieth century, American business was changing America as well as being changed by the evolution of American society. With the "formation of large industrial empires came new management problems and a growing problem with efficiency" (Napoli, 1981, p. 28). As efficiency became the watchword of new American business, psychologists would take up the challenges of increasing productivity, improving personnel selection, providing job analyses, and improving worker morale.

Business psychology—later to be called industrial psychology in the 1920s, and then industrial-organizational (I-O) psychology in the 1960s—can be said to have originated with Gale's advertising study in 1895. But Gale did not pursue that work. Instead, the first sustained program in business psychology was that of Walter Dill Scott, who published many articles on the psychology of advertising in *Mahin's Magazine,* a leading journal in the advertising field. Scott also wrote about his advertising work in other magazines, such as *Atlantic Monthly, Business World, Advertising World,* and *The Woman's Herald,* thus making business psychology known to a broad audience of potential employers and consumers. Scott promoted the psychology of suggestion, arguing that successful advertising suggested a course of action, that is, buying the product. He wrote, "Man has been called the reasoning animal but he could with greater truthfulness be called the creature of suggestion. He is reasonable, but he is to a greater extent suggestible" (Scott, 1903, p. 59). In applying suggestion to advertising, Scott advocated two techniques: the direct command (e.g., "Use Peterson's Tooth Powder") and the return coupon. Both techniques were thought to stimulate compulsive obedience.

In the subsequent theoretical debates in the advertising community on the nature of consumer behavior, other approaches displaced Scott's views (see Kuna, 1976, 1979), but his work gave psychology considerable visibility in the world of business and paved the way for many psychologists who would follow in advertising such as Harry Hollingworth, Daniel Starch, and John B. Watson.

Although business psychology can be said to have begun in the field of advertising, it quickly branched into other prominent areas. When increased emphasis on efficiency led to the "scientific management" of Frederick Winslow Taylor (1911), psychologists entered that arena as well. Efficiency meant not only better management and more effective advertising but also better training of workers, improved employee selection procedures, better ways to control employee performance, and better understanding of human actions in work. Prominent in these areas was Harvard psychologist Hugo Münsterberg (1863–1916), who argued in his book, *Psychology and Industrial Efficiency* (1913), that the key to workplace efficiency was matching job and worker and that successful matches generated satisfied employees, quality work, and high productivity. Münsterberg promoted psychology as the science of human efficiency, noting that psychology had the tools to create the perfect match by determining the mental traits required for any job and the mental traits of workers. That his ideas were well received by a broad public is evidenced by the fact that his book was for a time on the national list of best-sellers.

Psychologists began to develop mental tests to evaluate workers and jobs (ship captains, trolley car operators, saleswomen), work that was to prove especially important when they were asked to oversee the selection program for the United States armed forces during World War I. Business psychology had begun in the universities, but its practice soon moved to business settings as psychologists found full-time employment, particularly as personnel officers involved with selection, job analysis, and training. Such opportunities

expanded considerably after World War I, establishing the psychologist as a key player in the world of business.

The Counseling Psychologist

As noted earlier, with the proliferation of types of jobs around the turn of the twentieth century, people had more occupational choices than ever before. Vocational counseling, which had been a part of the business of nineteenth-century phrenologists, became even more important. The most influential figure in the vocational guidance movement of the early twentieth century was not a psychologist but an individual trained in engineering and law, Frank Parsons (1854–1908). He wrote his most important work in the waning days of his life, a book published after he died, entitled *Choosing a Vocation* (1909). Parsons's formula for successful guidance involved: (a) a clear understanding of the individual's talents, limitations, and interests, (b) knowledge about diverse jobs including what was required for success in those jobs, and (c) matching those two kinds of information for the best vocational guidance.

There were clear ties between Parsons's approach and the matching between jobs and people that was the focus of psychologists in personnel work in businesses. Parsons, as part of the progressive movement of the times, emphasized the reduction of human inefficiency—as reflected in the high turnover of workers—through the application of a careful program of career planning. Vocational guidance became a mantra of progressive reformers and soon found its way into the American mainstream with the formation of the National Vocational Guidance Association in 1913.

Quickly, the vocational guidance counselor was integrated into elementary and secondary schools across America, beginning a strong association between guidance and education. It also made its way into industry through personnel selection. Psychologists found the issues of person and career matching amenable to the new applied science of psychology and worked to develop reliable and valid measures of individual traits and abilities for use in guidance and selection.

Guidance counseling became even more prominent in schools after the passage of the National Vocational Education Act in 1917. Following the First World War, vocational guidance centers (or "clinics," as they were sometimes called) were established as well at colleges and universities. For example, Witmer founded a separate vocational guidance clinic at the University of Pennsylvania in 1920 that was headed by one of his doctoral graduates, Morris Viteles (1898–1996), who would later distinguish himself as an industrial psychologist.

In all of these vocational guidance centers and clinics, the key component of the arsenal of the guidance specialists was mental tests, including interest tests that were developed in the 1920s, and a growing number of aptitude and ability tests that were used not only in guidance but also for selection. This vocational role, both in personnel work and in guidance, remained relatively stable until after the Second World War. (See the chapters by Koppes and Baker in this volume.)

The School Psychologist

We have already noted that the origins of school psychology lie in the psychological clinic of Lightner Witmer. Thomas Fagan (1992) has written that:

> School psychology was one of many child-saving services originating in the period of 1890 to 1920. . . . [I]t originated in response to compulsory schooling, which provided the stage for development of separate special educational programs for atypical children. School psychology emerged in the middle of the child study movement. (p. 241)

The child study work of Hall focused attention on a broad spectrum of child behavior and education. Many of Hall's master's and doctoral students at Clark University worked in what could be described as school psychology, including three particularly influential pioneers: Henry Herbert Goddard (1866–1957), Lewis Terman (1877–1956), and Arnold Gesell (1880–1961).

Goddard was employed at the New Jersey Training School for Feebleminded Girls and Boys in Vineland when he began his research on mental retardation, searching for better tools for intellectual assessment and for methods of effective education and training of mentally handicapped children. Goddard was frustrated in his work at Vineland using the measurement tools he had learned at Clark University and from Cattell's work. Whereas those tools seemed appropriate for assessment of children of normal intelligence, they were not useful for the children at Vineland. In a 1908 trip to Europe, Goddard learned of a new approach to intelligence testing developed by French psychologist Alfred Binet (1857–1911). Goddard translated the test for English-language use, tested it on samples of public school children as well as the students at the Vineland Training School, and published his version of the test in 1909. Its popularity as an instrument of intellectual assessment spread rapidly, culminating in the version published by Terman in 1916 that became known as the Stanford-Binet Intelligence Test.

Goddard's role in school psychology, and more broadly in educational reform, cannot be overstated. He sought to apply the science of psychology to the questions then facing public schools, particularly regarding the educability of children labeled subnormal in intelligence. Through his research efforts, his training workshops for teachers, and the prominence of his ideas in American education, Goddard was instrumental in promoting special education opportunities in American schools (even though many of those efforts went beyond what he would have endorsed). More important for psychology, he established a place for psychologists in the schools as diagnosticians of mental capacity, a role that was often synonymous with the label of school psychologist in the twentieth century (Zenderland, 1998).

Terman, like Goddard, also focused on intellectual assessment. Although Terman conducted some research on mentally handicapped children (including some work published with Goddard using subjects at Vineland), his work with children came to be more focused on gifted students, and he is arguably best known (beyond the Stanford-Binet) for the longitudinal studies of children identified as gifted, the "genius studies," that began in California in 1921. His revision of the Binet test was better psychometrically than Goddard's across all intellectual levels but especially so in the higher ranges. Terman, like Goddard, enhanced the role of psychologist as assessor of intellectual functioning and as designer of curricula for special-needs children, particularly gifted children.

Gesell was the first person in the United States to hold the title of "school psychologist," according to Fagan (1992). He was hired by the Connecticut State Board of Education in 1915 to evaluate schoolchildren and make recommendations for those who needed special treatment. Gesell's duties in the beginning of his work were research oriented, but he later came to be consumed by a caseload of 502 schoolchildren (and his duties were similar to those of contemporary school psychologists). The significance of Gesell's appointment was that the title "school psychologist" was associated "with services to exceptional children, especially the mentally deficient, and it associated the functions of that title as primarily diagnostic testing for placement decisions in the newly created programs for the handicapped" (Fagan, 1987, p. 406). Although Gesell is perhaps the most prominent of the early school psychologists, he was not the only person performing those duties by 1915. Already schools were employing teachers in intellectual assessment roles as well as curriculum design for special children. Norma Estelle Cutts (1892–1988) played such a role as early as 1914 in the New Haven, Connecticut, schools after working with Goddard for a year at Vineland (Fagan, 1989). She was one of many individuals whom Goddard influenced to become school psychologists, most of them women who already had teaching experience. (See the chapter by Fagan in this volume.)

The Clinical Psychologist

At the beginning of the twentieth century, psychopathology was the domain of psychiatry and, to a lesser extent, neurology. Psychiatry, arguably the oldest of the medical specialties (excluding surgery), originated with the superintendents of mental asylums at the end of the eighteenth century. After a half century of asylum management, the superintendents formed an organization entitled the Association of Medical Superintendents of American Institutions for the Insane in 1844 and in the same year began publication of their journal, *The American Journal of Insanity*. The organization's name was later changed to the American Medico-Psychological Association in 1892 and in 1921 to the American Psychiatric Association; the journal name was changed as well in 1921 to the *American Journal of Psychiatry* (Grob, 1994). The abnormal mind was of interest to some, perhaps many, of the early psychologists, but the domains of diagnosis and treatment seemed clearly within the boundaries of medicine, and few psychologists saw any need to venture there. That would soon change.

Origins of any field are rarely, if ever, unequivocal—and so it is with clinical psychology. We have already discussed the contributions of Lightner Witmer with respect to school and clinical psychology. Not only did he establish the first psychology clinic in 1896, but as early as 1897 he had described a training program for psychologists to work in a field that he had named "clinical psychology," a field that would draw from the knowledge base in medicine, education, and psychology (particularly child psychology). An expanded description of this field and a rationale for its further development appeared in the inaugural issue of his journal, *The Psychological Clinic* (Witmer, 1907), a journal that largely published reports of the cases seen in Witmer's clinic.

Witmer was clearly interested in the difficulties that children exhibited in the classroom and believed that psychological science could offer solutions to behavioral problems of perception, learning, motivation, and emotion. He championed the need for accurate diagnosis based on psychological and medical tests (the latter were performed by associated physicians). Slowly others began to share his vision, and, by 1914, there were psychology clinics at 19 universities. Witmer's focus was on children (and chiefly on problems that impeded learning). Others soon broadened the scope of clinical psychology. But, the duties of these early clinical psychologists remained focused on diagnosis and recommendations

for treatment, with limited roles in actual treatment until after World War II.

Psychotherapy, a book published in 1909 by Hugo Münsterberg, represents an early psychology-based contribution to the clinical intervention literature. It was a non-Freudian textbook grounded in a theory of psychophysical parallelism, which argued that all psychical processes had a parallel brain process. His volume argued for the scientific study of the processes of psychotherapy and viewed psychotherapy as a clinical endeavor separate from "psychiatry."

Other influences came from physicians cognizant of the potential contributions of psychology. Morton Prince (1854–1929) was a neurologist interested in the problems of psychopathology and one who recognized the importance of psychology in the study and treatment of psychological disorders. His most famous book, *The Dissociation of a Personality* (1908), was a lengthy and insightful description of a case of multiple personality. His contributions to clinical psychology were considerable and include his founding of the *Journal of Abnormal Psychology* in 1906, which published the early work on experimental psychopathology, and his establishment of the Psychological Clinic at Harvard University in 1926, which he housed in the Department of Philosophy (where psychology was located) rather than in Harvard's medical school.

Another physician, William Healy (1869–1963), headed the Juvenile Psychopathic Institute, which opened in Chicago in 1909. Healy had studied with William James and had also been influenced by the work of Goddard at Vineland. His institute was to be both a research facility, investigating the causes of juvenile delinquency, and a treatment facility. He hired psychologist Grace Fernald (1879–1950) to work with him, and when she left, he replaced her with another psychologist, Augusta Bronner (1881–1966), whom he would later marry. Both Fernald and Bronner used the title "clinical psychologist" and played important roles in research, diagnosis, and treatment. Other juvenile courts and corrections facilities began to hire psychologists for similar roles (Levine & Levine, 1992).

Other stimulants to the development of clinical psychology before World War I included the work on mental assessment by Goddard and other advances in mental testing; the five addresses given by Sigmund Freud (1856–1939) at Clark University in 1909 that fostered considerable interest in psychoanalysis in America but more broadly in the nature of causation in mental illness; the mental hygiene movement begun around 1908 by former mental patient Clifford Beers (1876–1943) and psychiatrist Adolf Meyer (1866–1950), a movement that sought to understand the early causes of mental illness and how conditions might be changed (in families and society) to minimize psychological problems; and the popularity of the Emmanuel Movement begun by a Wundt doctoral student, Elwood Worcester (1862–1940), in his Boston church, a movement that spread across the United States emphasizing the alliance of medicine and psychology in treating mental disorders, a movement credited with the emergence of psychotherapy in America (Caplan, 1998).

All of these forces brought psychology into greater contact with issues of mental pathology and afforded new jobs for psychologists, largely as mental testers. As the demand for these diagnostic services grew, clinical psychologists petitioned the APA in 1915 for a certification program for qualified psychologists in consulting roles, a measure that was seen to protect the public and to preserve the jobs of consulting psychologists. When the APA declined to provide such certification, several psychologists, including J. E. Wallace Wallin (1876–1969) and Leta S. Hollingworth (1886–1939), formed in 1917 a new, short-lived organization entitled the American Association of Clinical Psychologists (AACP), arguably the first association of professional psychologists. The membership totaled only about 45 psychologists in its first year, some in university settings, some in applied jobs. The association was a clear statement of another of psychology's applied specialists coming of age: the clinical psychologist. (See the chapter by Routh and Reisman in this volume.)

WORLD WAR I AND THE GROWTH OF PSYCHOLOGICAL PRACTICE

The foundations for the modern practice of psychology were well in place before the beginning of the First World War. Psychologists could be found working in schools, businesses, hospitals, and social and clinical service agencies. The number of such individuals was still relatively small, particularly in comparison to their colleagues in colleges and universities. Two world wars would dramatically reverse that ratio. The first would promote the rapid development of the practice specialties; the second would open the floodgates for psychological practice, including psychologists as independent practitioners of psychotherapy.

It can be argued that American psychologists were unprepared for World War I. On April 6, 1917, two days after America's entry into the war, much of the leadership of American psychology—at least those located on the East Coast—were attending the annual meeting of E. B. Titchener's "experimentalists" at Harvard University (see Boring, 1938, 1967). In attendance was Robert M. Yerkes (1876–1956), who was the current president of the APA. Yerkes chaired a discussion about psychology's role in the war that led to an emergency meeting of the APA Council called for the end of April. At that meeting, Yerkes established a dozen committees that were charged with pursuing various roles for psychologists within the war effort. Only two of those really materialized. One involved a testing program of nearly two million military recruits, headed by Yerkes, that developed group intelligence tests, namely the Army Alpha and Army Beta. The second program was headed by Walter Dill Scott, who used his experience in developing job selection tests to assess the job skills of more than three million military personnel, a task accomplished by his staff's development of more than 100 separate selection instruments in a little more than 12 months. After the war, Scott was awarded the Distinguished Service Medal by the U.S. Army for this monumentally successful program. He was the only psychologist to be so honored in World War I (Napoli, 1981).

The exact number of American psychologists who participated in the war is not known, but the figure is likely between 250 and 300, counting those who served as consultants as well as those in uniform. Toward the end of the war, some were stationed at the 40 U.S. Army hospitals, where their assignments brought them into direct contact with issues of psychopathology. One example was Harry Hollingworth (1880–1956), a faculty member on leave from Barnard College who, as a captain in the army, was working at the army hospital in Plattsburgh, New York, examining approximately 1,200 soldiers suffering from "shell shock" and other psychological disorders. Based on those experiences, Hollingworth wrote a book entitled *The Psychology of Functional Neuroses* (1920). Although Hollingworth was not led into clinical psychology by his wartime experiences, other psychologists were.

All of the activities of psychologists during the war are far beyond the scope of this chapter. What is important to emphasize, though, is that the war efforts by psychologists had important implications for the public and for the discipline of psychology. The work of psychologists, especially in selection, was seen by the government and the public as a program of considerable success. Such favorable press brought many consulting opportunities to psychologists after the war, and psychologists were quick to take advantage of such applied opportunities. For example, Scott founded The Scott Company, a consulting firm of psychologists based in Pittsburgh, to do contract work for businesses and government agencies.

Further, the war work convinced psychologists of the value of their science, that is, that they had something significant to offer in the public sector that was grounded in fact, not myth. This newly gained disciplinary awareness for psychologists, the public's perception of the value of psychology as demonstrated by success in the war work, the growing economic prosperity of America in the 1920s, and the rapid social changes in American society after the war were all factors that led to the further development of the profession of psychology.

THE 1920s: THE DECADE OF POPULAR PSYCHOLOGY

American historians have written of the public euphoria in the United States that followed World War I. American forces had helped to win the war in Europe. There was general economic prosperity, and a growing belief in the American dream that anything was possible, with hard work. Writing for the American public in 1925, psychologist John B. Watson (1878–1958) promoted this nurturistic optimism:

> Give me a dozen healthy infants, well-formed, and my own specified world to bring them up in and I'll guarantee to take any one at random and train him to become any type of specialist I might select—doctor, lawyer, artist, merchant-chief and, yes, even beggar-man and thief, regardless of his talents, penchants, tendencies, abilities, vocations, and race of his ancestors. (Watson, 1925, p. 82)

Americans seemed delirious with the potential for psychology to improve their lives. The first popular psychology magazines (four of them) began publication in the decade. Countless self-help books were published, and newspapers carried daily columns of psychological advice. Touting the value of psychology for the public, journalist Albert Wiggam (1928) wrote:

> Men and women never needed psychology so much as they need it to-day. . . . You cannot achieve these things [effectiveness and happiness] in the fullest measure without the new knowledge of your own mind and personality that the psychologists have given us. (p. 13)

Public demand for psychological services grew rapidly, and consequently, many individuals, with little or no training in psychology, offered their services to the public as psychologists.

Consulting psychologists were especially concerned about such pseudopractitioners and petitioned the APA to create a certification program to identify psychologists qualified to consult with the public. Initially, the APA balked at the idea but relented in 1924, when it established such a program. Four years later, after fewer than 30 psychologists had received certification, the program was abandoned (Sokal, 1982b). There was no mechanism for enforcement of such a program, and the public seemed incapable of making distinctions between qualified psychologists and unqualified ones, or at least was uninterested in doing so. Nevertheless, psychology of all kinds prospered—and the professional opportunities in business, school, clinical, and counseling psychology grew at a rapid rate.

STRUGGLES FOR PROFESSIONAL IDENTITY

As early as 1915, consulting psychologists had petitioned the APA to recognize the growth of applied psychology by committing some program time at the annual meeting for discussion of professional issues. But APA leadership had balked, citing the APA's sole stated objective as an organization that existed for the advancement of psychology as a science.

When the American Association of Clinical Psychologists (AACP) had been founded in 1917, there was concern within the APA that the group would lead to a rupture in organized psychology. In negotiations between the two groups, the AACP agreed to dissolve in 1919 and reorganize as the Clinical Section of the APA. The Clinical Section identified three goals: "promoting better working relationships within clinical and within allied fields, developing professional standards for practitioners, and encouraging research and publication on topics in clinical psychology" (Napoli, 1981, p. 26).

Two years later, in 1921, the APA created a second section on consulting psychology, and the short-lived certification program would stem from the efforts of this group. The consulting/clinical psychologists recommended two additional APA sections, one on educational psychology and the other on industrial psychology, but those two requests were denied.

As the professional opportunities for psychologists grew and as problems in professional practice occurred, these psychologists made additional requests of the APA. They called on the APA to develop a code of professional ethics. They sought help in protecting the label "psychologist." They called for changes in graduate training that included additional applied psychology experiences, including internships (which had begun as early as 1908 but were still uncommon, see Routh, 2000). And, they asked that psychology departments hire more faculty who had significant practical experience. Except for some minimal gestures toward the applied group, the APA largely ignored those requests that were important for the professionalization of psychology, reminding the group of its mantra that the APA was a scientific association.

Throughout the 1920s, more than a dozen applied psychology groups were formed, most of them state associations. The largest of those was the New York State Association of Consulting Psychologists, which had begun in 1921. By 1930, it was clear to the professional psychologists that the

APA was not going to support their efforts. In that year New York University psychologist Douglas Fryer led a reorganization of the New York group, renamed it the Association of Consulting Psychologists (ACP), and extended its geographical boundaries for membership to include the entire United States. The ACP, thus, became the first "national" association for professional psychologists. In 1933, the ACP published its code of professional ethics, the first such document for psychologists. And, in 1937, it began publication of the *Journal of Consulting Psychology,* arguably the first professional psychology journal.

ACP struggled to establish itself as the national association for professional psychologists; however, it was dominated by New York psychologists. In 1935, a plan was initiated to broaden the ACP membership by creating a federation of societies. All the existing state associations were invited to join as well as the Clinical Section of the APA. Eventually the federation plan was abandoned, and it was decided to create a wholly new organization, the American Association for Applied Psychology (AAAP), which began in 1938. The ACP and the Clinical Section of the APA both disbanded and became part of AAAP. The ACP journal was continued by the AAAP—as its official organ.

The AAAP began with four sections: clinical, consulting, educational, and industrial psychology. Fryer served as the first president of AAAP and was followed in later years by such important applied psychologists as Walter Van Dyke Bingham (1880–1952) and Carl Rogers (1902–1987). The AAAP's success was manifested largely through its sections in which psychologists with similar needs could work together on issues of common concern. Each section wrote its own by-laws, elected its own officers, created its own committees, and planned its own program at the annual meeting of the AAAP.

> Even though most of the AAAP members retained their memberships in the older APA, many identified more strongly with the new organization than with APA because AAAP provided the professional identity, the collegial relations, and the professional assistance that APA had been unwilling to offer. (Benjamin, 1997, p. 728)

Although the AAAP was quite successful in serving the needs of professional psychologists, the organization lasted only slightly more than seven years. Its demise had nothing to do with the service it was providing for the growing profession of psychology. With the United States at war in 1942, there was federal government pressure on the various psychological organizations to come together with one voice for the national good. Negotiations among several groups (including the Society for the Psychological Study of Social Issues, or SPSSI, and the Psychometric Society) but principally steered by the two heavyweights, the APA and the AAAP, led to the establishment of a "new" American Psychological Association.

The new APA began with 18 charter divisions, a model borrowed from the sectional structure of the AAAP; a new journal that was intended to be a journal of "professional psychology," the *American Psychologist* (Benjamin, 1996); and a new central office in Washington, D.C. (Capshew, 1999). The new APA also had a new statement of objectives which read: "to advance psychology as a science, as a profession, and as a means of promoting human welfare" (Wolfe, 1946/1997, p. 721). The "professional" goal had come, of course, from the AAAP, and the "human welfare" goal from the SPSSI. The APA looked and sounded like a new kind of organization, one that had finally acknowledged the presence of the profession of psychology. However, professional psychologists would soon learn that they had little real support (or power) within the new association. It would be almost 30 years before that situation changed in any dramatic way.

POSTWAR GROWTH OF THE PRACTICE OF PSYCHOLOGY

Whereas American psychologists were caught napping by the First World War, they did not repeat that mistake for the second one. Both the APA and the AAAP had committees in place by 1939 to plan for psychology's role should the United States enter the war. As noted earlier, in the first war psychologists worked largely in two areas: examination of recruits and personnel selection. However, in the Second World War, the involvement of psychologists was substantially more diverse—and it included recruitment, selection, training, equipment design, propaganda, surveying attitudes in the United States and abroad, examining and testing prisoners of war, morale studies, intelligence work, and personality studies, including an analysis of Adolf Hitler (Capshew, 1999; Hoffman, 1992). The verdict on psychologists' performance in the war was an incredibly favorable one. The legacy of that performance was a growth in scientific and professional opportunities for psychologists that was unprecedented in psychology's history. The profession benefited particularly, and no group benefited more than clinical psychology.

Clinical Psychology

Early in the war, the federal government began planning to meet the mental health needs of returning veterans, which were judged to be substantial. Perhaps the government hoped to avoid the hard feelings among veterans that occurred as a result of their poor treatment following the First World War, ill feeling that had led to a massive march on Washington, D.C. It was evident in 1942 that psychiatrists were too few in number to provide the necessary clinical services, so the federal government mandated that the United States Public Health Service (USPHS) and the Veterans Administration (VA) significantly expand the pool of mental health professionals. That translated into increasing the availability of clinical psychologists.

The USPHS and VA worked with the new APA to expand doctoral training programs in clinical psychology and to identify programs of acceptable quality. The latter goal led to the formation of the APA's accreditation program for clinical psychology programs in 1946 and for counseling psychology programs in 1952. The former goal initiated a series of meetings with department heads of doctoral psychology programs who had extant clinical psychology programs or were interested in developing such programs. The USPHS promised funding to university graduate programs to support clinical psychology students, and the VA promised funding for practica and internship training (Moore, 1992). Because the GI bill had been altered to include benefits for graduate study, money was also available from that program to support doctoral training for veterans, and many chose to pursue advanced study in psychology, with much of that interest directed toward clinical psychology.

Although an accreditation process was already in place within the APA as of 1946, there was no agreed-upon model for clinical training. Discussions of such models dated to the 1890s with a proposal from Witmer, which was followed by subsequent curriculum and training proposals by APA's Clinical Section in 1918–1919 in a series of articles in the *Journal of Applied Psychology,* by the ACP, and by the AAAP. As a leader in the AAAP, clinical psychologist David Shakow (1901–1981) was the key figure in drafting a model curriculum for clinical training. He developed a proposal for the AAAP in 1941 that shaped all subsequent discussions, leading to the report of the Committee on Training in Clinical Psychology (CTCP), an APA committee founded in 1946 with Shakow as chair and funded by the VA and the USPHS. The committee's formidable charge was to

(a) formulate a recommended program for training in clinical psychology, (b) formulate standards for institutions giving training in clinical psychology, including both universities and internship and other practice facilities; (c) study and visit institutions giving instruction in clinical psychology and make a detailed report on each institution. (Baker & Benjamin, 2000, p. 244)

Shakow and his committee published their report in 1947 (American Psychological Association, 1947). Two years later it became the framework for the most famous report in the history of professional training in psychology, the "Boulder Report." That report was the result of the joint work of 73 individuals from psychology and related fields who came together in Boulder, Colorado, for two weeks in the summer of 1949 to produce a model of clinical training in psychology that became known as the "Boulder model" or "scientist-practitioner model" (Raimy, 1950). The architects of this model argued that it was both possible and desirable to train clinical psychologists as competent practitioners and scientists, a view that continues to be debated today.

Not only was there a new formal model for clinical training, but there was a new model for the clinical psychologist as practitioner (one that involved training as a psychotherapist, a role for psychologists that was strongly supported by the federal government). Clinical psychologists would break from their tradition in psychometrics to focus on the delivery of psychotherapy. In 1948, the federal government established the National Institute of Mental Health, which gave further impetus to both the training in and practice of clinical psychology (VandenBos, Cummings, & DeLeon, 1992). The turf disputes with psychiatry had been minor skirmishes before the war, but bigger battles were about to break out as psychologists began to be true competitors of psychiatrists.

As the numbers of psychologists who worked as practitioners grew, the pressures for certification, licensing, and even insurance reimbursement for clients again surfaced within the profession. Connecticut was the first state to enact a psychologist certification law in 1945. Over the next 30 years, professional psychologists worked state by state to get state legislatures to pass laws creating psychology licensing boards. These efforts were largely the responsibility of state psychological associations, although by 1970 the APA began providing some coordination and consultation. In the mid-1950s, the Board of Professional Affairs was created by the APA, with the mission to establish standards for professional practice, foster the application of psychological knowledge, and maintain satisfactory relations with other professions (American Psychological Association, 1957).

The struggles for equality were not only in the legislatures but also with insurance companies and employers. Employer-paid health insurance had emerged as an employee benefit during World War II. During the 1950s and 1960s, labor unions sought to achieve such coverage and expand it (and to include psychotherapy services). After years of urging by practitioners, the APA created an Ad Hoc Committee on Insurance and Related Social Developments in 1963 to meet with insurance industry officials in order to get psychologists included in reimbursement plans (and for such reimbursement to be at parity with that of psychiatrists). Leonard Small, Rogers Wright, Milton Theaman, and Nicholas Cummings were central in this undertaking. The committee also created model "freedom-of-choice" legislation, which individual state psychological associations could try to get adopted in their state (Cummings, 1979). Legislative language was such that if an insurance company reimbursed a psychiatrist for a particular service, it must also provide such reimbursement when the same service is provided by a qualified licensed psychologist.

Later, professional psychologists would use the courts as well in their struggle for equality. It took, for example, a lawsuit filed by the APA against the American Psychoanalytic Institute to establish the right of psychologists to be trained in psychoanalytic centers controlled by the institute (DeAngelis, 1989). The APA Practice Directorate, which was formed in the early 1990s by combining the Office of Professional Practice and the Office of Professional Affairs, evaluates cases and develops selected ones that further the independent practice of psychology. The directorate's efforts are partly funded by a yearly special assessment to all members who engage in practice activities. Divisions of the APA in which at least 50% of its members contribute to the assessment are identified as "practice Divisions."

Efforts outside of the APA also contributed to the development of standards of excellence for practitioners. The American Board of Examiners in Professional Psychology (ABEPP) was created in 1947 "to award diplomas for advanced competency in the field" (Riess, 1992, p. 769). Later the term "Examiners" was omitted, and at least five separate specialty boards exist today under the aegis of the parent organization.

Following the conference in Boulder, several other conferences were held to establish training guidelines for a clinical as well as for other professional subspecialties (see Cohen, 1992), but the 1973 "Vail Conference" (also in Colorado) gave credence to the burgeoning programs offering doctor of psychology (PsyD) degrees from universities as well as from freestanding schools (Korman, 1974). The history of the establishment of professional schools and the PsyD degree has been well documented by Peterson (1992) and Stricker and Cummings (1992). As of June 2001, there were 53 such schools accredited by the APA. Professional schools now graduate over 50% of all clinical students.

Counseling Psychology

As a profession, counseling psychology changed considerably following the war. Vocational guidance remained a duty, but that work would soon shift primarily to guidance counselors within secondary schools. And, the selection duties that had occupied many in vocational guidance became more exclusively the property of industrial psychologists. In place of these activities, "psychotherapy" came to counseling psychology, initially through the writings and teachings of Carl Rogers, who trained many counseling psychologists after the war in "non-directive" counseling and therapy techniques.

The 1950s proved to be a decade of crisis for counseling psychologists. It was a crisis of identity, or at least role confusion. Counseling psychologists who previously garnered most of their identity as vocational counselors had been called on in increasing numbers to provide a range of services to military veterans both in hospital settings and community service centers. Rehabilitation took on a broader meaning, and in addition to vocational planning, counselors were working on general issues of adjustment with service personnel seeking to integrate into the general society. Likewise, the role of student personnel workers in higher education began to focus more broadly on student adjustment.

Changes for the counseling profession in the 1950s were evidenced by several clear markers. "Counseling psychology" became the appellation of choice at the Northwestern Conference of 1951, a meeting specifically organized to explore changes in the field and to make plans for the future. Out of that conference came several initiatives that affected Division 17, the APA, and the VA.

In 1952, Division 17 changed its name from "Counseling and Guidance" to "Counseling Psychology." The Veterans Administration established two new psychological job descriptions: Counseling Psychologist (Vocational) and Counseling Psychologist. In that same year, the APA began accrediting doctoral programs in counseling psychology, partly in response to a doctoral training curriculum recommended by a Division 17 committee (APA, 1952). The final identifying component of a profession was added in 1954 with the establishment of a new publication, the *Journal of Counseling Psychology*.

It might seem that counseling psychology had arrived as a profession. Such professionals had an organizational home, a journal, doctoral training programs, and jobs. There were, however, continued difficulties in defining the field that led to a Division 17 Committee on Definition report in 1956 (American Psychological Association, 1956) and a "crisis" report on counseling psychology as a profession, written in 1960. This latter report was initiated by the APA's Education and Training (E&T) Board, which appointed a three-person committee to prepare a report on the status of counseling psychology as a professional specialty (Berg, Pepinsky, & Shoben, 1980).

The leadership of Division 17 was not pleased with the unilateral actions of the E&T Board. When the E&T report appeared, the division commissioned its own three-person committee, which drafted a much more optimistic report on the status of counseling psychology arguing that the profession was thriving, even if graduate programs were not. This 1961 report found that,

> The rate of growth of counseling psychology has been normal despite limited financial support for the development of graduate programs and the support of graduate students. . . . The social demand for well prepared counseling psychologists is great and continues to increase. The Division of Counseling Psychology has a deep professional obligation to meet this social need. (Tyler, Tiedeman, & Wrenn, 1980, p. 124)

Part of the dissatisfaction within counseling psychology was caused by its comparison with clinical psychology, a profession that was growing at a fantastic rate. By that yardstick, any field would have looked to be in trouble. There was concern from many in counseling that the field should clearly distinguish itself from clinical psychology, whereas others suggested merging the training of the two fields while maintaining differences in the nature of practice.

Traditional work in vocational guidance had been modified by the experiences of counseling psychologists in the VA and student personnel work in higher education. What emerged was a new specialty area that had as its focus the adjustment of the individual to the demands of everyday life, whether those demands were vocational, educational, or interpersonal. The emphasis on developmental processes of average individuals facing day-to-day life was seen as a clear contrast to the emphasis on psychopathology that was the bread and butter of the clinical psychologist.

Industrial Psychology

Other practice specialties also benefited from psychologists' record of accomplishment during the war. Historian Donald Napoli (1981) wrote this about the postwar growth of industrial psychology:

> The military had given psychologists a chance to prove the effectiveness of selection, classification, and aptitude testing, and psychologists met the challenge successfully. Civilian employers also offered new opportunities, which grew largely from the labor shortage produced by wartime mobilization. Business managers, beset by high rates of absenteeism and job turnover, took unprecedented interest in hiring the right worker and keeping him contented on the job. Management turned to psychologists . . . and the amount of psychological testing quickly increased. Surveys show that in 1939 only 14% of businesses were using such tests; in 1947 the proportion rose to 50%, and in 1952, 75%. (p. 138)

Another area of substantial development for the industrial psychologist that grew out of the wartime work was the field of human factors or engineering psychology. The military, in particular, continued to employ psychologists in its research on human–machine interactions, but businesses as well began to employ psychologists to design irons, telephones, arc welders, vending machines, chemical refineries, and the like. Human factors remained an important part of industrial psychology into the 1960s but gradually separated, a transition begun in the late 1950s when APA's Division 21 (Engineering Psychology) and the Human Factors Society were founded. It was replaced by psychologists interested in applying social psychological theories to the problems of organizations, leading to the growth of the "O" half of the I-O psychologist.

Prior to the war, most industrial psychologists served as consultants to businesses, thus working part-time as professionals. After the war, however, that pattern changed dramatically. Businesses offered full-time employment opportunities, and consequently graduate programs began to train the I-O practitioners to fill those jobs.

School Psychology

Unlike the other three practice specialties, the Second World War had much less impact on the practice of school psychology. Such practice has always been more circumscribed, as the label would imply. Furthermore, whereas the doctoral degree has been assumed to be the minimal level of training necessary for professional practice in the other three specialties, historically most school psychologists have practiced with a master's degree or specialty credential. Further, in the first half of the twentieth century, school psychologists came from many different educational backgrounds, sometimes with little training in psychology.

Fagan (1990) has divided the history of school psychology into "Hybrid years" (1890–1969) and "Thoroughbred years" (1970 to present). The Hybrid years describe a period when school psychology was "a blend of many kinds of educational and psychological practitioners loosely mobilized around a dominant role of psychoeducational assessment for special class placement" (p. 913). That role still exists in the Thoroughbred years, but the practitioner is more narrowly defined as a school psychologist, typically someone who has a master's or doctoral degree in school psychology from a nationally accredited program.

The first master's degree training program for school psychologists was initiated at New York University in 1928 and the first doctoral training program at the University of Illinois in 1953. The APA did not begin accrediting doctoral programs in school psychology until 1971, and only accredits at the doctoral level. Master's degree programs are accredited by the National Association of School Psychologists (NASP), an organization founded in 1969.

Like the other practice specialties, there have been significant postwar changes for school psychologists as they, too, have struggled to find their identity as a profession (see the report of the Thayer Conference, Cutts, 1955). Still, the Thoroughbred years have been ones of tremendous growth in training and practice for the field. Psychological services in the schools have increased dramatically since the 1970s, in part stimulated by America's baby boom, but also by federal legislation on education, particularly laws on special education such as the landmark Public Law 94-142, enacted in 1974, which mandated education for all children regardless of handicap.

A "PROFESSIONAL" JOURNAL WITHIN APA

When the new APA was formed in 1946, a new "professional" journal was established, the *American Psychologist.* Initially, many articles on professional training and professional job opportunities were published in the *AP.* After 10 years, the *AP* was serving a broader associationwide role, and the statement about "the professional journal" of psychology was quietly removed in 1957.

It would be 12 more years before practitioners got back a "professional" journal from the APA. In 1966, Donald K. Freedheim was asked by George W. Albee, who was then president of the Division of Clinical Psychology (12), to edit the newsletter of the division, which was a mimeographed publication. A magazine-like format, with a new logo, was developed. The format lent itself to having pictures, which enhanced the readability of the publication, but also helped to identify authors at conventions. With this new professional-looking publication, the editor invited contributions from members of other service divisions (e.g., school, industrial, counseling), as they were facing similar issues of standards of practice, training, and licensing that were of concern to the clinical members. Submissions from across the spectrum of professional fields in psychology grew, and there were clearly important issues that all the specialties shared.

The APA had a fine stable of scientific journals at the time but no publication that was appropriate for the sorts of

material important to the practicing community—policy issues, case histories, training and internship opportunities, and so forth. It was apparent that a truly professional practice–oriented journal was needed. The APA had just received a large grant from the National Science Foundation to develop new, innovative publications on an experimental basis. "The Clinical Psychologist" was about to be transformed into an "experimental publication" called *Professional Psychology,* with an editorial board made up of members from across subspecialty fields. The inaugural issue, fall 1969, contained "The Clinical Psychologist," and the cover of the journal retained the logo that had been developed for the newsletter. By the second issue of the quarterly, "The Clinical Psychologist" was pulled out to be published separately.

The transition from newsletter to journal was not always smooth. "The Clinical Psychologist" had carried book reviews, but none of the APA journals did. All APA-published reviews were in *Contemporary Psychology.* The *PP* editor believed it important to retain reviews for both the convenience of the readership and the clear fact that few practice-type publications would be reviewed in *CP.* After much discussion, the review section was allowed in the new journal, a major exception by the APA Publications and Communications Board (P&C Board). A similar, though less crucial, matter came up regarding authors' pictures, which had seldom appeared in APA journals, except in the *American Psychologist.* Not only were pictures maintained in *Professional Psychology,* but they started appearing in other APA journals as well, beginning with *Contemporary Psychology.* Another conflict emerged over the size of the publication, as the APA Journals Office wanted it to be in the standard 7-by-10-inch format then instituted for all other APA journals (except the *American Psychologist,* which was larger). The newsletter had been in a 6-by-9-inch format, and the *PP* editor believed that its successor should retain its distinct (and convenient) size, in part to distinguish it from the scientific journals. With the editor threatening to withdraw from the publication, the smaller format prevailed—at least for the seven-year term of the editor. After a year of being in experimental status, and submissions growing monthly, the quarterly was made an "official" APA publication—and the editor allowed to serve on the Council of Editors.

In 1983, the title of the journal expanded to *Professional Psychology: Research and Practice. PP* is currently published six times a year. During the editorial term of Patrick H. DeLeon (1995–2000), with Gary R. VandenBos serving as the managing editor, *Professional Psychology* made an even greater effort to address the interests of the practice community. After conducting three reader surveys during the first year (one of which involved an innovative nationwide telephone conference call hookup involving over 50 subscribers), *PP* readers made crystal clear that they wanted articles that "provide practical advice and concrete suggestions that could be implemented in everyday practice settings, rather than merely placing the new findings within the context of the existing published literature (and then commenting upon needed future research)" (DeLeon & VandenBos, 2000, p. 595).

PP's coverage included managed care, prescription privileges for psychologists, telehealth care, expanding roles for psychologists within the public policy (including legislative and administrative) arena, and behavioral health-service delivery within primary care. Each of these issues has become of major concern to the profession and to the nation's overall health-delivery system during the past decade. The readership numbers (individual and institutional) steadily increased to approximately 8,000, making *Professional Psychology* the second most popular subscribed to APA journal.

In retrospect, the concerted effort to promulgate APA Practice Directorate efforts and relevant federal public health initiatives (e.g., those of the U.S. Surgeon General), although perhaps highly unusual for an APA journal, have had an impact in educating the field regarding the changes evolving within their practice environments. Also, efforts to engage women and ethnic minorities in the editorial process (and thereby enrich the breadth of coverage) were particularly successful. The overall percentage of ethnic minority members in the APA at the time was 5.38%; in sharp contrast, in 1999 three of the five *Professional Psychology* associate editors were female, and two associate editors were members of ethnic minorities. Further, 34.7% of the editorial board were female and 14.7% were ethnic minorities. This was a significantly higher percentage of both categories of members than almost any other APA journal.

ELECTRONIC PUBLISHING INITIATIVES

In January 1995, the APA Web site was available to its members and the public. The total "hits" in the first three months was 22,474—a figure that today (in 2001) is reached every 30 minutes. Usage increased in every quarter of 1995, reaching 413,207 hits in the fourth quarter of that year; quarterly hits in 2001 ran at 90 million.

It is interesting to note that many people from a vast array of fields turn to the APA for information on how to reference electronic documents. The APA has a special "style page" on electronic citations. A million people access this specialized page on a relatively narrow topic every year. Nonpsychologist (and

nonstudent) use of the APA Web site remains strong. Almost 35% (or some four million annual users) of the APA Web site are *not* psychologists or students studying psychology.

In 1997, APA president-elect Martin Seligman proposed the establishment of an electronic journal called *Treatment,* to be published jointly with the American Psychiatric Association. For political reasons the "other APA" withdrew from the venture because of fear that psychologists might claim that reading the copublished journal would qualify them for prescribing medication. The American Psychological Association then decided to embark on the e-journal alone, which is now titled *Prevention and Treatment.* By the summer of 2001, under Seligman's editorship, the journal had 20,000 regular readers, with each article being "hit" an average of 35,000 times within the first year of release. Publications from the Practice Directorate, the e-journal, Web-based communications, videotapes, and over 70 new books each year constitute communications from the APA that are directed toward the practicing professional psychologist.

COMMUNITY INVOLVEMENT

During the 1990s, the APA became increasingly involved in several highly visible community activities that contributed to society's appreciation of the role of psychological services. In 1991, during the Gulf War, the APA joined with the American Red Cross in forming a network of psychologists to provide mental health services to families of members of the armed services. Since then the network has been activated following natural disasters, airline crashes, and terrorist attacks in Oklahoma City (1996) and in New York City and Washington, D.C., in September 2001.

In another effort, the Practice Directorate forged a partnership with Music Television (MTV) to develop a youth antiviolence initiative titled "Warning Signs," to help the nation's youth in identifying early signs of violent behavior and to emphasize the need to get help should they see any of them (Peterson & Newman, 2000). The campaign officially kicked off with a youth forum held in Los Angeles on April 22, 1999. The 30-minute documentary, coproduced by MTV and the APA, was the highest rated prosocial special in MTV's history, with 3.9 million youth watching the film. In that year, there were over 600 follow-up psychologist-led "Community Youth Forums on Violence" held across the nation, with more than 58,000 youths attending. In March 2000, the Practice Directorate launched "Warning Signs for Parents" as a logical follow-up; by the end of the year, nearly 150,000 copies of the accompanying publication had been distributed.

TWO ASSOCIATIONAL DEVELOPMENTS

The essence of a profession is daily involvement with patients or clients. The context in which this interaction occurs, including the very important issue of reimbursement for services rendered, falls within the jurisdiction of public policy (e.g., the political process). For psychology to become an active participant within primary care (or to expand its scope of practice to include prescriptive authority) requires institutional collective knowledge of the evolving "bigger picture" and ongoing interrelationships existing within society and the generic health care arena. Historically, professional psychology has, at most, seen itself as solely one of the mental health disciplines and has not concerned itself with broader public policy or public health issues (DeLeon, VandenBos, Sammons, & Frank, 1998). These two programmatic initiatives have significantly changed that perspective.

The APA Congressional Science Fellowship Program

In 1974, Pam Flattau served as the first APA Congressional Science Fellow, under the program established in conjunction with the American Association for the Advancement of Science (AAAS). Over a quarter of a century later, approximately 125 colleagues have had the opportunity to serve on Capitol Hill (or in the administration) as APA Fellows, Robert Wood Johnson Health Policy Fellows, or in other similar national programs. In this capacity, they experienced personal involvement in the public policy process. Initially, the APA focused only on providing the experience for recent doctoral graduates; as the program matured, however, a concerted effort was made to attract more senior fellows. The APA Fellows have included individuals from almost every psychological specialty area, including several who also possessed degrees in law (Fowler, 1996).

Over the years, a number of psychologists have gravitated to positions of high-level public policy responsibility. During President Lyndon Johnson's era of the "Great Society," John Gardner served as secretary of the Department of Health, Education, and Welfare. Psychologists have served as departmental assistant secretaries, subject to Senate confirmation; director of one of the National Institutes of Health (NIH), as well as of other federal research institutes; head of the federal Bureau of Prisons; commanders of federal health care facilities; and as Chief State Mental Health officials. In the 107th Congress (2001–2002), three psychologists were elected to U.S. House of Representatives, and 12 psychologists served in the various state legislatures during that same time.

With firsthand experience in the public policy process, psychologists have been influential in the gradual modification of statutes and implementation of regulations that recognize psychology's expertise. In the clinical arena, psychology's expertise is now independently recognized throughout the judicial system and under all federal and private reimbursement systems. Psychology's professional graduate students are supported under almost every federal training and service delivery initiative.

The underlying unanswered question remains, however: Has professional psychology matured sufficiently to establish its own programmatic agenda via the public policy process (VandenBos, DeLeon, & Belar, 1991)?

APAGS

In 1988, the APA Council of Representatives formally established the American Psychological Association of Graduate Students (APAGS). Over the years, psychology has continued to be one of, if not the, most popular undergraduate majors. By 2001, the APA membership (and affiliate) numbers had grown to 155,000, with the APAGS possessing 59,700 members.

An APAGS representative attends the open portions of the APA board of directors meetings (and another individual is seated on the floor of the Council of Representatives as a nonvoting member). Increasingly, as with other professions, the student voice is being heard. Several divisions, state associations, and council caucuses provide the APAGS with a voting seat on their boards of directors.

Student participation brings to the APA governance deliberations a unique focus upon the "here and now" practical consequences. The APAGS's presence constantly reminds those within the APA governance that their deliberations do have very real consequences on future generations of professional psychologists.

THE PRESCRIPTIVE AUTHORITY (RxP-) AGENDA

In November 1984, Senator Daniel K. Inouye addressed the annual meeting of the Hawaii Psychological Association and in closing suggested to them an entirely new legislative agenda that he proposed would fit nicely into their convention theme "Psychology in the 80's: Transcending Traditional Boundaries" (e.g., seeking prescriptive authority in order to better serve their patients). After his challenge, the executive committee of the Hawaii Psychological Association agreed to pursue legislation that would study the "feasibility of allowing licensed psychologists to administer and prescribe medication in the treatment of nervous, mental and organic brain diseases." At that time there was little enthusiasm for the proposal within the psychological community and extreme opposition within the local psychiatric community (DeLeon, Fox, & Graham, 1991). This, however, was to be the beginning of psychology's prescriptive authority (RxP-) quest.

In 1989, the APA Board of Professional Affairs (BPA) held a special retreat to explore the issues surrounding psychology obtaining RxP- authority. It concluded by strongly endorsing immediate research and study regarding the feasibility and the appropriate curricula in psychopharmacology so that psychologists might provide broader service to the public and more effectively meet the psychological and mental health needs of society. Further, the BPA also recommended that focused attention on the responsibility of preparing the profession to address current and future needs of the public for psychologically managed psychopharmacological interventions be made APA's highest priority. Interestingly, in the 1970s, the APA board of directors had appointed a special committee to review this very matter. The recommendation at that time was that psychology not pursue prescription privileges, primarily since the field was doing so well without that authority! (DeLeon, Sammons, & Fox, 2000).

At the APA annual convention in Boston in 1990, the motion to establish an ad hoc Task Force on Psychopharmacology was approved by a vote of 118 to 2. Their report back to council in 1992 concluded that practitioners with combined training in psychopharmacology and psychosocial treatments could be viewed as a new form of health care professional, expected to bring to health care delivery the best of both psychological and pharmacological knowledge. Further, the proposed new provider possessed the potential to dramatically improve patient care and make important new advances in treatment (Smyer et al., 1993).

On June 17, 1994, APA president Bob Resnick was formally recognized during the graduation ceremonies at the Walter Reed Army Medical Center for the first two Department of Defense (DoD) Psychopharmacology Fellows, Navy Commander John Sexton and Lt. Commander Morgan Sammons. This program had been directed by the Fiscal Year 1989 Appropriations bill for the Department of Defense (P.L. 100–463) (U.S. Department of Defense, 1988) and would ultimately graduate 10 fellows. Upon their graduation, each of these courageous individuals became active within the practitioner community, demonstrating to their colleagues that psychologists can indeed readily learn to provide high-quality psychopharmacological care. Several of the graduates have become particularly involved in providing consultation to evolving postdoctoral psychopharmacology training programs. All of the external evaluations of the clinical care was provided by the DoD Fellows (ACNP, Summer, 2000).

At its August 1995 meeting in New York City, the APA Council of Representatives formally endorsed prescriptive privileges for appropriately trained psychologists and called for the development of model legislation and a model training curriculum. The follow year in Toronto, the council adopted both a model prescription bill and a model training curriculum. Those seeking this responsibility should possess at least 300 contact hours of didactic instruction and have supervised clinical experience with at least 100 patients requiring psychotropic medication. In 1997, the APAGS adopted a "resolution of support" for the APA position. And, that same year, at the Chicago convention, the council authorized the APA College of Professional Psychology to develop an examination in psychopharmacology suitable for use by state and provincial licensing boards. This exam became available in the spring of 2000. As of the summer of 2001, approximately 50 individuals had taken the examination, which covers 10 predetermined distinct knowledge areas.

By late 2001, the APA Practice Directorate reported that RxP- bills had been introduced in 13 states and that the APA Council had demonstrated its support for the agenda by allocating contingency funding totaling $86,400 over 5 fiscal years. In its February 2001 reexamination of the top priorities for APA's future, the APA Council of Representatives had placed advocacy for prescription privileges as number six of 21 ranked priorities for the association. While no comprehensive bill has yet passed, the U.S. territory of Guam has passed legislation authorizing appropriately trained psychologists to prescribe in the context of a collaborative practice arrangement with a physician. During the spring of 2001, a psychologists' prescriptive authority bill only very narrowly missed passage in New Mexico, successfully making it through two House committees, the full House, and a Senate committee. Further, we would note that a reading of an amendment to the Indiana Psychology Practice Act, which passed in 1993, indicates that psychologists participating in a federal government–sponsored training or treatment program may prescribe. Thirty-one state psychological associations currently have prescription privileges task forces engaged in some phase of the RxP- agenda. Patrick H. DeLeon has had the pleasure of serving as the commencement speaker for three postdoctoral masters' psychopharmacology graduations (in Louisiana, Texas, and Florida). By the summer of 2001, cohorts of psychopharmacology classes had also graduated in Georgia (two separate classes), Hawaii, and New Mexico, with additional cohorts enrolled in several different states. The Prescribing Psychologists' Register (PPR) also reports having graduated a significant number of students. Psychology's RxP- agenda is steadily advancing (DeLeon, Robinson-Kurpius, & Sexton, 2001; DeLeon & Wiggins, 1996).

THE TWENTY-FIRST CENTURY

Unquestionably, the psychological practice environment of the twenty-first century will be dramatically different than it is today. The specifics of change are, of course, unpredictable. However, at least one major trend is clear. Our nation's health care system is just beginning to appreciate the applicability of technology, particularly computer and telecommunications technology, to the delivery of clinical services. The Institute of Medicine (IOM), which has served as a highly respected health policy "think tank" for administrations and the Congress since its inception in 1970, reports that

> Health care delivery has been relatively untouched by the revolution in information technology that has been transforming nearly every other aspect of society. The majority of patient and clinician encounters take place for purposes of exchanging clinical information. . . . Yet it is estimated that only a small fraction of physicians offer e-mail interaction, a simple and convenient tool for efficient communication, to their patients. (Institute of Medicine, 2001, p. 15)

The number of Americans who use the Internet to retrieve health-related information is estimated to be about 70 million. Currently, over half of American homes possess computers, and while information presently doubles every 5 years, it will soon double every 17 days, with traffic on the Web already doubling every 100 days (Jerome et al., 2000). And, at the same time, the IOM further reports that the lag between the discovery of more efficacious forms of treatment and their incorporation into routine patient care is unnecessarily long, in the range of about 15 to 20 years. Even then, adherence of clinical practice to the evidence is highly uneven.

The era of the "educated consumer" is upon us. How consumer expectations and the unprecedented explosion in communications technology will affect the delivery of psychological care is yet to be determined. Highly complex issues such as reimbursement for virtual therapy environments, automated diagnostic testing protocols, ensuring psychologically based enriched living and long-term care environments for senior citizens and the chronically ill, not to mention financial support for clinical graduate students, will all be debated in the public policy (e.g., political) arena. Professional psychology must become active participants in this critical— and ongoing—dialogue, in order to ensure the future of professional psychology, research in applied psychology, basic psychological research, and the public welfare in terms of health care and social services.

REFERENCES

American Psychological Association, Committee on Training in Clinical Psychology. (1947). Recommended graduate training program in clinical psychology. *American Psychologist, 2,* 539–558.

American Psychological Association. (1957). Proceedings of the sixty-fifth annual business meeting of the American Psychological Association. *American Psychologist, 12,* 696.

American Psychological Association. Division of Counseling and Guidance, Committee on Counselor Training. (1952). Recommended standards for training counseling psychologists at the doctoral level. *American Psychologist, 7,* 175–181.

American Psychological Association, Division of Counseling Psychology, Committee on Definition. (1956). Counseling psychology as a specialty. *American Psychologist, 11,* 282–285.

Baker, D. B. (1988). The psychology of Lightner Witmer. *Professional School Psychology, 3,* 109–121.

Baker, D. B., & Benjamin, L. T., Jr. (2000). The affirmation of the scientist-practitioner: A look back at Boulder. *American Psychologist, 55,* 241–247.

Benjamin, L. T., Jr. (1996). The founding of the *American Psychologist:* The professional journal that wasn't. *American Psychologist, 51,* 8–12.

Benjamin, L. T., Jr. (1997). The origin of psychological species: History of the beginnings of the American Psychological Association divisions. *American Psychologist, 52,* 725–732.

Benjamin, L. T., Jr. (in press). Science for sale: Psychology's earliest adventures in American advertising. In C. Haugtvedt, W. N. Lee, & J. Williams (Eds.), *Diversity in advertising.* Mahwah, NJ: Erlbaum.

Berg, I., Pepinsky, H. B., & Shoben, E. J. (1980). The status of counseling psychology: 1960. In J. M. Whiteley (Ed.), *The history of counseling psychology* (pp. 105–113). Monterey, CA: Brooks/ Cole.

Boring, E. G. (1938). The society of experimental psychologists, 1904–1938. *American Journal of Psychology, 51,* 410–423.

Boring, E. G. (1967). Titchener's experimentalists. *Journal of the History of the Behavioral Sciences, 3,* 315–325.

Caplan, E. (1998). *Mind games: American culture and the birth of psychotherapy.* Berkeley: University of California Press.

Capshew, J. H. (1999). *Psychologists on the march: Science, practice, and professional identity in America, 1929–1969.* New York: Cambridge University Press.

Cattell, J. M. (1890). Mental tests and measurements. *Mind, 51,* 373–381.

Cattell, J. M. (1893). Tests of the senses and faculties. *Educational Review, 5,* 257–265.

Cohen, L. D. (1992). The academic department. In D. K. Freedheim (Ed.), *History of psychotherapy: A century of change* (p. 731–764). Washington, DC: American Psychological Association.

Coon, D. J. (1992). Testing the limits of sense and science: American experimental psychologists combat spiritualism, 1880–1920. *American Psychologist, 47,* 143–151.

Cummings, N. A. (1979). Mental health and national health insurance: A case history of the struggle for professional autonomy. In C. A. Kiesler, N. A. Cummings, & G. R. VandenBos (Eds.), *Psychology and national health insurance: A sourcebook* (pp. 5–16). Washington, DC: American Psychological Association.

Cutts, N. E. (1955). *School psychologists at mid-century.* Washington, DC: American Psychological Association.

Davidson, E. S., & Benjamin, L. T., Jr. (1987). A history of the child study movement in America. In J. A. Glover & R. Ronning (Eds.), *Historical foundations of educational psychology* (pp. 41–60). New York: Plenum Press.

DeAngelis, T. (1989). Suit opens doors to analysis training. *APA Monitor, 20,* 16.

DeLeon, P. H., Fox, R. E., & Graham, S. R. (1991). Prescription privileges: Psychology's next frontier? *American Psychologist, 46,* 384–393.

DeLeon, P. H., Robinson-Kurpius, S. E., & Sexton, J. L. (2001). Prescriptive authority for psychologists: Law, ethics, and public policy. In M. T. Sammons & N. B. Schmidt (Eds.), *Combined treatments for mental disorders: A guide to psychological and pharmacological interventions* (pp. 33–52). Washington, DC: American Psychological Association.

DeLeon, P. H., Sammons, M. T., & Fox, R. E. (2000). Prescription privileges. In A. E. Kazdin (Ed.), *Encyclopedia of psychology* (Vol. 6, pp. 285–287). Washington, DC: American Psychological Association.

DeLeon, P. H., VandenBos, G. R., Sammons, M. T., & Frank, R. G. (1998). Changing health care environment in the United States: Steadily evolving into the 21st century. In A. S. Bellack & M. Hersen (Series Eds.) & A. N. Wiens (Vol. Ed.), *Comprehensive clinical psychology: Professional issues* (Vol. 2, pp. 393–401). London: Elsevier.

DeLeon, P. H., & VandenBos, G. R. (2000). News from Washington, DC. Reflecting and leading: Progress in professional practice in psychology. *Professional Psychology: Research and Practice, 31*(6), 595–597.

DeLeon, P. H., & Wiggins, J. G. (1996). Prescription privileges for psychologists. *American Psychologist, 51*(3), 225–229.

Fagan, T. K. (1987). Gesell: The first school psychologist. Part II: Practice and significance. *School Psychology Review, 16,* 399–409.

Fagan, T. K. (1989). Norma Estelle Cutts. (1892–1988). *American Psychologist, 44,* 1236.

Fagan, T. K. (1990). A brief history of school psychology in the United States. In A. Thomas & J. Grimes (Eds.), *Best practices in school psychology* (pp. 913–929). Washington, DC: National Association of School Psychologists.

Fagan, T. K. (1992). Compulsory schooling, child study, clinical psychology, and special education: Origins of school psychology. *American Psychologist, 47,* 236–243.

Fowler, R. D. (1996). Foreword: Psychology, public policy, and the congressional fellowship program. In R. P. Lorion, I. Iscoe, P. H. DeLeon, & G. R. VandenBos (Eds.), *Psychology and public policy: Balancing public service and professional need* (pp. ix–xiv). Washington, DC: American Psychological Association.

Gale, H. (1900). On the psychology of advertising. *Psychological Studies, 1,* 39–69.

Grob, G. N. (1994). *The mad among us: A history of the care of America's mentally ill.* Cambridge, MA: Harvard University Press.

Hoffman, L. E. (1992). American psychologists and wartime research on Germany, 1941–1945. *American Psychologist, 47,* 264–273.

Hollingworth, H. L. (1920). *The psychology of functional neuroses.* New York: D. Appleton.

Institute of Medicine. (2001). *Crossing the quality chasm: A new health system for the 21st century.* Washington, DC: National Academy Press.

Jerome, L. W., DeLeon, P. H., James, L. C., Folen, R., Earles, J., & Gedney, J. J. (2000). The coming of age of telecommunications in psychological research and practice. *American Psychologist, 55*(4), 407–421.

Korman, A. (1974). National conference on the levels and patterns of professional training in psychology: The major themes. *American Psychologist, 29,* 441–449.

Kuna, D. P. (1976). The concept of suggestion in the early history of advertising psychology. *Journal of the History of the Behavioral Sciences, 12,* 347–353.

Kuna, D. P. (1979). Early advertising applications of the Gale-Cattell order-of-merit method. *Journal of the History of the Behavioral Sciences, 15,* 38–46.

Levine, M., & Levine, A. (1992). *Helping children: A social history.* New York: Oxford University Press.

McReynolds, P. (1997). *Lightner Witmer: His life and times.* Washington, DC: American Psychological Association.

Moore, D. L. (1992). The Veterans Administration and the training program in psychology. In D. K. Freedheim (Ed.), *History of psychotherapy: A century of change* (pp. 776–800). Washington, DC: American Psychological Association.

Münsterberg, H. (1909). *Psychotherapy.* New York: Moffat, Yard.

Münsterberg, H. (1913). *Psychology and industrial efficiency.* Boston: Houghton Mifflin.

Napoli, D. S. (1981). *Architects of adjustment: The history of the psychological profession in the United States.* Port Washington, NY: Kennikat Press.

Parsons, F. (1909). *Choosing a vocation.* Boston: Houghton Mifflin.

Peterson, D. R. (1992). The doctor of psychology degree. In D. K. Freedheim (Ed.), *History of psychotherapy: A century of change* (pp. 829–849). Washington, DC: American Psychological Association.

Peterson, J. L., & Newman, R. (2000). Helping to curb youth violence: The APA-MTV, "warning signs" initiative. *Professional Psychology: Research and Practice, 31*(5), 509–514.

Prince, M. (1908). *The dissociation of a personality.* New York: Longman, Green.

Raimy, V. C. (Ed.). (1950). *Training in clinical psychology.* Englewood Cliffs, NJ: Prentice-Hall.

Riess, B. F. (1992). Postdoctoral training: Toward professionalism. In D. K. Freedheim (Ed.), *History of psychology: A century of change* (pp. 765–775). Washington, DC: American Psychological Association.

Routh, D. K. (2000). Clinical psychology training: A history of ideas and practices prior to 1946. *American Psychologist, 55,* 236–241.

Scott, W. D. (1903). *The theory of advertising.* Boston: Small, Maynard.

Smyer, M. A., Balster, R. L., Egli, D., Johnson, D. L., Kilbey, M. M., Leith, N. J., et al. (1993). Summary of the report of the ad hoc task force on psychopharmacology of the American Psychological Association. *Professional Psychology: Research and Practice, 24*(4), 394–403.

Sokal, M. M. (1982a). The Committee on the Certification of Consulting Psychologists: A failure of applied psychology in the 1920s. In C. J. Adkins Jr., & B. A. Winstead (Eds.), *History of applied psychology: Department of Psychology colloquium series, II* (pp. 71–90). Norfolk, VA: Old Dominion University.

Sokal, M. M. (1982b). James McKeen Cattell and the failure of anthropometric mental testing, 1890–1901. In W. R. Woodward & M. G. Ash (Eds.), *The problematic science: Psychology in nineteenth-century thought* (pp. 322–345). New York: Praeger.

Stricker, G., & Cummings, N. A. (1992). The professional school movement. In D. K. Freedheim (Ed.), *History of Psychotherapy:*

A century of change (pp. 801–828). Washington, DC: American Psychological Association.

Super, D. E. (1955). Transition: From vocational guidance to counseling psychology. *Journal of Counseling Psychology, 2,* 3–9.

Taylor, F. W. (1911). *The principles of scientific management.* New York: Harper and Brothers.

Tyler, L., Tiedeman, D., & Wrenn, C. G. (1980). The current status of counseling psychology: 1961. In J. M. Whiteley (Ed.), *The history of counseling psychology* (pp. 114–124). Monterey, CA: Brooks/Cole.

U.S. Department of Defense. (1988). Fiscal Year 1989 Department of Defense Appropriations Act, Pub, L. No. 100–463, 102 Stat. 2270 (October 1, 1988).

VandenBos, G. R., Cummings, N. A., & DeLeon, P. H. (1992). A century of psychotherapy: Economic and environmental influences. In D. K. Freedheim (Ed.), *History of psychotherapy: A century of change* (pp. 65–102). Washington, DC: American Psychological Association.

VandenBos, G. R., DeLeon, P. H., & Belar, C. D. (1991). How many psychologists are needed? It's too early to know! *Professional Psychology: Research and Practice, 22*(6), 441–448.

Watson, J. B. (1925). *Behaviorism.* New York: People's Institute.

Wiggam, A. E. (1928). *Exploring your own mind with the psychologists.* New York: Bobbs Merrill.

Witmer, L. (1897). The organization of practical work in psychology. *Psychological Review, 4,* 116–117.

Witmer, L. (1907). Clinical psychology. *The Psychological Clinic, 1,* 1–9. (Reprinted 1996 in *American Psychologist, 51,* 248–251.

Wolfle, D. (1997). The reorganized American Psychological Association. *American Psychologist, 52,* 721–724. (Original work published 1946)

Zenderland, L. (1998). *Measuring minds: Henry Herbert Goddard and the origins of American intelligence testing.* New York: Cambridge University Press.

CHAPTER 3

Biological Psychology

RICHARD F. THOMPSON AND STUART M. ZOLA

THE MIND   47
THE BRAIN   48
SENSORY PROCESSES   51
  Color Vision   51
  Pitch Detection   52
LEARNING AND MEMORY   53

MOTIVATION AND EMOTION   56
  Emotion   56
  Motivation   57
COGNITIVE NEUROSCIENCE   59
CONCLUSION   62
REFERENCES   62

The great questions of philosophy, the mind–body problem and the nature of knowledge, were also the questions that drove early developments in the pathways to modern psychology. This is especially true of biological or physiological psychology. Wilhelm Wundt, who founded experimental psychology, titled his major work *Foundations of Physiological Psychology* (1874/1908). William James, the other major figure in the development of modern psychology, devoted a third of his influential text *Principles of Psychology* (1890) to the brain and nervous system. Both Wundt and James studied medicine and philosophy, and both considered themselves physiologists. Their goal was not to reduce psychology to physiology but rather to apply the scientific methods of physiology to the study of the mind. The other driving force in early biological psychology was the study of the brain and nervous system.

The major topics in modern biological psychology are sensory processes, learning and memory, motivation and emotion, and most recently cognition—in short, behavioral and cognitive neuroscience. A number of other areas began as part of physiological psychology and have spun off to become fields in their own right. We treat the major topics in biological psychology separately in the text that follows. But first we sketch very briefly the recent philosophical and physiological roots.

THE MIND

The history of such issues as the mind–body problem and epistemology is properly the domain of philosophy, treated extensively in many volumes and well beyond the scope of this chapter and the expertise of these authors. Our focus in this brief section is on the history of the scientific study of the mind, which really began in the nineteenth century.

Perhaps the first experimental attacks on the nature of the mind were the observations of Weber as generalized by Gustav Fechner. Ernst Weber, a physiologist, was attempting in 1834 to determine whether the nerves that respond to the state of the muscles also contribute to judgments about weights. He found that the just noticeable difference (jnd) in weight that could be reliably detected by the observer was not some absolute amount but rather a constant *ratio* of the weight being lifted. The same applied to the pitch of tones and the length of lines.

Fechner realized that Weber had discovered a way of measuring the properties of the mind. Indeed, in his *Elements of Psychophysics* (1860/1966) he felt he had solved the problem of mind and body. He generalized Weber's observations to state that as the psychological measurement in jnd's increased arithmetically, the intensity of the physical stimulus increased geometrically—the relationship is logarithmic. Fechner, trained as a physicist, developed the classical psychophysical methods and the concepts of absolute and differential thresholds. According to Edwin Boring (1942), he had a nervous breakdown and resigned his chair at Leipzig in 1839. During the last 35 years of his life, he devoted himself to panpsychism, the view that mind and matter are one and thus that mind is all. He viewed the psychophysical law as the paradigm for the transformation of the material into the spiritual. In any event, the methods Fechner developed were of great help to such early experimental psychologists as Wundt and his student Tichener in their attempts to measure the attributes of sensation.

Tichener identified the elements of conscious experience as quality, intensity, extensity, protensity (duration), and attensity (clearness) (see Tichener, 1898). But for all their attempts at scientific observation, the basic approach of Wundt and Tichener was introspection, but other observers (e.g., Külpe at Bonn) had different introspections. Boring studied with Tichener and was for many years chair of the psychology department at Harvard. He attempted to recast Tichener's views in more modern terms (*The Physical Dimensions of Consciousness,* 1933) by emphasizing that the dimensions listed earlier related to discrimination of physical stimuli. His student S. S. Stevens showed that trained observers could reliably form judgments of sounds in terms of pitch, loudness, "volume," and "density" (see also Boring, 1950).

At Harvard, Stevens later introduced an important new method of psychophysics termed *direct magnitude estimation.* The subject simply assigned a number to a stimulus, a higher one to a more intense stimulus and a lower number to one that was less intense. Somewhat surprisingly this method gave very reliable results. Using this method, Stevens found that the proper relationship between stimulus intensity and sensation is not logarithmic, as Fechner had argued, but rather a power function: The sensation, that is, sensory magnitude, equaled the stimulus intensity raised to some power, the exponent ranging from less than to greater than one. This formulation proved very useful in both psychophysical and physiological studies of sensory processes (see Stevens, 1975).

The key point of all this work on psychophysics is that it is not necessary to be concerned at all about subjective experience or introspection. The observer simply pushes a button or states a word or number to describe his or her judgment of the stimulus. The more the observer practices, the more reliable the judgments become and the more different observers generate the same results. Psychophysics had become purely behavioral.

As Hilgard (1987) notes, Fechner was troubled by the question of where the transformation between stimulus and judgment occurs. Fechner distinguished between "inner" and "outer" psychophysics, *outer* referring to the relation between the mind and external stimuli and *inner* to the relation between the mind and excitation of the sensory apparatus. Fechner opted for a direct correspondence between excitation and sensation, a surprisingly modern view. Indeed, Stevens (1961) argued with evidence that the psychophysical transformation occurs at the receptor–first-order neurons, at least for intensity.

We take an example from the elegant studies of Mountcastle, Poggio, and Werner (1963). Here they recorded the action potentials of a neuron in the somatosensory thalamus of a monkey driven by extension of the contralateral knee. The relation between degrees of joint angle (θ) and frequency of neuron discharge (F) is $F = 13.9\theta^{0.429} + 24$, where 13.9 and 24 are constants determined by conditions. So the power exponent is 0.429, within the general range of exponents for psychophysical judgments of the relation between joint angle and sensation of movement. In other words, the relationship is established by ascending sensory neuron activity before the level of the cerebral cortex, presumably at the receptor–first-order neuron.

The modern era of psychophysics can perhaps be dated to a seminal paper by John Swets in 1961: *Is there a sensory threshold?* His answer was no. He and David Green developed the theory and methodology of signal detection theory (Green & Swets, 1966). There is always noise present with signals. When one attempts to detect a signal in noise, the criteria used will determine the outcome. This approach has proved immensely useful in fields ranging from the telephone to psychophysical studies in animals to detection of structural failures in aircraft wings to detection of breast cancer. But where is the mind in decision theory? It has disappeared. The initial hope that psychophysics could measure the mind has been reduced to considerations of observer bias. A similar conclusion led to the downfall of introspection.

THE BRAIN

Until the nineteenth century, the only method available to study brain function was the lesion, either in unfortunate humans with brain damage or brain lesions done in infrahuman animals. The key intellectual issue throughout the history of the brain sciences was localization. To state the question in simplistic terms: Are psychological traits and functions localized to particular regions of the brain or are they widely distributed in the brain?

The history of ideas about localization of brain function can be divided roughly into three eras. During the first era, which spans from antiquity to about the second century A.D., debate focused on the location of cognitive function, although the discussion revolved around the issue of the soul, that is, what part of the body housed the essence of being and the source of all mental life (for reviews, see Finger, 1994; Gross, 1987; Star, 1989). In an early and particularly prophetic Greek version of localization of function, the soul was thought to be housed in several body parts, including the head, heart, and liver, but the portion of the soul associated with intellect was located in the head (McHenry, 1969). The individual whom many historians have viewed as having the greatest influence during this era was Galen, an anatomist of Greek origin. Using animals, he performed experiments that provided evidence that the brain was the center of the nervous system and responsible for sensation, motion, and thinking (Finger, 1994; Gross, 1987).

In the second era (spanning the second to the eighteenth centuries), the debate focused on whether cognitive functions were localized in the ventricular system of the brain or in the brain matter itself. The influence of the church during this era cannot be overstated; for example, ethereal spirits (and ideas) were believed to flow through the empty spaces of the brain's ventricles. Nevertheless, by the fifteenth and sixteenth centuries, individuals such as da Vinci and Vesalius were questioning the validity of ventricular localization. Finally, during the seventeenth century, partly as a result of the strongly held views and prolific writings of Thomas Willis, and during the eighteenth century, with the publication of clinical descriptions of cognitively impaired patients accompanied by crude descriptions of brain damage (e.g., Baader), the view that intellectual function was localized in brain matter and not in the ventricles became solidified (Clenending, 1942).

The nineteenth century to the present makes up the third era, and here debate has focused on how mental activities (or cognitive processes) are organized in the brain. An early idea, which became known as the localizationist view, proposed that specific mental functions were carried out by specific parts of the brain. An alternative idea, which became known as the equipotential view, held that large parts of the brain were equally involved in all mental activity and that there was no specificity of function within a particular brain area (Clark & Jacyna, 1987).

Perhaps the most influential idea about localization of brain function derived from Franz Joseph Gall during the early nineteenth century. Gall had been influenced somewhat by the earlier ideas of Albrecht von Haller (Clarke & Jacyna, 1987). In the mid-eighteenth century, Haller had developed a doctrine of brain equipotentiality, or a type of *action commune*. He believed that the parts of a distinguishable anatomical component of the brain—the white matter, for instance—performed as a whole, each area of white matter having equivalent functional significance (Clarke & Jacyna, 1987). Indeed, one might characterize Gall's ideas as a reaction against the equipotential view of Haller. Gall's insight was that, despite its similarity in appearance, brain tissue was not equipotential but instead was actually made up of many discrete areas that had different and separate functions. Eventually, Gall was able to characterize 27 different regions, or organs, of the brain in a scheme that he called organology. Later, the term *phrenology* came to be associated with Gall's work. However, this term was coined by Gall's colleague, Spurzheim, with whom he had a falling out, and Gall himself never used the term (Zola-Morgan, 1995).

Gall's ideas about the localization of cognitive functions began to tear at the religious and social fabric of the nineteenth century. In particular, various governmental and religious authorities saw his notion that various mental faculties were represented in different places in the brain as in conflict with moral and religious views of the unity of the soul and mind. Gall's organology, and later versions of phrenology, faced similar critiques from philosophy and science. Clerics and metaphysicians were concerned with the larger theological implications of the phrenological system. For example, in Flourens's critique of phrenology in 1846 (dedicated to Decartes), Gall and his followers were declared guilty of undermining the unity of the soul, human immortality, free will, and the very existence of God (Harrington, 1991). Rolando, the famous Italian neuroanatomist, recognized the elegance of Gall's dissection techniques and his tracing of fiber tracts from the spinal cord to the cerebrum. However, he found no logical connection between the tracings of the fibers and the distinct organs in the convolutions of the brain proposed to house particular mental faculties.

Another scientific criticism had to do with the questionable way in which Gall had determined the locus and extent of each of the 27 organs. For example, Gall had localized the carnivorous instinct and the tendency to murder (organ 5) above the ear for three reasons: (a) This was the widest part of the skull in carnivores; (b) a prominence was found there in a student who was fond of torturing animals; and (c) this region was well developed in an apothecary who later became an executioner (Barker, 1897).

Another scientific issue critics raised during the nineteenth century was that Gall never specified the precise extent or the anatomical borders of any of the organs. This lack of rigor, it was argued, made it impossible to correlate a specific faculty with the size of an organ or cranial capacity (Sewall, 1839). Related criticisms involved Gall's seeming failure to acknowledge that there were variations in the thickness of the skull, that is, variations from one individual specimen to another and from one locus to another within the same skull (Sewall, 1839).

An oft-cited example of a specific contribution Gall made to our understanding of brain function is the idea that he anticipated the discovery by Broca in 1861 of a specific speech area of the brain (Ackernecht & Vallois, 1956; Bouillaud, 1848). However, we believe that a careful reading of the facts surrounding this discovery tells a somewhat different story. In fact, Broca never mentioned Gall's name in his 1861 report. Moreover, he referred to Gall's doctrine in a rather negative way. Nevertheless, Broca's work stands as a clear example of a modern idea of localization of function built on the foundation and fundamental idea, established by Gall a half century earlier, that specific parts of the brain mediate specific behaviors.

Both Gall and Bouillaud seemed to be vindicated in 1861 with the publication of the proceedings from a meeting of the Société d'Anthropologie de Paris. Broca, assisted by Alexandre Ernest Aubertin, Bouillaud's son-in-law and a strong believer in localization and in Bouillaud's hypothesis, presented the neuropathological findings from the brain of his patient, Monsieur Leborgne. [This patient subsequently was referred to by the name "Tan," the only utterance Broca ever heard Monsieur Leborgne make (Broca, 1861).]

Broca's finding from his patient Tan has been regarded by some historians as the most important clinical discovery in the history of cortical localization. Moreover, within the decade, what some historians regard as the most important laboratory discovery pertaining to cortical localization was reported when Gustav Fritsch and Eduard Hitzig (1870) discovered the cortical motor area in the dog and proved that cortical localization was not restricted to a single function (Finger, 1994). The discoveries of the speech area by Broca and the motor area by Fritsch and Hitzig were seen as vindication for Gall's ideas and reestablished him as the father of localization.

Following the pioneering study by Fritsch and Hitzig on the localization and organization of the motor area of the cerebral cortex, localization of function quickly won the day, at least for sensory and motor systems. In the last three decades of the nineteenth century, the general locations of the visual and auditory areas of the cortex were identified. The field of physiology, in particular neurophysiology—for example, in the work of Sir Charles Sherrington—together with clinical neurology and neuroanatomy, were exciting new fields at the beginning of the twentieth century.

At this time, the only experimental tools for studying brain organization and functions were ablation and electrical stimulation. Neuroanatomy was in its descriptive phase; thanks in part to the Golgi method, the monumental work of Ramon y Cajal was completed over a period of several decades beginning near the end of the nineteenth century. Neurochemistry was in its descriptive phase, characterizing chemical substances in the brain.

The first recording of a nerve action potential with a cathode-ray tube was done by Gasser and Erlanger in 1922, but the method was not much used until the 1930s. The human EEG was rediscovered in 1929 by H. Berger, and the method was applied to animal research and human clinical neurology, particularly epilepsy, in the 1930s by, for example, Alexander Forbes, Hallowell Davis, and Donald Lindsley.

The pioneering studies of Adrian in England (1940) and of Wade Marshall, Clinton Woolsey, and Philip Bard (1941) at Johns Hopkins were the first to record electrical evoked potentials from the somatic sensory cortex in response to tactile stimulation. Woolsey and his associates developed the detailed methodology for evoked potential mapping of the cerebral cortex. In an extraordinary series of studies, they determined the localization and organization of the somatic sensory areas, the visual areas and the auditory areas of the cerebral cortex, in a comparative series of mammals. They initially defined two projection areas (I and II) for each sensory field; that is, they found two complete functional maps of the receptor surface for each sensory region of the cerebral cortex, for example, two complete representations of the skin surface in the somatic-sensory cortex.

In the 1940s and 1950s, the evoked potential method was used to analyze the organization of sensory systems at all levels from the first-order neurons to the cerebral cortex. The principle that emerged was strikingly clear and simple—in every sensory system the nervous system maintained receptotopic maps or projections at all levels from receptors—skin surface, retina, basilar membrane—to cerebral cortex. The receptor maps in the brain were not point-to-point; rather, they reflected the functional organization of each system—fingers, lips, and tongue areas were much enlarged in the primate somatic cortex, half the primary visual cortex represented the forea, and so on.

The evoked potential method was very well suited to analysis of the overall organization of sensory systems in the brain. However, it could reveal nothing about what the individual neurons were doing. This had to await development of the microelectrode (a very small electrode that records the activity of a single cell). Indeed, the microelectrode has been the key to analysis of the fine-grained organization and "feature detector" properties (most neurons respond only to certain aspects, or features, of a stimulus) of sensory neurons. The first intracellular glass pipette microelectrode was actually invented by G. Ling and R. W. Gerard in 1949; they developed it to record intracellularly from frog muscle. Several investigators had been using small wire electrodes to record from nerve fibers, for example, Robert Galambos at Harvard in 1939 (auditory nerve; see Galambos & Davis, 1943) and Birdsey Renshaw at the University of Oregon Medical School in the 1940s (dorsal and ventral spinal roots). Metal electrodes were generally found to be preferable for extracellular single-unit recording (i.e., recording the spike discharges of a single neuron where the tip of the microelectrode is outside the cell but close enough to record its activity clearly). Metal microelectrodes were improved in the early 1950s; R. W. Davies at Hopkins developed the platinum-iridium glass-coated microelectrode, D. Hubel and T. Wiesel at Harvard developed the tungsten microelectrode, and the search for putative stimulus coding properties of neurons was on. The pioneering studies were those of Mountcastle and associates at Hopkins on the organization of the somatic-sensory system (Mountcastle, Davies, & Berman, 1957), those of Hubel and Wiesel (1959) at Harvard on the visual system (and Maturana and Lettvin's work at MIT on the optic nerve fibers of frogs, see Maturana, Lettrin, McCulloch, & Pitts, 1960), and those of Rose, Hind, Woolsey, and associates at Wisconsin on the auditory system (see Hind et al., 1960).

It was not until many years later that imaging methods were developed to study the organization and functions of the normal human brain (see following text). Heroic studies had been done on human brain functioning much earlier in neurosurgical procedures (heroic both for the surgeon and the patient, e.g., Penfield & Rasmussen, 1950). However, these patients typically suffered from severe epilepsy. The development of PET, fMRI, and other modern techniques is largely responsible for the explosion of information in the aspect of biological psychology termed *cognitive neuroscience* (see following and the chapter by Leahey in this volume).

SENSORY PROCESSES

We select two examples of sensory processes, color vision and pitch detection, that illustrate very well the historical development of the study of sensory systems. They are both extraordinary success stories in the field of biological psychology.

Color Vision

Color vision provides an illustrative case history of the development of a field in biological psychology with feet in both physics and physiology. Isaac Newton was perhaps the first scientist to appreciate the nature of color. The fact that a prism could break up white light into a rainbow of colors meant that the light was a mixture that could produce spectral colors. But Newton recognized that the light rays themselves had no color; rather, different rays acted on the eye to yield sensations of colors (1704/1931). Oddly, the great German literary figure Goethe asserted it was impossible to conceive of white light as a mixture of colors (1810/1970).

In physics there was an ongoing debate whether light was particle or wave (we know now it is both). Interestingly, Newton favored the particle theory. Thomas Young, an English physicist working a century later, supported the wave theory. Newton had developed the first color circle showing that complementary pairs of colors opposite to one another on the circle would mix to yield white light. Young showed that it was possible to match any color by selecting three

appropriate colors, red, green, and blue, and suggested there were three such color receptors in the eye. Helmholtz elaborated and quantified Young's idea into the Young-Helmholtz trichromatic theory. Helmholtz, incidentally, studied with Müller and Du Bois-Reymond. He received his MD in 1842 and published two extraordinary works, the three-volume *Treatis on Physiological Optics* (1856–1866/1924) and *On the Sensations of Tone* (1863/1954). He was one of the leading scientists in the nineteenth century and had a profound impact on early developments in psychology, particularly biological psychology.

The basic idea in the trichomatic theory is that the three receptors accounted for sensations of red, green, and blue. Yellow was said to derive from stimulation of both red and green receptors, and white was derived from yellow and the blue receptor. But there were problems. The most common form of color blindness is red-green. But if yellow is derived from red and green, how is it that a person with red-green color blindness can see yellow? In the twentieth century, it was found that there are four types of receptors in the human retina: red, green, blue (cones), and light-dark (rods). But what about yellow?

Hering (1878) developed an alternative view termed the "opponent-process" theory. He actually studied with Weber and with Fechner and received his MD just two years after Wundt in Heidelberg. Interestingly, Hering disagreed with Fechner about the psychophysical law, arguing that the relationship should be a power function, thus anticipating Stevens. Hering proposed that red-green and blue-yellow acted as opposites, along with white-black. In modern times, Dorothea Jameson and Leo Hurvich (1955) provided an elegant mathematical formulation of Herring's theory that accounted very well for the phenomena of color vision.

Russell De Valois, now in the psychology department at the University of California, Berkeley, provided the physiological evidence to verify the Herring-Jameson-Hurvich theory, using the monkey (see De Valois, 1960). Ganglion neurons in the retina that respond to color show "opponent" processes. One cell might respond to red and be inhibited by green, another will respond to green and be inhibited by red, yet another will respond to blue and be inhibited by yellow, and the last type will respond to yellow and be inhibited by blue. The same is true for neurons in the visual thalamus. De Valois's work provided an elegant physiological basis for the opponent-process theory of color vision. But Young and Helmholtz were also correct in proposing that there are three color receptors in the retina. It is the neural interactions in the retina that convert actions of the three color receptors into the opponent processes in the ganglion cells. It is remarkable that nineteenth-century scientists, working only with the facts of human color vision, could deduce the physiological processes in the eye and brain.

An interesting chapter in the development of color-vision theory is the work of Christine Ladd-Franklin (Hilgard, 1987). She completed her PhD in mathematics at Johns Hopkins in 1882 but was not awarded the degree because she was a woman. Later she spent a year in Müller's laboratory in Göttingen, where he gave her private lectures because, as a woman, she was not allowed to attend his regular lectures. She developed a most interesting evolutionary theory of color vision based on the color zones in the retina. The center of the fovia has all colors and the most detailed vision. The next outer zone has red and green sensitivity (as well as blue and yellow), the next outer zone to this has only blue and yellow sensitivity (and black-white), and the most peripheral regions have only black-white (achromatic) sensitivity.

She argued that in evolution, the achromatic sensitivity (rods) developed first, followed by evolution of blue and yellow receptors and finally red and green receptors. The fact that red-green color blindness is most common is consistent with the idea that it is the most recent to evolve and hence the most "fragile."

Modern molecular biology and genetics actually provide support for Ladd-Franklin's evolutionary hypothesis. The Old World monkey retina appears to be identical to the human retina: Both macaques and humans have rods and three types of cones. It is now thought that the genes for the cone pigments and rhodopsin evolved from a common ancestral gene. Analysis of the amino acid sequences in the different opsins suggest that the first color pigment molecule was sensitive to blue. It then gave rise to another pigment that in turn diverged to form red and green pigments. Unlike Old World monkeys, New World monkeys have only two cone pigments, a blue and a longer wavelength pigment thought to be ancestral to the red and green pigments of humans and other Old World primates. The evolution of the red and green pigments must have occurred after the continents separated, about 130 million years ago. The New World monkey retina, with only two color pigments, provides a perfect model for human red-green color blindness. Genetic analysis of the various forms of human color blindness, incidentally, suggests that some humans may someday, millions of years from now, have four cone pigments rather than three and see the world in very different colors than we do now.

The modern field of vision, encompassing psychophysics, physiology, anatomy, chemistry, and genetics, is one of the great success stories of neuroscience and biological psychology. We now know that there are more than 30 different visual areas in the cerebral cortex of monkeys and humans, showing degrees of selectivity of response to the various attributes of visual experience, for example, a "color" area, a "movement" area, and so on. We now have a very good understanding of phenomena of visual sensation and perception (see the chapter by Coren in this volume). The field concerned with vision has become an entirely separate field of human endeavor, with its own journals, societies, specialized technologies, and NIH institute.

Pitch Detection

As we noted, Helmholtz published a most influential work on hearing in 1863 (*On the Sensation of Tone*). The fundamental issue was how the nervous system codes sound frequency into our sensation of pitch. By this time, much was known about the cochlea, the auditory receptor apparatus. Helmholtz suggested that the basilar membrane in the cochlea functioned like a piano, resonating to frequencies according to the length of the fibers. The place on the membrane so activated determined the pitch detected; this view was called the place theory of pitch. The major alternative view was the frequency theory (Rutherford, 1886), in which the basilar membrane was thought to vibrate as a whole due to the frequency of the tone activating it. Boring (1926) presented a comprehensive theoretical analysis of these possibilities.

One of Boring's students, E. G. Wever, together with C. W. Bray, recorded from the region of the auditory nerve at the cochlea and found that the recorded electrical signal followed the frequency of the tone up to very high frequencies, many thousands of Hertz (Wever & Bray, 1930). So the frequency theory was vindicated. But there were problems. A single nerve fiber cannot fire at much greater than 1,000 Hertz. The attempted answer was the volley theory: Groups of fibers alternated in firing to code higher frequencies.

Wever and Bray's discovery is an interesting example of a perfectly good experiment fooled by biology. As it happens, there is a process in the cochlea much like the pizoelectric effect—a tone generates electrical activity at the same frequency as the tone, now termed the cochlear microphonic. It is thought to be an epiphenomenon, unrelated to the coding functions of the auditory system.

The solution to the question how the cochlea coded tone frequency was provided by Georg von Békésy. Born in Budapest, he received his PhD in physics in 1923 and was a professor at the University of Budapest from 1932 to 1946. In 1947, he accepted a research appointment in the psychology department at Harvard, where he worked until 1964. During his time at Harvard, he was offered a tenured professorship but did not accept it because he disliked formal teaching.

During his years of full-time research at Harvard, he solved the problem of the cochlea, for which he received the Nobel Prize in 1961. In 1964, he accepted a professorship at the University of Hawaii, where he remained until his death.

By careful microscopic study of the cochlea, Békésy determined the actual movements of the basilar membrane in response to tones (see Békésy, 1947). When William James Hall was built at Harvard to house the psychology department, a special floating room was constructed in the basement for Békésy's experiments. The entire room floated on an air cushion generated by a large air compressor. Furthermore, the experimental table floated within the floating room on its own compressor. For Békésy's experiments it was necessary to avoid all external building vibrations. (One of the authors, R.F.T., had the opportunity to use this facility when at Harvard.)

Békésy discovered that the traveling waves of the basilar membrane induced by a given tone establish a standing wave pattern that maximally displaces a given region for a given tone and different regions for different tones. The pattern of displacement is more complicated than the Helmholtz theory but nonetheless provided a triumph for the place theory.

Actually, another kind of physiological evidence provided strong support for the place theory in the 1940s. Woolsey and Walzl (1942) published an extraordinary study in which they electrically stimulated different regions of the auditory nerve fibers in the cochlea (the fibers are laid out along the basilar membrane) in an anesthetized cat and recorded evoked potentials in the auditory cortex. The place stimulated on the cochlea determined the region of the auditory cortex activated. An important practical outcome of all this work is the cochlear prosthesis developed for deaf individuals.

More recent studies recording the activity of single neurons in the auditory cortex have verified and extended these observations (e.g., Hind et al., 1960). When the ear is stimulated with low-intensity pure tones (anesthetized cat), neurons—in particular, narrow dorsal-ventral bands in the primary auditory cortex—respond selectively to tones of different frequency. The regions of the cochlea activated by pure tones are represented in an anterior-posterior series of narrow dorsal-ventral bands along the primary auditory cortex, a cochlea-topic representation.

Like the visual sciences, the modern field of the hearing sciences has become an entirely separate field with its own societies, journals, and NIH institute focusing on psychophysics and the neurobiology of the auditory system. We know a great deal less about the organization of auditory fields in the cerebral cortex in primates and humans, incidentally, than we do about the visual system. The human auditory areas must be very complex, given our extraordinary species-specific behavior of speech.

LEARNING AND MEMORY

Karl Lashley is the most important figure in the development of physiological psychology and the biology of memory in America. He obtained his PhD at Johns Hopkins University where he studied with John Watson and was heavily influenced by Watson's developing notions of behaviorism. While there he also worked with Sheherd Franz at a government hospital in Washington; they published a paper together in 1917 on the effects of cortical lesions on learning and retention in the rat. Lashley then held teaching and research positions at the University of Minnesota (1917–1926), the University of Chicago (1929–1935), and at Harvard from 1935 until his death in 1958. During the Harvard years, he spent much of his time at the Yerkes Primate Laboratory in Orange Park, Florida.

Lashley devoted many years to an analysis of brain mechanisms of learning, using the lesion-behavior method, which he developed and elaborated from his work with Franz. During this period, Lashley's theoretical view of learning was heavily influenced by two congruent ideas—localization of function in neurology and behaviorism in psychology.

Lashley describes the origins of his interest in brain substrates of memory and Watson's developing views of behaviorism in the following letter he wrote to Ernest Hilgard in 1935:

In the 1914, I think, Watson called attention of his seminar to the French edition of Bechterev, and that winter the seminar was devoted to translation and discussion of the book. In the spring I served as a sort of unpaid assistant and we constructed apparatus and planned experiments together. We simply attempted to repeat Bechterev's experiments. We worked with withdrawal reflexes, knee jerk, pupil. Watson took the initiative in all this, but he was also trying to photograph the vocal cord, so I did much of the actual experimental work. I devised drainage tubes for the parotid and submaxiallary ducts and planned the salivary work which I published. As we worked with the method, I think our enthusiasm for it was somewhat dampened. Watson tried to establish conditioned auditory reflexes in the rat and failed. Our whole program was then disrupted by the move to the lab in Meyer's clinic. There were no adequate animal quarters there. Watson started work with the infants as the next best material available. I tagged along for awhile, but disliked the babies and found me a rat lab in another building. We accumulated a considerable amount of experimental material on the conditioned reflex which has never been published. Watson saw it as a basis for a systematic psychology and was not greatly concerned with the nature of the reaction itself. I got interested in the physiology of the reaction and the attempt to trace conditioned reflex paths through the nervous system started my program of cerebral work. (Letter of May 14, 1935, K. S. Lashley to E. R. Hilgard, reproduced with the kind permission of E. R. Hilgard)

It was in the previous year, 1913, that Watson published his initial salvo in an article entitled "Psychology as the Behaviorist Views It." He was elected president of the American Psychological Association in 1914.

As we noted earlier, localization of function in the cerebrum was the dominant view of brain organization at the beginning of the twentieth century. In Watson's behaviorism, the learning of a particular response was held to be the formation of a particular set of connections, a series set. Consequently, Lashley argued, it should be possible to localize the place in the cerebral cortex where that learned change in brain organization was stored—the engram. (It was believed at the time that learning occurred in the cerebral cortex.) Thus, behaviorism and localization of function were beautifully consistent—they supported the notion of an elaborate and complex switchboard where specific and localized changes occurred when specific habits were learned.

Lashley set about systematically to find these learning locations—the engrams—in a series of studies culminating in his 1929 monograph, *Brain Mechanisms of Intelligence*. In this study, he used mazes differing in difficulty and made lesions of varying sizes in all different regions of the cerebral cortex of the rat. The results of this study profoundly altered Lashley's view of brain organization and had an extraordinary impact on the young field of physiological psychology. The locus of the lesions is unimportant; the size is critically important, particularly for the more difficult mazes. These findings led to Lashley's two theoretical notions of equipotentiality and mass action: that is, all areas of the cerebral cortex are equally important (at least in maze learning), and what is critical is the amount of brain tissue removed.

Lashley's interpretations stirred vigorous debate in the field. Walter Hunter, an important figure in physiological-experimental psychology at Brown University who developed the delayed response task in 1913, argued that in fact the rat was using a variety of sensory cues; as more of the sensory regions of the cortex were destroyed, fewer and fewer cues became available. Lashley and his associates countered by showing that removing the eyes has much less effect on maze learning than removing the visual area of the cortex. Others argued that Lashley removed more than the visual cortex. Out of this came a long series of lesion-behavior studies analyzing behavioral "functions" of the cerebral cortex. Beginning in the 1940s, several laboratories, including

Lashley's and those of Harry Harlow at the University of Wisconsin and Karl Pribram at Yale, took up the search for the more complex functions of association cortex using monkeys and humans.

Perhaps the most important single discovery in this field came from Brenda Milner's studies with patient H. M. who, following bilateral temporal lobectomy (removing the hippocampus and other structures), lives forever in the present. Work on higher brain functions in monkeys and humans is one of the key roots of modern cognitive neuroscience, to be treated later. Since Milner's work with H. M., the hippocampus has been of particular interest in biological psychology. Another facet of hippocampal study in the context of the biological psychology of memory is long-term potentiation (LTP), discovered by Bliss and Lomo (1973). Brief tetanic stimulation of monosynaptic inputs to the hippocampus causes a profound increase in synaptic excitability that can persist for hours or days. Many view it as a leading candidate for a mechanism of memory storage, although direct evidence is still lacking.

Yet another impetus to study of the hippocampus in the remarkable discovery of "place cells" by John O'Keefe (1979). When recording from single neurons in the hippocampus of the behaving rat, a give neuron may respond only when the animal is in a particular place in the environment (i.e., in a box or maze), reliably and repeatedly. There is great interest now in the possibility that LTP may be the mechanism forming place cells. A number of laboratories are making use of genetically altered mice to test this possibility.

Lashley's influence is felt strongly through the many eminent physiological psychologists who worked or had contact with him. We select two examples here—Austin Riesen and Donald O. Hebb. We discuss Roger W. Sperry's work next in the context of cognitive neuroscience. The basic problem of the development of perception fascinated Lashley and his students. How is it that we come to perceive the world as we do? Do we learn from experience or is it told to us by the brain? Riesen did pioneering studies in which he raised monkeys for periods of time in the dark and then tested their visual perception. They were clearly deficient.

This important work served as one of the stimuli for Hebb to develop a new theory of brain organization and function, which he outlined in *The Organization of Behavior* (1949). This book had an immediate and profound impact on the field. Hebb effectively challenged many traditional notions of brain organization and attempted to pull together several discordant themes—mass action and equipotentiality, effects of dark rearing on perception, the preorganization of sensory cortex, the lack of serious intellectual effects of removal of an entire hemisphere of the brain in a human child—into a coherent theory. Important influences of Gestalt notions can be seen in Hebb's theory. He is a connectionist but in a modern sense: Connections must underlie brain organization but there is no need for them to be in series.

One concept in Hebb's book has come to loom large (too large perhaps) in modern cognitive-computational neuroscience—the Hebb synapse:

> When an axon of Cell A is near enough to excite a cell B and repeatedly or persistently takes part in firing it, some growth process or metabolic change takes place in one or both cells such that A's efficiency, as one of the cells firing B, is increased. (1949, p. 62)

Lashley's pessimistic conclusions in his 1929 monograph put a real but temporary damper on the field concerned with brain substrates of memory. But other major traditions were developing. Perhaps the most important of these was the influence of Pavlov. His writings were not readily available to Western scientists, particularly Americans, until the publication of the English translation of his monumental work *Conditioned Reflexes* in 1927. It is probably fair to say this is the most important single book ever published in the field of behavioral neuroscience. Pavlov developed a vast and coherent body of empirical results characterizing the phenomena of conditioned responses, what he termed "psychic reflexes." He argued that the mind could be fully understood by analysis of the higher order learned reflexes and their brain substrates. As an example of his influence, Clark Hull, in his *Principles of Behavior* (1943), wrote as though he were a student of Pavlov.

W. Horsley Gantt, an American physician, worked with Pavlov for several years and then established a Pavlovian laboratory at Johns Hopkins. He trained several young psychologists, including Roger Loucks and Wulf Brogden, who became very influential in the field. Perhaps the most important modern behavioral analyses of Pavlovian conditioning are the works of Robert Rescorla and Allan Wagner (1972).

Although Pavlov worked with salivary secretion, most studies of classical conditioning in the West tended to utilize skeletal muscle response, à la Bechterev. Particularly productive have been Pavlovian conditioning of discrete skeletal reflexes (e.g., the eyeblink response), characterized behaviorally by Isadore Gormezano and Allan Wagner and analyzed neuronally by Richard Thompson and his many students, showing localization of the basic memory trace to the cerebellum (Thompson, 1986). Masao Ito and associates in Tokyo had discovered the phenomenon of long-term depression (LTD) in the cerebellar cortex (see Ito, 1984). Repeated conjunctive stimulation of the two major inputs to the cerebellum, mossy-parallel fibers and climbing fibers, yields a long-lasting decrease in the excitability of parallel fibers—Purkinje neuron synapses. Ito developed considerable evidence that this cerebellar process underlies plasticity of the vestibular-ocular reflex. Thompson and associates developed evidence, particularly using genetically altered mice, that cerebellar cortical LTD is one of the mechanisms underlying classical conditioning of eyeblink and other discrete responses.

Fear conditioning was characterized behaviorally by Neal Miller and analyzed neuronally by several groups, particularly Michael Davis (1992), Joseph LeDoux (2000), and Michael Fanselow (1994), and their many students. They showed that at least for classical conditioning of fear, the essential structure is the amygdala, which may contain the basic memory trace for this form of learning (but see just below). The process of LTP may serve to code the amygdalar fear memory.

Duncan's discovery in 1949 of the effects of electroconvulsive shock on retention of simple habits in the rat began the modern field of memory consolidation. Hebb and Gerard were quick to point out the implication of two memory processes, one transient and fragile and the other more permanent and impervious. James McGaugh and his associates (1989) have done the classic work on the psychobiology of memory consolidation. He and his colleagues demonstrated memory facilitation with drugs and showed that these effects were direct and not due to possible reinforcement effects of the drugs (and similarly for ECS impairment).

The amygdala is critical for instrumental learning of fear. McGaugh and his associates demonstrated that for both passive and active avoidance learning (animals must either not respond, or respond quickly, to avoid shock) amygdala lesions made immediately after training abolished the learned fear. Surprisingly, if these same lesions were made a week after training, learned fear was not abolished, consistent with a process of consolidation (see McGaugh, 2000). The apparent difference in the role of the amygdala in classical and instrumental learning of fear is a major area of research today.

Chemical approaches to learning and memory are recent. The possibility that protein molecules and RNA might serve to code memory was suggested some years ago by pioneers such as Gerard and Halstead. The RNA hypothesis was taken up by Hyden and associates in Sweden and by several groups in America. An unfortunate by-product of this approach was the "transfer of memory" by RNA. These experiments, done by investigators who shall remain nameless, in the end could not be replicated.

At the same time, several very productive lines of investigation of neurochemical and neuroanatomical substrates of learning were developing. In 1953, Krech and Rosenzweig began a collaborative study of relationships between brain chemistry and behavior. Krech did classic early work in animal learning (under his earlier name, Kreshevsky) and was a colleague of and collaborator with Tolman. Mark Rosenzweig received his PhD in physiological psychology at Harvard in 1949 and joined the psychology department at the University of California, Berkeley, in 1951. Soon after they began their joint work in 1953 they were joined by E. L. Bennett and later by M. C. Diamond. Their initial studies concerned brain levels of AChE in relation to the hypothesis behavior and included analysis of strain differences (see Krech, Rosenzweig, & Bennett, 1960). More recently, they discovered the striking differences in the brains of rats raised in "rich" versus "poor" environments. William Greenough (1984), at the University of Illinois, replicated and extended this work to demonstrate dramatic morphological changes in the structures of synapses and neurons as a result of experience.

The use of model biological systems has been an important tradition in the study of neural mechanisms of learning. This approach has been particularly successful in the analysis of habituation, itself a very simple form or model of learning. Sherrington did important work on flexion reflex "fatigue" in the spinal animal at the turn of the century. In 1936, Prosser and Hunter completed a pioneering study comparing habituation of startle response in intact rats and habituation of hindlimb flexion reflex in spinal rats. They established, for habituation, the basic approach of Sherrington, namely that spinal reflexes can serve as models of neural-behavioral processes in intact animals. Sharpless and Jasper (1956) established habituation as an important process in EEG activity. Modern Russian influences have been important in this field—the key studies of Evgeny Sokolov (1963), first on habituation of the orienting response in humans and more recently on mechanisms of habituation of responses in the simplified nervous system of the snail.

The defining properties of habituation were clearly established by Thompson and Spencer in 1966, and the analysis of mechanisms began. Several laboratories using different preparations—*Aplysia* withdrawal reflex; Kandel and his many associates (see Kandel, 1976); vertebrate spinal reflexes; Thompson, Spencer, Farel; crayfish tail flip escape; Krasne (1969), Kennedy—all arrived at the same underlying synaptic mechanism—a decrease in the probability of transmitter release from presynaptic terminals of the habituating pathway. Habituation is thus a very satisfying field; agreement ranges from defining behavioral properties to synaptic mechanisms. In a sense, the problem has been solved. Habituation also provides a most successful example of the use of the model biological systems approach to analysis of

neural mechanisms of behavioral plasticity (see Groves & Thompson, 1970).

Special mention must be made of the elegant and detailed studies by Eric Kandel and his many associates on long-lasting neuronal plasticity in the *Aplysia* gill-withdrawal circuit (Kandel, 1976; Hawkins, Kandel, & Siegelbaum, 1993). This simplified model system (together with work on the hippocampus) made it possible to elucidate putative processes that result in long-lasting synaptic plasticity, for example, biochemical models of memory formation and storage. Eric was awarded the Nobel Prize for Physiology and Medicine in 2000 in part for this work.

MOTIVATION AND EMOTION

Physiological and neural mechanisms of motivation and emotion have been a particular province of biological psychology and physiology in the twentieth century. In more recent years, the fields of motivation and emotion have tended to go separate ways (see Brown, 1961, 1979). However motivation and emotion have common historical origins. In the seventeenth and eighteenth centuries, instinct doctrine served as the explanation for why organisms were driven to behave (at least infrahuman organisms without souls). Darwin's emphasis on the role of adaptive behavior in evolutionary survival resulted in the extension of instinct doctrine to human behavior. Major sources of impetus for this were Freud's and McDougall's notions of instinctive human motivation. Watson rebelled violently against the notion of instinct and rejected it out of hand, together with all biological mechanisms of motivation. As Lashley (1938) put it, he "threw out the baby with the bath."

Emotion

The dominant theory of emotion in the first two decades of the century was that of James and Lange—"We feel afraid because we run" (see James, 1884). Actually, James focused more on the subjective experience of emotion, and Lange, a Danish anatomist, focused on the physiological phenomena, believing that subjective experience is not a proper topic for science. But between them they developed a comprehensive theory of emotion. The basic idea is that we first perceive an emotionally arousing situation or stimulus ("a bear in the woods" is a favorite example), which leads to bodily (physiological) changes and activities, which result in the experienced emotion.

This general view was challenged by the American physiologist Walter B. Cannon in the 1920s and 1930s. He actually agreed with James and Lange that the initial event had to be perception of an emotion-arousing situation but argued that the development of autonomic (sympathetic) responses—release of epinephrine and other bodily changes—occurred concomitantly with the subjective feelings (see Cannon, 1927). However, his primary interest was in the physiology, particularly the peripheral physiology. Cannon's view was championed by the distinguished Johns Hopkins physiologist Philip Bard, who stressed the key role of the brain, particularly the thalamus and hypothalamus, in both emotional behavior and experience (see Bard, 1934). Cannon, incidentally, also contributed the notion of homeostasis, which he developed from Bernard's concept of the *milieu interieur.*

A key issue in these theories was the role of sympathetic arousal or activation in the experience of emotion. This issue was tested in a classic study by Stanley Schachter and Jerome Singer at Columbia University in 1962. They injected human subjects with either effective doses of epinephrine or a placebo. The epinephrine activated the sympathetic signs of emotions (pounding heart, dry mouth, etc.). Both groups of subjects were told they were receiving a shot of a new vitamin. Stooges acted out euphoria or anger in front of the subjects. The subjects were either informed of what the injection might do, for example, the autonomic side effects, or not informed. Results were dramatic. Uninformed epinephrine subjects reported emotional experiences like those of stooges but informed epinephrine subjects did not report any emotion at all. Emotion is more than sympathetic arousal—cognitive factors are also important.

Experimental work on brain substrates of emotion may be said to have begun with the studies of Karplus and Kreidl in 1910 on the effects of stimulating the hypothalamus. In 1928, Bard showed that the hypothalamus was responsible for "sham rage." In the 1930s, S. W. Ranson and his associates at Northwestern, particularly H. W. Magoun, published a classic series of papers in the hypothalamus and its role in emotional behavior (Ranson & Magoun, 1939). In the same period, W. R. Hess (1957) and his collaborators in Switzerland were studying the effects of stimulating the hypothalamus in freely moving cats. A most important paper by H. Klüver and P. Bucy reported on "psychic blindness and other symptoms following bilateral temporal lobectomy in rhesus monkeys" in 1937. This came to be known as the Klüver-Bucy syndrome. The animals exhibited marked changes in motivation and aggressive behavior.

Pribram (Bucy's first resident in neurosurgery) developed the surgical methods necessary to analyze the Klüver-Bucy syndrome. This analysis led to his discovery of the functions of the inferotemporal cortex in vision and to the exploration of the suggestions of J. W. Papez (1937) and P. D. MacLean (1949)

that the structures of the limbic system (the "Papez" circuit) are concerned with motivation and emotion. However, modern neuroanatomy deconstructed the Papez circuit. The emphasis is now on the hypothalamus-pituitary axis, on descending neural systems, and on the amygdala.

Motivation

Today most workers in the field prefer the term *motivated behaviors* to emphasize the specific features of behaviors relating to hunger, thirst, sex, temperature, and so forth. Karl Lashley was again a prime mover. His 1938 paper, "Experimental Analysis of Instinctive Behavior," was the key. He argued that motivated behavior varies and is not simply a chain of instinctive or reflex acts, is not dependent on any one stimulus, and involves central state. His conclusions, that "physiologically, all drives are no more than expression of the activity of specific mechanisms" and that hormones "activate some central mechanism which maintains excitability and activity," have a very modern ring.

Several key figures in the modern development of the psychobiology of motivation are Clifford Morgan, Eliot Stellar, Kurt Richter, Frank Beach, Neal Miller, Philip Teitelbaum, and James Olds. Morgan went to graduate school at Rochester, where his professors included E. A. K. Culler and K. U. Smith and his fellow graduate students included D. Neff, J. C. R. Licklider, and P. Fitts. He then became an instructor at Harvard, where he first worked in Lashley's laboratory in 1939. He later moved to Johns Hopkins, where he remained until 1959. As a graduate student and later at Harvard, Morgan came to doubt Cannon's then current notion that hunger was the result of stomach contractions. Morgan did a series of studies showing this could not be a complete or even satisfactory account of hunger and feeding behavior. Eliot Stellar and Robert McCleary, then undergraduates at Harvard, worked with Morgan. They focused on hoarding behavior and completed a classic analysis of the internal and environmental factors controlling the behavior.

Lashley's general notion of a central mechanism that maintains activity was developed by Beach in an important series of papers in the 1940s and by Morgan in the first edition of his important text, *Physiological Psychology* (1943), into a central excitatory mechanism and ultimately a central theory of drive. This view was given a solid physiological basis by Donald B. Lindsley from the work he and H. W. Magoun, G. Moruzzi, and associates were doing on the ascending reticular activating system. Lindsley sketched his activation theory of emotion in his important chapter in the Stevens *Handbook* (1951). Hebb (1955) and Stellar (1954) pulled all these threads together into a general central theory of motivation.

Eliot Stellar worked with Clifford Morgan as an undergraduate at Harvard. After obtaining his doctorate in 1947 at Brown University, he spent several years at Johns Hopkins and joined the psychology department at the University of Pennsylvania in 1954. Stellar did extensive work on brain mechanism of motivation. He coauthored the revision of Morgan's text in 1950 and published his influential central theory of drive in 1954.

Philip Teitelbaum (1955) did the classic work on characterization of, and recovery from, the lateral hypothalamic "aphagia" syndrome. He discovered the striking parallel with the ontogenetic development of feeding behavior. In addition, he discovered more general aspects of the syndrome, for example, "sensory neglect."

Frank Beach received his doctorate from the University of Chicago under Lashley in 1940 and then joined the American Museum of Natural History in New York. He moved to Yale in 1946, and then to the University of California, Berkeley, in 1958. From the beginning, he focused on brain mechanisms of sexual behavior (see Beach, 1951). As the study of sexual behavior developed, hormonal factors came to the fore and the modern field of hormones and behavior developed. Beach played a critical role in the development of this field, as did the biologist W. C. Young of the University of Kansas. They and their students shaped the field as it exists today.

Even within the field of hormones and behavior, several fields have developed. Sexual behavior has become a field unto itself. Another important field is the general area of stress. The endocrinologist Hans Selye was an important intellectual influence. Kurt Richter, a pioneering figure in this field, took his BS at Harvard in 1917 and his doctorate at Johns Hopkins in 1921 and was a dominant influence at Hopkins. His early work was on motivation and feeding (see Richter, 1927). His pioneering "cafeteria studies" in rats are still a model (if given a wide choice of foods, they select a relatively balanced diet). Richter then focused on the adrenal gland, its role in diet and in stress. He also did pioneering work on circadian rhythms in mammals. The modern field of stress focuses on hormonal-behavioral interactions, particularly adrenal hormones, as in the work of Seymore Levine (1971).

Neal Miller represents a uniquely important tradition in biological psychology. From the beginning of his career, Miller was interested in physiological mechanisms of both motivation and learning. He took his doctorate at Yale in 1935 and stayed on at Yale for many years, with a year out in 1936 at the Vienna Psychoanalytic Institute. Throughout his career he has exemplified superb experimentation and an unusual ability to synthesize. He was a pioneer in early studies of punishing and rewarding brain stimulation and their roles in learning and in the study of conditioned fear (see Miller, 1948, 1961). In later years, his work focused on mechanisms of instrumental conditioning of autonomic responses—biofeedback techniques—and brain mechanisms of learning. The impact of his work is much wider than biological psychology, influencing learning theory, psychiatry, and clinical medicine as well.

James Olds, whose untimely death in 1976 cut short an extraordinary career, made the most important discovery yet in the field of motivation—rewarding electrical self-stimulation of the brain. He got his doctorate at Harvard and worked with Richard Solomon. Solomon, although primarily a behavioral student of learning, had considerable impact on biological psychology through his theoretical-experimental analysis of hypothetical central factors in learning. As a graduate student Olds read and was much influenced by Hebb's *Organization of Behavior* and obtained a postdoctoral fellowship with Hebb at McGill in 1953. He began work there with Peter Milner. In his own words:

> Just before we began our own work (using Hess's technique for probing the brain), H. R. Delgado, W. W. Roberts, and N. E. Miller at Yale University had undertaken a similar study. They had located an area in the lower part of the mid-line system where stimulation caused the animal to avoid the behavior that provoked the electrical stimulus. We wished to investigate positive as well as negative effects (that is, to learn whether stimulation of some areas might be sought rather than avoided by the animal).
>
> We were not at first concerned to hit very specific points in the brain, and, in fact, in our early tests the electrodes did not always go to the particular areas in the mid-line system at which they were aimed. Our lack of aim turned out to be a fortunate happening for us. In one animal the electrode missed its target and landed not in the mid-brain reticular system but in a nerve pathway from the rhinencephalon. This led to an unexpected discovery.
>
> In the test experiment we were using, the animal was placed in a large box with corners labeled A, B, C, and D. Whenever the animal went to corner A, its brain was given a mild electric shock by the experimenter. When the test was performed on the animal with the electrode in the rhinencephalic nerve, it kept returning to corner A. After several such returns on the first day, it finally went to a different place and fell asleep. The next day, however, it seemed even more interested in corner A.
>
> At this point we assumed that the stimulus must provoke curiosity; we did not yet think of it as a reward. Further experimentation on the same animal soon indicated, to our surprise, that its response to the stimulus was more than curiosity. On the second day, after the animal had acquired the habit of returning

to corner A to be stimulated, we began trying to draw it away to corner B, giving it an electric shock whenever it took a step in that direction. Within a matter of five minutes the animal was in corner B. After this the animal could be directed to almost any spot in the box at the will of the experimenter. Every step in the right direction was paid with a small shock; on arrival at the appointed place the animal received a longer series of shocks.

After confirming this powerful effect of stimulation of brain areas by experiments with a series of animals, we set out to map the places in the brain where such an effect could be obtained. We wanted to measure the strength of the effect in each place. Here Skinner's technique provided the means. By putting the animal in the "do-it-yourself" situation (i.e., pressing a lever to stimulate its own brain) we could translate the animal's strength of "desire" into response frequency, which can be seen and measured.

The first animal in the Skinner box ended all doubts in our minds that electric stimulation applied to some parts of the brain could indeed provide a reward for behavior. The test displayed the phenomenon in bold relief where anyone who wanted to look could see it. Left to itself in the apparatus, the animal (after about two to five minutes of learning) stimulated its own brain regularly about once very five seconds, taking a stimulus of a second or so every time. (1956, pp. 107–108)

We think now that this brain reward circuit Olds discovered underlies addictive behaviors. It includes the medial forebrain bundle (MRB) containing the ascending dopamine (and other neurotransmitters) projection system to the nucleus accumbens and prefrontal cortex. Activation of this system appears to be a common element in what keeps drug users taking drugs. This activity is not unique to any one drug; all addictive drugs affect this circuit.

Another direction of research in motivation and emotion relating to brain stimulation concerns elicited behaviors, particularly from stimulation in the region of the hypothalamus. This work is in some ways a continuation of the early work by Hess. Thus, Hess described directed attack, from hypothalamic stimulation in cats, as opposed to the "sham" rage of decerebrate animals and certain other brain stimulation studies ("sham" because the animal exhibited peripheral signs of rage without integrated behavior) (see Hess, 1957). John Flynn, in a most important series of studies, was able to elicit two quite different forms of attack behavior in cats—one a quiet predation that resembled normal hunting and the other a rage attack (Flynn, Vonegas, Foote, & Edwards, 1970). Elliot Valenstein analyzed a variety of elicited consumatory-like behaviors—eating, drinking, gnawing, and so forth—from hypothalamic stimulation and their possible relations to the rewarding properties of such stimulation (Valenstein, Cox, & Kakolweski, 1970).

Current focus in the study of motivated behaviors is on detailed physiological processes, particularly involving mechanisms of gene expression of various peptide hormones in the hypothalamus and their actions on the pituitary gland, and on descending neural systems from the hypothalamus that act on lower brain systems to generate motivated behaviors (see e.g., Swanson, 1991). But we still do not understand the neural circuitries underlying the fact that seeing the bear in the woods makes us afraid.

COGNITIVE NEUROSCIENCE

The term *cognitive neuroscience* is very recent, dating perhaps from the 1980s. The *Journal of Cognitive Neuroscience* was first published in 1989. Indeed, Posner and Shulman's comprehensive chapter on the history of cognitive science (1979) does not even mention cognitive neuroscience (human imaging techniques were not yet much in use then). The cognitive revolution in psychology is treated in the chapter by Leahey in this volume. Here we note briefly the biological roots of cognitive neuroscience (see Gazzaniga, 1995).

Karl Lashley was again a key figure. One of the most important aspects of cognitive neuroscience dates from the early days at the Orange Park laboratory, where young scientists like Chow and Pribram began studies of the roles of the association areas of the monkey cerebral cortex in learning, memory, and cognition.

The 1950s was an especially rich time of discovery regarding how cognitive function was organized in the brain. Pribram, Mortimer Mishkin, and Hal Rosvold at NIMH, using lesion studies in monkeys, discovered that the temporal lobe was critical for aspects of visual perception and memory. Work with neurologic patients also played a critical role in uncovering the neural substrates of cognition. One particular discovery became a landmark in the history of memory research. "In 1954 Scoville described a grave loss of recent memory which he had observed as a sequel to bilateral medial temporal resection in one psychotic patient and one patient with intractable seizures. In both cases . . . removals extended posteriorly along the medial surface of the temporal lobes . . . and probably destroyed the anterior two-thirds of the hippocampus and hippocampal gyrus bilaterally, as well as the uncus and amygdala. The unexpected and persistent memory deficit which resulted seemed to us to merit further investigation."

That passage comes from the first paragraph of Scoville and Milner's 1957 report, "Loss of Recent Memory after Bilateral Hippocampal Lesions." This publication became a landmark in the history of memory research for two reasons. First, the severe memory impairment (or amnesia) could be linked directly to the brain tissue that had been removed, suggesting that the medial aspect of the temporal lobe was an important region for a particular aspect of cognition, that is, memory function. Second, comprehensive testing of one of the patients (H. M.) indicated that memory impairment could occur on a background of otherwise normal cognition. This observation showed that memory is an isolatable function, separable from perception and other cognitive and intellectual functions.

The findings from patient H. M. (Scoville & Milner, 1957) identified a region of the brain important for human memory, that is, the medial portion of the temporal lobe. The damage was originally reported to have included the amygdala, the periamygdaloid cortex (referred to as the uncus in Scoville & Milner, 1957), the hippocampal region (referred to as the hippocampus), and the perirhinal, entorhinal, and parahippocampal cortices (referred to as the hippocampal gyrus). Recently, magnetic resonance imaging of patient H. M. has shown that his medial temporal lobe damage does not extend as far posteriorly as originally believed and that damage to the parahippocampal cortex is minimal (the lesion extends caudally from the temporal pole approximately 5 cm, instead of 8 cm, as originally reported; Corkin, Amaral, Gonzalez, Johnson, & Hyman, 1997).

While these observations identified the medial temporal lobe as important for memory, the medial temporal lobe is a large region including many different structures. To determine which structures are important required that studies be undertaken in which the effects of damage to medial temporal lobe structures could be evaluated systematically. Accordingly, soon after the findings from H. M. were reported, efforts were made to develop an animal model of medial temporal lobe amnesia. During the next 20 years, however, findings from experimental animals with intended hippocampal lesions or larger lesions of the medial temporal lobe were inconsistent and difficult to interpret.

In 1978, Mishkin introduced a method for testing memory in monkeys that captured an important feature of tests sensitive to human memory impairment (Mishkin, 1978). This method allowed for the testing of memory for single events at some delay after the event occurred. The task itself is known as the trial-unique delayed-nonmatching-to-sample task, and it measures object recognition memory. In Mishkin's study, three monkeys sustained large medial temporal lobe lesions that were intended to reproduce the damage in patient H. M. The operated monkeys and three unoperated monkeys were given the delayed-nonmatching-to-sample task in order to assess their ability to remember, after delays ranging from eight

seconds to two minutes, which one of two objects they had recently seen. The monkeys with medial temporal lobe lesions were severely impaired on the nonmatching task, consistent with the severe impairment observed in patient H. M. on delay tasks. Thus, lesions that included the hippocampal region, the amygdala, as well as adjacent perirhinal, entorhinal, and parahippocampal cortices caused severe memory impairment. This work, together with work carried out in the succeeding few years, established a model of human amnesia in nonhuman primates (Mishkin, Spiegler, & Saunders, 1982; Squire & Zola-Morgan, 1983). Although other tasks have been useful for measuring memory in monkeys (object discrimination learning, the visual paired-comparison task; see below), much of the information about the effects of damage to medial temporal lobe structures has come, until recently, from the delayed-nonmatching-to-sample task.

Once the animal model was established, systematic and cumulative work eventually identified the structures in the medial temporal lobe that are important for memory. The important structures are the hippocampal region and the adjacent perirhinal, entorhinal, and parahippocampal cortices (for reviews, see Mishkin & Murray, 1994; Zola-Morgan & Squire, 1993). The amygdala proved not to be a component of this memory system, although it can exert a modulatory action on the kind of memory that depends on the medial temporal lobe system (Cahill & McGaugh, 1998).

The medial temporal lobe is necessary for establishing one kind of memory, what is termed *long-term declarative* or *explicit memory*. Declarative memory refers to the capacity for conscious recollection of facts and events (Squire, 1992). It is specialized for rapid, even one-trial learning, and for forming conjunctions between arbitrarily different stimuli. It is typically assessed in humans by tests of recall, recognition, or cued recall, and it is typically assessed in monkeys by tests of recognition (e.g., the delayed-nonmatching-to-sample task). The medial temporal lobe memory system appears to perform a critical function beginning at the time of learning in order that representations can be established in long-term memory in an enduring and usable form (see also Eichenbaum, Otto, & Cohen, 1994).

Another important discovery that paralleled in time the work on the medial temporal lobe system involved the understanding that there is more than one kind of memory. Specifically, work with amnesic patients and with experimental animals who sustained lesions to specific brain regions showed that other kinds of abilities (including skills, habit learning, simple forms of conditioning, and the phenomenon of priming, which are collectively referred to as nondeclarative memory) lie outside the province of the medial temporal lobe memory system. Nondeclarative forms of memory are intact in amnesic patients and intact in monkeys with medial temporal lobe lesions. For example, classical delay conditioning of skeletal musculature depends on the cerebellum (Thompson & Krupa, 1994), conditioning of emotional responses depends on the amygdala (Davis, 1992; LeDoux, 2000), and habit learning (win-stay, lose-shift responding) depends on the neostriatum (Packard, Hirsh, & White, 1989; Salmon & Butters, 1995). Nondeclarative memory thus refers to a variety of ways in which experience can lead to altered dispositions, preferences, and judgments without providing any conscious memory content.

Further work with monkeys has demonstrated that the severity of memory impairment depends on the locus and extent of damage within the medial temporal lobe memory system. Damage limited to the hippocampal region causes significant memory impairment, but damage to the adjacent cortex increases the severity of memory impairment. It is important to note that the discovery that larger medial temporal lobe lesions produce more severe amnesia than smaller lesions is compatible with the idea that structures within the medial temporal lobe might make qualitatively different contributions to memory function. This is because anatomical projections carrying information from different parts of the neocortex enter the medial temporal lobe memory system at different points (Suzuki & Amaral, 1994).

Another important brain area for memory is the diencephalon. However, the critical regions in the diencephalon that when damaged produce amnesia have not at the time of writing been identified with certainty. The important structures appear to include the mediodorsal thalamic nucleus, the anterior nucleus, the internal medullary lamina, the mammillo-thalamic tract, and the mammillary nuclei. Because diencephalic amnesia resembles medial temporal lobe amnesia in many ways, these two regions together probably form an anatomically linked, functional system.

These findings in monkeys are fully consistent with the findings from human amnesia. Damage limited to the hippocampal region is associated with moderately severe amnesia (Rempel-Clower, Zola, & Squire, 1996; Zola-Morgan, Squire, Rempel, Clower, & Amarel, 1992), and more extensive damage that includes the hippocampal region as well as adjacent cortical regions is associated with more severe memory impairment (Corkin, 1984; Mishkin, 1978; Rempel-Clower et al., 1996; Scoville & Milner, 1957).

The same principle, that more extensive damage produces more severe impairment, has also been established for the hippocampus proper in the case of the rat (E. Moser, Moser, & Andersen, 1993; M. Moser, Moser, & Forrest, 1995). The dorsal hippocampus of the rat is essential for spatial learning in the water maze, and progressively larger lesions of this region produce a correspondingly larger impairment. Thus, in all three species it has turned out that the brain is organized such that memory is a distinct and separate cognitive function, which can be studied in isolation from perception and other intellectual abilities. Information is still accumulating about how memory is organized, what structures and connections are involved, and what functions they support. The disciplines of both psychology and neuroscience continue to contribute to this enterprise.

Roger Sperry was another key player in the origins of cognitive neuroscience. He received his doctorate in zoology at the University of Chicago and then joined Lashley for a year at Harvard and moved with Lashley to the Yerkes Primate Laboratory at Orange Park, where he stayed for some years. Sperry did his pioneering studies on the selective growth of brain connections during this time (see Sperry, 1951). Lashley was fascinated by the mind–brain issue—the brain substrates of consciousness (although he never wrote about it)—and often discussed this problem with his younger colleagues at Orange Park (Sperry, personal communication). In more recent years, Sperry and his associates at the California Institute of Technology tackled the issue with a series of commissurotomy patients—the human "split-brain" studies. This work proved to be extraordinary, perhaps the most important advance in the study of consciousness since the word itself was developed many thousands of years ago (Sperry, 1968).

Another key origin of the modern field of cognitive neuroscience is the study of humans with brain damage, as in Milner's work on H. M. noted earlier. Other influential scientists in the development of this field were Hans-Lukas Teuber and Brenda Milner. Karl Pribram also played a critical role. Teuber received his early training at the University of Basel, obtained his doctorate at Harvard, and studied with Karl Lashley. He became chairman of the psychology department at MIT in 1961. In the 1940s, he published an important series of papers in collaboration with Bender and others on perceptual deficits following penetrating gunshot wounds of the brain. Later he also investigated the effects of frontal lesions on complex performance in humans.

Brenda Milner received her undergraduate training at Cambridge; then after the war she came to Canada and studied for her PhD at McGill University under Hebb's supervision. Hebb arranged for her to work with Wilder Penfield's neurosurgical patients at the Montreal Neurological Institute. Her work on temporal lobe removal in humans, including H. M., really began modern study of the memorial functions of the hippocampus (see earlier). She also collaborated on studies with Roger Sperry and with Karl Pribram.

Another very important influence in modern cognitive neuroscience comes from the Soviet scientist Alexander

Luria, who died in 1977. Luria approached detection and evaluation of damage to higher regions of the human brain both as a clinician with extraordinary expertise in neurology and as a scientist interested in higher functions of the nervous system (e.g., his book *Language and Cognition,* 1981).

Yet another origin of cognitive neuroscience is recording the activity of the human brain, initially using the EEG. Donald Lindsley was a pioneer in this work. Lindsley did his graduate work at Iowa and worked with L. E. Travis, himself an important figure in psychophysiological recording. Lindsley then took a three-year postdoctoral at Harvard Medical School (1933–1935). The neurophysiologist Alexander Forbes was at Harvard doing pioneering studies on brain-evoked potentials and EEG in animals. The first human EEG recording laboratory was set up at Harvard, and Lindsley and other pioneering figures such as Hallowell Davis did the first EEG recording in America (Lindsley, 1936).

More recently, the method of averaging evoked potentials recorded from the human scalp made it possible to detect brain signals relevant to behavioral phenomena that could not be detected with individual trial recording. Donald Lindsley was a pioneer in this field as well, doing early studies on evoked potential correlates of attention. E. Roy John and others developed complex, comprehensive methods of quantitative analysis of EEG and evoked potential recordings.

But the techniques that have revolutionized the study of normal human brain organization and functions are of course the methods of imaging. The first such method was X-ray-computed tomography, developed in the early 1970s. The major innovation beyond simple X rays was complex mathematical and computer techniques to reconstruct the images.

Somewhat later, positron emission tomography (PET) was developed. It is actually based on a long used method in animal neuroanatomy—autoradiography. In this technique, a radioactive substance that binds to a particular type of molecule or brain region is infused and brain sections are prepared and exposed to X-ray film. For humans PET involves injecting radioactive substances, for example, radiolabeled oxygen (^{15}O), in water. Increased neuronal activity in particular regions of the brain causes a rapid increase in blood flow to the regions, as shown years earlier in work by Seymore Kety and others. Consequently, the radioactive water in the blood becomes more concentrated in active brain areas and is detectable by radioactivity detectors.

The most widely used method at present is magnetic resonance imaging (MRI). This is based on the fact that changes in blood flow cause changes in the blood's magnetic properties, which can be detected as changes in a strong imposed magnetic field. This method was first used in 1990 (Ogawa, Lee, Kay, & Tank). The current procedure is termed functional MRI (fMRI), involving very fast acquisition of images. A landmark publication in human brain imaging is the elegant book by two pioneers in the field, Michael Posner and Marcus Raichle, *Images of Mind* (1994). The fMRI procedures have several advantages, such as the fact that they are noninvasive—no radioactive substance is injected—and provide better spatial resolution than does PET imaging. Functional magnetic resonance imaging exploits variations in magnetic susceptibility that arise from molecular binding of oxygen to hemoglobin, which can be used to detect blood flow changes associated with neuronal activity. At the present time, these neuronal activity-related signals can be derived from areas of the brain with a spatial resolution of 1 to 2 mm. Moreover, the temporal resolution of this functional imaging technique is compatible with the time course needed to carry out most perceptual and cognitive operations. An important and promising strategy for the use of fMRI is its use in conjunction with other kinds of neurobiological techniques, including neurophysiology and anatomical and behavioral analyses. Thus, fMRI provides an extraordinary new window through which one can probe the neural machinery of cognition (Albright, 2000).

CONCLUSION

Physiological psychology, the field concerned with biological substrates of behavior and experience (mind), has to be the most important discipline in psychology and the life sciences. The two great questions in science are the nature of the universe and the nature of the mind. Over the past century, the field of physiological psychology has spun off a number of areas that are now separate fields in their own right: vision, audition, psychophysiology, behavioral genetics, behavioral neuroscience, and cognitive neuroscience. It seems that in this sense physiological psychology is destined to self-destruct. But to participate in the process is surely among the most exciting intellectual endeavors of our time.

REFERENCES

Ackernecht, E. H., & Vallois, H. V. (1956). *Franz Joseph Gall, inventor of phrenology and his collection* (C. St. Leon. Trans.). Madison, WI: Medical School, Department of History.

Adrian, E. D. (1940). Double representation of the feet in the sensory cortex of the cat. *Journal of Physiology, 98,* 16.

Albright, T. D. (2000). Functional magnetic resonance imaging of the brain in nonhuman primates: A prospectus for research on aging. In P. C. Stern & L. L. Cartensen (Eds.), *The aging mind.* Washington, DC: National Academy Press.

Bard, P. (1928). A diencephalic mechanism for the expression of rage with special reference to the sympathetic nervous system. *American Journal of Physiology, 84,* 490–513.

Bard, P. (1934). Emotion. I: The neuro-humoral basis of emotional reaction. In C. Murchison (Ed.), *A handbook of general experimental psychology.* Worcester, MA: Clark University Press.

Barker, L. F. (1897). The phrenology of Gall and Flechsig's doctrine of association centers in the cerebrum. *Bulletin of the Johns Hopkins Hospital, 8,* 7–14.

Beach, F. A. (1951). Instinctive behavior: Reproductive activities. In S. S. Stevens (Ed.). *Handbook of Experimental Psychology* (pp. 387–434). New York: Wiley.

Békésy, G. V. (1947). The variation of phase along the basilar membrane with sinusoidal vibration. *Journal of the Acoustical Society of America, 19,* 452–260.

Berger, H. (1929). Über das Elektrenkephalogramm des Menschen. *Archiv für Psychiatrie und Nervenkrankheiten, 87,* 555–543.

Bliss, T. V. P., & Lomo, T. (1973). Long-lasting potentiation of synaptic transmission in the dentate area of the anesthetized rabbit following stimulation of the perforant path. *Journal of Physiology, 232,* 331–356.

Boring, E. G. (1926). Auditory theory with special reference to intensity, volume and localization. *American Journal of Psychology, 37,* 157–188.

Boring, E. G. (1933). *The physical dimensions of consciousness.* New York: Century.

Boring, E. G. (1942). *Sensation and perception in the history of experimental psychology.* New York: Appleton-Century-Crofts.

Boring, E. G. (1950). *A history of experimental psychology* (2nd ed). New York: Appleton-Century-Crofts.

Bouillaud, J. (1848). *Recherches Cliniques Propres a Demontrer que le Sens du Langage Mouvements de la Parole Resident dans les Lobules Anterieurs du Cerveau.* Paris: Balliere.

Broca, P. (1861). Remarks on the seat of the faculty of articulate speech, followed by the report of a case of aphemia (loss of speech) (C. Wasterlain & D. A. Rottenberg, Trans.). *Bulletin of the Society of Anatomy Paris, 6,* 332–333, 343–357.

Brown, J. S. (1961). *The motivation of behavior.* New York: McGraw-Hill.

Brown, J. S. (1979). Motivation. In E. Hearst (Ed.), *The first century of experimental psychology* (pp. 231–272). Hillsdale, NJ: Erlbaum.

Cahill, L., & McGaugh, J. L. (1998). Mechanisms of emotional arousal and lasting declarative memory. *Trends in Neuroscience, 21,* 294–298.

Cannon, W. B. (1927). The James-Lange theory of emotions: A critical examination and an alternative theory. *American Journal of Psychology, 39,* 106–124.

Clark, E., & Jacyna, L. S. (1987). *Nineteenth-century origins of neuroscientific concepts.* Berkeley: University of California Press.

Clenending, L. (1942). *Source book of medical history.* New York: Dover.

Corkin, S. (1984). Lasting consequences of bilateral medial temporal lobectomy: Clinical course and experimental findings. *H. M. Seminars in Neurology, 4,* 249–259.

Corkin, S., Amaral, D. G., Gonzalez, R. G., Johnson, K. A., & Hyman, B. T. (1997). H. M.'s medial temporal lobe lesion: Findings from magnetic resonance imaging. *Journal of Neuroscience, 17,* 3964–3980.

Davis, M. (1992). The role of the amygdala in fear and anxiety. *Annual Review of Neuroscience, 15,* 353–376.

De Valois, R. L. (1960). Color vision mechanisms in monkey. *Journal of General Physiology, 43,* 115–128.

Duncan, C. P. (1949). The retroactive effect of electroshock on learning. *Journal of Comparative and Physiological Psychology, 42,* 34–44.

Eichenbaum, H., Otto, T., & Cohen, N. J. (1994). Two functional components of the hippocampal memory system. *Behavioral Brain Science, 17,* 449–518.

Fanselow, M. S. (1994). Neural organization of the defensive behavior system responsible for fear. *Psychonomic Bulletin Review, 1,* 429–438.

Fechner, G. T. (1966). *Elements of psychophysics* (Vol. 1; E. G. Boring & D. H. Howes, Eds.; H. E. Adler, Trans.). New York: Holt, Rinehart, and Winston. (Original work published 1860)

Finger, S. (1994). *Origins of neuroscience: A history of explorations into brain function* (pp. 32–62). New York: Oxford University Press.

Flynn, J. P., Vonegas, H., Foote, W., & Edwards, S. (1970). Neural mechanisms involved in a cat's attack on a rat. In R. E. Whalen, R. F. Thompson, M. Verzeano, & N. M. Weinberger (Eds.), *The neural control of behavior* (pp. 135–173). New York: Academic Press.

Fritsch, G., & Hitzig, E. (1870). Uber die elektrische Erregbarkeit des Grosshirns. *Archiv für Anatomie, Physiologie, und Wissenchaftliche Medizin, 37,* 200–332.

Galambos, R., & Davis, H. (1943). The response of single auditory-nerve fibers to acoustic stimulation. *Journal of Neurophysiology, 6,* 39–58.

Gasser, H. S., & Erlanger, J. (1922). A study of the action current of nerves with the cathode ray oscillograph. *American Journal of Physiology, 62,* 496–524.

Gazzaniga, M. S. (Ed.). (1995). *The cognitive neuroscience.* Cambridge, MA: MIT Press.

Goethe, J. W. V. (1970). *Theory of colours* (C. L. Eastlake, Trans.). Cambridge, MA: MIT Press. (Original work published 1810)

Green, D. M., & Swets, J. A. (1966). *Signal detection theory and psychophysics.* New York: Wiley.

Greenough, W. T. (1984). Structural correlates of information storage in the mammalian brain: A review and hypothesis. *Trends in Neuroscience, 7,* 229–233.

Gross, C. G. (1987). Early history of neuroscience. In G. Adelman (Ed.), *Encyclopedia of neuroscience* (pp. 843–846), Boston: Birkhäuser.

Groves, P. M., & Thompson, R. F. (1970). Habituation: A dual-process theory. *Psychological Review, 77,* 419–450.

Harrington, A. (1991). Beyond phrenology: Localization theory in the modern era. *The enchanted loom* (pp. 207–215). New York: Oxford University Press.

Hawkins, R. D., Kandel, E. R., & Siegelbaum, S. A. (1993). Learning to modulate transmitter release: Themes and variations in synaptic plasticity. *Annual Review of Neuroscience, 16,* 625–665.

Hebb, D. O. (1949). *The organization of behavior.* New York: Wiley.

Hebb, D. O. (1955). Drives and the CNS (conceptual nervous system). *Psychological Review, 62,* 243–254.

Helmholtz, H. F. V. (1924). *Treatise on physiological optics* (3rd ed., Vols. 1–3, J. P. Southall, Ed.). Rochester, NY: Optical Society of America. (Original work published 1856–1866)

Helmholtz, H. F. V. (1954). *On the sensations of tone* (4th ed., A. J. Ellis, Trans.). New York: Dover. (Original work published 1863)

Hering, E. (1878). *Zür Lehre vom Lichtsinne.* Vienna, Austria: Gerold.

Hess, W. R. (1957). *The functional organization of the diencephalons.* New York: Grune & Stratton.

Hilgard, E. R. (1987). *Psychology in America: A historical survey.* New York: Harcourt, Brace, and Jovanovich.

Hind, J. E., Rose, J. E., Davies, P. W., Woolsey, C. N., Benjamin, R. M., Welker, W. S., et al. (1960). Unit activity in the auditory cortex. In G. L. Rasmussen & W. F. Windle (Eds.), *Neural mechanisms of the auditory and vestibular systems* (pp. 201–210). Springfield, IL: Charles C. Thomas.

Hubel, D. H., & Wiesel, T. N. (1959). Receptive fields of single neurons in the cat's striate cortex. *Journal of Physiology, 148,* 574–591.

Hull, C. L. (1943). *Principles of behavior.* New York: Appleton-Century-Crofts.

Hunter, W. S. (1913). The delayed reaction in animals and children. *Behavior Monographs, 2*(6).

Ito, M. (1984). *The cerebellum and neuronal control.* New York: Appleton-Century-Crofts.

James, W. (1884). What is an emotion? *Mind, 7,* 206–208.

James, W. (1890). *Principles of psychology.* New York: Holt.

Jameson, D., & Hurvich, L. M. (1955). Some quantitative aspects of an opponents-colors theory. Vol. 1: Chromatic responses and spectral saturation. *Journal of the Optical Society of America, 45,* 546–552.

Kandel, E. R. (1976). *Cellular basis of behavior: An introduction to behavioral neurobiology.* San Francisco: Freeman.

Karplus, J. P., & Kreidl, A. (1910). Gehirn und sympathicus. II: Ein sympathicuszentrum im Zwischenhirn. *Pflüger Archives Geselshaft Physiologie, 135,* 401–416.

Klüver, H., & Bucy, P. C. (1937). Psychic blindness and other symptoms following bilateral temporal lobectomy in rhesus monkeys. *American Journal of Physiology, 119,* 352–353.

Krasne, F. B. (1969). Excitation and habituation of the crayfish escape reflex: The depolarization response in lateral giant fibers of the isolated abdomen. *Journal of Experimental Biology, 50,* 29–46.

Krech, D., Rosenzweig, M. R., & Bennett, E. L. (1960). Effects of environmental complexity and training on brain chemistry. *Journal of Comparative Physiology and Psychology, 53,* 509–519.

Lashley, K. S. (1929). *Brain mechanisms and intelligence.* Chicago: University of Chicago Press.

Lashley, K. S. (1938). Experimental analysis of instinctive behavior. *Psychological Review, 45,* 445–471.

LeDoux, J. E. (2000). Emotion circuits in the brain. *Annual Review of Neuroscience, 23,* 155–184.

Levine, S. (1971). Stress and behavior. *Scientific American, 224,* 26–31.

Lindsley, D. B. (1936). Brain potentials in children and adults. *Science, 83,* 254.

Lindsley, D. B. (1951). Emotion. In S. S. Stevens (Ed.), *Handbook of experimental psychology* (pp. 473–516). New York: Wiley.

Ling, G., & Gerard, R. W. (1949). The normal membrane potential of frog sartorius fibers. *Journal of Cellular and Comparative Physiology, 34,* 383–396.

Luria, A. R. (1981). *Language and cognition.* New York: Wiley.

MacLean, P. D. (1949). Psychosomatic disease and the "visceral brain": Recent developments bearing on the Papez theory of emotion. *Psychosomatic Medicine, 11,* 338–353.

Marshall, W. H., Woolsey, C. N., & Bard, P. (1941). Observations on cortical sensory mechanisms of cat and monkey. *Journal of Neurophysiology, 4,* 1–24.

Maturana, H. R., Lettvin, J. Y., McCulloch, W. S., & Pitts, W. H. (1960). Anatomy and physiology of vision in the frog (Rana pipiens). *Journal of General Physiology, 43,* 129–176.

McGaugh, J. L. (1989). Involvement of hormonal and neuromodulatory systems in the regulation of memory storage. *Annual Review of Neuroscience, 12,* 255–288.

McGaugh, J. L. (2000). Neuroscience: Memory: A century of consolidation. *Science, 287,* 248–251.

McHenry, L. C., Jr. (1969). *Garrison's history of neurology.* Springfield, IL: Charles C. Thomas.

Miller, N. E. (1948). Studies of fear as an acquirable drive. I: Fear as motivation and fear-reduction as reinforcement in the learning of new responses. *Journal of Experimental Psychology, 38,* 89–101.

Miller, N. E. (1961). Learning and performance motivated by direct stimulation of the brain. In D. E. Sheer (Ed.), *Electrical stimulation of the brain* (pp. 64–66). Austin: University of Texas Press.

Mishkin, M. (1978). Memory in monkeys severely impaired by combined but not separate removal of the amygdala and hippocampus. *Nature, 273,* 297–298.

Mishkin, M., & Murray, E. A. (1994). Stimulus recognition. *Current Opinion in Neurobiology, 4,* 200–206.

Mishkin, M., Spiegler, B. J., & Saunders, R. C. (1982). An animal model of global amnesia. In S. Corkin, K. L. Davis, & J. H. Growdon (Eds.), *Toward a treatment of Alzheimer's disease* (pp. 235–247). New York: Raven Press.

Morgan, C. T. (1943). *Physiological psychology.* New York: McGraw-Hill.

Morgan, C. T., & Stellar, E. (1950). *Physiological psychology.* New York: McGraw-Hill.

Moser, E., Moser, M., & Andersen, P. (1993). Spatial learning impairment parallels the magnitude of dorsal hippocampal lesions, but is hardly present following ventral lesions. *Journal of Neuroscience, 13,* 3916–3925.

Moser, M., Moser, E. L., & Forrest, E. (1995). Spatial learning with a minislab in the dorsal hippocampus. *Proceedings of the National Academy of Sciences, USA, 92,* 9697–9701.

Mountcastle, V. B., Davies, P. W., & Berman, A. L. (1957). Response properties of neurons of cat's somatic sensory cortex to peripheral stimuli. *Journal of Neurophysiology, 20,* 374–407.

Mountcastle, V. B., Poggio, G. F., & Werner, G. (1963). The relation of thalamic cell response to peripheral stimuli varied over an intensive continuum. *Journal of Neurophysiology, 26,* 807–834.

Newton, I. (1931). *Optiks* (F. Cajori, Ed.). New York: McGraw-Hill. (Original work published 1704)

Ogawa, S., Lee, L. M., Kay, A. R., & Tank, D. W. (1990). Brain magnetic resonance imaging with contrast dependent on blood oxygenation. *Proceedings of the National Academy of Sciences, USA, 87,* 9868–9872.

O'Keefe, J. (1979). A review of the hippocampal place cells. *Progress in Neurobiology, 13,* 419–439.

Olds, J. (1956). Pleasure centers in the brain. *Scientific American, 195,* 105–116.

Packard, M. G., Hirsh, R., & White, N. M. (1989). Differential effects of fornix and caudate nucleus lesions on two radial maze tasks: Evidence for multiple memory systems. *Journal of Neuroscience, 9,* 1465–1472.

Papez, J. W. M. (1937). A proposed mechanism of emotion. *Archives of Neurology and Psychiatry, 38,* 725–743.

Pavlov, I. P. (1927). *Conditioned reflexes* (G. V. Anrep, Trans.). London: Oxford University Press.

Penfield, W., & Rasmussen, T. (1950). *The cerebral cortex of man.* New York: Macmillan.

Pogliano, C. (1991). Between form and function: A new science of man. *The enchanted loom* (pp. 144–203). New York: Oxford University Press.

Posner, M. I., & Raichle, M. F. (1994). *Images of mind.* New York: Freeman.

Posner, M. I., & Shulman, G. L. (1979). Cognitive science. In E. Hearst (Ed.), *The first century of experimental psychology* (pp. 371–405). Hillsdale, NJ: Erlbaum.

Prosser, C. L., & Hunter, W. S. (1936). The extinction of startle responses and spinal reflexes in white rats. *American Journal of Physiology, 117,* 609–618.

Ranson, S. W., & Magoun, H. W. (1939). The hypothalamus. *Ergebnis der Physiology, 41,* 56–163.

Rempel-Clower, N., Zola, S. M., & Squire, L. R. (1996). Three cases of enduring memory impairment following bilateral damage limited to the hippocampal formation. *Journal of Neuroscience, 16,* 5233–5255.

Rescorla, R. A., & Wagner, A. R. (1972). A theory of Pavlovian conditioning: Variations in the effectiveness of reinforcement and nonreinforcement. In A. H. Black & W. F. Prokasy (Eds.), *Classical conditioning. II: Current research and theory* (pp. 64–99). New York: Appleton-Century-Crofts.

Richter, C. P. (1927). Animal behavior and internal drives. *Quarterly Review of Biology, 2,* 307–343.

Rutherford, W. (1886). The sense and hearing. *Journal of Anatomy and Physiology, 21,* 166–168.

Salmon, D. P., & Butters, N. (1995). Neurobiology of skill and habit learning. *Current Opinion in Neurobiology, 5,* 184–190.

Schachter, S., & Singer, J. E. (1962). Cognitive, social and physiological determinants of emotional state. *Psychological Review, 69,* 379–399.

Scoville, W. B., & Milner, B. (1957). Loss of recent memory after bilateral hippocampal lesions. *Journal of Neurology, Neurosurgery and Psychology, 20,* 11–21.

Sewall, T. (1839). *Examination of phrenology.* Boston: King.

Sharpless, S., & Jasper, H. H. (1956). Habituation of the arousal reaction. *Brain, 79,* 655–680.

Sokolov, E. M. (1963). Higher nervous functions: The orienting reflex. *Annual Review of Psychology, 25,* 545–580.

Sperry, R. W. (1951). Mechanisms of neural maturation. In S. S. Stevens (Ed.), *Handbook of experimental psychology* (pp. 236–280). New York: Wiley.

Sperry, R. W. (1968). Hemisphere deconnection and unity in conscious awareness. *American Psychologist, 23,* 723–733.

Squire, L. R. (1992). Declarative and nondeclarative memory: Multiple brain systems supporting learning and memory. *Journal of Cognitive Neuroscience, 4,* 232–243.

Squire, L. R., & Zola-Morgan, S. (1983). The neurology of memory: The case for correspondence between the findings for human and nonhuman primate. In J. A. Deutsch (Ed.), *The physiological basis of memory* (pp. 199–268). New York: Academic Press.

Star, S. L. (1989). *Regions of the mind: Brain research and the quest for scientific certainty.* Stanford, CA: Stanford University Press.

Stellar, E. (1954). The physiology of motivation. *Psychological Review, 61,* 5–22.

Stevens, S. S. (1961). To honor Fechner and repeal his law. *Science, 133,* 80–86.

Stevens, S. S. (1975). *Psychophysics* (G. Stevens, Ed.). New York: Wiley.

Suzuki, W. A., & Amaral, D. G. (1994). Perirhinal and parahippocampal cortices of the macaque monkey: Cortical afferents. *Journal of Comparative Neurology, 35,* 497–533.

Swanson, L. W. (1991). Biochemical switching in hypothalamic circuits mediating responses to stress. *Progress in Brain Research, 87,* 181–200.

Swets, J. A. (1961). Is there a sensory threshold? *Science, 134,* 168–177.

Teitelbaum, P. (1955). Sensory control of hypothalamic hyperphagia. *Journal of Comparative and Physiological Psychology, 50,* 486–490.

Thompson, R. F. (1986). The neurobiology of learning and memory. *Science, 233,* 941–947.

Thompson, R. F., & Krupa, D. J. (1994). Organization of memory traces in the mammalian brain. *Annual Review of Neuroscience, 17,* 519–550.

Thompson, R. F., & Spencer, W. A. (1966). Habituation: A model phenomenon for the study of neuronal substrates of behavior. *Psychological Review, 173,* 16–43.

Tichener, E. B. (1898). The postulates of structural psychology. *Philosophical Review, 7,* 449–465.

Valenstein, E. S., Cox, V. C., & Kakolweski, J. W. (1970). Reexamination of the role of the hypothalamus in motivation. *Psychological Review, 77,* 16–31.

Watson, J. B. (1913). Psychology as the behaviorist views it. *Psychological Review, 20,* 158–177.

Wever, E. G., & Bray, C. W. (1930). The nature of the acoustic response: The relations between sound frequency and frequency of impulses in the auditory nerve. *Journal of Experimental Psychology, 13,* 373–387.

Woolsey, C. N., & Walzl, E. M. (1942). Topical projection of nerve fibers from local regions of the cochlea to the cerebral cortex of the cat. *Bulletin of the Johns Hopkins Hospital, 71,* 315–344.

Wundt, W. (1908). *Grundzüge der physiologische psychologie* [Principles of physiological psychology] (6th ed., Vols. 1–3). Leipzig, Germany: Engelmann. (Original work published 1874)

Zola-Morgan, S. (1995). Localization of brain function: The legacy of Franz Joseph Gall (1758–1828). *Annual Review of Neuroscience, 18,* 359–383.

Zola-Morgan, S., & Squire, L. R. (1993). Neuroanatomy of memory. *Annual Review of Neuroscience, 16,* 547–563.

Zola-Morgan, S., Squire, L. R., Rempel, N. L., Clower, R. P., & Amaral, D. G. (1992). Enduring memory impairment in monkeys after ischemic damage to the hippocampus. *Journal of Neuroscience, 9,* 4355–4370.

CHAPTER 4

Comparative Psychology

DONALD A. DEWSBURY

EARLY HISTORY   68
FORERUNNERS OF COMPARATIVE PSYCHOLOGY   68
COMPARATIVE PSYCHOLOGY BEFORE
   WORLD WAR I   69
BETWEEN THE WORLD WARS   71
   Leaders of the Reconstruction   71
   New Blood for Comparative Psychology   71
   The State of Comparative Psychology between
      the Wars   73
COMPARATIVE PSYCHOLOGY SINCE WORLD WAR II   74
   Personnel   74
   Funding   75

Research Centers   75
Journals   76
Academic Societies   76
Soul-Searching   76
THREE IMPORTANT POSTWAR INFLUENCES   76
   European Ethology   77
   Sociobiology, Behavioral Ecology, and
      Evolutionary Psychology   77
   Comparative Cognition   78
CONCLUSION: PERSISTENT ISSUES   79
REFERENCES   81

Comparative psychology has been a part of American psychology since its emergence as a separate discipline. As early as 1875, William James wrote to Harvard University president Charles W. Eliot "that a real science of man is now being built up out of the theory of evolution and the facts of archaeology, the nervous system and the senses" (James, 1875/1935, p. 11). G. Stanley Hall (1901), founder of the American Psychological Association (APA), regarded the study of the evolution of the human soul as "the newest and perhaps richest field for psychology" (pp. 731–732). Future Yale University president James Rowland Angell (1905) wrote that "if the evolutionary doctrine is correct, there seems to be no reason why we should not discover the forerunners of our human minds in a study of the consciousness of animals" (p. 458). Although the field has changed greatly over more than a century, some of the problems addressed during this earlier era remain relevant today (Boakes, 1984; Dewsbury, 1984).

There is no universally accepted definition of comparative psychology, although there is general agreement concerning which research is included, excluded, or falls near its boundaries. Comparative psychology may be regarded as that part of the field of animal psychology, the psychology of nonhuman animals, not included within either physiological psychology or process-oriented learning studies. Such research generally is conducted on either species or behavioral patterns not generally utilized in those fields. Comparative psychology fits within the broad field of *animal behavior studies,* which includes research by scientists from many disciplines. Much research within comparative psychology includes no overt comparisons among species. The goals are to develop a complete understanding of general principles governing mind and behavior including its origins (evolutionary, genetic, and developmental), control (internal and external), and consequences (for the individual, the surrounding environment, and for subsequent evolution). Comparison is but one method of reaching such understanding. Comparative psychologists take seriously the effects of behavior on differential reproduction and, ultimately, evolutionary change. In an article on the contributions of comparative psychology to child study, a favorite approach of Hall's, Linus Kline (1904) used the term *zoological psychology* as a label for the field; this may be a more accurate descriptive title than *comparative* psychology because it highlights the connection of comparative psychology with zoology—especially so-called whole-animal biology.

In this chapter, I trace the history of comparative psychology from early cave paintings to the present. This entails first a consideration of the British forerunners of comparative psychology and the emergence of the field prior to World War I.

This was followed by a postwar period of decline, as younger comparative psychologists were unable to sustain careers, and then by a resurgence of activity between the world wars. The field has remained active since World War II and has been strongly influenced by developments in European ethology, sociobiology, and cognitive science.

EARLY HISTORY

Humans have a long history of interest in animal behavior. Perhaps the first evidence of this is from the cave paintings depicting animals in southern Europe dating from the Upper Paleolithic period, 35,000 to 10,000 years before the present. Domestication of animals began about 11,500 years ago in the Middle East and Asia (Singer, 1981). Among the ancient Greeks, Herodotus (c. 425 B.C.) described habits and behavior of animals and made observations on animal physiology. Interest in animals was brought to a new level by Aristotle (384–322 B.C.). He relied on observation and inductive reasoning, not just speculation, to develop a natural history of many species. Aristotle believed in the continuity of species, though he believed species to be fixed rather than evolving. He also proposed the notion of a *Scala naturae,* a single dimension along which all species could be ordered. Although this idea, transformed from dealing with the characteristics of the animals' souls to their level of intelligence, is still popular today, it is widely regarded as fallacious. Evolution is branching, and species do not lie along a single continuum.

During the long period from the ancient Greeks to the mid-nineteenth century, interest in animal behavior was strong in three areas. Such individuals as Frederick II of Hohenstaufen (1194–1250), John Ray (1627–1705), and Charles George Leroy (1723–1757), studied animal behavior in nature and developed the area of *natural history.* A second area was *applied animal behavior,* where domestication and selective breeding of livestock, dogs, and other species continued and was perfected. Falconers developed remarkable skills in the control of behavior (Mountjoy, 1980).

Finally, the relation between human and nonhuman animals became an area of interest to *philosophers.* The seventeenth-century French philosopher René Descartes is credited with popularizing the view that there is an absolute gulf between humans and all other species. According to Descartes, humans are the only ones to possess the immaterial rational soul that enables abstract reasoning and self-awareness; animals are automata that can carry on simple mental functions but cannot think or have language. Darwin's work would discredit this dichotomy. An interesting dichotomy developed between the British and continental

philosophers regarding the developmental origins of ideas. British philosophers such as John Locke and David Hume believed that all knowledge originated in experience. For Locke, the mind was a *tabula rasa,* or blank slate. Continental philosophers, such as Immanuel Kant, proposed the existence of an active mind with a priori properties, such as categories, that acted on experience to produce knowledge. This geographic difference can be seen in contrasting the British and continental approaches to the field of ethology in the twentieth century.

FORERUNNERS OF COMPARATIVE PSYCHOLOGY

The intellectual grounding for a comparative psychology was provided in the nineteenth century with the development of the theory of evolution. The notion that evolution had occurred did not originate with Charles Darwin but rather developed with the work of such individuals as Erasmus Darwin (his grandfather), Jean-Baptiste Pierre Antoinne de Monet de Lamarck, and Robert Chambers. Darwin provided a viable mechanism, the theory of natural selection, and established that no mystical forces affected the direction of evolutionary change. Change is the result of differential reproduction under prevailing circumstances. What was critical for comparative psychology was the solidification of the idea that human and nonhuman animal behavior is continuous and thus both can be studied and compared with similar methods. This need not imply that there are no important differences between humans and nonhuman animals (henceforth called *animals*), but only that there are similarities and that any differences will best be revealed through careful comparisons. Although his *Origin of Species* (1859) and *Descent of Man* (1871) are Darwin's best-known works, *The Expression of the Emotions in Man and Animals* (1872) was especially important for comparative psychology because it showed how a comparative study of behavior might be conducted. Among Darwin's many contributions to comparative psychology, we should remember that in the 1871 work Darwin laid out important principles of sexual selection, the manner in which individual males and females find mates and achieve reproductive success. Sexual selection has been an important topic in the field of comparative psychology in recent years.

Darwin's protégé was George John Romanes, an excellent scientist, who worked with jellyfish, starfish, and sea urchins (Romanes, 1885). He was also committed to demonstrating Darwin's principle of continuity in instinct and mind in humans and animals. In *Animal Intelligence* (1882), Romanes, like most of his contemporaries, relied heavily on anecdotes, reports of single instances of behavior provided by various associates. Although he tried to be careful in selecting these, some of them are rather far-fetched and have led to a vilification of Romanes and his methods. His reputation was further tarnished because, in his efforts to establish continuity, he tended to anthropomorphize (i.e., attribute human properties to animals). Romanes's many contributions are often neglected.

A more conservative approach to animal behavior was taken by another Englishman, C. Lloyd Morgan, in his book *An Introduction to Comparative Psychology* (1894). Although this was a multifaceted work, Morgan is best remembered for one sentence, which has come to be known as Lloyd Morgan's Canon:

> In no case may we interpret an action as the outcome of the exercise of a higher psychical faculty, if it can be interpreted as the outcome of the exercise of one which stands lower in the psychological scale. (p. 53)

Morgan clearly believed in a hierarchy of psychological processes, with some processes being higher, or more complex, than others. He suggested that we can only invoke the higher processes when behavior cannot be explained in terms of lower, or simpler, psychological processes. This principle is often confused with a related dictum, the law of parsimony (Dewsbury, 1984; Newbury, 1954). The terms "law of parsimony" and "Occam's razor" can be used interchangeably for most purposes. These terms refer to the assumptions made in providing an explanation rather than to the complexity of the psychological processes that are invoked. Thus, other things being equal, we should strive for explanations that do not multiply explanatory principles and that are simple explanations in that sense. Morgan (1894), by contrast, noted that "the simplicity of an explanation is no necessary criterion of its truth" (p. 54). It would be possible to construct an interpretation based on lower psychological processes but that introduces numerous additional assumptions and is thus consistent with Morgan's Canon but inconsistent with the law of parsimony or one that is parsimonious but in violation of the canon. The canon implies, for example, that we should be very careful in attributing consciousness to animals. By no means did Morgan wish to suggest that animals lack consciousness; rather, he meant that we could invoke such a process only when necessary to explain observations that could not be explained with psychologically lower complex processes.

Other investigations in the growing field of animal behavior studies were conducted by such Britishers as Douglas A. Spalding, Sir John Lubbock, and L. T. Hobhouse and Americans such as Lewis Henry Morgan, T. Wesley

Mills, George W. Peckham, and Elizabeth Peckham. Especially notable was the work of Charles H. Turner on the comparative psychology of crayfish, ants, spiders, bees, and other invertebrates. Turner was an African American scientist of the time who published significant research in major journals (see Cadwallader, 1984).

COMPARATIVE PSYCHOLOGY BEFORE WORLD WAR I

Building on these foundations, comparative psychology emerged as a significant, visible discipline during the late nineteenth and early twentieth centuries in the universities of the United States (see Dewsbury, 1992). Hall had been called to the presidency of Clark University and brought with him Edmund C. Sanford, who ran the laboratory. They taught courses and attracted students to comparative psychology. The laboratory course included work on microscopic animals, ants, fish, chicks, white rats, and kittens. Graduate student Linus Kline (1899), who did some of the teaching, suggested that "a careful study of the instincts, dominant traits and habits of an animal as expressed in its free life—in brief its natural history should precede as far as possible any experimental study" (p. 399). The best known of the early Clark studies were those on maze learning published by Willard S. Small (1901). Kline mentioned to Sanford that he had observed runways built by feral rats under the porch of his father's cabin in Virginia, and Sanford suggested the use of a Hampton Court maze as an analog of the learning required of rats in nature (Miles, 1930). Small and Kline constructed the mazes and other devices in which to study the learning process in rats. Thus, the early studies were designed to mimic situations the subjects faced under natural conditions. The Clark program was not limited to such studies. Under the influence of Hall, there was a strong developmental focus, as in Small's (1899) study of the development of behavior in rats and in Conradi's (1905) study of the development of song in English sparrows. James P. Porter (1906) analyzed the naturally occurring behavioral patterns of two genera of spiders.

Robert M. Yerkes, under the influence of William James and Hugo Münsterberg, was a mainstay of comparative psychology during this period at Harvard. He studied the behavior of a wide variety of invertebrates such as crayfish (Yerkes & Huggins, 1903) and published one of the early classics of the field, *The Dancing Mouse* (Yerkes, 1907), a comprehensive study of a mutant mouse strain. Yerkes and his students also studied a variety of behavioral patterns and species, including sensory function, such as Cole's (1910) study of the reactions of frogs to four chlorides; genetics and development, such as Yerkes and Bloomfield's (1910) study of the reactions of kittens to mice; and learning, such as Coburn and Yerkes's (1915) study of crows.

Edward Bradford Titchener dominated psychology at Cornell University. Although he is often portrayed as having opposed comparative psychology, he conducted a number of studies in the field early in his career (Dewsbury, 1997). A prize student at Cornell was his first PhD, Margaret Floy Washburn, who later became the second woman elected to the presidency of the APA. Her most notable contribution to comparative psychology was her book *The Animal Mind* (1908), that went through four editions and was the standard textbook in comparative psychology into the 1930s. Research at Cornell included a study of vision in fish (M. F. Washburn & Bentley, 1906) and one on learning in paramecia (Day & Bentley, 1911). Even Edwin G. Boring (1912), future historian of psychology, published a study of phototropisms in flatworms.

The pride of the program at the University of Chicago, directed by Angell, was John Broadus Watson. Although Watson became famous later in his career for his writings on behaviorism, he did work in comparative psychology during his younger years. His dissertation, *Animal Education* (Watson, 1903), was an early study in developmental psychobiology, as Watson tried to correlate the development of learning in rats with the development of the nervous system. Watson also studied imitation in monkeys and spent several summers studying noddy and sooty terns on the Dry Tortugas Islands off Florida (e.g., Watson & Lashley, 1915). This study anticipated some later research in ethology. Many psychologists who know only his writings on behaviorism are surprised by his earlier thinking on instinctive behavior (Watson, 1912). Most of the other students in animal psychology at Chicago worked on rats, although Clarence S. Yoakum (1909) studied learning in squirrels.

Edward L. Thorndike had a brief, but extremely influential, career in comparative psychology. After conducting some research with William James at Harvard, Thorndike moved to Columbia University, where he completed his PhD under James McKeen Cattell in 1898. After a year at Western Reserve University, he returned to Columbia, where he spent the remainder of his career, most of it as an educational psychologist. His dissertation, *Animal Intelligence* (Thorndike, 1898), was a classic study of cats learning to escape from puzzle boxes; Thorndike (1911) later expanded this work with the addition of several previously published articles. He believed that cats used simple trial and error to learn to operate manipulanda to escape from the compartments in which they had been enclosed; they kept emitting different behavioral

patterns until one was successful. Further, he believed that virtually all learning in all species followed the same laws of trial-and-error and reward (the law of effect). This provided little impetus for comparative analysis. Thorndike's major contribution was the development of precise methods for careful study of learning in the laboratory. In the tradition of C. L. Morgan, Thorndike generally sought to explain behavior in terms of relatively simple processes and eschewed notions of insight in creative problem solving. T. Wesley Mills took a very different approach, closer to that of Romanes than to that of Morgan. This led to a bitter exchange of mutually critical articles. Mills emphasized the importance of testing under natural conditions, writing of Thorndike's puzzle box experiments that one might "as well enclose a living man in a coffin, lower him, against his will, into the earth, and attempt to deduce normal psychology from his conduct" (Mills, 1899, p. 266). Thorndike (1899) defended his research as the only way "to give us an explanatory psychology and not fragments of natural history" (p. 415).

Karl S. Lashley, best known as a physiological psychologist, also had a lifelong interest in comparative psychology. He was influenced by Watson at Johns Hopkins and spent one summer working with him on the tern project. Lashley influenced comparative psychology not only through his research and integrative writings but also through his students. Harry M. Johnson was another Hopkins-trained comparative psychologist, as exemplified in his study of visual pattern discrimination in dogs, monkeys, and chicks (Johnson, 1914).

Other comparative psychologists in graduate school during this period included John F. Shepard at the University of Michigan, who did many studies of learning in ants and rats (see Raphelson, 1980), and William T. Shepherd at George Washington University, who worked on a variety of species (e.g., Shepherd, 1915).

Perhaps the most influential foreign-born comparative psychologist was Wolfgang Köhler, who completed a doctorate at the University of Berlin in 1909. Much of his career was devoted to the development and promotion of Gestalt psychology. His major work in comparative psychology was conducted on the island of Tenerife in the Canary Islands during World War I. Köhler's best-known studies were of problem solving with chimpanzees. These studies used such tasks as the stacking of boxes to reach a banana suspended above the animals' enclosure and stick problems in which the chimpanzees had to manipulate sticks of one sort or another to reach a banana that was placed outside of the enclosure where it could be reached with a stick but not without it (Köhler, 1925).

Little original theory was created during this period. The guiding theoretical framework came from the theory of evolution. Attention was devoted to building an empirical foundation for the field. The range of species studied was extensive. Although the study of learning came to be especially prominent, there was much research on sensory function, development, and social behavior as well. Although only a few comparative psychologists studied animal behavior in the field, many were aware of the place of their study subjects in nature and used that awareness in understanding behavior.

Although the foundations for a stable field of comparative psychology appeared to have been laid, it was not to be—at least not yet. A number of problems arose. The major difficulty lay in the place of comparative psychology, as a study of behavior in animals, in psychology, a discipline most viewed as the study of mind and behavior in humans. Despite its intellectual and historical connections with the rest of psychology, comparative psychology was perceived as a peripheral field. Pressures were brought to bear on those trained in comparative psychology to switch and move to other research areas, especially applied fields. At Harvard, for example, Münsterberg (1911) wrote of Yerkes to President Abbott Lawrence Lowell that "anyone interested in those animal studies alone is in no way a real psychologist, and really no longer belongs in the philosophy department." The situation was complicated because psychologists doing laboratory studies of animals required special facilities that were both expensive and viewed by some as undesirable because of odor and atmosphere. Some had philosophical objections to animal research. It became clear to many that the path to promotion was to leave comparative psychology for applied fields (Dewsbury, 1992). As a result, most comparative psychologists educated during these years followed such paths and left the field. The American entry into World War I and the loss of personnel to military endeavors exacerbated the situation.

BETWEEN THE WORLD WARS

The period running from the late 1910s and through the 1920s was a nadir for the field. With the old foundation for the field gone, a new one had to be constructed.

Leaders of the Reconstruction

Few psychologists were in the universities to engage in reconstruction. Harvey Carr and Walter Hunter, products of the Chicago program, remained active, as did Karl Lashley, who was influential in the careers of many aspiring comparative psychologists. After the war, Yerkes spent several years in Washington before Angell, then the president of Yale

University, brought him to New Haven in 1924. Yerkes and Lashley would be pivotal in the redevelopment of comparative psychology that would help to establish it as a field that has been strong ever since. Several other individuals who would lead the reformulation of comparative psychology were educated in other programs scattered about the country.

Although Yerkes functioned as an administrator in Washington until 1924, he never lost sight of his plan for a research station where nonhuman primates might be studied (Yerkes, 1916). In 1915, he took a half-year sabbatical to conduct research on primates in California. In 1923 he purchased two animals, Chim and Panzee, for study, primarily at his summer home in New Hampshire. The following summer, he studied primates in the colony of a private collector, Madame Rosalia Abreu in Havana, Cuba. All the while, he was publishing material on primate research (e.g., Yerkes, 1925) and lobbying various private foundations for funds for a primate facility. Finally, in 1925 the Rockefeller Foundation appropriated funds to support a primate facility in New Haven and, in 1929, for a feasibility study for a remote primate station. Later that year, $500,000 was granted and Yerkes established the Anthropoid Station of Yale University (later renamed the Yale Laboratories of Primate Biology when it was incorporated in 1935 and the Yerkes Laboratories of Primate Biology upon its founder's retirement). The facility would remain in Orange Park until 1965 and was a focal point of research on the great apes.

Lashley moved to the University of Minnesota in 1917 and, with an interlude of work in Washington, D.C., remained there until he moved to Chicago, first to the Behavior Research Fund of the Institute for Juvenile Research in 1926 and then to the University of Chicago in 1929. He moved to Harvard University in 1935, and in 1942, he became the second director of the Yerkes Laboratories of Primate Biology in Orange Park, Florida, from which he retired in 1955.

New Blood for Comparative Psychology

A cluster of comparative psychologists of lasting impact completed graduate training during the 1920s and 1930s. Perhaps the first of the new generation of comparative psychologists was Calvin P. Stone, who completed his PhD under Lashley at Minnesota in 1921. Stone went on to a long career at Stanford University, where he was noted for his studies of sexual behavior and the development of behavior, for his editorial work, and for mentoring numerous students.

Zing-Yang Kuo, a native of Swatow, Kwangton, China, completed a doctorate with Edward C. Tolman at the University of California at Berkeley in 1923. The primary issue with which Kuo grappled during his career was the nature of development and the relative roles of nature and nurture. At various stages of his career he concluded that there was either little evidence of genetic effects or that genetic and environmental influences were so intimately entwined that it was impossible to separate them. Although he was able to publish some articles throughout his career, his difficulty in finding employment in the United States and his involvement in administrative and political turmoil in China greatly limited his influence.

Carl J. Warden completed a PhD at the University of Chicago in 1922; he spent much of his career at Columbia University. Among his contributions to the field were his writings on the history of comparative psychology, textbooks, and research. The latter often entailed use of the Columbia Obstruction Box, in which a rat had to cross a shock grid in order to reach an incentive (e.g., Warden, 1931). The greater the intensity of the shock the animal was willing to endure, the greater was the animal's drive believed to be.

Henry W. Nissen completed a PhD with Warden at Columbia in 1929. He spent much of career working on primate behavior under the influence of Yerkes, first at Yale University and later at the Yerkes Laboratories of Primate Biology. He was the director of the latter facility from 1955 to 1958. Nissen is said to have known more about chimpanzees and their behavior than anyone else of his time but was a self-effacing psychologist whose influence was limited by his reticence. Nevertheless, his career was prominent enough to earn him election to the prestigious National Academy of Sciences of the United States.

A remarkable cluster of students worked with Lashley at the University of Chicago during the early 1930s (Dewsbury, in press-a). Norman R. F. Maier completed a PhD with Shepard at Michigan in 1928 and, after a year on the faculty at Long Island University, went to work with Lashley during 1929–1931. He then spent most of his career back at Michigan. In comparative psychology, Maier is best known for his studies of problem solving in which he suggested that rats do not learn to solve complex processes via the simple associative processes suggested by Thorndike but rather use a process of reasoning (e.g., Maier, 1937). This was part of a fairly substantial interest in cognitive approaches to behavior during the 1930s (Dewsbury, 2000). He was also interested in the abnormal behavior, including fixations and seizures, that sometimes occurred in his testing situations.

Theodore C. Schneirla also completed his doctorate with Shepard at Michigan in 1928. Shepard interested Schneirla in studies of the behavior of ants, which became the focus of Schneirla's career. In 1927, he moved to New York University, combining his duties there with a position at the American Museum of Natural History during much of his career. He went to work with Lashley in Chicago during 1930–1931. Schneirla was a primary exemplar of the role of field research in comparative psychology, as he made many trips to study the complex adaptive patterns of various species of ants at many sites. He also conducted notable laboratory research on learning in ants. Schneirla also engaged in theory construction. He advocated a concept of integrative levels, occupied by different species. With this concept, he called for caution in generalizing across widely diverse taxa. He also was a strong advocate of the epigenetic approach to development and opposed the notion that some behavioral patterns are innate. He believed that tendencies to approach toward and withdraw from stimuli of varying intensities played an important role in development (see Aronson, Tobach, Rosenblatt, & Lehrman, 1969).

Frank A. Beach completed an MA degree at the Kansas State Teachers College in Emporia before going to Chicago to complete his doctorate. He worked with Lashley during 1933–1934, taught high school for a year, and then returned to Chicago for further graduate work. Lashley was gone by then, but Beach followed him to Harvard in 1936. He completed the final requirements for the Chicago PhD in 1940. Beach spent his career at the American Museum of Natural History, Yale University, and the University of California, Berkeley. He is probably best known today for a series of incisive articles he wrote about the state of comparative psychology and the conceptual foundations thereof. The best-known example is his "The Snark Was a Boojum" (Beach, 1950). Beach argued that throughout the first half of the twentieth century, comparative psychologists had become interested in a more narrow range of behavioral patterns and progressively fewer species, primarily white rats. He suggested that this was not a healthy development. In "The Descent of Instinct" (1955), he criticized simplistic conceptions of the concept of instinct. His research program was a broadly based attack directed primarily at the determinants of reproductive behavior. He was interested in the neural bases, endocrine correlates, evolution, development, and situational determinants of reproductive and social behavioral patterns.

Isadore Krechevsky, later David Krech, studied first at New York University but completed his doctorate with Edward C. Tolman at the University of California at Berkeley. He then moved to the University of Chicago, initially with Lashley, where he remained from 1933 to 1937. A political activist, he had to change affiliations with some frequency because of difficulties with administrators, but he spent the last part of his career, beginning in 1947, at Berkeley. Krechevsky (1932) showed that as rats learn mazes, they appear to form "hypotheses," systematic runs of choices governed by different rules, each of which is tried as a solution is sought. As with Maier's work, this was part of the 1930s effort in comparative cognition.

The fifth important comparatively oriented student to work with Lashley at Chicago was Donald Olding Hebb. Hebb moved to Chicago in 1934 and accompanied his mentor to Harvard after one year. He received a Harvard PhD in 1936. He then filled positions in Canada and, in 1942, rejoined Lashley in Orange Park. In 1947, Hebb joined the faculty at McGill, from which he retired in 1974. Like Lashley, Hebb is best remembered for his contributions to physiological psychology. His *The Organization of Behavior* (1949) was important in the reinvigoration of physiological psychology after World War II and introduced the so-called Hebb synapse to psychology. Like Beach and Schneirla, Hebb worked toward reinterpretation of behavioral patterns that appeared to be innate (Hebb, 1953). His comparative interests are also apparent in his efforts to get studies of animal social behavior more recognition in the field of social psychology (Hebb & Thompson, 1954).

Two important comparative psychologists completed PhDs under Stone at Stanford. Harry F. Harlow completed the PhD in 1930 and spent the rest of his career at the University of Wisconsin. He spent much of his career studying learning in rhesus monkeys, where he developed an error factor theory, according to which the primary process during learning often involved the manner in which errors were eliminated. Harlow is best known, however, for his work on behavioral development. He found the social and reproductive behavior of rhesus monkeys reared in the absence of their parents and siblings to be greatly distorted. Deficits in learning were found to be much less severe. With many important students educated in his program and with his editorial and administrative work, Harlow was a very influential comparative psychologist.

The other Stanford-Stone graduate was C. Ray Carpenter, who completed his studies in 1932 with work on endocrine influences on pigeons. He is best known, however, as the "father" of primate field research. With the help of Yerkes, Carpenter began a series of field studies in locations such as Panama, Southeast Asia, and India (e.g., Carpenter, 1934). He established a colony of rhesus monkeys on the island of Cayo Santiago, off Puerto Rico. This was the first sophisticated work on primates in their native habitats. This field has exploded in recent years with the work of such scientists as Jane Goodall and George Schaller. Many people are surprised to learn of the role of a psychologist in establishing the subdiscipline of primate field research. Carpenter spent much of his career at the Pennsylvania State University, where he also devoted much effort to documenting studies of primates and other species on film.

Other comparative psychologists completing graduate work during this era included Curt P. Richter (Johns Hopkins, 1921), Carl Murchison (Johns Hopkins, 1923), Leonard Carmichael (Harvard, 1924), Lucien H. Warner (Columbia, 1926), Otto L. Tinklepaugh (Berkeley, 1927), Winthrop N. Kellogg (Columbia, 1929), and Meredith P. Crawford (Columbia, 1935).

The State of Comparative Psychology between the Wars

The comparative psychologists educated during the 1920s and 1930s placed comparative psychology on a firm footing. Unlike the pre–World War I cadre, this group was successful in securing research support and in educating a next generation of comparative psychologists who would carry on the tradition. Nevertheless, much was not well. This group of comparative psychologists, which appears to coalesce as a coherent unit when viewed in retrospect, did not appear so when viewed in its time. There were a number of reasons for this.

Disciplines and subdisciplines become recognizable and influential with the development of a set of institutional landmarks including departments, textbooks, courses, research facilities, organizations, meetings, and journals. During this period, comparative psychology was well established in many departments, and courses were a staple in many places. In other respects, however, it lacked elements that foster cohesion.

Textbooks

The 1930s saw the greatest burst of publication for textbooks in the history of the field. Margaret Floy Washburn's *The Animal Mind* had been dominant since 1908. Her fourth edition appeared in 1936. The most influential book of the era was Maier and Schneirla's *Principles of Animal Psychology* (1935). The textbook provided a comprehensive overview of the field, beginning with 11 chapters organized according to animal taxa. Material concerning receptor equipment, sensitivity, conduction, and the action system is provided for each group. The second part of the book is concerned with natively determined behavior, sensory function, and neural mechanisms in mammals. Part III addresses learning and mental processes.

The most comprehensive of the works was the three-volume *Comparative Psychology: A Comprehensive Treatise* (1935, 1936, 1940) by Warden, T. N. Jenkins, and Warner. The first volume deals with principles and methods; the second volume with plants and invertebrates; and the third volume with vertebrates.

A tradition of edited textbooks in the field began with F. A. Moss's (1934) *Comparative Psychology*. The 15 chapters included information on maturation, motivation, sensory function, learning, individual differences, animal social psychology, and a set of related topics. This work was followed by similar volumes from various editors at regular intervals in 1942, 1951, 1960, and 1973.

An interesting approach was taken by Normal L. Munn (1933) with his *An Introduction to Animal Psychology*. The book is concerned solely with the behavior of laboratory rats and provides a comprehensive review of many characteristics of rats.

Other Characteristics

In some respects, the textbooks were the only bright spot in the institutionalization of comparative psychology during the period between the wars. One problem was that of definition, a difficulty that still affects the field today. There was clearly a cadre of comparative psychologists of the sort included by my definition. The term *comparative psychology,* however, was used in a variety of ways. Often, it referred to all animal psychology. Important work was being done in the fields of animal learning and cognition during this period. Much of the work, however, was done within a more process-oriented framework than most work in comparative psychology as defined here. Similarly, numerous physiological studies were conducted. The true comparative tradition was obscured, in part, because the field lacked a clearly differentiating name, clear definition, and less permeable boundaries.

A landmark was the beginning of the publication of the *Journal of Comparative Psychology* in 1922. The field had had other journals, including the *Journal of Comparative Neurology and Psychology* (1904–1910), the *Journal of Animal Behavior* (1911–1917), and *Psychobiology* (1917–1920). With the *Journal of Comparative Psychology,* however, the field finally appeared to have a named journal to provide unity for the discipline. However, it was not to be. The journal became one of animal psychology and the primary vehicle for the publication of research in all fields of animal psychology, thus muddying the definitional problem even further. Indeed, during the 1920s, the *Journal of Comparative Psychology* included a significant number of studies of human behavior (Dewsbury, 1998).

A complete perspective on comparative psychology requires consideration of its flaws as well as its accomplishments. Some of the writings of the time appear to be racist, at least by contemporary standards. The early volumes of the *Journal of Comparative Psychology* included numerous articles on race differences regarding performance on intelligence tests, emotional traits, and physical development. In addition, Watson (1919) wrote that "psychologists persistently maintain that *cleanliness* is instinctive, in spite of the filth of the negro, of the savage, and of the child" (p. 260), and Yerkes (1925) wrote that "certainly these three types of ape [chimpanzees, orangutans, and gorillas] do not differ more obviously than do such subdivisions of mankind as the American Indian, the Caucasian, and the Negro" (p. 56). There are many aspects of the history of comparative psychology that are worthy of pride; a balanced view must include aspects lacking in such worth.

Perhaps underlying the looseness of organization of comparative psychology was a lack of identity among the leaders in the field. Although all would probably have accepted the title of comparative psychologist, there was no sense of unity or effort to differentiate their work from that of other animal psychologists who often were included as "comparative psychologists." There was no unifying theory of the sort developed by the followers of B. F. Skinner. There was no agenda of the sort later promulgated by the European ethologists. Most comparative psychologists of the era were independent-minded individuals concerned with doing their research, reporting it at existing meetings, and publishing it in mainline journals. There were no efforts to form new organizations or otherwise band together to define the developing tradition with any precision. As a result, the individual researchers gained respect and prestige for their efforts but they lacked real influence as a group. The subdiscipline that seems so clear in retrospect was not developed as an entity.

COMPARATIVE PSYCHOLOGY SINCE WORLD WAR II

The story of comparative psychology since World War II is one of developments within the field and response to influences from outside. The war caused some interruption in the efforts that could be devoted to comparative psychology. The improved funding environment and the growth of universities after the war, however, fueled rapid growth.

Personnel

Most critical was the availability of personnel. With stable positions, most of the prewar generation of comparative psychologists were able to develop active laboratories and produce a continued output of research. As universities grew and fellowships became available, this generation, in turn, produced a new generation of comparative psychologists. In 40 years at the University of Wisconsin, Harlow alone supervised 35 PhDs, including such names as Abraham Maslow, Donald R. Meyer, John M. Warren, Gerald E. McClearn, Allen M. Schrier, Leonard A. Rosenblum, and Stephen J. Suomi (Suomi & Leroy, 1982). During his career, Beach supervised 41 predoctoral and postdoctoral students (McGill, Dewsbury, & Sachs, 1978). Schneirla left a legacy of influential students including Daniel S. Lehrman, Jay S. Rosenblatt, and Ethel Tobach. Similar programs were developed elsewhere. Then, of course, these students found jobs, built laboratories, and began educating yet another generation. Comparative psychology still had a problem in that many who published animal research early in their careers left to become prominent in other fields of psychology. Examples include Maslow, William Bevan, Jerome S. Bruner, William K. Estes, Eugene Galanter, Eleanor J. Gibson, Jerome Kagan, Quinn McNemar, M. Brewster Smith, and Dael L. Wolfle. Comparative psychology was always a small part of the big picture of American psychology. Nevertheless, there was a solid cadre of comparative psychologists carrying on the tradition.

Funding

Critical to the growth of comparative psychology was the availability of funding. Prior to World War II, most funding for research came either from local sources or from private foundations, with prospective recipients making the rounds seeking research support. An exception was the Rockefeller Foundation–funded Committee for Research in Problems of Sex (Aberle & Corner, 1953). The explosive growth of support for scientific research not only increased the funding available but changed the pattern to one that involved the submission of research proposals that were subsequently subject to peer review.

I have analyzed funding patterns for comparative psychology for 1948–1963 at both the National Institute of Mental Health (NIMH) and the National Science Foundation (NSF) (Dewsbury, in press-b). According to my analysis, the NIMH awarded a total of 117 grants in comparative psychology for approximately $5.6 million during this period. The mean grant was for 2.5 years with an annual budget of under $20,000. The NSF program in psychobiology, not begun until 1952, awarded 72 grants in comparative psychology for a total of over $1.4 million with a mean size much smaller than those from the NIMH. The top-10 grant getters at the NIMH were Harlow, Lehrman, John Paul Scott, Richter, Eckhard Hess, Nissen, Beach, William Mason, M. E. Bitterman, and Schneirla. Half of those—Beach, Harlow, Lehrman, Nissen, and Richter—were elected to the National Academy of Sciences of the United States. Nissen, Schneirla, and Richter

also were among the top-10 grant getters in comparative psychology at the NSF. The leading research topic in the NIMH grants was behavioral development. The NSF grants were less concentrated, with a greater emphasis on sensation and perception and general studies of behavior. This input of funding helped to create a great surge of research in comparative psychology, still small relative to the rest of psychology but substantial relative to that which had come before.

Research Centers

Although most comparative psychologists were scattered about the country in various universities, this funding enabled the development of several centers for research. The Yerkes Laboratories of Primate Biology in Orange Park, Florida, were pivotal. Yerkes remained as director from its founding in 1930 until 1941 (Yerkes, 1943). He was succeeded in turn by Lashley and Nissen. Arthur J. Riopelle and Geoffroy Bourne were the final two directors in Orange Park. When the federal government established a program of Regional Primate Centers, Emory University, which then owned the Laboratories, moved them to their home campus in Atlanta. In addition to its directors, many other scientists such as Roger Sperry, Kenneth Spence, Austin Riesen, Paul Schiller, Hebb, Mason, and many others worked in Orange Park. From 1930 to 1965, the total budget was over $2.5 million. During the early years, the funding came almost exclusively from university and private foundation sources. This was reversed, and during the last five years for which data are available, over two-thirds of the funds came from the federal government. With greatly increased funding, the facility has thrived in Atlanta, albeit with a more biomedical emphasis.

Harlow established and directed a primate laboratory at the University of Wisconsin. With the founding of a Regional Primate Research Center in Madison in 1964, Harlow assumed its directorship as well. Behavior programs also thrived in regional primate research centers in New England, Louisiana, Oregon, Washington state, and Davis, California.

The behavior program at the Jackson Laboratory in Bar Harbor, Maine, was founded by John Paul Scott, who was educated as a geneticist but functioned in departments of psychology during much of his career. Joined by John L. Fuller, Walter C. Stanley, John A. King, and others, the program received substantial grant support and became a center for research on inbred strains of house mice and five breeds of dogs. It was also the site of two important conferences that helped to coalesce the field of animal behavior studies.

Another focal point developed in the New York City area. In 1937, Beach moved to the American Museum of Natural History, where he founded the Department of Animal

Behavior in 1942. Schneirla and Lester R. Aronson joined him in the department; Schneirla succeeded Beach as curator when Beach left for Yale University in 1946. Students such as Tobach, Rosenblatt, and Howard Topoff graduated and remained in the New York area. After graduating, one prominent student in the program, Daniel S. Lehrman, moved to the Newark, New Jersey, campus of Rutgers University, where he founded the Institute of Animal Behavior in 1959. This, too, became an important center for education and research. The focus of this whole group was on an epigenetic approach to development, and this New York epigeneticist group produced numerous students and programs in the field.

Journals

Beginning in 1947, the *Journal of Comparative Psychology* adopted a name more descriptive of its coverage: the *Journal of Comparative and Physiological Psychology*. That title remained until 1983, when it was split into three journals even more descriptive of the three prominent parts of animal psychology at the time: *Behavioral Neuroscience,* the *Journal of Experimental Psychology: Animal Behavior Processes,* and the reformulated *Journal of Comparative Psychology*.

The scope of the growth of animal psychology can be seen in an analysis of the articles appearing in the *Journal of Comparative and Physiological Psychology* in 1963 as compared with 1949 (Dewsbury, in press-b). The number of articles published increased by a factor of nearly 3.5 from 60 to 208. There were few footnote credits to federal funding sources in 1949; by 1963, just 14 years later, it had risen eightfold.

Comparative psychologists published in other American journals as well. Some comparative psychologists found American journals uncongenial and published in the growing stable of European journals, including *Animal Behaviour, Behaviour,* and the *Zeitschrift für Tierpsychologie* (now *Ethology*).

Academic Societies

No one academic society has emerged as the primary home for comparative psychologists. The APA remains the leading organization of psychologists, but its Division of Behavioral Neuroscience and Comparative Psychology (Division 6) is but a small part of the APA. Some psychologists have given allegiance to other psychological organizations such as the Psychonomic Society or the American Psychological Society. The Animal Behavior Society in North American, the Association for the Study of Animal Behavior in Great Britain, and the International Ethological Congress have become the leading organizations in the field of animal behavior studies.

Many comparative psychologists participate in these. The International Society for Comparative psychology, founded in 1983, has great possibilities that have not yet been realized.

Soul-Searching

Comparative psychologists have often assessed the state of their discipline and often criticized the directions taken. Three major articles stand out. In his famous "The Snark Was a Boojum," mentioned earlier, Beach (1950) argued that comparative psychology had begun as the study of a wide range of topics in a wide range of species but had degenerated into the study of learning in rats. He stressed the need for a resurrection of the breadth that had earlier characterized the field. Although Beach's analysis was flawed (Dewsbury, 1998), it was quite influential.

In the second major critique, Hodos and Campbell (1969) criticized comparative psychologists' perspective on evolutionary history. They argued that comparative psychologists still utilized the concept of a *Scala naturae,* derived from Aristotle, that implies that all species can be placed along a single great chain of being. They pointed to the branching nature of evolutionary history and to the need for a more realistic selection of species in comparative analyses.

In "Reflections on the Fall of Comparative Psychology: Is There a Lesson for Us All?" Lockard (1971) detailed 10 myths that he thought plagued the field. He incorporated the problems discussed by both Beach (1950) and Hodos and Campbell (1969) and added that comparative psychologists had devoted too little effort to the study of individual differences, species differences, genetics and evolution, and field research. Lockard advocated a more realistic biological approach for comparative psychology.

All three were effective critiques that provoked much discussion and appear to have helped to stimulate change. However, all three appear to have been overstatements of the problems. This may have been caused, in part, by the lack of a clear differentiation of true comparative psychology from other important, but different, parts of animal psychology. A survey published in 1980 revealed that comparative psychologists remained divided with regard to both the definition and status of the field (Demarest, 1980).

THREE IMPORTANT POSTWAR INFLUENCES

There were three major influences on comparative psychology after World War II. The first was from the important field developed by European zoologists that became know as ethology. The second stemmed from the elaboration of

Darwinian principles that led to sociobiology, behavioral ecology, and evolutionary psychology. Finally, the so-called cognitive revolution had important effects on the field.

European Ethology

Three major influences have affected and reshaped comparative psychology since World War II. The first was the full-blown arrival of European ethology. Ethology is as difficult to define as comparative psychology. It is a school of animal behavior studies that was developed in Europe by Konrad Lorenz, Niko Tinbergen, and their associates (Thorpe, 1979). According to a common, though greatly exaggerated, way of differentiating ethology from comparative psychology, the former developed in European zoology with birds, fish, and insects as subjects in observational studies and field experiments designed to understand instinct and evolution. Comparative psychology is said to have developed within North American comparative psychology with mammals, especially laboratory rats, as subjects in laboratory research emphasizing experimental control and statistical analysis designed to understand learning and development. Although these differences in emphasis are instructive, the extent to which they are exaggerations of comparative psychology should be apparent to the reader. On the other side, Lorenz himself conducted little field research.

Although European ethologists and American comparative psychologists had numerous interactions prior to World War II, it was only after the war that contact became extensive. The two disciplines that had each developed as "the objective study of behavior" along different lines came into direct conflict. Ethologists criticized psychologists for emphasizing laboratory research that may produce results irrelevant to the natural habitat; psychologists bemoaned the lack of experimental control in fieldwork of the ethologists.

The most critical issues, however, centered about behavioral development and the nature of instinctive behavior. The battle over instinct had gone on in the United States for most of the century, and during the 1950s, few psychologists accepted the concept; most emphasized the complex interaction of genes and environment in epigenesis. Based on their field observations, ethologists, by contrast, were quite comfortable with discussions of instinctive behavior (e.g., Lorenz, 1950). Lehrman (1953) wrote a scathing rebuttal to Lorenz's approach, with particular criticism directed at the instinct concept. On the one hand, the critique shocked ethologists and polarized the fields; on the other hand, however, it placed the issues out in the open where they could be debated and resolved. At a series of conferences, many of the differences were softened and mutual understanding increased. One

anecdote is revealing. Lehrman was discussing the issues in a rather stiff and formal disagreement with two ethologists, Gerard Baerends and Jan van Iersel, in a hotel room in Montreal. At one point, van Iersel's attention was distracted by a birdsong coming from the garden. Lehrman, a lifelong bird-watcher, replied that it was a hermit thrush. Van Iersel wanted to observe it, so the three went off on a birding expedition. When they returned to the debate, their shared feeling for animals lessened the hostility and fostered give-and-take discussion (Beer, 1975).

Although some psychologists, such as Schneirla, saw little value in ethology, others, like Lehrman and Beach, saw much. Beach and Carpenter facilitated interaction by agreeing to serve on the founding editorial board of the ethological journal *Behaviour*. Many students were attracted to the naturalism of the ethological analyses and traveled to Europe to work in ethological laboratories (Dewsbury, 1995). The two fields changed in each other's directions. Tinbergen moved from the Netherlands to Oxford University and developed a program with English-speaking ethologists. In general, they moved more toward the American position than did the German-speaking ethologists. The result of this activity was a more unified approach to animal behavior studies, with more psychologists even more concerned with naturally occurring behavior and principles that would be valid in nature and more ethologists concerned with control and experimental procedures. More and more psychologists participated in the biannual International Ethological Conferences, and more Europeans came to the United States for either short or extended periods of time. In the process, both fields benefited.

Sociobiology, Behavioral Ecology, and Evolutionary Psychology

The second major postwar influence came from the field that has become known as sociobiology. Many scientists had been studying behavior from an evolutionary perspective for many years. However, some of the implications of Darwinian theory had not been fully thought through; this led to some questionable interpretations. During the 1960s and early 1970s, theorists such as William D. Hamilton, John Maynard Smith, and Robert Trivers reinterpreted Darwinian principles. Although a number of principles were reevaluated, two were critical. One principle concerns the level at which natural selection acts. Much had been written about how behavior evolves for the good of the species or group. Thus, for example, reproduction had been thought to have evolved for the perpetuation of the species. On reinterpretation, it was concluded that natural selection works primarily at the level of the individual or gene, not the group or species. This had many important implications and permitted reinterpretation of many phenomena. If a nest of eggs is left unguarded in a colony of gulls, for example, other members of the colony will eat the eggs. This makes little sense if all were there to perpetuate the species but is easy to understand if competition was at the level of the individual, with each selected to get its genes into the next generation. It had been believed that, at high densities, some species temporarily curtail reproduction in order not to overexploit the available environmental resources. This became reinterpreted as a temporary "strategy" that could benefit the lifetime reproductive success of an individual by preserving energy during hard times. The extreme form of this approach was Richard Dawkins's (1976) selfish gene theory.

The second new principle concerned inclusive fitness. The term *fitness* refers to the relative contribution of different individuals to future gene pools. It was noted that an individual shares more genes with close relatives than with those to which one is unrelated. There are thus at least two ways in which one's genes can be transmitted to the next generation. One is through reproduction (direct fitness); the other is through facilitating the reproduction of close relatives (indirect fitness or kin selection). Inclusive fitness is, essentially, the sum of the two. Thus, what might appear to be altruistic behavior, which might lower one's fitness, might be adaptive in the long run. One might lower one's direct fitness but gain even more indirect fitness in the process. The bottom line became lifetime inclusive fitness.

These two principles, and some others associated with them, led many students of animal behavior, both inside and outside of psychology, to reorient their research programs. Many students became interested in the study of the evolutionary causes of behavior (ultimate causation) as opposed to the immediate and developmental causes (proximate causation). There were many studies of the role of kinship in behavior. A large number of species were found to modulate their behavior depending on the degree of kinship shared with others with which they interacted (e.g., Holmes & Sherman, 1982; R. H. Porter, 1988). Sexual selection, a topic emphasized by Darwin in 1871, became a major focus of research, with psychologists emphasizing studies of mate choice (e.g., Beauchamp, Yamazaki, & Boyse, 1985) and male–male competition for mates (e.g., LeBoeuf, 1974). Others sharpened evolutionary interpretations of phenomena of research on learning (e.g., Hollis, 1990; Kamil & Clements, 1990; Timberlake, 1990). Evolutionary perspectives had been a part of comparative psychology since its founding; now studies became more refined and were addressed more specifically to evolutionary principles.

This orientation had been somewhat diffuse until E. O. Wilson (1975) organized and named the field in his *Sociobiology: The New Synthesis*. Although Wilson predicted the demise of comparative psychology, the field was, in fact, strengthened by the new perspective. The first 26 chapters of Wilson's book provided a synthesis of much work related to the ultimate causation of animal behavior. In the final chapter, however, Wilson applied these principles to human behavior. This approach proved highly controversial. Although some careful research on human behavior stemmed from this approach (e.g., Daly & Wilson, 1978), other writings rested on less solid ground. A split developed between the controversial studies of human behavior and those less controversial studies of animals. The term *behavioral ecology* was coined, in part, so that students of animal behavior could distance themselves from some of the more speculative studies of humans.

More recently, sociobiology has been reborn as *evolutionary psychology*. An emphasis in the older sociobiology had been upon the ways in which existing patterns of human behavior enhanced fitness. In the newer perspective, the focus shifted to adaptiveness at the time that mechanisms of behavior evolved in the ancestors of humans, and it was recognized that many behavior patterns and tendencies, such as our attraction to sweet foods, might not be as adaptive under present conditions (e.g., Cosmides & Tooby, 1987).

Comparative Cognition

The third major influence on comparative psychology since World War II was from the "cognitive revolution." According to the received view, the hegemony of behaviorism precluded cognitive approaches to behavior prior to the 1960s and a major revolution occurred thereafter. In fact, however, research with a cognitive orientation has long been a part of comparative psychology (e.g., Dewsbury, 2000; Wasserman, 1993). Although a case can be made that there was no true revolution (Leahey, 1992), it is clear that in recent years cognitive perspectives have achieved a prominence in comparative psychology that had not been apparent previously.

This increased emphasis on cognitive perspectives was a part of the broad upsurge of interest in cognitive processes throughout psychology and related disciplines. Developments in information processing, computers, and mathematical logic fostered a reconstruction of psychology as a science of information as well as behavior. Some psychologists moved to overcome what they perceived as the counterproductive constraints imposed by more behavioristic theories. Interest was directed in the manner in which animals represent their worlds and the consequences of such representation for behavior.

Among the topics receiving renewed interest were attention, memory, timing, concept formation, counting, social cognition, and language (Roitblat, 1987; Shettleworth, 1998; Vauclair, 1996). The most publicized research in this field has been that of language learning. Although there had been earlier attempts to teach language to apes, such as that of Cathy and Keith Hayes at the Yerkes Laboratories (Hayes, 1951), three major approaches developed during the 1960s and 1970s. Gardner and Gardner (1969) taught American sign language to chimpanzee Washoe; Rumbaugh (e.g., Rumbaugh & Gill, 1976) studied acquisition of a computer-based language in chimpanzee Lana; and Premack (1971) used a system of sentence formation using pieces of plastic with chimpanzee Sarah. This groundbreaking research was both heavily criticized and staunchly defended. This produced a fallow period, due largely to an absence of funding, during which little language research was conducted. This period was followed by a reformulation and rebirth of studies of animal language, the most remarkable of which were of bonobo Kanzi, who learned a symbol-based language without overt training and became efficient in interpreting human speech (e.g., Savage-Rumbaugh et al., 1993). Other studies of language acquisition were conducted with an African grey parrot (Pepperberg, 1999), dolphins (Herman, 1987), and sea lions (Schusterman & Krieger, 1984).

Many of the studies in animal cognition were derived from, and closely related to, traditional research in animal learning. Other scientists made an effort to more completely revolutionize the field of animal cognition using language suggestive of conscious processes in animals. Leading the latter effort was American ethologist Donald R. Griffin (e.g., Griffin, 1976b); the field became known as cognitive ethology. Advocates of this approach contended that, with advances in methodology, there are now available methods that can provide windows to the minds of animals. According to Griffin (1976a), "the hypothesis that some animals are indeed aware of what they do, and of internal images that affect their behavior, simplifies our view of the universe by removing the need to maintain an unparsimonious assumption that our species is qualitatively unique in this important attribute" (p. 534). Critics disagreed, contending that no methods were yet available that enable scientists to observe the internal processes of animal minds.

Among the focal areas of research in cognitive ethology have been studies of self-recognition in mirrors (e.g., Gallup, 1985). According to Gallup, humans, chimpanzees, orangutans, and some gorillas are the only species to show evidence of self-recognition when presented with mirrors. The key evidence comes from "dot tests," in which a dot is painted onto the forehead of an anesthetized animal to see if the animal selectively touches the dot when awakened and presented with a mirror. Gallup believes that such behavior suggests awareness, self-awareness, and mind in chimpanzees. Critics

disagree (Heyes, 1994). In some ways, the field had returned to questions addressed a century ago. Psychologists disagree as to whether the results achieved during that century now permit a return to these questions in a more sophisticated manner or whether it is regressing to an earlier state.

CONCLUSION: PERSISTENT ISSUES

Looking back over a little more than a century of comparative psychology, a number of characteristics are apparent. The conceptual foundations of comparative psychology have changed greatly. Some of these changes have been generated from within the field; many more have been stimulated from related fields. Comparative psychologists have excelled in doing research and greatly expanded the body of data available. It is this mass of information, sometimes well organized and sometimes rather scattered, that has enabled a century of change. Comparative psychologists have been empiricists working to expand the observational and experimental foundation of the field; there are few postmodern comparative psychologists. In spite of the changes that have occurred, however, throughout the century there have been some persistent issues that have characterized the field.

Surely the first issue lies in the very definition of comparative psychology. Although comparative psychologists have written much about this problem, few have been truly bothered by it. Even lacking a clear definition, most comparative psychologists have ignored the fuzzy boundaries of the field and concentrated on the business of studying animals and building general principles of behavior.

Underlying the research effort have been issues of methodology. The field has been characterized by eclecticism, as most researchers have used whatever methods have appeared appropriate for the problem under study. Although some comparative psychologists, such as Carpenter, Schneirla, Yerkes, Mason, and others, have conducted field research, most have preferred the controlled conditions of the laboratory. Not all comparative psychologists make overt comparisons among species; the goal is not one of comparison for the sake of comparison but rather the development of principles of generality. Although some, such as Kline, Schneirla, and James V. McConnell, have studied invertebrates, most have concentrated on vertebrates, especially mammals. Some, such as Beach, Lehrman, and Carpenter, have concentrated on naturally occurring behavioral patterns; others have turned their attention to the study of learning and motivation in a comparative context. Although experimentation is the preferred method, many observational and correlational studies have been important. The anecdotes that characterized early research disappeared as laboratory methodology became more sophisticated but has begun to creep back into the field as some believe that the most remarkable feats of animals cannot be produced under controlled conditions but require unusual circumstances. Comparative psychologists have devoted much attention to the construction of apparatus appropriate to the problem at hand (Warden et al., 1935; D. A. Washburn, Rumbaugh, & Richardson, 1998).

The theory of evolution has provided the conceptual foundation of psychology since its founding. At times, it has been in the foreground, as in the early work of James, Angell, Hall, and James Mark Baldwin (1896), who along with two others, proposed the "Baldwin effect" as a means to explain apparent inheritance of acquired traits with more conventional evolutionary principles. Another examples is the APA presidential address of Calvin Stone (1943). At other times, it has been more implicit. Although the evolutionary focus of comparative psychology was not obvious to some observers during parts of the history of the field, the strong evolutionary approach has been increasingly visible since World War II.

Surely the most persistent issue in comparative psychology, and perhaps for all psychology, has been the nature-nurture problem. Throughout its history the pendulum has swung back and forth between emphases on genes and environment in the development of behavior. Such psychologists as William James and William McDougall postulated many instincts in humans and other species. This led to an anti-instinct revolt that was particularly strong during the 1920s. Virtually all comparative psychologists now recognize the importance of the continuous, dynamic interaction of genes and environment in the development of behavior. Some, such as Yerkes, Stone, Robert Tryon, and Jerry Hirsch, have conducted important studies of genetic influences. Such psychologists as Harlow, Eckhard Hess, and Gilbert Gottlieb have worked more on experiential factors. Virtually all agree on the importance of the dynamic interaction of both.

A key part of the nature-nurture problem is that problem of instinctive behavior. The fact is that individuals of many species develop either specific motor patterns or responsivity to specific stimuli in the absence of specific experience. For example, young sea turtles hatched on a beach in the absence of adults go toward the ocean, not the dune (Mellgren & Mann, 1998). The environment is critical for all behavior but appears not to provide the specificity in such instances. Whatever one may call it, the ontogeny of such behavioral patterns appears different, at least to some degree, from the ontogeny of many other behavioral patterns. Comparative psychologists still grapple with the problem of explaining such behavior.

Sensory-perceptual systems provide the stimuli for virtually all behavior and have been of interest in comparative psychology throughout its history. Six of the 13 chapters in M. F. Washburn's (1908) textbook were devoted to sensory systems. Watson, Lashley, Hess, and many others have contributed in this endeavor.

Many studies of basic behavioral patterns have been conducted. Included are such topics as orientation, activity, ingestive behavior, hoarding, nest building, exploration, and play. Many comparative psychologists have studied social behavior and imitation.

For sheer quantity of research articles, the study of learning may exceed all other problems in comparative psychology. Almost all comparative psychologists have conducted at least some research related to learning. Many studies have been of single species. Some, such as Bitterman (1965), Gossette (Gossette & Gossette, 1967), and Rumbaugh (Rumbaugh & Pate, 1984), have attempted systematic comparisons using particular learning problems. In recent years, many comparative psychologists have viewed learning in relation to the demands of the specific habitats in which the study species has evolved (e.g., Shettleworth, 1998). The question concerning the existence of a general learning process versus domain-specific mechanisms is actively debated.

At least from the time of Thorndike, the issue of animal cognition has been central. Is all learning the product of basic mechanisms, or are higher processes sometimes required to explain changes in animal behavior, as suggested by Köhler, Maier, and many recent cognitive psychologists and ethologists? Most of the issues addressed in the flourishing field of comparative cognition were also addressed, in one form or another, by earlier generations. In recent years, work based on the assumption that higher processes are operative has led to many fascinating findings in comparative psychology, including investigations based on a theory of mind (Premack & Woodruff, 1978), of production and comprehension of referential pointing (Call & Tomasello, 1994), and those suggesting that "chimpanzees are capable of modeling the visual perspectives of others" (Povinelli, Nelson, & Boysen, 1990). Such results suggest that, at the very least, these cognitive approaches might be of considerable heuristic value.

Throughout its history, comparative research, from Ivan Pavlov and John B. Watson to the present, has been attacked by animal activists of one sort or another (Dewsbury, 1990). Recent studies of animal cognition have produced an ironic twist. Some of the very research that activists condemn has revealed remarkable abilities in animals and similarities to humans that the activists then use to argue for the cessation of that research because of that similarity to humans.

Related to the issue of cognition is that of animal consciousness. In this area there seems to have been little progress since the days of Morgan (1894) and M. F. Washburn (1908). I see in many species, especially primates, behavior that, in myself, is correlated with certain states of consciousness. At a personal level, I fully believe that those animals have a consciousness that is similar to mine in at least some respects. However, despite the protestations of Griffin, I see no "windows on the mind" that will enable us to draw such conclusions in any scientifically meaningful way.

Throughout its history, comparative psychology has been a basic science, concerned with generating general principles rather than solving problems for immediate application. Nevertheless, many comparative studies have produced information of practical import. Primates trained to manipulate joysticks and other manipulanda have been used in the space program. Targeted research has been directed at a range of problems from controlling the tree snakes on Guam (Chiszar, 1990) to designing more challenging environments for captive zoo animals (Markowitz, 1982) to training animals for reintroduction into their natural habitats (e.g., Beck & Castro, 1994). Comparative psychologists have been concerned with the psychological well-being of primates in research laboratories (e.g., Novak & Suomi, 1988) and the use of therapy to treat behavioral problems in household pets (Tuber, Hothersall, & Voith, 1974).

The major paradox of comparative psychology is that it is basically the study of *nonhuman* animal mind and behavior within a discipline that is often defined as the study of the *human* mind and behavior. This issue was laid out near the beginning of the last century by Wilhelm Wundt (1901), who contrasted research conducted for its own sake with that conducted to shed light on human behavior. In the latter approach, Wundt suggested, "man is only considered as one, though, of course, the highest, of developmental stages to be examined" (p. 340). Near the middle of the century, Beach (1960) put it differently:

If we remove man from the central point in a comparative science of behavior, this may, in the long run, prove to be the very best way of reaching a better understanding of his place in nature and of the behavioral characteristics which he shares with other animals as well as those which he possesses alone or which are in him developed to a unique degree. (p. 18)

REFERENCES

Aberle, S. D., & Corner, G. W. (1953). *Twenty-five years of sex research: History of the National Research Council Committee for Research in Problems of Sex 1922–1947.* Philadelphia: Saunders.

Angell, J. R. (1905, January). Recent scientific contributions to social welfare: Contemporary psychology. *Chatauquan,* 453–459.

Aronson, L. R., Tobach, E., Rosenblatt, J. S., & Lehrman, D. S. (Eds.). (1969). *Selected writings of T. C. Schneirla.* San Francisco: Freeman.

Baldwin, J. M. (1896). A new factor in evolution. *American Naturalist, 30,* 536–553.

Beach, F. A. (1950). The snark was a boojum. *American Psychologist, 5,* 115–124.

Beach, F. A. (1955). The descent of instinct. *Psychological Review, 62,* 401–410.

Beach, F. A. (1960). Experimental investigations of species-specific behavior. *American Psychologist, 15,* 1–18.

Beauchamp, G. K., Yamazaki, K., & Boyse, E. A. (1985). The chemosensory recognition of genetic individuality. *Scientific American, 253*(1), 86–92.

Beck, B. B., & Castro, M. I. (1994). Environments for endangered primates. In E. F. Gibbons Jr., E. J. Wyers, E. Waters, & E. Menzel (Eds.), *Naturalistic environments in captivity for animal behavior research* (pp. 259–270). Albany, NY: SUNY Press.

Beer, C. G. (1975). Was Professor Lehrman an ethologist? *Animal Behaviour, 23,* 957–964.

Bitterman, M. E. (1965). The evolution of intelligence. *Scientific American, 212*(1), 92–100.

Boakes, R. (1984). *From Darwin to behaviourism.* Cambridge, England: Cambridge University Press.

Boring, E. G. (1912). Note on the negative reaction under light-adaptation in the planarian. *Journal of Animal Behavior, 2,* 229–248.

Cadwallader, T. C. (1984). Neglected aspects of the evolution of American comparative and animal psychology. In G. Greenberg & E. Tobach (Eds.), *Behavioral evolution and integrative levels* (pp. 15–48). Hillsdale, NJ: Erlbaum.

Call, J., & Tomasello, M. (1994). Production and comprehension of referential pointing by orangutans (*Pongo pygmaeus*). *Journal of Comparative Psychology, 108,* 307–317.

Carpenter, C. R. (1934). A field study of the behavioral and social relations of howling monkeys (*Alouatta palliata*). *Comparative Psychology Monographs, 10*(48), 1–168.

Chiszar, D. A. (1990). The behavior of the brown tree snake: A study in applied comparative psychology. In D. A. Dewsbury (Ed.), *Contemporary issues in comparative psychology* (pp. 101–123). Sunderland, MA: Sinauer.

Coburn, C. A., & Yerkes, R. M. (1915). A study of the behavior of the crow *Corvus americanus* Aud. by the multiple choice method. *Journal of Animal Behavior, 5,* 75–114.

Cole, L. W. (1910). Reactions of frogs to chlorides of sodium, potassium, ammonium, and lithium. *Journal of Comparative Neurology and Psychology, 20,* 601–614.

Conradi, E. (1905). Song and call-notes of English sparrows when reared by canaries. *American Journal of Psychology, 16,* 190–198.

Cosm ides, L., & Tooby, J. (1987). From evolution to behavior: Evolutionary psychology as the missing link. In J. Dupré (Ed.),

The latest on the best: Essays on evolution and optimality (pp. 277–306). Cambridge, MA: MIT Press.

Daly, M., & Wilson, M. (1978). *Sex, evolution, and behavior.* North Scituate, MA: Duxbury.

Darwin, C. (1859). *On the origin of species by means of natural selection, or the preservation of favoured races in the struggle for life.* London: John Murray.

Darwin, C. (1871). *The descent of man and selection in relation to sex.* London: John Murray.

Darwin, C. (1872). *The expression of the emotions in man and animals.* London: Appleton.

Dawkins, R. (1976). *The selfish gene.* Oxford, England: Oxford University Press.

Day, L. M., & Bentley, I. M. (1911). A note on learning in paramecium. *Journal of Animal Behavior, 1,* 67–73.

Demarest, J. (1980). The current status of comparative psychology in the American Psychological Association. *American Psychologist, 35,* 980–990.

Dewsbury, D. A. (1984). *Comparative psychology in the twentieth century.* Stroudsburg, PA: Hutchinson Ross.

Dewsbury, D. A. (1990). Early interactions between animal psychologists and animal activists and the founding of the APA Committee on Precautions in Animal Experimentation. *American Psychologist, 45,* 315–327.

Dewsbury, D. A. (1992). Triumph and tribulation in the history of American comparative psychology. *Journal of Comparative Psychology, 106,* 3–19.

Dewsbury, D. A. (1995). Americans in Europe: The role of travel in the spread of European ethology after World War II. *Animal Behaviour, 49,* 1649–1663.

Dewsbury, D. A. (1997). Edward Bradford Titchener: Comparative psychologist? *American Journal of Psychology, 110,* 449–456.

Dewsbury, D. A. (1998). Animal psychology in journals, 1911–1927: Another look at the snark. *Journal of Comparative Psychology, 112,* 400–405.

Dewsbury, D. A. (2000). Comparative cognition in the 1930s. *Psychonomic Bulletin and Review, 7,* 267–283.

Dewsbury, D. A. (in press-a). The Chicago five: A family group of integrative psychobiologists. *History of Psychology.*

Dewsbury, D. A. (in press-b). Comparative psychology: A case study of development of support for basic research by a Federal agency with an applied mission 1948–1963. In W. E. Pickren & S. F. Schneider (Eds.), *Psychology and the National Institute of Mental Health.* Washington, DC: American Psychological Association.

Gallup, G. G., Jr. (1985). Do minds exist in species other than our own? *Neuroscience and Biobehavioral Reviews, 9,* 631–641.

Gardner, R. A., & Gardner, B. T. (1969). Teaching sign language to a chimpanzee. *Science, 165,* 664–672.

Gossette, R. L., & Gossette, M. F. (1967). Examination of the reversal index (RI) across fifteen different mammalian and avian species. *Perceptual and Motor Skills, 24,* 987–990.

Griffin, D. R. (1976a). A possible window on the minds of animals. *American Scientist, 64,* 530–535.

Griffin, D. R. (1976b). *The question of animal awareness.* New York: Rockefeller University Press.

Hall, G. S. (1901). The new psychology. *Harper's Monthly Magazine, 103,* 727–732.

Hayes, C. H. (1951). *The ape in our house.* New York: Harper & Row.

Hebb, D. O. (1949). *The organization of behavior.* New York: Wiley.

Hebb, D. O. (1953). Heredity and environment in mammalian behaviour. *British Journal of Animal Behaviour, 1,* 243–254.

Hebb, D. O., & Thompson, W. R. (1954). The social significance of animal studies. In G. Lindzey (Ed.), *Handbook of social psychology* (Vol. 1, pp. 532–561). Cambridge, MA: Addison-Wesley.

Herman, L. M. (1987). Receptive competencies of language-trained animals. *Advances in the Study of Behavior, 17,* 1–60.

Heyes, C. M. (1994). Reflections on self-recognition in primates. *Animal Behaviour, 47,* 909–919.

Hodos, W., & Campbell, C. B. G. (1969). *Scala naturae:* Why there is no theory in comparative psychology. *Psychological Review, 76,* 337–350.

Hollis, K. L. (1990). The role of Pavlovian conditioning in territorial aggression and reproduction. In D. A. Dewsbury (Ed.), *Contemporary issues in comparative psychology* (pp. 197–219). Sunderland, MA: Sinauer.

Holmes, W. G., & Sherman, P. W. (1982). The ontogeny of kin recognition in two species of ground squirrels. *American Zoologist, 22,* 491–517.

James, W. (1935). Letter to Charles W. Eliot. In R. B. Perry (Ed.), *The thought and character of William James* (Vol. 2, pp. 10–11). Boston: Little, Brown. (Original work published 1875)

Johnson, H. M. (1914). Visual pattern discrimination in the vertebrates. II: Comparative visual acuity in the dog, the monkey, and the chick. *Journal of Animal Behavior, 4,* 340–361.

Kamil, A. C., & Clements, K. C. (1990). Learning, memory, and foraging behavior. In D. A. Dewsbury (Ed.), *Contemporary issues in comparative psychology* (pp. 7–30). Sunderland, MA: Sinauer.

Kline, L. W. (1899). Suggestions toward a laboratory course in comparative psychology. *American Journal of Psychology, 10,* 399–430.

Kline, L. W. (1904). Contributions of zoological psychology to child study. *Journal of Proceedings and Addresses of the National Education Association,* 776–782.

Köhler, W. (1925). *The mentality of apes.* London: Routledge & Keegan Paul.

Krechevsky, I. (1932). "Hypotheses" in rats. *Psychological Review, 39,* 516–532.

Leahey, T. H. (1992). The mythical revolutions of American psychology. *American Psychologist, 47,* 308–318.

LeBoeuf, B. J. (1974). Male-male competition and reproductive success in elephant seals. *American Zoologist, 14,* 163–176.

Lehrman, D. S. (1953). A critique of Konrad Lorenz's theory of instinctive behavior. *Quarterly Review of Biology, 28,* 337–363.

Lockard, R. B. (1971). Reflections on the rise and fall of comparative psychology: Is there a lesson for us all? *American Psychologist, 26,* 168–179.

Lorenz, K. Z. (1950). The comparative method in studying innate behavior patterns. In J. F. Danielli & R. Brown (Eds.), *Physiological mechanisms in animal behavior* (pp. 221–268). New York: Academic Press.

Maier, N. R. F. (1937). Reasoning in rats and human beings. *Psychological Review, 44,* 365–378.

Maier, N. R. F., & Schneirla, T. C. (1935). *Principles of animal psychology.* New York: McGraw-Hill.

Markowitz, H. (1982). *Behavioral enrichment in the zoo.* New York: Van Nostrand.

McGill, T. E., Dewsbury, D. A., & Sachs, B. D. (Eds.). (1978). *Sex and behavior: Status and prospectus.* New York: Plenum Press.

Mellgren, R. L., & Mann, M. A. (1998). Sea turtles. In G. Greenberg & M. M. Haraway (Eds.), *Comparative psychology: A handbook* (pp. 473–476). New York: Garland.

Miles, W. (1930). On the history of research with rats and mazes: A collection of notes. *Journal of General Psychology, 3,* 324–337.

Mills, W. (1899). The nature of intelligence and the methods of investigating it. *Psychological Review, 6,* 262–274.

Morgan, C. L. (1894). *An introduction to comparative psychology.* London: Walter Scott.

Moss, F. A. (Ed.). (1934). *Comparative psychology.* New York: Prentice-Hall.

Mountjoy, P. T. (1980). An historical approach to comparative psychology. In M. R. Denny (Ed.), *Comparative psychology: An evolutionary analysis of behavior* (pp. 128–152). New York: Wiley.

Munn, N. L. (1933). *An introduction to animal psychology: The behavior of the rat.* Boston: Houghton Mifflin.

Münsterberg, H. (1911, January 30). *Letter to President, A. L. Lowell* (Hugo Münsterberg papers). Boston: Boston Public Library.

Newbury, E. (1954). Current interpretation and significance of Lloyd Morgan's canon. *Psychological Bulletin, 51,* 70–74.

Novak, M. A., & Suomi, S. J. (1988). Psychological well-being of primates in captivity. *American Psychologist, 43,* 765–773.

Pepperberg, I. M. (1999). *The Alex studies: Cognitive and communicative abilities of grey parrots.* Cambridge, MA: Harvard University Press.

Porter, J. P. (1906). The habits, instincts, and mental powers of spiders, genera *Argiope* and *Eperia. American Journal of Psychology, 17,* 306–357.

Porter, R. H. (1988). The ontogeny of sibling recognition in rodents: Superfamily Muroidea. *Behavior Genetics, 18,* 483–494.

Povinelli, D. J., Nelson, K. E., & Boysen, S. T. (1990). Inferences about guessing and knowing by chimpanzees (*Pan troglodytes*). *Journal of Comparative Psychology, 104,* 203–210.

Premack, D. (1971). Language in chimpanzee? *Science, 172,* 808–822.

Premack, D., & Woodruff, G. (1978). Does the chimpanzee have a theory of mind? *Behavioral and Brain Sciences, 4,* 515–526.

Raphelson, A. C. (1980). Psychology at Michigan: The Pillsbury years, 1897–1947. *Journal of the History of the Behavioral Sciences, 16,* 301–312.

Roitblat, H. L. (1987). *Introduction to comparative cognition.* New York: Freeman.

Romanes, G. J. (1882). *Animal intelligence.* New York: Appleton.

Romanes, G. J. (1885). *Jelly-fish, star-fish, and sea-urchins.* New York: Appleton.

Rumbaugh, D. M., & Gill, T. V. (1976). Language and the acquisition of language-type skills by a chimpanzee (*Pan*). *Annals of the New York Academy of Sciences, 270,* 90–123.

Rumbaugh, D. M., & Pate, J. L. (1984). The evolution of cognition in primates: A comparative perspective. In H. L. Roitblat, T. G. Bever, & H. S. Terrace (Eds.), *Animal cognition* (pp. 569–587). Hillsdale, NJ: Erlbaum.

Savage-Rumbaugh, E. S., Murphy, J., Sevcik, R. A., Brakke, K. E., Williams, S. L., & Rumbaugh, D. M. (1993). Language comprehension in ape and child. *Monographs of the Society for Research in Child Development, 58*(233), 1–256.

Schusterman, R. J., & Krieger, K. (1984). California sea lions are capable of semantic comprehension. *Psychological Record, 34,* 3–23.

Shepherd, W. T. (1915). Tests on adaptive intelligence in dogs, and cats, as compared with adaptive intelligence in rhesus monkeys. *American Journal of Psychology, 26,* 211–216.

Shettleworth, S. J. (1998). *Cognition, evolution, and behavior.* Oxford, England: Oxford University Press.

Singer, B. (1981). History of the study of animal behaviour. In D. McFarland (Ed.), *The Oxford companion to animal behaviour* (pp. 255–272). Oxford, England: Oxford University Press.

Small, W. S. (1899). Notes on the psychic development of the young white rat. *American Journal of Psychology, 11,* 80–100.

Small, W. S. (1901). Experimental study of the mental processes of the rat–II. *American Journal of Psychology, 12,* 206–239.

Stone, C. P. (1943). Multiply, vary, let the strongest live and the weakest die–Charles Darwin. *Psychological Bulletin, 40,* 1–24.

Suomi, S. J., & Leroy, H. A. (1982). In memoriam: Harry F. Harlow (1905–1981). *American Journal of Primatology, 2,* 319–342.

Thorndike, E. L. (1898). Animal intelligence: An experimental study of the associative process in animals. *Psychological Review Monograph Supplement, 2*(4), 1–109.

Thorndike, E. L. (1899). A reply to "The nature of animal intelligence and the methods of investigating it." *Psychological Review, 6,* 412–420.

Thorndike, E. L. (1911). *Animal intelligence: Experimental studies.* New York: Macmillan.

Thorpe, W. H. (1979). *The origins and rise of ethology: The science of the natural behaviour of animals.* London: Praeger.

Timberlake, W. (1990). Natural learning in laboratory paradigms. In D. A. Dewsbury (Ed.), *Contemporary issues in comparative psychology* (pp. 31–54). Sunderland, MA: Sinauer.

Tuber, D. S., Hothersall, D., & Voith, V. L. (1974). Animal clinical psychology: A modest proposal. *American Psychologist, 29,* 762–766.

Vauclair, J. (1996). *Animal cognition: An introduction to modern comparative psychology.* Cambridge, MA: Harvard University Press.

Warden, C. J. (1931). *Animal motivation: Experimental studies on the albino rat.* New York: Columbia University Press.

Warden, C. J., Jenkins, T. N., & Warner, L. H. (1935). *Comparative psychology: A comprehensive treatise.* Volume I: Principles and methods. New York: Ronald.

Warden, C. J., Jenkins, T. N., & Warner, L. H. (1936). *Comparative psychology: A comprehensive treatise.* Volume III: Vertebrates. New York: Ronald.

Warden, C. J., Jenkins, T. N., & Warner, L. H. (1940). *Comparative psychology: A comprehensive treatise.* Volume II: Plants and invertebrates. New York: Ronald.

Washburn, D. A., Rumbaugh, D. M., & Richardson, W. K. (1998). Apparatus in comparative psychology. In G. Greenberg & M. M. Haraway (Eds.), *Comparative psychology: A handbook* (pp. 221–225). New York: Garland.

Washburn, M. F. (1908). *The animal mind.* New York: Macmillan.

Washburn, M. F., & Bentley, I. M. (1906). The establishment of an association involving color-discrimination in the creek chub. *Journal of Comparative Psychology and Neurology, 16,* 113–125.

Wasserman, E. A. (1993). Comparative cognition: Beginning the second century of the study of animal intelligence. *Psychological Bulletin, 113,* 211–228.

Watson, J. B. (1903). *Animal education: An experimental study of the psychical development of the white rat, correlated with the growth of its nervous system.* Chicago: University of Chicago.

Watson, J. B. (1912). Instinctive activity in animals. *Harper's Magazine, 124,* 376–382.

Watson, J. B. (1919). *Psychology from the standpoint of a behaviorist.* Philadelphia: Lippincott.

Watson, J. B., & Lashley, K. S. (1915). An experimental and historical study of homing. *Carnegie Institution Publication, 211,* 7–60.

Wilson, E. O. (1975). *Sociobiology: The new synthesis.* Cambridge, MA: Harvard University Press.

Wundt, W. (1901). *Lectures on human and animal psychology* (2nd ed., J. E. Creighton & E. B. Titchener, Trans.). London: Swan Sonnenschein.

Yerkes, R. M. (1907). *The dancing mouse.* New York: Macmillan.

Yerkes, R. M. (1916). Provision for the study of monkeys and apes. *Science, 43,* 231–234.

Yerkes, R. M. (1925). *Almost human.* London: Jonathan Cape.

Yerkes, R. M. (1943). *Chimpanzees: A laboratory colony.* New Haven, CT: Yale University Press.

Yerkes, R. M., & Bloomfield, D. (1910). Do kittens instinctively kill mice? *Psychological Bulletin, 7,* 253–263.

Yerkes, R. M., & Huggins, G. E. (1903). Habit formation in the crawfish *Cambarus affinis. Psychological Review Monograph Supplement, 17,* 565–577.

Yoakum, C. S. (1909). Some experiments upon the behavior of squirrels. *Journal of Comparative Neurology and Psychology, 19,* 565–568.

CHAPTER 5

Sensation and Perception

STANLEY COREN

THE PERCEPTUAL PROBLEM 86
SENSATION, PERCEPTION, REASON,
   AND COGNITION 87
PHYSICS AND VISUAL PERCEPTION 90
PHYSIOLOGY AND PERCEPTION 93
THE SCIENCE OF ILLUSION 99
THE RISE OF THE BEHAVIORAL LABORATORIES 101

THE PSYCHOPHYSICISTS AND THE
   CORRESPONDENCE PROBLEM 103
THE GESTALTISTS AND THE CORRESPONDENCE
   PROBLEM 105
THE PROGRESS OF PERCEPTUAL RESEARCH 106
BIBLIOGRAPHY 107
REFERENCES 108

The study of sensation and perception is diverse. Partly this is the result of the length of time that perceptual problems have been studied. The Greek philosophers, the pre-Renaissance thinkers, the Arabic scholars, the Latin Scholastics, the early British empiricists, the German physicists, and the German physicians who founded both physiology and psychology considered issues in sensation and perception to be basic questions. When Alexander Bain wrote the first English textbook on psychology in 1855 it was entitled *The Senses and the Intellect,* with the most extensive coverage reserved for sensory and perceptual functions. During the first half of his career, the major portion of both the theorizing and the empirical work of Wilhelm Wundt (who is generally credited with the founding of experimental psychology) were oriented toward sensation and perception.

The long history of sensory and perceptual research means that there is a huge database and that much information has accrued about the substantive issues concerning how the specific sensory systems operate and how we extract and interpret information from them. It would be possible to write a book just on the history of visual perception, or another on auditory perception, or yet another on the history of sensory and perceptual studies of the tactile, olfactory, or gustatory modalities. Even specific aspects of perception, such as the perception of pain, could generate its own full volume outlining the history of the major substantive findings and theoretical treatments of this single aspect of sensory experience. In addition to the large empirical database that has resulted from the long history of research in this area, the study of perception has been affected by many "schools" of thought. Each has its own major theoretical viewpoint and its own particular set of methodological techniques. Thus, we encounter psychophysicists, gestaltists, functionalists, structuralists, transactionalists, sensory physiologists, analytic introspectionists, sensory-tonic theorists, "new look" psychologists, efferent theorists, cognitive theorists, information processors, artificial intelligence experts, and computational psychologists, to name but a few. There are even theorists (such as some behaviorists) who deny the existence of, or at least deny our ability to study, the conscious event we call perception. How, then, can a single chapter give any coherent treatment of the issues associated with this fundamental aspect of psychology?

Fortunately, a broad overview shows that it is possible to see some unifying perspectives that have evolved through history. Common theoretical perspectives might be expected in this discipline, since most sensory and perception researchers are not exclusively bound to one sensory modality. Thus, we find Helmholtz and Hering studying both vision and audition, and George von Bekesy, who won the Nobel Prize for his work on hearing, also contributing to studies on vision and touch. Some researchers, such as Fechner, Stevens, Ames, Gibson, Wertheimer, Koffka, Helson, and others, have offered theoretical frameworks that are virtually modality independent and can be tested and explored using visual, auditory, or any other stimulus input. This is not to deny that there are issues that are important to a single sensory modality that do not generalize. One instance of a modality-specific issue might be the chain of events that leads from the absorption of a photon to a visual neural response and a conscious recognition of the stimulus. Instead, this is to suggest that there are global theoretical and methodological frameworks that encompass all sensory and perceptual research. To refer back to that very specific issue of visual detection, while the mechanism of how a photon is captured is specific to sight, all sensory modalities must deal with the ideas of detection and of sensory thresholds and their relationship to what the individual consciously perceives. It is also likely that the higher-level decisional processes, where the observer must decide if a stimulus is there or not, will be the same whether one is dealing with vision, audition, olfaction, or any other sensory system. Thus, we find that certain common issues and definitions cut across all sensory modalities. These methods, philosophical foundations, and psychological understandings have undergone a steady evolution during the history of this area of psychology.

This chapter will be written as an overview and will concentrate on some general themes rather than upon the data and findings from any one sensory modality. From this, hopefully, some idea of the context and scope of the study of perception and its relationship to other aspects of psychology and other sciences will emerge. Three global issues will reappear many times and in several guises during this history. The first deals with the *perceptual problem,* which is really the issue of the correspondence (or noncorrespondence) between our internal representation of the environment in consciousness and the objectively measured external physical situation. The second has to do with the borrowing of methods, viewpoints, and theoretical formulations from other sciences, such as physics and physiology. The third is the distinction between sensation and perception, which is really the distinction between stimulus-determined aspects of consciousness and interpretive or information-processing contributions to the conscious perceptual experience.

THE PERCEPTUAL PROBLEM

We must begin our discussion with some philosophical considerations. This is not merely because all of science began as philosophy, nor because only 50 years ago philosophy and psychology departments were often combined as the same academic entity in many universities. The reason that we begin with philosophy is that one must first understand that it takes a shift in philosophical viewpoint, away from our normal naive realistic faith in the ability of our senses to convey a picture of the world to us, for the very basic question of why we need a psychological discipline to study sensation and

perception to become meaningful. To the proverbial "man on the street," there is no perceptual problem. You open your eyes and the world is there. We perceive things the way we see them because that is the way they are. We see something as a triangular shape because it is triangular. We feel roughness through our sense of touch because the surface is rough. Thomas Reid summarized this idea in 1785 when he wrote

> By all the laws of all nations, in the most solemn judicial trials, wherein men's fortunes and lives are at stake, the sentence passes according to the testimony of eye or ear, witnesses of good credit. An upright judge will give fair hearing to every objection that can be made to the integrity of a witness, and allow it to be possible that he may be corrupted; but no judge will ever suppose that witnesses may be imposed upon by trusting to their eyes and ears. And if a sceptical counsel should plead against the testimony of the witnesses, that they had no other evidence for what they declared than the testimony of their eyes and ears, and that we ought not to put so much faith in our senses as to deprive men of life or fortune upon their testimony, surely no upright judge would admit a plea of this kind. I believe no counsel, however sceptical, ever dared to offer such an argument; and if it were offered, it would be rejected with disdain. (Essay 2, Chapter 5)

Unfortunately, the man on the street and Reid are both wrong, since perception is an act, and like all behavioral acts, it will have its limitations and will sometimes be in error. One need only look at the many varieties of visual-geometric illusions that introductory psychology textbooks delight in presenting to verify this. In these simple figures, you can see lines whose length or shape are systematically distorted and various element sizes and locations that are misconstrued in consciousness because of the effects of other lines drawn in near proximity to them. Such distortions are not artifacts of art or drawing. Even in nature there are perceptual distortions, illusions, and instances of noncorrespondence between the reality and the conscious perception. Take the size of the moon. Everyone has at some time or another experienced the moon illusion, where the moon on the horizon looks much larger than it does when it is high in the sky. Surely no one thinks that the moon really changes in size as it rises in the sky. That this is an illusion has long been known. In fact, Ptolemy (127–145) (whose Latin name in full was Claudius Ptolemaeus), the ancient astronomer, geographer, and mathematician who lived in Alexandria, devoted over one third of Book II of his *Optics* to the topic of "illusions." He classified various systematic visual misperceptions under the headings of size, shape, movement, position, and color and included the moon illusion as one of these topics.

The issue of error and illusion will be a recurring theme, since only after the possibility of perceptual error is recognized can the *perceptual problem* be defined. At the first level, the perceptual problem is simply the issue of how "what is out there" gets "in here," or more formally, how do the objects, object properties, relationships between items, and the metric of space and time come to be represented in consciousness? At a second level, this problem may be extended to pose the *correspondence problem,* which asks, "How accurate are these perceptions?" and "How well do they represent the external reality?" This is a fundamental issue that has nothing to do with simple sensory limitations. Obviously, in the absence of light we cannot expect the visual system to function, nor when the mechanical vibrations in the air are too weak do we expect the auditory system to register sounds. These situations, however, demonstrate *limitations,* which define the limits of the sensitivity of the sensory system and do not represent a failure of correspondence between perception and the external reality. However, once we allow for systematic distortions, where the perceived reality does not correspond to the physicist's measured reality, the argument for naive realism, that the eye merely "records" light and the ear simply "registers" sound, is no longer tenable. If illusion and distortion are possible, then the viewpoint that perception is a psychological act must be accepted.

SENSATION, PERCEPTION, REASON, AND COGNITION

The very first hurdle that had to be faced in the study of sensation and perception involved the definition of these processes and a determination of how they fit with other mental acts and processes. This is an issue that is fundamental; hence, it should not be surprising to find that long before data had been collected, at least well before empirical data in the form that we understand it today was available for analysis, philosophers were raising questions about the role that perception played in our mental life. During the era when Greece was the world's epicenter of intellectual activity, Greek writers and philosophers fell into two schools. One, characterized clearly by Plato (ca. 428–348 B.C.), argued that we should talk of perceiving objects *through* the senses but *with* the mind. The basic notion is that sensory inputs are variable and inaccurate, and at best provide only an imperfect copy of the objects and relationships in the world. We are saved by the mind, or more specifically Reason (yes, with a capitol *R*, since Reason is treated by the Greeks much like an individual in its own right, with special abilities, consciousness, and its own motivational system). Reason or intellect has the job of correcting the inaccuracies of the senses and providing us with a true and correct picture of the world. We are aided in

this endeavor by the fact that we are born with a preexisting concept of space, intensity, and time from which we can derive the lesser qualities of size, distance, position, color, and so forth.

In the 1770s the German philosopher Immanuel Kant would restate this view. According to Kant, the intellect creates those phenomena that we perceive by applying a set of specifiable and innate rules. The intellect's task is made simple because it has available an innate concept of space and time and several innate organizing categories and procedures that define quality, quantity, relation, and mode. The sensory systems simply provide whatever limited information they can, and our conscious reality is then shaped by our intellectual activity. The intellect fills in the holes and cleans up any minor discrepancies and inadequacies in the sensory representation. According to this view, the study of perception is simply part of the study of reason or cognition, and the study of senses, per se, would border on being a waste of valuable time and effort.

Plato's views were not unchallenged even during his life. At the very time when half of the cultivated population of Athens were flocking into the Grove of Hecatombs to listen to Plato's discourse on the rule of intellect, the other half of the population were going to the rival school of Aristippus (ca. 435–366 B.C.). This philosopher maintained that the senses are inherently accurate and thus responsible for our accurate view of the environment; hence, there should always be good correspondence between perception and reality. If there are any distortions, however, it is the mind or judgmental capacities that are limited and responsible for the discrepancies. This was not a new viewpoint. Protagoras (ca. 480–411 B.C.) captured the essence of this position when he said, "Man is nothing but a bundle of sensations." This doctrine, which would become known as Sensism, would owe its reincarnation to the philosopher Thomas Hobbes (1588–1679), who restated this view in 1651 when he wrote: "There is no conception in man's mind which hath not at first, totally or by parts, been begotten upon the organs of sense."

The height of the sensist doctrine can be found in the work of the associationist John Locke, who wrote more than 50 years after Hobbes about ideas. The very word "idea" is coined from the word *eidola,* which was supposed to be a copy of an object that was captured by the senses and sent to the mind. Eidolas were the basis of all sensory impressions and experience. An idea was a remembered or registered eidola, which could then be perceived by the mind, modified or associated with other ideas, and then laid down as a new idea or memory. Thus, in Locke's view of psychology, if we want to understand the mind, we must first have an accurate knowledge of the senses and perceptual processes. The mind is simply a *tabula rasa,* a blank tablet or white paper, and sensory processes write on that paper. Thus, his view was that perceptual experiences create everything that we know or conceive of. Jean Piaget (1896–1980) would bring this same concept into the twentieth century when, in his 1969 book *Mechanisms of Perception,* he considered the hypothesis that there is no difference between perception and intelligence.

Some attempts at compromise between these two extreme positions would be attempted. Perhaps one of the earliest came from Aristotle (384–322 B.C.). He began by arguing that there are some perceptual qualities that are immediately and accurately perceived by the senses. He noted that "Each sense has one kind of object which it discerns and never errs in reporting what is before it is color or sound (although it may err as to what it is that is colored or where it is, or what it is that is sounding or where it is)." There are, however, other qualities, such as movement, number, figural qualities, and magnitude, that are not the exclusive property of any one sense but are common to all. These qualities, according to Aristotelian doctrine, require intellectual meditation to assure accuracy of representation.

This compromise view would eventually lead to the separation of perceptual research into two domains, namely sensation and perception. Thomas Reid (1710–1796) is generally credited with making this distinction. A sensation is triggered by some impression on a sense organ that causes a change in experience. Thus, "I have a pain" is a statement that implies a sensation. It can have qualities such as a dull pain, burning pain, or sharp pain, and these are also indicative of a sensation. Perception, however, while depending on a sensation, is much more. It includes a conception of an object or a relationship that is being perceived, plus the immediate and irresistible conviction of the existence of objects or a spatial organization. Thus, "I have a pain in my toe because I stepped on a tack," represents a percept and requires intervention of mind or reason.

Reid's dichotomy is still with us and is the accepted compromise view (even the title of this chapter is evidence of that); however, modern usage has introduced a bit of a conceptual drift. Hermann von Helmholtz (1821–1894), who left his mark on much of the theoretical foundation of the discipline, began to introduce the mechanism by which a sensation became a perception. Although much of his contribution to our understanding had to do with the physiological basis of sensory experience, he felt that something more was required to actually produce our perception of the world. In what may be the book that had the greatest impact of any ever written on vision, the *Treatise on Physiological Optics* (published in three separate volumes during the 1850s and 1860s), he pro-

posed a process that he called *unconscious inference.* This is a mechanism by which individuals "derive" the objects in the environment using inferences made on the basis of their experience. Thus, perception is like problem solving, where the data used is the rather inadequate information furnished by the senses. Since most people share a common culture and environment, there will be a good level of agreement on the nature of objects and relationships in the world. Individual differences in personal histories, however, can potentially lead to quite different percepts among different people given the same stimulation. At the very minimum, the introduction of the factor of experience in shaping the final percept means that perception will have a developmental aspect and will certainly differ as a function of the age of the individual.

Helmholtz's view has a modern ring and uses terminology that psychologists are still comfortable with today. The general concept of an inductive process that shapes perception actually had a precursor in the writings of the ecclesiastic scholar St. Thomas Aquinas (1225–1274). In Aquinas's view all human knowledge is based upon the input of the senses. This sensory information, however, is believed to be the result of a simple transfer of an accurate picture of the external reality to an internal representation. However, this sensory input does not enter an empty, passive intellect. Rather, the sensory information is acted on by a second element, the *sensus communis,* or the center of common sense, which includes information from the individual's life history. This part of the mind actively organizes, mediates, and coordinates the sensory input. Thus, the senses provide an accurate picture of the world, and the higher perceptual or rational processes provide meaning, thus converting raw sensation into perceptual knowledge.

The sensation–perception distinction would undergo at least one more major transition. The stimulus would come from Adelbert Ames Jr. during the 1940s and 1950s, who, much like Helmholtz, began with interests in sensory physiology but felt that more was required. Ames refused to accept the basic postulate of Aquinas, that the sensory input is an accurate representation of the external world. He felt that the correspondence problem was much larger than previously suggested. The example he began with was the observation that the retinal image is inherently ambiguous. A square pattern of light on the retina could be caused by any of an infinite number of different squares at an infinite and indeterminate number of distances, and the same square image could be caused by one of an infinite number of squares of different sizes depending on their distance. This simple square image on the retina could also be caused by an infinite number of nonsquare objects, including an infinity of quadrilateral figures such as tilted trapezoids. Thus, shape, size, and distance, which are the basic elements we need to construct our conscious image of the external reality in visual perception, are not encoded in the sensory data in any manner readily accessible by the individual. How, then, do we construct our coherent perception out of our ambiguous sensory information? According to Ames, we do this by inference based on our experience and any other information that happens to be available. In other words, perception is our "best guess" as to what is out there. This is an update on Helmholtz's view that "such objects are always imagined as being present in the field of vision as would have to be there in order to produce the same impression on the nervous system, the eyes being used under normal conditions."

What Ames did was to demonstrate how much experiential and nonsensory information goes into our final conscious perception. We have some basic concepts such as our presumption that rooms are square or that shadows provide information about shapes. Since our hypotheses about common object shapes and sizes and certain ideas about possible and impossible objects and conditions are built up by our history of transactions with the environment, this viewpoint came to be known as *transactional psychology*. Our perceptions always conform to our presumptions about the world, and we will distort our conscious picture of reality to fit those presumptions. Fortunately, most of our presumptions, since they are based upon experience, are accurate; hence, we are not generally bothered by failures in correspondence. However, situations can be set up that show perceptual distortions based on this inferential process. One such is Ames's well-known *trapezoidal room*, where to conform with our firmly believed notions that rooms are squared with vertical walls and horizontal floors and ceilings, we distort the size of people viewed in this oddly shaped room. This is the better perceptual guess, since people can come in all sizes while room construction is fairly standard. This clearly demonstrates an inferential and nonsensory contribution to conscious perception.

The Ames and Helmholtz viewpoints would evolve into the "New Look" theories of perception (which permitted a broader spectrum of experiential and inferential contributions), then into information-processing theories (which focused on the deductive and analytic mechanisms used to form the percept), and finally to the modern conception of *cognition*. The name cognition, as used to label a very active field of inquiry in contemporary psychology, is itself quite old. It was first used by St. Thomas Aquinas when he divided the study of behavior into two broad divisions, *cognition,* meaning how we know the world, and *affect,* which was meant to encompass feelings and emotions. Today's definition of cognition is equally as broad as that of Aquinas. Although many investigators use the term to refer to memory, association,

concept formation, language, and problem solving (all of which simply take the act of perception for granted), other investigators include the processes of attention and the conscious representation and interpretation of stimuli as part of the cognitive process. At the very least, cognitive theories of perception attempt to integrate memory and reasoning processes into the perceptual act.

All of these viewpoints suggest that reasoning processes and experience can add to the perceptual experience and that there is much more to perception than is available in the stimulus array. There is, however, one theoretical approach that harkens back to the early sensist approaches and includes a relatively emphatic denial of contributions from reason or intellect. This position was offered by James J. Gibson (1908–1979) and is called *direct perception* (e.g., Gibson, 1979). Like the early sensist viewpoints, it begins with the premise that all the information needed to form the conscious percept is available in the stimuli that reach our receptors. For example, even though the image in our eye is continually changing, there are certain aspects of the stimulation produced by any particular object or environmental situation that are invariant predictors of certain properties, such as the actual size, shape, or distance of the object being viewed. These perceptual invariants are fixed properties of the stimulus even though the observer may be moving or changing viewpoints, causing continuous changes in the optical image that reaches the eye. This stimulus information is automatically extracted by the perceptual system because it is relevant to survival. Invariants provide information about *affordances*, which are simply action possibilities afforded or available to the observer, such as picking the object up, going around it, and so forth. Gibson argued that this information is directly available to the perceiver and was not dependent on any higher-level cognitive processing or computation.

For researchers who are interested in developing theories in the form of computer programs and those who are interested in creating computational systems that might allow machines to directly interpret sensory information in the same manner that a human observer might, direct perception is attractive. Typical of such theorists is David Marr (1982), who began with the general presumption made in direct perception that all of the information needed is in the stimulus inputs. Marr's approach adds to direct perception the process of piecing together information based on some simple dimensions in the stimulus, such as boundaries and edges, line endings, particular patterns where stimuli meet, and so forth, to define objects and spatial relationships. This process of interpretation or synthesis is believed to require a number of computations and several stages of analysis that often can be specified as mathematical equations or steps in a computer program; hence, the name *computational theories* is often used. These are computations associated with certain algorithms that are presumed to be innate or preprogrammed; thus, this is not an inferential process but rather application of a fixed processing algorithm, making this viewpoint somewhat reminiscent of the ideas of Kant.

While computational perception has a certain allure for the burgeoning field of cognitive science, and there are still some advocates of direct perception, the vast majority of perceptual researchers and theorists seem to have accepted a compromise position that accepts the distinction between sensation and perception. Correspondence between perception and reality is maintained because there is a rich source of information in the direct sensory inputs (in other words, sensation is reliable). However, there are some ambiguities that can be corrected by using experiential and inferential processes to derive the perceived object from the available sensory data (in other words, there are nonsensory contributions that shape the final conscious percept).

PHYSICS AND VISUAL PERCEPTION

The understanding of sensory events involves an understanding of physics. We rely on physics to define stimuli such as the electromagnetic radiation that we register as light, the mechanical vibrations that we call sound, the mechanical forces that result in touch, and so forth. The scientific contributions to our understanding of perception begins with physics, or at least with a protophysics, in which the only measurement instruments available were the eyes, ears, nose, and touch senses of the scientist. Since we learn about the world through the use of our senses, this inevitably leads to a belief that the world is what we perceive it to be—an idea that would ultimately come to be abandoned when it became clear that correspondence between percept and reality is not guaranteed.

The philosopher-scientists of earlier ages held a presumption consistent with the fact that our faith in the accuracy of our perception seems to be built into the very fabric of our lives as evidenced by homilies such as "Seeing is believing." Lucretius (ca. 98–55 B.C.), the Roman philosopher and poet known for his postulation of purely natural causes for earthly phenomena and who tried to prove that fear of the supernatural is consequently without reasonable foundation, stated this article of faith when he asked, "What can give us surer knowledge than our senses? With what else can we distinguish the true form from the false?" Thus, we see things as having a color because they are colored. We perceive that a person is larger than a cat because people are larger than cats, and so forth.

Thus, taking an inventory of our sensory experience is equivalent to taking an inventory of the state of the world. Since the main tool of the physicist was his own sensory apparatus, we find chapters of physics books are entitled "light" and "sound," which are sensory terms, rather than "electromagnetic wave phenomena" and "the propagation and properties of mechanical and pressure variations in an elastic medium."

You can see how far this attitude of belief in sensory data went by considering the medieval opinions about the use of eyeglasses. In the twelfth and thirteenth century, the art of grinding lenses was widely known. It was Roger Bacon (1220–1292) who, in 1266, first thought of using these lenses as an aid to vision by holding or fixing them in front of the eye to form spectacles. Such eyeglasses were in relatively common use during succeeding centuries; however, you will find little mention of these aids to vision in scientific works until the sixteenth century. The principle reason for this absence appears to be condemnation of their use on theoretical grounds. Since lenses distort the appearance of objects, they can be seen as creating illusions. This means that the use of eyeglasses can only lead to deception.

However mistaken this condemnation appears, it clearly reflects the concern of the medieval physicists and natural scientists that our vision must remain unmodified by any instrument if we are to obtain an accurate picture of the world. Before this negative view of the use of eyeglasses would be abandoned, the optics of refraction, which is common to both external glass lenses and the internal lens of the eye, would have to be recognized. Only then would there be acceptance that one was indeed *correcting* the inadequacy of internal physiological optics by the addition of those of the glass that the world was viewed through rather than distorting the semblance of the percept to the outside reality. It would be Galileo Galilei (1564–1642) who would eventually settle the issue. He inverted the reasoning of the medieval critics of eyeglasses by demonstrating that reality can be better known by images seen through a telescope (another combination of glass lenses) rather than by images seen through the naked eye. In this belief he is actually exhibiting the metaphysic behind the scientific revolution. In essence, this metaphysic is that it often takes more than just an observer's eye to know the nature of the external reality.

It may be useful to expand a bit on the optical issues associated with vision, since it is here that we can see that physics and physiology had a difficult time making their influence felt on the study of perception. In so doing we may also see just how clever, if still wrong, some of the early theories of vision were.

It all begins with a few simple observations. First, it is immediately obvious that the eye is the organ of sight; hence, any information pertaining to vision must enter the eye. Yet this leads us to an immediate paradox. How can I see objects in their correct size with this organ? Obviously some aspect of the perceived object must enter the eye. Classical theories asserted that multiple copies of the object (the eidolas that Locke spoke of) detach themselves, flying in all directions and entering the eye if it is looking in the right direction. Each eidolon is a perfect copy of the whole entity that produced it, since the external world is composed of entities that are perceived as wholes. It is in this way that the eye, and more importantly the *sensorium,* or perceiving mind that is behind the eye, gains knowledge of the object. Herein lies a problem. The commonly asked critical question is, How is it that an eidolon as large as that which you might get from a soldier, or even of a whole army, can enter through the pupil of the eye, which may be only 3 or 4 millimeters in diameter?

In a manner that is all too common in scientific theorizing, these early perceptual theorists simply assumed the final outcome and postulated anything that might be needed to make the conscious percept correspond to the external reality. The presumed answer is that the eidolon shrinks to a size appropriate for entering the pupil as it approaches the eye. The problem with simple presumption is that it rapidly leads to complications or contradictions. If the eidolon from an object is only a short distance from the eye, it must shrink very quickly in comparison to the eidola from farther objects, which must shrink at a slower rate to arrive at the eye the same size as all of the other eidola from similarly sized objects. This means that each copy of the object must know its destination prior to its arrival at the eye in order to shrink at the rate appropriate for entering the pupil. Even if we suppose that the shrinkage works, we are now left with the question of how the mind gains information about the true size and distance of objects. Remember that all of the shrunken eidola entering the pupil from all objects must be the same size to pass through the pupillary aperture. Thus, both a nearby soldier and a distant army must be 3 millimeters or less in size to enter a 3-millimeter-diameter pupil. This means that the received copy of the object contains no information about the actual size of the original objects from which they emanated.

In the absence of a knowledge of optics, and given the numerous difficulties associated with this *reception theory* of vision, an alternate theory took the field and held sway for millennia. To understand this theory, consider the way in which we learn the size and shape of things by touch alone. To tactually perceive the size and shape of a piece of furniture if I am blind folded or in the dark, I simply reach out with my hands and palpate it. Running my fingers over the surface gives me its shape; the size of the angle between my outstretched arms as I touch the outermost boundaries gives me its size, even

though that size may be much larger that the size of the hands or fingers that are doing the actual touching. It was reasoning like this that led to the *emission theory* of vision.

The emission theory suggests that light is actually emitted from the eye to make contact with objects. These light rays thus serve as the "fingers of the eye." Information returns along these same extended rays, in much the same way that tactile information flows back through extended arms. This is all consistent with the observation that we cease seeing when we close our eyes, thus preventing emission of the light rays; that what we see depends on the direction that we are looking; and that we can perceive objects that are much larger than the aperture size of our pupil.

This emission theory of vision anticipates another trend in perceptual theorizing, namely, that things that can be represented mathematically are more likely to believed as true, even though there is no evidence that the underlying mechanisms are valid. All that seems to be required is a predictive model. This was provided by an early believer in the emission theory, the great Greek mathematician Euclid (ca. 300 B.C.). All that Euclid needed to do was to appreciate that light travels in straight lines. Given this fact, and a knowledge of geometry, he was able to present a system of laws of optics that derive from simple principles and can predict the geometry of refraction and reflection of light. However, for Euclid, the scientific study of optics was not separable from the study of visual response. While considering the nature of vision, Euclid proposed the idea of the visual cone, which is a broad cone (or an angle when represented as a two-dimensional slice) with its apex at the eye. He also invented a way of representing the initial stages of the visual process that is still used in modern diagrams. Each light ray is drawn as a straight line that joins the object and the eye as it would if light were emitting like a long finger emerging from the pupil. This is shown in Figure 5.1. Notice that each object is defined by its visual angle. Euclid would use a diagram like this to explain why the more distant of two identical objects would appear smaller. As the figure demonstrates, the arrow *AB* is farther away from the eye and thus appears smaller than the closer arrow *CD* because the visual angle *AEB* is smaller than visual angle *CED*.

We have advanced well beyond Euclid, and obviously we now know that light is reflected from every point of an object and then reforms into an image after entering the eye. Despite this knowledge, even today, visual diagrams are routinely drawn as if the geometrical lines of emitted light actually existed. We do so, still ignoring the cautions of Bishop George Berkeley (1685–1753) that were given some 2,000 years after Euclid. Berkeley admonished "those *Lines* and *Angles* have no real Existence in Nature, being only *Hypotheses*

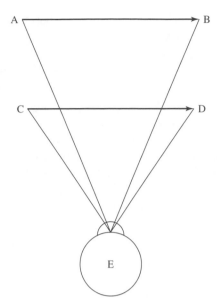

Figure 5.1   A figure after the style of Euclid, but still in use today, where the drawn lines describing the visual angles *AEB* and *CED* were originally meant to represent emissions from the eye.

fram'd by *Mathematicians,* and by them introduced into *Optics,* that they might treat of that *Science* in a *Geometrical* way" (Berkeley, 1709).

The first steps toward a more modern optics of vision comes from Alhazen (965–1040?), a scientist and natural philosopher who worked most of his life in Egypt and whose Arab name was Abu Ali al-Hasan ibn al-Haytham. He became fascinated by an illusion or failure of correspondence, namely the afterimages that one has after viewing bright objects. The existence of this failure of correspondence caused him ultimately to reject the emission theory. The fact that a residual effigy of an object remains after the object is removed, and even after the eyes were closed, suggested that this phenomenon was caused by light from the object having a persistent effect in the eye.

In the process of rejecting the emission theory, Alhazen modified the reception theory. Most importantly, he abandoned the idea that whole copies of objects reach the eye, an idea that had persisted because when people viewed their world, their phenomenological impression was that they were viewing a set of whole objects. Instead, he claimed that light, conceived of as a stream of minute particles, is thrown off by illuminated objects and is disseminated in all directions in straight lines. This light comes from each point on the object. Such tiny "point-eidola" would have no difficulties entering the pupil of the eye. It is here that he confronts the problem that frustrated those theorists who preceded him, namely that it seemed unnatural to assume that the copy of a unified entity should be broken up into pieces. If the

information coming from an object is actually decomposed into parts, how could it ever be put together again to recreate the whole? Furthermore, if so many of these points from so many points on the object entered the pupil simultaneously, it would be likely that they would mix in the eye and confuse the relation of one part to another. Alhazen solved this issue by the use of some information about refraction of light and a misinterpretation of anatomy that placed the crystalline lens of the eye in the center of the eye. According to this idea, the cornea and the lens of the eye effectively consist of concentric spherical surfaces, and only the projected rays of light that enter perpendicularly to these surfaces would be unbent by refraction. These rays produce a replicate image of the object according to the following logic. Of all the lines projecting from any point on an object, only one will be perpendicular to the cornea (the front surface of the eye). Only this ray is seen, and since from each object point there is only one effective ray, the complete set of rays preserves the topographic structure of their points of origin on the object.

Alhazen was basically a sensist in his approach, with the idea that we ought to be able to accurately perceive the world without the intervention of any higher, nonperceptual processes. This theoretical position was, however, impossible for object properties such as size, given the limited size of the final image, and also for location, since obviously the image is fixed at the location of the person's retina. Therefore, Alhazen was forced to allow a mental process to intervene, and he suggested that it was the mind that assigned an appropriate size and location to the object based on its image. However, he balked at the issue of orientation. Based on his knowledge of optics, he knew that an image passing through a simple lens was inverted and left–right reversed. To avoid dealing with this problem, he simply presumed that the light's final image to be analyzed by the mind was formed upright on the front surface of the crystalline lens of the eye. To ask a mental process to rotate the world 180 degrees plus correcting the left and right inversion of the image, and to do so instantaneously enough for us to coordinate properly in the world, was too much of leap of faith for him to accept.

Alhazen's analysis of light into points would set the stage for Kepler's correct description of the optics of the eye. Alhazen had failed when he had to deal with the inversion of the retinal image because he could not accept that much noncorrespondence between the input and the external world and others would show a similar weakness. Thus, Leonardo da Vinci (1452–1519), who was familiar with a pinhole version of the camera obscura and the inverted image that it casts on a screen, speaks in his fifteenth-century *Notebooks* of the eye as the window to the soul. He and others resorted to an odd sort of physical optics to solve the problem. They suggested that there must be a second inversion of the image in the eye, perhaps because the fundus or inside surface of the eye acts as a concave mirror that could then cast an upright image on the rear surface of the lens.

Johannes Kepler (1571–1630) was the first to describe the true nature of image formation in the eye in 1604. He depicted how a lens bends the multitude of rays approaching it from a point on one side of the lens in such a way that it causes the rays to converge and to meet in an approximation to a point on the other side of the lens. The order of object and image points is thus preserved, and an accurate, although inverted, image is formed of the object. By 1625, Scheiner would verify Kepler's theory. He removed the opaque layers at the back of a cow's eye and viewed the actual picture formed on the retina and found that it was inverted. Others would repeat this experiment, including Descartes, who described the results in detail. Kepler was not unaware of the problems that the inverted image had caused for previous theorists. However, he simply relegated its solution to what we would call physiological processing or psychological interpretation, much as Alhazen had relegated to the mind the assigning of size and location in space to objects some six centuries earlier.

An interesting example of how the study of physics became intertwined with the study of vision comes from Sir Isaac Newton (1642–1727). Newton, whose name is one of the most distinguished in the history of physics, had already started almost all of his important lines of thought before he was 30. During the short span of time from 1665 to 1666, while Newton was in his early 20s and was a student (but not yet a Fellow) at Trinity College in Cambridge University, he achieved the following ideas: (a) he discovered the binomial theorem; (b) he invented both differential and integral calculus; (c) he conceived his theory of gravitation and applied it to the behavior of the moon; and (d) he purchased a glass prism at the Stourbridge Fair for the purpose of studying the refraction of light. It was this last item that would turn him into a perceptual researcher.

Newton began his study of the refraction of light by prisms in an attempt to improve the telescope. Descartes had already shown that spherical lenses, because of their shape, cause aberrations in image formation, namely colored fringes. Experimenting with prisms first led Newton to the erroneous conclusion that all glass has the same refracting power, which would mean that it would forever be impossible to correct for this distortion. To get around this problem, he used the fact that there is no chromatic dispersion in reflected light. He therefore substituted a concave mirror for the lens and thus created the reflecting telescope. It was this invention that created his reputation and earned him an appointment to the Royal Society.

It is important to remember that Newton began with the belief system of a physicist and thus felt that the spectrum of colors that one got when passing light through a prism was a property of the glass. However, during his experimentation he was able to demonstrate that the spectrum could be recombined into white light if he used a second prism oriented in the opposite direction. This would be an impossibility, since all that a glass should be able to do is to add chromatic aberrations. He soon determined that what the prism was doing was differentially bending the light inputs, with shorter wavelengths bent to a greater degree. This means that the resulting light output is nothing more than a smear of light with gradually differing wavelength composition from one end to the other. Since we see an array of spectral colors, it led him to the conclusion that color is a perceptual experience that depends on the wavelength of the light hitting the eye. White light is then simply the perception resulting from a mixture of all of the colors or wavelengths. Thus, we have another case where only when the physics fails to explain the phenomena observed does the scientist resort to a perceptual explanation.

Other physicists would eventually contribute to knowledge of vision. Prominent among them would be Hermann Helmholtz, whose contributions to physics included development of the theory of conservation of energy and also understanding of wave motions and vortexes. Another was Ernst Mach, whose contribution to ballistics formed an important basis for our understanding of the mechanics of flight and who also would go on to study brightness perception in humans. However, in their contributions, they would use not only the principles of physics but data from the newly emerging fields of physiology and neurophysiology.

PHYSIOLOGY AND PERCEPTION

The physiological research that directly stimulated and guided the scientific study of sensation and perception was a product of the nineteenth century. However, the conceptual breakthrough that set the stage for these new findings was the acceptance of a mechanistic conception of the body that had been anticipated two centuries earlier. Henry Power, an English physician and naturalist who was elected to the Royal Society while it was still in its infancy, stated this emerging viewpoint in his *Experimental Philosophy* in 1664. Of perception he noted: "Originals in Nature, as we observe are producible by Art, and the infallible demonstration of Mechanicks," suggesting that principles of art (here to include mathematics and geometry) and mechanistic principles (here to include physics and physiology) should form the basis of the study of perceptual and mental processes. He then goes on to make it quite explicit that to understand mental phenomena we must understand "the Wheelwork and Internal Contrivance of such Anatomical Engines," including those that are responsible for perception (e.g., the eye and the ear).

This kind of thinking could encourage study of the body as a machine and leave the issue of soul to a more divine province. As an example, consider René Descartes (1596–1650), who accepted a dualistic approach. While sensory processing and response to stimulus inputs from the environment could be solely mechanical and could be studied empirically, Descartes felt that the higher levels of mental life, such as conscious perception, would require a soul and the intervention of God. According to Descartes, animals could process sensory inputs mechanically with no consciousness and no intelligence. He was convinced that this was a reasonable position after observing the statues in the royal gardens of Saint-Germain-en-Laye, the birthplace and home of Louis IV. These human-sized statues, constructed by the Italian engineer Thomas Francini, were automated and could behave in surprisingly lifelike ways. Each figure was a clever piece of machinery powered by hydraulics and carefully geared to perform a complex sequence of actions. For instance, in one grotto a figure of the mythological Greek musician Orpheus makes beautiful music on his lyre. As he plays, birds sing and animals caper and dance around him. In another grotto, the hero Perseus fights with a dragon. When he strikes the dragon's head, it is forced to sink into the water. The action of each figure was triggered when visitors stepped on particular tiles on the pathway. The pressure from their step tripped a valve, and water rushing through a network of pipes in the statue caused it to move.

In the *Treatise on Man* published in 1664, Descartes draws a parallel between the human body and the animated statues or automata in the royal gardens. He reasons that the nerves of the human body and the motive power provided by them are equivalent to the pipes and the water contained in the statues. He compares the heart to the source of the water, the various cavities of the brain with the storage tanks, and the muscles with the gears, springs, and pulleys that move the various parts of the statues. These statues do, of course, have the capability to respond to some aspects of stimulation from the outside world. In this case, the "stimulation" might be the pressure of the visitor's weight on a hidden lever beneath a tile, which causes a figure of Diana, who is caught bathing, to run away into the reeds to hide. If the visitor tries to follow her, pressure on another tile causes Neptune to rush forward, brandishing his trident protectively.

Using the figures in garden as his example, Descartes notes that in some ways the human body is like one of these mechanical contrivances, moving in predictable ways and governed by mechanical principles. Because he misunderstood what he was looking at by confusing the blood vessels that are found in the optic nerve with the nerve itself, he suggested that the optic nerve was simply a tube that contained "animal spirits" where motions are impressed by an image and are thus carried to the brain. He argued that there is nothing in animal behavior that could not be reproduced mechanically. While there appear to be complex activities going on in animals, these take place without any consciousness or thought. A number of activities that seem to require reason and intelligence, such as some of our protective reflexes, do not really require or use consciousness. An example is when you touch a hot surface. You usually withdraw your hand, without any voluntary or conscious command to your muscles to do so. In fact, most people who have experienced this find that their hand had already lifted from the hot surface before they were even conscious of the pain from their fingers. The consciousness of pain actually *follows* the protective withdrawal of the hand. According to Descartes, this is the level at which animals work. Their basic bodily functions and their basic apparent responsiveness to the environment are all without the need for consciousness, intelligence, self-awareness, or a soul. However, no matter how complex the movements of any machine might be, and no matter how variable and intricate the engineers have made its behavior, machines will always differ from a human being. The reason is that human beings have not only a body (controlled by mechanics) but also a soul (controlled by spirit). To have a soul or a mind is to have the capacity to think and to have consciousness and hence perception.

By the early nineteenth century, the study of the nervous system was beginning to advance. The world's first institute for experimental physiology was established by Johannes Müller (1801–1858) in Berlin. Müller's *Handbook of Physiology,* which summarized the physiological research of the period and contained a large body of new material from his own lab, was eagerly accepted, as is shown by its rapid translation and republication in English only five years later. Müller's conceptual breakthrough, the *Doctrine of Specific Nerve Energies,* was actually a direct attack on the image or eidola notion.

To see the problem facing Müller, one must first recognize that the classical view of the mind was that there exists within the brain something like a sentient being, a Sensorium, that wants to learn about the external world but can never come closer to it than the direct contact provided by the nerves.

Imagine that the Sensorium is a prisoner in the skull and wants to know about the Eiffel Tower. The only ways that it could learn about it would involve having pictures of the tower, or small copies of it (eidola) brought in, or failing that, at least a verbal description of it. Notice that the representation of the object to the mind is a real copy in kind. If there are no copies of the object, or if the nerves cannot carry them, then we could still have a symbolic representation of them, such as wordlike symbols, as long as these have a fixed functional relationship to the object so that the mind can recreate its properties by inference. However, there was already some data that suggested that images, or symbols representing images, were not being passed down the nerves. For instance, Charles Bell (1774–1842) pointed out that we perceive sensory qualities based on the specific nerve that is stimulated, not on the basis of the object providing the stimulation. If, for example, you put pressure on the eyeball, you will stimulate the retina; however, what you perceive will be light, not pressure.

Müller introduced the concept that the Sensorium is only directly aware of the states of the sensory nerves, not of the external object. Each nerve can only transmit information about one specific energy source, and there are five such nerve energies, one for each of the senses. Thus, a stimulus acting on a nerve that is tuned for visual energies will be perceived as visual, regardless of whether the actual stimulus was light, mechanical, or electrical stimulation. Finally, he suggested that the actual specificity is recognized only at the termination of the nerve in the brain. In doing this, he was incorporating the work of Pierre Flourens (1794–1867), who had demonstrated that specific locations in the brain controlled specific functions. Flourens based this upon data from animals that had had parts of the brain systematically destroyed and thus lost particular motor functions, as well as various visual and auditory reflexes. Later on this would be confirmed using human subjects who had head injuries due to war or accident and who also suffered from sensory impairments dependent on the location of the injury.

Müller's break with the eidola theory was not complete, however. He felt that each "adequate stimulus" impressed a wealth of information on the appropriate neural channel by exciting a *vis viva* (life force) or *vis nervosa* (neural power), which took an impression of all the information that would have been present had there been an actual eidola or image present. In this he was expressing the old physiological doctrine of vitalism, which maintained that living organisms were imbued with some special force that was responsible for life and consciousness but not subject to scientific analysis. This is very similar in tone to the concept of animal spirits postulated by Descartes.

It was Müller's students who would take the next steps. In addition to his writing and research, Müller was a splendid teacher who attracted many brilliant students. Among these was Hermann Helmholtz (1821–1895), who played a pivotal role in this history, and his classmates Émile du Bois-Reymond (1818–1896), who later collaborated with Helmholtz and gained fame by establishing the electrochemical nature of the nervous impulse; Rudolf Virchow (1821–1902), who later pioneered the cellular theory of pathology; and Ernst Brücke (1819–1893), who would later do work on the interactions between color and brightness but who would be best known as the most influential teacher of Sigmund Freud. Together these students rejected the idea that there was any life force that was so mysterious that it could not be analyzed, and so different that it did not follow the know rules of physics and physiology. As a rebellion against vitalism, they drew up a solemn article of faith in the mechanistic viewpoint, which stated that

> No other forces than the common physical-chemical ones are active within the organism. In those cases which cannot at the time be explained by these forces one has either to find the specific way or form of their action by means of the physical mathematical method, or to assume new forces equal in dignity to the physical-chemical forces inherent in mater, reducible to the force of attraction and repulsion. (Bernfeld, 1949, p. 171)

Then, with the passion generated by youthful fervor for a cause, they each signed the declaration with a drop of their own blood. It is ironic, in some ways, that a blood oath, so common in mysticism and magical rites, would be the beginning of a movement to purge spirits, demons, spirits, and the soul from psychology.

The full implications of specific nerve energies were not immediately apparent, but this idea would come to change the nature of perceptual research. In 1844, Natanson made the obvious mechanistic extension when he argued that every neural organ must have a function and conversely every function must have an organ. In sensory terms, he thought that there might be three different energies for touch, three for taste, three for vision, and an indeterminate number for smell. In that same year, A. W. Volmann attempted to criticize Müller on the ground that his theory would require not merely five specific energies but one for every sense-quality. This might require different channels for pressure, temperature, pain, every one of the 2,000 recognizable colors, every discriminable taste, and so forth. At the time, this seemed like almost a reductio ad absurdum, since it seemed to require an infinity of specific channels for the infinity of specific perceived sensory qualities. However, a solution would show itself.

The groundwork for saving the specific nerve energy theory had already been laid before the theory was announced. It appeared in a paper by Thomas Young (1773–1829), which went relatively unnoticed until it was rediscovered by Helmholtz. Young is best known for his linguistic research, particularly on the Egyptian hieroglyphs, and this included his work on translating the Rosetta Stone. However, when he accepted election into the Royal Society, instead of speaking about his linguistic and archaeological studies, he gave a paper on the perception of color in 1801. In it, he proposed that although there is a myriad of perceivable colors, it is possible to conceive that they all might be composed of mixtures of three different primaries. He speculated that these would be red, blue, and yellow, since artists are capable of mixing most colors using paints of only these hues. By extension, the visual system could do the same with three separate sets of specific neural channels, one for each of the primary colors. He had no empirical support for his speculations, however, and reasoned mostly from the artistic analogy.

Helmholtz had independently reached the same conclusion that only three primaries, hence three specific nerve energies, would be required. He would, however, modify the primaries to red, blue, and green. Helmholtz based his selection on some color-mixture studies conducted by another brilliant physicist, James Clerk Maxwell (1831–1879). Maxwell is best known for having demonstrated that light is an electromagnetic wave and for developing the fundamental equations describing electrical and magnetic forces and fields. This led to some of the major innovations made in physics in the twentieth century, including Einstein's special theory of relativity and quantum theory. Maxwell's color-mixture data was not based on the mixture of pigments that artists use, since such subtractive mixtures are often difficult to control and analyze. Instead, he used colored lights, generated by capturing small regions of a spectrum generated by passing sunlight through prisms and blocking off all but a small section. These additive mixtures are easier to control and to analyze.

Maxwell eventually "proved" the adequacy of three color primaries for full color perception in 1861. This was done by producing the first color photograph. Maxwell took a picture of a Scotch tartan–plaid ribbon using red, green, and blue filters to expose three separate frames of film. He then projected the images through the appropriate filters to recombine them to form the perception of a true colored image. This set the stage for color photography, color television, and color printing while at the same time demonstrating that three primaries would suffice to produce the full range of colors that humans can see.

Helmholtz next suggested that the specificity need not actually be in the nerves that are doing the conducting. All nerves might be equivalent as information channels; however, there might be specific receptors at the first stage of input that are tuned for specific sensory qualities. We now know that this was a correct assumption and that there are three cones with differential tuning to short wavelengths (blue), medium (green), and long wavelengths (red). This has been confirmed using microelectrode recording and also by using microspectroscopy and directly determining the absorption spectra of individual cones.

Helmholtz also recognized that in some modalities, such as hearing, the idea of only a few specific channels to carry the various sensory dimensions might not work. Certainly at the phenomenological level it is difficult to reduce the auditory sense to a small number of primary qualities. He thus suggested that further processing might be required at intermediate stages along the sensory pathways, and perhaps there may be specific centers in the brain that might selectively respond to specific sensory qualities. The first theory to formalize the idea of preprocessing sensory information to reduce the number of channels needed actually came from Hering, Helmholtz's major academic opponent. Ewald Hering (1834–1918) was a physiologist who would also go on to be known for his work in establishing the role the vagus nerve plays in breathing. Hering approached questions of perception from the point of view of a phenomenologist. This is, perhaps, not surprising, because he succeeded Johannes E. Purkinje (1787–1869), who was probably the best-known phenomenologist of his time. In addition to his work in microscopy, Purkinje is also known for his discovery of the wavelength-dependent brightness shifts that occur as the eye goes from a light to a dark adapted state (now called the *Purkinje shift*). This set of observations suggested to Purkinje that there might be two separate receptors in the eye, with different photic sensitivity. His speculation was eventually proven by discovery of rods and cones and the demonstration, by Max Johann Sigizmund Scultze (1825–1874), that rods functioned in low-light-level vision and cones in bright light.

Hering was himself a fine analytic phenomenologist like his predecessor Purkinje. He was not completely satisfied with the idea of three primaries as being sufficient to explain the phenomenon of color vision. It seemed to him, rather, that human observers acted as if there were four, rather than three, primary colors. For instance, when observers are presented with a large number of color samples and asked to pick out those that appear to be pure (defined as not showing any trace of being a mixture of colors), they tend to pick out four, rather than three, colors. These unique colors almost always include a red, a green, and a blue, as the Helmholtz-Young trichromatic theory predicts; however, they also include a yellow.

Hering also noted that observers never report certain color combinations, such as yellowish blue or a greenish red. This led him to suggest some hypothetical neural processes in which the four primaries were arranged in opposing pairs. One aspect of this opponent process would signal the presence of red versus green, and a separate opponent process would signal blue versus yellow. An example of such a process could be a single neuron whose activity rate increased with the presence of one color (red) and decreased in the presence of its opponent color (green). Since the cell's activity cannot increase and decrease simultaneously, one could never have a reddish green. A different opponent-process cell might respond similarly to blue and yellow. A third unit was suggested to account for brightness perception. This was called a black-white opponent process, after the fact that black and white are treated psychologically as if they were "pure colors." Evidence from colored afterimages seemed to support this theory.

One might have expected that Hering's notions would be met with enthusiasm, since the opponent-process concept would allow alternate forms of qualitative information to travel down the same pathway (e.g., red and/or green color), thus reducing the number of neural channels required to encode color from three under the trichromatic theory to two. Yet this idea was extremely unpopular. It appeared unconvincing because the theory was purely speculative, with only phenomenological evidence from a set of "illusions," namely afterimages and color contrast, to support it, and no proven physiological processes that demonstrated the required mode of operation. Furthermore, even as neurophysiology became more advanced in the early part of the twentieth century, the theory did not seem appealing, since it seemed to fly in the face of the newly discovered all-or-none neural response pattern. It implied some form of neural algebra, where responses are added to or subtracted from one another. Additive neural effects could easily be accepted; however, subtractive effects were as yet unknown.

The first hints that some neural activity could have subtractive or inhibitory effects came from the phenomenological data and an application of mathematical reasoning by physicist and philosopher Ernst Mach (1838–1916). Mach was a systematic sensist in that he felt that science should restrict itself to the description of phenomena that could be perceived by the senses. His philosophical writings did much to free science from metaphysical concepts and helped to establish a scientific methodology that paved the way for the theory of relativity. However, if the fate of science was to rest on the scientist's sensory systems, it was important to understand how the senses function and what their limitations are. This led him into a study of brightness phenomena, particularly of brightness contrast. At the time, brightness contrast was just another illusion or instance of noncorrespondence. It was demonstrated by noting that a patch of gray paper placed on a white background appears to be darker than an identical patch of gray paper placed on a dark background. This suggested to Mach that there was some form of inhibition occurring and that this inhibition could be between adjacent neural units. He suggested that the receptors responding to the bright surrounds inhibited the receptors responding to the gray paper in proportion to their activity, and this was more than the inhibition from the cells responding to the dimmer dark region surrounding the other patch, thus making the gray on white appear darker. This led to the prediction of the brightness phenomenon that now bears his name, *Mach bands*. This effect is seen in a light distribution that has a uniform bright region and a uniform dark region with a linear ramplike transition in light intensity between the two. At the top of the ramp a bright stripe is perceived, while at the bottom a dark stripe is seen. These stripes are not in the light distribution but can be predicted by an algebraic model in which neural intensities add to and subtract from those of adjacent neural units. This obviously suggests that some form of inhibition, such as that required by Hering's model of color vision, can occur in sensory channels.

Unfortunately, psychologists sometimes look at phenomenological data with the same suspicion that they might look at reports of extrasensory phenomena such as the perception of ghosts. Truth seems to depend on identifiable physiology rather than phenomenology; hence, neural inhibition remained unaccepted. The breakthrough would come with Ragnar A. Granit (1900–1991), who would usher in the era of microelectrode recording of sensory responses. Granit was inspired by the work of British physiologist Lord Edgar Douglas Adrian (1889–1977), who was the first to record electrical impulses in nerve fibers, including optic nerves, and eventually developed a method to use microscopic electrodes to measure the response to stimulation by the optic nerve. Granit's data began to show that when light is received by the eye, under some circumstances it could actually inhibit rather than excite neural activity. To confirm this in humans he helped to develop the electroretinogram (ERG) technique to measure mass activity in the retina.

Haldan Keffer Hartline (1903–1983), who would go on to share the 1967 Nobel Prize with Granit, was also fascinated by Lord Adrian's work. Hartline set about to use the microelectrode measures Granit developed to record electrical impulses in individual nerve cells. His goal was to extend that research into analysis of how the visual nerve system worked. He did much of his work with the horseshoe crab, which has a compound eye (like that of a fly) and has the advantage of having large individual cells that receive light (photoreceptor cells) and long, well-differentiated optic nerve fibers. In the 1930s he recorded electrical response from single fibers of the horseshoe crab's optic nerve and found that the neurons generated a response frequency that was proportional to the intensity of light shining on the photoreceptors. This is the sort of signal that had been expected. However, later work showed that under some circumstances shining a light on an adjacent receptor could decrease (inhibit) the response rate in a stimulated cell. This was the inhibitory response activity predicted by Mach and needed by Hering's theory. However, things became much more complicated when he began to study the more complex neural visual system of the frog. Now he found that optic nerve fibers were activated selectively, according to the type of light, and varied with brightness or movement. Further, under certain circumstances, increasing light stimulation might actually decrease neural response. This discovery convinced researchers that, even at the level of the retina, some sort of neural algebra could be taking place. Perhaps the sensory inputs were being processed and refined before being sent to higher neural centers.

At this same time, researchers were beginning to modify the doctrine of specific nerve energies because it still seemed to suffer from the major limitation pointed out by some of its early detractors. To put it into its simplest form, we perceive an indefinite number of different sensory qualities in each modality and we do not have an infinity of neural pathways. For example, in the visual realm, a stimulus will have a color, size, location, and state of motion. In addition, the stimulus will contain features such as contour elements that delineate its boundaries, and each of these will have a length and orientation. There may also be prominent defining elements such as angles or concave or convex curves, and so forth. The doctrine of specific nerve energies had evolved from simply positing a separate channel for each sensory modality to a supposition that there is a separate channel for each sensory quality or at least a limited set of qualities. While this is not practical at the input and transmission stages of perception, it is possible if we consider the end points or terminations in the brain and if, as Hartline seemed to be suggesting, there is some form of preprocessing that occurs before information is sent down specific channels.

In the 1950s Stephen Kuffler's laboratory at Johns Hopkins University was studying the visual response of retinal neurons using microelectrodes. It was in 1958 that two young researchers who had come to work with Kuffler met: David H. Hubel (b. 1926) and Torsten N. Wiesel (b. 1924). They decided to look at the response of single neurons in the visual cortex to see if they had any differential responses to stimuli

presented to the eye. In experiments with cats and monkeys, Hubel and Wiesel were able to show that varying the spatial location of a light spot caused variations in the response of the cortical cell in either an excitatory or inhibitory manner. By carefully mapping these changes in response to points of light, they later were able to demonstrate that there were complex cells in the brain that were "tuned" to specific visual orientations. This meant that they responded well to lines in one orientation and poorly or not at all to others with different degrees of inclination. Other cells responded to movement in a particular direction, and some were even tuned for particular speed of movement across the retina. There were even hypercomplex cells that responded to particular angles, concavity versus convexity, and lines of particular length. In a series of clever experiments, they also injected radioactively labeled amino acids into the brain under specific conditions of stimulation to show that there is a complex cytoarchitecture in the visual cortex. Feature-specific cells are vertically organized into columns and separated according to which eye is providing the input. The act of vision, then, involved a decomposition of an input into an array of features that then, somehow or other, would be resynthesized into the conscious percept.

Hubel and Wiesel's work was initially greeted with skepticism when it was announced in the 1960s. It seemed to be expanding the doctrine of specific nerve energies to a ridiculous degree. Adversaries suggested that, taken to the limit, one might argue that every perceived quality and feature in vision might require its own tuned neural analyzer. Thus, one might eventually find a "grandmother cell" or a "yellow Cadillac detector" that responds only to these particular stimuli. The strange truth here is that these critics were correct, and in the late 1970s, Charles Gross's laboratory at Princeton University began to find cortical neurons that are extremely specialized to identify only a small range of particular targets with special significance. For instance, one neuron in monkeys seems to produce its most vigorous response when the stimulus is in the shape of a monkey's paw. Gross, Rocha-Miranda, and Bender (1972) report that one day they discovered a cell in the cerebral cortex of a monkey that seemed unresponsive to any light stimulus. When they waved their hand in front of the stimulus screen, however, they elicited a very vigorous response from the previously unresponsive neuron. They then spent the next 12 hours testing various paper cutouts in an attempt to find out what feature triggered this specific unit. When the entire set of stimuli were ranked according to the strength of the response they produced, they could not find any simple physical dimension that correlated with this rank order. However, the rank order of stimuli, in terms of their ability to drive the cell, did correlate with their apparent similarity (at least for the experimenters) to the shadow of a monkey's hand. A decade later there were an accumulation of reports of finding cells that are tuned for specific faces, namely monkey faces in the monkey cortex and sheep faces in sheep cortex (e.g., Bruce, Desimone, & Gross, 1981; Kendrick & Baldwin, 1987). One wonders what Johannes Müller would think of his theory now.

THE SCIENCE OF ILLUSION

While Müller is best known to psychologists for his work on specific nerve energies, he is also an important contributor to philosophical shift in thinking that resulted in the definition of psychology as a separate science by influencing its founder. In 1826 Müller published two books, the first on physiology and the second the phenomenology of vision. This second volume contained discussions of a number of phenomena that Müller called *visual illusions*. These visual illusions were not the distortions in two-dimensional line drawings that we tend to use the label for today; rather, they were such things as afterimages and phantom limbs. Müller also included the fact that the impression of white may be produced by mixing any wavelength of light with its complement and the resulting percept contains no evidence of the individual components as another form of illusion. In other words, he was fascinated by the fact that there were some situations in which the conscious percept does not correspond with the external situation as defined by physical measurements. Müller's book posed some questions that would remain unanswered during his lifetime but would lead to a burst of empirical work a quarter of a century later.

In 1855, Oppel published three papers in which he included a number of size distortions that could be seen in figures consisting of lines drawn on paper. In his first paper, he noted a distortion that was small in magnitude but quite reliable and could be induced by lines drawn on paper. It appears in drawings such as that in Figure 5.2A and involves the perception that the upper divided extent appears to be slightly longer than the lower undivided space. By the third paper, he had developed more powerful distortions such as that shown in Figure 5.2C. Here the vertical line seems considerably longer than the horizontal line, and this apparent difference in length is usually in excess of 15 percent. Oppel cited Müller, crediting him with sparking the interest in this type of illusory phenomenon. Oppel was certainly not the first to recognize visual illusions as instances of noncorrespondence between perception and reality. Remember that Ptolemy, for example, had extensively discussed the moon illusion. Other researchers had noticed that the scale or shape of common

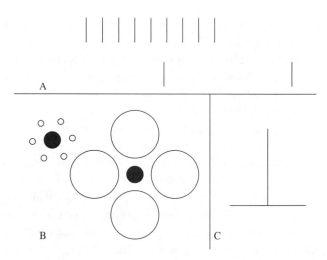

Figure 5.2 Instances of noncorrespondence and illusion: (A) the upper divided space appears to be slightly longer than the lower undivided space (the filled space–open space illusion); (B) the black circle surrounded by large circles appears smaller than the black circle surrounded by small circles (the Ebbinghaus illusion); (C) the vertical line appears longer than the horizontal line (the horizontal-vertical illusion).

items could be distorted in certain environments. For example, Smith (1738) noted that "Animals and small objects seen in valleys, contiguous to large mountains, appear extraordinarily small" (p. 314). For some reason, such descriptions simply do not create the same impact as a simple graphic display, such as Figure 5.2B, where the two black circles (which are simply surrogates for two animals) are the same size, yet the circle surrounded by large forms (which are mere the graphic analogues of mountains) seems to be somewhat smaller than its counterpart, which is surrounded by only small items.

It may well have been that having such portable demonstrations of the failure of vision to accurately represent reality generated more interest because more people could so readily and reliably see the effects. Perhaps these line figures appealed to the rising interest in experimentation. The juxtaposition of environmental elements that might cause illusions to appear (such as mountains or moons) cannot be arranged and rearranged at will. The major advantage of lines drawn on paper lies in their flexibility. To begin with, one can easily manipulate the array by bringing large and small objects in close proximity to one another in the picture plane. One can also select stimuli, such as circles, squares, or lines, that have no necessary and familiar size. One can manipulate stimulus elements along many dimensions, such as brightness, chromaticity, spatial proximity, identity, and so forth. Furthermore, one can verify the true dimensions of the perceptually distorted figural elements with tools as simple as a ruler.

With the opportunities for easy experimentation so readily available, perhaps it is not surprising that between 1855, when Oppel's papers appeared, and 1900, over 200 papers demonstrating and analyzing various visual distortions appeared. New illusion configurations began to appear in a vast unsystematic flood. There were new distortions described by the astronomer Johann Karl Friedrich Zöllner (1834–1882), the sociologist Franz Müller-Lyer (1857–1916), the physiologist Jacques Loeb (1859–1924), and the philosopher-psychologist Franz Brentano (1838–1917). Many psychologists whose main interests seem to lie far from perception also took their turn at producing illusion configurations. Included in this group are Charles Hubbard Judd (1873–1946) and Alfred Binet (1857–1911), both interested in education and child development; the philosophically oriented James Mark Baldwin (1861–1934) and William James (1842–1910); the clinician Joseph Jastrow (1863–1944); the founder of applied psychology, Hugo Münsterberg (1863–1916); as well as a host of workers interested in aesthetics, including Karl Stumpf (1848–1936) and Theodor Lipps (1851–1914). This is not to say that specialists in perception were excluded, since many of these joined this merry frenzy of exposing instances of noncorrespondence, including Wundt, Hering, Helmholtz, Titchener, and Ehrenfels, to name but a few.

It is difficult to believe, but it was in the midst of all of this activity of drawing lines on paper to produce illusory percepts that the science of psychology was born. Wilhelm Wundt (1832–1920) was probably the first person to call himself a psychologist and was certainly the first to found a formal administrative unit for psychological research. Oddly enough he embarked upon the development of exclusively psychological research because of all those line drawings that showed systematic distortions when carefully viewed. Wundt began by considering visual illusions as they were currently being described in his book *Contributions to the Theory of Sensory Perception,* various sections of which were published between 1858 and 1862. By the time he published his *Principles of Physiological Psychology* (in two parts, 1873 and 1874), his deliberations had forced him into a new philosophical and methodological position. For example, when he considered Oppel's strongest illusion, which demonstrated the fact that a vertical line looks longer than a horizontal line of equal length (as we saw in Figure 5.2C), he recognized that this perceived illusion could not be predicted by any of the known laws of physics, biology, or chemistry. To explain this phenomenon, then, we would need a new set of laws. These laws would be the laws that govern mental science. He suggested that we need a science of mental processes and we could name it "Psychology," as had been suggested earlier by the philosopher and mathematician Christian von Freiherr Wolff (1679–1754). Although he credited Wolff with the name, Wundt chose to ignore the fact that Wolff also

maintained that any science of mental life could not be based upon empirical research. Instead Wundt set out to create a new empirical science with its own methods and its own basic principles to study issues such as the noncorrespondence between the physical and the perceived world.

When Wundt first began his research, he had already accepted the concept that psychology should use a variety of experimental methods depending on the question being asked. One such technique was *analytic introspection.* Wundt initially adopted the atomistic viewpoint, which earlier in the century had proved to be so successful in physics, biology, and chemistry. It seemed reasonable to assume that consciousness could be viewed as the sum of some form of basic mental elements, much as physicists had come to view matter as the combination of basic elements called atoms and biologists had come to view living organisms as the combination of basic units called cells. Wundt's structuralist viewpoint argued that the total perceptual impression must similarly be composed of the sum of simple sensory impressions. Analytic introspection was one way of training observers to isolate these simple sensory impressions in consciousness and thus reveal the irreducible elements of conscious perception. There is a misperception about Wundt's methodology that was perpetrated by his student Edward Bradford Titchener (1867–1927). The fallacy is that analytic introspection was the main, and perhaps the only, technique of choice in Wundt's lab. This is not true, since Wundt advocated many methods, including observation without intervention, experimentation, and the use of objective indexes of mental processes such as discriminative responses to sensory stimuli and reaction time. Furthermore, well before his long career was through, the same stimulus configurations that brought him to consider psychology as a separate discipline would cause him to abandon analytic introspection.

If analytic introspection worked, then the observer should be able to reduce consciousness to basic sensory elements. If this is the case, then it seems reasonable to assume that visual illusion stimuli, when dealt with in this manner, would no longer produce any perceptual distortion. Thus, analytically viewing the items in Figure 5.2 should produce accurate assessments of all relevant sizes and lengths, and the illusions themselves should turn out to be nothing more than judgmental errors added to the basic sensory elements by not-so-careful observers. Unfortunately, such was not the case, and the illusions persisted, suggesting to Wundt that perhaps the atomistic view was untenable and the technique of analytic introspection might not be as useful as originally thought. Instead, he began to argue for a much more modern-sounding view of perception, which he called *creative synthesis.* According to this view, perception might be considered to be an amalgam between sensory and nonsensory elements. These nonsensory elements might arise through memories or associations established by an individual's experience or history, or information from other modalities. Thus, in Figure 5.2A, the eye might be expending more energy moving over the upper divided space (since it might be stopping and starting as it moved over the included elements). Since the movement of the eye over longer extents also normally requires more effort, it may be that the proprioception from this additional effort might interact with the visual impression to produce the perception of a longer extent. Such an idea (that is, the interaction of sensory factors with information from other modalities or nonsensory sources) would find ready acceptance with many current cognitive theories that attempt to integrate multimodal inputs as well as memory and reasoning processes into the perceptual act (c.f., Coren, 1986).

THE RISE OF THE BEHAVIORAL LABORATORIES

Although Helmholtz was doing experimentation on perceptual phenomena, he did not call himself a psychologist and would have claimed that he was studying physiology or physics rather than psychology. Hence, no one credits Helmholtz with having the first experimental lab in psychology. Helmholtz, however, did set the stage for the first labs by establishing a particular methodology that would find immediate acceptance and is still used today. Prior to his time, it was believed that sensory information was transmitted to whatever center needed to turn it into conscious awareness instantaneously. Helmholtz's friend, Émile du Bois-Reymond (1818–1896), had studied the chemical structure of nerve fibers and shown that the neural response was an electrochemical event. Helmholtz theorized that this meant that the nervous impulse might travel more slowly than anyone had previously imagined–perhaps even slow enough to be measured in a laboratory.

Unfortunately, to test his hypothesis, Helmoltz needed an instrument capable of measuring very small fractions of seconds, smaller than could be reliably detected by any existing timepiece. He devised such a "clock" from a simple laboratory galvanometer. A galvanometer is an instrument that detects the presence and strength of an electrical current by causing a needle to deflect, with the amount of deflection corresponding to the strength of the current. Helmholtz knew that when the current was first turned on it took a short, but measurable, amount of time to reach its maximum level and to cause the needle to reach its maximum deflection. If the current was turned off before it reached its maximum, the proportion of needle deflection registered was an accurate

measure of the very small amount of time the current had been on.

Now armed with this "galvanometric stopwatch," Helmholtz measured the speed of the neural impulse in a frog's leg. He knew that mild electrical stimulation of the motor nerve that ran the length of the leg would cause a twitch in the foot muscle, and by balancing the foot on a switch, this movement could be used to turn off a current. When the current was turned on the galvanometer was set in motion, but when the foot twitched it was turned off. He now compared the times when the nerve was stimulated at different locations along the nerve fiber. He found that a point four inches from the muscle took 0.003 seconds longer than a point only one inch away, meaning that the nerve impulse was traveling at about 83 feet per second.

The next step was to apply this technique to humans. He trained subjects to press a button whenever they felt a stimulus applied to their leg. Although the results were more variable than those for the frog, reaction times tended to be longer when the stimulus was applied to the toe than when applied to the thigh. Calculations showed that humans had a faster neural impulse travel speed than the frog, in excess of 165 feet per second, and perhaps up to around 300 feet per second.

It would take a few years for the significance of these experiments to register with the scientific world—partly because the results were too astonishing to believe. From a phenomenological perspective mental processes are subjectively experienced as occurring instantaneously, and physiologists believed that the neurological events associated with them should be instantaneous as well. The idea that it takes a finite time for events to occur was difficult to believe. Nonetheless, this new *reaction-time* methodology would allow the first true psychological laboratory to begin its testing program.

Wundt was quite aware of Helmhotz's work, since he had not only trained briefly with Helmholtz's mentor Johannes Müller but served as Helmholtz's assistant at Heidelberg. When Wundt established the first psychological laboratory at Leipzig in 1879, one of the major objective methodological tools that he would employ would be "mental chronometry," or reaction time, building on some earlier work of the Dutch physiologist Frans Cornelis Donders (1817–1881). Reaction-time methodology allowed Wundt to demonstrate a scientific basis for psychological research. The philosophic basis for this undertaking would come from Johann Friedrich Herbart (1776–1841), who suggested that the study of mental phenomena should be (a) empirical; (b) dynamic, in the sense that ideas and experiences can interact and vary over time; and (c) mathematical. To this substrate, Wundt added that the study of mental phenomena should use the technology, fundamental data, and empirical strategies that had been developed by physiology, since ultimately humans are simply physiological machines. It was in this context that Wundt developed the *subtractive method* to measure mental function.

An example of how the subtractive method works would be to first measure the reaction time for a simple task, say by tapping a key at the onset of a light (call this T_s). Next the observer is given a more complex task, say one in which he had to make a decision as to whether the light was red or green, tapping a key with his right hand for red and with his left hand for green (call this T_c). Since the more complex task takes more mental computation, T_c is longer than T_n, and Wundt reasoned that the actual time that the decisional process takes, T_d, could be computed by the simple subtraction $T_d = T_c - T_s$. This should give the researcher a metric. Reaction time should increase in direct proportion to the difficulty of the decision or the number of decisions that had to be made.

Although this methodology generated a lot of research, concerns began to be expressed by some researchers. N. Lange, working in Wundt's lab, found that attentional processes affected the length of the reaction time. Unattended or unexpected stimuli took longer to respond to, and paying attention to the response rather than to the stimulus also altered the reaction time. Other researchers, such as Oswald Klüpe (1862–1915), suggested that the method was not valid because the entire perceptual act is not simply the sum of simple sensory and decision times. Returning to the example above, suppose that we compare the time that it takes to detect a light (T_s) to the time that it takes to discern the locus of lights (e.g., whether a pair of lights were side by side or one above the other–T_l); now, following this decision we will also require the observer to add the color discrimination task that we described earlier (T_c). The addition of a second mental operation or sensory input was known as the *complication method*. Computing the decision time for the color task should produce the same value whether we base it on $T_c - T_l$ (where subjects are making two sequential decisions in a complication study) or $T_c - T_s$ (the single decision compared to the simple detection task), since the color decision (red versus green) added on to the first task is identical. Yet this was never the case, which suggested that mental activity was not a linear process and was not subject to simple algebraic analysis. Because of this, studies of reaction time came to be viewed as suspect, and their popularity declined during the first half of the twentieth century.

Reaction time would spring back into prominence as cognitive and information-processing approaches to perception became a problem of interest. The changes in reaction time with shifts in attention no longer would be viewed as a methodological artifact but rather could be used as a method of studying attention itself. Furthermore, the underlying conception that processing was a serial and linear process would be challenged, and reaction time would provide the vital measures. It was Saul Sternberg, in a series of visual search and recognition studies (e.g., Sternberg, 1967), and Ulric Neisser in his 1967 book *Cognitive Psychology*, who rebuilt the reputation of reaction-time methodology. They turned the apparent breakdown of the subtractive method into an investigative tool. Thus, in those instances in which addition of tasks or sensory inputs increases reaction time, we clearly have a serial processing system where the output from an earlier stage of processing becomes the input for the next stage of processing. Because of this serial sequence, processing times increase as the number of mental operations increases. However, in those instances where adding tasks, stimuli, or sensory channels does not increase the reaction time, we are dealing with a parallel and perhaps distributed processing network where many operations are occurring simultaneously. In this way, reaction-time methodology allows us to ascertain the pattern or network of processing and not simply the complexity of processing.

An example of parallel processing as it was originally conceptualized can be seen in a visual pattern recognition theory that emphasized feature extraction processes that all occur at the same time. It was originally called *pandemonium*, because, as a heuristic device, each stage in the analysis of an input pattern was originally conceived of as a group of *demons* shouting out the results of their analyses (Selfridge, 1959). According to the model, the contents of the retinal image are simultaneously passed to each of a set of *feature demons*, which actually are neurons that act like filters to detect specific features. All of these neurons do their processing at the same time, since copies of the original stimulus input are passed on to a number of neurons simultaneously. The response of these filtering neurons (the loudness with which the demons shout) is proportional to the fit of the stimulus to the filter's template. These outputs are judged simultaneously by a large set of *cognitive demons,* which are actually more complex filters or neurons that respond to a particular combination of features in proportion to their fit to the template. One of these will be a best fit, and thus respond most vigorously. At the final stage, a *decision demon* listens to the "pandemonium" caused by the yelling of the various cognitive demons. It chooses the cognitive demon (or pattern) that is making the most noise (responding most vigorously) as the one that is most likely to be the stimulus pattern presented to the sensory system and represents this as the final conscious percept. Such parallel-distributed processing theories have become popular because they are easily represented in a network form and thus can be implemented and tested as computer models. In this way, the reaction-time data confirms Herbart's contention that theories of psychology should be dynamic and can be mathematical.

THE PSYCHOPHYSICISTS AND THE CORRESPONDENCE PROBLEM

The ultimate battle over the conceptualization of perception would be fought over the correspondence problem. The issue has to do with the perceptual act, and the simple question is, "How well does the perceived stimulus in consciousness correspond or represent the external physical stimulus?" By the mid-1800s, the recognition that sensory systems were not passively registering an accurate picture of the physical world was becoming an accepted fact. The most common situations in which this became obvious were those that taxed the sensitivity of an observer. In these instances, stimuli might not be detected and intensity differences that might allow one to discriminate between stimuli might go unnoticed. These early studies were clearly testing the limitations of the receptivity of sensory organs and hence were consistent with both the physical and physiological view of the senses as mere stimulus detectors. However, as the data on just how sensitive sensory systems were began to be amassed, problems immediately arose.

Ernst Heinrich Weber (1795–1878) at the University of Leipzig did research on touch sensitivity. He noticed that the ability to discriminate between one versus two simultaneous touches and the ability to discriminate among different weights was not a simple matter of stimulus differences. As an example, take three coins (quarters work well) and put two in one envelope and one in the other. Now compare the weight of these two envelopes and you should have no difficulty discriminating which has two coins, meaning that the stimulus difference of the weight of one quarter is discriminable. Next take these two envelopes and put one in each of your shoes. When you now compare the weight of the shoes you should find it difficult, and most likely impossible, to tell which of them is one coin weight heavier, despite the fact that previously there was no difficulty making a discrimination based on the same weight difference. Physical measuring devices do not have this limitation. If you have a scale that can tell the difference between a 10-gram and 20-gram weight, it should have no difficulty telling the difference between a 110-gram and 120-gram weight, since it clearly can discriminate differences of 10 grams. Such cannot be said for sensory systems.

These observations would be turned into a system of measuring the correspondence between the perceived and the physical stimulus by Gustav Teodore Fechner (1801–1887). Fechner was a physicist and philosopher who set out to solve the mind–body problem of philosophy, but in so doing actually became, if not the first experimental psychologist, at least the first person to do experimental psychological research. Fechner got his degree in medicine at Leipzig and actually studied physiology under Weber. He accepted a position lecturing and doing research in the physics department at Leipzig, where he did research on, among other things, the afterimages produced by looking at the sun through colored filters. During the process of this, he damaged his eyes and was forced to retire in 1839. For years he wore bandages over his eyes; however, in 1843 he removed them, and reveling in the beauty of recovered sight he began a phenomenological assessment of sensory experience. On the morning of October 22, 1850, Fechner had an insight that the connection between mind and body could be established by demonstrating that there was a systematic quantitative relationship between the perceived stimulus and the physical stimulus. He was willing to accept the fact that an increase in stimulus intensity does not produce a one-to-one increase in the intensity of a sensation. Nonetheless, the increase in perceived sensation magnitudes should be predictable from a knowledge of the stimulus magnitudes because there should be a regular mathematical relationship between stimulus intensity and the perceived intensity of the stimulus. He described the nature of this relation in his classic book *The Elements of Psychophysics,* which was published in 1860. This book is a strange mixture of philosophy, mathematics, and experimental method, but it still had a major impact on perceptual research.

Fechner's description of the relationship between stimulus and perception began with a quantitative manipulation of Weber's data. What Weber had found was that the discrimination of weight differences was based on proportional rather than arithmetic difference. For example, suppose an individual can just barely tell the weight difference between 10 and 11 quarters in sealed envelopes; then this minimally perceptible difference between 10 and 11 represents a $\frac{1}{10}$ increase in weight (computed as the change in intensity of 1 quarter divided by the starting intensity of 10 quarters). This fraction, which would be known as the Weber fraction, then predicted the stimulus difference that would be just noticeable for any other starting stimulus. Thus, you would need a 10-quarter difference added to an envelope containing 100 quarters to be discriminated (e.g., 100 versus 110), a 5-quarter difference if the envelope contained 50 quarters, and so forth. Since these minimal weight changes are just barely noticeable, Fechner assumed that they must be subjectively equal. Now Fechner makes the assumption that these just noticeable differences can be added, so that the number of times a weight must be increased, for instance, before it equals another target weight, could serve as an objective measure of the subjective magnitude of the stimulus. Being a physicist gave him the mathematical skills needed to then add an infinite number of these just noticeable differences together, which in calculus involves the operation of integration. This resulted is what has come to be known as Fechner's law, which can be stated in the form of an equation of $S = W \log I$, where S is the magnitude of the sensation, W is a constant which depends on the Weber fraction, and I is the intensity of the physical stimulus. Thus, as the magnitude of the physical stimulus increases arithmetically, the magnitude of the perceived stimulus increases in a logarithmic manner. Phenomenologically this means that the magnitude of a stimulus change is perceived as being greater when the stimulus intensity is weak than that same magnitude of change is perceived when the starting stimulus is more intense. The logarithmic relationship between stimulus intensity and perceived stimulus magnitude is a better reflection of what people perceive than is a simple representation based on raw stimulus intensity; hence, there were many practical applications of this relationship. For instance, brightness measures, the density of photographic filters, and sound scales in decibels all use logarithmic scaling factors.

One thing that is often overlooked about Fechner's work is that he spoke of two forms of psychophysics. *Outer psychophysics* was concerned with relationships between stimuli and sensations, while *inner psychophysics* was concerned with the relationship between neural or brain activity and sensations. Unfortunately, as so often occurs in science, inner psychophysics, although crucial, was inaccessible to direct observation, which could create an insurmountable barrier to our understanding. To avoid this problem, Fechner hypothesized that measured brain activity and subjective perception were simply alternative ways of viewing the same phenomena. Thus, he hypothesized that the one realm of the psychological universe did not depend on the other in a cause-and-effect manner; rather, they accompanied each other and were complementary in the information they conveyed about the universe. This allowed him to accept the thinking pattern of a physicist and argue that if he could mathematically *describe* the relationship between stimulus and sensation, he had effectively *explained* that relationship.

Obviously, the nonlinearity between the change in the physical magnitude of the stimulus and the perceived magnitude of the stimulus could have been viewed as a simple failure in correspondence, or even as some form of illusion. Fechner, however, assumed that since the relationship was now predictable and describable, it should not be viewed as some form of illusion or distortion but simply as an accepted

fact of perception. Later researchers such as Stanley Smith Stevens (1906–1973) would modify the quantitative nature of the correspondence, suggesting that perceived stimulus intensities actually vary as a function of some power of the intensity of the physical stimulus, and that that exponent will vary as a function of the stimulus modality, the nature of the stimulus, and the conditions of observation. Once again the fact of noncorrespondence would be accepted as nonillusory simply because it could be mathematically described. Stevens did try to make some minimal suggestions about how variations in neural transduction might account for these quantitative relationships; however, even though these were not empirically well supported, he considered that his equations "explained" the psychophysical situation adequately.

While the classical psychophysicists were concerned with description and rarely worried about mechanism, some more modern researchers approached the question of correspondence with a mechanism in mind. For instance, Harry Helson (b. 1898) attempted to explain how context can affect judgments of sensation magnitudes. In Helson's theory, an organism's sensory and perceptual systems are always adapting to the ever-changing physical environment. This process creates an *adaptation level,* a kind of internal reference level to which the magnitudes of all sensations are compared. Sensations with magnitudes below the adaptation level are perceived to be weak and sensations above it to be intense. Sensations at or near the adaptation level are perceived to be medium or neutral. The classical example of this involves three bowls of water, one warm, one cool, and one intermediate. If an individual puts one hand in the warm water and one in the cool water, after a short time both hands will feel as if they are in water that is neither warm nor cool, as the ambient temperature of the water surrounding each hand becomes its adaptation level. However, next plunging both hands in the same bowl of intermediate temperature will cause the hand that was in warm to feel that the water in the bowl is cool and the hand that was in cool to feel that the same water is warm. This implies that all perceptions of sensation magnitude are relative. A sensation is not simply weak or intense; it is weak or intense compared to the adaptation level.

One clear outcome of the activity of psychophysicists was that it forced perceptual researchers to learn a bit of mathematics and to become more comfortable with mathematical manipulation. The consequence of this has been an acceptance of more mathematically oriented methods and theories. One of these, namely *signal detection theory,* actually is the mathematical implementation of a real theory with a real hypothesized mechanism. Signal detection theory conceptualized stimulus reception as analogous to signal detection by a radio receiver, where there is noise or static constantly present and the fidelity of the instrument depends on its ability to pick a signal out of the noisy environment. Researchers such as Swets, Tanner, and Birdsall (1961) noted that the situation is similar in human signal reception; however, the noise that is present is noise in the neural channels against which increased activity due to a stimulus must be detected. Furthermore, decisional processes and expectations as well as neural noise will affect the likelihood that a stimulus will be detected. The mathematical model of this theory has resulted in the development of an important set of analytic tools and measures, such as d' as a measure of sensitivity and β as a measure of judgmental criterion or decision bias.

This same trend has also led to the acceptance of some complex mathematical descriptive systems that were offered without physical mechanisms in mind but involve reasoning from analogy using technological devices as a model. Concurrent with the growth of devices for transmitting and processing information, a unifying theory known as *information theory* was developed and became the subject of intensive research. The theory was first presented by electrical engineer Claude Elwood Shannon (b. 1916) working at the Bell Labs. In its broadest sense, he interpreted information as including the messages occurring in any of the standard communications media, such as telephones, radio, television, and data-processing devices, but by analogy this could include messages carried by sensory systems and their final interpretation in the brain. The chief concern of information theory was to discover mathematical laws governing systems designed to communicate or manipulate information. Its principal application in perceptual research was to the problems of perceptual recognition and identification. It has also proved useful in determining the upper bounds on what it is possible to discriminate in any sensory system (see Garner, 1962).

THE GESTALTISTS AND THE CORRESPONDENCE PROBLEM

We have seen how psychophysicists redefined a set of failures of correspondence so that they are no longer considered illusions, distortions, or misperceptions, but rather are examples of the normal operation of the perceptual system. There would be yet another attempt to do this; however, this would not depend on mathematics but on phenomenology and descriptive psychological mechanisms.

The story begins with Max Wertheimer (1880–1943), who claimed that while on a train trip from Vienna for a vacation on the Rhine in 1910, he was thinking about an illusion he had seen. Suddenly he had the insight that would lead to Gestalt psychology, and this would evolve from his analysis

of the perception of motion. He was so excited that he stopped at Frankfurt long enough to buy a version of a toy stroboscope that produced this "illusion of motion" with which to test his ideas. He noted that two lights flashed through small apertures in a darkened room at long intervals would appear to be simply two discrete light flashes; at very short intervals, they would appear to be two simultaneously appearing lights. However, at an intermediate time interval between the appearance of each, what would be perceived was one light in motion. This perception of movement in a stationary object, called the *phi phenomenon*, could not be predicted from a simple decomposition of the stimulus array into its component parts; thus, it was a direct attack on associationist and structural schools' piecemeal analyses of experience into atomistic elements. Because this motion only appears in conscious perception, it became a validation of a global phenomenological approach and ultimately would be a direct attack of on the "hard-line" behaviorism of researchers such as John Broadus Watson (1878–1958), who rejected any evidence based on reports or descriptions of conscious perceptual experience. Wertheimer would stay for several years at the University of Frankfurt, where he researched this and other visual phenomena with the assistance of Kurt Koffka (1886–1941) and Wolfgang Köhler (1887–1967). Together they would found the theoretical school of Gestalt psychology. The term *gestalt* is usually credited to Christian Freiherr von Ehrenfels (1859–1932). He used the term to refer to the complex data that require more than immediate sense experience in order to be perceived. There is no exact equivalent to *gestalt* in English, with "form," "pattern," or "configuration" sometimes being suggested as close; hence, the German term has simply been adopted as it stands.

The basic tenants of Gestalt psychology suggest that perception is actively organized by certain mental rules or templates to form coherent objects or "wholes." The underlying rule is that "the whole is different from the sum its parts." Consider Figure 5.3. Most people would say that they see a square on the left and a triangle on the right. Yet notice that the individual elements that make up the square are four circular dots, while the elements that make up the triangle are actually squares. The gestalt or organized percept that appears in consciousness is quite different from the sum of its parts.

Few facts in perception are as well known as the gestalt laws of perceptual grouping, which include grouping by proximity, similarity, closure (as in Figure 5.3), and so forth. There had been a number of precursors to the gestalt laws of organization, and theorists such as Stumpf and Schumann had noticed that certain arrangements of stimuli are associated with the formation of perceptual units. These investigators, however, were fascinated with the fact that such added

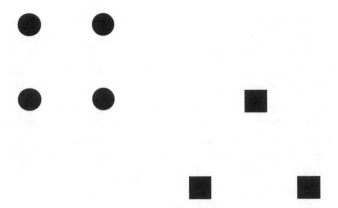

Figure 5.3　A square and a triangle appear as a function of the operation of the gestalt principle of perceptual organization labeled closure.

qualities as the squareness or triangularity that you see in Figure 5.3 represented failures in correspondence between the physical array and the conscious perception. For this reason they tended to classify such perceptual-grouping phenomena as errors in judgment analogous the visual-geometric illusions that we saw in Figure 5.2. They argued that it was just as illusory to see a set of dots cohering together to form a square as in Figure 5.3, when in fact there are no physical stimuli linking them, as it is to see two lines as different in length when in fact they are physically identical.

The gestalt theorists set out to attack this position with a theoretical article by Köhler (1913). This paper attacked the prevailing constancy hypothesis that maintained that every aspect of the conscious representation of a stimulus must correspond to some simple physical stimulus element. He argued that many nonillusory percepts, such as the perceptual constancies, do not perfectly correlate with the input stimulus. Perceptual organizational effects fall into the same class of phenomena. He argued that to label such percepts as "illusions" constitutes a form of "explaining away." He goes on to say, "One is satisfied as soon as the blame for the illusion so to speak, is shifted from the sensations, and a resolute investigation of the primary causes of the illusion is usually not undertaken" (Köhler, 1913, p. 30). He contended that illusory phenomena are simply viewed as curiosities that do not warrant serious systematic study. As he noted, "each science has a sort of attic into which things are almost automatically pushed that cannot be used at the moment, that do not fit, or that no one wants to investigate at the moment," (p. 53). His intention was to assure that the gestalt organizational phenomena would not end up in the "attic" with illusions. His arguments were clearly successful, since few if any contemporary psychologists would be so brash as to refer to gestalt organizations in perception as illusions, despite the fact that there is now evidence that the very act of organizing the percept does distort the metric of the surrounding perceived

space in much the same way that the configurational elements in Figure 5.2 distort the metric of the test elements (see Coren & Girgus, 1980).

THE PROGRESS OF PERCEPTUAL RESEARCH

Where are we now? The study of the perceptual problem and the issue of noncorrespondence remains an open issue, but it has had an interesting historical evolution. Wundt was correct in his supposition that psychology needed psychological laws, since physical and physiological laws cannot explain many of the phenomena of consciousness. What Wundt recognized was that the very fact of noncorrespondence between perception and the physical reality was what proved this fact and this same noncorrespondence is what often drives perceptual research. Köhler was wrong in saying that instances of noncorrespondence were relegated to the attic of the science. Instances of noncorrespondence or illusion are what serve as the motive power for a vast amount of perceptual investigation. It is the unexpected and unexplainable illusion or distortion that catches the attention and interest of researchers. The reason that there are no great insights found in the category of phenomena that are currently called illusions is that once investigators explain any illusion and find its underlying mechanism, it is no longer an illusion.

Consider the case of color afterimages, which Müller classified as an illusion in 1826. Afterimages would serve as stimuli for research by Fechner, Helmholtz, and Hering. Now that we understand the mechanisms that cause afterimages, however, these phenomena are looked on no longer as instances of illusion or distortion but rather as phenomena that illustrate the operation of the color coding system. Similarly, brightness contrast, which Luckiesh was still classifying as an illusion as late 1922, stimulated Hering and Mach to do research to explain these instances of noncorrespondence between the percept and the physical state. By 1965, however, Ratliff would no longer see anything illusory in these phenomena and would merely look upon them as perceptual phenomena that demonstrate, and are clearly predictable from, the interactions of neural networks in the retina.

The study of perception is fraught with the instances of noncorrespondence and illusion that are no longer illusions. The fact that a mixture color, such as yellow, shows no evidence of the component red or green wavelengths that compose it was once considered an example of an illusion. Later, once the laws of color mixture had been established, the expectation was built that we should expect fusion and blending in perception, which meant that the fact that the individual notes that make up a chord or a sound complex *could be* distinguished from one another and did not blend together into a seamless whole would also be considered to be an illusion. Since we now understand the physiology underlying both the visual and the auditory processes, we fail to see either noncorrespondence or illusion in either of these phenomena.

Apparent motion (Wertheimer's phi phenomena), perceptual organization, stereoscopic depth perception, singleness of vision, size constancy, shape constancy, brightness constancy, color constancy, shape from shading, adaptation to heat, cold, light, dark, touch and smell, the nonlinearity of judged stimulus magnitudes, intensity contrasts, brightness assimilation, color assimilation, pop-out effects, filling-in of the blind spot, stabilized image fading, the Purkinje color shift, and many more such phenomena all started out as "illusions" and instances of noncorrespondence between perception and reality. As we learn more about these phenomena we hear less about "illusion" or "distortion" and more about "mechanism" and "normal sensory processing."

The psychological study of sensation and perception remains extremely eclectic. Perceptual researchers still are quick to borrow methods and viewpoints from other disciplines. Physical, physiological, optical, chemical, and biochemical techniques and theories have all been absorbed into the study of sensory phenomena. It might be argued that a physiologist could study sensory phenomena as well as a psychologist, and, as the history of the discipline shows, if we are talking about matters of sensory transduction and reception, or single cell responses, this is sometimes true. David Hubel and Torston Wiesel were physiologists whose study of the cortical encoding and analysis of visual properties did as much to advance sensory psychology as it did to advance physiology. Georg von Bekesy (1899–1972), who also won the Nobel Prize for physiology, did so for his studies of the analysis of frequency by the ear, a contribution that is appreciated equally by physiology and psychology. Although some references refer to Bekesy as a physiologist, he spent two-thirds of his academic career in a psychology department and was initially trained as an engineer. Thus, sensory and perceptual research still represents an amalgam of many research areas, with numerous crossover theories and techniques.

It is now clear that on the third major theme, the distinction between sensation and perception, with a possible strong separation between the two in terms of theories and methodological approach, there is at least a consensus. Unfortunately the acceptance of this separation has virtually led to a schism that may well split this research area. Psychology has accepted the distinction between sensation (which is primary, physiological, and structural) and perception (which is based on phenomenological and behavioral data). These two areas have virtually become subdisciplines. Sensory research remains closely tied to the issue of capturing a stimulus and

transferring its information to the central nervous system for processing, and thus remains closely allied with the physical and biological sciences. Perceptual research is often focused on correspondence and noncorrespondence issues, where there are unexpected discrepancies between external and internal realities that require attention and verification, or where we are looking at instances where the conscious percept is either too limited or too good in the context of the available sensory inputs. It is more closely allied to cognitive, learning, and information-processing issues. Thus, while sensory research becomes the search for the specific physical or physiological process that can "explain" the perceptual data, perceptual research then becomes the means of explaining how we go beyond the sensory data to construct our view of reality. The importance of nonsensory contributions to the final conscious representation still remains an issue in perceptual research but is invisible in sensory research. The history of sensation and perception thus has seen a gradual separation between these two areas. Today, sensory researchers tend to view themselves more as neuroscientists, while perceptual researchers tend to view themselves more as cognitive scientists.

While the distinction between sensation and perception is necessary and useful, the task of the future may be to find some way of reuniting these two aspects of research. Certainly they are united in the organism and are interdependent aspects of behavior. I am reminded of a line by Judith Guest in her book *Ordinary People,* where she asked the question that we must ask about sensation and perception: "Two separate, distinct personalities, not separate at all, but inextricably bound, soul and body and mind, to each other, how did we get so far apart so fast?"

BIBLIOGRAPHY

(Some works used for background but not specifically cited in the text)

Boring, E. G. *Sensation and Perception in the History of Experimental Psychology.* New York: Appleton-Century-Crofts, 1942.

Coren, S., and J. S. Girgus. *Seeing is Deceiving: The Psychology of Visual Illusions.* Hillsdale, NJ: Erlbaum, 1978.

Hearnshaw, L. S. *The Shaping of Modern Psychology.* New York: Routledge, 1987.

Pastore, N. *Selective History of Theories of Visual Perception: 1650–1950.* New York: Oxford University Press, 1971.

Polyak, S. *The Vertebrate Visual System.* Chicago: Univesity of Chicago Press, 1957.

Sahakian, W. S. *History and Systems of Psychology.* New York: Wiley, 1975.

Spearman, C. *Psychology down the Ages.* London: Macmillan, 1937.

REFERENCES

Bain, A. (1855). *The senses and the intellect.* London: Longman, Green.

Berkeley, G. (1709). *An essay towards a new theory of vision.* London.

Bernfeld, S. (1949). Freud's scientific beginnings. *American Imago, 6,* 163–196.

Bruce, C., Desimone, R., & Gross., C. G. (1981). Visual neurons in a polysensory area in superior temporal sulcus in the macaque. *Journal of Neurophysiology, 46,* 369–384.

Coren, S. (1986). An efferent component in the visual perception of direction and extent. *Psychological Review, 93,* 391–410.

Coren, S., & Girgus, J. S. (1980). Principles of perceptual organization and spatial distortion: The Gestalt illusions. *Journal of Experimental Psychology: Human Perception and Performance, 6,* 404–412.

Descartes, R. (1972). *Treatise on man* (T. S. Hall, Trans.). Cambridge, MA: Harvard University Press. (Original work published 1664)

Fechner, G. T. (1960). *Elements of psychophysics.* New York: Holt, Rinehart, and Winston. (Original work published 1860)

Garner, W. R. (1962). *Uncertainty and structure as psychological concepts.* New York: Wiley.

Gibson, J. J. (1979). *The ecological approach to visual perception.* Boston: Houghton Mifflin.

Gross, C. G., Rocha-Miranda, E. C., & Bender, D. B. (1972). Visual properties of neurons in inferotemporal cortex of the macaque. *Journal of Neurophysiology, 35,* 96–111.

Hobbes, T. (1839). Human nature. In W. Molesworth (Ed.), *Hobbes English works.* Cambridge, England: Cambridge University Press. (Original work published 1651)

Kendrick, K. M., & Baldwin, B. A. (1987). Cells in the temporal cortex of a conscious sheep can responds differentially to the sight of faces. *Science, 236,* 448–450.

Köhler, W. (1971). Ber unbemrkete empfindugen und urteilstaschungen. In M. Henle (Ed.), *The selected papers of Wolfgang Köhler.* New York: Liveright. (Original work published 1913)

Marr, D. (1982). *Vision.* San Francisco: Freeman.

Neisser, U. (1967). *Cognitive psychology.* New York: Appleton-Century-Crofts.

Piaget, J. (1969). *Mechanisms of perception.* New York: Basic Books.

Reid, T. (1785). *Essays on the intellectual posers of man.* Edinburgh, Scotland: Macachian, Stewart.

Selfridge, O. G. (1959). Pandemonium: A paradigm for learning. In D. V. Blake & A. M. Uttley (Eds.), *Proceedings of the Symposium on the Mechanisation of Thought Processes* (pp. 511–529). London: Her Majesty's Stationery Office.

Smith, R. (1738). *A complete system of opticks.* Cambridge: Crowfield.

Sternberg, S. (1967). Two operations in character-recognition: Some evidence from reaction-time measurements. *Perception and Psychophysics, 2,* 45–53.

Swets, J. A., Tanner, W. P., & Birdsall, T. G. (1961). Decision processes in perception. *Psychological Review, 68,* 301–340.

CHAPTER 6

Cognition and Learning

THOMAS HARDY LEAHEY

THE PHILOSOPHICAL PERIOD   110
   The Premodern Period: Cognition before the
     Scientific Revolution   110
   The Scientific Revolution and a New Understanding
     of Cognition   114
   The Modern Period: Cognition after the
     Scientific Revolution   115
THE EARLY SCIENTIFIC PERIOD   118
   The Psychology of Consciousness   118
   The Verbal Learning Tradition   118

The Impact of Evolution   118
Animal Psychology and the Coming
   of Behaviorism   119
Behaviorism: The Golden Age of Learning Theory   120
THE MODERN SCIENTIFIC PERIOD   125
   The Three Key Ideas of Computing   125
   The Fruits of Computation: Cognitive Science   127
   Cognitive Psychology Today   131
REFERENCES   131

Trying to understand the nature of cognition is the oldest psychological enterprise, having its beginnings in ancient Greek philosophy. Because the study of cognition began in philosophy, it has a somewhat different character than other topics in the history of psychology. Cognition is traditionally (I deliberately chose an old dictionary) defined as follows: "Action or faculty of knowing, perceiving, conceiving, as opposed to emotion and volition" (*Concise Oxford Dictionary,* 1911/1964, p. 233). This definition has two noteworthy features. First, it reflects the traditional philosophical division of psychology into three fields: cognition (thinking), emotion (feelings), and conation, or will (leading to actions). Second, and more important in the present context, is the definition of cognition as *knowing.* Knowing, at least to a philosopher, is a success word, indicating possession of a justifiably true belief, as opposed to mere opinion, a belief that may or may not be correct or that is a matter of taste. From a philosophical perspective, the study of cognition has a normative aspect, because its aim is to determine what we *ought* to believe, namely, that which is true.

The study of cognition therefore has two facets. The first is philosophical, lying in the field of epistemology, which inquires into the nature of truth. The second is psychological, lying in the field of cognitive psychology or cognitive science, which inquires into the psychological mechanisms by which people acquire, store, and evaluate beliefs about the world. These two facets are almost literally two sides of a coin that cannot be pried apart. Once philosophers distinguished truth from opinion (epistemology), the question immediately arose as to how (psychology) one is to acquire the former and avoid the latter. At the same time, any inquiry into how the mind works (psychology) necessarily shapes investigations into the nature of truth (philosophy). The philosophers whose work is summarized below shuttled back and forth between inquiries into the nature of truth—epistemology—and inquiries into how humans come to possess knowledge.

This joint philosophical-psychological enterprise was profoundly and permanently altered by evolution. Prior to Darwin, philosophers dwelt on the human capacity for knowledge. Their standard for belief was Truth: People ought to believe what is true. Evolution, however, suggested a different standard, workability or adaptive value: People ought to believe what works in conducting their lives, what it is *adaptive* to believe. From the evolutionary perspective, there is little difference between the adaptive nature of physical traits and the adaptive nature of belief formation. It makes no sense to ask if the human opposable thumb is "true": It works for us humans, though lions get along quite well without them. Similarly, it may make no sense to ask if the belief "Lions are dangerous" is metaphysically true; what counts is whether it's more adaptive than the belief "Lions are friendly." After Darwin, the study of cognition drifted away from philosophy (though it never completely lost its connection) and became the study of learning, inquiring into how people and animals—another effect of evolution—acquire adaptive beliefs and behaviors.

I divide my history of cognition and learning into three eras. The first is the Philosophical Era, from Classical Greece up to the impact of evolution. The second is the Early Scientific Era, from the impact of evolution through behaviorism. The third is the Modern Scientific Era, when the psychological study of learning and cognition resumed its alliance with philosophy in the new interdisciplinary endeavor of cognitive science.

THE PHILOSOPHICAL PERIOD

During the Premodern period, inquiries into cognition focused on philosophical rather than psychological issues. The chief concerns of those who studied cognition were determining how to separate truth from falsity and building systems of epistemology that would provide sure and solid foundations for other human activities from science to politics.

The Premodern Period: Cognition before the Scientific Revolution

Thinking about cognition began with the ancient Greeks. As Greek thought took flight beyond the bounds of religion, philosophers began to speculate about the nature of the physical world. Political disputes within the *poleis* and encounters with non-western societies provoked debates about the best human way of life. These social, ethical, and protoscientific inquiries in turn raised questions about the scope and limits of human knowledge, and how one could decide between rival theories of the world, morality, and the best social order. The epistemological questions the ancient philosophers posed are perennial, and they proposed the first—though highly speculative—accounts of how cognition works psychologically.

The Classical World before Plato

By distinguishing between Appearance and Reality, the Greeks of the fifth century B.C.E. inaugurated philosophical and psychological inquiries into cognition. Various pre-Socratic philosophers argued that the way the world seems to us—Appearance—is, or may be, different from the way the world is in Reality. Parmenides argued that there is a fixed reality (Being) enduring behind the changing appearances of the world of experience. Against Parmenides, Heraclitus argued that Reality is even more fluid than our experience

suggests. This pre-Socratic distinction between Appearance and Reality was metaphysical and ontological, not psychological. Parmenides and Heraclitus argued about the nature of a "realer," "truer" world existing in some sense apart from the one we live in. However, drawing the distinction shocked Greeks into the realization that our knowledge of the world—whether of the world we live in or of the transcendental one beyond it—might be flawed, and Greek thinkers added epistemology to their work, beginning to examine the processes of cognition (Irwin, 1989).

One of the most durable philosophical and psychological theories of cognition, the *representational theory,* was first advanced by the Greek philosopher-psychologists Alcmaeon and Empedocles. They said that objects emit little copies of themselves that get into our bloodstreams and travel to our hearts, where they result in perception of the object. The famous atomist Democritus picked up this theory, saying that the little copies were special sorts of atoms called *eidola.* Philosophically, the key feature of representational theories of cognition is the claim that we do not know the external world directly, but only indirectly, via the copies of the object that we internalize. Representational theories of cognition invite investigation of the psychological mechanisms by which representations are created, processed, and stored. The representational theory of cognition is the foundation stone of Simon and Newell's symbol-system architecture of cognition (see following).

Once one admits the distinction between Appearance and Reality, the question of whether humans can know Reality—Truth—arises. Epistemologies can be then divided into two camps: those who hold that we are confined to dealing with shifting appearances, and those who hold that we can achieve genuine knowledge. (See Figure 6.1.) I will call the first group the Relativists: For them, truth is ever changing because appearances are ever changing. I will call the second group the Party of Truth: They propose that humans can in

Path Metaphysics	RATIONALISM (typically linked to IDEALISM)	EMPIRICISM
Party of TRUTH	Socrates Plato Stoics Descartes Kant	Alcmaeon Empedocles Locke Positivism
Party of RELATIVISM	Hegel Nietzsche	Sophists Hume Pragmatism

Figure 6.1 Four Epistemologies.

some way get beyond appearances to an enduring realm of Truth.

The first relativists were the Greek Sophists. They treated the distinction between Appearance and Reality as insurmountable, concluding that what people call truth necessarily depends on their own personal and social circumstances. Thus, the Greek way of life seems best to Greeks, while the Egyptian way of life seems best to Egyptians. Because there is no fixed, transcendental Reality, or, more modestly, no transcendental Reality accessible to us, we must learn to live with Appearances, taking things as they seem to be, abandoning the goal of perfect Knowledge. The Sophists' relaxed relativism has the virtue of encouraging toleration: Other people are not wicked or deluded because they adhere to different gods than we do, they simply have different opinions than we do. On the other hand, such relativism can lead to anarchy or tyranny by suggesting that because no belief is better than any other, disputes can be settled only by the exercise of power.

Socrates, who refused to abandon truth as his and humanity's proper goal, roundly attacked the Sophists. Socrates believed the Sophists were morally dangerous. According to their relativism, Truth could not speak to power because there are no Truths except what people think is true, and human thought is ordinarily biased by unexamined presuppositions that he aimed to reveal. Socrates spent his life searching for compelling and universal moral truths. His method was to searchingly examine the prevailing moral beliefs of young Athenians, especially beliefs held by Sophists and their aristocratic students. He was easily able to show that conventional moral beliefs were wanting, but he did not offer any replacements, leaving his students in his own mental state of *aporia,* or enlightened ignorance. Socrates taught that there are moral truths transcending personal opinion and social convention and that it is possible for us to know them because they were innate in every human being and could be made conscious by his innovative philosophical dialogue, the *elenchus.* He rightly called himself truth's midwife, not its expositor. Ironically, in the end Socrates' social impact was the same as the Sophists'. Because he taught no explicit moral code, many Athenians thought Socrates was a Sophist, and they convicted him for corrupting the youth of Athens, prompting his suicide.

For us, two features of Socrates' quest are important. Pre-Socratic inquiry into cognition had centered on how we perceive and know particular objects, such as cats and dogs or trees and rocks. Socrates shifted the inquiry to a higher plane, onto the search for general, universal truths that collect many individual things under one concept. Thus, while we readily see that returning a borrowed pencil and founding a democracy are just acts, Socrates wanted to know what Justice *itself* is. Plato extended Socrates' quest for universal moral truths to encompass all universal concepts. Thus, we apply the term "cat" to all cats, no two of which are identical; how and why do we do this? Answering this question became a central preoccupation of the philosophy and psychology of cognition.

The second important feature of Socrates' philosophy was the demand that for a belief to count as real knowledge, it had to be justifiable. A soldier might do many acts of heroic bravery but be unable to explain what bravery is; a judge might be esteemed wise and fair but be unable to explain what justice is; an art collector might have impeccable taste but be unable to say what beauty is. Socrates regarded such cases as lying awkwardly between opinion and Truth. The soldier, judge, and connoisseur intuitively embrace bravery, justice, and beauty, but they do not possess knowledge of bravery, justice, and beauty unless and until they can articulate and defend it. For Socrates, unconscious intuition, even if faultless in application, was not real knowledge.

Plato and Aristotle

Of all Socrates' many students, the most important was Plato. Before him, philosophy—at least as far as the historical record goes—was a hit or miss affair of thinkers offering occasional insights and ideas. With Plato, philosophy became more self-conscious and systematic, developing theories about its varied topics. For present purposes, Plato's importance lies in the influential framework he created for thinking about cognition and in creating one of the two basic philosophical approaches to understanding cognition.

Plato formally drew the hard and bright line between opinions—beliefs that might or might not be true—and knowledge, beliefs that were demonstrably true. With regard to perception, Plato followed the Sophists, arguing that perceptions were relative to the perceiver. What seemed true to one person might seem false to another, but because each sees the world differently, there is no way to resolve the difference between them. For Plato, then, experience of the physical world was no path to truth, because it yielded only opinions. He found his path to truth in logic as embodied in Pythagorean geometry. A proposition such as the Pythagorean theorem could be *proved,* compelling assent from anyone capable of following the argument. Plato was thus the first philosophical *rationalist,* rooting knowledge in reason rather than in perception. Moreover, Plato said, provable truths such as the Pythagorean theorem do not apply to the physical world of the senses and opinion but to a transcendental realm of pure Forms (ιδεα in Greek) of which worldly objects are imperfect copies. In summary, Plato taught that there is a transcendental and unchanging realm of Truth and that we can know it by the right use of reason.

Plato also taught that some truths are innate. Affected by Eastern religions, Plato believed in reincarnation and proposed that between incarnations our soul dwells in the region of the Forms, carrying this knowledge with them into their next rebirth. Overcome by bodily senses and desires, the soul loses its knowledge of the Forms. However, because worldly objects resemble the Forms of which they are copies, experiencing them reactivates the innate knowledge the soul acquired in heaven. In this way, universal concepts such as *cat* or *tree* are formed out of perceptions of individual cats or trees. Thus, logic, experience, and most importantly Socrates' *elenchus* draw out Truths potentially present from birth.

Between them, Socrates and Plato began to investigate a problem in the study of cognition that would vex later philosophers and that is now of great importance in the study of cognitive development. Some beliefs are clearly matters of local, personal experience, capturing facts that are not universal. An American child learns the list of Presidents, while a Japanese child learns the list of Emperors. Another set of beliefs is held pretty universally but seems to be rooted in experience. American and Japanese children both know that fire is hot. There are other universal beliefs, however, whose source is harder to pin down. Socrates observed that people tended to share intuitions about what actions are just and which are unjust. Everyone agrees that theft and murder are wrong; disagreement tends to begin when we try to say why. Plato argued that the truth of the Pythagorean theorem is universal, but belief in it derives not from experience—we don't measure the squares on 100 right-angled triangles and conclude that $a^2 \times b^2 = c^2$, $p < .0001$—but from universal logic and universal innate ideas. Jean Piaget would later show that children acquire basic beliefs about physical reality, such as conservation of physical properties, without being tutored. The source and manner of acquisition of these kinds of beliefs divided philosophers and divide cognitive scientists.

Plato's great student was Aristotle, but he differed sharply from his teacher. For present purposes, two differences were paramount. The first was a difference of temperament and cast of mind. Plato's philosophy had a religious cast to it, with its soul–body dualism, reincarnation, and positing of heavenly Forms. Aristotle was basically a scientist, his specialty being marine biology. Aristotle rejected the transcendental world of the Forms, although he did not give up on universal truths. Second, and in part a consequence of the first, Aristotle was an empiricist. He believed universal concepts were built up by noting similarities and differences between the objects of one's experience. Thus, the concept of

cat would consist of the features observably shared by all cats. Postulating Forms and innate ideas of them was unnecessary, said Aristotle. Nevertheless, Aristotle retained Plato's idea that there is a universal and eternal essence of *catness,* or of any other universal concept. He did not believe, as later empiricists would, that concepts are human constructions.

Aristotle was arguably the first cognitive scientist (Nussbaum & Rorty, 1992). Socrates was interested in teaching compelling moral truths and said little about the psychology involved. With his distrust of the senses and otherworldly orientation, Plato, too, said little about the mechanisms of perception or thought. Aristotle, the scientist, who believed all truths begin with sensations of the external world, proposed sophisticated theories of the psychology of cognition. His treatment of the animal and human mind may be cast, somewhat anachronistically, of course, in the form of an information-processing diagram (Figure 6.2).

Cognitive processing begins with sensation of the outside world by the *special senses,* each of which registers one type of sensory information. Aristotle recognized the existence of what would later be called the problem of sensory integration, or the binding problem. Experience starts out with the discrete and qualitatively very different sensations of sight, sound, and so forth. Yet we experience not a whirl of unattached sensations (William James's famous "blooming, buzzing, confusion") but coherent objects possessing multiple sensory features. Aristotle posited a mental faculty—today cognitive scientists might call it a mental module—to handle the problem. *Common sense* integrated the separate streams of sensation into perception of a whole object. This problem of object perception or pattern recognition remains a source of controversy in cognitive psychology and artificial intelligence. Images of objects could be held before the mind's eye by *imagination* and stored away in, and retrieved from, *memory*. So far, we have remained within the mind of animals, Aristotle's

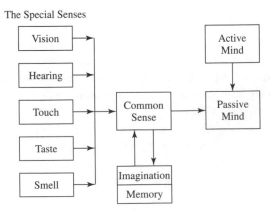

Figure 6.2 The structure of the human (sensitive and rational) soul according to Aristotle.

sensitive soul. Clearly, animals perceive the world of objects and can learn, storing experiences in memory. Humans are unique in being able to form universal concepts; dogs store memories of particular cats they have encountered but do not form the abstract concept *cat.* This is the function of the human soul, or *mind.* Aristotle drew a difficult distinction between active and passive mind. Roughly speaking, *passive mind* is the store of universal concepts, while *active mind* consists in the cognitive processes that build up knowledge of universals. Aristotle's system anticipates Tulving's (1972) influential positing of episodic and semantic memory. Aristotle's memory is Tulving's episodic memory, the storehouse of personal experiences. Aristotle's passive mind is Tulving's semantic memory, the storehouse of universal concepts.

The Hellenistic, Roman, and Medieval Periods

The death of Aristotle's famous pupil Alexander the Great in 323 B.C.E. marked an important shift in the nature of society and of philosophy. The era of the autonomous city-state was over; the era of great empires began. In consequence, philosophy moved in a more practical, almost psychotherapeutic (Nussbaum, 1994) direction. Contending schools of philosophy claimed to teach recipes for attaining happiness in a suddenly changed world. Considerations of epistemology and cognition faded into the background.

Nevertheless, the orientations to cognition laid down earlier remained and were developed. Those of Socrates' students who gave up on his and Plato's ambition to find transcendental truths developed the philosophy of skepticism. They held that no belief should be regarded as certain but held only provisionally and as subject to abandonment or revision. The Cynics turned Socrates' attack on social convention into a lifestyle. They deliberately flouted Greek traditions and sought to live as much like animals as possible. While cynicism looks much like skepticism—both attack cultural conventions as mere opinions—it did not reject Socrates' quest for moral truth. The Cynics lived what they believed was the correct human way of life free of conventional falsehoods. The Neoplatonists pushed Plato's faith in heavenly truth in a more religious direction, ultimately merging with certain strands of Christian philosophy in the work of Augustine and others. Of all the schools, the most important was Stoicism, taught widely throughout the Roman Empire. Like Plato, the Stoics believed that there was a realm of Transcendental Being beyond our world of appearances, although they regarded it as like a living and evolving organism, transcendent but not fixed eternally like the Forms. Also like Plato, they taught that logic—reason—was the path to transcendental knowledge.

Hellenistic and medieval physician-philosophers continued to develop Aristotle's cognitive psychology. They elaborated on his list of faculties, adding new ones such as *estimation,* the faculty by which animals and humans intuit whether a perceived object is beneficial or harmful. Moreover, they sought to give faculty psychology a physiological basis. From the medical writings of antiquity, they believed that mental processes are carried out within the various ventricles of the brain containing cerebrospinal fluid. They proposed that each mental faculty was housed in a distinct ventricle of the brain and that the movement of the cerebrospinal fluid through each ventricle in turn was the physical basis of information processing through the faculties. Here is the beginning of cognitive neuroscience and the idea of localization of cerebral function.

Summary: Premodern Realism

Although during the premodern period competing theories of cognition were offered, virtually all the premodern thinkers shared one assumption I will call *cognitive realism.* Cognitive realism is the claim that when we perceive an object under normal conditions, we accurately grasp all of its various sensory features.

Classical cognitive realism took two forms. One, *perceptual realism,* may be illustrated by Aristotle's theory of perception. Consider my perception of a person some meters distant. His or her appearance comprises a number of distinct sensory features: a certain height, hair color, cut and color of clothing, gait, timber of voice, and so on. Aristotle held that each of these features was picked up by the corresponding special sense. For example, the blue of a shirt caused the fluid in the eye to become blue; I see the shirt as blue because it is blue. At the level of the special senses, perception reveals the world as it *really* is. Of course, we sometimes make mistakes about the object of perception, but Aristotle attributed such mistakes to common sense, when we integrate the information from the special senses. Thus, I may mistakenly think that I'm approaching my daughter on campus, only to find that it's a similar-looking young woman. The important point is that for Aristotle my error is one of judgment, not of sensation: I really did see a slender young woman about 5′9″ tall in a leopard-print dress and hair dyed black; my mistake came in thinking it was Elizabeth.

Plato said little about perception because he distrusted it, but his *metaphysical realism* endorsed conclusions similar to, and even stronger than, Aristotle's. Plato said that we identify an individual cat as a cat because it resembles the Form of the Cat in heaven and lodged innately in our soul. If I say that a small fluffy dog is a cat, I am in error, because the dog really resembles the Form of the Dog. Moreover, Plato posited the existence of higher-level forms such as the Form of Beauty or the Form of the Good. Thus, not only is a cat a cat because it resembles the Form of the Cat, but a sculpture or painting is objectively beautiful because it resembles the Form of Beauty, and an action is objectively moral because it resembles the Form of the Good. For Plato, if I say that justice is the rule of the strong, I am in error, for tyranny does not resemble the Form of the Good. We act unjustly only to the extent our knowledge of the Good is imperfect.

Premodern relativism and skepticism were not inconsistent with cognitive realism, because they rested on distrust of human thought, not sensation or perception. One might believe in the world of the Forms but despair of our ability to know them, at least while embodied in physical bodies. This was the message of Neoplatonism and the Christian thought it influenced. Sophists liked to argue both sides of an issue to show that human reason could not grasp enduring truth, but they did not distrust their senses. Likewise, the skeptics were wary of the human tendency to jump to conclusions and taught that to be happy one should not commit oneself wholeheartedly to any belief, but they did not doubt the truth of individual sensations.

The Scientific Revolution and a New Understanding of Cognition

The Scientific Revolution marked a sharp, almost absolute, break in theories of cognition. It presented a new conception of the world: the world as a machine (Henry, 1997). Platonic metaphysical realism died. There were no external, transcendental standards by which to judge what was beautiful or just, or even what was a dog and what was a cat. The only reality was the material reality of particular things, and as a result the key cognitive relationship became the relationship between a perceiver and the objects in the material world he perceives and classifies, not the relationship between the object perceived and the Form it resembles. Aristotle's perceptual realism died, too, as scientists and philosophers imposed a veil of ideas between the perceiver and the world perceived. This veil of ideas was consciousness, and it created psychology as a discipline as well as a new set of problems in the philosophy and psychology of cognition.

The Way of Ideas: Rejecting Realism

Beginning with Galileo Galilei (1564–1642), scientists distinguished between *primary* and *secondary* sense properties (the terms are John Locke's). Primary sense properties are those that actually belong to the physical world-machine;

they are objective. Secondary properties are those added to experience by our sensory apparatus; they are subjective. Galileo wrote in his book *The Assayer:*

> Whenever I conceive any material or corporeal substance I immediately . . . think of it as bounded, and as having this or that shape; as being large or small [and] as being in motion or at rest. . . . From these conditions I cannot separate such a substance by any stretch of my imagination. But that it must be white or red, bitter or sweet, noisy or silent, and of sweet or foul odor, my mind does not feel compelled to bring in as necessary accompaniments. . . . Hence, I think that tastes, odors, colors, and so on . . . reside only in the consciousness [so that] if the living creature were removed all these qualities would be wiped away and annihilated.

The key word in this passage is *consciousness.* For ancient philosophers, there was only one world, the real physical world with which we are in direct touch, though the Platonists added the transcendental world of the Forms, but it, too, was external to us. But the concept of secondary sense properties created a New World, the inner world of consciousness, populated by mental objects—*ideas*—possessing sensory properties not found in objects themselves. In this new representational view of cognition—the Way of Ideas—we perceive objects not directly but indirectly via representations—ideas—found in consciousness. Some secondary properties correspond to physical features objects actually possess. For example, color corresponds to different wavelengths of light to which retinal receptors respond. That color is not a primary property, however, is demonstrated by the existence of color-blind individuals, whose color perception is limited or absent. Objects are not colored, only ideas are colored. Other secondary properties, such as being beautiful or good, are even more troublesome, because they seem to correspond to no physical facts but appear to reside only in consciousness. Our modern opinion that beauty and goodness are subjective judgments informed by cultural norms is one consequence of the transformation of experience wrought by the Scientific Revolution.

Cartesian Dualism and the Veil of Ideas

For psychology, the most important modern thinker was René Descartes (1596–1650), who created an influential framework for thinking about cognition that was fundamental to the history of psychology for the next 350 years. Descartes' dualism of body and soul is well known, but it also included the new scientific distinction of physical and mental worlds. Descartes assumed living bodies were complex machines no different from the world-machine. Animals lacked soul and consciousness and were therefore incapable of cognition. As machines, they responded to the world, but they could not think about it. Human beings were animals, too, but inside their mechanical body dwelled the soul, possessor of consciousness. Consciousness was the New World of ideas, indirectly representing the material objects encountered by the senses of the body. Descartes' picture has been aptly called the Cartesian Theater (Dennett, 1991): The soul sits inside the body and views the world as on a theater screen, a veil of ideas interposed between knowing self and known world.

Within the Cartesian framework, one could adopt two attitudes toward experience. The first attitude was that of natural science. Scientists continued to think of ideas as partial reflections of the physical world. Primary properties corresponded to reality; secondary ones did not, and science dealt only with the former. However, the existence of a world of ideas separate from the world of things invited exploration of this New World, as explorers were then exploring the New World of the Western Hemisphere. The method of natural science was observation. Exploring the New World of Consciousness demanded a new method, introspection. One could examine ideas as such, not as projections from the world outside, but as objects in the subjective world of consciousness.

Psychology was created by introspection, reflecting on the screen of consciousness. The natural scientist inspects the objective natural world of physical objects; the psychologist introspects the subjective mental world of ideas. To psychologists was given the problem of explaining whence secondary properties come. If color does not exist in the world, why and how do we see color? Descartes also made psychology important for philosophy and science. For them to discover the nature of material reality, it became vital to sort out what parts of experience were objective and what parts were subjective chimeras of consciousness. From now on, the psychology of cognition became the basis for epistemology. In order to know what people can and ought to know, it became important to study how people actually do know. But these investigations issued in a crisis when it became uncertain that people know—in the traditional Classical sense—anything at all.

The Modern Period: Cognition after the Scientific Revolution

Several intertwined questions arose from the new scientific, Cartesian, view of mind and its place in nature. Some are philosophical. If I am locked up in the subjective world of consciousness, how can I know anything about the world

with any confidence? Asking this question created a degree of paranoia in subsequent philosophy. Descartes began his quest for a foundation upon which to erect science by suspecting the truth of every belief he had. Eventually he came upon the apparently unassailable assertion that "I think, therefore I am." But Descartes' method placed everything else in doubt, including the existences of God and the world. Related to the philosophical questions are psychological ones. How and why does consciousness work as it does? Why do we experience the world as we do rather than some other way? Because the answers to the philosophical questions depend on the answers to the psychological ones, examining the mind—doing psychology—became the central preoccupation of philosophy before psychology split off as an independent discipline.

Three philosophical-psychological traditions arose out of the new Cartesian questions: the modern *empiricist, realist,* and *idealist* traditions. They have shaped the psychology of cognition ever since.

The Empiricist Tradition

Notwithstanding the subjectivity of consciousness, empiricism began with John Locke (1632–1794), who accepted consciousness at face value, trusting it as a good, if imperfect, reflection of the world. Locke concisely summarized the central thrust of empiricism: "We should not judge of things by men's opinions, but of opinions by things," striving to know "the things themselves." Locke's picture of cognition is essentially Descartes'. We are acquainted not with objects but with the *ideas* that represent them. Locke differed from Descartes in denying that any of the mind's ideas are innate. Descartes had said that some ideas (such as the idea of God) cannot be found in experience but are inborn, awaiting activation by appropriate experiences. Locke said that the mind was empty of ideas at birth, being a *tabula rasa,* or blank slate, upon which experience writes. However, Locke's view is not too different from Descartes', because he held that the mind is furnished with numerous mental abilities, or faculties, that tend automatically to produce certain universally held ideas (such as the idea of God) out of the raw material of experience. Locke distinguished two sources of experience, sensation and reflection. Sensation reveals the outside world, while reflection reveals the operations of our minds.

Later empiricists took the Way of Ideas further, creating deep and unresolved questions about human knowledge.

The Irish Anglican bishop and philosopher George Berkeley (1685–1753) began to reveal the startling implications of the Way of Ideas. Berkeley's work is an outstanding example of how the new Cartesian conception of consciousness invited psychological investigation of beliefs heretofore taken for granted. The Way of Ideas assumes with common sense that there is a world outside consciousness. However, through a penetrating analysis of visual perception, Berkeley challenged that assumption. The world of consciousness is three dimensional, possessing height, width, and depth. However, Berkeley pointed out, visual perception begins with a flat, two-dimensional image on the retina, having only height and width. Thus, as someone leaves us, we *experience* her as getting farther away, while *on the retina* there is only an image getting smaller and smaller.

Berkeley argued that the third dimension of depth was a secondary sense property, a subjective construction of the Cartesian Theater. We infer the distance of objects from information on the retina (such as linear perspective) and from bodily feedback about the operations of our eyes. Painters use the first kind of cues on canvases to create illusions of depth. So far, Berkeley acted as a psychologist proposing a theory about visual perception. However, he went on to develop a striking philosophical position called immaterialism. Depth is not only an illusion when it's on canvas, it's an illusion on the retina, too. Visual experience is, in fact, two dimensional, and the third dimension is a psychological construction out of bits and pieces of experience assembled by us into the familiar three-dimensional world of consciousness. Belief in an external world depends upon belief in three-dimensional space, and Berkeley reached the breathtaking conclusion that there is no world of physical objects at all, only the world of ideas. Breathtaking Berkeley's conclusion may be, but it rests on hardheaded reasoning. Our belief that objects exist independently of our experience of them—that my car continues to exist when I'm indoors—is an act of faith. Jean Piaget and other cognitive developmentalists later extensively studied how children develop belief in the permanence of physical objects. This act of faith is regularly confirmed, but Berkeley said we have no knockdown *proof* that the world exists outside the Cartesian Theater. We see here the paranoid tendency of modern thought, the tendency to be skeptical about every belief, no matter how innocent—true—it may seem, and in Berkeley we see how this tendency depends upon psychological notions about the mind.

Skepticism was developed further by David Hume (1711–1776), one of the most important modern thinkers, and his skeptical philosophy began with psychology: "[A]ll the sciences have a relation . . . to human nature," and the only foundation "upon which they can stand" is the "science of human nature." Hume drew out the skeptical implications of the Way of Ideas by relentlessly applying empiricism to every commonsense belief. The world with which we are acquainted is world of ideas, and the mental force of association

holds ideas together. In the world of ideas, we may conceive of things that do not actually exist but are combinations of simpler ideas that the mind combines on its own. Thus, the chimerical unicorn is only an idea, being a combination of two other ideas that do correspond to objects, the idea of a horse and the idea of a horn. Likewise, God is a chimerical idea, composed out of ideas about omniscience, omnipotence, and paternal love. The self, too, dissolves in Hume's inquiry. He went looking for the self and could find in consciousness nothing that was not a sensation of the world or the body. A good empiricist, Hume thus concluded that because it cannot be observed, the self is a sort of psychological chimera, though he remained uncertain how it was constructed. Hume expunged the soul in the Cartesian Theater, leaving its screen as the only psychological reality.

Hume built up a powerful theory of the mechanics of cognition based on association of ideas. The notion that the mind has a natural tendency to link certain ideas together is a very old one, dating back to Aristotle's speculations about human memory. The term "association of ideas" was coined by Locke, who recognized its existence but viewed it as a baleful force that threatened to replace rational, logical, trains of thought with nonrational ones. Hume, however, made association into the "gravity" of the mind, as supreme in the mental world as Newton's gravity was in the physical one. Hume proposed three laws that governed how associations formed: the law of similarity (an idea presented to the mind automatically conjures up ideas that resemble it); the law of contiguity (ideas presented to the mind together become linked, so that if one is presented later, the other will automatically be brought to consciousness), and the law of causality (causes make us automatically think of their effects; effects make us automatically think of their causes). After Hume, the concept of association of ideas would gain ground, becoming a dominant force in much of philosophy and psychology until the last quarter of the twentieth century. Various philosophers, especially in Britain, developed rival theories of association, adumbrating various different laws of associative learning. The physician David Hartley (1705–1757) speculated about the possible neural substrates of association formation. Associative theory entered psychology with the work of Ebbinghaus (see below).

Human psychology seemed to make scientific knowledge unjustifiable. Our idea of causality—a basic tenet of science—is chimerical. We do not see causes themselves, only regular sequences of events, to which we add a subjective feeling, the feeling of a necessary connection between an effect and its cause. More generally, any universal assertion such as "All swans are white" cannot be proved, because they have only been confirmed by experience so far. We might one day find that some swans are black (they live in New Zealand). To critics, Hume had reached the alarming conclusion that we can know nothing for certain beyond the immediate content of our conscious sensations. Science, religion, and morality were all thrown in doubt, because all assert theses or depend on assumptions going beyond experience and which may therefore some day prove erroneous. Hume was untroubled by this conclusion, anticipating later postevolutionary pragmatism. Beliefs formed by the human mind are not provable by rational argument, Hume said, but they are reasonable and useful, aiding us mightily in everyday life. Other thinkers, however, were convinced that philosophy had taken a wrong turn.

The Realist Tradition

Hume's fellow Scottish philosophers, led by Thomas Reid (1710–1796), offered one diagnosis and remedy. Berkeley and Hume challenged common sense, suggesting that external objects do not exist, or, if they do, we cannot know them or causal relationships among them with any certainty. Reid defended common sense against philosophy, arguing that the Way of Ideas had led philosophers into a sort of madness. Reid reasserted and reworked the older realist tradition. We see objects themselves, not inner representations of them. Because we perceive the world directly, we may dismiss Berkeley's immaterialism and Hume's skepticism as absurd consequences of a mistaken notion, the Way of Ideas. Reid also defended a form of nativism. God made us, endowing us with mental powers—faculties—upon which we can rely to deliver accurate information about the outside world and its operations.

The Idealist Tradition

Another diagnosis and remedy for skepticism was offered in Germany by Immanuel Kant (1724–1804), who, like Reid, found Hume's ideas intolerable because they made genuine knowledge unreachable. Reid located Hume's error in the Way of Ideas, abandoning it for a realist analysis of cognition. Kant, on the other hand, located Hume's error in empiricism and elaborated a new version of the Way of Ideas that located truth inside the mind. Empiricists taught that ideas reflect, in Locke's phrase, "things themselves," the mind conforming itself to objects that impress (Hume's term) themselves upon it. But for Kant, skepticism deconstructed empiricism. The assumption that mind reflects reality is but an assumption, and once this assumption is revealed—by Berkeley and Hume— the ground of true knowledge disappears.

Kant upended the empiricist assumption that the mind conforms itself to objects, declaring that objects conform themselves to the mind, which imposes a universal, logically necessary structure upon experience. Things in themselves— noumena—are unknowable, but things as they appear in consciousness—phenomena—are organized by mind in such a way that we can make absolutely true statements about them. Take, for example, the problem addressed by Berkeley, the perception of depth. Things in themselves may or may not be arranged in Euclidean three-dimensional space; indeed, modern physics says that space is non-Euclidean. However, the human mind imposes Euclidean three-dimensional space on its experience of the world, so we can say truly that phenomena are necessarily arrayed in three-dimensional space. Similarly, the mind imposes other Categories of experience on noumena to construct the phenomenal world of human experience.

A science fiction example may clarify Kant's point. Imagine the citizens of Oz, the Emerald City, in whose eyes are implanted at birth contact lenses making everything a shade of green. Ozzites will make the natural assumption that things *seem* green because things *are* green. However, Ozzites' phenomena are green because of the contact lenses, not because things in themselves are green. Nevertheless, the Ozzites can assert as an absolute and irrefutable truth, "Every phenomenon is green." Kant argued that the Categories of experience are logically necessary preconditions of any experience whatsoever by all sentient beings. Therefore, since science is about the world of phenomena, we can have genuine, irrefutable, absolute knowledge of that world and should give up inquiries into Locke's "things themselves."

Kantian idealism produced a radically expansive view of the self. Instead of concluding with Hume that it is a construction out of bits and pieces of experience, Kant said that it exists prior to experience and imposes order on experience. Kant distinguished between the Empirical Ego—the fleeting contents of consciousness—and the Transcendental Ego. The Transcendental Ego is the same in all minds and imposes the Categories of understanding on experience. The self is not a construction out of experience; it is the active constructor of experience. In empiricism the self vanished; in idealism it became the only reality.

Summary: Psychology Takes Center Stage

Nineteenth-century philosophers elaborated the empiricist, realist, and idealist philosophical theories of cognition, but their essential claims remained unchanged. The stage was set for psychologists to investigate cognition empirically.

THE EARLY SCIENTIFIC PERIOD

Contemporary cognitive scientists distinguish between *procedural* and *declarative* learning, sometimes known as *knowing how* and *knowing that* (Squire, 1994). Although the distinction was drawn only recently, it will be useful for understanding the study of cognition and learning in the Early Scientific Period. A paradigmatic illustration of the two forms of learning or knowing is bicycle riding. Most of us know *how* to ride a bicycle (procedural learning), but few of us know the physical and physiological principles *that* are involved (declarative learning).

The Psychology of Consciousness

With the exception of comparative psychologists (see following), the founding generation of scientific psychologists studied human consciousness via introspection (Leahey, 2000). They were thus primarily concerned with the processes of sensation and perception, which are discussed in another chapter of this handbook. Research and theory continued to be guided by the positions already developed by philosophers. Most psychologists, including Wilhelm Wundt, the traditional founder of psychology, adopted one form or another of the Way of Ideas, although it was vehemently rejected by the gestalt psychologists, who adopted a form of realism proposed by the philosopher Franz Brentano (1838–1917; Leahey, 2000).

The Verbal Learning Tradition

One psychologist of the era, however, Hermann Ebbinghaus (1850–1909), was an exception to the focus on conscious experience, creating the experimental study of learning with his *On Memory* (1885). Ebbinghaus worked within the associative tradition, turning philosophical speculation about association formation into a scientific research program, the verbal learning tradition. Right at the outset, he faced to a problem that has bedeviled the scientific study of human cognition, making a methodological decision of great long-term importance. One might study learning by giving subjects things such as poems to learn by heart. Ebbinghaus reasoned, however, that learning a poem involves two mental processes, comprehension of the meaning of the poem and learning the words in the right order. He wanted to study the latter process, association formation in its pure state. So he made up nonsense syllables, which, he thought, had no meaning. Observe that by excluding meaning from his research program, Ebbinghaus studied procedural learning exclusively, as would the behaviorists of the twentieth century.

Ebbinghaus's nonsense syllables were typically consonant-vowel-consonant (CVC) trigrams (to make them pronounceable), and for decades to come, thousands of subjects would learn hundreds of thousands of CVC lists in serial or paired associate form. Using his lists, Ebbinghaus could empirically investigate traditional questions philosophers had asked about associative learning. How long are associations maintained? Are associations formed only between CVCs that are adjacent, or are associations formed between remote syllables?

Questions like these dominated the study of human learning until about 1970. The verbal learning tradition died for internal and external reasons. Internally, it turned out that nonsense syllables were not really meaningless, undermining their raison d'etre. Subjects privately turned nonsense into meaning by various strategies. For example, RIS looks meaningless, but could be reversed to mean SIR, or interpreted as the French word for rice. Externally, the cognitive psychologists of the so-called cognitive revolution (Leahey, 2000) wanted to study complex mental processes, including meaning, and rejected Ebbinghaus's procedures as simplistic.

The Impact of Evolution

From the time of the Greeks, philosophers were concerned exclusively with declarative cognition. Recall the warrior, jurist, and connoisseur discussed in connection with Socrates. Each was flawless in his arena of competence, the battlefield, the courtroom, and the art gallery, knowing how to fight, judge, and appreciate. Yet Socrates denied that they possessed real knowledge, because they could not state the principles guiding their actions. Exclusive concern with declarative cognition was codified in its modern form by Descartes, for whom knowledge was the preserve of human beings, who uniquely possessed language in which knowledge was formulated and communicated. Action was the realm of the beast-machine, not the human, knowing soul.

Evolution challenged philosophers' preoccupation with declarative knowledge. To begin with, evolution erased the huge and absolute gap Descartes had erected between human mind and animal mindlessness. Perhaps animals possessed simpler forms of human cognitive processes; this was the thesis of the first comparative psychologists and of today's students of animal cognition (Vauclair, 1996). On the other hand, perhaps humans were no more than complex animals, priding themselves on cognitive powers they did not really possess; this was the thesis of many behaviorists (see below).

Second, evolution forced the recognition that thought and behavior were inextricably linked. What counted in Darwin's struggle for existence was survival and reproduction, not thinking True thoughts. The American movement of pragmatism assimilated evolution into philosophy, recognizing the necessary connection between thought and behavior and formulating evolution's new criterion of truth, usefulness. The first pragmatist paper, "How to Make Our Ideas Clear," made the first point. C. S. Peirce (1838–1914) (1878) wrote that "the whole function of thought is to produce habits of action," and that what we call beliefs are "a rule of action, or, say for short, a habit." "The essence of belief," Peirce argued, "is the establishment of a habit, and different beliefs are distinguished by the different modes of action to which they give rise." Habits must have a practical significance if they are to be meaningful, Peirce went on: "Now the identity of a habit depends on how it might lead us to act. . . . Thus we come down to what is tangible and conceivably practical as the root of every real distinction of thought . . . there is no distinction so fine as to consist in anything but a possible difference in practice." In conclusion, "the rule for attaining [clear ideas] is as follows: consider what effects, which might conceivably have practical bearings, we conceive the object of our conceptions to have. Then, our conception of these effects is the whole of our conception of the object" (Peirce, 1878/1966, p. 162).

William James (1842–1910) made the second point in *Pragmatism* (1905, p. 133):

> True ideas are those that we can assimilate, validate, corroborate and verify. False ideas are those that we can not. That is the practical difference it makes for us to have true ideas. . . . The truth of an idea is not a stagnant property inherent in it. Truth happens to an idea. It becomes true, is made true by events. Its verity is in fact an event, a process.

Peirce and James rejected the philosophical search for transcendental Truth that had developed after Plato. For pragmatism there is no permanent truth, only a set of beliefs that change as circumstances demand.

With James, philosophy became psychology, and scientific psychology began to pursue its own independent agenda. Philosophers continued to struggle with metaphysics and epistemology—as James himself did when he returned to philosophy to develop his radical empiricism—but psychologists concerned themselves with effective behavior instead of truth.

Animal Psychology and the Coming of Behaviorism

In terms of psychological theory and research, the impact of evolution manifested itself first in the study of animal mind and behavior. As indicated earlier, erasing the line between humans and animals could shift psychological thinking in either of two ways. First, one might regard animals as more humanlike than Descartes had, and therefore as capable of some forms of cognition. This was the approach taken by the first generation of animal psychologists beginning with George John Romanes (1848–1894). They sought to detect signs of mental life and consciousness in animals, attributing consciousness, cognition, and problem-solving abilities to even very simple creatures (Romanes, 1883). While experiments on animal behavior were not eschewed, most of the data Romanes and others used were anecdotal in nature.

Theoretically, inferring mental processes from behavior presented difficulties. It is tempting to attribute to animals complex mental processes they may not possess, as we imagine ourselves in some animal's predicament and think our way out. Moreover, attribution of mental states to animals was complicated by the prevailing Cartesian equation of mentality with consciousness. The idea of unconscious mental states, so widely accepted today, was just beginning to develop, primarily in German post-Kantian idealism, but it was rejected by psychologists, who were followers of empiricism or realism (Ash, 1995). In the Cartesian framework, to attribute complex mental states to animals was to attribute to them *conscious* thoughts and beliefs, and critics pointed out that such inferences could not be checked by introspection, as they could be in humans. (At this same time, the validity of human introspective reports was becoming suspect, as well, strengthening critics' case again the validity of mentalist animal psychology; see Leahey, 2000.)

C. Lloyd Morgan (1852–1936) tried to cope with these problems with his famous canon of simplicity and by an innovative attempt to pry apart the identification of mentality with consciousness. Morgan (1886) distinguished objective inferences from projective—or, as he called them in the philosophical jargon of his time, ejective—inferences from animal behavior to animal mind. Imagine watching a dog sitting at a street corner at 3:30 one afternoon. As a school bus approaches, the dog gets up, wags its tail, and watches the bus slow down and then stop. The dog looks at the children getting off the bus and, when one boy gets off, it jumps on him, licks his face, and together the boy and the dog walk off down the street. Objectively, Morgan would say, we may infer certain mental powers possessed by the dog. It must possess sufficient perceptual skills to pick out one child from the crowd getting off the bus, and it must possess at least recognition memory, for it responds differently to one child among all the others. Such inferences are objective because they do not involve analogy to our own thought processes. When we see an old friend, we do not consciously match up the face we see with a stored set of remembered faces, though it is plain that such a recognition process must occur. In making an objective inference, there is no difference between our viewpoint with respect to our own behavior and with respect to the dog's, because in each case the inference that humans and dogs possess recognition memory is based on observations of behavior, not on introspective access to consciousness.

Projective inferences, however, are based on drawing unprovable analogies between our own consciousness and putative animal consciousness. We are tempted to attribute a subjective mental state, happiness, to the watchful dog by analogy with our own happiness when we greet a loved one who has been absent. Objective inferences are legitimate in science, Morgan held, because they do not depend on analogy, are not emotional, and are susceptible to later verification by experiment. Projective inferences are not scientifically legitimate because they result from attributing our own feelings to animals and may not be more objectively assessed. Morgan's distinction is important, and although it is now the basis of cognitive science, it had no contemporary impact.

In the event, skepticism about mentalistic animal psychology mounted, especially as human psychology became more objective. Romanes (1883, pp. 5–6) attempted to deflect his critics by appealing to our everyday attribution of mentality to other people without demanding introspective verification: "Skepticism of this kind is logically bound to deny evidence of mind, not only in the case of lower animals, but also in that of the higher, and even in that of men other than the skeptic himself. For all objections which could apply to the use of [inference] . . . would apply with equal force to the evidence of any mind other than that of the individual objector" (pp. 4–5).

Two paths to the study of animal and human cognition became clearly defined. One could continue with Romanes and Morgan to treat animals and humans as creatures with minds; or one could accept the logic of Romanes's rebuttal and treat humans and animals alike as creatures without minds. Refusing to anthropomorphize humans was the beginning of behaviorism, the study of learning without cognition.

Behaviorism: The Golden Age of Learning Theory

With a single exception, E. C. Tolman (see following), behaviorism firmly grasped the second of the two choices possible within the Cartesian framework. They chose to treat humans and animals as Cartesian beast-machines whose behavior could be fully explained in mechanistic causal terms without reference to mental states or consciousness. They thus dispensed with cognition altogether and studied procedural learning alone, examining how behavior is changed by exposure to physical stimuli and material rewards and

punishments. Behaviorists divided on how to treat the stubborn fact of consciousness. Methodological behaviorists admitted the existence of consciousness but said that its private, subjective nature excluded it from scientific study; they left it the arts to express, not explain, subjectivity. Metaphysical behaviorists had more imperial aims. They wanted to explain consciousness scientifically, ceding nothing to the humanities (Lashley, 1923).

Methodological Behaviorism

Although methodological behaviorists agreed that consciousness stood outside scientific psychology, they disagreed about how to explain behavior. The dominant tradition was the stimulus-response tradition originating with Thorndike, and carried along with modification by Watson, Hull, and his colleagues, and the mediational behaviorists of the 1950s. They all regarded learning as a matter of strengthening or weakening connections between environmental stimuli and the behavioral response they evoked in organisms. The most important rival form of methodological behaviorism was the cognitive-purposive psychology of Tolman and his followers, who kept alive representational theories of learning. In short, the stimulus-response tradition studied how organisms react to the world; the cognitive tradition studied how organisms learn about the world. Unfortunately, for decades it was not realized that these were complementary rather than competing lines of investigation.

Stimulus-Response Theories.   By far the most influential learning theories of the Golden Age of Theory were stimulus-response (S-R) theories. S-R theorizing began with Edward Lee Thorndike's (1874–1949) connectionism. Thorndike studied animal learning for his 1898 dissertation, published as *Animal Learning* in 1911. He began as a conventional associationist studying association of ideas in animals. However, as a result of his studies he concluded that while animals make associations, they do not associate ideas: "The effective part of the association [is] a direct bond between the situation and the impulse [to behavior]" (Thorndike, 1911, p. 98).

Thorndike constructed a number of puzzle boxes in which he placed one of his subjects, typically a young cat. The puzzle box was a sort of cage so constructed that the animal could open the door by operating a manipulandum that typically operated a string dangling in the box, which in turn ran over a pulley and opened the door, releasing the animal, who was then fed before being placed back in the box. Thorndike wanted to discover how the subject learns the correct response. He described what happens in a box in which the cat must pull a loop or button on the end of the string:

> The cat that is clawing all over the box in her impulsive struggle will probably claw the string or loop or button so as to open the door. And gradually all the other nonsuccessful impulses will be stamped out and the particular impulse leading to the successful act will be stamped in by the resulting pleasure, until, after many trials, the cat will, when put in the box, immediately claw the button or loop in a definite way. (Thorndike, 1911, p. 36)

Thorndike conceived his study as one of association-formation, and interpreted his animals' behaviors in terms of associationism:

> Starting, then, with its store of instinctive impulses, the cat hits upon the successful movement, and gradually associates it with the sense-impression of the interior of the box until the connection is perfect, so that it performs the act as soon as confronted with the sense-impression. (Thorndike, 1911, p. 38)

The phrase *trial-and-error*—or perhaps more exactly trial-and-success—learning aptly describes what these animals did in the puzzle boxes. Placed inside, they try out (or, as Skinner called it later, emit) a variety of familiar behaviors. In cats, it was likely to try squeezing through the bars, clawing at the cage, and sticking its paws between the bars. Eventually, the cat is likely to scratch at the loop of string and so pull on it, finding its efforts rewarded: The door opens and it escapes, only to be caught by Thorndike and placed back in the box. As these events are repeated, the useless behaviors die away, or extinguish, and the correct behavior is done soon after entering the cage; the cat has learned the correct response needed to escape.

Thorndike proposed three laws of learning. One was the *law of exercise,* which stated that use of a response strengthens its connection to the stimuli controlling it, while disuse weakens them. Another was the *law of readiness,* having to do with the physiological basis of the law of effect. Thorndike proposed that if the neurons connected to a given action are prepared to fire (and cause the action), their neural firing will be experienced as pleasure, but that if they are inhibited from firing, displeasure will be felt.

The most famous and debated of Thorndike's laws was the *law of effect:*

> The Law of Effect is that: Of several responses made to the same situation, those which are accompanied or closely followed by satisfaction to the animal will, other things being equal, be more firmly connected with the situation, so that, when it recurs, they will be more likely to recur; those which are accompanied or closely followed by discomfort to the animal will, other things being equal, have their connections with that situation weakened, so that, when it recurs, they will be less likely to occur. The greater the satisfaction or discomfort, the greater the strengthening or weakening of the bond. (Thorndike, 1911, p. 244)

Thorndike seems here to state a truism not in need of scientific elaboration, that organisms learn how to get pleasurable things and learn how to avoid painful things. However, questions surround the law of effect. Is reward *necessary* for learning? Reward and punishment surely affect behavior, but must they be present for learning to occur? What about a reward or punishment makes it change behavior? Is it the pleasure and pain they bring, as Thorndike said, or the fact that they inform us that we have just done the right or wrong action? Are associations formed gradually or all at once?

Thorndike laid out the core of stimulus-response learning theory. It was developed by several generations of psychologists, including E. R. Guthrie (1886–1959) and most notably by Clark Hull (1884–1952), his collaborator Kenneth Spence (1907–1967), and their legions of students and grand-students. Hull and Spence turned S-R theory into a formidably complex logico-mathematical structure capable of terrifying students, but they did not change anything essential in Thorndike's ideas. Extensive debate took place on the questions listed above (and others). For example, Hull said reward was necessary for learning, that it operated by drive reduction, and that many trials were needed for an association to reach full strength. Guthrie, on the other hand, said that mere contiguity between S and R was sufficient to form an association between them and that associative bonds reach full strength on a single trial. These theoretical issues, plus those raised by Tolman, drove the copious research of the Golden Age of Theory (Leahey, 2000; Leahey & Harris, 2001).

When S-R theorists turned to human behavior, they developed the concept of mediation (Osgood, 1956). Humans, they conceded, had symbolic processes that animals lacked, and they proposed to handle them by invoking covert stimuli and responses. Mediational theories were often quite complex, but the basic idea was simple. A rat learning to distinguish a square-shaped stimulus from a triangular one responds only to the physical properties of each stimulus. An adult human, on the other hand, will privately label each stimulus as "square" or "triangle," and it is this mediating covert labeling response that controls the subject's observable behavior. In this view, animals learned simple one-stage S-R connections, while humans learned more sophisticated S-r-s-R connections (where *s* and *r* refer to the covert responses and the stimuli they cause). The great attraction of mediational theory was that it gave behaviorists interested in human cognitive processes a theoretical language shorn of mentalistic connotations (Osgood, 1956), and during the 1950s and early 1960s mediational theories dominated the study of human cognition. However, once the concept of information became available, mediational theorists—and certainly their students—became information processing theorists (Leahey, 2000).

Edward Chace Tolman's Cognitive Behaviorism. E. C. Tolman (1886–1959) consistently maintained that he was a behaviorist, and in fact wrote a classic statement of methodological behaviorism as a psychological program (Tolman, 1935). However, he was a behaviorist of an odd sort, as he (Tolman, 1959) and S-R psychologists (Spence, 1948) recognized, being influenced by gestalt psychology and the neorealists (see below). Although it is anachronistic to do so, the best way to understand Tolman's awkward position in the Golden Age is through the distinction between procedural and declarative learning. Ebbinghaus, Thorndike, Hull, Guthrie, Spence, and the entire S-R establishment studied only procedural learning. They did not have the procedural/declarative distinction available to them, and in any case thought that consciousness—which formulates and states declarative knowledge—was irrelevant to the causal explanation of behavior. S-R theories said learning came about through the manipulation of physical stimuli and material rewards and punishments. Animals learn, and can, of course, never say why. Even if humans might occasionally figure out the contingencies of reinforcement in a situation, S-R theory said that they were simply describing the causes of their own behavior the way an outside observer does (Skinner, 1957). As Thorndike had said, reward and punishment stamp in or stamp out S-R connections; consciousness had nothing to do with it.

Tolman, on the other hand, wanted to study cognition—declarative knowledge in the traditional sense—but was straitjacketed by the philosophical commitments of behaviorism and the limited conceptual tools of the 1930s and 1940s. Tolman anticipated, but could never quite articulate, the ideas of later cognitive psychology.

Tolman's theory and predicament are revealed by his "Disproof of the Law of Effect" (Tolman, Hall, & Bretnall, 1932). In this experiment, human subjects navigated a pegboard maze, placing a metal stylus in the left or right of a series of holes modeling the left-right choices of an animal in a multiple T-maze. There were a variety of conditions, but the most revealing was the "bell-right-shock" group, whose subjects received an electric shock when they put the stylus in the correct holes. According to the Law of Effect these subjects should not learn the maze because correct choices were followed by pain, but they learned at the same rate as other groups. While this result seemed to disprove the law of effect, its real significance was unappreciated because the concept of information had not yet been formulated (see below). In Tolman's time, reinforcers (and punishers) were thought of only in terms of their drive-reducing or affective properties. However, they possess informational properties, too. A reward is pleasant and may reduce hunger or thirst, but rewards typically provide information that one has made the correct choice, while punishers are unpleasant and ordinarily convey that one has made the wrong choice. Tolman's "bell-right-shock" group pried apart the affective and informational qualities of pain by making pain carry the information that the subject had made the right choice. Tolman showed—but could not articulate—that it's the informational value of behavioral consequences that cause learning, not their affective value.

Nevertheless, Tolman tried to offer a cognitive theory of learning with his concept of cognitive maps (Tolman, 1948). S-R theorists viewed maze learning as acquiring a series of left-right responses triggered by the stimuli at the various choice points in the maze. Against this, Tolman proposed that animals and humans acquire a representation—a mental map—of the maze that guides their behavior. Tolman and his followers battled Hullians through the 1930s, 1940s, and into the 1950s, generating a mass of research findings and theoretical argument. Although Tolman's predictions were often vindicated by experimental results, the vague nature of his theory and his attribution of thought to animals limited his theory's impact (Estes et al., 1954).

Metaphysical Behaviorism

Metaphysical behaviorists took a more aggressive stance toward consciousness than methodological behaviorists. They believed that scientific psychology should explain, not shun, consciousness. Two reasons guided them. First, they wanted to achieve a comprehensive scientific account of everything human, and since consciousness is undoubtedly something humans have, it should not be ceded to the humanities (Lashley, 1923). Second, stimuli registered only privately in a person's experience sometimes affects behavior (Skinner, 1957). If I have a headache, it exists only in my private consciousness, but it alters my behavior: I take aspirin, become irritable, and tell people I have a headache. Excluding private stimuli from psychology by methodological fiat would produce incomplete theories of behavior. (This is not the place to discuss the various and subtle ways metaphysical behaviorists had of explaining or dissolving consciousness. I will focus only on how such behaviorists approached learning and cognition.) Metaphysical behaviorism came in two forms, physiological behaviorism and radical behaviorism.

Physiological Behaviorism.   The source of physiological behaviorism was Russian objective psychology, and its greatest American exponent was Karl Lashley, who coined the term "methodological behaviorism," only to reject it (Lashley, 1923, pp. 243–244):

> Let me cast off the lion's skin. My quarrel with [methodological] behaviorism is not that it has gone too far, but that it has hesitated . . . that it has failed to develop its premises to their logical conclusion. To me the essence of behaviorism is the belief that the study of man will reveal nothing except what is adequately describable in the concepts of mechanics and chemistry. . . . I believe that it is possible to construct a physiological psychology which will meet the dualist on his own ground . . . and show that [his] data can be embodied in a mechanistic system. . . . Its physiological account of behavior will also be a complete and adequate account of all the phenomena of consciousness . . . demanding that all psychological data, however obtained, shall be subjected to physical or physiological interpretation.

Ultimately, Lashley said, the choice between behaviorism and traditional psychology came down to a choice between two "incompatible" worldviews, "scientific versus humanistic." It had been demanded of psychology heretofore that "it must leave room for human ideals and aspirations." But "other sciences have escaped this thralldom," and so must psychology escape from "metaphysics and values" and "mystical obscurantism" by turning to physiology.

For the study of learning, the most important physiological behaviorist was Ivan Petrovich Pavlov (1849–1936). Although Pavlov is mostly thought of as the discoverer of classical or Pavlovian conditioning, he was first and foremost a physiologist in the tradition of Sechenov. For him, the phenomena of Pavlovian conditioning were of interest because they might reveal the neural processes underlying associative learning—he viewed all behavior as explicable via association—and his own theories about conditioning were couched in neurophysiological terms.

The differences between Pavlov's and Thorndike's procedures for studying learning posed two questions for the associative tradition they both represented. Pavlov delivered an unconditional stimulus (food) that elicited the behavior, or unconditional response (salivation), that he wished to study. He paired presentation of the US with an unrelated conditional stimulus (only in one obscure study did he use a bell); finding that gradually the CS came to elicit salivation (now called the conditional response), too. Thorndike had to await the cat's first working of the manipulandum before rewarding

it with food. In Pavlov's setup, the food came first and caused the unconditional response; in Thorndike's, no obvious stimulus caused the first correct response, and the food followed its execution.

Were Pavlov and Thorndike studying two distinct forms of learning, or were they merely using different methodologies to study the same phenomenon? Some psychologists, including Skinner, believed the former, either on the operationist grounds that the procedures themselves defined different forms of learning, or because different nervous systems were involved in the two cases (Hearst, 1975). Although this distinction between instrumental (or operant) and classical, or Pavlovian (or respondent) conditioning has become enshrined in textbooks, psychologists in the S-R tradition believed S-R learning took place in both procedures. The debate was never resolved but has been effaced by the return of cognitive theories of animal learning, for which the distinction is not important.

The second question raised by Pavlov's methods was intimately connected to the first. Exactly what was being associated as learning proceeded? In philosophical theory, association took place between ideas, but this mentalistic formulation was, of course, anathema to behaviorists. Thorndike began the S-R tradition by asserting that the learned connection (his preferred term) was directly between stimulus and response, not between mental ideas of the two. Pavlovian conditioning could be interpreted in the same way, saying that the animal began with an innate association between US and UR and created a new association between CS and CR. Indeed, this was for years the dominant behaviorist interpretation of Pavlovian conditioning, the stimulus substitution theory (Leahey & Harris, 2001), because it was consistent with the thesis that all learning was S-R learning.

However, Pavlovian conditioning was open to an alternative interpretation closer to the philosophical notion of association of ideas, which said that ideas that occur together in experience become linked (see above). Thus, one could say that as US and CS were paired, they became associated, so that when presented alone, the CS evoked the US, which in turn caused the CR to occur. Pavlov's own theory of conditioning was a materialistic version of this account, proposing that the brain center activated by the US became neurally linked to the brain center activated by the CS, so when the latter occurred, it activated the US's brain center, causing the CR. American behaviorists who believed in two kinds of learning never adopted Pavlov's physiologizing and avoided mentalism by talking about S-S associations. It was sometimes said that Tolman was an S-S theorist, but this distorted the holistic nature of his cognitive maps. As truly cognitive theories of learning returned in the 1970s, Pavlovian and even instrumental learning were increasingly interpreted involving associations between ideas—now called "representations" (Leahey & Harris, 2001), as in the pioneering cognitive theory of Robert Rescorla (1988).

Radical Behaviorism.   A completely different form of metaphysical behaviorism was developed by B. F. Skinner (1904–1990). Skinner extended to psychology the philosophy of neorealism propounded by a number of American philosophers after 1910 (Smith, 1986). The neorealists revived the old realist claim that the Way of Ideas was mistaken, that perception of objects was direct and not mediated by intervening ideas. Tolman, too, built his early theories on neorealism but later returned to the Way of Ideas with the concept of the cognitive map (Smith, 1986). Skinner never wavered from realism, working out the radical implication that if there are no ideas, there is no private world of consciousness or mind to be populated by them. Introspective psychology was thus an illusion, and psychology should be redefined as studying the interactive relationship between an organism and the environment in which it behaves. The past and present environments provide the stimuli that set the occasion for behavior, and the organism's actions operate (hence the term *operant*) on the environment. Actions have consequences, and these consequences shape the behavior of the organism.

Skinner's thinking is often misrepresented as a S-R psychology in the mechanistic tradition of Thorndike, John B. Watson (1878–1958), or Clark Hull. In fact, Skinner rejected—or, more precisely, stood apart from—the mechanistic way of thinking about living organisms that had begun with Descartes. For a variety of reasons, including its successes, its prestige, and the influence of positivism, physics has been treated as the queen of the sciences, and scientists in other fields, including psychology, have almost uniformly envied it, seeking to explain their phenomena of interest in mechanical-causal terms. A paradigmatic case in point was Clark Hull, who acquired a bad case of physics-envy from reading Newton's *Principia,* and his logico-mathematical theory of learning was an attempt to emulate his master. Skinner renounced physics as the model science for the study of behavior, replacing it with Darwinian evolution and selection by consequences (Skinner, 1969). In physical-model thinking, behaviors are caused by stimuli that mechanically provoke them. In evolution, the appearance of new traits is unpredictable, and their fate is determined by the consequences they bring. Traits that favor survival and reproduction increase in frequency over the generations; traits that hamper survival and reproduction decrease in frequency. Similarly, behaviors are emitted, and whether they are retained (learned) or lost

(extinguished) depends on the consequences of reinforcement or nonreinforcement.

As a scientist, Skinner, like Thorndike, Hull, and Tolman, studied animals almost exclusively. However, unlike them Skinner wrote extensively about human behavior in a speculative way he called interpretation. His most important such work was *Verbal Behavior* (1957), in which he offered a theory of human cognition. Beginning with Socrates, the central quest of epistemology was understanding the uniquely human ability to form universal concepts, such as *cat, dog,* or *Truth.* From Descartes onward, this ability was linked to language, the unique possession of humans, in which we can state universal definitions. In either case, universal concepts were the possession of the human mind, whether as abstract images (Aristotle) or as sentences (Descartes). Skinner, of course, rejected the existence of mind, and therefore of any difference between explaining animal and human behavior. Mediational theorists allowed for an attenuated difference, but Skinner would have none of it. He wrote that although "most of the experimental work responsible for the advance of the experimental analysis of behavior has been carried out on other species . . . the results have proved to be surprisingly free of species restrictions . . . and its methods can be extended to human behavior without serious modification" (Skinner, 1957, p. 3). The final goal of the experimental analysis of behavior is a science of human behavior using the same principles first applied to animals.

In *Verbal Behavior,* Skinner offered a behavioristic analysis of universal concepts with the technical term *tact,* and drew out its implications for other aspects of mind and cognition. A tact is a verbal operant under the stimulus control of some part of the physical environment, and the verbal community reinforces correct use of tacts. So a child is reinforced by parents for emitting the sound "dog" in the presence of a dog (Skinner, 1957). Such an operant is called a tact because it "makes contact with" the physical environment. Tacts presumably begin as names (e.g., for the first dog a child learns to label "dog"), but as the verbal community reinforces the emission of the term to similar animals, the tact becomes generalized. Of course, discrimination learning is also involved, as the child will not be reinforced for calling cats "dog." Eventually, through behavior shaping, the child's "dog" response will occur only in the presence of dogs and not in their absence. For Skinner, the situation is no different from that of a pigeon reinforced for pecking keys only when they are illuminated any shade of green and not otherwise. Skinner reduced the traditional notion of reference to a functional relationship among a response, its discriminative stimuli, and its reinforcer.

Skinner's radical analysis of tacting raises an important general point about his treatment of human consciousness, his notion of private stimuli. Skinner believed that earlier methodological behaviorists such as Tolman and Hull were wrong to exclude private events (such as mental images or toothaches) from behaviorism simply because such events are private. Skinner held that part of each person's environment includes the world inside her or his skin, those stimuli to which the person has privileged access. Such stimuli may be unknown to an external observer, but they are experienced by the person who has them, can control behavior, and so must be included in any behaviorist analysis of human behavior. Many verbal statements are under such control, including complex tacts. For example: "My tooth aches" is a kind of tacting response controlled by a certain kind of painful inner stimulation.

This simple analysis implies a momentous conclusion. How do we come to be able to make correct private tacts? Skinner's answer was that the verbal community has trained us to observe our private stimuli by reinforcing utterances that refer to them. It is useful for parents to know what is distressing a child, so they attempt to teach a child self-reporting verbal behaviors. "My tooth aches" indicates a visit to the dentist, not the podiatrist. Such responses thus have Darwinian survival value. It is these self-observed private stimuli that constitute consciousness. It therefore follows that human consciousness is a product of the reinforcing practices of a verbal community. A person raised by a community that did not reinforce self-description would not be conscious in anything but the sense of being awake. That person would have no self-consciousness.

Self-description also allowed Skinner to explain apparently purposive verbal behaviors without reference to intention or purpose. For example, "I am looking for my glasses" seems to describe my intentions, but Skinner (1957) argued: "Such behavior must be regarded as equivalent to *When I have behaved in this way in the past, I have found my glasses and have then stopped behaving in this way*" (p. 145). Intention is a mentalistic term Skinner has reduced to the physicalistic description of one's bodily state. Skinner finally attacked the citadel of the Cartesian soul, thinking. Skinner continued to exorcise Cartesian mentalism by arguing that "thought is simply *behavior*." Skinner rejected Watson's view that thinking is subvocal behavior, for much covert behavior is not verbal yet can still control overt behavior in a way characteristic of "thinking": "*I think I shall be going* can be translated *I find myself going*" (p. 449), a reference to self-observed, but nonverbal, stimuli.

Skinner's radical behaviorism was certainly unique, breaking with all other ways of explaining mind and behavior. Its impact, however, has been limited (Leahey, 2000). At the dawn of the new cognitive era, *Verbal Behavior* received a severe drubbing from linguist Noam Chomsky (1959) from which its theses never recovered. The computer model of mind replaced the mediational model and isolated the radical behaviorists. Radical behaviorism carries on after Skinner's death, but it is little mentioned elsewhere in psychology.

THE MODERN SCIENTIFIC PERIOD

The modern era in the study of cognition opened with the invention of the digital electronic computer during World War II. The engineers, logicians, and mathematicians who created the first computers developed key notions that eventually gave rise to contemporary cognitive psychology.

The Three Key Ideas of Computing

Feedback

One of the standard objections to seeing living beings as machines was that behavior is purposive and goal-directed, flexibly striving for something not yet in hand (or paw). James (1890) pointed to purposive striving for survival when he called mechanism an "impertinence," and Tolman's retention of purpose as a basic feature of behavior set his behaviorism sharply apart from S-R theories, which treated purpose as something to be explained away (Hull, 1937). Feedback reconciles mechanism and goal-oriented behavior.

As a practical matter, feedback had been employed since the Industrial Revolution. For example, a "governor" typically regulated the temperature of steam engines. This was a rotating shaft whose speed increased as pressure in the engine's boiler increased. Brass balls on hinges were fitted to the shaft so that as its speed increased, centrifugal force caused the balls to swing away from the shaft. Things were arranged so that when the balls reached a critical distance from the shaft—that is, when the boiler's top safe pressure was reached—heat to the boiler was reduced, the pressure dropped, the balls descended, and heat could return. The system had a purpose—maintain the correct temperature in the boiler—and responded flexibly to relevant changes in the environment—changes of temperature in the boiler.

But it was not until World War II that feedback was formulated as an explicit concept by scientists working on the problem of guidance (e.g., building missiles capable of tracking a moving target; Rosenblueth, Wiener, & Bigelow, 1943/1966). The standard example of feedback today is a thermostat. A feedback system has two key components, a sensor and a controller. The sensor detects the state of a relevant variable in the environment. One sets the thermostat to the critical value of the variable of interest, the temperature of a building. A sensor in the thermostat monitors the temperature, and when it falls below or above critical value, the controller activates the heating or cooling system. When the temperature moves back to its critical value, the sensor detects this and the controller turns off the heat pump. The notion of feedback is that a system, whether living or mechanical, detects a state of the world, acts to alter the state of the world, which alteration is detected, changing the behavior of the system, in a complete feedback loop. A thermostat plus heat pump is thus a purposive system, acting flexibly to pursue a simple goal. It is, of course at the same time a machine whose behavior could be explained in purely causal, physical, terms. Teleology and mechanism are not incompatible.

Information

The concept of information is now so familiar to us that we take it for granted. But in fact it is a subtle concept that engineers building the first computers recognized by the middle of the twentieth century (MacKay, 1969). We have already seen how Tolman could have used it to better understand the nature of reward and punishment. Before the advent of the computer, information was hard to separate from its physical embodiment in parchment or printed pages. Today, however, the separation of information from physical embodiment is a threat to publishers because the content of a book may be scanned and digitized and then accessed by anyone for free. Of course, I could lend someone a book for free, but then I would no longer have its information, but if I share the information itself on a disk or as a download, I still have it, too. The closest the premodern world came to the concept of information was the *idea,* but looking back from our modern vantage point we can see that philosophers tended to assume ideas had to have some kind of existence, either in a transcendent realm apart from the familiar material world, as in Plato, or in a substantial (though nonphysical) soul, Descartes' *res cogitans.* Realists denied that ideas existed, the upshot being Skinnerian radical behaviorism, which can tolerate the idea of information no more than the idea of a soul.

The concept of information allows us to give a more general formulation of feedback. What's important to a feedback system is its use of information, not its mode of physical operation. The thermostat again provides an example. Most traditional thermostats contain a strip of metal that is really two metals with different coefficients of expansion. The strip then bends or unbends as the temperature changes, turning the heat pump on or off as it closes or opens an electrical circuit. Modern buildings, on the other hand, often contain sensors in each room that relay information about room tem-

perature to a central computer that actually operates the heat pump. Nevertheless, each system embodies the same informational feedback loop.

This fact seems simple, but it is in fact of extraordinary importance. We can think about *information as such,* completely separately from *any* physical embodiment. My description of a thermostat in the preceding section implicitly depended on the concept of information, as I was able to explain what *any* thermostat does without reference to how any *particular* thermostat works. My description of the older steam engine governor, however, depended critically on its actual physical operation.

In any information system we find a kind of dualism. On the one hand, we have a physical object such as a book or thermostat. On the other hand, we have the information it holds or the information processes that guide its operation. The information in the book can be stored in print, in a computer's RAM, on a hard-drive, in bubble memory, or be floating about the World Wide Web. The information flows of a thermostat can be understood without regard to how the thermostat works. This suggests, then, that mind can be understood as information storage (memory) and processes (memory encoding and retrieval, and thinking). Doing so respects the insight of dualism, that mind is somehow independent of body, without introducing all the problems of a substantial soul. Soul is information.

The concept of information opened the way for a new cognitive psychology. One did not need to avoid the mind, as methodological behaviorists wanted, nor did one have to expunge it, as metaphysical behaviorists wanted. Mind was simply information being processed by a computer we only just learned we had, our brains, and we could theorize about information flows without worrying about how the brain actually managed them. Broadbent's *Perception and Communication* (1958), Neisser's *Cognitive Psychology* (1967), and Atkinson and Shiffrin's "Human Memory: A Proposed System and Its Control Processes" (1968) were the manifestos of the information-processing movement. Broadbent critically proposed treating stimuli as information, not as physical events. Neisser's chapters described information flows from sensation to thinking. Atkinson and Shiffrin's model of information flow (Figure 6.3) became so standard that it's still found in textbooks today, despite significant changes in the way cognitive psychologists treat the details of cognition (Izawa, 1999).

Information from the senses is first registered in near-physical form by sensory memory. The process of pattern recognition assigns informational meaning to the physical stimuli held in sensory memory. Concomitantly, attention focuses on important streams of information, attenuating or

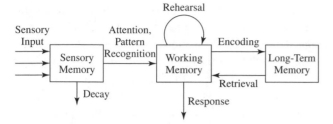

Figure 6.3 The standard model of information processing.

blocking others from access to consciousness. Organized information is stored briefly in working, or short-term, memory, and some manages to get stored in long-term, or permanent, memory. There is, of course, loss and distortion of information along the way, so that what's remembered is very seldom a veridical record of what happened.

Only one aspect of contemporary cognitive psychology was missing from Neisser and Atkinson and Shiffrin, the computational metaphor of mind, then just making headway in psychology.

The Program: Computation

In the information-processing perspective developed by Broadbent, Neisser, and Atkinson and Shiffrin, the notion of *processing* remained vague. Information itself is passive: It has to be transformed and manipulated in order to effect behavior. This problem was solved by the development of another concept that today we take for granted, the computer program. Again, the idea seems obvious, but did not come into existence until the 1930s in the work of Alan Turing (Hodge, 2000) and John von Neumann (MacRae,.1999).

Previously, all machines, including the calculators built by Blaise Pascal, Gottfried Leibniz, and Charles Babbage, were dedicated, single-purpose machines whose mechanical workings defined the function they carried out. Computers, however, are general-purpose machines, capable of performing a variety of tasks. Their operations are determined not by their mechanical workings but by their programs, a series of instructions the computer carries out. Because they manipulate information, programs are independent of their physical substrate. A program written in BASIC (or any other computer language) will run on any computer that understands BASIC, whatever its physical makeup, whether it be an Apple, PC, or a mainframe. As Turing (1950) pointed out, a human being following a sequence of steps written on slips of paper is functionally equivalent to a computer.

The computational approach to mind was complete and is known in philosophy as *functionalism*. The mind is essentially a computer program implemented in a meat-machine (Clark, 2001) rather than a silicon-and-metal machine. The

program of the mind acts on and controls the flow of information through the human information-processing system the way a computer's program controls the flow of information through a computer. The program arrives at decisions and controls the system's—the body's—behavior. The mind is what the brain does (Pinker, 1998). Cognitive psychology becomes a form of reverse engineering. In reverse engineering, computer scientists take a chip and without opening it up, study its input-output functions and try to deduce what program controls the chip's processing. Often this is done to imitate an existing chip without violating the patent holder's rights. In psychology, experiments reveal the human mind's input-output functions, and psychological theories attempt to specify the computational functions that intervene between input and output.

The Fruits of Computation: Cognitive Science

Mind Design and the Architectures of Cognition

Ironically, the first application of the computer conception of mind arose not in psychology but in computer science, when Alan Turing (1950) proposed that computer programs might emulate human intelligence. Turing put forward no new analysis of cognition but provided a now famous test by which computer intelligence might be recognized. A person interacts as in a chat room with two entities, one of which is a human being and the other of which is a computer program. Turing said that the program would have to be called intelligent when the person could not tell if his or her conversational partner was human or computer. As yet, no program has passed the Turing test in the form Turing originally suggested.

Obviously, constructing artificial intelligences has great practical value. For cognitive psychology, the value of mind design (Haugeland, 1981, 1985) is that it forces theorists to think deeply and precisely about the requirements for intelligent cognition. In an influential book, Marr (1982) specified three hierarchically arranged levels at which computational analysis takes place. In the case of artificial intelligence, the levels define the job of making a mind, while in the case of psychology—which studies an already evolved intelligence—they define three levels of reverse-engineering psychological theory. The levels are most readily described from the standpoint of artificial intelligence.

- The *cognitive level* specifies the task the AI system is to perform.
- The *algorithm level* specifies the computer programming that effects the task.

• The *implementation level* specifies how the hardware device is to carry out the program instructions.

The cognitive level is a detailed analysis of what a system must be able to know and do in order to perform a specified job. In certain respects, this is psychologically the most revealing level, because so much of what we know and do involves consciousness not at all. It is easy for me to walk downstairs and retrieve a book, and I can often do it while my conscious mind is engaged in thinking about writing this chapter. However, we find that building a robot to do the same thing reveals deep problems that my mind/brain solves effortlessly. Even recognizing an open doorway requires complexities of scene analysis that no robot can yet carry out.

Once one has specified the cognitive requirements of a task, the next job is writing the program that can get the job done. This is the algorithm level, defining the exact computational steps the system will perform. In psychology, this is the level of psychological theory, as we attempt to describe how our existing human program operates. An artificial system, on the other hand may achieve the same results with a very different program. For example, a human chess master and a chess-playing program such as Deep Blue solve the cognitive-level problems of chess very differently. A computational psychological theory of chess playing needs to replicate the mental steps of the human player; the computational AI theory does not.

Finally, one implements the program in a working physical system. In AI, this means building or programming an intelligent system; in psychology it means working out the neuroscience about the workings of the human meat machine. Within Marr's broad framework, two different approaches to mind design—two architectures of cognition—came into existence, the symbol-system hypothesis and connectionism.

The Symbol-System Hypothesis

Herbert Simon and his colleague Allan Newell first drew the connection between human and computer cognition at the RAND Corporation in 1954 (Simon, 1996). Simon was by training an economist (he won the 1981 Nobel Prize in that field). As a graduate student, Simon had been greatly influenced by the writings of E. C. Tolman, and was well schooled in formal logic. Previously, computers had been seen as glorious, if flexible, number crunchers, calculators writ large. Simon saw that computers could be more fruitfully and generally viewed as symbol manipulators.

By the early twentieth century, logicians had established the concept of interpreted formal systems, in which propositions stated in language could be reduced to abstract formal statements and manipulated by formal rules. For example, the statement "If it snows, then school will be closed" could be represented by $p \supset q$, where p = "it snows," q = "school closes," and $\supset$ = the logical relation if . . . then. If one now learns that it is snowing, one may validly infer that school will be closed. This inference may be represented as the formal argument *modus ponens:*

1. $p \supset q$
2. p
3. therefore, q

The significance of the translation into abstract, formal symbols is that we can see that it is possible to reason through a situation without knowledge of the content of the propositions. *Modus ponens* is a valid inference whether the topic is the connection between snow and school closings or whether a pair of gloves fits a murder suspect and the verdict ("If the gloves don't fit, you must acquit.") Mathematics is a formal system in which the variables have quantitative values; logic is a formal system in which the variables have semantic values. In both systems, valid reasoning is possible without knowledge of the variables' value or meaning.

Simon proposed, then, that human minds and computer programs are both *symbol systems* (Simon, 1980). Both receive informational input, represent the information internally as formal symbols, and manipulate them by logical rules to reach valid conclusions. Simon and Newell turned the notion into the pioneering computer simulation of thought, the General Problem Solver (Newell, Shaw, & Simon, 1958). Simon's symbol-system hypothesis established the first of the two architectures of cognition inspired by the analogy between human being and computer, and it was firmly ensconced in psychology and artificial intelligence by the late 1970s. It gave rise to the creation of a new discipline, cognitive science, devoted to the study of *informavores,* creatures that consume information (Pylyshyn, 1984). It brought together cognitive psychologists, computer scientists, philosophers, and—especially in the 1990s, the decade of the brain—neuroscientists. (Space precludes a treatment of cognitive neuroscience. See Gazzinaga, Ivry, and Mangun [1998] for an excellent survey.)

The Connectionist, Subsymbolic, Hypothesis

From the dawn of the computer era, there had been two approaches to information processing by machines, serial processing and parallel processing. In a serial processing system, for example in home PCs and Apples, a single central processing unit (CPU) processes the steps of a program one at a time, albeit very quickly. The flow diagrams of information-processing psychology implicitly assumed that the human mind was a serial processor. Figure 6.3, for example, shows that multiple streams of input to sensory memory are reduced to a single stream by attention and pattern recognition. Likewise, the symbol-system hypothesis was predicated on a serial processing architecture, the human CPU executing one logical step at a time.

In parallel processing, multiple data streams are processed simultaneously by multiple processors. In the most interesting of these systems, distributed cognition systems (Rumelhart, McClelland, & PDR Research Group, 1986), there are large numbers of weak processors, in contrast to serial systems' single powerful processor.

Obviously, parallel-processing computers are potentially much more powerful than single CPU machines, but for a long time obstacles stood in the way of constructing them. Parallel machines are more physically complex than sequential machines, and they are vastly more difficult to program, since one must somehow coordinate the work of the multiple processors in order to avoid chaos. With regard to self-programming machines, there is the special difficulty of figuring out how to get feedback information about the results of behavior to interior ("hidden") units lying between input and output units. Since sequential machines were great successes very early on, and the power of the parallel architecture seemed unnecessary, work on parallel-processing computers virtually ceased in the 1960s.

In the 1980s, however, developments in both computer science and psychology converged to revive the fortunes of parallel-processing architectures. Although serial processors continued to gain speed, designers were pushing up against the limits of how fast electrons could move through silicon. At the same time, computer scientists were tackling jobs demanding ever-greater computing speed, making a change to parallel processing desirable. For example, consider the problem of computer vision, which must be solved if effective robots are to be built. Imagine a computer graphic made up of 256×256 pixels. For a serial computer to recognize such an image, it would have to compute one at a time the value of $256 \times 256 = 65,536$ pixels, which might take more time than allowed for a response to occur. On the other hand, a parallel-processing computer containing 256×256 interconnected processors can assign one to compute the value of a single pixel and so can process the graphic in a tiny fraction of a second.

In psychology, continued failings of the symbolic paradigm made parallel, connectionist processing an attractive alternative to serial symbol systems. Two issues were especially important for the new connectionists. First of all,

traditional AI, while it had made advances on tasks humans find intellectually taxing, such as chess playing, was persistently unable to get machines to perform the sorts of tasks that people do without the least thought, such as recognizing patterns. Perhaps most importantly to psychologists, the behavior that they had most intensively studied for decades—learning—remained beyond the reach of programmed computers, and the development of parallel machines that could actually learn was quite exciting. That the brain could solve these problems while supercomputers could not suggested that the brain was not a serial machine.

The other shortcoming of symbolic AI that motivated the new connectionists was the plain fact that the brain is not a sequential computing device. If we regard neurons as small processors, then it becomes obvious that the brain is much more like a massively parallel processor than it is like a PC or an Apple. The brain contains thousands of interconnected neurons, all of which are working at the same time. As Rumelhart et al. (1986) announced, they aimed to replace the computer model in psychology with the brain model. The interconnected processors of connectionist models function like neurons: Each one is activated by input and then "fires," or produces output, depending on the summed strengths of its input. Assembled properly, such a network will learn to respond in stable ways to different inputs just as organisms do: Neural nets, as such processor assemblages are often called, learn.

Connectionism suggested a new strategy for explaining cognition. The symbol-system approach depends, as we have seen, on the idea that intelligence consists in the manipulation of symbols by formal computational rules. Like the symbol-system approach, connectionism is computational, because connectionists try to write computer models that emulate human behavior. But connectionist systems use very different rules and representations (Dreyfus & Dreyfus, 1986; Smolensky, 1988): weighted mathematical connections between neuronlike units rather that logical manipulation of symbols that map on to propositions.

Connectionist systems differ critically from symbolic systems at Marr's implementation and algorithm levels. Analysis at the cognitive level is indifferent between the two architectures. However, at the implementation level, the nature of the hardware (or wetware, in the case of the brain) becomes crucial, because the implementation consists in executing a program with a real machine or real person, and different computers implement the same cognitive task in different ways. One of the two main issues that separate the symbol-system architecture of cognition from its connectionist rival concerns whether or not psychological theories of learning and cognition need be concerned with the implementation level. According to the symbol-system view, the implementation of programs in a brain or a computer may be safely ignored at the cognitive and algorithm levels, while, according to the connectionist view, theorizing at higher levels must be constrained by the nature of the machine that will carry out the computations.

The second main issue concerns the algorithmic level of intelligence. William James (1890) first addressed the fundamental problem. James observed that when we first learn a skill, we must consciously think about what to do; as we become more experienced, consciousness deserts the task and we carry it out automatically, without conscious thought. One of the attractions of the symbolic paradigm is that it fits our conscious experience of thought: We think one thought at a time to the solution of a problem. The symbolic paradigm assumes that once a task becomes mastered and unconscious, we continue to think one thought at a time with consciousness subtracted. On the other hand, connectionism suggests that nonconscious thought may be very different from conscious thought.

Smolensky (1988) analyzed the architecture of cognition from the perspective of how thoughtful processes become intuitive actions. Smolensky's framework distinguishes two levels, the conscious processor and the intuitive processor. The conscious processor is engaged when we consciously think about a task or problem. However, as a skill becomes mastered, it moves into the intuitive processor; we just "do it" without conscious thought. Driving an automobile over a familiar route requires little if any conscious attention, which we turn over to listening to the radio or having a conversation with a passenger. Moreover, not everything the intuitive processor performs was once conscious. Many of the functions of the intuitive processor are innate, such as recognizing faces or simple patterns, while some abilities can be learned without ever becoming conscious, such as pure procedural learning in the absence of declarative learning, such as bicycle riding.

When it becomes automatic, driving or bicycling is performed by the intuitive processor, but what happens during the transition from conscious thought to intuition is a difficult issue to resolve. To see why, we must distinguish between *rule-following* and *rule-governed* behavior.

Physical systems illustrate how rule-governed behavior need not be rule-following behavior. The earth revolves around the sun in an elliptical path governed by Newton's laws of motion and gravity. However, the earth does not follow these laws in the sense that it computes them and adjusts its course to comply with them. The computer guiding a spacecraft does follow Newton's laws, as they are written into its programs, but the motions of natural objects are governed by physical laws without following them by internal processing.

The following example suggests that the same distinction may apply to human behavior. Imagine seeing a cartoon drawing of an unfamiliar animal called a "wug." If I show you two of them, you will say, "There are two wugs." Shown two pictures of a creature called "wuk," you will say, "There are two wuks." In saying the plural, your behavior is governed by the rule of English morphology that to make a noun plural, you add an -s. Although you probably did not apply the rule consciously, it is not implausible to believe that you did as a child. However, your behavior was also governed by a rule of English phonology that an -s following a voiced consonant (e.g., /g/) is also voiced—wugz—while an -s following an unvoiced consonant (such as /k/) is also unvoiced—wuks. It is unlikely you ever consciously knew this rule at all.

Having developed the distinction between rule-governed and rule-following behaviors, we can state the algorithm-level distinction between the symbol-system and the connectionist architectures of cognition. All psychologists accept the idea that human behavior is rule governed, because if it were not, there could be no science of human behavior. The issue separating the symbol-system hypothesis from connectionism concerns whether and when human behavior is rule following. According to the symbol system view, both the conscious processor and the intuitive processor are rule-following and rule-governed systems. When we think or decide consciously, we formulate rules and follow them in behaving. Intuitive thinking is likewise rule following. In the case of behaviors, that were once consciously followed, the procedures of the intuitive processor are the same as the procedures once followed in consciousness, but with awareness subtracted. In the case of intuitive behaviors, the process is truncated, with rules being formulated and followed directly by the intuitive processor. Connectionists hold that human behavior is rule following only at the conscious level. In the intuitive processor, radically different processes are taking place (Smolensky, 1988). Advocates of the symbol-system view are somewhat like Tolman, who believed that unconscious rats use cognitive maps as conscious lost humans do. Connectionists are like Hull, who believed that molar rule-governed behavior is at a lower level, the strengthening and weakening of input-output connections. After all, Thorndike called his theory connectionism 80 years ago.

The intuitive processor lies between the conscious mind—the conscious processor—and the brain that implements human intelligence. According to the symbol-system account, the intuitive processor carries out step-by-step unconscious thinking that is essentially identical to the step-by-step conscious thinking of the conscious processor, and so Clark (1989) calls the symbol-system account the *mind's-eye view* of cognition. According to connectionism, the intuitive processor carries out nonsymbolic parallel processing similar to the neural parallel processing of the brain, and Clark calls it the *brain's-eye view* of cognition.

Historically, connectionism represents more than simply a new technical approach to cognitive psychology. From the time of the ancient Greeks, Western philosophy assumed that having knowledge is knowing rules and that rational action consists in the following of rules. Human intuition has been deprecated as at best following rules unconsciously, and at worst as based on irrational impulse. Consistent with this view, psychology has been the search for the rule-governed springs of human behavior. But connectionism might vindicate human intuition as the secret of human success and rehabilitate a dissident tradition in philosophy—represented, for example, by Friedrich Nietzsche—that scorns being bound by rules as an inferior way of life (Dreyfus & Dreyfus, 1986). In addition, psychologists and philosophers are coming to believe that thought guided by emotion is wiser than pure logic (Damasio, 1994).

In the late 1980s, connectionism and the symbol-system view of learning and cognition acted as rivals, seemingly recreating the great theoretical battles of behaviorism's Golden Age. However, around 1990 a *modus vivendi* reunified the field of cognitive science. The two architectures of cognition were reconciled by regarding the human mind as a hybrid of the two (Clark, 1989). At the neural level, learning and cognition must be carried out by connectionist-type processes, since the brain is a collection of simple but massively interconnected units. Yet as we have learned, physically different computational systems may implement the same programs. Therefore, it is possible that, although the brain is a massively parallel computer, the human mind in its rational aspects is a serial processor of representations, especially when thought is conscious. The more automatic and unconscious (intuitive) aspects of the human mind are connectionist in nature. Connectionist theories thus have a valuable role to play in being the vital interface between symbol-system models of rational, rule-following thought, and intuitive, nonlinear, nonsymbolic thought.

Cognitive Psychology Today

The computer metaphor of mind dominates the psychological study of cognition. There are more computational models of information processes than can be briefly summarized. However, four large problems remain outstanding.

- *Consciousness.* The stubborn fact of consciousness remains, and the computer model of mind has been of little help, because computers are not conscious (though see Dennett, 1991). Why are we conscious? Does consciousness play any causal role in our mental economy or behavior? Little real progress has been made since behaviorist days.

- *Meaning.* How do physical symbols get their meaning; why does GIFT mean a present in English but poison in German? Ebbinghaus and S-R behaviorists avoided the question. Mediational behaviorists said meaning was carried by covert r-s connections, and Skinner offered an explanation in terms of tacting. The symbol system hypothesis finesses the issue by saying thinking is governed by formal logical rules (syntax), not meaning (semantics). Connectionism, like S-R psychology, tries to dissolve meanings into nonmeaningful units of response. The problem has not been solved.

- *Development.* Why and how do children throughout the world grow up with similar, if not identical, cognitive processes and a store of common beliefs, despite differences in environment?

- *Evolution.* Given that the human mind was constructed by evolution, are there important limits on human cognition, and certain thoughts it's easy to think while there may be others that are difficult or impossible to think?

Space prevents full discussion of these issues, and solving them lies in the future. See Clark (2001), Leahey (2000, 2001), and Leahey and Harris (2001) for more.

REFERENCES

Ash, M. G. (1995). *Gestalt psychology in German culture: Holism and the quest for objectivity.* Cambridge, England: Cambridge University Press.

Atkinson, R. C., & Shiffrin, R. M. (1968). Human memory: A proposed system and its control processes. In K. Spence & J. Spence (Eds.), *The psychology of learning and motivation* (Vol. 2, pp. 89–195). New York: Academic Press.

Broadbent, D. E. (1958). *Perception and communication.* Elmsford, NY: Pergamon Press.

Chomsky, N. (1959). Review of Skinner's *Verbal behavior. Language, 35,* 26–58.

Clark, A. (1989). *Microcognition: Philosophy, cognitive science, and parallel distributed processing.* Cambridge, MA: MIT Press.

Clark, A. (2001). *Mindware: An introduction to the philosophy of cognitive science.* New York: Oxford University Press.

Damasio, A. (1994). *Descartes' error: Emotion, reason, and the human brain.* New York: Putnam.

Dennett, D. D. (1991). *Consciousness explained.* Boston: Little, Brown.

Dreyfus, H., & Dreyfus, S. (1986). *Mind over machine: The power of human intuition and expertise in the era of the computer.* New York: Free Press.

Ebbinghaus, H. (1885/1964). *On memory.* New York: Dover.

Estes, W., Koch, S., MacCorquodale, K., Meehl, P., Mueller, C., Schoenfeld, W., et al. (1954). *Modern learning theory.* New York: Appleton-Century-Crofts.

Fowler, H. W., & Fowler, F. G. (1911). *The concise dictionary of current English,* 1964, Revised by E. McIntosh. Oxford: At the Clarendon Press.

Gazzinaga, M., Ivry, R., & Mangun, G. (1998). *Cognitive neuroscience: The biology of the mind.* New York: Norton.

Haugeland, J. (Ed.). (1981). *Mind design.* Cambridge, MA: MIT Press.

Haugeland, J. (1985). *Artificial intelligence: The very idea.* Cambridge, MA: MIT Press.

Hearst, E. (1975). The classical-instrumental distinction: Reflexes, voluntary behavior, and categories of associative learning. In W. K. Estes (Ed.), *Handbook of learning and cognitive processes* (Vol. 2, pp. 181–224). Hillsdale, NJ: Erlbaum.

Henry, J. (1997). *The scientific revolution and the origins of modern science.* New York: St. Martin's Press.

Hodge, A. (2000). *Alan Turing: The enigma.* New York: Walker.

Hull, C. L. (1937). Mind, mechanism, and adaptive behavior. *Psychological Review, 44,* 1–32.

Irwin, T. (1989). *Classical thought: A history of western philosophy–I.* Oxford, England: Oxford University Press.

Izawa, C. (Ed.). (1999). *On human memory: Evolution, progress, and reflections on the 30th anniversary of the Atkinson–Shiffrin model.* Mahwah, NJ: Erlbaum.

James, W. (1890). *Principles of psychology* (Vols. 1–2). New York: Henry Holt.

James, W. (1905/1955). *Pragmatism.* New York: Meridian.

Lashley, K. (1923). The behavioristic interpretation of consciousness. *Psychological Review, 30,* 237–272, 329–353.

Leahey, T. H. (2000). *A history of psychology: Main currents in psychological thought* (5th ed.). Upper Saddle River, NJ: Prentice-Hall.

Leahey, T. H. (2001). *A history of modern psychology* (3rd ed.). Upper Saddle River, NJ: Prentice-Hall.

Leahey, T. H., & Harris, R. J. (2001). *Learning and cognition* (5th ed.). Upper Saddle River, NJ: Prentice-Hall.

MacKay, D. M. (1969). *Information, mechanism, and meaning.* Cambridge, MA: MIT Press.

Mackintosh, N. J. (1985). Varieties of conditioning. In N. Weinberger, J. McGaugh, & G. Lynch (Eds.), *Memory systems of the brain: Animal and human cognitive processes.* New York: Guilford Press.

MacRae, N. (1999). *John von Neumann.* Washington, DC: American Mathematical Society.

Marr, D. (1982). *Vision.* San Francisco: Freeman.

Morgan, C. L. (1886). On the study of animal intelligence. *Mind, 11,* 174–185.

Neisser, U. (1967). *Cognitive psychology.* New York: Appleton-Century-Crofts.

Newell, A., Shaw, J. C., & Simon, H. A. (1958). Elements of a theory of problem solving. *Psychological Review, 65,* 151–166.

Nussbaum, M. (1994). *Therapies of desire: Theory and practice in Hellenistic ethics.* Princeton, NJ: Princeton University Press.

Nussbaum, M., & Rorty, A.-O. (Eds.). (1992). *Essays on Aristotle's de anima.* Oxford, England: Oxford University Press.

Osgood, C. E. (1956). Behavior theory and the social sciences. *Behavioral Science, 1,* 167–185.

Peirce, C. S. (1878). How to make our ideas clear. *Popular Science Monthly, 12,* 1–15.

Pinker, S. (1998). *How the mind works.* New York: Norton.

Pylyshyn, Z. W. (1984). *Computation and cognition: Toward a foundation for cognitive science.* Cambridge, MA: MIT/Bradford.

Rescorla, R. (1988). Pavlovian conditioning: It's not what you think. *American Psychologist, 43,* 151–160.

Romanes, G. J. (1883). *Animal intelligence.* New York: Appleton & Co.

Rosenblueth, A., Wiener, N., & Bigelow, J. (1943). Behavior, purpose, and teleology. *Philosophy of Science, 10,* 18–24.

Rumelhart, D. E., McClelland, J. L., & The PDP Research Group. (1986). *Parallel distributed processing: Explorations in the microstructure of cognition* (Vol. 1). Cambridge, MA: Cambridge University Press.

Simon, H. (1980). The social and behavioral sciences. *Science, 209,* 72–78.

Simon, H. (1996). *Models of my life.* Cambridge. MA: MIT Press.

Skinner, B. F. (1957). *Verbal behavior.* New York: Appleton-Century-Crofts.

Skinner, B. F. (1969). *Contingencies of reinforcement.* New York: Appleton-Century-Crofts.

Smith, L. (1986). *Behaviorism and logical positivism: A revised account of their alliance.* Stanford, CA: Stanford University Press.

Smolensky, P. (1988). On the proper treatment of connectionism. *Behavioral and Brain Sciences, 11,* 1–74.

Spence, K. (1948). Postulates and methods of "behaviorism." *Psychological Review, 55,* 67–78.

Squire, L. (1994). Declarative and nondeclarative memory: Multiple brain systems supporting learning and memory. In D. L. Schachter & E. Tulving (Eds.), *Memory systems 1994* (pp. 203–232). Cambridge, MA: MIT Press.

Thorndike, E. L. (1911). *Animal intelligence.* New York: Hafner.

Tolman, E. C. (1935). *Psychology vs. immediate experience.* Berkeley: University of California Press. (Reprinted from *Behavior and psychological man,* pp. 94–114, by E. Tolman 1951.)

Tolman, E. C. (1948). Cognitive maps in rats and men. *Psychological Review, 55,* 189–209.

Tolman, E. C. (1959). Principles of purposive behaviorism. In S. Koch (Ed.), *Psychology: Study of a science* (Vol. 2, pp. 92–157). New York: McGraw-Hill.

Tolman, E. C., Hall, C. S., & Bretnall, E. P. (1932). A disproof of the law of effect and a substitution of the laws of emphasis, motivation, and disruption. *Journal of Experimental Psychology, 15,* 601–614.

Tulving, E. (1993). What is episodic memory? *Current Directions in Psychological Science, 2,* 67–70.

Turing, A. M. (1950). Computing machinery and intelligence. *Mind, 59,* 433–460.

Vauclair, J. (1996). *Animal cognition: An introduction to modern comparative psychology.* Cambridge, MA: Harvard University Press.

CHAPTER 7

Intelligence

ROBERT J. STERNBERG

EXPERT OPINIONS ON THE NATURE
OF INTELLIGENCE   136
Intelligence Operationally Defined   136
The 1921 Symposium   136
**Intelligence as Arising from Individual Differences:
The Differential Model   137**
THE SEMINAL VIEWS OF GALTON AND BINET   137
**Intelligence Is Simple: Galton's Theory of
Psychophysical Processes   138**
Intelligence Is Complex: Binet's Theory of Judgment   139
MODELS OF THE NATURE OF INTELLIGENCE   140
Psychometric Models   140
Hierarchical Theories   142
Guilford's Structure-of-Intellect Model   143
Guttman's Radex Model   143

INTELLIGENCE AS ARISING FROM COGNITIVE
STRUCTURES AND PROCESSES   144
Cognitive Structures   144
Cognitive Processes   146
BIOLOGICAL BASES OF INTELLIGENCE   148
CULTURE AND SOCIETY   150
SYSTEMS MODELS   150
The Nature of Systems Models   150
CONCLUSION: RELATIONS AMONG THE VARIOUS
MODELS OF THE NATURE OF INTELLIGENCE   151
Different Names   151
Fighting for "Truth"   151
Dialectical Synthesis   151
REFERENCES   152

Anyone who has seriously studied the history of the United States or of any other country knows that there is not one history of the country but many histories. The history as told by some Native Americans, for example, would look quite different from the history as told by some of the later settlers, and even within these groups, the stories would differ. Similarly, there is no one history of the field of intelligence but rather many histories, depending on who is doing the telling. For example, the largely laudatory histories recounted by Carroll (1982, 1993), Herrnstein and Murray (1994), and Jensen (in press) read very differently from the largely skeptical histories recounted by Gardner (1983, 1999), Gould (1981), or Sacks (1999). And of course, there are differences within these groups of authors.

These differences need mentioning because, although all fields of psychology are subject to being perceived through ideological lenses, few fields seem to have lenses with so many colors and, some might argue, with so many different distorting imperfections as do the lenses through which is seen the field of intelligence. The different views come from ideological biases affecting not only what is said but also what is included. For example, there is virtually no overlap in the historical data used by Carroll (1993) versus Gardner (1983) to support their respective theories of intelligence.

Although no account can be truly value free, I try in this chapter to clarify values in three ways. First, I attempt to represent the views of the investigators and their times in presenting the history of the field. Second, I critique this past work but make it clear what my own personal opinions are by labeling evaluative sections "Evaluation." Third, I try to represent multiple points of view in a dialectical fashion (Hegel, 1807/1931; see R. J. Sternberg, 1999a), pointing out both the positive and negative sides of various contributions. This representation recognizes that all points of view taken in the past can be viewed, with "20/20 hindsight," as skewed, in much

Preparation of this chapter was supported by Grant REC-9979843 from the National Science Foundation and by a grant under the Javits Act Program (Grant No. R206R000001) as administered by the Office of Educational Research and Improvement, U.S. Department of Education. Grantees undertaking such projects are encouraged to express freely their professional judgment. This chapter, therefore, does not necessarily represent the position or policies of the National Science Foundation, Office of Educational Research and Improvement, or the U.S. Department of Education, and no official endorsement should be inferred.

the same way that present points of view will be viewed as skewed in the future. A dialectical form of examination will serve as the basis for the entire chapter. The basic idea is that important ideas, good or bad, eventually serve as the springboard for new ideas that grow out of unions of past ideas that may once have seemed incompatible.

The emphasis in this chapter is on the history of the field of intelligence, particularly with reference to theories of intelligence. Readers interested in contemporary theory and research are referred to the chapter "Contemporary Theories of Intelligence" in Volume 7 of this handbook (R. J. Sternberg, 2002). Such theories and research are mentioned only in passing in this chapter. Readers interested primarily in measurement issues might consult relevant chapters in R. J. Sternberg (1982, 1994, 2000).

Perhaps the most fundamental dialectic in the field of intelligence arises from the question of how we should conceive of intelligence. Several different positions have been staked out (Sternberg, 1990a). Many of the differences in ideology that arise in accounts of the history of the field of intelligence arise from differences in the model of intelligence to which an investigator adheres. To understand the history of the field of intelligence, one must understand the alternative epistemological models that can give rise to the concept of intelligence. But before addressing these models, consider simply the question of how psychologists in the field of intelligence have defined the construct on which they base their models.

EXPERT OPINIONS ON THE NATURE OF INTELLIGENCE

Historically, one of the most important approaches to figuring out what intelligence is has relied on the opinions of experts. Such opinions are sometimes referred to as *implicit theories,* to distinguish them from the more formal *explicit theories* that serve as the bases for scientific hypotheses and subsequent data collections. Implicit theories (which can be those of laypersons as well as of experts) are important to the history of a field for at least three reasons (R. J. Sternberg, Conway, Ketron, & Bernstein, 1981). First, experts' implicit theories are typically what give rise to their explicit theories. Second, much of the history of intelligence research and practice is much more closely based on implicit theories than it is on formal theories. Most of the intelligence tests that have been used, for example, are based more on the opinions of their creators as to what intelligence is than on formal theories. Third, people's everyday judgments of each other's intelligence always have been and continue to be much more strongly guided by their implicit theories of intelligence than by any explicit theories.

Intelligence Operationally Defined

E. G. Boring (1923), in an article in the *New Republic,* proposed that intelligence is what the tests of intelligence test. Boring did not believe that this operational definition was the end of the line for understanding intelligence. On the contrary, he saw it as a "narrow definition, but a point of departure for a rigorous discussion . . . until further scientific discussion allows us to extend [it]" (p. 35). Nevertheless, many psychologists and especially testers and interpreters of tests of intelligence have adopted this definition or something similar to it.

From a scientific point of view, the definition is problematical. First, the definition is circular: It defines intelligence in terms of what intelligence tests test, but what the tests test can only be determined by one's definition of intelligence. Second, the definition legitimates rather than calling into scientific question whatever operations are in use at a given time to measure intelligence. To the extent that the goal of science is to disconfirm existing scientific views (Popper, 1959), such a definition will not be useful. Third, the definition assumes that what intelligence tests test is uniform. But this is not the case. Although tests of intelligence tend to correlate positively with each other (the so-called *positive manifold* first noted by Spearman, 1904), such correlations are far from perfect, even controlling for unreliability. Thus, what an intelligence test tests is not just one uniform thing. Moreover, even the most ardent proponents of a general factor of intelligence (a single element common to all of these tests) acknowledge there is more to intelligence than just the general factor.

The 1921 Symposium

Probably the most well-known study of experts' definitions of intelligence was one done by the editors of the *Journal of Educational Psychology* ("Intelligence and Its Measurement," 1921). Contributors to the symposium were asked to write essays addressing two issues: (a) what they conceived intelligence to be and how it best could be measured by group tests, and (b) what the most crucial next steps would be in research. Fourteen experts gave their views on the nature of intelligence, with such definitions as the following:

1. The power of good responses from the point of view of truth or facts (E. L. Thorndike).
2. The ability to carry on abstract thinking (L. M. Terman).
3. Sensory capacity, capacity for perceptual recognition, quickness, range or flexibility of association, facility and imagination, span of attention, quickness or alertness in response (F. N. Freeman).

4. Having learned or ability to learn to adjust oneself to the environment (S. S. Colvin).

5. Ability to adapt oneself adequately to relatively new situations in life (R. Pintner).

6. The capacity for knowledge and knowledge possessed (B. A. C. Henmon).

7. A biological mechanism by which the effects of a complexity of stimuli are brought together and given a somewhat unified effect in behavior (J. Peterson).

8. The capacity to inhibit an instinctive adjustment, the capacity to redefine the inhibited instinctive adjustment in the light of imaginally experienced trial and error, and the capacity to realize the modified instinctive adjustment in overt behavior to the advantage of the individual as a social animal (L. L. Thurstone).

9. The capacity to acquire capacity (H. Woodrow).

10. The capacity to learn or to profit by experience (W. F. Dearborn).

11. Sensation, perception, association, memory, imagination, discrimination, judgment, and reasoning (N. E. Haggerty).

Others of the contributors to the symposium did not provide clear definitions of intelligence but rather concentrated on how to test it. B. Ruml refused to present a definition of intelligence, arguing that not enough was known about the concept. S. L. Pressey described himself as uninterested in the question, although he became well known for his tests of intelligence.

Of course, there have been many definitions of intelligence since those represented in the journal symposium, and an essay even has been written on the nature of definitions of intelligence (Miles, 1957). One well-known set of definitions was explicitly published in 1986 as a follow-up to the 1921 symposium (R. J. Sternberg & Detterman, 1986). R. J. Sternberg and Berg (1986) attempted a comparison of the views of the experts in 1986 (P. Baltes, J. Baron, J. Berry, A. Brown and J. Campione, E. Butterfield, J. Carroll, J. P. Das, D. Detterman, W. Estes, H. Eysenck, H. Gardner, R. Glaser, J. Goodnow, J. Horn, L. Humphreys, E. Hunt, A. Jensen, J. Pellegrino, R. Schank, R. Snow, R. Sternberg, E. Zigler) with those of the experts in 1921. They reached three general conclusions.

First, there was at least some general agreement across the two symposia regarding the nature of intelligence. When attributes were listed for frequency of mention in the two symposia, the correlation was .50, indicating moderate overlap. Attributes such as adaptation to the environment, basic mental processes, higher-order thinking (e.g., reasoning, problem solving, and decision making) were prominent in both symposia.

Second, central themes occurred in both symposia. One theme was the one versus the many: Is intelligence one thing or is it multiple things? How broadly should intelligence be defined? What should be the respective roles of biological and behavioral attributes in seeking an understanding of intelligence?

Third, despite the similarities in views over the 65 years, some salient differences could also be found. Metacognition—conceived of as both knowledge about and control of cognition—played a prominent role in the 1986 symposium but virtually no role at all in the 1921 symposium. The later symposium also placed a greater emphasis on the role of knowledge and the interaction of mental processes with this knowledge.

Definitions of any kind can provide a basis for explicit scientific theory and research, but they do not provide a substitute for these things. Thus, it was necessary for researchers to move beyond definitions, which they indeed did. Many of them moved to models based on individual differences.

Intelligence as Arising from Individual Differences: The Differential Model

McNemar (1964) was one of the most explicit in speculating on why we even have a concept of intelligence and in linking the rationale for the concept to individual differences. He queried whether two identical twins stranded on a desert island and growing up together ever would generate the notion of intelligence if they never encountered individual differences in their mental abilities.

Perhaps without individual differences, societies would never generate the notion of intelligence and languages would contain no corresponding term. Actually, some languages, such as Mandarin Chinese, in fact have no concept that corresponds precisely to the Western notion of intelligence (Yang & Sternberg, 1997a, 1997b), although they have related concepts that are closer, say, to the Western notion of wisdom or other constructs. Whatever may be the case, much of the history of the field of intelligence is based upon an epistemological model deriving from the existence of one or more kinds of individual differences.

THE SEMINAL VIEWS OF GALTON AND BINET

If current thinking about the nature of intelligence owes a debt to any scholars, the debt is to Sir Francis Galton and to Alfred Binet. These two investigators—Galton at the end of the nineteenth century and Binet at the beginning of the twentieth century—have had a profound impact on thinking about intelligence, an impact that has carried down to the present day. Many present conflicts of views regarding the nature of intelligence can be traced to a dialectical conflict between Galton and Binet.

Intelligence Is Simple: Galton's Theory of Psychophysical Processes

Intelligence as Energy and Sensitivity

The publication of Darwin's *Origin of Species* (1859) had a profound impact on many lines of scientific endeavor. One was the investigation of human intelligence. The book suggested that the capabilities of humans were in some sense continuous with those of lower animals and hence could be understood through scientific investigation.

Galton (1883) followed up on these notions to propose a theory of the "human faculty and its development." Because he also proposed techniques for measuring the "human faculty," his theory could be applied directly to human behavior.

Galton proposed two general qualities that he believed distinguish the more from the less intellectually able. His epistemological rooting, therefore, was in the individual-differences approach. The first quality was *energy,* or the capacity for labor. Galton believed that intellectually gifted individuals in a variety of fields are characterized by remarkable levels of energy. The second general quality was *sensitivity*. He observed that the only information that can reach us concerning external events passes through the senses and that the more perceptive the senses are of differences in luminescence, pitch, odor, or whatever, the larger would be the range of information on which intelligence could act. Galton's manner of expression was direct:

> The discriminative facility of idiots is curiously low; they hardly distinguish between heat and cold, and their sense of pain is so obtuse that some of the more idiotic seem hardly to know what it is. In their dull lives, such pain as can be excited in them may literally be accepted with a welcome surprise. (p. 28)

For seven years (1884–1890), Galton maintained an anthropometric laboratory at the South Kensington Museum in London where, for a small fee, visitors could have themselves measured on a variety of psychophysical tests. What, exactly, did these kinds of tests look like?

One such test was weight discrimination. The apparatus consisted of shot, wool, and wadding. The cases in which they were contained were identical in appearance and differed only in their weights. Participants were tested by a sequencing task. They were given three cases, and with their eyes closed, they had to arrange them in proper order of weight. The weights formed a geometric series of heaviness, and the examiner recorded the finest interval that an examinee could discriminate. Galton suggested that similar geometric sequences could be used for testing other senses, such as touch and taste. With touch, he proposed the use of wirework of various degrees of fineness, whereas for taste, he proposed the use of stock bottles of solutions of salt of various strengths. For olfaction, he suggested the use of bottles of attar of rose mixed in various degrees of dilution.

Galton also contrived a whistle for ascertaining the highest pitch that different individuals could perceive. Tests with the whistle enabled him to discover that people's ability to hear high notes declines considerably as age advances. He also discovered that people are inferior to cats in their ability to perceive tones of high pitch.

It is ironic, perhaps, that a theory that took off from Darwin's theory of evolution ended up in what some might perceive as a predicament, at least for those who subscribe to the notion that evolutionary advance is, in part, a matter of complexity (Kauffman, 1995). In most respects, humans are evolutionarily more complex than cats. Galton's theory, however, would place cats, which are able to hear notes of higher pitch than humans, at a superior level to humans, at least with respect to this particular aspect of what Galton alleged to be intelligence.

Cattell's Operationalization of Galton's Theory

James McKeen Cattell brought many of Galton's ideas across the ocean to the United States. As head of the psychological laboratory at Columbia University, Cattell was in a good position to publicize the psychophysical approach to the theory and measurement of intelligence. Cattell (1890) proposed a series of 50 psychophysical tests. Four examples were:

1. *Dynamometer pressure.* The dynamometer-pressure test measures the pressure resulting from the greatest possible squeeze of one's hand.
2. *Sensation areas.* This test measures the distance on the skin by which two points must be separated in order for them to be felt as separate points. Cattell suggested that the back of the closed right hand between the first and second fingers be used as the basis for measurement.
3. *Least noticeable difference in weight.* This test measures least noticeable differences in weights by having participants judge weights of small wooden boxes. Participants were handed two such boxes and asked to indicate which was heavier.

4. *Bisection of a 50-cm line.* In this test, participants were required to divide a strip of wood into two equal parts by means of a movable line.

Wissler Blows the Whistle

A student of Cattell's, Clark Wissler (1901), decided to validate Cattell's tests. Using 21 of these tests, he investigated among Columbia University undergraduates the correlations of the tests with each other and with college grades. The results were devastating: Test scores neither intercorrelated much among themselves, nor did they correlate significantly with undergraduate grades. The lack of correlation could not have been due entirely to unreliability of the grades or to restriction of range, because the grades did correlate among themselves. A new approach seemed to be needed.

Evaluation

Even those later theorists who were to build on Galton's work (e.g., Hunt, Frost, & Lunneborg, 1973) recognize that Galton was overly simplistic in his conception and measurement of intelligence. Galton was also pejorative toward groups whom he believed to be of inferior intelligence. Yet one could argue that Galton set at least three important precedents.

A first precedent was the desirability of precise quantitative measurement. Much of psychological measurement, particularly in the clinical areas, had been more qualitative, or has been based on dubious rules about translations of qualitative responses to quantitative measurements. Galton's psychometric precision set a different course for research and practice in the field of intelligence. His combination of theory and measurement techniques set a precedent: Many future investigators would tie their theories, strong or weak, to measurement operations that would enable them to measure the intelligence of a variety of human populations.

A second precedent was the interface between theory and application. Galton's Kensington Museum enterprise set a certain kind of tone for the intelligence measurement of the future. No field of psychology, perhaps, has been more market oriented than has been the measurement of intelligence. Testing of intelligence has been highly influenced by market demands, more so, say, than testing of memory abilities or social skills. It is difficult to study the history of the field of intelligence without considering both theory and practice.

A third precedent was a tendency to conflate scores on tests of intelligence with some kind of personal value. Galton made no attempt to hide his admiration for hereditary geniuses (Galton, 1869) nor to hide his contempt for those at the lower end of the intelligence scale as he perceived it (Galton,

1883). He believed those at the high end of the scale had much more to contribute than did those at the low end. The same kinds of judgments do not pervade the literatures of, say, sensation or memory. This tendency to conflate intelligence with some kind of economic or social value to society and perhaps beyond society has continued to the present day (e.g., Herrnstein & Murray, 1994; Schmidt & Hunter, 1998).

Intelligence Is Complex: Binet's Theory of Judgment

In 1904, the minister of Public Instruction in Paris named a commission charged with studying or creating tests that would ensure that mentally defective children (as they then were called) would receive an adequate education. The commission decided that no child suspected of retardation should be placed in a special class for children with mental retardation without first being given an examination "from which it could be certified that because of the state of his intelligence, he was unable to profit, in an average measure, from the instruction given in the ordinary schools" (Binet & Simon, 1916a, p. 9).

Binet and Simon devised a test based on a conception of intelligence very different from Galton's and Cattell's. They viewed judgment as central to intelligence. At the same time, they viewed Galton's tests as ridiculous. They cited Helen Keller as an example of someone who was very intelligent but who would have performed terribly on Galton's tests.

Binet and Simon's (1916a) theory of intelligent thinking in many ways foreshadowed later research on the development of metacognition (e.g., Brown & DeLoache, 1978; Flavell & Wellman, 1977; Mazzoni & Nelson, 1998). According to Binet and Simon (1916b), intelligent thought comprises three distinct elements: direction, adaptation, and control.

Direction consists in knowing what has to be done and how it is to be accomplished. When we are required to add three numbers, for example, we give ourselves a series of instructions on how to proceed, and these instructions form the direction of thought.

Adaptation refers to one's selection and monitoring of one's strategy during task performance. For example, in adding to numbers, one first needs to decide on a strategy to add the numbers. As we add, we need to check (monitor) that we are not repeating the addition of any of the digits we already have added.

Control is the ability to criticize one's own thoughts and actions. This ability often occurs beneath the conscious level. If one notices that the sum one attains is smaller than either number (if the numbers are positive), one recognizes the need to add the numbers again, as there must have been a mistake in one's adding.

Binet and Simon (1916b) distinguished between two types of intelligence: ideational intelligence and instinctive intelligence. *Ideational intelligence* operates by means of words and ideas. It uses logical analysis and verbal reasoning. *Instinctive intelligence* operates by means of feeling. It refers not to the instincts attributed to animals and to simple forms of human behavior but to lack of logical thinking. This two-process kind of model adumbrates many contemporary models of thinking (e.g., Evans, 1989; Sloman, 1996), which make similar distinctions.

What are some examples of the kinds of problems found on a Binet-based test (e.g., Terman & Merrill, 1937, 1973; R. L. Thorndike, Hagen, & Sattler, 1986)? In one version 2-year-olds are given a three-hole form board and required to place circular, square, and triangular pieces into appropriate indentations on it. Another test requires children to identify body parts on a paper doll. Six years later, by age 8, the character of the test items changes considerably. By age 8, the tests include vocabulary, which requires children to define words; verbal absurdities, which requires recognition of why each of a set of statements is foolish; similarities and differences, which requires children to say how each of two objects is the same as and different from the other; and comprehension, which requires children to solve practical problems of the sort encountered in everyday life. At age 14, there is some overlap in kinds of tests with age 8, as well as some different kinds of tests. For example, in an induction test, the experimenter makes a notch in an edge of some folded paper and asks participants how many holes the paper will have when it is unfolded. On a reasoning test, participants need to solve arithmetic word problems. Ingenuity requires individuals to indicate the series of steps that could be used to pour a given amount of water from one container to another.

The early Binet and Simon tests, like those of Cattell, soon were put to a test, in this case by Sharp (1899). Although her results were not entirely supportive, she generally accepted the view of judgment, rather than psychophysical processes, as underlying intelligence. Most subsequent researchers have accepted this notion as well.

Evaluation

Binet's work was to have far more influence than Galton's. Binet set many trends that were to be influential even up to the present day.

First, the kinds of test items Binet used are, for the most part, similar to those used in the present day. From the standpoint of modern test constructors, Binet "largely got it right." Indeed, a current test, the fourth edition of the Stanford-Binet Intelligence Scale (R. L. Thorndike, Hagen, & Sattler, 1986) is a direct descendant of the Binet test. The Wechsler tests (e.g., Wechsler, 1991), although somewhat different in their conceptualization, owe a great deal to the conceptualization and tests of Binet.

Second, Binet grounded his tests in competencies that are central to schooling and perhaps less central to the world of adult work. Such grounding made sense, given the school-based mission with which Binet was entrusted. Although intelligence-test scores correlate both with school grades and with work performance, their correlation with school grades is substantially higher, and they correlate better with job-training performance than with work performance (see reviews in Mackintosh, 1998; Wagner, 2000).

Third, intelligence tests continue today, as in Binet's time, to be touted as serving a protective function. The goal of Binet's test was to protect children from being improperly classified in school. Today, test users point out how test scores can give opportunities to children who otherwise would not get them. For example, children from lower-level or even middle-level socioeconomic class backgrounds who would not be able to pay for certain kinds of schooling may receive admissions or scholarships on the basis of test scores. At the same time, there is a dialectic in action here, whereby opponents of testing, or at least of certain kinds of testing, argue that the conventional tests do more damage than good (Gardner, 1983; Sacks, 1999), taking away opportunities rather than providing them to many children.

An important aspect of Binet's theory has been lost to many. This was Binet's belief that intelligence is malleable and could be improved by "mental orthopedics." To this day, many investigators are interested in raising levels of mental functioning (see review by Grotzer & Perkins, 2000). But many other investigators, even those who use Binet-based tests, question whether intelligence is malleable in any major degree (e.g., Jensen, 1969, 1998).

MODELS OF THE NATURE OF INTELLIGENCE

A number of different types of models have been proposed to characterize intelligence. What are the main models, and how are they similar to and different from one another?

Psychometric Models

The early efforts of intelligence theorists largely built upon the Binetian school of thought rather than the Galtonian school of thought. The most influential theorist historically, and perhaps even into the present, was also among the first, a British psychologist named Charles Spearman.

Spearman's Two-Factor Theory

Spearman (1904, 1927) proposed a two-factor theory of intelligence, a theory that is still very much alive and well today (e.g., Brand, 1996; Jensen, 1998). The theory posits a general factor (g) common to all tasks requiring intelligence and one specific factor (s) unique to each different type of task. Thus, there are two types of factors rather than, strictly speaking, two factors.

Spearman (1904) got this idea as a result of looking at data processed by a statistical technique of his own invention, namely, *factor analysis*, which attempts to identify latent sources of individual (or other) differences that underlie observed sources of variation in test performance. Spearman observed that when he factor-analyzed a correlation matrix, the two kinds of factors appeared—the general factor common to all of the tests and the specific factors unique to each particular test.

Spearman (1927) admitted to not being sure what the psychological basis of g is but suggested that it might be mental energy (a term that he never defined very clearly). Whatever it was, it was a unitary and primary source of individual differences in intelligence-test performance.

The Theories of Bonds and of Connections

Theory of Bonds. Spearman's theory was soon challenged and continues to be challenged today (e.g., Gardner, 1983; R. J. Sternberg, 1999b). One of Spearman's chief critics was British psychologist Sir Godfrey Thomson, who accepted Spearman's statistics but not his interpretation. Thomson (1939) argued that it is possible to have a general psychometric factor in the absence of any kind of general ability. In particular, he argued that g is a statistical reality but a psychological artifact. He suggested that the general factor might result from the working of an extremely large number of what he called *bonds*, all of which are sampled simultaneously in intellectual tasks. Imagine, for example, that each of the intellectual tasks found in Spearman's and others' test batteries requires certain mental skills. If each test samples all of these mental skills, then their appearance will be perfectly correlated with each other because they always co-occur. Thus, they will give the appearance of a single general factor when in fact they are multiple.

Although Thomson did not attempt to specify exactly what the bonds might be, it is not hard to speculate on what some of these common elements might be. For example, they might include understanding the problems and responding to them.

Theory of Connections. Thorndike, Bregman, Cobb, and Woodyard (1926) proposed a quite similar theory, based on Thorndike's theory of learning. They suggested that

> in their deeper nature the higher forms of intellectual operations are identical with mere association or connection forming, depending upon the same sort of physiological connections but requiring *many more of them*. By the same argument the person whose intellect is greater or higher or better than that of another person differs from him in the last analysis in having, not a new sort of physiological process, but simply a larger number of connections of the ordinary sort. (p. 415)

According to this theory, then, learned connections, similar to Thomson's bonds, are what underlie individual differences in intelligence.

Thurstone's Theory of Primary Mental Abilities

Louis L. Thurstone, like Spearman, was an ardent advocate of factor analysis as a method of revealing latent psychological structures underlying observable test performances. Thurstone (1938, 1947) believed, however, that it was a mistake to leave the axes of factorial solutions unrotated. He believed that the solution thus obtained was psychologically arbitrary. Instead, he suggested rotation to what he referred to as *simple structure,* which is designed to clean up the columns of a factor pattern matrix so that the factors display either relatively high or low loadings of tests on given factors rather than large numbers of moderate ones. Using simple-structure rotation, Thurstone and Thurstone (1941) argued for the existence of seven primary mental abilities.

1. *Verbal comprehension*—the ability to understand verbal material. This ability is measured by tests such as vocabulary and reading comprehension.
2. *Verbal fluency*—the ability involved in rapidly producing words, sentences, and other verbal material. This ability is measured by tests such as one that requires the examinee to produce as many words as possible in a short amount of time beginning with a certain letter.
3. *Number*—the ability to compute rapidly. This ability is measured by tests requiring solution of numerical arithmetic problems and simple arithmetic word problems.

4. *Memory*—the ability to remember strings of words, letters, numbers, or other symbols or items. This ability is measured by serial- or free-recall tests.

5. *Perceptual speed*—the ability rapidly to recognize letters, numbers, or other symbols. This ability is measured by proofreading tests, or by tests that require individuals to cross out a given letter (such as *A*) in a string of letters.

6. *Inductive reasoning*—the ability to reason from the specific to the general. This ability is measured by tests such as letters series ("What letter comes next in the following series? b, d, g, k, ...") and number series ("What number comes next in the following series? 4, 12, 10, 30, 28, 84, . . .").

7. *Spatial visualization*—the ability involved in visualizing shapes, rotations of objects, and how pieces of a puzzle would fit together. This ability is measured by tests that require mental rotations or other manipulations of geometric objects.

The argument between Spearman and Thurstone was not resoluble on mathematical grounds, simply because in exploratory factor analysis, any of an infinite number of rotations of axes is acceptable. As an analogy, consider axes used to understand world geography (Vernon, 1971). One can use lines of longitude and latitude, but really any axes at all could be used, orthogonal or oblique, or even axes that serve different functions, such as in polar coordinates. The locations of points, and the distances between them, do not change in Euclidean space as a result of how the axes are placed. Because Thurstone's primary mental abilities are intercorrelated, Spearman and others have argued that they are nothing more than varied manifestations of *g:* Factor-analyze these factors, and a general factor will emerge as a second-order factor. Thurstone, of course, argued that the primary mental abilities were more basic. Such arguments became largely polemical because there really neither was nor is any way of resolving the debate in the terms in which it was presented. Some synthesis was needed for the opposing thesis of *g* versus the antithesis of primary mental abilities.

Hierarchical Theories

The main synthesis to be proposed was to be hierarchical theories—theories that assume that abilities can be ordered in terms of levels of generality. Rather than arguing which abilities are more fundamental, hierarchical theorists have argued that all of the abilities have a place in a hierarchy of abilities from the general to the specific.

Holzinger's Bifactor Theory

Holzinger (1938) proposed a bifactor theory of intelligence, which retained both the general and specific factors of Spearman but also permitted group factors such as those found in Thurstone's theory. Such factors are common to more than one test but not to all tests. This theory helped form the basis for other hierarchical theories that replaced it.

Burt's Theory

Sir Cyril Burt (1949), known primarily for this widely questioned work on the heritability of intelligence, suggested that a five-level hierarchy would capture the nature of intelligence. At the top of Burt's hierarchy was "the human mind." At the second level, the "relations level," are *g* and a practical factor. At the third level are associations, at the fourth level is perception, and at the fifth level is sensation. This model has not proven durable and is relatively infrequently cited today.

Vernon's Theory of Verbal : Educational and Spatial : Mechanical Abilities

A more widely adopted model has been that of Vernon (1971), which proposes the general factor, *g*, at the top of the hierarchy. Below this factor are two group factors, *v:ed* and *k:m*. The former refers to verbal-educational abilities of the kinds measured by conventional test of scholastic abilities. The latter refers to spatial-mechanical abilities (with *k* perhaps inappropriately referring to the nonequivalent term *kinesthetic*).

Cattell's Theory of Fluid and Crystallized Abilities

More widely accepted than any of the previous theories is that of Raymond Cattell (1971), which is somewhat similar to Vernon's theory. This theory proposes general ability at the top of the hierarchy and two abilities immediately beneath it, fluid ability, or g_f, and crystallized ability, or g_c. Fluid ability is the ability to think flexibly and to reason abstractly. It is measured by tests such as number series and figural analogies. Crystallized ability is the accumulated knowledge base one has developed over the course of one's life as the result of the application of fluid ability. It is measured by tests such as vocabulary and general information.

More recent work has suggested that fluid ability is extremely difficult to distinguish statistically from general ability (Gustafsson, 1984, 1988). Indeed, the tests used to measure fluid ability are often identical to the tests used to measure what is supposed to be pure *g*. An example of such a test would be the Raven Progressive Matrices (Raven, Court, & Raven, 1992), which measures people's ability to fill in a missing part of a matrix comprising abstract figural drawings.

Horn (1994) has greatly expanded upon the hierarchical theory as originally proposed by Cattell. Most notably, he has suggested that g can be split into three more factors nested under fluid and crystallized abilities. These three other factors are visual thinking (g_v), auditory thinking (g_a), and speed (g_s). The visual thinking factor is probably closer to Vernon's k:m factor than it is to the fluid ability factor.

Carroll's Three-Stratum Theory

Today, perhaps the most widely accepted hierarchical model is one proposed by Carroll (1993) that is based on the re-analysis of (more than 450) data sets from the past. At the top of the hierarchy is general ability; in the middle of the hierarchy are various broad abilities, including fluid and crystallized intelligence, learning and memory processes, visual and auditory perception, facile production, and speed. At the bottom of the hierarchy are fairly specific abilities.

Guilford's Structure-of-Intellect Model

Although many differential theorists followed the option of proposing a hierarchical model, not all did. J. P. Guilford (1967, 1982; Guilford & Hoepfner, 1971) proposed a model with 120 distinct abilities (increased to 150 in 1982 and to 180 in later manifestations). The basic theory organizes abilities along three dimensions: operations, products, and contents. In the best-known version of the model, there are five operations, six products, and four contents. The five operations are cognition, memory, divergent production, convergent production, and evaluation. The six products are units, classes, relations, systems, transformations, and implications. The four contents are figural, symbolic, semantic, and behavioral. Because these dimensions are completely crossed with each other, they yield a total of $5 \times 6 \times 4$ or 120 different abilities. For example, inferring a relation in a verbal analogy (such as the relation between BLACK and WHITE in BLACK : WHITE :: HIGH : LOW) would involve cognition of semantic relations.

Guilford's model has not fared well psychometrically. Horn and Knapp (1973) showed that random theories could generate support equal to that obtained by Guilford's model when the same type of rotation was used that Guilford used—so-called "Procrustean rotation." Horn (1967) showed that equal support could be obtained with Guilford's theory, but with data generated randomly rather than with real data. These demonstrations do not prove the model wrong: They

show only that the psychometric support that Guilford claimed for his model was not justified by the methods he used.

Guttman's Radex Model

The last psychometric model to be mentioned is one proposed by Louis Guttman (1954). The model is what Guttman referred to as a radex, or radial representation of complexity. The radex consists of two parts.

The first part is what Guttman refers to as a simplex. If one imagines a circle, then the simplex refers to the distance of a given point (ability) from the center of the circle. The closer a given ability is to the center of the circle, the more central that ability is to human intelligence. Thus, g could be viewed as being at the center of the circle, whereas the more peripheral abilities such as perceptual speed would be nearer to the periphery of the circle. Abilities nearer to the periphery of the circle are viewed as being constituents of abilities nearer the center of the circle, so the theory has a hierarchical element.

The second part of the radex is called the circumplex. It refers to the angular orientation of a given ability with respect to the circle. Thus, abilities are viewed as being arranged around the circle, with abilities that are more highly related (correlated) nearer to each other in the circle. Thus, the radex functions through a system of polar coordinates. Snow, Kyllonen, and Marshalek (1984) used nonmetric multidimensional scaling on a Thurstonian type of test to demonstrate that the Thurstonian primary mental abilities actually could be mapped into a radex.

Evaluation

Psychometric theories of intelligence have been enormously influential, particularly in North America and in the United Kingdom. In many respects, they have served the field well. First, they have provided a zeitgeist for three generations of researchers. Second, they have provided a systematic means for studying individual differences. Arguably, no other paradigm has provided any means that has been nearly as systematic or, really, successful in so many respects. Third, the theories cross well between theory and application. Few theories have proven to have as many and as diverse practical applications. Finally, they have provided a model for how theory and measurement can evolve in synchrony.

At the same time, there have been problems with the differential approach. First, although factor analysis, as a method, is neither good nor bad, it has frequently been subject to misuse (Horn & Knapp, 1973; Humphreys, 1962;

McNemar, 1951). Second, factor analyses have sometimes been not so much misintepreted as overinterpreted. What one gets out of a factor analysis is simply a psychometric transformation of what one puts in. It is possible to support many different possible theories by choosing one's tests with a certain goal in mind. The resulting factors simply reflect the choice of tests and their interrelationships. Third, in exploratory factor analysis, the rotation issue has proven to be a thorny one. Any rotation is mathematically correct and equivalent in Euclidean space. Arguments over which theory is correct often have boiled down to little more than arguments over which rotation is psychologically more justified. But no adequate basis has been found for supporting one rotation as psychologically preferred over all others. Fifth and finally, the whole issue of deriving a theory of intelligence from patterns of individual differences has never received fully adequate examination by differential psychologists. Evolutionary theorists (e.g., Pinker, 1997; see R. J. Sternberg & Kaufman, 2001) would argue that intelligence needs to be understood in terms of commonalities, not differences. Of course, experimental psychologists have made the same claim for many decades, preferring to view individual differences as noise in their data. Perhaps the best solution is some kind of synthesis, as recommended by Cronbach (1957). Jean Piaget, disheartened with his observations from work in Binet's laboratory, provided a synthesis of sorts. He combined measurement with a more cognitive framework for understanding intelligence.

INTELLIGENCE AS ARISING FROM COGNITIVE STRUCTURES AND PROCESSES

Cognitive Structures

Piaget (1952, 1972), among others, has staked out an alternative position to the differential one. Piaget, who was never very interested in individual differences, viewed intelligence as arising from cognitive schemas, or structures that mature as a function of the interaction of the organism with the environment.

Equilibration

Piaget (1926, 1928, 1952, 1972), like many other theorists of intelligence, recognized the importance of adaptation to intelligence. Indeed, he believed adaptation to be its most important principle. In adaptation, individuals learn from the environment and learn to address changes in the environment. Adjustment consists of two complementary processes: assimilation and accommodation. *Assimilation* is the process of absorbing new information and fitting it into an already existing cognitive structure about what the world is like. The complementary process, *accommodation,* involves forming a new cognitive structure in order to understand information. In other words, if no existing cognitive structure seems adequate to understand new information, a new cognitive structure must be formed through the accommodation process.

The complementary processes of assimilation and accommodation, taken together in an interaction, constitute what Piaget referred to as equilibration. *Equilibration* is the balancing of the two, and it is through this balance that people either add to old schemas or form new ones. A *schema,* for Piaget, is a mental image or action pattern. It is essentially a way of organizing sensory information. For example, we have schemas for going to the bank, riding a bicycle, eating a meal, visiting a doctor's office, and the like.

Stages of Intellectual Development

Piaget (1972) suggested that the intelligence of children matures through four discrete stages, or periods of development. Each of these periods builds upon the preceding one, so that development is essentially cumulative.

The first period is the *sensorimotor period,* which occupies birth through roughly 2 years of age. By the end of the sensorimotor period, the infant has started to acquire object permanence, or the realization that objects can exist apart from him or herself. In early infancy, the infant does not ascribe a separate reality to objects. Thus, if a toy is hidden under a pillow or behind a barrier, the infant will not search for the toy because as far as he or she is concerned, it no longer exists when it goes out of sight. By the end of the period, the infant knows that a search will lead to finding the object.

The second period is the *preoperational period,* which emerges roughly between ages 2 and 7. The child is now beginning to represent the world through symbols and images, but the symbols and images are directly dependent upon the immediate perception of the child. The child is still essentially egocentric: He or she sees objects and people only from his or her own point of view. Thus, to the extent that thinking takes place, it is egocentric thinking.

The third period is the *concrete-operational period,* which occupies roughly ages 7 through 11. In this period, the child is able to perform concrete mental operations. Thus, the child now can think through sequences of actions or events that previously had to be enacted physically. The hallmark of concrete-operational thought is reversibility. It now is possible for the child to reverse the direction of thought. The child comes to understand, for example, that subtraction is the reverse of addition and division is the reverse of multiplication. The child can go to the store and back home again or trace out a route on a map and see the way back.

The period is labeled as one of "concrete" operations because operations are performed for objects that are physically present. A major acquisition of the period is conservation, which involves a child's recognizing that objects or quantities can remain the same despite changes in their physical appearance. Suppose, for example, that a child is shown two glasses, one of which is short and fat and the other of which is tall and thin. If a preoperational child watches water poured from the short, fat glass to the tall, thin one, he or she will say that the tall, thin glass has more water than the short, fat one had. But the concrete-operational child will recognize that the quantity of water is the same in the new glass as in the old glass, despite the change in physical appearance.

The period of *formal operations* begins to evolve at around 11 years of age and usually will be fairly fully developed by 16 years of age, although some adults never completely develop formal operations. In the period of formal operations, the child comes to be able to think abstractly and hypothetically, not just concretely. The individual can view a problem from multiple points of view and can think much more systematically than in the past. For example, if asked to provide all possible permutations of the numbers 1, 2, 3, and 4, the child can now implement a systematic strategy for listing all of these permutations. In contrast, the concrete-operational child will have essentially listed permutations at random, without a systematic strategy for generating all of the possible permutations. The child can now think scientifically and use the hypothetico-deductive method to generate and test hypotheses.

Vygotsky and Feuerstein's Theories

Whereas Piaget has emphasized primarily biological maturation in the development of intelligence, other theorists interested in structures, such as Vygotsky (1978) and Feuerstein (1979), have emphasized more the role of interactions of individuals with the environment. Vygotsky suggested that basic to intelligence is *internalization*, which is the internal reconstruction of an external operation. The basic notion is that we observe those in the social environment around us acting in certain ways and we internalize their actions so that they become a part of ourselves.

Vygotsky (1978) gave as an example of internalization the development of pointing. He suggested that, initially, pointing is nothing more than an unsuccessful attempt to grasp something. The child attempts to grasp an object beyond his reach and, initially, is likely to fail. When the mother sees the child attempting to grasp an object, she comes to his aid and is likely to point to the object. He thereby learns to do the same. Thus, the child's unsuccessful attempt engenders a reaction from the mother or some other individual, which leads to his being able to perform that action. Note that it is the social mediation rather than the object itself that provides the basis for the child's learning to point.

Vygotsky also proposed the important notion of a *zone of proximal development,* which refers to functions that have not yet matured but are in the process of maturation. The basic idea is to look not only at developed abilities but also at abilities that are developing. This zone is often measured as the difference between performance before and after instruction. Thus, instruction is given at the time of testing to measure the individual's ability to learn in the testing environment (Brown & French, 1979; Feuerstein, 1980; Grigorenko & Sternberg, 1998). The research suggests that tests of the zone of proximal development tap abilities not measured by conventional tests.

Related ideas have been proposed by Feuerstein (1979, 1980). Feuerstein has suggested that much of intellectual development derives from the mediation of the environment by the mother or other adults. From Feuerstein's point of view, parents serve an important role in development not only for the experiences with which they provide children but also for the way they help children understand these experiences. For example, what would be important would be not so much encouraging children to watch educational television or taking children to museums but rather helping children interpret what they see on television or in museums.

Evaluation

By any standard, Piaget's contribution to the study of intelligence was profound. First, his theory stands alone in terms of its comprehensiveness in accounting for intellectual development. There is no competition in this respect. Second, even the many individuals who have critiqued Piaget's work have honored the work by deeming it worthy of criticism. To the extent that a theory's value is heuristic, in its giving way to subsequent theories, Piaget's work is almost without peer. And much research today, especially in Europe, continues in the tradition of Piaget. Neo-Piagetians, although they have changed many of the details, still build upon many Piagetian theoretical ideas and tasks for studying development. Third, even the most ardent critics of Piaget would concede that many of his ideas were correct. Many of those ideas, such as of centration, conservation, and equilibration, remain alive today in a wide variety of forms. Fourth, Piaget provided an enormous database for developmental psychologists to deal with today as earlier. Replications generally have proven to be successful (Siegler, 1996). Yet the theory of Piaget has not stood the test of time without many scars. Consider some of the main ones.

First, Piaget's interpretations of data have proven to be problematical in many different respects. The list of such critiques is very long. For example, there is evidence that infants achieve object permanence much earlier than Piaget had thought (e.g., Baillargeon, 1987; Bowers, 1967, 1974; Cornell, 1978). There also is evidence that conservation begins earlier than Piaget suspected (Au, Sidle, & Rollins, 1993). As another example, difficulties that Piaget attributed to reasoning appear in some instances actually to have been due to memory (e.g., Bryant & Trabasso, 1971).

Second, it now appears that children often failed Piagetian tasks not because they were unable to do them but because they did not understand the task in the way the experimenter intended. The research of Piaget points out how important it is to make sure one understands a problem not only from one's own point of view as experimenter but also from the child's point of view as participant. For example, being asked whether a collection of marbles contains more blue marbles or more marbles can be confusing, even to an adult.

Third, many investigators today question the whole notion of stages of development (e.g., Brainerd, 1978; Flavell, 1971). Piaget fudged a bit with the concept of *horizontal décalage,* or nonsimultaneous development of skills within a given stage across domains, but many investigators believe that development is simply much more domain specific than Piaget was willing to admit (e.g., Carey, 1985; Keil, 1989). As another example, children master different kinds of conservation problems at different ages, with the differences appearing in a systematic fashion (Elkind, 1961; Katz & Beilin, 1976; S. A. Miller, 1976), with conservation of number appearing before conservation of solid quantity, and conservation of solid quantity before that of weight.

Fourth, many investigators have found Piaget's theory to characterize children's competencies more than their performance (e.g., Green, Ford, & Flamer, 1971). Indeed, Piaget (1972) characterized his model as a competency model. For this reason, it may not be optimally useful in characterizing what children are able to do on a day-to-day basis.

Fifth, although Piaget believed that cognitive development could not be meaningfully accelerated, the evidence suggests the contrary (Beilin, 1980). Piaget probably took too strong a position in this regard.

Finally, some have questioned the emphasis Piaget placed on logical and scientific thinking (e.g., R. J. Sternberg, 1990b). People often seem less rational and more oriented toward heuristics than Piaget believed (Gigerenzer, Todd, & ABC Research Group, 1999).

Vygotsky's theory is, at the turn of the century, more in vogue than Piaget's. It better recognizes the important role of the social-cultural environment in intellectual development. And it also suggests how conventional tests may fail to unearth developing intellectual functions that give children added potential to succeed intellectually. Vygotsky's theory is rather vague, however, and much of the recent development has gone considerably beyond anything Vygotsky proposed. Perhaps if Vygotsky had not died tragically at an early age (38), he would have extensively amplified on his theory.

Cognitive Processes

A related position is that of cognitive theorists (e.g., Anderson, 1983; G. A. Miller, Galanter, & Pribram, 1960; Newell & Simon, 1972), who seek to understand intelligence in terms of the processes of human thought and also the architecture that holds together these processes. These theorists may use the software of a computer as a model of the human mind, or in more recent theorizing, use the massively parallel operating systems of neural circuitry as a model (e.g., Rumelhart, McClelland, & PDP Research Group, 1986). Much of the history of this field is relatively recent, simply because much of the "early" development of the field has occurred in recent times. The field today, for example, has advanced quite far beyond where it was 30 years ago. At the same time, the origins of the field go back to early in the twentieth century and even further, depending upon how broad one is in labeling work as related to this approach.

The Origins of the Process-Based Approach in Spearman's Principles of Cognition

Although some psychologists in the nineteenth century were interested in information processing (e.g., Donders, 1868/1869), the connection between information processing and intelligence seems first to have been explicitly drawn by Charles Spearman (1923), the same individual known for initiating serious psychometric theorizing about intelligence.

Spearman (1923) proposed what he believed to be three fundamental qualitative principles of cognition. The first, *apprehension of experience,* is what today might be called the encoding of stimuli (see R. J. Sternberg, 1977). It involves perceiving the stimuli and their properties. The second principle, *eduction of relations,* is what today might be labeled inference. It is the inferring of a relation between two or more concepts. The third principle, *eduction of correlates,* is what today might be called application. It is the application of an inferred rule to a new situation. For example, in the analogy WHITE : BLACK :: GOOD : ?, apprehension of experience would involve reading each of the terms. Eduction of relations would involve inferring the relation between WHITE and BLACK. And eduction of correlates would involve applying the inferred relation to complete the analogy with *BAD*. Tests that measure these attributes without contamination from many other sources, such as the Raven Progressive Matrices tests, generally provide very good measures of psychometric *g*.

The Cognitive-Correlates Approach

Lee Cronbach (1957) tried to revive interest in the cognitive approach with an article on "the two disciplines of scientific psychology," and efforts to revive this approach in the 1960s proceeded by fits and starts. But serious revival can probably be credited in large part to the work of Earl Hunt. Hunt (1978, 1980; Hunt et al., 1973; Hunt, Lunneborg, & Lewis, 1975) was the originator of what has come to be called the *cognitive-correlates approach* to integrating the study of cognitive processing with the study of intelligence (Pellegrino & Glaser, 1979).

The proximal goal of this research is to estimate parameters representing the durations of performance for information-processing components constituting experimental tasks commonly used in the laboratories of cognitive psychologists. These parameters are then used to investigate the extent to which cognitive components correlate across participants with each other and with scores on psychometric measures commonly believed to measure intelligence, such as the Raven Progressive Matrices tests. Consider an example.

In one task—the Posner and Mitchell (1967) letter-matching task—participants are shown pairs of letters such as "A A" or "A a." After each pair, they are asked to respond as rapidly as possible to one of two questions: "Are the letters a physical match?" or "Are the letters a name match?" Note that the first pair of letters provides an affirmative answer to both questions, whereas the second pair of letters provides an affirmative answer only to the second of the two questions. That is, the first pair provides both a physical and a name match, whereas the second pair provides a name match only.

The goal of such a task is to estimate the amount of time a given participant takes to access lexical information—letter names—in memory. The physical-match condition is included to subtract out (control for) sheer time to perceive the letters and respond to questions. The difference between name and physical match time thus provides the parameter estimate of interest for the task. Hunt and his colleagues found that this parameter and similar parameters in other experimental tasks typically correlate about −.3 with scores on psychometric tests of verbal ability.

The precise tasks used in such research have varied. The letter-matching task has been a particularly popular one, as has been the short-term memory-scanning task originally proposed by S. Sternberg (1969). Other researchers have preferred simple and choice reaction time tasks (e.g., Jensen, 1979, 1982). Most such studies have been conducted with adults, but some have been conducted developmentally with children of various ages (e.g., Keating & Bobbitt, 1978).

The Cognitive-Components Approach

An alternative approach has come to be called the *cognitive-components approach* (Pellegrino & Glaser, 1979). In this approach, participants are tested in their ability to perform tasks of the kinds actually found on standard psychometric tests of mental abilities—for example, analogies, series completions, mental rotations, and syllogisms. Participants typically are timed, and response time is the principal dependent variable, with error rate and pattern-of-response choices serving as further dependent variables. This approach was suggested by R. J. Sternberg (1977; see also Royer, 1971).

The proximal goal in this research is, first, to formulate a model of information processing in performance on the types of tasks found in conventional psychometric tests of intelligence. Second, it is to test the model at the same time as parameters for the model are estimated. Finally, it is to investigate the extent to which these components correlate across participants with each other and with scores on standard psychometric tests. Because the tasks that are analyzed are usually taken directly from psychometric tests of intelligence or are very similar to such tasks, the major issue in this kind of research is not whether there is any correlation at all between cognitive task and psychometric test scores. Rather, the issue is one of isolating the locus or loci of the correlations that are obtained. One seeks to discover which components of information processing are the critical ones from the standpoint of the theory of intelligence (Carroll, 1981; Pellegrino & Glaser, 1979, 1980, 1982; Royer, 1971; R. J. Sternberg, 1977, 1980, 1983; R. J. Sternberg & Gardner, 1983).

Consider the analogies task mentioned above. The participant might be presented with an analogy such as WHITE : BLACK :: GOOD : (A) BAD, (B) BETTER. The task is to choose the better of the two response options as quickly as possible. Cognitive-components analysis might extract a number of components from the task, using an expanded version of Spearman's theory (R. J. Sternberg, 1977). These components might include (a) the time to *encode* the stimulus terms, (b) the time to *infer* the relation between WHITE and BLACK, (c) the time to *map* the relation from the first half of the analogy to the second, (d) the time to *apply* the inferred relation from GOOD to each of the answer options, (e) the time to *compare* the two response options, (f) the time to *justify* BAD as the preferable option, and (g) the time to *respond* with (A).

The Cognitive-Training Approach

The goal of the *cognitive-training approach* is to infer the components of information processing from how individuals perform when they are trained. According to Campione, Brown, and Ferrara (1982), one starts with a theoretical analysis of a task and a hypothesis about a source of individual differences within that task. It might be assumed, for example, that components A, B, and C are required to carry out Task X and that less able children do poorly because of a weakness in component A. To test this assertion, one might train less able participants in the use of A and then retest them on X. If performance improves, the task analysis is supported. If performance does not improve, then either A was not an important component of the task, participants were originally efficient with regard to A and did not need training, or the training was ineffective (see also Belmont & Butterfield, 1971; Belmont, Butterfield, & Ferretti, 1982; Borkowski & Wanschura, 1974).

The Cognitive-Contents Approach

In the *cognitive-contents approach,* one seeks to compare the performances of experts and novices in complex tasks such as physics problems (e.g., Chi, Feltovich, & Glaser, 1981; Chi, Glaser, & Rees, 1982; Larkin, McDermott, Simon, & Simon, 1980), the selection of moves and strategies in chess and other games (Chase & Simon, 1973; DeGroot, 1965; Reitman, 1976), and the acquisition of domain-related information by groups of people at different levels of expertise (Chiesi, Spilich, & Voss, 1979). The notion underlying such research can be seen as abilities being forms of developing expertise (R. J. Sternberg, 1998). In other words, the experts have developed high levels of intellectual abilities in particular domains as results of the development of their expertise. Research on expert-novice differences in a variety of task domains suggests the importance of the amount and form of information storage in long-term memory as key to expert-novice differences.

Evaluation

The information-processing approach to understanding intelligence has been very productive in helping to elucidate the nature of the construct. First, it has been uniquely successful in identifying processes of intelligent thinking. Second, it has not been bound to individual differences as a source of determining the bases of human intelligence. It can detect processes, whether or not they are shared across individuals. Third, it is the approach that seems most conducive to the use of conventional experimental methods of analysis, so that it is possible to gain more control in experimentation by the use of these methods than by the use of alternative methods.

The approach has also had its weaknesses, though. First, in many cases, information-processing psychologists have not been terribly sensitive to individual differences. Second, information-processing psychologists often have been even less sensitive to contextual variables (see Neisser, 1976; R. J. Sternberg, 1997). Third, although information-processing analyses are not subject to the rotation dilemma, it is possible to have two quite different models that nevertheless account for comparable proportions of variation in the response-time or error-rate data, thereby making the models indistinguishable. In other words, difficulties in distinguishing among models can plague this approach every bit as much as they can plague psychometric models (Anderson, 1983). Finally, the approach simply never produced much in the way of useful tests. Even more than a quarter of a century after its initiation, the approach has little to show for itself by way of useful or at least marketable products. Perhaps this is because it never worked quite the way it was supposed to. For example, R. J. Sternberg (1977) and R. J. Sternberg and Gardner (1983) found that the individual parameter representing a regression constant showed higher correlations with psychometric tests of abilities than did parameters representing well-defined information-processing components.

BIOLOGICAL BASES OF INTELLIGENCE

Some theorists have argued that notions of intelligence should be based on biological notions, and usually, on scientific knowledge about the brain. The idea here is that the base of intelligence is in the brain and that behavior is interesting in large part as it elucidates the functioning of the brain.

One of the earlier theories of brain function was proposed by Halstead (1951). Halstead suggested four biologically based abilities: (a) the integrative field factor (C), (b) the abstraction factor (A), (c) the power factor (P), and (d) the directional factor (D). Halstead attributed all four of these abilities primarily to the cortex of the frontal lobes. Halstead's theory became the basis for a test of cognitive functioning, including intellectual aspects (the Halstead-Reitan Neuropsychological Test Battery).

A more influential theory, perhaps, has been that of Donald Hebb (1949). Hebb suggested the necessity of distinguishing among different intelligences. *Intelligence A* is innate potential. It is biologically determined and represents the capacity for development. Hebb described it as "the possession of a good brain and a good neural metabolism" (p. 294). *Intelligence B* is the functioning of the brain in which development has occurred. It represents an average level of performance by a person who is partially grown. Although some inference is necessary in determining either intelligence, Hebb suggested that inferences about intelligence A are far less direct than inferences about intelligence B. A further distinction could be made with regard to *Intelligence C,* which is the score one obtains on an intelligence test. This intelligence is Boring's intelligence as the tests test it.

A theory with an even greater impact on the field of intelligence research is that of the Russian psychologist Alexander Luria (1973, 1980). Luria believed that the brain is a highly differentiated system whose parts are responsible for different aspects of a unified whole. In other words, separate cortical regions act together to produce thoughts and actions of various kinds. Luria (1980) suggested that the brain comprises three main units. The first, a unit of arousal, includes the brain stem and midbrain structures. Included within this first unit are the medulla, reticular activating system, pons, thalamus, and hypothalamus. The second unit of the brain is a sensori-input unit, which includes the temporal, parietal, and occipital lobes. The third unit includes the frontal cortex, which is involved in organization and planning. It comprises cortical structures anterior to the central sulcus.

The most active research program based on Luria's theory has been that of J. P. Das and his colleagues (e.g., Das, Kirby, & Jarman, 1979; Das, Naglieri, & Kirby, 1994; Naglieri & Das, 1990, 1997). The theory as they conceive of it is referred to as PASS theory, referring to *planning, attention, simultaneous processing,* and *successive processing.* The idea is that intelligence requires the ability to plan and to pay attention. It also requires the ability to attend simultaneously to many aspects of a stimulus, such as a picture, or, in some cases, to process stimuli sequentially, as when one memorizes a string of digits to remember a telephone number. Other research and tests also have been based on Luria's theory (e.g., Kaufman & Kaufman, 1983).

An entirely different approach to understanding intellectual abilities has emphasized the analysis of hemispheric specialization in the brain. This work goes back to a finding of an obscure country doctor in France, Marc Dax, who in 1836 presented a little-noticed paper to a medical society meeting in Montpelier. Dax had treated a number of patients suffering from loss of speech as a result of brain damage. The

condition, known today as aphasia, had been reported even in ancient Greece. Dax noticed that in all of more than 40 patients with aphasia, there had been damage to the left hemisphere of the brain but not the right hemisphere. His results suggested that speech and perhaps verbal intellectual functioning originated in the left hemisphere of the brain.

Perhaps the most well-known figure in the study of hemispheric specialization is Paul Broca. At a meeting of the French Society of Anthropology, Broca claimed that a patient of his who was suffering a loss of speech was shown postmortem to have a lesion in the left frontal lobe of the brain. At the time, no one paid much attention. But Broca soon became associated with a hot controversy over whether functions, particular speech, are indeed localized in the brain. The area that Broca identified as involved in speech is today referred to as Broca's area. By 1864, Broca was convinced that the left hemisphere is critical for speech. Carl Wernike, a German neurologist of the late nineteenth century, identified language-deficient patients who could speak but whose speech made no sense. He also traced language ability to the left hemisphere, though to a different precise location, which now is known as Wernicke's area.

Nobel Prize–winning physiologist and psychologist Roger Sperry (1961) later came to suggest that the two hemispheres behave in many respects like separate brains, with the left hemisphere more localized for analytical and verbal processing and the right hemisphere more localized for holistic and imaginal processing. Today it is known that this view was an oversimplification and that the two hemispheres of the brain largely work together (Gazzaniga, Ivry, & Mangun, 1998).

Evaluation

The biological approach has provided unique insights into the nature of intelligence. Its greatest advantage is its recognition that, at some level, the brain is the seat of intelligence. In modern times, and to a lesser extent in earlier times, it has been possible to pinpoint areas of the brain responsible for various functions. The approach is now probably among the most productive in terms of the sheer amount of research being generated.

The greatest weakness of the approach is not so much a problem of the approach as in its interpretation. Reductionists would like to reduce all understanding of intelligence to understanding of brain function, but it just will not work. If we want to understand how to improve the school learning of a normal child through better teaching, we are not going to find an answer in the foreseeable future through the study of the brain. Culture affects what kinds of behavior are viewed as more or less intelligent within a given cultural setting, but again, the biology of the brain will not settle the question of what behavior is considered intelligent within a given culture or why it is considered to be so.

Another weakness of the approach, or at least of its use, has been invalid inferences. Suppose one finds that a certain evoked potential is correlated with a certain cognitive response. All one really knows is that there is a correlation. The potential could cause the response, the response could cause the potential, or both could be based upon some higher-order factor. Yet, reports based on the biological approach often seem to suggest that the biological response is somehow causal (e.g., Hendrickson & Hendrickson, 1980). Useful though the biological approach may be, it always will need to be supplemented by other approaches.

CULTURE AND SOCIETY

A rather different position has been taken by more anthropologically oriented investigators. Modern investigators trace their work back at the very least to the work of Kroeber and Kluckhohn (1952), who studied culture as patterns of behavior acquired and transmitted by symbols. Much of the work in this approach, like that in the cognitive approach, is relatively recent.

The most extreme position is one of radical cultural relativism, proposed by Berry (1974), which rejects assumed psychological universals across cultural systems and requires the generation from within each cultural system of any behavioral concepts to be applied to it (the so-called *emic* approach). According to this viewpoint, therefore, intelligence can be understood only from within a culture, not in terms of views imposed from outside that culture (the so-called *etic* approach). Even in present times, psychologists have argued that the imposition of Western theories or tests on non-Western cultures can result in seriously erroneous conclusions about the capabilities of individuals within those cultures (Greenfield, 1997; R. J. Sternberg et al., 2000).

Other theorists have taken a less extreme view. For example, Michael Cole and his colleagues in the Laboratory of Comparative Human Cognition (1982) argued that the radical position does not take into account the fact that cultures interact. Cole and his colleagues believe that a kind of conditional comparativism is important, so long as one is careful in setting the conditions of the comparison.

Cole and his colleagues gave as an example a study done by Super (1976). Super found evidence that African infants sit and walk earlier than do their counterparts in the United States and Europe. But does such a finding mean that African infants are better walkers, in much the same way that North American psychologists have concluded that American children are better thinkers than African children (e.g., Herrnstein & Murray, 1994)? On the contrary, Super found that mothers in the culture he studied made a self-conscious effort to teach babies to sit and walk as early as possible. He concluded that the African infants are more advanced because they are specifically taught to sit and walk earlier and are encouraged through the provision of opportunities to practice these behaviors. Other motor behaviors were not more advanced. For example, infants found to sit and walk early were actually found to crawl later than did infants in the United States.

Evaluation

The greatest strength of cultural approaches is their recognition that intelligence cannot be understood fully outside its cultural context. Indeed, however common may be the thought processes that underlie intelligent thinking, the behaviors that are labeled as intelligent by a given culture certainly vary from one place to another, as well as from one epoch to another.

The greatest weakness of cultural approaches is their vagueness. They tend to say more about the context of intelligent behavior than they do about the causes of such behavior. Intelligence probably always will have to be understood at many different levels, and any one level in itself will be inadequate. It is for this reason, presumably, that systems models have become particularly popular in recent years. These models attempt to provide an understanding of intelligence at multiple levels.

SYSTEMS MODELS

The Nature of Systems Models

In recent times, systems models have been proposed as useful bases for understanding intelligence. These models seek to understand the complexity of intelligence from multiple points of view and generally combine at least two and often more of the models described above. For example, Gardner (1983, 1993, 1999) has proposed a theory of multiple intelligences, according to which intelligence is not just one thing but multiple things. According to this theory, there are 8 or possibly even 10 multiple intelligences—linguistic, logical-mathematical, spatial, musical, bodily-kinesthetic, interpersonal, intrapersonal, naturalist, and possibly existential and spiritual. R. J. Sternberg (1985, 1988, 1997, 1999b) has proposed a theory of successful intelligence, according to which intelligence can be seen in terms of various kinds of information-processing components combining in different ways to generate analytical, creative, and practical abilities. Ceci (1996) has proposed a bioecological model of intelligence, according to which intelligence is understood in the interaction between the biology of the individual and the ecology in which the individual lives. These theories are described in more detail in "Contemporary Theories of Intelligence" (see Volume 7 of this handbook).

Evaluation

The complexity of systems models is both a blessing and a curse. It is a blessing because it enables such models to recognize the multiple complex levels of intelligence. It is a curse because the models become more difficult to test. Indeed, one of the most popular models, that of Gardner (1983), was proposed some time ago. But as of when this chapter is being written, there has not been even one empirical test of the model as a whole, scarcely a commendable record for a scientific theory. This record compares with thousands of predictive empirical tests of psychometric or Piagetian models and probably hundreds of tests of information-processing models. R. J. Sternberg's (1997) triarchic theory has been predictively empirically tested numerous times (see, e.g., R. J. Sternberg et al., 2000), but because most of these tests have been by members of Sternberg's research group, the results cannot be considered definitive at this time.

CONCLUSION: RELATIONS AMONG THE VARIOUS MODELS OF THE NATURE OF INTELLIGENCE

There are different ways of resolving the conflicts among alternative models of the nature of intelligence.

Different Names

One way of resolving the conflicts is to use different names for different constructs. For example, some researchers stake their claim on a certain number of intelligences or intellectual abilities. Is intelligence, fundamentally, 1 important thing (Spearman, 1904), or 7 things (Gardner, 1983), or maybe 10 things (Gardner, 1999), or perhaps 120 things (Guilford, 1967), or even 150 or more things (Guilford, 1982)? Some

might say that those who are splitters are actually talking of "talents" rather than intelligence, or that they are merely slicing the same "pie" everyone else is eating, but very thinly.

Sometimes different names are used to reflect the same construct! For example, what once was the Scholastic Aptitude Test later became the Scholastic Assessment Test and still later became simply the SAT, an acronym perhaps belatedly asserted to stand for nothing in particular. The change in the name of the test points out how, over time and place, similar or even identical constructs can be given names in order to reflect temporally or spatially local sensibilities about what constitutes desirable or even acceptable terminology. Many similar efforts, such as referring to what usually is called *intelligence* as *cognitive development* (R. L. Thorndike, Hagen, & Sattler, 1986), point out the extent to which the history of intelligence is in part a battle over names.

In a sense, the history of the field of intelligence bifurcates. Some investigators, perhaps starting with Boring (1923), have suggested we define intelligence as what intelligence tests measure and get on with testing it; other investigators, such as Spearman (1904, 1927) and Thurstone (1938) view the battle over what intelligence is as determining what should be tested.

Fighting for "Truth"

A second response to the differences among theories has been for researchers to stake their ground and then slug it out in a perceived fight for the truth. Some of these battles became rather bitter. Underlying these battles was the notion that only one model or theory embedded under a model could be correct, and therefore the goal of research should be to figure out which one that is.

Dialectical Synthesis

A third response has been to seek some kind of dialectical synthesis among alternative models or theories embedded under these models. There have been different kinds of syntheses.

One Kind of Approach or Methodology Eventually Should Be Replaced by Another

Some investigators have argued that their approach is the best the field can do at the time, but that the approach later will be replaced. For example, Louis L. Thurstone suggested that factor analysis is useful in early stages of investigation, laboratory research, later on. In other words, the differential approach could be replaced by a more cognitively based one. Thurstone (1947), who was largely a psychometric theorist, argued that

> The exploratory nature of factor analysis is often not understood. Factor analysis has its principal usefulness at the borderline of intelligence. It is naturally superseded by rational formulations in terms of the science involved. Factor analysis is useful, especially in those domains where basic and fruitful concepts are essentially lacking and where crucial experiments have been difficult to conceive. . . . But if we have scientific intuition and sufficient ingenuity, the rough factorial map of a new domain will enable us to proceed beyond the exploratory factorial stage to the more direct forms of psychological experimentation in the laboratory. (p. 56)

Coexistence

Other investigators argued for coexistence. Charles Spearman, for example, had both a differential theory of intelligence (Spearman, 1927) and a cognitively based one (Spearman, 1923) (both of which were described earlier). Cronbach (1957) argued for the merger of the fields of differential and experimental psychology.

Synthetic Integration

Perhaps the best way to achieve a certain coherence in the field is to recognize that there is no one right "model" or "approach" and that different ones elucidate different aspects of a very complex phenomenon. Models such as the systems models are useful in attempting integrations, but they fall short in integrating all that we know about intelligence. Eventually, the time may come when such large-scale integrations can be achieved in ways that are theoretically meritorious and empirically sound. In the meantime, it is likely that many different conceptions of intelligence will compete for the attention of the scientific as well as the lay public.

REFERENCES

Anderson, J. R. (1983). *The architecture of cognition.* Cambridge, MA: Harvard University Press.

Au, T. K., Sidle, A. L., & Rollins, K. B. (1993). Developing an intuitive understanding of conservation and contamination: Invisible particles as a plausible mechanism. *Developmental Psychology, 29,* 286–299.

Baillargeon, R. L. (1987). Young infants' reasoning about the physical and spatial properties of a hidden object. *Cognitive Development 2*(3), 179–200.

Beilin, H. (1990). Piaget's theory: Alive and more vigorous than ever. *Human Development, 33,* 362–365.

Belmont, J. M., & Butterfield, E. C. (1971). Learning strategies as determinants of memory deficiencies. *Cognitive Psychology, 2,* 411–420.

Belmont, J. M., Butterfield, E. C., & Ferretti, R. (1982). To secure transfer of training, instruct self-management skills. In D. K. Detterman & R. J. Sternberg (Eds.), *How and how much can intelligence be increased?* (pp. 147–154). Norwood, NJ: Ablex.

Berry, J. W. (1974). Radical cultural relativism and the concept of intelligence. In J. W. Berry & P. R. Dasen (Eds.), *Culture and cognition: Readings in cross-cultural psychology* (pp. 225–229). London: Methuen.

Binet, A., & Simon, T. (1916a). *The development of intelligence in children.* Baltimore: Williams & Wilkins. (Original work published 1905)

Binet, A., & Simon, T. (1916b). *The intelligence of the feeble-minded* (E. S. Kite, Trans.). Baltimore: Williams & Wilkins.

Boring, E. G. (1923, June 6). Intelligence as the tests test it. *New Republic,* 35–37.

Borkowski, J. G., & Wanschura, P. B. (1974). Mediational processes in the retarded. In N. R. Ellis (Ed.), *International review of research in mental retardation, 7.* New York: Academic Press.

Bowers, T. G. R. (1967). The development of object-permanence: Some studies of existence constancy. *Perception and Psychophysics, 2,* 411–418.

Bowers, T. G. R. (1974). *Development in infancy.* New York: Freeman.

Brainerd, C. J. (1978). The stage question in cognitive-developmental theory. *Behavioral and Brain Sciences, 1,* 173–182.

Brand, C. (1996). *The g factor: General intelligence and its implications.* Chichester, England: Wiley.

Brown, A. L., & DeLoache, J. S. (1978). Skills, plans, and self-regulation. In R. Siegler (Ed.), *Children's thinking: What develops?* Hillsdale, NJ: Erlbaum.

Brown, A. L., & French, A. L. (1979). The zone of potential development: Implications for intelligence testing in the year 2000. In R. J. Sternberg & D. K. Detterman (Eds.), *Human intelligence: Perspectives on its theory and measurement* (pp. 217–235). Norwood, NJ: Ablex.

Bryant, P. E., & Trabasso, T. (1971). Transitive inferences and memory in young children. *Nature, 232,* 456–458.

Burt, C. (1949). Alternative methods of factor analysis and their relations to Pearson's method of "principal axis." *British Journal of Psychology, Statistical Section, 2,* 98–121.

Campione, J. C., Brown, A. L., & Ferrara, R. (1982). Mental retardation and intelligence. In R. J. Sternberg (Ed.), *Handbook of human intelligence* (pp. 392–490). New York: Cambridge University Press.

Carey, S. (1985). *Conceptual change in childhood.* Cambridge, MA: MIT Press.

Carroll, J. B. (1981). Ability and task difficulty in cognitive psychology. *Educational Researcher, 10,* 11–21.

Carroll, J. B. (1982). The measurement of intelligence. In R. J. Sternberg (Ed.), *Handbook of human intelligence* (pp. 29–120). New York: Cambridge University Press.

Carroll, J. B. (1993). *Human cognitive abilities: A survey of factor-analytic studies.* New York: Cambridge University Press.

Cattell, J. M. (1890). Mental tests and measurements. *Mind, 15,* 373–380.

Cattell, R. B. (1971). *Abilities: Their structure, growth and action.* Boston: Houghton Mifflin.

Ceci, S. J. (1996). *On intelligence . . . more or less.* Cambridge, MA: Harvard University Press.

Chase, W. G., & Simon, H. A. (1973). The mind's eye in chess. In W. G. Chase (Ed.), *Visual information processing* (pp. 215–281). New York: Academic Press.

Chi, M. T. H., Feltovich, P. J., & Glaser, R. (1981). Categorization and representation of physics problems by experts and novices. *Cognitive Science, 5,* 121–152.

Chi, M. T. H., Glaser, R., & Rees, E. (1982). Expertise in problem solving. In R. J. Sternberg (Ed.), *Advances in the psychology of human intelligence* (Vol. 1, pp. 7–75). Hillsdale, NJ: Erlbaum.

Chiesi, H. L., Spilich, G. J., & Voss, J. F. (1979). Acquisition of domain-related information in relation to high and low domain knowledge. *Journal of Verbal Learning and Verbal Behavior, 18,* 257–273.

Cornell, E. H. (1978). Learning to find things: A reinterpretation of object permanence studies. In L. S. Siegel & C. J. Brainerd (Eds.), *Alternatives to Piaget: Critical essays on the theory.* New York: Academic Press.

Cronbach, L. J. (1957). The two disciplines of scientific psychology. *American Psychologist, 12,* 671–684.

Darwin, C. (1859). *The origin of species.* London: Murray.

Das, J. P., Kirby, J. R., & Jarman, R. F. (1979). *Simultaneous and successive cognitive processes.* New York: Academic Press.

Das, J. P., Naglieri, J. A., & Kirby, J. R. (1994). *Assessment of cognitive processes: The PASS theory of intelligence.* Needham Heights, MA: Allyn & Bacon.

DeGroot, A. D. (1965). *Thought and choice in chess.* The Hague: Mouton.

Donders, F. C. (1868–1869). Over de snelheid van psychische processen. Onderzoekingen gedaan in het Physiologisch Laboratorium der Utrechtsche Hoogeschool. *Tweede reeks, II,* 92–120.

Elkind, D. (1961). Children's discovery of the conservation of mass, weight, and volume: Piaget replication study II. *Journal of Genetic Psychology, 98,* 219–227.

Evans, J. (1989). *Bias in human reasoning: Causes and consequences.* Hove, England: Erlbaum.

Feuerstein, R. (1979). *The dynamic assessment of retarded performers: The learning potential assessment device theory, instruments, and techniques.* Baltimore: University Park Press.

Feuerstein, R. (1980). *Instrumental enrichment: An intervention program for cognitive modifiability.* Baltimore: University Park Press.

Flavell, J. H. (1971). Stage related properties of cognitive development. *Cognitive Psychology, 2,* 421–453.

Flavell, J. H., & Wellman, H. M. (1977). Metamemory. In R. V. Kail Jr., & J. W. Hagen (Eds.), *Perspectives on the development of memory and cognition* (pp. 3–33). Hillsdale, NJ: Erlbaum.

Galton, F. (1869). *Heredity genius: An inquiry into its laws and consequences.* London: Macmillan.

Galton, F. (1883). *Inquiry into human faculty and its development.* London: Macmillan.

Gardner, H. (1983). *Frames of mind: The theory of multiple intelligences.* New York: Basic Books.

Gardner, H. (1993). *Multiple intelligences: The theory in practice.* New York: Basic Books.

Gardner, H. (1999). Are there additional intelligences? The case for naturalist, spiritual, and existential intelligences. In J. Kane (Ed.), *Education, information, and transformation* (pp. 111–131). Upper Saddle River, NJ: Prentice-Hall.

Gazzaniga, M. S., Ivry, R. B., & Mangun, G. (1998). *Cognitive neuroscience: The biology of the mind.* New York: Norton.

Gigerenzer, G., Todd, P. M., & The ABC Research Group. (1999). *Simple heuristics that make us smart: Evolution and cognition.* New York: Oxford University Press.

Gould, S. J. (1981). *The mismeasure of man.* New York: Norton.

Green, D. R., Ford, M. P., & Flamer, G. B. (1971). *Measurement and Piaget.* New York: McGraw-Hill.

Greenfield, P. M. (1997). You can't take it with you: Why abilities assessments don't cross cultures. *American Psychologist, 52*(10), 1115–1124.

Grigorenko, E. L., & Sternberg, R. J. (1998). Dynamic testing. *Psychological Bulletin, 124,* 75–111.

Grotzer, T. A., & Perkins, D. A. (2000). Teaching of intelligence: A performance conception. In R. J. Sternberg (Ed.), *Handbook of intelligence* (pp. 492–515). New York: Cambridge University Press.

Guilford, J. P. (1967). *The nature of human intelligence.* New York: McGraw-Hill.

Guilford, J. P. (1982). Cognitive psychology's ambiguities: Some suggested remedies. *Psychological Review, 89,* 48–59.

Guilford, J. P., & Hoepfner, R. (1971). *The analysis of intelligence.* New York: McGraw-Hill.

Gustafsson, J. E. (1984). A unifying model for the structure of intellectual abilities. *Intelligence, 8,* 179–203.

Gustafsson, J. E. (1988). Hierarchical models of the structure of cognitive abilities. In R. J. Sternberg (Ed.), *Advances in the psychology of human intelligence* (Vol. 4, pp. 35–71). Hillsdale, NJ: Erlbaum.

Guttman, L. (1954). A new approach to factor analysis: The radix. In P. F. Lazarsfeld (Ed.), *Mathematical thinking in the social sciences* (pp. 258–348). New York: Free Press.

Halstead, W. C. (1951). Biological intelligence. *Journal of Personality, 20,* 118–130.

Hebb, D. O. (1949). *The organization of behavior: A neuropsychological theory.* New York: Wiley.

Hegel, G. W. F. (1931). *The phenomenology of the mind* (2nd ed., J. D. Baillie, Trans.). London: Allen & Unwin. (Original work published 1807)

Hendrickson, A. E., & Hendrickson, D. E. (1980). The biological basis for individual differences in intelligence. *Personality and Individual Differences, 1,* 3–33.

Herrnstein, R. J., & Murray, C. (1994). *The bell curve.* New York: Free Press.

Holzinger, K. J. (1938). Relationships between three multiple orthogonal factors and four bifactors. *Journal of Educational Psychology, 29,* 513–519.

Horn, J. L. (1967). On subjectivity in factor analysis. *Educational and Psychological Measurement, 27,* 811–820.

Horn, J. L. (1994). Theory of fluid and crystallized intelligence. In R. J. Sternberg (Ed.), *The encyclopedia of human intelligence* (Vol. 1, pp. 443–451). New York: Macmillan.

Horn, J. L., & Knapp, J. R. (1973). On the subjective character of the empirical base of Guilford's structure-of-intellect model. *Psychological Bulletin, 80,* 33–43.

Humphreys, L. (1962). The organization of human abilities. *American Psychologist, 17,* 475–483.

Hunt, E., Frost, N., & Lunneborg, C. (1973). Individual differences in cognition: A new approach to intelligence. In G. Bower (Ed.), *The psychology of learning and motivation* (Vol. 7, pp. 87–122). New York: Academic Press.

Hunt, E. B. (1978). Mechanics of verbal ability. *Psychological Review, 85,* 109–130.

Hunt, E. B. (1980). Intelligence as an information-processing concept. *British Journal of Psychology, 71,* 449–474.

Hunt, E. B., Lunneborg, C., & Lewis, J. (1975). What does it mean to be high verbal? *Cognitive Psychology, 7,* 194–227.

Intelligence and its measurement: A symposium. (1921). *Journal of Educational Psychology, 12,* 123–147, 195–216, 271–275.

Jensen, A. R. (1969). How much can we boost IQ and scholastic achievement? *Harvard Educational Review, 39,* 1–123.

Jensen, A. R. (1979). *g:* Outmoded theory of unconquered frontier? *Creative Science and Technology, 2,* 16–29.

Jensen, A. R. (1982). Reaction time and psychometric *g.* In H. J. Eysenck (Ed.), *A model for intelligence.* Heidelberg, Germany: Springer-Verlag.

Jensen, A. R. (1998). *The g factor: The science of mental ability.* Westport, CT: Praeger/Greenwood.

Jensen, A. R. (in press). Psychometric *g:* Definition and substantiation. In R. J. Sternberg & E. L. Grigorenko (Eds.), *General factor of intelligence: Fact or fiction.* Mahwah, NJ: Erlbaum.

Katz, H., & Beilin, H. (1976). A test of Bryant's claims concerning the young child's understanding of quantitative invariance. *Child Development, 47,* 877–880.

Kaufman, A., & Kaufman, N. (1983). Kaufman Assessment Battery for Children. Circle Pines, MN: American Guidance Service.

Kauffman, S. (1995). *At home in the universe: The search for laws of self-organization and complexity.* New York: Oxford University Press.

Keating, D. P., & Bobbit, B. (1978). Individual and developmental differences in cognitive processing components of mental ability. *Child Development, 49,* 155–169.

Keil, F. C. (1989). *Concepts, kinds, and cognitive development.* Cambridge, MA: MIT Press.

Kroeber, A. L., & Kluckhohn, C. (1952). *Culture: A critical review of concepts and definitions* [Papers, Peabody Museum of Archaeology and Ethnology Vol. 47, pp. viii, 223]. Cambridge, MA: Harvard University.

Laboratory of Comparative Human Cognition. (1982). Culture and intelligence. In R. J. Sternberg (Ed.), *Handbook of human intelligence* (pp. 642–719). New York: Cambridge University Press.

Larkin, J. H., McDermott, J., Simon, D. P., & Simon, H. A. (1980). Expert and novice performance in solving physics problems. *Science, 208,* 1335–1342.

Luria, A. R. (1973). *The working brain.* New York: Basic Books.

Luria, A. R. (1980). *Higher cortical functions in man* (2nd ed.). New York: Basic Books.

Mackintosh, N. J. (1998). *IQ and human intelligence.* Oxford, England: Oxford University Press.

Mazzoni, G., & Nelson, T. O. (1998). *Metacognition and cognitive neuropsychology: Monitoring and control processes.* Mahwah, NJ: Erlbaum.

McNemar, Q. (1951). The factors in factoring behavior. *Psychometrika, 16,* 353–359.

McNemar, Q. (1964). Lost: Our intelligence? Why? *American Psychologist, 19,* 871–882.

Miles, T. R. (1957). On defining intelligence. *British Journal of Educational Psychology, 27,* 153–165.

Miller, G. A., Galanter, E. H., & Pribram, K. H. (1960). *Plans and the structure of behavior.* New York: Holt, Rinehart and Winston.

Miller, S. A. (1976). Nonverbal assessment of Piagetian concepts. *Psychological Bulletin, 83,* 405–430.

Naglieri, J. A., & Das, J. P. (1990). Planning, attention, simultaneous, and successive cognitive processes as a model for intelligence. *Journal of Psychoeducational Assessment, 8,* 303–337.

Naglieri, J. A., & Das, J. P. (1997). *Cognitive assessment system.* Itasca, IL: Riverside.

Neisser, U. (1976). General, academic, and artificial intelligence. In L. Resnick (Ed.), *Human intelligence: Perspectives on its theory and measurement* (pp. 179–189). Norwood, NJ: Ablex.

Newell, A., & Simon, H. A. (1972). *Human problem solving*. Englewood Cliffs, NJ: Prentice-Hall.

Pellegrino, J. W., & Glaser, R. (1979). Cognitive correlates and components in the analysis of individual differences. In R. J. Sternberg & D. K. Detterman (Eds.), *Human intelligence: Perspectives on its theory and measurement* (pp. 61–88). Norwood, NJ: Ablex.

Pellegrino, J. W., & Glaser, R. (1980). Components of inductive reasoning. In R. E. Snow, P.-A. Federico, & W. E. Montague (Eds.), *Aptitude, learning, and instruction: Cognitive process analyses of aptitude* (Vol. 1, pp. 177–217). Hillsdale, NJ: Erlbaum.

Pellegrino, J. W., & Glaser, R. (1982). Analyzing aptitudes for learning: Inductive reasoning. In R. Glaser (Ed.), *Advances in instructional psychology* (Vol. 2). Hillsdale, NJ: Erlbaum.

Piaget, J. (1926). *The language and thought of the child*. New York: Harcourt, Brace.

Piaget, J. (1928). *Judgment and reasoning in the child*. London: Routledge & Kegan Paul.

Piaget, J. (1952). *The origins of intelligence in children*. New York: International Universities Press.

Piaget, J. (1972). *The psychology of intelligence*. Totowa, NJ: Littlefield Adams.

Pinker, S. (1997). *How the mind works*. New York: Norton.

Popper, K. R. (1959). *The logic of scientific discovery*. London: Hutchinson.

Posner, M. I., & Mitchell, R. F. (1967). Chronometric analysis of classification. *Psychological Review, 74,* 392–409.

Raven, J. C., Court, J. H., & Raven, J. (1992). *Manual for Raven's Progressive Matrices and Mill Hill Vocabulary Scales*. Oxford, England: Oxford Psychologists Press.

Reitman, J. (1976). Skilled perception in GO: Deducing memory structures from interresponse times. *Cognitive Psychology, 8,* 336–356.

Royer, F. L. (1971). Information processing of visual figures in the digit symbol substitution task. *Journal of Experimental Psychology, 87,* 335–342.

Rumelhart, D. E., McClelland, J. L., & The PDP Research Group. (1986). *Parallel distributed processing: Explorations in the microstructure of cognition: Foundations* (Vol. 1). Cambridge, MA: MIT Press.

Sacks, P. (1999). *Standardized minds: The high price of America's testing culture and what we can do to change it*. Reading, MA: Perseus Books.

Schmidt, F. L., & Hunter, J. E. (1998). The validity and utility of selection methods in personnel psychology: Practical and theoretical implications of 85 years of research findings. *Psychological Bulletin, 124,* 262–274.

Sharp, S. E. (1899). Individual psychology: A study in psychological method. *American Journal of Psychology, 10,* 329–391.

Siegler, R. S. (1996). *Emerging minds: The process of change in children's thinking*. New York: Oxford University Press.

Sloman, S. A. (1996). The empirical case for two systems of reasoning. *Psychological Bulletin, 119,* 3–22.

Snow, R. E., Kyllonen, P. C., & Marshalek, B. (1984). The topography of ability and learning correlations. In R. J. Sternberg (Ed.), *Advances in the psychology of human intelligence* (Vol. 2, pp. 47–103). Hillsdale, NJ: Erlbaum.

Spearman, C. (1904). General intelligence, objectively determined and measured. *American Journal of Psychology, 15*(2), 201–293.

Spearman, C. (1923). *The nature of intelligence and the principles of cognition* (2nd ed.) London: Mcmillan.

Spearman, C. (1927). *The abilities of man*. London: Macmillan.

Sperry, R. W. (1961). Cerebral organization and behavior. *Science, 133,* 1749–1757.

Sternberg, R. J. (1977). *Intelligence, information processing, and analogical reasoning: The componential analysis of human abilities*. Hillsdale, NJ: Erlbaum.

Sternberg, R. J. (1980). Factor theories of intelligence are all right almost. *Educational Researcher, 9,* 6–13, 18.

Sternberg, R. J. (1982). Natural, unnatural, and supernatural concepts. *Cognitive Psychology, 14,* 451–488.

Sternberg, R. J. (1983). Components of human intelligence. *Cognition, 15,* 1–48.

Sternberg, R. J. (1985). *Beyond IQ: A triarchic theory of human intelligence*. New York: Cambridge University Press.

Sternberg, R. J. (1988). Mental self-government: A theory of intellectual styles and their development. *Human Development, 31*(4), 197–224.

Sternberg, R. J. (1990a). *Metaphors of mind: Conceptions of the nature of intelligence*. New York: Cambridge University Press.

Sternberg, R. J. (1990b). Thinking styles: Keys to understanding student performance. *Phi Delta Kappan, 71,* 366–371.

Sternberg, R. J. (Ed.). (1994). *Encyclopedia of human intelligence*. New York: Macmillan.

Sternberg, R. J. (1997). *Successful intelligence*. New York: Plume.

Sternberg, R. J. (1998). Abilities are forms of developing expertise. *Educational Researcher, 27,* 11–20.

Sternberg, R. J. (1999a). Successful intelligence: Finding a balance. *Trends in Cognitive Sciences, 3,* 436–442.

Sternberg, R. J. (1999b). The theory of successful intelligence. *Review of General Psychology, 3,* 292–316.

Sternberg, R. J. (Ed.). (2000). *Handbook of intelligence*. New York: Cambridge University Press.

Sternberg, R. J. (2002). Contemporary theories of intelligence. In I. B. Weiner (Series Ed.) & W. M. Reynolds & G. M. (Vol. Eds.), *Comprehensive handbook of psychology. Vol. 7: Educational psychology*. New York: Wiley.

Sternberg, R. J., & Berg, C. A. (1986). Quantitative integration: Definitions of intelligence: A comparison of the 1921 and 1986 symposia. In R. J. Sternberg & D. K. Detterman (Eds.), *What is intelligence? Contemporary viewpoints on its nature and definition* (pp. 155–162). Norwood, NJ: Ablex.

Sternberg, R. J., Conway, B. E., Ketron, J. L., & Bernstein, M. (1981). People's conceptions of intelligence. *Journal of Personality and Social Psychology, 41,* 37–55.

Sternberg, R. J., & Detterman, D. K. (1986). *What is intelligence?* Norwood, NJ: Ablex.

Sternberg, R. J., Forsythe, G. B., Hedlund, J., Horvath, J., Snook, S., Williams, W. M., et al. (2000). *Practical intelligence.* New York: Cambridge University Press.

Sternberg, R. J., & Gardner, M. K. (1983). Unities in inductive reasoning. *Journal of Experimental Psychology: General, 112,* 80–116.

Sternberg, R. J., & Kaufman, J. C. (Eds.). (2001). *The evolution of intelligence.* Mahwah, NJ: Erlbaum.

Sternberg, S. (1969). Memory-scanning: Mental processes revealed by reaction-time experiments. *American Scientist, 4,* 421–457.

Super, C. M. (1976). Environmental effects on motor development: The case of African infant precocity. *Developmental Medicine and Child Neurology, 18,* 561–567.

Terman, L. M., & Merrill, M. A. (1937). *Measuring intelligence.* Boston: Houghton Mifflin.

Terman, L. M., & Merrill, M. A. (1973). *Stanford–Binet Intelligence Scale: Manual for the third revision.* Boston: Houghton Mifflin.

Thomson, G. H. (1939). *The factorial analysis of human ability.* London: University of London Press.

Thorndike, E. L., Bregman, E. D., Cobb, M. V., & Woodyard, E. I. (1926). *The measurement of intelligence.* New York: Teachers College Press.

Thorndike, R. L., Hagen, E. P., & Sattler, J. M. (1986). *Stanford–Binet Intelligence Scale: Guide for administering and scoring the fourth edition.* Chicago: Riverside.

Thurstone, L. L. (1938). *Primary mental abilities.* Chicago: University of Chicago Press.

Thurstone, L. L. (1947). *Multiple factor analysis.* Chicago: University of Chicago Press.

Thurstone, L. L., & Thurstone, T. C. (1941). *Factorial studies of intelligence.* Chicago: University of Chicago Press.

Vernon, P. E. (1971). *The structure of human abilities.* London: Methuen.

Vygotsky, L. S. (1978). *Mind in society: The development of higher psychological processes.* Cambridge, MA: Harvard University Press.

Wagner, R. K. (2000). Practical intelligence. In R. J. Sternberg (Ed.), *Handbook of human intelligence* (pp. 380–395). New York: Cambridge University Press.

Wechsler, D. (1991). *Manual for the Wechsler Intelligence Scales for Children* (3rd ed.). San Antonio, TX: Psychological Corporation.

Wissler, C. (1901). The correlation of mental and physical tests. *Psychological Review, Monograph Supplement 3*(6).

Yang, S., & Sternberg, R. J. (1997a). Conceptions of intelligence in ancient Chinese philosophy. *Journal of Theoretical and Philosophical Psychology, 17*(2), 101–119.

Yang, S., & Sternberg, R. J. (1997b). Taiwanese Chinese people's conceptions of intelligence. *Intelligence, 25*(1), 21–36.

CHAPTER 8

Emotion

GEORGE MANDLER

PREMODERN HISTORY OF EMOTION   157
THEMES IN A MODERN HISTORY OF EMOTION   159
TWO DISTINCT PSYCHOLOGIES OF EMOTION   159
    Peripheral/Organic Approaches to Emotion   160
    Central/Mental Approaches to Emotion   165
    The Conflict Theories   167

A FUTURE HISTORY   171
    William James's Question   171
    How Many Theories?   172
REFERENCES   172

Emotion: A jungle, not a garden. One dictionary definition of a jungle describes it as a confused mass of objects, whereas a garden is a rich, well-cultivated region. The history of emotion is confused and disordered, and cultivation has been at best haphazard. I will attempt to tell the story of how the jungle grew, hoping to do some cultivating and weeding in the process. When we emerge from the jungle, the reader may have some notion how to proceed with further cultivation.

The attempt to understand human emotions has been split by two apparently contradictory tendencies. On the one hand, emotion as a topic has been traditionally part of any psychology of mind—it was not possible to try to explain people without explaining emotion. On the other hand, there has been from the beginning a lack of agreement as to what exactly is meant by "emotion," nor is there any discernible centripetal movement toward a consensual definition in contemporary thought. The result is that even if one believes in the notion of human progress, there is little evidence of a focus or consensus in the psychology of emotion. Themes are often repeated and old battles resurrected, but emotion lags behind such psychological success stories as found in memory, vision, early development, hearing, attention, and so forth. There is a web of directions, not a single path, in the history of emotion.

I shall briefly sketch the prehistory of emotion, describing some of the highlights that led up to the nineteenth century and the adoption by psychologists of modern, "scientific" attitudes and goals. The advent of a determinedly scientific psychology and the age of modernism occupy prominent late-nineteenth-century positions that coincide with a major shift in the psychology of emotion—the contribution of William James. Consequently, I let James lead us into the modern age and its two dominant—and as yet unreconciled—traditions of the organic and mental approaches to emotion. I end with a discussion of the contemporary scene and its precursors. A more extended treatment of such topics in the history of emotion as animal studies, the neurophysiology of emotion, phenomenology, and literary allusions may be found in such important secondary sources as Gardiner et al. (1937) and Ruckmick (1936). For a discussion of emotions in the context of literature and social history, but not psychology, see Elster (1999).

PREMODERN HISTORY OF EMOTION

Discussions of the emotions in pre-Socratic and later Greek thought centered, like so many of its discussions of complex human consciousness, on their relation to the mysteries of human life and often dealt with the relevance of the emotions to problems of ethics and aesthetics. Secondarily, their concerns addressed questions of the control and use of the emotions. That approach often stressed the distracting influences of the emotions—a theme that has continued in a minor key to modern times. To the extent that this distracting effect was due to the bodily, somatic symptoms of the emotions, the

Greeks approached emotion with a form of double-entry bookkeeping, dealing both with psychic and somatic aspects of emotional phenomena (Brett, 1928). Aristotle was the exception to his times when he considered feelings as natural phenomena, and his descriptions of the individual passions remain a model of naturalistic observation. But Aristotle did not allow for simple, pure affective processes. As he so often did, Aristotle sounded a more modern note when his description of emotion required the cognitive elements of a percept, an affective component of pleasantness/unpleasantness, and a conative (motivational) effort (Hammond, 1902).

Post-Aristotelian philosophy devoted much effort to various analyses of the emotions, yet Aristotle continued to dominate much of the thought of the Middle Ages well into the fifteenth century. The age of the Scholastics was often preoccupied with commentary and theological speculations and frequently relegated emotions to an expression of animal spirits, very distinct from the moral spirit and intellect with which the ancients had wrestled. The main contribution to the history of thought about emotion came from the great systematizer, Thomas Aquinas. He also asserted that emotions disturb thought and should be controlled, but his classifications barely survived to the Renaissance. On the whole, the period of theological dominance was best described in the late sixteenth century by Suarez (1856): *Pauca dicunt et in variis locis* ("They say little and do so in various places").

The Renaissance came late in the history of the emotions, though there was an early whiff of fresh air in the early-sixteenth-century work of the Spanish philosopher Juan Luis Vives, who explored and described the different passions (emotions) with empirical concern and clarity. However, the important shift came with René Descartes and his publication in 1649 of his *Les passions de l'âme (The Passions of the Soul)* (Descartes, 1649). In the spirit of his day, he started afresh, postulating six primary passions, with all the rest constructed of those six: wonder, love, hate, desire, joy, and sadness. This fundamentalist approach to constructing emotions is still with us, though Descartes' love, desire, and wonder have been substituted by other, more contemporary, states such as disgust, guilt, and shame.

Later in the seventeenth century Baruch Spinoza (1677/1876) broke with the still popular view of the emotions as bothersome intrusions and insisted that they be seen as natural and lawful phenomena. He is one of the major expositors of the notion that the passions are essentially conative, that is, derived from motivational forces, just as Aristotle and Hobbes had asserted before him. For Spinoza the passions—pleasure, pain, and desire—are all derived from the drive to self-preservation, to maintain one's own existence. By the late eighteenth century, Immanuel Kant definitively made feelings into a special class of psychical processes—a third mental faculty added to the other two of knowing and appetition (Kant, 1800). Kant, who dominated the early nineteenth century in philosophy in general, also did so in the realm of feelings and emotion. His view of feelings/emotions as a separate faculty was maintained well into the twentieth century, as was his distinction between (temporary) emotions and (lasting) passions.

With the nineteenth century, classification became a major theme of the new scientism, and the emotions followed suit. For example, Wilhelm Wundt's system went from simple to complex feelings and then to true emotions. Complex emotions were analyzed in terms of a half dozen or more types and tokens of feelings (Wundt, 1891). Two other major contributors to the nineteenth-century classificatory ambience were Alexander Bain and James McCosh. Bain, arguably the last great figure of British associationism, contributed to the enumerative wars by naming love, anger, and fear as primary emotions, but he also muddied the waters by needless multiplication of the list of emotions and introducing such unusual entries as emotions of property, power, and knowledge (Bain, 1859/1875). Another classifier popular in the United States was McCosh, a member of the Scottish school of psychology, who divided the field into appetences (the desire for specific objects), ideas, excitements, and organic affections (pleasant and unpleasant bodily reactions) (McCosh, 1880).

All these rather evanescent attempts were brought to an end by the James-Lange-Sergi theory, to which I shall return shortly. But first it is necessary to describe the landscape of the new century that William James introduced, to show how multifaceted the psychology of emotion became and how confused it may have looked, just as we enter another century with as many, and sometimes as different, theoretical positions as marked the twentieth.

The best illustration of the confusion of the new century is shown in three volumes of symposia on "Feelings and Emotions" (Arnold, 1970; Reymert, 1928, 1950). The 101 contributions to the three volumes represent one or two dozen different theories of emotion. Are we to follow each of these many strands through the century? Can we select one or two preeminent survivors? Probably not, because too many of these different strands still have respectable defenders today. All we can do is to pay attention to those that appear to be cumulative, persistent, and important. Some sense of the sweep of the past 70 years is conveyed by the participants in the three symposia. The 1928 volume conveys a definite sense of history. It is full of the great names: Spearman, Claparède, Bühler, McDougall, Woodworth, Carr, Cannon, Bekhterev, Pieron, Janet, Adler, and many more. The 1950 volume has a modern flavor; there are glimpses of the cold war and of the hope for psychology and its applications just after World War II. The 1970 volume seems to be in a place-holding position. Many of the names that will make a difference in the late twentieth century appear, but no discernible theme is apparent. There is also some philosophical speculation, strangely out of place, written by both philosophers and psychologists with a charming disregard of past or present evidence. The best summary of the dilemma of the field was provided by Madison Bentley in the 1928 volume. He knew then what many psychologists still fail to accept today, that there is no commonly or even superficially acceptable definition of what a psychology of emotion is about. And he concludes: "Whether emotion is today more than the heading of a chapter, I am still doubtful."

THEMES IN A MODERN HISTORY OF EMOTION

Modern concerns with problems of emotion date from the publication of William James's and Carl Lange's papers. William James's major contribution to psychology in his theory of emotion really had very little to do with the problem of emotion as such. At the end of the nineteenth century, psychology was still obsessed with its own "atomic" theory. Complex ideas and thoughts were made up of nuclear ideas, feelings, and thoughts. We find this fundamental notion in Wundt just as much as we found it in John Locke. If anything characterizes modern theoretical attitudes, it is an approach common to practically all of the various schools, trends, and points of view. Nearly all would subscribe to the notion that the role of modern psychology is to describe the processes and mechanisms that produce thoughts, ideas, actions, and feelings. Whether the stress is on the production of these "mental" events or on the production of behavior and action, the important point is that the basic building blocks are theoretical mechanisms and processes rather than atomic, undefined mental contents. It was William James who promoted the change from the content to a process approach. It is this approach that motivated his insistence that emotional consciousness is "not a primary feeling, directly aroused by the exciting object or thought, but a secondary feeling indirectly aroused" (James, 1894, p. 516), though he does consider as primary the "organic changes . . . which are immediate reflexes following upon the presence of the object" (p. 516). He contrasts his position with that of Wundt, who insisted that a feeling (*Gefühl*) was an unanalyzable and simple process corresponding to a sensation.

The fundamental distinction between feeling or emotion as a secondary derivative process and the view that feelings are unanalyzable provides one of the main themes running through the history of the psychology of emotion. Over 100 years later, we still find some psychologists who search for "fundamental" emotions whose origin is often found in the common language and subtle linguistic distinctions among feelings, emotions, and affects. James considered such attempts purely "verbal."

Another theme that defined the psychology of emotion, particularly in the United States, was the behaviorist insistence that conscious experience be abandoned as a proper subject of psychology. One of the results was that emotional behavior tended to be the sole target of emotion research during the second quarter of the twentieth century and that emotion in human and in nonverbal animals was studied at the same level. That made it possible to investigate emotional behavior in the cat and rat and to generalize that to human emotions. Finally, both the focus on observables and the James-Lange emphasis on visceral events made research on emotion almost exclusively a program of investigating visceral events and their concomitants.

Theories of emotion suffered the same fate as other theoretical endeavors in psychology. In the nineteenth century and before, they were primarily concerned with the explanation of conscious events. With the advent of Freud, the Würzburg school and its discovery of imageless thought, the Gestalt school in Germany, theoretical notions and particularly the emphasis on nonconscious events abounded. The movement to the (theoretical) unconscious went into decline in the United States during the behaviorist interlude to be resurrected with renewed energy after mid–twentieth century. The "new" cognitive psychology—actually just a theory-rich psychology—postulated that conscious events were a secondary phenomenon and that most of the interesting theoretical events were not conscious at all but rather the unobservable background of activations and interactions (sometimes mapped into a neuropsychology) that made action and thought possible.

TWO DISTINCT PSYCHOLOGIES OF EMOTION

There are two major traditions in the study of emotion. They are distinguished by a relative emphasis on central as opposed to peripheral processes, the former concerned with central nervous system mechanisms, the latter with peripheral reactions and particularly autonomic nervous system responses (see Schachter, 1970). A similar distinction is essentially a Cartesian one between mental and organic causes of emotion. Paul Fraisse (1968) calls the distinction *"les deux faces de l'émotion"*—the two aspects, or Janus-like faces, of emotion. One face is mental and intellectual—the organic events are seen as consequences of psychic events. While much of this line of thinking is tied to a belief in fundamental unanalyzable feelings, it was also the forerunner of another development—the conflict theories—that has a lengthy history going back at least 150 years to Johann Friedrich Herbart (1816), who saw emotion as a mental disorder caused by discrepancies (or what we would call today "conflicts") among perceptions or ideas. The other face of emotion is organic. It also has a long history, primarily among the sensualists of the eighteenth century who wanted all experience to be built of nothing but sensory impressions and who stressed the effect of organic reactions on mental emotional consequences. The organic theorists insisted on physiological events, rather than thoughts, as the determiners of emotion.

In the course of discussing the organic/peripheral theories, we shall have repeated occasion to refer to autonomic and/or visceral changes. Unless otherwise noted, this usually refers to activities of the sympathetic nervous system (SNS). The autonomic nervous system (ANS) is, in contrast to the central nervous system, the other major subdivision of the body's nervous armamentarium. The ANS consists of the SNS and the parasympathetic nervous system. The latter is primarily concerned with energy storage and conservation and is the evolutionarily older of the two (Pick, 1970); the former deals with energy expenditure, reaction to emergencies, and stress and is characterized, *inter alia,* by increased heart rate and sweating. Discussions of visceral responses, here and elsewhere, usually deal with sympathetic activity.

I shall follow Fraisse's distinctions and argument and start with the organic/peripheral and then return to the mentalist/central position.

Peripheral/Organic Approaches to Emotion

James, Lange, and Sergi

William James's presentation of his theory of emotion came in three installments: First, in an 1884 article in *Mind,* then in 1890 in Chapter 25 of his *Principles of Psychology,* and finally in 1894 in the extensive reply to his critics (James, 1884, 1890, 1894). I start with his bald statement in the 1884 article: "My thesis is . . . that the bodily changes follow directly the PERCEPTION of the exciting fact, and that our feeling of the same changes as they occur IS the emotion" (p. 189). James's emphasis on "organic" experience is illustrated when he notes that we might see a bear and decide it would be best to run away, or receive an insult and consider it appropriate to strike back, but "we would not actually feel afraid or angry." In illustration, he noted that it would be impossible to think of an emotion of fear if "the feelings neither of quickened heart-beats nor of shallow breathing, neither of trembling lips nor of weakened limbs, neither of goose-flesh not of visceral stirring, were present" (1894, p. 194). The bodily changes James wants to consider include running, crying, facial expressions, and even more complicated actions such as striking out. Whereas James did say that certain emotions were tied to specific visceral patterns, he did not confine himself to them. His insistence on general bodily changes sets him apart from Lange, who had said that emotions were the consequences of certain "vaso-motor effects." By 1894, James specifically rejected that position when he noted that "Lange has laid far too great stress on the vaso-motor factor in his explanation" (p. 517). James kept looking for crucial tests of his theory, but even in cases of congenital analgesia (who have no known pain sensations), he found it impossible to be certain of their emotional consciousness. He was concerned with the verbal problems and traps in existing and popular efforts to establish a taxonomy of emotion: "It is plain that the limit to [the number of emotions that could be enumerated] would lie in the introspective vocabulary of the seeker . . . and all sorts of groupings would be possible, according as we choose this character or that as a basis. . . . The reader may then class the emotions as he will" (1890, p. 485). Lange said very much the same thing and, antedating Wittgenstein by several decades, spoke of the reasons for the overlap among various conceptions of emotions as due to certain "family resemblances" that one can find in "popular speech as well as in scientific psychology."

Lange's little book appeared in Danish in 1885, and it was the German translation by Kurella that James saw shortly thereafter and that has formed the basis of all further expositions of Lange's work (Lange, 1885, 1887). Lange's book was not translated into English until 1922, when it appeared in a volume edited by Knight Dunlap, together with James's paper in *Mind* and the 1890 chapter (Dunlap, 1922).

Exactly what was it that Carl Lange said about emotion? He started his treatise by saying that the old conceptions of the emotions were wrong and must be reversed. But Lange was somewhat reluctant to state exactly what that reverse implies. In the clearest passage on that topic, he said that his theory holds "that the various emotional disturbances are due to disturbances in the vascular innervation that accompanies the affections, and which, therefore, makes these vaso-motor disturbances the only primary symptoms" (in Dunlap, 1922, p. 60). In his introductory passage, Lange had started out to explore the effects of the emotions on bodily functions but had found that goal to be very difficult, if not impossible, to achieve, "simply because the question had been put in reverse order."

There is a problem of interpretation of James's and Lange's "perceptual" antecedent of visceral disturbance. We are told repeatedly that particular perceptions produce certain bodily effects, which then in turn are perceived and experienced as "emotions." What we are not told is how these perceptions of external events produce the bodily effects. James says that external events can give rise to bodily, visceral changes without any awareness of the meaning and without interpretation of these events. For example, he finds it "surprising" that one can have mental events without conscious accompaniments, which then precede the bodily reaction. But then the theory falls apart because it is the intervening mental event that gives rise to the organically determined emotion. There is nothing surprising about this in 2002 with our current concern with cognitions, the "intervening" interpretive events.

If James is given some of the major credit for introducing a constructivist analytic modern psychology, it is because he was the most visible carrier of the idea. Others had similar notions. The most visible, apart from Lange, was the Italian psychologist Giuseppe Sergi, who wrote extensively on emotion and published his own *Nuova teoria della emozioni* in 1894 and 1896 independently of James and Lange (Sergi, 1894, 1896). Sergi insisted that the brain added only the conscious aspect to the emotions, all other aspects being the result of vasomotor changes. Dunlap (1922) specifically singles out the Australian Alexander Sutherland as the third discoverer of the James-Lange theory, although Sutherland, a philosopher, did not publish his independent version until 1898 (Sutherland, 1898), a version that was neither as clear nor as persuasive as James's. An even better candidate for a priority claim might be the philosopher Jacob Henle, whom James quotes repeatedly and approvingly. But these were the "others"—history is often unkind.

To understand the tenor of the times, consider Wundt's critique of the James-Lange theory (Wundt, 1891). Dealing with Lange's theory, Wundt called it a psychological pseudo-explanation that tries to explain away psychic facts with physiological observations. Instead, Wundt starts with the unanalyzable feelings that alter the stream of ideas. For example, the unanalyzable feelings of "fear" or "joy" can influence the current stream of ideation, encouraging some, discouraging some, or inhibiting other ideas. This altered stream of ideas produces a secondary feeling as well as organic reactions. And the organic reactions produce sensory feelings that are added to or fused with the preceding feeling (or sensation) and thus intensify the conscious feeling. Modern counterparts of Wundt are continuing a search for specific fundamental emotions. Instead of looking for fundamental emotions, others, such as Arnold (1960), considered "appraisals" as primary, in terms of their unanalyzability. First comes the appraisal of something as "good" or "bad," then

follows the rest of the emotional train. Apart from the theological implications for the a priori ability to make judgments of "good" and "bad," psychological theory in the twentieth century places more emphasis on the conditions and processes that give rise to such judgments.

The American attack on James came primarily from E. B. Titchener, who also started with fundamental feelings, though in a more complex form and with a somewhat less unanalyzable quality. The feeling is "in reality a complex process, composed of a perception or idea and affection, in which affection plays the principal part" (Titchener, 1896, p. 214). As far as the formation of an emotion is concerned, Titchener postulated that a train of ideas need be interrupted by a vivid feeling, that this feeling shall reflect the situation in the outside world (as distinct from inner experience), and that the feeling shall be enriched by organic sensations, set up in the course of bodily adjustment to the incident. The emotion itself, as experienced, consists of the stimulus association of ideas, some part of which are always organic sensations. For Titchener, sensations are truly based on external events and not "cognitive"; emotions occur in the presence of specific situations and conflicts.

None of the criticisms of James, piecemeal as they were, had much of an effect. The important and devastating attack came over a quarter century later from Walter B. Cannon (1914, 1927, 1929). Cannon used the attack on James to further his own relatively uninfluential neurophysiological theory, which postulated thalamically produced "feelings." What did have impact was his evaluation of the James-Lange theory, which set the tone for the succeeding 50 years of psychological theory. Cannon's major points were addressed to the question of visceral feedback as the basis for emotional behavior. Niceties as to whether Cannon's target should be Lange's emotional behavior or James's emotional experience were forgotten in the light of the devastating and elegant content of Cannon's attack. It consisted of five major points: (1) Even when the viscera are separated from the central nervous system, that is, when visceral arousal cannot be perceived, some emotional behavior may still be present. (2) There does not seem to be any reasonable way to specify visceral changes that James had maintained should differ from emotion to emotion. (3) The perception and feedback from autonomic nervous system discharge is so diffuse and indistinct that one must assume that the viscera are essentially insensitive and could not possibly serve the differentiation function that James's position requires. (4) Autonomic nervous system responses are very slow, and their slow onset, on the order of 1–2 seconds, would suggest that emotion should not occur within shorter intervals. (5) When visceral changes are produced by artificial means—for example, by the injection of adrenaline—emotional states do not seem to follow as a matter of course.

History has been kinder to Cannon than to James. Cannon's first point turned out to be essentially correct. However, there is evidence that separating the viscera from the central nervous system significantly interferes with at least the acquisition of emotional behavior. Arguments have also been made that even in the absence of the viscera, there are other systems, including the skeletal system, that may subserve the Jamesian functions. Cannon was quite right as far as points (2) and (3) are concerned; there is no evidence that different emotional states or behaviors are antecedently caused by different visceral states. Much heat has been generated by this argument in subsequent years, but still no causal evidence is available. Evidence that has been cited about the differential conditioning of various autonomic functions, or even differential responding in different parts of the autonomic system, is not relevant to this argument, since the Jamesian argument is about different *causally* implicated patterns of the autonomic system—different emotions are caused by different organic patterns. As far as point (4) is concerned, the argument is somewhat similar to point (1). Cannon is right in general, but other mechanisms such as conditioned skeletal responses and autonomic imagery may serve to bridge the gap and explain the phenomena, such as rapid reactions to painful stimuli or autonomic "perceptions" with very short reaction times, that the subjective evidence suggests. As for Cannon's fifth point, the evidence cited below shows that visceral changes produced by artificial means are not sufficient to produce emotional states, but that their presence certainly is an important condition for emotional experience in conjunction with other cognitive factors. In any case, Cannon's five criticisms were important enough to generate extensive and influential research on the points of disputation between James-Lange and Cannon.

The Post-James Period

The half century following James was primarily dominated by his approach but with a lingering concern about the kind of mental events that were responsible for the conditions that produced organic, and especially visceral, reactions and the nature of the perceptions that made for specific emotional qualities. All of these were attempts to find some way of bringing in the central nervous system. By 1936, Ruckmick had stressed the interaction of visceral and cognitive factors, and later Hunt, Cole, and Reis had specified how different emotions may be tied to specific environmental-cognitive interactions (J. Hunt, Cole, & Reis, 1958; Ruckmick, 1936). The major antecedent for the next significant change in direction of emotion theory was an essentially anecdotal study

by the Spanish physician Gregorio Marañon (1924), who found that when he injected a large number of patients with adrenaline, approximately one-third of them responded with a quasi-emotional state. The rest reported little or no emotional response and simply reported a physiological state of arousal. However, the patients who reported emotional reactions typically noted that they felt "as if" they were afraid or "as if" something very good was about to happen. In other words, they did not report the full range of emotional experience but something closely akin to it. Whenever Marañon discussed a recent emotional experience with his patients, such as a death in the family, the patients reported full rather than "as if" or "cold" emotion.

In part, these observations were the prolegomena for the Schachter and Singer experiments (1962) that changed the emotional landscape. Stanley Schachter (1971) put forward three general propositions: (a) Given a state of physiological arousal for which an individual has no immediate explanation, he will describe his state in terms of whatever cognitions are available. (b) Given a state of physiological arousal for which an individual has a completely appropriate explanation, no evaluative needs will arise and the individual is unlikely to label his feelings in terms of (any) cognitions available. (c) Given the same cognitive circumstances, the individual will react emotionally or describe his feelings as emotions only to the extent that he experiences a state of physiological arousal. In other words, both physiological arousal and cognitive evaluation are necessary, but neither is a sufficient condition for the production of emotional states.

The main contribution of Schachter's group in the 1960s was in opening up a new era of investigation and theory. It redefined the psychology of emotion just as James had done 70 years earlier. The contribution was not so much the ingenious experiments but a straightforward statement of a visceral-cognitive theory. Visceral action was setting the stage for emotional experience, but so was a cognitive evaluation, and emotion was the product of the two. Perhaps more important was the statement that general autonomic arousal rather than a specific pattern was the visceral concomitant of emotional experience. The consequences of this position have been a large number of experimental studies showing the influence of visceral and cognitive factors ranging from the instigation of aggressive behavior to the occurrence of romantic love.

In the first set of experiments, Schachter and Singer (1962) gave subjects injections of adrenaline under the cover story that these were vitamin compounds that would affect visual skills. Following the injection, subjects were either informed of the consequences of the injection (i.e., they were given correct information about the effects of adrenaline, but without having been told that they were given an adrenaline injection), or they were not given any information about the effects of adrenaline, or they were misinformed.

In the informed condition, they were told that they would feel symptoms of sympathetic nervous system discharge. In the misinformed condition, they were given a description of parasympathetic symptoms, none of which would be expected as a result of the adrenaline injection. Following the injection and the various types of information, the subject was left in a waiting room together with another person who was ostensibly another experimental subject but who was actually a "stooge" of the experimenters. Then the stooge would engage either in euphoric behavior (playing with paper airplanes, playing basketball with the wastebasket, and engaging in other happy behavior) or in angry behavior (becoming more and more insulting, asking personal and insulting questions, and eventually leaving the room in anger).

The results were essentially in keeping with the two-factor theory. The degree of information about the physiological consequences of the injection was negatively correlated with the degree of self-reported emotional state and with the degree of emotional behavior induced by the stooge's behavior. Thus, the misinformed group, which presumably had the highest evaluative need because the information they had been given about the physiological effects and their actual experiences were uncorrelated, showed the greatest degree of self-reported euphoria as well as anger. The informed group, with no "need" to explain their state, showed the lowest degree of induced emotion. The ignorant group fell in between the two other groups. The impact of these experiments was theoretical rather than empirical. In fact, no exact replication of these experiments is available, and a variety of misgivings have been aired about them.

With the Schachter experiments, the pure organic tradition came to an end, at least for the time being. Once it had been shown that the influence of visceral response depended on cognitive factors, purely organic theories had played out their role. The line from James and Lange was switched to a more cognitive track. However, even if purely organic theories seemed untenable, visceral-cognitive interactions still involved visceral response. I turn now to other evidence on the role of the autonomic nervous system in the production and maintenance of the emotions.

Emotions and Variations in Peripheral/Visceral Activity

A number of research areas are relevant to the James-Lange position on the importance of visceral activity. The most obvious is to produce an organism without a sympathetic nervous system, which should produce an absence of emotional behavior. Some animal preparations using immuno-sympathectomies (Levi-Montalcini & Angeletti, 1961) have been studied, but the results have been equivocal (Wenzel, 1972).

The most fervently pursued area of research has been in the hunt for visceral patterning. Once James had intimated and Lange had insisted that for every discrete emotion there existed a discrete pattern of visceral response, the search was on for specifying these discrete visceral antecedents of emotion. Unfortunately, some 90 years of search have proven fruitless.

Before examining some of the purported positive pieces of evidence, we must be clear about the theoretical position involved. Specifically, it must be shown that some specific emotional experience is the consequence of (is caused by) a specific pattern of visceral response. For our current understanding of causal analyses, any experiment claiming to support that position must show at least that the visceral pattern occurs prior to the occurrence of the emotional experience. Mere demonstrations of correlation between emotion and visceral response are interesting but do not address the issue.

The most widely cited study purporting to support the physiological specificity notion is an experiment by Ax (1953). Ax exposed subjects either to a fear-provoking or to an anger-provoking situation and measured patterns of physiological response to these two experimental "stimuli." Both situations produced elevated levels of sympathetic nervous system response with some significant differences on a number of visceral indicators. I do not need to argue that this does not show any causal effects of visceral patterns. In fact, the question is: What does it show? We do not know, in the absence of extensive internal analyses and subjects' reports, what specific "emotion" the subjects experienced.

To put the study in the proper historical perspective, it was done when psychology was still in the grip of the behavioristic approaches to emotion when "fear" and "anger" were defined by what was done to the subjects, not by what they perceived. In addition, the difference in visceral patterning was shown as the average pattern of response for the two groups of subjects. The kind of patterns that Ax found could have been a combination of a variety of patterns from each individual subject. Thus, with hindsight, we cannot even come to any correlational conclusion about this study. More important, subsequent attempts either to replicate or modify the study have either failed to replicate the study or to provide any evidence for the causal effect of visceral patterns.

The conclusions of a 30-year-old survey still hold: "Investigators have been unable to find an identifiable physiological change that corresponds to changes from one specific emotion to another," but "there is an unspecific relation between the emotional state and physiological state" (Candland et al.,

1977, pp. 31–32). There is no doubt that fulfillment of the James-Lange dream would have been a very pleasant conclusion to the search for specific emotions. But, although the hope remained, it was not to be. Dreams die hard. To those who still insist on a patterning approach, we are only left with Bertrand Russell's probably apocryphal response to the question of how he would react to being confronted with God after his death: "Lord, you did not give us enough evidence!"

What about an "unspecific relation" between viscera and emotion, that is, a general autonomic response? Schachter's studies provided one piece of evidence. The same physiological antecedent potentiated different emotions. It is also the case that widely different emotions show relatively little difference in physiological patterns. Here we need not go into the question of whether or not these patterns are antecedent to the emotional expression. If, with very different emotions, the patterns are similar, the argument can be made that it is highly unlikely the different emotions depend on different patterning. In 1969, Averill showed that both sadness and mirth are associated with measurable visceral responses and that both of them seem to involve primarily sympathetic nervous system patterns. Averill found that two divergent emotional states produce highly similar sympathetic states of arousal (Averill, 1969). Patkai (1971) found that adrenaline excretion increased in both pleasant and unpleasant situations when compared with a neutral situation. She concludes that her results "support the hypothesis that adrenalin release is related to the level of general activation rather than being associated with a specific emotional reaction" (Patkai, 1971). Frankenhaeuser's laboratory (e.g., Frankenhaeuser, 1975) has produced additional evidence that adrenaline is secreted in a variety of emotional states.

William James believed that patients who have no visceral perception, no feedback from visceral responses, would provide a crucial test of his theory. Parenthetically, we might note that this is a peculiar retreat from James's position stressing any bodily reaction to the position of Lange, which emphasized visceral response. In any case, James insisted that these people would provide the crucial evidence for his theory—namely, they should be devoid of, or at least deficient in, their emotional consciousness. In that sense, William James initiated the study of biofeedback. He thought that variations in the perception of visceral response are central to the emotional life of the individual, and that control over such variations would provide fundamental insights into the causes of emotions.

The sources of the biofeedback movement in modern times are varied, but there are three lines of research that have addressed James's problem, and it is to these that we now turn. One of them involved individuals who were victims of a cruel natural experiment—people with spinal injuries that had cut off the feedback from their visceral systems. The second approach has assumed that individuals may differ in the degree to which they perceive and can respond to their own visceral responses. The third approach, in the direct tradition of what is today commonly called biofeedback, involves teaching individuals to control their autonomic level of response and thereby to vary the feedback available.

The first area of research, the "anatomical restriction" of autonomic feedback, is related to the animal studies with auto-immune sympathectomies mentioned earlier. In human subjects, a study by Hohmann (1966) looked at the problem of "experienced" emotion in patients who had suffered spinal cord lesions. He divided these patients into subgroups depending on the level of their lesions, the assumption being that the higher the lesion the less autonomic feedback. In support of a visceral feedback position, he found that the higher the level of the spinal cord lesion, the greater the reported decrease in emotion between the preinjury and the postinjury level. A subsequent study by Jasnos and Hakmiller (1975) also investigated a group of patients with spinal cord lesions, classified into three categories on the basis of lesion level—from cervical to thoracic to lumbar. There was a significantly greater reported level of emotion the lower the level of spinal lesion.

As far as the second approach of individual responsiveness in autonomic feedback is concerned, there are several studies that use the "Autonomic Perception Questionnaire" (APQ) (Mandler, Mandler, & Uviller, 1958). The APQ measures the degree of subjective awareness of a variety of visceral states. The initial findings were that autonomic perception was related to autonomic reactivity and that autonomic perception was inversely related to quality of performance; individuals with a high degree of perceived autonomic activity performed more poorly on an intellective task (Mandler & Kremen, 1958). Borkovec (1976) noted that individuals who show a high degree of autonomic awareness generally were more reactive to stress stimuli and are more affected by anxiety-producing situations. Perception of autonomic events does apparently play a role in emotional reactivity.

Two studies by Sirota, Schwartz, and Shapiro (1974, 1976) showed that subjects could be taught to control their heart rate and that voluntary slowing of the rate led to a reduction in the perceived noxiousness of painful shock. They concluded that their results "lend further credence to the notion that subjects can be trained to control anxiety and/or pain by learning to control relevant physiological responses" (Sirota et al., 1976, p. 477). Finally, simulated heart rate feedback—playing a heart rate recording artificially produced and purported to be a normal or accelerated heart rate—affected judgmental evaluative behavior, and Ray and Valins showed that similar simulated heart rate feedback changed subjects' reactions to feared stimuli (Valins, 1966, 1970; Valins & Ray, 1967). The work on variations of autonomic feedback indicates that the perception of autonomic or visceral activity is a powerful variable in manipulating emotional response.

Given that the nineteenth century replayed the ancient view that organic/visceral responses are bothersome and interfering, and at best play some incidental mediating role, the mid–twentieth century provided evidence that that old position does not adequately describe the functions of the visceral reactions. The currently dominant notion about the function and evolution of the sympathetic nervous system has been the concept of homeostasis, linked primarily with W. B. Cannon. In a summary statement, he noted: "In order that the constancy of the internal environment may be assured, therefore, every considerable change in the outer world and every considerable move in relation to the outer world, must be attended by a rectifying process in the hidden world of the organism" (Cannon, 1930). However, visceral response may also, in addition to its vegetative functions, color and qualitatively change other ongoing action. It may serve as a signal for action and attention, and signal actions that are important for the survival of the organism (Mandler, 1975). Finally, the autonomic system appears to support adaptive responses, making it more likely, for example, that the organism will respond more quickly, scan the environment more effectively, and eventually respond adaptively.

Most of the work in this direction was done by Marianne Frankenhaeuser (1971, 1975). Her studies used a different measurement of autonomic activity: the peripheral appearance of adrenaline and noradrenaline (the catecholamines). Frankenhaeuser (1975) argued that the traditional view of catecholamine activity as "primitive" and obsolete may be mistaken and that the catecholamines, even in the modern world, play an adaptive role "by facilitating adjustment to cognitive and emotional pressures." She showed that normal individuals with relatively higher catecholarnine excretion levels perform better "in terms of speed, accuracy, and endurance" than those with lower levels. In addition, good adjustment is accompanied by rapid decreases to base levels of adrenaline output after heavy mental loads have been imposed. High adrenaline output and rapid return to base levels characterized good adjustment and low neuroticism.

In the course of this survey of the organic tradition, I have wandered far from a purely organic point of view and have probably even done violence to some who see themselves as cognitive centralists rather than organic peripheralists. However, the line of succession seemed clear, and the line of development was cumulative. Neither the succession nor the cumulation will be apparent when we look at the other face of emotion—the mental tradition.

Central/Mental Approaches to Emotion

Starting with the 1960s, the production of theories of emotion, and of accompanying research, multiplied rapidly. In part, this was due to Schachter's emphasis on cognitive factors, which made possible a radical departure from the James-Lange tradition. The psychological literature reflected these changes. Between 1900 and 1950, the number of references to "emotion" had risen rather dramatically, only to drop drastically in the 1950s. The references to emotion recovered in the following decade, to rise steeply by the 1980s (Rimé, 1999).

Historically, the centralist/mental movements started with the unanalyzable feeling, but its main thrust was its insistence on the priority of psychological processes in the causal chain of the emotions. Whether these processes were couched in terms of mental events, habits, conditioning mechanisms, or sensations and feelings, it was these kinds of events that received priority and theoretical attention. By mid-twentieth century, most of these processes tended to be subsumed under the cognitive heading—processes that provide the organism with internal and external information. The shift to the new multitude of emotion theories was marked by a major conference on emotion at the Karolinska Institute in Stockholm in 1972 (Levi, 1975). It was marked by the presence of representatives of most major positions and the last joint appearance of such giants of human physiology of the preceding half century as Paul MacLean, David Rioch, and Jose Delgado. In order to bring the history of emotion to a temporary completion, it is necessary to discuss some of the new arrivals in mid-century. I shall briefly describe the most prominent of these.

Initially, the most visible position was Magda Arnold's, though it quickly was lost in the stream of newcomers. Arnold (1960) developed a hybrid phenomenological-cognitive-physiological theory. She starts with the appraisals of events as "good" or "bad," judgments that are unanalyzable and are part of our basic humanness. She proceeds from there to the phenomenology of emotional "felt tendencies" and accompanying bodily states, and concludes by describing the possible neurophysiology behind these processes. Also in the 1960s, Sylvan Tomkins (1962–1992), the most consistent defender of the "fundamental emotions" approach, started presenting his theory. Tomkins argued that certain eliciting stimuli feed into innate neural affect programs, which represent primary affects such as fear, anger, sadness, surprise, happiness, and others. Each of these primary affects is linked to a specific facial display that provides feedback to the central brain mechanisms. All other affects are considered secondary and represent some combination of the primary affects. Izard (1971, 1972) presents an ambitious and comprehensive theory that incorporates neural, visceral, and subjective systems with the deliberate aim to place the theory within the context of personality and motivation theory. Izard also gives pride of place to feedback from facial and postural expression, which is "transformed into conscious form, [and] the result is a discrete fundamental emotion" (Izard, 1971, p. 185). Mandler (1975) presented a continuation of Schachter's position of visceral/cognitive interactions with an excursion into conflict theory, to be discussed below.

Frijda (1986) may be the most wide-ranging contemporary theorist. He starts off with a working definition that defines emotion as the occurrence of noninstrumental behavior, physiological changes, and evaluative experiences. In the process of trying a number of different proposals and investigating action, physiology, evaluation, and experience, Frijda arrives at a definition that's broad indeed. Central to his position are action tendencies and the individual's awareness of them. The tendencies are usually set in motion by a variety of mechanisms. Thus, Frijda describes emotion as a set of mechanisms that ensure the satisfaction of concerns, compare stimuli to preference states, and by turning them into rewards and punishments, generate pain and pleasure, dictate appropriate action, assume control for these actions and thereby interrupt ongoing activity, and provide resources for these actions (1986, p. 473). The question is whether such mechanisms do not do too much and leave nothing in meaningful action that is not emotional. At least one would need to specify which of the behaviors and experiences that fall under such an umbrella are to be considered emotional and which not. But that would again raise the elusive problem as to what qualifies as an emotion.

Ortony, Clore, and Collins (1988) define emotions as "valenced reactions to events, agents, or objects, with their particular nature being determined by the way in which the eliciting situation is construed" (p. 13). Such a definition is, of course subject to James's critique; it is abstracted from the "bodily felt" emotions. Richard Lazarus and his coworkers define emotion as organized reactions that consist of cognitive appraisals, action impulses, and patterned somatic reactions (Folkman & Lazarus, 1990; Lazarus, Kanner, & Folkman, 1980). Emotions are seen as the result of continuous appraisals and monitoring of the person's well-being. The result is a fluid change of emotional states indexed by cognitive, behavioral, and physiological symptoms. Central is the notion of cognitive appraisal, which leads to actions that cope with the situation.

Many of the mental/central theories are descendants of a line of thought going back to Descartes and his postulation of fundamental, unanalyzable emotions. However some 300 years later there has been no agreement on what the number of basic emotions is. Ortony and Turner (1990) note that the number of basic emotions can vary from 2 to 18 depending on which theorist you read. If, as is being increasingly argued nowadays, there is an evolutionary basis to the primary emotions, should they not be more obvious? If basic emotions are a characteristic of all humans, should the answer not stare us into the face? The emotions that one finds in most lists are heavily weighted toward the negative emotions, and love and lust, for example, are generally absent (see also Mandler, 1984).

Facial Expression and Emotions

If there has been one persistent preoccupation of psychologists of emotion, it has been with the supposed Darwinian heritage that facial expressions express emotion. Darwin's (1872) discussion of the natural history of facial expression was as brilliant as it was misleading. The linking of Darwin and facial expression has left the impression that Darwin considered these facial displays as having some specific adaptive survival value. In fact, the major thrust of Darwin's argument is that the vast majority of these displays are vestigial or accidental. Darwin specifically argued against the notion that "certain muscles have been given to man solely that he may reveal to other men his feelings" (cited in Fridlund, 1992b, p. 119).

With the weakening of the nineteenth-century notion of the unanalyzable fundamental emotion, psychologists became fascinated with facial expressions, which seemed to be unequivocal transmitters of specific, discrete emotional states. Research became focused on the attempt to analyze the messages that the face seemed to be transmitting (see Schlosberg, 1954). However, the evaluation of facial expression is marked by ambivalence. On the one hand, there is some consensus about the universality of facial expressions. On the other hand, as early as 1929 there was evidence that facial expressions are to a very large extent judged in terms of the situations in which they are elicited (Landis, 1929).

The contemporary intense interest in facial expression started primarily with the work of Sylvan Tomkins (see above), who placed facial expressions at the center of his theory of emotion and the eight basic emotions that form the core of emotional experience. The work of both Ekman and Izard derives from Tomkins's initial exposition. The notion that facial displays express some underlying mental state forms a central part of many arguments about the nature of emotion. While facial expressions can be classified into about half a dozen categories, the important steps have been more analytic and have looked at the constituent components of these expressions. Paul Ekman has brought the analysis of facial movement and expression to a level of sophistication similar to that applied to the phonological, phonemic, and semantic components of verbal expressive experiences (Ekman, 1982; Ekman & Oster, 1979). Ekman attributes the origin of facial expressions to "affect programs" and claims that the only truly differentiating outward sign of the different emotions is found in these emotional expressions.

Another point of view has considered facial expressions as primarily communicative devices. Starting with the fact that it is not clear how the outward expression of inner states is adaptive, that is, how it could contribute to reproductive fitness, important arguments have been made that facial displays are best seen (particularly in the tradition of behavioral ecology) as communicative devices, independent of emotional states (Fridlund, 1991, 1992a; Mandler, 1975, 1992). Facial displays can be interpreted as remnants of preverbal communicative devices and as displays of values (indicating what is good or bad, useful or useless, etc.). For example, the work of Janet Bavelas and her colleagues has shown the importance of communicative facial and other bodily displays. The conclusion, in part, is that the "communicative situation determines the visible behavior" (Bavelas, Black, Lemery, & Mullett, 1986). In the construction of emotions, facial displays are important contributors to cognitions and appraisals of the current scene, similar to verbal, imaginal, or unconscious evaluative representations.

The Conflict Theories

The conflict theories are more diverse than the other categories that we have investigated. They belong under the general rubric of mental theories because the conflicts involved are typically mental ones, conflicts among actions, goals, ideas, and thoughts. These theories have a peculiar history of noncumulativeness and isolation. Their continued existence is well recognized, but rarely do they find wide acceptance.

One of the major exponents of this theme in modern times was the French psychologist Frédric Paulhan. He started with the major statement of his theory in 1884, which was presented in book form in 1887; an English translation did not appear until 1930 (Paulhan, 1887, 1930). The translator, C. K. Ogden, contributed an introduction to that volume that is marked by its plaintive note. He expressed wonderment that so little attention had been paid to Paulhan for over 40 years. He complained that a recent writer had assigned to

MacCurdy (1925) the discovery that emotional expressions appear when instinctive reactions are held up. Ogden hoped that his reintroduction of Paulhan to the psychological world would have the proper consequences of recognition and scientific advance. No such consequences have appeared. It is symptomatic of the history of the conflict theories that despite these complaints, neither Ogden nor Paulhan mention Herbart (1816), who said much the same sort of thing.

Paulhan's major thesis was that whenever any affective events occur, we observe the same fact: the arrest of tendency. By arrested tendency Paulhan means a "more or less complicated reflex action which cannot terminate as it would if the organization of the phenomena were complete, if there were full harmony between the organism or its parts and their conditions of existence, if the system formed in the first place by man, and afterwards by man and the external world, were perfect" (1930, p. 17). However, if that statement rehearses some older themes, Paulhan must be given credit for the fact that he did not confine himself to the usual "negative" emotions but made a general case that even positive, pleasant, joyful, aesthetic emotions are the result of some arrested tendencies. And he also avoided the temptation to provide us with a taxonomy of emotions, noting, rather, that no two emotions are alike, that the particular emotional experience is a function of the particular tendency that is arrested and the conditions under which that "arrest" occurs.

The Paulhan-Ogden attempt to bring conflict theory to the center of psychology has an uncanny parallel in what we might call the Dewey-Angier reprise. In 1894 and 1895, John Dewey published two papers on his theory of emotion. In 1927, Angier published a paper in the *Psychological Review* that attempted to resurrect Dewey's views. His comments on the effect of Dewey's papers are worth quoting: "They fell flat. I can find no review, discussion, or even specific mention of them at the time or during the years immediately following in the two major journals" (Angier, 1927). Angier notes that comment had been made that Dewey's theory was ignored because people did not understand it. He anticipated that another attempt, hopefully a more readable one, would bring Dewey's conflict theory to the forefront of speculations about emotion. Alas, Angier was no more successful on behalf of Dewey than Ogden was in behalf of Paulhan. Dewey's conflict theory, in Angier's more accessible terms, was: Whenever a series of reactions required by an organism's total "set" runs its course to the consummatory reaction, which will bring "satisfaction" by other reactions, there is no emotion. Emotion arises only when these other reactions (implicit or overt) are so irrelevant as to resist ready integration with those already in orderly progress toward fruition. Such resistance implies actual tensions, checking of impulses, interference, inhibition, or conflict. These conflicts constitute the emotions; without them there is no emotion; with them there is. And just as Paulhan and Ogden ignored Herbart, so did Dewey and Angier ignore Herbart and Paulhan. Yet, I should not quite say "ignore." Most of the actors in this "now you see them, now you don't" game had apparently glanced at the work of their predecessors. Maybe they had no more than browsed through it.

The cumulative nature of science is true for its failures as well as for its successes. There was no reason for Paulhan to have read or paid much attention to Herbart, or for Dewey or Angier to have read Paulhan. After all, why should they pay attention to a forgotten psychologist when nobody else did? It may be that conflict theories appeared at inappropriate times, that is, when other emotion theories were more prominent and popular—for example, Dewey's proposal clashed with the height of James's popularity. In any case, it is the peculiar history of the conflict theories that they tend to be rediscovered at regular intervals.

In 1941, W. Hunt suggested that classical theories generally accepted a working definition of emotion that involved some emergency situation of biological importance during which "current behavior is suspended" and responses appear that are directed toward a resolution of the emergency (W. Hunt, 1941). These "classical" theories "concern themselves with specific mechanisms whereby current behavior is interrupted and emotional responses are substituted" (p. 268). Hunt saw little novelty in formulations that maintained that emotion followed when an important activity of the organism is interrupted. Quite right; over nearly 200 years, that same old "theme" has been refurbished time and time again. I will continue the story of the conflict theories without pausing for two idiosyncratic examples, behaviorism and psychoanalysis, which—while conflict theories—are off the path of the developing story. I shall return to them at the end of this section.

The noncumulative story of conflict theories stalled for a while about 1930, and nothing much had happened by 1941, when W. Hunt barely suppressed a yawn at the reemergence of another conflict theory. But within the next decade, another one appeared, and this one with much more of a splash. It was put forward by Donald O. Hebb (1946, 1949), who came to his conflict theory following the observations of rather startling emotional behavior. Hebb restricted his discussion of emotion to what he called "violent and unpleasant emotions" and to "the transient irritabilities and anxieties of ordinary persons as well as to neurotic or psychotic disorder" (1949, p. 235). He specifically did not deal with subtle emotional experiences nor with pleasurable emotional experiences.

Hebb's observations concerned rage and fear in chimpanzees. He noted that animals would have a paroxysm of terror at being shown another animal's head detached from the body, that this terror was a function of increasing age, and also that various other unusual stimuli, such as other isolated parts of the body, produced excitation. Such excitation was apparently not tied to a particular emotion; instead, it would be followed sometimes by avoidance, sometimes by aggression, and sometimes even by friendliness. Hebb assumed that the innate disruptive response that characterizes the emotional disturbance is the result of an interference with a phase sequence—a central neural structure that is built up as a result of previous experience and learning. Hebb's insistence that phase sequences first must be established before they can be interfered with, and that the particular emotional disturbance follows such interference and the disruptive response, identifies his theory with the conflict tradition. Hebb's theory does not postulate any specific physiological pattern for any of these emotional disturbances such as anger, fear, grief, and so forth, nor does he put any great emphasis on the physiological consequences of disruption.

The next step was taken by Leonard Meyer (1956), who, in contrast to many other such theorists, had read and understood the literature. He properly credited his predecessors and significantly advanced theoretical thinking. More important, he showed the application of conflict theory not in the usual areas of fear or anxiety or flight but in respect to the emotional phenomena associated with musical appreciation. None of that helped a bit. It may well be that because he worked in an area not usually explored by psychologists, his work had no influence on any psychological developments.

Meyer started by saying that emotion is "aroused when a tendency to respond is arrested or inhibited." He gave John Dewey credit for fathering the conflict theory of emotion and recognized that it applies even to the behaviorist formulations that stress the disruptive consequences of emotion. Meyer noted that Paulhan's "brilliant work" predates Dewey's, and he credited Paulhan with stating that emotion is aroused not only by opposed tendencies but also when "for some reason, whether physical or mental [a tendency], cannot reach completion." So much for Meyer's awareness of historical antecedents. Even more impressive is his anticipation of the next 20 years of development in emotion theory. For example, he cited the conclusion that there is no evidence that each affect has its own peculiar physiological composition. He concluded that physiological reactions are "essentially undifferentiated, and become characteristic only in certain stimulus situations. . . . Affective experience is differentiated because it involves awareness and cognition of the stimulus situation which itself is necessarily differentiated." In other words: An undifferentiated organic reaction becomes differentiated into a specific emotional experience as a result of certain cognitions. As an example, Meyer reminded his readers that the sensation of falling through space might be highly unpleasant, but that a similar experience, in the course of a parachute jump in an amusement park, may become very pleasurable.

In short, Meyer anticipated the development of the cognitive and physiological interactions that were to become the mainstays of explanations of emotions in the 1960s and 1970s (e.g., Schachter). Most of Meyer's book is concerned with the perception of emotional states during the analysis and the appreciation of music. His major concern is to show that felt emotion occurs when an expectation is activated and then temporarily inhibited or permanently blocked.

The last variant of the "conflict" theme to be considered has all the stigmata of its predecessors: The emotional consequences of competition or conflict are newly discovered, previous cognate theories are not acknowledged, and well-trodden ground is covered once again. The theorist is Mandler and the year was 1964. The theory is one of conflicting actions, blocked tendencies, and erroneous expectations. But there is no mention of Dewey, of Paulhan, and certainly not of Meyer. The basic proposition (Mandler, 1964) was that the interruption of an integrated or organized response sequence produces a state of arousal, which will be followed by emotional behavior or experience. This theme was expanded in 1975 to include the interruption of cognitive events and plans. The antecedents of the approach appeared in a paper by Kessen and Mandler (1961), and the experimental literature invoked there is not from the area of emotion; rather, it is from the motivational work of Kurt Lewin (1935), who had extensively investigated the effect of interrupted and uncompleted action on tension systems.

In contrast to other conflict theories—other than Meyer's—in Mandler, the claim is that interruption is a sufficient and possibly necessary condition for the occurrence of autonomic nervous system arousal, that such interruption sets the stage for many of the changes that occur in cognitive and action systems, and finally, that interruption has important adaptive properties in that it signals important changes in the environment. Positive and negative emotions are seen as following interruption, and, in fact, the same interruptive event may produce different emotional states or consequences depending on the surrounding situational and intrapsychic cognitive context. Some empirical extensions were present in Mandler and Watson and, for example, confirmed that an appetitive situation can produce extreme emotional behavior in lower animals when they are put into a situation where no appropriate behaviors are available to them (Mandler & Watson, 1966). Other extensions were further elaborations of the Schachter dissociation of arousal

and cognition, with discrepancy between expectation and actuality producing the arousal.

Just as interruption and discrepancy theory asked the question that Schachter had left out—"What is the source of the autonomic arousal?"—so it was asked later by LeDoux in 1989: "How is it that the initial state of bodily arousal . . . is evoked? . . . Cognitive theories require that the brain has a mechanism for distinguishing emotional from mundane situations prior to activating the autonomic nervous system" (LeDoux, 1989, p. 270). LeDoux suggested that separate systems mediate affective and cognitive computations, with the amygdala being primarily responsible for affective computation, whereas cognitive processes are centered in the hippocampus and neocortex. The (conscious) experience of emotion is the product of simultaneous projections of the affective and cognitive products into "working memory." In Mandler, it is discrepancy/interruption that provides a criterion that distinguishes emotional from mundane situations. Discrepant situations are rarely mundane and usually emotional; in other words—and avoiding the pitfall of defining emotions—whenever discrepancies occur, they lead to visceral arousal and to conditions that are, in the common language, frequently called emotional. Such constructivist analyses see the experience of emotion as "constructed" out of, that is, generated by, the interaction of underlying processes and relevant to a variety of emotional phenomena (Mandler, 1993, 1999).

Behaviorism and Psychoanalysis

I hesitated in my recital of conflict theories and decided to pause and postpone the discussion of two strands of theory that are—in today's climate—somewhat out of the mainstream of standard psychology. Both behaviorist and psychoanalytic theories of emotion are conflict theories, and both had relatively little effect on the mainstream of emotional theory—the former because it avoided a theoretical approach to emotion, the latter because all of psychoanalytic theory is a theory of emotion, as well as a theory of cognition, and adopting its position on emotion implied accepting the rest of the theoretical superstructure. Behaviorists had their major impact on theories of motivation, and the majority of their work relevant to emotion addressed animal behavior and the conditioning of visceral states. However, behaviorist approaches do fall under the rubric of mental theories, defined as applying to psychological, as opposed to physiological, processes. In their approach to emotion, behaviorists stress the primacy of psychological mechanisms, distinguished from the organic approach.

There is another reason to consider behaviorism and psychoanalysis under a single heading. Particularly in the area of emotion, these two classes of theories exhibited most clearly the effects of sociocultural-historical factors on psychological theories. Both, in their own idiosyncratic ways, were the products of nineteenth-century moral philosophy and theology, just as the unanalyzable feeling was congruent with nineteenth-century idealism. The influence of moral and religious attitudes finds a more direct expression in a theory of emotion, which implies pleasure and unpleasure, the good and the bad, rewards and punishments.

In the sense of the American Protestant ethic, behaviorism raises the improvability of the human condition to a basic theorem; it decries emotion as interfering with the "normal" (and presumably rational) progress of behavior. It opposes "fanciness" with respect to theory, and it budges not in the face of competing positions; its most dangerous competitor is eclecticism. Behaviorism's departure from classical Calvinism is that it does not see outward success as a sign of inward grace. Rather, in the tradition of the nineteenth-century American frontier, it espouses a Protestant pragmatism in which outward success is seen as the result of the proper environment. Conflict is to be avoided, but when it occurs, it is indicative of some failure in the way in which we have arranged our environment. The best examples of these attitudes can be found when the psychologist moves his theories to the real world, as Watson (1928) did when he counseled on the raising of children. While quite content to build some fears into the child in order to establish a "certain kind of conformity with group standards," Watson is much more uncertain about the need for any "positive" emotions. He was sure that "mother love is a dangerous instrument." Children should never be hugged or kissed, never be allowed to sit in a mother's lap; shaking hands with them is all that is necessary or desirable. A classical example of the behaviorist attitude toward emotion can be found in Kantor (1921), who decries emotional consequences: They are chaotic and disturb the ongoing stream of behavior; they produce conflict. In contrast, Skinner (1938) noted the emotional consequences that occur during extinction; he understood the conflict engendered by punishment, and his utopian society is based on positive reinforcement.

I have discussed the classical behaviorists here for two reasons. One is that underneath classical behaviorist inquiries into emotion is a conflict theory; it is obvious in Kantor, and implied in Watson and Skinner. But there is also another aspect of conflict in behaviorist approaches to emotion; it is the conflict between an underlying rational pragmatism and the necessity of dealing with emotional phenomena, which are frequently seen as unnecessary nuisances in the development and explanation of behavior. There is no implication that emotions may be adaptively useful. For example, apart from mediating avoidance behavior, visceral responses are rarely conceived of as entering the stream of adaptive and useful behavior.

One of the major aspirations of the behaviorist movement was that the laws of conditioning would provide us with laws about the acquisition and extinction of emotional states. Pavlovian (respondent, classical) procedures in particular held out high hopes that they might produce insights into how emotions are "learned." It was generally assumed that emotional conditioning would provide one set of answers. However, the endeavor has produced only half an answer. We know much about the laws of conditioning of visceral responses, but we have learned little about the determinants of human emotional experience (see Mowrer, 1939). The most active attempt to apply behaviorist principles in the fields of therapy and behavior modification is increasingly being faced with "cognitive" incursions.

In the area of theory, one example of neobehaviorist conflict theories is Amsel's theory of frustration (1958, 1962). Although Amsel is in the first instance concerned not with emotion but rather with certain motivational properties of nonreward, he writes in the tradition of the conflict theories. Amsel noted that the withdrawal of reward has motivational consequences. These consequences occur only after a particular sequence leading to consummatory behavior has been well learned. Behavior following such blocking or frustration exhibits increased vigor, on which is based the primary claim for a motivational effect. Amsel noted that anticipatory frustration behaves in many respects like fear. This particular approach is the most sophisticated development of the early behaviorists' observations that extinction (nonreward) has emotional consequences.

Psychoanalysis was in part a product of a nineteenth-century interpretation of the Judeo-Christian ethic. The great regulator is the concept of unpleasure (Unlust); Eros joins the scenario decades later. At the heart of the theory lies the control of unacceptable instinctive impulses that are to be constrained, channeled, coped with. Freud did not deny these impulses; he brought them out into the open to be controlled—and even sometimes liberated. However at the base was sinning humanity, who could achieve pleasure mainly by avoiding unpleasure. Psychoanalytic theory therefore qualifies as a conflict theory. I have chosen not to describe psychoanalytic theory in great detail for two reasons. First, as far as the mainstream of psychological theories of emotion is concerned, Freud has had a general rather than specific impact. Second, as I have noted, all of psychoanalytic theory presents a general theory of emotion. To do justice to the theory in any detail would require a separate chapter.

However briefly, it is not difficult to characterize Freud's theory as a conflict theory. In fact, it combines conflict notions with Jamesian concerns. Curiously, after rejecting psychological theories and particularly the James-Lange theory of emotion, Freud characterizes affect, and specifically anxiety, by a formulation that is hardly different from James's. Freud talks about specific feelings, such as unpleasantness, efferent or discharge phenomena (primarily visceral), and perception of these discharge phenomena (Freud, 1926/1975). However, in general, affect is seen as a result of the organism's inability to discharge certain "instinctive reactions." The best description of the psychoanalytic theory in terms of its conflict implications was presented by MacCurdy (1925). MacCurdy describes three stages that are implicit in the psychoanalytic theory of emotion. The first, the arousal of energy (libido) in connection with some instinctual tendency; second, manifestations of this energy in behavior or conscious thought if that tendency is blocked; and third, energy is manifested as felt emotion or affect if behavior and conscious thoughts are blocked and inhibited.

Not unexpectedly, psychoanalytic notions have crept into many different contemporary theories. The most notable of these is probably that of Lazarus and his associates, mentioned earlier, and their descriptions of coping mechanisms, related to the psychoanalytic concerns with symptoms, defense mechanisms, and similar adaptive reactions (Lazarus, Averill, & Opton, 1970).

This concludes our sampling of a history that is some 2,500 years old, that has tried to be scientific, and that has reflected modern culture and society for the past 100-plus years. What can one say about the possible future speculations about emotion that might arise from that past?

A FUTURE HISTORY

First, I want to revisit a question that has been left hanging, namely, exactly what is an emotion? And I start with William James, who pointedly asked that question.

William James's Question

William James initiated the modern period in the history of psychology by entitling his 1884 paper "What Is an Emotion?" Over a hundred years later we still do not have a generally acceptable answer. Did he confuse "a semantic or metaphysical question with a scientific one" (McNaughton, 1989, p. 3)? As we have seen, different people answer the question differently, as behooves a well-used umbrella term from the natural language. Emotion no more receives an unequivocal definition than does intelligence or learning. Within any language or social community, people seem to

know full well, though they have difficulty putting into words, what emotions are, what it is to be emotional, what experiences qualify as emotions, and so forth. However, these agreements vary from language to language and from community to community (Geertz, 1973) .

Given that the emotions are established facts of everyday experience, it is initially useful to determine what organizes the common language of emotion in the first place, and then to find a reasonable theoretical account that provides a partial understanding of these language uses. But as we have seen, these theoretical accounts themselves vary widely. In recent years theoretical definitions of emotions have been so broad that they seem to cover anything that human beings do, as in the notion that emotions are "episodic, relatively short-term, biologically based patterns of perception, experience, physiology, action, and communication that occur in response to specific physical and social challenges and opportunities" (Keltner & Gross, 1999).

Is there anything that is essential to the use of the term "emotion," some aspect that represents the core that would help us find a theoretical direction out of the jungle of terms and theories? Lexicographers perform an important function in that their work is cumulative and, in general, responds to the nuances and the changing customs of the common language. What do they tell us? Webster's *Seventh New Collegiate Dictionary* (1969) says that *emotion* is "a psychic and physical reaction subjectively experienced as strong feeling and physiologically involving changes that prepare the body for immediate vigorous action," and that *affect* is defined as "the conscious subjective aspect of an emotion considered apart from bodily changes." Here is the traditional definition, which responds to the advice of our elder statesmen Darwin and James that visceral changes are a necessary part of the emotions. But they are not sufficient; we still require the affective component. Assuming that "affect" falls under a broad definition of cognition, including information, cogitation, subjective classification and other mental entities, the advantage of an affective/cognitive component is that it makes all possible emotions accessible.

Whatever evaluative cognitions arise historically and culturally, they are potentially part of the emotional complex. Thus, emotions different from the Western traditions (e.g., Lutz, 1988) become just as much a part of the corpus as transcultural fears and idiosyncratically Western romantic love. However, even such an extension covers only a limited section of the panoply of emotions, and the arousal/cognition approach may not be sufficient.

It is unlikely that the question of a definition of the commonsense meaning of emotion will easily be resolved. And so I close this section by returning to a quote from Charles

Darwin, who had thought so fruitfully about the expression of emotion and who knew that "expression" involved more than the face and that the viscera were crucial in the experience of emotion: "Most of our emotions are so closely connected with their expression that they hardly exist if the body remains passive. . . . [As] Louis XVI said when surrounded by a fierce mob, 'Am I afraid? Feel my pulse.' So a man may intensely hate another, but until his body frame is affected, he cannot be said to be enraged" (Darwin, 1872, p. 239).

How Many Theories?

Given that different lists of emotions and definitions seem to appeal to different sets of emotions, one might have to consider the possibility that the emotion chapter contains so many disparate phenomena that different theories might be needed for different parts of the emotion spectrum. Such a possibility was hinted at even by William James, who, in presenting his theory of emotion, noted that the "only emotions . . . [that he proposed] expressly to consider . . . are those that have a distinct bodily expression" (James, 1884, p. 189). He specifically left aside aesthetic feelings or intellectual delights, the implication being that some other explanatory mechanism applies to those. On the one hand, many current theories of human emotion restrict themselves to the same domain as James did—the subjective experience that is accompanied by bodily "disturbances." On the other hand, much current work deals primarily with negative emotions—and the animal work does so almost exclusively. Social and cognitive scientists spend relatively little time trying to understand ecstasy, joy, or love, but some do important and enlightening work in these areas (see, for example, Berscheid, 1983, 1985; Isen, 1990). Must we continue to insist that passionate emotional experiences of humans, ranging from lust to political involvements, from coping with disaster to dealing with grief, from the joys of creative work to the moving experiences of art and music, are all cut from the same cloth, or even that that cloth should be based on a model of negative emotions? There are of course regularities in human thought and action that produce general categories of emotions, categories that have family resemblances and overlap in the features that are selected for analysis (whether it is the simple dichotomy of good and bad, or the appreciation of beauty, or the perception of evil).

These families of occasions and meanings construct the categories of emotions found in the natural language. The emotion categories are fuzzily defined by external and internal situations, and the common themes vary from case to case and have different bases for their occurrence. Sometimes an emotional category is based on the similarity of external conditions, as in the case of some fears and environmental threats. Sometimes an emotional category may be based on a collection of similar behaviors, as in the subjective feelings of fear related to avoidance and flight. Sometimes a common category arises from a class of incipient actions, as in hostility and destructive action. Sometimes hormonal and physiological reactions provide a common basis, as in the case of lust, and sometimes purely cognitive evaluations constitute an emotional category, as in judgments of helplessness that eventuate in anxiety. Others, such as guilt and grief, depend on individual evaluations of having committed undesirable acts or trying to recover the presence or comfort of a lost person or object. All of these emotional states involve evaluative cognitions, and their common properties give rise to the appearance of discrete categories of emotions.

It can also be argued that different theories and theorists are concerned with different aspects of an important and complex aspect of human existence. Thus, animal research is concerned with possible evolutionary precursors or parallels of some few important, usually aversive, states. Others are more concerned with the appraisal and evaluation of the external world, while some theories focus on the cognitive conjunction with autonomic nervous system reactions. And the more ambitious try to put it all together in overarching and inclusive systems.

It may be too early or it may be misleading to assume common mechanisms for the various states of high joy and low despair that we experience, or to expect complex human emotions to share a common ancestry with the simple emotions of humans and other animals. The question remains whether the term *emotion* should be restricted to one particular set of these various phenomena. Until such questions are resolved, there is clearly much weeding to be done in the jungle, much cultivation in order to achieve a well-ordered garden.

REFERENCES

Amsel, A. (1958). The role of frustrative nonreward in noncontinuous reward situations. *Psychological Bulletin, 53,* 102–119.

Amsel, A. (1962). Frustrative nonreward in partial reinforcement and discrimination learning. *Psychological Review, 69,* 306–328.

Angier, R. P. (1927). The conflict theory of emotion. *American Journal of Psychology, 39,* 390–401.

Arnold, M. B. (1960). *Emotion and personality.* New York: Columbia University Press.

Arnold, M. B. (1970). *Feelings and emotions: The Loyola Symposium.* New York: Academic Press.

Averill, J. R. (1969). Autonomic response patterns during sadness and mirth. *Psychophysiology, 5,* 399–414.

Ax, A. F. (1953). The physiological differentiation of fear and anger in humans. *Psychosomatic Medicine, 15,* 433–442.

Bain, A. (1875/1859). *The emotions and the will* (3rd ed.). London: Longmans, Green.

Bavelas, J. B., Black, A., Lemery, C. R., & Mullett, J. (1986). I show how you feel: Motor mimicry as a communicative act. *Journal of Personality and Social Psychology, 50,* 322–329.

Bentley, M. (1928). Is "emotion" more than a chapter heading? In M. L. Reymert (Ed.), *Feelings and emotions: The Wittenberg Symposium* (pp. 17–23). Worcester, MA: Clark University Press.

Berscheid, E. (1983). Emotion. In H. H. Kelley, E. Berscheid, A. Christensen, J. H. Harvey, T. L. Huston, G. Levinger, et al. (Eds.), *Close relationships* (pp. 110–168). San Francisco: Freeman.

Berscheid, E. (1985). Interpersonal attraction. In G. Lindzey & E. Aronson (Eds.), *Handbook of social psychology* (pp. 413–484). New York: Random House.

Borkovec, T. D. (1976). Physiological and cognitive processes in the regulation of fear. In G. E. Schwartz & D. Shapiro (Eds.), *Consciousness and self-regulation: Advances in research* (pp. 261–312). New York: Plenum Press.

Brett, G. S. (1928). Historical development of the theory of emotions. In M. L. Reymert (Ed.), *Feelings and emotions: The Wittenberg Symposium* (pp. 388–397). Worcester, MA: Clark University Press.

Candland, D. K., Fell, J. P., Keen, E., Leshner, A. I., Plutchik, R., & Tarpy, R. M. (1977). *Emotion.* Monterey, CA: Brooks/Cole.

Cannon, W. B. (1914). The interrelations of emotions as suggested by recent physiological researches. *American Journal of Psychology, 25,* 256–282.

Cannon, W. B. (1927). The James-Lange theory of emotions: A critical examination and an alternative theory. *American Journal of Psychology, 39,* 106–124.

Cannon, W. B. (1929). *Bodily changes in pain, hunger, fear and rage.* New York: Appleton-Century-Crofts.

Cannon, W. B. (1930). The Linacre lecture on the autonomic nervous system: An interpretation. *Lancet, 218,* 1109–1115.

Darwin, C. (1872). *The expression of the emotions in man and animals.* London: John Murray.

Descartes, R. (1649). *Les passions de l'âme.* Amsterdam: Chez Louys Elzevier.

Dewey, J. (1894). The theory of emotion. I: Emotional attitudes. *Psychological Review, 1,* 553–569.

Dewey, J. (1895). The theory of emotion. II: The significance of emotions. *Psychological Review, 2,* 13–32.

Dunlap, K. (1922). *The emotions—by C. G. Lange & W. James.* Baltimore: Williams & Wilkins.

Ekman, P. (Ed.). (1982). *Emotion in the human face.* New York: Cambridge University Press.

Ekman, P., & Oster, H. (1979). Facial expressions of emotion. *Annual Review of Psychology, 30,* 527–554.

Elster, J. (1999). *Alchemies of the mind: Rationality and the emotions.* New York: Cambridge University Press.

Folkman, S., & Lazarus, R. S. (1990). Coping and emotion. In N. S. Stein, B. L. Leventhal, & T. Trabasso (Eds.), *Psychological and biological approaches to emotion* (pp. 313–332). Hillsdale, NJ: Erlbaum.

Fraisse, P. (1968). Les Emotions. In P. Fraisse & J. Piaget (Eds.), *Traité de psychologie experimentale* (pp. 102–191). Paris: Presses Universitaires.

Frankenhaeuser, M. (1971). Behavior and circulating catecholamines. *Brain Research, 31,* 241–262.

Frankenhaeuser, M. (1975). Experimental approaches to the study of catecholamines and emotion. In L. Levi (Ed.), *Emotions: Their parameters and measurement.* New York: Raven Press.

Freud, S. (1975). Inhibitions, symptoms, and anxiety. *The standard edition of the complete psychological works of Sigmund Freud.* London: Hogarth Press. (Original work published 1926)

Fridlund, A. J. (1991). Evolution and facial action in reflex, social motive, and paralanguage. *Biological Psychology, 32,* 3–100.

Fridlund, A. J. (1992a). The behavioral ecology and sociality of human faces. In M. S. Clark (Ed.), *Review of personality and social psychology* (pp. 90–121). Beverly Hills, CA: Sage.

Fridlund, A. J. (1992b). Darwin's anti-Darwinism in *The expression of the emotions in man and animals.* In K. T. Strongman (Ed.), *International review of studies on emotion* (pp. 117–137). Chichester, England: Wiley.

Frijda, N. H. (1986). *The emotions.* Cambridge, England: Cambridge University Press.

Gardiner, H. M., Metcalf, R. C., & Beebe-Center, J. G. (1937). *Feeling and emotion: A history of theories.* New York: American Book.

Geertz, C. (1973). *The interpretation of cultures: Selected essays.* New York: Basic Books.

Hammond, W. A. (Ed.). (1902). *Aristotle's psychology: A treatise on the principles of life (De anima and Parva naturalia).* London: S. Sonnenschein.

Hebb, D. O. (1946). On the nature of fear. *Psychological Review, 53,* 259–276.

Hebb, D. O. (1949). *The organization of behavior.* New York: Wiley.

Herbart, J. F. (1816). *Lehrbuch zur Psychologie.* Königsberg und Leipzig, Germany: A. W. Unzer.

Hohmann, G. W. (1966). Some effects of spinal cord lesions on experienced emotional feelings. *Psychophysiology, 3,* 143–156.

Hunt, J. M., Cole, M. W., & Reis, E. S. (1958). Situational cues distinguishing anger, fear, and sorrow. *American Journal of Psychology, 71,* 136–151.

Hunt, W. A. (1941). Recent developments in the field of emotion. *Psychological Bulletin, 38,* 249–276.

Isen, A. M. (1990). The influence of positive and negative affect on cognitive organization: Some implications for development. In N. S. Stein, B. L. Leventhal, & T. Trabasso (Eds.), *Psychological and biological approaches to emotion* (pp. 75–94). Hillsdale, NJ: Erlbaum.

Izard, C. E. (1971). *The face of emotion.* New York: Appleton-Century-Crofts.

Izard, C. E. (1972). *Patterns of emotion.* New York: Academic Press.

James, W. (1884). What is an emotion? *Mind, 9,* 188–205.

James, W. (1890). *The principles of psychology.* New York: Holt.

James, W. (1894). The physical basis of emotion. *Psychological Review, 1,* 516–529.

Jasnos, T. M., & Hakmiller, K. L. (1975). Some effects of lesion level and emotional cues on affective expression in spinal cord patients. *Psychological Reports, 37,* 859–870.

Kant, I. (1800). *Anthropologie in pragmatischer Hinsicht* (2nd ed.). Königsberg, Germany: F. Nicolovius.

Kantor, J. R. (1921). An attempt toward a naturalistic description of emotion. *Psychological Review, 2,* 19–42, 120–140.

Keltner, D., & Gross, J. J. (1999). Functional accounts of emotions. *Cognition and Emotion, 13*(5), 467–480.

Kessen, W., & Mandler, G. (1961). Anxiety, pain, and the inhibition of distress. *Psychological Review, 68,* 396–404.

Landis, C. (1929). The interpretation of facial expression in emotion. *Journal of General Psychology, 2,* 59–72.

Lange, C. (1885). *Om Sindsbevaegelser.* Kjöbenhavn.

Lange, C. (1887). *Ueber Gemüthsbewegungen.* Leipzig, Germany: Theodor Thomas.

Lazarus, R. S., Averill, J. R., & Opton, E. M. J. (1970). Toward a cognitive theory of emotion. In M. B. Arnold (Ed.), *Feelings and emotions* (pp. 207–232). New York: Academic Press.

Lazarus, R. S., Kanner, A. D., & Folkman, S. (1980). Emotions: A cognitive-phenomenological analysis. In R. Plutchik & H. Kellerman (Eds.), *Theories of emotion* (pp. 189–217). New York: Academic Press.

LeDoux, J. E. (1989). Cognitive-emotional interactions in the brain. *Cognition and Emotion, 3,* 267–289.

Levi, L. (1975). *Emotions: Their parameters and measurement.* New York: Raven Press.

Levi-Montalcini, R., & Angeletti, P. W. (1961). Biological properties of a nerve growth promoting protein and its antiserum. In S. S. Kety & J. Elkes (Eds.), *Regional neurochemistry* (pp. 362–377). New York: Pergamon Press.

Lewin, K. (1935). *A dynamic theory of personality.* New York: McGraw-Hill.

Lutz, C. (1988). *Unnatural emotions: Everyday sentiments on a Micronesian atoll and their challenge to Western theory.* Chicago: University of Chicago Press.

MacCurdy, J. T. (1925). *The psychology of emotion.* London: Kegan Paul, Trench, Trubner.

Mandler, G. (1964). The interruption of behavior. In E. Levine (Ed.), *Nebraska symposium on motivation: 1964* (pp. 163–219). Lincoln: University of Nebraska Press.

Mandler, G. (1975). *Mind and emotion.* New York: Wiley.

Mandler, G. (1979). Emotion. In E. Hearst (Ed.), *The first century of experimental psychology* (pp. 275–321). Hillsdale, NJ: Erlbaum.

Mandler, G. (1984). *Mind and body: Psychology of emotion and stress.* New York: Norton.

Mandler, G. (1990). A constructivist theory of emotion. In N. S. Stein, B. L. Leventhal, & T. Trabasso (Eds.), *Psychological and biological approaches to emotion* (pp. 21–43). Hillsdale, NJ: Erlbaum.

Mandler, G. (1992). Emotions, evolution, and aggression: Myths and conjectures. In K. T. Strongman (Ed.), *International Review of Studies on Emotion* (pp. 97–116). Chichester, England: Wiley.

Mandler, G. (1993). Thought, memory, and learning: Effects of emotional stress. In L. Goldberger & S. Breznitz (Eds.), *Handbook of stress* (pp. 40–55). New York: Free Press.

Mandler, G. (1999). Emotion. In B. M. Bly & D. E. Rumelhart (Eds.), *Cognitive science* (pp. 367–384). San Diego, CA: Academic Press.

Mandler, G., & Kremen, I. (1958). Autonomic feedback: A correlational study. *Journal of Personality, 26,* 388–399.

Mandler, G., Mandler, J. M., & Uviller, E. T. (1958). Autonomic feedback: The perception of autonomic activity. *Journal of Abnormal and Social Psychology, 56,* 367–373.

Mandler, G., & Watson, D. L. (1966). Anxiety and the interruption of behavior. In C. D. Spielberger (Ed.), *Anxiety and behavior* (pp. 263–288). New York: Academic Press.

Marañon, G. (1924). Contribution à l'étude de l'action emotive de l'adrénaline. *Revue française d'Endocrinologie, 2,* 301–325.

McCosh, J. (1880). *The emotions.* New York: Scribner.

McNaughton, M. (1989). *Biology and emotion.* Cambridge, England: Cambridge University Press.

Meyer, L. B. (1956). *Emotion and meaning in music.* Chicago: University of Chicago Press.

Mowrer, O. H. (1939). Stimulus-response analysis of anxiety and its role as a reinforcing agent. *Psychological Review, 46,* 553–565.

Ortony, A., Clore, G. L., & Collins, A. (1988). *The cognitive structure of emotions.* New York: Cambridge University Press.

Ortony, A., & Turner, T. J. (1990). What's basic about basic emotions? *Psychological Review, 97,* 315–331.

Patkai, P. (1971). Catecholamine excretion in pleasant and unpleasant situations. *Acta Psychologia, 35,* 352–363.

Paulhan, F. (1887). *Les phénomènes affectifs et les lois de leur apparition.* Paris: F. Alcan.

Paulhan, F. (1930). *The laws of feeling.* London: Kegan Paul, Trench, Trubner.

Pick, J. (1970). *The autonomic nervous system.* Philadelphia: Lippincott.

Reymert, M. L. (1928). *Feelings and emotions: The Wittenberg Symposium.* Worcester, MA: Clark University Press.

Reymert, M. L. (1950). *Feelings and emotions: The Mooseheart Symposium.* New York: McGraw-Hill.

Rimé, B. (1999). President's column. *Emotion Researcher, 13*(3), 1–7.

Ruckmick, C. A. (1936). *The psychology of feeling and emotion.* New York: McGraw-Hill.

Schachter, S. (1970). The assumption of identity and peripheralist-centralist controversies in motivation and emotion. In M. B. Arnold (Ed.), *Feelings and emotions* (pp. 111–121). New York: Academic Press.

Schachter, S. (1971). *Emotion, obesity, and crime.* New York: Academic Press.

Schachter, S., & Singer, J. E. (1962). Cognitive, social and physiological determinants of emotional state. *Psychological Review, 69,* 379–399.

Schlosberg, H. (1954). Three dimensions of emotion. *Psychological Review, 61,* 81–88.

Sergi, G. (1894). *Principi di psicologie. Dolore e piacere; storia naturale dei sentimenti.* Milano, Italy: Fratelli Dumolard.

Sergi, G. (1896). Sulla nuova teoria della emozioni. *Rivista di Sociologica, 3,* 23–38.

Sirota, A. D., Schwartz, G. E., & Shapiro, D. (1974). Voluntary control of human heart rate: Effect on reaction to aversive stimulation. *Journal of Abnormal Psychology, 83,* 261–267.

Sirota, A. D., Schwartz, G. E., & Shapiro, D. (1976). Voluntary control of human heart rate: Effect on reaction to aversive stimulation: A replication and extension. *Journal of Abnormal Psychology, 85,* 473–477.

Skinner, B. F. (1938). *The behavior of organisms.* New York: Appleton-Century-Crofts.

Spinoza, B. (1876). *The ethics of Benedict de Spinoza: Demonstrated after the method of geometers.* New York: Van Nostrand. (Original work published 1677)

Suarez, F. (1856). *Opera omnia.* Paris: Vives.

Sutherland, A. (1898). *The origin and growth of the moral instinct.* London: Longmans, Green.

Titchener, E. B. (1896). *An outline of psychology.* New York: Macmillan.

Tomkins, S. (1962/1992). *Affect, imagery, and consciousness.* New York: Springer.

Valins, S. (1966). Cognitive effects of false heart-rate feedback. *Journal of Personality and Social Psychology, 4,* 400–408.

Valins, S. (1970). The perception and labeling of bodily changes as determinants of emotional behavior. In P. Black (Ed.), *Physiological correlates of emotion* (pp. 229–259). New York: Academic Press.

Valins, S., & Ray, A. A. (1967). Effects of cognitive desensitization on avoidance behavior. *Journal of Personality and Social Psychology, 7,* 345–350.

Watson, J. B. (1928). *Psychological care of infant and child.* New York: Norton.

Webster's seventh new collegiate dictionary. (1969). Springfield, MA: Merriam.

Wenzel, B. M. (1972). Immunosympathectomy and behavior. In G. Steiner & E. Schonbaum (Eds.), *Immunosympathectomy* (pp. 199–219). Amsterdam: Elsevier.

Wundt, W. (1891). Zur Lehre von den Gemüthsbewegungen. *Philosophische Studien, 6,* 335–393.

CHAPTER 9

Personality

NICOLE B. BARENBAUM AND DAVID G. WINTER

CASE STUDIES AND LIFE HISTORIES IN
   PERSONALITY PSYCHOLOGY: A HISTORY
   OF AMBIVALENCE   177
INDIVIDUAL LIVES AND INDIVIDUAL
   DIFFERENCES: THE MULTIDISCIPLINARY
   STUDY OF PERSONALITY (1900–1930)   179
   The "Culture of Personality"   179
   Psychiatry and Psychopathology   180
   Sociology and Social Work   181
   The Mental Hygiene Movement   182
   American Psychology   183
PROMOTING THE STUDY OF INDIVIDUAL LIVES:
   GORDON ALLPORT AND HENRY MURRAY   185

Gordon Allport and Case Studies: "The Most Revealing
   Method of All"   185
Henry Murray's Personology and the Study of Lives   187
The Study of Individual Lives in the 1930s and
   1940s . . . and Later   189
REASSESSING THE HISTORY OF AMBIVALENCE TOWARD
   THE STUDY OF INDIVIDUAL LIVES   191
   Revival of the Study of Individual Lives in
   Personality Psychology   192
   Context and Complexity in Personality Psychology   195
REFERENCES   196

CASE STUDIES AND LIFE HISTORIES IN PERSONALITY PSYCHOLOGY: A HISTORY OF AMBIVALENCE

> Psychology is proud of its laboratories, with their apparatus for careful experimentation and measurement. It is proud also of its array of tests for measuring the individual's performance in many directions. It is pleased when its data can be handled by mathematical and statistical methods. (Woodworth, 1929, pp. 7–8)

When Robert S. Woodworth revised his influential introductory psychology text in 1929, he expanded his final chapter on "personality"—"the individual as a whole, and his social adjustments" (Woodworth, 1929, p. 552), citing several recent studies involving personality tests. Woodworth also revised his treatment of "the methods of psychology" (p. 6), including a new discussion of the "case history method" (p. 8). However, the status of this method in Woodworth's hierarchy of methods was clear: It belonged at the bottom. Woodworth first described the experimental method, "preferred as the most trustworthy way of observing the facts"

under controlled conditions (p. 6); this method included the use of tests, as in testing "the object is to hold conditions constant, so that many individuals can be observed under the same conditions and fairly compared" (p. 6). When conditions cannot be fully controlled, Woodworth noted, psychology "has to resort to" a second method; this "genetic method" (p. 8) involves observations of developmental processes (during this period, "genetic" was frequently used as a synonym for "developmental"; see, e.g., Warren, 1934, p. 114). If psychologists wish to understand developments that have already occurred, however, they are left with a substitute:

> We find a genius, or an insane person, a criminal, or a "problem child" before us, and we desire to know how he came to be what he is. Then the best we can do is to adopt a substitute for the genetic method, by reconstructing his history as well as we can from his memory, the memories of his acquaintances, and such records as may have been preserved. This *case history* method has obvious disadvantages, but, as obviously, it is the only way to make a start towards answering certain important questions. (Woodworth, 1929, p. 8)

Having pointed out that the case history was primarily a clinical method used to help people with abnormal behavior and that "the cause of misfits and failures is certainly an important matter for study," Woodworth asked, "Would it not be

The authors would like to thank William McKinley Runyan for his helpful suggestions.

still more desirable to trace the development of the successful people, the great people, the lovely people, the splendid people of all sorts?" (1929, p. 10). To illustrate his point, and to introduce important topics in psychology, he presented a "biographical sketch" of Gene Stratton-Porter, "a successful writer of popular novels, and also of nature studies, essays and poems" (p. 10). After mentioning several topics suggested by Stratton-Porter's life history, however, Woodworth made sure to caution his readers that "a single case is not enough to warrant any general conclusions" (p. 19). "We have given so much space to the case history method in this introduction," he continued,

> not because it is the preferred method in psychology, for it is the least rather than the most preferred, but because it can give us what we want at the outset, a bird's-eye view of the field, with some indication of the topics that are deserving of closer examination. (p. 19)

In the ensuing 12 chapters of the text, Woodworth examined the "deserving" topics but made no further reference to the case of Gene Stratton-Porter.

Preceding by several years the full establishment of the field of personality psychology in the mid-1930s, Woodworth's text (first published in 1921) outsold all others for 25 years (Boring, 1950), and his definitions of methodological concepts served as prototypes for other textbook authors (Winston, 1988). Indeed, Woodworth's attention to personality, his role in designing what is generally considered the first personality inventory (the Personal Data Sheet; Woodworth, 1919, 1932), and his ambivalent treatment of the case history method—as the least preferred method, but the one best suited to "give us what we want at the outset" (Woodworth, 1929, p. 19)—have a distinctly modern ring. In recent years, personality researchers with an interest in case studies, life histories, and psychobiography have raised intriguing questions regarding the ambivalence of American personality psychologists toward the study of individual lives (Elms, 1994; McAdams, 1988, 1997; McAdams & West, 1997; Runyan, 1997). For example, McAdams and West observe that "from the beginning, personality psychologists have had a love/hate relationship with the case study" (p. 760). Such ambivalence, they suggest, is inconsistent with the views of Gordon Allport (1937b) and Henry Murray (1938), whose canonical texts defined the new field of personality psychology in the 1930s: "It is ironic that the field defined as the scientific study of the individual person should harbor deep ambivalence about the very business of examining cases of individual persons' lives" (McAdams & West, 1997, p. 761). (Personality psychologists other than Allport

and Murray shared this definition of the field. For example, in a third text that signaled the emergence of the new field, Stagner remarked, "The object of our study is a single human being" [1937, p. viii].)

Ambivalence regarding the study of individual lives also seems incompatible with personality theorists' "dissident role in the development of psychology" (C. S. Hall & Lindzey, 1957, p. 4; see McAdams, 1997) and their concern with "the study of the whole person," which Hall and Lindzey (p. 6) consider "a natural derivative of [the] clinical practice" of early personality theorists such as Freud, Jung, and Adler. Yet Hall and Lindzey's major text, *Theories of Personality* (1957), "gave almost no attention to the study of individual persons or lives" (Runyan, 1997, p. 41). Runyan suggests that personality psychologists in the 1950s and 1960s lost sight of the study of individual lives, the "central focus" of Allport and Murray, turning instead to "psychometric concerns and the experimental study of particular processes" (p. 41; see also Lamiell on the dominance of the individual differences approach, which he considers "ill-suited to the task of advancing theories of individual behavior/psychological functioning" [1997, p. 118], the goal of personality psychology). Craik (1986) notes that biographical and archival approaches were featured regularly in studies of personality during the 1930s and early 1940s but showed a "pattern of interrupted development in the post–World War II era followed by a vigorous contemporary re-emergence" (p. 27).

While observers generally agree regarding personality psychologists' ambivalence toward the study of individual lives, the historical course of this ambivalence remains somewhat unclear. Have personality psychologists had a relatively constant "love/hate relationship" with studies of individual lives "from the beginning" (McAdams & West, 1997, p. 760), or have they shown interest in such studies during some historical periods (e.g., the 1930s and 1940s) and neglected them during others (e.g., the 1950s and 1960s)? At what point did psychometric methods become predominant in personality research? And how can we explain the "puzzling history" (Runyan, 1997, p. 41) of American personality psychologists' tendency to neglect the study of individual lives? What historical, cultural, institutional, and personal factors have contributed to their ambivalence? Runyan suggests a number of factors but emphasizes the need for "more detailed research on the intellectual and institutional history of personality psychology" (p. 42).

In this chapter, we consider several pieces of this historical puzzle. We begin by examining the formative period of personality research between 1900 and 1930. As Parker (1991) suggests, this period has received scant attention in historical reviews of American personality psychology, largely due to the prevailing belief that "personality quite suddenly became a field in the middle of the 1930s" (Sanford, 1985, p. 492). In fact, psychologists developed an interest in personality much earlier, and their methodological choices, shaped by developments within the broader field of psychology and in the larger culture, influenced the field in important ways (Danziger, 1990, 1997; Parker, 1991; Shermer, 1985). In our own historical review of the field (Winter & Barenbaum, 1999), we argue that early research in personality reveals a tension between two central tasks of personality psychology—"*the study of individual differences*" and "*the study of individual persons as unique, integrated wholes*" (p. 6; emphasis in original)—and that the individual differences approach was already well-established in psychological studies of personality by the time the subfield of personality psychology was institutionalized in the 1930s. Here, we examine in more detail aspects of this formative period that contributed to the predominance of the psychometric approach and to personality psychologists' ambivalence regarding intensive studies of individual lives. We suggest that personality psychologists' attitudes toward case studies and life histories were influenced by work not only in psychology but also in neighboring disciplines that adopted alternative investigative practices. In particular, we compare the reception of case studies and life histories in psychiatry, sociology, and psychology during the early decades of the twentieth century.

To illustrate the lasting effects of these methodological choices, we trace the efforts of Allport and Murray to promote the study of individual lives in personality psychology, and we examine psychologists' responses to their work. Finally, we reconsider the question of the historical course of personality psychologists' ambivalence regarding the study of individual lives and suggest an interpretation of the revival of interest in case studies, life histories, and psychobiography in recent years. Rather than simply documenting the history of case studies and life histories in personality psychology, we focus in this chapter on contextual factors shaping American personality psychologists' attitudes toward these methods. Our account builds upon a number of earlier sources: historical reviews of case studies (e.g., Bromley, 1986; Forrester, 1996; McAdams & West, 1997), life histories and psychobiography (e.g., Bertaux, 1981; McAdams, 1988; Plummer, 1983; Runyan, 1982, 1988b, 1997); handbook chapters on the history of personality theories and research (e.g., McAdams, 1997; Pervin, 1990; Winter & Barenbaum, 1999); and historical studies of the early development of personality psychology (Burnham, 1968a; Danziger, 1990, 1997; Nicholson, 1996, 1997, 1998, 2000; Parker, 1991; Shermer, 1985).

INDIVIDUAL LIVES AND INDIVIDUAL DIFFERENCES: THE MULTIDISCIPLINARY STUDY OF PERSONALITY (1900–1930)

Gordon Allport's (1921) review of "personality" research, generally considered the first of its kind in an American psychological journal, was "an early indication that this word was beginning to have a technical meaning" (Parker, 1991, p. 113). Other indicators of institutional recognition (such as publication trends in journals and textbooks, contents of professional meetings, and changes in academic curricula) began to emerge during the mid-1920s, and personality research "became a relatively secure specialty area in American psychology by the mid-1930s" (Parker, 1991, p. 164; see also Burnham, 1968a). In the following section we discuss the broader cultural context that influenced the emergence of the new subfield.

The "Culture of Personality"

Personality . . . is by far the greatest word in the history of the human mind. . . . [It] is the key that unlocks the deeper mysteries of Science and Philosophy, of History and Literature, of Art and Religion, of all man's Ethical and Social relationships. (Randall, 1912, pp. xiii–xiv)

Cultural historians suggest that during the early decades of the twentieth century, societal changes associated with industrialization, urbanization, and mass education evoked among Americans "a strong sense of the urgency of finding one's self" (Burnham, 1968b, p. 367; see also Thornton, 1996). During the "turn-of-the-century decade," according to Susman (1979), "interest grew in personality, individual idiosyncrasies, personal needs and interests. . . . There was fascination with the very peculiarities of the self, especially the sick self" (pp. 216–217). The popular press featured dramatic descriptions of cases of psychopathology, such as the *Ladies' Home Journal* article entitled "How One Girl Lived Four Lives: The Astounding Case of Miss Beauchamp" (Corbin, 1908), a popularized version of Morton Prince's (1906) famous case of "dissociated personality." Seeking to relieve fears of depersonalization, Americans consulted self-improvement manuals that emphasized the cultivation of a unique, fascinating "personality"—a term that "became an important part of the American vocabulary" (Susman, 1979, p. 217). This new emphasis on "personality" is evident in the previous quote from John Randall. Randall represented the New Thought, or Mind Cure, movement, which was important in the transition from a "culture of character," a nineteenth-century ideal emphasizing duty and moral qualities, to a "culture of personality" (Susman, 1979, p. 216), emphasizing self-development and self-presentation.

The 1920s saw "the culmination on a mass scale of public interest in personal, introspective accounts of private experiences" and the development of "a mass market for popularized personal documents" (Burnham, 1968b, p. 368). Americans read magazines such as *True Story* (Krueger, 1925), first published in 1919 (Ernst, 1991), and *Personality: A Magazine of Biography,* published from 1927 to 1928 and edited by Ralph Henry Graves, who in 1934 published a biography of Henry Ford—an emblematic figure of the "culture of personality" (Susman, 1979, p. 223). They sought advice from publications on popular systems of character analysis such as graphology, the interpretation of personality from handwriting (see Thornton, 1996, who suggests that graphologists' romantic view of handwriting as a reflection of the unique individual offered more comfort to Americans than did psychologists' measures of individual differences). The "new psychology," which borrowed concepts of hidden human motives from psychoanalysis, became "one of the characteristic fads of the age" (Burnham, 1968b, p. 352). "Candid and confessional autobiographical fragments were central in popular expositions of psychoanalysis," and case reports "had all the appeal—and more—of true confessions" (p. 368). Public fascination with psychoanalysis was symbolized in 1924 by the appearance of Freud on the cover of *Time* magazine (Fancher, 2000).

Academic and professional cultures, too, reflected a concern with personality. James C. Johnston, for example, noted "the wide vogue" of biography (1927, p. x), "the literature of personality" (pp. xi–xii), and argued for the establishment of separate departments of biography, such as those that had been recently established at Carleton College and at Dartmouth (see the introduction to Johnston's book by biographer Gamaliel Bradford, 1927). Personality became a central concept in academic and professional fields such as psychopathology and psychiatry (Taylor, 2000), sociology (Barenbaum, 2000), education (Danziger, 1990), and social work (Richmond, 1922; V. P. Robinson, 1930), and in the mental hygiene movement (Cohen, 1983), as well as in psychology (Nicholson, 1997, 1998, 2000). Following Freud's visit to America in 1909, many of these fields began to reflect the influence of psychoanalysis (see, e.g., Danziger, 1997; Hale, 1971; Lubove, 1965; Shakow & Rapaport, 1964).

It is important to note the multidisciplinary nature of personality studies during the formative period of personality psychology. (Craik, 1986, makes a similar point but uses the term "interdisciplinary" instead of "multidisciplinary"; we use the latter term to suggest that research on personality was conducted in many disciplines, whether or not it involved cross-disciplinary collaboration.) At this time, the boundaries between psychology and disciplines such as sociology and psychiatry were unclear. For example, both psychology and sociology developed subfields of "social psychology" during this period (see the chapter by Morawski & Bayer in this volume), and social psychologists in both disciplines considered personality a primary topic of research (Barenbaum, 2000). Indeed, as late as the 1930s, according to Smith (1997), "there was little clear separation between sociology and psychology" in personality research, despite a general tendency toward separation of sociological and psychological social psychology (see also Good, 2000); researchers in both fields were "driven by the common interest in knowledge to make possible the individual's social adjustment" (Smith, 1997, p. 765).

In the following sections, we examine methodological choices regarding the study of individual lives in several areas in which personality became a central concept during the first three decades of the twentieth century—psychiatry and psychopathology, sociology and social work, the interdisciplinary mental hygiene movement, and psychology. There are, of course, other areas we might have included. For example, in anthropology, life history research aroused some interest following the publication of Radin's (1926) *Crashing Thunder,* but it became popular only in the 1930s and 1940s (Hudson, 1973). We have chosen to treat in more depth the reception of case studies and life histories between 1900 and 1930 in areas closely related to psychology.

Psychiatry and Psychopathology

The term "personality" appeared rarely in the general psychological literature before the second decade of the twentieth century, and during the first decade it "typically had a colloquial meaning that was synonymous with 'soul' or 'self'" (Parker, 1991, p. 40). Between 1910 and 1920, however, it began to appear in discussions of "psychiatric and abnormal psychology topics" (p. 42) and in reviews of books on psychoanalysis (Parker's observations are based on a survey of articles in the *Psychological Bulletin* and the *Psychological Review* between 1900 and 1920). It is important to remember that during this period, abnormal and clinical psychology were not central areas of academic psychology, as they are today. Some American psychologists were interested in psychopathology and psychotherapy (Hale, 1971; Taylor, 1996, 2000); one notable example is William James, who was trained in medicine and taught a course in psychopathology at Harvard beginning in 1893 (Taylor, 1996). (Woodworth, 1932, mentions having taken James's course as a graduate student.) In general, however, abnormal psychology was considered to be a medical subfield rather than an area of psychology, and the profession of clinical psychology was still in its infancy (see the chapter by Benjamin, DeLeon, & Freedheim in this volume; Napoli, 1981).

"Personality" appeared early as a topic of psychiatry and abnormal psychology in publications such as the *Journal of Abnormal Psychology,* founded in 1906 by Morton Prince, "eminent Boston physician and lecturer at Tufts College Medical School" (G. W. Allport, 1938, p. 3). For several years, the editorial board of the journal consisted entirely of persons with medical training; only Hugo Münsterberg and Boris Sidis were also trained in psychology (Shermer, 1985). Prince was a leading figure in the "Boston school" of psychopathology and psychotherapy (Hale, 1971), a group composed primarily of physicians, some of whom were also trained in experimental psychology (Taylor, 2000). The Boston psychopathologists were among the first professionals to be influenced by psychoanalysis (Fancher, 2000; Hale, 1971); indeed, the first issue of the *Journal of Abnormal Psychology* contained an article on psychoanalysis (Putnam, 1906). Between 1910 and 1925 the journal served as the official organ of the American Psychopathological Association (G. W. Allport, 1938), which consisted of physicians and psychologists with an interest in psychotherapy (Hale, 1971).

Between 1906 and 1920, the *Journal of Abnormal Psychology* featured more articles on "personality" than any other psychological journal. (This statement is based on a count of items in the historic PsycINFO database featuring the term "personality" in titles or abstracts.) In 1921, the journal was expanded to include a focus on social psychology and was renamed *The Journal of Abnormal Psychology and Social Psychology;* the editorial announcing this change pointed to "personality" as a central topic in both fields (Editors, 1921). Although Prince remained the nominal editor, he soon transferred most of the editorial responsibility for the journal to his new "Coöperating Editor," social psychologist Floyd Allport. In 1925, the journal was renamed *The Journal of Abnormal and Social Psychology* (G. W. Allport, 1938); in 1960, it became *Journal of Abnormal and Social Psychology.* In 1965, the journal split into the *Journal of Abnormal Psychology* and the *Journal of Personality and Social Psychology.*

Articles on personality in early issues of the *Journal of Abnormal Psychology* bore such titles as "My Life as a Dissociated Personality" (Anonymous, 1908) and "A Case of Disordered Personality" (Dewey, 1907), indicating their reliance on personal accounts and case studies. Between 1906 and 1916, nearly all of the empirical studies published in the journal presented data on individuals rather than groups. Although the proportion of group studies began to increase during the second decade of publication, the proportion of individual studies remained higher until 1925, averaging 75% during

Prince's last four years as active editor and 65% during Floyd Allport's term as cooperating editor (see Shermer, 1985; we discuss in a later section a change in publication trends beginning in 1925). This emphasis on case studies reflected the investigative practices of medical and psychiatric researchers and psychoanalysts. Around the turn of the twentieth century, the case study, familiar to medical practitioners since the days of Hippocrates, had been introduced as a pedagogical tool by Walter B. Cannon (1900; see Forrester, 1996; Taylor, 1996) and by Richard C. Cabot (see Forrester, 1996; Lubove, 1965), borrowing from law and from social casework, respectively. Case studies were of course central in psychoanalysis; a clear example is Freud's (1910/1957a) discussion of the case of "Anna O." in his first lecture in the United States in 1909. Case studies appeared regularly in psychiatric and psychoanalytic journals such as the *American Journal of Psychiatry* and the *Psychoanalytic Review* throughout the 1920s.

Sociology and Social Work

Sociologists also contributed to the personality literature during the early decades of the twentieth century (Barenbaum, 2000; Becker, 1930) and maintained an active interest in personality thereafter (Bernard, 1945). Their contributions have received little systematic attention in historical discussions of personality psychology. (For exceptions, see Burnham, 1968a, on the influence of sociology and social philosophy on the development of personality psychology; Runyan, 1982, on sociological contributions to the study of life histories; and Smith, 1997, on personality research as a focus of sociological and psychological social psychologists during the 1930s.)

The adoption in 1921 of a system for classifying abstracts of recent literature published in the *American Journal of Sociology* was one indication of sociologists' interest in personality. The "tentative scheme" included as a first category "Personality: The Individual and the Person" ("Recent Literature," 1921, p. 128; in contrast, the *Psychological Index* and *Psychological Abstracts* did not include "personality" in their classification schemes until 1929 and 1934, respectively). A subcategory for "Biography" (p. 128) as well as the category "Social Pathology: Personal and Social Disorganization" and two methodological subcategories, "Case Studies and Social Diagnosis" and "Life-Histories and Psychoanalysis" (p. 129), reflected sociologists' attention to studies of individual lives, an interest they shared with social workers, psychiatrists, and psychoanalysts.

Case study and life history methods, including the use of personal documents, drew attention in sociology following the publication of Thomas and Znaniecki's (1918–1920)

landmark study, *The Polish Peasant in Europe and America,* which was based on letters and autobiographical material. Promoting the use of empirical methods, the study served as a model for sociologists at the University of Chicago, the most influential institution in sociology in the 1920s and 1930s (Bulmer, 1984). Following Thomas's departure from Chicago in 1918, other prominent members of the sociology department, including Robert E. Park, Ernest W. Burgess, Clifford R. Shaw, and Herbert Blumer, continued to promote case studies and life histories (Bulmer, 1984), extending their influence through the Social Science Research Council (SSRC); we discuss these developments in a later section. Examples of works by Chicago sociologists include Shaw's (1930) *The Jack-Roller: A Delinquent Boy's Own Story* and Krueger's (1925) dissertation on autobiographical documents and personality.

A debate concerning the relative merits of case study and statistical methods during this period reflected sociologists' growing interest in quantitative methods, partly a result of their collaboration with researchers in neighboring disciplines, such as economics and psychology. Psychologist L. L. Thurstone, for example, was an important influence on such sociologists as Samuel Stouffer (1930), who became a proponent of statistical methods in sociology (Bulmer, 1984). The debate was a frequent topic of meetings of the Society for Social Research, an "integral part" of the Chicago sociology department composed of faculty and graduate students engaged in serious research (p. 114). Although Chicago sociologists were at the center of the debate, those at other institutions also participated (see, e.g., Bain, 1929; Lundberg, 1926).

According to Platt, the debate was a "hot" issue from the 1920s until the Second World War (1996, p. 36; see also Ross, 1991). During the 1930s, members of the Chicago sociology department demonstrated their allegiance to one method or the other at their student-faculty picnic, "where baseball sides were picked on the basis of case study versus statistics" (Platt, 1996, pp. 45–46). Bulmer (1984) notes, however, that an "emphasis on the complementarity of research methods was characteristic of the Chicago school" (p. 121) and that several participants in the debate actually advocated the use of both approaches. During this period many sociologists hoped to discover general laws by comparing and classifying individual cases, and this view eventually contributed to a blurring of the distinction between case study and statistical methods (Platt, 1992). Burgess (1927) compared sociologists' increasing interest in quantitative methods with psychologists' "heroic efforts to become more scientific, that is to say, statistical" (p. 108); in contrast, he noted that social workers and psychiatrists had introduced the case study method into social science.

Sociologists' use of case studies was derived in part from the close connection between sociology and social work:

> Sociology and social work took a long time to become disentangled; in the 1920s people called social workers were equally or even more likely to carry out empirical research, and university sociologists very frequently drew on their case data whether or not it had been collected for research purposes. (Platt, 1996, p. 46)

Social workers' interest in personality during this period is illustrated by social work theorist Mary Richmond's insistence that the "one central idea" of social casework was "the development of personality" (1922, p. 90). Richmond and other social workers (e.g., Sheffield, 1920) wrote influential works on case study methods.

In the sociological literature of this period, the term "case study" referred not only to the number of cases and the intensiveness with which they were studied but also to a "special kind" of data (Platt, 1996, p. 46). "Case study" was often used interchangeably with "life history" and "personal documents"; these methods were seen as giving "access to the subjects' personal meanings, while alternatives [were] seen as dry, narrow and giving access only to external data" (p. 46). Exemplifying this usage, sociologist John Dollard applied his *Criteria for the Life History* (1935) to several different types of "life history," defined as "an autobiography, biography or clinical history" or "even a social service case history or a psychiatric document" (p. 265). Dollard's work also reflected sociologists' interest in refining and standardizing case methods.

The Mental Hygiene Movement

Inspired by a case study—the autobiography of a former patient (Beers, 1908)—the mental hygiene movement was organized in 1909 to reform the treatment of patients in mental institutions. The movement soon became a powerful coalition of psychiatrists, educators, and social workers who attributed various social and personal problems to individual maladjustment (see Cohen, 1983; Danziger, 1990, 1997; Lubove, 1965; Parker, 1991). Expanding their goals to include the identification of potential cases of maladjustment, mental hygiene workers made "personality" the focus of their preventive and therapeutic efforts, which frequently involved interdisciplinary teams of experts undertaking intensive case studies of "troublesome" children in settings such as child guidance clinics (W. Healy, 1915; Jones, 1999). Psychiatrists typically screened clients for medical disorders and conducted psychotherapy, and social workers contributed case histories based on their investigations of clients and their families. Psychologists' role in these interdisciplinary teams "generally came down to the construction and application of scales that would subject 'personality' to the rigors of measurement and so convert it from merely an object of social intervention to an object of science" (Danziger, 1990, p. 164). The movement thus supported psychologists as purveyors of expert scientific knowledge of personality in the form of test scores.

American Psychology

Twentieth-century American experimenters wanted general laws, not remarkable phenomena involving special persons. (Porter, 1995, p. 211)

In the preceding sections, we have referred to the identification of psychologists with psychometric and statistical approaches to personality. Here, we examine several interrelated factors in the development of these approaches, and in psychologists' resistance toward studies of individuals, during the early decades of the twentieth century.

Scientific Ethos

As many historians have suggested, psychometric approaches reflected the positivistic, "natural science" ethos that had prevailed in American psychology since the late 1800s (see, e.g., Danziger, 1990; see the chapter by Fuchs & Milar in this volume; Hornstein, 1988; Porter, 1995). Psychologists were particularly concerned with producing "objective" knowledge and eliminating sources of "subjectivity":

For experimental psychologists, being scientific meant creating distance. It meant opening up a space, a "no man's land," between themselves and the things they studied, a place whose boundary could be patrolled so that needs or desires or feelings could never infiltrate the work itself. Every aspect of the experimental situation was bent toward this goal—the "blind subjects," the mechanized recording devices, the quantified measures, and statistically represented results. (Hornstein, 1992, p. 256)

From this perspective, case studies and life histories, relying on subjective reports or interpretations, appeared unscientific.

The tendency to consider case studies unscientific was already clear just after the turn of the century in comments on the work of two respected psychologists who drew heavily on personal documents. While observing that the "personal confessions" in William James's (1902) *The Varieties of Religious Experience* were "extraordinary in range and fulness

[sic]," Coe (1903, p. 62) suggested that James's results would be "doubly valuable" if they were supplemented by "an experimental and physiological study of the same types" (p. 63) and commented on the "romanticism, not to say impressionism" (p. 65) in his method. G. Stanley Hall's *Adolescence* (1904), which was illustrated with quotations from autobiographies, literature, and answers to questionnaires, drew similar criticism. "Dr. Hall is as much an artist as a scientist," commented one reviewer, adding, "It is to be regretted that much of the *questionnaire* data . . . has not been secured or tabulated according to the most approved statistical and scientific methods" (Kirkpatrick, 1904, p. 692).

Practical Demands

During the first two decades of the twentieth century, as American psychologists became increasingly concerned with practical problems, "the primary goal of psychology became the prediction and control of the 'other,' a science of the acts (and by a short extension, the behavior) of people rather than of their mental experiences" (Tweney & Budzynski, 2000, p. 1015; see also the chapter by Benjamin et al. in this volume). Psychologists developed "mental tests" for selection, diagnosis, and placement in an effort to establish their professional expertise in solving problems associated with educational institutions, labor unions, and immigration, and with the national war effort in 1917 and 1918 (Danziger, 1990; Parker, 1991; Sokal, 1984; Vernon, 1933). Designed to screen soldiers vulnerable to shell shock, Woodworth's Personal Data Sheet was probably the first objective self-report personality "inventory" based on the mental test format (see Camfield, 1969; Woodworth, 1919, 1932).

Following World War I, opportunities expanded for psychologists to administer mental tests in military, managerial, industrial, and educational settings (Danziger, 1990; O'Donnell, 1985; Samelson, 1985; Sokal, 1984). In the early 1920s, however, critics began to question the predictive utility of intelligence tests (Parker, 1991) and suggested that measures of personality or character traits would improve the prediction of performance (e.g., Fernald, 1920). Although early measures of character and personality took various forms, the less "efficient" methods were soon replaced by tests based on the mental test model of adding scores on separate multiple-choice or true/false items to get a total (see Parker, 1991). According to the psychometric approach to personality, individual differences, conceived as coefficients in prediction equations, could be used to predict and control behavior. (Years later, Raymond B. Cattell's "specification equation" [1957, pp. 302–306] would become perhaps the most fully developed example of such prediction equations.)

Institutional Factors

The predominance of the psychometric approach in psychological research on personality was reflected in the *Journal of Abnormal and Social Psychology* after Prince offered to donate the journal, once oriented primarily toward practicing psychiatrists, to the American Psychological Association in 1925. The transfer of ownership took place on April 1, 1926 (G. W. Allport, 1938). Once social psychologist Henry T. Moore of Dartmouth replaced Floyd Allport as cooperating editor, the practice of publishing case studies declined dramatically, conforming with publication trends in mainstream psychological journals where the proportion of reports featuring individual data had been declining steadily since the 1910s (Shermer, 1985). During Floyd Allport's first year as cooperating editor (1921–1922), the instructions appearing inside the front cover of each issue of the journal continued to direct authors to send articles to Prince. Allport's closer collaboration with Prince apparently resulted in only a small change in selection standards after he moved from Harvard to the University of North Carolina and assumed full editorial responsibility in 1922 (see also G. W. Allport, 1938; Shermer, 1985). The announcement of Moore's appointment requested that contributors submit articles to him (Editors, 1925), and he appears from the beginning of his tenure to have selected articles according to "psychological" standards. Thus, the proportion of empirical papers based on the study of individual cases dropped from an average of 65%, under Floyd Allport, to 30% under Moore (see Shermer, 1985): "Their place was taken by statistical studies based on group data" (Danziger, 1990, p. 165). (Moore himself conducted group studies using psychometric tests; see, e.g., Moore, 1925).

By the late 1920s, psychologists (e.g., G. W. Allport & Vernon, 1930; Murphy & Murphy, 1931) and sociologists (e.g., Bernard, 1932; Young, 1928) reviewing the personality literature were explicitly identifying the psychometric approach with psychology, and life histories and case studies with sociology and psychiatry. Although several of these authors expressed positive views of studies of individual lives, their recommendations that psychologists explore such methods appear to have had little impact (see, e.g., Parker, 1991). Like Woodworth (1929), other authors of psychological texts and reference works during the late 1920s and early 1930s tended to view the case study as a "clinical" method (Roback, 1927a; Warren, 1934) and to express doubts concerning its scientific status. For example, Symonds (1931) defined the case study as "a comprehensive study of the individual," but remarked, "It should be emphasized at the outset that the *case study* is not a research method. Primarily its function is to study the individual with a view toward helping him." Case study data might be used in research, he suggested, but

only if they consisted of "facts . . . obtained in a reliable, objective manner" using "scientifically valid methods" (p. 555).

In striking contrast to the sociological literature of the period, psychological studies of personality reveal little concern regarding the development of methods to study individual lives. The difference reflects a lack of institutional support for case methods in psychology, as compared to the support in sociology at the University of Chicago. One brief report of a methodological debate concerning case study and statistical approaches to personality, which took place in a "round table" on personality at the meeting of the American Psychological Association in 1930, suggests that case studies were quickly dismissed as insufficiently reliable (Ruckmick, 1931). One of the participants was L. L. Thurstone (Brigham, 1931), who represented the statistical point of view in the sociological debates at Chicago concerning case studies (Bulmer, 1984). Thurstone's allegiance to the experimental perspective in psychology is revealed in his remark concerning personality research:

> One of my principal interests in psychology to which I have returned several times has been the study of personality. . . . My conflict here was that, on the one hand, the center of psychology probably was the study of personality, but, on the other hand, I was unable to invent any experimental leverage in this field. That was the reason why I turned to other problems that seemed to lend themselves to more rigorous analysis. (1952, p. 318)

Professional Concerns

Our account of the early development of personality psychology differs from that of C. S. Hall and Lindzey (1957), who emphasize the influence of early personality theories based on clinical practice. However, Hall and Lindzey's perspective reflects the post–World War II boom in clinical psychology (Capshew, 1999; Herman, 1995) and a corresponding focus in the clinical and personality areas on psychoanalysis and competing theories of personality (see, e.g., Rosenthal, 1958). In contrast, during the 1920s and 1930s, American psychologists were more concerned with meeting practical demands for personality measures than with theory (Murphy, 1932; Vernon, 1933) and were particularly skeptical of psychoanalysis (see, e.g., Danziger, 1997; Hale, 1971; Triplet, 1983).

As many historians have observed, the enormous popularity of psychoanalysis in American culture during this period posed a threat to psychologists—particularly those working in applied areas—who were concerned with establishing their own professional expertise and differentiating themselves from pseudoscientists (see, e.g., Hornstein, 1992; Napoli, 1981). Many psychologists attempted to dismiss psychoanalysts as they dismissed the army of popular pseudopsychologists who advertised psychoanalysis for a dollar or promised to "show you how to talk with God" (Crider, 1936, p. 371). Accusing their competitors of being unscientific, they cited their own training in the use of rigorous scientific methods and quantitative techniques (Freyd, 1926; Morawski & Hornstein, 1991; Napoli, 1981). Personality researchers promoted tests as experimental methods (Terman, 1924; Woodworth, 1929) and ignored or criticized methods that appeared subjective. They considered the case studies of psychiatrists and psychoanalysts "unscientific and old-fashioned" (Hale, 1971, p. 115), and perhaps too similar to the sensational cases reported in the popular press (see, e.g., Burnham, 1968b). Roback, for example, found Freud's case studies more artistic than scientific (1927b) and suggested that many authors selected case material to "furnish interesting reading" or "prove a certain point" (1927a, p. 421). Indeed, Freud had expressed his own ambivalence toward case studies: "It still strikes me myself as strange that the case histories I write should read like short stories and that, as one might say, they lack the serious stamp of science" (1893–1895/1955, p. 160).

PROMOTING THE STUDY OF INDIVIDUAL LIVES: GORDON ALLPORT AND HENRY MURRAY

By 1930, studies of personality were flourishing, but personality was still considered a topic of several areas of psychology (e.g., abnormal, educational, and social) rather than a separate area. Gordon Allport played a central role in systematizing and defining the subfield of personality psychology and separating it from social psychology (Barenbaum, 2000; Nicholson, 1998, in press; Winter & Barenbaum, 1999), and Henry Murray was influential in expanding the boundaries of the study of personality to include experimental investigations of psychoanalytic concepts (Triplet, 1983; Winter & Barenbaum, 1999). Both Allport (1937b) and Murray (1938) promoted the intensive study of individual lives, an approach to the study of personality that their colleagues in psychology had generally overlooked. In doing so, each man drew upon his training in disciplines outside the mainstream of American psychology. In this section, we examine their efforts and assess the status of case studies and life histories in personality psychology in the 1930s and 1940s.

Gordon Allport and Case Studies: "The Most Revealing Method of All"

When Goethe gave it as his opinion that personality is the supreme joy of the children of the earth, he could not have foreseen the joyless dissection of his romantic ideal one hundred years hence. (G. W. Allport, 1932, p. 391)

Gordon Allport (1897–1967) is well known as an advocate of the idiographic approach to personality, a focus on the particular individual (e.g., G. W. Allport, 1937b; Pandora, 1997). Interestingly, however, his use of this approach has been both exaggerated and minimized. Labeled a "militant idiographer" by Boring (in an editorial introduction to G. W. Allport, 1958, p. 105) and accused by some critics of rejecting the nomothetic approach—the search for general laws via the study of common dimensions of personality (see, e.g., Skaggs, 1945), Allport in fact advocated and used both approaches (e.g., G. W. Allport, 1928, 1937b; G. W. Allport & Vernon, 1931). Other critics, noting that Allport published only one case study (1965), have commented on his "ambivalence regarding the approach that he had so long championed" (Cohler, 1993, p. 134; see also Capps, 1994; Holt, 1978; Peterson, 1988).

Interdisciplinary Roots: American Psychology, Social Ethics, and German Psychology

Trained in psychology at Harvard in the late 1910s and early 1920s, Allport was influenced by the prevailing experimental, scientific ethos and contributed to the psychometric approach to personality (Nicholson, 1996, 2000, in press). However, he also studied social ethics, an area that involved "field training and volunteer social service" (G. W. Allport, 1967, p. 6). Allport (1968) described social ethics professor Richard C. Cabot, who used case studies and biographies extensively in his teaching (G. W. Allport, 1937a), as a teacher who had influenced his thinking. It is not clear, however, whether he actually completed a course with Cabot. Allport (1951) mentioned having dropped one of Cabot's courses when he learned of the assignment to write up 25 cases in one semester. (The course was probably Cabot's seminar in case history method, which - Allport's future wife, Ada Gould, took in 1922; see Barenbaum, 1997a.) Allport's (1922) dissertation, an experimental study of personality traits, included individual case profiles and a chapter on the application of his methods to an individual client of a social service agency (possibly a client of Ada Gould, who was a social worker at the time; see Cherry, 1996).

Another disciplinary influence on Allport's interest in case studies was his encounter during a postdoctoral year in Germany (in 1923) with a qualitative, interpretive approach to the study of personality (e.g., G. W. Allport, 1923, 1924; see also Danziger, 1990). He studied with Eduard Spranger, a disciple of the philosopher Wilhelm Dilthey, who had promoted psychology as a "human science" (*Geisteswissenschaft*), emphasizing biographical studies (G. W. Allport, 1924). Allport also studied with William Stern, known not only for his psychology of individual differences but also for his interest in "the unity of the personality" (G. W. Allport, 1923, p. 613). Allport's interest in the case method and in personal documents (e.g., G. W. Allport, 1942) may have been encouraged by Stern, who advocated the use of biographical and historical methods (1911) and published a psychological analysis of his own adolescent diaries (1925; cited in G. W. Allport, 1942).

Promoting "the Intuitive Method"

After returning from Europe, Allport struggled to reconcile the empirical and quantitative American approach to personality with the more theoretical and qualitative German approach (G. W. Allport, 1962b). He became particularly interested in the German method known as *Verstehen,* which he translated as "the intuitive method" (G. W. Allport, 1929) or "case method" (Roe, 1962)—"the understanding of the concrete personality in its cultural setting" (G. W. Allport, 1929, p. 15). Contrasting the intuitive method with the psychometric approach, Allport remarked, "It was inevitable that mental testing should appear. By these methods persons can be compared with persons, *but can never in the wide world be understood in and of themselves*" (n.d., p. 11; emphasis in original [Courtesy of the Harvard University Archives]; see also G. W. Allport, 1924, p. 133; 1929, p. 16, for further elaborations of this point, which was one of Allport's cardinal principles). By this, Allport meant that only the intuitive method, by its focus on the whole person rather than the measurement of separate traits, could reveal the interaction or *organization* of traits within the person. (We discuss this point further below.)

In 1928, Allport conducted "an experiment in teaching by the intuitive method" (G. W. Allport, 1929, p. 14), basing an introductory psychology course on the autobiography of William Ellery Leonard (1927) and requiring that students prepare a case study (G. W. Allport, 1929). It is probably in this context that Allport began to develop his suggestions for preparing case studies (G. W. Allport, 1937b). He continued to teach by the case method throughout his career, using autobiographies (e.g., Leonard, 1927; Wells, 1934), personal documents, and other case materials and assigning the preparation of case studies (Barenbaum, 1997b; Cherry, 2000).

Allport's early publications promoting "the study of the undivided personality" (G. W. Allport, 1924) and the intuitive method (G. W. Allport, 1929) apparently had little impact on American psychologists. His suggestion that "personality never possesses an exclusively objective character" and his emphasis on intuition were clearly incompatible with the view of psychology as an objective "natural science." His critique of the psychometric method was an unwelcome reminder of psychologists' subjectivity:

> Personality is in reality always perceived by some person whose own experience is the background for the perception. That is to say, in actual life the apprehension of personality is conditioned by three factors, (a) the behavior sets of the person studied, (b) the behavior sets of the person studying, and (c) the conditions under which the study is made, including the relation which exists between the two persons. The psychograph [i.e., a profile of trait scores] oversimplifies the problem by assuming that the investigation of personality need only consider the first of these conditions. (1924, pp. 132–133)

Although Allport stressed the need for both "natural science" and intuitive methods in the study of personality, statements such as the following were no doubt unpersuasive to his scientifically minded colleagues: "The psychology of personality must be broad enough to embrace both the particular and general aspects of its subject. Even if this obligation requires that it be *both* art and science, there is still no escape" (1929, p. 20; emphasis in original).

Promoting "Scientific Case Studies"

In the early 1930s, Allport adopted a new strategy in his efforts to promote the case study. Employing more scientific rhetoric and echoing the prevailing view that the method was "unsatisfactory," he suggested nevertheless that "the concrete individual has eluded study by any other approach" and remarked that "in the future there will undoubtedly be attempts to standardize the case study in some way which will reduce its dependence upon the uncontrolled artistry of the author" (G. W. Allport & Vernon, 1930, p. 700; see also G. W. Allport, 1933; Nicholson, 1996). Toward this end, Allport and his students designed experimental studies of "intuitive" processes and attempted to improve the scientific respectability of case studies by addressing methodological issues related to the question, "How shall a psychological life history be written?" (G. W. Allport, 1967, p. 3). For example, Cantril (1932; cited in G. W. Allport, 1937b) showed that "optimum comprehension and memory-value result from the use of general characterization followed by specific illustration" (p. 393n).

Allport's (1937b) text reflected this change in strategy. Unlike other authors of psychological texts (e.g., Stagner, 1937), who treated the case study as a clinical method, Allport treated it as a research method. Noting that the case study "has not ordinarily been recognized as a psychological method," he described it as "the most revealing method of all" and devoted several pages to six "suggestions for the preparation of a case study" (1937b, p. 390)—for example, "*Deal only with a personality that is known*" (p. 391; emphasis in original). He cited the work of several students relating to the ability to judge personality and to the most effective method of describing personality. He discussed the "generalization of case studies" in "the construction of psychological laws" (p. 395)—a "nomothetic" application that would bolster their scientific status. But he noted that even a general law could be one that explained *"how uniqueness comes about"*; for example, the principle of functional autonomy, which suggests that motives become independent of their origins in "infantile" or "archaic" drives (p. 194; emphasis in original), accounts for unique personal motives. Allport also pointed out psychologists' neglect of laws that applied to particular individuals: "The course of each life is a lawful event, even though it is unlike all others of its class" (p. 558). The study of individual lives, he suggested, would enable psychologists to make better predictions of individual behavior, one of the goals of scientific psychology.

Allport saw the case study as the psychologist's "final affirmation of the individuality and uniqueness of every personality" (G. W. Allport, 1937b, p. 390). Clinicians and sociologists, he argued, had developed the method with a focus on "maladjustments" or on "social influences surrounding the individual" (p. 390) rather than on personality itself. Focusing within the person, he chose to overlook "the factors *shaping* personality" (p. viii; emphasis in original). This neglect of cultural and social contexts reflected the emerging personality ideal (Nicholson, 1998, in press) and the psychological Zeitgeist (for example, Allport's text was more successful than that of Stagner, 1937, who emphasized social and cultural factors; see Barenbaum, 2000). Ironically, however, it may have resulted in case studies that were one-sided (see our discussion of context later in the chapter).

Henry Murray's Personology and the Study of Lives

Like Allport, Henry Murray (1893–1988) developed an approach to personality that emphasized both the study of individual differences and the integrative understanding of individual persons. Also like Allport, Murray brought to personality psychology interests, skills, and experiences drawn from a variety of other fields—perspectives that led him to emphasize the study of individuals. Indeed, for Murray, the study of individual life histories *was* the psychology of personality, or (as he preferred to call it) "personology" (1938, p. 4). (Although "personology," either as a term or as a [sub]field, has by and large not entered general use, there is a small "Society for Personology," founded by Murray disciples, which is dedicated to the life history approach to the study of personality.)

Interdisciplinary Roots: Medicine, Literature, and "Depth Psychology"

Murray was born to wealth and privilege (Anderson, 1988; Murray, 1967). He was trained as a physician, concerned with diagnosing and treating individual persons. Even in medical school, his interest in case studies went well beyond what was required. For example, he wrote a thoroughly researched, formal medical history and an extensive narrative account (both unpublished) of the life and circumstances of a prostitute who was dying of syphilis (see F. G. Robinson, 1992, pp. 63–65).

Murray's strong literary and artistic interests also reinforced his emphasis on the study of individuals. A chance encounter during an ocean voyage in 1924 led him to read *Moby-Dick;* thus began a lifetime's passionate interest in the life and writings of Herman Melville (F. G. Robinson, 1992, pp. 81–82, 109–110, 133–140, and passim). Over the next six decades, Murray published an introduction to Melville's *Pierre* as well as reviews of several books about Melville.

An almost casual dinner-party discussion led Murray to buy Carl Jung's recently published *Psychological Types* (1923/1971). Two years later, he visited Jung in Zurich, meeting and socializing daily for three weeks (F. G. Robinson, 1992). Thus began a fascination with "depth psychology" (Jung and Freud; also Otto Rank, Alfred Adler, and others; see Murray, 1938, pp. 24–25) that was decisive in leading him away from medicine and physiology to psychology as a life vocation. While Murray did not incorporate Jung's specific types into his conceptual scheme of personality (Murray, 1938, pp. 238, 726–727), the concept of *type,* involving *categories of whole persons* rather than tables of component "elements," did create a path, for Murray (1955) and other personality psychologists, toward the study of molar units—that is, the whole lives of individual persons. By focusing on persons rather than variables, then, type is a quasi-dimensional, quantitative method that maintains the individual person perspective while also permitting comparison (Platt, 1992, describes sociologists' similar efforts to classify and compare cases). Jung's typology is probably the best-known example, but from time to time other personality theorists have suggested typologies (for example, Freud, 1908/1959, on the anal character type, 1916/1957b, on character types, 1931/1961, on libidinal types; Rank, 1931/1936, on the "artist," "neurotic," and "average" types; and Block, 1971, on normal personality types). And although the concept of type is not currently fashionable in personality research, there are signs that its usefulness is being recognized—or rediscovered (see Thorne & Gough, 1991; York & John, 1992).

The "Explorations" Project

At the Harvard Psychological Clinic during the 1930s, Murray gathered an extraordinary group of more than two dozen collaborators, including a sociologist, an anthropologist, a physician, a poet, and psychologists of widely varying backgrounds and approaches. They produced the landmark

Explorations in Personality (Murray, 1938), a study of 51 young men by his interdisciplinary team and one of the first major systematic research studies of normal personality.

Variable-Centered Concepts. *Explorations in Personality* is most often cited nowadays for its list of 20-plus motives or "needs." For example, this catalog of motives formed the basis of numerous personality questionnaire measures, such as the Stern Activities Index, the Edwards Personal Preference Schedule (EPPS), and the Jackson Personality Research Form (PRF). David McClelland and his colleagues developed thematic apperceptive measures of three major motives (achievement, affiliation, and power) from Murray's list of needs (see Winter, 1998b).

Actually, motives were only one part of an extensive, 101-page catalog of "variables of personality" (Murray, 1938, pp. 142–242), which also included other concepts (discussed below) such as need-integrates, general traits or attributes, "miscellaneous internal factors," and numerous other variables such as values, sentiments, interests, "gratuities," abilities, and complexes. (At the conclusion of the description of these variables, Murray wrote, "No one who has had the patience to read through this section can be expected to come away from it now with a clear head" [1938, p. 230].)

Person-Centered Procedures. In addition to its wealth of dimensional contributions, the *Explorations* project also presented an elaborate series of procedures, developed or adapted by Murray and his collaborators, for describing and assessing individual persons (Murray, 1938, pp. 397–603). Some (such as tests of hypnotic susceptibility or level of aspiration) yielded simple scores, like traditional dimensional tests. Many other procedures, however, lent themselves more to configurational or narrative interpretation: for example, a group conference with the person being studied, informal conversations, an autobiography, the Thematic Apperception Test (TAT), and a Dramatic Productions Test (developed by Erik Erikson; see Homburger, 1937).

The final stage in the assessment of each person was thoroughly centered on the unique and complex structure of the individual. After all information on a person had been collected, a "biographer" prepared a "psychograph," defined as an "abstract biography" (Murray, 1938, pp. 605–606) or "reconstruction of the subject's personality from birth" (p. 29); this definition, which emphasized the person-centered approach, was quite different from the nomothetic definition of "psychograph" as a profile of trait scores (see, e.g., F. H. Allport & G. W. Allport, 1921; for an application of both approaches to the description of an individual person, see McClelland, 1951,

especially pp. 589, 591). A five-person diagnostic council then discussed the person, often for five or six hours, and voted on final ratings for that person on all personality variables. (The reliance on a diagnostic council's discussion, rather than more quantitative, and thus dimensional, methods was one reason why Harvard psychologists Karl Lashley and Edwin Boring voted against tenure for Murray; see F. G. Robinson, 1992, p. 225). Only one such case, that of "Earnst" (written by Robert White), was actually presented in *Explorations,* but it was presented at considerable length: At 88 pages, it took up 11% of the book's entire text. Because of space limitations, other cases had to be eliminated from the final version of the book (Robinson, 1992).

Person-Centered Concepts. While most of the variables in Murray's catalog lent themselves to elaboration in a nomothetic direction, several concepts were particularly appropriate to the intensive study of individual lives. For example, the concept of *need-integrate* referred to the compound of a motive along with its customary emotions, preferred modes of action, and familiar related goal objects (1938, pp. 109–110). While the motive itself (e.g., achievement, affiliation, power) may be universal—that is, present in varying amounts in most people—the remaining components of emotion, action modes, and objects would be different for different people. Thus, the need-integrate concept individualizes the more nomothetic concept of motive. (Murray used the term "complex" in a similar fashion.)

Murray defined *gratuity* as a "gratuitous end situation," that is, an unnaturally easy goal-attainment due to factors such as inheritance or luck. Such gratuities are "common in the lives of the over-privileged" (1938, pp. 62, 112n; see also p. 228). The gratuity concept has the potential to link individual personalities to the opportunities, demands, and resources of their environments, thereby making it possible to incorporate race and class privilege (or, conversely, race and class oppression) into the personality portrait.

Several concepts refer to the hierarchical and temporal arrangement of people's motives; for example, *regnancy,* where one motive dominates others (Murray, 1938, pp. 45–49); relations of *fusion, subsidiation,* and *conflict* among different motives at any one time (pp. 86–89); and *time-binding* or *ordination* (p. 49; see also Murray, 1959), by which processes different motives are arranged into long-term temporal sequences, "strategies," or *serial proceedings* (Murray, 1959). These concepts make it possible to chart, with a relatively small number of basic motives and other personality characteristics, an almost infinite range of individuality over the life course.

Murray conceptualized the forces and stimuli of the environment in terms of perceived and actual *press.* In Murray's view, an environmental press typically elicited an individual need; this sequence was termed a *thema*. Thus, for example: press Rejection → need Affiliation. (Alternatively, for some people the thema might be: press Rejection → need Rejection.) At the most abstract level was the concept of unity-thema, an underlying press → needs reaction system that is the "key to [each individual's] unique nature. . . . *By the observation of many parts one finally arrives at a conception of the whole and, then, having grasped the latter, one can re-interpret and understand the former*" (Murray, 1938, p. 604–605; emphasis in original).

The Study of Individual Lives in the 1930s and 1940s . . . and Later

We have suggested that during the first three decades of the twentieth century, psychologists were reluctant to adopt methods of studying individual personalities. Were these methods more widely accepted in the 1930s and 1940s (see, e.g., Craik, 1986)? In this section we examine the reception of Allport's and Murray's texts and reassess the status of case studies and life histories in personality psychology during this period.

Reception of Allport's and Murray's Texts

As we have seen, Allport's early publications promoting case methods were generally overlooked by personality psychologists; in contrast, his Ascendance-Submission (G. W. Allport, 1928) and Study of Values (G. W. Allport & Vernon, 1931) tests were very successful (see, e.g., Bernreuter, 1933; Duffy, 1940). Reviewers of Allport's (1937b) book recognized it as a foundational text for the new field of personality psychology (e.g., Cantril, 1938; Hollingworth, 1938; Jenkins, 1938), but his emphasis on the study of the individual drew sharp criticism. J. P. Guilford, for example, considered it "a revolt against science" (1938, p. 416; see also Bills, 1938; Paterson, 1938; Skaggs, 1945). Similarly, Richard M. Elliott (1939) approved of Murray's (1938) efforts to combine psychoanalytic and experimental approaches, his procedures (especially the Thematic Apperception Test), and his catalog of variables, but he criticized Murray's neglect of psychometric research and of statistics. Elliott found the case study of Earnst too speculative.

Elliott's criticism reflected his own ambivalence regarding the study of individual lives in personality psychology. Around 1938, he had begun teaching a course entitled Biographical Psychology, relying on biographies, autobiographies, and fiction and requiring that his students prepare a biographical study. However, he referred to the course as a clinical offering, described it as highly unorthodox, and was greatly relieved to learn that his students were also taking more traditional psychology courses (Elliott, 1952).

Allport: Ambivalence or Accommodation?

Although Allport may have had some ambivalence regarding case studies (see, e.g., Barenbaum, 1997a; Cohler, 1993; Nicholson, 1996, in press), his unpublished record suggests that his failure to publish more than one case study was largely an accommodation to the prevailing climate in psychology, which continued to be unsupportive of such methods. His correspondence reveals that he hoped to follow his text with a volume on the methodology of case studies and life histories, including case materials for use in courses in psychology and social work (e.g., G. W. Allport, 1937a). In addition to the case of Jenny Masterson (G. W. Allport, 1965; Anonymous, 1946), he collected extensive materials on a second case that remained unpublished (Barenbaum, 1997a). In 1938 and 1940, Allport conducted seminars on the life history and the case method, working with his students to expand his list of "rules and criteria for the writing of scientific case studies" and design research concerning "reliability, validity, and the most effective methods for utilizing raw accounts of personality" (G. W. Allport, 1940a; see Barenbaum, 1997a). Examples of this research include studies by Cartwright and French (1939) and Polansky (1941). Although Allport (1967) later suggested that the rules for case studies had proved unsatisfactory and were therefore never published, in fact he submitted them to his publisher, along with several sample cases. When the publisher doubted that such a volume would be marketable (Allport, 1941; MacMurphey, 1941), describing himself as "the victim of an obsession" (courtesy of the Harvard University Archives), replied that he had to complete it whether or not it could be published (the rules were eventually published by Garraty, 1981).

Instead, he accepted a request to write a monograph on the use of personal documents in psychology (G. W. Allport, 1942) for the SSRC, noting that "to the best of my knowledge I am the only psychologist who has worked extensively with the methodological problem you raise" (1940a). He saw the monograph, written amidst the increasing press of work related to the U.S. involvement in World War II, as a beginning: "To render the logic of the case method acceptable to hard-headed American empiricists is a long and difficult job" (1941; quoted in Hevern, 1999, p. 14). Allport argued that personal documents provided knowledge of "concrete individuals. . . . in their natural complexity," an "essential first step" in psychology (1942, p. 56), and that they could "aid in meeting . . . the three critical tests of science: *understanding, prediction,* and *control*" (p. 191; emphasis in original).

Although the appearance of several monographs on personal documents and life histories (e.g., G. W. Allport, 1942; Dollard, 1935) suggests that these topics were salient in personality psychology during the 1930s and 1940s (Craik, 1986), these monographs reflected the interests of several members of the SSRC, and their influence on personality psychologists appears to have been minimal. Platt (1996) notes that Chicago sociologist Ernest W. Burgess, who had a particular interest in case study methods, chaired the SSRC's Committee on Appraisal of Research, which sponsored appraisals of the use of personal documents in several disciplines (G. W. Allport, 1942; Gottschalk, Kluckhohn, & Angell, 1945). She finds, however, that during this period sociologists' interest in case studies, life histories, and personal documents was declining and that attention to these methods virtually disappeared following World War II (Platt, 1992, 1996). Plans for a third volume were apparently canceled; Allport (1943a) had suggested that it either present a summary of German theories of *Verstehen* or review research, such as Murray's, that related case studies to psychometric and experimental methods.

Hevern (1999) observes that although Allport's monograph (G. W. Allport, 1942) outsold other SSRC volumes, his promotion of the case method was generally overlooked by mainstream psychologists. In contrast, Allport's argument that the idiographic use of personal documents could meet the three tests of science (understanding, prediction, and control) was widely cited by clinical psychologists in the debate regarding clinical and statistical prediction that coincided with the rapid expansion of clinical psychology during the 1940s and 1950s (Barenbaum, 1998; see Meehl, 1954). Ironically, the debate focused more on clinical predictions based on psychometric data than on the idiographic methods—involving subjective meanings—that Allport hoped to promote (see G. W. Allport, 1962a).

Although his work on the American war effort interfered with his plans, Allport continued to collect personal documents in hopes of interpreting and publishing them (e.g., G. W. Allport, 1945). Throughout his career he supported case studies "behind the scenes," using them in his teaching and increasing their visibility during his term as editor of the *Journal of Abnormal and Social Psychology* (1938–1949). In the 1940 volume, he featured a symposium on "psychoanalysis as seen by analyzed psychologists" (G. W. Allport, 1940c, p. 3). In 1943, he initiated a special "clinical supplement" consisting of case studies (G. W. Allport, 1943b), following it with regular clinical issues in 1944 and 1945. Beginning in April 1946, each issue included a section of case reports.

Allport described his solicitation and publication of case studies as "the one distinctive contribution that I have made during my term of editorial service" (G. W. Allport, 1949, p. 440). He also supported the work of authors such as Jean Evans, a reporter whose case studies appeared first in the *Journal* (1948, 1950) and later in a book (1954). In her foreword, Evans expressed her appreciation to "Dr. Gordon W. Allport, whose idea it was in the first place that such a book should be written" (p. xvii).

Publication Trends

Continuing an earlier trend, the number of studies of individuals published both in general psychology journals and in "personality" journals (the *Journal of Abnormal and Social Psychology* and *Character and Personality*) declined during the 1930s and 1940s (G. W. Allport, 1940b; Shermer, 1985). Although early volumes of *Character and Personality* featured studies using biographical and archival methods (Craik, 1986), this journal was atypical. Founded in 1932 by Robert Saudek, a European graphologist (Roback, 1935), it was originally international in scope and emphasized "psychodiagnostics," or character reading based on expressive behavior (G. W. Allport, 1937b), an approach that received little attention from American researchers. Allport was on the editorial board of the journal, which published the studies of several students from his life history seminar (Cartwright & French, 1939; Polansky, 1941). By 1945, however, the newly renamed *Journal of Personality* had changed to reflect the interests of American personality psychologists. The new direction was signaled by the omission from the title of "character," an older term preferred by many European psychologists (see Roback, 1927a). The proportion of studies of individuals declined sharply between the 1930s and the 1950s (Shermer, 1985).

Even among clinical psychologists, the status of case studies remained marginal. Allport's retirement as editor of the *Journal of Abnormal and Social Psychology* was followed by another dramatic decrease in the number of studies of individuals published in the journal (Shermer, 1985). Commenting on a pioneering book of clinical case studies (Burton & Harris, 1947), Dollard noted that it relied heavily on test material and was not "the much-needed book of illuminating case histories for the teacher of Abnormal Psychology" (1948, p. 541).

What Happened to Murray's "Personological" Concepts?

It seems clear that Murray's theory and methods, as originally developed in *Explorations in Personality* and later extended and elaborated (e.g., Murray, 1959, 1968, 1977; Murray & Kluckhohn, 1953), offered an extensive array of methods and concepts that could enrich the study-of-individuals approach to personality psychology. Yet in any account of Murray's enduring impact on the field, these methods and concepts usually (and fairly) take second place to his more nomothetic concepts and procedures, such as the TAT. How can we account for this discrepancy? One important factor was undoubtedly Murray's lifelong tendency—present in his biographical work on Melville as well as his psychology—to revise, rework, and "fuss" with his most important works—ultimately leaving them fragmentary and incomplete (see F. G. Robinson, 1992, *passim*). Many other personality psychologists, nomothetically inclined, were eager to develop his list of variables; no one took up the task of working out "need-integrate," "gratuity," or "serial proceeding" in sufficient detail so as to make their usefulness—and thereby the usefulness of the individual lives approach—apparent. What Murray left undone, especially in the conceptual domain of the study of individuals, often remained (to a great extent) undone.

Individualized Assessment Ventures

Murray's approach has survived in certain intellectual "niche" positions: for example, in the work of Robert White (a Murray protégé and a former member of Allport's life history seminar; see G. W. Allport, 1967) on the "study of lives" (White, 1952, 1963, 1972). Murray's approach has continued to be important in certain kinds of assessment situations. During World War II, he and several colleagues developed an assessment program, loosely modeled on the *Explorations* project, for selecting personnel (i.e., spies serving behind enemy lines, mostly) for the U.S. Office of Strategic Services, forerunner of the Central Intelligence Agency (Office of Strategic Services [OSS] Assessment Staff, 1948). After the war, Donald MacKinnon, a Murray protégé, used the OSS assessment system as a model for establishing the Institute for Personality Assessment and Research (IPAR) at the University of California, Berkeley (MacKinnon, 1967). (In the early 1990s, perhaps as a sign of ambivalence about the "person" versus dimensional approaches, and in response to funding opportunities, the institute was renamed Institute for Personality and Social Research [IPSR].) At the same time, "assessment centers," loosely based on many of Murray's principles, came to play an important role in selection and development of senior executives in U.S. corporations (Bray, 1982, 1985; Campbell & Bray, 1993). In contrast, nomothetic questionnaire-based assessment predominates in the selection and guidance of lower-level workers, and at all levels of education.

Why the difference? Person-centered assessment is clearly expensive and time-consuming. Probably these costs can only be justified in a few situations, where choosing the right or wrong person has important financial or social consequences—for example, the right spy, the most effective corporate senior officer. In a very real sense, therefore, personality assessment (and personality psychology generally) remains stratified, more or less along lines of social power and social class: person-centered for elites (and for criminals and others who threaten or challenge elite power; see our discussion of vivid persons, below), nomothetic for the masses.

REASSESSING THE HISTORY OF AMBIVALENCE TOWARD THE STUDY OF INDIVIDUAL LIVES

It is difficult to understand the history of ambivalence toward the study of individual lives in personality psychology if we accept historical accounts that attribute the origins of the field to clinically-derived theories, on the one hand (e.g., C. S. Hall & Lindzey, 1957), or to the publication of Allport's and Murray's texts, on the other hand (e.g., Sanford, 1985). Each of these historical reconstructions emphasizes the "dissident" role of personality theorists, overlooking broader contextual influences on the direction of personality research, as well as the development of the psychometric tradition before 1930. Adopting a longer time perspective, we have seen that the psychometric approach was predominant in personality research by the time the field was institutionalized in the mid-1930s and that the decline of interest in studies of individual lives between the 1930s and the 1950s continued a general trend in psychology (dubbed "the triumph of the aggregate"; Danziger, 1990, p. 68) that began as early as the 1910s.

Adopting a multidisciplinary perspective, we have suggested that the marginal status of case studies and life histories in personality psychology was related to their identification as preferred methods in psychiatry and in abnormal psychology (at a time when this field was primarily a medical specialty), and in sociology, where they were associated with the emergence of empirical research. In contrast, psychologists interested in personality adopted psychometric measures as efficient means of meeting practical goals. Psychologists working in "applied" areas were particularly attracted to quantitative methods that could establish their scientific expertise and differentiate them from their "pseudo-scientific" competitors. These preferences persisted during the emergence of personality psychology as a separate sub-discipline in the 1930s, despite calls for more attention to case study methods.

Gordon Allport's and Henry Murray's efforts to promote studies of individual lives were initially less successful than their efforts to systematize the new subfield. While generally agreeing that the goal of personality psychology was to understand the individual person, other authors of personality texts during this period, like Woodworth (1929) before them, used case studies for illustrative purposes (see McAdams & West, 1997) but continued to describe them as clinical methods rather than as research methods. Although several students and colleagues of Allport and Murray explored methods of studying individual lives, attention to these methods during the 1930s and 1940s reflected primarily the interests of sociologists (particularly those involved with the SSRC) and European psychologists rather than a more general acceptance of these methods by American personality psychologists.

Without these external supports, methods of studying individual lives received even less attention from personality psychologists during the post–World War II period, which saw an increase in the use of survey and quantitative techniques in the social sciences (Platt, 1992, 1996). Although Allport's monograph on personal documents (G. W. Allport, 1942) fueled controversy regarding clinical versus statistical prediction during the 1940s and 1950s, it appears to have had more of an impact on clinical psychologists than on personality researchers (e.g., O'Connell, 1958). The post–World War II expansion of clinical psychology contributed to the continuation of the prediction debate, but, ironically, drew attention away from Allport's goal of developing idiographic research methods in personality psychology. As Allport observed later, "We stop with our wobbly laws of personality and seldom confront them with the concrete person" (G. W. Allport, 1962a, p. 407).

Revival of the Study of Individual Lives in Personality Psychology

There are signs of a resurgence of interest in the study of individual lives on the part of personality psychologists. Psychobiography, a topic of special interest to political psychologists and many historians, had continued to grow and flourish since its beginnings in the early twentieth century. Erikson's studies of Luther (1958) and Gandhi (1969) were widely viewed as models of how to study individuals through the combined lenses of personality psychology and history. Other examples include studies of Woodrow Wilson (George & George, 1956), George Bush and Mikhail Gorbachev (Winter, Hermann, Weintraub, & Walker, 1991a, 1991b), four U.S. foreign policy advisors (Elms, 1986), U.S. president Bill Clinton (Suedfeld, 1994), and Adolf Hitler (W. Langer, 1972).

(Much of Langer's work was based on earlier studies of Hitler by Murray, whose work was not acknowledged by Langer; see F. G. Robinson, 1992, pp. 275–278, also Murray, 1943.) Several books and articles contain lists of psychobiographical studies (Cocks & Crosby, 1987, especially pp. 217–222; Craik, 1988; Crosby & Crosby, 1981; Elms, 1994; Friedman, 1994; Glad, 1973; Greenstein, 1969, especially p. 72; Howe, 1997; McAdams & Ochberg, 1988; Runyan, 1982, 1988a, 1988b, 1990, 1997; Simonton, 1999; and Stone & Schaffner, 1988). Greenstein (1969, chap. 3) provides a model for the tasks of description and analysis in constructing individual psychobiographical case studies, and Winter (2000) reviews recent developments.

Beginning in the 1980s, however, this wave of interest in psychobiography began to enter the mainstream, as personality psychologists explored how psychobiography and studies of individual persons could enrich their field. Runyan (1981) used the question of why nineteenth-century Dutch painter Vincent van Gogh cut off his ear as the basis for a discussion of how to gather and evaluate evidence, and how to decide among rival explanations of specific actions of particular individuals. In *Life Histories and Psychobiography: Explorations in Theory and Method,* Runyan (1982) reviewed methodological problems, addressed criticisms, and suggested guidelines for the evaluation and preparation of case studies, life histories, and psychobiographical studies. West (1983) edited a special issue of the *Journal of Personality* devoted to idiographic methods. A few years later, McAdams and Ochberg (1988) edited another special issue of the same journal, on psychobiography and life narratives, with papers devoted to analysis of earlier work, methodological suggestions, and studies of particular individuals.

Over the next decade, several collections of case studies appeared—often inspired by external intellectual influences and trends; for example, feminist theory (e.g., Franz & Stewart, 1994; Romero & Stewart, 1999) or hermeneutic-interpretive and narrative methods (e.g., Josselson & Lieblich, 1993–1999). At the same time, several new personality textbooks (e.g., McAdams, 1990; Winter, 1996) gave considerable attention to individual persons, while many existing texts expanded their use of case study material in new editions.

In many cases, these studies used quantitative scores from traditional nomothetic variables to elucidate personality change and development over time (e.g., Espin, Stewart, & Gomez, 1990; Stewart, Franz, & Layton, 1988). Sometimes the use of quantative data helped to resolve paradoxical behaviors (e.g., the study of Richard Nixon by Winter & Carlson, 1988) or explain surprising outcomes (e.g., the study of Bill Clinton by Winter, 1998a). And studies by Stolorow and Atwood (1979), Alexander (1990), and Demorest and Siegel (1996) turned personality on its head by arguing that personality theories have personal and subjective origins in the lives of their creators.

In 1997, Nasby and Read (1997) published a truly landmark case study of Dodge Morgan, who at the age of 54 sold his electronics business for $41 million, commissioned construction of a sailboat, and then completed a 150-day nonstop solo circumnavigation of the earth (see Morgan, 1989, for his own account of the voyage). Nasby and Read integrated a rich and diverse array of quantitative and qualitative data: numerous personality tests, administered before and after (and in some cases during) the voyage; Morgan's voyage log, content-analyzed for a variety of themes and personality characteristics; and Morgan's letters and later memoir (1989) of the voyage.

Motives That Drive Psychologists to Study Individuals

Considering all these trends together, it seems that—even when highly abstract and nomothetic perspectives such as the five-factor model of traits are enjoying great popularity—there is also a revival of interest in studies of individual persons within contemporary personality psychology. It is worthwhile to speculate about some reasons for the coexistence of these two very different trends.

Vivid Persons.   First, the world is populated with many vivid and arresting persons, people who compel our attention because their lives depart so extensively from the ordinary courses. History and today's headlines are full of people whose behaviors—hence their personalities—cry out for explanation and understanding because they are so strange or at least do not "make sense" by fitting into a coherent pattern. Thus, the enigma of Adolf Hitler's personality continues to drive interpretations, psychological and otherwise, more than 55 years after his death, as testified to by the comprehensive review of Hitler biographies and psychobiographies by Rosenbaum (1998), Kershaw (1999), and L. L. Langer (1999).

To take three more contemporary examples: What features of the personality of Theodore Kaczynski led him to become the "Unabomber," mailing meticulously-designed explosive packages to a miscellaneous group of people (e.g., technology executives and at least one psychologist) as a protest against the effects of technology? Why did Timothy McVeigh in 1995 blow up the Murrah Federal Building in Oklahoma City, killing 168 people (including 15 little children in a day-care center) and injuring more than 500 others? And finally, what personality dynamics led the mysterious figures of Mohamed Atta and his cohort to commit suicide and mass

murder by hijacking jet airliners to fly into the World Trade Center towers, the Pentagon, and whatever target they intended for the plane that crashed in rural Pennsylvania on September 11, 2001 (Yardley, 2001)?

Often, however, there are people who will never make headlines or draw lengthy obituaries; yet they fascinate and perplex their friends and acquaintances. Thus, Gordon Allport was drawn to the personality of his college roommate's mother, Jenny Gove Masterson (a pseudonym that Allport used in place of her real name), as they corresponded over a period of 11 years. (As Winter, 1993, suggests, perhaps this was because she resembled in some ways his own mother and cast him in the role of "good son," in comparison to her own son. Unconsciously, Allport may even have experienced his roommate as a kind of "double.") After Jenny's death, Allport used the letters as case materials in his teaching and later published them, first as journal articles (Anonymous, 1946) and then, near the end of his own life, as a book (Allport, 1965). At least two of his students attempted quantitative analyses of Jenny's personality, based on some of her letters (Baldwin, 1942; Paige, 1966). In the book version of her letters, Allport discussed a variety of personality interpretations of Jenny. Clearly, for Allport, Jenny was an exceptionally vivid person, someone who drew his attention and mobilized his most strenuous explanatory powers. As he put it in the preface: "Invariably she pins me down with the unspoken challenge, 'And what do you make of *me*?'" (Allport, 1965, p. x; emphasis in original). In such circumstances, everyone feels compelled to explain (thus graduate students—in psychology, anyway—often feel this compulsion with respect to their mentors!). To Allport, the psychologist "has a curiosity that drives him further, sometimes even to the point of indelicacy" (p. 157).

When we try to explain such vivid and compelling people with the usual resources of the personality psychologist's "toolbox" of nomothetic variables, the results can be quite unsatisfying—a hollow portrait. For example, a description of the Unabomber's personality in terms of the popular five-factor model of traits might run as follows: low surgency (at least in face-to-face interactions), low agreeableness, high conscientiousness, and high neuroticism. (His level on factor 5, openness to experience, can be debated. Was it high, as reflected in the broad erudition in his "manifesto," or was it perhaps low because of the rigidity of his ideas?) While this trait profile may be consistent with his behavior, it actually tells us very little. For one thing, such a profile probably fits several million middle-aged American males—most of whom have not tried to kill other people. (Recall how many people rush to apply the unhelpful descriptive cliché of "loner" to assassins and those who carry out mass shootings.)

Further, it is difficult to construct any strong explanatory links between such broad and general terms as "introversion" or "neuroticism," on the one hand, and the highly differentiated and specific actions of a Unabomber, a Hitler, or a Jenny, on the other.

"Synthesizing" the Individual Personality?   The most traditional and widespread criticism of the individual lives approach to personality is that it does not permit generalization (for discussions of several common criticisms, see Runyan, 1982, 1983, and McAdams and West, 1997). Staub (1980) put it succinctly: "If we focus on the uniqueness of every human being, we cannot generalize from one person to another . . . [and] the aim of science is to discover laws . . . applicable at least to some, if not to all people" (p. 3). Such an argument can easily be turned on its head, as follows: The object of science is to formulate general principles that enable us to understand concrete examples or instances. However, the present state of personality psychology is such that we are not really close to being able to "synthesize" a conception of a person from knowledge of that person's scores on *any* list of component personality variables alone. At a minimum, we need to know how these variables are structured.

Consider the following example (which is hypothetical, but based on some real people we have known). A factor analysis can describe how variables are grouped across large groups of people. Thus, in most five-factor trait models, "aggressive" and "kindly" might define two opposite poles of an *agreeableness* factor (and perhaps to some extent also two poles of an independent *surgency* factor). Nevertheless, while these two traits are somewhat opposed at the group level, it is not difficult to imagine individual persons who are both "kindly" and "aggressive." Such persons could express this opposed pair of traits in a variety of quite different ways, depending on how they are structured within the person. For example, they could *alternate* between being kindly and aggressive, thereby appearing inconsistent with respect to both traits. Or they could *differentiate as to other people,* acting (consistently) kindly toward some people and (consistently) aggressive toward others. Or one trait could *subsume and incorporate* the other, so that the person acts "kindly, but in an aggressive way" or else "aggressive, albeit in a kindly fashion." Embodied in real persons, each of these possibilities would lead to strikingly different patterns of behavior and effects on other people; yet each could be based on the same two trait scores.

Reconceptualizing the Goals of Personality Psychology. Another response to the criticism that case studies do not permit generalization is to take seriously Allport's suggestion that personality psychology has more than one goal. In Allport's view, these goals include not only the discovery of general laws but also the discovery of laws pertaining to particular individuals and, more broadly, the understanding of particular individuals (e.g., G. W. Allport, 1937b, 1962a). Recently, Runyan (1997, p. 44) has proposed a conceptual framework for personality psychology consisting of *four* major objectives: the development of general theories (e.g., psychoanalysis), the study of individual and group differences (e.g., the "Big Five" trait factors), the analysis of "specific processes and classes of behavior" (e.g., dreams, motives), and the understanding of individual persons and lives. Arguing that these four goals are interrelated but at least partially independent of one another, Runyan suggests, "Work on all four tasks is necessary, and the fact that inquiry at one level does not automatically answer questions at the other levels is not a telling criticism" (p. 50).

Questioning of "Science."   The Staub quotation cited above, which is critical of the individual lives approach, is based upon a particular (rather monolithic) conception of what science "is," as well as a high valuation of that conception. Without entering into the debate about those issues, we do note that in the last decades of the twentieth century, "science" as it has traditionally been practiced has come under intellectual, social, and political criticism from a variety of perspectives. Postmodernists have argued that the objectivity of "objective" science is an illusion; followers of Foucault claim that science is always practiced in the service of power; and feminists would refine that claim to be "in the service of male power." And indeed, from its very beginnings, mainstream personality psychology has eagerly sought recognition and funding by catering to the interests of the ruling class: selecting good executives, deselecting poor soldiers, managing industrial workers, and supplying labels used to identify and control the behavior of members of less powerful, and potentially "troublesome," groups (see above; also Danziger, 1990, 1997; Parker, 1991; Winter & Barenbaum, 1999). Thus it was inevitable that the mainstream quantitative, nomothetic approach in personality should be a target for more general criticisms of science (or at least of "scientism") and that an alternative (less "scientific") approach would be looked upon more favorably by the critics.

Yet we must not go too far. All personality psychologists who use the individual lives approach would insist that they are rigorous scholars; they would also vigorously deny that in their interpretations "anything goes," or that, in the derisive words of Gergen, "The case study simply allows the investigator freedom to locate the facts lending support to . . . preformulated convictions" (1977, p. 142). Most would maintain that they are practicing science, and many would argue for the possibility of (in Allport's words) "a science treating individuals" (G. W. Allport, 1937b, p. 21). And in fact, some of the critics of mainstream personality psychology are really friendly critics, trying to improve the true scientific credentials by taking account of these alternative perspectives (see, e.g., Stewart, 1993, on how feminist theories can improve personality research).

Thus, personality psychology is not immune to intellectual trends and fashions (albeit perhaps somewhat sluggish and belated in its responsiveness). Currently, approaches that involve narrative and other qualitative methods, as reflected in the existence and importance of the *Handbook of Qualitative Research* (Denzin & Lincoln, 2000), are enjoying relatively high prestige in the academic community, particularly in many social science fields. (For example, sociology has seen a revival of interest in case studies and personal documents; see Platt, 1992, 1996; Plummer, 1983.) Thus, it is only natural that such trends should give impetus to a renewed focus on the individual lives approach (e.g., McAdams, Josselson, & Lieblich, 2001), particularly when they can be combined with quantitative methods (see, e.g., J. M. Healy & Stewart, 1991).

Importance of Social Context. A final reason for the renewed interest in the individual lives approach to personality is a recognition of the importance of people's social contexts in shaping and channeling their personality characteristics and dynamics. Psychologists have long recognized the powerful effects of immediate situations or microcontexts; for example, things that can be manipulated in laboratory experiments. Even more striking in their effects, however, are macrocontexts, or enduring features of social structure and culture—*gender, age, social class, culture,* and *history.* For example, consider such personality variables as power motivation, optimistic explanatory style, extraversion, and conscientiousness. Each is clearly defined. Each has considerable construct validity, which means that it is associated with a recognized and characteristic set of observable behaviors. Yet imagine how differently each would have been expressed on the morning of June 6, 1944, by the following two people, in the following two situations: (1) a white 20-year-old American man storming Utah Beach during the World War II invasion of Normandy in France, and (2) a middle-aged Japanese American woman in an internment camp set up in the Utah desert at the beginning of the war by the U.S. government for citizens and residents of Japanese ancestry. Taking account of the enormous context differences, we could probably recognize abstract similarities in the expression of power motivation, optimistic explanatory style, extraversion,

and conscientiousness across the two situations. And within each situation, we could recognize differences between people who were high versus low in power motivation, conscientiousness, and so forth.

When we consider the many different features of people's social contexts, each interacting with all the others, it is immediately apparent that taken together, they transform and channel the expression of nomothetic "standardized" personality variables in an indefinitely large number of ways. (Of course, the different personality variables interact with and thereby transform each other, as well.) As a result, the concepts of "personality variables" and even "personality" are most appropriately understood not as autonomous, free-floating entities located "within" people but rather as "bundles" of potentialities, expressed in many and varied (but still recognizable) ways in combination with features of the social micro- and macrocontexts. The study and assessment of personality, then, become the much broader study and assessment of *personality-in-contexts;* this, in turn, means the study and assessment of individual lives. In other words, recognition of the importance of social context facilitates recognition of the value of the individual lives approach.

Context and Complexity in Personality Psychology

Some psychologists have recognized, at least in principle, the importance of context in the expression of personality. Kurt Lewin (1935) long ago articulated the principle that behavior is a joint function of the personality (P) and the environment (E); in formulaic terms: $B = f(P, E)$. This principle is often expressed by including a person-situation interaction term in an ANOVA or regression. However, Lewin's simple formula and these interaction terms are really little more than programmatic methodological aspirations or statements of faith; as they stand, they are of little use in the full analysis of complex person-environment transactions in the real world. From our perspective, Lewin's formula is misleadingly simple: Personality itself is also a function of complex and differentiated environments, past and present, as well as immediate situations. For example, might Jenny's personality have been different if she had been more financially secure (M. B. Allport, 1965)?

Atkinson (1957) developed a model for relating motivation and behavior by considering the effects of context-related variables such as expectancy and incentive as they interacted with approach and avoidance motives. While the model was usefully applied to the analysis of certain situations, mostly involving the achievement motive (Atkinson & Feather, 1966; McClelland, 1985; McClelland & Winter, 1969, pp. 15–19), it, too, remained a largely programmatic model.

In developing his list of personality variables, Murray made a deliberate analogy to organic chemistry (1938, p. 142). His list of motives and traits was seen as a limited number of *elements* capable of combining with each other and environmental press, producing an almost infinite number of complex and unique individual personality-environment "compounds"—that is, individual lives. On the other hand, subsequent personality psychologists mostly confined their attention to the short list of personality elements rather than the enormous variety of person-environment compounds. This would be analogous to chemists focusing only on the abstract characteristics of carbon, hydrogen, oxygen, and nitrogen, considered in isolation—appropriate for the early weeks of secondary school chemistry, perhaps, but hardly organic chemistry!

Taking Murray's metaphor seriously would lead personality psychology in the direction of studying these many and varied individual lives, just as organic chemists attend to the many and varied emergent properties of an enormous number of organic compounds. (As mentioned above, Murray actually introduced several concepts, such as need-integrate, regnancy, ordination, and gratuity, that could facilitate the study of personality-in-context in individual lives, but these concepts were never seriously developed and elaborated, either by Murray or by later generations of personality psychologists.) A similar perspective has emerged recently from the discovery that human complexity is generated by a surprisingly small number of genes:

> The key to complexity is not more genes, but more combinations and interactions generated by fewer units of code—and many of these interactions (as emergent properties, to use the technical jargon) must be explained at the level of their appearance, for they cannot be predicted from the separate underlying parts alone. So organisms must be explained as organisms, and not as a summation of genes. (Gould, 2001)

At the beginning of the twenty-first century, then, we have come to recognize that personality involves complex interactions among elements and contexts in ways that, over time, are to some extent irreversible (or at least only reversible with greater difficulty than acquisition) and cannot be adequately described with simplistic, positivistic conceptions of science. We believe that these complexities—of personality and of psychological science—have energized a renewed interest in the individual lives approach to understanding personality. At the same time, we believe that no one should underestimate the difficulty of studying lives with traditional and valuable standards of scientific objectivity and rigor—to develop, as Allport suggested, a true science of the single case. Perhaps in the next century, the field will benefit from the increased popularity and accessibility of chaos theory (also called complexity theory) and its associated mathematical concepts (e.g., Nowak & Vallacher, 1998) as alternatives to classical psychometric procedures and rules.

Finally, we suggest that to understand contexts and the way they shape the level and expression of personality dimensions within individual lives will involve us in making acquaintance with and giving serious study to many other disciplines: for example, anthropology, sociology, gender studies, political science, history, economics, religion, even architecture and geography. To do justice to the whole range of human experience, we believe, the study of individual lives in personality psychology must become again, as it originally was, an interdisciplinary endeavor.

REFERENCES

Alexander, I. E. (1990). *Personology: Method and content in personality assessment and psychobiography.* Durham, NC: Duke University Press.

Allport, F. H., & Allport, G. W. (1921). Personality traits: Their classification and measurement. *Journal of Abnormal Psychology and Social Psychology, 16,* 6–40.

Allport, G. W. (1921). Personality and character. *Psychological Bulletin, 18,* 441–455.

Allport, G. W. (1922). *An experimental study of the traits of personality, with application to the problem of social diagnosis.* Unpublished doctoral dissertation, Harvard University.

Allport, G. W. (1923). The Leipzig congress of psychology. *American Journal of Psychology, 34,* 612–615.

Allport, G. W. (1924). The study of the undivided personality. *Journal of Abnormal and Social Psychology, 19,* 132–141.

Allport, G. W. (1928). A test for ascendance-submission. *Journal of Abnormal and Social Psychology, 23,* 118–136.

Allport, G. W. (1929). The study of personality by the intuitive method: An experiment in teaching from *The locomotive god. Journal of Abnormal and Social Psychology, 24,* 14–27.

Allport, G. W. (1932). [Review of the book *Diagnosing personality and conduct*]. *Journal of Social Psychology, 3,* 391–397.

Allport, G. W. (1933). The study of personality by the experimental method. *Character and Personality, 1,* 259–264.

Allport, G. W. (1937a, September 29). Letter to R. C. Cabot. Gordon W. Allport Papers, Harvard University Archives, Cambridge, MA.

Allport, G. W. (1937b). *Personality: A psychological interpretation.* New York: Henry Holt.

Allport, G. W. (1938). *The Journal of Abnormal and Social Psychology:* An editorial. *Journal of Abnormal and Social Psychology, 33,* 3–13.

Allport, G. W. (1940a, December 23). Letter to A. T. Poffenberger. Gordon W. Allport Papers, Harvard University Archives, Cambridge, MA. Quoted by permission of Ardys Allport.

Allport, G. W. (1940b). The psychologist's frame of reference. *Psychological Bulletin, 37,* 1–28.

Allport, G. W. (1940c). Symposium: Psychoanalysis as seen by analyzed psychologists [Editor's note]. *Journal of Abnormal and Social Psychology, 35,* 3.

Allport, G. W. (1941, January 22). Letter to R. H. MacMurphey. Gordon W. Allport Papers, Harvard University Archives, Cambridge, MA.

Allport, G. W. (1942). *The use of personal documents in psychological science.* New York: Social Science Research Council.

Allport, G. W. (1943a, April 8). Letter to A. T. Poffenberger. Gordon W. Allport Papers, Harvard University Archives, Cambridge, MA.

Allport, G. W. (1943b). This clinical supplement: Editorial note. *Journal of Abnormal and Social Psychology, 38,* 3–5.

Allport, G. W. (1945, February 26). Letter to M. V. Vaughan. Gordon W. Allport Papers, Harvard University Archives, Cambridge, MA.

Allport, G. W. (1949). Editorial note. *Journal of Abnormal and Social Psychology, 44,* 439–442.

Allport, G. W. (1951, January 11). Letter to J. Evans. Gordon W. Allport Papers, Harvard University Archives, Cambridge, MA.

Allport, G. W. (1958). The science of whole lives [Review of the book *The person in psychology: Reality or abstraction?*]. *Contemporary Psychology, 3,* 105.

Allport, G. W. (1962a). The general and the unique in psychological science. *Journal of Personality, 30,* 405–422.

Allport, G. W. (1962b, October 29). *My encounters with personality theory.* Transcript of talk presented at Boston University School of Theology, Gordon W. Allport Papers, Harvard University Archives, Cambridge, MA.

Allport, G. W. (1965). *Letters from Jenny.* New York: Harcourt, Brace, & World.

Allport, G. W. (1967). Gordon W. Allport. In E. G. Boring & G. Lindzey (Eds.), *A history of psychology in autobiography* (Vol. 5, pp. 1–25). New York: Appleton-Century-Crofts.

Allport, G. W. (1968). *The person in psychology: Selected essays.* Boston: Beacon Press.

Allport, G. W. (n.d.). *Intuition as a method in psychology.* Unpublished manuscript, undated [internal evidence suggests 1927], Gordon W. Allport Papers, Harvard University Archives, Cambridge, MA.

Allport, G. W., & Vernon, P. E. (1930). The field of personality. *Psychological Bulletin, 27,* 677–730.

Allport, G. W., & Vernon, P. E. (1931). *A study of values.* Boston: Houghton Mifflin.

Allport, M. B. (1965, May 11). Letter to G. W. Allport. Gordon W. Allport Papers, Harvard University Archives, Cambridge, MA.

Anderson, J. W. (1988). Henry A. Murray's early career: A psychobiographical exploration. *Journal of Personality, 56,* 139–171.

Anonymous. (1908). My life as a dissociated personality. *Journal of Abnormal Psychology, 3,* 240–260.

Anonymous. (1946). Letters from Jenny. *Journal of Abnormal and Social Psychology, 41,* 315–350, 449–480.

Atkinson, J. W. (1957). Motivational determinants of risk-taking behavior. *Psychological Review, 64,* 359–372.

Atkinson, J. W., & Feather, N. T. (1966). *A theory of achievement motivation.* New York: Wiley.

Bain, R. (1929). The validity of life histories and diaries. *Journal of Educational Sociology, 3,* 150–164.

Baldwin, A. L. (1942). Personal structure analysis: A statistical method for investigating the single personality. *Journal of Abnormal and Social Psychology, 37,* 163–183.

Barenbaum, N. B. (1997a). The case(s) of Gordon Allport. *Journal of Personality, 65,* 743–755.

Barenbaum, N. B. (1997b, June). *"The most revealing method of all": Gordon Allport and case studies.* Paper presented at the annual meeting of Cheiron, Richmond, VA.

Barenbaum, N. B. (1998, June). *Idiographic and nomothetic: Gordon Allport's "introduction" of personality psychology as historical and natural science.* Paper presented at the annual meeting of Cheiron, San Diego, CA.

Barenbaum, N. B. (2000). How social was personality? The Allports' "connection" of social and personality psychology. *Journal of the History of the Behavioral Sciences, 36,* 471–487.

Becker, H. P. (1930). Distribution of space in the *American Journal of Sociology,* 1895–1927. *American Journal of Sociology, 36,* 461–466.

Beers, C. W. (1908). *A mind that found itself: An autobiography.* New York: Longmans, Green.

Benjamin, L. T., DeLeon, P. H., & Freedheim, D. K. (2002). Psychology as a profession. In I. B. Weiner (Gen. Ed.) & D. K. Freedheim (Vol. Ed.), *Handbook of psychology: History of psychology, Vol. 1.* New York: Wiley.

Bernard, L. L. (1932). Social psychology in the United States. *Sociologus, 8,* 257–280.

Bernard, L. L. (1945). The teaching of sociology in the United States in the last fifty years. *American Journal of Sociology, 50,* 534–548.

Bernreuter, R. G. (1933). The theory and construction of the personality inventory. *Journal of Social Psychology, 4,* 387–405.

Bertaux, D. (1981). *Biography and society: The life history approach in the social sciences.* Beverly Hills, CA: Sage.

Bills, A. G. (1938). Changing views of psychology as science. *Psychological Review, 45,* 377–394.

Block, J. (1971). *Lives through time.* Berkeley, CA: Bancroft Books.

Boring, E. G. (1950). *A history of experimental psychology* (2nd ed.). New York: Appleton-Century-Crofts.

Bradford, G. (1927). The significance of biography. In J. C. Johnston, *Biography: The literature of personality* (pp. xv–xxi). New York: Century.

Bray, D. W. (1982). The assessment center and the study of lives. *American Psychologist, 37,* 180–189.

Bray, D. W. (1985). Fifty years of assessment centres: A retrospective and prospective view. *Journal of Management Development, 4*(4), 4–12.

Brigham, C. C. (1931). Proceedings of the thirty-eighth annual meeting of the American Psychological Association, Iowa City, Iowa, December 29, 30, 31, 1930. *Psychological Bulletin, 28,* 181–250.

Bromley, D. B. (1986). *The case-study method in psychology and related disciplines.* Chichester, England: Wiley.

Bulmer, M. (1984). *The Chicago school of sociology: Institutionalization, diversity and the rise of sociological research.* Chicago: University of Chicago Press.

Burgess, E. W. (1927). Statistics and case studies as methods of sociological research. *Sociology and Social Research, 12,* 103–120.

Burnham, J. C. (1968a). Historical background for the study of personality. In E. F. Borgatta & W. W. Lambert (Eds.), *Handbook of personality theory and research* (pp. 3–81). Chicago: Rand McNally.

Burnham, J. C. (1968b). The new psychology: From narcissism to social control. In J. Braeman, R. H. Bremner, & D. Brody (Eds.), *Change and continuity in twentieth-century America: The 1920's* (pp. 351–398). Columbus: Ohio State University Press.

Burton, A., & Harris, R. E. (1947). *Case histories in clinical and abnormal psychology.* New York: Harper & Brothers.

Camfield, T. M. (1969). *Psychologists at war: The history of American psychology and the First World War.* Unpublished doctoral dissertation, University of Texas, Austin.

Campbell, R. J., & Bray, D. W. (1993). Use of an assessment center as an aid in management selection. *Personnel Psychology, 46,* 691–699.

Cannon, W. B. (1900). The case method of teaching systematic medicine. *Boston Medical and Surgical Journal, 142,* 31–36.

Cantril, H. (1938). [Review of the book *Psychology of personality*]. *Psychological Bulletin, 35,* 107–109.

Capps, D. (1994). An Allportian analysis of Augustine. *International Journal for the Psychology of Religion, 4,* 205–228.

Capshew, J. H. (1999). *Psychologists on the march: Science, practice, and professional identity in America, 1929–1969.* New York: Cambridge University Press.

Cartwright, D., & French, J. R. P. (1939). The reliability of life-history studies. *Character and Personality, 8,* 110–119.

Cattell, R. B. (1957). *Personality and motivation structure and measurement.* Yonkers, NY: World.

Cherry, F. (1996). *Entangled lives: "Letters from Jenny," the Allports and the Watsons.* Unpublished manuscript, Carleton University, Ottawa, Ontario, Canada.

Cherry, F. (2000). The nature of *The nature of prejudice. Journal of the History of the Behavioral Sciences, 36,* 489–498.

Cocks, G., & Crosby, T. L. (1987). *Psycho/history: Readings in the method of psychology, psychoanalysis, and history.* New Haven, CT: Yale University Press.

Coe, G. A. (1903). [Review of the book *The varieties of religious experience*]. *Philosophical Review, 12,* 62–67.

Cohen, S. (1983). The mental hygiene movement, the development of personality and the school: The medicalization of American education. *History of Education Quarterly, 23,* 123–149.

Cohler, B. J. (1993). Describing lives: Gordon Allport and the "science" of personality. In K. H. Craik, R. Hogan, & R. N. Wolfe (Eds.), *Fifty years of personality psychology* (pp. 131–146). New York: Plenum Press.

Corbin, J. (1908, November). How one girl lived four lives: The astounding case of Miss Beauchamp. *Ladies' Home Journal, 25,* 11–12, 68–69.

Craik, K. H. (1986). Personality research methods: An historical perspective. *Journal of Personality, 54,* 18–51.

Craik, K. H. (1988). Assessing the personalities of historical figures. In W. M. Runyan (Ed.), *Psychology and historical interpretation* (pp. 196–218). New York: Oxford University Press.

Crider, B. (1936). Who is a psychologist? *School and Society, 43,* 370–371.

Crosby, F., & Crosby, T. L. (1981). Psychobiography and psychohistory. In S. L. Long (Ed.), *Handbook of political behavior* (Vol. 1, pp. 195–254). New York: Plenum Press.

Danziger, K. (1990). *Constructing the subject: Historical origins of psychological research.* New York: Cambridge University Press.

Danziger, K. (1997). *Naming the mind: How psychology found its language.* Thousand Oaks, CA: Sage.

Demorest, A. P., & Siegel, P. F. (1996). Personal influences on professional work: An empirical case study of B. F. Skinner. *Journal of Personality, 64,* 243–261.

Denzin, N. K., & Lincoln, Y. S. (2000). *Handbook of qualitative research* (2nd ed.). Thousand Oaks, CA: Sage.

Dewey, R. (1907). A case of disordered personality. *Journal of Abnormal Psychology, 2,* 141–154.

Dollard, J. (1935). *Criteria for the life history.* New Haven, CT: Yale University Press.

Dollard, J. (1948). [Review of the book *Case histories in clinical and abnormal psychology*]. *Psychological Bulletin, 45,* 540–541.

Duffy, E. (1940). A critical review of investigations employing the Allport-Vernon Study of Values and other tests of evaluative attitude. *Psychological Bulletin, 37,* 597–612.

Editors. (1921). Editorial announcement. *Journal of Abnormal Psychology and Social Psychology, 16,* 1–5.

Editors. (1925). Announcement. *Journal of Abnormal and Social Psychology, 20,* 6.

Elliott, R. M. (1939). The Harvard *Explorations in personality* [Review of the book *Explorations in personality: A clinical and experimental study of fifty men of college age*]. *American Journal of Psychology, 52,* 453–462.

Elliott, R. M. (1952). Richard M. Elliott. In E. G. Boring, H. S. Langfeld, H. Werner, & R. M. Yerkes (Eds.), *A history of psychology in autobiography* (Vol. 4, pp. 75–95). New York: Russell & Russell.

Elms, A. C. (1986). From House to Haig: Private life and public style in American foreign policy advisers. *Journal of Social Issues, 42*(2), 33–53.

Elms, A. C. (1994). *Uncovering lives: The uneasy alliance of biography and psychology.* New York: Oxford University Press.

Erikson, E. H. (1958). *Young man Luther.* New York: Norton.

Erikson, E. H. (1969). *Gandhi's truth.* New York: Norton.

Ernst, R. (1991). *Weakness is a crime: The life of Bernarr Macfadden.* Syracuse, NY: Syracuse University Press.

Espin, O. M., Stewart, A. J., & Gomez, C. A. (1990). Letters from V: Adolescent personality development in sociohistorical context. *Journal of Personality, 58,* 347–364.

Evans, J. (1948). Johnny Rocco. *Journal of Abnormal and Social Psychology, 43,* 357–383.

Evans, J. (1950). Miller. *Journal of Abnormal and Social Psychology, 45,* 359–379.

Evans, J. (1954). *Three men: An experiment in the biography of emotion.* New York: Alfred A. Knopf.

Fancher, R. E. (2000). Snapshots of Freud in America, 1899–1999. *American Psychologist, 55,* 1025–1028.

Fernald, G. G. (1920). Character vs. intelligence in personality studies. *Journal of Abnormal Psychology, 15,* 1–10.

Forrester, J. (1996). If *p*, then what? Thinking in cases. *History of the Human Sciences, 9*(3), 1–25.

Franz, C. E., & Stewart, A. J. (1994). *Women creating lives: Identities, resilience, and resistance.* Boulder, CO: Westview.

Freud, S. (1955). Fräulein Elisabeth von R. In J. Strachey (Ed. & Trans.), *The standard edition of the complete psychological works of Sigmund Freud* (Vol. 2, pp. 135–181). London: Hogarth Press. (Original work published 1893–1895)

Freud, S. (1957a). Five lectures on psycho-analysis. In J. Strachey (Ed. & Trans.), *The standard edition of the complete psychological works of Sigmund Freud* (Vol. 11, pp. 7–55). London: Hogarth Press. (Original work published 1910)

Freud, S. (1957b). Some character types met with in psychoanalytic work. In J. Strachey (Ed. & Trans.), *The standard edition of the complete psychological works of Sigmund Freud* (Vol. 14, pp. 309–333). London: Hogarth Press. (Original work published 1916)

Freud, S. (1959). Character and anal erotism. In J. Strachey (Ed. & Trans.), *The standard edition of the complete psychological works of Sigmund Freud* (Vol. 9, pp. 169–175). London: Hogarth Press. (Original work published 1908)

Freud, S. (1961). Libidinal types. In J. Strachey (Ed. & Trans.), *The standard edition of the complete psychological works of Sigmund Freud* (Vol. 21, pp. 215–220). London: Hogarth Press. (Original work published 1931)

Freyd, M. (1926). What is applied psychology? *Psychological Review, 33,* 308–314.

Friedman, W. (1994). Woodrow Wilson and Colonel House and political psychobiography. *Political Psychology, 15,* 35–59.

Fuchs, A. H., & Milar, K. S. (2002). Psychology as a science. In I. B. Weiner (Gen. Ed.) & D. K. Freedheim (Vol. Ed.), *Handbook of psychology: History of psychology, Vol. 1.* New York: Wiley.

Garraty, J. A. (1981). Gordon Allport's rules for the preparation of life histories and case studies. *Biography, 4,* 283–292.

George, A. L., & George, J. L. (1956). *Woodrow Wilson and Colonel House: A personality study.* New York: John Day.

Gergen, K. J. (1977). Stability, change, and chance in understanding human development. In N. Datan & H. Reese (Eds.), *Life-span developmental psychology: Dialectical perspectives on experimental research* (pp. 135–157). New York: Academic Press.

Glad, B. (1973). Contributions of psychobiography. In J. N. Knutson (Ed.), *Handbook of political psychology* (pp. 296–321). San Francisco: Jossey-Bass.

Good, J. M. M. (2000). On the disciplining of social psychology: A case study of boundary relations in the history of the human sciences. *Journal of the History of the Behavioral Sciences, 36,* 383–403.

Gottschalk, L. R., Kluckhohn, C., & Angell, R. C. (1945). *The use of personal documents in history, anthropology, and sociology.* New York: Social Science Research Council.

Gould, S. J. (2001, February 19). Humbled by the genome's mysteries. *New York Times on the Web* [Online]. Retrieved from www.nytimes.com/2001/02/19/opinion/19GOUL.html

Graves, R. H. (1934). *The triumph of an idea: The story of Henry Ford.* Garden City, NY: Doubleday, Doran, & Co.

Greenstein, F. I. (1969). *Personality and politics.* Chicago: Markham.

Guilford, J. P. (1938). [Review of the book *Personality: A psychological interpretation*]. *Journal of Abnormal and Social Psychology, 33,* 414–420.

Hale, N. G. (1971). *Freud and the Americans: The beginnings of psychoanalysis in the United States, 1876–1917.* New York: Oxford University Press.

Hall, C. S., & Lindzey, G. (1957). *Theories of personality.* New York: Wiley.

Hall, G. S. (1904). *Adolescence: Its psychology and its relations to physiology, anthropology, sociology, sex, crime, religion and education* (Vols. 1–2). New York: D. Appleton.

Healy, J. M., Jr., & Stewart, A. J. (1991). On the compatibility of quantitative and qualitative methods for studying individual lives. In R. Hogan (Series Ed.), A. J. Stewart, J. M. Healy Jr., & D. J. Ozer (Vol. Eds.), *Perspectives in personality: Approaches to understanding lives, Vol. 3, Part B* (pp. 35–57). Bristol, PA: Jessica Kingsley.

Healy, W. (1915). *The individual delinquent: A text-book of diagnosis and prognosis for all concerned in understanding offenders.* Boston: Little, Brown.

Herman, E. (1995). *The romance of American psychology: Political culture in the age of experts.* Berkeley: University of California Press.

Hevern, V. W. (1999, August). *Allport's (1942) Use of personal documents: A contemporary reappraisal.* Paper presented at the annual meeting of the American Psychological Association, Boston.

Hollingworth, H. L. (1938). [Review of the book *Personality: A psychological interpretation*]. *Psychological Bulletin, 35,* 103–107.

Holt, R. R. (1978). *Methods in clinical psychology: Projective assessment, Vol. 1.* New York: Plenum Press.

Homburger, E. [Erikson, E. H.] (1937). Configurations in play: Clinical notes. *Psychoanalytic Quarterly, 6,* 139–214.

Hornstein, G. A. (1988). Quantifying psychological phenomena: Debates, dilemmas, and implications. In J. G. Morawski (Ed.), *The rise of experimentation in American psychology* (pp. 1–34). New Haven, CT: Yale University Press.

Hornstein, G. A. (1992). The return of the repressed: Psychology's problematic relations with psychoanalysis, 1909–1960. *American Psychologist, 47,* 254–263.

Howe, M. J. A. (1997). Beyond psychobiography: Towards more effective syntheses of psychology and biography. *British Journal of Psychology, 88,* 235–248.

Hudson, C. (1973). The historical approach in anthropology. In J. J. Honigmann (Ed.), *Handbook of social and cultural anthropology* (pp. 111–141). Chicago: Rand McNally College Publishing.

James, W. (1902). *The varieties of religious experience: A study in human nature.* New York: Longmans, Green.

Jenkins, J. G. (1938). [Review of the book *Personality: A psychological interpretation*]. *American Journal of Psychology, 51,* 777–778.

Johnston, J. C. (1927). *Biography: The literature of personality.* New York: Century.

Jones, K. W. (1999). *Taming the troublesome child: American families, child guidance, and the limits of psychiatric authority.* Cambridge, MA: Harvard University Press.

Josselson, R., & Lieblich, A. (Eds.). (1993–1999). *The narrative study of lives* (Vols. 1–6). Newbury Park, CA: Sage.

Jung, C. G. (1971). Psychological types. In H. Read, M. Fordham, G. Adler, & W. McGuire (Eds.), *The collected works of C. G. Jung* (Vol. 6, pp. 1–495). Princeton, NJ: Princeton University Press.

Kershaw, I. (1999). *Hitler, 1889–1936: Hubris.* New York: Norton.

Kirkpatrick, E. A. (1904). [Review of the book *Adolescence*]. *Journal of Philosophy, Psychology and Scientific Methods, 1,* 687–693.

Krueger, E. T. (1925). *Autobiographical documents and personality.* Unpublished doctoral dissertation, University of Chicago.

Lamiell, J. T. (1997). Individuals and the differences between them. In R. Hogan, J. Johnson, & S. Briggs (Eds.), *Handbook of personality psychology* (pp. 117–141). San Diego, CA: Academic Press.

Langer, L. L. (1999, February). Satan's biographers. *Atlantic Monthly,* 98–104.

Langer, W. (1972). *The mind of Adolf Hitler: The secret wartime report.* New York: Basic Books.

Leonard, W. E. (1927). *The locomotive-god.* New York: Century.

Lewin, K. (1935). *A dynamic theory of personality.* New York: McGraw-Hill.

Lubove, R. (1965). *The professional altruist: The emergence of social work as a career, 1880–1930.* Cambridge, MA: Harvard University Press.

Lundberg, G. A. (1926). Case work and the statistical method. *Social Forces, 5,* 61–65.

MacKinnon, D. W. (1967). Assessing creative persons. *Journal of Creative Behavior, 1,* 291–304.

MacMurphey, R. H. (1941, January 21). Letter to G. W. Allport. Gordon W. Allport Papers, Harvard University Archives, Cambridge, MA.

McAdams, D. P. (1988). Biography, narrative, and lives: An introduction. *Journal of Personality, 56,* 1–18.

McAdams, D. P. (1990). *The person: An introduction to personality psychology.* San Diego, CA: Harcourt Brace Jovanovich.

McAdams, D. P. (1997). A conceptual history of personality psychology. In R. Hogan, J. Johnson, & S. Briggs (Eds.), *Handbook of personality psychology* (pp. 3–39). San Diego, CA: Academic Press.

McAdams, D. P., Josselson, R., & Lieblich, A. (Eds.). (2001). *Turns in the road: Narrative studies of lives in transition.* Washington, DC: American Psychological Association.

McAdams, D. P., & Ochberg, R. L. (Eds.). (1988). Psychobiography and life narratives [Special issue]. *Journal of Personality, 56*(1).

McAdams, D. P., & West, S. G. (1997). Introduction: Personality psychology and the case study. *Journal of Personality, 65,* 757–783.

McClelland, D. C. (1951). *Personality.* New York: Sloane.

McClelland, D. C. (1985). How motives, skills, and values determine what people do. *American Psychologist, 40,* 812–825.

McClelland, D. C., & Winter, D. G. (1969). *Motivating economic success.* New York: Free Press.

Meehl, P. E. (1954). *Clinical vs. statistical prediction: A theoretical analysis and a review of the evidence.* Minneapolis: University of Minnesota Press.

Moore, H. T. (1925). Innate factors in radicalism and conservatism. *Journal of Abnormal and Social Psychology, 20,* 234–244.

Morawski, J. G., & Bayer, B. M. (2003). Social. In L. B. Weiner (Gen. Ed.) & D. K. Freedheim (Vol. Ed.), *Handbook of psychology: History of psychology, Vol. 1.* New York: Wiley.

Morawski, J. G., & Hornstein, G. A. (1991). Quandary of the quacks: The struggle for expert knowledge in American psychology, 1890–1940. In J. Brown & D. K. van Keuren (Eds.), *The estate of social knowledge* (pp. 106–133). Baltimore: Johns Hopkins University Press.

Morgan, D. M. (1989). *The voyage of the American promise.* Boston: Houghton Mifflin.

Murphy, G. (1932). *An historical introduction to modern psychology* (4th Rev. ed.). New York: Harcourt, Brace.

Murphy, G., & Murphy, L. B. (1931). *Experimental social psychology*. New York: Harpers.

Murray, H. A. (1938). *Explorations in personality: A clinical and experimental study of fifty men of college age*. New York: Oxford University Press.

Murray, H. A. (1943). *Analysis of the personality of Adolph [sic] Hitler, with predictions of his future behavior and suggestions for dealing with him now and after Germany's surrender*. Unpublished manuscript, Henry A. Murray Papers, Harvard University Archives, Cambridge, MA.

Murray, H. A. (1955). American Icarus. In A. Burton & R. E. Harris (Eds.), *Clinical studies of personality* (Vol. 2, pp. 615–641). New York: Harper.

Murray, H. A. (1959). Preparations for the scaffold of a comprehensive system. In S. Koch (Ed.), *Psychology: A study of a science* (Vol. 3, pp. 7–54). New York: McGraw-Hill.

Murray, H. A. (1967). Henry A. Murray. In E. G. Boring & G. Lindzey (Eds.), *A history of psychology in autobiography* (Vol. 5, pp. 283–310). New York: Appleton-Century-Crofts.

Murray, H. A. (1968). Components of an evolving personological system. In D. L. Sills (Ed.), *International encyclopedia of the social sciences* (Vol. 12, pp. 5–13). New York: Macmillan-Free Press.

Murray, H. A. (1977). Indispensables for the making, testing, and remaking of a personological system. In R. W. Rieber & K. Salzinger (Eds.), *The roots of American psychology: Historical influences and implications for the future* (pp. 323–331). New York: New York Academy of Sciences.

Murray, H. A., & Kluckhohn, C. K. M. (1953). Outline of a conception of personality. In C. K. M. Kluckhohn, H. A. Murray, & D. M. Schneider (Eds.), *Personality in nature, culture, and society* (Rev. ed., pp. 3–32). New York: Knopf.

Napoli, D. S. (1981). *Architects of adjustment: The history of the psychological profession in the United States*. Port Washington, NY: Kennikat Press.

Nasby, W., & Read, N. W. (1997). The life voyage of a solo circumnavigator: Integrating theoretical and methodological perspectives. *Journal of Personality, 65,* 785–1068.

Nicholson, I. A. M. (1996). *Moral projects and disciplinary practices: Gordon Allport and the development of American personality psychology*. Unpublished doctoral dissertation, York University, North York, Ontario, Canada.

Nicholson, I. A. M. (1997). To "correlate psychology and social ethics": Gordon Allport and the first course in American personality psychology. *Journal of Personality, 65,* 733–742.

Nicholson, I. A. M. (1998). Gordon Allport, character, and the "culture of personality," 1897–1937. *History of Psychology, 1,* 52–68.

Nicholson, I. A. M. (2000). "A coherent datum of perception": Gordon Allport, Floyd Allport, and the politics of "personality." *Journal of the History of the Behavioral Sciences, 36,* 463–470.

Nicholson, I. A. M. (in press). *Inventing personality: Gordon Allport and the science of selfhood*. Washington, DC: American Psychological Association.

Nowak, A., & Vallacher, R. M. (1998). *Dynamical social psychology*. New York: Guilford Press.

O'Connell, D. C. (1958). Idiographic knowledge. *Journal of General Psychology, 59,* 21–33.

O'Donnell, J. M. (1985). *The origins of behaviorism: American psychology, 1870–1920*. New York: New York University Press.

Office of Strategic Services Assessment Staff. (1948). *Assessment of men*. New York: Rinehart.

Paige, J. M. (1966). Letters from Jenny: An approach to the clinical analysis of personality structure by computer. In P. J. Stone, D. C. Dunphy, M. S. Smith, & D. M. Ogilvie (Eds.), *The General Inquirer: A computer approach to content analysis* (pp. 431–451). Cambridge, MA: MIT Press.

Pandora, K. (1997). *Rebels within the ranks: Psychologists' critique of scientific authority and democratic realities in New Deal America*. Cambridge, England: Cambridge University Press.

Parker, J. D. A. (1991). *In search of the person: The historical development of American personality psychology*. Unpublished doctoral dissertation, York University, North York, Ontario, Canada.

Paterson, D. G. (1938). A provocative treatise [Review of the book *Personality: A psychological interpretation*]. *Journal of Higher Education, 9,* 464–465.

Pervin, L. A. (1990). A brief history of modern personality theory. In L. Pervin (Ed.), *Handbook of personality theory and research* (pp. 3–18). New York: Guilford Press.

Peterson, C. (1988). *Personality*. San Diego, CA: Harcourt, Brace.

Platt, J. (1992). "Case study" in American methodological thought. *Current Sociology, 40,* 17–48.

Platt, J. (1996). *A history of sociological research methods in America 1920–1960*. Cambridge, England: Cambridge University Press.

Plummer, K. (1983). *Documents of life: An introduction to the problems and literature of a humanistic method*. London: Allen & Unwin.

Polansky, N. A. (1941). How shall a life-history be written? *Character and Personality, 9,* 188–207.

Porter, T. M. (1995). *Trust in numbers: The pursuit of objectivity in science and public life*. Princeton, NJ: Princeton University Press.

Prince, M. (1906). *The dissociation of a personality*. New York: Longmans, Green.

Putnam, J. J. (1906). Recent experiences in the study and treatment of hysteria at the Massachusetts General Hospital, with remarks on Freud's method of treatment by "psycho-analysis." *Journal of Abnormal Psychology, 1,* 26–41.

Radin, P. (1926). *Crashing Thunder: The autobiography of an American Indian*. New York: Appleton.

Randall, J. H. (1912). *The culture of personality*. New York: Dodge.

Rank, O. (1936). Life fear and death fear. In *Will therapy: An analysis of the therapeutic process in terms of relationship* (J. J. Taft, Trans.) (pp. 119–133). New York: Knopf. (Original work published 1931)

Recent literature. (1921). *American Journal of Sociology, 27,* 128–144.

Richmond, M. E. (1922). *What is social case work? An introductory description.* New York: Russell Sage Foundation.

Roback, A. A. (1927a). *The psychology of character, with a survey of temperament.* New York: Harcourt, Brace.

Roback, A. A. (1927b). [Review of the book *Collected papers. Vol. 3: Case histories*]. *Journal of Abnormal and Social Psychology, 22,* 346–347.

Roback, A. A. (1935). Dr. Robert Saudek. *Character and Personality, 3,* 263–269.

Robinson, F. G. (1992). *Love's story told: A life of Henry A. Murray.* Cambridge, MA: Harvard University Press.

Robinson, V. P. (1930). *A changing psychology in social case work.* Chapel Hill: University of North Carolina Press.

Roe, A. (1962). [Interview with Gordon W. Allport]. Anne Roe Papers, American Philosophical Society, Philadelphia.

Romero, M., & Stewart, A. J. (Eds.). (1999). *Women's untold stories: Breaking silence, talking back, voicing complexity.* Florence, KY: Taylor & Francis/Routledge.

Rosenbaum, R. (1998). *Explaining Hitler: The search for the origins of his evil.* New York: Random House.

Rosenthal, R. (1958). Training clinical students in personality theory. *American Psychologist, 13,* 605–606.

Ross, D. (1991). *The origins of American social science.* Cambridge, England: Cambridge University Press.

Ruckmick, C. R. (1931). Thirty-eighth annual meeting of the American Psychological Association. *American Journal of Psychology, 43,* 292–294.

Runyan, W. M. (1981). Why did Van Gogh cut off his ear? The problem of alternative explanations in psychobiography. *Journal of Personality and Social Psychology, 40,* 1070–1077.

Runyan, W. M. (1982). *Life histories and psychobiography: Explorations in theory and method.* New York: Oxford University Press.

Runyan, W. M. (1983). Idiographic goals and methods in the study of lives. *Journal of Personality, 51,* 413–437.

Runyan, W. M. (1988a). A historical and conceptual background to psychohistory. In W. M. Runyan (Ed.), *Psychology and historical interpretation* (pp. 3–60). New York: Oxford University Press.

Runyan, W. M. (1988b). Progress in psychobiography. *Journal of Personality, 56,* 295–326.

Runyan, W. M. (1990). Individual lives and the structure of personality psychology. In A. I. Rabin, R. A. Zucker, R. A. Emmons, & S. Frank (Eds.), *Studying persons and lives* (pp. 10–40). New York: Springer.

Runyan, W. M. (1997). Studying lives: Psychobiography and the conceptual structure of personality psychology. In R. Hogan,

J. Johnson, & S. Briggs (Eds.), *Handbook of personality psychology* (pp. 41–69). San Diego, CA: Academic Press.

Samelson, F. (1985). Organizing for the kingdom of behavior: Academic battles and organizational policies in the twenties. *Journal of the History of the Behavioral Sciences, 21,* 33–47.

Sanford, N. (1985). What have we learned about personality? In S. Koch & D. E. Leary (Eds.), *A century of psychology as science* (pp. 490–514). Washington, DC: American Psychological Association.

Shakow, D., & Rapaport, D. (1964). *The influence of Freud on American psychology.* New York: International Universities Press.

Shaw, C. R. (1930). *The jack-roller: A delinquent boy's own story.* Chicago: University of Chicago Press.

Sheffield, A. E. (1920). *The social case history: Its construction and content.* New York: Russell Sage Foundation.

Shermer, P. (1985). *The development of research practice in abnormal and personality psychology: 1906–1956.* Unpublished master's thesis, York University, North York, Ontario, Canada.

Simonton, D. K. (1999). Significant samples: The psychological study of eminent individuals. *Psychological Methods, 4,* 425–451.

Skaggs, E. B. (1945). Personalistic psychology as science. *Psychological Review, 52,* 234–238.

Smith, R. (1997). *The Norton history of the human sciences.* New York: Norton.

Sokal, M. M. (1984). James McKeen Cattell and American psychology in the 1920s. In J. Brozek (Ed.), *Explorations in the history of psychology in the United States* (pp. 273–323). Lewisburg, PA: Bucknell University Press.

Stagner, R. (1937). *Psychology of personality.* New York: McGraw-Hill.

Staub, E. (1980). *Personality: Basic aspects and current research.* Englewood Cliffs, NJ: Prentice-Hall.

Stern, W. (1911). *Die differentielle Psychologie in ihren methodischen Grundlagen* [Differential psychology in its methodological foundations]. Leipzig, Germany: Barth.

Stewart, A. J. (1993, August). *Doing personality research: How can feminist theories help?* Address presented at the annual meeting of the American Psychological Association, Toronto, Ontario, Canada.

Stewart, A. J., Franz, C. E., & Layton, L. (1988). The changing self: Using personal documents to study lives. *Journal of Personality, 56,* 41–74.

Stolorow, R. D., & Atwood, G. E. (1979). *Faces in a cloud: Subjectivity in personality theory.* New York: Aronson.

Stone, W. F., & Schaffner, P. E. (1988). *The psychology of politics* (2nd ed.). New York: Springer-Verlag.

Stouffer, S. A. (1930). *An experimental comparison of statistical and case history methods of attitude research.* Unpublished doctoral dissertation, University of Chicago.

Suedfeld, P. (1994). President Clinton's policy dilemmas: A cognitive analysis. *Political Psychology, 15,* 337–349.

Susman, W. I. (1979). "Personality" and the making of twentieth-century culture. In J. Higham & P. K. Conklin (Eds.), *New directions in American intellectual history* (pp. 212–226). Baltimore: Johns Hopkins University Press.

Symonds, P. M. (1931). *Diagnosing personality and conduct.* New York: Century.

Taylor, E. (1996). *William James on consciousness beyond the margin.* Princeton, NJ: Princeton University Press.

Taylor, E. (2000). Psychotherapeutics and the problematic origins of clinical psychology in America. *American Psychologist, 55,* 1029–1033.

Terman, L. M. (1924). The mental test as a psychological method. *Psychological Review, 31,* 93–117.

Thomas, W. I., & Znaniecki, F. (1918–1920). *The Polish peasant in Europe and America* (Vols. 1–5). Chicago: University of Chicago Press.

Thorne, A., & Gough, H. G. (1991). *Portraits of type: An MBTI research compendium.* Palo Alto, CA: Consulting Psychologists Press.

Thornton, T. P. (1996). *Handwriting in America: A cultural history.* New Haven, CT: Yale University Press.

Thurstone, L. L. (1952). L. L. Thurstone. In E. G. Boring, H. S. Langfeld, H. Werner, & R. M. Yerkes (Eds.), *A history of psychology in autobiography* (Vol. 4, pp. 295–321). New York: Russell & Russell.

Triplet, R. G. (1983). *Henry A. Murray and the Harvard Psychological Clinic, 1926–1938: A struggle to expand the disciplinary boundaries of academic psychology.* Unpublished doctoral dissertation, University of New Hampshire, Durham.

Tweney, R. D., & Budzynski, C. A. (2000). The scientific status of American psychology in 1900. *American Psychologist, 55,* 1014–1017.

Vernon, P. E. (1933). The American v. the German methods of approach to the study of temperament and personality. *British Journal of Psychology, 24,* 156–177.

Warren, H. C. (Ed.). (1934). *Dictionary of psychology.* Boston: Houghton Mifflin.

Wells, H. G. (1934). *Experiment in autobiography: Discoveries and conclusions of a very ordinary brain (since 1866).* New York: Macmillan.

West, S. G. (Ed.). (1983). Personality and prediction: Nomothetic and idiographic approaches [Special issue]. *Journal of Personality, 51*(3).

White, R. W. (1952). *Lives in progress: A study of the natural growth of personality* (3rd ed.). New York: Dryden Press.

White, R. W. (Ed.). (1963). *The study of lives: Essays on personality in honor of Henry A. Murray.* New York: Atherton Press.

White, R. W. (1972). *The enterprise of living: Growth and organization in personality* (3rd ed.). New York: Holt, Rinehart, and Winston.

Winston, A. S. (1988). Cause and experiment in introductory psychology: An analysis of R. S. Woodworth's textbooks. *Teaching of Psychology, 15,* 79–83.

Winter, D. G. (1993). Gordon Allport and "Letters from Jenny." In K. H. Craik, R. Hogan, & R. N. Wolfe (Eds.), *Fifty years of personality psychology* (pp. 147–163). New York: Plenum Press.

Winter, D. G. (1996). *Personality: Analysis and interpretation of lives.* New York: McGraw-Hill.

Winter, D. G. (1998a). A motivational analysis of the Clinton first term and the 1996 presidential campaign. *Leadership Quarterly, 9,* 367–376.

Winter, D. G. (1998b). "Toward a science of personality psychology": David McClelland's development of empirically derived TAT measures. *History of Psychology, 1,* 130–153.

Winter, D. G. (2000). *Assessing leaders' personalities: Historical survey of academic research studies.* Unpublished paper, University of Michigan, Ann Arbor, Department of Psychology.

Winter, D. G., & Barenbaum, N. B. (1999). History of modern personality theory and research. In L. A. Pervin & O. P. John (Eds.), *Handbook of personality: Theory and research* (2nd ed., pp. 3–27). New York: Guilford Press.

Winter, D. G., & Carlson, L. (1988). Using motive scores in the psychobiographical study of an individual: The case of Richard Nixon. *Journal of Personality, 56,* 75–103.

Winter, D. G., Hermann, M. G., Weintraub, W., & Walker, S. G. (1991a). The personalities of Bush and Gorbachev measured at a distance: Follow-up on predictions. *Political Psychology, 12,* 457–464.

Winter, D. G., Hermann, M. G., Weintraub, W., & Walker, S. G. (1991b). The personalities of Bush and Gorbachev measured at a distance: Procedures, portraits, and policy. *Political Psychology, 12,* 215–245.

Woodworth, R. S. (1919). Examination of emotional fitness for warfare. *Psychological Bulletin, 15,* 59–60.

Woodworth, R. S. (1921). *Psychology: A study of mental life.* New York: Henry Holt.

Woodworth, R. S. (1929). *Psychology* (Rev. ed.). New York: Henry Holt.

Woodworth, R. S. (1932). Robert S. Woodworth. In C. Murchison (Ed.), *A history of psychology in autobiography* (Vol. 2, pp. 359–380). Worcester, MA: Clark University Press.

Yardley, J. (2001, October 10). A portrait of the terrorist: From shy child to single-minded killer. *New York Times,* p. B9.

York, K. L., & John, O. P. (1992). The four faces of Eve: A typological analysis of women's personality at midlife. *Journal of Personality and Social Psychology, 63,* 494–508.

Young, K. (1928). The measurement of personal and social traits. *Journal of Abnormal and Social Psychology, 22,* 431–442.

CHAPTER 10

Developmental Psychology

ROSS D. PARKE AND K. ALISON CLARKE-STEWART

THE BEGINNING YEARS (1880–1914)   206
   The Founders   206
   Characteristics of the Early Theories   207
A PERIOD OF INSTITUTIONALIZATION AND
   FRAGMENTATION (1915–1940)   208
   The Institutes of Child Development   208
   A Triad of Towering Theorists   208
   An Appraisal of the Era   209
THE ERA OF EXPANSION (1940–1960)   210
   Fusing Learning Theory and Psychoanalysis   210
   An Operant Orientation   210
   Reflections on the Era of Expansion   211
THE RISE OF CONTEMPORARY THEMES (1960–1985)   211
   The Return of Cognition   211
   The Discovery of Precocity   211

Redefining Social Learning Theory   211
From Social Interaction to
   Social Relationships   212
Embracing Emotion   212
Advances in Theory and Method   213
THE CURRENT PERIOD (1985–PRESENT)   213
   Return to the Biology of Development   213
   Deepening the Study of Cognitive Development   214
   Appreciation of the Role of Culture
   in Development   214
   Appraisal of the Current Era   215
A GLANCE INTO THE FUTURE   217
REFERENCES   217

The onset of the twenty-first century heralds a new era for developmental psychologists, whose work is being enriched by new findings from such fields as behavioral and molecular genetics, cognitive science, cultural studies, sociology, epidemiology, history, psychiatry, and pediatrics. At the same time, many of our current questions owe a clear debt to our forebears. These earlier theorists influenced thinking and research in ways that are still evident today, and a review of their contributions reminds us that many questions in our field are recurring ones. Issues that have disappeared and reappeared in slightly different guises at various stages of the field's history are still part of the contemporary scene. It's not that developmentalists simply recycle problems, but progress often proceeds to a point and comes to a halt until developments in other fields, new conceptualizations and formulations of a problem, or methodological and design advances reenergize the issue and bring it to a new level of understanding and investigation. By stimulating interest in the historical roots of our discipline, we hope both to sharpen our appreciation of our forebears and to develop a source of hypotheses that may now be ripe for investigation in the current scientific climate.

We can give only the broadest outline of the history of the field of developmental psychology. There are many complexities that we have had to ignore. We hope that this overview will whet the reader's appetite for further exploration. Fuller reviews of our historical roots are available in Parke, Ornstein, Rieser, and Zahn-Waxler (1994) and Cairns (1998), and a reprint series of original articles and volumes by earlier theorists is available in Wozniak (1993a, 1993b, 1994, 1995).

We have divided the history of developmental psychology into five time periods—the beginning years of developmental psychology (1880–1914), the period of institutionalization and fragmentation (1915–1940), the era of expansion (1940–1960), the rise of contemporary themes (1960–1985), and the current period (1985 to present). Across these periods, we discuss recurring issues of theory and method to illustrate the ways in which there has been both constancy and change in developmental psychologists' views of the central issues of the field. We argue that, in many regards, there have been major strides in the subtlety of the distinctions and the sophistication of the measurements and designs brought to bear on developmental questions. At the same time, there is much consistency between the perspectives of our ancestors of a century ago and the views of contemporary developmental theorists.

Another thesis is that the agenda of contemporary developmental psychology has more in common with the field's agenda from the turn of the century than with the agenda of the middle era (1920–1960). This middle period, with its emphasis on behaviorist and normative development, its focus on experimental child psychology and social learning theory, was a sharp departure from the origins of the field. What Cairns noted two decades ago is still true today: "An overview of the past suggests that today's investigators are as much determined by history as they are makers of it. The major issues of the present appear to be, in a large measure, the same ones that thoughtful contributors to the science have addressed in the past" (Cairns, 1983, p. 90).

Why are we returning to the concerns of our distant past? One reason is that our forebears were wise in their choice of questions and raised enduring issues. Another reason is that, in the middle period, developmentalists took some detours away from the original goals of the field in their enthusiasm for establishing a separate science on the basis of positivistic principles. The field's behavioristic focus promoted a proliferation of excellent methods and technological advances but ignored basic questions of biology, consciousness, and cognition. Today, as the beneficiaries of both the early and the middle eras, we are in a position to ask again the old questions and address them in more methodologically sophisticated ways.

THE BEGINNING YEARS (1880–1914)

The beginning years of the field of development can be characterized in two ways. One way is to describe the figures who first forged the field; the other way is to describe their positions in terms of modern theoretical distinctions.

The Founders

When the field of child psychology was established as a separate and distinctive field, two sets of influential individuals were involved. One group provided the institutional and organizational support for the new discipline of psychology; the second group provided ideas and methods for the new science of developmental psychology. G. Stanley Hall led the first group; James Mark Baldwin, Sigmund Freud, and Albert Binet formed the second.

The intellectual figure who anticipated the emergence of the distinctive field of developmental psychology and who influenced the thinking of all these early figures was not a psychologist, however, but the biologist, naturalist, and architect of evolutionary theory, Charles Darwin (1809–1882). Darwin provided the intellectual foundation for a science of development by arguing that human development was governed by a set of discoverable natural laws. This central thesis, in combination with Darwin's own early experimental studies of infants' emotional and perceptual abilities, paved the way for later scientific analysis of children's development.

G. Stanley Hall (1844–1924) was a cofounder and first president of the American Psychological Association and the founder of the first professional journal on development, *Pedagogical Seminary*. In 1909, Hall, as president of Clark University, invited Sigmund Freud to an international conference involving American and European psychologists and psychoanalysts. This was a landmark meeting; it introduced Freud and his psychoanalytic ideas to an American audience, and those ideas shaped the thinking of developmental scholars in the United States for the next half century. As a theorist and methodologist, Hall made more limited contributions (see Ross, 1972; White, 1992). He did introduce the questionnaire as a way to explore the contents of children's minds—in fact, between 1894 and 1914 he published 194 questionnaires (White, 1992)—but his nonrandom sampling strategies, his imprecise wording of questions, and his nonstandardized mode of administering the questionnaires made the work more suggestive than definitive. Hall and his contemporaries at the turn of the century had limited knowledge of sampling techniques and issues of generalizability, and they chose samples of convenience; unfortunately, these highly selected samples were of unknown representativeness. Hall is perhaps best known for his recognition that adolescence is a unique period of development with a variety of concomitant shifts in biology, cognition, and social relationships (Hall, 1904).

Hall's contemporary, James Mark Baldwin (1860–1934), was less of a facilitator but more of a theorist. He held positions at the University of Toronto, where he established the first experimental psychology laboratory in North America, and later at Princeton University and Johns Hopkins University. Although he was a talented experimentalist, it was his theoretical work that secured his position in the history of developmental psychology. In his extensive theoretical writings, he articulated a variety of themes, which in retrospect appear surprisingly contemporary (Baldwin, 1894, 1895, 1897). First, he developed a stage theory of development, which was remarkably similar to Piaget's. As Piaget would later do, Baldwin set out a series of stages of development for mental processes, which were to a substantial extent based on observations of his own children. Even more than Piaget, he recognized the interplay between social and cognitive development and championed the study of the self and the need to examine different units of analysis (individual, dyad, and group). Unfortunately, Baldwin's contribution was limited because of the short duration of his career, which ended abruptly as the result of a personal scandal. In 1908, he was forced to resign from Johns Hopkins after being caught in a raid on a house of prostitution. He spent the rest of his career in Mexico and Europe, where he continued to write about development as well as world peace. A second reason for his limited influence was his failure to develop empirical paradigms to test his ideas. As is always the case in science, theory without a clear way of evaluating the underlying notion is of limited value to the field. In spite of his lack of data, his ideas are remarkably modern. It is now recognized that "Baldwin stands alongside William James as one of the primary intellectual forces involved in the founding of American psychology as a science" (Cairns, 1994, p. 129).

At the time, however, it was Sigmund Freud (1856–1939) who influenced American developmental psychology. Freud offered both a theory of development based on psychosexual stages and a method of study, psychoanalysis (Freud, 1900, 1905, 1910). Freud taught at the University of Vienna but devoted himself largely to clinical work with neurotic patients and to a prolific writing career. In spite of the fact that he did not treat children, he developed a theory of early development based on the recollections of childhood by his adult clients. In many ways, Freud set the agenda for the next 50 years of developmental psychology by defining content domains (aggression, sex roles, morality) and articulating central themes (the importance of early experience, the formative impact of early family relationships for later developmental outcomes).

Alfred Binet (1857–1911) was the most underappreciated figure of this era (Siegler, 1992). Despite his lack of formal training in psychology, Binet was a prolific contributor with over 200 books, articles, and reviews on a wide range of psychological subjects to his credit. Binet is, of course, best known for his contributions to the assessment of intelligence (Binet & Simon, 1905), but he was much more than the father of IQ testing. He anticipated a number of Piaget's views, for example, that cognitive development is a constructive process, that its purpose is adaptation to the physical and social worlds, that children assimilate new experiences to existing ways of thinking, and that intelligence pervades all activities. Moreover, he made major contributions to various areas of memory, particularly suggestibility and eyewitness testimony, children's memory for prose, and the role of memory in mental calculation expertise (Binet, 1894, 1900). Binet designed and conducted a variety of memory experiments. At the same time, he recognized the need to apply convergent methodological approaches to solve psychological problems. "Our psychology is not yet so advanced that we can limit our analyses to information attained in the laboratory" (Binet, quoted in Cairns, 1983). It is interesting

that Binet's demonstrations of the feasibility of an experimentally based science of child development predated Watson's more famous experiments on conditioning of emotion by nearly 20 years. "Binet was the first to provide convincing evidence for the proposition that a science of human development was possible" (Cairns, 1983, p. 51). For a variety of reasons—primarily, perhaps, his lack of a university position—Binet's contributions were largely forgotten until recently (Cairns, 1983; Siegler, 1992).

Characteristics of the Early Theories

Theories of development may be characterized, most centrally, by whether they posit that development is the consequence of internal (nature) or external (nurture) forces. Overton and Reese (1973) describe this dichotomy as *organismic* versus *mechanistic*. The organismic view is characterized by a focus on biological or endogenous accounts of development. It has as its basic metaphor "the organism, the living, organized system presented to experience in multiple forms. . . . In this representation, the whole is organic rather than mechanical in nature" (Reese & Overton, 1970, pp. 132–133). The mechanistic view is characterized by a focus on environmental mechanisms, and development is seen as essentially an externally controlled or driven process. The machine is often used as the metaphor for this developmental model of development. In the early era, Baldwin, Freud, Hall, and Binet all endorsed an organismic approach. As Cairns noted of Baldwin: "His aim was to outline 'a system of genetic psychology' that would attempt to achieve a synthesis of the current biological theory of organic adaptation with the doctrine of the infant's development" (Baldwin, 1895, p. vii, cited by Cairns, 1983, p. 54).

Another way in which theories of development can be described is in terms of their breadth. The scope of the early theories was notably broad. Not only did they include emotions and cognitions, sex and sensation, but a century ago, theorists in the grand tradition assumed that large portions of the developmental landscape could be accounted for in terms of a limited number of general, universal principles. They were not unaware of cross-cultural variation, but they viewed other cultures as living laboratories that could provide opportunities to evaluate the operation of fundamental laws of development. Freud's use of anthropological data in *Totem & Taboo* (Freud, 1918) was an attempt to describe unconscious motivation in other cultures. This was a prime example of our ancestors' eagerness to seek confirmation of their theories in other cultures. Their understanding of those cultures, however, was quite limited.

Limited, too, was their understanding of their own culture. Contemporary developmental psychologists recognize that societal conditions in a variety of spheres—medical, education, economic, political, and social—influence both development itself and research and theory about development. They have seen how historical conditions can shape choices of problems and theoretical interpretations. The most celebrated example, of course, is the influence of Victorian Vienna on psychoanalysis (Lerner, 1986). The repressive views concerning sex and sexuality held by European society in the early 1900s quite clearly contributed to the symptoms exhibited by Freud's patients and the focus on sexual feelings and processes in Freud's theory. However, Freud himself and the other early theorists showed little awareness of the need to acknowledge the role of societal and historical influences in their theories of development.

As an emerging discipline, not surprisingly, developmental psychology was also an interdisciplinary enterprise. The early theorists looked to philosophy, biology, pedagogy, and sociology for ideas. Hall was particularly influenced by philosophy, religion, education, and evolutionary biology. Baldwin reached out to religion. Freud incorporated anthropology. At the same time, there was a strong push to disassociate the emerging field from its roots—especially its philosophical roots—and to establish the new field as a separate discipline, especially a scientific one. Baldwin's theories as well as Binet's experimental demonstrations represented clear departures from the introspectionist approach of the past.

In brief, by 1914, American psychology had become established as an independent discipline, developmental psychology as a separate science was beginning to emerge, and the major themes of development that occupied us for the next century were being defined. In the next phase, the institutionalization of developmental psychology as a distinctive subfield within mainstream psychology began.

A PERIOD OF INSTITUTIONALIZATION AND FRAGMENTATION (1915–1940)

Two major themes characterize the next period in the history of developmental psychology. First, this was a period of establishment of major research institutes. Second, it was an era both of extraordinary theoretical and empirical advances in developmental psychology and of multiple voices and raucous cacophony.

The Institutes of Child Development

Reflecting societal concerns about ways to improve the rearing of children, a number of research institutes were established around the United States, including those at the University of Iowa, the University of Minnesota, Teachers College at Columbia, Yale, and the University of California, Berkeley. The goals of these new institutes were research, teaching, and dissemination. The programs were modeled after the successful agricultural research stations. As Mrs. Cora Bussey Hillis, an early supporter of these activities, envisioned, "if research could improve corn and hogs, it could improve children" (Sears, 1975, p. 19).

The institutes not only created a professional workforce of child developmentalists but also initiated some of the major longitudinal projects of the century. Some of these projects were highly specialized; others were more general. At Yale, Arnold Gesell (1880–1961) began his intensive studies of children's motor development, while John Anderson at Minnesota provided detailed descriptions of personality development (Anderson, 1937). At Berkeley, two sets of longitudinal studies began in the late 1920s and early 1930s focusing on a variety of aspects of development—intellectual, social, and motor (see Bayley, 1949; Elder, 1974). Sontag (1944), at the Fels Research Institute, also started a longitudinal study in the 1930s that lasted until the 1970s. The Fels project also used a broadband approach involving assessments of social, emotional, motoric, and physical development. These studies were largely atheoretical and descriptive; they provided important normative guidelines concerning early developmental timetables.

A Triad of Towering Theorists

But theory in developmental psychology was not dead. On the contrary, this was an era of fragmentation, and markedly different theoretical approaches to the study of development were all competing for support. In the United States, behaviorism under the leadership of John B. Watson (1878–1958) was a force to be reckoned with, with its strict views that children's development was the consequence of conditioning by the environment. According to Watson, children learn everything, from skills to fears. All behavior begins as a simple reflex and is conditioned over time. Fears are most easily conditioned through pairing with loud noise; love is created by fondling; even verbal behavior and thinking begin as babbling, then grow in complexity as they are conditioned to objects in the environment. Watson's (1913, 1924) experimental demonstrations of conditioning, most famously of little Albert, did much to place the newly emerging field of child development on a solid scientific footing.

Meanwhile, other viewpoints were emerging as significant challenges to a behavioral view of development. Most directly in opposition to Watson's position was Gesell's maturational approach to development, which suggested that development unfolds in a series of steps, fixed and predetermined in order. Only under extreme conditions, such as famine, war, or poverty, are children thrown off this biologically programmed timetable. According to Gesell, the tendency to grow is the strongest force in life, and the inevitableness and surety of maturation are the most impressive characteristics of early development. "The inborn tendency toward optimum development is so inveterate that [the child] benefits liberally from what is good in our practice, and suffers less than he logically should from our unenlightenment" (Gesell, 1928, p. 360). Gesell's years of careful observation produced a corpus of work that was not only a highly sophisticated account of motor development but an early version of a dynamic systems view of development (Thelen, 1993).

At the same time, Jean Piaget (1896–1980) was emerging as an influential theorist in Europe and offered a further contrast with prevailing American views. Piaget offered not only a rich description of children's cognitive progress from infancy to adolescence but the first fully developed theory of stages of cognitive development. In a series of books, Piaget outlined four major stages of cognitive development, the stages of sensorimotor development (0 to 2 years), preoperational development (2 to 6 years), concrete operations (6 to 12 years), and formal operations. Children were observed to pass through these stages in a fixed and sequential order as they moved toward increasingly abstract modes of thought. His theory and empirical demonstrations over the span of more than half a century place him with Freud in the forefront of child development theorists of the twentieth century. Although there have been challenges to his originality with credible claims that much of his theory was anticipated by Baldwin (Cahan, 1984), his uncanny ability to design tasks to test his theoretical propositions secured his scientific reputation.

An Appraisal of the Era

The marked differences among the three theorists in this period, Watson, Gesell, and Piaget, are brought into perspective by noting their positions on key developmental questions. Their basic positions concerning what causes development were in stark contrast. Watson was the archetypical mechanistic theorist who believed that development occurred from the outside in. He believed that the goal of theory was not to understand behavior but to predict and control it. He viewed learning and conditioning principles as the processes through which these ends were met. In contrast, Gesell was a theorist who was organismic in his viewpoint on the causes of development, championing maturational processes as the key to

development. His goal was to provide a systematic account of development, not necessarily to control or predict the direction of development. Piaget balanced the importance of both internal, biological processes of development and external resources to support it. He posited biological adaptational processes as the explanatory mechanism for development, and his theoretical aim was understanding, not prediction or control. Although these three theorists diverged in their assessment of the nature of developmental processes, they did agree that there are universal and historically independent processes that account for development.

The three theorists also differed in their assumptions about the course of development. Piaget was clearly a committed stage theorist who endorsed the concept of discontinuity across development. Watson, on the other hand, viewed development as continuous. Gesell recognized both continuity and discontinuity across development. For Gesell, there are periods of reorganization at different points across development but considerable continuity in terms of underlying processes. Siegler and Crowley's (1992) microgenetic approach might well have been championed by Gesell, with its recognition that there is an uneven progression across development as new skills and strategies are acquired and integrated in the child's repertoire.

The big-three theorists of this era also took somewhat different approaches to conducting research. Watson performed laboratory "experiments," which actually, because of their lack of control, are more accurately referred to as demonstrations. Gesell and Piaget, in contrast, raised systematic observation to a new level. Piaget watched, with much profit, his own infants (Piaget, 1926), while Gesell made a career of cataloging motor movements of other people's children (Gesell, 1928). Both incorporated subtle structured interventions into their observations—a pile of three red blocks, a matchbox, a screen—to probe with infinite patience the minute changes in abilities evident over the course of a week or a month in a child's life.

A final way in which the triad of theorists differed was in their view of how—or whether—the principles of developmental psychology should be applied to "real world" issues. Piaget was basically uninterested in applied issues—in spite of an abundance of efforts by others to apply his theory to education settings in the 1960s and 1970s. He called these concerns "the American question." In contrast, Watson was a strong proponent of applying learning principles to the rearing of children. Through a series of popular books addressed to parents, Watson tried to shape the thinking of a generation of parents. "Parents, whether they know it or not," he stated with authority, "start intensive training of their children at birth. By 3 years of age, the child's whole emotional life plan has been laid down. His parents have determined whether he is to grow into a happy person, a whining, complaining neurotic, an overbearing slave driver, or one whose every move in life is controlled by fear." What was most damaging, according to Watson, was too much "mother love." Watson's advice on how to run an efficient, no-nonsense household, in which infants were fed and napped on schedule like efficient little machines, and no time was lost nor bad habits created by hugging and kissing, had a widespread influence on American parents. In spite of his maturationalist leanings, Gesell, too, was a prolific and influential voice in the "advice to parents" movement. Over a period of 40 years, Gesell and his colleagues (Gesell & Ilg, 1946; Gesell, Ilg, & Ames, 1956) offered not only normative guidelines to help parents anticipate the developmental trajectories of their children but also specific advice concerning child-rearing tactics, toys, and tomes for children of different ages (see Clarke-Stewart, 1978, 1998). The outreach efforts of both Watson and Gesell were consistent with the tenor of the time and the American belief that the new developmental science could and should be harnessed to improve the lives of children.

To summarize, this period of our history was best characterized as a battle among theoretical titans. A science of development had clearly been launched, but there was little agreement about the theoretical details.

THE ERA OF EXPANSION (1940–1960)

In the third period of our history, developmental psychology returned to the fold of mainstream psychological thinking, as it had been at the turn of the century. Major strides were achieved by extending the basic tenets of learning theory to the puzzles of development.

Fusing Learning Theory and Psychoanalysis

Classic learning theory, which dominated American psychology from the 1930s through the 1950s, was creatively combined with Freud's theory of development to generate a new era of research and theorizing in child psychology. At Yale, several young psychologists, including John Dollard, Neal Miller, Leonard Doob, Robert Sears, and later anthropologist John Whiting, combined forces to fuse Hullian learning concepts with Freudian psychoanalytic theory (e.g., Dollard, Doob, Miller, Mowrer, & Sears, 1939). Their goal was to translate Freud's propositions into testable form by recasting them in learning-theory terms. Freud had provided the focus of the research on such issues as aggression, sex typing,

and dependency; Hull provided the learning mechanisms, such as primary and secondary drives, drive reduction, and stimulus-response associations. In one example of the learning-psychoanalytic fusion, the Yale psychologists proposed that infants' early attachment to their mother derived from the association of the mother with reduction of the hunger drive through feeding. Mothers, in short, assumed secondary reinforcement value as a result of being paired with hunger reduction for the infant. Decades of effort followed, in which these researchers sought to evaluate the relations between early child-rearing practices and later personality development. Such Freudian-based concerns as the timing of weaning and toilet training and whether the infant was bottle- or breast-fed dominated the scientific activity (Sears, 1944, 1975).

The major paradigm for this era is illustrated by the classic study of child rearing organized by Robert Sears and his colleagues Eleanor Maccoby and Harry Levin (Sears, Maccoby, & Levin, 1957). These investigators interviewed over 300 mothers about their child-rearing practices (weaning, toilet training, discipline) and the child's behavior (aggression, dependency, sex roles, moral development). Modest relations between child-rearing practices and child outcomes were found in this and related studies (Sears, Rau, & Alpert, 1966; Sears, Whiting, Nowlis, & Sears, 1953; Whiting & Child, 1953), but the enterprise as a theoretical guide was largely unsupported. Not only were the fundamental hypotheses probably incorrect, but the methods themselves came under serious criticism (M. R. Yarrow, Campbell, & Burton, 1964). Critics noted not only that constructs were poorly defined but also that the basic method of using mothers' recall of their earlier practices was fraught with error. As Robbins (1963) showed, mothers often report child-rearing practices that are more in agreement with current "experts" than they are with their actual practices. Although the enterprise served to bring theoretical rigor to the study of development and move us beyond description to learning-based explanations of development, the theoretical limitations of the Freudian framework were bound to doom their efforts.

An Operant Orientation

Another extension of learning theory that emerged during this era was operant learning theory. This approach was developed by B. F. Skinner (1904–1990) at Harvard University. In contrast to Hullian theory, with its drive-centered focus, Skinner's theory emphasized contingent reinforcement of behavior as the central learning mechanism. Although Skinner was not a developmental theorist, his thinking had a profound impact on developmental psychology. Such influential developmental researchers as Bijou, Baer, and Gewirtz were all influenced by Skinner (Bijou & Baer, 1961; Gewirtz, 1969). The modern behavior modification approach to the control and shaping of children's behavior in classrooms, homes, and institutional settings owes a direct debt to Skinner and his theory of operant learning.

Reflections on the Era of Expansion

Under the guidance of the learning titans of this era, developmentalists once again became a part of mainstream psychology. A mechanistic orientation characterized the theorizing of the period, whether under the guidance of Hullian-influenced Sears or of operant-oriented Skinner. Theorists searched for broad, universal principles of development, with little concern for either culture or secular influences, although Sears did document social-class differences in child-rearing practices in one of his studies (Sears et al., 1957). Neither Sears nor Skinner was a prominent provider of descriptions or prescriptions for parents in the tradition of Watson and Gesell, but they both had an abiding American faith in the potential of developmental science to help children. Skinner's invention of the baby box and teaching machine and Sears's hope that his studies of child rearing would provide scientific guidelines for future parents illustrate their commitment to an applied developmental psychology.

In sum, during this era, developmental psychology became recognized as part of mainstream psychology, but it had not yet reached a mature state. In the case of Sears, there was still too much borrowing from the past, and in the case of Skinner, there was not enough recognition of the uniqueness of children that might require distinctive and separate approaches.

THE RISE OF CONTEMPORARY THEMES (1960–1985)

In the era from 1960 to 1985, a number of themes rather than a number of theorists guided research and theory in developmental psychology. These themes were the return of a concern about cognition, the discovery of precocity, the redefining of social learning, the refinement of the study of social interaction, and the emergence of an interest in emotion.

The Return of Cognition

Several significant events transformed our thinking about development in this quarter century. The Russians launched Sputnik, and Americans began to worry about their educational system. Coincidentally, there was a rediscovery of

Piaget by American psychologists. J. McVicker Hunt (1906–1991) published his influential treatise, *Intelligence and Experience* (1961), which reintroduced Piagetian thinking to Americans. A few years later, a systematic overview of Piaget's theory was offered by John Flavell in his book *The Developmental Psychology of Jean Piaget* (1963). Piaget's views of nature and nurture as both necessary and interactive quickly became prevalent in developmental psychology. A flurry of empirical work that both supported and challenged Piagetian theory appeared in the 1960s and 1970s. This revitalized interest in cognitive development coincided with the onset of the cognitive revolution (Miller, Galanter, & Pribram, 1960) in mainstream psychology, so it is not surprising that cognitive development returned as a major theme of research.

The Discovery of Precocity

In part the result of Piaget's early work on infant cognitive and perceptual development and in part the consequence of new experimental techniques for assessing infant visual, auditory, and olfactory capacities (e.g., Fantz, 1963; Lipsitt, 1963), there was a resurgence of interest in documenting infant sensory and perceptual competence. Studies of infants challenged traditional views and ushered in an era of discovering the "competent infant." In contrast to earlier views of infants as limited, helpless, and incompetent, these new studies revealed an infant who was biologically prepared for social, perceptual, and cognitive encounters with the external environment. Babies were revealed to be capable of visual and auditory discriminations (e.g., color, form, pitch) from a much younger age than earlier theorists had assumed. In turn, this prepared the way for a closer look at biological contributions to early development. A similar set of advances concerning the remarkable capacity of infants to learn was also reported (Lipsitt, 1963; Papousek, 1961; Sameroff, 1970).

Redefining Social Learning Theory

On the socialization front, there was a serious challenge to the Freud-Hull approach to social development. Albert Bandura and Richard Walters, in their 1963 volume *Social Learning and Personality Development,* forcefully rejected the assumptions of the previous era. Instead of endorsing a drive-based theory of development, they proposed that observational learning or modeling was the major way that children acquire new behaviors and modify old ones. As subsequently developed by Bandura (1969, 1977), cognitive social learning theory drew much of its theoretical foundation from developments in the new cognitive science, with its insights into attention and memory. Not only were drives and drive reduction unnecessary for learning, according to Bandura, but reinforcement was unnecessary either for the acquisition of new responses or the modification of old responses. Along with new mechanisms for learning, Bandura dismissed the Freudian baggage of the earlier Sears era. Instead, a more eclectic theory of socialization, which drew from sociology, anthropology, and other disciplines, served as a guide. In a series of influential experimental studies, Bandura and his colleagues revitalized the study of social development by reintroducing experimental approaches in studies of the observational learning of aggression (e.g., Bandura, Ross, & Ross, 1961). Unfortunately, like most learning theory approaches, the focus was more on learning and less on development (see Grusec, 1992).

From Social Interaction to Social Relationships

An area of intense focus in this period was the social interactive processes and the ways in which these face-to-face processes develop into social relationships (Hartup & Rubin, 1986; Hinde, 1979). A prominent issue was the understanding of social interaction patterns among infants, children, and their social partners. Emphasis on the mutual regulation of the partners' behavior, concern about detailed description, and quantification of the tempo and flow of the interactive interchange clearly separated the current work from its earlier antecedents (Cohn & Tronick, 1987; Field, 1991). In addition, developmental psychologists in this era went beyond studying the process of interaction per se to use interaction as a window into social relationships (Hinde, 1979).

The most influential theory exemplifying this theme was John Bowlby's (1907–1990) theory of attachment (1969, 1973, 1980). This theory offered a new account of the ways in which infants come to form close relations with their caregivers. Instead of a fusion between the constructs of Hull and Freud, it represented a marriage between ethology and psychoanalysis. Bowlby proposed that attachment has its roots in a set of instinctual infant responses that are important for the protection and survival of the species. The infant responses of crying, smiling, sucking, clinging, and following elicit the parental care and protection that the baby needs and promote contact between the child and the parents. Just as the infant is biologically prepared to respond to the sights, sounds, and nurturance provided by caregivers, parents are biologically prepared to respond to these eliciting behaviors on the part of the infant. As a result of these biologically programmed

responses, both parent and infant develop a mutual attachment. From this perspective, attachment is a relationship, not simply a set of behaviors of either the parent or the infant (Sroufe & Fleeson, 1986).

Moreover, in this era, there was an increasing appreciation of the range of characters who play a prominent role in children's social relationships. The definition of family expanded to include not only the mother–infant dyad but fathers, siblings, and grandparents as well (Dunn & Kendrick, 1982; Lamb, 1975; Tinsley & Parke, 1984).

There was also a growing appreciation of the embeddedness of children and families in a variety of social systems outside the family, including peers, school, and kin-based networks (Bronfenbrenner, 1986, 1989; Cochran & Brassard, 1979), which led to an interest in peer and other relationships outside the family (Asher & Gottman, 1981). This focus on relationships was part of a more general reorientation away from a focus on the individual as the unit of analysis to dyadic and larger units of analysis.

Embracing Emotion

One of the most dramatic shifts during this period was the renewed interest in the development of emotions in infancy. Topics such as social smiling, stranger anxiety, and fear of heights were of interest in the 1960s (Gibson & Walk, 1960), but the motivation for conducting such studies was to use emotions to index something else—usually perceptual or cognitive process (Campos & Barrett, 1985). The timing of the development of emotions and the role of emotions in social interaction were of little interest at that time. In the 1970s and 1980s, however, the role of affect became an issue of increasing concern throughout psychology (e.g., Campos, Barrett, Lamb, Goldsmith, & Stenberg, 1983). The developmental origins of both the production and recognition of emotions, as well as the role of emotional expressions in the regulation of social interaction, became central concerns of developmental psychologists, especially infancy researchers.

In light of research by Ekman (Ekman & Friesen, 1978) and Izard (1982), the older assumption that facial response patterns are not specific to discrete emotional states was discounted. Evidence suggested that facial expressions may be, at least in part, governed by genetically encoded programs and universally recognized (Ekman & Friesen, 1978). The recognition that emotional expressions have a role in the regulation of social behavior, another important development in this era, was exemplified in studies of face-to-face interaction of parents and infants (e.g., Brazelton, Koslowski, & Main, 1974; Stern, 1977, 1985; Tronick, 1989).

Advances in Theory and Method

In this period, from 1960 to 1985, we see signs of maturity in the field of developmental psychology. Instead of theories suggesting that development is either exclusively internally driven or entirely environmental in origin, the theories in this period included elements of both. In addition, under the guidance of Bronfenbrenner (1979), a commitment to contextualism was evident. Lerner (1986), a major proponent of this viewpoint, defines this position as follows: A contextual model assumes that there is constant change at all levels of analysis and that each level is embedded within all others. Thus, changes in one promote changes in all. Central to the position is the interaction between the organism and its context (Sameroff, 1975). Ethology, ecological systems theory, and socio-cultural theory are examples of the contextual model.

Explanatory processes, too, were multifaceted in this period and included cognitive, social interactional, and affective processes. The grand claims of earlier eras were less evident, and more limited theories, which explained smaller bands of behavior rather than the full array of development achievements, began to emerge. A glimmer of recognition that theories may not be universally applicable appeared in this period, and interest in cross-cultural work intensified (Greenfield, 1974; Harkness & Super, 1983). The role of historical and secular changes, such as the Great Depression, as influences on development were recognized for the first time (Elder, 1974). There was a return to an interest in applying basic knowledge to practical problems of child rearing and education unseen since the days of Gesell and Watson (e.g., research on the effects of early preschool experience on children's development by Ramey & Haskins, 1981). There was a shift toward a lifespan view of development, and, consistent with this shift, a reevaluation of the role of critical periods in development. Although considerable evidence to support the critical period hypothesis as it related to infant social development was collected (e.g., Harlow & Harlow, 1962; Sackett, 1968; L. J. Yarrow, 1961), it also became apparent in this period that simple yes-or-no questions about whether early experience played a role in particular domains were inadequate to guide our thinking. Rather, it was important to understand the processes through which experiences exerted their influence on structure and function and when they exerted that influence.

THE CURRENT PERIOD (1985–PRESENT)

In the current period, several themes characterize research and theory in developmental psychology. These include the rise of interest in the genetic and neurological underpinnings of behavior, interest in the interdependency of cognition and emotion, recognition of the role of culture, and a move toward a mature interdisciplinary developmental science.

Return to the Biology of Development

Of considerable importance in the current period is the lively interest of developmental psychologists in biology. This interest has been expressed in many ways. One way is the investigation of psychophysiological responses associated with different emotions and different social situations, such as separation of a child from the mother or the entrance of a stranger into the room (Field, 1987). These studies provide additional evidence in support of the specificity-of-emotion hypothesis (i.e., that different emotions may have different elicitors and distinct psychophysiological patterns; Campos et al., 1983).

A second way the current interest in the biological bases of behavior is expressed is through the study of genetics. This return to biology resulted, in part, from advances in the field of behavior genetics, which produced a more sophisticated understanding of the potential role that genetics can play not only in the onset of certain behaviors but in the unfolding of behavior across development (Plomin, DeFries, & McLearn, 1990). This work has generally taken the form of determining the possible genetic origins of certain traits, such as extroversion and introversion, and other aspects of temperament, as well as the age of onset of emotional markers such as smiling and fear of strangers. For example, Plomin and DeFries (1985) found that identical twins exhibit greater concordance than fraternal twins in the time of onset and amount of social smiling. Similarly, identical twins are more similar than fraternal twins in social responsiveness (Plomin, 1986). At the same time, behavior genetic researchers are documenting the clear and necessary role of the environment in this process. Plomin's (1994) reformulation of genetic questions has led to a call for studies of nonshared-environment effects and represents a good example of how behavior genetics has stimulated new designs for the assessment of both genetic and environmental influences. Rather than returning to an old-fashioned nature-nurture debate, the new behavior genetics is spurring the development of better measures of the environment that will enable us to assess the interactions of nature and nurture in more meaningful ways. Clearly, environmental influences matter; they simply need to be measured better. One of the ironies of recent years is that some of the most compelling evidence that environmental effects are important comes from behavior genetics. At the same time, advances in the measurement and conceptualization of *specific* environmental influences has come largely from the work of socialization scholars interested in parental disciplinary styles and socialization techniques and who generally used between-family than within-family designs (Baumrind, 1973; Radke-Yarrow & Zahn-Waxler, 1984). In fact, the reorientation of research to a nonshared emphasis remains controversial, and there is considerable debate about the implications and interpretation of nonshared effects (Baumrind, 1993; Hoffman, 1991; Scarr, 1993). Recently there has been a rise of interest in the role of molecular genetics in developmental research (Plomin & Rutter, 1998; Reiss, Neiderhiser, Hetherington, & Plomin, 2000) with the goal of identifying how specific genes or clusters of genes are linked with developmental outcomes.

Other ways that developmentalists in the current period focus on the biological bases of behavior is studying hormones and behavior during infancy and adolescence (Gunnar, 1987) and looking for the biological bases for temperament in infancy (Rothbart & Bates, 1998). They also study biological constraints on behavior development; for example, developmental implications of immature sensory systems have been related to the social world of infants (e.g., Aslin, 1998), the implication of immature limb systems have been related to locomotion (Thelen & Ulrich, 1991), and the implications of the immature cortex have been related to infant search behavior (Diamond, 1990, 1991). As these last studies indicate, recent advances in cognitive neuroscience have also begun to influence developmental psychology (Diamond, 1990; Greenough, Black, & Wallace, 1987), and this is another sign of developmental psychologists' return to biology. Finally, the resurgence of interest in the types of evolutionary approaches to the study of human development represents a return to Darwin's early efforts to apply evolutionary principles to human development (Bjorklund & Pellegrini, 2000; Hinde, 1991). Although controversial (Hinde, 1991), this theorizing clearly illustrates one of the myriad ways in which psychologists are returning to questions that were raised by our forebears.

Deepening the Study of Cognitive Development

As part of the current vigorous study of cognitive development, researchers have returned to issues of consciousness, reflection, intention, motivation, and will (Flavell, 1999). There has been a reemergence of interest in the interplay between conscious and unconscious processes, an indication of a willingness to tackle problems that preoccupied our field's founders but were set aside for nearly a century. Several investigators (Greenwald, 1992; Kihlstrom, Barnhardt, & Tataryn, 1992) have developed methods that

permit examination of the impact of unconscious processes on a variety of cognitive and perceptual processes and allow methodologically defensible excursions into such classic clinical issues as repression and self-deception. These methods could be adapted usefully for developmental studies and would provide interesting approaches to a range of current issues, from eyewitness testimony to early affective memories. In turn, such applications would have important implications for an understanding of effects of early experience and attachment.

There is also a strong interest in the interplay between cognition and emotion, as reflected in the activity surrounding children's understanding of emotion (Harris, 1989; Saarni, 1999). Most recently, the range of emotions under investigation has expanded to include self-conscious emotions such as shame, guilt, pride, empathy, and envy, topics that were anticipated by Freud and others but were of little interest for many years (Denham, 1998; Eisenberg, 1991; Lewis, 1992).

Appreciation of the Role of Culture in Development

One of the major shifts in our thinking about development in the current era is our recognition of the central role played by culture. Since the 1980s, more attention has been given to contributions of culture to our theoretical explanations of development (e.g., Gauvain, 2001; Rogoff, 1990). One example is the cross-cultural studies of infant–parent attachment, in which wide disparities were found in the distribution of infants in terms of their attachment classifications. Although the measures show securely attached infant–mother relations in 57% of American samples, the rate drops to 33% in samples tested in northern Germany (Grossman, Grossman, Spangler, Suess, & Unzner, 1985). These and other findings underscore the need to consider cultural influences in our developmental theories.

Similarly, there have been advances, albeit limited, in our understanding of intracultural and socioeconomic differences in the United States (Parke & Buriel, 1998). Although African American children have received the most attention, other groups, including Latino and Asian American children, are beginning to be more commonly included in developmental investigations (McLoyd, Cauce, Takeuchi, & Wilson, 2000; Steinberg, Dornbusch, & Brown, 1992). These variations across ethnic lines represent important opportunities to explore the universality of psychological processes and to provide naturally occurring variations in the relative salience of key determinants of social, emotional, and cognitive development. These studies may provide a better basis for guiding policies, programs, and culturally sensitive interventions on behalf of children. As our culture becomes increasingly diverse, it is important that we begin to make a serious commitment to an exploration of this diversity, both theoretically and through systematic empirical inquiry. The search for a balance between processes that are universal and those that are particular to racial, and ethnic, and socioeconomic groups probably represents one of the greatest challenges of the new century.

Appraisal of the Current Era

The current era represents significant continuity with the prior period and can best be characterized as eclectic in terms of theoretical models, developmental assumptions, and methodological approaches. As is characteristic of a more mature science, methods and models are not perceived as dogmatic dicta but instead are flexible guides to help formulate and answer new questions and address new issues as they arise.

The retreat from grand theory that began in the 1980s has continued, and in its place, a variety of minitheories aimed at limited and specific aspects of development has emerged. However, there is evidence of an attempt to link together these minitheories. The idea of general processes as explanations of development has been given up because we have learned that they are not so general; instead, it is increasingly evident that processes depend on the specifics of the situation, the task, and the subjects' understanding of the task or situation (Flavell, 1985, 1999; Siegler, 1991). It is now recognized that the domains of childhood—social, emotional, physical, and cognitive—are interdependent and that they overlap and influence each other mutually.

Attention to secular trends and historical contexts has accelerated as the social contexts of children's lives come under increased scrutiny (Elder, Modell, & Parke, 1994). Shifts in medical practices, employment patterns, and child-care arrangements are all issues of lively debate and vigorous research activity (Clarke-Stewart, 1992a, 1992b; Conger & Elder, 1994). Moreover, researchers are giving serious consideration to the role that shifts in technology (e.g., computers) have on children's development; part of the puzzle is to determine whether secular trends produce changes in the timing of onset of developmental phenomena or whether developmental processes themselves are significantly altered. Current thinking suggests that certain behavioral characteristics are relatively independent of historical variations, while others are more susceptible to these influences (Horowitz, 1987).

Collaboration between disciplines is increasingly common as the multidetermined nature of development is increasingly appreciated. Not only are sociologists, anthropologists, and historians part of new developmental research teams, but so are neurologists, geneticists, lawyers, and epidemiologists. It is likely that the interesting issues and questions of the new century will arise at the boundaries between disciplines. The dichotomy between applied and basic research is fading rapidly, and child developmentalists are returning in increasingly large numbers to their applied roots. For example, research on mental-health issues among children is prominent, and work on how to improve children's early development through intervention programs continues to flourish (Coie & Jacobs, 1993).

In terms of developmental assumptions, developmentalists have become less interested in strong forms of discontinuity organized around stage constructs. Rather, there is growing recognition that the course of development may vary markedly even for presumably related concepts. But there is also recognition that the entire issues of qualitative or quantitative change may depend on one's point of observation. As Siegler indicated, "When viewed from afar, many changes in children's thinking appear discontinuous; when viewed from close-up, the same changes often appear as part of a continuous, gradual progression" (1991, p. 50).

Researchers in the 1980s and 1990s have taken seriously a life-span developmental perspective (Baltes, 1987). In part, this view emerges from a recognition that the social context provided by caregivers varies as a function of the location of the adults along their own life-course trajectory (Parke, 1988). The earlier view was that variations in parenting behavior were relatively independent of adult development. Evidence of this shift comes from a variety of sources, including studies of the impact of the timing of parenthood and the effects of maternal (and paternal) employment, job satisfaction, and work involvement on children's development (Parke & Buriel, 1998). In addition, there is a serious return to the study of aging (Baltes, 1987; Salthouse, 1985), especially the study of speed of processing, memory, and intelligence (e.g., Hertzog, 1989) and social behavior (e.g., Brubaker, 1990; Hanson & Carpenter, 1994).

Consistent with the shift toward a life-span view is the reevaluation of the role of critical periods in development. Recent evidence suggests that a modified version of sensitive, if not critical, periods is likely to emerge in contrast to a view of unlimited plasticity across development (Bornstein, 1989). For example, Rieser, Hill, Talor, Bradfield, and Rosen (1992) have demonstrated that adult skill in spatial representation seems to require early perceptual learning experiences that involve self-produced movement. Johnson and Newport (1989) found evidence for a sensitive period in grammatical mastery in acquiring a second language. The question for this century is to discover which aspects of behavior are likely to be altered by environmental events at specific points in development and which aspects remain more plastic and open to influence across wide spans of development.

In terms of units of analysis, researchers have begun to conceptualize the unit of analysis as dyads within the family system, such as the parent–child dyad, the husband–wife dyad, and the sibling dyad (Belsky, 1984; Cowan & McHale, 1996; Parke, 1988). Moreover, units beyond the dyad have been recognized as important as well. Several researchers have recently begun to investigate triads (Hinde & Stevenson-Hinde, 1988; Kreppner, 1988) as well as the family as units of analysis (Dickstein et al., 1998).

At present, this shift toward units beyond the individual is evident in cognitive as well as social development and is due, in part, to the revival of interest in Vygotskian theory. Lev Vygotsky (1896–1934), a Russian psychologist, championed the view that mental functioning is a kind of action that may be exercised by individuals or by dyads or larger groups (Wertsch, 1991). His view was one in which mind is understood as "extending beyond the skin." "Mind, cognition and memory . . . are understood not as attributes or properties of individuals but as functions that may be carried out intermentally or intramentally" (Wertsch & Tulviste, 1992, p. 549). Such terms as *socially shared cognition* (Resnick, Levine, & Teasley, 1991), *socially distributed cognition* (Hutchins, 1991), and *collaborative problem solving* (Rogoff, 1990) reflect the increasing awareness that cognition can be a social as well as an individual enterprise.

In terms of methods, variety best describes the contemporary period. In the 1990s, the use of longitudinal designs increased markedly, motivated in part by an increased interest in issues of developmental stability and change. Two types of longitudinal studies are evident. Short-term longitudinal studies, in which a particular issue is traced over a short time period of a few months to a year, are currently popular (Clarke-Stewart, Gruber, & Fitzgerald, 1994; Hetherington & Clingempeel, 1992). These studies are of value for detecting short-term stability or for tracking development across a time period of assumed rapid change in an emerging developmental process or structure.

Other longitudinal studies have a long-term character and have continued from infancy through childhood and into adolescence. For example, a number of investigators have followed families from infancy to the preadolescent or adolescent years (Sameroff, 1994; Sroufe, 1996). This strategy has permitted a more definitive evaluation of a variety of theoretical issues, especially those concerning the effect of early experience, including the role of sensitive and critical periods on later development. Nonetheless, because of the expense

and difficulty of longitudinal research, cross-sectional designs still predominate among developmental investigations. Often researchers will use both strategies, and, in an area that is not yet well developed either theoretically or empirically, cross-sectional studies often precede longitudinal pursuit of an issue. A commitment to multiple design strategies rather than a near-exclusive reliance on a single design is characteristic of the current area.

In terms of experimental designs, a greater openness to multiple strategies is evident. Laboratory-based experimental studies and field-based experimental investigations coexist with nonexperimental observational field studies. Data-collection strategies come in a variety of forms as well. In spite of its less than stellar history, the self-report measure has reentered our methodological repertoire; parent, teacher, and peer reports are now commonly used. Another noteworthy trend reflects in part the openness of researchers to multimethod strategies as opposed to strict adherence to one approach. Observational methods are widely used along with verbal reports. Evidence, not just speculation, may be driving the field to this new openness to a wide range of methods. Some researchers have found that ratings of behavior yield better prediction of later social behavior (Bakeman & Brown, 1980) and later cognitive assessments (Jay & Farran, 1981) than do more microanalytic and more expensive measures of parent–child interaction.

Finally, our sampling methods have come of age. Shifts in awareness of the importance of sampling have led to an increase in use of large representative national samples in developmental research. Although this has typically been the domain of sociologists and survey researchers, in the early 1990s, developmentalists have shown an increased awareness of the potential value of supplementing their usual small-sample strategies with these large-sample approaches. One prominent example is the use of the National Longitudinal Study of Youth (NLSY) for the examination of developmental issues, including divorce, achievement, and day care (Brooks-Gunn, Phelps, & Elder, 1991). These surveys have several advantages, including a large number of subjects, more representative samples, a multifaceted range of variables, and longitudinal designs. In turn, these characteristics permit testing of more complex models of development that require large numbers of subjects. In addition, these studies allow examination of connections across content-based domains as well as encouraging interdisciplinary cooperation. Finally, they permit testing of the cultural generality of the models.

Newer, more innovative approaches that combine levels of sampling are becoming increasingly common as well. As a supplement to a large-scale survey approach, researchers are selecting subsamples of subjects for more intensive examination of a particular process of interest. For example, Beitel and Parke (1998) conducted a survey of 300 families to assess maternal attitudes toward father involvement in infant care. To supplement this approach, in which a self-report questionnaire was used, a subsample of 40 families was observed in their homes as a way of validating the self-report data. Similarly, Reiss et al. (2000) generated a nationally representative sample of stepfamilies, and in a second stage of their work, they observed these families in interaction tasks in the home. These combined approaches increase the generalizability of findings and, at the same time, allow us to illuminate basic social processes.

A GLANCE INTO THE FUTURE

Where are we going next? Today, a proliferation of minitheories has replaced single dominant positions or theoretical frameworks, and each of these smaller-scale theories accounts for a limited set of issues. This domain-specific nature of theory is one of the hallmarks of our current state of the field. It represents a disenchantment with grand theories both of a century ago and of our more recent past. Part of the reason for the current proliferation of smaller and more modest paradigms is the lack of a new overarching paradigm to replace the disfavored grand theories.

The next stage of our development as a field involves the creation of such a new overarching paradigm or framework to help us with our integrative efforts. There are signs that a new integration may be emerging in the form of a systems perspective that will bring together biological, social, cognitive, and emotional minitheories into a more coherent framework (Fogel & Thelen, 1987; Sameroff, 1994). Although the promise of a general dynamic systems theory is appealing and has been applied with considerable success to the motor development domain, especially by Thelen (1989), it remains to be seen whether the stringent requirements of this approach for precise parameter estimation and measurement can be met in other domains (Aslin, 1993). Whether we have reached the stage of being able to quantify social behavior or children's theories of mind with sufficient precision to make this approach useful, beyond being merely metaphoric, is an open question.

We are cautiously optimistic that a systems approach is a promising one and has proven useful both in organizing data and in pointing to new research directions in recent family research, as well as in research on the organization and functioning of social contexts. Perhaps we need to develop a family of systems-theory integrations that would be hierarchically organized and would represent the levels of analysis that are intrinsic to different areas of development, just as we have long recognized that biological, biochemical, and social levels of inquiry may each have its own set of integrative principles (Sameroff, 1994). Multiple integrative approaches may be needed to cover different parts of the development terrain. The goal is to retain the advances that our retreat to minitheories has brought but, at the same time, to begin to put the "whole child" back together again. Our forebears had the vision to see this as the goal, and we should be in a better position to achieve it now than they were a century ago.

REFERENCES

Anderson, H. H. (1937). Domination and integration in the social behavior of young children in an experimental play situation. *Genetic Psychology Monographs, 19,* 343–408.

Asher, S. R., & Gottman, J. M. (Eds.). (1981). *The development of children's friendships.* New York: Cambridge University Press.

Aslin, R. N. (1993). The strange attractiveness of dynamic systems to development. In L. B. Smith & E. Thelen (Eds.), *A dynamic systems approach to development* (pp. 385–400). Cambridge, MA: MIT Press.

Aslin, R. N. (1998). The developing brain comes of age. *Early Development and Parenting, 7,* 125–128.

Bakeman, R., & Brown, J. V. (1980). Early interaction: Consequences for social and mental development at three years. *Child Development, 51,* 437–447.

Baldwin, J. M. (1894). *Mental development in the child and the race.* London: Routledge/Thoemmes Press.

Baldwin, J. M. (1895). The origin of a "thing" and its nature. *Psychological Review, 6,* 551–573.

Baldwin, J. M. (1897). *Social and ethical interpretations in mental development: A study in social psychology.* New York: Macmillan.

Baltes, P. B. (1987). Theoretical propositions of life span development psychology: On the dynamics of growth and decline. *Developmental Psychology, 23,* 611–626.

Bandura, A. (1969). Social learning of moral judgments. *Journal of Personality and Social Psychology, 3,* 275–279.

Bandura, A. (1977). *Social learning theory.* Englewood Cliffs, NJ: Prentice Hall.

Bandura, A., Ross, D., & Ross, S. A. (1961). Transmission of aggression through imitation of aggressive models. *Journal of Abnormal and Social Psychology, 3,* 575–582.

Bandura, A., & Walters, R. H. (1963). *Social learning and personality development.* New York: Holt, Rinehart and Winston.

Baumrind, D. (1973). The development of instrumental competence through socialization. In A. D. Pick (Ed.), *Minnesota Symposia on Child Psychology* (Vol. 7, pp. 33–46). Minneapolis: University of Minnesota Press.

Baumrind, D. (1993). The average expectable environment is not good enough: A response to Scarr. *Child Development, 5,* 1299–1317.

Bayley, N. (1949). Consistency and variability in the growth of intelligence from birth to eighteen years. *Journal of Genetic Psychology, 75,* 165–196.

Beitel, A., & Parke, R. D. (1998). Maternal and paternal attitudes as determinants of father involvement. *Journal of Family Psychology, 12,* 268–288.

Belsky, J. (1984). The determinants of parenting: A process model. *Child Development, 55,* 83–96.

Bijou, S. W., & Baer, D. M. (1961). *Child development: A systematic and empirical theory* (Vol. 1). New York: Appleton-Century-Crofts.

Binet, A. (1894). *Introduction a la psychologie experimentale.* Paris: Alcan.

Binet, A. (1900). *La suggestibilite.* Paris: Schleicher Freres.

Binet, A., & Simon, T. (1905). Application of the new methods to the diagnosis of the intellectual level among normal and subnormal children in institutions and in the primary schools. *L'annee Psychologique, 12,* 245–336.

Bjorklund, D. F., & Pellegrini, A. I. (2000). Child development and evolutionary psychology. *Child Development, 71,* 1687–1708.

Bornstein, M. H. (1989). Sensitive periods in development: Structural characteristics and causal interpretations. *Psychological Bulletin, 2,* 179–197.

Bowlby, J. (1969). *Attachment and loss. Volume I: Attachment.* New York: Basic Books.

Bowlby, J. (1973). *Attachment and loss. Volume II: Separation: Anxiety and anger.* New York: Basic Books.

Bowlby, J. (1980). *Attachment and loss. Volume III: Loss: Sadness and depression.* New York: Basic Books.

Brazelton, T. B., Koslowski, B., & Main, M. (1974). The origins of reciprocity: Early mother-infant interaction. In M. Lewis & L. A. Rosenblum (Eds.), *The effect of the infant on its caregiver* (pp. 49–76). New York: Wiley.

Bronfenbrenner, U. (1979). *The ecology of human development.* Cambridge, MA: Harvard University Press.

Bronfenbrenner, U. (1986). Ecology of the family as a context for human development: Research perspectives. *Developmental Psychology, 22,* 723–742.

Bronfenbrenner, U. (1989). Ecological systems theory. In R. Vasta (Ed.), *Annals of child development* (pp. 187–249). Greenwich, CT: JAI Press.

Brooks-Gunn, J., Phelps, E., & Elder, G. H. (1991). Studying lives through time: Secondary data analyses in developmental psychology. *Developmental Psychology, 6,* 899–910.

Brubaker, T. (Ed.). (1990). *Family relationships in later life.* Newbury Park, CA: Sage.

Cahan, E. D. (1984). The genetic psychologies of James Mark Baldwin and Jean Piaget. *Developmental Psychology, 20,* 128–135.

Cairns, R. B. (1983). The emergence of development psychology. In W. Kessen (Ed.), *Handbook of child psychology. Vol. 1: History, theory, and methods* (pp. 41–102). New York: Wiley.

Cairns, R. B. (1994). The making of a developmental science: The contributions and intellectual heritage of James Mark Baldwin. In R. D. Parke, P. A. Ornstein, J. J. Riesen, & C. Zahn-Waxler (Eds.), *A century of developmental psychology* (pp. 127–143). Washington, DC: American Psychological Association.

Cairns, R. B. (1998). Developmental psychology. In W. Damon (Series Ed.) & R. Lerner (Vol. Ed.), *Handbook of child psychology: Theoretical models of human development, Vol. 1* (5th ed., pp. 25–106). New York: Wiley.

Campos, J. J., & Barrett, K. C. (1985). Toward a new understanding of emotions and their development. In C. E. Izard & J. Kagan (Eds.), *Emotions, cognition, and behavior* (pp. 229–263). New York: Cambridge University Press.

Campos, J. J., Barrett, K. C., Lamb, M. E., Goldsmith, H. H., & Stenberg, C. (1983). Socio-emotional development. In W. Damon (Series Ed.), M. M. Haith, & J. J. Campos (Vol. Eds.), *Handbook of child psychology: Infancy and developmental psychobiology, Vol. 2* (5th ed., pp. 783–916). New York: Wiley.

Clarke-Stewart, K. A. (1978). Popular primers for parents. *American Psychologist, 33,* 359–369.

Clarke-Stewart, K. A. (1992a). Consequences of child care for children's development. In A. Booth (Ed.), *Child care in the 1990s: Trends and consequences* (pp. 63–82). Hillsdale, NJ: Erlbaum.

Clarke-Stewart, K. A. (1992b). Consequences of child care—one more time: A rejoinder. In A. Booth (Ed.), *Child care in the 1990s: Trends and consequences* (pp. 116–124). Hillsdale, NJ: Erlbaum.

Clarke-Stewart, K. A. (1998). Historical shifts and underlying themes in ideas about rearing young children in the United States: Where have we been? Where are we going? *Early Development and Parenting, 7,* 101–117.

Clarke-Stewart, K. A., Gruber, C. P., & Fitzgerald, L. M. (1994). *Children at home and in day care.* Hillsdale, NJ: Erlbaum.

Cochran, M. M., & Brassard, J. A. (1979). Child development and personal social networks. *Child Development, 50,* 601–616.

Cohn, J. F., & Tronick, E. Z. (1987). Mother-infant face-to-face interaction: The sequence of dyadic states at 3, 6, and 9 months. *Developmental Psychology, 23,* 68–77.

Coie, J. D., & Jacobs, M. R. (1993). The role of social context in the prevention of conduct disorder. *Development and Psychopathology, 1/2,* 263–275.

Conger, R. D., & Elder, G. H., Jr. (1994). *Families in troubled times.* New York: Aldine de Gruyter.

Cowan, P. A., & McHale, P. A. (Eds.). (1996). *Understanding how family-level dynamics affect children's development: Studies of two-parent families.* San Francisco: Jossey-Bass.

Denham, S. A. (1998). *Emotional development in young children.* New York: Guilford Press.

Diamond, A. (1990). The development and neural bases of memory functions as indexed by the AB and delayed response tasks in human infants and infant moneys. *Annals of the New York Academy of Sciences, 608,* 267–317.

Diamond, A. (1991). Frontal lobe involvement in cognitive changes during the first year of life. In K. R. Gibson & A. C. Petersen (Eds.), *Brain maturation and cognitive development: Comparative and cross-cultural perspectives* (pp. 127–180). Hawthorne, NY: Aldine de Gruyter.

Dickstein, S., Seifer, R., Hayden, L. C., Schiller, M., Sameroff, A. J., Keitner, G., et al. (1998). Levels of family assessment: Impact of maternal psychopathology on family functioning. *Journal of Family Psychology, 21,* 23–40.

Dollard, J., Doob, L. W., Miller, N. E., Mowrer, O. H., & Sears, R. R. (1939). *Frustration and aggression.* New Haven, CT: Yale University Press.

Dunn, J., & Kendrick, C. (1982). *Siblings: Love, envy and understanding.* New York: Academic Press.

Eisenberg, N. (1991). Meta-analytic contributions to the literature on prosocial behavior. *Personality and Social Psychology Bulletin, 3,* 273–282.

Ekman, P., & Friesen, W. (1978). *Facial action coding system.* Palo Alto, CA: Consulting Psychological Press.

Elder, G. H. (1974). *Children of the Great Depression.* Chicago: University of Chicago Press.

Elder, G. H., Modell, J., & Parke, R. D. (Eds.). (1994). *Children in time and place.* New York: Cambridge University Press.

Fantz, R. (1963). Pattern vision in newborn infants. *Science, 140,* 296–297.

Field, T. M. (1987). Affective and interactive disturbances infants. In J. D. Osofsky (Ed.), *Handbook of infant development* (2nd ed., pp. 972–1005). New York: Wiley.

Field, T. M. (1991). *Infancy.* Cambridge, MA: Harvard University Press.

Flavell, J. H. (1963). *The developmental psychology of Jean Piaget.* New York: Nostrand.

Flavell, J. H. (1985). *Cognitive development* (2nd ed.). Englewood Cliffs, NJ: Prentice-Hall.

Flavell, J. H. (1999). Cognitive development: Children's knowledge of the mind. *Annual Review of Psychology, 50,* 21–45.

Fogel, A., & Thelen, E. (1987). Development of early expressive and communicative action: Reinterpreting the evidence from a dynamic systems perspective. *Developmental Psychology, 23,* 747–761.

Freud, S. (1900). The interpretation of dreams. In J. Strachey (Ed.), *The standard edition of the complete psychological works of Sigmund Freud* (Vols. 4–5, pp. 1–715). London: Hogarth Press.

Freud, S. (1905). Three essays on the theory of sexuality. In J. Strachey (Ed.), *The standard edition of the complete psychological works of Sigmund Freud* (Vol. 7, pp. 123–230). London: Hogarth Press.

Freud, S. (1910). The origin and development of psychoanalysis. *American Journal of Psychology, 2,* 181–218.

Freud, S. (1918). *Totem & taboo: Resemblances between the psychic lives of savages and neurotics.* New York: Moffat, Yard.

Gauvain, M. (2001). *The social context of cognitive development.* New York: Guilford Press.

Gesell, A. (1928). *Infancy and human growth.* New York: Macmillan.

Gesell, A., & Ilg, F. L. (1946). *The child from five to ten.* New York: Harper.

Gesell, A., Ilg, F. L., & Ames, L. B. (1956). *Youth: The years from ten to sixteen.* New York: Harper.

Gewirtz, J. (1969). Mechanisms of social learning: Some roles of stimulation and behavior in early human development. In D. A. Goslin (Ed.), *Handbook of socialization theory and research* (pp. 157–212). Chicago: Rand McNally.

Gibson, E. J., & Walk, R. R. (1960). The "visual cliff." *Scientific American, 202,* 2–9.

Greenfield, P. M. (1974). Comparing dimension categorization in natural and artificial contexts: A developmental study among the Zinacantecos of Mexico. *Journal of Social Psychology, 2,* 157–171.

Greenough, W. T., Black, J. E., & Wallace, C. S. (1987). Experience and brain development. *Child Development, 3,* 539–559.

Greenwald, A. G. (1992). New look 3: Unconscious cognition reclaimed. *American Psychologist, 6,* 766–779.

Grossman, K., Grossman, K. E., Spangler, G., Suess, G., & Unzner, I. (1985). Maternal sensitivity and newborns' orientation responses as related to quality of attachment in northern Germany. In I. Bretherton & E. Waters (Eds.), *Growing points of attachment theory and research. Monographs of the Society for Research in Child Development, 50*(1–2, Serial No. 209), 233–256.

Grusec, J. E. (1992). Social learning theory and developmental psychology: The legacies of Robert R. Sears and Albert Bandura. *Developmental Psychology, 28,* 776–786.

Gunnar, M. R. (1987). Psychological studies of stress and coping: An introduction. *Child Development, 58,* 1403–1407.

Hall, G. S. (1904). *Adolescence.* New York: Appleton-Century-Crofts.

Hanson, R. O., & Carpenter, B. N. (1994). *Relationships in old age.* New York: Guilford Press.

Harkness, S., & Super, C. M. (1983). The cultural construction of child development: A framework for the socialization of affect. *Society for Psychological Anthropology, 4,* 221–231.

Harlow, H. F., & Harlow, M. K. (1962). Social deprivation in monkeys. *Scientific American, 207,* 137–146.

Harris, P. L. (1989). *Children and emotion: The development of psychological understanding.* Oxford, England: Blackwell.

Hartup, W. W., & Rubin, Z. (Eds.). (1986). *Relationships and development.* Hillsdale, NJ: Erlbaum.

Hertzog, C. (1989). Influences of cognitive slowing on age differences in intelligence. *Developmental Psychology, 25,* 636–651.

Hetherington, E. M., & Clingempeel, G. (Eds.). (1992). Coping with marital transitions. *Monographs of the Society for Research in Child Development, 57*(No. 2–3, Serial No. 227).

Hinde, R. A. (1979). *Towards understanding relationships.* London: Academic Press.

Hinde, R. A. (1991). When is an evolutionary approach useful? *Child Development, 62,* 671–675.

Hinde, R. A., & Stevenson-Hinde, J. (1988). Interpersonal relationships and child development. In S. Chess & A. Thomas (Eds.), *Annual progress in child psychiatry and child development* (pp. 5–26). New York: Oxford University Press.

Hoffman, L. W. (1991). The influence of the family environment on personality: Accounting for sibling differences. *Psychological Bulletin, 110,* 187–203.

Horowitz, F. D. (1987). *Exploring developmental theories: Toward a structural/behavioral model of development*. Hillsdale, NJ: Erlbaum.

Hunt, J. M. (1961). *Intelligence and experience*. New York: Ronald Press.

Hutchins, E. (1991). The social organization of distributed cognition. In L. B. Resnick & J. M. Levine (Eds.), *Perspectives on socially shared cognition* (pp. 283–307). Washington, DC: American Psychological Association.

Izard, C. E. (1982). *Measuring emotions in infants and children*. New York: Cambridge University Press.

Jay, D., & Farran, D. C. (1981). The relative efficacy of predicting IQ from mother-child interactions using ratings versus behavioral count measures. *Journal of Applied Developmental Psychology, 2*, 165–177.

Johnson, J. S., & Newport, E. L. (1989). Critical period effects in second language learning: The influence of maturational state on acquisition of English as a second language. *Cognitive Psychology, 21*, 60–99.

Kihlstrom, J., Barnhardt, T. M., & Tataryn, D. J. (1992). The psychological unconscious. *American Psychologist, 47*, 788–791.

Kreppner, K. (1988). Changes in dyadic relationships within a family after the arrival of a second child. In R. Hinde & J. Stevenson-Hinde (Eds.), *Relationships within families* (pp. 143–167). London: Cambridge University Press.

Lamb, M. D. (1975). Fathers: Forgotten contributors to child development. *Human Development, 4*, 245–266.

Lerner, R. M. (1986). *Concepts and theories of human development* (2nd ed.). New York: Random House.

Lewis, M. (1992). Self-conscious emotions and the development of self. In T. Shapiro & R. N. Emde (Eds.), *Affect: Psychoanalytic perspectives* (pp. 45–73). Madison, CT: International Universities Press.

Lipsitt, L. P. (1963). Learning in the first year of life. In L. P. Lipsitt & C. C. Spiker (Eds.), *Advances in child development and behavior* (Vol. 1, pp. 147–195). New York: Academic Press.

McLoyd, V. C., Cauce, A. M., Takeuchi, D., & Wilson, L. (2000). Marital processes and parental socialization in families of color: A decade review of research. *Journal of Marriage and the Family, 62*, 1070–1093.

Miller, G. A., Galanter, E., & Pribram, K. H. (1960). *Plans and the structure of behavior*. New York: Holt, Rinehart and Winston.

Overton, W. F., & Reese, H. W. (1973). Models of development: Methodological implications. In J. R. Nesselroade (Ed.), *Life-span developmental psychology: Methodological issues* (pp. 65–86). New York: Academic Press.

Papousek, H. (1961). Conditioning during postnatal development. In Y. Brackbill & G. G. Thompson (Eds.), *Behavior in infancy and early childhood* (pp. 259–284). New York: Free Press.

Parke, R. D. (1988). Families in life-span perspective: A multilevel developmental approach. In E. M. Hetherington, R. M. Lerner, & M. Perlmutter (Eds.), *Child development in life-span perspective* (pp. 159–190). Hillsdale, NJ: Erlbaum.

Parke, R. D., & Buriel, R. (1998). Socialization in the family: Ecological and ethnic perspectives. In W. Damon (Series Ed.) & N. Eisenberg (Vol. Ed.), *Handbook of child psychology: Social, emotion, and personality development* (Vol. 3, pp. 463–552). New York: Wiley.

Parke, R. D., Ornstein, P. A., Rieser, J. J., & Zahn-Waxler, C. (1994). The past is prologue: An overview of a century of developmental psychology. In R. D. Parke, P. A. Ornstein, J. J. Rieser, & C. Zahn-Waxler (Eds.), *A century of development psychology* (pp. 10–70). Washington DC: American Psychological Association.

Parke, R. D., & Tinsley, B. J. (1987). Family interaction in infancy. In J. D. Osofsky (Ed.), *Handbook of infant development* (Vol. 2, pp. 599–641). New York: Wiley.

Piaget, J. (1926). *The language and thought of the child*. New York: Harcourt, Brace.

Plomin, R. (1986). *Development, genetics and psychology*. Hillsdale, NJ: Erlbaum.

Plomin, R. (1994). Genetic research and identification of environmental influences. *Journal of Child Psychology and Psychiatry, 35*, 817–834.

Plomin, R., & DeFries, J. C. (1985). *Origins of individual differences in infancy: The Colorado adoption project*. Orlando, FL: Academic Press.

Plomin, R., DeFries, J. C., & McLearn, G. E. (1990). *Behavioral genetics: A primer* (2nd ed.). New York: Freeman.

Plomin, R., & Rutter, M. (1998). Child development, molecules and what to do with genes once they are found. *Child Development, 4*, 1223–1242.

Radke-Yarrow, M., & Zahn-Waxler, C. (1984). Roots, motives and patterns in children's prosocial behavior. In E. Staub, D. Bar-Tal, J. Karylowski, & J. Reykowski (Eds.), *Development and maintenance of prosocial behavior* (pp. 81–99). New York: Plenum Press.

Ramey, C. T., & Haskins, R. (1981). The modification of intelligence through early experience. *Intelligence, 1*, 5–19.

Reese, H., & Overton, W. (1970). Models of development and theories of development. In L. R. Goulet & P. B. Baltes (Eds.), *Life span developmental psychology: Research and theory* (pp. 109–137). New York: Academic Press.

Reiss, D., Neiderhiser, J. M., Hetherington, E. M., & Plomin, R. (2000). *The relationship code: Deciphering genetic and social influences on adolescent development*. Cambridge, MA: Harvard University Press.

Resnick, L. B., Levine, J. M., & Teasley, S. D. (Eds.). (1991). *Perspectives on socially shared cognition*. Washington, DC: American Psychological Association.

Rieser, J. J., Hill, E. W., Talor, C. R., Bradfield, A., & Rosen, R. (1992). Visual experience, visual field size, and the development of nonvisual sensitivity to the spatial structure of outdoor neighborhoods explored by walking. *Journal of Experimental Psychology: General, 2*, 210–221.

Robbins, L. C. (1963). The accuracy of parental recording of aspects of child development and child rearing practice. *Journal of Abnormal and Social Psychology, 66*, 261–270.

Rogoff, B. (1990). *Apprenticeship in thinking.* New York: Oxford University Press.

Ross, D. (1972). *G. Stanley Hill: The psychologist as prophet.* Chicago: University of Chicago Press.

Rothbart, M., & Bates, J. E. (1998). Temperament. In W. Damon (Series Ed.) & N. Eisenberg (Vol. Ed.), *Handbook of child psychology: Social, emotion, and personality development* (Vol. 3, pp. 105–176). New York: Wiley.

Saarni, C. (1999). *The development of emotional competence.* New York: Guilford Press.

Sackett, G. P. (1968). The persistence of abnormal behavior in monkeys following isolation rearing. In R. Porter (Ed.), *The role of learning in psychotherapy* (pp. 26–39). London: Churchill.

Salthouse, T. A. (1985). *A theory of cognitive aging.* Amsterdam: North-Holland.

Sameroff, A. J. (1970). Changes in the nonnutritive sucking response to stimulation during infancy. *Journal of Experimental Child Psychology, 1,* 112–119.

Sameroff, A. J. (1975). Early influences on development: Fact or fancy? *Merrill-Palmer Quarterly, 4,* 267–294.

Sameroff, A. J. (1994). Developmental systems and family functioning. In R. D. Parke & S. G. Kellam (Eds.), *Exploring family relationships with other social contexts* (pp. 199–214). Hillsdale, NJ: Erlbaum.

Scarr, S. (1993). Biological and cultural diversity: The legacy for development. *Child Development, 5,* 1333–1353.

Sears, R. R. (1944). Experimental analysis of psychoanalytic phenomena. In J. M. Hunt (Ed.), *Personality and the behavior disorders* (Vol. 1, pp. 306–332). New York: Ronald Press.

Sears, R. R. (1975). Your ancients revisited: A history of child development. In E. M. Hetherington (Ed.), *Review of child development research* (Vol. 5, pp. 1–73). Chicago: University of Chicago Press.

Sears, R. R., Maccoby, E. E., & Levin, H. (1957). *Patterns of child rearing.* Evanston, IL: Row, Peterson.

Sears, R. R., Rau, L., & Alpert, R. (1966). *Identification and child rearing.* Stanford, CA: Stanford University Press.

Sears, R. R., Whiting, J. W. M., Nowlis, V., & Sears, P. S. (1953). Some child-rearing antecedents of aggression and dependency in young children. *Genetic Psychology Monographs, 47,* 135–234.

Siegler, R. S. (1991). *Children's thinking* (2nd ed.). Englewood Cliffs, NJ: Prentice-Hall.

Siegler, R. S. (1992). The other Alfred Binet. *Developmental Psychology, 28,* 179–190.

Siegler, R. S., & Crowley, K. (1992). Microgenetic methods revisited. *American Psychologist, 10,* 1241–1243.

Sontag, L. W. (1944). Differences in modifiability of fetal behavior and physiology. *Psychosomatic Medicine, 6,* 151–154.

Sroufe, L. A. (1996). *Emotional development: The organization of emotional life in the early years.* New York: Cambridge University Press.

Sroufe, L. A., & Fleeson, J. (1986). Attachment and the construction of relationships. In W. W. Hartup & Z. Rubin (Eds.), *Relationships and development* (pp. 51–72). Hillsdale, NJ: Erlbaum.

Steinberg, L., Dornbusch, S. M., & Brown, B. B. (1992). Ethnic differences in adolescent achievement: An ecological perspective. *American Psychologist, 6,* 723–729.

Stern, D. N. (1977). *The first relationship.* Cambridge, MA: Harvard University Press.

Thelen, E. (1989). The (re)discovery of motor development: Learn things from an old field. *Developmental Psychology, 6,* 946–949.

Thelen, E. (1993). Self-organization in developmental processes: Can systems approaches work? In M. H. Johnson (Ed.), *Brain development and cognition: A reader* (pp. 555–591). Malden, MA: Blackwell.

Thelen, E., & Ulrich, B. D. (1991). Hidden skills: A dynamic analysis of treadmill stepping during the first year. *Monographs of the Society for Research in Child Development, 56*(No. 1, Serial No. 223).

Tinsley, B. J., & Parke, R. D. (1984). Grandparents are support and socialization agents. In M. Lewis (Ed.), *Beyond the dyad* (pp. 161–195). New York: Plenum Press.

Tronick, E. (1989). Emotions and emotional communication in infants. *American Psychologist, 44,* 112–119.

Watson, J. B. (1913). Psychology as the behaviourist views it. *Psychological Review, 2,* 158–177.

Watson, J. B. (1924). *Psychology, from the standpoint of a behaviorist* (2nd ed.). Philadelphia: Lippincott.

Wertsch, J. V. (1991). *Voices of the mind: A sociocultural approach to mediated action.* Cambridge, MA: Harvard University Press.

Wertsch, J. V., & Tulviste, P. (1992). Lev Semyonovich Vygotsky and contemporary developmental psychology. *Developmental Psychology, 28,* 557–548.

White, S. H. (1992). G. Stanley Hall: From philosophy to developmental psychology. *Developmental Psychology, 28,* 25–34.

Whiting, J. W. M., & Child, I. (1953). *Child training and personality.* New Haven, CT: Yale University Press.

Wozniak, R. H. (Ed.). (1993a). *Experimental and comparative roots of early behaviourism: Studies of animal and infant behaviour.* London: Routledge/Thoemmes Press.

Wozniak, R. H. (Ed.). (1993b). *Theoretical roots of early behaviourism: Functionalism, the critique of introspection, and the nature and evolution of consciousness.* London: Routledge/Thoemmes Press.

Wozniak, R. H. (Ed.). (1994). *Reflex, habit and implicit response: The early elaboration of theoretical and methodological behaviourism.* London: Routledge/Thoemmes Press.

Wozniak, R. H. (Ed.). (1995). *Mind, adaptation and childhood.* London: Routledge/Thoemmes Press.

Yarrow, L. J. (1961). Maternal deprivation: Toward an empirical and conceptual re-evaluation. *Psychological Bulletin, 58,* 459–490.

Yarrow, M. R., Campbell, J. D., & Burton, R. V. (1964). Reliability of maternal retrospection: A preliminary report. *Family Process, 1,* 207–218.

CHAPTER 11

Social Psychology

JILL G. MORAWSKI AND BETTY M. BAYER

SOCIAL HEAVENS AND THE NEW CENTURY 224
   **The Social as Dynamic and Moral: James
     and Baldwin 225**
   Scientific Specificity and the Social 226
A SOCIAL PSYCHOLOGY TO SERVE PSYCHOLOGY
   AND SOCIETY 227
WORK DURING THE INTERWAR YEARS 229
   Progressive Science 229
   Making and Finding Social Relevance 230
MIDCENTURY ON: FROM POST–WORLD WAR II
   AND POST-MECHANISM TO POST-POSITIVISM 232

World War II Era 232
   Cold War, Cybernetics, and Social Psychology 234
SOCIAL MOVEMENTS AND MOVEMENTS FOR CHANGE
   IN SOCIAL PSYCHOLOGY 236
   Individual–Social World Dualism Revisited 236
   A Social Psychology of Social Psychology 237
   "Social Psychology in Transition" 238
TRANSITING THE MODERN TO POSTMODERN ERA 239
REFERENCES 242

In an early appraisal of American social psychology, Albion Small (1916) traced the springs of that intellectual enterprise to the Civil War, when people "whose thought-world had been stirred to its depths by the war found themselves in 1865 star-gazing in social heavens that had never looked so confused nor so mysterious" (p. 724). The war had dispelled American's naive beliefs that "a constitution and laws enacted in the pursuance thereof would automatically produce human welfare," thus forcing recognition "that work was ahead to bring American conditions into tolerable likeness of American ideals" (pp. 724–725). Social psychology, according to Small, was born of those social conditions, a maturation of intellectual consciousness, including a growing independence from European thought and, as his astronomical metaphor intimates, an appreciation of the "social" as a phenomenon appropriate to scientific study. Another early historical appraiser, Fay Karpf (1932), wrote that only with these preconditions "did an American intellectual self-conscientiousness begin to assert itself in the fields directly of significance for social psychology" (p. 213).

This wide-angled perspective on the history of social psychology appreciates the multiple and diverse efforts undertaken in at least a half a dozen disciplines to render rational, coherent explanations of social action and the relations between the individual and society. It is a history that ultimately must attend to classic texts as varied in their rendition

of the social world as, for example, Edward Ross's (1901) *Social Control,* William I. Thomas and Florian Znaniecki's (1920), *The Polish Peasant in Europe and America,* George Herbert Mead's (1934) *Mind, Self, and Society,* and William James's (1890) *Principles of Psychology.* With an even more comprehensive gaze, historians also need to register more recent "extracurricular" social psychology, which includes texts as wide ranging as Richard Sennet's (1974) *Fall of Public Man,* Betty Friedan's (1963) *The Feminine Mystique,* and Lewis Thomas's (1974) *Lives of a Cell.* On another plane, that of discipline boundaries, historical accounting must measure social psychology's multiplicity: its nascent emergence across the social sciences and its eventual blossoming in sociology and psychology (Karpf, 1934; Loy, 1976). This prospective inclusive history would consider, too, the numerous blueprints for systematic theory, including pragmatism, behaviorism, psychoanalysis, cognition, discourse, symbolic interaction, social learning, evolution, phenomenology, dramaturgy, balance, and gestalt. In one sense this would yield a historical telling that reverberates with setting the distinctly *psychological* terms of modernity, principally the discipline's detection and naming of what comes to be taken as the "psychological" in the social life of Americans. In another sense social psychology's story, broadly told, would contribute to explicating late-twentieth-century America's shift from belief in a distinctly modern individual to a postmodern subject.

This transition involves the scientific inscription of multiple social selves, cybernetic loops between self and other, and a reworking of psychology's subject. Perhaps it was in recognizing these civilian engagements of social psychology—its contributions to defining psychological personhood—that Gordon Allport revised his initial history of social psychology with the opening claim that "Social psychology is an ancient discipline. It is also modern—ultramodern and exciting" (1985, p. 1).

In recognizing the material and political influences on the intellectual conceptions of the social and individual, such historical understanding comprehends how "the history of social psychology is inseparable from much of the political history of the twentieth century and from argument about power, justice, freedom and obligation" (Smith, 1997, p. 747). Social psychology's evolution must be understood, therefore, as plural, multisited, and morally and politically inspired. Such a historical perspective situates social psychology as one, albeit crucial, project to understand human nature through scientific method, and ultimately, to apply that scientific knowledge to the enhancement of human welfare.

Contrasted with this situated historical perspective is a narrative accounting of social psychology that charts the field's rise and contributions on progressive terms (Allport, 1954; Jones, 1985). In this progressive history crucial laboratory experiments are named to serve as pivotal points in social psychology's development as scientific. Disregarded in these scientifically internalist accounts are political and moral as well as disciplinary conditions that compelled particular models of the individual and the social. Similarly eschewed are empirical projects initiated but abandoned, alternative models and research practices, and challenges to the scientific status quo. In preparing this chapter, we were at once pulled in one direction by the need to trace fruition of these progressive intellectual commitments within experimental work, and tugged in another by the desire to generate an earnest account of the sociopolitical dynamics and the vibrant intellectual enterprises that yielded multiple, sometimes controversial conceptions of social psychology. Without giving the chapter over to one or the other historical narrative, we seek to chart those culminating forces in social psychology's subject matter, its continuing struggles over research methods, and its stronghold in the public imagination of twentieth-century American life. Factors influencing social psychology's emergence, development, and paradigmatic commitments, considered in conjunction with the social identity and demeanor of the social psychologist, frame our review, as does social psychology's broader concern with the nature of what is taken as the individual and the social.

The first section begins this charting of emergences in a variety of proposals published in the final decade of the nineteenth century and the first decade of the twentieth. Factors that shaped the contours of social psychology, choices that delimited ideal methods, the nature of what is taken as social, and the demeanor of the social psychologist are reviewed in the second section. In the third part, several classic projects undertaken prior to and during World War II are described: These cases illuminate the interdependence of science, culture, and politics, charting the postwar emergence of a society yearning to be understood in psychological terms (Herman, 1995) and of a field increasingly self-aware of its reflexive entanglements with the very subjects it sought to study. The final two sections describe social movements and intellectual endeavors from the 1960s to the end of the century, highlighting cybernetic influences and wider Western intellectual debates on the nature of knowledge as well as more specific theories that ultimately served to transform time and again social psychology's subject.

SOCIAL HEAVENS AND THE NEW CENTURY

If the social confusions rent by the Civil War prompted new observations of the "social heavens," as Small conjectured, then subsequent social changes certainly heightened the sense that the "social" urgently needed to be observed, understood, and even corrected or improved. Stirring the social order, too, were heightened industrialization, urbanization, and immigration along with dramatic economic swings during the final decades of the nineteenth century. In heeding such enormous changes, "the role of knowledge must be seen as potentially crucial, not only in bringing about social change, but in defining identities appropriate to a changed reality" (Rosenberg, 1979, p. 443). Social phenomena as wide-scale as economic trends and international wars, along with those as minute as smiling behaviors and marital relations, captured the attention of political scientists, sociologists, economists, and psychologists alike. As researchers proceeded to generate novel theories and elaborate prolegomena for research programs, their energies were dedicated to locating the causes of social processes and cataloging their variations.

In America the social scientific mission, while displaying a theoretical pluralism, nevertheless shared several premises about society and individuals as social beings. These projects drew upon new notions of human nature inspired by evolutionary theory, studies of the unconscious, and major reconceptualizations of the physical universe. No longer was it assumed that human nature could be understood using notions of the autonomous individual, moral sentiments, rational cognitions, and the unilinear causality of human action. In recognizing that human nature was more complex than these classic notions supposed, social scientists came to understand human action as not inherently moral, rational, autonomous, or self-conscious but rather socially interdependent, multicausal, nonrational, and amoral (Haskell, 1977). Religion, morality, and philosophy consequently became inadequate for explaining human nature; however, although human nature was seen as complex, it was not deemed unknowable, and the second premise of the new social scientific projects entailed an unconditional belief that scientific method alone could produce valid knowledge about the social world. Finally, the discovery of the complex and partially subterranean currents of human nature along with faith in scientific rationality were, in the minds of most American social scientists, inextricably intertwined with commitments to social reform and human betterment (Leary, 1980; Morawski, 1982). For John Dewey (1900), then newly elected president of the American Psychological Association, the promise of a science of the laws of social life was inseparable from social change. He wrote that social psychology itself "is the recognition that the existing order is determined neither by fate nor by chance, but is based on law and order, on a system of existing stimuli and modes of reaction, through knowledge of which we can modify the practical outcome" (p. 313). For William McDougall (1908) social psychology would produce the "moralisation of the individual" out of the "creature in which the non-moral and purely egoistic tendencies are so much stronger than any altruistic tendencies" (p. 18). Two decades later Knight Dunlap (1928) essentially identified the field with social remediation, calling social psychology "but a propaedeutic to the real subject of ameliorating social problems through scientific social control" (p. xx).

American social science, including what was to take form as social psychology, stepped onto a platform built of a sturdy scientific rationality and a curiously optimistic anticipation of scientifically guided social control. As J. W. Sprowls reflected in 1930, "American politics, philanthropy, industry, jurisprudence, education, and religion have demanded a science of control and prediction of human behavior, not required by similar but less dynamic institutional counterparts in other countries" (p. 380). The new understandings of human nature as complex, amoral, and not entirely rational, however, could have yielded other intellectual renderings. Many European scholars constructed quite different theories, self-consciously reflecting upon the complexities of the unconscious and the implications of nonlinear causality and refusing to set aside two challenging but fundamental manifestations of human sociality: language and culture. They directed their science of social phenomena toward the aims of historical and phenomenological understanding, notably toward hermeneutics and psychoanalysis (Bauman, 1978; Steele, 1982).

By contrast, purchased on a stand of positivist science and optimistic reformism, American intellectuals confronted the apparent paradox of championing the rationality of progressive democratic society while at the same time asserting the irrationality of human action (see Soffer, 1980). These scientists consequently faced an associated paradox of deploying rational scientific procedures to assay the irrationality of human conduct. Despite these paradoxes, or maybe because of them, American social psychologists engineered their examinations of the microdynamics of social thought and action by simultaneously inventing, discovering, and reproducing social life in methodically regulated research settings. The paradoxes were overwritten by a model of reality consisting of three assertions: the unquestionable veracity of the scientific (experimental) method, the fundamental lawfulness of human nature, and the essential psychological base of human social life.

The early psychological perspectives on the social dynamics of human nature were neither universally nor consistently tied to these three premises about human nature, and for that reason many of these bold pilot ventures are omitted from conventional textbook histories of psychology's social psychology. Given that the individual was a central analytic category in their discipline, psychologists were drawn toward understanding the nature of the social in terms of its fundamental relations to the individual. By the last decade of the nineteenth century they began to generate a variety of theoretical perspectives, alternatively defining the social dimensions of the individual as mental functions, consciousness, evolutionary products (or by-products), human faculties, or historically emergent properties. A sampling of these psychological conceptions advanced around the turn of the century illustrates the remarkable varieties of intellectual options available for developing a psychological social psychology.

The Social as Dynamic and Moral: James and Baldwin

For William James, whose 1890 landmark introductory psychology textbook, *The Principles of Psychology,* offers provocative treatises on the social, humans are intrinsically gregarious. This fundamental sociality includes "an innate propensity to get ourselves noticed, and noticed favorable by our kind" (James, 1890, I, p. 293). Although evolutionary theorists already had postulated a biological basis of sociality in terms of selection and survival, James interjected a radical addendum into that postulate. While he, too, defined the social self as a functional property, his social was not a singular self but rather plural selves: "Properly speaking, a *man has as many social selves as there are individuals who recognize him* and carry an image of him in their mind" (p. 294). When he added that "To wound any one of these images is to wound him," plurality became the essence of the individual. James claimed, for instance, that the personal acquaintances of an individual necessarily result in "a division of the man into several selves; and this may be a discordant splitting, as where one is afraid to let one set of his acquaintances know him as he is elsewhere; or it may be a perfectly harmonious division of labor, as where one tender to his children is stern to the soldiers or prisoners under his command" (p. 294). James's social self is complex, fragile, interdependent, and diachronic: The social self is "a *Thought,* at each moment different from that of the last moment, but *appropriative* of the latter, together with all that the latter called its own" (p. 401). The social self constitutes an object that is not readily accessible to scrutiny using scientific methods or explicable in simple deterministic laws of action.

James's mercurial, complex social psychological actor bears striking similarities to James Mark Baldwin's (1897) social individual rendered just 7 years later in *Social and Ethical Interpretations in Mental Development: A Study in Social Psychology.* Baldwin asserted the fundamental nature of the individual and posited that psychological phenomena could be explained *only* in relation to the social. In other words, the individual self can take shape only because of and within a social world. Baldwin's conceptualized "self" at once has agency to act in the world as well as being an object of that world. Delineating a "dialectic of personal growth" (p. 11), wherein the self develops through a response to or imitation of other persons, Baldwin challenged late-nineteenth-century notions of an authentic or unified self and proposed, instead, that "*A man is a social outcome rather than a social unit.* He is always in his greatest part, also some one else. Social acts of his—that is, acts which may not prove anti-social—are his *because they are society's first;* otherwise he would not have learned them nor have had any tendency to do them" (p. 91).

Baldwin's self was more deeply rooted in society than was James's; yet, they shared an overriding distrust of society and consequently created a central place for ethics in their social psychologies. And like James, Baldwin was a methodological pluralist, insisting that social psychology demanded multiple methods: historical and anthropological, sociological and statistical, and genetic (psychological and biological). Baldwin ultimately held that individual psychology is, in fact, social psychology because the individual is a social product and could be understood only by investigating every aspect of society, from institutions to ethical doctrines. It is in this broader conception of the individual as a fundamentally social being that Baldwin differs most strikingly from James: His model directly suggested psychology's social utility through its enhanced knowledge of the individual in society, and in this sense he shared closer kinship with John Dewey in the latter's call for a practical social psychology (Collier, Minton, & Reynolds, 1991). However, in a gesture more nineteenth century than twentieth, Baldwin placed his intellectual faith in human change not in psychology's discovery of techniques of social regulation but rather in a Darwinian vision of the evolution of ethics.

Scientific Specificity and the Social

James's and Baldwin's theories of the social self were embedded in their respective programmatic statements for psychology more generally. Other psychologists prepared more modest treatises on the social self. Among the studies contained in psychology journals of the last decade of the century are various studies depicting social psychology as anthropological-historical, as evolutionary and mechanistic, and as experimental science. For instance, Quantz (1898) undertook a study of humans' relations to trees, describing dozens of myths and cultural practices to demonstrate the virtues of a social evolutionary explanation of customs, beliefs, and the individual psyche. Using historical and anthropological records, he theorized that humans evolved to use reason except under certain social circumstances, where we regress to lower evolutionary status. Such historical researches were held to inform human conduct; for instance, understanding how social evolution is recapitulated in individual development leads us to see how "an education which crowds out such feelings, or allows them to atrophy from disuse, is to be seriously questioned" (p. 500). In contrast to Quantz's descriptive, historical approach but in agreement with his evolutionary perspective, Sheldon (1897) reported a study of the social activities of children using methods of quantification and standardization to label types of people (boys and girls, different social classes) and forms of sociality (altruism, gang behavior). Incorporating both a mechanistic model of control and evolutionary ideas about social phenomena (sociality), Sheldon detected the risks of social-psychological regression to less evolved forms and, consequently, strongly advocated scientifically guided social regulation of human conduct. Soon after, Triplett's (1898) study of competition bore no obvious evolutionary theorizing (or any other theory) but advanced an even stronger mechanistic model and scientific methodology. With its precise control, manipulation, and measurement of social variables, Triplett's experiment compared a subject's performance winding a fishing reel when undertaking the task alone or in competition with others. His experimental report offers no theoretical appreciation of the concepts of "social" or the relation of the individual to society; instead, what is social is simply operationalized as the residual effect when all other components of an action are factored out. Triplett baldly concluded, "From the above facts regarding the laboratory races we infer that the bodily presence of another contestant participating simultaneously in the race serves to liberate latent energy not ordinarily available" (p. 533). Here the social has no unique properties, appears to abide by determinist laws, and requires no special investigative methods or theories.

The research projects of Quantz, Sheldon, and Triplett along with the theoretical visions of James and Baldwin serve not to register some distinct originating moment in psychology's social psychology but rather to exemplify the diversity of theories and methodologies available as the new century commenced. Evolution, ethics, history, and mechanics supplied viable theoretical bases for social psychology, and historical, observational, and experimental techniques likewise furnished plausible methods of inquiry. These promising foundations of a discipline were engaged in the investigation of varied social phenomena, but these protosocial psychologists were especially attentive to two objects: the crowd or "mob" mind and "suggestion," a hypothesized property that purportedly accounted for considerable social behaviors.

A decade later the field had garnered enough scholarly interest to become the subject of two textbooks. William McDougall's (1908) *Introduction to Social Psychology* engaged Darwinian theory to propose the idea of the evolution of social forms and, more specifically, the construct of instincts or innate predispositions. According to McDougall, instincts— "the springs of human action" (p. 3)—consist of cognitive, emotional, and behavioral components that have evolved to constitute the fundamental dynamics of social behaviors and interactions. The same year, Edward A. Ross's (1908) *Social Psychology,* taking a more sociological orientation, proffered an interpretation of society as an aggregate of individual social actions. Ross called his combination of sociological and psychological precepts a "psycho-sociology."

Numerous accounts record 1908, the year of the textbooks, as the origin of the discipline. In fact, the first two decades of the century witnessed a proliferation of studies, theories, and pronouncements on the field. Some historians consequently labeled this interval of social psychological work as the age of schools and theories; they list among the new theory perspectives those of instinct, imitation, neo-Hegelian or Chicago, psychoanalytic, behaviorist, and gestalt (Faris, 1937; Frumkin, 1958; Woodard, 1945). Others have depicted the era as conflictual, fraught with major controversies and theoretical

problems (Britt, 1937a, 1937b; Deutsch & Krauss, 1965; Faris, 1937; Woodard, 1945). As one historical commentator remarked, "It was around 1911 or 1912 that things really began to happen. The second decade of the century witnessed all kinds of ferment" (Faris, 1937, p. 155). George Herbert Mead's inventive theory of the social self and Charles Horton Cooley's conceptualization of groups mark the ingenuity circulating throughout this ferment (Karpf, 1932; Meltzer, 1959; Scheibe, 1985).

For many, eventual resolution of these varied perspectives materialized with a metatheoretical conviction that social psychology was essentially reductive to psychology. In the words of one commentator, there emerged "a settled conviction that patterns as matters of individual acquisition will explain all psychological phenomena, social and individual. As investigation proceeds, the once widely accepted notion that individual psychology is one thing, and social psychology another, has found a place in the scrapheap of exploded psychological presuppositions" (Sprowls, 1930, p. 381). Along with the benefits of a largely established niche within universities and colleges, the discipline of psychology afforded would-be researchers of social life a set of scientific practices that positioned them at the forefront of the social science's search for objective methods and purportedly value-free discourse (Ross, 1979).

A SOCIAL PSYCHOLOGY TO SERVE PSYCHOLOGY AND SOCIETY

In the years surrounding World War I and the more prosperous 1920s, many of these innovative ideas about social psychology did, in fact, end up in a scrap heap, replaced by the belief that psychology provided an appropriate and rich home for social psychology. Psychology offered tantalizing research methods—objective methods. More importantly, psychology manifested a conviction that through this scientific perspective, mental life could be explained as deterministic and lawful (O'Donnell, 1979). By this time psychology was relatively well established as a professional discipline with a progressive scientific association, journals, textbooks, and independent departments in many colleges and universities (Camfield, 1969; Fay, 1939; O'Donnell, 1985). Professional security, however, was just one resource that psychology offered social psychological inquiry. Figuring more prominently among its investigative resources was psychology's overarching conception of the individual and the potential utility of scientific knowledge.

By the 1920s the discipline of psychology had generated a program for interrogating human nature that coupled the late-nineteenth-century recognition that humans were at once more complex and less rational than previously was believed with a growing sense that both individuals and society needed scientific guidance. Moral sentiments, character, individual autonomy, and self-reliance now seemed inadequate for the social scientific task of understanding the dynamics, complexity, and interdependence of human thought and actions (Haskell, 1977; Ross, 1979). American psychologists were proposing something distinctly more modern about mental life: The functionalist idea of individual adaptations to a continually changing environment, an idea nurtured by evolutionary theory, promised a coherent model for penetrating beyond proximate causes, perceiving dynamic action rather than static structures, and observing complex connectedness rather than unilinear causation. In turn, this functionalist viewpoint opened a conceptual place for behaviorism with its hypothesized mechanisms for explaining microscopic processes of adaptation within the individual. Using a double discourse of the *natural* and the *mechanistic* (Seltzer, 1992), psychology afforded a rich, if sometimes contradictory, conception of the individual as at once a natural organism produced through evolution and as operating under mechanistic principles. This "mechanical man" of behaviorism (Buckley, 1989) was promising both as an object of scientific scrutiny and as a target of social control despite the fact that it seemed at odds with the white middle-class sense of psychological complexity: Americans were envisioning self as personality realized through presentation of self, consumption, fulfillment, confidence, sex appeal, and popularity (Lears, 1983; Morawski, 1997; Susman, 1985). The popularization of psychoanalysis promoted understandings of the self as deep, dynamic, and nonrational and, consequently, heightened anxieties about managing this self (Pfister, 1997).

The apparent tensions between deterministic notions of mental life and a dynamic if anxious conception of often irrational human tendencies, however, proved productive for the social and political thinking in the first three decades of the century. The Progressive Era, spanning 1900 to 1917, yielded a series of social reforms marked by firm beliefs in the possibility of efficient and orderly progress and equality—in social betterment (Gould, 1974; Wiebe, 1967) and the centrality of scientific guidance of social and political life (Furner, 1975; Haber, 1964; Wiebe, 1967). Although World War I caused considerable disillusionment about the possibility of rational human conduct, it also provided concrete evidence of both the efficacy and need for scientific expertise to design social controls—to undertake "social engineering" (Graebner, 1980; Kaplan, 1956; Tobey, 1971). Even the acrimonious social commentator Floyd Dell (1926) lauded the new

scientific professionals who "undertake therapeutically the tasks of bringing harmony, order and happiness into inharmonious, disorderly and futile lives" (p. 248). Psychologists' active involvement in the war effort, largely through construction and administration of intelligence tests, demonstrated their utility just as it provided them with professional contacts for undertaking postwar projects (Camfield, 1969; Napoli, 1975; Sokal, 1981; Samelson, 1985). It was in this spirit that John Dewey (1922), an early proponent of psychological social psychology, announced that ensuring democracy and social relations depended on the growth of a "scientific social psychology" (p. 323). Likewise, Floyd Allport (1924) devoted a major part of his famous textbook, *Social Psychology,* to "social control," which he believed essential for the "basic requirements for a truly democratic social order" (p. 415). Knight Dunlap (1928) pronounced that social psychology was "but a propadeutic to the real subject" of ameliorating social problems through techniques of control, and Joseph Jastrow (1928), another psychologist interested in social psychology, urged psychologists studying the social to join "the small remnant of creative and progressive thinkers who can see even this bewildering world soundly and see it whole. Such is part of the psychologist's responsibility" (p. 436). Social psychology, then, would examine precisely those dimensions of human life that were critical to matters of social control and, if investigated at the level of individual actors, would prescribe circumscribed remedies for pressing social problems.

What distinguished the emerging social psychology from earlier propositions was a set of assumptions materializing within scientific psychology more generally: *a belief in the irrational, amoral bases of human nature; a mechanistic, reductionist model of human thought and behavior; the scientific aspirations to prediction and control; and a firm conviction that the resultant scientific knowledge would provide an ameliorative guide to social practice.* Reductionist and mechanistic models conceptualized social phenomena as events at the level of the individual, while the associated scientific aspirations to prediction and control prescribed the use of experimental methods of inquiry. Notably absent from this umbrella program were construals of moral agency, dynamic selfhood, culture, and the dialectic relations between the individual and society that were theorized just a short time earlier.

This rising social psychology, however, harbored several complications and paradoxes. First, psychologists, including the newly self-defined social psychologists, recognized a dilemma of their own complicity: They too inhabit a social world and sometimes act in irrational, emotional ways, but scientific expertise demanded something different, primarily rationality and emotional detachment (Morawski, 1986a, 1986b). Second, the idea of having superior understandings of the social world and the specific knowledge of what constitutes optimal social relations and institutions are unequivocally evaluative claims; yet these claims stood alongside an earnest belief that science is value free, disinterested, and objective. Twinning these latter two incompatible commitments yielded a conflict between utopian or "Baconian" morality, where science serves as an instrument of human improvement, and a "Newtonian" morality, where science serves the rational pursuit of true understandings of nature (Leary, 1980; Toulmin, 1975). Third, the commitment to rigorous, predictive science demanded that discrete variables be investigated under assiduously controlled conditions (typically in the laboratory). Ironically, these experimental conditions actually produced new social phenomena (Suls & Rosnow, 1988), and "The search for precise knowledge created a new subject matter isolated from the wider society; but the justification for the whole research was supposedly its value to this wider world" (Smith, 1997, pp. 769–770). Experimental social psychology, explaining social phenomena in terms of the individual, was soon to dominate the field but did not entirely escape these three tensions; they would continue to surface intermittently. While triumphant, the experimental psychological program for social psychology was not without its critics, some of whom would propose alternative scientific models.

WORK DURING THE INTERWAR YEARS

Progressive Science

Evolutionary notions of social instinct and mechanical notions of radical behaviorism were entertained by social psychologists and the laity alike through the 1920s, albeit with considerable disagreement about their appropriateness. By World War II social psychology comprised a productive research program that in relatively little time had yielded credible models of how individuals interact with others or function in the social world. Appropriating the behaviorist worldview that was rapidly ascending in psychology, Floyd Allport defined social psychology as *"the science which studies the behavior of the individual in so far as his behavior stimulates other individuals, or is itself a reaction to their behavior; and which describes the consciousness of the individual in so far as it is a consciousness of social objects and social relations"* (1924, p. 12). Many scholars have deemed

Allport's *Social Psychology* foundational for an experimental social psychology that emphatically took the individual to be the site of social phenomena. (For an account of the discipline's "origin myths," including Allport's work, see Samelson, 1974, 2000.) This "asocial" social psychology followed its parent, psychology, in its ever-growing fascination with experimentation and statistical techniques of investigation (Danziger, 1990; Hornstein, 1988; Winston, 1990; Winston & Blais, 1996), increasing considerably after World War II (Stam, Radtke, & Lubek, 2000). Allport's text was largely one of boundary charting for the researchers who explored the new field. However, it also is important to see that during the interwar period Allport's introduction comprised but one scientific stream in "a set of rivulets, some of them stagnating, dammed up, or evaporating . . . and others swept up in the larger stream originating elsewhere, if still maintaining a more or less distinctive coloration" (Samelson, 2000, p. 505).

One of these rivulets flowed from the Progressive Era desiderata that social scientific experts devise scientific techniques of social control and took more precise form through the rubric of the individual's "personal adjustment" to the social world (Napoli, 1975). Linking social psychology to the emerging field of personality (Barenbaum, 2000) on the one hand, and to industrial psychology with its attendant commercial ventures on the other, the idea of personal adjustment undergirds substantial research on attitudes, opinions, and the relations between individual personality and social behavior. Employing the first scale to measure masculinity and femininity, a scale that became the prototype for many such tests, for instance, Terman and Miles (1936) were able to observe the relations between an individual's psychological sex identification and problems in their social functioning such as marital discord (Morawski, 1994). Another example of such adjustment research is seen in what has come to be called the "Hawthorne experiment" (purportedly the first objective social psychology experiment in the "real world"), which investigated not individual personality but the individual's adjustment within groups to changes in workplace conditions. The experiment is the source of the eponymous "Hawthorne effect," the reported finding that "the workers' attitude toward their job and the special attention they received from the researchers and supervisors was as important as the actual changes in conditions themselves, if not more so" (Collier, Minton, & Reynolds, 1991, p. 139). Archival examination of the Hawthorne experiments indicates a rather different history: These "objective" experiments actually entailed prior knowledge of the effects of varying workplace conditions, suppression of problematic and contradictory data, and class-based presumptions about workers, especially female employees, as less rational and subject to "unconscious" reactions (Bramel & Friend, 1981; Gillespie, 1985, 1988). Such unreported psychological dynamics of the experimental situation, dynamics later to be called "artifacts" (Suls & Rosnow, 1988), went undocumented in these and other experimental ventures despite the fact that some psychologists were describing them as methodological problems (Rosenzweig, 1933; Rudmin, Trimpop, Kryl, & Boski, 1987).

In 1936 Muzafer Sherif extended social psychology to psychologists themselves, who, he suggested, are "no exception to the rule about the impress of cultural forces." Sherif admonished social psychologists for such disregard—for their "lack of perspective"—arguing that "Whenever they study human nature, or make comparisons between different groups of people, without first subjecting their own norms to critical revision in order to gain the necessary perspective, they force the absolutism of their subjectivity or their community-centrism upon all the facts, even those laboriously achieved through experiment" (p. 9).

Making and Finding Social Relevance

Another stream of research entailed the study of "attitudes," which in 1935 Gordon Allport called "the most distinctive and indispensable concept in American social psychology" (p. 798). Scientific study of attitudes shared kinship with Progressive ideals to scientifically assess beliefs and opinions of the populace and ultimately was to have political and commercial uses, especially in advertising and marketing (Lears, 1992). It is through controlled, quantitative attitude studies that social psychologists significantly refined their experimental techniques of control and numeric exactitude, notably through development of sampling techniques, psychometric scales, questionnaire formats, and technical approaches to assessing reliability and validity (Katz, 1988). In his 1932 review of social psychology L. L. Bernard wrote, "Scale and test making is almost a science in itself utilized by social psychologists in common with the educationists [sic], the industrial and business management people, and in fact by most of the vocational interests in the United States" (p. 279). Bernard detected the wide-scale market value of these psychological technologies, especially their compatibility with and rising ethos of quantification: "There is a strong tendency in this country to find a method of measuring all forms of behavior and nothing is regarded as a demonstrated fact in social psychology or elsewhere until it has been measured or counted and classified" (p. 279).

In the 1930s social psychology's original aim of aiding social welfare, albeit muted by intensive efforts to realize the challenging goal of experimentation on social processes, became more pronounced. Throughout the remainder of the century social psychology would exhibit similar swings back and forth between worldly or political aspirations and scientific ones (Apfelbaum, 1986, p. 10). A swing was indeed occurring in this decade: Psychologist-turned-journalist Grace Adams (1934) chided psychologists for their failure to predict the stock market crash of 1929 culminating in worldwide depression, but soon after social psychologists persevered in probing the depression's complex social effects. The commitment to investigations that more or less directly serve social betterment grew wider in the 1930s and 1940s. However visible these reformist efforts, historians disagree about the political philosophy underlying the research: Whereas some scholars assume the philosophical basis was simply objective science applied to nonlaboratory conditions, others see a more engaged politics, including a benignly democratic, elitist "democratic social engineering" or "New Deal" liberalism (Graebner, 1980; Richards, 1996; van Elteren, 1993). The political atmosphere certainly included a sense of professional survival as evidenced by psychologists' mobilization to create an organization devoted to studying social problems, the Society for the Psychological Study of Social Issues (Finison, 1976, 1979; Napoli, 1975).

Aggression was a prime social problem identified in the 1930s, and the researchers who formulated what was to become a dominant view in aggression research, the frustration-aggression hypothesis, retrospectively produced a list of events that precipitated the research. In addition to the depression, the list included the Spanish Civil War, racism and the caste system of the South, anti-Semitism in Germany, and labor unrest and strikes. Combining the odd bedfellows of behavior theory and Freudian psychoanalysis, a group of Yale University psychologists hypothesized "that the occurrence of aggressive behavior always presupposes the existence of frustration and, contrariwise, that the existence of frustration always leads to some form of aggression" (Dollard, Doob, Miller, Mowrer, & Sears, 1939). Extended to studies of concrete situations—frustrated laboratory rats, poor southerners, unemployed husbands, and adolescents—the frustration-aggression hypothesis constituted a truly "socially relevant" social psychology. The hypothesis pressed a view of the social individual as not always aware of his or her actions, as motivated by factors about which he or she was not fully conscious.

Political and professional affairs inspired social psychologists to engage more directly in social-action-related research; also influencing such research was the formation of a more ethnically diverse research community, including Jewish émigrés who had fled Germany and whose backgrounds entailed dramatically different personal experiences and intellectual beliefs. Franz Samelson (1978) has suggested that these new ethnic dimensions, including researchers more likely sensitized to prejudice, were influential in shaping research on racial prejudice, discrimination, and stereotypes and the consequential move away from American psychology's biologically based notion of race difference. In the case of Kurt Lewin, heralded by many as the most important social psychologist of the century, his own experiences, coupled with the influence of European socialism, shaped his studies of labor conditions that considered foremost the perspective of the workers and attended to the broader context in which events, including labor, transpire (van Elteren, 1993). The influence of émigré social psychologists is evident in the scientific investigations of the psychology of fascism and anti-Semitism; most notable of this socially responsive work is the authoritarian personality theory (Samelson, 1985), discussed more in a later section.

Some streams of intellectual activity, to extend Samelson's metaphor of the field's watercourse, eventually evaporate or are dammed. Despite economic scarcity or perhaps because of it, the 1930s proved a fertile period of innovations, although most of these noncanonical ideas did not survive long. Katherine Pandora (1997) has recovered and documented one such innovative gesture in the interwar work of Garner Murphy, Lois Barclay Murphy, and Gordon Allport through which they "rejected the image of the laboratory as an ivory tower, contested the canons of objectivity that characterized current research practice, and argued against reducing nature and the social worlds to the lowest possible terms" (1997, p. 3). They also questioned the prevailing conceptions of democracy and the moral implications of social scientific experts' interest in adjusting individuals to their social environment. These psychologists' differences with the status quo were sharp, as witnessed by Gordon Allport's claim that "To a large degree our division of labor is forced, not free; young people leaving our schools for a career of unemployment become victims of arrested emotional intellectual development; our civil liberties fall short of our expressed ideal. Only the extension of democracy to those fields where democracy is not at present fully practiced—to industry, education and administration, and to race relations for examples—can make possible the realization of infinitely varied purposes and the exercise of infinitely varied talents" (Allport, quoted in Pandora, 1997, p. 1). His stance on the relation of the individual to society, and on the state of society, stands in stark contrast to the elitist models of social control, personal adjustment, and democratic social engineering that inhered in

most social psychology. Their dismissal of the dominant meaning of the two central terms of social psychology, the "individual" and "social," as well as their critiques of conventional laboratory methods, enabled them to propose what Pandora calls "experiential modernism": the historically guided "search for scientific forms of knowing that would unsettle conventional ways of thinking without simultaneously divorcing reason from feeling, and thus from the realm of moral sentiments" (p. 15).

Another attempt to alter mainstream social psychology is found in Kurt Lewin's endeavors to replace the discipline's individualist orientation with the study of groups qua groups, to apply gestalt principles instead of thinking in terms of discrete variables and linear causality, and to deploy experiments inductively (to illustrate a phenomenon) rather than to use them deductively (to test hypotheses) (Danziger, 1992, 2000). Other now largely forgotten innovations include J. F. Brown's (1936; Minton, 1984) proposal for a more economically based and Lewinian social psychology, and Gustav Icheiser's phenomenological theories along with his social psychology of the psychology experiment (Bayer & Strickland, 1990; Rudmin, Trimpop, Kryl, & Boski, 1987). By the time of the United States' entrance into World War II in 1941, social psychology had acquired both a nutrient-rich professional niche within psychology and a set of objective techniques for probing individuals' thoughts and actions when interacting with other individuals. While social psychology's ability to generate scientific knowledge still was regarded suspiciously by some psychologists, social psychologists nevertheless became actively involved in war-related research. They confidently took the helm of government-sponsored studies of propaganda, labor, civilian morale, the effects of strategic bombing, and attitudes. The war work proved to have so strengthened social psychologists' solidarity that one participant claimed, "The Second World War has brought maturity to social psychology" (Cartwright, quoted in Capshew, 1999, p. 127). After the war psychological experts were challenged to generate both relevant and convincingly objective research and form alliances with those in positions of power (Harris, 1998). However promising to the field's future, that organizational gain was achieved at the cost of damming up some of the field's investigative channels, narrowing further the acceptable options for theory and methods alike. This scientific service experience also permeated the core conceptions of human kinds, and during the postwar years the conception of the individual–social world relation would evolve significantly from the Progressive and interwar scenario of more or less mechanical actors needing adjustment to efforts to refine the machinery of society.

MIDCENTURY ON: FROM POST–WORLD WAR II AND POST-MECHANISM TO POST-POSITIVISM

World War II Era

For many historians of social psychology, the two world wars often bracket significant shifts within the discipline. Both world wars brought with them pronounced expansions of psychology, ones that eventually found their way into nearly every facet of daily life (Capshew, 1999; Herman, 1995). In reflecting on changes wrought by the war years to social psychology, Kurt Lewin (1947/1951) speculated that new developments in the social sciences might prove "as revolutionary as the atom bomb" (p. 188). What he seemed to have in mind is how the social sciences informed one another in treating social facts as a reality as worthy of scientific study as are physical facts. He also observed developments in research tools and techniques and a move among the social sciences away from classification systems to the study of "dynamic problems of changing group life" (p. 188). What Lewin could not have imagined at the time, however, were those very depths to which the "atomic age" would rearrange sociopolitical life and the field of social psychology. In his own time Lewin's optimism for social psychology counterbalanced Carl Murchison's more gloomy tone in the 1935 edition of *The Handbook of Social Psychology*: "The social sciences at the present moment stand naked and feeble in the midst of the political uncertainty of the world" (p. ix). The turnaround in these intervening years was so dramatic that Gardner Lindzey was moved to declare in the 1954 *Handbook* that Murchison's edition was not simply "out of print" but "out of date." Lindzey measured out social psychology's advance by the expansion of the handbook to two volumes. But more than quantity had changed. Comparing the table of contents over these years is telling of social psychology's changing face. In 1935 natural history and natural science methods applied to social phenomena across species; the history of "man" and cultural patterns were strikingly predominant relative to experimental studies. By 1954 social psychology was given a formal stature, deserving of a history chapter by Gordon Allport, a section on theories and research methods in social psychology, and a second volume of empirical, experimental, and applied research.

On many counts, during and after World War II experimental social psychology flourished like never before under military and government funding and a newfound mandate of social responsibility, which, in combination, may have served to blur the line between science and politics writ large, between national and social scientific interests (Capshew, 1999; Finison, 1986; Herman, 1995). Questions turned to matters of morale (civilian and military), social relations (group and intergroup dynamics), prejudice, conformity, and so on (Deutsch, 1954; Lewin, 1947/1951), and they often carried a kind of therapeutic slant to them in the sense of restoring everyday U.S. life to a healthy democracy. To quote Herman (1995), "Frustration and aggression, the logic of personality formation, and the gender dynamics involved in the production of healthy (or damaged) selves were legitimate sources of insight into problems at home and conflicts abroad" (p. 6). Psychologists' work with civilians and the military, with organizations and policy makers, parlayed into new relations of scientific psychological practice, including those between "scientific advance, national security, and domestic tranquility" and between "psychological enlightenment, social welfare, and the government of a democratic society" (Herman, 1995, p. 9). As Catherine Lutz (1997) writes, military and foundation funding of social psychological research, such as Hadley Cantril's on foreign and domestic public opinion or the Group Psychology Branch of the Office of Naval Research, once combined with the "culture and political economy of permanent war more generally, shaped scientific and popular psychology in at least three ways—the matters defined as worthy of study, the epistemology of the subject that it strengthened, and its normalization of a militarized civilian subjectivity" (pp. 247–248).

New Ways of Seeing Individual and Social Life

Amongst historians there exists fair consensus on a reigning social psychology of this moment as one of an overriding sensibility of social engineering or a "psychotechnology" in the service of a "liberal technocratic" America (e.g., Graebner, 1986; Rose, 1992; also see Ash, 1992). But such an exclusive view overlooks how certain theoretical influences that in concert with the times helped to shape the terms of the subject matter, the field itself, and how the individual–social world relation was to be construed. For Solomon Asch (1952), for example, subject matters, such as conformity, were sites revealing of the "intimate unity of the personal and social" in a single act of yielding or asserting one's independence (p. 496). Elsewhere the personal and social became reworked through Kenneth B. Clark's research on race and segregation, work that was vital to the decision in *Brown v. Board of Education;* and, Gordon Allport's (1954) *The Nature of Prejudice* revealed how prejudice, hatred, and aggression rippled out across the personal and situational to the social and national. Another significant case is found in what has come to be called the authoritarian personality. Early Marxist-Freudian integrations in the study of political passivity or "authoritarian character" structure in Germany by Reich and Fromm and subsequently in America by Horkheimer and the "Berkeley group" yielded the 1950 edited volume *The Authoritarian Personality* (Adorno, Frenkel-Brunswik, Levinson, & Sanford, 1950). Even though "Reich's original problem" was refitted to "a liberal, empiricist, individual-psychology framework" (Samelson, 1985, p. 200), study of authoritarian personality, like other examples mentioned, made visible the equation of "politics and psychology and the convergence of personal and social analysis" (Herman, p. 60). The "authoritarian episode," writes Graham Richards (1997), "was an expression of a complex but fundamental set of ideological conflicts being waged within and between industrialised white cultures: capitalism vs. communism, democracy vs. totalitarianism, liberalism vs. puritanism" (pp. 234–235). Insofar as authoritarian personality hinged individual personality to political ideologies and national character to intergroup and international tensions (including racism in the United States and leadership studies in small groups), then Lewinian small group research's physical and mathematical language of space, field, forces, and tensions served to link public and private spheres of home and work with liberal ideals of a technocratic America (Deutsch, 1954; Gibb, 1954; Ash, 1992; van Elteren, 1993). Together, these levels of analysis (the individual, group, etc.) and social psychological phenomena offered different ways to conceive of the traffic between the individual and the social world. They also functioned to remap how the social was construed to reside in or be created by the individual, as well as the function of these new ways of seeing individual and social life for all.

Still, once entered into, social psychology offers no Ariadne's thread to guide historians through its disciplinary passageways of subject matters, epistemological shifts, and changing notions of subjectivity. Just as cultural, social, economic, and political life in the United States was in flux, so the more familiar and routine in social psychology was being tossed up and rearranged. Gender and race rearrangements during and after the war in the division of work, in labor union negotiations, and in domestic affairs signal incipient counterculture and social movements ready to burst through the veneer of a culture of "containment" (Brienes, 1992; May, 1988). Much as some historians broaden out this moment's sensibility as "not just nuclear energy that had to be contained, but the social and sexual fallout of the atomic age itself" (May, p. 94), so others add that the "tide of black migration, coupled with unprecedented urban growth and prosperity, reinvigorated African American culture, leading to radical developments in music, dance, language and fashion" (Barlow, 1999, p. 97). American life was being recreated, with the tug of desires for stability—cultural accommodation and civil defense—exerting as much force as the drive

for change—cultural resistance and civil rights. Margot Henriksen (1997) writes of this tension as one between consent and dissent wherein for blacks "Western powers' racism and destructiveness came together explicitly in the Holocaust and implicitly in the atomic bombings of Hiroshima and Nagasaki" (p. 282). These entanglements of postwar anxieties, struggles, and dreams reverberated in America's popular imagination, such as Frank Capra's early postwar film *It's a Wonderful Life,* Frank Conroy's characterizations of 1950s America as "in a trance" and young Americans as the "silent generation," Salinger's age of anxiety in *The Catcher in the Rye,* the new science fiction genre film *The Day the Earth Stood Still,* the rebel "beat generation" of Jack Kerouac, bebop jazz, and a "wave of African American disc jockeys introduc[ing] 'rhyming and signifying'" (Barlow, p. 104; Breines, 1992; Henriksen, 1997).

Social psychological works appealed for new approaches to leadership and peace, group relations (at home and work), cohesiveness, ways to distinguish good democratic consensus (cooperation) from bad (compliance, conformity, and the more evil form of blind obedience), prejudice, trust, and surveillance (as, for example, in research by Allport, Asch, Gibb, Milgram, Thibaut, and Strickland). Tacking back and forth between social and cultural happenings marking this era and the field's own internal developments, social psychology did not simply mirror back the concerns of the age but rather was carving out its place in American life as it translated and built psychological inroads to America's concerns of the day.

Approaching problems of the day provoked as well cross-disciplinary interchange for many social psychologists, such as Kurt Lewin, Solomon Asch, Leon Festinger, Gordon Allport, and Theodore Newcomb. One way this need was formalized for small group research was through centers, such as those at Harvard University, MIT, or the University of Michigan. Another way interdisciplinary interchange became influential within social psychology was through the Macy Foundation Conferences, which brought together researchers from, for example, mathematics, anthropology, neuropsychology, and social psychology for discussion on communication and human relations, which came to be regarded as the area of cybernetics (Fremont-Smith, 1950). Amongst researchers attending the Macy Conferences were those who, such as Alex Bavelas, Gregory Bateson, and Margaret Mead, would come to construe social psychology's small group concepts and dynamics through cybernetic notions of communication patterns, the flow of information and human relations (Heims, 1993). Together, the concerns of the day urged along disciplines on questions of moral certainty and epistemological truth as military technologies of information theory and communication began to give rise to the cybernetic age and its corresponding challenges to notions of human subjectivity.

Cold War, Cybernetics, and Social Psychology

When Solomon Asch (1952) well noted the very conditions of life and beliefs in society as part and parcel of the "historical circumstances [under which] social psychology [made] its appearance" in midcentury America (p. 4), he might have added how the culmination of these forces made for a profound overhaul of psychology's object—the human. The Macy Foundation Conferences, for example, incited talk of "electronic brains" and fantasies of robots, as well as of "communication," "cybernetics," and "information," all of which assumed their collective place in social psychology's imagination of the human subject for decades to come (Bayer, 1999a; also see Heims, 1993). This makeover is about assessing how, as John Carson (1999) argues of psychology's object, the human mind, social psychology's object of the individual becomes "fashioned into different investigative objects" (p. 347). By the mid-1950s, "Information theory and computer technology, in addition to statistical methods, suggested a new way to understand people and to answer the question of the mind's relation to matter" (Smith, 1997, p. 838). The older mechanistic notion of man-as-machine was giving way to one of man-as-an-information-processor in which the human becomes a composite of input-output functions understood as a "homeostatic self-regulating mechanism whose boundaries were clearly delineated from the environment" (Hayles, 1999, p. 34; also see Bayer, 1999a; Edwards, 1996; Smith, 1997). Seen as forged out of a combination of cognitive psychology, behaviorism, gestalt, information theory, mathematics, and linguistics, this version of the nature of "man" allowed for "man" and machine (computer) to go beyond metaphors of mechanical man into the realm of *relations between* man and machine (Edwards). Cybernetics was thus "a means to extend liberal humanism" by "fashioning human and machine alike in the image of an autonomous, self-directed" and "self-regulating" individual (Hayles, p. 7). Movement between man and machine was eased by the idea of communication denoting relation, not essence; indeed, *relation* itself came to signify the direction of social psychology—interpersonal, group, intergroup—as much as in communication studies (Hayles, p. 91; Samelson, 1985). This transformation of social psychology's object also entailed a change to small groups as its unit of study (Heims, p. 275; also see Back, 1972; Danziger, 1990), an idea resonant with an emerging idealized notion of open communication in small communities.

Within small group laboratories, cybernetics and information theory brought men and machines together by including each in the loop of communication-control-command-information (C^3I) interactions. Robert Bales, for example, translated Parson's sexual division of labor into a language of communication codes of instrumental and expressive interactions such that together in the context of small groups they functioned as a "mutually supporting pair" serving "stabilizing" or "homeostatic like functions" (Bales, 1955, p. 32). For Alex Bavelas (1952) messages carried information about status and relationship to the group and patterns of communication about networks, efficiency, and leadership. Bavelas's work thus marks the beginning of the sea change from Lewin's "Gestalt psychology to . . . 'bits' of information" (Heims, 1993, p. 223).

That human and machine could interface via information codes or messages in small groups eased the way as well to using certain technologies as message communicators, such as Crutchfield's (1955) vision of an electronic communication apparatus for small group research, featuring a system of light signals with a controlling switchboard allowing the experimenter to control and communicate messages among group members. Electronic apparatuses "stood in" for other experimental group participants, creating the impression of the presence of other participants sending messages to one another in a small group. But, just as significantly, these apparatuses helped to fashion a human-as-information-processor subjectivity (Bayer, 1998a). Such electronic devices, along with a host of other technologies, such as audio recordings and one-way mirrors, began to characterize small group laboratory research as the outer world of everyday social life was increasingly recreated inside the social psychology laboratory (Bayer & Morawski, 1992; Bayer, 1998a). Simulated laboratory small groups offered at least one way to reconcile small group research with social psychology's demands for scientific experimental rigor and to serve as a kind of laboratory in which to reconstrue communication as a social psychology of social relations (Graebner, 1986; Pandora, 1991).

In retrospect, small group research of the 1950s to the 1990s seemed deeply invested in mapping a "contested terrain of the social relations of selves" (Bayer & Morawski, 1991, p. 6), for which the language of communication and control served as much to set the terms of management relations as it did to masculinize communication in corporate culture, or the thinking man's desk job (Bayer, 2001). Bales's research, for example, tailored the gender terms of social psychology's communication, control, and command interchanges by converting Parsonian sex roles into communication labor that sorted group members' contributions into either the "best liked man" or the "best ideas man"—a mutually supporting pair in corporate management. That the typical instrumental gender role moved between private and public life was in keeping with a Parsonian view of normal social arrangements. Less routine here was the translation of social-emotional relations, the work expected of women and thought to be suited to domestic life, into a kind of communication labor needed in masculine corporate culture. Despite small group researchers' reliance at times on women, as in Lewin's work with women and nutrition during times of scarcity or Parson's familial gender division, small group research in the field and the laboratory tended, in the early decades, to study the group life of men in the public domain (Bayer & Morawksi, 1991). Over subsequent decades, however, small group research became a site of gender-difference testing, almost serving as a barometer of the gender politicization of work spaces and women's movement into them (e.g., Eagly, 1987; Eagly, Karau, & Makhijani, 1995).

Cybernetics and the "Inside-Outside Problem" in Times of Suspicion and Surveillance

While the cybernetic age clearly had a hand in renewed study of boundaries between inner and outer, or the "inside-outside" problem (Heider, citing F. Allport, 1959, p. 115; Edwards, 1996; Hayles, 1999), equally mediating were postwar and McCarthy times in U.S. life heightening a psychological sensibility around inner-outer spaces. This period was itself, to quote M. Brewster Smith (1986), marked by a "crescendo of domestic preoccupation with loyalty and internal security" (p. 72). Drawing on the work of Paul Virillo, Hayles writes that "in the post–World War II period the distinction between inside and outside ceased to signify in the same way," as "cybernetic notions began to circulate . . . and connect up with contemporary political anxieties" (p. 114). Worries over the "inability to distinguish between citizen and alien, 'loyal American' and communist spy" (Hayles, p. 114) are concerns about distinguishing between appearances and reality, between self and other, between surface and depth, outer and inner realms. Whereas David Riesman (1969) wrote that this period resulted in a shift from inner to an other-directed society, Richard Sennett (1974/1976) later countered with observations that in fact the reverse order characterized midcentury American selves. American society had become increasingly marked by its stress on inner-directed conditions, by what he saw as a "confusion between public and intimate life" (p. 5). Side by side, these interpretations tell of a magnified concern by social psychologists and citizens alike around borders and boundaries. Rearrangements in social divisions of private and public life, of inner- and other-directedness in postwar America, had at their heart a reconfiguring of inner-outer boundaries.

The Case of Balance Theories

It may be of little surprise, given the above, that balance or consistency theories garnered a fair bit of social psychological attention at this time. The individual–social world relation was depicted as a kind of juggling of internal states and external conditions, or personal versus situational attributions played off of one another. Against the backdrop of social and political upheaval, then, psychological balance theories offered a feeling of equipoise at some level, whether of one's own inner and outer life or one's relation to others or to surrounding beliefs, during this heated mix in America of politics, sex, and secrets. Balance theories may thus be thought of as exerting a kind of intuitive double-hold—first through the cybernetic revision of homeostatic mechanisms and second through an everyday social psychology that sought perhaps to balance the day-to-day teeter-tottering of psychological security and insecurity. Arguably outgrowths of cybernetics and wider cultural preoccupations, cognitive consistency theories, such as Leon Festinger's cognitive dissonance theory, Frtiz Heider's balance theories, and John Thibaut and Harold Kelley's social exchange theories, held out a subjectivity of rational control in a time of the country appearing out of control.

It is possible to regard social psychology's mix of balance theories and cybernetic influences during the period 1945 to the 1960s as reflecting not quite competing versions of the human. On the one hand, as Hayles outlines them, there circulated the notion of "man" as a "homeostatic self-regulating mechanism whose boundaries were clearly delineated from the environment and, [on the other], a more threatening, reflexive vision of a man spliced into an informational circuit that could change him in unpredictable ways" (Hayles, 1999, p. 34; also see Bayer, 1999b). The former version resonates with early balance or consistency theories for how they tried to reconcile psychological life with observable reality. The latter, more reflexive version carried within it the beginnings of a critique of objectivist epistemology. Such reflexive notions of the subject helped to recast behaviorist notions of simple, reductionist input-output mechanisms and other correspondence theories of the subject in which representations of the world were assumed to map neatly onto internal experience. Instead, experience itself was thought to organize or bring into being the outside—or social—world (Hayles, 1999). That attributions might arise out of common cultural beliefs without objective or empirical real-world referents gestures toward a more constructionist intelligibility in social psychology, as found in theory and research on self and social perception work by Daryl Bem and Harold Kelly in his attribution research. By the 1970s Gergen was to note that had works such as these been "radically extended," they would have posed a "major threat to the positivist image of human functioning" (1979, p. 204). One could add to this research on sense-making the high drama of laboratory simulations, including Milgram's 1960s experiments on obedience (and his film *Obedience*) and Zimbardo's 1970s prison study that augmented—however inadvertently—views of social roles as performative.

From Rational Calculator to Error-Prone Subject

One might usefully think of the influence of computers, cybernetic notions, and laboratory simulation techniques as technologies of the social psychological subject. That is, as Gerd Gigerenzer (1991) argues, researchers' tools function as collaborators in staging versions of human nature or the human mind, what he called *tools-to-theory* transformations. Looking at the case of the institutionalization of the statistic ANOVA (Analysis of Variance) and Kelley's attribution theory, for example, Gigerenzer demonstrated how the statistic became a version of human as an "intuitive statistician." Across these tool-to-theory transformations relying on computers, statistics, and information theory—cybernetics— notions of the human as a rational calculator were one side of the coin of the social psychological subject. On its flip side was an opposing version arising in the 1970s when political events and social history conspired to make known man as a fallible information processor. Irving Janis's analyses of the Pearl Harbor and Bay of Pigs fiascos, for example, cast a stone into the seeming calm waters of group cohesion by revealing its downside—groupthink (Janis & Mann, 1977). By the 1970s "man" was virtually awash in characterizations as an error-prone decision maker who fell victim to a host of biases and heuristics, such as in research by Daniel Kahneman and Amos Tversky. Prior to the 1970s, as Lola Lopes (1991) found, most of the research depicted a rather good decision-making subject. By the 1980s, however, when *Time* magazine named the computer "Man of the Year," "man" himself would be characterized in *Newsweek* as "woefully muddled information processors who often stumble along ill-chosen shortcuts to reach bad conclusions" (Lopes, p. 65; Haraway, 1992). This rhetoric of irrationality caught on inside the discipline as well, reframing areas such as social perception, influence, and prejudice wherein miscalculation, misperception, and other social psychological information errors were taken to be the devil in the details of daily interactions. Overlooked here as with the overemphasis on internal causes in attribution research was, as Ichheiser argued, the power of the American ideology of individualism in predisposing individuals and social psychologists to look for personal rather than social-historical causes (Bayer & Strickland, 1990).

This oversight was in fact a crucial one, especially in light of the penetrating challenges to social psychology's subject matters, its reigning positivist epistemology, and notions of subjectivity from various social movements.

SOCIAL MOVEMENTS AND MOVEMENTS FOR CHANGE IN SOCIAL PSYCHOLOGY

Individual–Social World Dualism Revisited

Changes in social psychology's vision of man, including ways to conceptualize the individual, social relations, and the "ensuing riddle of their relationship"—or, "the endless problem of how the individual stood *vis-à-vis* the world"—would meet additional challenges from social movements such as second wave feminism, black civil rights, and gay and lesbian rights, as well as from war protests (Riley, 1988, p. 15; Richards, 1997). That social psychology suffered theoretically and research-wise on the social side of its psychological equation was a significant part of the storm social psychology would have to weather in the 1970s. But, the problem went beyond the nature of the relation of this dualism's polar opposites. Instead, the dualism itself, as that of the nature-nurture divide, would eventually be undermined (Henriques, Hollway, Urwin, Venn, & Walkerdine, 1984/1998; Richards, 1997; Parker & Shotter, 1990).

Whence the Social?

For some social psychologists, the desire for a *social* social psychology formed out of what was considered the disappearing "social" in social psychology, which, even in the case of small group research, seemed to have collapsed into the individual. Ivan Steiner (1974) posed the disappearance of "the social" as a conundrum given that social movements of the 1960s might have led one to expect a more "groupy" social psychology. In examining dissonance theory, attribution theory, attitude research, and self-perception theory, Steiner found even further evidence of social psychology's individualistic orientation. Not only had the social moved inside the individual, but social psychology appeared to have lost sight of its compass, all of which, he thought, might account for the "gloomy" "self-reproach" and near "despair" among social psychologists (Steiner, p. 106). It is curious that social psychology's object, the human, had become, at least in some experimental quarters, a rather gloomy-looking soul too— error prone and, if not alienated from himself, given to failures in helping (e.g., Darley & Latane, 1968). Against various "denunciations of laboratory research to damning criticisms of the ethical and methodological qualities of . . . investigative strategies, and even to suggestions that [social psychologists] forsake . . . scientific tradition in favor of participation in social movements," however, Steiner initially held out hope (p. 106). He saw signs of change in social movements; the new decision-making research, such as that of Irving Janis's concept of groupthink; Eliot Aronson's interest in T-groups; and, the faint rustle of reviving interest in Hadley Cantril's 1941 *The Psychology of Social Movements* (in which mental and social context formed the crucial framework for chapters on, for example, the lynch mob, the kingdom of father divine, the Oxford group, the Townsend plan, and the Nazi party). These signs were read as indicative of a rising tide of "collective action" that might displace the "self-reliant individualism" of the 1960s (Steiner, 1974)—only to be regrettably reinterpreted a decade later as a *mis*reading of the power of the individualist thesis (Steiner, 1986).

Whence the Real-World Relevance?

Inside the discipline, critical voices grew increasingly strong on the shortcomings of group research and experimental methods in social psychology, as well as concern over social psychology's impoverished theoretical status. Experimental set-ups that grew out of information theory and translated into laboratory simulations came to be regarded as overly contrived, relying on "button pressing, knob turning, note writing, or telephonic circuits loaded with white noise" (Steiner, 1974, p. 100). The very invented nature of experimental laboratory groups was described in the 1960s as "a temporary collection of late adolescent strangers given a puzzle to solve under bizarre conditions in a limited time during their first meeting while being peered at from behind a mirror" (Fraser & Foster, 1984, p. 474). These groups came to be referred to as "nonsense" groups (Barker, cited in Fraser & Foster), and laboratory experiments as "experiments in a vacuum" (Tajfel, 1972). Alternative approaches to groups began to gather their own critical reviews, both for their ultimately individualistic focus and for a rather narrow cognitive emphasis. Even Henri Tajfel's alternative of Social Categorization Approach and Social Identity Theory, while proposed as putting the "social" back into the study of groups, began to reveal itself as part of the information-processing model in which "error becomes a theoretical catch-all for what cannot be explained within individual-society dualism: the absence of the 'correct' response" (Henriques et al., 1984/1998, p. 78). In this framework, racial prejudice, for example, wound up being treated as a problem in information processing without "addressing either the socio-historical production of racism or the psychic mechanism through which it is reproduced in white people's feelings and their relations to black people" (p. 78).

Crisis—What Crisis?

These criticisms of social psychology's individualistic thesis and nonsense laboratory groups combined with fierce debate about social psychology's laboratory uses of deception and its positivist scientific practices for a full blown disciplinary self-analysis—or crisis of knowledge in social psychology, as it has come to be known. For some, social psychology's laboratory of "zany manipulations," "trickery," or "clever experimentation" was regarded as ensuring the "history of social psychology . . . [would] be written in terms not of interlocking communities but of ghost towns" (Ring, 1967, p. 120; see also, for example, Kelman, 1967; Rubin, 1983). For others, experimental artifacts appeared almost impossible to contain as the laboratory increasingly revealed itself as a site wherein social psychological meanings were as likely to be created in situ as to reveal wider general laws of individual and social life (Suls & Rosnow, 1988; also see Rosenzweig, 1933). In a wider sense, the field was regarded as having gone through several phases of development as a science to arrive at what Kurt Back (1963) identified as a "unique position" of being able to encompass a "social psychology of knowledge as a legitimate division of social psychology," which would take into account "the problem of the scientist, of his shifting direction, his relation to the trends of the science and of society, and his assessment of his own efforts is itself a topic of social psychology" (p. 368).

A Social Psychology of Social Psychology

Not quite mirroring one another, social psychology's troubles around its individual–social world relation were becoming as fraught as the internal–external divide constituting the imagined interior of its subject. Julian Henriques (1984/1998), for one, argues that "for psychology the belief in rationality and in perfect representation come together in the idea of scientific practice" such that with an individual subject prone to errors "the path is set for empiricist science to intervene with methodologies which can constrain the individual from the non-rational as, for example, Allport has social psychology protecting individuals against the lure of communist misinformation and society against subversion" (p. 80). Other analyses had begun to show in different ways problems with social psychology's individual–social world and person–situation dualisms. With these problems came the appearance of splinters in social psychology's positivist desires for knowledge outside history, culture, and time. Social psychology's image of positivist "man" was further uncovered to be commensurate with the Western ideology of possessive individualism, an "important ingredient of political liberalism" and "predominant ideology of modern capitalism," as Joachim Israel (1979) and others traced out (e.g., Sampson, 1977) in dissonance theory, level of aspiration work, and social comparison group research. "Domination-recognition" struggles provided another case in point, regarding which Erika Apfelbaum and Ian Lubek (1976) asked whether social psychology played a repressive role. Their concern was that social psychology detracted attention from identity processes, such as those among women and blacks, and so eclipsed recognition of those relational spaces where power shapes a group's chances for visibility and its capacity to claim an identity of its own (also see Apfelbaum, 1979/1999). Other critical historical studies elaborated this central critique of social psychology's subjects and subject matters, such as Lita Furby's (1979) and Karen Baistow's (2000) examination of the cultural, historical, and political particulars of the concept of locus of control.

The Case of Locus of Control

Furby and Baistow both recognize several main features of concepts articulated through notions of internal psychological control, such as locus of control, level of aspiration, learned helplessness, and self-efficacy. First, emphases on internal control reflect the discipline's class-based interests in "maintaining a prevailing control ideology that is as internal as possible" (Furby, p. 180) and contributed to a fashioning of a "self-management subject" (Baistow). Second, emphases on self-determinism fit well with prevailing Protestant ethic beliefs in the value of internal control, an integral ingredient of capitalist ideology. Third, while for Furby this promulgation of a self-determining subject indicates a repressive role of psychology's social control interventions, Baistow takes this one step further to show a more productive potential of psychology's self-control ideologies. Drawing on Nikolas Rose's (1992) extension of Foucauldian analysis to psychology, Baistow (2000) shows how, for example, increased senses of internality could eventuate in challenges to the status quo, such as black civil rights protests and the rise of black militancy. In these cases, increasingly widespread notions of locus of control introduced as solutions to problems of disadvantaged groups may have helped to make possible empowerment talk, now "commonplace in political rhetoric in the USA and the UK in recent years and a seemingly paradoxical objective of government policy and professional activities" (p. 112). Contrary, then, to being overly individualized and depoliticized psychological notions of control, locus of control discourses became instead politicized through their use in collective action to transform being powerless into empowerment (Baistow, 2000).

"Social Psychology in Transition"

Reconnecting the Dots between the Personal and the Political

In addition to these critical histories of central social psychological concepts were those entered by women, feminist, and black psychologists who provided detailed appreciations and evidence on the social, cultural, historical, and political contingencies of social psychology's production of knowledge on the one hand, and of social psychological life on the other. Where many of these works dovetailed was on the fallacy of attributing to nature what was instead, in their view, thoroughly social. Psychologist Georgene H. Seward's 1946 book *Sex and the Social Order,* for example, revealed the historical contingencies of distinct sex-typed roles for women and men by showing how these distinctions often dissolved in times of economic or political turmoil. Just years later, philosopher Simone de Beauvoir (1952) published *The Second Sex,* whose central tenet, "woman is made, not born," struck a chord with Seward's argument as well as those who followed in subsequent decades. Betty Friedan's (1963) *The Feminine Mystique* rendered the "woman question" anew through its language of humanistic psychology identifying sex-role typing as stunting women's growth while forgoing a language of rights in favor of post-war cultural discourse that neither wholly eschewed domesticity nor wholly endorsed a single-minded pursuit of careers for women (see Meyerowtiz, 1993). Dorothy Dinnerstein, a student of Solomon Asch, published the feminist classic *The Mermaid and the Minotaur* in 1976, a book she had been working on since the late 1950s and that stemmed from her thinking through the "pull between individuality and the social milieu." The nature of her questions and concerns carried clear cold war preoccupations as well as feminist ones, influenced by de Beauvoir and Norman Brown, in her attempts to "resolve the contradictions between the Freudian and the Gestalt vision of societal processes" (p. xii) and those of gender arrangements. Kenneth B. Clark's (1966a, 1966b) research on psychological hurt and social-economic-political oppression of blacks, like his writing on civil rights, and the dilemma of power and the "ethical confusion of man" brought together the psychological and political. By the late 1960s the black psychology movement voiced concern over the discipline's ethnocentrism and internal racism (Richards, 1997).

In her social psychology textbook, Carolyn Wood Sherif (1976) acknowledged both movements, asking if there could indeed be a valid social psychology that neglected social movements, for social movements and social change surely transform social psychological phenomena. By now, Naomi Weisstein, as Sherif (1979/1987) reflected in her chapter on bias in psychology, had "almost a decade ago . . . fired a feminist shot that ricocheted down the halls between psychology's laboratories and clinics, hitting its target dead center" (p. 58). Weisstein (1971) showed that psychology's understanding of woman's nature was based more in myth than in fact—and patriarchal myth at that. She argued further that without attention to the social context and knowledge of social conditions, psychology would have little to offer on the woman question. For, if anything, decades of research on experimental and experimenter bias had repeatedly demonstrated that instead of offering an unfettered view of the nature of womanhood, laboratory experiments had themselves been revealed as sites of social psychological processes and phenomena in-the-making.

It is interesting that the forces of feminist and black psychologists would combine with results from the social psychology of laboratory experiments for what by the 1970s became known within the discipline as a full-blown crisis. This period of intense self-examination from the ground of social psychology's paradigm on up is all too readily apparent in hindsight to be about social psychology's transition from the height of its modernist commitments in midcentury America to what is often now called postmodernism.

TRANSITING THE MODERN TO POSTMODERN ERA

A number of markers can be identified to indicate this transition of social psychology from the age of modernism into postmodernism, a transition that is still very much a part of U.S. culture, politics, and daily life. In wider Western social psychology endeavors one of the markers of this passage would most likely be the conference organized by Lloyd Strickland and Henri Tajfel, held at Carleton University and attended by psychologists from Europe, the U.K., and North America, and from which was published the 1976 book *Social Psychology in Transition*. Disciplinary parameters considered to be in transition included the view of social psychology's subjects and topics as historically constituted (e.g., Gergen, 1973) and of the laboratory as out-of-sync with notions of an "acting, information-seeking, and information-generating agent" (Strickland, 1976, p. 6). Others tackled

more epistemological and ontological matters facing social psychology, querying everything from what constituted science in social psychology to more ontological concerns. In addressing priorities and paradigms, the conference volume accorded with then current views on Kuhnian notions of paradigm shifts and with a more profound concern about what constituted the human. Additional signposts are found in works addressing psychology as a "moral science of action" (e.g., Shotter, 1975), revisiting phenomena through frameworks of the sociology of knowledge, as discussed in an earlier section (e.g., Buss, 1979), and critically engaging the reflexive nature of the field—that is, how "psychology helps to constitute sociopsychological reality [and] . . . is itself constituted by social process and psychological reality" (Gadlin & Rubin, 1979, pp. 219–220). The field's growing recognition of its cultural and historical relativity pointed time and again to how social psychologists need to contend with a subject and with subject matters that are for all intents and purposes more historical, cultural, social, and political than not (e.g., Strickland, 2001).

One could think of these shifts in social psychology as working out the critical lines of its crisis, from a focus on "bias" through to the sociology of social psychological knowledge and social construction to more recent formulations of a critical sociohistorical grounding of social psychological worlds. But this would be a mistake. Questions of the human, science, epistemology, the social, and the psychological each opened in turn appreciation of how the "crisis" resided less inside of psychology than with practices and institutions of "western intellectual life" (Parker & Shotter, 1991). In what followed, the scientific laboratory in psychology as in other sciences was revealed to be anything but ahistorical, contextless, or culture free—the place of a "culture of no culture" (Haraway, 1997), as were notions of scientific objectivity as a "view from nowhere" (Nagel, 1986). One consequence of these examinations has been an increase in epistemological exploration almost unimagined during crisis conversations, ones as much concerned with how to warrant our claims to social psychological knowledge as with how to think through what counts as human and "for which ways of life" (Haraway, 1997; Smith, 1997; see also Bayer, 1999a).

Of course, these very rethinkings and redoings of the science of psychology have often served as lightening rods within the field for acting out contentious views and divisiveness. But when they are constructive interchange, they offer productive signs of hope. Particularly interesting is how these very reworkings find their way, though often unacknowledged and modified, across this great divide, evidencing their influence and implied presence as more central to social psychology's conventional directions than consciously wished.

Shelley Taylor (1998), for example, addresses variations on the "social being in social psychology" and advances made in social psychology in past decades. On the social being, Taylor attends to social psychology's more diverse subject pool beyond a database of college students (e.g., Sears, 1986), and the area's more complex views of persons who "actively construe social situations" and of social contexts as themselves invariably complex. While the changes she notes seem more consonant with social construction than with positivist assumptions, Taylor nonetheless pursues the conventionalist line, albeit morphing it to accommodate ideas on "context," "social construction," "multiple effects," and "multiple processors." One cannot help but hear influences from postmodernist debate on the nature of the "subject," including an implied reflexive relation ostensibly not amenable to quantification (Hayles). Seemingly at odds with positivist assumptions and with liberal humanist notions of the subject, Taylor's review everywhere evidences how science in social psychology undergoes transformation itself. Her view of scientific social psychology contrasts as much with earlier overviews of social psychology in which the methodology was assumed unchanged and unaltered by cultural historical conditions even as social psychology's "insights" were to "gradually work their way into our cultural wisdom" (Jones, 1985, p. 100) as it does with feminist and critical psychologists who explicitly engage "transformative projects" (Morawski, 1994). As Morawski writes, such "everyday histories of science, especially of psychology, presume that empiricism means much the same thing as it did fifty, or one hundred fifty, years ago" (p. 50), relying, as they do, on linear, transhistorical "narratives of progression or stability." But changes in the language of these narratives and of the views of the subject as of science, culture, and so on betray the storyline of these narratives. As we have attempted to show, the history of social psychology, its scientific practices, and reigning views of the human have been anything but stable, linear or progressive, or science-as-usual for those who claim the conventional or alternative practices of social psychological research.

It is well worth keeping Morawki's words on history and historiographical practices in mind as they hold across our theoretical, methodological, epistemological, and ontological differences. Whether practitioners of social construction (e.g., Gergen, 1994); discourse social psychology (e.g., Potter & Wetherell, 1987; Wilkinson & Kitzinger, 1995); feminist social psychology (Wilkinson, 1996; Sherif; Morawski; Bayer); Russian/Soviet social psychology (Strickland, 1998); or conventional social psychology, we are engaged in what is most usefully thought of as transformative

projects. Ian Hacking (1999) writes of this in the sense of a "looping effect"— "classifications that, when known by people or by those around them, and put to work in institutions, change the ways in which individuals experience themselves—and may even lead people to evolve their feelings and behavior in part because they are so classified" (p. 104). Ideas on looping effects hold as well for the individual–social world divide where the framing itself may show its historical wear and tear as much as Graham Richards writes in his history of race and psychology of the coherence of the "nature-nurture" polarity "crumb[ling] after 1970" and that even the "'interactionist' position must now be considered too crude a formulation" given how the "notion of them being distinguishable . . . has been undermined" (pp. 252–253). Likewise for the individual–social world dualism, which having been reformulated and remade carries its own history of social psychology, from splitting subjects off from the world through to moving the "social" more and more into our subjects' interior life and to bringing past psychology into current phenomena (e.g., MacIntyre, 1985). Nikolas Rose (1990, 1992) reverses typical construals of the "social" in social psychology by placing psychology in the social arena, where it serves as a relay concept between politics, ethics, economics, and the human subject. Here the social is as much a part of individual subjectivity as notions of political and democratic life have themselves come to be understood in psychological ways. For Rose (1992) the matter is less about the "social construction of persons" and more attuned to how "if we have become profoundly psychological beings . . . we have come to think, judge, console, and reform ourselves according to psychological norms of truth" (p. 364).

Social psychology's cornerstone of the individual–social world relation has itself therefore undergone remakings, ones that must be considered, especially where we are oft-tempted to line up social psychologists as falling on one or the other side of the divide, switching positions, or indeed lamenting the loss of the social in areas such as small group social psychology or the field itself. Indeed, Floyd Allport's (1961) move to the individual–group as the "master" problem in social psychology as much as Ivan Steiner's (1986) lament of his failed prediction of a "groupy" social psychology might usefully be rethought in terms of the changing nature of the dualism itself, signified perhaps by talk of relations, communication, information processing, and perception in years past (Bayer & Morawski, 1991), and by the terms of voice, stories, local histories, and discourses in matters of gender, race, and culture today.

Insofar as the history of social psychology is tied up in the history of this dualism, and insofar as wider critical discussions on the "crisis" have served to recast matters of epistemology within disciplines, then we might well take this one step further to consider how the timeworn narrative of a sociological social psychology versus a psychological social psychology simply no longer makes good sense—historical or otherwise. Social psychology in the twenty-first century is perhaps no more uniform than it was in the mid-1950s, or at its outset, but this diversity of interests and approaches, including discursive, feminist, sociocultural, hermeneutic, ecological, critical, narrative, and the newer technocultural studies, is part and parcel of this working out of boundaries and problematics. To overlook this history is to run into the same trouble of assuming social psychology weathered storms of debate and change, arriving in the twenty-first century stronger but basically unchanged. Or, conversely, that social psychology's history is one of increasing emphasis on the individual, going from social to asocial, and a narrowing of defined scientific practices (Samelson). But as Franz Samelson (2000) found, neither of these histories suffices, for each eclipses the broader and more local engaging questions. And, as Jill Morawski (2000) writes in her assessment of "theory biographies," few of psychology's leading lights seemed to confine themselves to some hypothetical, tidy box of social psychological theory and research. Seen historically, their work addressed connections of theory and practice, theory and value, and theory and social control consequences, however intended or unintended. Equally significant is the irony Samelson finds in textbook and "success" histories' omission of the "fact that some of their respected heroes and innovators later in life found their old approaches wanting and forswore them totally, at the same time as novices in the field were being taught to follow in the old (abandoned) footsteps" (p. 505). Such is the case of Leon Festinger, who, pursuing questions on human life, turned to historical inquiry via other fields. Further, the history of social psychology, as Smith notes, gives the lie to social psychology losing sight of or turning away from that broader project, whether expressly or not, of "larger intellectual difficulties fac[ing] the human sciences" and of being "fundamentally a political and moral as well as scientific subject" (Smith, p. 747).

Social psychology has never been quite as contained, narrow, asocial, or apolitical as construed in some of its historical narratives or reviews. Inasmuch as social psychology sought to engage its lifeworld of social meanings and doings, it can hardly be thought of as residing anywhere but in the very midst of these self- and world-making practices. Its theories, "like life elsewhere," writes Morawski (2000), were "born of cultural contradictions, fixations, opportunities, and tensions," and have been as much transformed as transformative in effect (p. 439). And just as there is no "going back" in our life histories (Walkerdine, 2000), so it goes for social psychology as it confronts a changing twenty-first-century world in which notions of culture, the global, and of human life itself are everywhere being debated and transformed. Epistemological matters remain as central to these questions as they did long before the formal inception of the field. Whereas much of social psychology has been wrought through industrial world terms, as have many of its critical histories, the challenge before us is about life in postindustrial times, challenges of human-technology interfaces only imagined in the 1950s, and of life-generating and life-encoding technologies, such as cloning and the Human Genome Projects redrawing the bounds around personal, cultural, social, political, and economic life and what it means to be human (Haraway, 1997). Not unlike how social-political reorderings called social psychology into being (Apfelbaum, 1986), so we must consider how globalization, the Internet, and other technologies fundamentally change the nature of social psychology today. Protests against agencies such as the IMF and the World Bank are inviting reexamination of what is taking place in human and environmental rights as the economics and location of the workplace, not to mention judicial life, become less clearly demarcated by national boundaries. The economy of production has been morphing into one of marketing, to a "brand name" economy of obsessional corporate proportions (Klein, 2000). Time and space alterations, like those of human–technology boundaries, confront social psychology anew with matters of the body and embodiment and with changes in human-technology connections (Bayer, 1998b). Social psychology, like other human sciences, will most likely "go on being remade as long as ways of life go on being remade," and, perhaps best regarded—and embraced— as Smith characterizes the human sciences (p. 861): "The human sciences have had a dramatic life, a life lived as an attempt at reflective self-understanding and self-recreation" (p. 870). Who knows, should social psychology take its lived historical subjects and subjectivities seriously, and should this be accompanied by recognition of the social, political, moral, and technocultural warp and woof of life lived here in what William James called the "blooming, buzzing confusion," we may exercise the courage, as Morawski (2002) says of earlier theorists' efforts, to not only meet the world halfway but to engage it in creatively meaningful ways. An imaginable course is suggested by Smith's claim that the "history of human sciences is itself a human science" (p. 870). That would indeed be to make social psychology history.

REFERENCES

Adams, G. (1934). The rise and fall of psychology. *Atlantic Monthly, 153,* 82–92.

Adorno, T. W., Frenkel-Brunswik, E., Levinson, D. J., & Sanford, R. N. (Eds.). (1950). *The Authoritarian personality.* New York: Harper & Brothers.

Allport, F. H. (1924). *Social psychology.* Boston: Houghton Mifflin.

Allport, F. H. (1961). The contemporary appraisal of an old problem. *Contemporary Psychology, 6,* 195–196.

Allport, G. W. (1935). In C. A. Murchison (Ed.), *Attitudes: Handbook of social psychology* (Vol. 2, pp. 798–844). New York: Russell and Russell.

Allport, G. W. (1954a). The historical background of social psychology. In G. Lindzey (Ed.), *Handbook of social psychology* (Vol. 1, pp. 3–56). Cambridge, MA: Addison-Wesley.

Allport, G. W. (1954b). *The nature of prejudice.* Garden City, NY: Doubleday Anchor Books.

Allport, G. W. (1985). The historical background of social psychology. In G. Lindzey & E. Aronson (Eds.), *Handbook of social psychology* (2nd ed., Vol. 1, p. 1). New York: Random House.

Apfelbaum, E. (1986). Prolegomena for a history of social psychology: Some hypotheses concerning its emergence in the 20th century and its raison d'etre. In K. S. Larsen (Ed.), *Dialectics and Ideology in psychology* (pp. 3–13). Norwood, NJ: Ablex.

Apfelbaum, E. (1999). Relations of domination and movements for liberation: An Analysis of power between groups. *Feminism and Psychology, 9,* 267–272. (Original work published 1979)

Apfelbaum, E., & Lubek, I. (1976). Resolution versus revolution? The theory of conflicts in question. In H. L. Strickland, F. E. Abood, & K. J. Gergen (Eds.), *Social psychology in transition* (pp. 71–94). New York: Plenum Press.

Asch, S. E. (1952). *Social psychology.* Englewood Cliffs, NJ: Prentice-Hall.

Ash, M. (1992). Cultural contexts and scientific change in psychology. *American psychologist, 47*(2), 198–207.

Back, K. W. (1963). The proper scope of social psychology. *Social Forces, 41,* 368–375.

Back, K. W. (1972). *Beyond words: The story of sensitivity training and the encounter movement.* New York: Russell Sage Foundation.

Baistow, K. (2000). Problems of powerlessness: Psychological explanations of social inequality and civil unrest in post-war America. *History of the Human Sciences, 13*(3), 95–116.

Baldwin, J. M. (1897). *Social and ethical interpretations in mental development: A study in social psychology.* New York: Macmillan.

Bales, R. F. (1955). How people interact in conferences. *Scientific American, 192*(3), 31–35.

Barenbaum, N. B. (2000). How social was personality? The Allports' connection of social and personality psychology. *Journal of the History of the Behavioral Sciences, 36*(4), 471–487.

Barlow, W. (1999). *Voice over: The making of Black radio.* Philadelphia: Temple University Press.

Bauman, Z. (1978). *Hermeneutics and social science.* New York: Columbia University Press.

Bavelas, A. (1952). Communication patterns in problem-solving groups. In H. von Foerster (Ed.), *Cybernetics: Circular causal, and feedback mechanisms in biological and social systems* (pp. 1–44). New York: Josiah Macy Jr. Foundation.

Bayer, B. M. (1998a). Between apparatuses and apparitions: Phantoms of the laboratory. In B. M. Bayer & J. Shotter (Eds.), *Reconstructing the psychological subject* (pp. 187–213). London: Sage.

Bayer, B. M. (1998b). Re-enchanting constructionist inquiries. In B. M. Bayer & J. Shotter (Eds.), *Reconstructing the psychological subject* (pp. 1–20). London: Sage.

Bayer, B. M. (1999a). Psychological ethics and cyborg body politics. In A. Gordo-López & I. Parker (Eds.), *Cyberpsychology* (pp. 113–129). London: Macmillan.

Bayer, B. M. (1999b). Technovisions and the remaking of scientific identity. In W. Maiers, B. Bayer, B. Duarte Esgalhado, R. Jorna, & E. Schraube (Eds.), *Challenges to theoretical psychology* (pp. 341–349). York, Ontario, Canada: Captus University Press.

Bayer, B. M. (2001). Plugged in: Psychology, technology and popular culture. In J. R. Morss, N. Stephenson, & H. van Rappard (Eds.), *Theoretical issues in psychology* (pp. 23–34). Boston: Kluwer Press.

Bayer, B. M., & Morawski, J. (1991). *Father knows best? Gender relations in the family and small group research, 1950–1990.* Paper presented at the 99th annual convention of the American Psychological Association, San Francisco.

Bayer, B. M., & Morawski, J. (1992, June). *Experimenters and their experimental performances: The case of small group research, 1950–1990.* Paper presented at the annual convention of the Canadian Psychological Association, Quebec, Canada.

Bayer, B. M., & Strickland, L. H. (1990). Gustav Ichheiser on sociopsychological misperception in international relations. *Political Psychology, 11*(4), 699–719.

Bernard, L. L. (1932). Social psychology in the United States. *Sociologies 8,* 257–279.

Bramel, D., & Friend, R. (1981). Hawthorne, the myth of the docile worker, and class bias in psychology. *American Psychologist, 36,* 867–878.

Breines, W. (1992). *Young, White, and miserable: Growing up female in the fifties.* Boston: Beacon Press.

Britt, S. H. (1937a). Past and present trends in the methods and subject matter of social psychology. *Sociological Forces, 15,* 462–469.

Britt, S. H. (1937b). Social psychologists or psychological sociologists: Which? *Journal of Abnormal and Social Psychology, 32,* 314–318.

Brown, J. F. (1936). *Psychology and the social order: An introduction to the dynamic study of social fields.* New York: McGraw-Hill.

Buckley, K. W. (1989). *Mechanical man: John Broadus Watson and the beginnings of behaviorism.* New York: Guilford Press.

Buss, A. R. (1979). The emerging field of the sociology of psychological knowledge. In A. Buss (Ed.), *Psychology in social context* (pp. 1–24). New York: Irvington.

Camfield, T. (1969). *Psychologists at war: The history of American psychology.* Austin: University of Texas.

Cantril, H. (1941). *The psychology of social movements.* New York: Wiley.

Capshew, J. H. (1999). *Psychologists on the march: Science, practice and professional identity in America, 1929–1969.* Cambridge, England: Cambridge University Press.

Carson, J. (1999). Minding matter/mattering mind: Knowledge and the subject in nineteenth-century psychology. *Studies in History and Philosophy of Biological and Biomedical Sciences, 30*(3), 345–376.

Clark, K. (1966a). The civil rights movement: Momentum and organization. In T. Parsons & K. B. Clark (Eds.), *The American Negro* (pp. 595–625). Cambridge, MA: Houghton Mifflin.

Clark, K. (1966b). Introduction: The dilemma of power. In T. Parsons & K. B. Clark (Eds.), *The American Negro* (pp. xi–xxviii). Cambridge, MA: Houghton Mifflin.

Collier, G., Minton, H. L., & Reynolds, G. (1991). *Currents of thought in American social psychology.* New York: Oxford University Press.

Crutchfield, R. S. (1955). Conformity and character. *American Psychologist, 10,* 191–198.

Danziger, K. (1990). *Constructing the subject: Historical origins of psychological research.* New York: Cambridge University Press.

Danziger, K. (1992). The project of an experimental social psychology: historical perspectives. *Science in Context, 5,* 309–328.

Danziger, K. (2000). Making social psychology experimental: A conceptual history, 1920–1970. *Journal of the History of the Behavioral Sciences, 36*(4), 329–347.

Darley, J., & Latane, B. (1968). Bystander intervention in emergencies: Diffusion of responsibility. *Journal of Personality and Social Psychology, 8,* 377–383.

de Beauvoir, S. (1952). *The second sex.* New York: Vintage Books.

Dell, F. (1926). *Intellectual vagabondage: An apology for the intelligentsia.* New York: George H. Doran.

Deutsch, M. (1954). Field theory in social psychology. In G. Lindzey (Ed.), *Handbook of social psychology* (Vol. 1, pp. 181–222). Cambridge, MA: Addison-Wesley.

Deutsch, M., & Krauss, R. (1965). Trends in social psychology. *Theories in social psychology* (pp. 212–216). New York: Basui.

Dewey, J. (1900). Psychology and social practice. *Psychological Review, 7,* 105–124.

Dewey, J. (1922). *Human nature and conduct.* New York: Holt.

Dinnerstein, D. (1976). *The mermaid and the minotaur: Sexual arrangements and human malaise.* New York: Harper & Row.

Dollard, J., Doob, L. W., Miller, N. E., Mowrer, O. H., & Sears, R. R. (1939). *Frustration and aggression.* New Haven, CT: Yale University Press.

Dunlap, K. (1928). The applications of psychology to social problems. In C. Murchison (Ed.), *Psychologies of 1925* (pp. 353–379). Worchester, MA: Clark University Press.

Eagly, A. H. (1987). *Sex differences in social behavior: A social-role interpretation.* Hillsdale, NJ: Erlbaum.

Eagly, A. H., Karau, S. J., & Makhijani, M. G (1995). Gender and the effectiveness of leaders: A meta-analysis. *Psychological Bulletin, 117*(1), 125–145.

Edwards, P. N. (1996). *The closed world: Computers and the politics of discourse in cold war America.* Cambridge, MA: MIT Press.

Faris, E. (1937). Nature of human nature. In F. H. Allport (Ed.), *Historical background* (p. 161). New York: McGraw-Hill.

Fay, J. W. (1939). *American psychology before William James.* New Brunswick, NJ: Rutgers University Press.

Finison, L. J. (1976). Unemployment, politics, and the history of organized psychology. *American Psychologist, 31*(11), 747–755.

Finison, L. J. (1986). The psychological insurgency: 1936–1945. *Journal of Social Issues, 42*(1), 21–33.

Fraser, C., & Foster, D. (1984). Social groups, nonsense groups and group polarization. In H. Tajfel (Ed.), *The social dimension: European developments in social psychology* (Vol. 2, pp. 473–497). Cambridge, England: Cambridge University Press.

Fremont-Smith, F. (1950). Introductory discussion. In H. von Foerster (Ed.), *Cybernetics: Circular causal, and feedback mechanisms in biological and social systems* (pp. 9–26). New York: Josiah Macy Jr. Foundation.

Friedan, B. (1963). *The feminine mystique.* New York: Norton.

Frumkin, R. M. (1958). Social psychology. In J. S. Rouiek (Ed.), *Contemporary sociology* (pp. 270–285). New York: Philosophical Library.

Furby, L. (1979). Individualistic bias in studies of locus of control. In A. R. Buss (Ed.), *Psychology in social context* (pp. 169–190). New York: Irvington.

Furner, M. O. (1975). *Advocacy and objectivity: A crisis in the professionalization of American social science.* Lexington: University of Kentucky Press.

Gadlin, H., & Rubin, S. (1979). Interactionism. In A. R. Buss (Ed.), *Psychology in social context* (pp. 213–238). New York: Irvington.

Gergen, K. (1973). Social psychology as history. *Journal of Personality and Social Psychology, 26,* 309–320.

Gergen, K. (1979). The positivist image in social psychological theory. In A. R. Buss (Ed.), *Psychology in social context* (pp. 193–212). New York: Irvington.

Gergen, K. (1994). *Realities and relationships.* Cambridge, MA: Harvard University Press.

Gibb, C. A. (1954). Leadership. In G. Lindzey (Ed.), *Handbook of social psychology* (Vol. 11, pp. 877–920). Cambridge, MA: Addison-Wesley.

Gigerenzer, G. (1991). From tools to theories: A heuristic of discovery in cognitive psychology. *Psychological Review, 98*(2), 254–267.

Gillespie, R. P. (1985). Manufacturing knowledge: A history of the Hawthorne experiments. Unpublished doctoral dissertation, University of Pennsylvania, Philadelphia.

Gillespie, R. P. (1988). The Hawthorne experiments and the politics of experimentation. In J. G. Morawski (Ed.), *The rise of experimentation in American psychology* (pp. 114–137). New Haven, CT: Yale University Press.

Gould, L. (1974). *The progressive era.* Syracuse, NY: Syracuse University Press.

Graebner, W. (1980). The unstable world of Benjamin Spock: Social engineering in a democratic culture, 1917–1950. *Journal of American History, 67*(3), 612–629.

Graebner, W. (1986). The small group and democratic social engineering. *Journal of Social Issues, 42,* 137–154.

Haber, S. (1964). *Efficiency and uplift: Scientific management in the progressive era, 1890–1920.* Chicago: University of Chicago Press.

Hacking, I. (1999). *The social construction of* what? Cambridge, MA: Harvard University Press.

Haraway, D. (1992). The promises of monsters: A regenerative politics for in-appropriated others. In L. Grossberg, C. Nelson, & P. A. Treichler (Eds.), *Cultural studies* (pp. 295–337). New York: Routledge.

Haraway, D. (1997). *Modest witness at second millennium: Female man meets OncoMouse.* New York: Routledge.

Harris, B., & Nicholson, I. (1998). Perils of a public intellectual. *Journal of Social Issues, 54,* 79–118.

Haskell, T. L. (1977). *Emergence of a professional social science: The American Social science association and the nineteenth-century crisis of authority.* Urbana, University of Illinois Press.

Hayles, N. K. (1999). *How we became posthuman.* Chicago: University of Chicago Press.

Heider, F. (1959). On Lewin's methods and theory. In G. Klein (Ed.), *Psychological Issues* (pp. 108–123). New York: International Universities Press.

Heims, S. (1993). *Constructing a social science for postwar America.* Cambridge, MA: MIT Press.

Henriksen, M. A. (1997). *Dr. Strangelove's America: Society and culture in the atomic age.* Berkeley: University of California Press.

Henriques, J. H., Hollway, W., Urwin, C., Venn, C., & Walkerdine, V. (1998). *Changing the subject: Psychology, social regulation and subjectivity.* London: Routledge. (Original work published 1984)

Herman, E. (1995). *The romance of American psychology: Political culture in the age of experts.* Berkeley: University of California Press.

Hornstein, G. (1988). Quantifying psychological phenomena: Debates, dilemmas, and implications. In J. Morawski (Ed.), *The rise of experimentation in American psychology* (pp. 1–34). New Haven, CT: Yale University Press.

Israel, J. (1979). From level of aspiration to dissonance (Or, what the middle class worries about). In A. R. Buss (Ed.), *Psychology in social context* (pp. 239–257). New York: Irvington.

James, W. (1890). *The principles of psychology.* New York: Holt.

Janis, I., & Mann, L. (1977). *Decision making: A psychological analysis of conflict, choice, and commitment.* New York: Free Press.

Jastrow, J. (1928). Lo, the psychologist! In M. L. Reymert (Ed.), *Feelings and emotions: The Wittenburg symposium* (pp. 434–438). Worcester, MA: Clark University Press.

Jones, E. E. (1985). Major developments in social psychology during the past five decades. In G. Lindzey & E. Aronson (Eds.), *Handbook of social psychology* (3rd ed., Vol. 1, pp. 47–107). New York: Random House.

Kaplan, S. (1956). Social engineers as saviors: Effects of World War I on some American liberals. *Journal of the History of Ideas, 17,* 347–369.

Karpf, F. B. (1932). *American social psychology.* New York: McGraw-Hill.

Katz, D. (1988). The development of social psychology as a research science. In H. J. O'Gorman (Ed.), *Surveying social life: Papers in honor of Herbert H. Hyman* (pp. 217–235). Middletown, CT: Wesleyan University Press.

Kelman, H. C. (1967). Human use of human subjects: The problem of deception in social psychological experiments. *Psychological Bulletin, 67,* 1–11.

Klein, N. (2000). *No logo: Taking aim at the brand bullies.* Toronto, Ontario, Canada: Vintage.

Lears, J. (1992). The ad man and the grand inquisitor: Intimacy, publicity, and the managed self in America, 1880–1940. In G. Levine (Ed.), *Constructions of the self* (pp. 107–141). New Brunswick, NJ: Rutgers University Press.

Lears, T. J. J. (1983). From salvation to self-realization: Advertising and the therapeutic roots of consumer culture, 1880–1930. In R. W. Fox & T. J. J. Lears (Eds.), *The culture of consumption: Critical essays in American history, 1880–1980* (pp. 3–38). New York: Pantheon.

Leary, D. L. (1980). The intentions and heritage of Descartes and Locke: Toward a recognition or the moral basis of modern psychology. *Journal of General Psychology, 102,* 283–310.

Lewin, K. (1951). Frontiers in group dynamics. In D. Cartwright (Ed.), *Field theory in social science* (pp. 130–154). New York: Harper & Brothers. (Original work published 1947)

Lindzey, G. (1954). *Handbook of social psychology.* Cambridge, MA: Addison-Wesley.

Lopes, L. (1991). The rhetoric of irrationality. *Theory and Psychology, 1*(1), 65–82.

Loy, P. (1976). Trends in the history of contemporary social psychology: A quantitative analysis. Unpublished doctoral dissertation, University of New Hampshire Press, Durham.

Lutz, C. (1997). Epistemology of the bunker: The brainwashed and other new subjects of permanent war. In J. Pfister & N. Schnog (Eds.), *Inventing the psychological: Toward a cultural history of emotional life in America* (pp. 245–267). New Haven, CT: Yale University Press.

MacIntyre, A. (1985). How psychology makes itself true–or false. In S. Koch & D. E. Leary (Eds.), *A century of psychology as science* (pp. 897–903). New York: McGraw-Hill.

May, E. T. (1988). *Homeward bound: American families in the cold war era.* New York: Basic Books.

McDougall, W. (1908). *Introduction to social psychology.* London: Methuen.

Mead, G. H. (1934). *Mind, self, and society from the standpoint of a social behaviorist.* Chicago: University of Chicago Press.

Meltzer, B. N. (1959). *The social psychology of George Herbert Mead.* Kalamazoo, MI: Western Michigan University.

Meyerowitz, J. (1993). Beyond the feminine mystique: A reassessment of postwar mass culture, 1946–1958. *Journal of American History, 79,* 1455–1482.

Minton, H. L. (1984). J. F. Brown's social psychology of the 1930's: A historical antecedent to the contemporary crisis in social psychology. *Personality and Social Psychology Bulletin, 10*(1), 31–42.

Morawski, J. (1982). Assessing psychology's moral heritage through our neglected utopias. *American Psychologist, 37,* 1082–1095.

Morawski, J. (1985). The measurement of masculinity and femininity: Engendering categorical realities. *Journal of Personality, 53,* 196–223.

Morawski, J. (1986a). Contextual discipline: The unmaking and remaking of sociality. In R. L. Rosnow & M. Georgoudi (Eds.), *Contextualism and understanding in behavioral science: Implications for research and theory* (pp. 47–56). New York: Praeger.

Morawski, J. (1986b). Organizing knowledge and behavior at Yale's Institute of Human Relations. *Isis, 77,* 219–242.

Morawski, J. (1994). *Practicing feminisms, reconstructing psychology.* Ann Arbor: University of Michigan Press.

Morawski, J. (1997). Educating the emotions: Academic psychology, textbooks, and the psychology industry, 1890–1940. In J. Pfister & N. Schnog (Eds.), *Inventing the psychological: Toward a cultural history of emotional life in America* (pp. 217–244). New Haven, CT: Yale University Press.

Morawski, J. (2000). Gifts bestowed, gifts withheld: Assessing psychological theory with a Kochian attitude. *American Psychologist, 56*(5), 433–440.

Murchison, C. (1935). *Handbook of social psychology.* Worcester, MA: Clark University Press.

Nagel, T. (1986). *The view from nowhere.* Oxford, England: Oxford University Press.

Napoli, D. S. (1975). *Architects of adjustment: The practice and professionalization of American psychology 1920–1945.* Unpublished doctoral dissertation, University of California, Davis.

O'Donnell, J. M. (1979). The crisis of experimentalism in the twenties: E. G. Boring and his use of historiography. *American Psychologist, 34,* 289–295.

O'Donnell, J. M. (1985). *The origin of behaviorism: American psychology, 1870–1920.* New York: New York University Press.

Pandora, K. (1991, June). *Dissenting from pure experimentalism: The natural history model and pragmatist psychologists during the 1930s.* Paper presented at the annual meeting of Cheiron, Slippery Rock, PA.

Pandora, K. (1997). *Rebels within the ranks: Psychologists' critique of scientific authority and democratic realities in New Deal America.* Cambridge, England: Cambridge University Press.

Parker, I., & Shotter, J. (Eds.). (1990). *Deconstructing social psychology.* London: Routledge.

Pfister, J. (1997). On conceptualizing the cultural history of emotional and psychological life in America. In J. Pfister & N. Schnog (Eds.), *Inventing the psychological: Toward a cultural history of emotional life in America* (pp. 17–59). New Haven, CT: Yale University Press.

Potter, J., & Wetherell, M. (1987). *Discourse and social psychology.* London: Sage.

Quantz, J. O. (1898). Dendro-Psychoses. *American Journal of Psychology, 9*(4), 449–506.

Richards, G. (1996). *Putting psychology in its place.* London: Routledge.

Richards, G. (1997). *Race, racism and psychology: Towards a reflexive history.* London: Routledge.

Riesman, D. (1969). *The lonely crowd.* New Haven, CT: Yale University Press.

Riley, D. (1988). *Am I that name? Feminism and the category of "women" in history.* Minneapolis: University of Minnesota.

Ring, K. (1967). Experimental social psychology: Some sober questions about some frivolous values. *Journal of Experimental Social Psychology, 3,* 113–123.

Rose, N. (1990). Psychology as a "social" social science. In I. Parker & J. Shotter (Eds.), *Deconstructing social psychology* (pp. 103–116). London: Routledge.

Rose, N. (1992). Engineering the human soul: Analyzing psychological expertise. *Science in Context, 5*(2), 351–369.

Rosenberg, C. (1979). Toward an ecology of knowledge: On disciplines, context and history. In A. Oleson & J. Voss (Eds.), *The organization of knowledge in the United States* (pp. 440–455). Baltimore: Johns Hopkins University Press.

Rosenzweig, S. (1933). The experimental situation as a psychological problem. *Psychological Review, 40,* 337–354.

Ross, D. (1979). The development of the social sciences. In A. Oleson & J. Voss (Eds.), *The organization of knowledge in modern America, 1860–1920* (pp. 107–138). Baltimore: Johns Hopkins University Press.

Ross, E. A. (1901). *Social control: A survey of the foundations of order.* New York: Macmillan Company.

Ross, E. A. (1908). *Social psychology.* New York: Macmillan.

Rubin, Z. (1983). Taking deception for granted. *Psychology Today, 17,* 74–75.

Rudmin, F. R., Trimpop, R., Kryl, I. P., & Boski, P. (1987). Gustav Ichheiser in the history of social psychology: An early phenomenology of social attribution. *British Journal of Social Psychology, 26*(2), 165–180.

Samelson, F. (1974). History, origin myth and ideology: Discovery of social psychology. *Journal for the Theory of Social Behavior, 4*(2), 217–231.

Samelson, F. (1978). From race psychology to studies in prejudice: Some observations on the thematic reversal in (social) psychology. *Journal of the History of the Behavioral Sciences, 14,* 265–278.

Samelson, F. (1979). Putting psychology on the map: Ideology and intelligence testing. In A. R. Buss (Ed.), *Psychology in social context* (pp. 103–167). New York: Irvington.

Samelson, F. (1985). Authoritarianism from Berlin to Berkeley: On social psychology and history. *Journal of Social Issues, 42*(1), 191–208.

Samelson, F. (2000). Whig and anti-Whig histories–and other curiosities of social psychology. *Journal of the History of the Behavioral Sciences, 36*(4), 499–506.

Sampson, E. E. (1977). Psychology and the American ideal. *Journal of Personality and Social Psychology, 35*(11), 767–782.

Scheibe, K. E. (1985). Historical perspectives on the presented self. In B. Schlenker (Ed.), *The self in social life* (pp. 33–64). New York: McGraw-Hill.

Sears, David O. (1986). College sophomores in the laboratory: Influences of a narrow database on social psychology's view of human nature. *Journal of Personality and Social Psychology, 51,* 515–530.

Seltzer, M. (1992). *Bodies and machines.* New York: Routledge.

Sennett, R. (1976). *The fall of public man: On the social psychology of capitalism.* New York: Vintage Books. (Original work published 1974)

Seward, G. H. (1954). *Sex and the social order.* London: Penguin Books. (Original work published 1946)

Sheldon, H. P. (1897). The institutional activities of American children. *American Journal of Psychology, 9*(4), 425–448.

Sherif, C. W. (1976). *Orientation in social psychology.* New York: Harper & Row.

Sherif, C. W. (1987). Bias in psychology. In S. Harding (Ed.), *Feminism and methodology* (pp. 37–56). Bloomington: Indiana University Press. (Original work published 1979)

Sherif, M. (1936). *The psychology of social norms.* New York: Harper & Brothers.

Shotter, J. (1975). *Images of man in psychological research.* London: Methuen.

Small, A. W. (1916). Fifty years of sociology in the United States. *American Journal of Sociology, 21*(6), 721–864.

Smith, M. B. (1986). McCarthyism: A personal account. *Journal of Social Issues, 42*(4), 71–80.

Smith, R. (1997). *The Norton history of the human sciences.* New York: Norton.

Soffer, R. N. (1980). *Ethics and society in England: The revolution in the social sciences, 1870–1914.* Berkeley: University of California Press.

Sokal, M. M. (1981). The origins of the psychological corporation. *Journal of the History of the Behavioral Sciences, 17,* 54–67.

Sprowls, J. W. (1930). Recent social psychology. *Psychological Bulletin, 27,* 380–393.

Stam, H. J., Radtke, L., & Lubek, I. (2000). Strains in experimental social psychology: A textural analysis of the development of experimentation in social psychology. *Journal of the History of the Behavioral Sciences, 36*(4), 365–382.

Steele, R. S. (1982). *Freud and Jung: Conflict of interpretation.* London: Routledge & Kegan Paul.

Steiner, I. (1974). Whatever happened to the group in social psychology? *Journal of Experimental Social Psychology, 10,* 94–108.

Steiner, I. (1986). Paradigms and groups. *Advances in Experimental Social Psychology, 19,* 251–289.

Strickland, L. (1976). Priorities and paradigms: The conference and the book. In H. L. Strickland, F. E. Abood, & K. J. Gergen (Eds.), *Social psychology in transition* (pp. 3–11). New York: Plenum Press.

Strickland, L. (Ed.). (1998). *V. M. Bekhterev's suggestion and its role in social life* (T. Dobreva-Martinova, Trans.). New Brunswick: Transaction.

Strickland, L. (2001). Editor's Forward. *V. M. Bekhterev's collective reflexology: The complete edition* (L. H. Strickland, & E. Lockwood, Trans.). New Brunswick, NJ: Transaction.

Suls, J. M., & Rosnow, R. L. (1988). Concerns about artifacts in psychological experiments. In J. Morawski (Ed.), *The rise of experimentation in American psychology* (pp. 163–187). New Haven, CT: Yale University Press.

Susman, W. (1985). *Culture as history: The transformation of American society in the twentieth century.* New York: Pantheon.

Tajfel, H. (1972). Experiments in a vacuum. In J. Israel & H. Tajfel (Eds.), *The context of social psychology: A critical assessment* (pp. 69–119). London: Academic Press.

Taylor, S. (1998). The social being in social psychology. In D. Gilbert, S. T. Fiske, & G. Lindzey (Eds.), *The handbook of social psychology* (4th ed., Vol. 1, pp. 58–95). Boston: McGraw-Hill.

Terman, L. M., & Miles, C. C. (1936). *Sex and personality: Studies in masculinity and femininity.* New York: McGraw-Hill.

Thomas, L. (1974). *Lives of a cell.* New York: Viking Press.

Thomas, W. I., & Znaniecki, F. (1920). *The Polish peasant in Europe and America.* Chicago: University of Chicago Press.

Tobey, R. C. (1971). *The American ideology of national sciences, 1919–1930.* Pittsburgh, PA: University of Pittsburgh Press.

Toulmin, S. E. (1975). The twin moralities of science. In N. H. Steneck (Ed.), *Science and society: Past, present and future* (pp. 111–135). Ann Arbor: University of Michigan Press.

Toulmin, S. E., & Leary, D. E. (1985). The cult of empiricism in psychology and beyond. In S. Koch & D. E. Leary (Eds.), *A century of psychology as science* (pp. 594–617). New York: McGraw-Hill.

Triplett, N. (1897–1898). The dynamogenic factors in peacemaking and competition. *American Journal of Psychology, 9*(4), 507–533.

van Elteren, V. (1993). From emancipating to domesticating the workers: Lewinian social psychology and the study of the work process till 1947. In H. J. Stam, M. P. Leendert, W. Thorngate, & B. Kaplan (Eds.), *Recent trends in theoretical psychology: Selected proceedings of the fourth biennial conference of the International Society for Theoretical Psychology* (p. 3). New York: Springer-Verlag.

Walkerdine, V. (2000). Conclusion. In C. Squire (Ed.), *Culture in psychology* (pp. 175–178). London: Routledge.

Weisstein, N. (1971). Psychology constructs the female. In V. Gornick & B. K. Moran (Eds.), *Women in sexist society: Studies in power and powerlessness* (pp. 207–224). New York: New American Library.

Weisstein, N. (1993). Psychology constructs the female; or, the fantasy life of the male psychologist (with some attention to the fantasies of his friends, the male biologist and the male anthropologist). *Feminism and Psychology, 3*(2), 195–210. (Original work published 1971)

Wiebe, R. (1967). *The search for order, 1877–1920.* New York: Hill and Wang.

Wilkinson, S. (Ed.). (1996). *Feminist social psychologies: International perspectives.* Buckingham, England: Open University Press.

Wilkinson, S., & Kitzinger, C. (Eds.). (1995). *Feminism and discourse: Psychological perspectives.* London: Sage.

Winston, A. (1990). Robert Sessions Woodworth and the Columbia Bible: How the psychological experiment was redefined. *American Journal of Psychology, 103*(3), 391–401.

Winston, A., & Blais, D. J. (1996). What counts as an experiment? A transdiciplinary analysis of textbooks, 1930–1970. *American Journal of Psychology, 109*(4), 599–616.

Woodard, J. (1945). Social psychology. In G. Gurvich & W. E. Moore (Eds.), *Twentieth century sociology* (pp. 220–249). New York: Philosophical Library.

CHAPTER 12

Psychology of Women and Gender

JEANNE MARECEK, ELLEN B. KIMMEL, MARY CRAWFORD, AND RACHEL T. HARE-MUSTIN

SETTING THE STAGE   250
SECOND-WAVE FEMINISM AND PSYCHOLOGY   250
FRAMEWORKS FOR STUDYING WOMEN
    AND GENDER   251
    The First Wave (c. 1876–1920)   251
    The Second Wave (c. 1970–the Present)   252
CLINICAL PRACTICE, COUNSELING, AND
    FEMINIST THERAPY   256
    Biases in Diagnosis and Clinical Judgment   257
    Feminist Approaches to Therapy   258
ORGANIZATIONS AND ACTIVISM   260
    The National Council of Women Psychologists   260
    Society for the Psychological Study of
        Social Issues   260
    The Association for Women in Psychology   260

The Society for the Psychology of Women of the American
    Psychological Association (Division 35)   261
The APA Committee on Women in Psychology   261
The APA Women's Programs Office   261
Other Activities   262
The Section on Women and Psychology of the Canadian
    Psychological Association   262
The Psychology of Women Section of the British
    Psychological Association   262
SUMMING UP AND LOOKING AHEAD   262
    Research, Scholarship, and Pedagogy   262
    Feminist Clinical and Counseling Practice   263
    Confronting the Backlash   263
CONCLUSION   264
REFERENCES   264

In 1910, Helen Thompson Woolley rendered the following assessment of psychology's claims about women: "There is perhaps no field aspiring to be scientific where flagrant personal bias, logic martyred in the cause of supporting a prejudice, unfounded assertions, and even sentimental rot and drivel, have run riot to such an extent as here" (p. 340). Now, over 90 years since Woolley's assessment, that charge no longer stands. Galvanized by the second wave of feminism, the field of psychology of women and gender has produced a large and diverse body of research, theory, and methodological critique and innovation. Born in the late 1960s, the field is young in comparison to many other fields of psychology; thus, its history is short.

The field of psychology of women and gender is pluralist and multifaceted. Psychologists have posed questions about sex and gender in virtually every area of psychology. They have allegiances to a broad range of intellectual frameworks, and they espouse diverse modes of inquiry and approaches to clinical practice. Feminism has always centered on ending the subordination of women, but today feminism encompasses a wide spectrum of additional ideas, theories, and practices. Among feminist psychologists, this spectrum is fully represented. A key strength of the field is that diverse points

of view are brought into interaction, leading to productive intellectual interchange and new developments. Moreover, many feminist psychologists have close connections (or joint appointments) with women's studies programs. These connections infuse feminist psychology with the knowledge and perspectives of other disciplines, such as history, sociology, and philosophy of science. An interdisciplinary stance has prompted some to formulate innovative research questions and to experiment with research approaches from other disciplines. For some, an interdisciplinary stance has also fostered a critical consciousness of the powers and limits of psychology's epistemological, theoretical, and methodological commitments.

Feminist psychologists have continually engaged in ongoing critical conversations about how best to study gender and how best to do psychology—whether as researchers, practitioners, teachers, or activists. Indeed, skepticism about conventional ways of doing psychology has been a hallmark of feminist psychology. Feminists have noted that psychological knowledge has often served the interests of social groups of which psychologists are part. Historically, most psychologists have been white, middle or upper-middle class, and male. Feminists also have analyzed the intellectual habits that led psychologists to relegate knowledge about women to the margins and to regard questions about gender as having little import or significance.

SETTING THE STAGE

In a later section, we describe work on women and gender from earlier eras of psychology. As we note, there was a lack of support for such work, and those who engaged in it found their efforts difficult to sustain. The creation of a field of study as it exists today had to await two developments: a critical mass of scholars devoted to questions of gender and the political impetus of the second wave of feminism, which emerged in the 1960s.

Until the late 1960s, graduate programs in psychology admitted few women. Most were admitted to masters degree programs but not to doctoral programs. The more selective the school, the fewer women were granted access. The more prestigious the specialty within psychology, the more obstacles to women's participation were created. Women were mostly channeled into applied work in child psychology, school psychology, and counseling. Training requirements and the typical academic career trajectory suited men's life pattern; they were not readily compatible with the family and domestic responsibilities that women were expected to shoulder.

For those women who managed to complete advanced training in psychology, occupational barriers remained. Women who entered academia were likely to be pigeonholed in adjunct appointments and teaching positions, preserving the prestigious and lucrative research positions for men. Women were overrepresented in departments and institutions where research was not possible. Women who entered applied fields, such as clinical and counseling psychology, also faced occupational discrimination and invidious stereotypes. In clinical psychology, most doctoral-level therapists were men. Women who were therapists had to confront the accepted wisdom that male therapists were more competent and more prepared to deal with serious clinical disorders. Thus, a common pattern was that of a male therapist assisted by a female cotherapist. Also, many believed that female therapists lacked the authority and stature to work effectively with male clients. This stereotype limited women's access to Veterans Administration hospitals and thus to many internship opportunities for clinical trainees. Ironically, a substantial number of women had made important contributions to clinical theory and practice, as well as to the field of psychological assessment, during the 1940s and 1950s. Nonetheless, as documented in a number of surveys, invidious judgments about women's abilities as clinicians persisted well into the 1970s.

SECOND-WAVE FEMINISM AND PSYCHOLOGY

Women in psychology who were committed to the ideals of equality between the sexes and solidarity among women started to mobilize near the end of the 1960s. Many had engaged in social activism—in the civil-rights movement, the antiwar movement, and the women's liberation movement—in addition to their work as researchers, therapists, and teachers. Transformation of the structure of society and, more immediately, of the structure of the profession was on their horizon. For example, at the Employment Bureau of the 1970 American Psychological Association (APA) convention, a group of women protested rampant sexism in interviewing and hiring practices. Another early initiative of fledgling feminist organizations in psychology was a push for blind review of scholarly work. In a blind review, an author's identity is concealed from reviewers who are judging work submitted for publication or presentation, a procedure that limits the possibility that knowledge about the author's identity will bias the judgments of the work under review. The policy of blind review was adopted by a number of journals; some still maintain it. Moreover, scholarly work on the topics of women and sexism was often regarded as trivial or "too political" by psychologists. In response, feminists engaged in a number of projects aimed at challenging sexist ideology and practices in psychology. They produced documents that offered guidelines for nonsexist therapy, counseling, research, and language usage. They also mounted a campaign for amendments to the ethical code that would protect women in therapy and women students from sexual abuse and harassment.

At the same time as feminists were trying to change psychology as a whole, feminist psychology was coalescing as an independent field. One way that this can be charted is to note the expansion of course offerings and textbooks. Before 1970, psychology departments offered virtually no courses on women or gender. Two decades later, an APA survey showed that 51 percent of U.S. psychology departments offered undergraduate courses on women and gender; 172 departments offered graduate courses (Women's Programs Office, 1991). There were no textbooks in the field until 1971. By the end of the century, there were dozens, representing varying points of view and emphases.

Although questions about sex differences and women's psychology have been posed throughout the history of psychology, we argue that the study of women and gender as an organized field of psychology extends back only to about 1970. Thus, the history that we recount is short relative to that of most other fields of psychology. The remainder of this chapter is devoted to describing the new field of psychology of women and gender. First, we take up research and scholarship on women and gender. Next, we consider the contributions of feminist clinicians and clinical researchers. In both domains, efforts have been two-pronged. On the one hand, they involve critiques of conventional constructs, research methods, and practices. On the other hand, they involve the development of new forms of scholarship and practice that incorporate feminist insights and feminist values. In the third section, we describe some of the organizations, activities, and projects that have sustained and advanced the field.

Our review covers only English-language work. It is centered on the United States but includes developments in Canada, the United Kingdom, Australia, and New Zealand as well. We focus on broad themes and not every individual contribution to the field is mentioned.

FRAMEWORKS FOR STUDYING WOMEN AND GENDER

Criticisms of psychology's treatment of women and people of color have been voiced intermittently throughout the history of psychology. As early as 1876, Mary Putnam Jacobi, a physician, challenged the then-popular notion that hormonal changes associated with the menstrual cycle handicapped women mentally and physically. Jacobi pointed out that research on the limitations of women was rarely conducted by women themselves but rather by men, who often attributed sex differences to nature (Sherif, 1979). In effect, Jacobi argued that psychological knowledge is socially situated, that is, that interpretations of data reflect the perspectives and interests of the researcher.

The First Wave (c. 1876–1920)

Only a small cohort of American women held higher degrees in psychology in the early years of the twentieth century. Some women in this cohort questioned prevailing beliefs about innate sex differences in personality and ability. For instance, Helen Thompson Woolley conducted the first laboratory study of sex differences in mental traits, developing innovative measures in the process. Woolley stressed the overall similarity of the sexes, critiqued biases in earlier research, and discussed possible environmental determinants of observed differences. Indeed, she argued that the experimental method was of little use for studying sex differences because it was not possible to find male and female research subjects with equivalent social training and experiences. As we noted earlier, Woolley did not mince her words in assessing psychology's claims about women and sex differences.

Inspired by Woolley's work, Leta Stetter Hollingworth offered a rebuttal of the variability hypothesis, the belief that males were the more variable sex and thus responsible for the evolutionary progress of the human species (Hollingworth, 1914, 1916). Hollingworth argued against the claim that women's genetic makeup made them less likely than men to be highly creative or intelligent (Shields, 1975). Woolley and Hollingworth pioneered the use of empirical research to challenge assertions about women's natural limitations. The research and theory they developed was necessarily reactive rather than proactive. That is, they worked to refute claims about female inferiority that they themselves did not originate. Because their ability and their very right to do research and develop theory were in doubt, they were able to gain credibility only insofar as they addressed the questions posed by the psychological establishment.

Few women of this era gained access to positions at research universities or funds for research, and few were able to train graduate students who might have spread their ideas or continued in their footsteps (Rosenberg, 1982). By the 1920s, there was no longer an active women's movement to lend political support to their ideas. Therefore, first-wave feminism had no lasting impact on psychology. Most of the "foremothers" of feminist psychology remained unknown until second-wave feminist psychologists reclaimed the early history of women in psychology (Bernstein & Russo, 1974).

Opportunities for women remained limited during the interwar years (Morawski & Agronick, 1991). Women were channeled into applied fields, especially those connected with children. Women in academia often held adjunct status or unstable research positions. An important response to women's secondary status in psychology was the founding of the National Council of Women Psychologists in 1941, which we describe later.

An even greater resistance to women in the professions marked the decades following World War II. This resistance was part of the broad cultural pressure on women to have large families and to engage in full-time homemaking. The number of women professionals declined during the 1940s and 1950s. Indeed, many social critics and mental health professionals pressed women into domestic roles by a variety of dubious pronouncements issued under the guise of science. For example, they blamed mothers for a variety of psychological disorders, behavior problems, and social ills in their children (Caplan & Hall-MacCorquodale, 1985). They extolled marriage, motherhood, and subordination to men's interests as criteria of maturity and fulfillment for women. Nonetheless, there were resisters like Karen Horney, Clara Thompson, and Georgene Seward.

The Second Wave (c. 1970–the Present)

The second wave of feminism sparked strong challenges to psychology's ideas about women. Feminists in psychology openly challenged psychology's choice of research topics, its theoretical constructs and research methods, and its theories about women's mental health, its modes of diagnosis, and its therapeutic interventions. From a feminist perspective, many aspects of psychological knowledge have been androcentric (that is, male-centered). Historically, men have been studied much more often than women have. For example, classic studies of personality by Murray (1938) and Allport (1954), as well as McClelland's landmark study of achievement motivation (McClelland, Atkinson, Clark, & Lowell, 1953), excluded women. Moreover, psychological theories about many aspects of cognition, social behavior, emotion, and motivation have been influenced by cultural biases against women (Crawford & Unger, 1994). Women's behavior has often been judged against an unacknowledged norm based on white, middle-class men. Women's behavior, more often than men's, has been seen as biologically determined, with researchers overlooking the different social situations of women and men.

Feminist psychologists quickly moved beyond critique to focus on generating new knowledge about women and gender. The psychology of women and gender is now a varied enterprise that encompasses virtually every specialty area and intellectual framework within psychology, that spans international boundaries, and that has produced a large body of research and scholarship. Our goal in this chapter is to describe and evaluate representative approaches to research in the field.

Recovering the Past

One early approach was to find the "great women" of the past, that is, women who had made early contributions to psychology that had gone unrecognized or been forgotten (Scarborough & Furumoto, 1987). In addition to Helen Thompson Woolley and Leta Stetter Hollingworth, several women made substantive contributions to psychology prior to the present period. Among them are Louise Bates Ames, Mary Whiton Calkins, Edna Heidbreder, Else Frenkel-Brunswik, Marguerite Hertz, Karen Machover, Anne Roe, and Bluma Zeigarnik. Historical studies began to correct the "woman-less" image that psychology had maintained. However, studying exceptional women, past and present, can be viewed as tokenism. It has been criticized as an "add-women-and-stir" approach that leaves male-centered norms and power structures unexamined. When notable women's lives are examined

in their social context, however, this work can shed light not just on individual ability and effort but also on the conditions of work in the profession that govern women's accomplishments and lack thereof. For many decades, for example, women psychologists faced structural obstacles that included lack of employment opportunities, overtly sexist attitudes and practices of gatekeepers to the profession, and social values that made women responsible for family care.

Woman as Problem

Given psychology's focus on the individual and its emphasis on inner qualities and traits, psychologists, including feminist psychologists, have been especially susceptible to the fallacy of accounting for women's social position solely in terms of personal deficiencies. This approach has been called the woman-as-problem framework (Crawford & Marecek, 1989). There are many examples: In the area of motivational problems or conflicts, women have been said to suffer from fear of success (Horner, 1970), the Cinderella complex, and the impostor phenomenon (Clance, Dingman, Reviere, & Stober, 1995). They were characterized as lacking crucial skills such as assertiveness (Lakoff, 1975). And they were urged to view therapy as a form of compensatory resocialization that would rectify their deficiencies. The problems faced by women in corporate management have also been characterized in terms of individual deficits. This individual-deficit model represented women as lacking in business skills, leadership ability, and appropriate interpersonal skills; it neglected structural and institutional aspects of sex discrimination (Nieva & Gutek, 1981).

Research within the woman-as-problem framework has sought to explain psychological problems or deficits of women in terms of socialization or upbringing. Certainly, gender-role socialization has been a useful explanatory device. However, it emphasizes distal causes of gender differences, such as early socialization; this may lead to neglecting immediate causes. For example, women may speak "unassertively" as an adaptive response to the immediate social situation, not because they lack the skills to speak more assertively. Cues in that situation may indicate that assertive behavior is unwelcome or will be penalized. Moreover, the emphasis on early socialization fails to challenge the use of men's behavior as the norm against which women are measured. That is, women's behavior is judged as problematic in comparison to an idealized representation of men's behavior. For example, the "new assertive woman" who was held up as the ideal speaker in assertiveness-training manuals of the 1970s exhibited the characteristics attributed to masculine speakers in North American culture (Crawford, 1995).

Despite its drawbacks, the woman-as-problem framework has remained prominent in the field of psychology of women. It has extended to the realm of self-help psychology, with its largely female audience and its offerings based on the premise that women's problems are of their own making (Worell, 1988). Perhaps this framework has been so popular because it fits comfortably within both conventional psychology and popular culture. It is individualist, it fosters research on sex differences, and—unlike the study of power relations between the sexes or structural obstacles to equality—it does not call for social change.

Sex Differences and Similarities

In the decades preceding the second wave of feminism, psychologists had assumed profound differences between men and women in cognitive capacities, emotions, personality traits, values, and inclinations. These presumptions furnished support for the norm of male superiority and justified a range of inequities between men and women. Thus, one of the first projects of feminists in psychology was a program of corrective research, aimed at reexamining purported differences between men and women. In 1974, Eleanor Maccoby and Carol Jacklin published a review of sex-difference research in psychology that soon became a classic. Surveying over 1,400 studies covering more than 80 psychological traits and skills, they found reliable evidence for sex differences in only four areas. Indeed, many of the studies were so flawed that nothing could be concluded from them.

Studies of the psychological differences and similarities between men and women still continue. However, a number of important methodological and conceptual advances have been made. Feminist researchers have pointed out repeatedly that a sex-difference finding does not signify a difference that is inherent or biologically determined. A great deal of feminist research has examined the power of roles, norms, and expectations to influence behavior, as well as the penalties incurred for role violations. Indeed, the correlational design of most sex-difference studies makes it impossible to draw any conclusions about causality. Another significant advance is the adaptation of meta-analysis for use in investigations of sex differences (Hyde & Linn, 1988). Like a narrative review of the literature, meta-analysis collates the results of selected studies into a single integrated summary. Meta-analysis, however, cumulates the results statistically. Meta-analysis also calculates the size of a gender difference (Johnson & Eagly, 2000).

Feminist psychologists challenged psychology's conception and measurement of masculinity and femininity. Anne Constantinople (1973) pointed out that standard psychological inventories were constructed with masculinity and femininity as opposite ends of a single, bipolar continuum. The test format rendered them mutually exclusive. Constantinople argued against this built-in assumption, pointing out that an individual could embrace both masculine and feminine traits and behaviors. Going a step further, Sandra Bem (1974) argued that optimal psychological functioning and personal adjustment required that an individual possess both masculine and feminine qualities, that is, embrace an androgynous sex-role identity. Bem designed the Bem Sex Role Inventory, a scale of masculinity and femininity that permitted respondents to endorse both masculine and feminine attributes (or neither). Bem's ideas, her inventory, and an alternate measure of sex-related attributes, the Personal Attributes Questionnaire (Spence & Helmreich, 1978) framed much feminist research, as well as feminist approaches to therapy, for the next several years. Although the field has now moved beyond the conception of androgyny, the work in this era laid the foundation for subsequent theorizing on gender identity.

In the early 1980s, a new line of feminist inquiry emerged. Instead of pursuing comparisons of men and women, some researchers shifted their focus to women's unique emotional capacities, identities, and relational needs. *In a Different Voice* (Gilligan, 1982) is a prominent example of this line of endeavor. By putting women at the center of inquiry, researchers could reexamine and reevaluate feminine qualities that had been ignored, disdained, or viewed as deficiencies or signs of immaturity. Gilligan's initial investigations, for example, put forward the notion of a distinctive feminine mode of moral decision making, one that emphasized what she called an ethic of care.

Questions about male-female differences and similarities remain unresolved, even after many thousand empirical studies. Hare-Mustin and Marecek (1990) used the terms *alpha bias* to indicate an inclination or tendency among some researchers to maximize differences and *beta bias* to indicate an inclination to minimize or overlook differences. They pointed out that the focus on gender-as-difference diverts attention away from a focus on gender as domination. That is, questions about the differences between men and women distract researchers from examining the power relations between them and the way in which gender serves as a vehicle for distributing power and resources. In addition, the focus on male-female differences presumes that each gender is homogenous. It distracts attention from differences among women associated with ethnicity, class, age, and other social categories. It also distracts researchers from interrogating relations of power among women. Thus, Hare-Mustin and Marecek, as well as some other researchers, have called for feminist psychologists to lay aside the question of gender differences (cf., for example, the essays collected by Kitzinger, 1994).

The Feminist Study of Women's Lives

Many feminist researchers have investigated the experiences of diverse groups of women and girls, situating their research in specific historical and cultural contexts. Often these researchers have chosen to study women as intentional actors, relying on such methods as open-ended interviews and focus groups rather than measurement of abstract psychological constructs. They have examined diverse experiences of women in contemporary society: poor and working-class young women coping with cuts in welfare (Fine & Weis, 1998); dual-career professional couples (Gilbert, 1993); women living amidst political turmoil and state-sponsored terrorism (Lykes, 1989); lesbian and gay teenagers and their peer and family networks (Russell, Bohan, & Lilly, 2000); rural working-class girls (L. M. Brown, 1998); suburban and urban teenagers' sexual desire (Tolman & Szalacha, 1999); and women coping with physical illness and impairment (Ussher, 2000). Others have examined the lives and experiences of women during particular historical episodes, such as the internment of Japanese Americans in the United States during World War II and the civil-rights movement of the 1950s (Franz & Stewart, 1994; Romero & Stewart, 1999). Particularly notable has been the large body of research on violence against girls and women, including rape and sexual assault, incest, wife battering, and sexual harassment (e.g., Gordon & Riger, 1989; Gutek, 1985; Herman, 1992; Koss, 1993; Walker, 1979; Yllo & Bograd, 1988).

Feminist researchers' concern with the particulars of women's experiences and situations sets them apart from the mainstream of psychological research. From the 1940s onward, research in mainstream journals has relied more and more on college student samples, even though such samples are not representative of the population at large with regard to age, social class, ethnicity, marital status, maturity, and many other aspects of experience (Sears, 1986). Yet, although feminist psychology has incorporated studies of women at diverse points in the life cycle, we still know little about many aspects of women's lives: sexuality and sexual desire, childbirth and motherhood, inequality in the relationships of heterosexual couples, and midlife and aging. The gaps in knowledge about women are especially acute when it comes to women who are not white and women who are not middle class. As Pamela Reid (1993) has pointed out, women who are ethnic minorities, poor, or working class are given little attention by researchers except when they are seen as creating social problems. For example, there is abundant research on out-of-wedlock pregnancy among African American teenagers but little research on areas of strength and resilience such as skills for coping with racism, commitment to academic achievement and labor force participation, and spirituality and church membership. Although minority and working-class heterosexual couples often have unconventional divisions of domestic responsibilities and child care, this too has not been studied. In short, feminist psychology has not yet adequately addressed the diversity of women's lives, despite ongoing efforts to do so. The knowledge base, though it is expanding, is still shaped by the priorities of academic institutions and funding agencies, allowing limited scope for innovation.

Psychology of Gender

In an early paper, Rhoda Unger (1979) introduced psychologists to the term *gender,* which she defined as "those characteristics and traits socio-culturally considered appropriate to males and females." The term was intended to set social aspects of maleness and femaleness apart from biological mechanisms, so that the former could be submitted to scientific scrutiny. Important in its time, Unger's definition of gender is only one of several in use today. Some have argued for putting aside the definition of gender as a set of traits of individuals in favor of a view of gender as a socially prescribed set of relations. Reviewing research on sex and gender, Kay Deaux (1985) concluded that the research to that date had been severely limited by the assumption that gender could be fully understood as either a biological category, a finite list of sex differences, or a set of stable personality traits. The model she developed with Brenda Major (Deaux & Major, 1987) conceptualized gender as an interactive process.

Feminist theorists have articulated a number of additional ways to conceptualize gender that go beyond the individual difference model. Gender has been seen as a complex set of principles—a meaning system—that organizes male-female relations in a particular social group or culture (Bem, 1993; Hare-Mustin & Marecek, 1988). Gender has also been viewed as a marker of status, hierarchy, and social power (Henley, 1977). Others have conceptualized gender as the set of practices that create and enact masculinity and femininity in mundane social contexts and in social institutions such as language and law (Bohan, 1993; West & Zimmerman, 1987). Gender has even been conceptualized as the "incorrigible" set of beliefs that underlie the social construction of the binary sex categories, male and female (Kessler & McKenna, 1978).

These alternative ways to conceptualize gender have opened new areas of research. The question is no longer simply "How do women differ psychologically from men?" Instead researchers are asking more radical questions: How are women and men perceived, treated, and rewarded differently in social interactions? What are the habits, language practices, and social institutions by which masculinity and femininity are constituted? How are gender distinctions sustained in particular social groups? How do they come to be seen as natural and inevitable? Construing gender as a system of social relations opens the way to considering gender in relation to ethnicity, class, and other dimensions of social organization and hierarchy (Landrine, 1995; Reid, 1993).

Feminist Epistemology

Some feminist psychologists have explored epistemological and methodological alternatives to conventional ways of producing knowledge in psychology (Hare-Mustin & Marecek, 1990; Kimmel & Crawford, 2000; Morawski, 1994). Chief among them are redefining objectivity; reflexively exploring the investigator's subjectivity and social position; attention to power relations within the research process; and openness to methodological pluralism.

Redefining Objectivity. Feminist commentary about science has called into question the notion of objectivity, that is, the possibility of knowledge uninfluenced by values (Harding, 1986). All of us necessarily perceive, think, and speak from a standpoint generated by our social location and experience. The scientific method does not prevent an investigator from influencing the research process and its outcome. From the time of Helen Thompson Woolley to the present, feminists in psychology have questioned the assumption that facts and values could be separated. As feminist critics reconsidered the research process, they uncovered the profound effects of researchers' standpoints at every stage from formulating questions to designing studies to interpreting data (McHugh, Koeske, & Frieze, 1986).

Some feminists see knowledge production as a historical process embedded in the particular situations of the participants in that process—the researchers and the researched. Research practices, procedures, and outcomes are situated in the social, political, economic, and ideological contexts of their time. Thus, investigations can yield only a particular, limited truth (Haraway, 1988). Jill Morawski (1994) offers a thoughtful reconceptualization of objectivity, subjectivity, and other constructs such as validity, reliability, and generalization. Rather than denying that human values and perspectives influence the research process, many feminists strive to discern and acknowledge their standpoint. For example, they report who sponsors their research and who will benefit from the findings (accountability), and they disclose their social position, politics, and values (partiality).

Exploring Reflexivity and Subjectivity. Some feminists have also advocated reflexivity (Wilkinson, 1988).

Reflexivity is a broad concept. It can refer to a researcher's disciplined reflection on how her identity and social location influence her work. It can also refer to a critical analysis of the relationships among researchers and participants. And, it can refer to a critical perspective on the discipline of psychology. We give examples of each kind of reflexivity in turn.

Personal reflexivity is a continuing process of reflection on the part of the researcher about how her multiple identities (her social class, gender, age, status, feminist stance, ethnicity, and so on) influence her work. Psychology has long denied that the social identity of researchers affects their choice of research topics, theories, methods, and interpretation of research results. By contrast, in taking a reflexive stance, a researcher acknowledges these connections, is willing to explore them, and recognizes that she is not exempt from the psychological processes she studies in others. For example, Deborah Belle (1994) reflected on how her position as a young, middle-class, white professional affected her relationship with and understanding of the low-income white and African American women she was interviewing. Pondering the similarities and differences between herself and her respondents led Belle to insights about the limited utility of conceiving of race and class merely as categories of individual difference, the complex significance of social networks for poor women, and the inadequacy of equating poverty with current household income.

Reflexivity also encompasses analysis of the social relationships among various participants in the research enterprise. Most researchers work in groups with differing levels of experience and skill, and most work in the context of hierarchical institutions. These social configurations affect the research process. Frances Grossman and her colleagues (2000) explored how their needs for equality and intimacy affected their research on adult women who had experienced childhood sexual abuse. These needs affected both their understanding of women's accounts of abuse and their collaboration.

Reflexivity also refers to a critical stance toward the discipline. Early second-wave theorists such as Naomi Weisstein (1971) and Carolyn Sherif (1979) exemplify this critical stance. This form of reflexivity continues to the present. Richard Walsh-Bowers (1999), for example, has recently analyzed some underlying assumptions of the APA publication manual. Critically examining its implicit definitions of what counts as research and the roles of researchers and participants, he discussed the manual's function in socializing its users into the culture of the discipline.

Methodological Pluralism. Both first- and second-wave feminists criticized psychology's research methods. With the second wave, however, has come a more fundamental criticism, not merely of flaws and biases in the application of the methods but of the methods themselves. Psychology, some feminist critics have charged, overrelies on laboratory experimentation, which strips away social context (Parlee, 1979). Some feminists have pointed out that psychology has a long but hidden tradition of inquiry that goes beyond laboratory experimentation (Marecek, Fine, & Kidder, 1997). Field research, observational techniques, content analysis, participant-observation, focus groups, and case studies are a few examples. A growing number of feminist researchers use these approaches as well as new modes of inquiry, such as discourse analysis, that draw on postmodern thought. The call for methodological pluralism has had some effects, at least in some feminist circles. *Feminism and Psychology,* published in the United Kingdom and intended for an international readership, routinely publishes work using innovative approaches. Special issues of *Psychology of Women Quarterly* in 1989 and 1999 have focused on innovative methods and theory.

CLINICAL PRACTICE, COUNSELING, AND FEMINIST THERAPY

During the 1960s, the mental health professions came under strong criticism from various social movements, including the women's movement. At that time, psychoanalytic theories held sway among most psychotherapists, including most clinical psychologists. Feminists assailed these theories on a number of grounds. They charged that they restricted women to domestic roles; they established heterosexuality, marriage, and motherhood as criteria for normality and maturity; they reduced women's ambitions and achievements to pathological expressions of penis envy; and they blamed a wide array of psychological problems and social ills on mothers. Mental health professionals claimed the authority of science to back their assertions about normality and abnormality, but feminists pointed out that these assertions often were based on cultural ideology.

One of the most powerful early critics was Naomi Weisstein, who took clinical and personality theories to task. "Psychology," she said, "has nothing to say about what women really are like, what they need, and what they want, essentially because psychology does not know" (1971, pp. 207, 209). Another influential critique was that of Inge Broverman and her colleagues (Broverman, Broverman, Clarkson, Rosenkrantz & Vogel, 1970). Using an adjective checklist, they showed that the traits that therapists ascribed to the ideal man resembled those they ascribed to a mentally healthy person, while traits ascribed to the ideal woman resembled those ascribed to "a typical mental patient." In

Women and Madness, Phyllis Chesler (1972) charged that the therapy professions placed women in a double bind: Women who violated norms of femininity were stigmatized, yet such norms (e.g., emotional expressiveness and dependence) were also used as indicators of mental disorders such as hysteria and dependent personality disorder.

Another concern feminists raised during the 1960s and 1970s was that men dominated the mental health field. Men held most of the powerful positions in professional organizations, educational institutions, and mental health research settings. Most clinical psychologists were men, yet most consumers of psychotherapy were women. Feminists charged that therapy relationships, which usually consisted of a male therapist and a female patient, replicated the cultural norm of male dominance and female subordination. Rather than helping women to move beyond passivity and dependence, such therapy perpetuated women's reliance on men's judgments of their normality and women's dependence on male approval and validation. Feminists believed that if women shared control of the field and brought women-centered perspectives to clinical psychology, patterns of knowledge and clinical care for women would improve.

The early criticisms that feminists made touched off what became a sustained movement to reform knowledge and practice in clinical and counseling psychology. The concerns raised—that cultural biases permeate scientific constructs; that therapists too readily ignore the social context or underestimate its influence; that sexism and other biases are embedded in diagnostic constructs and practices; that power differences in therapy can work against clients' interest—still thread through feminist clinical psychology today. In response to these concerns, feminists have developed alternate theories and conducted innovative research. They have also developed feminist-inspired therapies and diagnostic practices. Feminists have also worked to improve the conditions of work for women who are therapists. They have addressed the rights of therapy clients and promoted changes in the APA ethical code in order to provide better protection for clients.

The scope of feminist knowledge in clinical psychology is wide, and feminists have devised many approaches to understanding and treating individual women and girls, heterosexual and same-sex couples and families, and men. There are three journals concerned with feminist practice and women-centered therapies: *Women and Therapy,* the *Journal of Feminist Family Therapy,* and *Affilia.* In addition, *Feminism and Psychology* and *Psychology of Women Quarterly* frequently publish research on clinical disorders of women, such as eating disorders and depression, as well as on aspects of diagnosis and treatment. Researchers and practitioners have developed a sophisticated understanding of how gender shapes stressful life experiences, patterns of distress and dysfunction, and coping efforts. They have also examined practices of diagnosis, assessment, and treatment (Worell & Remer, 1992).

Biases in Diagnosis and Clinical Judgment

The history of mental health treatments is replete with examples of diagnostic classifications that reflected and reproduced cultural stereotypes about women, as well as ethnic minority group members, immigrants, and poor people. From the middle of the nineteenth century until well into the twentieth, for example, women and girls whose sexual desire was deemed excessive risked being diagnosed with nymphomania (Groneman, 1994). In some cases, clitoridectomy was the treatment. Neurasthenia, a condition involving diffuse symptoms of low mood, nervousness, and fatigue, was diagnosed in large numbers of American women. The treatment was a prolonged period of enforced bed rest and social isolation, during which reading, writing, and other forms of intellectual stimulation were banned.

Our own times have spawned a jumble of diagnostic categories. The *Diagnostic and Statistical Manual of the American Psychiatric Association (DSM)* (American Psychiatric Association, 1994) lists the diagnoses that are officially recognized. Feminists and other critics are concerned that the scope of the *DSM* has widened appreciably each time it has been revised. The first edition, published in 1952, contained 198 entries. The fourth one, published in 1994, contains 340. The power of mental health professionals to judge, categorize, and label has come to encompass more and more domains of human experience. In addition, unofficial diagnostic classifications proliferate freely in popular culture and psychotherapy vernacular—Sex Addiction, Battered Woman Syndrome, Codependency, Abortion Trauma Syndrome, Internet Addiction, and ACOA (Adult Child of an Alcoholic), to name a few. Although such diagnoses have no official status and little or no systematic research to substantiate them, they, too, exert considerable cultural influence.

Feminists have looked askance at the burgeoning list of diagnoses and pseudodiagnoses. These categories impose a particular way of understanding one's own and others' suffering. They make psychological disorders akin to physical disorders, seeming to exist separately from the social context in which they arise and to be unrelated to its politics and values.

Feminists have raised additional concerns about several specific diagnostic categories. Along with other progressive social groups, they mobilized in the early 1970s to expunge homosexuality from the list of psychiatric diagnoses in the *DSM*. (Ultimately, the membership of the American Psychiatric Association voted to remove homosexuality from the *DSM*. However, a category called "ego-dystonic homosexuality" was substituted instead.) The 1980 edition reflected this change. Many feminists have been concerned that the diagnostic criteria for Premenstrual Dysphoric Disorder do not distinguish it from premenstrual distress, a condition experienced in some degree by as many as 80% of women. Mary Parlee's (1994) elegant account of the struggle over this diagnostic category reveals how the economic interests of pharmaceutical companies and the biomedical profession handily overruled the scientific and social-scientific evidence.

Borderline Personality Disorder (BPD) is another diagnostic category of special concern, if only because three times as many women as men receive this diagnosis (Becker, 1997). This diagnosis carries with it a variety of negative expectations: Individuals with BPD are said to be difficult and troublesome therapy clients, unlikely to make progress. Yet the criteria for BPD are vague: for example, "inappropriate" anger, "marked" reactivity of mood, "markedly unstable" self-image. It is left to therapists to judge whether clients' behavior reaches the threshold for diagnosis. Also, the symptoms overlap with the symptoms of other disorders. A diagnosis of BPD is often mistakenly given to women who have experienced sexual or physical abuse and who should be diagnosed as suffering from post-traumatic stress disorder (Herman, 1992). This diagnostic error prevents women from receiving appropriate treatment.

Apart from formal diagnoses, therapists continually make judgments in the course of treatment: They set goals for therapy, they evaluate clients' progress, and they specify what is healthy functioning for individuals, couples, and families. Feminists have investigated how gender meanings and ethnic and class differences inflect these judgments. Judgments about healthy sexual functioning, for example, rest on the theory of the Human Sexual Response Cycle put forward by Masters and Johnson in 1966. Indeed, the *DSM* diagnostic categories of sexual dysfunction, though purportedly atheoretical, rest on this implicit foundation. As Leonore Tiefer (1995) has shown, this theory privileges forms of sexual behavior preferred by men and overlooks or trivializes many sources of pleasure that women say are important. Also, counselors and therapists who work with clients from impoverished backgrounds may unwittingly presume that such individuals have access to resources for coping and to avenues of judicial redress that in fact are limited to affluent and white members of society (Fine, 1983). Some feminists have challenged definitions of autonomy and its centrality as a criterion of mental health. Autonomy may not be possible for individuals in subordinated positions. Nor is it universally regarded as desirable; in many cultural groups, collective responsibility takes precedence over self-sufficiency (Hare-Mustin & Marecek, 1986).

Feminist critiques have been accompanied by a variety of efforts to change clinical training and practice. In 1977, the Division of Counseling Psychology undertook a 2-year program of conferences and special issues of *The Counseling Psychologist* designed to provide information and skills about women and girls and to counter sex bias in therapy and counseling. Around the same time, the APA constituted a Task Force on Sex Bias and Sex Role Stereotyping, which produced and promulgated guidelines for nonsexist therapy (American Psychological Association, 1978). In 1979, the APA and the National Institutes of Mental Health convened an interdisciplinary conference of mental health specialists to identify priorities for clinical research on women. *Women and Psychotherapy,* the volume resulting from that conference, served as a core text in the area of women and psychotherapy for many years (Brodsky & Hare-Mustin, 1980). Feminists "broke the silence" surrounding sexual contact in psychotherapy (Hare-Mustin, 1974). They argued that because of the inevitable power differences in therapy relationships, sexual involvement between therapist and client could not be consensual. As a result of pressure by feminist groups, the APA eventually altered its ethical code to include an explicit injunction against sexual contact between therapist and client.

Feminist Approaches to Therapy

The term *feminist therapy* came into use in the early 1970s. The first feminist therapists deliberately positioned themselves outside the system in freestanding therapy collectives. One therapist has described the early days of feminist therapy as "raggedy, boisterous, know-it-all, risky, and heady" (Adelman, 1995). In those times, some volunteered their services without pay. Others raised funds to be able to offer therapy without charge or on a sliding-fee scale. Now, feminist therapy has for the most part moved beyond its separatist, grassroots beginnings and its underground aspect. Therapists who identify themselves as feminist therapists or who specialize in women's issues work in a variety of settings, including universities, public and private hospitals and clinics, private agencies, and independent practice.

Although there are a number of frameworks for feminist therapy, certain concepts unite feminist approaches to therapy. First and foremost is an ethical commitment to promoting equality and social justice. Other key concepts are attention to the social context, particularly to inequities in the distribution of power and resources; respect for diversity and cultural difference; valuing ways of being and social roles associated with women; and a commitment to collaboration and power sharing in therapy relationships.

Women in Context

Feminists bring to clinical practice a focus on the gender system—the institutions, social practices, language, and normative beliefs that constitute maleness and femaleness as we know them and that create and normalize power inequities. The first feminist therapists incorporated consciousness raising as part of therapy with women. Consciousness raising helped women see how "the personal is political," that is, how private troubles were connected to social roles and expectations and women's subordinate status (Brodsky, 1977; Lerman, 1976). Feminist therapists and researchers view gender as a central feature of social life and personal identity; thus, they seek to understand clients' difficulties and strengths in relation to the gender system (L. S. Brown, 1994; Lerner, 1988). This angle of vision goes beyond cataloguing symptoms and syndromes. It sometimes dislodges conventional meanings of behavior and may even overturn customary judgments about what is healthy or unhealthy.

The influence of the sociocultural context on women's psychological well-being can be seen with special clarity in the case of eating problems. In the United States, more than 90% of those with clinical eating disorders are women. Women's eating problems are neither timeless nor universal; they are specific to contemporary Western societies (especially North America). One line of feminist work has identified a prevailing "culture of thinness," that is, the glamorization of ultrathin female bodies in the mass media. The culture of thinness promotes an intense preoccupation with body shape and size, feelings of shame and chronic dissatisfaction with one's body, and rigorous dieting in order to achieve an ideal body (Rodin, Silverstein, & Striegel-Moore, 1984). Other feminist work has drawn attention to motifs and themes associated with women's body size, virtuous self-restraint, and self-denial (Bloom, Gitter, Gutwill, Koegel, & Zaphiropoulos, 1994). Another line of work has tied women's eating problems to social processes of objectification, which set a woman's body parts and sexuality apart from her personhood (Frederickson & Roberts, 1997). Sexualized scrutiny, sexual evaluation, and sexual objectification are continually present in women's lives, both in actual interpersonal encounters and in media images (Kaschak, 1992). Not surprisingly, many women and girls come to adopt attitudes of self-scrutiny and self-evaluation, resulting in shame, anxiety, and distortions in body image. Eating problems may also arise as a means to relieve severe emotional strain—for example, adolescent struggles over coming out as a lesbian or childhood experiences of sexual abuse (Thompson, 1995). As Thompson points out, gender is implicated in a multiplicity of ways in women's eating problems.

Clinical researchers and practitioners have a unique vantage point for examining the corrosive effects of intimate violence—wife beating, coercive sexual relations, sexual abuse—on women and girls (Walker, 1999). Violence against women is a concrete manifestation of the unequal power relations between men and women, as well as a crucial mechanism of social control. Feminist theorists have probed the intricate connections between love, attachment, and violence and examined the cultural imperatives of masculinity and femininity (Goldner, 1999; McLean, Carey, & White, 1996). They also have offered accounts of the multiple ways that women experience, interpret, and react to male violence in their lives (Haaken, 1998; Lamb, 1996, 1999). Feminist therapists have pioneered treatment programs for women who have experienced negative effects of intimate violence, sexual abuse, and rape; for couples seeking to break patterns of violence in their relationships; and for abusive men and boys (e.g., Courtois, 1996; Goldner, Penn, Sheinberg, & Walker, 1990; Herman, 1992).

Many problems that heterosexual couples bring to treatment involve power disparities (Hare-Mustin, 1991). Power disparities include the lopsided distribution of household and family work and leisure time and the implicit privileging of men's points of view, needs, and interests. There is a long line of feminist research concerning women's domestic arrangements and depression, agoraphobia, and other clinical disorders (e.g., Radloff, 1975). From a feminist perspective, family life is embedded within the larger society, not a private domain set apart from it. Thus, feminists who are family therapists have called attention to problems within families resulting from such societal factors as women's diminished earning power, the simultaneous idealization and blaming of mothers, the lack of facilities and support for caring for children or for frail or sick family members, and the stigma faced by families without men, such as female-headed households and lesbian families (Goodrich, 1991).

Diversity and Cultural Difference

Gender is not the only axis of social hierarchy. To be a woman may involve subordination, but all women are not subordinated equally or in the same way. Racism, ethnic prejudice, heterosexism, and homophobia affect clients' experiences and contribute to the problems that bring them to therapy. Feminist researchers have begun to compile a knowledge base that encompasses the diversity of women's experiences across cultural and class backgrounds (e.g., Chin, 2000; Comas-Diaz,

1987; Espín, 1997; Greene, White, Whitten, & Jackson, 2000). The goal of this work is not to describe the psychology (let alone, the psychopathology) of "the" Hispanic woman, "the" African American teenager, or "the" lesbian. Rather it is to comprehend the experiences of women with varying relations to privilege in society (Hurtado, 1989): the problems they bring to therapy, the strengths and resources available to them, and the barriers confronting them.

Valuing Women's Ways of Being

In *Toward a New Psychology of Women,* Jean Baker Miller (1976) addressed women's experiences of subordination in the intimate setting of marriage and family life. Although her observations were limited mainly to white, middle-class, heterosexual women, she argued that women in general were endowed with special capacities for intuition, empathy, and relatedness, as well as a propensity for nurturing and caring for others. Miller celebrated these universal feminine characteristics as "closer to psychological essentials" and "therefore, the bases of a more advanced form of living" (p. 27). Subsequently, others put forward a variety of related claims about women's experience and personality. The prime example is a model of women's development originally called the self-in-relation model and now named the relational/cultural model (Jordan, Kaplan, Miller, Stiver, & Surrey, 1991). The model holds that childhood experiences, particularly mother–daughter interactions, give rise to a uniquely feminine psychology, one that is sustained by and seeks out emotional connections. Although some scholars have raised doubts about the model (Marecek, 2001; Westkott, 1989), the self-in-relation model has been a popular framework for many feminist-identified therapists and counselors.

Collaboration and Power Sharing in Therapy

Attention to the power relations between therapists and clients has been a distinctive feature of feminist therapy. Feminist therapists were among the first to disseminate materials to clients and potential clients informing them about the nature of therapy, how to go about selecting a therapist, and their rights as consumers. Feminist therapists have experimented with a variety of other ways to put the therapy relationship on a more equal footing. One is the practice of self-disclosure, for example, the disclosure that the therapist has struggled with issues akin to those the client faces. Other disclosures may show clients that their therapists are ordinary and fallible human beings. There are both ethical and theoretical considerations that govern the use of self-disclosure;

the literature on feminist therapy discusses these in detail (Wyche & Rice, 1997). More generally, feminist therapists strive to find ways to affirm clients' competence and their right and responsibility to make choices about their lives.

In sum, feminist approaches to clinical psychology have offered new perspectives on clinical disorders of women and girls. Feminists have challenged diagnostic and treatment practices, ethical codes, and theoretical constructs that have worked against women's interests. Feminist therapists have offered new ideas about the conduct of therapy and new models for treating problems common to women. Many of their ideas were iconoclastic when feminist therapy began in the early 1970s; now they are widely accepted. For example, it is no longer radical for therapists to encourage women to work outside the home. It is no longer radical to raise questions about equality and fairness with couples in marital therapy. It is now unexceptional to view single life and lesbian relationships as fulfilling lifestyle choices.

ORGANIZATIONS AND ACTIVISM

For many feminist psychologists, exposing inequity and injustices that women face is the very core of their work. They also hold an ethic that uncovering abuses of power must be accompanied by actions aimed at reform and redress. This has required organizational structures that support and foster research, practice, and activism. Several organizations have provided venues for addressing issues of importance in the field of the psychology of women and gender.

The National Council of Women Psychologists

The National Council of Women Psychologists (NCWP) was founded in 1941. During World War II, women were not allowed to be part of the defense system of the country. Mildred Mitchell, who worked for the U.S. military, Gladys Schwesinger, and other women protested the exclusion of women (Capshew & Laszlo, 1986; Frances M. Culbertson, personal communication, March 1, 2001). They founded the NCWP to develop and promote emergency services that women psychologists could render. After the war, the group continued to carry out projects that promoted the careers of women psychologists, such as a newsletter of employment opportunities. In 1947, the name was changed to the International Council of Women Psychologists and membership opened to women outside the United States. The organization remained a women's organization until 1960; at that point, men were admitted and the group became the International Council of Psychologists.

Society for the Psychological Study of Social Issues

Founded in 1937, the Society for the Psychological Study of Social Issues (SPSSI) was one of the earliest groups to advocate for social action research. Despite its commitment to social justice, however, SPSSI did not focus on women's issues until the 1970s. With the women's movement of the 1970s, the number of women in the discipline increased and SPSSI's membership changed. During the 1980s and 1990s, women assumed leadership roles in SPSSI. The *Journal of Social Issues,* as well as SPSSI's workshops, conferences, and meeting programs, have addressed issues of women and gender (Katz, 1991). Moreover, many other topics that SPSSI has addressed, such as poverty, homelessness, pornography, and immigration, are directly relevant to women's lives.

The Association for Women in Psychology

In March 1969, a group of women in the Psychologists for Social Action formed a Women's Consortium. They organized a symposium for the 1969 APA convention called "Woman as Subject," as opposed to "woman as sex object." Although the symposium was not sponsored by any division and was publicized only via flyers posted in the public areas of the hotel, 400 people, mostly women, attended (Berman, 1995). Two other groups of women independently organized paper sessions and workshops, also unofficially. During these sessions, a petition was circulated demanding that the APA examine and rectify sexist discrimination in the organization and in psychology departments. Another petition called for the APA to pass a resolution stating that abortion (then illegal in most states) was a civil right of pregnant women. A core group of about 35 psychologists (women and men) continued to meet in the months following the convention, and they laid the groundwork for a new organization, the Association for Women in Psychology (AWP). AWP's purpose was defined in an initial statement: "AWP is dedicated to maximizing the effectiveness of, and the professional opportunities for, women psychologists, and to exploring the contributions which psychology can, does, and should make to the definition, investigation, and modification of current sex role stereotypes" (Association for Women in Psychology, 1970, p. 1).

In 1970, the AWP presented 32 resolutions and 18 motions to the APA at the annual APA convention. These were designed to overhaul the way the APA and university departments of psychology operated (Tiefer, 1991). In response, the APA appointed a Task Force on the Status of Women, chaired by Helen S. Astin. The Task Force Report documented inequities within the field. Among other recommendations, it recommended that a division be created to address deficiencies in psychological knowledge about women. Despite much skepticism and covert resistance in the APA, the division, Division 35, was formally approved in 1973 (see below).

The AWP did not dissolve with the establishment of the division; instead, it continued to exist as a parallel organization independent of the APA. Its activities continued to focus on efforts to reshape the APA. In addition, its members endeavored to devise methods to govern themselves that did not recapitulate the hierarchical structures of the organizations they were trying to change (Tiefer, 1991). Most important, the AWP provided a venue for sharing feminist ideas and knowledge and for supporting and mentoring its members. For example, the AWP provided lesbian psychologists their earliest organizational home. In 1973, the organization expanded its by-laws to incorporate the following statement of purpose: "Helping women create individual sexual identities through which they may freely and responsibly express themselves, provided such expression does not oppress other individuals" (AWP newsletter, 1973, p. 1).

The AWP has sustained itself to the present, with a national and international membership that includes individuals from psychology and related disciplines. The AWP holds annual national conventions, as well as regional meetings, and initiates and funds numerous projects.

The Society for the Psychology of Women of the American Psychological Association (Division 35)

The Society for the Psychology of Women (formerly called the Division of the Psychology of Women) has the purpose of "promoting research and the study of women, and encouraging the integration of this information about women with current psychological knowledge and beliefs in order to apply the gained knowledge to the society and its institutions" (American Psychological Association Division of the Psychology of Women, 1989, p. 1).

The mission of Division 35 is multidimensional (Mednick & Urbanski, 1991). Its founders viewed social action research as important. They also recognized that in order to influence the discipline and society, the field of the psychology of women and gender had to become a recognized academic field. The division has also supported the development of clinical knowledge and principles of clinical practice consistent with feminist ideals. Another important goal has been placing women in leadership positions in the APA governance structure. The division's representatives to APA's governing Council of Representatives formed a Women's Caucus in the Council. This caucus has supported proposals that furthered the interests of women and minority groups.

The division established a peer-reviewed journal, *Psychology of Women Quarterly,* in 1976. The journal has come to occupy a visible and respected position. By 1999, it ranked 16th out of 109 psychology journals in terms of the number of times its articles were cited in scholarly publications. Division 35 also sponsors a program of formal and informal sessions and social events at the annual APA convention, continuing-education workshops on teaching and other topics, and a yearly midwinter conference. In addition, the division gives annual awards for excellence in feminist research, practice, and service. In 1993, the division organized the first National Conference on Education and Training in Feminist Practice (defined broadly to include research, writing, clinical practice, clinical supervision, and leadership), held in Boston. *Shaping the Future of Feminist Psychology* (Worell & Johnson, 1997) is a summation of the conference.

Division 35 was one of the first divisions that gave priority to including psychologists from racial, ethnic, and other minority groups in its membership. It also took steps to assure that its leadership represented the diversity of women in psychology. The division has also worked to ensure that women from ethnic minority groups were considered for leadership positions in the APA. It has supported APA activities that advance the interests of racial and ethnic minorities and their full representation within organized psychology. The division has had a Section on Women of Color for many years; among other activities, the section has promoted research on and by women of color.

The APA Committee on Women in Psychology

The Committee on Women in Psychology (CWP) began as the task force headed by Helen Astin in 1970; it was accorded status as a continuing committee of the APA in 1973. The committee has worked to increase the visibility of scholarship on women and gender, highlight the contributions of women in psychology, end discrimination against women psychologists, and promote leadership by women. More broadly, the committee has worked to promote the psychological well-being of women. The CWP has actively pursued its goals through symposia, conferences, task forces, and liaisons with government agencies and professional groups. The CWP annually makes awards to women who have been distinguished leaders in psychology.

The APA Women's Programs Office

The volume and magnitude of the projects initiated by the CWP in its early years quickly exceeded what a volunteer committee could accomplish. In response, the APA established the

Women's Programs Office in 1977. The office coordinates resources for research and collects information and reference material. It also gathers statistical data concerning women's employment in the various scientific and professional fields. The office has compiled directories of graduate programs that offer training in the psychology of women and gender. It has also compiled bibliographies of research reports and pamphlets for the general public.

Other Activities

A number of divisions of the APA have sections or committees focused on women's issues. One of the first ones to establish such a subgroup was the Division of Counseling Psychology. Among divisions that have active sections are the Society for Clinical Psychology, the Division of Psychotherapy, and the Division of Psychoanalysis. The groups publish newsletters, sponsor symposia and programs at the APA conventions and other conferences, and present awards.

The Southeastern Psychological Association (SEPA) was the site of a vibrant organization of women during the 1970s. In 1972, at the behest of several feminist psychologists, the incoming president, Charles Speilberger, and the Executive Committee appointed the first SEPA Commission on the Status of Women, chaired by Ellen Kimmel. Not only did that group report on the status of women (Kimmel, 1974), it also initiated a number of activities that are still in place today, including a visiting scholars program and student research awards. The commission was so effective in enhancing the participation and status of women that the SEPA expanded its charge to include other underrepresented groups in addition to women, renaming it the Committee on Equality of Opportunity.

Another important organization is the Feminist Therapy Institute, established in 1983, which has held conferences and workshops, sponsored publications, and led feminists in protesting against diagnoses detrimental to women.

Finally, an innovative series of small conferences, developed and sustained by Faye Crosby, has brought psychologists together in informal settings around topics on women, gender, and feminism. The conference series is called Nag's Heart, a name that evolved from its forerunner, a conference series in social psychology held at Nag's Head, North Carolina.

The Section on Women and Psychology of the Canadian Psychological Association

The turbulence of the 1970s was felt within the Canadian Psychological Association (CPA) just as in its American counterpart. In 1975, upon the recommendation of its president, Mary Wright, the CPA established a Task Force on the Status of Women in Canadian Psychology. The task force presented almost 100 recommendations to the board of directors in 1976. Included among them was a recommendation to establish a special-interest group on the psychology of women. This special-interest group, now called the Section on Women and Psychology (SWAP), is the second largest of the CPA's 26 sections (Pyke, 1993). SWAP holds a daylong institute prior to the annual CPA convention for the presentation of scholarly research and discussions on the psychology of women. SWAP also publishes a newsletter. The CPA has formally approved several initiatives undertaken by SWAP. These include guidelines on the elimination of sexual harassment, the conduct of nonsexist research, and the provision of sex-fair counseling and therapy.

The Psychology of Women Section of the British Psychological Association

The Psychology of Women Section of the British Psychological Association (BPA) was established in 1988. The goals of the section are to provide a forum for research, teaching, and practice on the psychology of women and to eliminate gender inequality in the BPA and the field of psychology (Psychology of Women Section, 2000). The section holds conferences and symposia annually, provides support for other events, and works within the BPA to influence policy and promote research on the psychology of women and gender. One project that the section has undertaken is an investigation of the portrayal of women in British undergraduate psychology courses.

In sum, a number of organizations have been founded to further the development of the field of psychology of women and gender. Although we have not provided an exhaustive description of their activities, all have made important contributions to feminist psychology and, in turn, to changing the field of psychology and the way its practices affect society.

SUMMING UP AND LOOKING AHEAD

The endeavors of feminist researchers, teachers, practitioners, and activists have reshaped the contours of the discipline and the status of women in profession. In this final section, we survey what has been accomplished and what, in our best guess, lies ahead.

Research, Scholarship, and Pedagogy

When the field of psychology of women and gender was in its infancy, the question of sex differences loomed large. Today, the range of questions has expanded. One significant trend has been the shift away from studying women as if they constituted a single, undifferentiated category. Researchers turn their sights on specific groups of women and girls, situated in specific circumstances. Another trend is increased attention to the lives of women beyond the borders of the United States and to interconnections between women in the United States and women worldwide. Issues include trafficking of women and girls for prostitution, the systematic rape of women as part of warfare, and the growing use of women as a pool of cheap and mobile labor in the transnational economy. A third trend is a focus on strength and resilience, that is, how women cope and prevail despite hardship, discrimination, life crises, and physical illness or disability (Romero & Stewart, 1999; Johnson, Roberts, & Worell, 1999).

The research methods employed in the psychology of women and gender also continue to evolve. Many feminist psychologists have moved beyond prevailing experimental methodology. Their methods of inquiry include open-ended interviewing and focus groups, textual analysis, field-based research and participatory action research, and the family of approaches called discourse analysis. These methods have proven invaluable for studying how gendered power relations are reproduced in everyday practice and talk. They also enable researchers to study the multivalent meanings of gender that research participants hold. These methods are important tools for understanding people not only as passive recipients of social influences but also as effective agents. The use of alternate research methods has brought increased attention to questions about the relationship between methods of inquiry and research outcomes. Although qualitative approaches are not new to psychology, they have been long out of vogue in the United States. As they are resurrected and refurbished, we can expect to learn more about how they work. Moreover, the powers and limits of all approaches will be thrown into sharper relief.

Finally, the turn toward theory is another significant trend in feminist psychology. Some feminists have found the critical psychology movement compatible with their stance (Wilkinson, 1997). They are alert to the ways in which psychology, even feminist psychology, may share in and legitimate the status quo. For example, critical feminist psychologists have upbraided social psychology for failing to incorporate social, cultural, historical, and even group contexts in its understanding of social processes (Apfelbaum, 1999). Others have noted that the uncritical use of psychological language shunts moral and political concerns to the side. For example, when the psychological consequences of horrific events are reformulated as the medicalized diagnosis of Post-traumatic Stress Disorder, they lose their moral and political import. The social, cultural, and historical forces that shaped the event (and perhaps allowed perpetrators to go unpunished) are pushed into the background.

Feminist Clinical and Counseling Practice

As we have noted, feminists have situated women's problems and strengths within the context of the larger social, political, and cultural forces surrounding them. Today, clinicians work under strong conservative pressures from pharmaceutical companies, managed-care companies, and a biologically oriented psychiatric profession. Among other things, they press to redefine psychological disorders as biological aberrations to be controlled by medication. Although feminists are not against the use of medication, this medicalized framework is diametrically opposed to the feminist emphasis on the social context. Thus far, organized psychology's responses to conservative pressures and corporate interests have fallen short of what feminists would wish.

Confronting the Backlash

Many of the changes promoted by the women's movement have become accepted practice: equal pay for equal work; women working outside the home; the repudiation of wife beating. These changes are no longer identified with feminism. At the same time, the term *feminism* has come to be disparaged, even vilified, by the mass media. By the 1990s, the backlash against feminism in popular culture was intense (Faludi, 1991). Moreover, the legal gains that women had made in such areas as affirmative action and reproductive rights have eroded. State support for poor women and their families has been severely curtailed by the welfare reforms of 1996.

In popular culture, there has been an upsurge of claims that masculinity and femininity, as well as sexual orientation, are biologically determined and perhaps genetically encoded. For example, *Men are from Mars, Women are from Venus* (Gray, 1992) amounts to propaganda for male-female difference and an apologia for male privilege. Yet, many—even some therapists—have accepted it as credible clinical theory. Extreme and profligate claims about the evolutionary bases of male dominance and sexual access have become the fad in popular science. Media reports of sex differences in mathematics achievement have announced a "math gene," ignoring the influence of social roles and differential opportunities and expectations regarding boys' and girls' math performance (Eccles & Jacobs, 1986). By now, feminists have amassed a good deal of evidence to counter many such claims. The task remains, however, to translate that evidence into a form that will be effective and persuasive.

Every movement for social change meets resistance. The field of the psychology of women and gender is no exception. Such resistance is an inevitable reaction to any struggle for change. In psychology, the resistance includes disdain for work on "women's" topics and for feminist journals. Women, the majority of humankind, are still considered a special population; research on women is seen as failing to contribute to psychological knowledge about human behavior. An analysis of psychology journal articles showed that when researchers used an all-female (versus an all-male) sample, they were more likely to provide a justification for a single-sex sample and to point out that their results could not be generalized to the other sex (Ader & Johnson, 1994). Finally, many feminist psychologists value collaboration and interdisciplinary work, research with applied potential, and the use of innovative research approaches. All of these draw further antipathy.

CONCLUSION

Has the psychology of women and gender significantly altered the field of psychology? With regard to psychological knowledge, some see fundamental transformations (e.g., Worell & Johnson, 1997). Others argue that only weakened, nonthreatening versions of feminist ideas have been assimilated into the field as a whole (e.g., Burman, 1997). We argue that although the alliance between psychology and feminism has been uneasy, feminism has put on the table for psychology a number of provocative problems and challenges. To varying degrees, it has changed the field with respect to them. Feminist researchers have put forth a strong claim that gender is an important constituent of social life. They have contested certain technologies of research, some key epistemological assumptions, and the ethics of certain research practices. To us, the importance of feminist psychology is not that it can correct the omissions and biases of mainstream psychology and produce objective truths. That is impossible. Rather, feminist psychology can serve to help all psychologists become more self-aware of their perspectives, politics, and practices and to ask how these shape the production of knowledge.

Feminists in clinical practice have offered new perspectives on disorders of women and new ideas about the conduct of therapy. They have protested flawed diagnostic and treatment practices, ethical breaches, and outmoded theoretical constructs. Sometimes these protests have succeeded in provoking change. Even when they did not succeed, they raised awareness that policies and practices in the mental health field are not the outcome of a pristine and unassailable scientific consensus but rather a concatenation of scientific evidence, popular beliefs, and the vested interests of many parties.

Conditions for women faculty members, students, and therapists have improved vastly since 1970, in large part because of feminist activism. Knowledge about women and gender is now available to students of psychology at both undergraduate and graduate levels. Moreover, with barriers to women's participation removed by the federal legislation of the 1970s, women were soon enrolling in psychology graduate programs in large numbers. In 1971, women were awarded fewer than 25 percent of doctorates in psychology; by 1999, they received 66 percent. Furthermore, many women have attained recognition for their academic accomplishments—they are professors, department chairs, program directors, and editors of journals. Many now have influence in the publication process, as well as the awarding of tenure and promotion, grants, and awards. Only two women held the presidency of APA from its inception in 1892 up to 1970; five women have held the presidency since 1970. (Mary Calkins held the presidency in 1905; Margaret Washburn, in 1921. The five recent women presidents are Florence Denmark, Janet Spence, Bonnie Strickland, Dorothy Cantor, and Norine G. Johnson.) Many other women have held positions on boards and committees and been elected to offices in divisions. All these developments signal substantial changes in psychology as a whole over the past 30 years.

At its best, feminist psychology has generative capacity: It challenges the guiding assumptions of the culture, raises fundamental questions about social life, and provokes the reexamination of what is taken for granted. By viewing the knowledge, methods, and practices of psychology with a critical eye, feminist psychologists have provided generative theory for the discipline. Their work incites debate, offers new forms of social action, and ultimately can help to transform social reality. Psychology has benefited from feminist psychology.

REFERENCES

Adelman, J. (1995). Looking backward, moving forward. In E. F. Williams (Ed.), *Voices of feminist therapy.* Luxembourg Belgium: Harwood.

Ader, D. N., & Johnson, S. B. (1994). Sample description, reporting and analysis of sex in psychological research: A look at APA and APA division journals in 1990. *American Psychologist, 49,* 216–218.

Allport, G. W. (1954). *The nature of prejudice.* Cambridge, MA: Addison-Wesley.

American Psychiatric Association. (1994). *Diagnostic and statistical manual of mental disorders* (4th ed.). Washington, DC: Author.

American Psychological Association, Division of the Psychology of Women. (1989). *Handbook of the division of the psychology of women.* Washington, DC: Author.

American Psychological Association Task Force on Sex Bias and Sex Role Stereotyping in Psychotherapeutic Practice. (1978). Guidelines for therapy with women. *American Psychologist, 33,* 1122–1123.

Apfelbaum, E. (1999). Relations of dominance and movements for liberation: An analysis of power between groups. *Feminism and Psychology, 9,* 267–272.

Association for Women in Psychology. (1970, Summer). *Newsletter* (p. 1). Pittsburgh, PA: Author.

Becker, D. (1997). *Through the looking glass: Women and Borderline Personality Disorder.* Boulder, CO: Westview Press.

Belle, D. (1994). Attempting to comprehend the lives of low-income women. In C. E. Franz & A. J. Stewart (Eds.), *Women creating lives: Identities, resilience, and resistance* (pp. 37–50). Boulder, CO: Westview Press.

Bem, S. L. (1974). The measurement of psychological androgyny. *Journal of Consulting and Clinical Psychology, 42,* 155–162.

Bem, S. L. (1993). *The lenses of gender.* New Haven, CT: Yale University Press.

Berman, J. S. (1995). From Chicago to Rainbow Bridge: In search of changing woman. In E. F. Williams (Ed.), *Voices of feminist therapy* (pp. 11–24). Luxembourg, Belgium: Harwood Academic.

Bernstein, M. D., & Russo, N. F. (1974). The history of psychology revisited: Or, up with our foremothers. *American Psychologist, 29,* 130–134.

Bloom, C., Gitter, A., Gutwill, S., Kogel, L., & Zaphiropoulos, L. (1994). *Eating problems: A feminist psychoanalytic treatment model.* New York: Basic Books.

Bohan, J. S. (1993). Regarding gender: Essentialism, constructionism, and feminist psychology. *Psychology of Women Quarterly, 17,* 5–21.

British Psychological Association. (2000–2001). *Psychology of Women Section.* Web address: www.bps.org.uk

Brodsky, A. M. (1977). Therapeutic aspects of consciousness-raising groups. In E. I. Rawlings & D. K. Carter (Eds.), *Psychotherapy of women.* Springfield, IL: Charles C. Thomas.

Brodsky, A. M., & Hare-Mustin, R. T. (1980). *Women and psychotherapy.* New York: Guilford Press.

Broverman, I. K., Broverman, D. M., Clarkson, F. E., Rosenkrantz, P. S., & Vogel, S. R. (1970). Sex-role stereotypes and clinical judgments of mental health. *Journal of Consulting and Clinical Psychology, 34,* 1–7.

Brown, L. M. (1998). *Raising their voices: The politics of girls' anger.* Cambridge, MA: Harvard University Press.

Brown, L. S. (1994). *Subversive dialogues: Theory in feminist therapy.* New York: Basic Books.

Burman, E. (1997). *Deconstructing feminist psychology.* London: Sage.

Caplan, P. J., & Hall-MacCorquodale, I. (1985). Mother-blaming in major clinical journals. *American Journal of Orthopsychiatry, 55,* 345–353.

Capshew, J. H., & Laszlo, A. C. (1986). We would not take no for an answer: Women psychologists and gender politics during World War II. *Journal of Social Issues, 42,* 157–180.

Chesler, P. (1972). *Women and madness.* New York: Doubleday.

Chin, J. (Ed.). (2000). *Relationships among Asian American women.* Washington, DC: American Psychological Association.

Clance, P. R., Dingman, D., Reviere, S. L., & Stober, D. R. (1995). Impostor phenomenon in an interpersonal/social context: Origins and treatment. *Women and Therapy, 16,* 79–96.

Comas-Diaz, L. (1987). Feminist therapy with mainland Puerto Rican women. *Psychology of Women Quarterly, 11,* 461–474.

Constantinople, A. (1973). Masculinity-femininity: An exception to a famous dictum? *Psychological Bulletin, 80,* 389–407.

Courtois, C. A. (1996). *Healing the incest wound: Adult survivors in therapy.* New York: Norton.

Crawford, M. (1995). *Talking difference.* London: Sage.

Crawford, M., & Marecek, J. (1989). Psychology reconstructs the female, 1968–1988. *Psychology of Women Quarterly, 13,* 147–166.

Crawford, M., & Unger, R. (1994). Gender issues in psychology. In A. M. Colman (Ed.), *Companion encyclopedia of psychology* (pp. 1007–1027). New York: Routledge.

Deaux, K. (1985). Sex and gender. *Annual Review of Psychology, 36,* 49–81.

Deaux, K., & Major, B. (1987). Putting gender into context: An interactive model of gender-related behavior. *Psychological Review, 94,* 369–389.

Eccles, J. S., & Jacobs, J. E. (1986). Social forces shape math attitudes and performance. *Signs, 11,* 367–380.

Espín, O. M. (1997). *Latina realities.* Boulder, CO: Westview Press.

Faludi, S. (1991). *Backlash: The undeclared war against American women.* New York: Crown.

Fine, M. (1983). Coping with rape: Critical perspectives on consciousness. *Imagination, Cognition, and Personality: A Scientific Study of Consciousness, 3,* 249–264.

Fine, M., & Weis, L. (1998). *The unknown city: Lives of poor and working class young adults.* Boston: Beacon Press.

Franz, C. E., & Stewart, A. J. (Eds.). (1994). *Women creating lives: Identities, resilience, and resistance.* Boulder, CO: Westview Press.

Frederickson, B. L., & Roberts, T.-A. (1997). Objectification theory: Toward understanding women's lived experiences and mental health risks. *Psychology of Women Quarterly, 21,* 173–206.

Gilbert, L. A. (1993). *Two careers/one family: The promise of gender equality.* Thousand Oaks, CA: Sage.

Gilligan, C. (1982). *In a different voice.* Cambridge, MA: Harvard University Press.

Goldner, V. (1999). Morality and multiplicity: Perspectives on the treatment of violence in intimate life. *Journal of Marital and Family Therapy, 25,* 325–336.

Goldner, V., Penn, P., Sheinberg, M., & Walker, G. (1990). Love and violence: Gender paradoxes in volatile attachments. *Family Process, 29,* 343–364.

Goodrich, T. J. (Ed.). (1991). *Women and power: Perspectives for therapy.* New York: Norton.

Gordon, M. T., & Riger, S. (1989). *The female fear: The social cost of rape.* Urbana: University of Illinois Press.

Gray, J. (1992). *Men are from Mars, women are from Venus.* New York: HarperCollins.

Greene, B., White, J. C., Whitten, L., & Jackson, L. C. (Eds.). (2000). *Psychotherapy with African American women: Innovations in psychodynamic perspective and practice.* New York: Guilford Press.

Groneman, C. (1994). Nymphomania: The historical construction of female sexuality. *Signs, 19,* 337–367.

Grossman, F. K., Kruger, L., & Moore, R. P. (2000). Reflections on a feminist research project: Subjectivity and the wish for intimacy and equality. In E. B. Kimmel & M. Crawford (Eds.), *Innovations in feminist psychological research* (pp. 117–135). New York: Cambridge University Press.

Gutek, B. A. (1985). *Sex and the workplace.* San Francisco: Jossey-Bass.

Haaken, J. (1998). *Pillar of salt.* New Brunswick, NJ: Rutgers University.

Haraway, D. (1988). Situated knowledges: The science question in feminism and the privilege of partial perspective. *Feminist Studies, 14,* 575–599.

Harding, S. (1986). *The science question in feminism.* Ithaca, NY: Cornell University Press.

Hare-Mustin, R. T. (1974). Ethical considerations in the use of sexual contact in psychotherapy. *Psychotherapy, 11,* 308–310.

Hare-Mustin, R. T. (1991). Sex, lies, and headaches: The problem is power. In T. J. Goodrich (Ed.), *Women and power: Perspectives for therapy* (pp. 63–85). New York: Norton.

Hare-Mustin, R. T., & Marecek, J. (1986). Autonomy and gender: Some questions for therapists. *Psychotherapy, 23,* 205–212.

Hare-Mustin, R. T., & Marecek, J. (1988). The meaning of difference: Gender theory, postmodernism, and psychology. *American Psychologist, 43,* 455–464.

Hare-Mustin, R. T., & Marecek, J. (1990). *Making a difference: Psychology and the construction of gender.* New Haven, CT: Yale University Press.

Henley, N. M. (1977). *Body politics.* Englewood Cliffs, NJ: Prentice Hall.

Herman, J. (1992). *Trauma and recovery.* New York: Basic Books.

Hollingworth, L. S. (1914). Variability as related to sex differences in achievement. *American Journal of Sociology, 19,* 510–530.

Hollingworth, L. S. (1916). Social devices for impelling women to bear children. *American Journal of Sociology, 22,* 19–29.

Horner, M. S. (1970). Femininity and successful achievement: A basic inconsistency. In J. M. Bardwick, E. Douvan, M. S. Horner, & D. Gutman (Eds.), *Feminine personality and conflict* (pp. 45–74). Belmont, CA: Brooks/Cole.

Hurtado, A. (1989). Relating to privilege: Seduction and rejection in the subordination of White women and women of color. *Signs: Journal of Women in Culture and Society, 14,* 833–855.

Hyde, J. S., & Linn, M. (1988). Sex differences in verbal ability: A meta-analysis. *Psychological Bulletin, 104,* 53–69.

Johnson, B. T., & Eagly, A. H. (2000). Quantitative synthesis of social psychological research. In H. T. Reis & C. Judd (Eds.), *Handbook of research methods in social and personality psychology* (pp. 496–528). New York: Cambridge University Press.

Johnson, N. G., Roberts, M. C., & Worell, J. (Eds.). (1999). *Beyond appearance: A new look at adolescent girls.* Washington, DC: American Psychological Association.

Jordan, J. V., Kaplan, A. G., Miller, J. B., Stiver, I. P., & Surrey, J. (1991). *Women's growth in connection.* New York: Guilford Press.

Kaschak, E. (1992). *Engendered lives.* New York: HarperCollins.

Katz, P. (1991). Women, psychology, and social issues research. *Psychology of Women Quarterly, 15,* 665–675.

Kessler, S., & McKenna, S. (1978). *Gender: An ethnomethodological approach.* New York: Wiley.

Kimmel, E. B. (1974). The status of women in the southeast: A case study. *American Psychologist, 29,* 519–540.

Kimmel, E. B., & Crawford, M. (Eds.). (2000). *Innovations in feminist psychological research.* New York: Cambridge University Press.

Kitzinger, C. (1994). Should psychologists study sex differences? *Feminism and Psychology, 4,* 501–546.

Koss, M. P. (1993). Rape: Scope, impact, interventions, and public policy responses. *American Psychologist, 48,* 1062–1069.

Lakoff, R. (1975). *Language and woman's place.* New York: Harper & Row.

Lamb, S. (1996). *The trouble with blame: Victims, perpetrators, and responsibility.* Cambridge, MA: Harvard University Press.

Lamb, S. (1999). *New versions of victims: Feminists struggle with the concept.* New York: New York University Press.

Landrine, H. (1995). *Bringing cultural diversity to feminist psychology: Theory, research, and practice.* Washington, DC: American Psychological Association.

Lerman, H. (1976). What happens in feminist therapy? In S. Cox (Ed.), *Female psychology: The emerging self.* Chicago: Science Research Associates.

Lerner, H. G. (1988). *Women in therapy.* New York: Harper & Row.

Lykes, M. B. (1989). Dialogue with Guatemalan Indian women: Critical perspectives on constructing collaborative research. In

R. Unger (Ed.), *Representations: Social constructions of gender* (pp. 167–185). Amityville, NY: Baywood.

Maccoby, E. E., & Jacklin, C. (1974). *The psychology of sex differences.* Palo Alto, CA: Stanford University.

Marecek, J. (2001). Disorderly constructs: Feminist frameworks for clinical psychology. In R. Unger (Ed.), *Handbook of the psychology of women and gender* (pp. 303–316). New York: Wiley.

Marecek, J., Fine, M., & Kidder, L. H. (1997). Working between worlds: Qualitative methods and social psychology. *Journal of Social Issues, 53,* 29–44.

McClelland, D. C., Atkinson, J. W., Clark, R. A., & Lowell, E. L. (1953). *The achievement motive.* East Norwalk, CT: Appleton-Century-Crofts.

McHugh, M. D., Koeske, R. D., & Frieze, I. H. (1986). Issues to consider in conducting nonsexist psychological research: A guide for researchers. *American Psychologist, 41,* 879–890.

McLean, C., Carey, M., & White, C. (1996). *Men's ways of being.* Boulder, CO: Westview Press.

Mednick, M. T. S., & Urbanski, L. (1991). The origins and activities of APA's division of the psychology of women. *Psychology of Women Quarterly, 15,* 651–663.

Miller, J. B. (1976). *Toward a new psychology of women.* Boston: Beacon Press.

Morawski, J. G. (1994). *Practicing feminisms: Reconstructing psychology.* Ann Arbor: University of Michigan Press.

Morawski, J. G., & Agronick, G. (1991). A restive legacy: Experimental and cognitive psychology. *Psychology of Women Quarterly, 15,* 567–579.

Murray, H. A. (1938). *Explorations in personality: A clinical and experimental study of fifty men of college age.* London: Oxford University.

Nieva, V. F., & Gutek, B. A. (1981). *Women and work: A psychological perspective.* New York: Praeger.

Parlee, M. B. (1979). Psychology of women. *Signs, 5,* 121–133.

Parlee, M. B. (1994). The social construction of premenstrual syndrome: A case study in scientific discourse as cultural contestation. In M. G. Winkler & L. B. Cole (Eds.), *The good body: Asceticism in contemporary culture* (pp. 91–107). New Haven, CT: Yale University Press.

Pyke, S. W. (1993). The more things change. *Canadian Psychology, 33,* 2.

Radloff, L. S. (1975). Sex differences in depression: The effects of occupation and marital status. *Sex Roles, 1,* 249–265.

Reid, P. T. (1993). Poor women in psychological research: Shut up and shut out. *Psychology of Women Quarterly, 17,* 133–150.

Rodin, J., Silverstein, L. R., & Striegel-Moore, R. H. (1984). Women and weight: A normative discontent. In T. B. Sonderegger (Ed.), *Psychology and gender: Nebraska Symposium on Motivation, 1984* (pp. 267–307). Lincoln: University of Nebraska Press.

Romero, M., & Stewart, A. J. (Eds.). (1999). *Women's untold stories: Breaking silence, talking back, voicing complexity.* New York: Routledge.

Rosenberg, R. (1982). *Beyond separate spheres: The intellectual roots of modern feminism.* New Haven, CT: Yale University Press.

Russell, G. M., Bohan, J. S., & Lilly, D. (2000). Queer youth: Old stories, new stories. In S. Jones (Ed.), *A sea of stories: The shaping power of narratives in gay and lesbian cultures* (pp. 69–92). New York: Haworth.

Scarborough, E., & Furumoto, L. (1987). *Untold lives: The first generation of American women psychologists.* New York: Columbia University Press.

Sears, D. O. (1986). College sophomores in the laboratory: Influences of a narrow data base on psychology's view of human nature. *Journal of Personality and Social Psychology, 51,* 515–530.

Sherif, C. W. (1979). Bias in psychology. In J. A. Sherman & E. T. Beck (Eds.), *The prism of sex: Essays in the sociology of knowledge* (pp. 93–133). Madison: University of Wisconsin Press.

Shields, S. A. (1975). Functionalism, Darwinism, and the psychology of women: A study in social myth. *American Psychologist, 30,* 739–754.

Spence, J. T., & Helmreich, R. L. (1978). *Masculinity and femininity: Their psychological dimensions, correlates, and antecedents.* Austin: University of Texas.

Thompson, B. W. (1995). *A hunger so wide and deep.* Minnesota: University of Minnesota Press.

Tiefer, L. (1991). A brief history of the Association for Women in Psychology. *Psychology of Women Quarterly, 15,* 635–649.

Tiefer, L. (1995). *Sex is not a natural act and other essays.* Boulder, CO: Westview Press.

Tolman, D. T., & Szalacha, L. A. (1999). Dimensions of desire: Bridging qualitative and quantitative methods in a study of female adolescent sexuality. *Psychology of Women Quarterly, 23,* 9–42.

Unger, R. K. (1979). Toward a redefinition of sex and gender. *American Psychologist, 34,* 1088–1094.

Ussher, J. (Ed.). (2000). *Women's health: Contemporary international perspectives.* London: British Psychological Association.

Walker, L. E. (1979). *The battered woman.* New York: Harper Colophon.

Walker, L. E. (1999). Psychology and domestic violence around the world. *American Psychologist, 54,* 21–29.

Walsh-Bowers, R. (1999). Fundamentalism in psychological science: The publication manual as "Bible." *Psychology of Women Quarterly, 23,* 375–392.

Weisstein, N. (1971). *Psychology constructs the female.* Boston: New England Free Press.

West, C., & Zimmerman, D. H. (1987). Doing gender. *Gender and Society, 1,* 125–151.

Westkott, M. C. (1989). Female relationality and the idealized self. *American Journal of Psychoanalysis, 49,* 239–250.

Wilkinson, S. (1988). The role of reflexivity in feminist psychology. *Women's Studies International Forum, 11,* 493–502.

Wilkinson, S. (1997). Feminist psychology. In D. Fox & I. Prilleltensky (Eds.), *Critical psychology: An introduction* (pp. 247–264). London: Sage.

Women's Programs Office. (1991). *Graduate faculty interested in psychology of women.* Washington, DC: American Psychological Association.

Woolley, H. T. (1910). Psychological literature: A review of the recent literature on the psychology of sex. *Psychological Bulletin, 7,* 335–342.

Worell, J. (1988). Women's satisfaction in close relationships. *Clinical Psychology Review, 8,* 477–498.

Worell, J., & Johnson, N. G. (Eds.). (1997). *Shaping the future of feminist psychology: Education, research, and practice.* Washington, DC: American Psychological Association.

Worell, J., & Remer, P. (1992). *Feminist perspectives in therapy: An empowerment model for women.* New York: Wiley.

Wyche, K. F., & Rice, F. J. (1997). Feminist therapy: From dialogue to tenets. In J. Worell & N. G. Johnson (Eds.), *Shaping the future of feminist psychology: Education, research, and practice* (pp. 57–71). Washington, DC: American Psychological Association.

Yllo, K., & Bograd, M. (Eds.). (1988). *Feminist perspectives on wife abuse.* Beverly Hills, CA: Sage.

CHAPTER 13

Educational Psychology

CLAIRE ELLEN WEINSTEIN AND PAMELA J. WAY

CONTRIBUTIONS OF EARLY PHILOSOPHERS 269
EUROPEAN INFLUENCES IN THE EIGHTEENTH
    AND NINETEENTH CENTURIES 270
EARLY DEVELOPMENTS IN AMERICA 271
FURTHER DEVELOPMENTS IN THE
    TWENTIETH CENTURY 271
TRACING PROGRESS THROUGH THE
    WRITTEN RECORD 272
THE EFFECTS OF INSTRUCTIONAL PSYCHOLOGY 273

THE INFLUENCES OF COGNITIVE PSYCHOLOGY 273
THE DISCIPLINE OF EDUCATIONAL
    PSYCHOLOGY TODAY 274
GOALS FOR THE FUTURE: THE RESEARCH AND
    DEVELOPMENT OF QUESTIONS, MODELS,
    ISSUES, AND APPLICATIONS 274
THE FUTURE 276
REFERENCES 276

The history of educational psychology traces a path from its origins in concerns about cultural improvement and transmission of cultural norms to philosophical issues in general education and psychology (Berliner, 1993; Charles, 1976; Glover & Ronning, 1987; Good & Levin, 2001; Grinder, 1989; Hilgard, 1996; Mayer, 2001; Walberg & Haertel, 1992; Wittrock & Farley, 1989; Zimmerman & Schunk, in press). The effects of this amalgam of antecedent contributions on its birth and development are still evident in the difficulties encountered when attempting a strict definition of educational psychology that clearly separates it from other psychological disciplines (see Berliner & Calfee, 1996). We will return to this issue later in this chapter.

Although it is not difficult to identify the emergence of educational psychology as a recognized discipline, it is somewhat more difficult to determine educational psychology's precise lineage. It has been suggested that educational psychology may have first emerged as part of a kind of folk tradition in which adults educated their children (Berliner, 1993). This certainly makes sense intuitively, and it is quite easy to imagine not only our own grandmothers and grandfathers teaching our parents a variety of life skills but also parents and grandparents from many previous generations passing down what they considered to be the requisite knowledge and cultural norms of their day. It also seems likely that this knowledge was passed down in a dynamic rather than static way, incorporating the abilities, skills, weaknesses, and frames of reference of each generation of teacher and student.

As Berliner (1993) notes, part of the traditional Jewish Passover service is the duty of the leader of the service to tell the story of Passover to each of his sons in turn. The father, however, must tell each son the story in such a way as to emphasize the particular son's own strengths and weaknesses. So, for example, the wise son may hear the entire story with additional commentaries, while the recalcitrant son may hear the story with an emphasis on obeying authority.

Although the folk tradition of educational psychology has probably existed since the earliest times of humans on the earth and continues to this day, most formal histories of educational psychology trace its origins to ancient philosophers and statesmen. Here we find not only the historical roots of educational practices but also the historical roots of the psychology of learning and memory.

CONTRIBUTIONS OF EARLY PHILOSOPHERS

Aristotle is sometimes pointed to as a founder of educational psychology (Berliner, 1993; Charles, 1976; Kaur, 1972). Aristotle's book *De Memoria et Reminiscentia (On Memory and Reminiscence)*, incorporates views of learning, association, and retention (Charles, 1976). In this book, written in 350 B.C.E., Aristotle notes that memory is a function of presentation; that is, memory is directly related to the context in which the learning occurred. There are very few, if any, modern-day educational psychologists who would disagree with this observation. Others who often share the title of founder with Aristotle include Democritus (460–370 B.C.E.), Quintilian (A.D. 35–100), and Comenius (1592–1671).

Each of these philosophers made contributions to philosophy in general and education in particular. For example, Democritus voiced the opinion that education is advantageous and that the home environment has a substantial impact on learning; Quintilian felt that good teachers, when combined with a worthwhile curriculum, might help control behavioral problems; and Comenius noted that memorization is not the same as understanding and that teachers' own learning is optimized when they have the opportunity to teach others (Berliner, 1993). Additionally, both Aristotle and Quintilian felt that teachers should make the effort to tailor learning to the individual, taking into account the individual differences of their students (Berliner, 1993).

Although each of these early philosopher-educators can be considered forefathers of modern-day educational psychologists, it may be the views of Juan Luis Vives (1492–1540) that would resonate most closely with today's educational psychologist. His 1531 book, *De Tradendis Disciplinus (The Art of Teaching)*, has been called the first major book on psychology. In this book, Vives says, "We must first examine, for each type of instruction, the question of what, how, to what extent, by whom and where it should be taught." Vives goes on to note that the teacher should be the student's guide and should help individual students make decisions about their studies based on the student's own interests and abilities (Ibanez, 1994).

EUROPEAN INFLUENCES IN THE EIGHTEENTH AND NINETEENTH CENTURIES

In the late eighteenth and the nineteenth centuries, there were strong European influences on the early development path of educational psychology as a discipline (Grinder, 1989; Hilgard, 1996). Hilgard (1996) identified four Europeans who he felt influenced both conceptions and practices in instruction, teaching, and learning: Rousseau (1712–1788) from France, Pestalozzi (1746–1827) from Switzerland, and Herbart (1776–1841) and Froebel (1782–1852), both from Germany. Rousseau's book *Émile* (1762/1979) emphasized that children discover things for themselves and described some of the instructional implications of this fundamental assumption. Pestalozzi (1820/1977), a Swiss lawyer by training, developed a model school that incorporated many of the ideas that are current today in educational psychology. For example, he stressed that students must be active learners,

that education involved personal growth in addition to simple knowledge acquisition, that psychology could be used as a guide for developing and implementing instructional methods, and that schools should be warm, nurturing environments.

While Rousseau and Pestalozzi made important contributions to our thinking about students, schools, subject matter, and instruction, their ideas were primarily based on their moral and ethical views and their experience. It remained for Johann Friedrich Herbart of Germany to call for a more "scientific" approach to studying educational conceptions and practices.

In 1824, Johann Herbart published *Psychology as Science*, regarded as one of the first treatises suggesting that educational conceptions and educational practices could be studied scientifically and that the instructional process itself was different from the subject matter being taught. Herbart was the first to provide a psychological rather than philosophical or moral substratum for his ideas and applications. Like Vives, Herbart believed that educational programs should be developed based on the interests, aptitudes, and abilities of students. Herbart's followers, the Herbartians, developed a system of teaching that followed a "logical progression" of five steps that could be applied to nearly any subject matter: (a) prepare the student's mind for the coming lesson (e.g., arouse students' interests and relate the new material to familiar ideas); (b) present the lesson (e.g., use appropriate means such as using storytelling with young children); (c) compare, or associate the new lesson with material previously learned (e.g., use concrete things and experiences); (d) generalization or abstraction (e.g., express ideas conceptually by using principles and general rules); and, finally, (e) require that the students use, or apply, the new material appropriately (e.g., have students practice using varied examples) (Berliner, 1993; Grinder, 1989; Hilgard, 1996).

The work of Friedrich Froebel had a very direct effect on educational thinking and practice in the United States (Hilgard, 1996). Froebel, the founder of the kindergarten movement, was a bit of a romantic and thought of kindergarten as a place to train children in cooperative living. He also wanted to foster creativity and active learning in children. In 1873 the first public kindergarten was established in St. Louis, and by 1880, America had over 400 private kindergartens. At the same time, the public school system and the idea of compulsory school attendance emerged. Many of these ideas about universal education and its purposes were influenced by the optimistic views of society and the ideas of these European philosophers and statesmen. The transition to a greater psychological basis for educational conceptions and practices was also developing during this time in America.

EARLY DEVELOPMENTS IN AMERICA

The subtle transition from philosophy and somewhat utopian worldviews to newer conceptions of psychology as the framework for understanding and applying educational variables was introduced to America with William James's (1842–1910) 1891 lecture series at Harvard on the "new psychology." These lectures were eventually turned into a book, *Talks to Teachers on Psychology*. This book is sometimes regarded as the first popular educational psychology text, and there is evidence that this lecture series helped to spark the growth of educational psychology as a movement in America. James spoke of psychology as a science and teaching as an art, but one that could benefit from an understanding of psychological laws and human behavior. In addition, long before the so-called cognitive revolution in psychology, James introduced the idea that consciousness could control the direction of its own attention, thus setting the stage for later work in cognition and metacognition (Berliner, 1993; Hilgard, 1996; Wittrock & Farley, 1989).

One of James's students, G. Stanley Hall (1844–1924), earned the first PhD in psychology awarded in America. Although his degree was in psychology, Hall is most often remembered as an educator, a label he came by quite naturally. Hall, as well as his mother and father, taught school for some time. He went on to develop the first research lab in America at Johns Hopkins, where he introduced another first—fellowships for graduate students (Berliner, 1993). In Hall's lab at Clark University (where he also served as president), he and his students systematically researched and documented problems in higher education, thus establishing the first formal graduate program specializing in education. This program was designed to furnish leaders to what was called a new educational movement in America, a movement that would facilitate the study of and research in education for years to come (Berliner, 1993).

FURTHER DEVELOPMENTS IN THE TWENTIETH CENTURY

Although his early works emphasized his interests in the intersection of philosophy and psychology, John Dewey's (1859–1952) later work and publications focused more on educational philosophies and educational practices (Hilgard,

1996). He had his greatest influence on the field after his move to Columbia in 1904. His books *Interest and Effort in Education* (1913) and *Schools of Tomorrow* (1915) were extremely popular and influential. Much of his work on engaging children's interest and the need for them to be active learners can be traced to the influence of the European work described earlier, but he went way beyond what had been proposed through the end of the 1800s. A number of his ideas about educational practice and ways to conceptualize educational processes are still current. However, it remained for others to try to refine the field and give it a more "scientific" base.

Edward Thorndike was an established researcher when he directed his attention to educational contexts, processes, and outcomes. In a landmark study with Woodworth, he attacked the doctrine of formal discipline (very popular at the time) and demonstrated that simply "exercising the mind" resulted in only slight learning gains. In 1901, he and Woodworth published a paper demonstrating problems of transfer of learning and the need for "identical elements." He published his first educational psychology textbook in 1903 and, in 1913–1914, published a classic three-volume educational psychology text.

In 1910, in an essay entitled "The Contribution of Psychology to Education," appearing in the first issue of the *Journal of Educational Psychology,* Thorndike described the role he believed that psychology could and should play in education (Thorndike, 1910). Briefly, Thorndike suggested that psychology could assist in making the aims of education more definable and measurable and that education should promote changes in the intellects, ideals, and behaviors of students.

In the founding issue of the *Journal of Educational Psychology,* the editors ambitiously planned for future issues to focus on the topics of mental development, heredity, adolescence and child study, individual differences, and issues related to testing and measurement. Within each of these topics, matters involving general psychology, sensation, instinct, attention, habit, memory, technique and economy of learning, and perceptual processes could be explored (Charles, 1976).

Although the discipline's primary journal was founded in 1910, it was not until 1922 that the American Psychological Association (APA) surveyed its members to determine the need for an educational psychology division within the APA (O'Donnell & Levin, 2001). It was determined, however, that there was insufficient interest in educational psychology as a discipline at that time. It was not until 1946 that enough APA members cited "psychology in education" as a key concern for psychologists that educational psychology was assigned division status as Division 15. Only three years later, in 1949, Dael Wolfle, the APA executive secretary, claimed that educational psychology had "lost its momentum," and in the early 1950s the suggestion was made to combine educational psychology with Division 12, Clinical Psychology (O'Donnell & Levin, 2001).

Notwithstanding these problems, the discipline of educational psychology seemed quite defined in its early years. Practitioners focused on problems in education and looked for resolutions to those problems. However, these years were marred by considerable criticism of educational psychology and of educational psychologists, and it was much more likely that a psychologist working in education would refer to himself or herself as a psychologist than as an educational psychologist (Sutherland, 1988). Ironically, perhaps, America's consternation over Russia's advances in science and technology spurred a new interest in research and funding of education, which in turn spurred a renewed interest in educational psychology. Thus, Division 15 showed more than a seven fold increase between the years 1959 and 1967, growing from only 525 members to almost 4,000, making it one of the largest divisions within the American Psychological Association (Charles, 1976).

In the 11 years between 1977 and 1988, however, Division 15 membership declined by almost 40% (Farley, 1989). Although this decline was substantial, the 1,400-member loss still left Division 15 with more total members than many other APA divisions, and still in the top 10 in terms of total division membership. As Farley notes, this membership loss was largely due to many factors, including the creation of closely related or component divisions within the APA that drew members away from Division 15, as well as membership drifts to special societies such as the Psychonomics Society. In particular, the more education-centered organization, the American Educational Research Association (AERA), also drew members away from the APA. Many faculty and graduate students have also elected to pursue membership in one or more additional organizations that reflect their individual theoretical, research, or population interests.

These organizations are as likely to be traditionally psychology based (e.g., American Psychological Society, Society for Industrial and Organizational Psychology) as they are to be traditionally education based (e.g., National Association of Developmental Education, the National Reading Conference). Rather than reflecting disagreement or an outgrowth of factions within educational psychology, this diversity of organizational membership instead reflects the growing recognition by contemporary educational psychologists that we are qualified—perhaps uniquely so—to serve a wide variety of public interests.

TRACING PROGRESS THROUGH THE WRITTEN RECORD

One way of tracing the history of a discipline is to examine that discipline's documents. In the case of educational psychology, there are two primary document resources: professional journals and academic textbooks. One of the first reviews of textbooks was by Worcester (1927). Worcester's 1927 review found an "amazing lack of agreement" in the content of educational psychological texts. One author, for example, used 30% of the textbook space for psychology and tests in primary-school subjects, while other authors neglected these topics entirely. There was also marked dissimilarity in the discussions of laboratory practices of educational psychologists, with some focusing on, for example, testing of individual differences, statistical methods, and studies of memory, while others investigated transfer of learning and intelligence testing. Most of the approximately 37 different textbooks used among the labs were, in practice, general psychology texts (Worcester, 1927). And, as Charles (1976) notes, things were not much different even 25 years later. A 1949 comparison of texts used in educational psychology classes revealed that while one author devoted a full 20% to the topic of intelligence testing, another author devoted a scant 1.5% to this same topic.

Content analyses have also been performed on the founding journal in the field of educational psychology, the *Journal of Educational Psychology*. In an examination of 641 articles reviewed by decade from 1910 to 1990, O'Donnell and Levin (2001) delimited different "central themes." They found that articles in the teaching category decreased from 30% to a mere 0.03% and that articles in the intelligence-testing category dropped from 13.3% to 0.0%. Articles in the learning category, however, increased by almost 47 percentage points—from 13.3% to 60%. Ball (1984), in a content analysis of articles published during the first 75 years of the *Journal of Educational Psychology*, found similar trends.

Ball notes that while there has continued to be a strong research content core, the emphasis of the research has shifted over the years. For example, in the early days of the *Journal of Educational Psychology*, the emphasis was on practical issues related to teachers and teaching; the 1940s and 1950s ushered in increased interest in personal and social issues; and the 1970s and beyond reflected a growth in theoretical rather than strictly practical areas, especially in motivation and psycholinguistics. Ball (1984) also noted a trend toward both more multi-authored articles and longer articles; additionally, he noted that the number of women in the field had increased substantially.

THE EFFECTS OF INSTRUCTIONAL PSYCHOLOGY

The beginnings of instructional psychology as a field of study are often traced to World War II and its demand for rapidly trained soldiers and officers who could operate more technically advanced equipment. When Arthur Melton developed the Air Force Human Resources Lab (AFHRL), he and the people he trained and worked with, such as Robert Glazer and Robert Gagne, helped to develop guidelines for learning, retention, and transfer of new knowledge and skills based on psychological principles. After the war, AFHRL remained a vibrant research and development center, although many of its researchers and developers went into academic positions. Their work continued as the postwar era's GI bill gave low-cost loans and scholarships to returning military personnel to further their education. Methods were needed to deal with this more diverse and expanded population of students in America's high schools, community colleges, and universities.

Another boost to funding and interest in instructional psychology occurred when the Russians launched an unmanned space vehicle, *Sputnik*, in 1957. Along with the fears that America was losing its technological superiority was a call for massive increases in science and mathematics curricula and courses, and effective teaching/learning methods. Building on techniques developed during World War II, new types of audio-visual aids were developed, such as motion picture projectors and audiotapes (Glaser, 1962). Given the dominance of behaviorism in psychology during much of this period, it also witnessed the development of programmed-instruction teaching machines and, ultimately, computer-assisted instruction. However, this is also the period during which the trend began toward adapting classroom practices to the needs of individual students (Gage, 1964). The field of educational psychology, which absorbed instructional psychology, was definitely on center stage. However, there was a lingering feeling that even with the modern technologies, perhaps we were missing a big piece of the learning/education/transfer puzzle.

THE INFLUENCES OF COGNITIVE PSYCHOLOGY

Cognitive psychology has had a major influence on the development of educational psychology. In a seminal chapter in the *Annual Review of Psychology,* 1977, Wittrock and Lumsdaine pointed out the importance of a cognitive perspective and the somewhat bankrupt contributions of behaviorism for further development in instructional and educational psychology. The chapter had a strong impact on educational psychologists. Educational psychology was finally on the road to being a discipline within psychology whose focus was on the psychology of all components of educational processes and practice. No longer was it only an application of other areas within psychology (although these other areas continue to influence it).

One reason the cognitive psychology revolution is viewed by many as an improvement over the days of experimenting with rats and pigeons is that it helped to focus researchers' attention on realistic rather than artificial contexts. This shift provided researchers with the opportunity to examine students in their own environment—the classroom (Mayer, 2001). As Mayer notes, psychology needed something real to study, and education provided it. This has, of course, proven to be a symbiotic relationship, because psychology was able to provide to education established scientific methodological frameworks that education had previously lacked. Mayer's view of the historical relationship between education and psychology in the twentieth century seems to be quite apt: First, there was a time during which psychologists developed theories and left it to educators to apply the theories; next came a period during which psychology resolutely focused on theoretical issues that were unrelated to educational issues, and education resolutely focused primarily on practical issues; and, now, we have an era in which psychology and education seem to be working more hand-in-hand, combining the strengths of both groups to work for the mutual benefit of each group, as well as for the public (Mayer, 1992, cited in Mayer, 2001).

Even though the advent of cognitive psychology in the 1970s encouraged researchers to examine more realistic contexts and situations, many researchers still tended to deconstruct their findings into isolated parts. Rather than viewing students as a whole, they often broke students' behaviors into components, which might then be used to construct new models, or even to reconstruct old models (Paris & Paris, 2001). Even the didactic methods and suggestions derived from this work were often nothing more than isolated pieces of advice. For example, common didactic methods for improving students' academic success included options such as summarizing text, direct instruction for using specific strategies, and a tendency to instruct students to employ the same tactics and strategies across subjects and situations. And, in spite of the rationale that cognitive psychology afforded for using realistic situations, much of the research was still conducted in laboratory contexts. It was only quite recently that these methods changed.

Now, for example, the emphasis is more on examining text from within the reader's frame of reference than it is on merely summarizing text; making strategies adaptive, functional, and tailored to the individual learner is considered to be as important as simply teaching specific strategies; and, finally, strategies should be dynamic rather than static across different disciplines—elaboration strategies in math, for example, are quite different from elaboration strategies in a literature class. Perhaps most importantly, however, is the acknowledgment that it is impossible to examine whether or not specific techniques and strategies are effective unless they are tested in the classroom or other educational settings using students' own curricula (Paris & Paris, 2001).

THE DISCIPLINE OF EDUCATIONAL PSYCHOLOGY TODAY

Another approach to tracing a discipline's history is to examine the current state of the discipline, for all disciplines are, ultimately, a culmination of precedents. In educational psychology, this current state can be represented by looking at a small sampling of recent definitions, directives, theories, methodologies, and applications in the field of educational psychology.

Some of the definitions of educational psychology today are broad: Berliner (1993), for example, states: "Our fundamental goal should be to understand and improve education in our society." Other definitions are more specific: Good and Levin (2001) assert, "The heart of work in educational psychology is to produce theoretical and well-researched psychological knowledge that has the potential for enhancing learning and socialization in various settings."

The directives to practicing educational psychologists come from both institutions and individuals. The mission of the APA's Division 15, Educational Psychology, is "to provide a collegial environment for psychologists with interests in research, teaching, or practice in educational settings at all levels to present and publish papers about their work in the theory, methodology, and applications to a broad spectrum of teaching, training, and learning issues" (American Psychological Association, 2000).

And, somewhat in contrast to the early days of educational psychology, with its emphasis on the purely practical components of teachers and teaching, Pintrich (2000b) directs educational psychologists, now and in the future, to do work that merges the primarily applied goals of the past with the present and future goals of furthering the more theoretical, scientific, and fundamental understandings of learning, development, cognition, and motivation. Furthermore, Pintrich charges that, as scientists, educational psychologists should also work to gather and provide sound evidence to support our conclusions and conceptual models (Pintrich, 2000b). Although there are some who believe that the discipline of

educational psychology is too often in a state of flux, others commend the ability of the discipline to change itself in ways appropriate to meeting the changing needs and demands of society (O'Donnell & Levin, 2001).

Mayer (2001) suggests that educational psychology has substantial strengths whose energies can be directed toward making considerable contributions to both the psychology of the subject matter itself and the teaching of cognitive strategies. This is congruent with the message in Pintrich's farewell address after his fifth year as editor of *Educational Psychologist*. In this address, Pintrich reviewed several themes he saw as emergent in the field of educational psychology. Although he cited a focus on the individual learner as one of these themes, Pintrich emphasized that educational psychologists could no longer consider the dimensions of cognition, motivation, and social interaction in isolation from the individual (Pintrich, 2000b).

This being said, however, what is the current state of educational psychology? What contributions are educational psychologists making now? Who are these changes affecting? Most importantly, perhaps, is the question about what directions educational psychology and its practitioners will take in the future. Again, a look at the direction of recent research in the area provides clues that can be used to help answer these questions.

GOALS FOR THE FUTURE: THE RESEARCH AND DEVELOPMENT OF QUESTIONS, MODELS, ISSUES, AND APPLICATIONS

Several recent trends in educational psychology show great promise for the present as well as for the future. One of these trends is greater emphasis on the development of models that can be used not only to explain and predict students' successes but to aid students directly in achieving academic success. Many of the existing and evolving models have been designed and developed to provide an easily negotiated bridge between the theoretical and the concrete. Thus, although these models do explain and predict in the same way as more traditional models, they can also be used within a curricular or other setting to foster student success. Another difference is that many of the current models are constructed such that the individual components within the model can be assimilated and integrated with the other components of the model. The focus is not on the individual elements as much as it is upon the emergent properties that are apparent when the components are interacting. These emergent properties are similar to the concept of the gestalt: The whole is greater than a simple sum of the parts.

Many of these newer models focus on conceptions of broad theoretical and applied interests in the area of self-regulation. Some of these models are instructional, emphasizing the development of self-regulation skills through specific instruction; other models provide teachers with directions for implementing specific tools and strategies (Zimmerman, 1998).

An example of a model based on this integrative approach to student learning that incorporates both the cognitive and motivational aspects of learning was developed by Pintrich and his associates (Hofer, Yu, & Pintrich, 1998). This model, which draws on the earlier work of Garcia and Pintrich (1994), is based on a four-by-four matrix. The resulting cells, cognitive knowledge/beliefs, cognitive and metacognitive strategies for regulation, motivational/self-knowledge beliefs, and motivational strategies for regulation, can be conceptually separated from each other. More importantly, perhaps, the cells can be combined and recombined by students as they learn the specific strategies congruent with each cell (Hofer et al., 1998).

An example of a conceptual model being widely used in practice is the Model of Strategic Learning (Weinstein, Husman, & Dierking, 2000). Variations of this model have been used successfully in university "learning to learn" courses for more than 20 years. This model focuses on variables impacting strategic learning, that is, learning that is goal driven. Weinstein's Model of Strategic Learning has at its core the learner: a unique individual who brings to each learning situation a critical set of variables, including his or her personality, prior knowledge, and school achievement history. Around this core are four broad components focusing on factors that, in interaction, can tremendously influence the degree to which students set and reach learning and achievement goals. These four components are referred to as skill (i.e., learning strategies and prior knowledge and skills), will (i.e., motivation and positive affect toward learning), self-regulation (i.e., metacognitive comprehension monitoring and time management) and the academic environment (i.e., available resources and social support). Although instruction is encouraged in each of the elements, the interaction among the elements for different learning tasks and goals is most important.

The models developed by Pintrich, Weinstein, Zimmerman, and their associates also provide a useful illustration for another trend in educational psychology. As previously mentioned, many current models in educational psychology use theoretical underpinnings as a base from which to expand to real-life and real-world educational and training settings. However, these real-life and real-world settings are no longer composed solely of formal educational settings, nor do they incorporate only the typically aged K–12 or college student.

A recently published book, *Handbook of Self-Regulation* (2000), incorporates chapters on the relationship between personality factors and self-regulation (Kuhl, 2000; Matthews, Schwean, Campbell, Saklofske, & Mohamed, 2000); communal models of self-regulation (as opposed to the Western, traditionally individualistic models of self-regulation) (Jackson, MacKenzie, & Hobfoll, 2000); the use of self-regulatory strategies in organizational settings (Vancouver, 2000); the examination of the relationship between self-regulation and health behaviors (Brownlee, Leventhal, & Leventhal, 2000; Maes & Gebhardt, 2000); and the function of self-regulation in clinical settings for the treatment of distress (Endler & Kocovski, 2000) and chronic illnesses (Creer, 2000). Although it could be argued that what has changed is more a matter of terminology than of substance—in the early 1900s, for example, "will psychologists" used the terms *volition* and *will-power* in much the same way as we now use the term self-regulation—what has changed is that in the 2000s we are attempting to identify and describe the components of self-regulation empirically, using sound research and statistical methodology in favor of earlier, often faulty methods of introspection and self-report (Kuhl & Beckman, 1985). We are also focusing on these components in interaction in these varied educational settings.

Perhaps one of the most important trends in educational psychology has been the move away from viewing the learner as a generic template and toward viewing the learner as an individual, each with his or her own cognitive, metacognitive, affective, and motivational strengths and weaknesses. Part of the task here is for educational psychologists to work to expand and move beyond the current concept of education, which tends to focus on the core of learning, cognition, and motivation, to a model of education that also encompasses an individual's affect, values, caring, mental health, adjustment, coping, and adaptation (Pintrich, 2000b).

One way educational psychologists have succeeded in expanding the core concepts of learning, cognition, and motivation has been to use these constructs as nuclei around which more detailed constructs are built and can revolve. Already mentioned is the idea of a strategic learner, a student or trainee of any age, in any setting, who becomes skilled at learning to learn. In contrast to many earlier conceptions of education, it is now accepted that meaningful learning is not simply the ability to memorize chunks of material but the ability to learn, develop, transfer, and use a wide variety of strategies that can be adapted to both content and context in the service of learning, achievement, and performance goals. Any student's desire to learn, practice, and apply these strategies, however, must also be accompanied by an appropriate motivational system (Pintrich, 2000a). Not surprisingly, therefore, research in motivational theories has grown tremendously over the past decade, and it is common for many current publications and textbooks in the field of educational psychology to include substantial text devoted to both the theory and practice of motivation and the regulation of motivation (Alexander, 2000).

Much of the contemporary conflict within the discipline of educational psychology can be better understood when differences in epistemological stances are taken into account (O'Donnell & Levin, 2001). As O'Donnell and Levin suggest, there are essentially two epistemological stances, resulting in two different research traditions. Some educational psychologists take the positivistic or postpositivist position. These researchers emphasize explanation, prediction, and control, and research often focuses on hypotheses and experiments. Researchers with a preference for critical theory and constructivism have more interest in arriving at an understanding of the construct under study. Because the method used in this research is frequently qualitative, the increased understanding of the construct often occurs on the part of both the researcher and the participant (McCaslin & Hickey, 2001; O'Donnell & Levin, 2001). As Pintrich (2000b) notes, educational psychologists should, however, be well beyond the quantitative-qualitative debate. Instead, our concern should now be on providing valid and reliable evidence that supports our conceptual models and conclusions.

THE FUTURE

In American society now more than ever, educational psychology is moving into the public's consciousness and into the classroom. For example, typing the term "strategic learning" into a public computer search engine (i.e., not PsychINFO or a similar database) yields more than 5,000 hits; the term "self-regulated learning" produces almost 3,200 additional hits.

The future of educational psychology is bright and full of exciting challenges. The dawn of the Information Age is challenging our most fundamental conceptions of learning, instruction, assessment, and appropriate outcomes in relation to education and training. The importance of core research and development areas in educational psychology, such as motivation, self-regulation and strategic learning is expanding rapidly. These are exciting times to be an educational psychologist.

REFERENCES

Alexander, P. (2000). Humble beginnings, ambitious ends: Special issue on motivation and the educational process. *Contemporary Educational Psychology, 25,* 1–2.

American Psychological Association. (2000). *Membership dues statement* (No. 7). Washington, DC: Author.

Ball, S. (1984). Educational psychology as an academic chameleon: An editorial assessment after 75 years. *Journal of Educational Psychology, 76*(6), 993–999.

Berliner, D. C. (1993). The 100-year journey of educational psychology: From interest to disdain, to respect for the practice. In T. K. Fagan & G. R. VandenBos (Eds.), *Exploring applied psychology: Origins and critical analyses* (pp. 41–78).Washington, DC: American Psychological Association.

Berliner, D. C., & Calfee, R. C. (Eds.). (1996). *Handbook of educational psychology.* New York: Macmillan Library Reference USA.

Brownlee, S., Leventhal, H., & Leventhal, E. A. (2000). Regulation, self-regulation, and construction of the self in the maintenance of physical health. In M. Boekaerts, P. R. Pintrich, & M. Zeidner (Eds.), *Handbook of self-regulation* (pp. 369–416). San Diego, CA: Academic Press.

Charles, D. C. (1976). A historical overview of educational psychology. *Contemporary Educational Psychology, 1,* 76–88.

Creer, T. L. (2000). Self-management of chronic illness. In M. Boekaerts, P. R. Pintrich, & M. Zeidner (Eds.), *Handbook of self-regulation* (pp. 601–630). San Diego, CA: Academic Press.

Dewey, J. (1913). *Interest and effort in education.* New York: Houghton Mifflin.

Dewey, J., & Dewey, E. (1915). *Schools of tomorrow.* New York: Dutton.

Endler, N. S., & Kocovski, N. L. (2000). Self-regulation and distress in clinical psychology. In M. Boekaerts, P. R. Pintrich, & M. Zeidner (Eds.), *Handbook of self-regulation* (pp. 569–600). San Diego, CA: Academic Press.

Farley, F. (1989). Challenges for the future of educational psychology. In F. Farley & M. C. Wittrock (Eds.), *The future of educational psychology* (pp. 19–29). Hillsdale, NJ: Erlbaum.

Gage, N. L. (1964). Theories of teaching. In E. R. Hilgard (Ed.), *Theories of learning and instruction* (63rd yearbook of the National Society for the Study of Education, Pt. 1, pp. 268–285). Chicago: University of Chicago Press.

Garcia, T., & Pintrich, P. R. (1994). Regulating motivation and cognition in the classroom: The role of self-schemas and self-regulatory strategies. In D. H. Schunk & B. J. Zimmerman (Eds.), *Self-regulation of learning and performance: Issues and educational applications* (pp. 127–153). Hillsdale, NJ: Erlbaum.

Glazer, R. (1962). *Training research and education.* Pittsburgh, PA: University of Pittsburgh Press.

Glover, J. A., & Ronning, R. R. (1987). *Historical foundations of educational psychology.* New York: Plenum Press.

Good, T. L., & Levin, J. R. (2001). Educational psychology yesterday, today, and tomorrow: Debate and direction in an evolving field. *Educational Psychologist, 36*(2), 69–72.

Grinder, R. E. (1989). Educational psychology: The master science. In F. Farley & M. C. Wittrock (Eds.), *The future of educational psychology* (pp. 3–18). Hillsdale, NJ: Erlbaum.

Hilgard, E. R. (1996). History of educational psychology. In D. C. Berliner & R. C. Calfee (Eds.), *Handbook of educational psychology* (pp. 990–1004). New York: Macmillan Library Reference USA.

Hofer, B. K., Yu, S. L., & Pintrich, P. R. (1998). Teaching college students to be self-regulated learners. In D. H. Schunk & B. J. Zimmerman (Eds.), *Self-regulated learning: From teaching to self-reflective practice* (pp. 57–85). New York: Guilford Press.

Ibanez, R. M. (1994). Juan Luis Vives (1492–1540). *Prospects: The quarterly review of comparative education, 3,* 743–759.

Jackson, T., MacKenzie, J., & Hobfoll, S. E. (2000). Communal aspects of self-regulation. In M. Boekaerts, P. R. Pintrich, & M. Zeidner (Eds.), *Handbook of self-regulation* (pp. 275–302). San Diego, CA: Academic Press.

Kaur, A. (1972). History of educational psychology in the U.S.A. during 1880–1940. *Indian Educational Review, 7*(1), 123–140.

Kuhl, J. (2000). A functional-design approach to motivation and self-regulation: The dynamics of personality systems and interactions. In M. Boekaerts, P. R. Pintrich, & M. Zeidner (Eds.), *Handbook of self-regulation* (pp. 111–170). San Diego, CA: Academic Press.

Kuhl, J., & Beckman, J. (1984). Introduction and overview. In J. Kuhl & J. Beckman (Eds.), *Action control: From cognition to behavior* (pp. 1–8). New York: Springer.

Maes, S., & Gebhardt, W. (2000). Self-regulation and health behavior: The health behavior goal model. In M. Boekaerts, P. R. Pintrich, & M. Zeidner (Eds.), *Handbook of self-regulation* (pp. 343–368). San Diego, CA: Academic Press.

Matthews, G., Schwean, V. L., Campbell, S. I., Saklofske, D. H., & Mohamed, A. A. R. (2000). Personality, self-regulation, and adaptation: A cognitive-social framework. In M. Boekaerts, P. R. Pintrich, & M. Zeidner (Eds.), *Handbook of self-regulation* (pp. 171–201). San Diego, CA: Academic Press.

Mayer, R. E. (2001). What good is educational psychology? The case of cognition and instruction. *Educational Psychologist, 36*(2), 83–88.

McCaslin, M., & Hickey, D. T. (2001). Educational psychology, social constructivism, and educational practice: A case of emergent identity. *Educational Psychologist, 36*(2), 133–140.

O'Donnell, A. M., & Levin, J. R. (2001). Educational psychology's healthy growing pains. *Educational Psychologist, 36*(2), 73–82.

Paris, S. G., & Paris, A. H. (2001). Classroom applications of research on self-regulated learning. *Educational Psychologist, 36*(2), 89–101.

Pestalozzi, J. H. (1977). How Gertrude teaches her children. In D. N. Robinson (Ed.), *J. H. Pestalozzi: Significant contributions to the history of psychology, 1750–1920* (Series B, Vol. 2, pp. 17–391). Washington, DC: University Publications of America. (Original work published 1820)

Pintrich, P. R. (1994). Continuities and discontinuities: Future directions for research in educational psychology. *Educational Psychologist, 29*(3), 137–148.

Pintrich, P. R. (2000a). An achievement goal theory perspective on issues in motivation terminology, theory, and research. *Contemporary Educational Psychology, 25,* 92–104.

Pintrich, P. R. (2000b). Educational psychology at the millennium: A look back and a look forward. *Educational Psychologist, 35*(4), 221–226.

Rousseau, J. J. (1979). *Emile* or, *On education* (A. Bloom, Trans.). New York: Basic Books. (Original work published 1762)

Sutherland, M. (1988). Educational psychology: The distracted handmaiden. *Educational and Child Psychology, 5*(1), 13–18.

Thorndike, E. L. (1903). *Educational psychology.* New York: Teachers College Press.

Thorndike, E. L. (1910). The contribution of psychology to education. *Journal of Educational Psychology, 1,* 5–12.

Thorndike, E. L. (1913a). *Educational psychology. Vol. 1: The original nature of man.* New York: Teachers College Press.

Thorndike, E. L. (1913b). *Educational psychology. Vol. 2: The psychology of learning.* New York: Teachers College Press.

Thorndike, E. L. (1914). *Educational psychology. Vol. 3: Mental work and fatigue, and individual differences and their causes.* New York: Teachers College Press.

Thorndike, E. L., & Woodworth, R. S. (1901). The influence of one mental function upon the efficiency of other functions. *Psychological Review, 8,* 247–261, 384–395, 553–564.

Vancouver, J. B. (2000). Self-regulation in organizational settings: A tale of two paradigms. In M. Boekaerts, P. R. Pintrich, & M. Zeidner (Eds.), *Handbook of self-regulation* (pp. 303–342). San Diego, CA: Academic Press.

Walberg, H. J., & Haertel, G. D. (1992). Educational psychology's first century. *Journal of Educational Psychology, 84,* 6–19.

Weinstein, C. E., Husman, J., & Dierking, D. R. (2000). Self-regulation interventions with a focus on learning strategies. In M. Boekaerts, P. R. Pintrich, & M. Zeidner (Eds.), *Handbook of self-regulation* (pp. 728–749). San Diego, CA: Academic Press.

Wittrock, M. C., & Farley, F. (Eds.). (1989). *The future of educational psychology.* Hillsdale, NJ: Erlbaum.

Wittrock, M. C., & Lumsdaine, A. A. (1977). Instructional psychology. *Annual Review of Psychology, 28,* 417–459.

Worcester, D. A. (1927). The wide diversities of practice in first courses in educational psychology. *Journal of Educational Psychology, 18,* 11–20.

Zimmerman, B. J. (1998). Developing self-fulfilling cycles of academic regulation: An analysis of exemplary instructional models. In D. H. Schunk & B. J. Zimmerman (Eds.), *Self-regulated learning: From teaching to self-reflective practice* (pp. 1–19). New York: Guilford Press.

Zimmerman, B. J., & Schunk, D. H. (Eds.). (in press). *History of psychology in biography.* Mahwah, NJ: Erlbaum.

CHAPTER 14

Assessment Psychology

IRVING B. WEINER

ORIGINS OF ASSESSMENT PSYCHOLOGY 279
EVALUATING INTELLECTUAL ABILITY 280
    The Binet Scales 280
    Group-Administered Tests 281
    The Wechsler Scales 281
    The Kaufman Scales 282
    Brief Methods 282
    Frequency of Test Use 282
IDENTIFYING PERSONALITY CHARACTERISTICS
AND PSYCHOPATHOLOGY 283
    Relatively Structured Tests 283
    Relatively Unstructured Tests 286
    Interview Methods 289
    Behavioral Methods 291

MONITORING NEUROPSYCHOLOGICAL
    FUNCTIONING 292
    Bender Gestalt 292
    Neuropsychological Test Batteries 293
MEASURING ACHIEVEMENT, APTITUDES,
    AND INTERESTS 294
    Wide-Range Achievement Test 294
    Strong Interest Inventory 295
    Kuder Occupational Interest Survey 295
    Holland Self-Directed Search 295
LOOKING AHEAD 296
REFERENCES 297

In Act I, Scene ii of *Julius Caesar,* Caesar observes one of his colleagues from afar and says to Marc Antony, "Yon Cassius has a lean and hungry look; He thinks too much: such men are dangerous . . . seldom he smiles . . . such men as he never be at heart's ease whiles they behold a greater than themselves, and therefore they are very dangerous." In penning these words, William Shakespeare captured the essence of psychological assessment, which consists of translating observations of a person into inferences about the person's nature and how he or she is likely to behave in various situations. In more formal terms, assessment psychology is the field of behavioral science concerned with methods of identifying similarities and differences among people in their personal characteristics, functioning capacities, and action tendencies. Assessment methods are accordingly designed to identify what people are like and how they can be expected to conduct themselves, specifically with respect to their disposition to think, feel, and act in certain ways.

This chapter begins by identifying the origins of assessment psychology and then traces the development of assessment methods for serving four purposes: the evaluation of intellectual ability; the identification of personality characteristics and psychopathology; the monitoring of neuropsychological functioning; and the measurement of aptitudes, achievement, and

interests. The chapter concludes with comments concerning issues currently confronting assessment psychology and bearing on its future prospects.

ORIGINS OF ASSESSMENT PSYCHOLOGY

Over time in recorded history and for diverse reasons, methods of assessment have been used to classify, select, diagnose, advise, and plan services for people in all walks of life. Just as Caesar used observation to classify Cassius as an overly ideational and envious person not to be trusted, Gideon in a Bible story from the Book of Judges chose his troops for battle by observing how they drank water from a stream. Those soldiers who used one hand to bring water to their mouth while keeping their other hand on their weapon were chosen to fight; those who put down their weapon and used both hands to drink were sent home.

Informal decision-making procedures of this kind define the province of assessment psychology, but the transformation of such informal procedures into the standardized methodology that constitutes contemporary assessment psychology became possible only following a scientific prehistory during which the fledgling discipline of psychology gradually began to address individual differences. Scientific attention to individual differences was inspired by Charles Darwin (1859), who in *The Origin of Species* encouraged systematic study of how varying characteristics between species and within members of species could influence which of them survive and prosper. Intrigued by these notions of evolution and heredity, and interested particularly in the origins of human genius, Sir Francis Galton (1869, 1883) proposed that differences between people in their intellectual ability could be measured by their performance on sensory-motor tasks like reaction time, grip strength, weight discrimination, and visual acuity. Galton established a laboratory in London to study psychophysical variations in performance, and his creativity and initiative in this work led to the emergence of scientific study of human capacities. With good reason, Boring (1950, p. 487) in his *History of Experimental Psychology* credited Galton as being the founder of individual psychology.

Subsequent progression from individual psychology to assessment psychology came with the contribution of James McKeen Cattell (1860–1944), who as a graduate student in 1883 presented himself at Wilhelm Wundt's laboratory in Leipzig and asked to be taken on as an assistant. The founding of Wundt's laboratory in 1879 marks the inception of psychology as a scientific discipline, and Wundt's goals as a scientific psychologist were to formulate universal principles of behavior that would account for response patterns common to all people. Like other behavioral scientists past and present operating with this nomothetic perspective, Wundt had little affinity for measuring differences among people, which he regarded as a troublesome error variance. Fortunately for assessment psychology, he nevertheless allowed Cattell to conduct dissertation research on individual variations in reaction time. Returning home after completing his doctorate in Leipzig, Cattell sought to extend the methods of Galton, whose laboratory he had visited briefly while lecturing at Cambridge in 1888. He did so with enormous energy and success while serving as head of the Psychology Laboratory at Columbia University from 1891 to 1917. Cattell (1890) introduced the term *mental test* to the psychological literature, and, during a long career that included serving as the fourth president of the American Psychological Association (APA), he pioneered mental testing and generated scientific interest in psychological tests. More than anyone else, Cattell deserves the title "father" of assessment psychology.

In the twentieth-century wake of Cattell's generativity, the formal pursuit of methods of identifying similarities and differences among people was more often than not stirred by some practical purpose needing to be served. Assessment consequently developed as an *applied* rather than a basic field

in psychology. Its theoretical underpinnings and the extensive research it has generated not withstanding, assessment psychology has been taught, learned, and practiced mainly as a means of facilitating decisions based in part on the needs, desires, capacities, and behavioral tendencies observed in persons being assessed.

EVALUATING INTELLECTUAL ABILITY

The history of intellectual assessment can be traced sequentially through five developments: the emergence of the Binet scales, the construction of group-administered tests, the evolution of the Wechsler scales, the appearance of the Kaufman scales, and the quest for brief methods of measuring intelligence. The sections that follow discuss each of these instruments and describe surveys concerning the frequency with which these and other tests are used.

The Binet Scales

In 1904, the Minister of Public Instruction in Paris became concerned about the presence in public school classrooms of "mentally defective" children who could not benefit from regular instruction. The Minister's information indicated that these "subnormal" children were detracting from the quality of the education that elementary school teachers were able to provide their other students and required special educational programs tailored to "subnormal" children's needs and capabilities. Acting on this information necessitated some method of identifying intellectually subnormal children, which led the Minister to appoint a commission charged with developing such a method. Among those asked to serve on the commission was Alfred Binet (1875–1911), a distinguished experimental psychologist of the day well known for his interest in higher mental processes and his research on the nature of intelligence (Binet, 1903).

Binet accepted appointment to this commission and, in collaboration with physician colleague Theodore Simon (1873–1961), designed a series of verbal and perceptual motor tasks for measuring whether students' mental abilities fell substantially below expectation for their age. The Binet-Simon instrument debuted in 1905 (Binet & Simon, 1905), was revised in 1908 to arrange these tasks according to mental age level, and was expanded in 1911 to include adult as well as childhood levels of expectation. Word spread rapidly concerning the utility of this new instrument, which was soon translated into several English versions. The most important of these translations emerged from an extensive revision and standardization project directed by Lewis Terman (1877–1956) at

Stanford University and was published in 1916 as the Stanford Revision and Extension of the Binet-Simon Intelligence Scale, soon to become known as the Stanford-Binet (Terman, 1916). Subsequent modifications and restandardization over the years produced several further versions of this measure, the most recent of which was published as the Fourth Edition Stanford-Binet in 1986 (Thorndike, Hagen, & Sattler, 1986).

Central to the conceptual basis and empirical standardization of the Stanford-Binet is a focus on normative age-related expectations for performance on its component tasks, which makes it possible to translate successes and failures on these tasks into a mental-age equivalent. While Terman was collecting his standardization data, William Stern (1871–1938) advanced the notion that a "mental quotient" could be calculated for respondents by dividing their chronological age by their mental age and multiplying the result by 100 (Stern, 1914). Terman endorsed this notion and included Stern's calculation in the 1916 Stanford-Binet. However, he decided to rename this number an "intelligence quotient," introducing the term *IQ* into the language of psychology and into vocabularies worldwide.

Group-Administered Tests

Just one year after publication of the Stanford-Binet, public duty once more shaped the development of intelligence testing. The entry of the United States into World War I in 1917 generated a pressing need to draft and train a large number of young men who could quickly be transformed from city boys and farm boys into the "doughboys" who served in the trenches. It would facilitate this process to have a measure of intelligence that could be administered to large numbers of recruits at a single sitting and help screen out those whose intellectual limitations would prevent them from functioning competently in the military, while also identifying those with above average abilities who could be trained for positions of responsibility. Robert Yerkes (1877–1956), then president of the American Psychological Association, responded to the war effort by chairing a Committee on the Psychological Examination of Recruits, on which Terman was asked to serve. Coincidentally, one of Terman's graduate students, Arthur Otis (1886–1963), had been working to develop a group intelligence test. Otis shared his work with Yerkes' committee, which drew heavily on it to produce what came to be known as the *Army Alpha test*. The Army Alpha test was the first group-administered intelligence test and, as noted by Haney (1981), it was constructed quickly enough to be given to almost two million recruits by war's end.

As a language-based instrument that required respondents to read instructions, however, the Army Alpha was not suitable for assessing recruits who were illiterate or, being re-cent immigrants to the United States, had little command of English. This limitation of the Army Alpha led to creation of the Army Beta, which was based on testing procedures previously developed for use with deaf persons and consisted of nonverbal tasks that could be administered through pantomime instructions, without use of language. The Army Beta's attention to groups with special needs foreshadowed later attention to culture-related sources of bias in psychological assessment and to the importance of multicultural sensitivity in developing and using tests (see Dana, 2000; Suzuki, Ponterotto, & Meller, 2000). Following the war, group testing of intelligence continued in the form of several different measures adapted for civilian use, one of the first, fittingly enough, was the Otis Classification Test (Otis, 1923).

The Wechsler Scales

The Stanford-Binet was the first systematically formulated and standardized measure of intelligence, and for many years it was by far the most commonly used method of evaluating intelligence in young people and adults as well. The kinds of tasks designed by Binet have continued to the present day to provide the foundation on which most other tests of intelligence have been based. Beginning in the late 1930s, however, a new thread in the history of intelligence testing was woven by David Wechsler (1896–1981), then chief psychologist at Bellevue Hospital in New York City. Wechsler saw shortcomings in defining intelligence by the ratio of mental age to chronological age, especially in the evaluation of adults, and he developed instead a method of determining IQ on the basis of comparing test scores with the normative distribution of these scores among people in various age groups. The instrument he constructed borrowed subtests from the Stanford-Binet, the Army Alpha and Beta, and some other existing scales, and thus it was not new in substance. What was new was the statistical formulation of IQ as having a mean of 100 and a standard deviation of 15, which in turn led to the widely accepted convention of translating IQ scores into percentile ranks.

Also innovative was Wechsler's belief that intellectual capacities constitute an integral feature of personality functioning, from which it followed that a well-designed intelligence test could provide useful information beyond the implications of an overall IQ score. Wechsler postulated that the pattern of relative strengths and weaknesses across subtests measuring different kinds of mental abilities could be used to identify normal and abnormal variations in numerous cognitive characteristics and coping capacities. Published as the Wechsler-Bellevue, Wechsler's (1939) test gradually replaced the Stanford-Binet as the most widely used measure of adult intelligence. In addition, because of the profile of subtest scores it offered, compared to the single IQ score or mental age equivalent available from the Stanford-Binet, the Wechsler-Bellevue found applications in clinical health settings as a measure not only of intellectual ability but also of features of neuropsychological impairment and disordered thinking.

A revised Wechsler-Bellevue-II appeared in 1946, and three further revisions of the test were published as the Wechsler Adult Intelligence Scale (WAIS), the most recent being the WAIS-III (Wechsler, 1997). The basic format and individual subtests were also extended downward to provide versions for use with young people: the Wechsler Intelligence Scale for Children (WISC) (Wechsler, 1949), the most recent version of which is the WISC-III (Wechsler, 1991), and the Wechsler Preschool and Primary Scale of Intelligence (WPPSI) (Wechsler, 1967), with its most recent version being the WPPSI-R (Wechsler, 1989).

The Kaufman Scales

Although numerous other intelligence tests employing Binet's mental age concept or Wechsler's statistical approach have appeared, none has approached the visibility or popularity of these two measures. Perhaps most notable after Binet and Wechsler among intelligence test developers is Alan Kaufman, who in addition to writing extensively about the assessment of intelligence (Kaufman, 1990, 1994) developed his own general intelligence measures for children—the Kaufman Assessment Battery for Children (K-ABC) (Kaufman & Kaufman, 1983)—and for adolescents and adults—the Kaufman Adolescent and Adult Intelligence Test (KAIT; Kaufman & Kaufman, 1993). Kaufman's measures differed in two important respects from their predecessors. First, reflecting a theoretical rather than an empirical approach, tasks were chosen not by testing how trial participants would respond to them, but by formulating certain constructs concerning the nature of intellectual functioning and using tasks that were considered likely to assess these constructs. Second, Kaufman included subtests designed to provide achievement as well as IQ scores, including assessment of abilities in reading and arithmetic.

Brief Methods

Along with developing full-length measures, Kaufman stimulated contemporary efforts to construct brief tests of intelligence. A quest for brief methods has long been common to all types of psychological assessment, and intelligence testing provided especially fertile ground for developing short forms of existing measures and constructing new measures that were

short to begin with. The structure of Wechsler's scales offered examiners obvious possibilities for replacing the full WAIS or WISC with a selection of subtests they believed would be sufficient for their purposes. As reviewed by Campbell (1998) and Kaufman (1990), many such beliefs became formalized as short forms comprising from two to six subtests and achieving varying success in estimating Wechsler IQ. The most promising compromises between saving time and obtaining sufficient data have been (a) the utilization of seven-subtest short forms for the WAIS-R and the WAIS-III, which have shown correlations in the high .90s with Full Scale IQ and provide dependable estimates of Verbal and Performance IQ as well (Ryan & Ward, 1999; Ward, 1990); and (b) the selection of an eight-subtest short form of the WISC-III that yields dependable estimates of both the IQ and Index Scores calculated for this measure (Donders, 1997).

Kaufman influenced these developments by constructing a new measure, the Kaufman Brief Intelligence Test (K-BIT), which includes tasks measuring verbal facility and nonverbal reasoning and provides a composite score that can be used to estimate intellectual functioning for persons age 4 to 90 (Kaufman & Kaufman, 1990). The K-BIT became sufficiently popular among practitioners to stimulate construction of numerous other new measures consisting of a small number of traditional kinds of subtests, the most visible of these being the Wechsler Abbreviated Scale of Intelligence (WASI; Psychological Corporation, 1999) and the Wide-Range Intelligence Test (WRIT; Glutting, Adams, & Sheslow, 1999).

Frequency of Test Use

The frequency information given about the use of the Stanford-Binet and Wechsler scales derives from extensive survey data. Attention to the frequency with which various tests are used has characterized assessment psychology at least as far back as surveys conducted in 1934 and 1946 (see Loutit & Browne, 1947). Sundberg (1961) expanded on these earlier surveys with a nationwide sampling of test usage across a variety of clinical agencies and institutions, and his methodology was later repeated on a larger scale (Brown & McGuire, 1976; Lubin, Larsen, & Matarazzo, 1984; Lubin, Wallis, & Paine, 1971; and Piotrowski & Keller, 1989).

Other informative surveys have queried individual psychologists rather than agencies concerning the frequency with which they use various tests, including large samples of clinical psychologists (Archer & Newsom, 2000; Camara, Nathan, & Puente, 2000; Watkins, Campbell, Nieberding, & Hallmark, 1995), neuropsychologists (Butler, Retzlaff, & Vanderploeg, 1991; Camara et al., 2000; Lees-Haley, Smith, Williams, & Dunn, 1995), school psychologists (Kamphaus,

Petoskey, & Rowe, 2000; Stinnett, Havey, & Oehler-Stinnett, 1994; Wilson & Reschly, 1996), and forensic psychologists doing criminal evaluations (Borum & Grisso, 1995), personal injury evaluations (Boccaccini & Brodsky, 1999), and custody evaluations (Ackerman & Ackerman, 1997; LaFortune & Carpenter, 1998). Surveys have recently been undertaken outside of the United States as well, as illustrated in a report by Muñiz, Prieto, Almeida, and Bartram (1999) on test use in Spain, Portugal, and Latin American countries. Without always repeating these reference citations, subsequent comments in this chapter about test use frequency are based on the findings they report.

IDENTIFYING PERSONALITY CHARACTERISTICS AND PSYCHOPATHOLOGY

Standardized assessment of personality characteristics and psychopathology emerged from four separate threads of history differentiated by their distinctive procedures. A first thread involves relatively structured procedures in which respondents reply to a fixed number of specific questions by selecting their answer from a prescribed list of alternatives (e.g., Question: "Do you feel unhappy?" Answers: "Most of the time," "Occasionally," "Hardly ever"). Such relatively structured measures are commonly referred to as self-report methods, given that the data they provide constitute what people are able and willing to say about themselves.

A second thread consists of relatively unstructured procedures in which respondents are presented with somewhat ambiguous test stimuli and given rather vague instructions concerning what they should say about or do with these stimuli (e.g., shown a picture of a boy looking at a violin, the respondent is asked to make up a story that has a beginning and an end and includes how the boy is feeling and what he is thinking about). Measures of this kind have traditionally been called "projective" tests, because they invite respondents to attribute characteristics to test stimuli that are based on their own impressions rather than known fact (e.g., "The boy is feeling sad") or give them considerable latitude to complete tasks in whatever manner they prefer (asked by respondents about how they should proceed on these measures, examiners typically answer with statements like "It's up to you" or "Any way you like").

However, most so-called projective tests have some clearly defined as well as ambiguous aspects and include specific as well as vague instructions (a violin *is* a violin, and "What will happen to him?" is a precise request for information). Accordingly, instead of being labeled "projective" measures, these relatively unstructured assessment instruments are probably more appropriately classified as belonging to a category of "performance-based" measures, as has been proposed by the American Psychological Association Work Group on Psychological Assessment (Kubiszyn et al., 2000; Meyer et al., 2001). By contrast with self-report data, the data obtained by performance-based measures consist not of what people say about themselves, but of the manner in which they deal with various tasks they are given to do.

A third thread in the history of methods for assessing personality characteristics and psychopathology comprises interview procedures. Assessment interviews are similar to self-report measures, in that respondents are asked directly what the assessor wants to know. Unlike relatively structured tests, however, which are typically taken in written form and involve little interaction with the examiner, interviews are interactive oral procedures in which the participants engage in a conversational exchange. Moreover, assessment interviews include a performance-based as well as a self-report component, in that interviewers typically base their impressions not only on what respondents say about themselves, but also on how they say it and how they conduct themselves while being interviewed.

The fourth thread consists of behavioral procedures that epitomize performance-based assessment. In behavioral assessment, the manner in which respondents conduct themselves is not an ancillary source of information, but instead constitutes the core data being obtained. Respondents are asked to perform tasks selected or designed to mimic certain real-world situations as closely as possible, and their performance on these tasks is taken as a representative sample of behavior that should be predictive of how they will act in the real-world situation. Gideon's previously mentioned method of selecting his troops exemplifies assessment based on observing behavior in representative circumstances. As elaborated next, behavioral assessment, like the other three threads of personality assessment history, has a unique lineage with respect to how, why, and by whom it became established.

Relatively Structured Tests

The entry of the United States into World War I influenced assessment psychology by creating an urgent need to evaluate not only the intellectual level of draftees, as noted earlier, but their emotional stability as well. Reports from France in 1917 indicated that the war effort was being hampered by the presence in the ranks of mentally fragile soldiers who could not tolerate the psychological stress of combat. In response to these reports, Robert Woodworth (1869–1962), a prominent experimental psychologist who had done his doctoral work with Cattell and later succeeded him as department head at

Columbia, designed the Personal Data Sheet (Woodworth, 1920). The Personal Data Sheet consisted of a written list of questions concerning presumed symptoms of psychological disturbance (e.g., "Are you happy most of the time?"), which were to be answered by checking "Yes" or "No." Although intended for use as a screening device to deselect emotionally unstable draftees, Woodworth's measure was not completed in time to serve this purpose. Following the war, however, the Personal Data Sheet was put to civilian use as a measure of adjustment, and as such it was the first formal self-report personality assessment questionnaire to become generally available.

Although limited in scope and superficial in design, Woodworth's measure served as the model on which later generations of adjustment and personality inventories were based. Before continuing with that history, there is an historical footnote to World War I that should be noted. The development of the Personal Data Sheet as a model for an enduring tradition in assessment psychology (i.e., personality inventories), like the development of the Binet-Simon and Army Alpha before it as models of other enduring traditions (i.e., individual and group intelligence tests), bears witness to the impetus of war and public need in evoking formal methods of psychological assessment. The tides of war inevitably have their dark side, however, for those caught in the civilian crossfire as well as for those coming under military attack. In an event with broad sociopolitical implications, James McKeen Cattell, after 26 years as a senior faculty member at Columbia University was, according to Boring (1950, p. 535), dismissed from his position in 1917 after taking a pacifist stance with respect to the United States entry into World War I.

Returning to the history of self-report measures, the next major development following the Personal Data Sheet was the publication by Robert Bernreuter (1901–1995) of a new Personality Inventory (Bernreuter, 1931). Unlike Woodworth's measure, which yielded just a single score for overall level of adjustment, the Bernreuter was a multidimensional self-report instrument with separate scales for several different personality characteristics, such as neurotic tendencies, ascendance-submission, and introversion-extraversion. This was the first multidimensional personality assessment measure to appear and, although the era in which it was widely used and recognized is long past, the Bernreuter's place in history is assured by its having set the stage for a bevy of similarly designed instruments that came to constitute a cornerstone of assessment psychology. Among these many multidimensional personality questionnaires, six currently prominent instruments are notable for illustrating different motivations and methodologies that have been involved in developing such measures: the Minnesota Multiphasic Personality Inventory (MMPI), the California Psychological Inventory (CPI), the Millon Clinical Multiaxial Inventory (MCMI), the Sixteen Personality Factors Questionnaire (16PF), the NEO Personality Inventory (NEO-PI), and the Personality Assessment Inventory (PAI).

MMPI

The Minnesota Multiphasic Personality Inventory was constructed during the late 1930s by Starke Hathaway (1903–1995), a psychologist, and J. Charnley McKinley, a psychiatrist, while they worked together at the University of Minnesota hospitals. Hathaway and McKinley undertook this task for the purpose of developing a group-administered pencil-and-paper measure that would assist in assigning patients to diagnostic categories. The measure they produced was first published in finished form in 1943 (Hathaway & McKinley, 1943) and has since then become the most widely used and researched of all personality assessment instruments. The manner in which Hathaway and McKinley constructed the MMPI was noteworthy for their total reliance on empirical keying in the selection of test items. Empirical keying was a radical departure from the logical keying approach that had characterized construction of the Woodworth and Bernreuter tests and other early adjustment scales and trait measures as well. In logical keying, items are selected or devised on the basis of some reasonable expectation or subjective impression that they are likely to measure a particular personality characteristic. Empirical keying, by contrast, involves selecting items according to how well in fact they differentiate among groups of people previously identified as having various psychological disorders or personality characteristics.

The original MMPI of Hathaway and McKinley was expanded over the years by the addition of many new scales and subscales, and an extensive revision and re-norming process produced the MMPI-2 (Butcher, Dahlstrom, Graham, Tellegen, & Kaemmer, 1989) and an adolescent version, the MMPI-A (Butcher et al., 1992). Having been developed with patient populations and for clinical purposes, the MMPI/MMPI-2/MMPI-A is generally regarded as being more suited for evaluating psychological disturbance than for elucidating normal variations in personality characteristics. Nevertheless, the instrument has proved valuable in a variety of contexts and is often used by psychologists doing forensic, neuropsychological, and personnel evaluations as well as mental health assessments.

CPI

A significant spin-off of the MMPI resulted from the efforts of Harrison Gough, who was interested less in identifying patterns of psychopathology among patients than in assessing personality characteristics in nonclinical populations. Using a combination of empirical and logical keying methods, and borrowing from the MMPI many items that were interpersonal in nature and not symptom-oriented, Gough began in 1948 to develop scales that were published as the California Psychological Inventory, currently in its third edition (Gough, 1957; Gough & Bradley, 1996). Whereas the MMPI scales had been named with diagnostic labels (e.g., depression, schizophrenia), Gough named his scales with commonly used terms that most people would be likely to recognize and understand (e.g., independence, responsibility). The essence of Gough's purpose was captured in a review by Thorndike (1959), who referred to the CPI as "the sane man's MMPI."

Whereas the MMPI has been used primarily in clinical, forensic, and health care settings, the CPI has been applied mainly in counseling, educational, and organizational settings, as a way of facilitating decisions concerning career choice, academic planning, personnel selection, and the resolution of normal range adjustment problems. The CPI has also found considerable use as a research tool in studies of personality dimensions associated with achievement, leadership, and creativity.

MCMI

In a mode similar to Gough's, Theodore Millon developed the Millon Clinical Multiaxial Inventory using a combination of empirical and logical keying procedures. As a major difference from both the MCMI and the MMPI, however, Millon's scales were derived from a comprehensive theory of personality and psychopathology that he had formulated prior to turning his attention to developing a measuring instrument (Millon, 1969). First published in 1977 (Millon, 1977), the MCMI was standardized on patients receiving mental health care and, like the MMPI, is intended for purposes of psychodiagnostic screening and clinical assessment, rather than for use with nonpatient populations. Unlike the MMPI, however, which was designed primarily to measure symptomatic concerns corresponding to Axis I disorders in the *Diagnostic and Statistical Manual (DSM)* of the American Psychiatric Association (2000), the MCMI is scaled mainly to reflect disorders in personality function as categorized on Axis II of the *DSM*. Although some

symptom-related scales are included in the MCMI, and some personality disorder scales are available for the MMPI, these are not usually regarded as a strength of either, and many practitioners have found some advantage in using both instruments together in complementary fashion.

The original MCMI has been revised twice, with the current version, the MCMI-III, having been published in 1994 (Millon, 1994; see also Millon, 1996). Millon also extended his test downward to include an adolescent form, originally known as the Millon Adolescent Personality Inventory (MAPI) and currently in revised form as the Millon Adolescent Clinical Inventory (MACI) (Millon & Davis, 1993; Millon, Green, & Meagher, 1982).

16PF

As an approach to constructing self-report inventories entirely different from the empirical and logical keying that characterized the MMPI, CPI, MCMI, and their predecessors, Raymond Cattell (1905–1998; no relation to J. McK. Cattell) began in the 1940s to apply factor analytic methods to personality test construction. After drawing on a large pool of adjectives describing personality characteristics to build a long list of trait names, he obtained ratings on these traits from samples of nonpatient adults. By factor analyzing these ratings, he extracted 15 factors that he identified as "the source traits of personality." To these 15 factors, he added a short measure of intelligence to produce the Sixteen Personality Factors Questionnaire (16PF), which was originally published in 1949 and most recently revised in 1993 (R. B. Cattell, Cattell, & Cattell, 1993).

From Cattell's perspective, his factors captured the entire domain of trait characteristics that underlie human personality and, in common with Gough, he intended his test to serve as a measure of normal personality functioning, and not of the presence or extent of psychopathology. Nevertheless, as demonstrated by Karson and O'Dell (1989), the 16-PF can be used by practitioners to identify aspects of personality in disturbed as well as normally functioning persons.

NEO-PI

Cattell's factor analytic approach from the 1940s, in addition to being still visible in continued use of the 16-PF, had a contemporary renaissance in the work of Paul Costa and Robert McCrae. Like Millon, Costa and McCrae were guided in their test construction by a theoretical formulation of personality functioning, in this case the Five Factor Model (FFM), sometimes referred to as the "Big Five." The FFM emerged from various factor analyses of personality test and rating scale data that recurrently identified four to six factors to which individual differences in personality could be attributed (see Digman, 1990). Selecting self-report items related to their preferred five-factor formulation, Costa and McCrae developed a questionnaire that yields scores along five trait dimensions, which they called "domain scales": neuroticism, extraversion, openness, agreeableness, and conscientiousness. Their effort resulted in the 1985 publication of the NEO Personality Inventory, currently available in revised form as the NEO PI-R (Costa & McCrae, 1992).

Like the 16-PF, the NEO PI-R was intended as a measure of normal personality characteristics but has proved useful in evaluating personality problems in disturbed persons (see Piedmont, 1998). Although time has yet to tell how the NEO PR-I will eventually fare with respect to its frequency of use, there is already an extensive literature on the Five Factor Model to suggest that it will become well-established assessment instrument.

PAI

The last of these six self-report questionnaires to become well-known assessment instruments is the Personality Assessment Inventory developed by Leslie Morey (1991, 1996). The PAI is intended to provide information relevant to clinical diagnosis, treatment planning, and screening for adult psychopathology, and in this respect it is closely modeled after the MMPI. Drawing on methodology used in constructing other inventories, however, Morey formulated his scales in terms of theoretical constructs and used rational as well as quantitative criteria in selecting his items. The PAI clinical scales are primarily symptom-oriented and, as in the case of the MMPI, more likely to assist in Axis I than Axis II diagnosis. In addition, however, the PAI features several scales directly related to aspects of treatment planning.

Relatively Unstructured Tests

Unlike formal tests of intelligence and self-report methods of assessing personality, which arose in response to public needs, relatively unstructured personality assessment methods came about largely as the product of intellectual curiosity. The best known and most widely used of these are the Rorschach Inkblot Method (RIM) and a variety of picture-story, figure drawing, and sentence completion methods, the most prominent of these being the Thematic Apperception Test (TAT), the Draw-a-Person (DAP), and the Rotter Incomplete Sentences Blank (RISB).

Rorschach Inkblot Method

As a schoolboy in late nineteenth-century Switzerland, Hermann Rorschach (1884–1922) was known among his classmates for his skill at a popular parlor game of the day, which consisted of making blots of ink and suggesting what they look like. Rorschach's parlor game creativity reflected his artistic bent, because he was a talented painter and craftsman. Some of his work is permanently displayed in the Rorschach Archives and Museum in Bern, Switzerland. Later on, serving as a staff psychiatrist in a large mental hospital, Rorschach pondered whether he could learn something about his patients' personality characteristics and adaptive difficulties by studying the perceptual style they showed in looking at inkblots. His curiosity and scientific bent led him to develop a standard series of inkblots and to collect responses to them from several hundred patients and from nonpatient respondents as well. Rorschach's analyses of the data he obtained culminated in the 1921 publication of *Psychodiagnostics* (Rorschach, 1921/1942), which introduced the Rorschach Inkblot Method (RIM) in the form that the test stimuli have retained since that date.

Following Rorschach's death at age 37, just one year after his monograph appeared, many different systems were developed both in the United States and around the world for administering, coding, and interpreting Rorschach protocols. Recognizing the potential clinical and psychometric benefit of integrating the most informative and dependable features of these various systems into a standardized procedure, John Exner (1993) developed the Rorschach Comprehensive System, which since its original publication in 1974 has become the predominant way of administering and coding this instrument. The currently most common approach to interpreting Rorschach data combines attention to respondents' perceptual style in formulating what they see in the inkblots with analyses of the thematic imagery contained in their responses and the behavioral style with which they produce these responses (see Weiner, 1998). These three data sources are then used as a basis for inferring adaptive strengths and weaknesses in how people manage stress, exercise their cognitive functions, deal with affect, view themselves, and regard other people.

Periodically issues have been raised in the literature concerning the psychometric soundness and utility of Rorschach assessment, and this matter is presently the subject of some debate. With due respect for differences of opinion, however, the weight of empirical evidence documents the validity of the RIM when used appropriately for its intended purposes (Hiller, Rosenthal, Bornstein, Berry, & Brunell-Neuleib, 1999; Meyer & Archer, 2001; Rosenthal, Hiller, Bornstein, Berry, & Brunell-Neuleib, 2001; Viglione & Hilsenroth, 2001;

Weiner, 2001), and the previously referenced surveys of test usage attest its continued widespread use in practice settings.

Picture-Story Methods

During the mid-1930s, Henry Murray (1893–1988), a psychoanalytically trained physician with a doctorate in biochemistry who was then serving as director of the Harvard Psychological Clinic, formulated a theory of personality that stressed the role of idiographic needs and attitudes in determining individual differences in human behavior. In collaboration with Christiana Morgan, Murray also considered the possibility of identifying needs and attitudes, especially those that people were reluctant to admit or unable to recognize, by examining the fantasies they produced when asked to tell stories about pictures they were shown. These notions led to a seminal article about picture-story methods of studying fantasy (Morgan & Murray, 1935), a classic and highly influential book called *Explorations in Personality* (Murray, 1938), and eventually the publication of the Thematic Apperception Test (TAT) (Murray, 1943/1971).

To the extent that the content of imagined stories can provide clues to a respondent's inner life, TAT data are expected to shed light on the particular hierarchy of a person's needs and the nature of his or her underlying conflicts, concerns, and interpersonal attitudes. As was the case for the inkblot method following Rorschach, Murray's picture-story method gave rise to numerous systems of coding and interpretation. The approaches that became most commonly employed in clinical practice were variations of an "inspection technique" proposed by Leopold Bellak that consists of reading through respondents' stories to identify repetitive themes and recurring elements that appear to fall together in meaningful ways (see Bellak & Abrams, 1997). The popularity of such a strictly qualitative and uncoded approach to TAT data has limited efforts to demonstrate the psychometric soundness of the instrument or to develop a substantial normative database for it.

On the other hand, several quantified TAT scales designed to measure specific personality characteristics for clinical or research purposes have shown that the instrument can generate reliable and valid findings when it is used in a standardized manner. Three noteworthy cases in point are scoring systems developed by McClelland, Atkinson, and their colleagues to measure needs for achievement, affiliation, and power (Atkinson & Feather, 1966; McClelland, Atkinson, Clark, & Lowell, 1953); a defense preference scale developed by Cramer (1999); and a measure of capacity for adaptive interpersonal relationships, the Social Cognition and Object Relations Scale (SCORS) developed by Westen, Lohr, Silk, Kerber, and Goodrich (1985).

The original TAT also spawned numerous extensions and spin-offs of the picture-story method intended to broaden its scope. Two variations developed by Bellak to expand the age range for respondents are the Children's Apperception Test (CAT), which portrays animal rather than human characters in the pictures, and the Senior Apperception Test (SAT), which depicts primarily elderly people and circumstances common in the lives of older persons (see Bellak & Abrams, 1997). As an effort to enhance multicultural sensitivity, the TAT approach was used to develop the Tell-Me-A-Story-Test (TEMAS), which portrays conflict situations involving African American and Latino characters and has been found to elicit fuller responses from minority respondents than the all-Caucasian TAT pictures (Costantino, Malgady, & Rogler, 1988). Finally of note is the Roberts Apperception Test for Children (RATC), which was designed specifically to improve on the TAT and CAT as measures for use with children by portraying children and adolescents in everyday interactions, rather then either adult or animal figures; by providing an alternate set of cards showing African American young people in similar scenes; and by using a standardized scoring system (McArthur & Roberts, 1990).

Together with the emergence of specific quantifiable scores for the TAT, the publication of the RATC signaled movement in picture-story assessment toward achieving psychometric respectability, much in the manner that Exner's Comprehensive System for Rorschach assessment moved the inkblot method in that direction. Although the TAT still lags well behind the RIM and most relatively structured assessment instruments in empirical validation, it has long been and remains one of the most frequently used methods for assessing personality functioning. Moreover, as found in a literature survey by Butcher and Rouse (1996), the volume of research articles published on the TAT in the 20-year-period from 1974 to 1994 numbered 998, which was third largest among personality measures, exceeded only by the MMPI (4,339 articles) and the Rorschach (1,969 articles).

Figure Drawing Methods

It is difficult to say who first suggested that what people choose to draw and how they draw it reveal features of their personality, whether the drawing is a prehistoric sketch found on the wall of a cave, a painting by a great master, or the doodles of an ordinary citizen. Whoever it was, it was long before Florence Goodenough (1886–1959) introduced the first formal application of figure drawings in psychological assessment in 1926. Seeking a nonverbal measure of intellectual development in children, Goodenough (1926), developed the Draw-a-Man test, in which intellectual maturity is measured by the amount of accurate detail in a young person's drawing of a human figure. The Draw-a-Man was later revised by Harris (1963), who suggested having respondents draw pictures of a woman and of themselves, in addition to drawing a man, and expanded Goodenough's scoring system and standardization. Most recently the Goodenough-Harris was further updated by Naglieri (1988) to include representative norms for assessing cognitive development in young people age 5 to 17.

The Draw-a-Man was adapted for purposes of personality assessment by Karen Machover (1902–1996), who in 1948 rechristened the measure as the Draw-a-Person (DAP) and introduced the notion that human figure drawings convey in symbolic ways aspects of a respondent's underlying needs, attitudes, conflicts, and concerns. She believed that for persons of all ages and not just children, significant meaning can be attached to structural features of drawings (e.g., where figures are placed on the page) and the manner in which various parts of the body are drawn (e.g., a disproportionately large head). Whereas Machover's approach to DAP interpretation consisted of qualitative hypotheses concerning the symbolic significance of figure drawing characteristics, subsequent developments that were focused mainly on refining this instrument for use in evaluating young people provided quantitative scoring schemes for the instrument. Notable among these were a formulation of 30 specific indicators of emotional disturbance (Koppitz, 1968) and the construction of a Screening Procedure for Emotional Disturbance (SPED; Naglieri, McNeish, & Bardos, 1991). The DAP-SPED is an actuarially derived and normatively based system comprising 55 scorable items and intended as a screening test for classifying young people age 6 to 17 with respect to their likelihood of having adjustment difficulties that call for further evaluation.

Particular interest in the assessment of young people was reflected in several other variations of Goodenough's original method, two of which have become fairly widely used. One of these is the House-Tree-Person (HTP) test devised by Buck (1948), in which children are asked to draw a picture of a house and a tree as well as a person, in the expectation that drawings of all three objects provide symbolic representations of important aspects of a young person's world. The other is the Kinetic Family Drawing (KFD) formalized by Burns and Kaufman (1970), in which respondents are instructed to draw a picture of their whole family, including themselves, doing something.

Also of note is a commonly used procedure suggested by Machover in which people taking any of these figure drawing tests are asked in addition to make up a story about the people they have drawn or to answer specific questions about

them (e.g., "What is this person like?"). When this procedure is followed, figure drawings take on some of the characteristics of picture-story techniques, and, like picture stories, they are despite recent efforts at quantification most commonly interpreted in practice by an inspection technique in which personality characteristics are inferred primarily from subjective impressions of noteworthy or unusual features of the figures drawn. As a consequence, figure drawings remain a largely unvalidated assessment method that has remained popular despite having thus far shown limited psychometric soundness (see Handler, 1995).

Sentence Completion Methods

Sentence completion methods of assessing personality and psychopathology originated in the earliest efforts to develop tests of intelligence. Herman Ebbinghaus (1897), the pioneering figure in formal study of human memory, developed a sentence completion test for the purpose of measuring intellectual capacity and reasoning ability in children, and Binet and Simon included a version of Ebbinghaus' sentence completion task in their original 1905 scale. Sentence completions have been retained in the Stanford-Binet, and a variety of sentence completion tasks have also found use to the present day as achievement test measures of language skills.

The extension of the sentence completion method to assess personality as well as intellectual functioning was stimulated by Carl Jung (1916), the well-known Swiss psychoanalyst and one-time close colleague of Freud who founded his own school of thought, known as "analytic psychology," and whose writings popularized his use of a "word association" technique for studying underlying aspects of a person's inner life. This technique was formalized in the United States by Grace Kent and Aaron Rosanoff (1910), who developed a standard 100-item list called the Free Association Test and compiled frequency tables for different kinds of responses given by a sample of 1,000 nonpatient adults.

The apparent richness of word association tasks in revealing personality characteristics suggested to many assessors that replacing the word-word format with full sentences written as completions to brief phrases (e.g., "I like . . ."; "My worst fear is . . .") would result in an even more informative assessment instrument. Numerous sentence completion tests were constructed during the 1920s and 1930s and used for a variety of purposes, but with little systematic effort or standardization. The first carefully constructed and validated measure of this kind was developed in the late 1930s by Amanda Rohde and, like other performance-based tests of personality, was intended to "reveal latent needs, sentiments, feelings, and attitudes which subjects would be unwilling or unable to recognize or to express in direct communication" (Rohde, 1946, p. 170). The Rohde Sentence Completion Test served as a model for many similar instruments developed subsequently, and, as described by Rohde (1948), use of those that were available during the 1940s was stimulated by the impact of World War II. It has already been noted that the impetus for designing performance-based personality assessment instruments was largely intellectual curiosity rather than civilian or military needs, and such was the case with sentence completion tests. However, as a brief self-administered measure that provided relatively unstructured assessment of personality characteristics, the sentence completion was found to be extremely helpful in evaluating and planning treatment for the vast number of psychological casualties seen in military installations during the war and cared for in its aftermath in Veterans Administrations Hospitals.

For many years, the best known and most widely used sentence completion has been the Rotter Incomplete Sentences Blank (RISB), which was developed by Julian Rotter in the late 1940s and first published in 1950, and for which adult, college, and high school forms are available (Rotter, Lah, & Rafferty, 1992). The authors provide a scoring system for the RISB that yields an overall adjustment score, but in practice the instrument is most commonly interpreted by the inspection method that characterizes the typical application of picture-story and figure-drawing instruments; that is, examiners read the content of the items and form impressions of what respondents' completions might signify concerning their personality characteristics. Beyond published studies demonstrating modest validity of the RISB as a measure of adjustment, there has been little accumulation of empirical evidence to support inferring any specific personality characteristics from it, nor has there been much progress in documenting the reliability of RISB findings and establishing normative standards for them.

Interview Methods

As elaborated in Volume 10 of this Handbook, psychological assessment is a data-gathering process that involves integrating information gleaned not only from the types of tests discussed thus far, but also from interview methods, behavioral observations, collateral reports, and historical documents. Of these, interviewing and observing people are the most widely used assessment methods for attempting to learn something about them. Although being discussed here in relation to identifying personality characteristics and psychopathology, interview methods are also commonly employed in assessing intellectual and neuropsychological functioning and aptitudes, achievement, and interests. Unlike psychological testing, interviewing is not a method uniquely practiced by psychologists, but rather an evaluative procedure employed by many different kinds of professionals for various purposes and by people in general who have some reason to assess another person, like a father interviewing a suitor for his daughter's hand to gauge his suitability as a son-in-law.

By including both a self-report component, consisting of what people say about themselves, and a performance-based component, consisting of how they go about saying it, assessment interviews provide abundant clues to what a person is like. As a source of important assessment information, no battery of psychological tests can fully replace oral interactions between respondents and skilled interviewers, and most assessment professionals consider the interview an essential element of a psychological evaluation. In their historical development, formal interview methods emerged first in a relatively unstructured format and subsequently in relatively structured formats as well.

Relatively Unstructured Formats

More than most persons using interviews for evaluative purposes, psychologists and other mental health professionals have traditionally favored relatively unstructured interviewing methods. The popularity of unstructured inquiry can be credited to the influence of two of the most significant figures in the history of psychotherapy, Sigmund Freud (1856–1939) and Carl Rogers (1902–1987). Freud (1913/1958) recommended a *free association* method for conducting psychoanalytic treatment sessions that consists of instructing people to report whatever thoughts or feelings come to mind. Rogers (1942, 1951) proposed a *nondirective* method for conducting client-centered therapy in which the therapist's interventions consist mainly of reflecting clients' statements back to them. Although based on markedly different ways of conceptualizing human behavior and the psychotherapeutic process, free association and nondirective methods share in common an open-ended approach that provides minimal guidance to people concerning what or how much they should say.

Although developed for treatment purposes, free association and nondirective techniques subsequently proved valuable as well for obtaining information in assessment interviews. Even though both techniques must usually be supplemented with focused questions to clarify specific points of information, they typically elicit ideas, attitudes, and recollections that would not have emerged in response to direct questioning. The psychoanalytic tradition has generated a substantial literature on psychodynamic approaches to assessment interviewing, perhaps the best known and most highly respected of which is Sullivan's (1954) *The Psychiatric Interview*. Rogers' attention to the interviewing process fostered not only advances in practice but also new developments in research. Unlike tests, which entail a test form or written protocol that remains available for future review, interviews do not produce any written record other than whatever process notes may be made during or following them. Recognizing that such notes are largely inadequate for research purposes, Rogers, while serving as Director of the Counseling Center at the University of Chicago, began making tape recordings of clinical interviews as a means of obtaining reliable data concerning their exact content. In the research program developed by Rogers and his colleagues, tape recordings were examined for various patterns of verbal interaction between interviewer and interviewee during treatment sessions. This research on interactive processes in clinical interviews stimulated extensive studies of what became known as the "anatomy of the interview" (Matarazzo & Wiens, 1972; Pope, 1979), and Rogers' innovative work was seminal as well in fostering systematic psychotherapy research.

Because open-ended interviews require some supplementation to serve assessment purposes adequately, various formal procedures and guidelines have been inserted over time into otherwise unstructured interviews. The most notable of these is the Mental Status Examination (MSE), first proposed in 1902 by Adolf Meyer (1866–1950), a distinguished psychiatrist best known for championing a humane and "common-sense" approach to seriously disturbed persons that included thorough inquiry into their personal history and current circumstances. The MSE took form as a series of specific questions and tasks intended to provide a brief but standardized assessment of a person's attention, memory, reasoning ability, social judgment, fund of knowledge, and orientation in time and space. As elaborated by Trzepacz and Baker (1993), a contemporary MSE also includes observations concerning a person's general appearance, interpersonal conduct, prevailing mood, sense of reality, thought processes, self-awareness, and intellectual level.

The MSE has become a standard mental health assessment tool that is considered an integral part of diagnostic evaluations by most psychiatrists and is often used by psychologists as well, especially when they are not including any other formal tests among their procedures. Paralleling the previously mentioned interest in short forms of intelligence tests, the MSE has been particularly popular in an 11-item version developed in the 1970s as the Mini Mental Status Examination (Folstein, Folstein, & McHugh, 1975). Whatever the length of an MSE, however, the information it provides emerges in fuller and more reliable form in a psychodiagnostic test battery, and psychological assessors who are including formal testing among their evaluation procedures rarely find use for it.

Along with the development of the MSE as a semi-formal addendum, relatively unstructured assessment interviews have been shaped by numerous interviewing outlines or schedules that identify topics to be covered (e.g., nature and history of presenting complaint, educational and occupational history) and specific items of information that should regularly be obtained (e.g., basic demography, current medications, and history of substance use, suicidal behavior, and physical or sexual abuse). Such interview guides have long been standard topics in interviewing textbooks for mental health professionals (e.g., Craig, 1989; Morrison, 1993; Othmer & Othmer, 1994). From a historical perspective, one of the most comprehensive and psychologically sensitive but frequently forgotten contributions of this kind was made by George Kelley (1905–1966), who is known primarily for developing personal construct theory and a personality assessment instrument he based on it, the Role Construct Repertory Test. In a classic book, *The Psychology of Personal Constructs,* Kelley (1955) included several chapters on conducting assessment interviews that provide excellent guidance by today's standards as well as those of a half century ago.

Relatively Structured Formats

However rich the information obtainable from unstructured interviews, and despite the flexibility of an unstructured approach in adapting to unpredictable variations in how interviewees may present themselves, these formats lack sufficiently standardized procedures to ensure replicable and reliable data collection. Mounting concerns that the unreliability of diagnostic interviews in clinical settings were impeding mental health research led in the 1970s to the development of the Research Diagnostic Criteria (RDC), which comprised a set of clearly specified descriptive behavioral criteria for assigning participants in research studies to one of several diagnostic categories (Spitzer, Endicott, & Robins, 1978). This descriptive behavioral approach noticeably improved the interrater reliability achieved by diagnostic interviewers, and the RDC format, including many of its specific criteria, was subsequently incorporated into the *Diagnostic and Statistical Manual (DSM)* of the American Psychiatric Associations, beginning with *DSM-II* in 1980 and extending to the present *DSM-IV-TR* (American Psychiatric Association, 2000).

The RDC criteria also lent themselves well to formulating questions to be asked in diagnostic interviews, and they soon gave rise to a new genre of assessment methods, a relatively structured interview that consists entirely or in large part of specific items of inquiry. Simultaneously with the publication of the RDC criteria, Endicott and Spitzer (1978) introduced the best known and most frequently used instrument of this kind, the Schedule for Affective Disorders and Schizophrenia (SADS). Intended to assist in identifying a broad range of symptomatic disorders in addition to affective disorders and schizophrenia, the SADS is a semistructured interview guide that requires professional judgment and serves clinical as well as research purposes. Following on its heels came the Diagnostic Interview Schedule (DIS), which is entirely structured and was designed for use by nonprofessional interviewers in research studies (Robins, Helzer, Croughan, & Ratcliff, 1981). Both of these measures were extended downward for use with young people, as the Kiddie SADS (K-SADS; Puig-Antich & Chambers, 1978) and the Diagnostic Interview for Children (DISC; Costello, Edelbrock, & Costello, 1985). The most comprehensive measure of this kind to emerge has been the Structured Clinical Interview for the *DSM* (SCID), which includes forms for identifying personality as well as symptomatic disorders (Spitzer, Williams, & Gibbon, 1987; see also R. Rogers, 2001).

Behavioral Methods

The prescientific history of psychology aside, the formal implementation of behavioral methods for assessing personality is usually traced to the World War II activities of the United States Office of Strategic Services (OSS), the predecessor organization to the Central Intelligence Agency. Once again the winds of war instigated advances in the methods of behavioral science, just as they have in the biological and physical sciences. To aid in selecting operatives for covert intelligence missions, the OSS observed how recruits behaved in a variety of contrived problem-solving and stress-inducing situations and on this basis predicted the likely quality of their performance in the field (Office of Strategic Services Assessment Staff, 1948; see also Handler, 2001). A gap of more than 20 years followed before the OSS methods led to a clearly defined approach to assessment, mainly because the emergence of systematic behavioral assessment techniques had to await new ways of conceptualizing personality for assessment purposes.

Of many contributions to the literature that reconceptualized personality in ways that fostered the development of behavioral assessment, two can be singled out for their clarity and influence. In 1968, Walter Mischel published *Personality and Assessment* (Mischel, 1968), a book in which he argued that personality traits are semantic fictions, that continuity in behavior across time and place exists only as a function of similarity across situations, and that assessment of behavior should accordingly focus on its situational determinants. A few years later, Goldfried and Kent (1972) drew a sharp distinction between "traditional" and "behavioral" assessment

procedures with respect to how personality is viewed. From a traditional assessment perspective, these authors pointed out, personality consists of characteristics that lead people to behave in certain ways, and understanding a person's actions is a product of examining his or her underlying tendencies or dispositions. From a behavioral perspective, by contrast, personality "is defined according to the likelihood of an individual manifesting certain behavioral tendencies in the variety of situations that comprise his day-to-day living" (Goldfried & Kent, 1972, p. 412). Behaviorally speaking, then, personality is not an *a priori* set of concrete action tendencies that people have and carry around with them, but is rather a convenient abstraction for summarizing after the fact how people have been observed to interact with their environment.

These innovative conceptions of personality, echoed in numerous other books and articles, led during the 1970s and 1980s to a dramatic growth of interest in developing assessment methods in which the obtained data would consist of representative samples of behavior that could be objectively evaluated for their implications after the fact, as contrasted with test responses to be interpreted inferentially as signs of underlying states or traits they are presumed before the fact to measure. The core techniques used to achieve this purpose of behavioral assessment included (a) observational ratings of person's responses in natural and contrived situations, as suggested by the OSS methods and by situations devised by Paul (1966) to assess the effectiveness of systematic desensitization; (b) observed conduct in role-playing exercises, based on procedures developed by Rotter and Wickens (1948); (c) self-report instruments focused on specific behavioral interactions, as had earlier been exemplified by measures like Geer's (1965) Fear Survey Schedule; (d) psychophysiological measurements, which were suggested by the successful employment of such techniques in the then emerging field of behavioral medicine research (see Kallman & Feuerstein, 1977); and (e) behavioral interviews specifically focused on how people respond to certain kinds of situations in their lives.

The late 1980s saw gradual moderation of the original conceptual underpinnings of behavioral assessment and considerable broadening of its focus. It is currently widely recognized that people are not as "trait-less" as Mischel argued, nor are traditional and behavioral methods of assessment as distinct and mutually exclusive as Goldfried and Kent originally suggested. In the case of Mischel's argument, behavioral assessors rediscovered Lewin's classic maxim that how people behave is an interactive function of their dispositional nature and the environmental circumstances in which they find themselves, and the advent of cognitive perspectives in behavioral approaches encouraged behavioral assessors to attend to what people are thinking and feeling as well what they are doing. As for the Goldfried and Kent distinction, behavioral assessors recognized that they could extend the practical applications of their approach by supplementing behavioral observations with judicious utilization of clinical judgment. As reflected in the behavioral assessment literature that ushered in the 1990s, strictly behavioral methods became appreciated as having some limitations, and traditional methods as having some strengths; correspondingly, behavioral assessment evolved into a multifaceted process comprising a broader range of techniques and levels of evaluation than had been its legacy (see Bellack & Hersen, 1988; Ciminero, Calhoun, & Adams, 1986; Haynes & O'Brien, 2000).

MONITORING NEUROPSYCHOLOGICAL FUNCTIONING

As summarized by Boll (1983), neuropsychology emerged both as a discipline and as an area of professional practice. As a discipline, neuropsychology is the field of science concerned with the study of relationships between brain functions and behavior. As applied practice, neuropsychology consists primarily of using various assessment procedures to measure the development and decline of brain functions and their impairment as a consequence of head injury, cerebrovascular accidents (stroke), neoplastic disease (tumors), and other illnesses affecting the central nervous system, of which Alzheimer's disease is the most prevalent. The historical highlights of formal neuropsychological assessment cluster around the development of the Bender Visual Motor Gestalt Test and the subsequent emergence of neuropsychological test batteries.

Bender Gestalt

Best known among the earliest formal psychological assessment methods constructed to measure brain functions was the Bender Visual Motor Gestalt Test, first described by Lauretta Bender (1897–1987) in 1938 (Bender, 1938). Historical lore has it that Bender, then a psychiatrist at Bellevue Hospital in New York, became intrigued by psychomotor differences she observed among children as they made chalk drawings on the city sidewalks in preparation for playing hopscotch. She noted that some of the children were more skillful than others in executing these drawings. By and large, older children were better at it than younger ones, but some older children appeared to have persistent difficulty in drawing the hopscotch designs accurately. These observations led Bender to conclude that Gestalt principles of visual organization

and perception, as reflected in the drawing of designs, could be applied to identifying individual differences in maturation and detecting forms of organic brain disease and psychopathology. Selecting for her test nine designs that had been developed by Wertheimer, she presented in her 1938 text illustrations of how these designs were likely to be copied by normally developing children age 4 to 11 and by normal, brain-damaged, and emotionally disturbed adults.

The Bender Gestalt test has fared both well and poorly since 1946, when the stimulus cards were first published separately from Bender's book and made generally available for professional use. Among important refinements of the test, Pascal and Suttell (1951) developed an extensive scoring system for identifying brain dysfunction in adults, and Koppitz (1975) undertook a large standardization study in the 1960s to construct a scoring scheme that would measure both cognitive maturation and neuropsychological impairment in children. Lacks (1998) later proposed a simplified 12-item criterion list that has proved fairly accurate in differentiating brain-damaged from neuropsychologically intact adults. The Bender Gestalt also became and has remained very popular among assessment psychologists as a screening device for brain dysfunction in adults and for developmental delay in young people. In the recent test use surveys mentioned previously, this instrument was ranked fifth in frequency of use among samples of clinical psychologists (Camara et al., 2000) and experienced professionals conducting child custody evaluations (Ackerman & Ackerman, 1997), and seventh among forensic examiners experienced in neuropsychology (Lees-Haley et al., 1995).

On the other hand, with respect to its faring poorly, the Bender was reported as being used by only 27% of sampled members of the International Neuropsychological Society (Butler et al., 1991), and a sample of the National Academy of Neuropsychologists membership ranked the Bender 25th in frequency among the measures they use (Camara et al., 2000). The apparent disrepute of the Bender among mainstream neuropsychologists, despite its extensive research base, may have several origins. These include (a) its having been developed prior to the emergence of neuropsychological assessment as a well-defined practice specialty, which began in the 1950s; (b) its having typically been interpreted by practitioners on the basis of their subjective impressions rather than one of the available scoring systems for it; and (c) its frequently having been given more credence than was warranted as a definitive and stand-alone indicator of cognitive insufficiency or brain dysfunction. Particularly relevant in this last regard is the fact that, although the Bender provides useful information concerning aspects of visual organization and perceptual-motor coordination, it does not encompass the broad range of cognitive processes that constitute neuropsychological functioning. Sufficiently broad measurement to warrant neuropsychological inferences awaited the development of test batteries designed for this purpose.

Neuropsychological Test Batteries

The inception of broadly based and multifaceted test batteries for assessing neuropsychological functioning can be credited to the efforts of Ward Halstead (1908–1969), who in 1935 established a laboratory at the University of Chicago for the purpose of studying the effects of brain damage. Halstead's observations convinced him that brain damage produces a wide range of cognitive, perceptual, and sensorimotor deficits that cannot be identified by any single psychological test. He accordingly devised numerous tasks for measuring various aspects of cerebral functioning. In subsequent collaboration with one of his graduate students, Ralph Reitan, he gradually reduced the number of these tasks to seven for which empirically determined cutoff scores showed good promise for distinguishing normal from impaired brain functioning. This set of tasks became formalized as the Halstead-Reitan Neuropsychological Test Battery (HRB) in the 1950s and continues to have a major place in neuropsychological assessment (see Reitan & Wolfson, 1993). Developed originally with adults, the HRB was later extended downward for children age 9 to 15 (Halstead Neuropsychological Test Battery for Children and Allied Procedures) and age 5 to 9 (Reitan-Indiana Neuropsychological Test Battery for Children).

The primarily quantitative approach to neuropsychological assessment represented by the HRB stimulated considerable research and attracted to assessment practice a substantial contingent of brain-behavior scientists who might not otherwise have become directly involved in clinical work. Also exerting a lasting influence on assessment methods was a qualitative approach to identifying neuropsychological impairment, which stemmed from the work of Alexander Luria (1902–1977) in the Soviet Union. Luria believed that more could be learned from behavioral features of how people deal with test materials than from the scores they earn, and he accordingly emphasized measures designed to maximize opportunities for respondents to demonstrate various kinds of behavior he considered relevant in diagnosing brain dysfunction.

In Luria's approach, conclusions are based less on psychometric data than on an examiner's observations and inferences. Although Luria's testing methods and his theoretical formulation of functional systems in the brain date from the 1930s, it was not until his work was first translated into English in the 1960s that his seminal contributions to neuropsychology first became widely appreciated. The initial organization of his procedures into a formal test manual was published in the 1970s (Christensen, 1975), and further standardization and validation of his measures during the 1980s resulted in publication of the Luria-Nebraska Neuropsychological Battery (LNNB; Golden, Purisch, & Hammeke, 1985).

The face of neuropsychological assessment and the uses to which it is put have gradually changed since the early work that led to the Halstead-Reitan and Luria-Nebraska batteries. Consistent with the underlying premise of both batteries that identification of brain dysfunction requires assessment of a range of cognitive functions, many specifically focused measures of concept formation, memory, psychomotor, language, and other related capacities were designed for use instead of or as supplements to these batteries. The specific measures most commonly used by contemporary neuropsychologists include the Wechsler Memory Scale, the Boston Naming Test, the Verbal Fluency Test, the Wisconsin Card Sorting Test, the California Verbal Learning Test, the Rey-Osterreith Complex Figure Test, the Stroop Neuropsychological Screening Test, and two components of the HRB, the Finger Tapping Test and the Trail Making Test (Butler et al., 1991; Camara et al., 2000; for further information concerning these and other neuropsychological assessment instruments, see Lezak, 1995; Spreen & Strauss, 1998).

Along with benefiting from the availability of increasingly refined measures, neuropsychological examiners began as early as the 1950s to move beyond what had been their original focus in applied practice, which was helping to determine whether a patient's complaints were "functional" in nature (i.e., psychologically determined) or "organic" (i.e., resulting from central nervous system dysfunction). Instead of inferring from test data merely the likelihood of a patient's having a brain lesion, skilled neuropsychologists became proficient in identifying which side of the brain and which lobe were likely to contain the lesion. Over time, however, the development of sophisticated radiographic techniques for determining the presence, location, and laterality of brain damage rendered neuropsychological tests all but superfluous for this purpose, except as screening measures. Concurrently, on the other hand, contemporary neuropsychological assessment became increasingly valuable in professional practice by reverting to the purpose Halstead originally had in mind back in the 1930s: namely, evaluating an individual's strengths and weaknesses across a broad range of perceptual, cognitive, language, and sensorimotor functions.

With its current focus on the measurement of functioning capacities, neuropsychological assessment provides useful information concerning what people can be expected to do in educational, occupational, and other everyday life activities. Armed with this information, psychologists and the people to whom they consult can predict degrees of success and failure in these activities, identify what kinds of skill improvements are needed to enhance success level, and propose types of intervention or training that will be likely to enhance these deficient skills in the particular person being evaluated. In addition to basing performance predictions and treatment plans on the nature and extent of functioning deficits associated with brain damage from whatever source, neuropsychological examiners can use retesting data to monitor changes in functioning capacity over time. Refined measures of neuropsychological functioning can help to assess the rate and amount of declining capacity in conditions that involve progressive deterioration, and they can likewise quantify the pace of progress in persons recovering from brain disease or injury. Neuropsychological assessment has consequently become common practice in diverse applied settings ranging from forensic consultation to rehabilitation planning.

MEASURING ACHIEVEMENT, APTITUDES, AND INTERESTS

As noted in previous sections of the chapter, intellectual and personality assessment emerged largely out of a perceived necessity for administrators to make decisions about people, specifically with respect to their educational requirements and their eligibility for military service. By contrast, methods of assessing achievement, aptitudes, and interests were developed primarily to help people make decisions about themselves. To be sure, measures of what a person is able to do or is interested in doing can be used to determine class placement in the schools or personnel selection in organizations. More commonly, however, these measures have been used to help people plan their educational and vocational future on the basis of what appear to be their abilities and interests.

Early formulations identified tests of achievement as ways of measuring the effects of learning, as distinguished from "native ability" that was independent of learning and measured by aptitude and intelligence tests. There remains a general consensus that aptitude tests serve to predict a person's potential for improved performance following education or training in some endeavor, whereas achievement tests serve to evaluate the performance level attained at a particular point in time. It is also widely agreed, however, that "aptitude test" scores are influenced by learning and life experience as well as inborn talents, and that "achievement test" scores identify future potential as well as present accomplishment. Accordingly, what respondents display on both kinds of tests

is the extent to which they have developed certain kinds of abilities, and little purpose is served by rigid distinctions between these types of measures (see Anastasi & Urbina, 1997, chap. 17). With this in mind, the discussion that follows traces briefly the development of four measures of achievement/aptitude and interest that have deep roots in the history of assessment psychology and enjoy continued widespread use: the Wide-Range Achievement Test, the Strong Interest Inventory, the Kuder Occupational Interest Survey, and the Holland Self-Directed Search.

Wide-Range Achievement Test

In the United States, formal achievement testing began in the schools during the early 1920s. Tests of specific competencies (e.g., spelling) had been developed prior to that time, but group-administered batteries for assessing a broad range of academic skills began with the 1923 publication of the Stanford Achievement Test (SAT), which was designed for use with elementary school students. This was followed in 1925 by the Iowa High School Content Examination, later called the Iowa Test of Basic Skills, designed for use with older students. Contemporary versions of the Stanford and Iowa scholastic achievement measures remain widely used for group testing in elementary and secondary schools.

Individual assessment of academic skills can be traced to the late 1930s, when Joseph Jastak (1901–1979), then at Columbia University, became acquainted with David Wechsler's work on developing scales for the Wechsler-Bellevue. Jastak came to the conclusion that fully adequate assessment of cognitive functioning required supplementing Wechsler's scales with some measures of basic learning skills, especially reading, writing, and calculating. To this end, he began constructing measures that involved recognition and pronunciation of words, a written spelling test, and a written arithmetic test. An instrument comprising these three measures was published as the Wide-Range Achievement Test (WRAT) in 1946 (Jastak, 1946). Later versions of this instrument, consisting of essentially the same reading, spelling, and arithmetic tests as the original, have appeared as the WRAT-R (Jastak & Wilkinson (1984) and the WRAT3 (Wilkinson, 1993).

In common with most of the other measures discussed in this chapter, the WRAT has been remarkable for its longevity and widespread use. Its normative data make it applicable for age 5 through adulthood, and it has become a standard assessment tool not only in academic settings but in clinical and neuropsychological practice. The previously cited survey of test usage by Camara et al. (2000) show the WRAT as the seventh most frequently used test by clinical psychologists and ninth most frequently used test by neuropsychologists.

Strong Interest Inventory

During the academic year 1919–1920, E. K. Strong Jr. (1884–1963) attended a graduate seminar on interest measurement while attending the Carnegie Institute of Technology. What he learned in this seminar peaked his curiosity about whether interests could be measured in ways that would predict what kinds of occupations a person would find enjoyable. In pursuit of this goal, Strong first developed a list of statements about various activities that test respondents could endorse as something they liked or disliked to do. He then keyed these statements to different occupations on the basis of how people employed in these occupations responded to them. This latter procedure introduced empirical keying methodology to interest measurement, just as Hathaway and McKinley would later introduce it to personality measurement in constructing the MMPI. Several years of developmental work resulted in the publication of the Strong Vocational Interest Blank (SVIB) (Strong, 1927). For persons taking this test, the results provided direct information concerning the extent to which their patterns of interests were similar to or different from those of people working as lawyers, teachers, production managers, and the like.

Like other self-report inventories that have found an enduring place in assessment psychology, the SVIB has been extensively revised since its original publication. The number of occupations in its empirical base has been increased substantially, its initially strictly empirical approach to interpreting the implications of its scale scores has been amplified by theoretical perspectives on the classification of occupational interests, and its name has evolved into the Strong Interest Inventory (SII) (Hansen & Campbell, 1985; Harmon, Hansen, Borgen, & Hammer, 1994). Stable since its inception, however, has been the status of Strong's instrument as the most frequently used among all interest inventories.

Kuder Occupational Interest Survey

Frederic Kuder (1903–2000) set about measuring occupational interests differently from Strong in two respects. First, instead of presenting individual items to be endorsed as "like" or "dislike," he constructed groups of three alternative activities and asked respondents to indicate which of each triad they would most prefer to do. Second, instead of scoring respondents' preferences for their relevance to specific occupations, he developed scales for relating them to general areas of interest, including Outdoor, Mechanical, Computational, Scientific, Persuasive, Artistic, Literary, Musical, Social Service, and Clerical. A measure embodying these characteristics was published as the Kuder Personal Preference Record

(Kuder, 1939) with scales for seven areas of interest. As an alternative to the Strong, the Kuder pointed less directly to specific occupations that respondents should consider but provided more information about personal characteristics that would be likely to have a bearing on whether they would enjoy certain kinds of work.

Kuder's measure was expanded in subsequent revisions to feature 20 broad interest areas, a downward extension for use with elementary and high school students, and its current name, the Kuder Occupational Interest Survey (KOIS; Kuder & Zytowski, 1991). Paralleling the evolution of the SVIB from a strictly occupationally scaled measure to one that incorporates as well a theoretically based classification of occupational interests, the KOIS now includes some occupational as well as basic interest scores.

Holland Self-Directed Search

Like Strong and Kuder before him, John Holland began his work on measuring vocational interests as an empiricist, concerned with collecting data on likes, dislikes, and preferences that would have predictive value for successful occupational choice. Early on, however, he opted for a rational-empirical approach to scale construction in which variables are selected on the basis of some guiding concepts and empirical testing with criterion groups is employed only secondarily to refine and revise item content. Holland's guiding concepts were rooted in his belief that occupational preferences derive from a person's self-concept and personality style, and the first product of his approach was the Vocational Preference Inventory (VPI; Holland, 1953). The VPI yielded scale scores related to broad aspects of personality styles or attitudes, and in subsequent revisions the core VPI scales evolved into the following six: Realistic (R), Investigative (I), Artistic (A), Social (S), Enterprising (E), and Conventional (C) (Holland, 1985). Some additional empirically derived scales were added to the instrument, but the RIASEC group became the model on which Holland elaborated an influential personality-based theory of career choice and satisfaction (Holland, 1966). Holland postulated that every individual's personality comprises some combination of these six styles, and he maintained that the extent to which each style is present provides a personality description that has direct implications for career planning.

Holland later used this model to design the Self-Directed Search (SDS), which generates scale scores for the RIASEC components and offers suggestions concerning the kinds of occupations for which persons with various scale combinations might find themselves suitable (Holland, 1979; Holland, Fritzsche, & Powell, 1994). A unique feature of the

SDS is a manual that instructs respondents not only in how to self-administer the test but also in how to interpret the results for themselves. Although in actual practice SDS results are typically reviewed with an assessment professional, the self-interpretation guidelines have the advantage of enriching a respondent's engagement in and understanding of a vocational counseling process.

LOOKING AHEAD

Having opened with the words of one English author, this chapter can fittingly close with the words of another: "It was the best of times; it was the worst of times," wrote Charles Dickens in beginning *A Tale of Two Cities.* Assessment psychology has arrived at the best and worst of times following a long and distinguished history. As has been noted, the roots of scientific and professional interest in assessing individual differences reach almost as far back as the inception of psychology as a science and preceded its initial applications in applied practice. Advances in assessment methods were psychology's main way of responding to public and national needs during the first half of the twentieth century, and applied psychology was largely defined during this time by assessment conducted in clinical, educational, and organizational settings. Students interested in practicing or studying aspects of applied psychology were routinely trained in assessment methods of various kinds, and being a competent assessor was generally considered an integral part of being a competent psychological practitioner.

As reviewed elsewhere in the present volume and in Volume 10 of this Handbook, applied psychology and the place of assessment in it changed dramatically during the second half of the twentieth century. Practicing psychologists embraced many new roles as therapists and consultants, and their primary work settings evolved from a narrow range of institutions into a broad panoply of attractive opportunities in independent practice and in forensic, health care, governmental, and other agencies that came to appreciate the knowledge and skills that psychologists can bring to bear. Consonant with these new directions in practice, assessment came to play a lesser part than before in what applied psychologists did, and many practitioners chose not to include assessment among the services they offered.

Despite reducing the predominance of assessment, however, these practice changes did not bring bad times with them. To the contrary, the beginning of the twenty-first century is in many respects the best of times for assessment psychology, which more than ever before is a progressive, dynamic, intriguing, challenging, and potentially rewarding

field of scientific and professional endeavor. A recent survey by the American Psychological Association Practice Directorate has indicated that, after psychotherapy, assessment is the second most frequent service provided by psychologists across various practice settings. Respondents to this survey working in independent practice or in health care or government settings reported spending 15% to 23% of their time doing assessment, and there appears to be a stable cadre of persons in both academic and practice positions who identify themselves primarily as assessment psychologists (Phelps, Eisman, & Kohout, 1998). Organizations like the Society for Personality Assessment with more that 2,500 members and the National Academy of Neuropsychologists with more than 3,000 members are flourishing, as are practice specialties in which assessment plays a central role, including not only neuropsychology but forensic psychology and school psychology as well.

The thriving test publishing business bears further witness to widespread use of many different kinds of assessment methods. There is a steady stream of new instruments, revisions of older instruments, updated normative reference data, and advances in computer-based test interpretation with which assessment psychologists must keep current. Competence in assessment cannot be maintained by employing yesterday's methods; only by incorporating rapidly emerging improvements in assessment methods can practitioners meet ethical standards for competent practice (see Weiner, 1989).

The present-day vigor of assessment psychology is reflected not only in its applications but in a burgeoning literature as well. There are more quality journals, textbooks, and handbooks concerned with assessment available now than at any time in the past. The subscriber-selected journals presently abstracted in the American Psychological Association's *PsycSCAN: Clinical Psychology* include in alphabetical order *Assessment, Journal of Clinical and Experimental Neuropsychology, Journal of Clinical Neuropsychology, Journal of Personality Assessment,* and *Psychological Assessment,* and also widely referenced are the journals *Archives of Clinical Neuropsychology, Behavioral Assessment,* and *Journal of Behavioral Assessment.* The literature includes an international array of publications as well (e.g., the *European Journal of Psychological Assessment,* official organ of the European Association of Psychological Assessment, and the *International Journal of Testing,* official organ of the International Test Commission), and published research findings are constantly expanding knowledge concerning the psychometric foundations of psychological assessment methods and the benefits that derive from their appropriate use. Noteworthy in this latter regard are detailed reports by the previously mentioned American Psychological

Association Psychological Assessment Work Group that document the validity of a broad range of assessment methods and their utility in clinical health care and other applied settings (Kubiszyn et al., 2000; Meyer et al., 2001).

And yet these are also trying times for assessment, due primarily to negative forces operating from outside psychology and from within our own ranks as well. From the outside, psychological assessment practice has been buffeted by the priorities placed by managed care agencies on delivering health services in the quickest and least expensive way possible. Such priorities severely restrict support for complex and time-consuming evaluation procedures conducted by doctoral level professionals. In common with other health care professionals specializing in evaluation procedures, assessment psychologists doing primarily clinical work have had their practices curtailed by the advent of managed care, and there has in recent years been some decline in the frequency with which comprehensive multimethod assessments using full-length measures are conducted (Eisman et al., 2000; Piotrowski, 1999; Piotrowski, Belter, & Keller, 1998).

Within psychology's ranks, contemporary trends in graduate education have compromised the caliber of assessment training provided in many psychology programs. Striving to achieve breadth and diversity in a crowded curriculum, graduate faculty have been prone to undervalue assessment skills, to disregard the unique significance of assessment for psychology's professional identity, and to consider internship centers responsible for assessment training. These attitudes have been reflected in reduced course offerings and decreased requirements in assessment, sometimes consisting of little more than exposure to the mechanics of a few selected tests, without hands-on experience in integrating assessment data collected from multiple sources into carefully crafted written reports. Recent surveys of internship directors identify considerable dissatisfaction on their part with the assessment training students are receiving in many graduate programs, and they report that the majority of graduate students arriving at their centers come poorly prepared to conduct evaluations (see Clemence & Handler, 2001; Stedman, Hatch, & Schoenfeld, 2000).

What lies ahead for assessment psychology? Although definitely wounded by managed care, the field does not appear to have sustained any life-threatening injuries. The chapters in Volume 10 of the Handbook attest the continuing breadth and vitality of the field, in productive research as well as useful applications, and practitioners on the average appear to have had moderate success in finding sufficient demand for their services. Hence, although health maintenance organizations have posed a distinct threat to the viability of comprehensive assessment and disrupted the professional

lives of many psychologists, there is reason to believe that both quality assessment and its practitioners are succeeding in weathering this storm.

Of greater concern than managed care is the matter of how and where the next generation of potential researchers and practitioners will be trained in assessment psychology. No matter how well-intended, the argument that assessment training belongs in internships rather than in graduate programs poses a more serious threat to the future of assessment psychology than issues of how fees for service will be paid. Taking assessment out of the graduate curriculum separates it from its academic base and discourages students from becoming involved in or enthusiastic about assessment-related research. Relegating assessment training to the internship—which means in many cases that the internship center must provide basic instruction in assessment methods before interns can even begin to conduct comprehensive evaluations—restricts the time available for students to develop even minimal competence as assessors. A further argument sometimes heard, that assessment competence is a specialized skill to be acquired by interested students in postdoctoral programs or workshops, is even more ill-advised. Assessment being learned mainly as a postdoctoral specialty would divorce the field even further from its research base and subtract it even further from the core content of psychology with which graduate students are made familiar.

Needed now and in the years ahead, then, to perpetuate the scientific and professional advancement of assessment psychology, is enlightened orchestration of graduate education. Graduate programs should be carefully crafted to acquaint students with the nature of assessment psychology and its place in psychology's history; to provide opportunities for students to become involved in assessment research and to gain appreciation for the practical value of good assessment; and, for students in applied areas, to include pre-internship experience in conducting multimethod psychological evaluations and integrating the data obtained from them. Only then will assessment psychology be able in the future as in the past to contribute to expanded understanding of human behavior and the delivery of helpful psychological services.

REFERENCES

Ackerman, M. J., & Ackerman, M. C. (1997). Custody evaluation practices: A survey of experienced professionals (revisited). *Professional Psychology, 28,* 137–145.

American Psychiatric Association. (2000). *Diagnostic and statistical manual of mental disorders* (4th ed., text rev.). Washington, DC: Author.

Anastasi, A., & Urbina, S. (1997). *Psychological testing* (7th ed.). Upper Saddle River, NJ: Prentice-Hall.

Archer, R. P., & Newsom, C. R. (2000). Psychological test usage with adolescent clients: A survey. *Assessment, 7,* 227–235.

Atkinson, J. W., & Feather, N. T. (1966). *A theory of achievement motivation.* New York: Wiley.

Bellack, A. S., & Hersen, M. (Eds.). (1988). *Behavioral assessment: A practical handbook* (3rd ed.). New York: Pergamon Press.

Bellak, L., & Abrams, D. M. (1997). *The T.A.T., C.A.T., & S.A.T. in clinical use* (6th ed.). Boston: Allyn & Bacon.

Bender, L. (1938). *A visual motor Gestalt test and its clinical uses* (Research Monographs No. 3). New York: American Orthopsychiatric Association.

Bernreuter, R. G. (1931). *The Personality Inventory.* Palo Alto, CA: Consulting Psychologists Press.

Binet, A. (1903). *L'etude expérimental de l'intelligence* [The experimental study of intelligence]. Paris: Schleicher.

Binet, A., & Simon, T. (1905). Methodes nouvelles pour le diagnostic du niveau intellectual des anormaux [New methods for the diagnosis of abnormal intellectual level]. *L'Annee Psychologique, 11,* 193–244.

Boccaccini, M. T., & Brodsky, S. L. (1999). Diagnostic test usage by forensic psychologists in emotional injury cases. *Professional Psychology, 30,* 253–259.

Boll, T. J. (1983). Neuropsychological assessment. In I. B. Weiner (Ed.), *Clinical methods in psychology* (2nd ed., pp. 282–330). New York: Wiley.

Boring, E. G. (1950). *A history of experimental psychology.* New York: Appleton-Century-Crofts.

Borum, R., & Grisso, T. (1995). Psychological test use in criminal forensic evaluations. *Professional Psychology, 26,* 465–473.

Brown, W. R., & McGuire, J. M. (1976). Current psychological assessment practices. *Professional Psychology, 7,* 475–484.

Buck, J. N. (1948). The H-T-P technique: A qualitative and quantitative method. *Journal of Clinical Psychology, 4,* 317–396.

Burns, R. C., & Kaufman, S. H. (1970). *Kinetic Family Drawings (K-F-D): An introduction to understanding children through kinetic drawings.* New York: Brunner/Mazel.

Butcher, J. N., Dahlstrom, W. G., Graham, J. R., Tellegen, A., & Kaemmer, B. (1989). *Minnesota Multiphasic Personality Inventory (MMPI-2): Manual for administration and scoring.* Minneapolis: University of Minnesota Press.

Butcher, J. N., & Rouse, S. V. (1996). Personality: Individual differences and clinical assessment. *Annual Review of Psychology, 47,* 87–111.

Butcher, J. N., Williams, C. L., Graham, J. R., Archer, R., Tellegen, A., Ben-Porath, Y. S., et al. (1992). *MMPI-A manual for administration, scoring, and interpretation.* Minneapolis: University of Minnesota Press.

Butler, M., Retzlaff, P., & Vanderploeg, R. (1991). Neuropsychological test usage. *Professional Psychology, 22,* 510–512.

Camara, W. J., Nathan, J. S., & Puente, A. E. (2000). Psychological test usage: Implications in professional psychology. *Professional Psychology, 31,* 141–154.

Campbell, J. M. (1998). Internal and external validity of seven Wechsler Intelligence Scale for Children: 3rd ed. short forms in a sample of psychiatric inpatients. *Psychological Assessment, 10,* 431–434.

Cattell, J. M. (1890). Mental tests and measurements. *Mind, 15,* 373–380.

Cattell, R. B., Cattell, A. K., & Cattell, H. E. (1993). *Sixteen Personality Factors Questionnaire* (5th ed.). Champaign, IL: Institute for Personality and Abilities Testing.

Christensen, A. L. (1975). *Luria's neuropsychological investigation: Text, manual, and test cards.* New York: Spectrum.

Ciminero, A. R., Calhoun, K. S., & Adams, H. E. (Eds.). (1986). *Handbook of behavioral assessment* (2nd ed.). New York: Wiley.

Clemence, A. J., & Handler, L. (2001). Psychological assessment on internships: A survey of training directors and their expectations for students. *Journal of Personality Assessment, 76,* 18–47.

Costa, P. T., Jr., & McCrae, R. R. (1992). *Revised NEO Personality Inventory (NEO PI–R) and NEO Five-Factor Inventory (NEO-FFI).* Odessa, FL: Psychological Assessment Resources.

Costantino, G., Malgady, R. G., & Rogler, L. H. (1988). *TEMAS (Tell-Me-A-Story) manual.* Los Angeles: Western Psychological Services.

Costello, E. J., Edelbrock, C. S., & Costello, A. J. (1985). Validity of the NIMH Diagnostic Interview Schedule for Children: A comparison between psychiatric and pediatric referrals. *Journal of Abnormal Child Psychology, 13,* 579–595.

Craig, R. J. (Ed.). (1989). *Clinical and diagnostic interviewing.* Northvale, NJ: Aronson.

Cramer, P. (1999). Future directions for the Thematic Apperception Test. *Journal of Personality Assessment, 72,* 74–92.

Dana, R. H. (Ed.). (2000). *Handbook of cross-cultural and multicultural personality assessment.* Mahwah, NJ: Erlbaum.

Darwin, C. (1859). *The origin of species.* London: Murray.

Digman, J. M. (1990). Personality structure: Emergence of the Five-Factor Model. *Annual Review of Psychology, 41,* 417–440.

Donders, J. (1997). A short form of the WISC-III for clinical use. *Psychological Assessment, 9,* 15–20.

Ebbinghaus, H. (1897). Über eine neue methode zur prüfung geistiger fähigkeiten und ihre anwendung bei schulkindern [On a new method for the testing of intellectual capacity and its application by school children]. *Zeitschrift fur Psychologie und Physiologie der Sinnesorgane, 13,* 451–457.

Eisman, E. J., Dies, R. R., Finn, S. E., Eyde, L. D., Kay, G. G., Kubiszyn, T. W., et al. (2000). Problems and limitations in using psychological assessment in the contemporary health care delivery system. *Professional Psychology, 31,* 131–140.

Endicott, J., & Spitzer, R. L. (1978). A diagnostic interview: The schedule for affective disorders and schizophrenia. *Archives of General Psychiatry, 35,* 837–844.

Exner, J. E., Jr. (1993). *The Rorschach: A comprehensive system.* Vol. I. *Basic foundations* (3rd ed.). New York: Wiley.

Folstein, M. F., Folstein, S. E., & McHugh, P. R. (1975). Mini-mental state. *Journal of Psychiatric Research, 12,* 189–198.

Freud, S. (1958). On beginning the treatment (further recommendations on the technique of psychoanalysis-I). In J. Strachey (Ed. & Trans.), *The standard edition of the complete psychological works of Sigmund Freud* (Vol. 12, pp. 123–144). London: Hogarth Press. (Original work published 1913)

Galton, F. (1869). *Hereditary genius: An inquiry into its laws and consequences.* London: Macmillan.

Galton, F. (1883). *Inquiry into human faculty and its development.* London: Macmillan.

Geer, J. H. (1965). The development of a scale to measure fear. *Behaviour Research and Therapy, 3,* 45–53.

Glutting, J., Adams, W., & Sheslow, D. (1999). *Wide Range Intelligence Test.* Wilmington, DE: Wide Range.

Golden, C. J., Purisch, A. D., & Hammeke, T. A. (1985). *Luria-Nebraska Neuropsychological Battery: Forms I and II Manual.* Los Angeles: Western Psychological Services.

Goldfried, M. R., & Kent, R. N. (1972). Traditional vs. behavioral assessment: A comparison of methodological and theoretical assumptions. *Psychological Bulletin, 77,* 409–420.

Goodenough, F. L. (1926). *Measurement of intelligence by drawings.* New York: Harcourt, Brace & World.

Gough, H. G. (1957). *California Psychological Inventory manual.* Palo Alto, CA: Consulting Psychologists Press.

Gough, H. G., & Bradley, P. (1996). *CPI manual* (3rd ed.). Palo Alto, CA: Consulting Psychologists Press.

Handler, L. (1995). The clinical use of drawings. In C. Newmark (Ed.), *Major psychological assessment instruments* (pp. 206–293). Boston: Allyn & Bacon.

Handler, L. (2001). Assessment of men: Personality assessment goes to war by the Office of Strategic Services assessment staff. *Journal of Personality Assessment, 76,* 558–578.

Haney, W. (1981). Validity, vaudeville, and values: A short history of social concerns over standardized testing. *American Psychologist, 36,* 1021–1034.

Hansen, J. C., & Campbell, D. P. (1985). *Manual for the SVIB–SII* (4th ed.). Stanford, CA: Stanford University Press.

Harmon, L. W., Hansen, J. C., Borgen, F. H., & Hammer, A. L. (1994). *Strong Interest Inventory: Applications and technical guide.* Palo Alto, CA: Consulting Psychologists Press.

Harris, D. B. (1963). *Children's drawings as a measure of intellectual maturity.* New York: Harcourt, Brace & World.

Hathaway, S. R., & McKinley, J. C. (1943). *The Minnesota Multiphasic Personality Inventory manual.* New York: Psychological Corporation.

Haynes, S. N., & O'Brien, W. O. (2000). *Principles of behavioral assessment.* New York: Kluwer Academic/Plenum.

Hiller, J. B., Rosenthal, R., Bornstein, R. F., Berry, D. T. R., & Brunell-Neuleib, S. (1999). A comparative meta-analysis of Rorschach and MMPI validity. *Psychological Assessment, 11,* 278–296.

Holland, J. L. (1953). *Manual for the Vocational Preference Inventory.* Palo Alto, CA: Consulting Psychologists Press.

Holland, J. L. (1966). *The psychology of vocational choice.* Waltham, MA: Blaisdell.

Holland, J. L. (1979). *The Self-Directed Search professional manual.* Palo Alto, CA: Consulting Psychologists Press.

Holland, J. L. (1985). *Vocational Preference Inventory: Professional manual.* Odessa, FL: Psychological Assessment Resources.

Holland, J. L., Fritzsche, B. A., & Powell, A. B. (1994). *The Self-Directed Search (SDS) Technical manual.* Odessa, FL: Psychological Assessment Resources.

Jastak, J. (1946). *Wide Range Achievement Test.* Wilmington, DE: C. L. Story.

Jastak, J., & Wilkinson, G. (1984). *Wide Range Achievement Test-Revised.* Wilmington, DE: Jastak Associates.

Jung, C. G. (1916). The association method. *American Journal of Psychology, 21,* 219–269.

Kallman, W. M., & Feuerstein, M. (1977). Psychophysiological procedures. In A. R. Ciminero, K. S. Calhoun, & H. E. Adams (Ed.), *Handbook of behavioral assessment* (pp. 329–366). New York: Wiley.

Kamphaus, R. W., Petoskey, M. D., & Rowe, E. W. (2000). Current trends in psychological testing of children. *Professional Psychology, 31,* 155–164.

Karson, S., & O'Dell, J. W. (1989). The 16 PF. In C. S. Newmark (Ed.), *Major psychological assessment instruments* (Vol. 2, pp. 45–66). Boston: Allyn & Bacon.

Kaufman, A. S. (1990). *Assessing adolescent and adult intelligence.* Boston: Allyn & Bacon.

Kaufman, A. S. (1994). *Intelligent testing with the WISC-III.* New York: Wiley.

Kaufman, A. S., & Kaufman, N. L. (1983). *Interpretive manual for the Kaufman Assessment Battery for Children.* Circle Pines, MN: American Guidance Service.

Kaufman, A. S., & Kaufman, N. L. (1990). *Kaufman Brief Intelligence Test.* Circle Pines, MN: American Guidance Service.

Kaufman, A. S., & Kaufman, N. L. (1993). *Interpretive manual for the Kaufman Adolescent and Adult Intelligence Test.* Circle Pines, MN: American Guidance Service.

Kelley, G. A. (1955). *The psychology of personal constructs.* New York: Norton.

Kent, G. H., & Rosanoff, A. (1910). A study of association in insanity. *American Journal of Insanity, 67,* 37–96, 317–390.

Koppitz, E. M. (1968). *Psychological evaluation of children's human figure drawings.* New York: Grune & Stratton.

Koppitz, E. M. (1975). *The Bender Gestalt Test for young children. Vol. 2: Research and applications*. New York: Grune & Stratton.

Kubiszyn, T. W., Finn, S. E., Kay, G. G., Dies, R. R., Meyer, G. J., Eyde, L. D., et al. (2000). Empirical support for psychological assessments in clinical health care settings. *Professional Psychology, 31,* 119–130.

Kuder, G. F. (1939). *Kuder Preference Record: Form A*. Chicago: University of Chicago Press.

Kuder, G. F., & Zytowski, D. G. (1991). *Kuder Occupational Interest Survey Form DD: General manual* (3rd ed.). Monterey, CA: CTB Macmillan/McGraw-Hill.

Lacks, P. (1998). *Bender Gestalt screening for brain dysfunction* (2nd ed.). New York: Wiley.

LaFortune, K. A., & Carpenter, B. N. (1998). Custody evaluations: A survey of mental health professionals. *Behavioral Sciences and the Law, 16,* 207–224.

Lees-Haley, P. R., Smith, H. H., Williams, C. W., & Dunn, J. T. (1995). Forensic neuropsychological test usage: An empirical survey. *Archives of Clinical Neuropsychology, 11,* 45–51.

Lezak, M. D. (1995). *Neuropsychological assessment* (3rd ed.). New York: Oxford University Press.

Loutit, C. M., & Browne, C. G. (1947). Psychometric instruments in psychological clinics. *Journal of Consulting Psychology, 11,* 49–54.

Lubin, B., Larsen, R. M., & Matarazzo, J. D. (1984). Patterns of psychological test usage in the United States: 1935–1982. *American Psychologist, 39,* 451–454.

Lubin, B., Wallis, R. R., & Paine, C. (1971). Patterns of psychological test usage in the United States: 1935–1969. *Professional Psychology, 2,* 70–74.

Matarazzo, J. D., & Wiens, A. N. (1972). *The interview: Research on its anatomy and structure*. Chicago: Aldine-Atherton.

McArthur, D. S., & Roberts, G. E. (1990). *Roberts Apperception Test for Children manual*. Los Angeles: Western Psychological Services.

McClelland, D. C., Atkinson, J. W., Clark, R. A., & Lowell, E. L. (1953). *The achievement motive*. New York: Appleton-Century-Crofts.

Meyer, G. J., & Archer, R. P. (2001). The hard science of Rorschach research: What do we know and where do we go? *Psychological Assessment, 13,* 486–562.

Meyer, G. J., Finn, S. E., Eyde, L. D., Kay, G. G., Moreland, K. L., Dies, R. R., et al. (2001). Psychological testing and psychological assessment: A review of evidence and issues. *American Psychologist, 56,* 128–165.

Millon, T. (1969). *Modern psychopathology: A biosocial approach to maladaptive learning and functioning*. Philadelphia: Saunders.

Millon, T. (1977). *Millon Clinical Multiaxial Inventory*. Minneapolis, MN: National Computer Systems.

Millon, T. (1994). *Manual for the MCMI–III*. Minneapolis, MN: National Computer Systems.

Millon, T. (1996). *The Millon inventories*. New York: Guilford Press.

Millon, T., & Davis, R. (1993). *Millon Adolescent Clinical Inventory (MACI)*. Minneapolis, MN: National Computer Systems.

Millon, T., Green, C. J., & Meagher, R. B., Jr. (1982). *Millon Adolescent Personality Inventory manual*. Minneapolis, MN: National Computer Systems.

Mischel, W. (1968). *Personality land assessment*. New York: Wiley.

Morey, L. C. (1991). *The Personality Assessment Inventory professional manual*. Odessa, FL: Psychological Assessment Resources.

Morey, L. C. (1996). *An interpretive guide to the Personality Assessment Inventory (PAI)*. Odessa, FL: Psychological Assessment Resources.

Morgan, C. D., & Murray, H. A. (1935). A method for investigating fantasies. *Archives of Neurology and Psychiatry, 34,* 389–406.

Morrison, J. (1993). *The first interview: A guide for clinicians*. New York: Guilford Press.

Muñiz, J., Prieto, G., Almeida, L., & Bartram, D. (1999). Test use in Spain, Portugal, and Latin American countries. *European Journal of Psychological Assessment, 15,* 151–157.

Murray, H. A. (1938). *Explorations in personality*. New York: Oxford University Press.

Murray, H. A. (1971). *Thematic Apperception Test manual*. Cambridge, MA: Harvard University Press. (Original work published 1943)

Naglieri, J. A. (1988). *Draw-a-Person: A quantitative scoring system*. New York: Psychological Corporation.

Naglieri, J. A., McNeish, T. J., & Bardos, A. N. (1991). *Draw-a-Person: Screening procedure for emotional disturbance*. Austin, TX: ProEd.

Office of Strategic Services Assessment Staff. (1948). *Assessment of men*. New York: Rinehart.

Othmer, E., & Othmer, S. C. (1994). *The clinical interview using DSM-IV. Vol. 1: Fundamentals*. Washington, DC: American Psychiatric Association.

Otis, J. A. (1923). *Otis Classification Test*. Yonkers, NY: World.

Pascal, G. R., & Suttell, B. J. (1951). *The Bender Gestalt Test: Quantification and validity for adults*. New York: Grune & Stratton.

Paul, G. L. (1966). *Insight vs. desensitization in psychotherapy*. Stanford, CA: Stanford University Press.

Phelps, R., Eisman, E. J., & Kohout, J. (1998). Psychological practice and managed care: Results of the CAPP practitioner survey. *Professional Psychology, 29,* 31–36.

Piedmont, R. L. (1998). *The Revised NEO Personality Inventory: Clinical and research applications*. New York: Plenum Press.

Piotrowski, C. (1999). Assessment practices in the era of managed care: Current status and future directions. *Journal of Clinical Psychology, 55,* 787–796.

Piotrowski, C., Belter, R. W., & Keller, J. W. (1998). The impact of "managed care" on the practice of psychological testing: Preliminary findings. *Journal of Personality Assessment, 70,* 441–447.

Piotrowski, C., & Keller, J. W. (1989). Psychological testing in outpatient mental health facilities: A national study. *Professional Psychology, 20,* 423–425.

Pope, B. (1979). *The mental health interview: Research and application.* New York: Pergamon Press.

Psychological Corporation. (1999). *Wechsler Abbreviated Scale of Intelligence.* San Antonio, TX: Author.

Puig-Antich, J., & Chambers, W. (1978). *The schedule for affective disorders and schizophrenia for school age children.* New York: New York State Psychiatric Institute.

Reitan, R. M., & Wolfson, D. (1993). *The Halstead-Reitan Neuropsychological Test Battery: Theory and clinical interpretation.* Tucson, AZ: Neuropsychology Press.

Robins, L. N., Helzer, J. E., Croughan, J. L., & Ratcliff, K. S. (1981). National Institute of Health Diagnostic Interview Schedule. *Archives of General Psychiatry, 38,* 381–389.

Rogers, C. R. (1942). *Counseling and psychotherapy.* Boston: Houghton Mifflin.

Rogers, C. R. (1951). *Client-centered therapy.* Boston: Houghton Mifflin.

Rogers, R. (2001). *Handbook of diagnostic and structure interviewing.* New York: Guilford Press.

Rohde, A. R. (1946). Explorations in personality by the sentence completion method. *Journal of Applied Psychology, 30,* 169–181.

Rohde, A. R. (1948). A note regarding the use of the sentence completion test in military installations since the beginning of World War II. *Journal of Consulting Psychology, 12,* 190–193.

Rorschach, H. (1942). *Psychodiagnostics: A diagnostic test based on perception.* New York: Grune & Stratton. (Original work published 1921)

Rosenthal, R., Hiller, J. B., Bornstein, R. F., Berry, D. T. R., & Brunell-Neuleib, S. (2001). Meta-analytic methods, the Rorschach, and the MMPI. *Psychological Assessment, 13,* 449–551.

Rotter, J. B., Lah, M. I., & Rafferty, J. E. (1992). *Manual: Rotter Incomplete Sentences Blank* (2nd ed.). Orlando, FL: Psychological Corporation.

Rotter, J. B., & Wickens, D. D. (1948). The consistency and generality of ratings of social aggressiveness made from observations of role playing situations. *Journal of Consulting Psychology, 12,* 234–239.

Ryan, J. J., & Ward, L. C. (1999). Validity, reliability, and standard errors of measurement for two seven-subtest forms of the Wechsler Adult Intelligence Scale–III. *Psychological Assessment, 11,* 207–211.

Spitzer, R. L., Endicott, J., & Robins, E. (1978). Research diagnostic criteria: Rationale and reliability. *Archives of General Psychiatry, 35,* 773–782.

Spitzer, R. L., Williams, J. B. W., & Gibbon, M. (1987). *Structured clinical interview for DSM-III-R.* New York: New York State Psychiatric Institute.

Spreen, O., & Strauss, E. (1998). *A compendium of neuropsychological tests* (2nd ed.). New York: Oxford.

Stedman, J. M., Hatch, J. P., & Schoenfeld, L. S. (2000). Preinternship preparation in psychological testing and psychotherapy: What internship directors say they expect. *Professional Psychology, 31,* 321–326.

Stern, W. (1914). *The psychological methods of testing intelligence.* Baltimore: Warwick & York.

Stinnett, T. A., Havey, J. M., & Oehler-Stinnett, J. (1994). Current test usage by practicing school psychologists: A national survey. *Journal of Psychoeducational Assessment, 12,* 331–350.

Strong, E. K., Jr. (1927). *Vocational Interest Blank.* Stanford, CA: Stanford University Press.

Sullivan, H. S. (1954). *The psychiatric interview.* New York: Norton.

Sundberg, N. D. (1961). The practice of psychological testing in clinical services in the United States. *American Psychologist, 16,* 79–83.

Suzuki, L. A., Ponterotto, J. G., & Meller, P. J. (Eds.). (2000). *The handbook of multicultural assessment* (2nd ed.). New York: Wiley.

Terman, L. M. (1916). *The measurement of intelligence.* Boston: Houghton Mifflin.

Thorndike, R. L. (1959). The California Psychological Inventory: A review. In O. K. Buros (Ed.), *Fifth mental measurements yearbook* (pp. 742–744). Highland Park, NJ: Gryphon Press.

Thorndike, R. L., Hagen, E. P., & Sattler, J. M. (1986). *Stanford-Binet Intelligence Scale: Guide for administering and scoring the 4th ed.* Chicago: Riverside.

Trzepacz, P. T., & Baker, R. W. (1993). *The psychiatric mental status examination.* New York: Oxford University Press.

Viglione, D. J., & Hilsenroth, M. J. (2001). The Rorschach: Facts, fictions, and future. *Psychological Assessment, 13,* 452–471.

Ward, L. C. (1990). Prediction of Verbal, Performance, and Full Scale IQs from seven subtests of the WAIS–R. *Journal of Clinical Psychology, 46,* 436–440.

Watkins, C. E., Jr., Campbell, V. L., Nieberding, R., & Hallmark, R. (1995). Contemporary practice of psychological assessment by clinical psychologists. *Professional Psychology, 26,* 54–60.

Wechsler, D. (1939). *Measurement of adult intelligence.* Baltimore: Williams & Wilkins.

Wechsler, D. (1949). *Manual for the Wechsler Intelligence Scale for Children.* New York: Psychological Corporation.

Wechsler, D. (1967). *Manual for the Wechsler Preschool and Primary Scale of Intelligence.* New York: Psychological Corporation.

Wechsler, D. (1989). *Manual for the Wechsler Preschool and Primary Scale of Intelligence–Revised.* New York: Psychological Corporation.

Wechsler, D. (1991). *Manual for the Wechsler Intelligence Scale for Children* (3rd ed.). New York: Psychological Corporation.

Wechsler, D. (1997). *WAIS–III administration and scoring manual.* San Antonio, TX: Psychological Corporation.

Weiner, I. B. (1989). On competence and ethicality. *Journal of Personality Assessment, 53,* 827–831.

Weiner, I. B. (1998). *Principles of Rorschach interpretation.* Mahwah, NJ: Erlbaum.

Weiner, I. B. (2001). Advancing the science of psychological assessment: The Rorschach Inkblot Method as exemplar. *Psychological Assessment, 13,* 423–432.

Westen, D., Lohr, N., Silk, K., Kerber, K., & Goodrich, S. (1985). *Object relations and social cognition TAT scoring manual.* Ann Arbor: University of Michigan.

Wilkinson, G. S. (1993). *Wide Range Achievement Test–3.* Wilmington, DE: Wide Range.

Wilson, M. S., & Reschly, D. J. (1996). Assessment in school psychology training and practice. *School Psychology Review, 25,* 9–23.

Woodworth, R. S. (1920). *Personal data sheet.* Chicago: Stoelting.

CHAPTER 15

Abnormal Psychology

WINIFRED B. MAHER AND BRENDAN A. MAHER

PRELIMINARY ISSUES 303
  Popular Myths of Psychopathology 304
  Early Attempts at Classification 305
  Legal Views of the Mentally Ill 306
THEORY AND PRACTICE IN THE
  CLASSICAL PERIOD 307
  Classical Medical Theory 307
  Medical and Other Treatments 307
THE MIDDLE AGES TO THE
  EIGHTEENTH CENTURY 310
  Hospitals 311
  The Anatomy of Melancholy 311
  From Animal Spirits to Animal Electricity 312
  From Magnetism and Mesmerism to Hypnosis 313
  Moral Management and the Association Model 314
EIGHTEENTH TO MID-NINETEENTH CENTURY 315
  Asylums of the Era 315
  Advent of Nosological Systems 315
  Brain Pathology Model of Psychopathology and
    Nervous Diseases 316
  Phrenology 317
  Brain Hemisphere Theories 317
LATE NINETEENTH INTO TWENTIETH
  CENTURY 318

Theory of the Evolution of the Brain
  and Psychopathology 318
Social Darwinism 319
Degeneracy Theory 319
Eugenics 320
Early Role of Hypnosis 320
Sigmund Freud and Psychoanalysis 322
Morton Prince and Multiple Personality 324
THE TWENTIETH CENTURY 325
  Treatment Approaches 325
  Experimental Psychopathology 326
  Typologies of Mental Illness 328
  Organic versus Functional Psychoses 329
  Theories of Origin and Research in
    Antisocial Personality 330
  Behaviorism and Behavior Therapy 330
  Recent Approaches 330
  Progress in the Biological Understanding
    of Psychopathology 332
INTO THE TWENTY-FIRST CENTURY 333
REFERENCES 333

In this chapter we present a history of abnormal psychology, now commonly called psychopathology. This must be a partial history, because, although contemporary psychopathology science and practice are amply archived in scientific journals, epidemiological surveys, hospital reports, and government statistics, little of the field's history is well documented. Modern scientific method was not applied to the investigation of disease until the nineteenth century, and it was applied even later to the study of psychopathology. Knowledge was authenticated by the teacher's experience, not by producing objective empirical evidence, impartially gathered, and opened to criticism. Theories about psychopathology and the ways to treat it during earlier periods of history were developed by physicians, philosophers, theologians, and lawyers. Our knowledge is derived from their extant writings, medical treatises, church and legal documents, historical narratives, diaries, and literature.

PRELIMINARY ISSUES

Historians of this field face several major problems, including the definitions of psychopathology and the availability and authenticity of information about the past. Also, any written history of psychopathology must consider how culture and class difference affect definition and treatment of psychopathology, as well as the influences of contemporary external factors in other fields, principally medicine, science, and law.

Broadly speaking, practical definitions of psychopathology include behavior that (a) appears injurious to the interests of the person concerned and/or to others, (b) lacks a rational relationship to the realities of the environment in which it occurs, and (c) has behavioral characteristics that deviate significantly from the norm of the culture. What may appear pathologically deviant in one culture may appear desirable in another. One example is self-flagellation, in which an individual flogs himself with whips until blood flows from his body. Some cultures regard this as a worthy religious practice; in the downtown section of a modern American city, it would most likely be judged pathological.

We must also note that in many cases, the accidental discovery of an effective treatment has spurred the scientific research necessary to understand why the treatment worked. The treatment led to the theory, not vice-versa. In other cases, a treatment derived by logical inference from a theory may survive many years of unimpressive results. Treatment is also constrained by the resources that the patient or the society can command. The poor are treated differently from the rich, a situation not unknown in any branch of medicine and not a form of discrimination directed uniquely at the mentally ill.

The reports of physicians who became famous enough to achieve recognition are not always reliable sources of information. Fame and fortune, then as now, awaited the clinician who could claim cures where none had achieved them before. Clinician self-interest in such cases was a sure obstacle to reliable information about the actual successes and failures of novel treatments. We shall see this phenomenon recur time and time again, from Paracelsus to Mesmer and from psychoanalysis to prefrontal lobotomy. Such a history makes for interesting reading, but it makes difficulties for the historian.

Finally, one of the greatest problems facing the historian is the fact that only exceptional events tend to be recorded while the mass of ordinary events does not, thereby leaving a misleading record of what actually happened most of the time to most of the people. From such a process has arisen a popular history of psychopathology, leaving the serious historian to clarify what did not happen as well as to recount what did.

Popular Myths of Psychopathology

The popular theme in psychopathology is that over the centuries we have become increasingly knowledgeable and humane in our treatment of mental illness. Past beliefs about the origins of psychopathology are seen as mostly unintelligent, and earlier treatment methods as inhumane and ineffective.

An amalgam of these histories runs somewhat thus: From the beginning of mankind, people believed that abnormal behavior was caused by spirit or demon possession. Until approximately the eighteenth century, mental illness elicited superstitious reactions, hostility, maltreatment, and even persecution by the community at large. One exception allowed in this grim scenario is said to have occurred in Greece in the fifth century B.C., when, thanks to one notable physician, Hippocrates, a rational and scientific approach to abnormal psychology abruptly appeared and briefly flourished.

Some texts extend this period to the time of Galen (ca. A.D. 130–200), a Greek physician at the court of the Roman Emperor Marcus Aurelius. They tend to claim that after the collapse of the Roman Empire the fledgling naturalistic, scientific approach to understanding psychopathology was eclipsed by a resurgence of rampant superstition, usually attributed to the retrograde influence of the Christian church. Early in the fifteenth century, so the myth goes, it was a common practice to segregate the mentally ill by putting them on "ships of fools." Before this time Europe had virtually no mental hospitals although thousands of asylums were built to confine lepers, and once leprosy disappeared, the mentally ill were confined in them. Finally, during the eighteenth century, Philippe Pinel (1745–1826) liberated the insane from their chains in the Salpêtrière in Paris and enlightened individuals began moral treatment of the insane in small establishments. Unfortunately, so the story goes, during the nineteenth century these relatively benign institutions grew into giant warehouses where, again, the mentally ill were maltreated. Finally, as a result of the efforts of psychiatrists and psychologists, knowledge of the causes of incrementally improved, culminating in humane scientific understanding and treatment, and the maltreatment of the mentally ill ended.

In fact, improvements in the care of the mentally ill have arisen in part as a result of advances in scientific knowledge, in part by improvement in socioeconomic conditions which, in turn, stem in large part from technological innovations. How people with mental illness were treated in the past depended then, as now, on their social position and their financial resources. It appears that many individuals who posed no danger to themselves or others often had the support and care of their families, were extended shelter by the religious community, or permitted to support themselves by begging.

Treatments accorded in the past must be compared not to conditions today, but to the general conditions of those times. Although past housing conditions for mentally ill people were deplorable by modern standards, so were housing conditions during the same time period for sane poor people. Insane people were sometimes cruelly treated and sane persons accused of heresy, witchcraft, treason, even petty thievery, were also subjected to great cruelties. Demons and other supernatural causes were invoked when naturalistic explanations were inadequate and rational treatments of no avail. We tentatively suggest that before the invention of the microscope, which enabled scientists to see germs, the belief that demons inhabiting the body were responsible for serious bodily and mental ills was not irrational.

Many of these mythical histories have a professional or political agenda. The thesis that the times prior to the eighteenth century were characterized by demonological explanations of mental illness and cruel mistreatment of the mentally ill can be traced primarily to textbooks of psychiatry that promulgated the value of Freudian ideas. The claim that during the fifteenth century the mentally ill were placed on "ships of fools" and sent out to sea derives from Michel Foucault's, *Madness and Civilization: A History of Insanity in the Age of Reason* (1961/1965). Foucault presented his speculations about the historical treatment of the mentally ill to illustrate his conjecture that, in order to define themselves, the dominant group in a culture must exclude others who do not share the aspects they consider most important, reason, in the case of the mentally ill. The fictitious nature of Foucault's ship of fools has been thoroughly demonstrated (Maher & Maher, 1982).

No documentary evidence records prehistoric belief systems; nevertheless, the lack of evidence has not deterred writers of the history of psychopathology from making assertions about the beliefs held by prehistoric peoples regarding the cause and treatment of mental illness. Many such histories open with the statement that prehistoric man believed that deviant behavior was caused by demon-possession and so cut a hole in the skull of a mentally ill person in order to let the demon escape. A photograph of a prehistoric skull with a roughly circular hole in it is presented as evidence for this allegation. This popular myth of the trephined (or trepanned) skull has in it all of the elements of guesswork plus ignorance and indifference to actual evidence that characterize such myths.

Archaeologists have unearthed a large number of such skulls and dated them to the Neolithic period. The holes in the skulls are usually symmetrical and are thought to have been intentionally incised by the surgical technique of trepanning. Thickening of the bone around the margins of the holes in many of these skulls suggests healing and that the patient survived the operation for some time. We do not know the mental state of the patient and no direct evidence explains why the hole was cut. (See MacCurdy (1924) for more on trephining.)

Although we cannot prove wrong the assertion made about the trepanned skulls, neither can we prove it correct. It is based on an *a priori* assumption about prehistoric man first advanced by the French neurologist, Paul Broca (1824–1880), when Neolithic trepanned skulls were found in the 1870s. Broca "felt that primitive man had made these holes in skulls in order to liberate evil spirits who might be causing headaches or epilepsy" (Ackerknecht, 1982, pp. 8–9). It is likely that Broca was influenced by a widely accepted theory of stages advanced by Auguste Comte (1798–1857), the French philosopher/sociologist who founded the school of positivism. Comte (1830–1842),

proposed an inevitable progression in mental development of peoples through three major stages. The first stage is the superstitious theological stage, which progresses through (1) animism (the belief that each object has its own will), (2) polytheism (the belief that demons, spirits, and deities impose themselves on objects), and (3) monotheism (the belief that one God imposes his will on all things).

In the second metaphysical stage it is believed that natural events are caused by occult physical forces. In the third scientific stage, positive knowledge of natural causes replaces superstition and metaphysics, and humans turn to the study of laws "of relations of succession and resemblances" in order to understand events in the natural world. It followed that primitive humans at the animistic stage of reasoning about the world would not react in the same way as civilized humans. Subsequently, interpretations of Darwin's theory of evolution by natural selection published in 1859 reinforced the assumption that prehistoric peoples would have been too intellectually primitive to perform trepanation as a rational surgical technique.

Early Attempts at Classification

For many centuries, the dominant view held that mental illness, although differing in symptoms and severity, is fundamentally one general disorder called melancholy. However, in the seventeenth century, a view began to develop that mental illness is an umbrella term encompassing a number of distinguishable mental diseases. Robert Burton (1651/1927) wrote, "Some confound melancholy and madness, others say melancholy is madness differentiated not in kind but in extent or degree, some acknowledge a multitude of kinds and leave them indefinite." This view became popular after the discovery that mental illness as well as physical diseases differ not only by symptoms but also by cause.

In the nineteenth century, attempts were undertaken to identify and classify types of mental illness on the basis of clusters of symptoms, etiology, course, and response to treatment. The view that psychopathology is a general pathology again emerged in the middle of the twentieth century when learning theorists proposed that psychopathology represents maladaptive responses to stress, and psychoses differ from neuroses on a dimension of severity, unless the pathology had been clearly determined to be caused by a demonstrable lesion of the nervous system.

Today it is again generally held that diagnostically distinct psychopathological disorders exist that differ in symptoms, etiology, course, and response to different kinds of treatment. In 1952, the American Psychiatric Association published the first edition of *The Diagnostic and Statistical Manual of Mental*

Disorders (DSM), which listed 60 diagnostic categories. In subsequent editions the categories have been revised and the number enlarged; the 1968 second edition described 145 mental disorders, the 1977 third edition described 230, and the fourth 1994 edition described about 450.

Legal Views of the Mentally Ill

The legal system has classified psychopathology based on different premises. They include the concept of responsibility for one's actions and the duty of society to protect those who cannot protect themselves. The concept of responsibility is the cornerstone of western law.

Throughout history legislation has been enacted to protect the insane, as well as to protect society from those who are disruptive or violent. Western law pertaining to the mentally ill has its beginnings in the Roman law of Twelve Tables, codified from traditional practices in the fifth century B.C., which provided for the appointment of guardians empowered with authority over those regarded as incompetent to manage their affairs. According to Neaman (1975), the Roman laws of guardianship were designed to protect people and property. The insane and the immature could not legally acquire possessions, nor legally consent and dissent, because they were presumed to lack the capacity to know what they were doing. In cases where an insane person had committed a crime, Roman law held that "an insane person, as well as an infant, is legally incapable of malicious intent and the power to insult, and therefore the action for injuries cannot be brought against them" (p. 90).

Throughout recorded history, laws have been devised to minimize the social impact of mental disorder. Legal records dating from the earliest times indicate that throughout Europe and Great Britain the family and, if family resources were inadequate or unavailable, the community was responsible for the care, maintenance, and supervision of incompetent or deranged individuals. Such persons, if they were harmless to themselves or others, were kept at home, allowed to roam and beg, or were maintained by charity extended by members of the community and the church. Some disruptive mentally ill individuals may have been driven away by their families or community—but we have no idea at all of their numbers. In many places and times, the legal guardians of the insane were held responsible for their actions and for conserving their property. Insane persons considered likely to injure themselves or others could be imprisoned. The antiquity of such measures is indicated by the fact that mental disorders were termed "surveillance diseases" in old Icelandic law (Retterstol, 1975).

Laws that define culpability for criminal actions, as a matter of whether or not individuals are of sound mind and hence responsible for their actions, are based on the doctrine of "free will," a concept developed by St. Augustine (354–430 A.D.) and abandoned in scientific psychology. The doctrine held that the will is governed by the rational intellect, which enables the individual to tell right from wrong, to make judgments, and to choose to act based on rational considerations. Without rational intellect, the individual is not free to act responsibly. It was assumed that the rational intellect is not developed in children before the age of seven, fails to develop in "natural fools," and is lost in the insane. Therefore, children, "natural fools," and the insane are incapable of free will, and cannot be held responsible for the consequence of their actions. Although children, natural fools, and madmen could not be punished for their crimes, it was deemed necessary to supervise and restrain them so they would not pose a problem to society. The principle of diminished responsibility was taken into consideration in assessing the guilt of insane persons for criminal acts and in depriving them of certain civil rights or obligations. Juries readily pardoned guilty persons they considered demonstrably insane both before and after the crime. Proofs of insanity most commonly used in courtrooms were attempted suicide, violent or irrational behavior, and abnormal behavior accompanied by sickness.

Neugebauer (1978) reviewed extensive legislation enacted in medieval England intended to protect the person, property, and civil rights of the mentally ill. The laws distinguished between persons suffering from congenital subnormality and presumably incurable ("natural fools") and those, once normal, who became mentally deranged (*non compos mentis*), for whom recovery might be possible. The Prerogative Regis, dating from the thirteenth century, designated the king as custodian of lands belonging to "natural fools" and any profit therefrom rendered to the rightful heirs; the lands of persons considered *non compos mentis* were to be conserved and returned to the persons if they should come to right mind. Judgment of mental disability relied on common sense methods such as determining ability to perform simple intellectual tasks.

In the nineteenth century the concept of responsibility, and hence culpability in the case of crime, provided the basis for England's McNaughten Rules to handle the legal disposition of criminals judged to be insane. These rules were established after the 1843 trial of Daniel McNaughten in London, which he was found McNaughten not guilty on grounds of insanity for the murder of Edward Drummond, secretary to Sir Robert Peel, the British prime minister. The rules hold that persons who commit crimes while insane are not responsible for them because they lack the rational faculty for telling the difference between right and wrong, and, although such persons must be restrained, they should be treated for their insanity and not punished for the crime. The McNaughten Rules are still applied in Great Britain and in some states of the United States. (See chapter by Brigham & Grisso in this volume.)

THEORY AND PRACTICE IN THE CLASSICAL PERIOD

The humoral/pneumatic theory of disease, which originated in fifth century B.C. Greece and was elaborated by Galen in Rome in the second century, was the dominant medical theory in the Western world until the eighteenth century—an extraordinary longevity.

Classical Medical Theory

What we know about theories of medical practitioners in ancient Greece we have derived from the *Hippocratic Corpus,* a collection of 60 to 70 medical writings that includes theoretical papers on the nature of disease in general and of various illnesses in particular. It contains specifics of diagnosis, descriptions of therapies, case histories intended to teach theory and practice to physicians, and papers apparently written as lectures intended to publicize a physician's work as well as to present to laymen information about how to maintain health. The whole of the *Corpus* is often attributed to the Greek physician Hippocrates (ca. 460–367 B.C.) but, varieties of style of the papers make it evident that they were written over a long time span by various people (Lloyd, 1978).

The theories of disease presented in the *Corpus* are biological and materialistic. No clear demarcation exists between "physical" and "psychological" disease; all disease was attributed to some sort of imbalance in the natural state of the body, which provided an explanation of the hidden cause of diseases. Certain papers emphasized the importance of the humors (fluids) in the body. They conjectured that by a blending process called "pepis" or "coction," various bodily organs convert food into humors, but reached no consensus as to the number or origin of the principal humors although bile and phlegm were usually mentioned. Diagnosis was based on close observation of specific symptoms, especially of every secretion, and changes in the patient's vital forces, nutrition, body heat, mood, and memory.

The theory of humors, elaborated by Galen in the second century, became the basis of medical theory and practice until the eighteenth century. The four humors considered essential for life were blood, phlegm, choler (yellow bile), and melancholer (black bile). They were concocted by various bodily organs from the primal elements taken into the body from the heat of the sun, air breathed, and substances ingested. The humors varied in their qualities along the two axes of hot–cold and moist–dry. Health required a balance of the relative proportions of the humors, and anything that interfered with proper coction of the humors resulted in disease. Three types of madness were distinguished—phrenitis, mania, and melancholia. Phrenitis was diagnosed when fever and delirium were present. Mania was characterized by extreme excitement similar in the absence of fever. Melancholia was differentiated from phrenitis by lack of either excitement or fever and was usually attributed to an excess or corruption of black bile (melancholer). Melancholia could be engendered by psychological stress and could lead to serious physical illness and even death. (The term *melancholia* referred to a specific pathology now called depression. The term *melancholy* evolved to denote a wide spectrum of psychopathology.)

The Doctrine of Pneuma

Since living creatures die when they are deprived of air, it followed that the life force must require a substance in the air breathed, which led to the hypothesis of "pneuma," a superfine material essential to life and growth, in which motion is inherent. It was conjectured that pneuma, distinguished from the psyche or soul, is present at the very beginning of life, assists all physiological and psychological functions, and is renewed by breathing and digestion. Because blood pulses as if impelled by a vital force, it was assumed that pneuma is transported by the blood throughout the body, and further assumed that pneuma is stored in the ventricles of the brain (Brett, 1963). The paper "The Sacred Disease" in the *Hippocratic Corpus* states that the air breathed in leaves behind in the ventricles of the brain "its vigour and whatever pretains to consciousness and intelligence [and,] the movement of the limbs" (Lloyd, 1978, p. 250)—for example, pneuma. "Therefore, when the blood-vessels are shut off from this supply of air by the accumulation of phlegm . . . the patient loses his voice and his wits" (Ibid, p. 243); hence, the brain is the seat of the "sacred" disease (probably epilepsy). Note that at the time, and for many centuries after, the brain tissue itself was not believed to have any psychological function.

Medical and Other Treatments

Treatment consisted of bloodletting and herbal drugs with emetic or purgative properties to remove excess or corrupt humors, and of herbal extracts, nourishing food, and stimulating drinks to augment depleted humors. It was generally believed that opposites are cures for opposites, hence cold packs and cooling drinks for fever, hot drinks and warm blankets for chills, herbal extracts with narcotic properties (such as opium) for agitation and excitement, and extracts with stimulating properties for lethargy. If a disease is caused by a morbid agent, the process of coction normally expels the morbid agent in the feces, urine, and sweat, and the physician helped by administering appropriate laxatives, diuretics, or sudorifics. Diet, exercise, and adequate sleep, subsumed under the concept of "regimen," was considered of paramount importance both in managing disease and maintaining both mental and physical health (Lloyd, 1978).

Theories that attributed psychopathology to the failure to use reason to control emotion, restrain impulse, and regulate conduct date back at least as far as Plato (428–348 B.C.). He is credited with having introduced the concept of the tripartite soul, which, elaborated by Aristotle, persisted for centuries. The function of the rational soul is to seek knowledge and truth; it is intended to govern the spirited soul (mediating sensation and movement), which in turn is intended to govern the appetitive soul (the nutritive and reproductive functions). Eros is the energetic force for all activity and, at its lowest level, is sexual desire. The rational soul can seek knowledge only if Eros is sublimated to higher ends (Plato, 1894a).

The soul, in this line of thinking, can become diseased as a result of bodily disease: "For where the acid and briny phlegm and other bitter and bilious humours wander about in the body, and . . . mingle their own vapours with the motions of the soul . . . they produce all sorts of diseases, and being carried to the three places of the soul, whichever they may severally assail, they create infinite varieties of ill-temper and melancholy. . . ." In Plato's view "excessive pains and pleasures are justly to be regarded as the greatest disease to which the soul is liable . . ." and can cause madness (Plato, 1894b). The intensity of sexual drive can cause mental disorder in both men and women. The idea that sexual deprivation in females is the cause of "all varieties of disease" served down through the centuries to explain hysteria, accompanied by the assumption that hysteria can be cured by sexual intercourse. The view that the passions, or affective excitement (particularly that arising from the sexual passion), are a significant cause of psychopathology first described by Plato, was held until the nineteenth century and appears in *Studies on Hysteria* by Breuer and Freud (1895/1955).

As Rome became the center of power in the Mediterranean world, the various schools of Greek medicine gradually transferred there from Alexandria. By the time the Roman empire had been established, Greek physicians dominated Roman medicine. Physicians separated into various sects, each basing its system of treatment on a different aspect of Greek medical philosophy. Some physicians retained the theory of humors. The pneumatists believed that disturbed pneuma flow in the body caused disease. The methodists, who based their theory on atomism, attributed disease to an abnormal constriction or relaxation of the solid particles of the body. The empirical school renounced theory in favor of devising treatments based on observation. The eclectics took whatever seemed useful to them from the other schools.

Aulus Cornelius Celsus, a first century Roman writer, compiled an encyclopedia of which *De Medicina,* the portion on medicine, survives. The work largely derived from the Hippocratic *Corpus.* It was printed in 1478, translated into English in 1756, and was used by physicians as a medical text into the eighteenth century (Celsus, 1935).

Celsus made the usual distinction between insanity and the delirium of patients suffering from high fever. Some insane persons are sad, others hilarious; some are more readily controlled and rave in words only; others are rebellious and act with violence. Of the latter, some do harm only by impulse whereas others, although appearing sane, seize the occasion for mischief, and their insanity must be detected by the result of their acts. Patients should have pleasant surroundings, be provided with interesting but not overstimulating diversions, and should not be left alone or among people whom they do not know. They should be agreed with, rather than opposed, with the object of turning their mind slowly and imperceptibly from irrational talk to something better. For insane persons duped by phantoms, Celsus recommended purging with black hellebore, a poisonous herb believed to purge black choler. Those who are hilarious should be given white hellebore (another poisonous herb) as an emetic. Massage should be used sparingly with patients who are overcheerful. Insane persons who are deceived by the mind may benefit if forced by fear to consider what they are doing; for example starvation or flogging might force the patient, little by little, to fix his or her attention and learn. (Such treatments, we note, suggest modern methods of aversive conditioning and attempts to train attentional focusing.)

Galen of Pergamon (ca. A.D. 130–201) was considered the greatest of the eclecticist physicians. (We note that Hippocrates' reputation is largely based on Galen's frequent citations as the authority of his own views.) He integrated the doctrine of pneuma into an elaboration of the theory of four humors in which different diseases are caused by different imbalances of the normal equilibrium of the humors and their specific qualities ("dyscrasia"). Galen emphasized that because individuals have characteristic patterns for metabolizing the elements of food, they differ in temperament, which accounts for individual differences in susceptibility to different kinds of disease. Temperament is evident in body type, and it follows that prognosis is improved if the body type is identified.

By Galen's time the existence of nerves had been recognized. Herophilus (ca. 355–280 B.C.) and his contemporary Erasistratus (ca. 330–250 B.C.) had traced some of the nerves to the brain and concluded that nerves must provide the "conduits" for the passage of pneuma to and from the brain, hence nerves must be hollow. They theorized that sensation occurs when pneuma that conveys impressions of the external world flows through the nerves toward pneuma stored in the ventricles of the brain. The flow outward from the brain is directed by the psyche through the nerves to various muscles, inflating them to initiate action. Galen developed the final form of this doctrine to construct a theory of psychophysiology that in its general outline remained influential through the eighteenth century.

According to Galen, pneuma, the basic principle of life, and originates from the general "world spirit." As pneuma ascends through the body to the brain it is progressively refined into natural spirit, vital spirit, and animal spirit. The quality of pneuma could be adversely affected by a variety of agents, including "vicious humors," toxins, poor diet, inadequate sleep. Severe pain and, notably, excessive passions (such as sexual lust, rage, greed, grief, fear, and great joy) interfere with attention, memory, imagination and thought, and could eventuate in melancholy or mania. As had Plato and the Stoic philosophers before him, Galen viewed emotional states as a form of mental disorder, and commented that "the passions have increased in the souls of the majority of men to such a point that they are incurable diseases" (Jackson, 1969, p. 380). Hence a salubrious climate, proper diet, good digestion, adequate sleep, proper exercise, and freedom from perturbation of the soul by the passions are essential to preserve health. Galen recommended that those with mental health disturbed by passions receive education designed to promote self-understanding, governance of the expression of the passions, and capacity to delay acting when in a passionate state in order to reflect and choose a rational course of action. Such education ideally should be provided by a mature man, himself free from passion.

Galen identified three types of melancholia: one in which the brain is directly affected by overheated blood and black bile, one in which the brain is secondarily affected by blood corrupted by black bile throughout the whole body, and one ("hypochondriasis"), in which the brain is secondarily affected by black bile in the abdominal organs (the hypochondrium), particularly in the stomach, which Galen believed to be intimately connected to the brain. Hypochondriasis is characterized by severe digestive disturbances and flatulence; because proper coction of humors was assumed to depend on good digestion, it followed that digestive disorders would be a significant cause of melancholy. The notion of hypochondriacal melancholy was still current in the seventeenth century (see Burton, 1654/1927) and being described in the eighteenth century. By the twentieth century, hypochondriasis had come to mean a morbid concern about one's health.

Melancholy tends to occur in individuals constitutionally inclined to the disorder. Galen observed that melancholy was more common in men but tended to be more serious in women, and that it occurred sometimes in young persons, was uncommon in persons in the prime of life, and was so common in older people that it could be considered an almost inevitable result of advancing age. Individuals who suffer from melancholy are usually, but not always, sad and fearful; some wish to die, others fear death. Symptoms of melancholy described by Galen included incoherent speech, mutism, amnesia, and elaborate delusions. A melancholy patient might be delusional, yet be otherwise sane. Instances of delusions mentioned by Galen include the conviction of a patient that he was made of glass and feared being broken, the belief of another patient that he had no head, and beliefs of being poisoned or chased by demons. Galen's case histories were plagiarized throughout the course of medical and psychiatric history—and were, perhaps, plagiarized by Galen from others before him.

Galen recommended the traditional treatments of bloodletting, purgations, herbal remedies, and a regimen of exercise and nutritious diet, and suggested that sexual intercourse could be beneficial. He is known for his emphasis on the use of drugs (which came to be called "galenicals") in the treatment of disease, although most of the drugs he used were not original with him. Galen discussed hysteria, believed caused by disease of the uterus, which was not considered a form of madness because psychological symptoms were not an essential aspect of the disorder. Although Galen believed that the uterus could be displaced from its normal position, he rejected the ancient idea that the uterus could be freed from its attachments to move about the body. Like earlier medical theorists, Galen believed that hysteria was a disease of unmarried women and widows as a result of their being deprived of sexual intercourse.

Galen's writings were synthesized and elaborated by later Greek authors. Although the medical schools of Athens and Alexandria continued to function at least until the seventh century and some medical treatises, largely based on Galen's teaching were written, interest in scientific medicine declined in Western Europe after the fall of the Roman Empire. Waning interest may have derived from decreasing numbers of students going to medical school in Alexandria and the dramatic increase in those entering the priesthood during the early years of the spread of Christianity. After the fall of Alexandria in 642, knowledge of Greek medicine and other aspects of Greek learning were preserved by Byzantine and Arab authors who translated and further elaborated them. These writings were later translated into Latin in Europe, and as a consequence Galen's doctrines came to dominate medical theory in the western world until well into the eighteenth century.

The humoral theory provided a basis for understanding individual differences in character and patterns of behavior. Although Galen is credited with having emphasized the significance of temperament, Leicester (1974) points out that he did not name the temperamental types applied in the twelfth century by Honorius of Autun who identified them as sanguine, melancholic, choleric, and phlegmatic. By this time temperament had come to refer to characteristic psychological dispositions. Both bodily characteristics and personal traits were believed to be determined within broad limits by an individual's characteristic balance of humors; therefore, to assess body type was to obtain information usefully correlated with character. Although the humoral theory was finally abandoned, the concept of balance of bodily processes as an explanation for a wide range of complex psychological and physiological phenomena is still useful today. For example, the concept of pneuma or animal spirits was a forerunner of our current knowledge that the impulses of the brain are electrical and transmitted by nerve fibers through the biochemical substances known as neurohumors, most recently called neurotransmitters. Classical ideas about melancholer and its correlation with melancholia are precursors of current hypotheses about the causes of serious depressive and schizophrenic disorders.

THE MIDDLE AGES TO THE EIGHTEENTH CENTURY

Sometime in the sixth century, monks began copying and translating available Greek manuscripts. Libraries of important abbeys contained summaries of Galen and other Greek physicians. Until approximately the twelfth century, monks in some monasteries as well as local healers and itinerant doctors provided any medical treatment in the Hippocratic-Galenic tradition. From the eighth to the thirteenth century, Arab and Jewish scholars were preeminent in medicine and science. What came to be known as "Galenism," was based on Arabic syntheses and elaborations of his theories,

dominated Byzantine and Arabic medical theory. Many of these treatises were translated into Latin in the twelfth century and were used as medical texts in Western Europe universities established by the Roman Catholic Church. They were, in fact, a major source of medical knowledge for physicians in Western Europe through the seventeenth century. In addition, many Middle Eastern doctors migrated to Europe bringing knowledge of Arabic science with them. Clark (1984) states that recent research has indicated that by the late sixteenth century, with the tremendous increase in literacy at the time (and, we add, by word of mouth) the average European had at least a partial knowledge of the accepted medical theory and practice.

A major tenet of Christianity was the importance of compassion and charity toward the unfortunate. Hospices were established to provide shelter and succor for the destitute— the orphaned, the aged, the disabled, the chronically ill (including the mentally ill), and the destitute. Hospitals were founded, originally attached to monasteries, where the insane, who were usually regarded as sick, were accepted.

Many fundamental concepts of human nature, derived from classical philosophy, were incorporated into the developing Christian theology. St. Augustine (354–430), who was greatly influenced by Neoplatonism, attempted to reconcile Plato's theories with Christian theology and St. Thomas Aquinas (1225–1274), incorporated aspects of Aristotelian philosophy into Christian theology. Christianity, gradually became a single unifying ideology in Western Europe and its doctrines came to have a pervasive influence on all aspects of human life.

The dualism of an immortal soul in a mortal body is central to Christian theology. Christian doctrine held that salvation of the soul requires renunciation of the pleasures of this world, which are temptations to sin. Unpleasant and painful experiences, including psychological suffering, could be interpreted as punishment from God for sin. People with clearly psychological disorders ("soul sickness") were often treated by a priest with prayers and counseling. Handbooks were issued for priests with advice on how to deal with psychological problems. They included guidelines for counseling, moral advice, recognition of responsibility.

Although faith healing and demonology increased with the spread of Christianity, it did not replace medical treatment among those who had access to and could afford it. The importance of demonological theories to the understanding of psychopathology throughout the Middle Ages and Renaissance has been greatly overemphasized. It was usually assumed that demons could only cause symptoms indirectly by corrupting the humors and animal spirits of the body. Demonology was not invoked for most illness and deaths, including epidemic disease, but only when the usual theories were not adequate to explain a particular illness (see Clark, 1984).

Hospitals

The London hospital of St. Mary of Bethlehem (later known as Bethlem, or Bedlam) was founded in 1247. Originally intended to provide accommodations for visiting clergy, it later became a hospital, which, like most other hospitals, cared for a certain number of mental patients. John Stow's 1890 *Survey of London* stated that ". . . it was an Hospitall for distracted people. . . . In this place people that bee distraight in wits, are by the smite of their friends receyved and kept as afore, but not without charges. . . ." (Clay, 1909, p. 31). By the fourteenth century, the church had established hospitals throughout Western Europe, some with limited accommodation for the mentally ill. By the fifteenth century, asylums for the mentally ill were founded. In the sixteenth century, hospitals established by religious groups began to be replaced by hospitals under secular management with the objective of providing for the sick and needy at public expense. Affluent lunatics were boarded out with clergymen or physicians, thus giving rise to the first private "madhouses." In England and Germany, insane persons considered not dangerous wore badges that signified they were entitled to seek alms. In England, at least as early as the sixteenth century, inmates confined in Bethlehem Hospital were released to beg when they were considered no longer likely to harm themselves or others (Aubrey, 1813/1972).

Certain shrines became noted as centers for mental healing. In Belgium, during the eleventh and twelfth centuries, the shrine of St. Dymphna, which had been erected on the site of Dymphna's martyrdom at Geel, became particularly known for miraculous cures of epileptics and other "lunatics." From the second half of the fourteenth century, the shrine gradually became a place of pilgrimage specifically for mental patients.

Europe's population approximately doubled during the sixteenth and seventeenth centuries. Poverty conditions worsened and begging reached unprecedented levels, with large numbers organized into gangs. This exacerbated a growing resentment on the part of citizens expected to give charity to those who asked for it. Almsgiving came to be considered the promotion of a social evil and therefore immoral. Resources were unified under the governance of local or national authorities with the aim of eliminating begging by organizing public assistance. In France, a royal edict issued in 1656 by King Louis XIV ordained the confinement of beggars, tramps, vagabonds, freethinkers, prostitutes, and the insane.

The Hôpital General of Paris was established to segregate socially dependent or disruptive individuals from society. La Bicêtre, for men, and the Salpêtrière, for women, often described as asylums for the insane, were both large general hospitals for the poor with only a few wards for the insane. There were many paths into institutions other than that of mental illness. A 1690 regulation decreed that children (up to age 25) of artisans and other poor inhabitants of Paris who "used their parents badly," refused to work because of laziness, or, in the case of girls, were debauched, were to be confined—the boys in the Bicêtre, the girls in the Salpêtrière (Rosen, 1968).

The first European institutions specifically for lunatics were established during the eighteenth century. The methods of treatment were those traditional from the classical period—bloodletting, emetics, purgatives, and blisters raised on the patients' bodies in order to draw off corrupted humors. St. Patrick's Hospital was founded in 1746 in Dublin with the legacy left by Jonathan Swift (1667–1745), dean of St. Patrick's. Swift, known for his satire *Gulliver's Travels,* was deeply concerned about the problems of mental illness. He willed most of his estate for the foundation of a "House for Fools and Mad." Lunatic asylums were founded somewhat later in other large cities.

The Anatomy of Melancholy

Robert Burton (1577–1640), an English clergyman, wrote *The Anatomy of Melancholy,* first published in 1621. Burton undertook the task of "anatomizing" melancholy, a term that embraced all kinds of madness. He compiled all the descriptive and conjectural writings on the nature, causes, and cures of melancholy, accumulated from the classical period to his own time. His book, which went through numerous editions, was highly regarded as a medical treaties into the eighteenth century and is an invaluable source for information regarding the history of ideas about mental illness and its treatment. Largely derived from Galen and modified by Christian theology, his work testifies to the longevity of the humoral/pneumatic theory.

Burton, as had Galen, stated that the passions may be called diseases, and are a frequent cause of melancholy. Other causes include defective heredity; bad nursing in infancy; too rigorous, severe, remiss, or indulgent education by bad parents, step-mothers, and teachers; and loss of liberty, servitude, poverty, and death of friends. He wrote that although melancholy is difficult to treat, it may be cured or at least mitigated if it is not hereditary, if it is treated early, and if the patient is willing to be helped. The physician should seek to relieve the patient's mind of worries, fears, and suspicions, "for the body cannot be cured till the mind be satisfied ... but if satisfaction may not be had ... then ... drive out one passion with another, or by some contrary passion" (Burton, 1651/1927, p. 476).

Mystical Bedlam by Michael MacDonald (1981) is another source for information about concepts of abnormal psychology in seventeenth century England. MacDonald researched case histories recorded by Napier, a seventeenth-century astrological physician, of some 2,000 "obscure rustics" that Napier had treated. Napier's diagnoses classified mental disorders as types of sickness variously explained by traditional cosmological and religious beliefs, and as results of individual experiences and social actions.

Increasing city populations and sizes likewise increased the importance attached to the physical consequences of living in crowded urban environments and assumptions that the humors are affected by toxins and miasmas. George Cheyne's *The English Malady,* published in 1734, refers to depression or melancholy, then regarded as a peculiarly British ailment not only by the English but also by the French. Cheyne attributed the alleged prevalence of melancholy among the English to the conditions of urban life with special reference to London: ". . . the infinite number of fires, . . . the clouds of stinking breaths and perspirations, . . . the stinking butcherhouses, stables, dunghills . . . and mixture of such variety of all kinds of atoms are more than sufficient to putrefy . . . which in time, must alter, weaken, destroy the healthiest constitutions of men. . . ." (quoted in Harms, 1967, pp. 59–60). The recommendation that asylums be built in the country comes as no surprise.

From Animal Spirits to Animal Electricity

In the sixteenth century Andreas Vesalius (1514–1564) reported that nerves appear solid and therefore could not serve as conduits for pneuma. In the seventeenth century, William Harvey (1578–1657) discovered the circulation of the blood. He demonstrated that the heart is a pump that propels blood through the body by mechanical action. This ended the need for the theory that vital spirits provide the impetus for the pulsing of the blood. However, the concept of animal spirits was not abandoned based on these discoveries, but continued in use to explain psychological function and mental illness beyond the seventeenth century. The neurology of the French philosopher, René Descartes (1596–1650), depended on the notion of animal spirits being shunted along tubular nerves from the sense organs to the brain. In 1660, Highmore (cited in Lopez-Piñero, 1983) described animal spirits as minutest fiery particles, rarefied in the heart by fermentation and,

mixed with blood, transmitted through the arteries to the brain where they are separated from the blood and stored in the channels and ventricles of the brain for use under the direction of the soul. Thomas Willis (1684) published a fairly accurate description of nerves and his theories about convulsive diseases. He conjectured that animal spirits formed in the brain produce motions by explosive action. When this explosive action is excessive, convulsions and mental disease result.

After Isaac Newton (1642–1726) published his *Philosophiae Naturalis Principia Mathematica* in 1687, the concept of animal spirits was redefined as a vital gravitational force (*elan vita*). The Italian anatomist Luigi Galvani (1737–1798) reported that electrical energy is propagated along the nerves and generates muscular movement, a discovery that finally led to the abandonment of the belief that animal spirits move through tubular nerves. However, the doctrine of animal spirits was not wholly replaced as a physiological explanation for sensation and action and the notion of "animal electricity" (*vis nervosa*) replaced that of animal spirits. Clarke and Jacyna (1987) comment as follows:

> It is a remarkable fact that a concept of how a nerve functioned should have survived almost intact from Greco-Roman antiquity to the nineteenth century, but this was the case with the doctrine of the hollow nerve. . . . The basic supposition was that messages could travel along the lumen of the hollow nerve, and although subjected to various modifications, the theory was still alive in the early 1800s. Because it was universally accepted for so many centuries, owing chiefly to the authority of Galen, we can conclude that it must have satisfied the majority of scientists and physicians. (p. 160)

The theory was finally overthrown by research on animal electricity first reported by Galvani in 1791.

The declining influence of the humoral theory was accompanied by an increasing interest in so-called nervous disease. This rather loosely defined concept distinguished between insanity and less disabling disturbances found with some frequency in the general population.

In Britain, nervous diseases were assumed to be more common in the leisured classes as a result of insufficient fresh air, lack of exercise, adultery, abuse of medicine, excessive study, and others previously listed by Burton (1651/1927) as causes of melancholy. Robert Whytt (1765) complained,

> . . . the disorders which are the subject of the following observations have been treated by authors under the names of flatulent, hypochondriac, or hysteric. Physicians have bestowed the character of nervous on all those disorders whose nature and cause they were ignorant of. (p. III)

Despite Whytt's caveat, William Cullen (1784), the influential nosologist, considered all diseases, but especially psychic diseases, to be neuroses. For many years the term *neurosis,* first coined by Cullen, referred to a biological disorder of the nervous system, but one not localized to a specific part of the nervous system. According to Cullen, life is maintained by brain energy flowing from the central nervous system to muscles and solid organs; disease results if the energy is inadequate. The debate about the presence or absence of a neurological disorder underlying the neuroses continued well into the late nineteenth century.

From Magnetism and Mesmerism to Hypnosis

The sixteenth century saw the development of magnetism, a theory and treatment of disease concurrent with, but outside that of traditional medicine. William Gilbert (1544–1603), English scientist and physician to the queen of England, discovered the physical force of magnetism. Gilbert's discovery gave rise to the notion of a cosmic magnetic life force that permeates the universe and controls psychological and physiological functioning, and magnets gained popularity as a means of manipulating this force to cure physical and mental disease. During the eighteenth century this cosmic force was redefined as the force of gravity posited by Newton and was regarded as a vital principle of life. The practice of magnetism to treat disease, rationalized by Newton's theory, became particularly popular in Germany and Austria. The notion relating magnetic force's influence on the balance of bodily spirits received renewed emphasis with the popularity of Franz Anton Mesmer (1734–1815) whose theory of disease and its cure combined century-old notions from humoral theory with the idea of occult natural forces borrowed from Newtonian physics. Mesmer identified a "subtle and mobile fluid" as the medium of the force of universal gravity and the primeval agent of nature. He described it as bathing the entire universe, surrounding and penetrating all bodies that exist and particularly exercised on the nervous system. All illness, physical and psychological, results from an imbalance of the fluid's distribution within the body. Certain privileged individuals are capable of directing this fluid in the bodies of sick people to restore its balance. Mesmer established a medical practice in Vienna and began using magnets to treat disease in 1774, but soon discovered that he did not need magnets—he could produce the same effects by passing his hands downward over his patient's body toward the feet, even at a distance. He concluded that he, himself, must have an accumulation of "animal magnetism" in his body that he could transmit to the patient.

Mesmer moved to Paris and in 1778 established a treatment salon. His famous tub, placed in the center of the salon, contained wine bottles filled with "magnetized" water covered with an iron lid pierced through with holes. From each of the holes issued a long movable iron rod that the patients applied to the parts of their body afflicted with pain or disease. The patients sat in a circle around the tub as close together as possible; they held each other by the hand and pressed their knees together in order to facilitate the passage of the magnetic fluid from one to another. Well built, handsome young men circled the patients, pouring onto them fresh streams of invisible "magnetic" fluid from the tips of their fingers; they also rubbed the patients down their spines and gazed into their eyes. All this passed in silence except for occasional swelling notes from a glass harmonica or a hidden singer. After an hour or two of this, one or more of the patients began to convulse in epileptic-like fits. At this point, Mesmer himself appeared, dressed in a richly embroidered silk robe and waving a wand, and the remaining patients, some sobbing, others laughing or screaming, all subsided into somnambulistic trances. When the patients regained consciousness, they described feeling streams of cold or burning vapor passing through their bodies and reported that their ailments were cured (Tinterow, 1970). Mesmer's therapeutic technique, known as mesmerism gained great popularity, but was vigorously criticized by the leading members of the academic, scientific, and medical establishments of the day, and by the clergy, some of whom claimed he was in league with satanic forces (Darnton, 1968).

In 1784, by order of King Louis XVI, a joint commission was appointed from the Faculty of Medicine in Paris and the Royal Academy of Science to investigate the claims of the Mesmerists. Benjamin Franklin presided over the commission (chosen because of his investigations of electricity), which included the French scientists Lavoisier and Guillotin. The commission did not question Mesmer's results but did dispute the claim that Mesmerists could manipulate a magnetic fluid. They concluded that Mesmer's claimed forces did not exist and that the Mesmerists' apparent successes could be explained by suggestion and imagination.

Although the commission's report invalidated the extravagant claims made by Mesmer and his followers, the facts of his apparent cures were left unexplained. James Braid (1795–1860), a British surgeon, like most reputable physicians, had dismissed the mesmerists' practice as mere chicanery and the behavior of their mesmerized subjects as voluntary simulation. However, after attending several public exhibitions of mesmerism he became convinced the phenomena he was observing were real. Braid experimented with family members and friends and discovered that he was able to induce a trance state. He identified a trance as nervous sleep and coined the term *hypnosis* for the induced state (see *Braidism,* Oxford English Dictionary).

Moral Management and the Association Model

Although Philippe Pinel is often credited with having initiated reform in institutions for the insane, agitation for reform had begun before him in many countries where general institutional conditions had been deteriorating. In 1796, in response to widespread publicity generated by investigations of deplorable institution conditions, the English philanthropist, William Hack Tuke (1732–1822) persuaded the Society of Friends, to found the Retreat at York, planned as a therapeutic environment for mentally ill Quakers. Tuke instituted a system known as moral management, based on humanitarian care, moral (i.e., psychological) treatment, minimal restraint, and constructive activities.

The principles of moral management followed the concepts of eighteenth century moral philosophers, and the British concept of "associationism," that psychological states and processes are sequentially determined by prior experience and governed by the laws of association. Individual differences were explained as a consequence of differing particular sequences of experiences, especially those of education. This view led to the optimistic belief that, based on proper education, it would be possible to plan a utopian society to achieve a universal social harmony.

Associationism owed a debt to John Locke (1632–1704) who, in his *An Essay Concerning Human Understanding* (1700) stated that all our ideas come from experience, first from sensation and secondly from reflection upon the ideas furnished by sensation. Locke believed that in ordinary thought, one idea normally succeeds another by "natural" or rational connections. But, according to Locke, occasionally ideas become fortuitously associated by their contiguity, which explains how even reasonable people may come to hold unreasonable beliefs. Locke suggested that mental disorders are extreme instances of such unreasonable beliefs. Although this "association model" of psychopathology attributed sensory defects and abnormalities of movement to structural defects in the nervous system, it explained insanity—peculiar ideas, aberrant and incoherent thought processes, inappropriate emotions, and bizarre behaviors—as attributable to chains of irrational associations established by unfortunate learning situations. Sanity was considered a matter of coherent, rational thought processes and of self-control, with the proper use of the will in the service of reason to control emotions and to guide action. (This view has a long

history—Plato held it and stressed the importance of inner governance.) Insanity results from unfortunate experiences, lack of discipline, and self-indulgence, hence it can be cured by reeducation (Plato, 1894a).

The association model provided the rationale for moral management. People affected with insanity, according to this view, should be removed from the pernicious influence of their homes and environments. They should be placed in a well-ordered social milieu designed to gently but firmly rehabilitate them to the norms of society by an orchestration of therapeutic relearning experiences and provision of firm moral guidance in order restore mental health.

Small asylums, modeled on the York Retreat, sprang up in Britain and the United States. Managers were often physicians but also ministers, because insanity was attributed to psychological, not biological, causes. Persons who provided therapy for the insane had come to be known as "alienists" because they dealt with the problems of the alienated mind. Physical restraint and drugs were minimized in favor of kindly supervision and methods designed to reeducate and to instill appropriate behavior and self-discipline. Religious services were available, although patients who tended to religious brooding might not be permitted to attend. Practitioners made little attempt to determine specific causes for the psychopathology. These measures, intended to induce habits of self-control, did not always work, as many patients were self-destructive or violent to others, which made restraint necessary at times.

William Battie (1704–1776), an English alienist and an early advocate of moral management, was the first in Britain to teach psychiatry to medical students. In his *A Treatise on Madness* (1758), Battie made a distinction between "original" (i.e., organic) and "consequential" (or acquired) madness. He believed that mental disorder could be cured if patients were treated in an asylum where they were isolated from family and friends, were attended by asylum staff rather than their own servants, and were managed by efforts to check their "unruly appetites" and divert their "fixed imaginations."

Philippe Pinel (1745–1826), the French alienist, founded a school of psychiatry at the Salpêtrière, where he trained a generation of psychiatrists, including Esquirol, who spread his ideas throughout Europe. Pinel has been considered the founder of modern psychiatry because he wrote the first textbook of psychiatry, *Traité Médico-Philosophique sur la Manie* (Pinel, 1806). Pinel is also credited with having inaugurated the humane care of the institutionalized insane, based the claim that he removed the chains from the insane patients at the Bicêtre. Weiner (1979) points out that, in fact, this was done by Pussin, who successfully replaced chains with straitjackets for incurable mental patients at Bicêtre. Pinel subsequently had Pussin transferred to the Salpêtrière to help him reorganize the hospital.

In Italy, Vincenzo Chiarugi (1759–1820), superintendent of the hospital of Bonifazio published his three volumes, *On Insanity and its Classification* (1793/1987). He issued hospital regulations in which he stated that mental patients should be given humanitarian care, restraint should be kept to a minimum, physicians should visit the wards daily, and a program of recreation and work should be initiated. He attributed insanity to congenital factors and to environmental influences. John Conolly (1794–1866), a British physician, practiced enlightened treatment methods for the mentally ill, including minimal use of restraints when he became resident physician at the Hanwell Asylum in 1839 (Scull, 1985).

EIGHTEENTH TO MID-NINETEENTH CENTURY

Asylums of the Era

Early nineteenth-century British asylums, conducted according to principles of moral management, offered cures for madness and acquired a reputation for achieving them. During the same period private madhouses multiplied that accepted a few mentally ill patients for payment. Many were owned or managed by clergymen or physicians and often remained in the same family for generations. Some were owned by reputable physicians, of whom William Battie was one.

However, many private madhouses and asylums were badly managed, and complaints about the conditions in these places led to a parliamentary inquiry. Findings of inhumane treatment led to government legislation aimed at providing proper care and treatment, and establishing an efficient system of inspection and licensing of public and private institutions. The belief that the social engineering that organized and maintained a productive economy could solve the problems of human need engendered the hope that persons put in hospitals (and prisons) could be cured, or at least improved, and rehabilitated to society. These institutions were, in the main, general hospitals and workhouses intended to provide minimal housing and care for paupers, those unable to fend for themselves or unwilling to work.

As it became obvious that mentally deranged or incompetent persons presented special problems, institutions were built to house them. The inmates of these "lunatic asylums" included habitual drunkards, petty offenders, vagrants, sufferers of organic diseases (in particular general paresis), as well as the mad. Over time, the increasing number of individuals judged to require institutionalization resulted in enormous expansion of these asylums. As a typical example, the West Riding Asylum in Wakefield, England was built in 1818 to care for 150 patients but within 80 years, it held almost 1,500. Moves to provide help funded by the state were encumbered by problems of indifference. Under pressure of increasing admissions plus accumulation of hopeless cases, asylum architecture, initially designed to provide environmental stimuli calculated to rouse pleasant and ordered emotions, was altered. The size of public institutions eventually reflected not patient needs but cost to the public, and the institutions tended to become custodial warehouses. Harsh measures were often used and asylum staff as well as patients lived a dismal existence (Russell, 1988).

Advent of Nosological Systems

In the latter half of the eighteenth century, nosological systems organized diseases, described in detail, according to the model of systematic botany established by Linnaeus, the Swedish botanist, physician and founder of modern taxonomy. William Cullen (1710–1790), a professor of medicine at the University of Edinburgh, was the most influential classifier of disease of the time. The section on medicine in the first edition of *The Encyclopædia Britannica* (1771), utilizes his system. The discussion of neuroses or nervous diseases states that melancholy and madness are related, melancholy being the primary disease and madness an augmentation of melancholy. Both are caused by an excessive congestion of blood in the brain.

Jean Étienne Dominique Esquirol (1772–1840), Pinel's student and successor at the Salpêtrière, was one of the first to apply statistical methods to clinical studies and tabulate psychological causes. He elaborated the concept of monomania, a type of insanity that does not involve loss of reason, to designate an abnormally active, garrulous individual with "delirium" or disturbed thought process confined to a fairly circumscribed cluster of ideas or interests. The condition sometimes appears abruptly and abruptly ceases, and often does not necessitate hospitalization (Esquirol, 1838). His student, Jules Philippe Joseph Falret (1824–1902) published a paper in 1854 on "circular insanity," which he described as a clinically coherent and diagnostically distinct illness, characterized by an alteration between manic excitement and depression, typically with brief periods of reason (Sedler & Dessain, 1983). The *DSM-III* description of bipolar affective disorder is remarkably similar to Falret's description of circular insanity; it appears to be a specific disease with a cluster of typical symptoms, a particular course and prognosis, and a particular response to certain somatic treatments (such as, lithium, or electrical shock treatment).

Descriptive psychiatry with classification of data did not develop until, with the growth of institutions and the increasing professionalization of psychiatry, a sufficient number of mental patients were gathered for observation over a period of time. In the second half of the nineteenth century, more than 15 national and international psychiatric societies were organized and almost fifty journals of psychiatry appeared in the United States and Europe. Classifying types of mental illness began by establishing standard ways of describing symptoms and symptom clusters.

Emil Kraepelin (1856–1926) developed the first widely accepted classification of mental disorders and is considered the founder of modern psychiatric nosology. Kraepelin systematically collected and described facts, on the basis of which he classified types of severe mental disorder. His *Compendium der Psychiatrie* went through eight editions between 1883 and 1914, growing to a multivolume textbook of psychiatry. Kraepelin divided the major psychoses into manic-depressive psychoses and dementia praecox, and subclassified dementia praecox into three types: catatonia (characterized by mutism and maintenance of a bodily posture for long periods of time), hebephrenia (characterized by inappropriate, often silly, speech and behavior), and paranoia (characterized by delusions of persecution and/or grandeur). He concluded that persons suffering from manic-depressive disorder can recover, whereas those with dementia praecox deteriorate, and hence hypothesized that dementia praecox may be of metabolic origin. Kraepelin emphasized the physiological causes of mental disorders and considered the personal side of a patient's illness as incidental to understanding psychopathology. He presented ordered groups of observations, with clear detail and fully documented statistical tables, in order to establish that serious mental illness, like other diseases, has a predetermined course and outcome (Kraepelin 1915). No consistent, central system of diagnosis was established within the United States until the appearance of the *Diagnostic and Statistical Manual: Mental Disorders (DSM),* first published in 1952 by the American Psychiatric Association. Although this was a step forward, criticisms attacked its inherent inconsistency because the categories included disorders defined on the basis of etiology, on the basis of behavioral symptomology, and on the basis of presumed psychodynamics. However, the process of defining classification had begun, and revisions have followed throughout the latter half of the twentieth century. Eugen Bleuler (1857–1939), a Swiss psychiatrist, professor, and director of Burghölzli Asylum, Zurich, from 1898 to 1927, originated the term *schizophrenia* ("split-mind") in 1908 as a generic label for the category of mental illnesses that Kraepelin had called dementia praecox. Bleuler believed that schizophrenia represents a split between a person's emotional life and faculty of reasoning that results from morbid thought processes that disturb the emotional integrity of the self, and that schizophrenia is amenable to psychotherapy.

By the 1870s, the field of medicine had entered the era of modern scientific experimentation. Claude Bernard, French physician and physiologist considered the founder of experimental medicine, published his classic *Introduction to Experimental Medicine* in 1865, which established the value of experimental methods for determining mechanisms regulating the activity of bodily systems and their relation to physical pathology. Medical advances, such as Pasteur's germ theory were based on the use of the pathogen model of disease, sometimes loosely known as the "medical model."

Knowledge of the role of pathogens and the accompanying social benefits of immunological procedures established this model as the most effective strategy and has profoundly influenced approaches to psychopathology. In so doing it has created vigorous controversy. Applied to the understanding of psychopathology the model assumes that disordered behaviors are symptoms of a particular pathology, the hidden cause of which must be discovered. The first step is to sort mentally ill people into groups based on clusters of symptoms (syndromes) common to each group. The second step is to determine the particular pathogen that has caused the disease in order to solve the problem of etiology. The third step, once a psychopathology has been diagnosed and its etiology established, is to determine the appropriate treatment for the condition. The hidden pathogen may be biological (genes, for example) or may be past stressful experience. In the psychoanalytic model, the pathogen is an unconscious conflict, hidden from the patient and allegedly requiring the skill of the analyst to discover. The critical difference between this metaphorical use of the term *pathogen* and its original meaning is that the analyst's discovery cannot be visibly demonstrated to all who look, but its presence is inferred on theoretical grounds.

Brain Pathology Model of Psychopathology and Nervous Diseases

By the end of the eighteenth century and during the early nineteenth century, the development of new technologies to study the brain and nervous system produced findings that were to provide the foundations of modern neurology. The medical community accepted the role of electrical impulses transmitted within central nervous system tissue in the mediation of behavior, and old beliefs about the role of the blood and generalized *vis nervosa* faded from the scene. It had become clear that the central nervous system integrates the sensory and motor systems of the higher organisms. The brain's importance as the organ of human thought and behavior was firmly established and led to the emphasis on disorders of the brain and nervous system to account for psychopathology. Accumulating evidence of human psychological and physical variability also produced a shift in emphasis to neurological causes of insanity. Such evidence, it was argued, could not be attributed solely to different experiences in basically similar human beings. The variety and extremes of mental disorder exceeded the apparent explanatory capacity of the associationist psychology.

These changes led to development of the brain pathology model of psychopathology, which held that psychopathology represents, not unfortunate psychological processes learned by the individual in the social milieu, but malfunction and morbidity of the central nervous system variously caused by hereditary faults, disease, malnutrition, toxins, and stress. For example, Moseley (1838) stated that ". . . disease in the organ of the brain and not in the mind is the cause of nervous complaints and insanity is now admitted." He believed that the brain could be affected by environmental and psychological factors as well as by toxic agents (e.g., if not exercised, the brain, like other organs, becomes relaxed and sinks into a condition of incompetency). The predisposing causes of insanity that he lists are similar to the causes of melancholy suggested by Robert Burton in the seventeenth century. An extreme of this view was to trace all psychopathology to hypothetical lesions in the brain. Writing some 40 years after Moseley, Henry Maudsley, whose major works appeared between 1867 and 1879, believed all psychopathology was caused by brain disease.

Franz Joseph Gall (1758–1828), whose major work was published between 1822 and 1825, opposed the prevailing view that the mind is a unitary thinking thing. He asserted that it consists of interacting separate psychological faculties, each with a separate locus in the brain, one of each in the two cerebral hemispheres (a theory he called organology). He agreed with the view that each side of the brain can serve as a complete organ, one side providing a backup for the other. He held that derangement of thinking and behavior are caused by disease of particular parts of the brain, notably gross under- or overdevelopment of particular cerebral organs, or to an imbalance between cerebral organs. Gall maintained that all humans are vulnerable to malfunction of the brain that can result in insanity, although some people have a greater constitutional disposition to insanity than others (Gall, 1825/1835, Vol. 1, p. 281).

Phrenology

Johann Gaspar Spurzheim (1776–1832) had begun to collaborate with Gall in 1800, but Gall later severed their relationship because of his objections to modifications that Spurzheim began introducing in Gall's theory. Spurzheim

called his variant *phrenology,* a term that Gall never used (Clark & Jacyna, 1987, p. 222). Phrenology attracted numerous adherents in both England and the United States, including influential philosophers and physicians specializing in psychiatry. Isaac Ray (1807–1881), an American physician and well-received writer on forensic psychiatry, was for some years an advocate of phrenology. Spurzheim's phrenology was used to rationalize discrimination and prejudice on the basis of presumed biological racial and class differences. Victor Hilts (1982) points out that, although Gall did not use hereditarian arguments, phrenologists such as Spurzheim began to promote the social policy of eugenics well before the appearance of the social Darwinists. They popularized hereditarian ideas in the conviction that social progress depends on the improvement of human biological endowment through selective breeding, and warned of the possibility of racial degeneration if this were not accepted as a moral duty.

Brain Hemisphere Theories

Discovery of the brain's division into two hemispheres led to an interpretation of psychopathology as caused by a breakdown in the activity integration between the two hemispheres. Esquirol (1838) attributed impairment to the duality of the brain, whose two hemispheres, "if not equally activated, do not act simultaneously." Benjamin Rush (1745–1813) speculated that the mind, like vision, is a double organ, which could account for cases of somnambulism in which patients seemed to experience two independent states of consciousness. And the French neurologist, Marie François Xavier Bichat, explained that the brain has two hemispheres because the organism must interact with the external world in a unified way with both sides of the body (Harrington, 1987).

In 1844, during the autopsy of an apparently normal man, Arthur Ladbroke Wigan reported that the man possessed only one cerebral hemisphere, evidence that a person requires only one to function normally. Wigan concluded that ". . . each cerebrum is a distinct and perfect whole," capable of independent thought and volition, and suggested that the healthy brain synchronizes the actions of the two hemispheres, with one of the two dominant and controlling the volitions of the other. He speculated that in mental disease "one cerebrum becomes sufficiently aggravated to defy the control of the other," and then the two hemispheres act independently, their separate wills conflicting, and their separate thoughts being confused. For such cases, Wigan (1844) suggested that "a well-managed education" might serve to "establish and confirm the power of concentrating the energies of both brains on the same subject at the same time."

Neuroscience research overturned view that the cerebral hemispheres are identical in the latter half of the nineteenth century. Results of neurological research, including autopsies performed on patients with psychological deficits related to brain tumors and traumas, correlation of behavioral changes with ablation of particular structures of the central nervous system, direct electrical stimulation of areas of the exposed brain in living subjects and the corresponding techniques of measuring degree and locus of electrical activity of the brain evoked by systematic stimulation of areas of the body, all lent support for the theory that different psychological functions are localized in separate areas of the brain.

LATE NINETEENTH INTO TWENTIETH CENTURY

Theory of the Evolution of the Brain and Psychopathology

J. Hughlings Jackson (1835–1911), an English neurologist who specialized in neuropathology, confirmed Broca's discovery of the speech center, finding in most cases that aphasia in right-handed persons is associated with disease of the left cerebral hemisphere. In 1863, he observed epileptic convulsions that progress through the body in a series of spasms; such convulsions are now known as "Jacksonian epilepsy." He theorized that the lower functional levels of the human mind are dynamically and unconsciously present in all healthy individuals and are temporarily released from control of the higher cortical centers whenever the cortex is relatively inactive, as during sleep, and in cases of cortical damage. Jackson concluded that the behavioral symptoms of brain damage are determined by the functioning of one or more lower centers that have been freed from the inhibitory control normally imposed on them by the higher brain centers. He pointed out that this evolutionary sequence can be observed in individual mental development and suggested that in old age, in various neurological diseases, and in most forms of insanity there occurs a general reversal of this developmental/ evolutionary process (Jackson, 1887).

The Clinico-Anatomic Method

The discovery of cerebral localization of motor, sensory, and even integrative psychological functions supported the thesis that psychological functions are localized in the brain. If particular psychological functions are localized in different parts of the brain, it follows that various manifestations of psychopathology might be caused by diseases of specific parts of the brain. In this view, the domain of psychopathol-

ogy represents various specific diseases to be described in order to establish descriptive categories. The diseases can then be related to specific underlying diagnosable neurological pathologies. This is conceptually a "pathogen model" of psychopathology. This view was largely hereditarian but not necessarily so, as organically based psychopathology could be caused by innate or acquired brain dysfunctions.

General Paresis

By the late nineteenth century large numbers of mentally ill persons were crowded in the large public institutions, some suffering from alcoholism, others from old age and dementia, and still others were probably "natural fools." Still others suffered from various metabolic and neurological diseases and brain damage. Many suffered from general paresis (originally called "general paralysis of the insane" or GPI). Autopsy of the brains revealed widespread brain tissue destruction, but no one knew that general paresis had a specific pathology linked to syphilis until Krafft-Ebing established that this form of insanity is the tertiary stage of syphilis, a delayed, but not inevitable, result of a syphilitic infection. In 1897, he inoculated with the syphilis spirochete nine individuals with general paresis and no known history of syphilitic infection. None developed secondary symptoms. Researchers concluded that they must have been previously infected, although they had not developed the usual symptoms of syphilis. This finding established that an early infection with syphilis is the cause of general paresis. The symptoms, which begin to appear 15 to 20 years after the initial infection, include manic-like behavior, with euphoria, delusions of grandeur and persecution and depression, and disorders of speech and locomotion, similar to those found in some major psychiatric disorders. The hypothesis of syphilitic infection was not fully accepted until Noguchi and Moore produced definitive proof by finding evidence of the spirochete in the brains of syphilitics (Moore, 1910).

Brain Lesions and Psychopathology

Throughout the second half of the nineteenth century, many physicians attributed all mental derangement to cerebral pathology. Technical limitations mostly prevented physicians from establishing the nature and location of central nervous system pathology until after the patient had died, and so medical researchers turned to autopsies to confirm the supposition that brain pathology underlay psychopathology.

D. Hack Tuke (1881), in his presidential address to the Medico-Psychological Association, reviewed autopsy research into the physical correlates of mental pathology. He concluded that the morphological and histological study of the brains of idiots by Mierzejewski, Luys, and others were

> ... sufficient to prove, had we no other evidence, the fundamental truth of cerebro-mental pathology—the dependence of healthy mind on healthy brain.... We are surely justified in expecting that by a prolonged examination of every part of the brain structure, and the notation of the mental symptoms, we shall arrive in future at more definite results; that the locality of special disorders will be discovered, and that the correlation of morbid mental and diseased cerebral states will become more and more complete that the scientific classification of mental maladies may be one day based upon pathological as well as clinical knowledge, and psychology be founded, in part at least, upon our acquaintance with the functions of the brain (pp. 330–331).

Carl Wernicke (1848–1905), a German neurologist, also assumed that pathology of the brain causes mental disorders, the various symptoms being expressions of disorders of different localized cerebral functions. Wernicke analyzed symptoms of mental disorder as to whether their causes appeared to be pathology in the sensory, the intrapsychic, or the motor sphere of the brain. Meyer (1904) assessed Wernicke's work as pure empiricism with a rather artificial and not sufficiently founded brain pathology and psychopathology. And in 1914, David C. Thomson said, "The knowledge of the aetiology, pathology, and therapeutics of insanity has advanced, and can only advance, on the fundamental view that the symptom-complex insanity is a disorder or disease of the brain. I do not think this can be asserted too often in these days of fads and 'isms, such as faith-healing, Christian science, etc." (p. 558).

However, various failures to relate specific psychopathological symptoms to specific *loci* of pathology in the brain suggested that the cerebral problems in insanity were caused by dynamic disturbances in function rather than lesions in the brain structure. Nevertheless by the end of the nineteenth century most members of the medical profession subscribed to some variant of this view. They believed psychopathology was caused by some biological disorder, inherited or acquired, which affected the functioning of the central nervous system, either by agency of the blood or because of lesions or physiological malfunctioning, with increasing emphasis on heredity.

Social Darwinism

Perhaps the most important nineteenth-century development arose from the impact of Charles Darwin's work. Evolutionary theory and the conception of man as a descendant of earlier animal forms were not totally unknown before Darwin. However, the evidence he adduced was powerful and his exposition was cogent. The clear consequences his theory held for religious views of human nature and popular views of man's purpose in the cosmos created a dramatic and disturbing departure from the thinking of earlier centuries. Natural selection, with its message of competition and conflict was equally disturbing. Social Darwinism, a political interpretation of the principle of natural selection, was to have serious consequences for the public perception and treatment of the mentally ill. Social Darwinism assumed that human society was the product of inevitable and continuous conflict and competition. As a result, individuals formed a continuum of the "fit" (the intelligent, physically healthy, affluent, and powerful) at one end and the "unfit" (poor, diseased, retarded, insane, alcoholic, criminal, and powerless) at the other that extended to the different "races" of man. The elimination of unfit individuals or races was interpreted as part of man's inevitable process of progressive improvement with an accompanying moral imperative to eliminate any obstacles to this improvement.

Degeneracy Theory

One theory that was compatible with Social Darwinism was the theory of degeneration, which rested on the belief that a wide variety of social ills were evidence of a unitary hereditary defect. Physical disease (such as tuberculosis, deformed bone development, etc.) and insanity, alcoholism, unemployment, poverty, and crime seemed to go hand in hand. In families and communities in which any of these were prevalent, the others were likely to be found.

Dowbiggin (1985) reviewed the history of degeneracy theory in France. The psychiatrist Jacques-Joseph Moreau de Tours (1804–1884) asserted in 1859 that all insanity is caused by an actual alteration of the central nervous system, and that the major cause of insanity is genetic transmission from parents to children of a neuropathic predisposition. He argued that "large series of organs" such as the nervous system, rather than "isolated traits," are transmitted from parents to offspring, and that susceptibility to disease, particularly mental derangement, is caused by a morbid deviation from the healthy human type. However, autopsies of patients with mental disease had failed to discover specific lesions or pathological structures of the brain, suggesting that the causes of insanity might not be biological. This led to the theory that mental disease was caused by a hereditary degeneracy that results in a diffuse pathological functional disequilibrium of the nervous system not detectable by autopsy.

Dowbiggin pointed out that the theory of morbid heredity was compatible with the idea of free will. Dualism of soul and body was preserved by the thesis that madness results when pathological functioning of the nervous system deceives the mind of the patient, interfering with the exercise of his reason and thus his moral liberty. The exercise of free will and rationality of the mind is possible only in a healthy body, the body (specifically the nervous system) being the instrument of the mind. The sane person possesses rationality and free will; the insane patient lacks both as a result of a diseased body.

Not all proponents of the hereditary degeneracy theory were clear about what exactly began the process of degeneration. A significant body of opinion held that the problem lay in the unhealthy nature of city life. The steady movement of rural dwellers into the large cities had exacerbated the already intense overcrowding in city slums. Low standards of nutrition, difficulties in maintaining cleanliness, poor or nonexistent sanitation, promiscuity, heavy drinking, and crime were endemic in the warrens of London, New York, and the large cities of Europe. Many argued that all this weakened the constitution and morals of the previously healthy countryman, and that this acquired debility was somehow transmitted by hereditary to offspring, getting more intense with each succeeding generation.

During the second half of the nineteenth century, prominent French psychiatrists such as Morel and Moreau not only endorsed the belief that insanity was caused by hereditary transmission of a predisposition to nervous system pathology, but further proposed that this degeneracy, endemic among the lower classes, was the cause of political unrest in those strata. An ideal multipurpose theory that could account for phenomena as diverse as psychopathology and social unrest, degeneracy theory would form a central plank in the eugenic and racist platform.

In Germany, Darwinian ideas found a reception so enthusiastic that it rapidly transformed into an all-encompassing, mystical quasi-religious system of belief. The German biologist, Ernst Haeckel, a leading proponent of this movement, proposed that forces in nature were moving always to the improvement of the species, affecting man in precisely the same way as any other animal. It was the moral duty of the people to further nature's purposes and to take active steps to prevent the decay of degeneracy. This notion of a moral imperative to further the alleged purposes of nature would appear in the development and spread of eugenic ideas in Europe and North America, culminating in the murder of thousands of mentally ill in the gas chambers of Nazi Germany (Düffler, 1996).

Eugenics

The concept of eugenics was first developed in England by a cousin of Charles Darwin's, Francis Galton (1822–1911), who proposed that measures be taken to prevent the spread of hereditary defect in society. Galton's ideas included financial allowances for children born to "superior" parents and discouragement or prohibition of marriage and reproduction among those of lesser quality (Galton, 1909). In one essay, Galton proposed that the value of a prospective child might be calculated in terms of its future economic contribution or cost to society, and this would determine what amount might be spent to encourage the potential parents to reproduce. In the case of severe degenerate defect, sterilization might be considered. As the presence of a degenerate taint might not be visible in a particular individual, a history of disorder in one's ancestors would be adequate grounds for the application of eugenic measures.

Galton's ideas found a particular promoter in Karl Pearson, a professor of eugenics at the University of London, who opened a eugenics laboratory and became the driving force in the eugenics society that Galton founded. Pearson also presented the eugenics program in a series of publications (Pearson, 1909, 1910, 1911). These ideas found support in the United States, where some states legalized sterilization of mentally retarded people. Goddard's (1912) then-famous study of the Kallikak family reinforced the argument for sterilization.

Early Role of Hypnosis

After Mesmer was discredited in 1784, reputable study of hypnotic phenomena in France languished until the 1870s and the work of Jean-Martin Charcot (1825–1893), a physician and director of research in neurological disorders at the Salpêtrière. Harrington (1987) presents a history of neomesmerism in late nineteenth century French psychiatry, and the background to Charcot's involvement with hypnosis.

In 1876, Victor Burq, a physician, sent to Claude Bernard, then president of the Sociéte de Biologie of Paris, an account of how he had cured women who suffered from hysterical hemianesthesia by applying metallic discs to the afflicted side of their bodies (a procedure known as "metalloscopy"), with a request that Bernard arrange for his work to be investigated and validated. Bernard appointed a committee, consisting of Charcot, Jules Bernard Luys, and Amédée Dumontpallier. A year later, the committee reported that they had confirmed that Burq's claimed metallic effects were genuine, although it was not clear if these effects were lasting. Furthermore they had found that the symptoms of hysterical hemianesthesia could be transferred from one side of the body to the other with application of metal disks (and later, magnets). When sensation was restored to a region on one side of the body, symmetrical regions on the healthy side lost normal sensibility. It was suggested that the metals effected a dynamic transfer of a functional lesion responsible for the anesthesia from one hemisphere of the brain to the other. These findings stimulated further research by Alfred Binet, Charles Féré, Joseph Babinski, and others, and led to Charcot's interest in hypnosis.

Jean Marie Charcot

Charcot undertook research in the use of hypnosis with a selected group of hysterical female patients. They were typically put in the first stage of hypnosis, a cataleptic trance, by the use of a bright light or a sudden noise. The second stage, lethargy, was induced by having the patients shut their eyes, and the third stage, somnambulism, by instructing the patient to move about. Charcot believed that hysteria was caused by a morbid organization of the nervous system, and he described the hysterical crisis as comprised of four stages: the epileptoid phase, the large movements phase, the passionate attitudes phase, and the termination stage of delirium and muscular resolution. The similarity between symptoms of hysteria and those that can be induced by hypnotic suggestion led Charcot to theorize that hypnosis is a form of experimental hysteria, and that susceptibility to hypnotic suggestion can only be found in hysterical patients. He conjectured that the hysterical symptoms are a consequence of autosuggestions generated within a region of the patient's mind isolated from waking consciousness.

Charcot repeatedly performed experiments on dozens of hypnotically susceptible patients, some of whom were paid a fee and maintained for this purpose in the hospital. One day a week, his clinic, with lectures on and demonstrations of hysterical patients, was open to the general public. His clinic became a highly fashionable event attracting a variety of socialites, actors, authors, and others who came to observe patients presenting dramatic portrayals of the "classical" states of lethargy, catalepsy, somnambulism, and seizures. Charcot was criticized for exploiting sick patients; conversely, Charcot faced charges that the patients learned their symptoms as they were rehearsed repeatedly in the sorts of responses he expected, because their welfare depended on their displaying the behaviors he sought to validate his theories. His patients have been described as vying with each other to produce the classical symptoms to make themselves more interesting.

One patient, Blanche Wittmann, nicknamed the Queen of Hysterics because of her talent in reproducing the three stages of hypnosis with a grand finale of a hysterical "crisis," is said to have confessed to Jules Janet, a brother of Pierre Janet, that even during the throes of a hypnotic trance she was aware of her "act." It was said that Charcot's interns and other assistants organized the experiments and demonstrations, prepared the patients, and conducted the hypnotic sessions, and that, because Charcot failed to check the conduct of the experiments, he was unaware of their inadequacies. Sigmund Freud studied with Charcot for six months in 1889. Other students of Charcot to achieve fame include Pierre Janet, Gilles de La Tourette, and Joseph Babinski (Harrington, 1987).

Bernheim and the Nancy School

About 1885, criticisms against metalloscopy research by Hippolyte Bernheim (1840–1919), a physician in Nancy, France, led to its being discredited, and further investigations were abandoned. At about the same time Bernheim learned that A. A. Liébault, a country doctor, was successfully using hypnosis to cure patients. Bernheim was impressed by Liébault's success in curing a case of sciatica by direct hypnotic suggestion—a case that had failed to respond to his conventional treatment. In 1882, they opened a clinic, known as the Nancy School. In a textbook published in 1884, Bernheim stated that susceptibility to hypnosis does not reflect a pathological functioning of a morbid nervous system; it has a mental etiology. He suggested that Charcot's "classic" three stages of hypnosis were artifacts of specific suggestions made to the patient and that Charcot's identification of hypnosis with hysteria was mistaken.

Bernheim believed that the phenomena of hypnotism can only be explained ideogenically; the hypnotist's suggestions to the hypnotized subject cause hypnotic phenomena and reflect normal psychological processes in a state of increased passivity-receptivity engendered by the suggestions. Hence hypnosis cures when the patient—in a state of increased suggestibility induced by the hypnotist—uncritically accepts new attitudes and beliefs. Statistics were compiled at the Nancy School to demonstrate the lack of marked difference in the proportion of men and of women susceptible to hypnosis, that young children are hypnotizable, and that all subjects are more or less influenced by hypnotic procedures, with only about 10% of persons showing no influence at all. Freud spent several weeks with Bernheim and Liébault in 1889 in order to perfect his hypnotic techniques. He also translated Bernheim's textbook into German.

Pierre Marie Félix Janet

Neurologist and psychologist Pierre Marie Félix Janet (1859–1947) was known for his studies of hysteria and neuroses and for his application of psychological theory to the clinical treatment of hysteria. He collaborated with Charcot at the Salpêtrière in demonstrating that no signs of actual neuropathy can be found in genuinely hysterical patients. In 1890 Janet succeeded Charcot as head of the psychological laboratory.

Janet assumed that mental pathology is determined by the functional features of the brain and a weakened and poorly integrated nervous system. In order to determine whether sexual factors are important in the etiology of hysteria, he examined 120 hysterical patients. He found a preeminently erotic disposition in only four and concluded that hysterical patients are generally too self-centered and emotionally restricted to be preoccupied with sexual interests. Janet emphasized the importance of psychogenic or "ideogenic" causes in the etiology of hysteria and criticize Freud's insistence on a universal psychosexual etiology of the neuroses. He traced hysterical symptoms to a system of "fixed ideas" that concentrated in one field of consciousness and controlled the patient's mental life. The fixed ideas "may develop completely during the attacks of hysteria and express themselves then by acts and words" (Janet, 1892/1977), and are also revealed in dreams, "natural somnambulisms," and hypnotic states. The fixed ideas, over which the patient has no control, arise from a persisting traumatic memory of a series of emotionally distressing events that the patient appears to have completely forgotten, but that can be remembered in a hypnotic state.

Janet claimed that when the patient was able to express the traumatic memories, the symptoms improved or disappeared. One of his therapeutic techniques involved asking his patients, usually under hypnosis, to describe the circumstances in which a symptom first occurred. Then, to eliminate the symptom, he gave the patient a direct hypnotic suggestion that the circumstances the patient recalled had not actually occurred. His success in treating hysterical patients with a combination of hypnosis and psychological analysis led him to devise a treatment plan for various types of hysterical symptoms. He stressed that each patient must be treated as a unique case, not in terms of a generalized psychological theory.

Sigmund Freud and Psychoanalysis

For most of the first half of the twentieth century, Sigmund Freud (1856–1939) and his speculations on the origin of psychopathology had perhaps a more pervasive influence on both professional and popular opinion in the United States than any other single theorist.

Freud received his medical degree from the University of Vienna in 1881, later deciding to specialize in neurology. In 1885 he studied for six months at Charcot's clinic at the Salpêtrière, where he was impressed by Charcot's theory that hysterical phenomena are generated by ideas isolated

psychically in some second region of the patient's mind that is separate from normal waking consciousness. In 1886, he began private practice, specializing in nervous diseases (predominantly hysteria). In this practice he used the conventional treatments for neurosis: massage, hydrotherapy, electrical stimulation, the rest cure, and hypnosis. Freud used hypnosis primarily to suggest to the patient that specific symptoms would disappear. He also used a "pressure technique" in which he placed his hand on the patient's forehead to elicit memories.

Breuer, Freud, and the First Version of the Psychoanalytic Theory of Psychopathology

Early in the 1890s, Freud and his colleague, Josef Breuer, began to collaborate in developing a psychoanalytic theory to explain hysteria. Their collaboration produced the first version of psychoanalytic theory, *On the Psychical Mechanism of Hysterical Phenomena: Preliminary Communication* (Breuer & Freud, 1895/1955), in which they identified an unconscious memory or complex of memories of a psychical trauma as the pathogen that causes hysteria. An event (or series of events) that causes distressing affect, such as fright, anxiety, shame, or physical pain, can result in a psychical trauma in a susceptible person, and if memory of the event is repressed it acts as a determining cause of hysterical symptoms. They hypothesized that if the distressing affect thus generated is discharged by energetic involuntary and/or voluntary reaction, the memory of the event fades. However if no appropriate reaction occurs, either because it is prohibited by social circumstances or the patient voluntarily suppresses (defends against) memory of affective ideas intolerable to the ego, the memory persists, inaccessible to consciousness, and retains its quota of affect, which is converted into pathological somatic symptoms.

Because patients are reluctant to talk about the event that originally precipitated a hysterical symptom or, much more often, are genuinely unable to remember it, the event cannot be discovered by questioning the patient. However, if the patient is hypnotized, the memory can be recovered. Freud and Breuer claimed that when the patient described the event that had provoked a hysterical symptom and expressed the affect that had accompanied it, the symptom immediately disappeared. They conceded that new symptoms may replace those eliminated, but considered their method superior to attempts to remove the symptoms by means of direct suggestion.

Much of this theory relied on one particular case. Breuer treated a young woman identified by the pseudonym Anna O., for numerous disabling somatic symptoms. He found that Anna went readily and often spontaneously into trance states, during which she recalled the circumstances in which a particular symptom first appeared, accompanied by an emotional reaction that had not occurred at the time, after which the symptom improved or even disappeared. Throughout his career, Freud continued to claim that Breuer had achieved a great therapeutic success with Anna O. However, research undertaken by Ellenberger (1972) revealed that this was not the case; almost immediately after Breuer ended her treatment, Anna O. was hospitalized in a sanitarium where she spent some time under medical treatment. She finally recovered and subsequently achieved recognition in the feminist movement in general and with her social work with unwed mothers in particular.

In 1895 Breuer and Freud published *Studies on Hysteria* (1895/1955), which included five case histories of hysteria (the case of Anna O. and four treated by Freud) and his *Psychotherapy of Hysteria*. In the preface to the book's first edition, Breuer and Freud stated that "Our view is that sexuality seems to play a principal part in the pathogenesis of hysteria as a source of psychical traumas and as a motive for defense, that is, for repressing ideas from consciousness" (p. xxix). But in order to protect the confidentiality of their patients they did not publish details of their observations in support of this view.

The Psychoanalytic Theory of Psychopathology, Second Version—Freud's Seduction Theory

In 1896, Freud published *The Aetiology of Hysteria* (Freud, 1896/1950a), in which he stated unequivocally that the unconscious memories that generate hysterical symptoms are inevitably of one or more premature actual sexual experiences in early childhood (stimulation of the genitals, coitus-like activities, etc.). Freud asserted that he could recognize the connection between an infantile sexual experience and every symptom in 18 cases of hysteria that he had treated, and that this was confirmed by therapeutic success with each patient when he brought them to recall the pathogenic memory. His discovery that infantile sexual experience is the origin of neuropathology, Freud claimed, was a revelation as momentous as the discovery of the source of the Nile. The alleged sexual experience was either an isolated instance of abuse by strangers or, much more frequently, seduction by a caretaker, near relation, or siblings who initiated the child into sexual intercourse and maintained a regular love-relation with him, often for years.

Freud had had great difficulty in eliciting memories of early sexual experience from his patients. He referred to the fact that his patients would reproduce the scenes only under the strongest compulsion, trying to hide the most violent sensations while doing so, and claiming that they had no real feeling of recollecting these scenes. However, he asserted that the incidents must have been real because the recollections by different patients displayed uniformity in certain details that must have followed identical experiences. Uniformity of recollection is, unfortunately, more consistent with the simple explanation that Freud's conviction of what the memory ought to be was determining the content of the memory.

Not long after publishing his seduction theory, Freud began to realize that some of his patients had not in fact actually been seduced, and in 1897, he discarded both the theory and his pressure technique. He substituted instead the method of free association and the procedure of interpretation, including the interpretation of dreams.

Freud claimed in his *On the History of the Psychoanalytic Movement* (1914/1950b) that he knew of no influence that drew "my interest to [dreams] or inspired me with any helpful expectations." He was, however, familiar with J. Hughlings Jackson's theory that during sleep, the higher mental processes no longer "keep down" the processes of the lower brain centers. He had quoted Jackson's statement, "Find out all about dreams, and you will have found out all about insanity." In Freud's view, dreams, like neurotic symptoms, provide a conduit for the indirect discharge of accumulated nervous excitations. In sleep, although the body is no longer attuned to external stimulation, internal stimulation continues since organic needs are always signaling their presence.

The Third Version of Freud's Psychoanalytic Theory of Psychopathology

When Freud discarded his seduction theory, he recognized that his patients had been right in expressing their disbelief in the recollections he had forced upon them. However Freud did not relinquish his belief in a universal sexual etiology for the neuroses; instead he modified his theory. "Analysis had led by the right paths back to these sexual traumas and yet they were not true. At that time I would gladly have given up the whole thing . . . perhaps I persevered only because I had no choice and could not then begin at anything else. . . ." (Freud, 1914/1950b, p. 299). If Freud's theory of the sexual etiology of neurosis, with its accompanying concepts of repressed memories and resistance to recovery of repressed memories, was invalid, it followed that his psychoanalytic method of treating patients by retrieving repressed memories was invalid. In that event, Freud would have had to abandon both his method of analysis and of therapy.

Freud rejected the possibility that in his psychoanalysis he might have led patients to report false memories of sexual seductions. Instead he concluded that the memories he had elicited were real—but not of real experiences. The memories were memories of infantile fantasies of sexual seduction created because they had wished either to be seduced or to seduce. Why, if the patients had fantasized sexual seduction in early childhood, had they repressed the memories of these fantasies? Freud answered this question with the further assumption that childhood sexual fantasies are always incestuous—hidden behind the fantasies of seduction were infantile wishes for erotic gratification with their parents that led to fear of parental wrath and punishment, and so the memories of the fantasies were repressed. Freud also had to explain why neurotic patients had incestuous sexual fantasies, and this he did with the generalization that all young children create such fantasies. Mentally healthy individuals would show the same resistances if presented with evidence that they had once had such fantasies. To Freud, the only difference between patients and nonpatients was that the analyst was in a position to bring pressure to bear on patients, so as to induce them to realize and overcome their resistances. In short, Freud claimed that criticism of his theory by others was itself evidence for the validity of the theory.

The Psychoses

Psychoanalytic theory was least developed in the matter of the major psychoses, especially schizophrenia and bipolar affective disorder. However, the central theme of psychoanalytic thinking about the psychoses, and the schizophrenias in particular, determined that they arise from a massive failure of repression of unconscious material.

From this perspective, schizophrenia symptoms are like dream-material intruding into and controlling consciousness in the waking state. Freud referred to psychosis as a waking dream. The central difference between the neuroses and the psychoses, according to Freud, was that the neurotic did not deny the existence of reality, whereas the psychotic did deny reality and tried to substitute something else for it.

Freud's extensive modifications were manufactured in order to shore up the suppositions from which the theory had originated. And for more than a hundred years, analysts indoctrinated with Freudian theory or its various modifications directed the course of therapy to the elucidation of childhood erotic fantasies and wishes. Freud elaborated his psychoanalytic theory, publishing extensively, until his death in 1939. Freud died in London, where he had moved from Vienna after the U.S. government intervened with the German Nazi government to permit him to do so.

Empirical Studies of Psychoanalytic Theory and Practice

The years following Freud's death saw increasing pressure for empirical evidence both for the hypotheses that underlay the theory and for the claims that psychoanalytic therapy provided an effective treatment for the neuroses. In a now famous, albeit controversial study, Hans Eysenck (1952), using data from the work of Denker (1946), compared outcomes of intensive psychoanalytic treatment, brief treatment by general practitioners, and no treatment at all for neuroses. Denker's study had reported that, although psychoanalysis had produced a 44% rate of significant improvement, other psychotherapies had produced 64%, and general practitioners had produced the best results with 72%. Eysenck's analysis implied that the more intensive and prolonged the therapy (psychoanalysis being the best example of this) the less likely was the patient to make a significant recovery.

Eysenck's study left reasonable grounds for criticism, in that he failed to match the groups for severity (or anything else), and he left the definitions of cure unreported. In spite of these criticisms, two key conclusions could reasonably be drawn: (a) up to that time, no systematic, methodologically adequate attempt had been made to test the efficacy of psychotherapy, and (b) the rate of improvement of the patients in Denker's study vastly exceeded anything reported by psychoanalysis. References to the reports of Freud himself on the success of his efforts provided to be seriously unreliable. The application of Freudian ideas to the major mental illnesses was to come later, and came fraught with problems.

One consequence of the rise of psychodynamic ideas and practices was that, given the avoidance of biological methods of either diagnosis or treatment, no *a priori* reason justified why the practitioner should have medical training. Freud himself was to remark that medical training was unnecessary for the practice of psychoanalysis. In the United States, however, until the second half of the century, psychotherapy was carefully regulated and defined as a medical technique, only to be provided by a psychologist or social worker under the supervision of a psychiatrist. Indeed in some jurisdictions the supervisor needed only to be a physician without formal psychiatric qualifications. (See chapters by Benjamin, DeLeon, Freedheim, & VandenBos and Routh & Reisman in this volume.)

Morton Prince and Multiple Personality

Boston neurologist Morton Prince (1854–1929) adapted the theories and methods of Freud and Janet to his own interests in the study of neuroses, the unconscious, and hypnosis. Prince was interested in both conversion hysteria and multiple personality, and his paper, written at the end of the nineteenth century and during the first several decades of the twentieth century, provided examples of both. His case history of Miss Beauchamp is cited as a classic example of multiple personality (Prince, 1975). The essential diagnostic feature of multiple personality is the apparent existence in the individual of two or more distinct personalities that alternate in dominance. Each personality appears complex and integrated, has memories unique to that personality, and displays patterns of behavior, emotional expression, and ways of interacting socially that differentiate it from the other personalities. The personalities seem often to be opposites; a retiring, highly moralistic person may on occasion behave in a self-advertising and outrageously amoral manner. The transition from one to another of the personalities is often sudden and associated with apparent psychosocial stress. The original personality has no knowledge of the others, whereas the sub-personalities are usually aware of each other.

The problem with all cases of multiple personality that have been highly publicized is that the extra personalities are initially brought forth by the psychotherapist, usually while the client is in a hypnotic trance and therefore suggestible. The names of the additional personalities may be suggested by the therapist. It is unclear whether each personality pre-existed or was constructed and shaped by the clinician.

Spanos (1986) suggested that multiple personality is not a disease, but a role learned in response to situations in which this behavior is useful and considered appropriate. He attributes the astonishing increase in frequency of reported multiple personalities to the increased use by mental health professionals who encourage patients to adopt this role. We note that the motivation to present multiple personality is particularly intense when a client has been accused of a serious crime and hopes to transfer responsibility for the crime to an alleged alternate personality.

THE TWENTIETH CENTURY

The twentieth century saw the development of major changes in the treatment of psychopathology and in the understanding of the biological and psychological processes that are involved in its development.

Treatment Approaches

One significant development involved attempts to treat the patient by direct intervention in the structure and function of the nervous system. Brain surgery was among the first of these interventions.

Brain Surgery

In 1890, Swiss psychiatrist G. Burkhardt, assuming that the causes of specific kinds of abnormal behavior were located in particular parts of the brain, removed parts of the cortex in patients with hallucinations and other symptoms, hoping to eliminate symptoms. He claimed that the treatment improved patients, but he came under criticism from his colleagues and abandoned the technique (Goldstein, 1950). Others performed surgery on mental patients, including an Estonian neurosurgeon who, in 1900, cut the connections between the frontal and parietal lobes, but with no detectable improvement in patient condition (Valenstein, 1986).

Not until the 1930s did brain surgery occur to any significant extent. In 1935, two Portuguese physicians, Egas Moniz and Almeida Lima, performed an operation using a procedure that came to be known as prefrontal lobotomy (Moniz, 1937). Walter Freeman and James Watts (1948) later modified the method in the United States. By 1950, more than 5,000 lobotomies had been performed in the United States. An estimated tens of thousands of such operations were performed worldwide between 1948 and 1952. The surgery was performed initially on patients with chronic schizophrenia, but was later extended to patients with other psychiatric disorders, as well as to criminals (Valenstein, 1986) and to hyperactive children (Masson, 1986). In the course of time other related forms of brain surgery such as transorbital lobotomy, and cingulotomy were developed.

These procedures, collectively referred to as "psychosurgery," became the focus of scientific and ethical controversy. Ethical concerns centered on the irreversible damage done to the psychological functioning of the patient and extended as far as the actual circumstances under which the operations were performed, sometimes in the physician's office on an outpatient basis, often by physicians who were not qualified neurosurgeons. On one occasion Freeman administered a transorbital lobotomy in a motel room, first anesthetizing the patient by administering electroconvulsive treatment (ECT) to produce coma (Valenstein, 1986). Freeman ultimately lost his surgical privileges at a California hospital following the death of a patient during surgery. By that time, psychosurgery was already in decline, partly because of the extreme ethical questions raised, and partly because emerging new medications provided safer, more effective and humane alternatives.

Fever Therapies

In 1887, Austrian psychiatrist Julius Wagner-Jauregg published a paper on the therapeutic effects of fever on cases of psychosis. For some years he conducted research on the effects of various febrile illnesses (e.g., tuberculosis) on patients with diagnosis of psychosis, reporting some successes and many failures. In 1917 he treated some general paresis patients with blood from a patient infected with malaria. Three of them died, and not until 1919 was he able to define the kind of malarial infection that would be beneficial. Others quickly accepted his technique, and in 1924 he received the Nobel Prize for this discovery.

The exact manner in which these effects occurred was a matter of speculation, many physicians concluding that the high heat of the fever itself killed the organisms causing the syphilitic infection. Other methods of generating high heat were employed, including hot baths, hot air, radiothermy, electric blankets, and so forth. The general success of the fever treatment prompted an attempt to apply it to cases of schizophrenia, manic-depressive psychosis, and other psychiatric syndromes. These were unsuccessful, and the use of malarial fever treatment in GPI was abandoned with the discovery of penicillin (Shorter, 1997).

Comas and Convulsions

The first extensive systematic use of treatments intended to induce convulsions and/or coma was reported by Manfred Sakel (1900–1957). While treating drug addicts in a Berlin sanitarium, Sakel accidentally gave an overdose of insulin to one patient who also had diabetes. The patient became comatose, but on recovery appeared to have lost her craving for drugs. Sakel began to apply insulin as a treatment for addiction. A later accidental overdose was given to a patient who was also psychotic. In this case, the patient's psychosis appeared to be much reduced, inspiring Sakel to develop insulin coma treatment for schizophrenia. He reported that he had observed many successful outcomes but, as usual, no independent objective evaluation of the improvement was conducted (Sakel, 1935). This procedure became widespread until it was displaced by the use of the synthetic chemical metrazol.

In 1935, a Hungarian physician J. L. Von Meduna (1896–1964) reported that he had discerned subtle differences in the brain cells of epilepsy and schizophrenia patients. He inferred that epilepsy and schizophrenia were antagonistic and that schizophrenia might be treated by inducing convulsions. On the basis of experiments with animals, Meduna (1935) decided to use camphor injections but soon switched to metrazol and reported impressive improvements in his patients. By the 1940s, metrazol shock (convulsion) therapy was widespread in the psychiatric hospitals of the United States. Some evidence indicated that metrazol was

effective with depressed patients, but not with schizophrenia patients, and it was ultimately replaced with electroconvulsive treatment (ECT). In the case of both insulin coma and metrazol-shock the basic initial observations had been accidental; no accepted theory existed regarding the biological mechanisms that might account for the reported effects and little appears to have been attempted to develop one.

In 1937 two psychiatrists, Cerletti and Bini (1938), presented an account of their use of ECT of sufficient strength to produce convulsions and coma in psychiatric patients, some of whom showed an improvement in clarity of thinking and general reality contact. Although the procedure was applied rather widely to psychotic patients and especially schizophrenia patients, the results were discouraging. Huston and Locher (1948), for example, found no difference in the rate of improvement in depressed patients treated with ECT compared with untreated patients. In addition, improvement in the untreated lasted longer than in the treated patients. Later studies of damage attributable to ECT (Alpers & Hughes, 1942) showed destructive effects to brain tissue. Again, no satisfactory theory accounted for the effects of the treatment. Gordon (1948) listed no fewer than 50 hypotheses, ranging from the belief that the patient had experienced the convulsion as death and rebirth, to the view that the shock acted as a stressor and stimulated stress-resistance mechanisms in bodily functioning (Maher, 1966, pp. 499–500). Today, ECT is used sparingly and then mainly with certain kinds of affective disorder.

Experimental Psychopathology

Experimental investigation of psychopathology was stimulated by the methods that were being developed to measure the psychological processes of healthy individuals in laboratories of experimental psychology in the latter part of the nineteenth century. Although its beginnings were modest, experimental investigations of psychopathology were to expand throughout subsequent decades.

Kraepelin

Investigation of psychopathology using the methods of scientific experimental psychology began with the work of Emil Kraepelin (1856–1926), who established a laboratory in Heidelberg in 1890, where he conducted experimental studies of psychiatric patients. His work attracted others to join his laboratory, notably British psychologist/anthropologist William Rivers, and American psychiatrist, August Hoch. Rivers (1895) and Hoch (1904) published translations of some of the work done at Heidelberg, but much of Kraepelin's experimental work, which was published from 1895 onward in his series of volumes *Psychlogischen Arbeiten,* still remains untranslated (Kraepelin, 1915).

Kraepelin's work was guided by the basic assumption that all psychopathological behaviors arise from some defect in nervous system function. The task was to measure nervous system functions as carefully and quantitatively as possible. The kind of defect discovered could help explain the clinical phenomena that had led to the diagnosis. Measuring procedures were limited to those that could be applied externally (i.e., without invasion of tissue). The use of experimental methods and quantitative measurement in medical research generally was still in an early stage. It is noteworthy that Kraepelin had no method for observing or measuring brain functions in the living human being. Modern methods of electroencephalography and brain imaging lay far in the future. Postmortem examination of the brain provided opportunity to measure structure, but not function.

Kraepelin and his colleagues regarded experimental psychology and experimental physiology as a unitary domain of study. The functions examined included motor movements, reaction time to various kinds of stimulus, memory, word associations, and mental work (simple calculations). Control comparisons were made between patients and nonpatients. The diagnostic categories of the patients involved included paresis, dementia praecox (schizophrenia), neurasthenia, and epilepsy. Although Kraepelin emphasized quantitative measurement, no statistical tests available could assess the reliability of the differences that he found, which limited him to reporting absolute differences. In this respect, too, his situation was the same as that generally prevalent in medical research at that time.

The investigation of psychophysical and physiological factors in mental illness became a continuing theme in the ensuing decades. Psychological laboratories were established in the early twentieth century at McLean Hospital in Massachusetts, the Worcester State Hospital, and the New York State Psychiatric Institute. Some laboratories were situated in academic institutions, notably at Yale University, where Edward Scripture conducted studies on reaction time in various diagnostic groups. Hunt (1936) and Shakow (1971) include useful reviews of the development of experimental psychopathology during this period.

With increasing hegemony of psychoanalysis in American academic psychiatry in the period immediately following World War II, experimental research into psychopathology experienced a decline. One triumphant analyst chronicled this change with the assertion that "psychological apparatus had found its way to the lumber rooms of psychiatric clinics, covered with dust and rusting away without having left

behind any gap in the resources of the research worker and the practitioner" (Maher & Maher, 1979).

The Conditioned Reflex

Russian physiologist Ivan Pavlov (1849–1936) was one of the most influential scientists of his time. Although his work was almost exclusively concerned with animals, he made significant contributions to human psychopathology. In 1914, in the course of conducting an experimental investigation of discrimination in a dog, Pavlov made a finding of significance to the understanding of neurosis. While investigating the dog's capacity to discriminate between different shapes, the shapes were progressively altered until no discrimination could be made. When the hitherto quiet dog was brought back into the laboratory room, it struggled when harnessed in its stand, whined, and bit at the apparatus. "In short," wrote Pavlov, "it presented all of the symptoms of a condition of acute neurosis." (Pavlov, 1927/1960, p. 291). Further research was undertaken with dogs differing in temperament, one type being extremely excitable, the other type extremely inhibitable. The results led Pavlov to conclude that experimental neurosis develops only in animals of extreme types, and the symptoms of neurosis differ in the two types and relate to the characteristics of the animals' different nervous organizations.

Coincidentally, a violent storm flooded Petrograd, and the dogs had to swim from the kennels to the laboratory. After this experience some of them displayed disturbed behavior similar to the "experimental neuroses" obtained in the laboratory. Pavlov concluded that ". . . a development of a chronic pathological state of the hemispheres can occur from . . . first a conflict between excitation and inhibition which the cortex finds itself unable to resolve; second the action of extremely powerful and unusual stimuli." (Pavlov, 1957, p. 318). Pavlov linked the phenomena seen in laboratory studies of animals with those seen in human psychopathology in a manner that was to influence experimental psychopathology for several decades to come.

Much later, Howard Liddell at Cornell University investigated the adaptive behavior of sheep and goats in which the thyroid had been removed. Using a mild shock, Liddell was interested in how long the animal would require to make a conditioned anticipatory response. Both animals with and without thyroid glands learned this quite readily. Because of time pressure to complete his experiments, he increased the number of trials at each testing session. This had the unexpected effect of producing an experimental neurosis in certain sheep. They showed excitement, alarm, struggled to escape, showed rapid heart rate and breathing, micturation and defecation, and so forth. The sheep from which the thyroid gland had been removed, however, did not show these effects. Liddell (1944) concluded that the critical element in the experimental neurosis was not the difficulty in making discriminations, but the emotional reaction to the threat posed by the electric shock. Although Liddell performed no human studies, he made the theoretical link with human neuroses explicit in his reports of his animal work. W. H. Gantt (1953) performed similar studies on dogs.

Experimental Neurosis and Approach-Avoidance Conflict

Other animal behavior studies were conducted within a Freudian framework. They centered on the hypothesis that a conflict between a motive toward pleasure (a "drive") and a fear of punishment (another "drive") constituted the core element of the psychodynamics of animal—and human—neurosis. Clark Hull at Yale performed much of the initial work. Hull took basic tenets of Pavlovian psychology and sought to integrate them with certain Freudian concepts, with a view to understanding how such conflicts might be reduced by suitable environmental manipulations (Miller, 1944). Within this framework other experimenters studied the effect of variables designed to reduce the anxiety component of the conflict, thereby permitting the emergence of the positive (approach) component. These studies were attempting to discern "therapeutic" factors that might be applied to neurotic human patients. Investigations using animals included the effects of displacement and escape, Berkun (1957), Elder, Noblin, and Maher (1961), Taylor and Maher (1959), and many others. The paradigm was applied to many aspects of human behavior, including verbal statements in psychotherapy (Murray & Berkun, 1955), and neurotic behavior in general (Phillips, 1956).

After 1960, this approach declined, partly because of developing doubt about Freudian explanations of psychopathology. Another reason was methodological constraints involved in generalizing from animals to humans and increasing criticisms of the approach-avoidance model itself (e.g., Atthowe, 1960; Maher, 1964). Although laboratory animal research of this kind declined, the application of these ideas to humans was to become one of the main themes of behavior therapy.

Typologies of Mental Illness

The notion, embodied in the humor theory, that mental illness proceeded from an imbalance of some internal biological factor, survived for centuries. Its decline did not lead to the abandonment of typology. New ones followed, each sharing the assumption that normal personality included basic types, each with specific biological balance, and each more liable to a specific kind of psychopathology should the balance be disturbed.

Pavlov

Pavlov provided one such typology. He theorized that behavior, both normal and pathological, is determined by the interaction of three basic properties of the nervous system. These are the strength of the excitatory and inhibitory processes, the equilibrium of these processes, and their mobility. Pavlov initially based the typology upon observations of dogs in his laboratory, but later extended it to humans.

Kretschmer and Sheldon

German psychiatrist and neurologist Ernst Kretschmer (1888–1964) presented a theory of personality in which he attempted to link psychological disorders to physical build. In his 1921 *Körperbau und Charakter* (published in English in 1925), he proposed three main body types: the asthenic (thin), the athletic, and the pyknic (stout). Based on observations of patients in mental hospitals, he concluded that schizophrenia is linked to the asthenic, and manic-depression to the pyknic body type. Although, some studies of psychiatric groups found some support for the classification, significant criticisms pointed to different reactions of others to people of varying body types, and the effect of these reactions upon later behavior.

The basic idea behind his typology was developed more quantitatively in the United States by William Sheldon (1942). Sheldon also proposed a threefold classification of components of body form derived from stages of embryological development: the endomorphic component, with a prominence of intestines and other visceral organs; the mesomorphic component, with a prominence of bone and muscle; and the ectomorphic, with delicacy of skin, fineness of hair, and sensitivity of the nervous system. In an individual, each component is measured on a scale of three and a body type assigned by the three digits for each component. Sheldon proposed temperamental classifications to correspond to the morphological types. He published on this theme from 1927 to 1971, and in his later publications he reported findings based on a study of patterns of psychosis as related to physical constitution.

Eysenck

Hans Eysenck (1947) developed a typology of personality based in large part upon the Pavlovian model, together with some elements of Jung. His typology was framed within the statistical factor-analysis approach then common in Britain, whereby temperamental factors were defined as continua. Eysenck recognized three major independent continua or axes. The most basic was extraversion-introversion, in which extraversion was defined as a balance where inhibitory activity dominated excitatory processes, and introversion was the reverse. The position of any individual on this axis could be determined by various laboratory measures and questionnaires. The other two axes were psychoticism and neuroticism, each of which was scaled from low to high. Any given disorder could be produced by the combination of magnitudes of the three axes. Thus, antisocial personality (the psychopath) was located in the high extraversion, moderate psychoticism, and low neuroticism; schizophrenia was located in the high psychoticism, high introversion, and moderate neuroticism combination. Most of the laboratory measures tested sensory and/or motor performance such as critical flicker fusion, reactive inhibition in motor pursuit tasks, and the like.

Nervous Diseases—Neurosis and Neurasthenia

The debate about neurological disorders underlying nervous diseases, in particular hysteria and hypochondria, continued well into the late nineteenth century. One important event in the debate was the introduction of the concept of neurasthenia (literally weakness of the nerves) by George Beard (1880). The term had already found it way into medical literature (e.g., Kraus, 1831). Charcot's 1888–1889 modification (as cited in Lópes-Piñero, 1983) mentioned two major neuroses, hysteria and neurasthenia. Both terms passed into the twentieth century, each carrying the implication of a separate hereditary biological basis. Many psychopathologists claimed a gender difference in these two disorders, hysteria being a female neurosis and neurasthenia a male neurosis.

Organic versus Functional Psychoses

As brain studies of psychotic patients failed to reveal characteristic patterns of neuropathology in most psychoses, researchers began to recognize two kinds of psychosis. One type, the organic psychosis, arose from demonstrable biological origins, such as direct injury, toxic damage, or other destructive processes acting on the brain; the other type, it was suggested, arose from intrapsychic conflicts essentially similar to those that produce the neuroses. By the end of World War II, psychoanalytic conceptions had begun to dominate psychiatric thinking and practice in the United States. Although applied mainly to treatment of neuroses, some

practitioners attempted to treat psychotic patients on the assumption that the major psychotic syndromes—schizophrenia, depression, and manic-depressive psychosis—were the outcomes of severe intrapsychic conflicts and might therefore yield to intensive psychoanalytic treatment. Freud had been pessimistic about the possibility of such treatment, not because he thought these disorders primarily organic in nature, but because he judged the patient to have regressed so far to an infantile level of psychic development that the analyst could not make the interpersonal contact necessary for psychoanalytic treatment. Nonetheless many followers of psychoanalytic doctrine did attempt to apply psychological treatments. These included milieu therapy, group therapy, individual psychotherapy, occupational therapy, and recreational therapy (Shapiro, 1981).

In this context the fundamental distinction between the "organic" psychoses and the "functional" psychoses arose. Organic psychoses included paresis, Alzheimer's disease, the toxic psychoses, and other psychotic syndromes associated with undeniable biological damage. The functional were those for which no biological basis had been found and included schizophrenia, manic-depressive psychosis (now bipolar affective disorder), and psychotic depression. By default, these were regarded as having intrapsychic origins.

However, techniques to detect brain pathologies in the living patient were crude. One was electroencephalography (EEG), another x-ray. By midcentury, Hill and Parr (1950) concluded that the EEG's practical value was to enable us to know something about organic cerebral disorder but little else. Information also came from cases of patients who had suffered externally inflicted damage to the brain and where the locus of the injury could be relatively easily identified. (German neuropsychiatrist Conrad Rieger employed a battery of such tests as early as 1888.) It was time-consuming to administer, consisting of forty different tests (Benton, 1991). In the aftermath of each of the two world wars much research into brain-damaged patients provided a knowledge base about the effects of injuries to specific psychological functions. World War I gave rise to numerous neuropsychological tests, mostly from German sources. A second major wave occurred after World War II, primarily in the United States.

German psychologist Kurt Goldstein made an important contribution to this research. In a seminal monograph, Goldstein and Scheerer (1941) reported studies of brain-damaged patients. Their results had led them to formulate the hypothesis that substantial brain damage produced a loss of "abstract attitude." Schizophrenia patients tested with the same tests used on brain-damaged patients performed in similar ways, supporting the view that the functional psychoses were essentially organic.

By the 1940s, neuropsychological assessment of psychotic patients employed a range of tests for the assessment of brain damage (Benton & Howell, 1941). They largely focused on cognitive functions such as memory, attention, and other components such as the subtests of general adult intelligence tests. The combination of neuropsychological tests, EEG and its derivatives, and clinical neurological examination provided the main tools for investigating brain psychopathology connections until well into the second half of the twentieth century. After that, new techniques of brain imaging were to revolutionize the strategies of research.

Theories of Origin and Research in Antisocial Personality

Much experimental research has been generated by clinical assumptions about the characteristics and etiology of antisocial personality disorder. Keep in mind that most of these studies have been restricted to subjects in prisons or in psychiatric facilities. Such subjects are not only more likely to be extreme in their manifestation of sociopathy, but the effect of imprisonment of hospitalization may have influenced the obtained results.

Early theories of motivation postulated that all organisms are driven by a need to reduce sensory stimulation. In 1949, Hebb suggested instead that behavior can be motivated to increase sensory stimulation. Quay (1965) hypothesized that sociopaths, compared to normal people, have a lower basal reactivity to stimulation and so need more intense sensory input in order to maintain a level of cortical function adequate for the subjective experience of pleasure. Hence, they require more intense levels of stimulation.

It has also been suggested that the antisocial behavior of sociopaths reflects their inability to delay gratification of emotions and inhibit their impulses to action. Research results are inconsistent in their support of this hypothesis.

Behaviorism and Behavior Therapy

Neopavlovian behaviorism, in the forms developed by Hull at Yale and Eysenck in the United Kingdom, devoted much effort to the understanding of the processes associated with disordered behavior. The logic underlying the application of behavioral principles to the task of changing behavior were relatively straightforward. Maladaptive behavior was acquired (i.e., learned) and maintained in the same way that any other behavior is learned, namely by the circumstances surrounding when it first occurred and its consequences. The maladaptive behavior was either followed by some desired consequence (a reward), or served to avert some undesirable

consequence (a punishment). This general principle warranted the deduction that treatment should consist of extinguishing the maladaptive behavior by removing its rewards while, at the same time, giving rewards to the patient whenever normal behavior was displayed. When the behavior was primarily avoidant, the principle was that repeated exposure to the feared stimulus without any aversive consequences would ultimately lead to extinction of fear and the emergence of more adaptive behavior.

The effectiveness of these techniques had been demonstrated in the animal laboratory, but their application to actual patients was another matter. Psychoanalytic doctrine had asserted that the overt behavior was a "symptom" of an underlying intrapsychic conflict, and that removing the symptom without solving the conflict could not be curative. Thus, it was claimed, the symptom might disappear when treated by behavioral methods, but that a new symptom would emerge to take its place. This hypothesized phenomenon was called "symptom substitution." From the behavioral perspective, the so-called symptom was the problem, not just an indicator of an invisible problem. Although later studies were to show that the psychoanalytic claim was unfounded, the hegemony of psychoanalysis in psychiatric practice effectively prevented any extensive use of behavioral methods with patients. Although Salter (1949) published his classic *Conditioned Reflex Therapy* in 1949, not until the deficiencies of psychoanalytic treatment had been demonstrated did the way open for applying behavioral treatment. This development did not occur until after midcentury, and occurred at first more widely in the treatment of children's behavior problems in the classroom and the home, where psychiatric influences were usually minimal.

Recent Approaches

The half century that spanned the period 1950 to 2000 saw major changes in almost every aspect of theory and practice in psychopathology. One of the first was the decline of psychoanalysis.

The Decline of Psychoanalysis

It is important to note that the influence of psychoanalysis within psychiatry in the United States far exceeded its influence in psychiatry in other countries. The combined membership of the psychoanalytic societies of Austria, Denmark, France, Germany, The Netherlands, Italy, Sweden, and Switzerland by 1961 amounted to only 250 people (Szasz, 1961). In these countries and Great Britain, the psychoanalyst need not have had medical training, whereas in the

United States psychoanalysis became a medical specialty and also the predominant theoretical viewpoint of psychiatrists. Theories generally do not so much decline because of their inherent defects as because they have been replaced by better alternatives. Psychoanalysis declined as an influence in psychology for several reasons. One was the rise in psychopharmacology, another was the spread of behaviorist techniques, and a third was the increasingly evident defects of the theory itself.

The Rise of Psychopharmacology

Public hospitals provided the most dramatic evidence for the development of medications that could effectively alleviate the symptoms of both the neuroses and the psychoses. Wortis (1959) reported a survey of the world's medical literature between 1930 and 1959. Before 1953, reports of pharmacological treatments comprised less than 10% of published papers. By 1959, they comprised more than 70%, and the number was rising rapidly. The World Health Organization (1958) issued a classification of psychopharmacological compounds that covered seven categories, of which the most significant category, the major tranquilizers chlorpromazine and reserpine, were effective with psychoses. Psychoanalysts complained that medication merely removed the symptoms without curing the patient. Because they believed that the basic cause was psychological, they asserted that biological treatments were therefore inherently limited to palliative effects. As psychoanalysis itself was not achieving even palliative effects with psychotic patients, the argument was unimpressive. A more important problem with the early medications was their frequent and unpleasant side effects. These included dryness of mouth, involuntary motor movements of the tongue and lips (tardive dyskinesia), occasional episodes of dizziness, and such. When the psychotic symptoms subsided, patients often discontinued taking the medication because of the side effects, and relapsed into their previous psychotic condition. Improved drugs and techniques of supervised administration and/or injection of long-lasting timed release compounds have been developed to eliminate this cyclical effect.

The Rise of Behavior Modification

The first to report extension of behavioral methods to hospitalized psychosis patients were Allyon and Haughton (1962). Their approach consisted primarily of controlled application of rewards to patients when they behaved in an adaptive (i.e., "normal") manner. The underlying concept was that traditional treatment gave attention and care when a patient's behavior was maladaptive but ignored the patient when behavior was adaptive ("normal") thereby serving to reinforce symptomatic behavior and to extinguish normal behavior. Rewarding normal behavior would provide a more rational approach to eliminating symptoms. Studies directed toward eliminating eating problems, mutism, and other symptoms, reported successes (e.g., Allyon, 1963, Allyon & Haughton, 1962) and led some public hospitals to develop large-scale "token reinforcement" programs.

Behavioral methods of this kind ran into criticism. One criticism was that they turned the professional ethical imperative to provide care and attention to the sick on its head and therefore compromised patients' rights. Another was that patient improvements often were specific to the hospital setting and failed to persist after the patient was discharged. But the main factor in limiting the spread of this approach was the success of the new medications.

Behavior therapy proved broadly successful in treating nonpsychotic problems such as systematic desensitization of phobias, eliminating fear of flying, smoking reduction, and training mentally retarded patients and passed into the repertoire of psychiatric practice.

The Rise of Anti-Psychiatry

A point of view arose that opposed the medical definition of psychopathological disorders. Known as "anti-psychiatry," it drew inspiration from several sources. One source was Erving Goffman's (1961) *Asylums,* which described the effects of hospital rules and disciplines on patient behavior, finding their behavior similar to the inmates of other "total institutions" such as convents, the military, and prisons. Scheff (1966) argued that the distinction between sane and insane is not a scientific one, but essentially a matter of social judgment and social labeling of the deviant.

Perhaps the single most influential book was *The Myth of Mental Illness* (Szasz, 1961), in which Thomas Szasz asserted that the mental illnesses had no established biological basis and that they were not really a proper subject for medical diagnosis and treatment. Terms such as disease, symptom, diagnosis, therapy, and the like were therefore metaphorical when applied to psychopathology. In support of his contention, he pointed out the failure to find a biological basis for the various mental illnesses. Instead, he said, the "patient" suffers from problems of living in a stressful world, and his behavior may be best understood as a form of both communication and coping. While much of the work was centered on the problematic status of hysteria as a disease, his criticisms were addressed to the medicalization of deviant behavior generally. He alleged that the diagnosis that somebody was "mentally ill" served to limit that person's freedom of action and to prevent his communications from being taken seriously. His argument went on to point out that the practice of involuntary hospitalization meant that individuals were being incarcerated against their will when they had not committed crimes. Taken together, these were charges that contemporary psychiatry was bad science, unreliable practice, and an abuse of civil rights.

In this context, civil rights issues of the mentally ill attained the same kind visibility as civil rights issues for minorities and for women. The first redress for discrimination against the mentally ill was deinstitutionalization. Patients were discharged from hospitals in large numbers, some to return to their families, but many to live as welfare recipients or, in some cases, to live homeless on the streets. The scale of deinstitutionalization was large, and the results varied from striking improvements in the functioning of some patients to tragedies of death from neglect in some of the homeless mentally ill. Discharge from the hospitals had become feasible mainly because of the efficacy of the new medications. The focus of caring for the mentally ill then shifted to problems of medication maintenance outside the hospital and provision of some degree of supervisory care in halfway houses or other residential arrangements that provided transitional care between the hospital and the private home. Training in the vocational and social skills necessary to obtain employment and to get along in society outside the hospital emerged as a more practical goal for psychological techniques than had been the case with psychotherapy.

The Third Force and the New Therapies

One component of the antipsychiatry viewpoint was development of therapies based upon avowedly nonscientific principles. A spectrum of therapeutic techniques, known sometimes as the "Third Force," and sometimes as "humanistic" arose. These included transactional analysis (Berne, 1961); rational psychotherapy (Ellis, 1958, 1962), logotherapy (Frankl, 1953), gestalt psychotherapy (Perls, 1969), and client-centered therapy (Rogers, 1951).

These approaches in general rejected the concept that human behavior could be studied scientifically. Many humanistic therapists followed the lead of Carl Rogers in abandoning the use of the medical term *patient* preferring instead to use *client*. He, and they, did however retain the use of the medical term *therapy,* and defined themselves as "therapists." These methods were not often applied to seriously disturbed clients. The more usual clientele were primarily persons with minor neuroses, mild anxieties, self-esteem problems, and the like.

The Return of Diagnosis

One consequence of the hegemony of psychoanalysis in U.S. psychiatry was the diminution of interest in formal diagnosis. Patient evaluations typically oriented to a description of the hypothesized psychodynamics supposed to underlie the clinically manifest behavior. The decision as to what diagnostic label to attach to the patient's case was often considered a bureaucratic requirement for statistical reports but of no great significance in patient treatment. In 1952, the American Psychiatric Association published the first *Diagnostic and Statistical Manual of Mental Disorders (DSM-I)*. The categories employed conceived of mental disorders largely as personality reactions to various factors; biological, psychological, and social. It was replaced in 1968 by *DSM-II,* to bring it into line with the Eighth edition of the *International Classification of Diseases (ICD-8)*.

In later years, further revisions included *DSM-III* in 1980, *DSM III-R* (revised) in 1987, and *DSM-IV* in 1994, and *DSM IV-TR* in 2000. These successive versions included an increasing number of disorders and increasingly detailed criteria for definition of diagnostic categories. Research into various forms of psychopathology based upon this classification system has permitted more confident comparison of patient samples from different hospitals and from different countries, an essential requirement if independent replication of findings is to be established.

Progress in the Biological Understanding of Psychopathology

Certainly the most significant advances in the study of psychopathology have occurred in the closing decades of the twentieth century. Progress has been made in developing techniques for measuring the structure and function of the living brain and in our understanding of the complexities of genetics.

Brain Measurement

At midcentury observation of the structure and function of the living brain was confined to measuring the electrophysiology of brain activity with the electroencephalogram (EEG) and x-ray photography. These were replaced by various kinds of brain imaging that depended on the availability of high-powered computers and upon new ways of scanning the brain's metabolic activity. The major forms of brain imaging (brain "scanning") are positron emission tomography (PET), computerized tomography (CT), single photon emission computed tomography (SPECT) and magnetic resonance imaging (MRI). All of these methods rely on the fact that brain activity requires energy and this energy comes from increased metabolic activity in the brain area doing the work.

PET and CT scans begin with an injection of briefly acting radio-active material into the blood stream to mark changes in blood flow and blood concentration, thereby indicating where the increased metabolic activity is taking place. These scan methods require keeping radioactive material in the laboratory, and the injections are somewhat intrusive. These methods also are expensive and are limited as to the clarity of the images of brain structure they provide.

For all of these reasons, use of these scans has been generally superseded by magnetic resonance imaging. Not until 1959 was MRI used for medical diagnosis, and not until the 1970s did it came into general use for body imaging. MRI could detect natural changes in blood oxygen levels (an index of metabolic activity) without using radioactive materials. High-speed scanning of the whole brain in a few milliseconds enabled the investigator to study rapid localized brain activity changes during mental activity. Additionally, improvements in EEG made it possible to study the rise and fall of electrophysiological activity at specific points in the brain in real time.

The New Genetics

With the discovery of the double-helix DNA, the genetics of psychopathology passed from dependence upon inference from studies of twins to direct identification of genetic anomalies. One of the first outcomes of genetic studies of the psychoses was the evidence that no one-gene–one-disorder relationship existed. In the case of schizophrenia alone, Gottesman and Moldin (1998) reported on several studies between 1994 and 1997 that implicated seven different chromosomal regions in the genetics of schizophrenia.

Paradoxically, the increased sophistication of method provided by brain imaging and genetic analysis has not suggested that we are nearing a clear answer to the historic questions about the biology of mental illness. Instead it has gradually revealed the complexity of interactions between brain areas, the heterogeneity of brain anomalies in the psychoses, and the heterogeneity of the genetic factors in what appear to be unitary diagnostic categories.

Experimental Psychopathology

Experimental psychological work in psychopathology in the tradition of Kraepelin, Shakow, and others had also dwindled by midcentury. Much of this reflected the influence of psychoanalysis, which asserted that the answers to questions of etiology were already known and that experimental research

was not only irrelevant to the question but antithetical to the analytic method. Experimental research in psychopathology revived from the 1950s onward, extending in various directions, both behavioral and biopsychological. Progress of experimental work in psychopathology mirrored ongoing changes within general psychology and the neural sciences. Experimental work itself was greatly facilitated by the development of desktop computers, which replaced earlier bulky equipment. Computer portability made it possible to bring the laboratory to the patient rather than vice versa, thereby extending the kinds of sample that could be obtained.

By the final decade of the twentieth century, experimental investigations of psychotic patients focused mainly on the association between brain structure and function, on one hand, and cognitive and emotional processes on the other. As an illustration of the changing emphases, we might note that by 1991 biological research on schizophrenia—a previously "functional" psychosis comprised four of the five volumes of the *Handbook of Schizophrenia* (Nasrallah, 1991). It was now regarded as an obviously biological disorder.

INTO THE TWENTY-FIRST CENTURY

Looking backward from the vantage point of the new millennium, we see certain themes recurring in cyclical form. The dilemma posed by the need to care for persons unable to care for themselves versus the need to respect individual rights and liberties to make personal decisions leads to a cycle in which society creates institutions to provide the necessary care and later discharges the patients on civil rights principles. Advances made in technologies for other purposes prove to have significant effects in forwarding our understanding of psychopathology investigations and treatments. The microscope, the x-ray, electroencephalography, and brain imaging are examples of this. The emphasis on genetics and brain function shifts in time to an emphasis on social/environmental factors in the genesis of behavior. Themes within psychology in general, mostly significant but sometimes faddish, find reflection in psychopathology research trends. What is clear is that with progress our questions are becoming more sophisticated, and our answers more complicated.

REFERENCES

Ackerknecht, E. H. (1982). *A short history of medicine* (Rev. ed.). Baltimore: Johns Hopkins University Press.

Alpers, B. J., & Hughes, J. (1942). Changes in the brain after electrically induced convulsions in cats. *Archives of Neurology and Psychiatry, 47,* 385–398.

American Psychiatric Association. (1952). *Diagnostic and statistical manual of mental disorders.* Washington, DC: Author.

Atthowe, J. M. (1960). Types of conflicts and their resolution. *Journal of Experimental Psychology, 59,* 1–9.

Aubrey, J. (1972). *Aubrey's brief lives.* (O. L. Dick, Ed.) Harmondsworth, England: Penguin. (Original work published 1813)

Allyon, T. (1963). Intensive treatment of psychotic behavior by stimulus satiation and food reinforcement. *Behavior Research and Therapy, 1,* 53–61.

Allyon, T., & Haughton, E. (1962). Control of the behavior of schizophrenic patients by food. *Journal of the Experimental Analysis of Behavior, 5,* 343–352.

Battie, W. (1758). *A treatise on madness.* London: Whiston.

Beard, G. M. (1880). *A practical treatise on nervous exhaustion (neurasthenia): Its causes, symptoms, and sequences.* New York: Wood.

Benton, A. L. (1991). Basic approaches to neuropsychological assessment. In S. R. Steinhauer, J. H. Gruzelier, & J. Zubin (Eds.), *Handbook of schizophrenia* (Vol. 5, pp. 505–524). Amsterdam: Elsevier.

Benton, A. L., & Howell, I. L. (1941). The use of psychological tests in the evaluation of intellectual function following head injury. *Psychosomatic Medicine, 3,* 138–143.

Berkun, M. M. (1957). Factors in the recovery from approach avoidance conflict. *Journal of Experimental Psychology, 54,* 65–73.

Berne, E. (1961). *Transactional analysis in psychotherapy.* New York: Grove Press.

Brett, G. S. (1963). *Psychology ancient and modern: Our debt to Greece and Rome.* New York: Cooper Square.

Breuer, J., & Freud, S. (1955). Studies on hysteria. In J. Strachey (Ed.), *The standard edition of the complete psychological works of Sigmund Freud* (Vol. 2, pp. 1–305). London: Hogarth Press. (Original work published 1895)

Burton, R. (1927). *Anatomy of melancholy* (6th ed., F. Dell & P. Jordan-Smith, Eds.). New York: Tudor. (Original work published 1651)

Celsus. (1935). *De medicina, Books I–IV* (W. G. Spencer, Trans.). Cambridge, MA: Harvard University Press.

Cerletti, U., & Bini, L. (1938). L'Elettroshock [Electric shock]. *Archivo Generale di Neurologia, 19,* 266–268.

Chiarugi, V. (1987). *On insanity and its classification* (G. Mora, Trans.). Canton, Mass: Science History Publications. (Original work published 1793)

Clark, S. (1984). The scientific status of demonology. In B. Vickers (Ed.), *Occult and scientific mentalities in the Renaissance.* Cambridge, England: Cambridge University Press.

Clarke, E., & Jacyna, L. S. (1987). *Nineteenth-century origins of neuroscientific concepts.* Berkeley: University of California Press.

Clay, R. M. (1909). *The medieval hospitals of England.* London: Methuen.

Comte, A. (1830–1842). *Cours de philosophie positive* [in 60 lessons] (Vols. 1–6). Paris: Bachelier.

Cullen, W. (1784). *First lines of the practice of physick* (4th ed., Vol. 3). Edinburgh, Scotland: Creech.

Darnton, R. (1968). *Mesmerism and the end of the enlightenment in France.* Cambridge, MA: Harvard University Press.

Denker, R. (1946). Results of treatment of psychoneuroses by the general practitioner: A follow-up study of 500 cases. *New York State Journal of Medicine, 46,* 2164–2166.

Dowbiggin, I. (1985). Degeneration and hereditarianism in French mental medicine 1840–90: Psychiatric theory as ideological adaptation. In W. F. Bynum, R. Porter, & M. Shepherd (Eds.), *The anatomy of madness, essays in the history of psychiatry: People and ideas* (Vol. 1, pp. 188–232). London: Tavistock.

Düffler, J. (1996). *Nazi Germany 1933–1945.* London: Arnold.

Elder, T., Noblin, C. D., & Maher, B. A. (1961). The extinction of fear as a function of distance versus dissimilarity from the original conflict situation. *Journal of Abnormal and Social Psychology, 63,* 530–533.

Ellenberger, H. F. (1972). The Story of Anna O: A critical review with new data. *Journal of the History of the Behavioral Sciences, 8,* 267–279.

Ellis, A. (1958). Rational psychotherapy. *Journal of General Psychology, 59,* 35–49.

Ellis, A. (1962). *Reason and emotion in psychotherapy.* New York: Lyle Stuart.

Encyclopedia Britannica. (1771). *Dictionary of arts and sciences compiled upon a new plan by a society of gentlemen in Scotland* (Vol. 3, p. 59). Edinburgh, Scotland: A. Bell & C. MacFarquhar.

Esquirol, J. E. D. (1838). *Des maladies mentales considérée sous les rapports médical, hygienique et médico-legal* [Mental illnesses considered in their medical, hygienic, and medico-legal aspects] (Vols. 1–2). Paris: Ballière.

Eysenck, H. J. (1947). *The dimensions of personality.* London: Routledge & Kegan Paul.

Eysenck, H. J. (1952). The effects of psychotherapy: An evaluation. *Journal of Clinical and Consulting Psychology, 16,* 319–324.

Foucault, M. (1965). *Madness and civilization: A history of insanity in the age of reason* (R. Howard, Trans.). New York: Mentor Book/New American Library.

Frankl, V. E. (1953). Logos and existence in psychotherapy. *American Journal of Psychotherapy, 7,* 8–15.

Freeman, W., & Watts, J. W. (1948). Pain mechanisms and frontal lobes: A study of prefrontal lobotomy for intractable pain. *Annals of Internal Medicine, 28,* 747–754.

Freud, S. (1950a). The etiology of hysteria. In *Collected papers: Early papers* (Vol. 1, J. Riviere, Trans.). London: Hogarth Press. (Original work published 1896)

Freud, S. (1950b). On the history of the psycho-analytic movement. In *Collected papers: Early papers* (Vol. 1, J. Riviere, Trans.). London: Hogarth Press. (Original work published 1914)

Gall, F. J. (1835). *Sur les fonctions du cerveau et sur celles de chacune de ses parties* [On the functions of the brain and each of its parts] (Vol. 1-6, W. Lewis, Jr., Trans.). Boston: Marsh, Capen & Lyon. (Original work published 1825)

Galton, F. (1909). *Essays in eugenics.* London: Eugenics Education Society.

Gantt, W. H. (1953). The principles of nervous breakdown: Schizokinesis. *Annals of the New York Academy of Sciences, 56,* 143–163.

Goddard, H. H. (1912). *The Kallikak family.* New York: Macmillan.

Goffman, E. (1961). *Asylums.* New York: Anchor Doubleday.

Goldstein, K. (1950). Prefrontal lobotomy: Analysis and warning. *Scientific American* (Vol. 183, pp. 44–47).

Goldstein, K., & Scheerer, M. (1941). Abstract and concrete behavior: An experimental study with special tests. *Psychological Monographs, 41,* 239.

Gordon, H. (1948). Fifty shock therapy theories. *Military Surgeon, 3,* 397–401.

Gottesman, I. I., & Moldin, S. O. (1998). Genotypes, genes, genesis, and pathogenesis in schizophrenia. In M. F. Lenzenweger & R. H. Dworkin (Eds.), *Origins and development of schizophrenia* (pp. 5–26). Washington, DC: American Psychological Association.

Harms, E. (1967). *Origins of modern psychiatry.* Springfield, IL: Charles C. Thomas.

Harrington, A. (1987). *Medicine, mind, and the double brain: A study in nineteenth-century thought.* Princeton, NJ: Princeton University Press.

Hebb, D. O. (1949). *The organization of behavior; a neuropsychological theory.* New York: Wiley.

Hill, D., & Parr, G. (Eds.). (1950). *Electroencephalograpy.* New York: Macmillan.

Hilts, V. (1982). Obeying the laws of hereditary descent: Phrenological views on inheritance and eugenics. *Journal of the History of the Behavioral Sciences, 8,* 62–77.

Hoch, A. (1904). A review of some psychological and physiological experiments done in connection with the study of mental diseases. *Psychological Bulletin, 1,* 241–257.

Hunt, J. M. (1936). Psychological experiments with disordered persons. *Psychological Bulletin, 33,* 1–58.

Huston, P. E., & Locher, L. M. (1948). Manic-depressive psychosis: Course when treated and untreated with electric shock. *Archives of Neurology and Psychiatry, 60,* 37–48.

Jackson, J. H. (1887). Remarks on the evolution and dissolution of the nervous system. *Journal of Mental Science, 33,* 25–48.

Janet, P. (1977). The mental state of hystericals. In *Significant contributions to the history of psychology* (Vol. 2). Washington, DC: University Publications of America. (Original work published 1892)

Kraepelin, E. (1915). *Klinische psychiatrie: Ein lehrbuch für studierende und årtze* [Clinical psychiatry: A textbook for students and physicians]. Leipzig, Germany: Barth.

Kraus, L. A. (1831). *Kritisch-etymologisches medicinisches lexikon, Theil I* [Critical etymological medical dictionary, Part I]. Vienna, Austria: Haykul & Lechner.

Leicester, H. M. (1974). *Development of biochemical concepts from ancient to modern times.* Cambridge, MA: Harvard University Press.

Liddell, H. S. (1944). Conditioned reflex method and experimental neurosis. In J. McV. Hunt (Ed.), *Personality and the behavior disorders* (Vol. 1). New York: Ronald.

Lloyd, G. E. R. (Ed.). (1978). *Hippocratic writings* (J. Chadwick, W. N. Mann, I. M. Lonie, & E. T. Withington, Trans.). Harmondsworth, England: Penguin Books.

Locke, J. (1700). On disorders of the mind. *An essay concerning humane understanding* (4th ed.). London: Awnsham and Churchill.

López-Piñero, J. M. L. (1983). *Historical origins of the concept of neurosis* (D. Berrios, Trans.). Cambridge, England: Cambridge University Press.

MacCurdy, G. G. (1924). *Human origins, a manual of prehistory: The new stone age and the ages of bronze and iron* (Vol. 2). New York: D. Appleton.

MacDonald, M. (1981). *Mystical bedlam: Madness, anxiety and healing in seventeenth-century England.* Cambridge, England: Cambridge University Press.

Maher, B. A. (1964). The application of the approach-avoidance conflict model to social behavior. *Journal of Conflict Resolution, 8,* 287–291.

Maher, B. A. (1966). *Principles of psychopathology.* New York: McGraw-Hill.

Maher, B. A., & Maher, W. B. (1979). Psychopathology. In E. Hearst (Ed.), *The first century of experimental psychology* (pp. 561–621). Hillsdale, NJ: Erlbaum.

Maher, W. B., & Maher, B. A. (1982). The ship of fools: Stultifera navis or Ignis fatuus. *American Psychologist, 37,* 756–761.

Masson, J. M. (1986). *A dark science.* New York: Farrar, Straus and Giroux.

Meduna, L. V. (1935). Versuche uber die biologische beeinflussung des ablaufes der schizphrenie [Experiments on biological influences on the course of schizophrenia]. *Zeitschrift fuer die Gesamte Neurologie und Psychiatrie, 152,* 235–262.

Meyer, A. (1904). A few trends in modern psychiatry. *Psychological Bulletin, 1,* 217–240.

Miller, N. E. (1944). Experimental studies of conflict. In J. M. Hunt (Ed.), *Personality and the behavior disorders* (Vol. 1, pp. 431–465). New York: Ronald.

Moniz, E. (1937). Psycho-chirugie [Psycho-surgery]. *Nervenartz, 10,* 113–118.

Moore, J. W. (1910). The syphilis-general paralysis question. *Review of Neurology and Psychiatry, 8,* 259–271.

Moseley, E. (1838). *Eleven chapters on nervous and mental complaints.* London: Simpkin, Marshall & Cole.

Murray, E. J., & Berkun, M. M. (1955). Displacement as a function of conflict. *Journal of Abnormal and Social Psychology, 51,* 47–56.

Nasrallah, H. A. (Ed.). (1991). *Handbook of schizophrenia* (Vols. 1–5). Amsterdam: Elsevier.

Neaman, J. S. (1975). *Suggestion of the devil.* New York: Anchor.

Neugebauer, R. (1978). Treatment of the mentally ill in medieval and early modern England: A reappraisal. *Journal of the History of the Behavioral Sciences, 14,* 158–169.

Pavlov, I. P. (1957). *Experimental psychology and other essays.* New York: Philosophical Library.

Pavlov, I. P. (1960). *Conditioned reflexes: An investigation of the physiological activity of the cerebral cortex.* (G. V. Anrep, Ed. & Trans.). New York: Dover. (Original work published 1927)

Pearson, K. (1909). The groundwork of eugenics. *Eugenic Laboratory.* London: Dulau.

Pearson, K. (1910). The scope and importance to the state of the science of national eugenics. *Eugenic Laboratory.* London: Dulau.

Pearson, K. (1911). The academic aspect of the science of national eugenics. *Eugenic Laboratory.* London: Dulau.

Perls, F. S. (1969). *Gestalt psychotherapy verbatim.* Lafayette, CA: Real People Press.

Phillips, E. L. (1956). *Psychotherapy: A modern theory and practice.* Englewood Cliffs, NJ: Prentice-Hall.

Pinel, P. (1806). *A treatise on insanity* [Traité médico-philosophique de la aliénation mentale] (D. D. Davis, Trans.). Sheffield, England: Todd. (Original work published 1801)

Plato. (1892). *The dialogues of Plato* (B. Jowett, Trans.). New York: Macmillan.

Plato. (1894). *The republic* (B. Jowett, Trans.). Oxford, England: Clarendon Press.

Prince, M. (1975). *Psychotherapy and multiple personality: Selected essays (1885–1925).* Cambridge, MA: Harvard University Press.

Quay, H. (1965). Psychopathic personality as pathological stimulus seeking. *American Journal of Psychiatry, 122,* 180–183.

Retterstol, N. (1975). Scandinavia and Finland. In J. G. Howells (Ed.), *World history of psychiatry* (pp. 207–237). London: Ballière Tindall.

Rivers, W. H. (1895). Experimental psychology in relation to insanity. *Journal of Mental Science, 41,* 591–599.

Rogers, C. R. (1951). *Client-centered therapy.* Boston: Houghton Mifflin.

Rosen, G. (1968). *Madness in society: Chapters in the historical sociology of mental illness.* London: Routledge & Kegan Paul.

Russell, R. (1988). The lunacy profession and its staff in the second half of the nineteenth century, with special reference to the West Riding Lunatic Asylum. In W. F. Bynum, R. Porter, & M. Shepherd (Eds.), *The anatomy of madness: The asylum and its psychiatry* (Vol. 3, pp. 297–315). London: Routledge.

Sakel, M. (1935). *Neue behandlung der schizophrenia* [A new treatment for schizophrenia]. Vienna, Austria: Moritz Perles.

Salter, A. (1949). *Conditioned reflex therapy.* New York: Capricorn.

Scheff, T. J. (1966). *Being mentally ill.* Chicago: Aldine.

Scull, A. (1985). A Victorian alienist: John Conolly, FRCP, DCL (1704–1866). In W. F. Bynum, R. Porter, & M. Shepherd (Eds.), *The anatomy of madness: Essays in the history of psychiatry: People and ideas* (Vol. 1, pp. 103–150). London: Tavistock.

Sedler, M. J., & Dessain, E. C. (1983). Falret's discovery: The origin of the concept of bipolar affective illness. *American Journal of Psychiatry, 140*(9), 1127–1133.

Shakow, D. (1971). Some observations on the psychology (and some fewer, on the biology) of schizophrenia. *Journal of Nervous and Mental Diseases, 153,* 300–316.

Shapiro, S. (1981). *Contemporary theories of schizophrenia: Review and synthesis.* New York: McGraw-Hill.

Sheldon, W. H. (1942). *The varieties of temperament: A psychology of constitutional differences.* New York: Harper.

Shorter, E. (1997). *A history of psychiatry.* New York: Wiley.

Spanos, N. (1986). Hypnosis, nonvolitional responding, and multiple personality: A social psychological perspective. In B. A. Maher & W. B. Maher (Eds.), *Progress in experimental personality research* (Vol. 14, pp. 1–62). Orlando, FL: Academic Press.

Szasz, T. S. (1961). *The myth of mental illness: Foundations of a theory of personal conduct.* New York: Harper & Row.

Taylor, J. A., & Maher, B. A. (1959). Escape and displacement experience as variables in recovery from approach-avoidance conflict. *Journal of Comparative and Physiological Psychology, 52,* 586–590.

Thomson, D. C. (1914). Presidential address. *Journal of Mental Science, 60,* 541–572.

Tinterow, M. M. (1970). *Foundations of hypnosis from Mesmer to Freud.* Springfield, IL: Charles C. Thomas.

Tuke, D. H. (1881). Presidential address. *Journal of Mental Science, 27,* 1881.

Valenstein, E. S. (1986). *Great and desperate cures.* New York: Basic Books.

Weiner, D. (1979). The apprenticeship of Phillipe Pinel. *American Journal of Psychiatry, 136,* 1128–1134.

Whytt, R. (1765). *Observations on the nature, causes, and cure of those disorders which have been commonly called nervous, hypochondriacal, or hysteric, to which are prefixed some remarks on the sympathy of the nerves.* Edinburgh, Scotland: Becket & De Hondt.

Wigan, A . L. (1844). *A new view of insanity: The duality of the mind.* London: Longman, Brown, Green, Longmans.

Willis, T. (1684). *Practice of physick* (S. Pordage, Trans.). London: Dring, Harper & Leigh.

World Health Organization. (1958). *Ataractic and hallucinogenic drugs in psychiatry* (Tech. Rep. Series No. 152). Geneva: Author.

Wortis, J. (1959). *History of insulin shock.* New York: Philosophical Library.

CHAPTER 16

Clinical Psychology

DONALD K. ROUTH AND JOHN M. REISMAN

LIGHTNER WITMER AND THE FOUNDING OF
   CLINICAL PSYCHOLOGY   338
A SCIENTIFIC ART?   339
AN ARTISTIC SCIENCE?   341
A SUSTAINING ZEITGEIST   341
ORGANIZATIONAL STRUGGLES AND
   TRAINING MODELS   344

A NURTURING ZEITGEIST   345
SUBSEQUENT PROFESSIONAL DEVELOPMENTS   347
TREATMENT INTERVENTIONS   348
CONCLUSIONS AND FUTURE TRENDS   352
REFERENCES   353

Clinical psychology may be defined as "a scientific and professional field that seeks to increase our understanding of human behavior and to promote the effective functioning of individuals" (Reisman, 1991, p. 3). Clinicians share with other psychologists a valuing of truth and a commitment to its determination, which they believe is best done through scientific methods. However, they are also committed to being of help to people, who often present urgent problems that require immediate assistance. They emphasize the value and uniqueness of each individual and so strive to provide services to all populations. Thus, they have faced, and no doubt will continue to face, the dilemma of addressing insistent and pressing human needs with measuring instruments and methods of treatment whose validities are questioned by others, as well as by clinicians themselves.

In this chapter, we are going to consider the history of clinical psychology through its various phases of development. We will view the field in the context of the changing milieu of attitudes and professional approaches that have characterized the area known as mental health. Throughout the relatively short history of the field, there have been differing views as to the roles of science and "art," as well as both favorable climates (which we have titled zeitgeists) and resistance within the field. We shall also review the changing requisites for training and qualifying clinicians and treatment approaches and take a brief view of current and possible future developments.

Surprisingly, the history of clinical psychology is almost as long as the history of scientific psychology itself. Scientific psychology is often said to have begun when Wilhelm Wundt founded the first psychological laboratory at the University of Leipzig in 1879; clinical psychology can be said to have originated when Lightner Witmer, who earned his doctorate under Wundt established the first psychological clinic at the University of Pennsylvania in 1896 (Routh, 1996; Routh & DeRubeis, 1998; Witmer, 1897). Since at that time psychology itself was still in an early stage of gaining academic, scientific, and public acceptance, many psychologists had misgivings about the prudence of establishing an applied field of their discipline. In fact, almost a century later many clinicians believe such misgivings continue to remain detectable.

The early clinical psychologists thought of themselves as researchers, psychometricians (or measurers), and reeducators in the areas of individual differences, the ways in which people differ from one another, such as intelligence (see the chapter by Sternberg in this volume), personality (see the chapter by Sternberg, the chapter by Barenbaum & Winter, and the chapter by Weinstein & Way, all in this volume), and abnormal behaviors (see the chapter by B. Mayer & A. Mayer in this volume). Because the histories of those topics are addressed in those and other related chapters within this volume (e.g., see the chapter by Mandler, the chapter by Morawski & Bayer, and the chapter by Marecek, Kimmel, Crawford, & Hare-Mustin) our task is made easier than it might have been. Yet it must also be pointed out and acknowledged that clinicians draw, more or less, from almost every area of psychology, and thus every chapter is of some relevance to the history of clinical psychology. So, recognizing the arbitrariness of what we are about, let us begin.

LIGHTNER WITMER AND THE FOUNDING OF CLINICAL PSYCHOLOGY

Wundt and many of the early psychologists regarded psychology as the scientific study of consciousness. As empiricists, they believed that all that we know comes to us through our senses. Accordingly, they were interested in how we experience the world through our senses, in the acuity of our senses, and so on. When, in about 1884, Galton sought to measure intelligence, it seemed reasonable to do so by means of reaction time, sensory discrimination, height, weight, and other anthropometric indices. James McKeen Cattell, who was among the first Americans to receive a doctorate from Wundt, was most interested in Galton's work and elaborated upon it.

Cattell (1890) introduced the term *mental test* and suggested administering a standardized battery of 10 tests, such as Least Noticeable Difference in Weight, Reaction-Time for Sound, and Judgment of Ten Seconds. Subsequently, in 1921, Cattell went on to found the Psychological Corporation, which has since become one of the world's largest suppliers of psychological tests, but before he did that he had as one of his students at the University of Pennsylvania a fledgling psychologist by the name of Lightner Witmer (1867–1956).

Prior to studying psychology, Witmer was teaching English at Rugby Academy, a prep school in Philadelphia, where one of his pupils had an articulation problem. Witmer had been considering a career in law or business, but this youngster's difficulties with speech aroused his interest. Upon investigating further, he concluded the problem derived from a head injury suffered at the age of 2 and speculated that with proper diagnosis and treatment, this youngster could have avoided years of frustration and embarrassment. That psychology might be of help to those who had such problems was a factor in leading Witmer to major in the new science.

After he received his doctorate in 1892, Witmer returned to the University of Pennsylvania and took over the psychology laboratory from Cattell, who left to assume a similar position at Columbia University. While teaching a course in psychology at Pennsylvania, Witmer was challenged by one of his students, Margaret Maguire, a teacher in the Philadelphia public schools, to use psychology to be of help to children with learning problems. Specifically, she asked Witmer to help a 14-year-old who seemed to be of normal intelligence yet was three grades retarded in spelling. Witmer put the adolescent through a diagnostic process and found a visual anomaly that was partially corrected by glasses. Then, by having the child tutored, some improvement was effected, though the situation was considerably more complex than originally presented (McReynolds, 1997; Witmer, 1907a).

Witmer was sufficiently encouraged by this success and sufficiently convinced that psychology could be helpful to persuade the university administration to back the creation of a psychology clinic in 1896. Later that year, at the American Psychological Association (APA) convention, he reported to his colleagues what he had done and urged them to do likewise. He spoke of a "clinical method," which would educate students through demonstrations and contacts with those who required the services of psychologists. Thus, the psychological clinic would be an agency for instruction, original research, and service to the community (Reisman, 1991; Witmer, 1897).

The treatments Witmer practiced and taught were essentially pedagogical. In so doing, he carried on in the tradition of such pioneers as J. Rodriguez Pereira, who taught the deaf to speak; J. M. G. Itard, who attempted to educate and civilize Victor, the Wild Boy of Aveyron; and Edouard Seguin, who set up the first school to train those with mental retardation (Routh, del Barrio, & Carpentero, 1996). However, it should also be recognized that Witmer, in common with many clinicians today, believed that a broad range of problems indicated the need for remediation and training. To Witmer, a juvenile delinquent was deficient in moral training or proper conduct, and he thought of a child who might be regarded as psychotic today as developmentally arrested in a variety of behaviors that required correction.

In assessing the person, Witmer at first relied upon observation and whatever psychometric devices were available, which were then not very many. He also availed himself of the services of social workers, teachers, and any other professional who might be indicated, such as neurologists, optometrists, and physicians. A few years after Alfred Binet developed the first age scale for measuring children's intelligence in France (Binet & Simon, 1905), Witmer incorporated a version of it into his clinical assessment procedures. Another important aspect of how Witmer viewed assessment was that he saw the attempted remediation of a problem as an opportunity to test his understanding of it. Thus, he regarded treatment as part of assessment and to be often decisive in determining the validity of one's diagnosis.

About a decade after the founding of the clinic, Witmer appealed to Philadelphia philanthropist Mrs. J. Lewis (Mary L.) Crozer for funds to establish a clinical journal. By then, Witmer was offering courses and a training program in this new field of psychology and appeared to be successfully serving the community. She agreed to give him the money, and in 1907, a journal called *The Psychological Clinic* began publication. For the next 30 years, until it ceased publication in 1937, Witmer served as its editor, frequent contributor, occasional book reviewer, and gossip columnist. In its first issue,

Witmer (1907b) wrote what is perhaps the most significant article in the history of clinical psychology (McReynolds, 1997).

Witmer called for the creation of the field of clinical psychology as an independent profession, though grounded in the science of psychology. While his experiences had been almost exclusively with children, he made it clear in the last paragraph of the article that clinical psychology could help others as well:

> I would not have it thought that the method of clinical psychology is limited necessarily to mentally and morally retarded children. . . . The methods of clinical psychology are necessarily invoked wherever the status of an individual mind is determined by observation and experiment, and pedagogical treatment applied to effect a change, i.e., the development of such individual mind. Whether the subject be a child or an adult, the examination and treatment may be conducted and their results expressed in the terms of the clinical method. (Witmer, 1907b)

Witmer also recognized that clinical psychology encroached to some extent upon the field of psychiatry. However, he believed that given the proper training, the clinical psychologist could make contributions that were distinctive and valuable. Such training was being provided under Witmer's direction in the psychological clinic and through formal graduate-level course work in developmental psychology, abnormal psychology, and mental and physical defects of school children.

By 1909, the staff of the psychological clinic consisted of Witmer as director, an assistant director, five trained PhDs as examiners, a social worker, and three assistant social workers. They were no longer alone. The Iowa Psychological Clinic was founded in 1913 by Carl Seashore and R. L. Sylvester (Routh, 1984), and a psychological clinic was also established at Clark University in 1913. Moreover, there were courses in clinical psychology and there would soon be clinics at the University of Minnesota and the University of Washington (Reisman, 1991).

Also by 1909, Witmer was urging a broader goal for clinicians and "orthogenics" as a new designation for the field. Orthogenics included all that is now meant by the terms primary, secondary, and tertiary prevention, as well as the human potential movement. This was to be a profession concerned with human development, both of the individual and the species. Whatever was determined to impede or distort development, including social conditions and public policies that might be damaging, was grist for the clinician's mill and should be identified and remedied. With regard to the nutritional, intellectual, and emotional deprivations of poor children, Witmer (1909–1910) stated, "The problem calls for

preventive social action. . . . We should offer the slum parent something better than a choice between race suicide and child murder."

He began to subtitle *The Psychological Clinic* as *A Journal of Orthogenics,* and each issue thereafter carried that subtitle and a definition of orthogenics: "While orthogenics concerns itself primarily with the causes and treatment of retardation and deviation, it is by definition the science of normal development, and comprehends within its scope all the conditions which facilitate, conserve, or obstruct the normal development of mind and body" (Witmer, 1925). Obviously, in view of the title of this chapter not too many people warmed up to orthogenics as a new designation, but Witmer's vision for the scope of the field he began has gained in acceptance over the years.

A SCIENTIFIC ART?

Scientific psychiatry is probably best regarded as originating around the nineteenth century, though like scientific psychology it can trace its origins back over 2,000 years to the philosophers and medical practitioners of ancient Greece. Hippocrates spoke of mania, melancholia, phrenitis, hysteria, and paranoia and thought of these as medical disorders, probably brought about by an excess of one type or another of humor, or bodily fluid (Routh, 1998). By and large, however, he recommended that patients with mental disorders be treated with kindness, soothing music, and rest. The Roman physician Galen (A.D. 129–198), promoted the view that the etiology of specific disorders lay with excess humors, such as black bile, yellow bile, blood, and phlegm, which led to the treatment of the mentally ill with purges, vomits, bleeding, and expectorants; these were the treatments widely used in Western societies to the end of the eighteenth century.

During the eighteenth century, there emerged on several fronts a different way of looking at people. The philosopher Jean-Jacques Rousseau (1712–1778) argued that people are naturally good but that they are corrupted by their society. If allowed to develop naturally, or freely to experience the world and the consequences of their behaviors, a natural goodness or nobility would be expressed. Rousseau argued it was the artificialities of the social order that drove people to despair and that a simple life, close to nature, was best. Clearly Rousseau's influence can be seen today in natural remedies and holistic medicine.

Moral treatment, treating the mentally disturbed with kindness and respect rather than with physical force, restraints, or harsh medications, began to be practiced toward the end of the eighteenth century. In France, Philippe Pinel (1745–1826), called the father of scientific psychiatry because he introduced case histories and maintained records for his patients and because he tried to develop a nosology, advocated humane treatment for the mentally ill. A famous picture of Pinel "striking off the chains" of an unfortunate patient is depicted in many books on abnormal psychology and psychiatry. Contrary to legend, Pinel was not the first to unchain the insane.

In England, a Quaker tea merchant, William Tuke (1732–1822), established the York Retreat, where kindness and decency in a rural setting were provided for the disturbed. In Italy, Vincinzo Chiarugi opposed restraints and cruel measures, and in the United States, Eli Todd urged physicians to practice moral treatment and established the Retreat in Hartford. Social reformers, such as Dorothea Dix, advocated the building of mental hospitals to provide humane care for the mentally ill, and during the nineteenth century more than 30 state institutions, as well as asylums in Europe, were erected as a direct result of her efforts.

By the middle of the nineteenth century, moral treatment was being employed at a number of mental hospitals amid enthusiastic reports of high recovery and discharge rates. During this same period, the profession of psychiatry was also growing. The Association of Medical Superintendents of asylums for the insane, the precursor of the American Psychiatric Association, was founded in 1844, about the same time as similar organizations were founded in France and England. Its major publication was the *American Journal of Insanity,* which became the *American Journal of Psychiatry,* now in 2002 is in its 159th consecutive year of publication.

Breakthroughs were occurring in the scientific determination of the etiologies of a variety of mental disorders. In 1826, the French physician Antoine L. Bayle found an association between general paresis of the insane, a psychotic condition that led to dementia and paralysis, and chronic inflammation of the meninges. Richard von Krafft-Ebing's experiments demonstrated that paresis was caused by syphilis. Sergei Korsakov reported the harmful effects of chronic alcoholism on brain functioning. Karl Wernicke studied the effects of lesions in different areas of the brain and different forms of language disturbances or aphasias. It seemed to Emil Kraepelin, and to many other psychiatrists, that what was needed was the determination of the syndromes of specific disorders, research into their etiologies and their natural courses, and the development of their specific treatments. For a detailed review of this period, see Alexander and Selesnik's *History of Psychiatry* (1966).

Therefore, toward the end of the nineteenth century, the attitude toward moral treatment changed. Mental hospitals began to be seen mainly as custodial institutions for the mentally ill, who required further scientific study until appropriate treatments could be determined. It was suggested that the improvement rates for moral treatment had not been scientifically determined and were probably grossly exaggerated. Lower rates of improvement with moral treatment were reported, and its defenders attributed these to a more intransigent and difficult patient population and to a newer generation of psychiatrists who lacked the zeal and conviction of earlier practitioners (Levine, 1981). Sound familiar? Additional research, it was generally agreed, for this and other questions, would soon settle matters.

The major neurosis at this time was hysteria, whose symptoms had an annoying similarity to those of many neurological disorders. Jean-Martin Charcot, a leading neurologist of his day, used a cast of hysterics who had been previously hypnotized to demonstrate to his colleagues that all the various symptoms of hysteria—paralyses, crying spells, anesthesias—could be produced and modified under hypnosis. Charcot concluded, incorrectly, that there was an intimate relationship between hysteria and hypnosis and thus those who could be hypnotized either had hysteria or were predisposed to develop this neurosis (Goetz, Bonduelle, & Gelfand, 1995). An interested spectator at some of Charcot's demonstrations in 1885 was the Viennese neurologist Sigmund Freud (1856–1939).

Freud had gone to Paris to learn the latest thinking about the treatment of hysteria. An older colleague of Freud's, Josef Breuer, had become involved in an interesting case, in which the patient suggested talking about problems. This talking seemed to be of help, and Charcot's hypnotic demonstrations supported Freud in his belief that whatever the etiology of hysteria, the symptoms could be treated and reduced by verbal means. By 1892, Freud abandoned hypnosis in favor of a "concentration" technique, in which the patient was directed to try to recall all memories in connection with a symptom. By 1895, Freud was talking about "psychical analysis," or "psychoanalysis," and his relationship with Breuer was close to an end (Breuer & Freud, 1895/1955; Gay, 1988).

Within the first decade of the twentieth century, Freud was rapidly developing psychoanalysis as a theory of personality, which he regarded as his contribution to psychology; as a method of treatment, which he believed was of limited use because of its expense, duration, and the few analysts available; and as a way of doing research. He had achieved international recognition and had adherents throughout Europe and in the United States. In 1909, the eminent developmental psychologist G. Stanley Hall invited Freud to come to Clark University to address a gathering of American psychologists who would be participating in the celebration of the school's 20th anniversary. One of the members of that audience was William James.

AN ARTISTIC SCIENCE?

William James (1842–1910), like many of the other early psychologists such as Wundt, had originally trained to be a physician. For 12 years, he labored to produce a psychology text that would serve to help him appraise the field, and in 1890 his magnum opus, *Principles of Psychology,* was published. It quickly became a classic, and despite the early stage of development of scientific psychology when it was written, much within it would be of interest to clinicians today. There was a chapter on the unconscious mind and the evidence for its existence: that ideas or thoughts that are seemingly forgotten must be existing somewhere if they can be recalled; sleepwalkers who have no memory for what they did; our ability to sense the boundaries of our beds while asleep and to awaken close to a desired time; posthypnotic suggestions and movements carried out automatically by hysterics. In contrast, the unconscious mind as it would soon be conceived by Freud affected human functioning all through the day and night, in dreams as well as in neurotic symptoms, in daily accidents and thoughts and memory lapses and decisions.

There was a lengthy discussion of the Self, which in James's view was the sum total of all that the person owned: a Material Self consisting of the person's clothing, property, body, and family; a Social Self composed of the many roles people played in different kinds of interactions; and a Spiritual Self, consisting of the person's conscience and will, values, and psychological faculties. And there was often conflict between these different aspects of self, which had to be resolved by simply deciding what should be given expression and what should be suppressed. According to James, it was simply impossible to give expression to all aspects of oneself.

James had a much more rational view of human behavior than Freud. In his own life, prior to becoming a psychologist, James had overcome feelings of depression by sheer strength of resolve. He asserted that people could control their emotions if they determined to do it and by exhibiting characteristics of the feeling they wished to have. In other words, to be happy, smile and act happy, and you will begin to experience happiness . . . or as Shakespeare eloquently put it in *Henry V* in exhorting troops to do battle bravely: "Stiffen the sinews, summon up the blood, Disguise fair nature with hard-favor'd rage" (act 3, scene 1).

An equally straightforward approach was recommended to build good habits and break bad ones. Just go to it, and allow no exceptions to the doing of the habit you wish to achieve and immediately stop doing the habit you want to break. For James, it made no sense to try to gradually wean yourself from doing what you supposedly wanted to stop doing.

Similarly, James argued in his discussion of the self that people had it in their power to raise their self-esteem. He reasoned that our feelings about ourselves are determined by our accomplishments divided by our aspirations. If we wished to feel better about ourselves, we could raise our self-esteem by achieving more of our goals or—and this was the easier course—by lowering our aspirations and pretensions.

These practical suggestions made sense to James, who was shortly to become a leading proponent of pragmatism, a philosophical system that stresses that the value or merit of a truth or undertaking lies in its practical consequences. However, in the opinion of those who favored psychology as a "pure" science, these practical matters were totally extraneous to the field. James was not so sure psychology was headed in the right direction, and in 1907 he became a professor of philosophy. Within six years, a movement called behaviorism was launched against the prevailing psychology of Wundt and introspection.

It was in 1913 that John B. Watson proclaimed psychology to be "a purely objective experimental branch of natural science. Its theoretical goal is the prediction and control of behavior." Using as his model the reflex, Watson argued that all psychology needed to be concerned about were stimuli and responses: given the stimuli, to determine the responses; given the responses, to discover the stimuli. Research using introspection was best avoided, and psychologists should endeavor to put their findings to practical use (Watson, 1913). In 1915, Watson became president of the American Psychological Association (APA), while the numbers of psychologists who regarded themselves as behaviorists grew with each year. Their focus was not on sensation or perception but on learning, and they were not averse to seeing the process of learning in all areas of human functioning.

A SUSTAINING ZEITGEIST

Another way of looking at the fact that Witmer was successful when he approached his university looking for funds for a psychology clinic and when he contacted a philanthropist for money to start a journal in clinical psychology is to say the zeitgeist was favorable. We have already considered a number of events that during the eighteenth and nineteenth centuries prepared the way for the development of this field, and here we shall note others that promoted its advance during the early part of the twentieth century.

However, it would be incorrect to suggest the going was smooth and easy. The APA, founded in 1892 with 31 members, had only about 300 by 1917; its purpose was solely to promote the advance of psychology as a science, and it was reluctant to become involved in what many of its members considered extraneous issues, such as what the qualifications of a psychological examiner were and whether clinical psychologists should be supported when their expertise was challenged by psychiatrists. Not surprisingly, while there may have been a need for the services of clinical psychologists in the society at large, at this stage in the development of the field there was little demand.

Accordingly, the training of clinicians was haphazard and without any uniformity. A few universities provided education for clinicians, but most professionals had to take what courses they could in college and seek further training on the job in mental hospitals and clinics. In the former setting, they thought of themselves as primarily researchers in abnormal functioning; in the latter, they regarded themselves as mainly psychometricians and educators with children. (It should be remembered that the first individually administered intelligence scale standardized on adults, the Wechsler-Bellevue, did not become available until 1939.) With these sobering qualifications stated, let us note some of the positive influences.

Morton Prince (1854–1929), a neurologist at Tufts Medical College, founded the *Journal of Abnormal Psychology* in 1906 and served as its editor for many years. He was particularly interested in hysteria and multiple personalities and thought that the same processes that govern learning can be used to explain abnormal behaviors. Neuroses, for example, were often perversions of associations, because neurotics often had difficulties in recalling the past. Psychotherapies, he concluded, are actually different ways of educating people to associate differently and thus adjust better to their environments (Prince, 1909–1910). While working in Boston, Prince met with a congenial circle of physicians and psychologists, including Boris Sidis and William James, to discuss psychopathology and its treatment. He was sympathetic to psychoanalysis and through his journal helped to make it known. In 1927, he founded the Harvard Psychological Clinic, and by making it a unit of the Department of Psychology, he sought to ensure that the study of personality and psychopathology was regarded as part of psychology rather than psychiatry.

William James received a visit in 1906 from a former mental patient who had written a book about his experiences in treatment. The book was titled *A Mind That Found Itself,* and its author was Clifford Beers (1908). James read the manuscript and wrote a letter of endorsement, which became part of the book's introduction and which served to bring others to Beers's support. Clifford Beers (1876–1943) wanted to establish a movement that would make the public aware of mental illness and willing to provide for its alleviation and treatment. This became known as the mental hygiene movement, and Beers founded the first of its many societies in Connecticut in 1908.

That same year a prominent social worker, Julia Lathrop, met with a psychiatrist, William Healy (1869–1963), in Chicago to consider what new approaches to juvenile delinquency might be of help. At that time, judges disposed of delinquents with nothing more than the results of a physical examination to guide them. Certainly their decisions could be better informed, and as a first step, research might be conducted to determine the causes of delinquency. Healy went off to get ideas by meeting with James and other psychologists and by visiting the clinics of Witmer and Goddard. Influenced by the favorable recommendation of William James, Julia Lathrop asked Healy to be the director of the new clinic, which, when it opened in 1909, was called the Juvenile Psychopathic Institute and today is known as the Institute for Juvenile Research. Its original staff consisted of Healy; a clinical psychologist, Grace Fernald (who later moved to California, where she developed innovative practices for remediating reading disorders in children and where a school was named in her honor by UCLA); and a secretary. Many consider it the first child-guidance clinic in the world.

A number of judges visited Healy's clinic, with the idea in mind to assess whether a similar operation could work with their courts. During the summers of 1912 and 1913, Healy taught a course at Harvard describing his work, and in 1917 he and Augusta Bronner, a clinical psychologist whom he married, moved to Boston to establish the Judge Baker Guidance Clinic. The focus of these clinics affiliated with the courts was to evaluate children by means of psychological tests, mainly intelligence tests, and other means in order to make recommendations to juvenile-court judges regarding the disposition of their cases. Healy, it should be added, thought of himself not only as a psychiatrist but also as a clinical psychologist; he developed two performance measures of intelligence, one of which, the Healy Picture Completion Test, was quite popular in its day.

During World War I, Robert Yerkes (1876–1956), a comparative psychologist at Yale (who later had primate laboratories, now at Emory University, named in his honor) and also a clinician who made the Binet into a point scale (Yerkes, Bridges, & Hardwick, 1915), chaired a committee of psychologists that was asked to develop a group-administered scale of intelligence for the army. This committee produced the Army Alpha, a verbal scale; the Army Beta, which was nonverbal and intended for those who could not read English; and the Personal Data Sheet, a neurotic inventory designed by Robert Woodworth that was one of the earliest personality questionnaires (Yerkes, 1919). Almost two million men were assessed with the Army Alpha and Beta tests, and Yerkes believed the prestige of psychology had been enhanced by its contributions to the war effort. (See Weiner's chapter on assessment in this volume for further details on the testing movement at this time.)

On December 28, 1917, an organization known as the American Association of Clinical Psychologists (AACP) was founded by J. E. Wallin, Leta Hollingworth, Rudolf Pintner, and three others. Aside from conviviality, the AACP came into being because clinicians wanted a group that would be forceful in addressing their concerns, such as mental tests being administered by nonqualified examiners and clinicians gaining legal recognition as experts in the determination of mental retardation and psychopathology.

Robert Yerkes, the president of the APA at the time and also a member of AACP, negotiated with the dissidents and convinced them their interests would be best served through the APA. Accordingly the AACP went out of existence in 1919 and became the Clinical Section of the APA, the first of what were to become the many divisions of that organization. About the only activity of the AACP during its brief life was to sponsor a symposium at the 1918 APA convention. The room was so jammed with people that it was not possible to present this program, but the papers were published the next year in the *Journal of Applied Psychology*. David Mitchell is regarded as the first to earn his living through private practice; he obtained his PhD from the University of Pennsylvania (Meltzer, 1966; Mitchell, 1919, 1931) and reported that his treatment approach involved strengthening and eliminating habits.

The number of child-guidance clinics began to grow during the 1920s with the support of the Commonwealth Fund, established by the Harkness family which also funded the National Committee for Mental Hygiene to seek the causes and prevention of juvenile delinquency. These clinics, usually staffed by psychiatrists, clinical psychologists, and social workers and concerned with the diagnosis and treatment of child problems of all sorts, from infancy through adolescence, served as additional sources of employment for clinicians. By 1930, there were about 500 clinics in the United States offering psychiatric services, of which about 125 were child guidance; by 1936, there were 676 psychiatric clinics and 87 psycho-educational clinics, the latter mostly affiliated with colleges and directed by psychologists.

In 1924, the psychiatrist Karl Menninger met with a group of colleagues at the Institute for Juvenile Research to form the American Orthopsychiatric Association. Its first president was William Healy. Although voting membership in the group was initially restricted to psychiatrists, this restriction was dropped within 2 years. Among the clinical psychologists in this organization were Lightner Witmer, Augusta

Bronner, Shepherd Franz (one of the first clinical neuropsychologists), Henry Goddard, and Edgar Doll (1920). The association soon began publication of a journal, *The American Journal of Orthopsychiatry,* which still focuses on interdisciplinary research and advocacy regarding the mental health problems of children and families.

John B. Watson returned from service in World War I and set about to determine what unconditioned stimuli produce what unconditioned emotional responses in infants. He was particularly interested in fear and was aware that Freud (1909/1959) had presented a case of a boy who had a phobia of horses, which through analysis was discovered to be a fear of his father. Watson found that loud noises and sudden loss of support elicit fear in infants and that by pairing a loud noise with a white rat, a fear response could not only be conditioned to the rodent but could be generalized to other furry objects (Watson & Raynor, 1920). Unfortunately the infant, Albert, became unavailable for Watson to extinguish the response. However, Mary Cover Jones (1924), subsequently a prominent developmental psychologist, did demonstrate that a child's fear of rabbits could be reconditioned by bringing a rabbit closer and closer while the boy ate lunch. Here was evidence, Watson believed, to suggest that some irrational fears in children might be brought about and treated through conditioning and without any need to invoke unconscious conflicts.

Nevertheless, psychoanalytic concepts were winning the day. They were gaining in popularity among mental health professionals. Morton Prince was moved to remark: "Freudian psychology had flooded the field like a full rising tide and the rest of us were left submerged like clams in the sands at low water" (quoted by Hale, 1971, p. 434). In 1924, William Alanson White, then president of the American Psychiatric Association, urged psychiatrists to incorporate psychoanalytic concepts into their thinking and to use analysis to gain fresh insights into mental illness. Psychologists were impressed not only by Freud's ideas but by the ideas of those who disagreed with Freud, such as Alfred Adler and his notions about the significance of birth order and the inferiority complex, and Carl Jung and his introvert/extrovert personality types. Moreover, there were new tests of personality, like the Rorschach and the TAT, which relied upon an appreciation and an understanding of unconscious functioning to be administered and interpreted. Further, there began to be a new way of looking at neurosis, as illustrated in the analyst Karen Horney's (1937) book, *The Neurotic Personality of Our Time.* Neuroses, Horney argued, are brought about by disturbances in interpersonal relations, and their symptoms are determined by their culture and period. The conditions that existed for Freud differ from those that are current. Were we to analyze our culture, we would find different kinds of confusion and conflict from those of turn-of-the-century Vienna. Therefore, we see fewer hysterics and more neuroses of character, whose symptoms involve difficulties in relating to people effectively. Similar ideas were being expressed by Franz Alexander, Erich Fromm, and Wilhelm Reich (see Munroe, 1955).

ORGANIZATIONAL STRUGGLES AND TRAINING MODELS

Clinicians persisted in trying to get the APA to address their professional concerns, but the APA still wavered. In 1931, the Clinical Psychology section of the APA tried to set standards for a training program in clinical psychology. A committee was appointed and within 4 years issued its report: Clinical psychology was defined as "that art and technology which deals with the adjustment problems of human beings"; it required of its practitioners the PhD and a year of supervised experience; an MA and a year's experience would qualify one to be an assistant psychologist (Report of Committee, 1935). Then considering its task finished, this committee disbanded.

Evidently tiring of frustration, in 1937 the Clinical Psychology section of the APA dissolved itself and became instead a section of a new organization known as the American Association of Applied Psychology (AAAP). This clinical section had 229 members at its founding (Routh, 1994, 1997). When the clinical section had first affiliated with APA, part of the agreement had been that the section would be allowed to continue its focus on the professional as well as the scientific aspects of the field. As time went on, the APA did not live up to this agreement, and the section's annual meeting became merely a place to read scientific papers. Also, the APA had agreed to set up a system for certifying "consulting psychologists" as qualified to offer their services to the public. Only 25 persons were ever so certified before the system was discontinued in 1927. The AAAP also incorporated the Association of Consulting Psychologists, which had been founded in 1931, and began publishing its *Journal of Consulting Psychology*. (It continues to enjoy a fine reputation as a premier publication for clinicians' research as the *Journal of Consulting and Clinical Psychology*.)

With all this unrest and with all the excitement psychoanalysis and its offshoots were generating in psychiatry and in the culture, it is small wonder that clinicians began to want to become more involved in treatment and saw their roles as researchers, psychometricians, and educators to be somewhat lacking in prestige, status, and pizzazz. Could treating enuresis by a bell and pad apparatus (Mowrer & Mowrer, 1938) compare in sophistication with determining why a child

unconsciously resisted the toilet-training efforts of parents? World events would shortly push that question a bit to the side and afford clinicians an unprecedented opportunity for the growth of their profession. But before we consider the momentous events that happened—U.S. participation in the Second World War from 1941 to 1945—let us take a closer look at the training of clinicians in the prewar period.

If we examine those clinical psychologists who achieved eminence in the field, as indicated by recognition from their colleagues through awards or election to office in professional organizations, we find that many of them earned their doctorates from only a handful of schools. A list of schools whose graduates became prominent clinical psychologists is shown in Table 16.1. As this table shows, the University of Pennsylvania, Columbia, and Harvard had large numbers of successful graduates, with Columbia alone accounting for more than twice as many as any other school (Routh, 2000). Yet even at many of these universities, such as Harvard, there was no prescribed course work or training to become a clinical psychologist. David Shakow, for example, took what relevant courses and training he could, which he described as a "do-it-yourself program" (Shakow, 1976), and his experiences were more the rule than the exception.

TABLE 16.1   Officers and Awardees of Clinical Psychology Organizations with Doctoral Degrees Prior to 1946

University	Number	Well-Known Examples
Columbia	25	S. J. Beck (1932), John E. Bell (1942), Augusta Bronner (1914), S. I. Franz (1899), Leta S. Hollingworth (1917), Anne Roe (1933), Carl R. Rogers (1931), David Wechsler (1925), Joseph Zubin (1932).
Harvard	9	Robert R. Holt (1944), James Grier Miller (1943), Saul Rosenzweig (1932), R. Nevitt Sanford (1934), David Shakow (1942), Robert W. White (1932).
Pennsylvania	9	Francis N. Maxfield (1912), David Mitchell (1913), Herman H. Young (1916).
Ohio State	6	Victor C. Raimy (1943).
Iowa	5	George A. Kelly (1931), Boyd R. McCandless (1941), Marie Skodak (1938).
Stanford	5	Robert G. Bernreuter (1931), E. Lowell Kelly (1930), Catherine Cox Miles (1925).
Clark	5	Arnold L. Gesell (1906), Frederick Kuhlmann (1903), Seymour B. Sarason (1942).
Minnesota	4	Starke R. Hathaway (1932), Carney Landis (1924), Paul E. Meehl (1945).

Note: The data is from *Clinical Psychology since 1917: Science, Practice, and Organization* (pp. 237–255), by D. K. Routh, 1994, New York: Plenum. Copyright 1994 by Kluwer Academic. Reprinted with permission. This table is reproduced from D. K. Routh (2000), p. 238.

The internship is generally regarded as one of the most significant experiences in the training of clinicians (Doll, 1920). The Training School at Vineland, an institution for persons with mental retardation, is considered the first non-university institution to offer an internship, beginning in 1908. Routh (2000) identified 26 psychology internships that were established before 1946. According to Morrow's (1946) personal communication from William Healy, psychology interns would stay "for at least a year, the tenures sometimes overlapping for considerable periods. These students engaged in psychometric examinations and in research and attended all staff meetings" (p. 168). What is of significance about this description is that prior to 1946, training in psychotherapy for clinical psychologists was more the exception than the rule.

A NURTURING ZEITGEIST

World War II represents a watershed in the history of clinical psychology. In its aftermath, clinical psychology received something it had not received before: enormous institutional support from the federal government, from universities, and from the APA for the training of clinical psychologists. In 1942, Robert Yerkes chaired a committee of the National Research Council, which sought to unite the AAAP and the APA by drafting a new constitution that would be acceptable to both groups. Such a constitution was drafted and provided for an APA dedicated "to advance psychology as a science and as a means of promoting human welfare." Henceforth, the APA would be involved in professional and scientific issues, and a new journal, *American Psychologist,* would give coverage to both concerns. In 1944, the APA accepted the new constitution, the AAAP transferred its membership of about 600 psychologists to the APA, and the dues went up. *American Psychologist* began publication in 1946. The new APA had a divisional structure, in which psychologists with similar interests could affiliate. Division 12 was the division (now known as the Society) of Clinical Psychology, and it for a time became APA's largest division.

Even before America's entry into the war, oppressive dictatorships in Europe had brought about an influx of psychologists to the United States who did much to invigorate and enrich American psychology. Many of the leading Gestalt psychologists, such as Max Wertheimer, Wolfgang Kohler, Kurt Koffka, Kurt Lewin, and many lay analysts (that is, those without MD degrees), such as Erik Erikson, Erich Fromm, and Hanns Sachs, immigrated to this country. Many who were recognized psychoanalysts in Europe found their practices impeded by the American Psychoanalytic Association, which

had a long history of opposition to lay analysts, despite Freud's precepts to the contrary (Freud, 1927). At training institutes under its aegis, the American Psychoanalytic Association would admit only physicians, unless a nonphysician first agreed to use his or her education only for purposes of research or self-enlightenment and not to train nonphysician colleagues in psychoanalysis. European psychologists such as Theodore Reik did not accept these restrictions. Instead, Reik founded his own psychoanalytic training institute in the United States, which welcomed psychologists and other mental health professionals.

As the war drew to a close, it was recognized that there were going to be enormous demands for clinical psychologists to provide their services to veterans. There were 16 million veterans of World War II and 4 million veterans of previous wars. The Veterans Administration (VA) estimated it alone would need 4,700 clinical psychologists and vocational counselors, and there was nothing close to that number of clinicians. A joint APA and AAAP committee, with David Shakow as chairman, began meeting in 1944 to address the problem. That committee decided that rather than develop new professional schools, it would be better to use existing universities and programs. A 4-year graduate course of instruction leading to the PhD degree was proposed: the first year to ground the student in psychology as a science, research methodology, and theory; clinical courses, practicums, and an internship would be in the second and third years; and the fourth year would involve finishing the doctoral dissertation.

All the planets and stars seemed to be in the proper alignment. The chief of the Division of Clinical Psychology and Neuropsychiatry at the VA was James G. Miller, who earned simultaneously both a PhD in psychology and an MD at Harvard; he recognized the value of clinical psychologists, supported their training in psychotherapy, and sought to give them equal status with psychiatrists (Hilgard, 1987). The APA endorsed the graduate program recommended by the committee and agreed to evaluate and monitor schools and training facilities to ensure they were meeting standards. Robert Felix, a psychiatrist who was the first director of the newly created National Institutes of Mental Health (NIMH), was also friendly toward psychology; in 1946, the NIMH began its program of training grants and was soon awarding over $200,000 a year to students in clinical psychology and making funds available for psychological research. Also in 1946, the APA published its first list of acceptable schools for graduate training in clinical psychology, realizing there was much more to be done in setting standards.

In 1947, Carl Rogers, as president of the APA, appointed David Shakow to chair yet another Committee on Training in

Clinical Psychology (Shakow, 1965). This committee recommended that courses for clinicians should include psychotherapy and psychodynamics, with coursework in related areas—for example, anthropology, medicine, and sociology—germane to the particular student. These recommendations appeared to extend the duration of graduate education beyond the bounds of what was seemly, so in 1949 the APA held a conference in Boulder, Colorado, to discuss training policies in clinical psychology.

The Boulder Conference had 73 attendees, most of whom were intimately involved in the graduate education of clinicians. It was the first national meeting to consider standards for their doctoral training. Basically, the conference decided to endorse a solid grounding in science and practice, and this scientist-practitioner role for the clinical psychologist came to be called the Boulder model. (It reflected David Shakow's own background, which included a lengthy research-clinical apprenticeship at Worcester State Hospital in Massachusetts, a personal psychoanalysis undertaken in part to prepare for research in that area, and a career dedicated largely to studies of motor performance and attentional deficits in schizophrenia, both before and after he became chief psychologist at NIMH.) Despite its endorsement of the scientist-practitioner model, the Boulder Conference also urged graduate schools to be flexible and innovative in their training (Benjamin & Baker, 2000; Raimy, 1950). Of most significance was that psychotherapy or treatment became an essential component in the training of the clinical psychologist.

Since it is rare to find unanimity about anything, not all clinicians welcomed this change in their profession. Hans Eysenck (1949), for one, spoke against it. He gave three reasons why it would be better for clinicians not to become therapists: Treatment is a medical problem; training in therapy reduces the time available for training in research and diagnosis; and becoming a psychotherapist biases the clinician from studying its effectiveness objectively. His comments, however, had little immediate impact, and most students of clinical psychology saw the learning of psychotherapy as the sine qua non of their graduate education.

While there was concern about standards and models, there was explosive growth in the profession. From a handful of universities offering graduate training in clinical psychology before the war, the number grew to 22 by 1947, 42 by 1949. Each of these programs reported it had far more applicants than it could accommodate. This interest in clinical psychology was spurred by a growing interest in psychological matters in the culture through movies, literature, newspaper accounts, art, self-help books, and so on. At the same time, clinical psychologists were beginning a national drive for legal recognition and protection of their field.

Within the states, legislators were being asked to enact licensing and certification laws for psychologists. A certification law restricts the use of the title "psychologist" by specifying the criteria that must be met by those who wish to use it. A licensing law restricts the performance of certain activities to members of a specific profession. Because some of the activities of clinicians overlap with some of the activities of other professions, the APA favored certification over licensing legislation. The first state to enact a certification law for psychologists was Connecticut in 1945; it restricted the title of psychologist to those who had a PhD and a year of professional experience. In 1946, Virginia enacted a certification law for clinical psychologists that required the PhD and 5 years of professional experience.

The passage of this legislation often encountered stiff resistance from the medical profession. Many psychiatrists, such as William Menninger, respected clinical psychologists and felt they had a major contribution to give to the psychiatric team through their diagnostic testing and research. According to this view, clinical psychologists could even do psychotherapy under medical supervision, but they should be barred from the private practice of treatment because they lacked the keen sense of responsibility felt by physicians for their patients (Menninger, 1950).

Recognizing that certification or licensure by the states would be a difficult, lengthy process, it was decided in 1946 to establish a kind of certification by the profession, and thus was created the American Board of Examiners in Professional Psychology (ABEPP). The board consisted of nine APA fellows who served 3-year terms, set and administered standards for professional competence, and awarded diplomas that signified professional recognition of the qualifications of the applicant. At its inception, these standards required the applicant to have: a doctorate in psychology; APA membership; satisfactory moral, ethical, and professional standing; 5 years of professional experience; and passing scores on written and oral evaluations that included samples of the applicant's diagnostic and therapeutic skills. In 1949, the first ABEPP written examinations were held. (Subsequently, in 1968, this group became the American Board of Professional Psychology, or ABPP).

By 1949, it was generally accepted that the roles of the clinical psychologist were psychotherapy, diagnosis, and research. Since the VA had been involved in so much of the training of clinicians and was a major employer, clinical psychology had gone from being largely a provider of services to children to being largely a provider of services to adults, of whom the majority were males. The membership of the APA had increased to 6,735, and there were 1,047 in the clinical division alone. About 149 graduate departments offered some training in clinical psychology to about 2,800 clinical majors. The profession was growing at a rapid and exhilarating pace.

SUBSEQUENT PROFESSIONAL DEVELOPMENTS

In 1918, Leta Hollingworth suggested the creation of a new doctoral degree, the PsyD, which could be awarded to psychologists who sought not to be scientists but practitioners of psychology (Hollingworth, 1918). A similar suggestion was made by Crane (1925–1926) with a similar imperceptible response. In 1947, a commission appointed by Harvard University published a report recommending that Harvard establish a PsyD program for clinical psychologists (University Commission to Advise on the Future of Psychology at Harvard, 1947). The report included the following statement, which proved to be somewhat prophetic and a bit comical: "If the best universities deliberately dodge the responsibility for training applied psychologists, the training will be attempted in proprietary schools but under conditions so deplorable that the universities will either be begged to assume responsibility or blamed for not doing so" (p. 33). However, by the time this report was published, the Harvard psychology department had already acted by spinning off a new Department of Social Relations, which included the psychology clinic and its staff and which continued to offer the PhD.

The first institution to offer a PsyD degree was the University of Illinois (Peterson, 1992). It began its PsyD program in 1968 as an alternative for clinical graduate students who might find it more appealing than its PhD program. The PsyD program had a greater focus on training for practice and did not require experimental research; instead, the student could present a detailed case history or a documented attempt at clinical intervention and be prepared to discuss its theoretical, practical, and research implications. Eventually this program was dropped at Illinois and its leading proponent, Donald Peterson, went to Rutgers University to become dean of its Graduate School of Applied and Professional Psychology. (One of the illustrious PsyD graduates of the Rutgers program was Dorothy W. Cantor, president of the APA in 1996.)

In the meantime, the California School of Professional Psychology opened its doors in 1969, offering a 6-year PhD program. Other universities, such as Baylor and Yeshiva, began to offer PsyD programs, and a number of proprietary schools of professional psychology were established, most of which offered the PsyD.

What seemed to spur the growth of PsyD programs was the Vail Conference held in Colorado in 1973 (Korman, 1974). That conference endorsed the practitioner-training model as an alternative to the scientist-practitioner one. But of course

there was more to it than that. After the first burst of postwar growth had waned, some universities (e.g., Chicago and Northwestern) had dropped their clinical programs and almost all colleges had far more applicants than they could accept; this alarmed some clinicians into thinking their profession would not be viable until there were independent schools for the training of clinical psychologists. The alarm proved unjustified, as the number of graduate training programs in clinical psychology at universities has continued to increase. As of June 2001, some 50 years after APA approval began, 202 programs were approved or regularly monitored for approval. (Courtesy of Tia Scales at the Education Directorate of the American Psychological Association.) In addition, 53 free-standing schools were producing clinicians (two were counseling programs). In August 1976, these schools banded together into an organization of their own, the National Council of Schools of Professional Psychology, in order to ensure that their interests were pursued and protected (Stricker & Cummings, 1992).

The trend toward state certification and licensure of psychologists reached something like a conclusion when Missouri in 1977 became the last state to enact licensing legislation—though concerns remained about the revocation of laws and legal challenges to them. Clinicians themselves used legal suits to gain admission privileges in hospitals and to be counted as part of medical staffs. Their goals were to compel medical insurance companies to reimburse them for their services and (in 1988 in *Welch et al. v. American Psychoanalytic Association et al.*) to force an end to the restrictions imposed on lay analysts and their training and practice. Often the APA was involved in this litigation, attesting to a growing involvement in professional issues both within that organization and among clinical psychologists.

In the days of NIMH training grants to PhD programs in clinical psychology, it was considered a policy failure for graduates to enter into independent private practice. Indeed, most of those PhDs took public-sector jobs, whether in teaching, at the VA, or in community mental health centers. That is no longer the case. More and more clinical psychologists are in private practice, and they have promoted the passage of freedom-of-choice legislation, mandating that if insurance companies pay psychiatrists for psychotherapy, they must do the same for clinical psychologists. In a world of managed care, clinical psychologists find themselves competing vigorously for their share of the market. To aid third-party payers in determining which psychologists merit reimbursement, a National Register of Health Service Providers was developed by Carl Zimet and others. To be listed in the register, a psychologist must hold a state license or certification, have successfully completed at least 1 year of internship, and must have 2 years of supervised experience in a health setting.

During the 1970s, the APA was forced to become definitive about what constituted a psychological training program. This came about when graduates of guidance or counseling or sundry other programs demanded to be certified or licensed as psychologists and brought suit if their qualifications were questioned. They asserted, unfortunately correctly, that the courses that went into a psychology education were unspecified. Therefore, the APA made it known that as of 1980 all graduate programs in psychology must require courses in the history and systems of psychology; the biological, social, developmental, and learned bases of behavior; and statistics and research design. Moreover, clinical students were also required to have instruction in psychological assessment and intervention, individual differences and psychopathology, practicum training, and a 1-year full-time internship.

So, what does all this suggest, aside from more regulation and specification than anyone would have thought possible or desirable a few years before? First, clinical psychologists were increasing their numbers and becoming a dominant force within American psychology and perhaps elsewhere as well. They were evident in Canada, the United Kingdom, and Scandinavia. Norway, for instance, was training about 100 psychologists a year at the doctoral level. These countries, unlike the United States, had publicly supported health systems, which were major employers of clinical psychologists.

Although the United States has continued to emphasize a rather lengthy, and somewhat indefinite, period of graduate education leading to the doctorate for clinical psychologists, a variety of other models exist elsewhere. In the United Kingdom, a 3-year program leading to a doctor of clinical psychology degree (D.Clin.Psy.) has emerged. In Germany, Hungary, Mexico, and Spain, the PhD is usually reserved for academicians and/or researchers; practitioners of clinical psychology study in undergraduate-graduate programs lasting up to 6 years, perhaps supplemented by postgraduate training in psychoanalysis or behavior therapy (Donn, Routh, & Lunt, 2000). Believing that it was about time that the largest psychological field of specialization had its own international organization, Routh (1998) and colleagues founded the International Society of Clinical Psychology in 1998. This organization holds its meetings with various larger international groups, such as the International Association of Applied Psychology, the International Council of Psychologists, the International Union of Psychological Science, or the European Federation of Professional Psychology Associations. (See the chapter by David & Buchanan in this volume for a full description of the international contacts in psychology.)

Second, with increasing numbers come divisions and splits. When there are few psychologists, the interests of one or two can be regarded as idiosyncrasies. When there are thousands of psychologists, the interests of 1% or 2% may constitute the beginning of a new field of specialization or a new social grouping. APA membership has increased from about 7,250 in 1950 to 16,644 in 1959 to 30,830 in 1970 to 50,933 in 1980 to about 150,000 in 2000. At one time, a school psychologist was a clinical psychologist who worked in a school setting, but eventually school psychology became a field of specialization in its own right (Fagan, 1996, and the chapter by Fagan in this volume). Similarly there are more and more areas of specialization within clinical psychology that could become separate fields, such as clinical neuropsychology, clinical child psychology, and health psychology. This differentiation is probably inevitable, but it is not without the possible consequence of fostering less unity among clinicians unless care is taken to ensure cohesiveness.

Third, there has been an increasing professionalization within clinical psychology. Until World War II, very few clinical psychologists were involved in private practice. The role of the clinician changed from one of diagnosis and research to diagnosis, treatment, and research. Correspondingly, along the way from its inception in 1892, the APA's aim—"to advance psychology as a science"—has changed: "to advance psychology as a science and as a means of promoting human welfare" and "to advance psychology as a science, as a profession, and as a means of promoting human welfare." As this is being written, the APA membership is being polled on whether "health" should be inserted into the aim of the association. Since many psychologists who objected to the growing professional interests of the APA left it in 1989 to form a more exclusively scientific American Psychological Society and since clinical psychologists constitute more than half the APA membership, the professionalization of the APA is not likely to be reversed. (See the chapter by Benjamin, DeLeon, Freedheim, & VandenBos and the chapter by Pickren & Fowler, both in this volume.) A concern here is that clinicians not become divorced from their scientific roots and function.

Treatment interventions can serve to illustrate much of what we have discussed, and it is to that topic that we turn.

TREATMENT INTERVENTIONS

By World War II, many of those who had broken with Freud (such as, Adler, Jung, and Rank) established personality theories, schools, and therapeutic systems of their own that were unified by the importance they ascribed to unconscious motivation in determining psychopathology. These "psychodynamic" psychotherapies were augmented by those of Horney, Sullivan, and Fromm, who, impressed by social forces and relationships, did much to make psychotherapy responsive to changing conditions. Among those just mentioned, Rank and Fromm were not physicians, and both had been trained in Europe. As time went on, Erik Erikson's (1950, 1959) integration of a psychosocial theory of development with Freud's psychosexual theory opened psychoanalysis to the concepts of many of the rebels: an oral stage of trust versus mistrust; an anal stage of autonomy versus shame and doubt; a phallic stage of initiative versus guilt; a latency stage of industry versus inferiority; an adolescent stage of identity versus identity diffusion; a young-adult stage of intimacy versus isolation; a middle-adult stage of generativity versus stagnation; and an old-age stage of integrity versus despair.

The first American psychologist to develop a form of psychotherapy that was highly influential was Carl Rogers (1902–1987), who received his PhD in 1931 from Teachers College, Columbia University, where Leta Hollingworth supervised his clinical experiences with children. He continued clinical work with children until 1940, when he left to become a professor of psychology at Ohio State University and later the University of Chicago. By then his clinical work was mostly with college students. Rogers was heavily influenced by social worker Jesse Taft and especially by child psychiatrist and former school psychologist Frederick Allen, who in turn were much affected by what they had learned from Otto Rank. Originally, Rogers called his system of psychotherapy "nondirective" (Rogers, 1942). Later he called it "client-centered therapy" (Rogers, 1951), and eventually he and his followers referred to it as "person-centered." No matter what it was called, it was distinguished by Rogers's willingness to subject it and its practitioners to scientific scrutiny.

Rogers pioneered the recording of therapy sessions so that they could be analyzed in detail for purposes of research, supervision, and training. He argued that psychotherapy could become a science and believed there was a discoverable orderliness as the sessions continued to a successful end. Hypothesis testing was one of the hallmarks of his approach, and he tried to make explicit what conditions were essential for personality change: the therapist's possession and manifestations of unconditional positive regard, accurate empathy, genuineness, and congruence (Rogers, 1957). A considerable research effort was undertaken to measure these attributes and determine if they indeed were related to effective therapy. The results of 20 years of research led to the conclusion that the relationship between these attributes and positive change in patients remained in doubt (Parloff, Waskow, & Wolfe, 1978).

This period, extending from the 1930s through the 1950s, was the high-water mark in the prestige of psychotherapy, especially psychodynamic psychotherapy. In the 1960s,

psychotherapy came under attack from four "revolutions" or "movements": (1) community psychology, which argued that psychotherapy was futile and not provided to those most in need of it, and that clinicians should direct their efforts toward preventing psychopathology through bringing about changes in deleterious social policies and conditions (see the chapter by Wilson, Hayes, Greene, Kelly, & Iscoe in this volume); (2) humanistic psychology, which emphasized the importance of present experiences, ongoing events, and confrontational approaches in groups, as contrasted with traditional approaches to the individual's exploration and integration of the past; (3) the increasing use of drugs, by physicians and by free spirits, to alter moods, regulate behaviors, and enhance self-esteem and experiences; and (4) behavior therapy.

It was the English clinician Hans Eysenck who was less than enthusiastic about clinical psychologists becoming psychotherapists and raised the question of whether scientific studies had demonstrated the effectiveness of psychotherapy (Eysenck, 1952). Culling the research and pulling together a motley group of studies, he concluded that they failed to demonstrate that control groups were significantly less likely to improve than groups that received psychotherapy. Although psychotherapists strongly disagreed with his conclusion and manner of arriving at it, the fact remained that it was their responsibility to prove otherwise.

In South Africa, psychiatrist Joseph Wolpe made use of Hullian concepts and learning principles to develop procedures that would reduce neurotic symptoms. In essence, he sought to elicit responses, such as relaxation, that would be incompatible with or inhibit a symptom, such as anxiety or fear. (This is similar to the previously discussed deconditioning or reconditioning approach of Mary Cover Jones.) After coming to the United States to spend a year at Stanford University's Center for Advanced Study in the Behavioral Sciences, Wolpe (1958) published a book, *Psychotherapy by Reciprocal Inhibition,* which was hailed by Eysenck as a promising advance in effective treatment.

Wolpe took a position at the University of Virginia Medical School, and in 1962, along with Salter and Reyna, sponsored a conference there that got the behavior therapy ball rolling (Wolpe, Salter, & Reyna, 1964). The clinical journals were soon filled with a variety of studies, many of them quite ingenious, demonstrating the effectiveness of behavioral approaches.

One of the first of these studies was one by Peter Lang and David Lazovik (1963) of college students who were identified by a questionnaire, the Fear Survey Schedule, as being afraid of snakes. The students were then given a Behavioral Avoidance Test (BAT) in which they were placed in a room with a nonpoisonous snake and encouraged to go as close as they could to it and, if they were willing, to pick it up. Each student completed a Fear Thermometer, a rating of how much fear was experienced. The therapy consisted of devising a hierarchy of imagined scenes involving snakes, with scenes arranged from neutral to the most fear arousing. Then the student was taught to relax, asked to imagine the least fear-arousing scene, asked to relax, and so on until the student became able to imagine scenes higher and higher in the hierarchy without feeling anxious, a procedure known as "systematic desensitization." Finally the BAT and Fear Thermometer were readministered, and it was found that these students had become significantly less afraid of snakes than randomly assigned students in a control group. Critics of such analogue studies noted that the results might have been less impressive had neurotic patients and their fears been tested.

Nevertheless, later research supported the effectiveness of desensitization procedures of various kinds in dealing with a variety of symptoms. For example, exposure with response prevention (allowing a patient to experience what happens when a compulsion is not permitted) is a kind of in vivo desensitization that has come to be regarded as appropriate in the treatment of obsessive-compulsive disorders (Foa & Goldstein, 1978).

Another major behavioral approach to treatment is behavior modification, or applied behavior analysis, which comes from the experimental work and writing of B. F. Skinner (1938). Although Skinner's experimental work was almost exclusively with animals, neither he nor his followers have been reluctant to apply his principles to humans, including clinical populations (Skinner, 1971). Sidney Bijou, who served as director of clinical training when Skinner chaired the psychology department at Indiana University, pioneered in the use of operant conditioning with persons with mental retardation (Bijou, 1996). Applied behavior analysis has become a mainstay of psychological treatment of persons with mental retardation and pervasive developmental disorders such as autism. It has been used to teach social and self-help skills like dressing, toileting, and proper table manners, as well as dealing with defiant, aggressive, and self-injurious behaviors.

Nathan Azrin at Anna State Hospital in Illinois demonstrated the utility of behavior modification with adult mental patients (Ayllon & Azrin, 1968) and the usefulness of token economies, in which the performance of desired behaviors earns tokens that can be exchanged for rewards (much as occurs in our society where money is given for work). Extensive research on token economies in mental hospitals was done by Gordon Paul and his colleagues (e.g., Paul & Lentz, 1977). Their research with long-term, regressed, and chronic

schizophrenics focused on developing such practical behaviors as making their beds, behaving well at mealtime, participating in the classroom, and socializing with others during free time. Paul's research showed that his program of behavior therapy and milieu therapy (moral treatment) improved symptoms when compared with the results of routine hospital management, and that behavior therapy was more effective than milieu therapy alone in bringing about the desired changes.

The principal assessment procedure advocated by Skinnerians is the functional analysis of behavior: a determination of what may be rewarding or maintaining undesirable behaviors and what may serve to reward or establish the performance of behaviors that are desired. A functional analysis requires observation, preferably in the setting where the behaviors are to be modified, in order to assess the frequency of their occurrence and their consequences. Gerald Patterson (1974) pioneered in the use of direct behavioral observations in natural settings to record the behavior of aggressive children and their families in their homes. His research led to a theory of coercion in which the child is seen as both the determiner and victim of episodes of escalating violence in the family and to controlled research on the behavioral treatment of child aggression.

Another major category of behavior therapy is cognitive therapy or cognitive behavior therapy. Two pioneers in this area were George A. Kelly and Albert Ellis. Kelly (1955) viewed his clients as resembling scientists in their attempts to make sense of the world around them. He used a diagnostic procedure called the Role Construct Repertory Test to ascertain their beliefs about themselves and others. The therapist then negotiated with the client about what changes might be desired and how these could be accomplished. Using fixed role therapy, the client was encouraged to rehearse or play-act the new role, first with the therapist, then with others. Albert Ellis (1958) developed rational emotive therapy; here the patient's opinions and attitudes are explored for irrational beliefs ("I can't make a mistake and must be perfect. My feelings are out of my control"), which the therapist then attempts to make more reasonable and rational.

Martin Seligman (1975) stimulated much research on the treatment of depression. Based upon previous research with dogs that were prevented from avoiding or escaping an electric shock, he noted that when they were in a situation where the shock could not be avoided, such animals simply gave up and endured the pain. They had learned to be helpless, and perhaps, he reasoned, the same process of ineffectiveness and feeling unable to cope occurred among humans who were depressed. This had obvious treatment implications, but further study indicated the need for the concept of attribution

(Abramson, Seligman, & Teasdale, 1978): Persons who are likely to become depressed attribute their failures to their own personality characteristics, while those who are not at risk for depression attribute failures to external, transitory, specific circumstances. Accordingly, the cognitive therapist might help a person to be less depressed by coming to see how failures occur in certain situations and dealing with those events more effectively.

Cognitive behavior therapy for treating panic disorders involves teaching the patient to interpret symptoms of acute anxiety as relatively harmless rather than as indications of a pending heart attack or psychotic episode (Craske, Brown, & Barlow, 1991). This was found to be more beneficial than treatment with the anti-anxiety drug Xanax (alprazolam). More recently, Marsha Linehan (1993) developed a procedure, called dialectical behavior therapy, that shows promise in the treatment of borderline personality disorder.

Social learning is yet another major approach in behavior therapy, which owes much to the work of Albert Bandura (1977). The emphasis here is on learning that occurs without obvious rewards, as when we learn what to do by observing the consequences of behaviors performed by others (vicarious learning); or when we imitate the behaviors of those we like, respect, or admire (modeling); or when we have internalized values and standards and reward or punish ourselves for our successes or failures in living up to them, a self-regulating process.

Susan Mineka and her colleagues (Mineka, Davidson, Cook, & Keir, 1984) demonstrated the acquisition of fears in rhesus monkeys through vicarious or observational learning. When adolescent monkeys were allowed to watch their parents, who had an intense fear of snakes, interact with toy snakes and real ones, they soon exhibited the same fear, even though they did not do so originally. Even at a 3-month follow-up, the fear was strongly evident. Similarly, much research was devoted to the consequences of watching violence in movies and television, particularly for producing antisocial, aggressive behaviors in children, which are apt to lead to such behaviors in adulthood (Huesmann, Eron, Lefkowitz, & Walder, 1984). A final example, Peter Lewinsohn's research (Lewinsohn, 1975, 1988; Teri & Lewinsohn, 1986), demonstrated a correlation between depression and a reduced number of rewards: Losses of any and every kind are risk factors for depression and frequently involve losses of rewards, and a depressed person is less affected by and is less apt to engage in behaviors that elicit social rewards. By helping the person to perform behaviors that generate social rewards, the depression can be alleviated.

Behavioral approaches in treatment have obviously increased rapidly in number and applications. It was not until 1955 that the first course in behavior modification was offered by Arthur Staats, and by the early 1970s about two-thirds of the psychology departments in the United States offered behavior therapy courses. It would be rare today for instruction in this topic to be neglected. Equally significant has been its acceptance in medical, psychiatric, and psychodynamic settings. This acceptance has come about because for almost any purpose—reducing stress (Lazarus, 1966), overcoming shyness, modeling appropriate behaviors in the hospital, or applying for a job—training procedures can be helpful. In some circumstances, such as teaching people with retardation or autism, behavioral techniques are among the few means available to provide assistance.

Considerable interest was generated in the study of Smith and Glass (1977), who through a relatively new statistical procedure, meta-analysis, sought to determine if psychotherapy was effective. By reexamining the data from 375 controlled studies of psychotherapy and counseling, they found that typical patients receiving therapy were rated higher than 75% of those in the control groups. They concluded this was evidence for the effectiveness of psychotherapy, though they did not find any support for the superiority of one type of psychotherapy over another.

An alternative or supplement to psychotherapy and behavior therapy is drug treatment. The first neuroleptic medications for the treatment of psychosis were introduced in France in 1952, and by the 1960s they had revolutionized psychiatric treatment. Psychiatry went from shock therapies and custodial care to a "revolving door" policy in mental hospitals that sent patients into halfway houses, where they could be maintained on drugs. This drug revolution—this change in emphasis from "warehousing" patients to avoiding the effects of institutionalization, from isolating them to returning them to society—stimulated the field of community psychology, which was also invigorated by the Community Mental Health Centers Act of 1963. The drugs, particularly chlorpromazine (Thorazine) and other phenothiazines, became widely used all over the world and led to great reductions in the numbers of patients requiring hospitalization. Such medications did not necessarily eliminate the psychosis, but they did reduce the severity of symptoms and so helped patients to be more acceptable to others. Some clinicians have been involved in the study of the long-term effects of taking neuroleptics, for example, tardive dyskinesia, a neurological syndrome that involves involuntary movements of the lips and tongue (Sprague, Kalachnik, & Shaw, 1989). Other clinical psychologists have conducted research on the use of both traditional neuroleptics and the newer drugs of this type, for example, risperidone, in the treatment of self-injurious behaviors and aggression in individuals with mental retardation (Schroeder, Rojahn, & Reese, 1997).

A second category of frequently used medications is antidepressants, including tricyclics (Tofranil) and selective serotonin reuptake inhibitors (Prozac). These medications have proven to be effective in many double-blind studies, though not more so than cognitive behavior therapy or manualized interpersonal psychotherapy, according to NIMH clinical trials. Nevertheless, they have brought about a fundamental change in the practice of outpatient psychiatry, which is much more involved with adjusting drug regimens and less involved with psychotherapy than it used to be (Shorter, 1997). Lithium seems an effective treatment for manic states and also has prophylactic value in managing bipolar disorder. Again, while clinicians have made contributions to this area (Jamison, 1992; Jamison & Akiskal, 1983), its administration was a medical responsibility. The same thing can be said about methylphenidate or Ritalin, the most frequently prescribed drug for children, used in the treatment of attention deficit hyperactivity disorder (ADHD). Clinical psychologists have been involved in evaluating the effects of stimulant drugs (Conners, Sitarenios, Parker, & Epstein, 1998) and in determining whether behavior therapy can be an effective treatment. Barkley (1990) used Ritalin to examine the parent–child relations in children with ADHD. The parents of these children tend to be overcontrolling but are less so when their child is on Ritalin, thus indicating they are responsive to their child's level of hyperactivity. However, not all clinical psychologists were content with restricting their role to research with drugs.

During the 1980s, a movement began to permit clinical psychologists with proper additional training to prescribe these medications. The government sponsored a demonstration project to show its feasibility, and with that accomplished a few university training programs began to offer courses that would prepare clinical psychologists to assume that role. Although the majority of clinical psychologists showed little interest in gaining prescription privileges (Piotrowski & Lubin, 1989), that interest may be more broadly kindled in the coming generations. An APA division for psychologists who do have an interest in prescribing psychotropic medications has been recently established. In 1995 APA Division 12, the Society of Clinical Psychology, set up a task force to identify empirically supported psychological interventions for various types of psychopathology. Such an identification has decided implications for health service insurers, who can use it to determine if practitioners are entitled to be reimbursed for their services. A listing of such treatments tends to endorse behavior therapy approaches more so than psychotherapy, which has led to understandable anguish among psychotherapists, who believe their effects are not fairly evaluated when overt symptoms are the major focus.

The criteria used for selecting empirically supported treatments has been much discussed (Chambless & Hollon, 1998), and an interdiciplinary movement is under way, including representatives of psychiatry, psychology, other mental health fields, managed care executives, and consumers, to develop treatment guidelines so that health care dollars can be rationally allocated.

CONCLUSIONS AND FUTURE TRENDS

It should be apparent that clinical psychology has come a long way since 1896. Its growth was slow during the early years of its development when it essentially focused on psychometrics, research, and pedagogical services to children. Although this was made clear in the chapter by Parke and Clarke-Stewart in this volume, we should at least mention that the major contribution of clinical psychologists at that time was in the measurement of intelligence. The age scale of Binet-Simon led to the revisions of Lewis Terman (the Stanford-Binet), longitudinal studies of gifted children (Terman, 1925) that are still being pursued, infant and adult scales that have contributed to our understanding of intellectual functioning throughout the life span, and fairly reliable and valid predictors of success in school, work, and psychotherapy.

Following World War II, clinical psychology grew rapidly until it became a dominant force in American psychology and an established and legally recognized profession with a respected place among the mental health disciplines. Its major contribution in the postwar period has been in treatment formulations, especially behavior therapy approaches.

Clinical psychology is now perhaps the most popular field of psychological specialization in the world (Sexton & Hogan, 1992). With increasing numbers of clinicians has come a trend toward more and more areas of specialization (e.g., school psychology, health psychology, clinical child psychology, pediatric psychology, clinical geropsychology, clinical neuropsychology, family psychology, psychological hypnosis, rehabilitation psychology), many of which have developed into fields of their own (Fagan, 1996; Wallston, 1997). In addition, the practices within the field have expanded, with more sophisticated evaluation techniques (see the chapter by Weiner in this volume), various therapeutic approaches (including use of the electronic medias), and the possibility of prescribing psychotropic medications (see the chapter by Benjamin, DeLeon, Freedheim, & VandenBos in this volume).

Such growth in numbers and differentiation is to be expected. Nevertheless, care should be exercised to ensure that psychologists are aware of their commonalties—their origins from a common history and their beliefs in a common set of values. That awareness, we hope, has been enhanced by the reading of this volume.

REFERENCES

Abramson, L. Y., Seligman, M. E. P., & Teasdale, J. D. (1978). Learned helplessness in humans: Critique and reformulation. *Journal of Abnormal Psychology, 87,* 49–74.

Alexander, F. G., & Selesnik, S. T. (1966). *History of psychiatry.* New York: Harper & Row.

Ayllon, T., & Azrin, N. H. (1968). *The token economy.* New York: Appleton-Century-Crofts.

Bandura, A. (1977). *Social learning theory.* Englewood Cliffs, NJ: Prentice-Hall.

Barkley, R. A. (1990). *Attention-deficit hyperactivity disorder: A handbook for diagnosis and treatment.* New York: Guilford Press.

Beers, C. (1908). *A mind that found itself, an autobiography.* New York: Longman, Green.

Benjamin, L. T., Jr., & Baker, D. B. (2000). Boulder at 50: Introduction to the section. *American Psychologist, 55,* 233–236.

Bijou, S. W. (1996). Reflections on some early events related to behavior analysis of child development. *Behavior Analyst, 19,* 49–60.

Binet, A., & Simon, T. (1905). A new method for the diagnosis of intellectual level of abnormal persons. *Annee Psychologique, 11,* 191–244.

Breuer, J., & Freud, S. (1955). Studies on hysteria. In J. Strachey (Ed.), *The standard edition of the complete psychological works of Sigmund Freud* (Vol. 2, pp. 1–305). London: Hogarth Press. (Original work published 1895)

Cattell, J. M. (1890). Mental tests and measurements. *Mind, 15,* 373–381.

Chambless, D. L., & Hollon, S. D. (1998). Defining empirically supported therapies. *Journal of Consulting and Clinical Psychology, 66,* 7–18.

Conners, C. K., Sitarenios, G., Parker, J. D. A., & Epstein, J. N. (1998). The revised Conners' Parent Rating Scale–Revised (CPRS-R): Factor structure, reliability, and criterion validity. *Journal of Abnormal Child Psychology, 26,* 257–268.

Crane, L. (1925–1926). A plea for the training of psychologists. *Journal of Abnormal and Social Psychology, 20,* 228–233.

Craske, M. G., Brown, A. T., & Barlow, D. H. (1991). Behavioral treatment of panic disorder: A two-year follow-up. *Behavior Therapy, 22,* 289–304.

Doll, E. A. (1920). The degree of Ph.D. and clinical psychology. *Journal of Applied Psychology, 4,* 88–90.

Donn, J. E., Routh, D. K., & Lunt, I. (2000). From Leipzig to Luxembourg (via Boulder and Vail): A history of clinical psychology training in Europe and the United States. *Professional Psychology: Research and Practice, 31,* 423–428.

Ellis, A. (1958). Rational psychotherapy. *Journal of General Psychology, 59,* 35–49.

Erikson, E. H. (1950). *Childhood and society.* New York: Norton.

Erikson, E. H. (1959). Identity and the life cycle. *Psychological Issues, 6*(1), entire issue.

Eysenck, H. J. (1949). Training in clinical psychology: An English point of view. *American Psychologist, 4,* 173–176.

Eysenck, H. J. (1952). The effects of psychotherapy: An evaluation. *Journal of Consulting Psychology, 16,* 319–324.

Fagan, T. K. (1996). A history of division 16 (school psychology): Running twice as fast. In D. Dewsbury (Ed.), *Unification through division: Histories of the divisions of the American Psychological Association* (Vol. 1, pp. 101–135). Washington, DC: American Psychological Association.

Foa, E. B., & Goldstein, A. J. (1978). Continuous exposure and complete response prevention in the treatment of obsessive-compulsive neurosis. *Behavior Therapy, 9,* 821–829.

Freud, S. (1926). The question of lay analysis. In J. Strachey (Ed.), *The standard edition of the complete psychological works of Sigmund Freud* (Vol. 20, pp. 77–172). London: Hogarth Press.

Freud, S. (1959). Analysis of a phobia in a five-year-old boy. In J. Strachey (Ed.), *The standard edition of the complete psychological works of Sigmund Freud* (Vol. 10, pp. 1–147). London: Hogarth Press. (Original work published 1909)

Gay, P. (1988). *Freud: A life for our time.* New York: Norton.

Goetz, C. G., Bonduelle, M., & Gelfand, T. (1995). *Charcot: Constructing neurology.* New York: Oxford University Press.

Hale, N. G., Jr. (1971). *Freud and the Americans. Vol. 1: The beginnings of psychoanalysis in the United States 1876–1917.* New York: Oxford University Press.

Hilgard, E. R. (1987). *Psychology in America.* New York: Harcourt, Brace, Jovanovich.

Hollingworth, L. S. (1918). Tentative suggestions for the certification of practicing psychologists. *Journal of Applied Psychology, 2,* 280–284.

Horney, K. (1937). *The neurotic personality of our time.* New York: Norton.

Huesmann, L. R., Eron, L. D., Lefkowitz, M. M., & Walder, L. O. (1984). Stability of aggression over time and generations. *Developmental Psychology, 20,* 1120–1134.

James, W. (1890). *Principles of psychology.* New York: Holt.

Jamison, K. R. (1992). *Touched with fire: Manic depressive illness and the artistic temperament.* New York: Basic Books.

Jamison, K. R., & Akiskal, H. S. (1983). Medication compliance in patients with bipolar disorder. *Psychiatric Clinics of North America, 6,* 175–192.

Jones, M. C. (1924). The elimination of children's fears. *Journal of Experimental Psychology, 7,* 382–390.

Kelly, G. A. (1955). *The psychology of personal constructs.* New York: Norton.

Korman, M. (1974). National conference on levels and patterns of professional training in psychology: The major themes. *American Psychologist, 29,* 441–449.

Lang, P., & Lazovik, A. D. (1963). Experimental desensitization of a phobia. *Journal of Abnormal and Social Psychology, 66,* 519–525.

Lazarus, R. S. (1966). *Psychological stress and the coping process.* New York: McGraw-Hill.

Levine, M. (1981). *The history and politics of community mental health.* New York: Oxford University Press.

Lewinsohn, P. M. (1975). Engagement in pleasant activities and depression level. *Journal of Abnormal Psychology, 84,* 644–654.

Lewinsohn, P. M. (1988). A prospective study of risk factors for unipolar depression. *Journal of Abnormal Psychology, 97,* 251–284.

Linehan, M. M. (1993). *Cognitive-behavior therapy of borderline personality disorder.* New York: Guilford Press.

McReynolds, P. (1997). *Lightner Witmer: His life and times.* Washington, DC: American Psychological Association.

Meltzer, H. (1966). Psychology of the scientist: XVII. Research has a place in private practice. *Psychological Reports, 19,* 463–472.

Menninger, W. C. (1950). The relationship of clinical psychology and psychiatry. *American Psychologist, 5,* 3–15.

Mineka, S., Davidson, M., Cook, M., & Keir, R. (1984). Observational conditioning of snake fear in rhesus monkeys. *Journal of Abnormal Psychology, 93,* 355–372.

Mitchell, D. (1919). The clinical psychologist. *Journal of Abnormal Psychology, 14,* 325–332.

Mitchell, D. (1931). Private practice. In R. A. Brotemarkle (Ed.), *Clinical psychology: Studies in honor of Lightner Witmer* (pp. 177–190). Philadelphia: University of Pennsylvania Press.

Morrow, W. R. (1946). The development of psychology internship training. *Journal of Consulting Psychology, 10,* 165–183.

Mowrer, O. H., & Mowrer, W. M. (1938). Enuresis: A method for its study and treatment. *American Journal of Orthopsychiatry, 8,* 436–459.

Munroe, R. (1955). *Schools of psychoanalytic thought.* New York: Dryden.

Parloff, M. B., Waskow, I. E., & Wolfe, B. (1978). Research on therapist variables in relation to process and outcome. In S. L. Garfield & A. E. Bergin (Eds.), *Handbook of psychotherapy and behavior change.* New York: Wiley.

Patterson, G. R. (1974). Interventions with boys with conduct problems: Multiple settings, treatments, and criteria. *Journal of Consulting and Clinical Psychology, 42,* 471–481.

Paul, G. L., & Lentz, R. J. (1977). *Psychosocial treatment of chronic mental patients: Milieu versus social learning programs.* Cambridge, MA: Harvard University Press.

Peterson, D. R. (1992). The doctor of psychology degree. In D. K. Freedheim (Ed.), *History of psychotherapy: A century of change* (pp. 829–849). Washington, DC: American Psychological Association.

Piotrowski, C., & Lubin, B. (1989). Prescription privileges: A view from health psychologists. *Clinical Psychologist, 42,* 83–84.

Prince, M. (1909–1910). The psychological principles and field of psychotherapy. *Journal of Abnormal Psychology, 4,* 72–98.

Raimy, V. C. (Ed.). (1950). *Training in clinical psychology.* New York: Prentice Hall.

Reisman, J. M. (1991). *A history of clinical psychology* (2nd ed.). New York: Hemisphere.

Report of Committee of Clinical Section of APA. (1935). *Psychological Clinic, 23,* 1–140.

Rogers, C. R. (1942). *Counseling and psychotherapy.* New York: Houghton.

Rogers, C. R. (1951). *Client-centered therapy.* Boston: Houghton Mifflin.

Rogers, C. R. (1957). The necessary and sufficient conditions of therapeutic personality change. *Journal of Consulting Psychology, 21,* 95–103.

Routh, D. K. (1984, May). When was the first psychology clinic in Iowa founded? *Iowa Psychologist, 29,* 3–7.

Routh, D. K. (1994). *Clinical psychology since 1917: Science, practice, and organization.* New York: Plenum Press.

Routh, D. K. (1996). Lightner Witmer and the first 100 years of clinical psychology. *American Psychologist, 51,* 244–247.

Routh, D. K. (1997). A history of division 12 (clinical psychology): Fourscore years. In D. Dewsbury (Ed.), *Unification through division: Histories of the divisions of the American Psychological Association* (Vol. 2, pp. 55–82). Washington, DC: American Psychological Association.

Routh, D. K. (1998). Hippocrates meets Democritus: A history of psychiatry and clinical psychology. In A. S. Bellack & M. Hersen (Eds.), *Comprehensive clinical psychology* (Vol. 1, pp. 1–48). New York: Pergamon Press.

Routh, D. K. (2000). Clinical psychology training: A history of ideas and practices prior to 1946. *American Psychologist, 55,* 236–241.

Routh, D. K., del Barrio, V., & Carpintero, H. (1996). European roots of the first psychology clinic in North America. *European Psychologist, 1,* 44–50.

Routh, D. K., & DeRubeis, R. (1998). *The science of clinical psychology: Accomplishments and future directions.* Washington, DC: American Psychological Association.

Schroeder, S. R., Rojahn, J., & Reese, M. R. (1997). Reliability and validity of instruments for assessing psychotropic medication effects on self-injurious behavior in mental retardation. *Journal of Autism and Developmental Disabilities, 27,* 89–102.

Seligman, M. E. P. (1975). *Helplessness: On depression, development, and death.* San Francisco: Freeman.

Sexton, V. S., & Hogan, J. S. (1992). Epilogue. In V. S. Sexton & J. D. Hogan (Eds.), *International psychology: Views from around the world* (pp. 467–477). Lincoln: University of Nebraska Press.

Shakow, D. (1965). Seventeen years later: Clinical psychology in the light of the 1947 Committee on Training in Clinical Psychology report. *American Psychologist, 20,* 353–362.

Shakow, D. (1976). Reflections on a do-it-yourself program in clinical psychology. *Journal of the History of the Behavioral Sciences, 12,* 14–30.

Shorter, E. (1997). *A history of psychiatry: From the era of the asylum to the age of Prozac.* New York: Wiley.

Skinner, B. F. (1938). *The behavior of organisms: An experimental analysis.* New York: Appleton-Century-Crofts.

Skinner, B. F. (1971). *Beyond freedom and dignity.* New York: Knopf.

Smith, M. L., & Glass, G. V. (1977). Meta-analysis of psychotherapy outcome studies. *American Psychologist, 32,* 752–777.

Sprague, R. L., Kalachnik, J. E., & Shaw, K. M. (1989). Psychometric properties of the Dyskinesia Identification System: Condensed User Scale. *Mental Retardation, 27,* 141–148.

Stricker, G., & Cummings, N. A. (1992). The professional school movement. In D. K. Freedheim (Ed.), *History of psychotherapy: A century of change* (pp. 801–828). Washington, DC: American Psychological Association.

Teri, L., & Lewinsohn, P. M. (1986). Individual and group treatment of unipolar depression: Comparison of treatment outcome and identification of predictors of successful treatment outcome. *Behavior Therapy, 17,* 215–228.

Terman, L. M. (1925). *Genetic studies of genius.* Stanford, CA: Stanford University Press.

University Commission to Advise on the Future of Psychology at Harvard. (1947). *The place of psychology in an ideal university.* Cambridge, MA: Harvard University Press.

Wallston, K. (1997). A history of division 38 (health psychology): Healthy, wealthy, and Weiss. In D. Dewsbury (Ed.), *Unification through division: Histories of the divisions of the American Psychological Association* (Vol. 2, pp. 239–267). Washington, DC: American Psychological Association.

Watson, J. B. (1913). Psychology as the behaviorist views it. *Psychological Review, 20,* 158–179.

Watson, J. B., & Raynor, R. (1920). Conditioned emotional reactions. *Journal of Experimental Psychology, 3,* 1–14.

Witmer, L. (1897). The organization of practical work in psychology. *Psychological Review, 4,* 116.

Witmer, L. (1907a). A case of chronic bad spelling: Anesia visualis verbalis, due to arrest of post-natal development. *Psychological Clinic, 1,* 53–64.

Witmer, L. (1907b). Clinical psychology. *Psychological Clinic, 1,* 1–9.

Witmer, L. (1909–1910). The restoration of children of the slums. *Psychological Clinic, 3,* 266–280.

Witmer, L. (1925). Psychological diagnosis and the psychonomic orientation of analytic science. *Psychological Clinic, 16,* 1–18.

Wolpe, J. (1958). *Psychotherapy by reciprocal inhibition.* Stanford, CA: Stanford University Press.

Wolpe, J., Salter, A., & Reyna, L. J. (Eds.). (1964). *The conditioning therapies: The challenge in psychotherapy.* New York: Holt, Rinehart and Winston.

Yerkes, R. M. (1919). Report of the Psychology Committee of the National Research Council. *Psychological Review, 26,* 83–149.

Yerkes, R. M., Bridges, J. W., & Hardwick, R. S. (1915). *A point scale for measuring mental ability.* Baltimore: Warwick & York.

CHAPTER 17

Counseling Psychology

DAVID B. BAKER

THE MODERN AGE   357
THE GUIDANCE MOVEMENTS   358
   A Plan for Guidance   358
   Guidance in Education and Psychology   358
THE RISE OF PSYCHOLOGICAL TESTING   359
WAR AND THE TRAINING OF PSYCHOLOGISTS   360

AN IDENTITY FOR COUNSELING PSYCHOLOGY   361
   Diversification   362
   The Question of Identity   362
   Moving Ahead   363
SUMMARY   363
REFERENCES   364

Beginnings, for the most part, tend to be arbitrary. Whether chosen for historical precision, maintenance of myth, convenience, or necessity, beginnings tell us something of how we want our story to be told. For the purposes of this chapter, the genesis of counseling psychology is viewed through the context of the Progressive Era of the early twentieth century. For purposes of convenience the chapter will start at the beginning of the twentieth century; the reader is asked to consider that the substantive story of the history of counseling psychology is a story of the twentieth century.

THE MODERN AGE

America in 1900 was embracing the modern. There was no longer a frontier but rather a growing industrial base that drove the economy. The technology of travel, the making of fuel from oil, and the building of structures from steel transformed the continent and the culture. The national industrial machine cleared a path east and west, north and south, transforming native lands and displacing and frequently exterminating wildlife and native peoples.

The culture of change brought many to the new urban centers of the industrial Northeast and Midwest. City life amazed with a dizzying array of new technologies, including telephones, radios, movies, electricity, and automobiles. Most believed these would improve individual lives and the collective good. Information, goods and services, and people could move more rapidly, and processes could be mechanized. Progress was synonymous with precision and efficiency, a

belief that became associated with the Progressive political movement (Mann, 1975; Watts, 1994).

Achieving precision meant avoiding waste, a concept that could be applied to products as well as people. In industry, efficiency was embodied in the work of Frederick Taylor, whose scientific study of jobs was designed to streamline human performance and increase production. Taylor believed his system would benefit management and the worker. The better-trained worker was likely to be more productive, thus increasing the possibility of promotion and improved wages. Gains in productivity would translate into greater profit for management, and at the end of the cycle, the consumer would benefit from a better and more cost-efficient product (Taylor, 1911).

Alongside industrial efficiency was a belief in the perfectibility of the individual and society. The search for perfectibility began with the young, and America, a young nation itself, became increasingly concerned with the promise of youth as the hope of the nation. Child saving, as it came to be known (Levine & Levine, 1992), was a movement that worked to protect children from the ravages of poverty, abuse, and neglect. The impulse toward child saving propelled the beginnings of the vocational guidance movement, a major precursor to the development of counseling psychology.

The city, while offering modern conveniences, was also a place of wretched poverty and deplorable conditions. Millions who sought refuge in America could find work in the industrial city, although it was low paying, low skilled, and frequently dangerous. Immigrants new to the culture and the language could easily be exploited, and this applied to all members of a family. Children from poor families were especially vulnerable, frequently leaving school before the age of 12 to do menial labor. Within the culture of child saving, these conditions created a strong rallying cry that resulted in greater protections for some of society's most at-risk people (Davidson & Benjamin, 1987).

What many wanted most was a chance for children to receive an adequate education, one that would last beyond the primary grades. Children's leaving school to drift aimlessly was seen as a tremendous waste of human potential and an inefficient use of human resources. The concern over leaving school was embedded within the larger context of the place of public education in American society, a debate that gave rise to a variety of visions for the future of the nation and its youth. Many saw the school system as failing the students it was charged with serving. They called for public education to complement the world outside of the classroom and provide tools for success in the new American urban industrial centers. For immigrant children, the system struggled to provide thoughtful alternatives; for Native American, Hispanic, and African American children, the system was and would remain limited, segregated, and largely indifferent.

A variety of alternatives were offered. Booker T. Washington called for national programs of industrial education for African American children, psychologist Helen Thompson Woolley conducted scientific studies of school leaving, and philanthropic reformers like Jane Addams established settlement homes (Baker, in press).

In Boston, Chicago, New York, and Philadelphia, settlement homes were a common feature of the progressive landscape at the start of the twentieth century (Carson, 1990). Wanting to respond to the plight of poor inner-city families, socially minded students, professors, clergy, and artists would take up residence in working-class neighborhoods, becoming part of and an influence on the social, educational, political, artistic, and economic life of the community. In this setting, the vocational guidance movement in America began in earnest.

THE GUIDANCE MOVEMENTS

In Boston, the Civic Service House opened in 1901. Funded by Pauline Agassis Shaw, a philanthropist with a strong commitment to children, the Civic Service House served the educational needs of immigrant adults. One goal of the Civic Service House was to provide a semblance of a college education to the working poor of the neighborhood (Brewer, 1942; A. F. Davis & McCree, 1969). Helping in this effort was a frequent guest of the Civic Service House, Boston attorney Frank Parsons. Well educated and socially minded, he

was an advocate for the rights and needs of those he believed were exploited by industrial monopolies.

A Plan for Guidance

Parsons was very much interested in how people chose their life's work, viewing vocational choice as a form of individual and social efficiency, a part of the Progressive ideal. Talking of the subject to students at the Civic Service House, Parsons found many who wanted personal meetings to discuss their vocational futures, so much so that in January 1908, he opened the Vocational Bureau at the Civic Service House under the motto "Light, Information, Inspiration, and Cooperation" (Brewer, 1942; Watts, 1994).

Parsons' (1909) own words reflect the spirit of the times and the themes that would come to be associated with vocational psychology and guidance:

> The wise selection of the business, profession, trade, or occupation to which one's life is to be devoted and the development of full efficiency in the chosen field are matters of the deepest moment to young men and to the public. These vital problems should be solved in a careful, scientific way, with due regard to each person's aptitudes, abilities, ambitions, resources, and limitations, and the relations of these elements to the conditions of success than if he drifts into an industry for which he is not fitted. An occupation out of harmony with the worker's aptitudes and capacities means inefficiency, unenthusiastic and perhaps distasteful labor, and low pay; while an occupation in harmony with the nature of the man means enthusiasm, love of work, and high economic values, superior product, efficient service, and good pay. (p. 3)

Parsons' beliefs were actualized in a program of individual guidance that he developed based on the triadic formulation of (a) knowledge of oneself, (b) knowledge of occupations, and (c) the relationship between the two. Parsons had to develop many of the methods he used or borrow from questionable practices such as physiognomy and phrenology. The matching of self and job traits retained popular appeal, and Parsons earned a place of historical distinction (Baker, in press). The legacy was shortened by Parsons' premature death in 1908.

Guidance in Education and Psychology

The institutionalization of vocational guidance began in 1917 with the transfer of the Vocational Bureau to the Division of Education at Harvard. Here educators and psychologists would frame some of the earliest debates about the nature of guidance and counseling, debates that have echoed throughout the history of counseling psychology.

Some on the Harvard faculty, such as John Brewer, saw vocational guidance as an educational function; others, such as Hugo Münsterberg, saw it as a province of the new applied psychology. Brewer argued that guidance was a part of the educational experience, a process by which the student is an active agent in seeking out experiences that help determine the appropriate choice of an occupation (Brewer, 1932). Psychologists such as Münsterberg (1910) viewed guidance as an activity well suited to the new applied psychology. Münsterberg, director of the psychological laboratory at Harvard and an early progenitor of applied psychology, was familiar with and supportive of Parsons' work but offered a warning:

> We now realize that questions as to the mental capacities and functions and powers of an individual can no longer be trusted to impressionistic replies. If we are to have reliable answers, we must make use of the available resources of the psychological laboratory. These resources emancipate us from the illusions and emotions of the self-observer. The well-arranged experiment measures the mental states with the same exactness with which the chemical or physical examination of the physician studies the organism of the individual. (p. 401)

Münsterberg was joined by colleagues such as Harry Hollingworth and Leta Hollingworth, psychologists who had advocated for the scientific study of vocational guidance. Like Münsterberg, they were wary of pseudoscientific means of assessing individual traits. They were so concerned with the problem that in 1916, Harry Hollingworth published the book *Vocational Psychology*. Designed to debunk such character-reading techniques as physiognomy, it promoted the benefits the new science of psychology could lend to the assessment of individual abilities. Leta Hollingworth, an early advocate for the psychological study of women and women's issues, added a chapter on the vocational aptitudes of women. The purpose of the chapter she wrote was

> to inquire whether there are any innate and essential sex differences in tastes and abilities, which would afford a scientific basis for the apparently arbitrary and traditional assumption that the vocational future of all girls must naturally fall in the domestic sphere, and consequently presents no problem, while the future of boys is entirely problematical and may lie in any of a score of different callings, according to personal fitness. (p. 223)

Reflective of much of her work on gender differences and mental abilities, she concluded that "so far as is at present known, women are as competent in mental capacity as men are, to undertake any and all human vocations" (p. 244).

The new applied psychology fit well with the Progressive Era theme of social efficiency. The scientific study of mental life encouraged greater understanding of adaptation to everyday life. Psychologists such as Lightner Witmer, E. Wallace Wallin, G. Stanley Hall, Augusta Bronner, William Healy, Maude Merrill, Lewis Terman, and Helen Woolley investigated various aspects of the childhood experience, each contributing in his or her own way to the child-saving movement and helping to create a body of knowledge that helped to shape social-science policy in the early decades of the twentieth century (Baker, 2001).

While psychologists were busy with the study of individual difference in mental abilities, educators continued to develop a national program of vocational guidance. Although Frank Parsons was well regarded for developing a system of vocational guidance, his was an individual method. In public education, greater numbers of students could and would be reached through the provision of group guidance. In 1907, Jesse B. Davis became principal of Grand Rapids High School in Michigan. Davis attempted to expose students to vocational planning through English composition. He reasoned that having high school students explore their vocational interests, ambitions, and character would empower them to make informed choices about their place in the flux of the new social order (J. B. Davis, 1914). Soon his ideas about vocational and moral development would be translated into a complete program of guidance (Brewer, 1942).

Between 1890 and 1920, vocational guidance would come of age in American culture and establish itself as a permanent fixture of the twentieth-century landscape. Individual efforts of people like Parsons and Davis were eclipsed by the formation of national organizations concerned with vocational guidance. In 1906, the National Society for the Promotion of Industrial Education (NSPIE) was formed largely through the efforts of progressive labor leaders and settlement home advocates, many with ties to the Civic Service House and its Vocational Bureau. The NSPIE provided an organized means of lobbying the federal government for changes in public schooling that would accommodate industrial education and vocational guidance (Stephens, 1970). In 1913, the National Vocational Guidance Association was founded and provided a clear identity for those associated with vocational guidance. With powerful political support and an impressive set of advocates, vocational guidance found its way into most educational systems in America by 1920.

THE RISE OF PSYCHOLOGICAL TESTING

The First World War saw much less interest in the choice of a meaningful career and much more interest in the selection of able soldiers. The role and influence of psychologists expanded greatly during this period as the new tools of the trade were offered to the testing and classification of recruits.

Shortly after the United States entered World War I in 1917, American Psychological Association (APA) president Robert Yerkes organized psychologists to assist with the war effort. Offering the services of psychology to the nation, Yerkes established a number of committees, including an examining committee that he headed and a committee on the classification of personnel under the direction of Walter Dill Scott. Scott was not new to the venture; as a member of the Division of Applied Psychology at the Carnegie Institute of Technology, he was a leader in the development and evaluation of selection methods. The program he introduced into the armed services proved to be highly successful in classifying recruits and bolstered the place of psychology, especially applied psychology, in America (Benjamin & Baker, in press; Napoli, 1981).

More than anything else, American psychologists demonstrated the efficacy of group testing. Measures of aptitude, adjustment, interest, and ability, while less publicized than the development of group measures of intelligence, soon found applications in guidance and counseling. Indeed, the 1920s and 1930s were witness to a testing craze in public education that provided work for secondary school counselors, educational psychologists, and test publishers. The scientific management of the student extended into higher education, and soon student personnel work would flourish on college campuses alongside the faculty who were developing the instruments of the new science (Baker, in press).

For all the possibilities, there were also limitations. Group testing, still in its infancy, had problems, none more apparent than the question of the reliability and validity of intelligence tests that failed to recognized cultural bias. The questionable use of questionable tests led to numerous claims of racial differences in intelligence and education that contributed to continued perpetuation of racial stereotyping and bias (Guthrie, 1998).

Like the First World War, the Great Depression of the 1930s provided hardships for American citizens and opportunities for applied psychology. With high rates of unemployment and the success of the classification work of Walter Dill Scott and colleague Walter Bingham at Carnegie Tech, federal assistance was available for large-scale studies of selection procedures in industry and education. The 1930s were a time of incredible development in the psychometrics of selection. Test of interest, aptitude, and ability were developed and studied by such well-known figures as E. K. Strong Jr., L. L. Thurstone, and E. L. Thorndike. The vocational guidance of the early century was transforming and branching out into areas such as student personnel work and industrial psychology (Super, 1955; Paterson, 1938).

The prototype of what eventually became counseling psychology can be found in these early activities and programs.

Of particular relevance was the Minnesota Employment Stabilization Research Institute at the University of Minnesota. A depression-era project, it was an early model of integration of science and practice, designed to scientifically study occupations and employment while simultaneously finding jobs for its unemployed subjects. The director of the program, Donald G. Paterson, would soon merge all the branches of vocational guidance, applied and scientific, into a program of counseling and guidance that would serve as a model for the later formalization of counseling psychology (Blocher, 2000).

The 1930s also saw a rise in the number of psychologists interested in applying testing and counseling to those with more severe forms of maladjustment. Most often these psychologists were found in hospitals and clinical settings, where they worked under the direction of a psychiatrist. Many were linked to clinical work with children like those associated with Lightner Witmer and his psychological clinic at the University of Pennsylvania (Baker, 1988; McReynolds, 1997). With the aid of psychometrics (largely measures of intelligence, individually administered) and the clinical laboratory, these psychologists sought to establish an identity for themselves, often defined in terms of clinical psychology. Indeed, they bore a resemblance to what we would now call school psychologists or clinical psychologists (Routh, 1994). However, in the 1930s and 1940s such labels were not in popular use, nor were there organized and systematic training programs for mental health professionals. All was about to change.

WAR AND THE TRAINING OF PSYCHOLOGISTS

The role of psychologists during the Second World War would greatly expand. Classification and other assessment activities remained an integral part of the work, but unlike during the First World War, when intellectual function was stressed, the concern shifted to the mental health of the fighting force. Mental health screening of new recruits indicated alarming rates of psychopathology, about 17% of draft-age men (Deutsch, 1949). When anticipated casualties from the war were added and when counts of occupied Veterans Administration (VA) beds were made, it was clear that psychiatric problems were the leading cause of casualty among soldiers. The United States Public Health Service (USPHS) and the Veterans Administration quickly realized that there were not enough trained mental health professionals to meet the burgeoning need. Through joint action, the USPHS and the VA developed a national plan of mental health. First and foremost was the establishment of a recognized mental health profession. The Mental Health Act of 1946 provided federal funds to the USPHS for an aggressive campaign of research, training, and service to combat mental illness, and in the process it created the National Institute of Mental Health (NIMH). The VA offered significant financial and organizational support to psychology by supporting the creation of accredited doctoral training programs in clinical and counseling psychology (Baker & Benjamin, in press).

The coordination of academic psychology, the APA, the VA, and the USPHS was swift and best represented by the convening of the Boulder Conference on Graduate Education in Clinical Psychology in 1949. For 15 days, 73 representatives of academic and applied psychology, medicine, nursing, and education debated and discussed the establishment of the professional psychologist. For many the most memorable outcome was the endorsement of the scientist-practitioner model of training. The conference, though, was about much more. In very broad terms, it gave national policy makers the assurance that professional applied psychology was prepared to meet the mental health needs of the nation (Benjamin & Baker, 2000).

It is important to note that few distinctions were made between specialty areas in psychology, and if anything the call was for an inclusive view. According to the report of the Boulder Conference (Raimy, 1950),

> the majority of the conference was clearly in favor of encouraging the broad development of clinical psychology along the lines that extend the field of practice from the frankly psychotic or mentally ill to the relatively normal clientele who need information, vocational counseling, and remedial work. Specialization in any of these less clearly defined branches has now become an open issue that must be faced sooner or later. (pp. 112–113)

The conferees went so far as to offer a vote of support for the recommendation that

> the APA and its appropriate division should study the common and diverse problems and concepts in the fields of clinical psychology and counseling and guidance with a view to immediate interfield enrichment of knowledge and methods. Consideration should also be given to the possibility of eventual amalgamation of these two fields. (p. 148)

Obviously such an amalgamation never occurred. The reorganization of the APA in 1945 brought clear divisions between those who identified themselves with clinical psychology and those who identified with counseling and guidance. Division 17, first known as the Division of Personnel and Guidance Psychologists (quickly changed to the Division of Counseling and Guidance), came into existence with the reorganization, due in large part to many faculty members at the University of Minnesota, including Donald Paterson, E. G. Williamson, and John Darley (Blocher, 2000).

Soon after Boulder, substantial federal dollars went to supporting the establishment of doctoral training programs in clinical and counseling psychology at universities across America. The Boulder vision of the professional psychologist was most closely associated with clinical psychology, and clinical training programs would be the first recognized by the USPHS and VA. Counseling psychologists eager to make their contribution and get their share of the funding windfall received support for training conferences of their own with funds supplied by the USPHS.

AN IDENTITY FOR COUNSELING PSYCHOLOGY

A conference titled "The Training of Psychological Counselors" was held at the University of Michigan in July 1948, and again in January of 1949. Under the direction of Michigan faculty member and counseling center director Edward Bordin, the participants sought to provide a training model that would address the unique contributions that counseling and guidance could make to a national program of mental health. The proposals offered at the Michigan meeting were passed along to Division 17, which along with the APA sponsored the Northwestern Conference in 1951. In an effort to produce a formal statement on the training of counseling psychologists, the participants at Northwestern University reviewed the recommendations of the Ann Arbor group and the Boulder Conference. Upon deliberation, they upheld the primacy of the PhD degree and advocated training in the fashion of the scientist-practitioner. In addition, they identified those aspects of counseling and guidance that made it unique. It was decided to change the name of the division from "counseling and guidance" to "counseling psychology," a move no doubt in concert with a desire to have the division look more similar to clinical psychology than educational guidance. In addressing the roles and functions of the counseling psychologist, the report (APA, 1952) stated:

> The professional goal of the counseling psychologist is to foster the psychological development of the individual. This includes all people on the adjustment continuum from those who function at tolerable levels of adequacy to those suffering from more severe psychological disturbances. Counseling psychologists will spend the bulk of their time with individuals within the normal range, but their training should qualify them to work in some degree with individuals at any level of psychological adjustment. Counseling stresses the positive and the preventative. It focuses upon the stimulation of personal development in order to maximize personal and social effectiveness and to forestall psychologically crippling disabilities. (p. 175)

Northwestern brought important dividends. The VA responded by creating two new positions for psychologists, Counseling Psychologist (Vocational) and Counseling Psychologist (Vocational Rehabilitation and Education). Under the leadership of Robert Waldrop, the VA sought to help universities establish counseling psychology doctoral training programs that would complement existing clinical psychology training programs. The APA followed suit and began to accredit counseling psychology doctoral training programs in 1951. Along with this would come the need for counseling psychologists to pass through those rites of passage that define a profession, including issues of professional ethics, licensure, and the like. All in all, it seemed that counseling psychology was starting to come into its own.

Diversification

Not only did the federal government help to create the profession of counseling psychology, it also supported students entering the field through training stipends provided by the VA and the USPHS and through benefits under provisions of the GI bill (Baker & Benjamin, in press). As counseling psychology moved closer to clinical psychology, it distanced itself from its earlier identification with the National Vocational Guidance Association, which together with others interested in guidance and student personnel work formed the American Personnel and Guidance Association (now known as the American Counseling Association). Many members of Division 17 shared membership in these associations, oftentimes serving as officers in each (Pepinsky, Hill-Frederick, & Epperson, 1978).

The number of settings and activities that counseling psychologists concerned themselves with seemed to explode. Many pursued the opportunities available through the VA, others remained closer to student personnel work, and still others, such as Donald Super, Anne Roe, and David Tiedeman, vigorously pursued programs of research centered around vocational development (Blocher, 2000).

The launch of the Russian satellite *Sputnik* on October 4, 1957, provided new opportunities for counseling psychology. Passage of the National Defense Education Act (NDEA) of 1958 again focused considerable attention upon the nation's schools. There were widespread concerns that the public schools were not producing enough students interested in math and science. The finger of blame pointed directly at progressive education, which was faulted for failing to provide a demanding enough curriculum that would bring out the best in American youth. Among other things, the NDEA authorized funds to identify public school students who might show promise in math and science. To identify those

students, a national program of testing would be necessary, a program that at its core would require significant numbers of school counselors who could identify and direct students with potential. Just as World War II had identified shortages of mental health professionals, NDEA identified shortages of school counselors and quickly supplied funding to colleges and universities to conduct counseling and guidance institutes. Approximately 80 institutes per year were conducted. These could be summer institutes of 6 to 8 weeks or yearlong sequences. Participants were generally drawn from the ranks of high school guidance counselors, who were attracted to the opportunities and the stipends the institutes offered (Tyler, 1960).

Institute staffs were mostly educational psychologists, counseling psychologists, and developmental psychologists. Topics of study included tests and measurement, statistics, and individual and group counseling methods. The use of group experiences was common, as was supervised practicum experience. The institutes were supported for 8 years from 1958 to 1966, at which time they continued under a variety of educational acts. The institutes provided employment for counseling psychologists and helped to increase the visibility of counseling psychology, but by and large the program increased demand for counselor educators, enhancing the presence of such programs on university campuses and making training requirements for graduate degrees in counseling and guidance more concrete. In the 8 years of the program, some 44,000 counselors were trained (Baker, 2000; Tyler, 1960).

The Question of Identity

Counseling psychology was perhaps moving along too many paths, and in 1959, the APA's Education and Training Board called for an evaluation of the status of the field. The initial report, authored by three counseling psychologists (Irwin Berg, Harold Pepinsky, and Joe Shobin) was not flattering. Criticisms were made about the lack of a research emphasis and the broad meaning of *counseling* (to read the report see Whitely, 1980). It was recommended that consideration be given to dissolving Division 17 and moving it under the auspices of Division 12, Clinical Psychology. This was not the sort of amalgamation the Boulder participants had envisioned. The report was never released, and after much protest on the part of Division 17, a new report was commissioned and published (also in Whitely, 1980). It presented a more encouraging view of counseling psychology and provided data to demonstrate that the profession was alive and well.

The whole affair contributed to serious questions of identity and the place and direction of counseling psychology.

In response, the division set about regrouping and taking stock. The result was the convening of the Greyston Conference. Named for the Greyston Mansion, a gift to Teachers College, Columbia University, the meeting was held over a 3-day period in January 1964. In an interview (Baker, 2001), one of the organizers and authors of the conference report, Albert S. Thompson, describes the nature and significance of the meeting:

> We wanted a group that would be representative of counseling psychologists. There were 60 and it certainly was an interesting group. When you think of it, they were a terrific group, 10 were previous presidents of Division 17 and 11 of them later became presidents. The conference was well organized and Don Super really gets the most credit for that. At the end of the conference we came up with 32 recommendations. Some were for Division 17, some for APA, some for universities, some for practicum and internship settings, and some for employers. Most were designed to be practical. I would like to go record to say that the recommendations did stimulate further developments such as American Board of Examiners of Professional Psychologists (ABEPP) certification, a brochure put out by Division 17 on what counseling psychology is, and criteria for internship. There was general agreement that counseling psychology had a special substance and emphasis in training, which were not necessarily included in the current preparation. (p. 318)

Greyston if nothing else helped to unite counseling psychologists in a spirit of shared mission. After Greyston, there was less talk about disbanding and more talk of identity. The brochure that Thompson referred to appeared in 1968 (Jordaan, Myers, Layton, & Morgan, 1968). The document, affirming the tenets of the Northwestern Conference, defined the counseling psychologist in terms of three central roles: the remedial/rehabilitative, the preventative, and the educational/developmental.

Moving Ahead

However, it was not that simple. The expansion of private practice, a decline in federal support of training and research, and retrenchment in academia contributed to continued self-doubt and a lingering unease about the future and direction of counseling psychology. Whiteley and Fretz (1980) invited a distinguished cohort to comment on the future of counseling psychology, and the forecast was gloomy. Counseling psychology's lack of a clear identification with a particular role, function, or setting made it difficult for many of the contributors to see a future that made any sense. But in spite of decades of an entrenched identity crisis, the division has grown. There are over 2,500 members (APA, 2001), 67 active

APA-accredited doctoral programs (APA, 2000), and two major journals (*The Journal of Counseling Psychology* and *The Counseling Psychologist*). Counseling psychologists are found in higher education, industry, government, and health care (private and nonprofit). As an organization, counseling psychology has a unified existence within Division 17, which provides a forum for debate, sets policy through coordinated meetings and conferences, reorganizes itself to the demands of the times, and recognizes its members through a variety of awards and honors (Blocher, 2000; Meara & Myers, 1999).

Since its inception, the division has worked on the issue of identity, the most recent definition of counseling psychology appearing in 1998 (APA, 1999):

> Counseling psychology is a general practice and health service-provider specialty in professional psychology. It focuses upon personal and interpersonal functioning across the life span and on emotional, social, vocational, educational, health-related, developmental and organizational concerns. Counseling psychology centers on typical or normal developmental issues as well as atypical or disordered development as it applies to human experience from individual, family, group, systems, and organizational perspectives. Counseling psychologists help people with physical, emotional and mental disorders improve well being, alleviate distress and maladjustment, and resolve crises. In addition, practitioners in the professional specialty provide assessment, diagnosis and treatment of psychopathology. (p. 589)

SUMMARY

Perhaps it is most important to know that counseling psychology does have a history, one that is embedded in the American experience of the twentieth century that stressed the triumph of turning raw materials into finished products with precision and efficiency. The application of this to the human experience, while a desired goal, was a messier proposition.

The genesis of counseling psychology can be found in the vocational guidance movement, a Progressive Era development that sought to add a humane element to the science of efficiency. Its adherents and practitioners saw in the progressive ideal a chance for a better and more satisfying life for all people of all ages.

Embracing the applied study of individual difference, these prototypes of the professional psychologist found their calling in the theory and practice of measurement of human abilities, aptitudes, and interests. Their work had applications in all corners of society, especially in those areas concerned with education and rehabilitation. Over time, these coalesced into an identify as a health service profession, aligned with a training model for professional psychology espoused by the American Psychological Association.

Psychotherapy continues to grow as an area of emphasis within counseling psychology, and counseling psychologists have long served as active contributors to theory, research, and practice. The same is true for vocational psychology and career development.

Like any organization or institution, counseling psychology has molded itself to the demands, challenges, changes, and opportunities of the times. It is interesting to note that as the new century begins, counseling psychology finds itself defining as a value the priority of multicultural inclusiveness. The template of inclusiveness is now laid over all aspects of counseling psychology research, teaching, training, and service. It is a point of view that expresses a concern for the well-being of all people, a concern much like that of 100 years ago.

REFERENCES

American Psychological Association. (1999). Archival description of counseling psychology (Division 17). *Counseling Psychologist, 27,* 589–592.

American Psychological Association. (2000). Accredited doctoral training programs in professional psychology: 2000. *American Psychologist, 55,* 1473–1486.

American Psychological Association. (2001). *Directory of the American Psychological Association.* Washington, DC: Author.

American Psychological Association, Division of Counseling and Guidance, Committee on Counselor Training. (1952). Recommended standards for training counselors at the doctoral level. *American Psychologist, 7,* 175–181.

Baker, D. B. (1988). The psychology of Lightner Witmer. *Professional School Psychology, 3,* 109–121.

Baker, D. B. (in press). Child saving and the emergence of vocational counseling. *Journal of Vocational Behavior.*

Baker, D. B., & Benjamin, L. T., Jr. (in press). Creating a profession: NIMH and the training of psychologists 1946–1954. In W. Pickren (Ed.), *Psychology and the National Institute of Mental Health.* Washington, DC: American Psychological Association.

Benjamin, L. T., Jr., & Baker, D. B. (2000). Boulder at 50: Introduction to the special section. *American Psychologist, 55,* 233–236.

Benjamin, L. T., Jr., & Baker, D. B. (in press). Walter Van Dyke Bingham: Portrait of an industrial psychologist. In G. Kimble & M. Wertheimer (Eds.), *Portraits of pioneers in psychology* (Vol. 5). Washington, DC: American Psychological Association.

Blocher, D. H. (2000). *The evolution of counseling psychology.* New York: Springer.

Brewer, J. M. (1932). *Education as guidance: An examination of the possibilities of a curriculum in terms of life activities, in elementary and secondary school and college.* New York: Macmillan.

Brewer, J. M. (1942). *History of vocational guidance.* New York: Harper & Brothers.

Carson, M. J. (1990). *Settlement folk: Social thought and the American settlement movement, 1885–1930.* Chicago: University of Chicago Press.

Davidson, E., & Benjamin, L. T., Jr. (1987). A history of the child study movement in America. In J. A. Glover & R. R. Ronning (Eds.), *Historical foundations of educational psychology* (pp. 187–208). New York: Plenum Press.

Davis, A. F., & McCree, M. L. (1969). *Eighty years at Hull House.* Chicago: Quadrangle Books.

Davis, J. B. (1914). *Vocational and moral guidance.* New York: Ginn and Company.

Deutsch, A. (1949). *The mentally ill in America: A history of their care and treatment from colonial times* (2nd ed.). New York: Columbia University Press.

Guthrie, R. V. (1998). *Even the rat was white: A historical view of psychology.* Boston: Allyn & Bacon.

Hollingworth, H. L. (1916). *Vocational psychology: Its problems and methods.* New York: D. Appleton and Company.

Jordaan, J. P., Myers, R. A., Layton, W. L., & Morgan, H. H. (1968). *The counseling psychologist.* New York: Teachers College Press.

Levine, M., & Levine, A. (1992). *Helping children: A social history.* New York: Oxford University Press.

Mann, A. (Ed.). (1975). *The progressive era* (2nd ed.). Hinsdale, IL: Dryden Press.

McReynolds, P. (1997). *Lightner Witmer: His life and times.* Washington, DC: American Psychological Association.

Meara, N. M., & Myers, R. A. (1999). A history of Division 17 (Counseling Psychology): Establishing stability amidst change. In D. A. Dewsbury (Ed.), *Unification through division: Histories of the divisions of the American Psychological Association* (Vol. 3, pp. 9–41). Washington, DC: American Psychological Association.

Münsterberg, H. (1910). Finding a life work. *McClures, 34,* 398–403.

Napoli, D. S. (1981). *Architects of adjustment: The history of the psychological profession in the United States.* Port Washington, NY: Kennikat Press.

Parsons, F. (1909). *Choosing a vocation.* Boston: Houghton–Mifflin.

Paterson, D. G. (1938). The genesis of modern guidance. *The Educational Record, 19,* 36–46.

Pepinsky, H. B., Hill-Frederick, K., & Epperson, D. L. (1978). Journal of Counseling Psychology as a matter of policies. *Journal of Counseling Psychology, 25,* 483–498.

Raimy, V. C. (Ed.). (1950). *Training in clinical psychology.* Englewood Cliffs, NJ: Prentice-Hall.

Routh, D. K. (1994). *Clinical psychology since 1917: Science, practice, and organization.* New York: Plenum Press.

Stephens, W. R. (1970). *Social reform and the origins of vocational guidance.* Washington, DC: Monograph of the National Vocational Guidance Association.

Super, D. E. (1955). Transition: From vocational guidance to counseling psychology. *Journal of Counseling Psychology, 2,* 3–9.

Taylor, F. W. (1911, May). The gospel of efficiency. III: The principles of scientific management. *American Magazine,* 101–113.

Tyler, L. E. (1960). *The National Defense Counseling and Guidance Training Institutes Program: A report of the first 50 institutes sponsored during the summer of 1959 by 50 colleges and universities under contract with the U.S. Office of Education authorized by the National Defense Education Act of 1958.* Washington, DC: Office of Education.

Watts, G. A. (1994). Frank Parsons: Promoter of a progressive era. *Journal of Career Development, 20,* 265–286.

Whiteley, J. M. (Ed.). (1980). *The history of counseling psychology.* Monterey, CA: Brooks/Cole.

Whiteley, J. M., & Fretz, B. R. (Eds.). (1980). *The present and future of counseling psychology.* Monterey, CA: Brooks/Cole.

CHAPTER 18

Industrial-Organizational Psychology

LAURA L. KOPPES

THE RISE OF INDUSTRIAL-ORGANIZATIONAL
   PSYCHOLOGY 367
   Labels and Definitions 367
   Scope of Content 368
   Education 370
   Employment 371
   Organized Industrial-Organizational Psychology 372
   Summary 372
CONFLUENCE OF DYNAMIC FORCES 373
   Socioeconomic Forces 374
   Business Forces 377

Legal Forces 379
Military Forces 380
Technological Forces 381
Psychological Forces 382
Intradisciplinary Forces 383
SUMMARY 384
CONCLUSION: WHAT HAVE WE LEARNED? 384
REFERENCES 385

The scope and present status of the science [Industrial Psychology], the rapidity of its development, can only be fully understood by considering *economic, social,* and *psychological* factors which have contributed to this development. (Viteles, 1932, p. 5)

While studying great discoveries and individuals in the history of industrial-organizational (I-O) psychology in the past several years, I found myself frequently asking, "*Why* were psychologists studying behavior in work settings and applying psychology to improve the workplace?" To answer this question, I realized that the evolution of I-O psychology must be examined within the overall social, cultural, and political contexts of the times, an approach referred to as a new history of psychology (Furumoto, 1988). Pate and Wertheimer (1993), for example, stated, "The history of a discipline such as psychology involves describing major discoveries, illuminating questions of priority, and identifying 'great individuals' in the context of a national or international Zeitgeist" (p. xv). This chapter is a nascent effort to describe the zeitgeist or social-historical context of I-O psychology by identifying various dynamic forces that shaped the rise of the discipline during the past 100 years in the United States.

The history presented in this chapter is not intended to be a comprehensive description of I-O psychology content or a duplication of historical accounts previously written (e.g., Austin & Villanova, 1992; Baritz, 1960; Colarelli, 1998;

Farr & Tesluk, 1997; Ferguson, 1962–1965; Hilgard, 1987; Katzell & Austin, 1992; Koppes, 1997; Landy, 1992, 1997; Meltzer & Stagner, 1980; Napoli, 1981; Thayer, 1997; Van De Water, 1997; Zickar, 2001). Katzell and Austin (1992) provided the most comprehensive review of I-O psychology's history, and I rely heavily on their work to present the rise of I-O psychology and to examine why I-O psychologists embraced various issues and questions. This chapter consists of two main sections. The first encapsulates I-O psychology's growth; the second describes the dynamic forces that shaped I-O psychology and reveals that the discipline's evolution was the result of confluences of several external and internal forces.

THE RISE OF INDUSTRIAL-ORGANIZATIONAL PSYCHOLOGY

The growth of I-O psychology can be ascertained from examining changes in labels and definitions, scope of content, education, employment, and organized I-O psychology.

Labels and Definitions

During the early years, I-O psychology was labeled *economic psychology* (Münsterberg, 1914) or *business psychology* (Kingsbury, 1923; Münsterberg, 1917). *Industrial psychology* was used infrequently before World War I but became more common after the war (Viteles, 1932). Other labels were *employment psychology* (Burtt, 1926) and *psychotechnology* (Jenkins, 1935). When the American Association of Applied Psychology (AAAP) formed in 1937, a section was created and labeled *Industrial and Business Psychology* (Section D). In 1945, the AAAP merged with the American Psychological Association (APA), and Division 14, Industrial and Business Psychology, was established. "Business" was dropped from the division's name in 1962. In 1973, "Organizational" was added to the name, and APA Division 14 became the Division of Industrial and Organizational Psychology. This label remained when Division 14 incorporated in 1982 as the Society for Industrial and Organizational Psychology, Inc. (SIOP), Division 14 of the APA.

In recollection of these name changes, APA-Division 14 (now SIOP) past president (1972–1973) Robert M. Guion recalled,

> In the late 1960s (the decade of the youthful revolt), youthful industrial psychologists . . . demanded a Division 14 name change to indicate a change in the focus of the field. They opted for the name "Division of Organizational Psychology." Vocal adherents did not want to eliminate the heritage. . . . There were enough traditionalists and enough "young Turks" to make compromise necessary. One name that was considered as more descriptive than any of the others was "Division of the Study of the Psychology of Behavior at Work." It was never seriously considered (it defies acronym), and thus I/O was born. I think this may have been the most important name-change debate in I/O history during the last half of the century. First of all, its abbreviation of general choice was I/O. The slash, /, is a printers' symbol for "or." Most of the next couple of decades were times of division, with people being either "I's" or "O's"—there is still not much real communication between the two components of the field. The name of the division and the subsequent Society, however, used the conjunction "and," implying integration of these two components. (Robert M. Guion, personal communication, July 27, 2000)

Renewed interest in renaming SIOP to accurately reflect the scope of the science and practice recently materialized (i.e., Church, 2000).

During the early years, definitions described the field almost exclusively as a technology with a focus on practical issues. For example, Kingsbury (1923) stated that business psychology or psychotechnology is "interested in acquiring facts and principles only in so far as they can be turned directly to account in the solution of practical problems, in industry, selling, teaching, or other fields of human behavior" (p. 5). Forty-five years later, Blum and Naylor (1968) defined the discipline as "simply the application or extension of psychological facts and principles to the problems concerning

human beings operating within the context of business and industry" (p. 4).

Over time, definitions included science (theories and research) and practice, and a wide range of work-related topics. In both editions of *the Handbook of Industrial and Organizational Psychology,* Dunnette stated,

> Industrial and Organizational Psychology *is* today an academic discipline, an emerging blend of research, theory and practice. The blend offers great promise, in the years ahead, for further developing and extending our knowledge of those behavioral processes which are critical to an understanding of interactions between persons and the institutions and organizations of a society. (Dunnette, 1976, p. 12, 1990, p. 23)

Although the definition has expanded, a common underlying theme persists: improving the workplace and work lives.

Scope of Content

A discipline is defined by the kinds of questions that are asked, which can be determined by examining the content of the field at different points in time. Changes in scope are evident from reviewing textbooks (e.g., Viteles, 1932) and chapters in the *Annual Review of Psychology* and the *Handbook of Industrial and Organizational Psychology* (Dunnette, 1976; Dunnette & Hough, 1990–1992; Triandis, Dunnette, & Hough, 1994). Table 18.1 contains the contents of Viteles's book. Table 18.2 contains a list of topics from the chapter titled "Industrial Psychology" in the first volume of the *Annual Review of Psychology* (Shartle, 1950). Similar topics were covered in chapters for the next 10 years. In 1961 and subsequent years, multiple chapters on related areas, such as personnel management, industrial social psychology, consumer psychology, personnel selection, program evaluation, group dynamics, and engineering psychology, were included. In 1964, the first chapter devoted to organizational psychology was published. Table 18.2 displays the broad range of topics related to I-O psychology from 1961 to 2000.

Dunnette (1976) provided several observations about changes in content by comparing the 1950 *Handbook of Applied Psychology* (Fryer & Henry, 1950) and the 1976 *Handbook of Industrial and Organizational Psychology* (Dunnette, 1976). He noted that the 1950 *Handbook* consisted of techniques and applications; scant attention was given to research, research methodology, or theories of individual or organizational behavior. In contrast, the 1976 *Handbook* contents, shown in Table 18.3, emphasized research strategies and methods, theories of behavior, and the psychological influences and forces of organizational characteristics on individuals. The earlier handbook covered all areas of applied psychology, whereas the latter included only I-O, reflecting

TABLE 18.1 *Industrial Psychology* (Viteles, 1932)

Table of Contents

Section 1: The foundations of industrial psychology.
Introduction to a study of industrial psychology.
The economic foundations of industrial psychology.
Social foundations of industrial psychology.
The psychological foundations of industrial psychology.
The rise and scope of industrial psychology.
The nature and distribution of individual differences.
The origin of individual differences.

Section 2: Fitting the worker to the job.
Basic factors in vocational selection.
Job analysis.
The interview and allied techniques.
Standardization and administration of psychological tests.
Standardization and administration of psychological tests (continued).
Tests for skilled and semiskilled workers.
Tests in the transportation industry.
Tests for office occupations, technical, and supervisory employees.

Section 3: Maintaining fitness at work.
Safety at work.
Psychological techniques in accident prevention.
Accidents in the transportation industry.
The acquisition of skill.
Training methods.
Industrial fatigue.
The elimination of unnecessary fatigue.
Machines and monotony.
Specific influences in monotonous work.
Motives in industry.
The maladjusted worker.
Problems of supervision and management.

TABLE 18.2 Topics Related to Industrial and Organizational Psychology Covered by *Annual Review of Psychology* in 1950 and 1961–2000

Topics	Number of Chapters
I. (1950). "Industrial Psychology"	1
Broader studies.	
Interview.	
Test procedures and norms.	
Job analysis and evaluation.	
Criteria of performance.	
Training.	
Motivation and morale.	
Communications and advertising.	
Human engineering.	
II. (1961–2000). *Annual Review of Psychology*	
Attitudes, attitude change, opinions, and motivation.	22
Attribution theory and research.	2
Behavioral decision theory.	5
Cognition (social cognition/cognitive science).	13
Community intervention.	7
Consumer psychology.	9
Counseling psychology, career development.	10
Culture/cross-cultural psychology.	6
Engineering psychology.	6
Environmental psychology.	5
Group dynamics/study of small groups/teams/intergroup relations.	13
Human abilities and individual differences.	5
Instructional psychology.	9
Judgment and decision/decision behavior.	3
Organizational behavior.	10
Organization development.	6
Organizational psychology.	3
Personality and personality measurement.	28
Personnel/human resource management.	4
Personnel selection, classification, test validation.	18
Personnel training and human resource development.	6
Psychology of men at work.	2
Program evaluation/research.	5
Scaling and test theory.	10
Statistics/statistical theory/data analysis.	14
Miscellaneous other topics (one chapter each).	13
Group awareness training.	
Industrial social psychology.	
Moral judgment.	
Motivation and performance.	
Performance evaluation in organizations.	
Psychology of deception.	
Psychology of law.	
Psychometric methods.	
Sex and gender.	
Sport psychology.	
Survey research.	
Test validation.	
Trust and distrust in organizations.	

an increase in specialization in the domains of applied psychology (Dunnette, 1976).

From 1990 to 1994, four volumes were written for the second edition of the *Handbook of Industrial and Organizational Psychology* (Dunnette & Hough, 1990–1992; Triandis, Dunnette, et al., 1994), compared to one volume in 1976. The content of the second edition, presented in Table 18.3, reveals significant advances in the field. Particularly noteworthy is the increased attention given to theory (e.g., motivation, learning, individual differences, judgment, and decision making) and research methods and measurements. Additional chapters on organizational psychology (e.g., leadership, groups, productivity, stress, conflict, organization development) are included. Most notably, an entire volume on cross-cultural topics was included.

The scope of the field has changed significantly since Morris Viteles wrote his first textbook. During the early years, the discipline's objective was to improve organizational goals (i.e., productivity and efficiency) primarily by applying psychology (i.e., practice) with an emphasis on individual differences. Later, the objective was to improve both organizational goals/efficiency and employee goals/efficiency by applying psychology *and* by theorizing and researching

psychology in the workplace (i.e., science), with consideration for individual *and* organizational factors. Today, many complex issues are addressed, and consequently, specializations have developed in the discipline. The I-O psychologist's impact has broadened, and currently the discipline pervades almost every aspect of organizations.

TABLE 18.3   Comparison of Major Areas of Coverage in the *Handbook of Industrial and Organizational Psychology,* **First Edition (1976) and the** *Handbook of Industrial and Organizational Psychology,* **Second Edition (1990–1994)**

Table of Contents

I. *Handbook of Industrial and Organizational Psychology* (1976) (1 vol.)
Theory development and theory application.
Research strategies and research methodology.
Theories of individual and organizational behavior.
Job and task analysis.
Attributes of persons.
Taxonomies.
Engineering psychology.
Occupational and career choice and persistence.
Individual and group performance measurement (development of criteria).
Validity and validation strategies.
Attributes of organizations.
Communication in organizations.
Organizational socialization processes.
Behavioral responses by individuals.
Job attitudes and satisfaction.
Problem solving and decision making.
Assessment of persons.
Selection and selection research.
Strategies for training and development.
Strategies of organization change.
Consumer psychology.
Cross-cultural issues.

II. *Handbook of Industrial and Organizational Psychology,* Second Edition
   (1990–1994) (4 vols.)
Volume 1
Blending the science and practice of industrial and organizational
   psychology: Where are we and where are we going?
The role of theory in industrial and organizational psychology.
Motivation theory and industrial and organizational psychology.
Learning theory and industrial and organizational psychology.
Individual differences theory in industrial and organizational psychology.
Judgment and decision-making theory.
Research methods in the service of discovery.
Research strategies and tactics in industrial and organizational psychology.
Quasi experimentation.
Item response theory.
Multivariate correlational analysis.
Modeling the performance prediction problem in industrial and
   organizational psychology.
Volume 2
Cognitive theory in industrial and organizational psychology.
Job analysis.
The structure of work: Job design and roles.
Human factors in the workplace.
Job behavior, performance, and effectiveness.
Personnel assessment, selection, and placement.
Recruitment, job choice, and post-hire consequences: A call for new
   research directions.

Adaptation, persistence, and commitment in organizations.
Training in work organizations.
Utility analysis for decisions in human resource management.
Physical abilities.
Vocational interests, values, and preferences.
Personality and personality measurement.
Volume 3
Aptitudes, skills, and proficiencies.
Developmental determinants of individual action: Theory and practice
   in applying background measures.
Theory and research on leadership in organizations.
Group influences on individuals in organizations.
Group performance and intergroup relations in organizations.
Organization-environment relations.
Consumer psychology.
Organizational productivity.
Employee compensation: Research and practice.
Stress in organizations.
Conflict and negotiation processes in organizations.
Organizational development: Theory, practice, and research.
Behavior change: Models, methods, and a review of evidence.
Alternative metaphors for organization design.
Strategic decision making.
Strategic reward systems.
Volume 4
Contemporary meta-trends in industrial and organizational psychology.
Cross-cultural industrial and organizational psychology.
Selection and assessment in Europe.
Technological change in a multicultural context: Implications for
   training and career planning.
An underlying structure of motivational need taxonomies:
   A cross-cultural confirmation.
Action as the core of work psychology: A German approach.
Time and behavior at work.
Cross-cultural leadership making: Bridging American and Japanese
   diversity for team advantage.
Aging and work behavior.
Age and employment.
Toward a model of cross-cultural industrial and organizational
   psychology.
The Japanese work group.
The nature of individual attachment to the organization: A review of
   East Asian variations.
Culture, economic reform, and the role of industrial and organizational
   psychology in China.
Culture embeddedness and the developmental role of industrial
   organizations in India.
Workplace diversity (in United States).

Education

Issues about training and education in I-O psychology were raised as early as 1918 when methods of technical training for consulting psychologists were discussed (Geissler, 1918). During those early years, most psychologists were trained in general experimental psychology; education in specialized industrial psychology was not possible. The first university program to train in the field was established in the 1920s at Carnegie Institute of Technology (now known as Carnegie-Mellon University), and Bruce V. Moore is credited with the first doctorate from this program in 1921 (Farr & Tesluk, 1997). Lillian Moller Gilbreth was acknowledged for completing the first dissertation related to industrial psychology at Brown University in 1915. She applied psychology and scientific management principles to the work of classroom teachers (Koppes, 1997; Koppes, Landy, & Perkins, 1993; Perloff & Naman, 1996).

In 1919, H. E. Burtt joined the faculty at Ohio State University, and along with psychometric specialist H. Toops formed the first doctoral specialization in industrial psychology after the one at Carnegie Institute of Technology (Katzell & Austin, 1992). In addition to Ohio State and Carnegie Tech, institutions that produced industrially oriented doctorates during the 1920s included the University of Minnesota and Stanford University. In 1930, Pennsylvania State College (now University) offered a doctorate in I-O psychology under B. V. Moore. Throughout the 1930s, additional universities trained students who were oriented toward I-O careers, including Purdue University, Columbia University, and New York University. Katzell and Austin (1992) noted that specialization in I-O psychology during these early years consisted mostly of a student's choice of a principal mentor and associated research and dissertation topics.

Immediately after World War II, the number of specialized I-O training programs escalated, including the creation of terminal master's programs. Existing programs, such as the one at Ohio State University, were expanded, and new programs were created (George Washington University in 1948, University of Maryland in 1961, Michigan State University in 1951) (Katzell & Austin, 1992). Additional new doctoral programs were established during the 1960s, such as those at Bowling Green State University in 1965, North Carolina State University in 1966, and the University of Akron in 1968 (Katzell & Austin, 1992).

Programs in specialized I-O psychology and related fields have proliferated in the past 30 years, which indicates continued progression in the discipline. The 1989 SIOP *Graduate Training Programs in Industrial/Organizational Psychology and Organizational Behavior* (Society for Industrial and Organizational Psychology, Inc., 1989) lists 51 doctoral programs and 36 master's programs in psychology departments, and 46 doctoral programs and 8 master's programs in business or related departments. The 1998 SIOP *Graduate Training Programs in Industrial-Organizational Psychology and Related Fields* (Society for Industrial and Organizational Psychology, Inc., 1998a) lists 62 doctoral programs and 70 master's programs in psychology departments, and 35 doctoral programs and 9 master's degree programs in business and related departments.

SIOP members have discussed several education and training issues, such as standards, accreditation, master's education/training, postdoctoral training, internships, and continuing education for licensure. Programs in I-O psychology are not accredited; however, SIOP created competency-based guidelines according to a scientist-practitioner model. The documents are titled the *Guidelines for Education and Training at the Master's Level in Industrial/Organizational Psychology* (Society for Industrial and Organizational Psychology, Inc., 1995) and the *Guidelines for Education and Training at the Doctoral Level in Industrial/Organizational Psychology* (Society for Industrial and Organizational Psychology, Inc., 1998b). Challenges about maintaining the scientist-practitioner model in a highly diverse and specialized field were expressed recently (Downey, 2000). In addition, concerns were raised about the future of I-O psychology programs because many academic I-O psychologists are seeking employment in business schools rather than psychology departments due to higher salaries for business-related faculty appointments (DeNisi, 2000; Downey, 2000).

Employment

When I-O psychology emerged, almost all psychologists were employed in academia, and psychologists who did applied work did so on a part-time basis. Some academic psychologists pursued part-time consulting work to supplement their meager academic salaries (Goodwin, 1999). Others sought applied work because the number of psychology doctoral graduates quickly outgrew the number of positions in psychology departments and laboratories. Cattell (1946) estimated that as late as 1917 only 16 of the more than 300 members of APA were working primarily in the various applications of psychology. Napoli (1981) revealed no full-time I-O psychologists from 1913 through 1917; however, there were individuals practicing I-O psychology, although their work was not labeled as such. In 1916, Walter Dill Scott was appointed professor of applied psychology at Carnegie Institute of Technology, the first appointment by that title in academia (Landy, 1997).

After World War I, additional employment opportunities became available in academia, the military, government, private industry, and consulting organizations (e.g., the U.S. Civil Service Commission, Kaufman Department Store, Macy's department store, Aetna Life Insurance, U.S. Rubber Company, Procter & Gamble, Milwaukee Electric Railway and Light Company) (Katzell & Austin, 1992). These opportunities paved the way for employment of women psychologists who faced barriers gaining employment in academia (Koppes, 1997). Katzell and Austin (1992) estimated that the total number of industrial psychologists by the end of the 1920s was approximately 50.

Employment in academia slowed during the 1930s, but employment in other areas improved. Between 1916 and 1938, the number of APA members in teaching positions increased fivefold, from 233 to 1,299; however, the number of members in applied positions grew almost 29 times, from 24 to 694 (Finch & Odoroff, 1939). In 1940, Darley and Berdie

(1940) found that those reporting to work in industry did not call themselves industrial psychologists.

After World War II, employment opportunities outside of academia exploded. Each branch of the armed services created centers of research activity to continue the benefits of World War II efforts. A number of psychological research organizations, consulting firms, and university research centers were formed. Private industry continued to hire I-O psychologists, and some companies established their own research groups. Areas of activities included job analysis and job evaluation, salaries and wages, selection and placement, promotions, training, performance appraisal, job satisfaction and morale, counseling and guidance, labor relations, industrial hygiene, accidents and safety, and equipment design (e.g., Canter, 1948). In 1959, McCollom found at least 1,000 psychologists who were employed full-time industry in the United States (McCollom, 1959).

Thirty years later, Howard (1990) reported that of the 1,739 SIOP members who responded to her survey and were employed full-time, 36% were employed in academic settings and 57% reported working in industry, including private organizations (21%), public organizations (7%), and consulting (29%). Eight percent responded that they worked in other settings (e.g., health service, research organizations). O'Connor and Ryan (1996) reported that of the 1,873 SIOP members who responded to their survey and were employed full-time, 39.1% indicated they worked in academic settings and 54.9% were employed in industry, including private organizations (15.1%), public organizations (7.1%), and consulting (32.7%). Six percent responded that they worked in other settings (e.g., health/clinical). Recently, the SIOP Administrative Office (Lee Hakel, personal communication, August 4, 2000) reported that of the 3,286 SIOP members (89.9% of total members) providing information about their employers, 36.1% were in academic positions, 17.1% held full-time positions in private organizations, 6.3% were in public organizations, 34.3% were in consulting, and 5.9% worked for health care or other employers (e.g., research organizations). Two notable shifts between 1990 and 2000 can be observed: (a) a decrease in the relative percentage of individuals employed in private organizations, and (b) an increase in the relative percentage of individuals working in external consulting. One possible explanation is the outsourcing of work and downsizing of private organizations (O'Connor & Ryan, 1996). Eminent I-O psychologists recently expressed concerns about the multitude of inexperienced consultants (C. H. Lawshe Jr., personal communication, June 1, 2000; Locke, 2000).

A prodigious number of employment opportunities in I-O psychology are apparent from examining the SIOP-APA Division 14 membership. This data, however, may underestimate the actual number of individuals and positions because many I-O psychologists, especially practitioners, do not join APA or SIOP (Finch & Odoroff, 1939; Katzell & Austin, 1992). A perusal of the job openings on the SIOP Web site and published in *The Industrial-Organizational Psychologist (TIP)* reveals a plethora of options, especially in the past decade. London and Moses (1990) observed that the role of I-O psychologists has evolved from that of technician-analyst to change agent or strategist.

Organized Industrial-Organizational Psychology

As applied psychology expanded and the demand for applied psychologists increased, interest in professional organizations flourished. Early organizations for I-O psychologists and their dates of formation can be found in Katzell and Austin (1992). Benjamin (1997) traced the development of professional groups for I-O psychologists, with specific attention to the evolution of SIOP. AAAP Section D: Industrial and Business was the professional organization for psychologists in industry during the early years. In 1945, the AAAP merged with APA, and Division 14, Industrial and Business, was formed with 130 members (fellows and associates). In 1985, shortly after SIOP incorporated in 1982 to achieve some independence from APA (Hakel, 1979), there were 2,499 members (fellows, members, and associates). When this chapter was written, there were 3,655 professional members (fellows, members, and associates) (Lee Hakel, personal communication, August 4, 2000). The overall purpose of the current society is not significantly different from the purpose established by the AAAP Section D in 1937; clear linkages between SIOP's and AAAP's objectives are obvious. The society changed with regard to structure, membership, and activities, primarily because of the expansion of the discipline and the growth of membership (Benjamin, 1997). For example, the organization evolved from one that was totally managed by volunteers to one now staffed professionally (Koppes, 2000).

Summary

I-O psychology shifted from a simple, narrowly defined technical field focused on individual issues for accomplishing organizational objectives to a complex, broad scientific and applied discipline emphasizing individual and organizational issues for achieving both individual and organizational goals. A challenge of the discipline is to maintain an identity as a rigorous scientific discipline while at the same time providing a growing range of professional services and applications.

A science–practice dichotomy has characterized the discipline since its inception. The roots of this dichotomy can be traced to the founders of psychology in the late 1800s and early 1900s, when tension existed between individuals wanting psychology to be a pure science (basic) separate from practical concerns and individuals wanting to apply psychology to practical matters (Hergenhahn, 1997). Applied psychologists did not advocate for an applied psychology instead of a pure psychology. These psychologists, along with their scientific contemporaries, viewed science as being first and applications as being second (Hergenhahn, 1997). The pure psychologists disapproved of applying psychology, however. Benjamin (1997) noted, "The purists railed against such premature ventures and warned these purveyors of suspect psychological knowledge to stay home and perfect their science" (p. 102).

One explanation for the tension between scientists and practitioners was the reward structure of the American scientific community during 1906–1944 (Sokal, 1995). James McKeen Cattell used a star system, in which asterisks were attached to the names of individuals he identified as the preeminent American scientists of the day in his *American Men of Science,* first published in 1906. Ten leading representatives, who were members of the National Academy of Science and contributors to *Science,* selected these individuals. This reward structure placed a high value on being a scientist. A second explanation was the questionable scientific integrity of applied research funded by corporations for legal and commercial gains. Results from these studies were often discredited (Benjamin, Rogers, & Rosenbaum, 1991). A third explanation for the tension was the incompatible values between scientists (pure psychologists), who pursue the advancement of knowledge, and practitioners (applied psychologists), who apply knowledge to solve problems (Hergenhahn, 1997).

During the early years, a prevalent distinction between science and practice within industrial psychology did not exist, as most industrial psychologists consulted part-time while working full-time in university positions and conducted research in field settings for the purposes of solving problems. The dichotomy gradually emerged as the number of individuals employed in universities, research institutions, and applied positions grew. In the published version of her APA Division 14 (now SIOP) presidential address entitled "Our Expanding Responsibilities," Marion Bills (1953) foresaw the developing gap between scientists and practitioners. She argued that psychologists working in industry were not given sufficient credit for their contributions to science. Bills stated,

> Perhaps our [psychologists in private industry] real function is that of a liaison officer between our experimental workers and management under which function our chief duty would be to keep them very well informed on both sides, and display the

ingenuity to connect them, even when in many cases the connection is far from obvious. (Bills, 1953, p. 145)

On several occasions, Bruce V. Moore, the first president of APA Division 14 (now SIOP), espoused his belief that industrial psychology as an applied discipline values equally research and implementation (Farr & Tesluk, 1997). Moore stated,

> [The] pure scientist has no basis for intellectual snobbery or contempt for the applied scientist. What both should avoid is busy work without thinking, or activity without relating it to theory, or the quick answer without adequate facts or basic research. . . . The extreme applied practitioner is in danger of narrow, myopic thinking, but the extremely pure scientist is in danger of being isolated from facts. (Cited in Farr & Tesluk, 1997, p. 484)

The scientist-practitioner tension prevails today, as evident by the attention it continues to receive (e.g., Dunnette & Hough, 1990; Holland, Hogan, & Sheton, 1999; Klimoski, 1992). Hackman (1985) identified factors that contribute to the current gap between I-O scientists and practitioners. These include corporate reward systems that compensate I-O psychologists for performing as professional practitioners rather than as scientists, differences in the conceptual and research paradigms of scientists and practitioners, and the failure of laboratory and field experiments to guide practice. J. P. Campbell (1992) noted, however, that the latent needs of the two parties are actually more similar than their surface dissimilarities would suggest. When he was 93 years old, Morris Viteles stated, "If it isn't scientific, it's not good practice, and if it isn't practical, it's not good science" (cited in Katzell & Austin, 1992, p. 826). The two poles must blend in order to address the complex work issues of organizations today.

CONFLUENCE OF DYNAMIC FORCES

Many historians contend that the rise of I-O psychology was the result of external forces. Psychologists were pulled by the demands and expectations of industry and of an ever-changing society and economy (e.g., Baritz, 1960). As early as 1913, Hugo Münsterberg, who is often referred to as the father of I-O psychology, stated, "Our aim is to sketch the outlines of a new psychology which is to intermediate between the modern laboratory psychology and the problems of economics: the psychological experiment is systematically placed at the service of commerce and industry" (Münsterberg, 1913, p. 3). More recently, Katzell and Austin (1992) observed, "The field's history reveals a proclivity for science and practice in I-O psychology to be shaped more by external forces than by theories, foresight or imagination. In short, I-O psychologists tend to be more reactive than proactive . . ." (p. 824).

Scholars also recognize that the discipline's progression resulted from internal forces or individual visionaries within the field who advocated and pushed for the application of psychology (e.g., Koppes, 1997; Landy, 1997; Van De Water, 1997). Entrepreneurial efforts by independent investigators moved the discipline forward because of their developments in theory, research, and practice. Most historians agree, however, that both internal and external influences shaped the discipline. For example, Van De Water (1997) noted, "A combination of internal and external forces helped transform industrial psychology from a few individuals' visions into a larger, self-perpetuating institution" (p. 487). To fully understand the sociohistorical context of I-O psychology, both external and internal forces must be considered.

Socioeconomic Forces

Socioeconomic forces refer to indicators of the economy (e.g., income, the gross national product, unemployment), societal views (e.g., with regard to workers, organizations, environment, health) and ideologies (e.g., social Darwinism and eugenics), and population demographics. Katzell and Austin (1992), for example, observed that I-O topics seem to be correlated with cycles of social or political concerns (e.g., labor relations with labor–management conflicts, job analysis with fair employment issues).

In the late nineteenth century, American society experienced rapid changes and developments because of industrialization, immigration, a high birth rate, education reform, and urban growth. A progressive drive for reform prevailed (Minton, 1988), and Americans were ready for the practical and useful. Multiple changes created problems for humanity (Napoli, 1981), and society looked toward science for practical solutions. In addition to these societal demands, institutional pressures and the desire to improve their institutional status to keep their discipline alive forced psychologists to popularize their science and demonstrate the value of psychology in solving problems and helping society (Burnham, 1987; Goodwin, 1999). Taking psychology outside academic laboratories and increasing psychological research on practical applications in education, medicine, criminology, business, and industry were expressions of psychologists' intense desire for social recognition and support (Camfield, 1973). One proponent of applied research stated that progress toward the development of an applied psychology offered "the hope of seeing greater socio-economic values placed upon the science in American community life" (cited in Camfield, 1973, p. 75). The intellectual, social, cultural, and economic milieu engendered the formation of an applied psychology.

As psychology's popularity increased, society and the business community became skeptical and disenchanted with the discipline because individuals not trained in psychology began practicing to gain financial rewards. Psychologists felt compelled to combat society's images of psychology as common sense or as occultism and superstition (Burnham, 1987) and society's stereotype of the psychologist as an "absent-minded professor, preoccupied with abstruse manners" (Burnham, 1987, p. 92). One response was to use experimentation to invalidate the claims of pseudoscientists (Van De Water, 1997). Methodological developments included measurement methods (mental tests, observations, case studies) and statistics for measuring and analyzing individual differences (regression, simple correlation, partial correlation) (Cowles, 1989). Furthermore, Gillespie (1988) noted that the decision to undertake social scientific research in the workplace during the 1920s was a political process, and "social and behavioral scientists believed that experimentation would guarantee objectivity of their findings and recommendations, and ensure their professional standing on an intellectual and moral plane above that of capitalists and workers" (p. 133).

During the 1920s, euphoria and prosperity swept the United States. Despite a short recession in 1921–1922, the gross national product rose 39% between 1919 and 1929 (Cashman, 1989). The growth of employment associated with the rise in the gross national product provided opportunities for industrial psychologists as full-time employees or consultants in industry. Companies were interested in psychological applications used during the war (i.e., selection and placement), and the primary concern was finding the right employee for the job. Articles and books on various aspects of personnel psychology described developments and issues (e.g., Link, 1919; Pond, 1927; Scott & Hayes, 1921).

Viteles (1932) noted a shift in the social philosophy of workers during the early part of the twentieth century. A policy of noninterference shifted to a policy that emphasized the employee's welfare. This policy of employee's welfare was reinforced during the economic depression, when 25% of the workforce was unemployed (Manchester, 1973–1974). The depression's adverse effects on individuals led to heightened sensitivity to and concern for the human condition and the humanization of work. Organizations and the U.S. government felt responsible for employee welfare; thus, social issues such as unemployment and adjustment of workers became prevalent. The greatest need was to find jobs for people to fill, so there was less need for and interest in personnel selection and training. More than 16% of the companies that had used personnel tests dropped them during the Great Depression (Katzell & Austin, 1992). None of the studies cited in an extensive review of the psychological literature on training in industry were published during the 1930s (Katzell & Austin, 1992; McGehee & Thayer, 1961). The social aspects of industrial psychology began to emerge as industrial psychologists developed an interest in improving an individual's well-being at work. According to Viteles (1932), "They [psychologists] have definitely accepted the viewpoint that industrial practices are to be judged not only by the criterion of economic return, but in terms of their effects on human beings" (p. 25).

The Minnesota Employment Stabilization Research Institute (MESRI) was established in 1931 to study the psychological and economics effects of unemployment (e.g., Paterson, 1932). The idea that individual differences could be shown by special aptitude tests, not just intelligence tests, was formulated; thus, aptitude tests (e.g., the Minnesota Clerical Test and the Minnesota Paper Form Board) were designed. A Minnesota perspective was created, which eventually developed into a theory of work adjustment (Dawis & Lofquist, 1984).

The U.S. Employment Service (USES), founded in 1917, was renewed with the Wagner-Peyser Act of 1933 (Lowenberg & Conrad, 1998). Along with the Minnesota Institute, this program tried to eliminate the crevasses between the unemployed and the few available jobs. The USES is known for developing the General Aptitude Test Battery (GATB) and completing the first large-scale systematic analysis of jobs, the *Dictionary of Occupational Titles,* published in 1939. This project moved I-O psychologists further toward realizing the importance of matching individual ability profiles with different job requirements (Lowenberg & Conrad, 1998). Various methods were used to achieve this match, such as selection and placement, vocational guidance, and a combination of processes called differential job placement (Dunnette, 1966).

A few early research studies on attitudes and morale were conducted during this time (e.g., Hoppock, 1935), and the measurement of attitudes was improved by the scaling techniques of Thurstone (1927) and Likert (1932). Attitude surveys and structured interviews were popular tools for management consulting (Houser, 1938). Kurt Lewin, a researcher at the University of Iowa Child Welfare Research Station from 1935 to 1944, commenced research on various psychological aspects of work such as leadership, productivity, satisfaction, group dynamics, employee participation, and resistance to change (Katzell & Austin, 1992).

During the depression, President Franklin D. Roosevelt's reform programs provided a favorable climate for organized labor; thus, corporate America had to respond to new labor laws and the growing muscle of unions. According to Gillespie (1988),

> The calm of the 1920s and early 1930s had been shattered by the militancy of new industrial unions of mass-production workers

and industrial relations had been reshaped by New Deal legislation that protected workers' rights to organize and bargain collectively with their employers. Personnel management flourished in this environment, and a function that had previously been the responsibility of middle managers was transformed overnight into the province of executives; henceforth, no managerial decisions could be made without considering their impact on labor relations. (p. 132)

Early efforts to minimize the distance between labor and management were made by psychologists employed by the Scott Company in 1919 and 1920, and some I-O psychologists were concerned with the labor-relations movement during the 1930s and after World War II (Gordon & Burt, 1981). The relationship between I-O psychology and labor unions has been described as one of mutual indifference, however (e.g., Gordon & Burt, 1981). One explanation for psychologists' limited involvement is that I-O psychologists are perceived as being aligned with management (Baritz, 1960; Gordon & Burt, 1991). APA Division 14 (now SIOP) past president (1970–1971) Herbert H. Meyer who worked numerous years in industry, offered another perspective:

> Unions have a vested interest in maintaining an adversarial relationship between workers and management. Thus instead of being cooperative and committed to organizational goals, union members are inclined to regard management as the enemy. And, incidentally, in unionized plants, I have found that managers are inclined to regard union employees as the enemy—a rather poor situation in which to engender cooperation and commitment.... [T]he desire of many progressive companies to stay non-union because of the costly work rules often associated with unionism provided for many opportunities for the employment of I/O psychologists. (Herbert H. Meyer, personal communication, July 20, 2000)

Unions are important in I-O psychology's history because they affected organizations' structures, policies, and the management of employees. Thus, the impact of labor unions on the development of I-O psychology needs further investigation.

The emphasis on employee welfare during the depression led to the development of personnel counseling as a popular organizational intervention for helping employees solve personal problems. Once viewed as the "new industrial psychology" (Cantor, 1945), personnel counseling programs disappeared from the domain of applied psychology and were dropped by several organizations by the 1960s (Highhouse, 1999). Highhouse suggested that industrial psychologists may have distanced themselves from personnel counseling because of poorly trained counselors employed by organizations. Reasons for the decline of personnel counseling programs include the questionable effectiveness of the programs and the lack of managerial support for programs addressing employees' personal problems (Highhouse, 1999). A renewed interest in worker adjustment, work–family conflicts, and other personal issues (e.g., mental health) has emerged in the past decade (e.g., Zedeck, 1992).

After World War II, the economy provided for prosperity, leisure, pleasure, affluence, education, and a heightened awareness of the good life. A new generation of American workers increasingly valued noneconomic outcomes and personal rewards (satisfaction, personal growth, self-fulfillment, actualization, self-expression) instead of traditional bread-and-butter rewards (Katzell, 1958). An increased emphasis on workers' attitudes and motivations and ways of improving life in organizations became salient, with particular attention to social and organizational contexts. The focus shifted to topics other than those directly tied to bottom-line performance, including the effects of work on individuals, motivation, job attitudes, life and job satisfaction, challenges of the job, and job characteristics (Katzell & Austin, 1992).

The postwar economy provided for an explosion of psychological applications and research opportunities. The focus was on both fitting people for the job and fitting the job for people. Military research centers were formed, psychological research organizations were created (e.g., American Institutes for Research), consulting firms were established (e.g., Richardson, Bellows, Henry, & Company), and research groups were formed within private companies (e.g., General Electric, Standard Oil of New Jersey) (Katzell & Austin, 1992). In addition, universities organized research centers to investigate aspects of I-O psychology. For example, in 1944, Lewin established the Research Center for Group Dynamics at Massachusetts Institute of Technology (MIT), where he collaborated with a similar group in London, the Tavistock Institute of Human Relations. Together the organizations created the journal *Human Relations* in 1947. Because of the work of Lewin and his colleagues, emphasis shifted toward human relations rather than the technical aspects of production. Shortly after Lewin's death in 1947, the Research Center for Group Dynamics was relocated to the University of Michigan. The center joined the Survey Research Center, which had been in existence since 1946 under the direction of Rensis Likert (Hilgard, 1987). Other university research centers that partially devoted their efforts to I-O psychology were located at Ohio State University with its leadership research program, Cornell University with its studies of satisfaction in work and retirement, Western Reserve University with its emphasis on personnel problems and occupational guidance, and Purdue University with its occupational research (Katzell & Austin, 1992).

Unrest surfaced in America's society during the 1950s and 1960s because of changes in values and attention to discriminatory and unfair practices. Society demanded equitable practices in organizations. As it had during the depression, the government intervened, and civil-rights legislation was created. The unrest and chaos continued throughout the 1960s and 1970s as the United States entered the Vietnam War, baby boomers entered the workforce, and international and foreign competition became a threat. According to Dipboye, Smith, and Howell (1994), the fabric of the American society was disintegrating. A new generation of employees was questioning the authority of organizations, and a general revulsion against fascism and authoritarianism stimulated interest in democracy and autonomy in the workplace (Dipboye et al., 1994). These changing societal views influenced organizations to rethink their way of dealing with employees. How the organization could best serve the individual became important. Theories about organizations as open, sociotechnical systems were developed, which stimulated research in areas of communication, conflict management, socialization, and organizational climate and culture. The development of interventions for facilitating organizational change and development (OD) resulted in an interface of I and O approaches. During the 1980s, known as the health decade, research was initiated on worker stress, health, and well-being (e.g., Ilgen, 1990).

Society's unrest and questioning raised consciousness about many social issues, which led to additional research and applications concerning job involvement, organizational commitment, antisocial behaviors, the psychological contract, and organizational citizenship behaviors. Muchinsky (2000) noted, "In the past 10–15 years, we have had to address new aspects of organizational behavior about which we had little knowledge. The depth and magnitude of these issues in the psychology of work have had a profound impact on the profession of I-O psychology" (p. 295).

A socioeconomic factor that affects the work of I-O psychologists is the demographics of the workforce. Two recent changes in the workforce are worth noting: diversity and quantity. The increasing diversity of the U.S. population creates a diverse workforce in terms of gender, age, ethnicity, race, and culture. There are now various subgroups of employees, with minority groups increasing as a proportion of the workforce, the bulk of the workforce (baby boomers) aging, and life expectancies increasing (Briggs, 1987; Cohen, 1995). Diversity in the workforce can also be attributed to a global marketplace because multinational organizations are hiring employees from an international labor market. A diverse workforce has implications for both practice and research in I-O psychology (see Triandis, Kurowoski, & Gelfand, 1994). For example, organizations need to identify ways to individualize reward systems and recruit and retain diverse employees. Theories, research methods, and applications will need to include individual differences with regard to age, gender, ethnicity, race, and culture.

In addition to diversity, the supply of workers is shrinking (Cascio, 1995; Cohen, 1995). The birth rate has declined for the past 20 to 30 years, and individuals are retiring earlier because of the prosperous economy during the 1990s (Aiman-Smith & Koppes, 2000). The shrinking labor force, record low unemployment associated with a strong economy, and accelerated global competition has engendered new topics for I-O psychologists (e.g., acquisitions/mergers, employee retention, work/family balance) and a revisiting of traditional issues (e.g., job analysis, selection, training and development, performance appraisal) (Cascio, 1995). I-O psychology does not exist in a vacuum; societal forces will continue to influence the discipline. Thus, additional research on socioeconomic forces is warranted.

Business Forces

Organizations must change their structures, technologies, and processes to adapt to their environments and to survive (Huber, 1984). Because I-O psychologists historically responded to business problems (e.g., Baritz, 1960), changes in business directly affected I-O psychology. I-O psychologists provided employers techniques and information for implementing an explicit scientific approach and developed techniques to help employers make decisions (Dipboye et al., 1994). When asked to identify an influence on the field, SIOP past president (1991–1992) Richard J. Klimoski responded,

> The changing nature of organizing—favoring large manufacturing enterprises right after the war, the rise of the large multidivisional firm, to the conglomerate, to the rise of service providers, to the multinational firm, to the development of virtual organizations. These affect such things as the need for I/O services, the kinds of problems studied, the kinds of job venues I/O types hold. (Richard J. Klimoski, personal communication, August 27, 2000)

The Industrial Revolution at the end of the nineteenth century created a prevailing faith in capitalism (Katzell & Austin, 1992). The primary business objectives were to improve efficiency, increase productivity, and decrease costs through standardization and simplification (Dipboye et al., 1994). Scientific management advocates addressed these objectives by designing work to improve efficiency (Taylor, 1947). Frank and Lillian Gilbreth, known for their time-and-motion studies, were concerned with individual needs in work settings. They believed that scientific management was more than machines, tools, procedures, and inventory control. "It meant, first of all, the *people* who did the jobs" (Gilbreth, 1970, p. 103). The primary importance of scientific management for I-O psychology was the study of work (Baritz, 1960) and the establishment of a precedent for scientists to enter organizations.

The emergence of capitalism and emphasis on efficiency forced companies to hire the most qualified employees; thus, selection and training were critical issues. Industrial psychologists used mental tests that had been successful in education and in the armed forces to select hardworking and committed employees (Katzell & Austin, 1992). According to Van De Water (1997), mental tests were the field's first technical product.

An emphasis on productivity during the late nineteenth and early twentieth centuries influenced organization leaders to explore ways to advertise, sell, and distribute their goods. Psychologists recognized the value of their discipline to these business issues as well. For example, Scripture (1895) wrote in his book *Thinking, Feeling, Doing* that advertisers could benefit from psychology with regard to attention and memory. A young psychologist, Walter Dill Scott, was approached by a group of businessmen to present a speech about the value of psychology for advertising in 1901. He did so on the condition that his name not be published because he feared the disdain of his colleagues. This concern soon dissipated, as Scott in 1903 published a book titled *The Theory of Advertising* (Ferguson, 1962–1965).

Interest in applying psychology to business problems provided opportunities for businesses and academic psychologists to collaborate. An important program for the development of I-O psychology was the Division of Applied Psychology at Carnegie Institute of Technology (now Carnegie-Mellon University), which was established in 1915 with Walter VanDyke Bingham as the director (Hilgard, 1987). In 1916, a new department was formed, the Bureau of Salesmanship Research, headed by Scott. Scott and his colleagues devised a multiple-component selection system for sales personnel that included a personal history blank (biodata), a standard interview, a reference form, and a mental alertness test (Katzell & Austin, 1992). Later, the bureau was renamed the Bureau of Personnel Research. Bingham created another program, the School of Life Insurance Salesmanship, which trained several thousand life insurance salesmen (Hilgard, 1987). Following World War I, the Carnegie Institute of Technology expanded its work to include sales training, with the establishment of the Research Bureau of Retail Training. Vocational interests were researched, and E. K. Strong along with Karl Cowdery eventually developed the Strong Vocational Interest Blank, now known as the Strong

Interest Inventory. The Carnegie program trained and prepared future applied psychologists, especially women, and paved the way for research, applications, and collaborative efforts with industry (Hilgard, 1987). Despite its success, the Division of Applied Psychology was dissolved in 1924 by a new university president who did not support the enterprise (Hilgard, 1987).

Following World War I, opportunities for psychology proliferated because of a heightened awareness of psychological applications and an increased concern for personnel issues by management (Baritz, 1960; Hilgard, 1987). Forward-looking executives wanted to extend techniques and programs developed for the army into private industry (Katzell & Austin, 1992). Consequently, consulting firms formed to respond to the needs of business and industry. Scott and colleagues at the Army's Committee on Classification and Personnel formed The Scott Company in 1919. The consultants used techniques such as mental ability group tests, "job standards for career progression and personnel planning, a performance rating system, oral trade tests and apprentice training materials, and a program of personnel administration" (Katzell & Austin, 1992, p. 807). The company advocated a future-oriented philosophy of cooperative labor relations that was adopted in the men's garment industry (Gordon & Burt, 1981). Mary Holmes Stevens Hayes, a psychologist, was hired as a consultant (one of the first woman professional consultants) (Koppes, 1997), and she collaborated with Scott in writing a book for professional personnel managers entitled *Science and Common Sense in Working with Men* (Scott & Hayes, 1921). The Scott Company disbanded in the early 1920s because of financial difficulties and because its founder left to become president of Northwestern University.

James McKeen Cattell organized the Psychological Corporation in 1921. Twenty influential psychologists were directors, and approximately 170 psychologists held stock (Cattell, 1923). The organization was formed for the "advancement of psychology and the promotion of the useful applications of psychology" (Cattell, 1923, p. 165). According to Burnham (1987), the Psychological Corporation was created to popularize psychology, and the founders tried to set standards for applied psychology. The corporation failed miserably under Cattell's leadership, however. Although Cattell espoused the application of psychology, he had never himself been an applied psychologist. Consequently, he provided little direction to those who worked under him (Sokal, 1981). Sokal (1981) noted that both Cattell's ineffective leadership and the context in which the corporation existed explain the company's failure. By the end of the 1920s, several applied psychology endeavors and the mental-testing movement had failed. Subsequent leaders (e.g., Bingham) of

the Psychological Corporation were successful in sharing and implementing psychological techniques for 50 years (Katzell & Austin, 1992). For example, the Differential Aptitude Test and the Bennett Test of Mechanical Comprehension are widely used today.

Private companies hired full-time psychologists to handle personnel problems (e.g., Kaufman Department Store, Aetna Life Insurance, Procter & Gamble, Milwaukee Railway and Light Company, Scoville Manufacturing Company) (Katzell & Austin, 1992). In 1919, R. H. Macy and Company in New York hired psychologist Elsie Oschrin Bregman to examine the company's personnel processes. Bregman (1922) wrote about disputes over the use of psychological tests for personnel purposes in industry. She described how the company took the lead in researching tests in the field: "[A]bout three years ago, an almost unprecedented experiment was begun. Almost never before had a psychological laboratory been equipped in an industrial organization, certainly not a department store, and a psychologist commissioned to experiment in his own field of science" (Bregman, 1922, p. 696). Research on personnel issues (e.g., selection, placement, fatigue, safety) in organizations flourished during the 1920s (e.g., Bregman, 1922; Pond, 1927). The Personnel Research Federation was created in 1921 under the auspices of the National Research Council to advance "scientific knowledge about men and women in relation to their occupations" (Bingham, 1928, p. 299).

A widely publicized research study conducted in an organization was the Hawthorne studies (e.g., Gillespie, 1988; Roethlisberger & Dickson, 1939). The original purpose of the study was to examine the relationship between illumination levels and productivity. A serendipitous finding was that work groups and attitudes had an effect on performance. (A detailed description of the study is presented by Roethlisberger and Dickson, 1939, and Gillespie, 1988.) These studies were important to the evolution of I-O psychology for several reasons. The researchers demonstrated the feasibility of conducting scientific research in organizational settings. Personnel management as a specialized function was recognized and legitimized (Gillespie, 1988). Supervisory personnel training as an important management activity was discovered (Gillespie, 1988). In addition, a human-relations movement arose in industrial psychology because of these studies. When Viteles revised his 1932 textbook, he found that the field had changed dramatically and in 1953 had to rename his book *Motivation and Morale in Industry* to better represent the discipline (Katzell & Austin, 1992).

Beginning in the 1950s and through the 1960s, the nation's manufacturing-based economy evolved into a service-based economy, changing the economic/business objective from efficiency to one of quality or customer service. During the late 1950s, more than 50% of the workforce consisted of service employees (Katzell & Austin, 1992). This shift created changes in the organization's structure and the nature of work, increasing attention to organizational characteristics and their impact on employee attitudes and behaviors. The socioeconomic forces described in the previous section combined with business changes inspired researchers to investigate job satisfaction, motivation, leadership, intergroup and intragroup relations, communication, and influence and power. The Research Center for Group Dynamics created the journal *Administrative Science Quarterly* in 1955 so researchers could share their work on various social topics.

Although numerous long-range research programs were conducted in several organizations, an important one worth noting here was begun at the American Telephone and Telegraph Company (AT&T) in 1956. The basic purpose of the study was to discover qualities related to managerial success and advancement in the company. Results revealed that test and inventory scores as well as staff judgments on several dimensions predicted salaries and advancement to middle management over several years (Howard & Bray, 1988). This research effort by Bray and his colleagues "stands out as one of the most carefully designed and comprehensive longitudinal studies ever conducted" (Dunnette, 1998, p. 140).

Flagging productivity in the 1960s and 1970s forced companies to look at new ways of managing. They examined their foreign competitors' successes and consequently changed from individualistic, authoritarian systems to structures emphasizing groups, teamwork, employee participation, and total quality management (1986–1987 SIOP past president Sheldon Zedeck, personal communication, July 6, 2000). With the advent of organization development (OD) as an attempt to better understand the process of group dynamics, the assumption that developing people would create healthier and more effective organizations changed to the assumption that developing organizations would create healthier and more effective people (Mirvis, 1988).

In the 1980s, stagnant productivity, threats to economic well-being, and American companies' failure to adapt to economic circumstances raised concerns about productivity, utility, and quality. Although the foundations for utility analyses had been offered earlier (e.g., Brogden, 1946), it was not until the 1980s that serious attention to utility analysis surfaced (Cascio, 1991). In addition, a renewed interest in OD reestablished the relationship between employees and organizations (Muchinsky, 2000). Some I-O psychologists view OD as a symbiosis of scientists and practitioners (e.g., Lowenberg & Conrad, 1998).

For the past two decades and for the next century, the external environment for organizations has been and will be turbulent because of globalization, increased competition, and rapid change. To survive, flexible organizations' responses include restructuring, mergers and acquisitions, downsizing (e.g., elimination of management positions in order to reduce size and costs), and new product lines. To be competitive, strategies for managing change and for creating a committed and satisfied workforce will need to be developed and implemented. Cascio (1995) suggested that training and development will emerge as the essential activity for companies in the twenty-first century. As they did at the beginning of I-O psychology, I-O psychologists will continue to respond to business needs. Some senior SIOP members recently expressed concerns that top management issues and business demands (e.g., strategic planning, financial incentives) rather than the pursuit of science will drive the work of I-O psychologists (Locke, 2000).

Legal Forces

There is no question that the legal and political climate in the United States influenced the evolution of I-O psychology. According to SIOP president (2001–2002) William H. Macey, "there were some clear watershed events in the last 35–40 years in the form of particular legislation . . . that clearly are singular in their impact on our discipline/profession" (William H. Macey, personal communication, August 19, 2000).

During the depression, the U.S. government strengthened its influence by creating New Deal legislation and programs to help the downtrodden employee. Both business leaders and psychologists became cognizant of worker issues; thus, attention to the social aspects of industrial psychology increased. Psychologist Mary Holmes Stevens Hayes was directly involved with the New Deal. In 1935, she conducted a research study (requested by the U.S. Congress) on problems of the unemployed, which served as the basis for the National Youth Administration (NYA), one of several New Deal programs created within the Works Progress Administration (Cashman, 1989). Hayes first led the Division of Guidance and Placement, one division of the NYA, and then in 1940, when the NYA was placed under the auspices of the Federal Security Agency, she was promoted to director of the Division of Youth (Koppes, 1997).

The civil-rights movement began in the early 1950s when the separate-but-equal doctrine in education was struck down in the case of *Brown v. Board of Education* (1954). Congressional hearings led to publications dealing with standards of testing, such as the *Technical Recommendations of Psychological Tests and Diagnostic Techniques* (American

Psychological Association, 1954) and the *Ethical Principles of Psychologists* (American Psychological Association, 1953). Antidiscrimination legislation, executive orders, and agency regulations ensued in the 1960s. Specifically, the Civil Rights Act (CRA) of 1964, Title VII, prohibited discrimination in employment because of race, color, religion, sex, or national origin (Gutman, 2000). In 1972, the CRA was amended to include educational institutions and state and federal agencies (Gutman, 2000).

During the 1970s, the social and legal emphasis was on ensuring that employers did not blatantly discriminate against minorities and women. In 1971, in the case of *Griggs v. Duke Power Co.* (1971), the Supreme Court ruled that selection devices must be job-related. Arvey (1979) noted that this ruling "opened the door for statistical methods in reviewing the consequential effects of employment practices" (p. 68). The Equal Employment Opportunity Commission (EEOC) and the Office of Federal Contract Compliance reacted by issuing guidelines that included validation standards defined by the American Psychological Association. Three key standards documents were written: *Uniform Guidelines on Employee Selection Procedures* (1978), *Standards for Educational and Psychological Testing* (American Educational Research Association, American Psychological Association, & National Council on Measurement in Education, 1999), and *Principles for the Validation and Use of Personnel Selection Procedures* (Society for Industrial and Organizational Psychology, Inc., 1987). Other legislation was subsequently passed to address discrimination based on age, gender, service in the Vietnam War, disability, and others (Barrett, 1996).

It was much harder for an aggrieved party to sue and win in the 1980s (Potter, 1989), which resulted in a succession of changes in the legal climate. I-O activities associated with fair employment practices generally declined because of less aggressive enforcement. Interests in test fairness and fair employment practices were renewed, however, with the passage of the American with Disabilities Act in 1990 and the Civil Rights Act of 1991, along with a continued increase in the number of lawsuits in the United States. The first executive order of the twenty-first century, issued by President Bill Clinton, forbids federal departments and agencies from discriminating in personnel decisions based on protected genetic information. Legislation was presented to implement similar protections in private organizations (Fox, 2000).

The legal requirements that emerged during the past 40 years and the increase in the number of lawsuits in the 1980s and 1990s contributed to the rapid growth of I-O psychology during these decades. Tenopyr (1992) noted that the civil-rights movement and criticisms of employee selection tools significantly advanced research in I-O psychology.

Science and scientific practices were reinforced, developed, and further refined (Lowenberg & Conrad, 1998). When asked to identify influences and related developments in the field, SIOP past president (1999–2000) Angelo S. DeNisi commented,

> Without a doubt I would include the passage of the Civil Rights Act of 1964. Before this Act, I/O psychologists were interested in test validity, but their interest was a scientific one, not a legal one. The CRA began a tidal wave of work on test validation, beginning with discussion of criterion issues, and culminating in the work on validity generalization and utility. Once we realized how important it was to be able to validate tests, the race was on to discover factors that led to lower than desired validities, and ways to validate tests more efficiently. This was really the impetus behind the VG [validity generalization] research program. Eventually, the line of research led to more serious discussions of intelligence and intelligence tests (i.e., the role of "g"); searches for alternatives to intelligence tests (e.g., research on the Big 5 Personality Factors); and research on alternative methods for delivering tests. (Angelo S. DeNisi, personal communication, August 15, 2000)

The emphasis on validity led to further development of meta-analysis, refinement of job analysis methods, and research on legally defensible performance appraisal systems. In addition, a new employment opportunity for I-O psychologists emerged: as expert witnesses in court. Other legislation, court cases, and congressional hearings have influenced I-O psychology research and practice. For example, the Senate confirmation hearings for Supreme Court Justice Clarence Thomas, marked by accusations by Anita Hill that he had sexually harassed her, stimulated research on sexual harassment in organizations, and the Occupational Safety and Health Act, instituted in 1971, raised awareness about safety and health issues in the workplace.

Although many I-O psychologists believe that legislation positively impacted the evolution of I-O psychology science and practice, some colleagues believe that legal forces inhibited the discipline's growth. Guion, for example, stated that the Civil Rights Act constrained selection research and practice (Locke, 2000). Further discussion of legal forces is necessary to better understand the legal context of I-O psychology's history.

Military Forces

The two world wars provided occasions for psychologists to demonstrate psychology's value to society during times when skepticism about the science existed (e.g., Capshew, 1999; Hill, 1955; von Mayrhauser, 1987). During both wars, the greatest need was to find people to fill jobs, so the emphasis was on recruitment, selection, and placement. G. Stanley Hall first suggested the use of psychology in the military in 1916 while addressing a joint session of the APA and the American Association for the Advancement of Science (Hergenhahn, 1997). When the United States declared war on Germany in April 1917, a group of psychologists led by Robert M. Yerkes (then president of APA) and others (from the National Academy of Sciences, the American Association for the Advancement of Science, and the APA) formed the Psychology Committee of the National Resource Council to evaluate a psychological examining program for recruits (von Mayrhauser, 1987). At the same time, W. D. Scott and W. V. Bingham, faculty at Carnegie Institute of Technology, formed the Committee on Classification and Personnel to aid the army in the selection of officers (von Mayrhauser, 1987). Douglas Fryer worked with a small program in the Morale Branch of the Surgeon General's Office to ease the adjustment of soldiers to army life.

Although many psychologists were involved with World War I, Yerkes and his colleagues received the most publicity for developing the Army Alpha and Army Beta group mental ability tests. These tests paved the way for large-scale intelligence testing and for later expansion of psychological testing into government, industry, and education (Katzell & Austin, 1992). After the war, the military increased spending to identify ways to improve the efficiency of the fighting forces, thus creating opportunities for psychological research and application under the auspices of the armed forces. In addition, the success of psychological applications during the war stimulated the interests of corporate leaders to use psychology in their businesses.

The Second World War, like the First World War, created the opportunity for psychologists to apply their techniques. The army sought the assistance of psychologists, who were ready to be involved (e.g., Capshew, 1999). Significant accomplishments included the Army General Classification Test (AGCT), situational stress tests, assessment centers, and simulation training. One of the first comprehensive applied psychology programs was the Aviation Psychology Program directed by J. C. Flanagan and published in 19 volumes (Flanagan, 1947–1949). APA Division 14 (now SIOP) past president (1976–1977) Paul W. Thayer recalled,

> World War II had an interesting effect on I/O. . . . It threw together a number of psychologists, some industrial, some experimental, some measurement, etc., in a variety of places. Wallace and Flanagan worked with some experimental types in the Army Air Corps (later the USAF), while McGehee and others were in the Navy. Wherry worked with the Army in D.C., and Shartle continued his work on job classification. . . . Experimental psychologists learned to respect what applied psychologists could

do, and vice versa. (Paul W. Thayer, personal communication, June 5, 2000)

After World War II, the economic and political division of the world along capitalistic-communist lines, the emergence of the Soviet Union as a superpower, and the threat of nuclear war increased military spending (Dipboye et al., 1994). Psychological research benefited from this spending as the military sought behavioral means to improve the effectiveness of the armed forces. Several research centers were created, such as the Army Research Institute (ARI), the Navy Personnel Research and Development Center (NPRDC), and the Air Force Human Resources Laboratory (AFHRL). Although military spending on research has decreased in the past 20 years, some projects prevailed. For example, J. P. Campbell (1990) described Project A, a large-scale project for the U.S. Army. This effort involved several psychologists over a 10-year period to research the selection and classification of military personnel and develop the Armed Services Vocational Aptitude Battery (ASVAB). Another example of military research is the extensive investigation of teams completed by the U.S. Navy's Training Systems Center (e.g., Swezey & Salas, 1992).

One outcome of the wars that indirectly influenced I-O psychology was the creation of the G.I. bill (e.g., Haydock, 1996). This bill allowed funded military personnel to attend college, increasing the number of students entering graduate programs. At 92 years of age, APA Division 14 (now SIOP) past president (1957–1958) Charles H. Lawshe Jr. recalled,

> Tiffin's book . . . was adopted by the U.S.A.F.I. (Armed Forces Institute) in a correspondence course for G.I.'s and was sent to them all over the world. With the cessation of hostilities these G.I.'s, now familiar with the book and with pockets full of cash applied for admission to graduate schools in drones. [sic] Purdue alone admitted 23 or 24 each year. . . . The result, a tremendous influx of many, many very bright students, all who eventually became available to be hired by industry. While it is no longer true, it seemed that almost every industry had its own "in house" industrial psychologist. (Charles H. Lawshe, Jr., personal communication, June 1, 2000)

The significant impact of the two world wars and the military on the development of I-O psychology has been documented (e.g., Britt & Morgan, 1946; Ferguson, 1962–1965; von Mayrhauser, 1989). The impact of other wars (e.g., Korea, Vietnam, the Gulf War) and military efforts on I-O psychology needs investigation.

Technological Forces

Technological forces include new processes and hardware revolutions with regard to computers, transportation, communication, medicine, administrative systems, and the like. Work may be redesigned or a job may become obsolete because of technological advances. For example, when the typewriter was introduced in the late 1800s, the occupation of copyist became obsolete and typist emerged as a new job (Dipboye et al., 1994). Recently, I-O psychologists (Howard, 1995) examined the influence of computer technologies on the functioning of organizations, which in turn affects the fundamental nature of work.

Craiger (1997) described two paradigm shifts in the history of computer technology and organizations. The first shift occurred from the 1950s to the 1980s when computers used for military purposes were converted to business purposes. Initially, only the most technically skilled individuals could use the complex technology; thus, computers were typically housed in management information systems departments. After IBM introduced the first stand-alone desktop personal computer in 1981, computers appeared at a rapid rate and allowed all employees to work directly with the technology; however, employees still worked in isolation, as the computers were not connected. The second paradigm shift occurred in the early 1980s when computer technology was installed throughout organizations. The ubiquity of computer technology inspired organizational leaders to reevaluate their business practices and organizational structures (Craiger, 1997). Then, the local area network (LAN) and client-server networks were introduced, allowing workers to share hardware, software, and information. Organizations adopting this network technology were called open-networked organizations. The primary work unit was transformed from individuals and typical department work groups to empowered work teams (Tapscott & Caston, 1993). The rise of information technology permitted organizations to (a) "have a *high-performance team* structure," (b) "function as *integrated* businesses despite high business unit autonomy," and (c) "to reach out and develop *new relationships with external* organizations—to become an 'extended enterprise'" (Tapscott & Caston, 1993, p. 14).

These changes in organizational functioning affect I-O psychology research and practice in several ways. Technology innovations have grown rapidly in human resources practices (Downey, 2000). More sophisticated selection tools have been developed, validated, and implemented (e.g., interview kiosks, computerized adaptive testing). New performance criteria and methods for evaluating performance (computer-aided performance appraisal) will need to be generated as a result of the open-networked organization (Craiger, 1997). Computer monitoring of efficiency and accuracy of employees (e.g., keyboard operators) and

surveillance technologies are currently in use (Dipboye et al., 1994). Computer-based training (CBT), Web training, and multimedia instructional formats have become a standard in college education and several organizations. Implications of technology on the design of jobs and teams will need investigation. With these technological advances, training for learning and adapting to changes in technology will become essential (Cascio, 1995).

Changes in technology also impact the research and statistical methods I-O psychologists use. Sophisticated statistical methodologies blossomed with the availability of computers and software in the 1980s and 1990s. SIOP past president (1995–1996) Michael A. Campion noted, "The advent of computers is certainly partially responsible for the advanced statistics we use" (Michael A. Campion, personal communication, September 22, 2000). Examples include item response theory, structural equation modeling, meta-analysis, event history analysis, and other methods for the study of change (Katzell & Austin, 1992). In addition, the Internet has changed communication patterns and research methods by making correspondence and information accessible. Most recently, SIOP leaders recognized the importance of technology for the discipline by devoting a portion of SIOP's 2001 annual conference to technological issues for the first time (SIOP Executive Committee Meeting Minutes, September, 24, 2000).

Psychological Forces

Psychological forces are developments in thought, theories, research, and practice in psychology generally. I-O psychology can trace its roots to the inception of psychology as a discipline at the end of the nineteenth century, the period described as the flowering of science (Roback, 1952). The intellectual zeitgeist consisted of positivism, materialism, and empiricism; consequently, scientists became interested in empirically investigating the mind and behavior. In his Germany laboratory, Wilhelm Wundt used the experimental method to control observations for studying objectively mind and behavior in order to separate psychology from philosophy as a scientific discipline (Hergenhahn, 1997).

During this time, functionalism, which is based on Darwinism and individual differences, was formulated. This school of thought emphasized the importance of adaptations, functions, and fitness as keys to survival (Angell, 1907). Psychologists became interested in how and why the mind adapts the individual to its environment. Functionalism served as the foundation for the mental-testing movement that took place at the turn of the twentieth century and the birth of a second psychology, or applied psychology. In addition to functionalism and the mental-testing movement, great emphasis was placed on empirical methods because psychologists felt compelled to legitimize their science and to address society's skepticism of the profession. Industrial psychology evolved from these developments in psychology (see Goodwin, 1999, or Hergenhahn, 1997, for a lengthier discussion of the development of American psychology).

Connections are apparent between I-O psychology and psychology perspectives such as behaviorism, neobehaviorism, gestalt, humanistic, and cognitive psychology. Behaviorism was a catalyst for conducting objective studies of behavior, developing practical applications, and including environmental or situational variables in theories of work behavior. For example, I-O theorists identified behaviors and situational conditions for effective leadership and developed behavioral measures for evaluating performance. One manifestation of Skinner's neobehaviorism was organizational behavior modification (Katzell & Austin, 1992). Similarities exist between the systems view of organizations and gestalt theory. The humanistic perspective inspired theorists and researchers to consider self-actualization and noneconomic motivators in the workplace. Lord and Maher (1991) described several developments in I-O psychology derived from the cognitive revolution. For example, cognitive theory has helped I-O psychologists understand cognitive processes in evaluating performance and designing jobs. Further exploration of the links between psychology and I-O psychology is needed.

Intradisciplinary Forces

In addition to external forces, individuals within I-O psychology contributed to the sustained growth of research and practice. According to SIOP past president (1986–1987) Sheldon Zedeck, "I-O psychologists have an intrinsic interest in solving problems" (Sheldon Zedeck, personal communication, July 6, 2000). Early in the history of I-O psychology, Hugo Münsterberg, James McKeen Cattell, Walter Dill Scott, Walter VanDyke Bingham, Frank and Lillian Gilbreth, Kurt Lewin, and others had the vision and initiative for developing ways their young, evolving discipline could be applied to business and societal needs (Koppes, 1997; Landy, 1997) and for identifying relevant topics for scientific research (Katzell & Austin, 1992). Münsterberg, for example, provided the foundation for every major development in industrial psychology in his books *Psychology and Industrial Efficiency* (1913) and *Business Psychology* (1917) (Moskowitz, 1977).

Too many individuals influenced I-O psychology to mention all the names here. Reviewing reference lists or the indexes of I-O textbooks and specialized I-O books reveals the vast number of contributors. Presidents of organized I-O psychology (APA Division 14 and SIOP) are elected because of their significant contributions, which are described in their autobiographies available on the SIOP Web site (www. siop.org). SIOP members are given the distinction of fellow because of their outstanding contributions to the discipline. SIOP awards are named after influential individuals (Koppes, 1999), and award recipients are recognized for their contributions. Other contributors are recognized in biographies and obituaries, which are published in *TIP*. In addition to individual accomplishments, I-O psychologists created ways to work together. For example, many I-O psychologists formed professional groups, such as the Dearborn Conference Group (Meyer, 1997) and the No-Name Group (Benjamin, 1997), to address concerns, discuss issues, and share research. I-O psychologists have also established consulting firms, which provide for collaborations between individuals and subsequent developments in research and practice (e.g., Center for Creative Leadership, Development Dimensions International, Jeanneret and Associates, Inc., Personnel Research Associates, Inc., Personnel Decisions Research Institute).

An indicator of developments in the field is the number of periodicals, books, and other sources that contain I-O-related research and applications. In addition to the resources mentioned in this chapter, over 25 different journals were formed, handbooks on related topics were created (e.g., Lorsch, 1987), two annual series were generated (e.g., *Research in Organizational Behavior* and *Research in Personnel and Human Resource Management*), and two series were established by SIOP to publish cutting-edge research and applications: *Organizational Frontiers of Industrial and Organizational Psychology* and *The Professional Practice Series*.

Numerous advances have been observed within the discipline. Katzell and Austin (1992) and Katzell (1994) identified metatrends such as the predominant use of sophisticated statistical analyses (e.g., structural equation modeling, meta-analysis) and more attention to outcomes not directly linked to the bottom line (e.g., stress and career development). Dunnette (1998) recognized accomplishments in his recent review of trends and emerging issues in I-O psychology:

> Most significant has been an increasingly fruitful blending of aspects of the science and practice of this field. Special attention has been directed towards systematic study of issues related to fair employment practices, and to broader recognition of the importance of meta-analysis for advancing knowledge as opposed to such simplistic approaches as statistical significance testing. Increased attention has been focused on the importance of genetic influences in areas of work behaviour.... Several important

trends in the field are . . . increased use of personality measures, 360° feedback instruments, and expanding the work performance domain to include aspects of contextual performance such as citizenship behaviours. (Dunnette, 1998, pp. 129–130)

Along with the discipline's successes, several criticisms have been made (e.g., Dunnette, 1966). Some I-O psychologists believe that practice has outstripped research. Others state that too much attention has been given to precision and objectivity. Researchers disagree with respect to how to analyze, define, measure, design, and evaluate research. Excess research has been conducted on predictors and validation techniques; a paucity of research exists on criteria. Theories, research methodologies, and data analyses are less applicable for dynamic issues and thus do not account for change. Few longitudinal studies have been conducted because they are cumbersome and expensive. A gap is increasing between I-O psychology and psychology (Highhouse & Zickar, 1997). In addition, progress has been slow because of reporting to people who are not in positions of authority (Locke, 2000) and being too close to the client (Baritz, 1960).

One specific criticism plaguing the discipline throughout its history is that I-O psychologists practice "dustbowl empiricism," which is the process of researching relationships between variables with scant or no attention to the logic or theory underlying those relationships. Landy (1997) noted, "As a sub-discipline, I/O psychologists have long had problems with theory development" (p. 472). One explanation is that the field's primary focus during the early years was to develop solutions to practical problems to legitimize applied psychology (Dunnette, 1976). Dustbowl empiricism may have characterized the discipline in the early years, and some psychologists may continue to believe that theory and research have not progressed; however, since the 1960s, a stronger orientation toward theory development and theory-related research can be observed. One explanation is that I-O psychologists demonstrated their usefulness, so their time and energy could be directed toward theory (Katzell & Austin, 1992). Other explanations for strides in theory and research include (a) a growing distinction between science and practice, (b) an increased use of laboratory experiments because of academic pressures to publish, (c) the growth of organizational psychology that has a theoretical slant, and (d) unsupported theories that led to revised theories.

SUMMARY

This analysis of I-O psychology's history demonstrates that the rise of the discipline during the past 100 years was the result of confluences of dynamic external (socioeconomic, business, legal, military, technology, psychology) and internal forces (individuals, theories, and applications) at various times. These forces, along with other influences (e.g., interdisciplinary fields), interacted in shaping both science and practice. Several trends from then to now can be summarized: (a) I-O psychologists are more proactive and less reactive, (b) both employee goals and organizational goals are now considered rather than only organizational goals, (c) the discipline is a blending of science and practice, (d) intricate and integrated approaches are used to understand humans in the workplace (i.e., broad theories and models take into consideration the complexity of cognition and behavior in organizations) instead of a simple view, (e) specialties within the discipline now exist, (f) an increasing objectivity and greater accuracy of measurement (statistics) are emphasized, (g) more and better trained I-O psychologists and teachers are available, (h) more research is conducted on employee behaviors (personality traits, organizational citizenship behaviors) and contexts (work teams, international contexts) rather than on theoretical constructs (e.g., motivation), and (i) the underlying theme, improving the workplace and work lives, remains steadfast in the discipline.

CONCLUSION: WHAT HAVE WE LEARNED?

A better understanding of what I-O psychologists did and why they did what they did was obtained from examining the sociohistorical context of the discipline. Have I-O psychologists made a difference in the workplace? According to Katzell and Austin (1992),

> I-O psychology has become a viable scientific discipline that has added much to society's knowledge about work behavior. . . . I/O psychology has become an important contributor to management. . . . I/O psychology has been contributing to the general well-being of American society. It has done so by helping to select people for work for which they are suited, training and developing them to be more effective in their work and careers, reducing bias in the employment of the disadvantaged, improving safety and comfort at work, and enhancing the quality of work life. (pp. 822–823)

What can the past teach about the future of I-O psychology? External and internal forces will continue to affect the work of I-O psychologists. Cascio (1995) identified several rapid changes relative to the world of work (e.g., global competition, explosion of information technology, reengineering of business processes) that have important implications for the science and practice in I-O psychology (i.e., job analysis, employee selection, training and development, performance appraisal, organizational development). When asked to identify factors that will influence future developments in I-O psychology, SIOP president (2001–2002) William H. Macey remarked,

> Technology is an easy answer. The shift in work (and educational) interpersonal relationships occurring because of technology implementation may be another. Also, in a related sense, the meaning of work itself will change and by definition so will our practice and science. . . . [A] disproportionate degree of our attention may change from science to technology. Also, the hard part of our profession will be in maintaining the scientific integrity of our work as we move quickly to apply new technology and media. (William H. Macey, personal communication, August 19, 2000)

These remarks indicate that I-O psychology may come full circle (from primarily technology to science and research, then back to technology), and the scientist-practitioner distinction will continue to prevail. Thus, it is imperative that for I-O psychologists to continue to make a difference, they need to know their history to understand what was done, what was not done, and why. After reviewing the first 50 years of the journal *Personnel Psychology,* editor John R. Hollenbeck (1998) stated, "the impact that one has on the future seems to be closely related to one's appreciation of the past. This makes it all the more fitting, therefore, to reflect on and study our past. . . ." (Editorial).

REFERENCES

Aiman-Smith, L., & Koppes, L. L. (Chairs). (2000, April). *Factors of change: Reflections and predictions from past presidents.* Invited symposium at the 15th annual conference of the Society for Industrial and Organizational Psychology, New Orleans, LA.

American Educational Research Association, American Psychological Association, & National Council on Measurement in Education. (1999). *Standards for educational and psychological testing.* Washington, DC: American Educational Research Association.

American Psychological Association. (1953). *Ethical principles of psychologists.* Washington, DC: Author.

American Psychological Association. (1954). *Technical recommendations of psychological tests and diagnostic techniques.* Washington, DC: Author.

American With Disabilities Act of 1990, 42 U.S.C.A. 12101 *et seq.*

Angell, J. R. (1907). The province of functional psychology. *Psychological Review, 14,* 61–91.

Arvey, R. D. (1979). *Fairness in selecting employees.* Reading, MA: Addison-Wesley.

Austin, J. T., & Villanova, P. (1992). The criterion problem: 1917–1992. *Journal of Applied Psychology, 77*(6), 836–874.

Baritz, L. (1960). *The servants of power.* New York: Wiley.

Barrett, R. S. (Ed.). (1996). *Fair employment strategies in human resource management.* Westport, CT: Quorum Books.

Benjamin, L. T., Jr. (1997). A history of Division 14 (Society for Industrial and Organizational Psychology). In D. A. Dewsbury (Ed.), *Unification through division: Histories of the divisions of the American Psychological Association* (Vol. 2, pp. 101–126). Washington, DC: American Psychological Association.

Benjamin, L. T., Rogers, A. M., & Rosenbaum, A. (1991). Coca-Cola, caffeine, and mental deficiency: Harry Hollingworth and the Chattanooga trial of 1911. *Journal of the History of the Behavioral Sciences, 27,* 42–55.

Bills, M. A. (1953). Our expanding responsibilities. *Journal of Applied Psychology, 37,* 142–145.

Bingham, W. B. (1928). The Personnel Research Federation in 1928: Annual report of the director. *Personnel Journal, 7,* 299–313.

Blum, M. L., & Naylor, J. C. (1968). *Industrial psychology: Its theoretical and social foundations.* New York: Harper & Row.

Bregman, E. O. (1922). A scientific plan for sizing up employees. *System,* 696–763.

Briggs, V. M., Jr. (1987). The growth and composition of the U.S. labor force. *Science, 238,* 176–180.

Britt, S. H., & Morgan, J. D. (1946). Military psychologists in World War II. *American Psychologist, 1,* 423–437.

Brogden, H. E. (1946). On the interpretation of the correlation coefficient as a measure of predictive efficiency. *Journal of Educational Psychology, 37,* 64–76.

Brown v. Board of Education, 347 U.S. 483 (1954).

Burnham, J. C. (1987). *How superstition won and science lost: Popularizing science and health in the United States.* New Brunswick, NJ: Rutgers University Press.

Burtt, H. E. (1926). *Principles of employment psychology.* New York: Harper.

Camfield, T. (1973). The professionalization of American Psychology, 1870–1917. *Journal of the History of Behavioral Sciences, 9,* 66–75.

Campbell, J. P. (1990). An overview of the army selection and classification project (Project A). *Personnel Psychology, 43,* 231–239.

Campbell, J. P. (1992, May). *The latent structure of science and practice: A confirmatory test.* Paper presented at the 7th annual conference of the Society for Industrial and Organizational Psychology, Montreal, Quebec, Canada.

Canter, R. R. (1948). Psychologists in industry. *Personnel Psychology, 1,* 145–161.

Cantor, N. (1945). *Employee counseling: A new viewpoint in industrial psychology.* New York: McGraw-Hill.

Capshew, J. H. (1999). *Psychologists on the march: Science, practice, and professional identity in America, 1929–1969.* New York: Cambridge University Press.

Cascio, W. F. (1991). *Costing human resources: The financial impact of behavior in organizations* (3rd ed.). Boston: PWS-Kent.

Cascio, W. F. (1995). Whither industrial and organizational psychology in a changing world of work? *American Psychologist, 50,* 928–939.

Cashman, S. D. (1989). *America in the twenties and thirties.* New York: New York University Press.

Cattell, J. M. (1923). Psychological corporation. *Annals of the American Academy of Political and Social Science, 110,* 165–171.

Cattell, J. M. (1946). Retrospect: Psychology as a profession. *Journal of Consulting Psychology, 10,* 289–291.

Church, A. H. (2000). From the editor: Lazing on a Sunday afternoon. *Industrial-Organizational Psychologist, 38*(1), 16–21.

Civil Rights Act of 1964, 42 U.S.C. §2000e-2000e 17.

Civil Rights Act of 1991, Publ. L. No. 102–166, 105 Stat. 1071.

Cohen, M. S. (1995). *Labor shortages as America approaches the twenty-first century.* Ann Arbor: University of Michigan Press.

Colarelli, S. M. (1998). Psychological interventions in organizations: An evolutionary perspective. *American Psychologist, 53*(9), 1044–1056.

Cowles, M. (1989). *Statistics in psychology: A historical perspective.* Hillsdale, NJ: Erlbaum.

Craiger, P. (1997). Technology, organizations, and work in the 20th century. *Industrial-Organizational Psychologist, 34*(3), 89–96.

Darley, J. G., & Berdie, R. (1940). The fields of applied psychology: A survey report to the committee on professional employment of the American Association for Applied Psychology. *Journal of Consulting Psychology, 4*(2), 41–52.

Dawis, R., & Lofquist, L. H. (1984). *A psychological theory of work adjustment: An individual differences model and its applications.* Minneapolis: University of Minnesota Press.

DeNisi, A. S. (2000, April). *SIOP in its second century: Challenges, threats, and opportunities.* Presidential address at the 15th annual conference of the Society for Industrial and Organizational Psychology, New Orleans, LA.

Dipboye, R. L., Smith, C. S., & Howell, W. C. (1994). *Understanding industrial and organizational psychology: An integrated approach.* New York: Harcourt Brace College Publishers.

Downey, R. G. (2000, April). *The new I-O millennium: Riding the wave or wipe out?* Panel discussion presented at the 15th annual conference of the Society for Industrial and Organizational Psychology, New Orleans, LA.

Dunnette, M. D. (1966). Fads, fashions, and folderol in psychology. *American Psychologist, 21,* 343–352.

Dunnette, M. D. (Ed.). (1976). *Handbook of industrial and organizational psychology.* Chicago: Rand McNally.

Dunnette, M. D. (1990). Blending the science and practice of industrial and organizational psychology: Where are we and where are we going. In M. D. Dunnette & L. M. Hough (Eds.), *Handbook of industrial and organizational psychology* (2nd ed., Vol. 1, pp. 492–576). Palo Alto, CA: Consulting Psychologists Press.

Dunnette, M. D. (1998). Emerging trends and vexing issues in industrial and organizational psychology. *Applied psychology: An international review, 47*(2), 129–153.

Dunnette, M. D., & Hough, L. (Eds.). (1990–1992). *Handbook of industrial and organizational psychology* (2nd ed., Vols. 1–3). Palo Alto, CA: Consulting Psychologists Press.

Farr, J. L., & Tesluk, P. E. (1997). Bruce V. Moore: First president of Division 14. *Journal of Applied Psychology, 82*(4), 478–485.

Ferguson, L. W. (1962–1965). *The heritage of industrial psychology* [14 pamphlets]. Hartford, CT: Finlay Press.

Finch, F. H., & Odoroff, M. E. (1939). Employment trends in applied psychology. *Journal of Consulting Psychology, 3,* 118–122.

Flanagan, J. C. (Ed.). (1947–1949). *The aviation psychology program in the Army Air Forces* (Vols. 1–19). Washington, DC: U.S. Government Printing Office.

Fox, H. R. (2000). First executive order of the 21st century addressed employment discrimination. *Industrial-Organizational Psychologist, 37*(4), 167–168.

Fryer, D. H., & Henry, E. R. (Eds.). (1950). *Handbook of applied psychology* (Vols. 1–2). New York: Rinehart.

Furumoto, L. (1988). The new history of psychology. In I. S. Cohen (Ed.), *The G. Stanley Hall Lecture Series* (Vol. 9, pp. 9–33). Washington, DC: American Psychological Association.

Geissler, L. R. (1918). A plan for the technical training of consulting psychologists. *Journal of Applied Psychology, 2,* 77–83.

Gilbreth, F., Jr. (1970). *Time out for happiness.* New York: Thomas Y. Crowell.

Gillespie, R. (1988). The Hawthorne experiments and the politics of experimentation. In J. G. Morawski (Ed.), *The rise of experimentation in American psychology* (pp. 114–137). New Haven, CT: Yale University Press.

Goodwin, C. J. (1999). *A history of modern psychology.* New York: Wiley.

Gordon, M. E., & Burt, R. (1981). A history of industrial psychology's relationship with American unions: Lessons from the past and directions for the future. *International Review of Applied Psychology, 30,* 137–156.

Griggs v. Duke Power Company, 401 U.S. 424 (1971).

Gutman, A. (2000). *EEO law and personnel practices* (2nd ed.). Thousand Oaks, CA: Sage.

Hackman, J. R. (1985). Doing research that makes a difference. In E. E. Lawler III, A. M. Mohrman Jr., S. A. Mohrman, G. E.

Ledford Jr., & T. G. Cummings (Eds.), *Doing research that is useful for theory and practice* (pp. 126–149). San Francisco: Jossey-Bass.

Hakel, M. D. (1979). Proposal to incorporate as the Society for Industrial and Organizational Psychology. *Industrial-Organizational Psychologist, 16*(4), 4–5.

Haydock, M. D. (1996). The G.I. Bill. *American History, 31*(4), 52–58.

Hergenhahn, B. R. (1997). *An introduction to the history of psychology* (3rd ed.). Pacific Grove, CA: Brooks/Cole.

Highhouse, S. (1999). The brief history of personnel counseling in industrial-organizational psychology. *Journal of Vocational Behavior, 55*, 318–336.

Highhouse, S., & Zickar, M. J. (1997). Where has all the psychology gone? *Industrial-Organizational Psychologist, 35*(2), 82–88.

Hilgard, E. R. (1987). *Psychology in America: A historical survey.* New York: Harcourt, Brace and Jovanovich.

Hill, C. (1955). Psychological research within the armed services. *American Psychologist, 10*, 238–242.

Holland, B., Hogan, R., & Sheton, P. (1999). From phrenology to fraud: The breakdown of science in the practice of industrial-organizational psychology. *Industrial-Organizational Psychologist, 36*(3), 35–36.

Hollenbeck, J. R. (Ed.). (1998). Personnel psychology's citation leading articles: The first five decades. *Personnel Psychology, 51*(4), Editorial.

Hoppock, R. M. (1935). *Job satisfaction.* New York: Harper.

Houser, J. D. (1938). *What people want from business.* New York: McGraw-Hill.

Howard, A. (1990). *The multiple facets of industrial/organizational psychology: Membership survey results.* Arlington Heights, IL: Society for Industrial/Organizational Psychology.

Howard, A. (Ed.). (1995). *The changing nature of work.* San Francisco: Jossey-Bass.

Howard, A., & Bray, D. W. (1988). *Managerial lives in transition: Advancing age and changing times.* New York: Guilford Press.

Huber, G. P. (1984). The nature and design of post-industrial organizations. *Management Science, 30*(8), 928–951.

Ilgen, D. R. (1990). Health issues at work. *American Psychologist, 45*, 273–283.

Jenkins, J. G. (1935). *Psychology in business and industry: An introduction to psychotechnology.* New York: Wiley.

Katzell, R. A. (1958). Looking around: Is individualism disappearing? *Harvard Business Review, 36*, 139–143.

Katzell, R. A. (1994). Contemporary meta-trends in industrial and organizational psychology. In H. C. Triandis, M. D. Dunnette, & L. M. Hough (Eds.), *The handbook of industrial and organizational psychology* (2nd ed., Vol. 4, pp. 1–89). Palo Alto, CA: Consulting Psychologists Press.

Katzell, R. A., & Austin, J. T. (1992). From then to now: The development of industrial-organizational psychology in the United States. *Journal of Applied Psychology, 77*, 803–835.

Kingsbury, F. A. (1923). Applying psychology to business. *Annals of the American Academy of Political and Social Sciences, 110*, 2–12.

Klimoski, R. J. (1992, May). *Revitalizing the interface between science and practice.* Presidential address given at the 7th annual conference of the Society for Industrial and Organizational Psychology, Montreal, Quebec, Canada.

Koppes, L. L. (1997). American female pioneers of industrial and organizational psychology during the early years. *Journal of Applied Psychology, 82*(4), 500–515.

Koppes, L. L. (1999). Ideals of science: Persons behind the SIOP awards. *Industrial-Organizational Psychologist, 36*(4), 75–86.

Koppes, L. L. (2000). A history of the SIOP administrative office. *Industrial-Organizational Psychologist, 38*(2), 48–54.

Koppes, L. L., Landy, F. J., & Perkins, K. N. (1993). First American female applied psychologists. *Industrial-Organizational Psychologist, 31*, 31–33.

Landy, F. J. (1992). Hugo Münsterberg: Victim or visionary? *Journal of Applied Psychology, 77*, 787–802.

Landy, F. J. (1997). Early influences on the development of industrial and organizational psychology. *Journal of Applied Psychology, 82*(4), 467–477.

Likert, R. (1932). A technique for the measurement of attitudes. *Archives of Psychology, 22*, 1–55.

Link, H. C. (1919). *Employment psychology.* New York: Macmillan.

Locke, E. A. (Chair). (2000, April). *Eminent I-O psychologists look back and forward.* Symposium presented at the 15th annual conference of the Society for Industrial and Organizational Psychology, New Orleans, LA.

London, M., & Moses, J. L. (1990). The changing roles of the industrial/organizational psychologist: From analyst/technician to change agent/strategist. *Industrial-Organizational Psychologist, 27*, 17–26.

Lord, R. G., & Maher, K. J. (1991). Cognitive theory in industrial and organizational psychology. In M. D. Dunnette & L. M. Hough (Eds.), *Handbook of industrial and organizational psychology* (2nd ed., Vol. 2, pp. 1–62). Palo Alto, CA: Consulting Psychologists Press.

Lorsch, J. W. (Ed.). (1987). *Handbook of organizational behavior.* Englewood Cliffs, NJ: Prentice-Hall.

Lowenberg, G., & Conrad, K. A. (1998). *Current perspectives in industrial/organizational psychology.* Needham Heights, MA: Allyn & Bacon.

Manchester, W. (1973–1974). *The glory and the dream* (Vols. 1–2). Boston: Little, Brown.

McCollom, I. N. (1959). Psychologists in industry in the United States. *American Psychologist, 14*, 704–708.

McGehee, W., & Thayer, P. W. (1961). *Training in business and industry.* New York: Wiley.

Meltzer, H., & Stagner, R. (Eds.). (1980). Industrial-organizational psychology: 1980 overview [Special issue]. *Professional Psychology, 11*, 347–546.

Meyer, H. H. (1997). An early stimulus to psychology in industry: A history of the Dearborn conference group. *Industrial-Organizational Psychologist, 34*(3), 24–27.

Minton, H. L. (1988). Charting life history: Lewis M. Terman's study of the gifted. In J. G. Morawski (Ed.), *The rise of experimentation in American psychology* (pp. 138–162). New Haven, CT: Yale University Press.

Mirvis, P. H. (1988). Organizational development. Part I: An evolutionary perspective. In W. A. Pasmore & R. W. Woodman (Eds.), *Research in organizational change and development* (Vol. 2, pp. 1–57). Greenwich, CT: JAI Press.

Moskowitz, M. J. (1977). Hugo Münsterberg: A study in the history of applied psychology. *American Psychologist, 32,* 824–842.

Muchinsky, P. M. (2000). *Psychology applied to work* (6th ed.). Belmont, CA: Wadsworth/Thomson Learning.

Münsterberg, H. (1913). *Psychology and industrial efficiency.* New York: Houghton Mifflin.

Münsterberg, H. (1914). *Psychology: General and applied.* New York: D. Appleton.

Münsterberg, H. (1917). *Business psychology.* Chicago: La Salle Extension University.

Napoli, D. S. (1981). *Architects of adjustment: The history of the psychological profession in the United States.* Port Washington, NY: Kennikat Press.

O'Connor, G. T., & Ryan, A. M. (1996). *Multiple facets of industrial-organizational psychology. II: Results of the 1995 membership survey.* Bowling Green, OH: Society for Industrial and Organizational Psychology.

Pate, J. L., & Wertheimer, M. (1993). Preface. In J. L. Pate & M. Wertheimer (Eds.), *No small part: A history of regional organizations in American psychology* (pp. xv–xvii). Washington, DC: American Psychological Association.

Paterson, D. G. (1932). The Minnesota unemployment research project. *Personnel Journal, 10,* 318–328.

Perloff, R., & Naman, J. L. (1996). Lillian Gilbreth: Tireless advocate for a general psychology. In G. A. Kimble, C. A. Boneau, & M. Wertheimer (Eds.), *Portraits of pioneers in psychology* (Vol. 2, pp. 106–116). Washington, DC: American Psychological Association.

Pond, M. (1927). Selective placement of metalworkers. *Journal of Personnel Research, 5,* 345–368, 405–417, 452–466.

Potter, E. E. (1989). Employer's burden of proof may be reduced in testing cases. *Industrial-Organizational Psychologist, 26,* 43–47.

Roback, A. A. (1952). *A history of American psychology.* New York: Collier-Macmillan.

Roethlisberger, F. J., & Dickson, W. J. (1939). *Management and the worker.* Cambridge, MA: Harvard University, Graduate School of Business Administration.

Scott, W. D., & Hayes, M. H. S. (1921). *Science and common sense in working with men.* New York: Ronald Press.

Scripture, E. W. (1895). *Thinking, feeling, doing.* New York: Chautauqua-Century Press.

Shartle, C. L. (1950). Industrial psychology. *Annual Review of Psychology, 1,* 151–172.

Society for Industrial and Organizational Psychology. (1987). *Principles for the validation and use of personnel selection procedures* (3rd ed.). College Park, MD: Author.

Society for Industrial and Organizational Psychology. (1989). *Graduate training programs in industrial/organizational psychology and organizational behavior.* College Park, MD: Author.

Society for Industrial and Organizational Psychology. (1995). *Guidelines for education and training at the master's level in industrial/organizational psychology.* Bowling Green, OH: Author.

Society for Industrial and Organizational Psychology. (1998a). *Graduate training programs in industrial-organizational psychology and related fields.* Bowling Green, OH: Author.

Society for Industrial and Organizational Psychology. (1998b). *Guidelines for education and training at the doctoral level in industrial/organizational psychology.* Bowling Green, OH: Author.

Sokal, M. M. (1981). The origins of the Psychological Corporation. *Journal of the History of the Behavioral Sciences, 17,* 54–67.

Sokal, M. M. (1995). Stargazing: James McKeen Cattell, American men of science, and the reward structure of the American scientific community, 1906–1944. In F. Kessel (Ed.), *Psychology, science and human affairs: Essays in honor of William Bevan* (pp. 64–86). Boulder, CO: Westview Press.

Swezey, R., & Salas, E. (1992). *Teams: Their training and performance.* Norwood, NJ: Ablex.

Tapscott, D., & Caston, A. (1993). *Paradigm shift: The new promise of information technology.* New York: McGraw-Hill.

Taylor, F. W. (1947). *Principles of scientific management.* New York: Harper. (Original work published 1911)

Tenopyr, M. L. (1992). Reflections of a pioneering woman in industrial psychology. *Professional Psychology: Research and Practice, 23*(3), 172–175.

Thayer, P. W. (1997). Oh! For the good old days! *Industrial-Organizational Psychologist, 34*(3), 17–20.

Thurstone, L. L. (1927). A law of comparative judgement. *Psychological Review, 34,* 273–286.

Triandis, H. C., Dunnette, M. D., & Hough, L. M. (1994). *The handbook of industrial and organizational psychology* (2nd ed., Vol. 4). Palo Alto, CA: Consulting Psychologists Press.

Triandis, H. C., Kurowoski, L. L., & Gelfand, M. J. (1994). Workplace diversity. In H. C. Triandis, M. D. Dunnette, & L. M. Hough (Eds.), *The handbook of industrial and organizational psychology* (2nd ed., Vol. 4, pp. 769–827). Palo Alto, CA: Consulting Psychologists Press.

Uniform Guidelines on Employee Selection Procedures. (1978). *Federal Register 43,* 38290–38315.

Van De Water, T. J. (1997). Psychology's entrepreneurs and the marketing of industrial psychology. *Journal of Applied Psychology, 82*(4), 486–499.

Viteles, M. S. (1932). *Industrial psychology.* New York: Norton.

von Mayrhauser, R. (1987). The manager, the medic, and the mediator: The clash of professional psychological styles and the wartime origins of group mental testing. In M. M. Sokal (Ed.), *Psychological testing and American society, 1890–1930* (pp. 128–157). New Brunswick, NJ: Rutgers University Press.

von Mayrhauser, R. (1989). Making intelligence functional: Walter Dill Scott and applied psychological testing in World War I. *Journal of the History of the Behavioral Sciences, 25,* 60–72.

Zedeck, S. (Ed.). (1992). *Work, families, and organizations.* San Francisco: Jossey-Bass.

Zickar, M. J. (2001). Using personality inventories to identify thugs and agitators: Applied psychology's contribution to the war against labor. *Journal of Vocational Behavior, 59,* 149–164.

CHAPTER 19

Forensic Psychology

JOHN C. BRIGHAM AND J. THOMAS GRISSO

WHAT IS FORENSIC PSYCHOLOGY?   391
EARLY ATTEMPTS TO APPLY PSYCHOLOGICAL
   OR PSYCHIATRIC KNOWLEDGE TO THE
   LEGAL SYSTEM   392
   Conceptualizations of Insanity   392
   Early Enthusiasts for Applying Psychology to the Law:
      Freud and Münsterberg   394
   Amicus Curiae Briefs   395
   Early Research and Expert Testimony on
      Eyewitness Memory   396
   Psychologists as Expert Witnesses: Historical Trends   396
   Pre-1955 Psychological Writings about Psychology
      and Law   397

EMERGENCE OF FORENSIC PSYCHOLOGY AS A
   RECOGNIZED SUBFIELD   398
   Signs of Maturation   398
   Forensic Clinical Evaluations   400
   New Roles for Psychologists: Expert Witness   401
   New Roles for Psychologists: Trial Consultant   403
CURRENT ISSUES IN FORENSIC PSYCHOLOGY   404
   Recent Trends in Scientific Amicus Briefs   404
   Advances in Forensic Psychology Research   406
FORENSIC PSYCHOLOGY IN THE
   TWENTY-FIRST CENTURY   408
REFERENCES   408

WHAT IS FORENSIC PSYCHOLOGY?

There are two ways to ask the question "What is forensic psychology?" One is to inquire about its current boundaries, and the other is to ask when it began. Both questions can be answered with a broad or a narrow perspective.

Concerning what forensic psychology is now, one perspective takes a broad view, equating the field roughly with what is often termed *psychology and law.* Consistent with this broad perspective, we can note that *forensic* comes from the Latin *forum* (a place of assembly, a court of law) and is defined as "pertaining to or employed in legal proceedings or argumentation" (*American Heritage Dictionary,* 1982). Taking this broad approach, forensic psychology began whenever psychological concepts were first applied to the legal system.

This broad definition is contained in the *Specialty Guidelines for Forensic Psychologists,* created by the Committee on Ethical Guidelines for Forensic Psychologists of the American Psychology-Law Society in 1991. The guidelines define the field as covering "all forms of professional conduct when acting, with definable foreknowledge, as a psychological expert on explicitly psychological issues in direct assistance to courts, parties to legal proceedings, correctional and forensic mental health facilities, and administrative, judicial,

and legislative agencies acting in a judicial capacity" (Committee on Ethical Guidelines, 1991, p. 657). In a similar vein, the American Board of Forensic Psychology on its Web site in 1998 gave a broad definition: "The application of the science and profession of law to questions and issues relating to psychology and the legal system." In *The Handbook of Forensic Psychology,* Bartol and Bartol (1999, p. 3) stated, "Forensic psychology is viewed broadly here. It is both (a) the research endeavor that examines aspects of human behavior directly related to the legal process . . . and (b) the professional practice of psychology within, or in consultation with, a legal system that encompasses both civil and criminal law and the numerous areas where they intersect. Therefore, forensic psychology refers broadly to the production and application of psychological knowledge to the civil and criminal justice systems." Later, these authors suggested that forensic psychology is "an umbrella term for psychology and law, correctional psychology, police psychology, and the psychology of juvenile and adult offending" (Bartol & Bartol, 1999, p. 19).

A similarly broad perspective was provided by Hess, a coeditor of *The Handbook of Forensic Psychology* (Hess & Weiner, 1999), who asserted that a functional definition of forensic psychology encompasses three ways in which psychology and law interact: "(a) the practice of psychology in legal settings, (b) the effects of the law on the practice of psychology, and (c) research and scholarly inquiry as applied to legal issues" (Hess, 1999, p. 24). Elsewhere, Hess noted the difficulty of defining forensic psychology, as he asked, "Is there a forensic psychology? Or, Is there a set of associated forensic psychologies? This is a crucial issue facing us" (Hess, 1996, p. 239).

The second popular definition of forensic psychology is more circumscribed, focusing on the clinical aspects. Many psychologists define forensic psychology more narrowly to refer to clinical psychologists who are engaged in clinical practice within the legal system. The distinction here is between psychologists who bring scientific information to the courts for their consideration in cases and psychologists who evaluate individuals and testify about them in reference to a legal question.

The second question, concerning when forensic psychology began, also has a broad and narrow definition. A broad perspective would see the starting point as that time when psychological concepts—that is, notions of psychological functioning—were first applied to address forensic questions. One might qualify this by requiring that these concepts were offered to courts by professionals. This definition would date forensic psychology at least back to the eighteenth century when physicians and neurologists testified in insanity cases. The narrower view would contend that forensic psychology cannot be said to have existed until there was a field called "psychology." It was not until the mid-twentieth century that psychologists were routinely allowed to testify about insanity and competency, roles that were the exclusive purview of psychiatrists until then (Bartol & Bartol, 1999).

If one adopts the broad perspective, where and when did forensic psychology begin? The beginnings of forensic psychology could be identified at least as far back as the ancient Greeks, as Hippocrates (ca. 480 B.C.E.) identified two forms of mental illness, melancholia and mania. The ancient Romans also wrote about "madness" as a medical and legal problem. Similarly, ancient Hebraic law stated that "idiots" and "lunatics" should not be held criminally responsible for their acts because they could not distinguish right from wrong (Maeder, 1985). The issue of madness received increasing scrutiny over the centuries. By the thirteenth century, the policy in England was to use the regular system of prosecution to determine guilt and then use "the King's mercy" as a possible basis for avoiding the execution of an insane convicted person. By the sixteenth century, in England the idea that a madman should be acquitted, not convicted, was widely accepted (Weinreb, 1986). The evolution of this linkage between the law and the psychological concept of insanity will be briefly outlined in the next section.

Where does all of this leave us? For historical completeness, we will begin our analysis with an overview of the early ideas about insanity held by legal systems. We leave it to the reader to interpret this as either the early beginnings of forensic psychology or a historical precursor to the later emergence of forensic psychology as a subfield within psychology.

EARLY ATTEMPTS TO APPLY PSYCHOLOGICAL OR PSYCHIATRIC KNOWLEDGE TO THE LEGAL SYSTEM

Conceptualizations of Insanity

While the ancient Greeks and Romans pioneered the use of notions of insanity in the law, later several widely publicized cases in Great Britain laid the groundwork for the treatment of insanity in the American and Canadian courts. *Rex v. Arnold* in 1723 involved the trial of Edward Arnold, also known as "Mad Ned" Arnold, who shot and wounded Lord Onslow, a nobleman closely aligned with the new British king, George I. Justice Tracy elucidated what has become known as the "wild beast" test, stating that in order for a person to be found not liable for an offense, he must be "a man that is totally deprived of his understanding and memory, and doth not know what he is doing, no more than an infant, than a brute, or a wild beast . . ." (Walker, 1968, p. 56). Arnold was found guilty and sentenced to death, but Lord Onslow interceded and Arnold remained in prison for life. Although the defense did not call any medical witnesses, the judge ruled that evidence about the defendant's behavior after the crime was admissible, thus paving the way for medical testimony in future trials about the results of examinations of the defendant performed after the crime. Finkel (1988, p. 3) asserted that this case was "the Anglo-American benchmark case most commonly cited as the historical beginning of the insanity defense."

In 1800, James Hadfield attempted to assassinate King George III. Hadfield had suffered a serious head wound while fighting for the British against the French six years earlier. As a result of his injury, part of his skull was missing, the membrane of his brain was exposed, and he had been discharged from the army due to insanity. Now he believed that he had been instructed by God to kill the "evil" king, and he stated that he knew he would be executed for his act. Since he knew what he was doing and the consequence that would follow, he was not insane according to the "wild beast" test. However, Hadfield's defense attorney, Thomas Erskine, argued instead that Hadfield was a "lunatic" whose actions were caused by a "morbid delusion." Given the grievousness of his grotesque injury, and the fact that all of the witnesses' testimony supported the notion of insanity, both sides agreed to stop the trial and invite the jury to find Hadfield not guilty due to insanity. The jury did so, and Hadfield was committed to an institution. This case overturned the "wild breast" standard by finding that one did not have to be *totally* devoid of reason to be found not guilty due to insanity. It showed that a person whose behavior is controlled by a delusion, even if he knows the difference between right and wrong, may be found insane. The principles established in the Hadfield case were used in the United States in 1835 in the Washington, DC, trial of a man who had shot at President Andrew Jackson (Rieber & Green, 1981).

In 1843, Daniel McNaughten (or M'Naghten), a woodturner and shopkeeper from Glasgow, Scotland, attempted to assassinate British prime minister Robert Peel. Instead, he mistakenly shot and killed the prime minister's secretary, Edward Drummond. In his only public statement about his motives, McNaughten said, "The Tories in my native city have compelled me to do this. They follow, persecute me wherever I go and have entirely destroyed my peace of mind. They followed me to France, into Scotland, and all over England. In fact they follow me wherever I go. I cannot sleep nor get no rest from them. I shall never be the man I was. I used to have good health and strength, but I have not now" (quoted in Moran, 1981, p. 10). McNaughten's statement formed the basis for an insanity defense at his trial.

When arrested, McNaughten had in his pocket a deposit slip for 750 pounds, a huge sum for a man in his position. These funds were used to hire what might be called the first legal defense "Dream Team," 150 years before the O. J. Simpson murder trial. McNaughten was defended by four barristers; they called nine medical experts who testified that he was insane or "partially insane." The prosecution did not attempt to counter the defense's medical testimony, and the prosecutor withdrew the Crown's case against McNaughten after the medical testimony had been given. Not surprisingly, the jury quickly came to a verdict (in less than 2 minutes!) of not guilty by reason of insanity (Finkel, 1988).

Queen Victoria, who had herself been shot at by an assassin three years earlier, was not amused, and neither was the House of Lords, which discussed the issue further. The eventual result was the "McNaughten rule" as established by the House of Lords, which specified that, "To establish a defense on the ground of insanity it must be clearly proved that, at the time of committing the act, the party accused was laboring under such a defect of reason, from disease of the mind, as not to know the nature and quality of the act he was doing, or if he did know it, that he did not know he was doing what was wrong" (Finkel, 1988, p. 21). This "McNaughten rule"

remains the standard for defining insanity in about half of the U.S. states.

A fascinating sidelight to this case concerns the chaotic political situation of the day and the mysterious 750 pounds. Where did a lowly shopkeeper get such a huge sum of money? Apparently, neither the defense nor the prosecution was overly curious at the time. Much later, Moran (1981, p. 4) suggested that the verdict was mainly the result of political considerations rather than McNaughten's mental state, contrary to the court's stated basis for the decision. McNaughten was *not* insane, Moran asserted. Given the great political turmoil of the times in McNaughten's home area (riots, general unrest and political intrigue, Tory spies and agents throughout England and Scotland), and McNaughten's known status as an orator and antigovernment sympathizer, his statement may have had the ring of truth to it. Finkel (1988, p. 18) suggested, "Perhaps he was striking back, defending himself against a series of escalating harassments that might, if unstopped, lead to his own murder? Was it an act of self-defense? A muchprovoked reaction? Or was the unexplained 750 pound note a payment for a political assassination that simply did in the wrong man?" How ironic if this landmark insanity verdict was based upon a false premise!

Shortly before this incident, Isaac Ray (1838/1983) had written *A Treatise on Medical Jurisprudence of Insanity,* which was regarded in England and the United States as the most influential book in this area at the time (Rieber & Green, 1981). Often described as the "father of forensic psychiatry," Ray wrote that no act done by a person in a state of insanity can be punished as an offense. This approach asserted that it was not necessary to show that the insanity *caused* the act or that the act was the product of an "irresistible impulse." This perspective was later incorporated in the definition of insanity introduced in the case of *Durham v. United States* (1954). However, this approach is now used in only one U.S. state, New Hampshire (Wrightsman, 2000).

The McNaughten rule had been adopted by the federal courts and most U.S. state courts by 1851 (Simon, 1983). While the McNaughten rule focused on *cognitive* factors (knowing, understanding), another approach recognized a *volitional* factor: whether or not the person, due to a mental disorder that produced an "irresistible impulse," was unable to prevent himself from committing an act. The irresistible impulse test was used in the United States just one year after the McNaughten case in England and was endorsed by the U.S. Supreme Court in 1897 in *Davis v. United States* (Garrison, 1998).

With respect to psychology's role in such proceedings, it was not until the mid-twentieth century, a half century after the establishment of psychology as a scientific discipline, that psychologists were regularly called as expert witness in such proceedings. Until this period, in cases involving the question of insanity, only licensed medical doctors were allowed to testify as experts. Finally, in 1940 the Michigan Supreme Court ruled in *People v. Hawthorne* that the trial court had erred in refusing to qualify as an expert a well-credentialed psychologist. The Court opined that a psychologist's ability to assess insanity should not be assumed to be inferior to that of a medical doctor (Bartol & Bartol, 1999).

Early Enthusiasts for Applying Psychology to the Law: Freud and Münsterberg

The early years of the twentieth century saw several significant attempts to inject the young discipline of psychology into the legal system. Two early leaders with very different perspectives, Sigmund Freud and Hugo Münsterberg (neither of whom was shy about asserting the value and applicability of his nascent field), argued that psychology, even in its present early state, had important applications for the law. In a 1906 speech to Austrian judges, Freud (1906/1959) asserted that knowledge of psychological processes was very important for their jobs. Freud suggested that procedures adapted from psychoanalysis, especially the word-association technique, could establish a "new method of investigation, the aim of which is to compel the accused person himself to establish his own guilt or innocence by objective signs" (p. 103). Freud suggested further that "The task of the therapist . . . is the same as that of the examining magistrate. We have to uncover the hidden psychical material; and in order to do this we have invented a number of detective devices, some of which it seems that you gentlemen of the law are now about to copy from us" (p. 108). Freud's optimism about the eagerness with which the law would embrace psychological principles and methods was not borne out, however.

In the early years of the twentieth century, another strong voice asserting that psychology was of great value for the law was that of Hugo Münsterberg. Münsterberg, a Harvard professor, had emigrated from Germany in 1892 at the invitation of William James. He became president of the American Psychological Association (APA) a decade later. Münsterberg had an arrogant manner and often adopted a pugnacious, somewhat sensationalized, self-promoting stand in his writings. In his controversial book, *On the Witness Stand* (1908), which was actually a collection of previously published magazine articles, Münsterberg argued in strong terms that lawyers should pay close attention to psychology. Münsterberg's arguments that psychology had much to offer the legal system, and the legal system's generally negative reaction to this assertion, illustrate the often acrimonious debate between psychologists and the legal community that continued intermittently for the rest of the century. He asserted that "the lawyer alone is obdurate" in failing to recognize the importance of applied psychology.

Münsterberg's assertions were so arrogant that they provoked a scathing response from legal scholar John Wigmore (1909), who created "transcripts" of a mythical libel trial in which Professor Münsterberg was sued for libel by the legal field for his assertions and was found guilty of claiming more than he could offer. The plaintiffs' lawyer, Mr. Tyro, criticized the lack of relevant research publications available (none had yet been published in English when Münsterberg's book was published), and noted that eminent European psychologists such as Sigmund Freud and Wilhelm Stern had cautioned against overzealous application of psychological findings. In 1906, Stern had written, "It is not yet time to speak of the practical use of this method; neither too great optimism nor too great skepticism is fitting. Thus far it has not yet passed beyond the laboratory stage. An extensive series of purely methodological work will be required before it can be thought of for application to the larger field of practice. . . . It is still premature to discuss its forensic use" (quoted in Wigmore, 1909, p. 414). Mr. Tyro accused Professor Münsterberg of committing "the whimsical mistake of bearing testimony against our innocent profession . . . for neglecting to use new and 'exact' methods which were and are so little 'exact' and so incapable of forensic use that even their well-wishers confess that thousands of experiments and years of research will be required before they will be practicable, if ever" (Wigmore, 1909, p. 415).

It should be noted that Wigmore criticized his own field as well. In his article, the trial judge, after receiving the jury's verdict in favor of the plaintiffs, pointed out that "No country in the world was probably so far behind in the scientific study of the criminal law as affected by the contributory sciences of sociology, anthropology, psychology, and medicine. In no [other] country had the legal profession taken so little interest in finding out or using what those other sciences were doing" (p. 433). Mr. Tyro expressed the desire that "their whole profession would expect and hope to go forward hereafter with the other profession [psychology] in joint endeavor to fruitful ends. They would put aside mutual distrust and public fault-finding." He urged the "friendly and energetic alliance of psychology and law, in the noble cause of justice" (p. 432).

After Wigmore's devastating critique, American psychologists "left the law rather severely alone," in the words of Hutchins (1927, p. 678) two decades later. Many years later, Bersoff (1999, p. 375) suggested that Münsterberg's work was so vilified by legal scholars "that it almost irreparably damaged the nascent attempt to apply the behavioral sciences to the law." Although it has been suggested (Kuna, 1978) that Münsterberg was more an opportunist than a trailblazer, some (e.g., Bartol & Bartol, 1999, p. 7) suggest that he still made a major contribution by drawing attention to the possibility of applying psychology to legal issues.

Amicus Curiae Briefs

At about the same time, the first legal amicus curiae ("friend of the court") brief that contained then-current social science (extralegal) knowledge about an issue was submitted to the Oregon Supreme Court by attorney (and later U.S. Supreme Court justice) Louis Brandeis, in *Muller v. Oregon* (1908). The brief argued that Oregon's statute limiting women to 10-hour workdays should be upheld because social science knowledge showed that longer workdays would be deleterious to women's health and well-being. The court's decision upheld the position taken in the brief. Subsequently, such briefs have been called "Brandeis briefs" or *science-translation briefs*. The original Brandeis brief remains the source of some controversy because of its references to "general 'female weakness'" and to "the periodical semi-pathological state of women" (quoted in Monahan & Loftus, 1982, p. 463). The "evidence" presented consisted largely of value statements and casual observations. This brief did not instantly start a trend, as presenting extralegal information to the courts did not become common until the late 1930s (Hafemeister & Melton, 1987).

The *Muller* (1908) case is generally recognized as the first historical example of using social science data as *social authority* (Monahan & Walker, 1987) in order to create or change a legal rule. The most famous case of this sort is probably *Brown v. Board of Education* (1954), the landmark ruling that made school segregation illegal. This was also the first application of social science to attack, rather than support, the actions of the state (Hafemeister & Melton, 1987). The science-translation brief was known as the "Social Science Statement." Because this was a case with extraordinary social, political, and societal ramifications, we will discuss it in some detail.

In the early 1950s, lawyers from the National Association for the Advancement of Colored People's Legal Defense and Education Fund, led by Thurgood Marshall (who later became a Justice on the U.S. Supreme Court), were working on several segregation cases that they hoped would reach the Supreme Court. Within psychology, a committee on intergroup relations, formed by the Society for the Psychological Study of Social Issues (SPSSI) shortly after World War II, prepared a statement on this issue for four school segregation cases that were moving toward the U.S. Supreme Court. The

Court agreed to hear the first two of the school segregation cases in 1952. Three members of the committee, Kenneth B. Clark, Isidor Chein, and Stuart Cook, drafted a statement submitted to the Supreme Court. This appendix to the plaintiffs' legal briefs, labeled the Social Science Statement, did not discuss specific research studies but referred to the relevant research in 35 footnotes. The Statement made three central arguments (Kluger, 1976): (a) Segregation was psychologically damaging to minority group children. It produced low self-esteem, self-hatred, frustration, and increased chances of delinquency. (b) Segregation was also harmful to majority group children, who experienced a distorted sense of reality, confusion, and "moral cynicism." (c) Desegregation could proceed smoothly if it were done quickly and firmly. The third argument relied heavily on studies of beneficial interracial contact in housing and employment situations. The Statement framed the argument strictly in scientific terms rather than political, legal, or moral ones. The Statement was subsequently signed by 32 other prominent social scientists. Included among the signatures were those of 14 past or future presidents of SPSSI (Jackson, 1998) and most of the psychologists who had been studying social prejudice since the 1930s.

During deliberations, the Supreme Court justices asked both sides to prepare new arguments on the issue of whether desegregation should be immediate and complete, or whether "an effective gradual adjustment" would be better. Psychology's response, written by Kenneth B. Clark (1953), concluded that immediate desegregation could be effective when imposed swiftly and with firm authority from above. Five conditions that would ensure effective desegregation were described: (a) a clear and unequivocal statement of policy by prestigious leaders; (b) firm enforcement of the new policy; (c) a willingness to deal strongly with violations; (d) a refusal to allow subterfuge or delay by local authorities; and (e) an appeal to individuals based on their religious principles of brotherhood and the American tradition of fair play and justice.

On May 14, 1954, the Supreme Court ruled unanimously that school segregation was a violation of the Fourteenth Amendment. This was the court's first major decision under its new chief justice, Earl Warren. Warren wrote that "modern authority" showed that the assumptions implicit in the 1896 *Plessy v. Ferguson* decision that had upheld so-called "separate but equal" facilities were not valid. All seven sources cited in support of this point (in footnote 11) had been discussed in the Social Science Statement.

But the psychologists' job was not yet over. After its 1954 *Brown* decision, the Court asked for yet another round of arguments focusing on the issue of immediate versus gradual desegregation. The resulting Social Science Memo, drafted by Clark, Cook, and others, urged a strict 1-year deadline for desegregation, although this point was troubling to several group members (Jackson, 1998). The Memo also pointed out that "There is a considerable body of evidence indicating that where the situation demands that an individual act as if he were not prejudiced, he will do so in spite of his continued prejudice" (quoted in Jackson, 1998, p. 170). The Supreme Court did not make a clear choice between "immediate" and "gradual." Instead, in May 1955, the court remanded the cases back to the federal district courts, which were ordered to desegregate the public schools "with all deliberate speed" (*Brown v. Board of Education*, 1955).

Although the Social Science Statement has been widely lauded as one of psychology's greatest contributions to society, it has remained controversial. Some observers argued that the Statement really had little or no effect on the Supreme Court; others criticized the uneven research support for the Statement (e.g., Cahn, 1955; Karst, 1960). The attacks on the validity of the Social Science Statement reminded one observer (Bersoff, 1986, p. 154) of Wigmore's (1909) rejoinder to Münsterberg (1908) more than four decades earlier.

Later, other psychologists (e.g., Gerard, 1983), perhaps frustrated by the uneven results of desegregation in the two decades after the *Brown* decisions, questioned whether the points made in the Statement were valid. In reply, Cook (1979, 1984) noted that the mixed nature of subsequent research results pertaining to the effects of desegregation were not surprising, because rarely did desegregation occur under conditions conducive to favorable outcomes for the children participating. Cook (1984, p. 831) suggested rather that there had been "an evident increase in the credibility of the social sciences as reflected by the extraordinary range of policy questions to which social science research is now being applied. This suggests that the social science role in public policy has been steadily growing and will continue to do so in the future."

Early Research and Expert Testimony on Eyewitness Memory

One area that Münsterberg (1908) touted as an important field of expertise was the study of witness memory and testimony. One of the first studies in this area was conducted in 1893 by J. McKeen Cattell at Columbia University, who asked students a series of memory questions similar to those that might be asked in a court of law. Cattell (1895) was surprised at the degree of inaccuracy that his respondents showed and by the tenuous relationship between their accuracy and their own certainty that they were correct. It has

been suggested that "Cattell's study probably was the genesis of modern forensic psychology" (Bartol & Bartol, 1999, p. 4) because it sparked the interest of other researchers, particularly those in Europe, in the psychology of testimony. Alfred Binet in France (e.g., Binet, 1900, 1905) and Wilhelm Stern in Germany (e.g., Stern, 1906, 1910) carried out a number of empirical studies on memory and testimony. In Belguim in 1911, psychologist J. Varendonck presented in court the results of several experiments indicating that children were inaccurate in their memory of important events (Bartol & Bartol, 1999). In the United States, Guy Whipple wrote a series of articles in the *Psychological Bulletin* that summarized (mostly European) research on observation and reported memories (Whipple, 1909, 1912, 1915, 1918). In the initial article in this series, Wigmore (1909, p. 154) lamented "the fact that English and American investigators are conspicuous by their absence" in studies of the psychology of testimony. The first recorded instance in which an American psychologist was proffered as an eyewitness expert was in *Criglow v. State*, a 1931 Arkansas case (Fulero, 1993). There was a resurgence of interest in the study of eyewitness memory and in expert testimony on the issue by research psychologists, beginning in the 1970s. We will briefly summarize that research later.

Psychologists as Expert Witnesses: Historical Trends

It was not until 1921 that an American psychologist served as an expert witness in a criminal case. In *State v. Driver*, a West Virginia trial court qualified a psychologist as an expert on juvenile delinquency, although the court rejected his testimony, which was based on results of psychological tests. The first psychologist to testify as an expert in a civil trial was Karl Marbe in Germany in 1922. Marbe discussed the result of reaction-time experiments in offering an opinion on the effect of alcohol on an engineer's responsibility in a train wreck (Bartol & Bartol, 1999). As a rule, psychological expert testimony was rejected in criminal cases involving the defendant's mental state. The lone area in which psychologists' observations seemed to be valued by the courts, even as far back as the early 1900s, was in the juvenile justice system; we will discuss this issue subsequently.

In the decade after World War I, the person most widely known in American psychology and law was probably William Marston, a student of Münsterberg's who was appointed professor of legal psychology at American University in 1922. Marston, who had both a law degree and a PhD, initially discovered a relationship between systolic blood pressure and lying and subsequently developed the polygraph (e.g., Marston, 1917, 1925). An attempt to introduce expert testimony based on polygraph results in 1923 was rejected, and the decision by the District of Columbia Circuit Court in *Frye v. United States* produced the venerable "Frye test" for the admissibility of scientific expert testimony. The court ruled that the proposed testimony must represent a position that is generally accepted within the relevant scientific community.

Marston (1920) also studied reaction times as indicators of deception and reported that there was a type of person whose reaction times during deception were shorter than while telling the truth. Marston consulted with police and attorneys on such matters, leading Bartol and Bartol (1999) to suggest that he was one of the first consultants to the criminal justice system, especially to law enforcement. Further, Marston (1924) conducted some of the first research on the jury system. In this research, he studied reactions to eyewitness testimony by staging a series of events, after which witnesses reported their memories in front of mock juries under conditions of free narration, direct examination, and cross-examination. In discussing such research, Marston made a point that would still be relevant to eyewitness research 75 years later. He noted that "Experimentation upon the completeness and accuracy of testimony, and of the findings of fact which might be based upon the testimony, probably had its origin in an unconscious, scientific wish to prove that our present juristic system is incapable of achieving a decent degree of justice." He added that "For such observations and reports, therefore, we must continue to depend upon human testimony. In light of this undeniable conclusion, it seems to me that the most profitable subjects of psychological discussion and experiment are to be found in the various possibilities of practical improvement in the elicitation and use of normal, average testimony, rather than in over-emphasizing its futility" (p. 29).

As we have seen, psychologists began to appear in some western European courtrooms as expert witnesses at the beginning of the twentieth century. There was some use of psychologists as expert witnesses in the United States from 1921 to 1950; they testified mostly about cognitive processes involved in witness memory or the psychology of crime and criminal personality. The 1950s was labeled the "forensic stage" by Loh (1981), because there was a dramatic increase in the involvement of psychologists in the legal system, testifying as expert witnesses in civil rights cases, about mental disorders, and on the effects of pretrial publicity (Greenberg, 1956). The regular use of clinical psychologists as expert witnesses on individual assessments of issues such as competency (to stand trial, to plead guilty, to waive rights), parental competency, insanity, child custody, and the like became commonplace only in the latter half of the twentieth century. In a 1956 *American Psychologist* article, McCary asserted

that "An important problem in psychology today is the legal status of the psychologist and his relationship to the courts. . . . The use of the expert witness is a fairly modern innovation in the field of legal evidence" (McCary, 1956, p. 8). McCary supported moves toward the certification or licensing of psychologists, noting that "As long as any quack can call himself a psychologist there is going to be resistance to granting the mantle of the expert witness to psychologists as a class" (p. 12).

The caution with which many courts regarded psychologists at the time may be illustrated by a 1955 decision of the Texas Court of Criminal of Appeals in *Watson v. State*. The judge wrote, "A psychiatrist is certainly best qualified to pass upon a question of mental illness. However, we have consistently accepted the testimony of medical doctors as experts. We think that also of those qualified to give an opinion, superior to that of a layman, would be a practicing psychologist" (p. 879). In addition to clinical psychologists making individual clinical judgments, social psychologists in this period began to appear as experts in cases involving pretrial publicity and civil rights (Greenberg, 1956; Loh, 1981).

The involvement of psychologists in the legal system had been only sporadic until the 1960s, when the social-political activism of the times, with its emphasis on "social relevance," encouraged many psychologists to focus their research efforts on the legal system. Interest in conducting legally relevant research accelerated in the early 1970s, when it grew at an even greater pace; indeed, in 1981 Loh (1981, p. 327) asserted that since 1974, "there have been more psychologists doing more empirical research on law-related matters that in all the preceding years combined." The rate of law-related empirical research has not slowed in the ensuing decades.

During this period, the scope of empirical inquiry expanded beyond the traditional areas of eyewitness testimony and evidence rules to encompass several fields relevant to procedural justice. Loh (1981) posited that there were four major areas: the effect of pretrial influences on the jury (e.g., pretrial publicity and pretrial identifications), selection of the jury, presentation of testimony and of the law to the jury (e.g., judicial instructions), and decision making by the jury.

Pre-1955 Psychological Writings about Psychology and Law

By about 1930, nearly 50 articles relating to forensic psychology (broadly defined) had appeared in American professional journals; about one-third were written by German psychologists. A survey of these "legal psychology" articles by Slesinger and Pilpel (1929) found that the psychology of testimony (11 articles) and the detection of deception (10 articles) were the most popular topics. Hutchins and Slesinger (1928a, 1928b, 1928c, 1929) carried out a series of studies on the law of evidence, looking at "consciousness of guilt," memory, spontaneous exclamations, and hearsay.

The first textbook in the area written by a psychologist was *Legal Psychology* by Howard Burtt (1931), also a student of Münsterberg's. In 1935, psychologist Edward Robinson wrote *Law and the Lawyers,* in which he argued that "every legal problem is at bottom a psychological problem and . . . every one of the many legal traditions about human nature which are to be found in legal training needs to be gone over from the standpoint of modern psychological knowledge" (Robinson, 1935, p. 51). This controversial book, like Münsterberg's, was received negatively by legal reviewers (e.g., Mechem, 1936), who asserted that psychology did not have the necessary knowledge to provide "plain psychological facts" (Robinson's term) that would be useful to the legal system. Robinson also recommended that psychological researchers investigate the behavioral premises implicit in legal doctrines. Loh (1981, p. 319) later pointed out that "This modest and sensible proposition, embedded as it was in his more impassioned diatribes against the conservatism of the law, was lost on his legal critics."

EMERGENCE OF FORENSIC PSYCHOLOGY AS A RECOGNIZED SUBFIELD

Signs of Maturation

Among the early signs that a field is beginning to mature is the emergence of professional organizations and publications that provide a source of intellectual support for the field, the identification of a specific knowledge domain that constitutes the field, and the development of professional training programs. The 1970s and 1980s saw significant development in all of these areas for forensic psychology and for psychology and law.

Professional Organizations

The American Psychology-Law Society was chartered in 1969, and it soon became the organizational support for enormous growth in psychology and law research and for forensic psychology practitioners (Grisso, 1991). From an initial 12 founders, the organization grew to over 100 members within its first year. Although most of its early members specialized in clinical forensic practice, during the 1970s the focus of the organization swung primarily to research and applications of social, developmental, and experimental psychology to legal issues.

When a number of members wished to develop a way to certify clinical forensic psychologists, the society provided the financial support for the development of a separate organization, the American Board of Forensic Psychology, in 1976. This board developed a process of examination leading to a diplomate in forensic psychology, and the board eventually became a specialty board of the American Board of Professional Psychology.

Led by John Monahan, several psychologists in the society successfully petitioned the American Psychological Association for a Division of Psychology and Law, which began in 1980. Within a few years the American Psychology-Law Society merged with the division, which is now formally named APA Division 41—the American Psychology-Law Society.

Journals and Textbooks

The 1970s saw the development of the first journals in law and psychology. The American Psychology-Law Society began publishing *Law and Human Behavior,* and the American Association of Correctional Psychologists developed *Criminal Justice and Behavior.* They were joined by the *Law and Psychology Review,* then in the 1980s by *Behavioral Sciences and the Law,* and finally the APA's new journal, *Psychology, Public Policy, and Law,* in the 1990s. Several new journals also appeared in Great Britain in the 1990s: *Criminal Behaviour and Mental Health, Legal and Criminological Psychology,* and *Psychology, Crime and Law.*

One of the first forensic psychology texts in this modern era of forensic psychology was Brodsky's *Psychologists in the Criminal Justice System* (1973). Few texts in psychology and law were available until the American Psychology-Law Society developed a book series in the mid-1970s, but by the 1980s the field had spawned enough texts to provide the field with a body of recognized knowledge that began to forge the field's identity.

Basic Knowledge Domain

As the field evolved, the question of what constituted the knowledge domain that defines forensic psychology became more salient. This was particularly important from the perspective of training forensic psychologists. A National Conference on Education and Training in Law and Psychology, popularly known as the Villanova Conference, addressed this issue in 1995. The conference participants identified five areas crucial for properly educating a competent scholar of psychology and law. The first was *substantive psychology,* a core knowledge of basic areas of psychology (e.g., developmental, social, cognitive, and abnormal psychology), as well as an understanding of important ethical and professional issues. The second area was *knowledge of research design and statistics.* Third was *basic legal knowledge,* the ability to "think like a lawyer," learning the basic tools of law and the core substance of the law itself. The fourth area was labeled *substantive legal psychology,* which involves an understanding of how social-scientific evidence is used in law. The final area, called *scholarship and training,* included the experience of conducting original dissertation research. The conference participants also noted that it would be especially helpful if additional opportunities were provided for students to obtain appropriate real-life experience in legislative, administrative, and judicial settings. It has been asserted that the competent psycholegal scholar must be "trilingual," familiar with scientific psychology, the law, and the psychology-law interface. This would seem to be a most challenging training situation (e.g., see Bersoff, Goodman-Delahunty, Grisso, Hans, Roesch, & Poythress, 1997).

Training

The 1970s and 1980s saw a proliferation of psychology and law training programs. The prototype was developed at the University of Nebraska by Bruce Sales in 1974, offering joint PhD and JD degrees in a blended graduate program involving the university's psychology department and law school. Several other joint-degree programs followed, but even greater was the increase in clinical graduate programs that allowed students to specialize in forensic psychology either formally or informally. By 1980, about one-third of the clinical psychology graduate programs in the United States included courses in psychology and law or forensic psychology in their curricula (Grisso, Sales, & Bayless, 1982). Shortly thereafter, postdoctoral programs in psycholegal studies as well as forensic clinical psychology began to evolve.

Currently a number of doctoral programs offer training in "forensic psychology," "psychology and law," or "social science and law." The latter two concentrations, which Brigham (1999) suggested could be called "legal psychology," may be located within social psychology programs, stand alone as an area in psychology, or serve as a specialty within a general psychology and law track. In contrast, graduate training labeled as "forensic" typically is located within a clinical psychology program. A survey of graduate student members of the American Psychology-Law Society in the late 1990s found that almost half (48%) of those who replied were in clinical programs, while 18% were in social psychology programs, 10% were in joint degree programs, and 8% were in applied graduate programs (Baldwin & Watts, 1996).

The way that forensic psychology is conceptualized will have a strong impact on the way graduate training programs are set up (e.g., see Bersoff et al., 1997; Ogloff, Tomkins, & Bersoff, 1996: Roesch, Grisso, & Poythress, 1986). As the twenty-first century began, there were at least five joint JD/PhD programs at universities in the United States. But while joint degree programs may represent the most direct route to achieving integration of psychology of law (Tomkins & Ogloff, 1990), such programs require from students massive amounts of time, effort, and tuition costs (to two schools within the university). Psycholegal scholars continue to debate whether it is necessary to achieve terminal degrees in both psychology and in law in order to be a competent psycholegal scholar, or whether this represents an instance of overkill. Another issue involves whether there are sufficient numbers of well-trained scholars to staff joint-degree programs or general psychology-law programs. Although such broad-based training seems to presuppose the presence of several faculty members with varied knowledge, it has been pointed out that it is a "cold fact that most departments have only one, if any, faculty member interested in social science applications to law" (Bersoff et al., 1997, p. 1304). Nevertheless, as has been stated elsewhere (Brigham, 1999), there is a growing need for well-trained psycholegal scholars to conduct policy development work, to train law-enforcement personnel, lawyers, and judges, to work on legislative committee staffs, and, as we discuss below, to work in various phases of the legal process (e.g., jury selection, expert testimony, trial consultation, dispute resolution).

As noted above, most training programs that call themselves "forensic psychology" are housed in clinical psychology graduate programs. Presumably, these programs are oriented toward applying the scientist-practitioner model to psycholegal issues. A survey by a working group from the Villanova Conference found that slightly over half of clinical internship programs offered major forensic rotations, mostly inpatient experiences with adult criminal forensic populations. Turning to the postdoctoral level, the working group was able to identify only about a dozen postdoctoral forensic training programs. They noted, though, that these programs should be oriented toward producing the future leaders in (clinical) forensic psychology (Bersoff et al., 1997).

Elsewhere, Brigham (1999) argued that it appears necessary to maintain two, or perhaps three, categories to describe psychologists involved in legal matters. A typology suggested by Heilbrun (in Brigham, 1999) includes three basic areas: clinical forensic psychology, experimental (researchers who consult with attorneys and/or give expert testimony in their research specialty), and legal psychologists (those with training in law and social science who work on broad psycholegal issues). At the level of ethical guidelines and professional responsibilities, the broadest definition of "forensic psychology" applies best. Any psychologist (e.g., clinical, social, cognitive, developmental) who works within the legal system should be held to the same high ethical and professional standards that are presented in the APA Code of Ethics and the AP-LS *Specialty Guidelines*. But the clinical/nonclinical distinction is still a meaningful one. For example, education, training, and licensing issues that are pertinent to clinical forensic psychologists may be irrelevant or inapplicable to nonclinical forensic psychologists (e.g., a one-year clinical internship). Further, clinicians and nonclincians differ in their orientation to the legal process and in the role they are likely to play in the courtroom. Clinicians are more likely to present assessments of specific individuals, while nonclinicians are more likely to present research-based social-fact evidence that applies to people in general.

Forensic Clinical Evaluations

Today many psychologists are employed full-time or part-time to provide clinical evaluations to courts and attorneys in addressing forensic issues. These evaluations are requested in criminal cases (e.g., competence to stand trial, insanity, sentencing), civil cases (e.g., disability claims, civil commitment, competence to consent to treatment, personal injury), and cases before juvenile, child and family, and probate courts (e.g., child abuse and neglect, parental competence, divorce custody, and various issues in delinquency cases).

The earliest involvement of psychologists in forensic clinical evaluations for courts, at least in significant numbers, was with regard to child and family cases that were before the courts. When the American system of juvenile justice began in the early 1900s, the original juvenile courts had court clinics attached to them to serve judges in understanding youths' needs. The earliest of these clinics was an institute developed in 1909 by William Healy, a neurologist, and Grace Fernald, a psychologist, to serve the Cook County (Chicago) Juvenile Court (Schetky & Benedek, 1992). Using a team approach, they provided comprehensive, multidisciplinary "studies" of youths to assist the court in arriving at rehabilitation plans. Psychologists' evaluation services to juvenile courts have continued relatively unabated to the present time. In the latter half of the twentieth century, psychologists have been the most frequent professional providers of evaluations for disposition recommendations and transfer to criminal court in delinquency cases, as well as parental capacities in divorce custody cases.

The evolution of clinical psychology in the mid-twentieth century brought many psychologists in contact with criminal populations through their employment in correctional programs (Brodsky, 1973). In addition, in their clinical roles in forensic inpatient hospitals, they began to perform psychological testing in forensic evaluation cases under the auspices of psychiatry. At least by the 1960s, some attorneys and courts were increasingly recognizing psychologists' potential as evaluation experts in criminal and civil cases. In *Jenkins v. United States* (1962), the Supreme Court decided that a psychologists' testimony should not be excluded as evidence regarding mental illness in cases involving competence to stand trial. The issue, the Court said, was not the individual's degree, but whether the person had adequate training and experience to form an expert opinion. This ruling opened the way for psychologists to step into that role as independent examiners.

This opportunity was seized by the founders of the American Psychology-Law Society (AP-LS), most of whom had primary interests in promoting forensic psychology as an evaluation resource for attorneys and courts (Grisso, 1991). No sooner had the group of 101 charter members convened, however, than they found that they were radically divided in their views of psychology's future as providers of forensic evaluations. The majority felt that psychology's empirical foundation and tradition of psychological testing offered the courts much more than did psychiatry and that psychologists should forge ahead in their efforts to provide evaluations for the courts. But a vocal minority (including the first president of the AP-LS, Jay Ziskin) urged restraint until the field could perform some research to support psychological experts' testimony. These dissenters pointed out that psychologists knew no more about the validity of their opinions—for example, about predictions of dangerousness or mental states related to criminal responsibility—than did clinicians in any other mental health profession (Grisso, 1991).

The more conservative minority was correct. At that time, only one major research study had been conducted on the evaluation of competence to stand trial (directed not by a psychologist, but a psychiatrist) (Laboratory for Community Psychiatry, 1973). There was no standard way to perform an evaluation for competence to stand trial, and the quality of most such evaluations in must states was woefully inadequate by today's standards. By the mid-1970s data were beginning to appear that indicated that when mental health professionals predicted that someone was going to engage in a violent behavior, they were wrong two out of three times (Monahan, 1981). Psychological and psychiatric analysis of the definition and assessment of criminal responsibility (insanity) offered no particular advances beyond those that could be found in medical treatises of the nineteenth century (Quen, 1994). And until the 1980s, the field had not a single textbook on forensic psychology, much less a textbook on the performance of specific forensic clinical evaluations.

Despite psychology's inability to make any claim of reliability or validity for most of its forensic evaluations, it required only two decades beyond the founding of AP-LS for psychologists' independent forensic evaluations to be commonplace in all areas in which clinical expertise was needed in criminal, civil, and juvenile courts. In many states, by the 1990s psychologists outnumbered psychiatrists as public-sector providers of forensic clinical evaluations for competence to stand trial and criminal responsibility (Grisso, Cocozza, Steadman, Fisher, & Greer, 1994). As we shall discuss later, the field also witnessed significant growth in research that eventually allowed psychologists to correct many of the inadequacies inherent in their forensic evaluations before the 1980s.

New Roles for Psychologists: Expert Witness

Standards of Admissibility for Expert Testimony

Three important court decisions, separated by over 50 years, and a federal evidence code introduced in 1975 have provided the basis for evaluating the admissibility of proposed scientific testimony. As noted earlier, in *Frye v. United States* (1923), the District of Columbia Circuit Court ruled that the results of an early polygraph test were not admissible because there was not general agreement within the relevant scientific community about the validity of polygraph results as an indicator of truthfulness. In the court's words, there was not a "commonly accepted explanatory theory" that applied to the polygraph. Hence, the "Frye test" of admissibility depends upon the general acceptance of a technique or finding within the scientific community. Over the ensuing years, other psychological expert testimony that has failed the Frye test has included more complex polygraph techniques and the use of hypnosis as a memory "refresher."

The Frye test was one of four criteria that were applied to proposed expert testimony in an influential decision by the Ninth Circuit Court of Appeals in *United States v. Amaral* (1973). The main issue in this case was whether the jury would receive "appreciable help" from proffered expert testimony on eyewitness research. (It should be noted that not much solid eyewitness research had been conducted up to this point.) The *Amaral* decision set out four criteria to determine helpfulness of the proposed expert testimony: (1) whether the expert was deemed qualified; (2) whether the testimony proffered was a "proper subject matter" for expert testimony, meaning that it would provide information that is not already part of jurors' "common knowledge" and would not invade the province of the jury; (3) whether the testimony conformed to a "generally accepted explanatory theory" (the Frye test);

and (4) whether the probative value of the testimony outweighed its possible prejudicial effect. Most subsequent decisions based on the *Amaral* criteria have come down against the admittance of expert testimony on the reliability of eyewitnesses (Brigham, Wasserman, & Meissner, 1999).

A new evidence code for federal cases, the Federal Rules of Evidence, was enacted in 1975 after extensive consideration by a prominent advisory committee, the U.S. Supreme Court, and both houses of Congress. The Federal Rules describe the criteria for admission of evidence for the entire federal court system; many states subsequently adopted similar codes. The central theme, as summarized by Woocher (1986, p. 48), is: "*Only* relevant evidence is admissible, and *all* relevant evidence is admissible in the absence of some countervailing policy" (italics in original). These relatively liberal criteria for admissibility are established in Rule 702, which declares that if scientific, technical, or other specialized knowledge would assist the trier of fact (judge, jurors) to understand the evidence or to determine a fact in issue, then a qualified expert may deliver expert testimony about the matter (Federal Rules of Evidence, 1975).

The U.S. Supreme Court dealt with the issue of the admissibility of scientific evidence in *Daubert v. Merrill Dow Pharmaceuticals, Inc.* (1993). In addressing the differences between the Federal Rules of Evidence and the more restrictive Frye test, the Court faced questions central to the potential conflict between science and the law. To what extent should judges be gatekeepers, screening out "junk science" from naive jurors who might otherwise be misled or overly awed by its scientific appearance? Conversely, to what extent should juries be permitted to serve their traditional role as fact finders by having access to any evidence that is potentially relevant?

In its decision, the Court focused on the acceptability of the *techniques* used to gather the scientific evidence rather than on its "general acceptance" within the scientific community (as in the Frye test). The Court discussed the importance of establishing that the testimony is based on research that adheres to the "scientific method" and is "not only relevant, but reliable" (what is described as "reliable" by the justices would be called "valid" by psychologists). The Court's decision discussed several standards for evaluating the research, including peer review of published work, its testability (or "falsifiability"), whether it has a recognized "rate of error," and whether it is consistent with recognized professional standards in the area.

Under this decision, judges must evaluate not only the conclusions but also the methods used by scientific experts. The Court opined that Rule 702 assigned to the trial judge the task of ensuring that the expert's testimony was both reliable and relevant to the case at hand. The Court stressed that the "overarching subject is the scientific validity" of the research in question rather than its general acceptance within the relevant scientific community. Thus, trial judges were assigned the role of gatekeeper, whose task is to decide, in effect, whether the proposed testimony represents methodologically sound research or is "junk science."

In *Kumho Tire v. Carmichael* (1999), the Supreme Court reaffirmed this aspect of the *Daubert* decision, ruling that trial judges should be granted broad latitude in determining which factors are applied in assessing the reliability of a given expert's testimony. The court also extended Rule 702 to include *all* expert testimony, whether it is "scientific," "technical," or represents "other specialized knowledge."

Because *Daubert* was a federal case rather than a state case, it has been left up to nonfederal jurisdictions whether to apply the *Daubert* standards or to retain the Frye test as the arbiter of admissibility. At present it is unclear what effect the *Daubert* decision will have on scientific psychological testimony or on clinical expert testimony. Regarding scientific testimony, it has been pointed out that, while the decision may open the door to innovative, valid new evidence that has not yet received widespread acceptance within the relevant scientific community, it also potentially opens the door for testimony based on questionable techniques that are unrecognized by the scientific community for good reasons, reasons that are not necessarily discernible by persons who are not trained in scientific methodology. Other observers have worried about whether the decision may be used to exclude the testimony of clinical psychologists expressing opinions about specific issues, especially on such controversial forensic issues as predicting dangerousness, rape, trauma, the presence of sex stereotyping, and child sexual abuse. Because interpretations of the *Daubert* standards have varied widely in the years since it was handed down, the question of its eventual impact remains open (Grove & Barden, 1999; Mark, 1999; Shuman & Sales, 1999).

Ethical and Professional Issues in Expert Testimony

As psychologists have appeared as expert witnesses with increasing frequency in recent years, attention to the ethical issues involved in such testimony has increased as well. When psychologists work in legal contexts, they may find themselves in situations involving unanticipated ethical or legal issues. Indeed, ethics complaints against psychologists who work in forensic contexts are among the most common made to licensing boards (Ogloff, 1999, p. 403). The Ethical Code of the American Psychological Association applies to forensic psychologists in all of their professional activities. However, it was not until the 1992 revision of the Ethical Code that issues pertaining to forensic psychology were directly addressed (Ethical Standards 7.01–7.06). The *Specialty Guidelines for Forensic Psychologists* (Committee on Ethical Guidelines for Forensic Psychologists, 1991), formulated by the American Psychology-Law Society, contain a more comprehensive analysis of ethical issues that forensic psychologists may face. However, while psychologists are obligated to adhere to the APA's ethical principles (American Psychological Association, 1992), the *Specialty Guidelines* do not represent an official statement of the APA and are "aspirational in nature" (Ogloff, 1999, p. 405).

The *Specialty Guidelines* are meant to apply to all psychologists within any subdiscipline of psychology (e.g., clinical, cognitive, developmental, social, experimental) who are engaged regularly as forensic psychologists. The guidelines discuss the issue of competence (i.e., the need to maintain current knowledge of scientific, professional, and legal developments within the area of claimed competence), types of relationships and potential conflicts of interest, and issues regarding confidentiality and privilege. The guidelines also note: "Forensic psychologists are aware that hearsay exceptions and other rules governing expert testimony place special ethical burden upon them" and they should "seek to minimize sole reliance upon such evidence" (Committee on Ethical Guidelines for Forensic Psychologists, 1991, p. 662). Further, the guidelines stress the importance of ensuring that forensic psychologists' public statements and professional testimony are communicated in ways that will promote understanding and avoid deception. The guidelines assert: "Forensic psychologists realize that their public role as 'expert to the court' or as 'expert representing the profession' confers upon them a special responsibility for fairness and accuracy in their public statements. . . . When testifying, forensic psychologists have an obligation to all parties to legal proceeding to present their findings, conclusions, evidence, or other professional products in a fair manner. This principle does not preclude forceful representation of the data and reasoning upon which a conclusion or professional product is based. It does, however, preclude an attempt, whether active or passive, to engage in partisan distortion or misrepresentation" (p. 664).

As several writers have pointed out (e.g., Keith-Spiegel & Koocher, 1985; Ogloff, 1999), psychologists working in the legal system may encounter ethical situations for which their training has not prepared them. One issue is: Who is the client? If the psychologist has been hired to examine a job applicant as part of an employment screening process, for example, the employer, not the job applicant, is the client. In such a case, the employer "owns" the confidentiality, and the psychologist must share the results with the employer (Ogloff, 1999, p. 407). Another issue of concern is the scope of the psychologist's competence and the danger that may arise from the temptation (perhaps encouraged by an attorney) to testify or work outside of the boundaries of one's competence. The APA Ethics Code declares that psychologists must provide services only within the boundaries of their competence, and the *Specialty Guidelines* note that "forensic psychologists have an obligation to present to the court, regarding the specific matters to which they will testify, the boundaries of their competence" (Specialty Guideline III[B]).

The politically charged issue of the use of intelligence tests with different ethnic groups is an instance where values, psychological data, and expert opinions have clashed in the courts. In a California case, *Larry P. v. Riles* (1972), the trial court heard expert testimony from many eminent psychologists and measurement experts. Some of the experts argued that the tests upon which school determinations were based were racially and culturally biased, while other experts concurred with the school system that there was no evidence that tests disfavored minorities because of an inherent bias in their construction. The trial judge ruled that individual intelligence tests discriminate against minority children and restricted their use in California. In contrast, in the later case of *PASE v. Hannon* (1980), in which many of the same experts testified, the trial judge found that such tests did *not* discriminate against minorities. What was particularly troubling to some (e.g., Bersoff, 1986) was the apparently questionable nature of the expert testimony. The judge in *Hannon* was very critical of the experts' testimony and wrote that "None of the witnesses in this case has so impressed me with his or her credibility or expertise that I would feel secure in basing a decision simply on his or her opinion" (quoted in Bersoff, 1986, p. 161). Bersoff asserted that "This perception of the behavior of the expert witnesses who testified before Judge Grady raises some formidable and disturbing, if not painful, ethical issues. If he is correct in that perception, each of the psychologists who offered opinions out of a 'doctrinaire commitment to a preconceived idea' rather than as a 'result of scientific inquiry' may be guilty of violating several important provisions of the Ethical Principles of Psychologists."

Another ethical issue that has received considerable attention in the past three decades is the duty to disclose information in order to protect or warn third parties. The California Supreme Court's final decision in *Tarasoff v. Regents of the University of California* (1976) may be the single court decision that is best known to psychologists. In this case, a therapist and university clinic were found liable for failing to protect an identifiable third party, Tatiana Tarasoff. She was the sometime girlfriend of a therapy client at the clinic who, during therapy, made serious threats toward her. The therapist told the campus police, who talked to the young man and concluded that he was not dangerous. Ms. Tarasoff was never told of the man's threats; two months later he stabbed her to death. The court ruled that the therapist "bears a duty to exercise reasonable care to protect the foreseeable victim of that danger [of violence]" (*Tarasoff*, 1976, p. 345). *Tarasoff* and related court decisions place some limitations on the therapy client's right to complete confidentiality. The legal test for knowing whether to report a threat is whether the psychologist knew or should have known (in a professional capacity) of the client's dangerousness (Keith-Spiegel & Koocher, 1985). All psychologists have an affirmative duty to report suspected cases of child sexual abuse and, in many jurisdictions, elder abuse as well. As a consequence, the necessity of being able to accurately assess risk for violence has assumed great importance to many forensic psychologists (Applebaum, 1985; Ogloff, 1999). For some, the fear of adverse legal complications or of malpractice litigation may have produced changes in practice, such as conducting "defensive psychotherapy" (Applebaum, 1988).

New Roles for Psychologists: Trial Consultant

Psychologists acting as trial consultants (who also may be called litigation consultants or jury consultants) are hired most often in civil cases, where substantial amounts of money may be involved, although their use is increasing in criminal cases as well. Probably the most visible trial-consultant role is as a jury consultant who attempts to aid one side to select a jury that is favorable to its position. The role of jury consultants in the murder trial of O. J. Simpson in 1994–1995 may be the most widely publicized instance. Other activities of trial consultants include pretrial evaluation of attorneys' presentations, mock-jury research, witness preparation, focus groups, and community surveys. They may advise their clients on important areas such as identifying the major issues in the trial, preparing witnesses for testimony, and advising on jury selection techniques. Consultants may also attempt to assist in developing effective opening statements, cross-examination techniques, and closing statements, or in carrying out survey research to assess whether the effects of pretrial publicity may necessitate a change of venue. Trial consultants also may make presentations to continuing-education seminars for attorneys that are intended to help them improve their courtroom presentation skills or jury selection techniques.

The systematic involvement of psychologists in so-called scientific jury selection began in the early 1970s in a series of politically charged trials involving persons prosecuted for actions protesting the war in Vietnam. Social psychologists Jay Schulman and Richard Christie participated in several highly visible trials, beginning with the trial of several Catholic priests and nuns, antiwar protesters who became known as the "Harrisburg 7" (*United States v. Ahmad,* 1973) and continuing with the group of antiwar protesters known as the "Gainesville 8" (*United States. v. Briggs,* 1973). In the Harrisburg 7 trial, the social scientists, assisted by corps of volunteers, conducted a survey of community members to find out which demographic variables (including age, education, religion, and gender) were associated with favorable attitudes toward war protesters. They then rated each prospective juror on a 1-to-5 scale in terms of favorability. The consultants also used "information networks" in the community, interviewing friends, neighbors, and employers, to gather more information about prospective jurors. In-court observations during voir dire provided the remaining information. The jury selection techniques based on this information were apparently successful, as the defendants were found not guilty. The researchers also carried out follow-up interviews with jurors after the verdict had been reached (Christie, 1976; Schulman, Shaver, Colman, Emrick, & Christie, 1973).

Another high-profile trial that used social scientists for the defense was the trial of U.S. Attorney General John Mitchell and former secretary of commerce Maurice Stans (also the former head of Richard Nixon's reelection committee) on charges of conspiracy to impede a Securities and Exchange Commission investigation of financier Robert L. Vesco in return for a $200,000 cash contribution to Nixon's reelection campaign. The defense was assisted in the selection of jurors by a public opinion survey, and the defendants were found not guilty. The survey was originally commissioned to support a motion for change of venue from New York City. When that motion was denied, the attorneys realized that, with some work, the survey findings might provide guidance in the selection of trial jurors. Additional information was obtained from interviews with neighbors, friends, and employers of the potential jurors (Christie, 1976).

Trial consultants are not licensed or certified in any state; therefore, anyone can proclaim himself or herself a trial consultant (Wrightsman, 2000). In the role of applied researcher, a trial consultant must follow professional standards for ethical research, which, according to Wrightsman (2000, p. 31), have the "form of a list of moral imperatives: 1. Thou shall not fake data. 2. Thou shall not plagiarize. 3. Thou shall not make false conclusions on the basis of your data." But given the fact that the trial consultant is an entrepreneur as well as a scientist, certain conflicts may arise. The AP-LS-sponsored *Specialty Guidelines* represent one attempt to provide general guidelines for dealing with such conflicts. One ambiguous

area concerns the sharing of data and ideas. It is a fundamental principle within the scientific community that empirical data and scientific ideas are shared among researchers. However, trial consultants, whether working alone or for an organization, may guard their ideas closely. For example, one consulting firm trademarked the term "shadow jury" and informed other consultants and researchers that they were to cease using the term "shadow jury" in their own work (Wrightsman, 2000, p. 32).

While some see the use of trial consultants as an improvement, a way to go beyond relying simply on attorneys' stereotypes and prejudices, others see it in a less positive light. For example, Marcia Clark, lead prosecutor in the O. J. Simpson criminal trial, asserted: "As far as I'm concerned, they are creatures of the defense. They charge a lot, so the only people who can afford them are wealthy defendants in criminal trials or fat-cat corporations defending against class-action suits" (M. Clark, 1997, p. 138).

CURRENT ISSUES IN FORENSIC PSYCHOLOGY

Recent Trends in Scientific Amicus Briefs

Areas Addressed by the Briefs

The past several decades, academic psychologists and psychological organizations, such as the American Psychological Association (APA), have been increasingly involved in the submission of "friend of the court" briefs to the courts on scientific issues. Science-translation briefs were submitted in cases involving gay rights (*Watkins v. United States Army,* 1988), "hypnotically-refreshed" testimony (*Rock v. Arkansas,* 1987), abortion (*Thornburgh v. American College of Physicians and Surgeons,* 1986), jury size (*Ballew v. Georgia,* 1978), prediction of dangerousness (*Barefoot v. Estelle,* 1983), treatment of mentally ill individuals (*Cleburne Living Center, Inc. v. City of Cleburne, Texas,* 1985), and gender stereotyping (*Price Waterhouse v. Hopkins,* 1989).

In *Bowers v. Hardwick* (1986), a case challenging sodomy statutes that criminalized certain sexual behaviors, the APA, in collaboration with the American Public Health Association, contributed an amicus brief containing a great deal of scientific and clinical data indicating that there was no evidence that homosexuality or method of intercourse is pathological in and of itself. The brief also noted the possible harmful psychological effects of deterring such conduct. Nevertheless, in a 5–4 decision, the Supreme Court upheld the sodomy statutes. The Court held that the Constitution does not confer a fundamental right upon consenting homosexuals to engage in oral or anal intercourse in private. In

Bersoff's words (1987, p. 57), this opinion "in its most favorable light, can only be described as archaic, medieval, and callous. Research was ignored in favor of history and morality."

The *Lockhart v. McCree* (1986) case was especially interesting to many forensic psychologists because it seemed to be one in which psychological research findings might be taken very seriously by the U.S. Supreme Court. Two decades earlier, the Court had upheld the legality of the process of "death qualification" in capital cases, in which potential jurors who had "scruples" against the death penalty (i.e., anti-death-penalty attitudes that would affect their ability to reach a guilty verdict, or would affect their willingness to ever vote for the death penalty) were automatically excluded from juries "for cause" (*Witherspoon v. Illinois,* 1968). In *Witherspoon,* the U.S. Supreme Court declined to rule that death-qualified juries were biased against defendants in the guilt process because the research data to that point, based upon just three empirical studies, were "tentative and fragmentary." The Court wrote that it might rule differently in the future if further research clearly demonstrated that death-qualified juries were not neutral with regard to guilt. In the two decades after the *Witherspoon* decision, a number of empirical psychological studies were carried out that appeared to clearly demonstrate that death-qualified juries were not neutral but were "conviction prone" (e.g., see Bersoff, 1987; Thompson 1989). The amicus brief submitted for the APA in *Lockhart* summarized the results of 15 empirical studies that led to the conclusions that: (a) death-qualified juries are conviction prone; (b) death-qualified juries are unrepresentative, thereby threatening the defendant's right to a jury composed of a fair cross-section of the community; and (c) death qualification interferes with the proper functioning of the jury.

In a narrow 5–4 decision, the U.S. Supreme Court upheld the death qualification process in *Lockhart v. McCree* (1986). Donald Bersoff, then general counsel for the APA, wrote that "it is now clear that even the most unassailable and methodologically perfect evidence would not have convinced the majority." But, he added,

> even though the majority eventually concluded that the social science evidence was not germane to its decision, it did not ignore it either. It gave it a respectful hearing and, it must be said, echoed the objective critique APA provided in its amicus brief. The Court's emphasis on the admitted lack of perfection in the studies was of far greater import to it, however, than it was to APA.

Ethical and Professional Issues

The decision whether a psychological organization should sponsor or create an amicus brief is a thorny one. Who should make this decision, what criteria should be used, and who should be asked to write the brief itself? In the late 1980s, the American Psychology-Law Society (AP-LS) initiated a pro bono brief project to collaborate with the APA in preparing briefs for cases involving important psychological issues (Roesch, Golding, Hans, & Reppucci, 1991). The first such brief was filed in *Maryland v. Craig* (1990), a U.S. Supreme Court case involving the acceptability of special procedures for the courtroom testimony of child witnesses. The brief, written by several leading psycholegal scholars and submitted on behalf of the APA, concluded that child victim-witnesses in sexual abuse trials were especially vulnerable and that the state "has a compelling interest in protecting a vulnerable child victim-witness." The brief suggested that "multiple sources of information, including expert testimony, should be sought in making the individualized determination whether there is a need to limit the defendant's right to face-to-face confrontation [by allowing the child to testify by means of closed-circuit television] when a particular child victim testifies" (Goodman, Levine, Melton, & Ogden, 1991, p. 29).

This brief stimulated immediate criticism from Underwager and Wakefield (1992), who argued that the brief's authors had misrepresented the value and relevance of much of the research that was cited. They also argued that the *Craig* brief's conclusions were inconsistent with those of an earlier APA-sponsored brief in *Kentucky v. Stincer* (1987). Three authors of the *Craig* brief replied that they had accurately described the best scientific evidence that was available. They wrote: "Psychology bears a social responsibility to provide the best available evidence on important questions of legal policy whenever it can do so (APA, Principle F). It should proceed with caution but it should not be disabled by a requirement for perfect evidence" (Goodman, Levine, & Melton, 1992, p. 249). The APA-sponsored brief in *Lockhart v. McCree* has also been criticized as possibly overstating the value of the relevant research (Elliot, 1991a, 1991b), and those criticisms were answered as well (e.g., Ellsworth, 1991). It seems likely that debates will continue, both within psychology and from those outside the field, about the relevance and applicability of evidence based upon psychological research studies.

Even when the U.S. Supreme Court chooses to pay attention to data included in a scientific brief, the Court may not always reach the conclusion that the brief's writers intended. A case in point is the issue of jury size. The APA submitted an amicus brief in *Williams v. Florida* (1970) presenting research that, the brief's writers felt, indicated that juries consisting of fewer than 12 members were undesirable because they were unlikely to maintain a representative cross-section of the community or to safeguard group deliberation processes. The Court apparently misread the data and declared that the difference in effects between 6- and 12-member juries to be only "negligible." The "naivete and ignorance of the Court" (Bersoff, 1986, p. 155) stimulated social scientists to conduct more research on the effects of jury size, especially differences between 6- and 12-person juries.

In a subsequent case, *Ballew v. Georgia* (1978), more scientific data (based on 18 studies) were submitted bearing on the differences between 6- and 12-member juries. The Court referred to these studies in its decision but ignored any difference between 6- and 12-person juries, focusing its attention on 5-member juries (which had *not* been studied in the research) and finding them unconstitutional. Although these jury-size cases are sometimes cited by psychologists as illustrating that the Supreme Court may pay close attention to empirical research, it is instructive that in a portion of the *Ballew* opinion, three justices expressed their "reservations as to the wisdom—as well as the necessity—of Mr. Justice Blackmun's heavy reliance on *numerology* [emphasis ours] derived from statistical studies" (p. 246). As Loh (1981, p. 340) summed it up, "The data were apparently used to ornament a decision reached on other legal and policy grounds. . . . The opinion used social science the way a drunk uses a lamp post, for support rather than illumination."

Perhaps researchers need to realize that attorneys and judges, who are not strongly socialized in the value of empirical research as psychological researchers are, will take a different perspective on the utility of empirical evidence. Bersoff (1986, pp. 155–156) stated it well: "It is relatively clear, then, that the relationship between experimental psychologists and the courts is less than perfect. In fact, if that relationship were to be examined by a Freudian, the analyst would no doubt conclude that it is a highly neurotic, conflict-ridden ambivalent affair (I stress affair because it is certainly no marriage). Like an insensitive scoundrel involved with an attractive but fundamentally irksome lover who too much wants to be courted, the judiciary shamelessly uses the social sciences. Courts cite the result of psychological research when they believe it will enhance the elegance of their opinions but empiricism is readily discarded when more traditional and legally acceptable bases for decision making are available."

Advances in Forensic Psychology Research

The past three decades saw a substantial growth in research directed specifically toward improving psychologists' capacities to provide courts with psychological information relevant to legal questions. Examples of these advances include research in eyewitness testimony, research to improve clinical forensic evaluations, and research on legal issues pertaining to children and adolescents.

Eyewitness Memory

The issue of the accuracy of eyewitness memory did not receive much attention from researchers from the 1920s until the late 1960s, when legal interest was sparked by three Supreme Court decisions relating to eyewitness evidence (*Gilbert v. California,* 1967; *Stovall v. Denno,* 1967; *United States v. Wade,* 1967) and by legal writers' suggestions that eyewitness errors had led to more convictions of innocent persons than all other judicial factors combined (e.g., Wall, 1965). Consequently, research interest increased dramatically in the 1970s (e.g., see Buckhout, 1974; Loftus, 1979; Yarmey, 1979 for reviews of this early work). By the end of this decade, Yarmey (1979, p. 228) argued that it was already the most advanced area of psycholegal research and the one "most able to make a significant contribution to the legal system." In fact, there was such an explosion of eyewitness research in the 1970s and early 1980s that Michael Saks, editor of *Law and Human Behavior,* felt compelled in a 1986 editorial to remind readers that "the law does not live by eyewitness testimony alone" (Saks, 1986, p. 279).

Eyewitness researchers studied aspects of the *acquisition (encoding) phase,* such as the witness's opportunity to observe the criminal, level of stress, presence of a weapon, age and race of the witness, and characteristics of the criminal. Studies also analyzed the *retention phase,* the period between witnessing an event and trying to retrieve the memory by making an identification. Researchers studied how the length of this interval affected memory accuracy and also looked at effects of events that happened during this period, such as potentially confusing or suggestive postevent information that might cause "unconscious transfer" or memory blending. Important aspects of the *retrieval phase* have included the type of identification procedure used (e.g., showup, simultaneous lineup, sequential lineup), the effect of suggestive instructions or procedures, and the overall relationship (or lack of it) between witnesses' accuracy and confidence in their identifications.

A great deal of pertinent research data have been accumulated about eyewitness memory, but despite the plethora of research (e.g., see Cutler & Penrod, 1995; Sporer, Malpass, & Koehnken, 1996, for summaries), judicial acceptance of the testimony of researchers on eyewitness memory has been slow in coming (Brigham, Wasserman, & Meissner, 1999). Many jurisdictions regularly rejected proposed "educational" expert testimony by eyewitness researchers, although by 1993 there had been at least 450 cases in 26 states in which eyewitness researchers had testified as experts (Fulero, 1993). It has been pointed out that "no such problem of admissibility was raised in the 1950s when clinical psychologists began to testify on mental disorders or when social psychologists first appeared to describe the debilitating personality consequences of segregation" (Loh, 1981 p, 332). One reason for the cool legal reception to eyewitness researchers is that the law requires particularized proof rather than general proof (e.g., average responses as shown by research), and the law is reluctant to assume that there is a one-to-one correspondence between *potential* unreliability of eyewitnesses (which is conceded) and its *actual* impact in a particular trial (which must be proven). Another issue is that many courts have assumed that awareness of the fallibility of eyewitness evidence is already within the "common knowledge" of most jurors, leaving no need for expert testimony (Brigham et al., 1999).

The type of issue studied may also make a difference. Wells (1978, 1993) asserted that psychologists should concentrate on studying *system variables,* that is, factors that are changeable within the system (e.g., police procedures, interrogation techniques, fairness of lineups), rather than *estimator variables,* whose impact in any particular situation can only be estimated (e.g., level of stress, weapon focus, race). Wells asserted that because of their potential usefuless for improving procedures, the results of system-variable research would be more readily accepted by the legal system than would estimator-variable research. It remains to be seen whether the legal system will become more receptive in the future to expert testimony about the memory of eyewitnesses, or whether the results of eyewitness research find their way into the legal system by other means (e.g., via science-translation briefs).

Clinical Forensic Evaluations

Little research was directed toward improving clinicians' evaluations for the courts until the 1980s. This changed dramatically across the next 20 years, heralded by seminal works published early in the 1980s. Among these were Monahan's (1981) treatise summarizing the serious limits of our abilities to assess and predict violent behavior, the first book to summarize what we did and did not know about competence to stand trial as a legal and forensic assessment issue (Roesch & Golding, 1980), the publication of a systematic model for the future development of instruments to assess a variety of legal competencies (Grisso, 1986), and the first comprehensive texts on the full range of forensic psychological evaluations for the courts in criminal, civil, and juvenile cases (Melton, Petrila, Poythress, & Slobogin, 1987; Weiner & Hess, 1987).

The importance of improving psychologists' abilities to assess the potential for future violence among offenders and persons with mental illnesses was driven also by legal cases during the 1980s. Most notable among these was *Barefoot v. Estelle* (1983), in which the U.S. Supreme Court acknowledged experts' inability to provide reliable predictions but, ironically, determined that they should continue to be consulted by the courts. Several large-scale research projects to improve our abilities to assess the risk of future violence began in the 1980s and had a major impact on practice when their results emerged in the 1990s. Among these were the work of researchers who developed and validated comprehensive violence risk assessment tools to provide estimates of likelihood of reoffending among prisoners (e.g., Quinsey, Harris, Rice, & Cormier, 1998), likelihood of future violence related to psychopathy (Hare, 1996), and likelihood of violence among persons with mental disorders after their release from psychiatric hospitals (Steadman et al., 1998).

Research to improve our conceptualization and assessment of abilities related to legal competencies grew exponentially throughout the 1980s and 1990s. Reviews of research on competence to stand trial (Roesch, Zapf, Golding, & Skeem, 1999) describe the development of important and basic information regarding the legal process for determining competence, as well as the validation of structured assessment tools for obtaining relevant psycholegal information on defendants in such cases (e.g., Poythress et al., 1999). Similar advances were made in substantial research projects culminating in data and assessment tools to improve evaluations of competence of patients to consent to treatment (e.g., Grisso & Appelbaum, 1998).

Child and Adolescent Psycholegal Issues

Research advanced in the 1980s and 1990s in a number of areas pertaining to children's capacities related to psycholegal questions. Among the most extensively researched of these questions was children's capacities to offer reliable testimony as eyewitnesses or as victims (e.g., Ceci & Hembrooke, 1998; Ceci, Toglia, & Ross, 1987). By the 1990s, developmental and experimental psychologists were able to provide significant information to courts regarding not only children's capacities to testify but also methods of investigation and questioning that would reduce the likelihood that children's reports would be contaminated by their experiences between the event and the trial.

Children's capacities to make decisions about matters affecting their welfare became a major issue in the courts in the late 1970s in the context of debates about youths' choices concerning abortion (e.g., *Bellotti v. Baird,* 1979), medical treatment (e.g., *Parham v. J.R.,* 1979), and waiver of Miranda rights (e.g., *Fare v. Michael C.,* 1979). Calls for research to address these issues (e.g., Melton, Koocher, & Saks, 1983) were answered by many researchers, and the need for further research in this area increased as more punitive delinquency laws of the 1990s strengthened the argument that youths had to be competent to stand trial (Grisso & Schwartz, 2000).

FORENSIC PSYCHOLOGY IN THE TWENTY-FIRST CENTURY

While we focused our attention on three areas above, the full range of topics that now fall under the rubric of forensic psychology is impressively broad. To illustrate, the second edition of *The Handbook of Forensic Psychology* (Hess & Weiner, 1999) contains sections on applying psychology to civil proceedings, applying psychology to criminal proceedings, communicating expert opinions, intervening with offenders, and professional issues (legal, ethical, and moral considerations; training in forensic psychology and the law). Among the civil proceedings discussed are mediating domestic law issues, personality assessment, educational disabilities, and civil competency. Among the criminal proceedings covered are assessing dangerousness and risk; evaluating eyewitness testimony; assessing jury competence; recommending probation and parole; assessing competency to stand trial, diminished capacity, and criminal responsibility; interacting with law enforcement; the "state of the art" of polygraph testing; and forensic uses of hypnosis. The section on interventions includes discussions of punishment, diversion, and alternative routes to crime prevention, substance abuse programs, psychotherapy with criminal offenders, and diagnosing and treating sexual offenders.

Research is currently being carried out within each of these areas, and the results are reported regularly in the forensically oriented journals mentioned earlier, as well as in mainstream psychology journals and, less frequently, in law reviews and other legal journals. In addition, many psychologists now take an active role in attempting to apply research findings and other relevant psychological knowledge to the legal system. In addition to the wide range of situations involving clinical psychological evaluations, these efforts may include writing research-based articles designed to inform both attorneys and social scientists, delivering expert testimony, creating science-translation briefs, consulting with attorneys, and making presentations as part of continuing-education programs for attorneys and judges.

The future of forensic psychology looks bright, as communication between leaders in both fields appears to be increasing in frequency and understanding. The potential for mutually beneficial cooperation between psychology and the legal system seems more promising than at any time since the optimistic (though inaccurate) predictions made by Freud and Münsterberg almost a century ago.

REFERENCES

American Heritage Dictionary. (1982). Boston: Houghton Mifflin.

American Psychological Association. (1992). Ethical principles of psychologists and code of conduct. *American Psychologist, 47,* 1597–1611.

Applebaum, P. S. (1985). *Tarasoff* and the clinicians: Problems in fulfilling the duty to protect. *American Journal of Psychiatry, 142,* 425–429.

Applebaum, P. S. (1988). The new preventive detention: Psychiatry's problematic responsibility for the control of violence. *American Journal of Psychiatry, 145,* 779–785.

Baldwin, M., & Watts, B. (1996). A survey of graduate education and training experiences in psychology and law. *American Psychology and Law Society News, 16,* 10–11.

Ballew v. Georgia, 435 U.S. 223 (1978).

Barefoot v. Estelle, 463 U.S. 880 (1983).

Bartol, C. R., & Bartol, A. M. (1999). History of forensic psychology. In A. K. Hess & I. B. Weiner (Eds.), *The handbook of forensic psychology* (2nd ed., pp. 3–23). New York: Wiley.

Bellotti v. Baird, 428 U.S. 132 (1979).

Bersoff, D. N. (1986). Psychologists and the judicial system: Broader perspectives. *Law and Human Behavior, 10,* 151–165.

Bersoff, D. N. (1987). Social science data and the Supreme Court: *Lockhart* as a case in point. *American Psychologist, 42,* 52–58.

Bersoff, D. N. (1999). Preparing for two cultures: Education and training in law and psychology. In R. Roesch, S. D. Hart, & J. R. P. Ogloff (Eds.), *Psychology and law: The state of the discipline* (pp. 375–401). New York: Kluwer Academic/Plenum Press.

Bersoff, D. N., Goodman-Delahunty, J., Grisso, T., Hans, V. P., Roesch, R., & Poythress, N. G. (1997). Training in law and psychology: Models from the Villanova conference. *American Psychologist, 52,* 1301–1310.

Binet, A. (1900). *La suggestibilite.* Paris: Schleicher.

Binet, A. (1905). La science du termoignage. *L'Annee Psychologique, 11,* 128–137.

Bowers v. Hardwick, 106 S. Ct. 2841 (1986).

Brigham, J. C. (1999). What is forensic psychology, anyway? *Law and Human Behavior, 23,* 273–298.

Brigham, J. C., Wasserman, A. W., & Meissner, C. A. (1999). Disputed eyewitness identification evidence: Important legal and scientific issues. *Court Review, 36*(2), 12–25.

Brodsky, S. (1973). *Psychologists in the criminal justice system.* Beverly Hills, CA: Sage.

Brown v. Board of Education, 347 U.S. 483 (1954).

Buckhout, R. (1974). Eyewitness testimony. *Scientific American, 231,* 23–31.

Burtt, H. E. (1931). *Legal psychology.* Indianapolis, IN: Bobbs-Merrill.

Cahn, E. (1955). Jurisprudence. *New York University Law Review, 30,* 150–169.

Cattell, J. M. (1895). Measurements of the accuracy of recollection. *Science, 2,* 761–766.

Ceci, S., & Hembrooke, H. (Eds.). (1998). *Expert witnesses in child abuse cases.* Washington, DC: American Psychological Association.

Ceci, S., Toglia, M., & Ross, D. (Eds.). (1987). *Children's eyewitness memory.* New York: Springer-Verlag.

Christie, R. (1976). Probability v. precedence: The social psychology of jury selection. In G. Bermant, C. Nemeth, & N. Vidmar (Eds.), *Psychology and the law: Research frontiers* (pp. 265–281). Lexington, MA: Lexington Books.

Clark, K. B. (1953). Desegregation: An appraisal of the evidence. *Journal of Social Issues, 9,* 1–15.

Clark, M. (1997). *Without a doubt.* New York: Viking Penguin.

Cleburne Living Center, Inc. v. City of Cleburne, Texas, 726 F.3d 191 (1985).

Committee on Ethical Guidelines for Forensic Psychologists. (1991). Specialty guidelines for forensic psychologists. *Law and Human Behavior, 15,* 655–665.

Cook, S. W. (1979). Social science and desegregation: Did we mislead the Supreme Court? *Personality and Social Psychology Bulletin, 15,* 420–437.

Cook, S. W. (1984). The 1954 Social Science Statement and school desegregation: A reply to Gerard. *American Psychologist, 39,* 819–831.

Cutler, B. L., & Penrod, S. D. (1995). *Mistaken identification: The eyewitness, psychology, and the law.* Cambridge: Cambridge University Press.

Daubert v. Merrell Dow Pharmaceuticals, Inc., 113 S. Ct. 2786 (1993).

Davis v. United States, 165 U.S. 373 (1897).

Durham v. United States, 214 F.2d 862 (1954).

Elliott, R. (1991a). Social science data and the APA: The *Lockhart* brief as a case in point. *Law and Human Behavior, 15,* 59–76.

Elliott, R. (1991b). Response to Ellsworth. *Law and Human Behavior, 15,* 91–94.

Ellsworth, P. C. (1991). To tell what we know or wait for Godot. *Law and Human Behavior, 15,* 77–90.

Fare v. Michael C., 442 U.S. 707 (1979).

Federal Rules of Evidence for the United States courts and magistrates. (1975). St. Paul, MN: West.

Finkel, N. J. (1988). *Insanity on trial.* New York: Plenum Press.

Freud, S. (1959). Psycho-analysis and the ascertaining of truth in courts of law. In E. Jones (Ed.), *Collected papers of Sigmund Freud* (Vol. 2, pp. 13–24). New York: Basic Books. (Original work published 1906)

Frye v. United States, 293 F. 1013 (D.C. Cir. 1923).

Fulero, S. M. (1993). *Eyewitness expert testimony: An overview and annotated bibliography, 1931–1988.* Unpublished manuscript, Sinclair College, Dayton, Ohio.

Garrison, A. H. (1998). The history of the M'Naughten insanity defense and the use of posttraumatic stress disorder as a basis of insanity. *American Journal of Forensic Psychology, 16,* 39–88.

Gerard, H. B. (1983). School desegregation: The social science role. *American Psychologist, 38,* 869–877.

Gilbert v. California, 388 U.S. 263, 87 S. Ct. 1951 (1967).

Goodman, G. S., Levine, M., & Melton, G. B. (1992). The best evidence produces the best law. *Law and Human Behavior, 16,* 244–251.

Goodman, G. S., Levine, M., Melton, G., & Ogden, D. W. (1991). The American Psychological Association brief in *Maryland v. Craig. Law and Human Behavior, 15,* 13–29.

Greenburg, J. (1956). Social scientists take the stand: A review and appraisal of their testimony in litigation. *Michigan Law Review, 54,* 953–970.

Grisso, T. (1986). *Evaluating competencies: Forensic assessments and instruments.* New York: Plenum Press.

Grisso, T. (1991). A developmental history of the American Psychology-Law Society. *Law and Human Behavior, 15,* 213–231.

Grisso, T., & Appelbaum, P. (1998). *Assessing competence to consent to treatment.* New York: Oxford University Press.

Grisso, T., Cocozza, J., Steadman, H., Fisher, W., & Greer, A. (1994). The organization of pretrial forensic evaluation services: A national profile. *Law and Human Behavior, 18,* 377–393.

Grisso, T., Sales, B., & Bayless, S. (1982). Law-related graduate courses and programs in psychology departments: A national survey. *American Psychologist, 37,* 267–278.

Grisso, T., & Schwartz, R. (Eds.). (2000). *Youth on trial: A developmental perspective on juvenile justice.* Chicago: University of Chicago Press.

Grove, W. M., & Barden, R. C. (1999). Protecting the integrity of the legal system: The admissibility of testimony from mental health experts under *Daubert/Kumho* analyses. *Psychology, Public Policy, and Law, 5,* 224–242.

Hafemeister, T. L., & Melton, G. B. (1987). The impact of social science research on the judiciary. In G. B. Melton (Ed.), *Reforming the law: The impact of developmental research* (pp. 27–59). New York: Guilford Press.

Hare, R. (1996). Psychopathy: A clinical construct whose time has come. *Criminal Justice and Behavior, 23,* 25–54.

Hess, A. K. (1996). Celebrating the twentieth anniversary of *Criminal Justice and Behavior:* The past, present, and future of forensic psychology. *Criminal Justice and Behavior, 23,* 236–250.

Hess, A. K. (1999). Defining forensic psychology. In A. K. Hess & I. B. Weiner (Eds.), *The handbook of forensic psychology* (2nd ed., pp. 24–47). New York: Wiley.

Hess, A. K., & Weiner, I. B. (Eds.). (1999). *The handbook of forensic psychology* (2nd ed.). New York: Wiley.

Hutchins, R. M. (1927). The law and the psychologists. *Yale Review, 16,* 678–690.

Hutchins, R. M., & Slesinger, D. (1928a). Some observations on the law of evidence: The competency of witnesses. *Yale Law Journal, 37,* 1017–1028.

Hutchins, R. M., & Slesinger, D. (1928b). Some observations on the law of evidence: Spontaneous exclamations. *Columbia Law Review, 28,* 432–440.

Hutchins, R. M., & Slesinger, D. (1928c). Some observations on the law of evidence: Memory. *Harvard Law Review, 41,* 860–873.

Hutchins, R. M., & Slesinger, D. (1929). Legal psychology. *Psychological Review, 36,* 13–26.

Jackson, J. H., Jr. (1998). Creating a consensus: Psychologists, the Supreme Court, and school desegregation, 1952–1955. *Journal of Social Issues, 54*(1), 143–177.

Jenkins v. United States, 307 F.2d 637 (D.C. Cir. 1962).

Karst, K. (1960). Legislative facts in constitutional litigation. *Supreme Court Review,* 75–112.

Keith-Spiegel, P., & Koocher, G. (1985). *Ethics in psychology: Professional standards and cases.* New York: Random House.

Kentucky v. Stincer, 482 U.S. 730 (1987).

Kluger, R. (1976). *Simple justice.* New York: Knopf.

Kumho Tire Co. v. Carmichael, 119 S. Ct. 1167 (1999).

Kuna, D. P. (1978). One-sided portrayal of Münsterberg. *American Psychologist, 33,* 700.

Laboratory of Community Psychology. (1973). *Competency to stand trial and mental illness* (DHEW Publication No. ADM77–103). Rockville, MD: Department of Health, Education and Welfare.

Larry P. v. Riles, 343 F. Supp. 1306 9N.D. Cal. 1972 (order granting preliminary injunction) *aff'd* 502 F.2d 963 (9th Cir. 1974); 459 F. Supp. 926 (N.D. Cal. 1979) appeal docketed No. 80–4027 (9th Cir., Jan. 17, 1980).

Lockhart v. McCree, 106 S. Ct. 1758 (1986).

Loftus, E. F. (1979). *Eyewitness testimony.* Cambridge, MA: Harvard University Press.

Loh, W. D. (1981). Perspectives on psychology and law. *Journal of Applied Social Psychology, 11,* 314–355.

Maeder, T. (1985). *Crime and madness: The origins and evolution of the insanity defense.* New York: Harper & Row.

Mark, M. M. (1999). Social science evidence in the courtroom: *Daubert* and beyond? *Psychology, Public Policy, and Law, 5,* 175–193.

Marston, W. M. (1917). Systolic blood pressure changes in deception. *Journal of Experimental Psychology, 2,* 117–163.

Marston, W. M. (1920). Reaction-time symptoms of deception. *Journal of Experimental Psychology, 3,* 72–87.

Marston, W. M. (1924). Studies in testimony. *Journal of Criminal Law and Criminology, 15,* 5–32.

Marston, W. M. (1925). Negative type, reaction-time symptoms of deception. *Psychological Review, 32,* 241–247.

Maryland v. Craig, 110 S. Ct. 3157 (1990).

McCary, J. L. (1956). The psychologist as an expert witness in court. *American Psychologist, 11,* 8–13.

Mechem, P. (1936). The jurisprudence of despair. *Iowa Law Review, 21,* 669–692.

Melton, G., Koocher, G., & Saks, M. (Eds.). (1983). *Children's competence to consent.* New York: Plenum Press.

Melton, G., Petrila, J., Poythress, N., & Slobogin, C. (1987). *Psychological evaluations for the courts.* New York: Guilford Press.

Monahan, J. (1981). *Predicting violent behavior: An assessment of clinical techniques.* Beverly Hills, CA: Sage.

Monahan, J., & Loftus, E. (1982). The psychology of law. *Annual Review of Psychology, 33,* 441–475.

Monahan, J., & Walker, L. (1987). Social framework: A new use of social science in law. *Virginia Law Review, 73,* 559–598.

Moran, R. (1981). *Knowing right from wrong: The insanity defense of Daniel McNaughten.* New York: Free Press.

Muller v. Oregon, 208 U.S. 412 (1908).

Münsterberg, H. (1908). *On the witness stand: Essays on psychology and crime.* New York: Doubleday.

Ogloff, J. R. P. (1999). Ethical and legal contours of forensic psychology. In R. Roesch, S. D. Hart, & J. R. P. Ogloff (Eds.), *Psychology and law: The state of the discipline* (pp. 405–422). New York: Kluwer Academic/Plenum Press.

Ogloff, J. R. P., Tomkins, A. J., & Bersoff, D. N. (1996). Education and training in psychology and law/criminal justice. *Criminal Justice and Behavior, 23,* 200–235.

Parham v. J. R. 442 U.S. 584 (1979).

PASE v. Hannon, 506 F. Supp. 831 (N.D. Ill. 1980).

People v. Hawthorne, 293 Mich. 15, 291 N.W. 205 (1940).

Plessy v. Ferguson, 163 U.S. 537 (1896).

Poythress, N., Nicholson, R., Otto, R., Edens, J., Bonnie, R., Monahan, J., et al. (1999). *The MacArthur Competence Assessment Tool for Criminal Adjudication.* Odessa, FL: Psychological Assessment Resources.

Price Waterhouse v. Hopkins, 109 S. Ct. 1775 (1989).

Quen, J. (1994). *The psychiatrist in the courtroom: Selected papers of Bernard L. Diamond, M.D.* Hillsdale, NJ: Analytic Press.

Quinsey, V., Harris, G., Rice, M., & Cormier, C. (1998). *Violent offenders: Appraising and managing risk.* Washington, DC: American Psychological Association.

Ray, I. (1983). *A treatise on the medical jurisprudence of insanity.* New York: DaCapo Press. (Original work published 1838)

Rex v. Arnold (Kingston upon Thames Assizes), 16 State Trials 695 (1812).

Rieber, R. W., & Green, M. (Eds.). (1981). *Milestones in the history of forensic psychology and psychiatry.* New York: DaCapo Press.

Robinson, E. S. (1935). *Law and the lawyers.* New York: Macmillan.

Rock v. Arkansas, 107 S. Ct. 2804 (1987).

Roesch, R., & Golding, S. (1980). *Competency to stand trial.* Urbana: University of Illinois Press.

Roesch, R., Golding, S., Hans, V. P., & Reppucci, N. D. (1991). Social science and the courts: The role of amicus briefs. *Law and Human Behavior, 15,* 1–11.

Roesch, R., Grisso, T., & Poythress, N. G. (1986). Training programs, courses, and workshops in psychology and law. In M. F. Kaplan (Ed.), *The impact of social psychology on procedural justice* (pp. 83–108). Springfield, IL: Thomas.

Roesch, R., Zapf, P., Golding, S., & Skeem, J. (1999). Defining and assessing competency to stand trial. In A. Hess & I. Weiner (Eds.), *The handbook of forensic psychology* (2nd ed., pp. 327–349). New York: Wiley.

Saks, M. J. (1986). The law does not live by eyewitness testimony alone. *Law and Human Behavior, 10,* 279–280.

Schetky, D., & Benedek, E. (1992). *Clinical handbook of child psychiatry and the law.* Baltimore: Williams & Wilkins.

Schulman, J., Shaver, P., Colman, R., Emrick, B., & Christie, R. (1973, May). Recipe for a jury. *Psychology Today,* 37–44, 79–84.

Shuman, D. W., & Sales, B. D. (1999). The impact of *Daubert* and its progeny on the admissibility of behavioral and social science evidence. *Psychology, Public Policy, and Law, 5,* 3–15.

Simon, R. (1983). The defense of insanity. *Journal of Psychiatry and Law, 11,* 183.

Slesinger, D., & Pilpel, M. E. (1929). Legal psychology: A bibliography and a suggestion. *Psychological Bulletin, 12,* 677–692.

Sporer, S. L., Malpass, R. S., & Koehnken, G. (Eds.). (1996). *Psychological issues in eyewitness identification.* Mahwah, NJ: Erlbaum.

Steadman, H., Mulvey, E., Monahan, J., Robbins, P., Appelbaum, P., Grisso, T., et al. (1998). Violence by people discharged from acute psychiatric facilities and by others in the same neighborhoods. *Archives of General Psychiatry, 55,* 393–401.

Stern, L. W. (1906). Zur psychologie der aussage. *Zeaschrift fur die qesamte Strafrech-swissenschaft, 23,* 56–66.

Stern, L. W. (1910). Abstracts of lectures on the psychology of testimony. *American Journal of Psychology, 21,* 273–282.

Stovall v. Denno, 388 U.S. 293 (1967).

Tarasoff v. Regents of the University of California, 17 Cal. 3d 425, 551 P.2d 334, 131 Cal. Rptr. 14 (1976).

Thompson, W. C. (1989). Death qualification after *Wainright v. Witt* and *Lockhart v. McCree. Law and Human Behavior, 13,* 185–215.

Thornburgh v. American College of Physicians and Surgeons, 106 U.S. (1986).

Tomkins, A. J., & Ogloff, J. R. P. (1990). Training and career options in psychology and law. *Behavioral Sciences and the Law, 8,* 205–216.

Underwager, R. W., & Wakefield, H. (1992). Poor psychology produces poor law. *Law and Human Behavior, 16,* 233–243.

United States v. Ahmad, 366 F. Supp. 1356 (1973).

United States v. Amaral, 488 F.2d, 1148 (9th Cir., 1973).

United States v. Briggs, Cr. No. 14950, Middle District of Pennsylvania, Harrisburg Division. (1973).

United States v. Durham, 214 F.2d 862 (1954).

United States v. Wade, 388 U.S. 218 (1967).

Walker, N. (1968). *Crime and insanity in England: The historical perspective, Vol. 1.* Edinburgh, Scotland: Edinburgh University Press.

Wall, P. C. (1965). *Eyewitness identification in criminal cases.* Springfield, IL: Charles C. Thomas.

Watkins v. United States Army, 837 F.2d 1428, rch'g en blanc granted, 847 F.2d 1362 (9th Cir. 1988).

Weiner, I., & Hess, R. (1987). *The handbook of forensic psychology.* New York: Wiley.

Weinreb, L. (1986). *Criminal law* (4th ed.). Mineola, NY: University Casebook Series.

Wells, G. L. (1978). Applied eyewitness testimony research: System variables and estimator variables. *Journal of Personality and Social Psychology, 36,* 1546–1557.

Wells, G. L. (1993). What do we know about eyewitness identifications? *American Psychologist, 48,* 553–571.

Whipple, G. M. (1909). The observer as reporter: A survey of the "psychology of testimony." *Psychological Bulletin, 6,* 153–170.

Whipple, G. M. (1912). Psychology of testimony and report. *Psychological Bulletin, 9,* 264–269.

Whipple, G. M. (1915). Psychology of testimony. *Psychological Bulletin, 12,* 221–224.

Whipple, G. M. (1918). The obtaining of information: Psychology of observation and report. *Psychological Bulletin, 15,* 217–248.

Wigmore, J. H. (1909). Professor Münsterberg and the psychology of testimony: Being a report of the case of *Cokestone v. Münsterberg. Illinois Law Review, 3,* 399–445.

Williams v. Florida, 399 U.S. 78 (1970).

Witherspoon v. Illinois, 391 U.S. 350 (1968).

Woocher, F. D. (1986). Legal principles governing expert testimony by experimental psychologists. *Law and Human Behavior, 10,* 47–61.

Wrightsman, L. S. (2000). *Forensic psychology.* Belmont, CA: Wadsworth.

Yarmey, A. D. (1979). *The psychology of eyewitness testimony.* New York: Free Press.

CHAPTER 20

School Psychology

THOMAS K. FAGAN

WHAT IS SCHOOL PSYCHOLOGY?   413
   Demographic Descriptions   413
   Training and Credentialing   413
   Employment Characteristics and Services   414
   Historical Periods Defined   414
THE HYBRID YEARS   414
   Factors Contributing to the Origins of Practice   414
   Professional Developments (1890–1920)   417
   **Emergence of School Psychology as a Distinct Field
     (1920–1940)   418**
   **Emerging Symbols of Professionalization
     (1940–1970)   420**

THE THOROUGHBRED YEARS (1970–PRESENT)   422
   Organizational Development   423
   Literary Development   424
   Training Development   424
   Credentialing Development   425
   Practice Characteristics   425
   Overview   426
A COMMENT ON THE FUTURE   426
ADDITIONAL RESOURCES   427
REFERENCES   428

WHAT IS SCHOOL PSYCHOLOGY?

School psychology is an applied psychology specialty that blends the knowledge bases of education and psychology into a professional practice that delivers services to clients of various ages, primarily those of school age (preschool to college), in a variety of settings, primarily public and private elementary and secondary schools. School psychology can be further defined along several dimensions, including professional association definitions, demographics, training, credentialing, employment characteristics, and services. A career publication states that "school psychologists work directly with public and private schools. They assess and counsel students, consult with parents and school staff, and conduct behavioral intervention when appropriate" (American Psychological Association, 1998, p. 7). The Division of School Psychology (Division 16) within the American Psychological Association (APA) describes itself as composed of scientist-practitioner psychologists whose major professional interests lie with children, families, and the schooling process. The National Association of School Psychologists (NASP) describes school psychologists as members of a team with educators, parents, and other mental health professionals who seek to ensure that children learn in safe, healthy, and supportive environments. A broad definition of school psychology appears in the Petition for Reaffirmation (1997).

Demographic Descriptions

Estimates are that there are at least 30,000 school psychologists in the United States, perhaps constituting one-third of all school psychologists on earth (Oakland, 2000). Practitioners in the field are approximately 70% female, predominantly Caucasian (at least 90%), have a median age of about 41 to 45 years, and have a median of 11 to 15 years of experience. School-based practitioners work within a psychologist-to-schoolchildren ratio of 1 to 1,800–2,000.

Training and Credentialing

Practitioners are prepared in more than 200 graduate-level school psychology programs. The programs are accredited by one or more of the following agencies: the APA (doctoral programs only) and the National Council for Accreditation of Teacher Education (NCATE; master's, specialist, and doctoral programs), and they are approved by state departments of education. Programs exist in departments of psychology in colleges of arts and sciences as well as various departments within colleges of education (e.g., departments of special education, educational psychology). At least two-thirds of all school psychologists hold a specialist degree (EdS) or its equivalent (master's degree plus 30 semester hours) or a higher degree; approximately 20% to 25% hold a doctoral degree (EdD, PhD, PsyD). Specialist-level programs typically require 60 to 70 semester hours, while doctoral programs typically require 100 or more. Both degrees require the equivalent of at least one school year of supervised internship (a minimum of 1,200 hours at the nondoctoral level and 1,500 hours at the doctoral level).

School psychologists are granted practice credentials (certificates or licenses) by each state's department of education (SDE) and/or by a separate state board of examiners in psychology (SBEP). The SDE credentials school psychologists for practice in the settings under its jurisdiction, typically all public schools but also possibly private schools, correctional schools, and residential schools. The SBEP credentials practitioners, often referred to as health service providers, for practice in settings under its jurisdiction, typically all nonschool settings within the state (e.g., mental health centers, hospitals, independent private practice). In some states the jurisdictional authority is less distinct.

Employment Characteristics and Services

School psychologists work predominately in school settings (at least 80%), under 9- or 10-month contracts (180–200 days). In 1999, their average salary was $49,000 per year. As school district employees, most are subject to the district's conditions and receive benefits and retirement packages similar to those of other district employees. Other school psychologists work in a variety of nonschool settings. Among them, 3% to 5% work full-time in private practice, and 3% to 4% in colleges or universities.

The referrals most commonly made to school psychologists come from children in the elementary school grades and are more often males than females. The referrals are associated with learning and behavioral difficulties that teachers and/or parents often suspect are related to one or more categories of disability within the regulations of the state education agency. Surveys of practitioners have consistently revealed that they spend at least 50% of their time in psychoeducational assessment activities related to special education referrals, perhaps 40% of their time in consultation and direct intervention activities, and the remaining 10% in research and evaluation, in-service instruction, and administrative duties.

Historical Periods Defined

Although derived from similar origins and early developments, contemporary school psychology is a specialty distinct from clinical, counseling, and educational psychology. The historical development of school psychology has been described as consisting of two broad periods, the Hybrid Years (1890–1969) and the Thoroughbred Years (1970–present) (Fagan & Wise, 2000). During the Hybrid Years,

school psychology was often a blend of educational and psychological practice; its dominant role was assessment to meet public education's need for diagnoses for special class placement. Even in the latter decades of this period, school psychology was a mix of practitioners trained and certified in various fields (e.g., clinical psychology, teacher education, and guidance counseling) as well as many whose training and experience were specifically in school psychology.

The Thoroughbred Years period differs from the previous period because of the rapid growth in the number of training programs, practitioners, and state and national associations, the expansion of literature, and increasing professional regulation from forces within and outside of the field. Collectively, these changes contributed to a stable professional entity known as school psychology. Since 1970, school psychologists have been more consistently employed in positions titled "school psychologist"; they work in states offering school psychology credentials to those who have completed training programs specifically in school psychology and accredited as such and whose trainers have been school psychologists. This greater uniformity has been modal in the Thoroughbred Years, although it could be observed in more advanced locales in the latter Hybrid Years, especially in urban and suburban areas (Mullen, 1967). The Thoroughbred period was not achieved simply because of an identity made possible by more purely bred school psychologists. The Hybrid Years had many persons who championed the cause and identity of school psychology despite their own backgrounds in clinical and educational psychology, teacher education, and guidance counseling. Among the notables were Harry Baker, Jack Bardon, Ethel Cornell, Susan Gray, Leta Hollingworth, Bertha Luckey, Grace Munson, Frances Mullen, T. E. Newland, Marie Skodak, and Percival Symonds.

THE HYBRID YEARS

The practice of school psychology did not start abruptly. Several factors contributed to the circumstances under which psychological services to schools emerged.

Factors Contributing to the Origins of Practice

Era of Reform

Several factors led to the origin of school psychology as a distinct discipline. Paramount among these was a post–Civil War era of reform marked by the rise of juvenile courts, the enactment of child labor laws, the growth of institutions serving children, the beginnings of the mental health, vocational guidance, and child study movements, and the enactment of compulsory school attendance laws for children. Collectively, these efforts reflected the improving status of children and youth in America and a growing commitment to the viewpoint that the welfare of our children was closely related to the long-term improvement of our society.

Compulsory Schooling

Compulsory schooling laws significantly influenced the conditions under which school psychological services developed. Over the course of American history, the responsibility for schooling had passed from parents in the home, to schooling outside of the home, and eventually to formally established, compulsory schooling. Even in the absence of compulsory attendance laws, school enrollments grew throughout the nineteenth century. The attendance reflected a growing need for education to help children and youth meet society's demand for educated employees to fill newer and more technologically demanding jobs. It also reflected the need to inculcate a sense of moral values and character to better ensure the survival of the nation. The concern for national survival was related to heightened U.S. immigration during this period. These and other forces spurred the compulsory schooling movement, and by 1920 all states had enacted such legislation. Thus, during the period 1890–1920, increasingly large numbers of children were thrust upon the public schools, many of whom had never before attended school in America or elsewhere before coming to America as immigrants. Between 1890 and 1930, public school enrollments increased from 12.7 to 25.7 million students, with secondary school enrollment increasing from 203,000 to 4.4 million. The average number of days in the school year increased from 135 to 173 (28%), and the average number of days attended increased from 86 (64% of 135 day year) to 143 (83% of 173 day year).

Special Education

The schools were not well prepared for such rapid change. The formal preparation of teachers was meager by contemporary standards, accreditation of programs and teacher credentialing were practically nonexistent, class sizes were large, facilities were often ill equipped and unhealthy, and large numbers of children had various mental, physical, and other disabilities that impaired their efforts to learn.

Estimates of the number of children with disabilities were large. For example, Wallin (1914) estimated that 12 million pupils were handicapped by one or more physical defects (e.g., defective vision or hearing, adenoids, teeth, lungs). Such conditions quickly led to medical inspections for school entrance. Noting the presence of other disabilities related to school learning (e.g., intelligence, memory, speech, sensation), Wallin called for psychological inspections as well. Wallin reasoned that if the child was to be compelled to attend school, then it was the state's responsibility to provide conditions under which the child could learn the material the state required him or her to learn. Compulsory schooling, which led to the mass education of children, in effect created the conditions under which other forms of educational treatments would be needed for children who failed to profit from the regular educational program. Thus was advanced the concept and practice of special education and the groundwork for what would become a growing separation of regular and special education throughout the twentieth century. The growth of special classes, usually segregated from the mainstream of regular education, was gradual but persistent. Dunn (1973) indicates that special education enrollment grew from 26,163 in 1922 to 356,093 in 1948 and to 2,857,551 by 1972. Today more than five million school children are in special education.

Rise of Experts

Compulsory schooling thus created a major community setting, the school, within which psychologists could choose to work. This was as significant to the future of school psychology as the promise of the Community Mental Health Centers Act of the 1960s was to clinical and counseling psychology. Moreover, the conditions of the children placed demands on educators that would require the addition of specialized personnel in several fields, including school psychology. These fields would soon be referred to collectively as pupil personnel services and would include attendance officers, truant officers, social workers, guidance counselors, vocational counselors, school health workers including nurses and physicians, speech and language clinicians, and psychologists. Schooling had not only become formalized outside of the home, but there were now various experts to assist an increasingly formally trained teaching force. Despite opposition from the scientific psychology community, the emergence of psychological science during this period influenced the rise of experts in applied psychology. Applied psychologists were part of a growing class of experts in many fields as knowledge expanded rapidly and one could no longer expect to manage the affairs of life without expert assistance. Real or illusory, this perception grew during the twentieth century, promoting the rise of psychological experts, specializations, and subspecializations.

Child Study Movement

Another potent factor in the origin of school psychological services was the child study movement. Influenced primarily by G. Stanley Hall, this movement served to sensitize parents and teachers to the importance of childhood and to the knowledge gained about children from research through observational and questionnaire methods. Hall was interested primarily in the normative aspects of the development of normal children and youth. By the beginning of the twentieth century, he had supervised or conducted dozens of normative research studies that helped to define the typical or normal child. The child study movement had chapters in several states, and conventions were held on child study topics. Hall founded several professional journals and is credited with founding the American Psychological Association (APA) in 1892 (Ross, 1972).

Educational Psychology

Hall's efforts and those of other psychologists of the period (e.g., E. L. Thorndike) fostered the emergence of educational psychology as a major field of psychological application. Educational psychology built upon the normative notions of child study and sought to provide educators broader understanding of how children learn, how curricula could be more efficiently arranged, and how schools could be better organized. Educational psychology also served to sensitize educators and parents to the contributions that psychology could make in the mass education movement (see e.g., Cubberly, 1909; Thorndike, 1912).

Clinical Psychology

Another highly potent factor was the emergence of clinical psychology. Although related to the child study movement, the emergence of clinical psychology is credited to Lightner Witmer, and its orientation was primarily idiographic. Witmer is considered to be the father of clinical psychology, having founded the first psychological clinic in this country at the University of Pennsylvania in 1896 (McReynolds, 1997). Where Hall was concerned about the typical development of schoolchildren, Witmer was most concerned with diagnosing and intervening on behalf of children who did not thrive in the regular educational environment of the mass education experiment. Witmer's efforts brought to the attention of educators and parents the importance of studying and designing interventions for individual children with one or more atypical characteristics. He worked in school settings on occasion and received numerous referrals from parents and educators. By

the early twentieth century, he was training persons to provide these services on a limited basis to schoolchildren. Though perhaps the first person to practice school psychology, Witmer never held that title, nor did he originate the term. Rather, the term "school psychologist" appears to have its origins in the German literature, first translated into English in 1911 (Stern, 1911).

Summary of Potent Factors

In summary, among the most potent factors creating the conditions for school psychological services were the changing status of children, the emphasis on the importance of childhood to saving adult society, and the central role of public schooling in that process. Indeed, almost every perceived failure or problem in society throughout the twentieth century led to curricular and other adjustments in our schools. These include food services for the poor, special reading programs, pupil personnel services, alcohol, drug, and tobacco prevention programs, special programs for teen pregnancy, delinquency and dropout prevention, and special education. Even curricula in home economics and driver education can be seen as reflecting societal needs.

In addition, the importance of children as emotional, as opposed to mainly financial, assets (see e.g., Zelizer, 1985) and the fact that they were housed for much of their childhood and youth in school buildings helped to create a new culture of childhood and adolescence that pervaded the twentieth century. The emergence of adolescence as a formal developmental stage and recognition of the significance of peer groups are, in part, a function of the mass education movement. Formal entry into adulthood for most children became delayed until the late teen years or longer, and it was educational facilities that served as warehouses for children and youth until such entry. Needless to say, the growth of elementary enrollments would lead to growth in secondary enrollments, then growth in the postsecondary colleges and universities, technical schools, and other forms of education. With this formal structure in place, the post–World War II baby boom would accelerate these developments. Applied psychologists would follow this trend, and by the late twentieth century, school psychologists were employed in preschool, elementary, secondary, and postsecondary educational settings.

The emergence of child study and clinical and educational psychology in the period 1890–1920 were symbiotic developments with the emergence of mass education. They were instrumental in advancing the organization of schools and their curricula and in drawing attention to the needs of atypical children through special educational programs. The disciples of pioneers like Hall and Witmer would bring together the knowledge and practices of these fields into school psychological services. Most notable among these disciples was Arnold Gesell, the first person to work with the title "school psychologist" within a part-time practice under the supervision of the state of Connecticut. His efforts built upon those of Witmer and Hall and helped to establish school psychology's connection to the individual psychoeducational diagnosis of children with school problems and their placement in special education. His practice from 1915 to 1919 bore numerous similarities to contemporary school psychology (Fagan, 1987).

Professional Developments (1890–1920)

In addition to the factors that led to the emergence of school psychology, several other professional developments between 1890 and 1920 contributed to the discipline's development.

Spread of Clinics

Witmer's clinical psychology and Hall's child study stimulated the rise of clinics in hospital, residential care, college and university, juvenile courts, and public school settings (Wallin, 1914). The first school-based clinic, the Department of Scientific Pedagogy and Child Study, was founded in 1899 in the Chicago public schools (Slater, 1980). Over time, this agency shifted from a nomothetic to a more idiographic clinical approach and still operates as the district's Bureau of Child Study. Cincinnati, Cleveland, Detroit, Los Angeles, New Orleans, New York, Philadelphia, Pittsburgh, Rochester, Seattle, St. Louis, and several other urban, and a few rural, school systems had clinics by the end of this period. The orientations of the school-based clinics were often nomothetic and idiographic; some carried names such as "bureau of educational research," while others were specifically clinical and referred to as psychological services. Thus, school psychological services developed from both idiographic clinical and nomothetic orientations. Contemporary school psychology continues to reflect both orientations as seen in the emphases on work with individuals and groups and the use of normative data and instruments within a clinical child study model. By the end of the period, several individual school districts had hired school psychologists to facilitate special educational placement of children, whether or not the district had a formal clinic.

Test Development

Perhaps no other factor contributed more to the early role and function of psychologists in schools than the development,

publication, and rapid popularity of normatively referenced psychological and educational tests. Emerging from procedures developed in laboratory settings, the use of tests gained ascendancy from the work of Alfred Binet, whose scales were widely used in this country following their modification and norming by Louis Terman in 1916. The Stanford Revision of the Binet-Simon Scales helped to define the segmentation of children for special education and was the hallmark of school psychology services for decades to come. Test development also occurred in academic achievement, vocational development, motor and sensory skills, and other areas. The testing movement was given additional impetus by the Army Alpha tests developed to select and classify recruits in World War I. These tests led to further development of group and individual tests in numerous skill areas, many of which were used with schoolchildren. The Binet scales were frequently used by Gesell and other school psychologists of the period. Psychoeducational tests, developed without the need for expensive and cumbersome laboratory instruments and procedures, provided a portability to psychological services that enhanced their development in several settings, especially in schools throughout the country (Fagan, 2000).

Organizational Development

Although founded in 1892, the APA had a small, predominantly doctoral level, membership, and avoided for several decades involvement in professional and applied psychology. Few school psychologists belonged to the APA, but perhaps some belonged to the National Education Association founded in 1870 (which added a section on child study in 1894). Of the 100 to 200 practitioners who provided psychological services in school settings during this period, most held no national membership, and few if any state-level or local organizations represented their interests. The American Association of Clinical Psychologists (AACP) was formed in 1917 to serve the interests of clinicians in various settings, but it was short-lived, disbanding in 1919 to become the clinical section of the APA, the first APA division.

Training and Credentialing

Formal programs of training and regulation through accreditation and state-level credentialing (licensing or certification) are among the major symbols of professionalization. At least for school psychology, and most of applied and clinical psychology, such symbols were absent in this period. Although there were a few clinical psychology training programs, including one developed by Lightner Witmer, no programs were specifically titled "school psychology." Child-study-related degrees under Hall at Clark University contributed to the knowledge of some who practiced in school settings, but this was not a "school psychology" program. Practical experiences were often available beyond the training programs in local clinics or institutions. The first formal internship appears to have been available as early as 1908 at the Vineland Training School in New Jersey (Morrow, 1946). Also absent were avenues for the formal granting of credentials to psychologists in school or other settings.

Literary Development

The availability of professional literature is among the few symbols of professionalization observable in this period, though no journals or books appear to have existed specifically for school psychologists. To the extent practitioners sought professional information, they would have read the available psychology journals (e.g., *American Journal of Psychology, Pedagogical Seminary, Psychological Bulletin*) and education journals (e.g., *School and Society, Journal of Educational Psychology*). Perhaps the most relevant journal was *The Psychological Clinic,* founded by Witmer in 1907.

Early Practice

This period lacked much theoretical development or a knowledge base for the diagnosis and treatment of children's disorders. Practitioners were operating largely from their own experience or that of mentors and used available laboratory and psychoeducational tests, including anthropometric measurements. Practice was oriented primarily toward observation and assessment of the child (e.g., a medical model) with consideration given to some extent to school-based and family influences. The dominant role of the school psychologist was assessment, with lesser emphasis on remediation or therapy and consultation. Research and evaluation, administration, and in-service education activities were also performed to some degree.

School psychologists were a mix of persons trained in psychology, teacher education, and related fields. They were hired by school boards to administer the newly developed Binet and other tests primarily to sort children into different educational programs and to foster the development of special education. Overall, the period 1890–1920 provided a prototype from which a more identifiable school psychology specialty would emerge. For all practical purposes, professional development in school psychology was meager throughout this period. Training, credentialing, literature, organizational development, and practice identity would advance considerably in the following decades.

Emergence of School Psychology as a Distinct Field (1920–1940)

The factors specific to school psychology's origins expanded during this period, and discernible trends for the future were established. Despite the financial woes of education during the Great Depression, employment opportunities for psychologists in schools expanded during this period. Although organizational representation continued to be unclear, school psychology literature contributed to the discipline's identity. Training opportunities and the emergence of specific credentials followed upon the growth of employment and special educational programs.

Organizational Development

Psychologists in New York State formed the New York Association of Consulting Psychologists in 1921. Interest in this group spread to other states, and in 1930 it was renamed the Association of Consulting Psychologists (ACP). In addition to several state affiliate groups, the ACP published a newsletter and, in 1937, founded the *Journal of Consulting Psychology* (now the *Journal of Consulting and Clinical Psychology*). In 1937, the ACP merged with the Clinical Section of the APA to form the American Association of Applied Psychologists (AAAP), which had specific sections for business and industry, clinical, consulting, and educational psychology (English, 1938). Psychologists practicing in school settings belonged to the clinical and/or educational sections. The dual representation reflected the origins of the field and its growing identity as a blend of both educational and clinical psychology. As yet, however, there was no clear identity for school psychologists in any national organization, and it is likely that most school psychological practitioners still did not belong to a national group. Even by 1940, there were no state-level organizations specifically for school psychologists, although many practitioners probably belonged to state affiliates of the AAAP (e.g., the Ohio Association of Applied Psychologists). Local psychology groups existed in some large cities as well.

Literary Development

With few exceptions, literature related to school psychology remained similar to that of the previous period. There were still no journals specifically about school psychology, and practitioners continued to read education and psychology journals. The addition of the AAAP's *Journal of Consulting Psychology* provided a more specific focus, however. It was also during this period that the first text about school psychology was published, *Psychological Service for School*

Problems by Gertrude Hildreth (1930). In addition, the first journal article including "school psychologist" in its title appeared early during this period (Hutt, 1923).

Training Program Development

For psychology trainees desiring to work in the schools, recommended curricula were available at several colleges and universities. In the late 1920s, New York University established the first programs specifically titled "school psychology" leading to undergraduate and graduate degrees and even the doctorate (Fagan, 1999). In the late 1930s, Pennsylvania State University also established graduate sequences for school psychologists, although a specific school psychology doctoral program was not available until much later. By the end of the period, few training programs were specifically titled "school psychology," and most personnel continued to be trained in general experimental psychology, educational and clinical psychology, and teacher-education-related programs.

Credentialing Development

Governmental recognition of psychologists providing services to public schools emerged in this period. The development of standardized tests to facilitate the proper placement and education of children made it necessary to impose some form of regulation on those who administered the tests. By 1925, the New York City public school system was offering a licensing examination for persons holding a master's degree from an institution recognized by the state's board of regents and who had at least 1 year of experience in mental measurement. Although specific evidence of credentialing is lacking, it is probable that several other major cities were also implementing some regulation. In some locales, especially smaller cities and rural settings, such regulation required no more than a teaching certificate and a special course in Binet testing; the experts were often referred to as "Binet examiners." The title "school psychologist" was growing in use but was not widespread.

State-level credentials for school psychologists were first approved in New York and Pennsylvania in the mid-1930s. Although the requirements did not include graduation from a training program in school psychology per se, recommended programs of preparation appropriate to such practice were included, as were expectations for fieldwork experience. Graduate-level work (which might lead to the master's degree) was expected in addition to an undergraduate degree. In Pennsylvania, practitioners were called "school psychological examiners" or "school psychologists" (depending on experience); in New York, they were called "school psychologists."

Characteristics of Practice

Specific practice information is provided in Hildreth (1930) and in her diary entries when she was a school psychologist for the Okmulgee, Oklahoma, schools (1922–1923). (The Educational Testing Service maintains her papers.) These and other retrospective accounts reveal an expansion of services from the previous period, though services were still dominated by the psychoeducational assessment role. Newly developed tests of achievement, as well as the Binet scales, revised in 1937 to include two forms (L and M), were in widespread and frequent use. Practitioners were also involved in group testing, academic remediation, adjustment services for children with social and emotional problems, and consultation, while administrative, in-service education, and research duties continued to take up small percentages of time. Watson's behaviorism had a discernible impact on educators, although it is unlikely that many practitioners were providing behavior modification services. In comparison to psychoeducational assessment services, therapeutic interventions, behavioral or psychodynamic, were not common among applied psychologists of this period (Loutit, 1939).

The 1935 New York State certification requirements specified the duties of the school psychologist:

> Subject to the direction and supervision of the superintendent of schools, to examine children for ungraded classes, classes of mentally retarded or gifted children and other special classes in which mental ability of the pupils is the main factor; diagnose learning difficulties of children and suggest remedial treatment; investigate causes of personality and social maladjustment; supervise the diagnostic and remedial measures and procedures used by teachers and supervisors in overcoming learning difficulties or social maladjustments of pupils, and advise and assist teachers and supervisors in the application of such measures; give pupils individual instruction in overcoming learning difficulties or other maladjustments and advise supervisors, teachers and parents with regard to the kind of instruction given to said pupils; confer with teachers and parents with regard to the learning and behavior problems of children; advise teachers, principals and the superintendent of schools with regard to all matters relating to psychological problems of children; and to related work as required. (Cooper, 1935, pp. 14–15)

The services described were probably more comprehensive than most school psychologists were able to provide at that time, especially in rural areas and in states less professionally advanced than New York. The Bureau of Child Guidance in the New York City schools and the Bureau of Child Study in the Chicago public schools are examples of comprehensive urban service delivery for that period (City of New York,

Board of Education, 1938; City of Chicago, Board of Education, 1941). These sources give clear indication that psychological workers were often providing remediation, counseling, and in-service instruction in addition to conducting regular and special education assessments.

Service delivery was increasingly provided by district-based psychologists. However, services through school and community clinics or research bureaus were common in large and medium-sized cities, and some rural areas were served through traveling clinics. In the latter model, services were provided by small teams of workers (e.g., a psychiatrist, a psychologist, and a social worker) traveling to small districts and providing evaluations, recommendations, and consultation on a periodic basis. Such services lacked the continuity that could be provided by a district served by its own school psychologist. By the end of the period, as many as 500 school psychologists may have been employed in connection with the schools.

Emerging Symbols of Professionalization (1940–1970)

Despite the general expansion of school psychology from 1920 to 1940, only a few symbols of professionalization were evident (training and credentialing), and they appeared in only a few locales. Even a code of ethics had yet to be officially adopted, although the APA would celebrate its 50th birthday in 1942. The period 1940 to 1970 would see the further expansion of these symbols and the emergence of others in the form of organizational identity, literature, professional recognition, and accreditation. By the mid-1960s, the field was rapidly expanding through training, credentialing, and employment that set the stage for the Thoroughbred Years to follow.

Organizational Developments

Participating in a broad effort to consolidate psychology groups to assist with government efforts during World War II, the AAAP, along with several smaller groups, merged with the APA in 1945. The new APA had 19 divisions, including the former divisions of the AAAP and Division 16, specifically for school psychologists (Fagan, 1993). Although the division struggled for survival during its first several years, it provided a national organizational identity for practicing school psychologists that had not been available in the AAAP. The division was weak in comparison to those serving clinical, educational, and counseling psychology. In part, this was because its members were divided in their loyalty to other divisions (many had previously belonged to the educational or clinical sections of AAAP) and because the division accepted as members only practicing school psychologists. The membership requirement limited the number of academics that could join the division, which also reduced its research contributions and scientific image. Owing to these weaknesses and the general lack of a clear identity, the division did not share in the professional advancements of clinical and counseling psychology until the late 1960s. For example, the division did not achieve the status of awarding a diploma in school psychology as part of the American Board of Professional Psychology (ABPP) until 1968, nor did it share in accreditation until the beginning of the next period.

Despite these weaknesses, the division accomplished many things. In 1953, the APA adopted a code of ethics, and the division was active in adapting the code to the needs of school practitioners. The division's convention programs and professional institutes were highly successful. It broadened membership to include academics and improved the status of nondoctoral members. A highlight of the period was the Thayer Conference of 1954, the proceedings of which were widely distributed (Cutts, 1955). The conference forged an identity for school psychology. It specified two levels of training and credentialing, with nondoctoral personnel expected to be under the supervision of doctoral-level school psychologists and to carry titles such as "school psychological examiner." Subsequently, standards for preparation at two levels and efforts to accredit programs at two levels were implemented but with little success.

Unlike clinical and counseling psychology, school psychology within the APA was unable to shed its nondoctoral practitioner advocacy, despite an allegiance to the doctoral requirement for full status as a psychologist. By the 1960s, fewer than 10% of the field's practitioners held doctoral degrees, and most positions were filled by persons with master's degrees who wanted better national and state-level representation than the APA or its state affiliates provided. The first separate state association for school psychologists was formed in Ohio in 1943. By 1970, 17 states had separate associations for school psychologists. In 1968, the Ohio School Psychologists Association organized a conference in Columbus, Ohio, attended by representatives of several states who chose to establish in 1969 a separate national group, the National Association of School Psychologists (NASP). In the same year, the Division of School Psychologists changed its name to School Psychology in order to reflect a broader representation of school psychology as a field of study in addition to persons who worked as school psychologists.

Literary Developments

More literature specific to school psychology was produced in this period than in all the previous periods combined. In addition to the Thayer Conference proceedings, a special issue of the *Journal of Consulting Psychology* (Symonds, 1942) focused on practice in the schools. The primary events, however, were the founding of the *Journal of School Psychology* in 1963 and *Psychology in the Schools* in 1964. School psychology finally had a literature of its own. The Division of School Psychology had a newsletter, as did the state associations, but their content and circulation were much narrower than these journals provided. Several books about school psychology were published in the 1960s. Many of these were philosophical in nature, describing the authors' viewpoints on the appropriate roles and functions of school psychologists and their training needs. The literature reflected the growing interest in the field, the need for texts in emerging training programs, and a continuing effort to clarify the field's identity (Fagan, 1986).

Training Developments

Although there were only a few programs at the beginning of this period, at least 18 (including 5 doctoral programs) were identified by the time of the Thayer Conference, and about 100 programs specifically on school psychology existed by 1970. However, APA accreditation of school psychology programs was not accomplished until 1971. Thus, during this period, programs were developed in the absence of official APA curriculum standards, although some programs used the guidelines being developed by Division 16 in its effort to achieve accreditation. Programs were more often developed to comply with the requirements for certification and licensure put forth by state-level education and psychology boards. By the end of this period, school psychology programs were widespread in the more populous states, especially east of the Mississippi River, and approximately 3,000 students were in training. Locally developed and uncoordinated efforts provided internships for trainees in most states, although a few, like Ohio, developed a statewide system of paid internships by the mid-1960s.

Credentialing Developments

As demand for practitioners grew, the need to regulate their services and preparation increased. State education agency credentialing of school psychological examiners and school psychologists grew quickly. Following the examples of New York and Pennsylvania, other states began credentialing school psychologists so that by the mid-1940s, 13 states had done so. That number increased to 23 states by 1960, and perhaps 40 by the end of the period. Few of these states followed the two levels of training, titles, and practice recommended by Division 16, choosing instead to require training below the doctoral degree, sometimes to include a bachelor's degree with additional graduate work or a master's degree with specific training, and in some instances requiring a teaching credential and/or experience. By the end of the period, however, the master's degree with training in school psychology was typical of credentialing requirements from state education agencies, and few states were requiring prior training as a teacher.

Credentialing for nonschool practice (e.g., community clinics, independent private practice) followed closely upon the success of the state education agencies. The first psychology credentialing by a state board of examiners in psychology (SBEP) occurred in 1945 in Connecticut. By 1960, 15 states achieved this, and 40 states had done so by 1969. These laws tended to follow closely the APA's expectations for the doctoral degree, with some states allowing the title "psychologist" at the master's level. Most states employed the term "psychological examiner" or "associate" for nondoctoral persons and restricted their practice or placed their work under doctoral supervision. The differing requirements of the SDE and SBEP restricted or barred the practice of most school-based school psychologists in nonschool settings. This set the stage for numerous state-level conflicts in the future.

Practice Characteristics

School psychology practice remained similar to the previous period, although its roles and functions in the area of therapeutic interventions and consultation expanded somewhat. Whereas World War I had launched the contributions of psychological testing, World War II launched the contributions of psychotherapy to war veterans and indirectly to school psychological practice. The period 1940–1970 brought to the fore the theories of Carl Rogers, Fritz Perls, Albert Ellis, and others in addition to the dynamic Freudian therapies. In addition, Skinnerian theory was advancing the position of behavioral psychology and its applications in behavior modification. The growth of therapeutic psychology was also heightened by the Community Mental Health Centers Act of 1963, which encouraged widespread development of community-based clinics for therapy in addition to psychological assessment.

The therapeutic expansion spilled over into the practice of school psychology, albeit on a much narrower scale than the traditional psychoeducational assessment role for special education eligibility. However, even the traditional role was broadened by the influx of new scales, such as the Wechsler intelligence scales; numerous personality assessment measures, including projective techniques; psychomotor and psycholinguistic scales; and the Binet scales, which were revised to a single form (L-M.). Their use was enhanced by the official recognition of learning disability as a special education category in the late 1960s.

The approach to practice was also expanding. The latter portion of the Hybrid Years was characterized by renewed interest in environmental influences on development and education. Child study expanded from its traditional focus on the child to a broader conceptualization of factors including the ecology of the school and family variables. School failure and child social and emotional problems were no longer viewed simply as failures of the child. Rather, such problems were also being attributed to teacher, classroom, family, and environmental factors.

The post–World War II baby boom quickly raised school enrollments and heightened the need for psychological assistance in developing special educational programs. Special education enrollments grew from 310,000 to 2 million during this period, increasing the demand for school psychologists. By 1950, there were about 1,000 practitioners, but by the end of the period the number had grown to 5,000. Practitioners worked primarily in school settings (public, private, residential), with only a fraction working in nonschool settings or independent private practice. With baby boom enrollments and mothers increasingly working out of their homes, day care and Head Start programs were established. As schools expanded kindergarten and other preschool programs, school psychology practice spread to those settings. School psychologists continued to be in demand because they were perceived as specialists employed to assist the school system in sorting children into more appropriate educational programs and services and providing interventions and consultation to children, their families, and educators.

Overview

The historical origins of school psychology from both psychology and education were clearly observable in the structure of the field by the end of the Hybrid Years. Two separate associations were now representing school psychologists at the national level. Separate state-level organizations affiliated with the NASP were established, whereas the state psychological associations affiliated with the APA. School psychology had achieved a literature distinct from mainstream psychology's literature, reflecting its need to have information and an identity that focused on psychological applications to schools and the problems of schooling.

Training programs were developing in psychology departments in colleges of arts and sciences but more rapidly in various departments of colleges of education. To the extent that program accreditation was discernible, it was emerging at the doctoral level from the APA and at the master's and doctoral levels from the National Council for Accreditation of Teacher Education (NCATE). Two systems of credentialing in school psychology were in place, one regulated by state departments of education and the other by state boards of examiners in psychology.

The prototypical developments of the early Hybrid Years had evolved into a distinct structure of school psychology by the end of the period. This structure would grow in strength and complexity during the Thoroughbred Years, but the two worlds of school psychology (education and psychology) and the two levels of training, titles, and practice would haunt the field for the remainder of the century and into the next.

THE THOROUGHBRED YEARS (1970–PRESENT)

The past 30 years of school psychology's development are characterized by strengthened identity, consolidation of national and state-level organizations, and acquisition of the symbols of full professionalization. Significant influencing factors include external and internal regulation of training and practice. Among the most influential has been the enactment of federal legislation regarding the management of information and the rights of persons with disabilities. Public Law 93-380, the Federal Educational Rights and Privacy Act of 1974, substantially changed the manner in which public and private agencies collected, maintained, and disseminated information, including school psychological records. Public Law 94-142, the Education for All Handicapped Children Act of 1975, mandated a special education in the least restrictive environment, including psychological services for all eligible children of school age. Subsequent amendments to this law broadened the age range of eligible children and the categories of special education. The most recent amendment was Public Law 105-17, the Individuals with Disabilities Education Act of 1997. These laws and their subsequent national and state-level regulations reflected a growing influence of the federal government in public education, an arena previously left largely up to state and local governments. The ripple effect of such external regulation on school psychology is observable in the content of training curricula, credentialing requirements, organizational advocacy and governmental relations, literary content, and practice.

Some of the external and internal regulation was in response to the changing structure of U.S. society. Increased immigration contributed to a more culturally diverse school population. School psychologists were particularly involved in programs of bilingual education, the teaching of tolerance, and especially the development of nondiscriminatory assessment practices. Maternal employment out of the home and the rapid rise of single-parent families, largely as a result of divorce, also had an impact on schooling and psychological services. These were related to concerns for "latchkey" and "at-risk" children that necessitated school psychological services along lines of intervention and consultation (see later discussion of practice).

Finally, the practitioner workforce was also growing in cultural diversity, but by the turn of the twenty-first century it was still predominantly Caucasian. Efforts to improve minority representation have been moderately successful. Women were always well represented in school psychology, perhaps always at least 30% of practitioners. Many held high-ranking administrative positions in school districts and directed departments of psychological services. Female representation in the field increased rapidly after the 1960s and was more than 70% by the late 1990s. In the Thoroughbred Years, women quickly acquired positions of leadership in the NASP, the APA, and state associations, as well as editorships and training program faculty positions.

Organizational Development

Professional progress related to school psychology organizations is one of the most dramatic historical developments of the Thoroughbred Years. The NASP, with fewer than 1,000 members in its first year, grew to more than 21,000 by the year 2000 and dominated the organizational development of the period. However, it struggled in its first decade to establish a base beyond itself in public advocacy and governmental relations. Instead, the period 1970–1980 was characterized by internal achievements, including a code of ethics, standards for training, credentialing, and service provision, publications, conventions, and practitioner representation. Although its efforts in governmental relations were noteworthy, particularly those efforts connected to the federal legislation mentioned above, in the 1980s such efforts gained in stature. In the 1990s, these efforts blossomed with a strong Washington, DC, presence after the NASP established its headquarters in the DC area (Fagan, Gorin, & Tharinger, 2000).

Among the NASP's many accomplishments in this period, two are paramount in contributing to professionalization. The first was its persistent effort with the NCATE to jointly and separately recognize training programs that met NASP standards. This was achieved within the NCATE's revised procedures for unit accreditation and for programs that were in institutions that did not participate in NCATE accreditation. By the late 1980s, the NASP had reached an agreement with the NCATE to identify NASP-approved programs at both the doctoral and specialist degree levels. By 1999, approximately half of all training programs were so approved (Fagan & Wells, 2000). The second was the success of its National Certification in School Psychology (NCSP) program, which gave individual practitioners recognition for completing training consistent with the NASP's standards. More than 50% of NASP members held the NCSP during the 1990s.

Within a decade of its founding, NASP became the dominant representative group for school psychologists at the national level, although it shared in several collaborative efforts with the APA and its Division of School Psychology. Descriptions of NASP history are found in *School Psychology Digest* (volume 8, number 2), *School Psychology Review* (volume 18, number 2), Fagan (1993, 1994), Fagan and Bose (2000), and Fagan, Gorin, and Tharinger (2000).

The Division of School Psychology still could not capture a representative practitioner membership. However, most trainers, especially those connected to doctoral programs, held membership in the division, often also holding membership in NASP. The division's total membership persisted in the range of 2,300–2,800 throughout the period. As an official governance unit within the APA and accepting APA policies with regard to doctoral training, credentialing, and practice, the division consolidated its advocacy for doctoral school psychology, succeeded in gaining a stronger representation on key APA boards and committees, and gained approval for doctoral program accreditation, resulting in the first accreditation of a program at the University of Texas in 1971. The growth of APA-accredited school psychology programs was slow but steady beyond 1980, and by 1999 there were more than 50 accredited programs (Fagan & Wells, 2000). Accounts of the division's history appear in Fagan (1993, 1996) and Fagan, Gorin, and Tharinger (2000).

The policies of the NASP and the APA included sharp differences regarding the legitimacy of the nondoctoral practitioner. These differences were at the center of most controversies among the NASP, the APA, and the APA's Division of School Psychology. They influenced policies and negotiations on matters of training, credentialing, titles, and practice. For example, accreditation conflicts between the NCATE and the APA led to the establishment in 1978 of the APA-NASP Task Force, now titled the Interorganizational Committee (IOC). Although such differences have yet to be resolved, the

IOC has been an effective vehicle for several collaborative efforts between these organizations.

Although NASP was a dominant force in many areas and held a commanding membership representation of school psychologists (perhaps 70%), the Division of School Psychology continued to be an important representative of school psychology to the broader arena of American psychology within the APA. In addition, the division was the dominant force in doctoral-level program accreditation and advocacy efforts exclusively on behalf of doctoral school psychology. By the 1990s, the NASP and APA Division 16 had achieved a more comfortable relationship, despite their major policy differences (Fagan, Gorin, & Tharinger, 2000).

With the assistance of NASP, state associations for school psychologists thrived. While there were just 17 associations at the end of the Hybrid Years, there were at least 50 by the late 1990s, almost all of which had formally affiliated with NASP. In almost every state, two systems of organizational representation now existed via the state psychological association and the state school psychological association. In a few states, the school psychology affiliate was a part of the state psychological association. In most states, however, they were entirely separate and often in bitter competition over practice privileges and credentialing. Every state's psychological association was affiliated with the APA. The network of NASP state affiliates allowed the NASP a ready avenue for promoting its positions, products, and advocacy efforts throughout the country. The Division of School Psychology had little or no effectiveness in doing this because state psychological associations did not affiliate directly with APA divisions, and in most states few school psychologists belonged to the state psychological association. The differences in the effectiveness of such networks for the NASP and the division were observable in the aftermath of their jointly sponsored futures conferences in 1980 and 1981 (see Brown, Cardon, Coulter, & Meyers, 1982; Ysseldyke & Weinberg, 1981).

Organizational developments outside the United States were also occurring. Originating in the early 1970s, the international school psychology movement led to the establishment of the International School Psychology Association in 1982. Relatedly, the Canadian Association of School Psychology (CASP) was founded in 1985. Both groups conduct annual meetings and have affiliate organizations (see Fagan & Wise, 2000, chapters 9 and 10).

Literary Development

Literary development followed quickly upon the expansion of the 1960s. The NASP founded its *School Psychology Digest* (now the *School Psychology Review*) in 1972 as a member subscription journal, and it has one of the largest circulations of all psychology journals. The Division of School Psychology-APA founded *Professional School Psychology* (now *School Psychology Quarterly*) in 1986. The division's journal was an indirect outgrowth of its monograph series in the 1970s. Both groups improved the content and size of their newsletters and provided other products in print and nonprint media. The NASP developed an array of products specifically for school psychology training programs and practitioners, and the APA conducted a broad expansion of its publications. Both groups published codes of ethics, standards, and reference materials (e.g., membership, training, and credentialing directories). Division 16 produced several "Conversation Series" interviews on videotape that were used in training programs in the 1990s. Also of interest to literary expansion in the United States was the founding of *School Psychology International* in 1979 and the *Canadian Journal of School Psychology* in 1985.

Numerous books on school psychology and related topics were published, including those that were revised periodically, for example, *Best Practices in School Psychology* (Thomas & Grimes, 1995) and *The Handbook of School Psychology* (Reynolds & Gutkin, 1999). In contrast to earlier periods, there were a considerable number of books on consultation, intervention, and service delivery alternatives.

Communication among school psychologists was spurred as well by the widespread use of computers with Internet and electronic mail capacity. Organizations, journals, school systems, university programs, and many school psychologists disseminated information via Web sites and listservs.

National efforts were reflected at the state association level as well. The state school psychology associations produced a mass of literature and products of their own, including widely disseminated newsletters. Whereas school psychologists during the Hybrid Years had suffered a dearth of communication, the Thoroughbred Years approached communication overload, especially in print and Internet communication. In addition, practitioners with subspecialty interests often garnered information beyond the core school psychology sources. It was indeed the "information age" for all of psychology.

Training Development

Training programs expanded rapidly in the 1970s, and for the remainder of the period between 200 and 230 institutions were offering programs at the master's, specialists, and doctoral levels. Program standards were proffered by the NASP that were in contrast to those of the APA. Both organizations offered procedures for program approval and accreditation.

By 2000, the NCATE, with the NASP as a constituent member, was the largest accreditor of nondoctoral programs, although the APA maintained a stronger presence among doctoral programs and related internship and postdoctoral training sites. The Thoroughbred Years were characterized by much greater consistency in training curricula, the standards for which were increasingly interlocked with the credentialing expectations of the state education and psychology boards.

Doctoral programs offered subspecializations (e.g., neuropsychology, preschool) to coincide with the broadening interests and practices of school psychologists and their diverse practice settings. Many subspecializations were represented in special-interest groups within the NASP and the APA. Some even had their own publications. As the number of subspecializations expanded, there was concern that the traditional specialties of clinical, counseling, and school psychology might lose their identities because subspecialization often merged the interests of two or more specialty groups (e.g., school and child-clinical psychology along lines of pediatric applications).

Credentialing Development

By the mid-1970s, all states had credentialing for school psychologists from their respective state departments of education (SDE) and/or state boards of examiners in psychology (SBEP). The two credentialing structures had standards that differed along lines of doctoral and nondoctoral preparation, titles, and practice settings. The differences created several state-level skirmishes over practice privileges in nonschool settings. Some states (e.g., California, Connecticut, Illinois, Ohio) achieved nonschool practice privileges for nondoctoral practitioners as an outcome of state-level legislative skirmishes. Nevertheless, by the end of the period, credentialing for school-based practice was almost entirely regulated by SDEs with nondoctoral degree training requirements, whereas nonschool practice was almost entirely regulated by SBEPs with doctoral degree requirements. Nonpractice recognition credentials continued to be available from the APA in the form of the diploma from the American Board of School Psychology (ABSP) and from the NASP in the form of National Certification in School Psychology (NCSP).

Practice Characteristics

Concern for the appropriate roles and functions of school psychologists was a dominant theme in the literature of the Thoroughbred Years. Throughout the twentieth century, school psychology practitioners expressed concern at being

identified as "gatekeepers" for special education by virtue of their expertise with psychoeducational tests. Calls for change, even reform, of the school psychologists' roles permeated the Thoroughbred Years. In the early 1970s, the thrust was for school psychologists to become more system focused and to be child advocates within the system. This thrust was related to the general zeitgeist of the 1970s to "change the system," whether it was the system of our schools, special education, school psychology, or government. It was a rebellious period in American history, and school psychology was no exception. The systems and organizational psychology approach to school psychology was popular (see e.g., Maher, Illback, & Zins, 1984), but the historical legacy of school psychology was reaffirmed in the service expectations required by federal legislation for children suspected of being eligible for special education. In retrospect, this legislation and its reauthorizations, although creating thousands of new school psychology jobs, pitted the field against itself: The longtime desire to expand roles and functions clashed with the need to provide mandated traditional services for job survival.

Local, state, and national surveys of how school psychologists spent their time consistently revealed that half to two-thirds of their time was devoted to psychoeducational assessment related to eligibility for special education. These results were observed even during a period of public education and school psychology reform in the last two decades of the century (Reschly, 1998). Comparisons are uncertain, but the psychoeducational assessment role during the Hybrid Years was probably more intense than recent studies have revealed. Nevertheless, it is clear that the assessment role dominated practice throughout the twentieth century. Of course, uniformity of practice was never observed. Evidence for consultation, intervention, research and evaluation, and other roles has always been available. The Thoroughbred Years were fraught with literature, expert opinion, and organizational positions that did broaden the roles of school psychologists, even if not to the extent many desired. For its part, the assessment role was broadened through improved technical adequacy of normative tests, an emphasis on criterion-referenced methods, nondiscriminatory practices, team approaches to service delivery, and mandatory reevaluations.

The model of child study continued to evolve and broaden. Throughout the century, a gradual but persistent expansion of the factors involved in referrals is discernible (Fagan, 1995). In addition to the long-standing focus on the child, assessment and intervention functions expanded in the Thoroughbred Years to more consistently include classroom and teacher variables, parental and family variables, and broader theoretical perspectives on traditional testing (e.g., neuropsychological and cognitive theories). Skinnerian behaviorism, traceable to the influences of Thorndike and Watson in child study many decades before, had a strong impact on school psychology. Its offshoot, cognitive behavior modification, found even greater acceptance by emphasizing cognitive interactional variables of the child and the environment. Broader forms of theoretical application, including reciprocal determinism, constructivist developmental psychology, and ecological psychology, seemed well established by the turn of the twenty-first century. School psychologists, supported by the work of other pupil personnel specialists (e.g., guidance counselors, speech and language clinicians, social workers) were conducting more comprehensive assessments that were better connected to interventions than observed in the Hybrid Years.

The "gatekeeper" perception had been countered by team approaches, especially prereferral approaches, and by the persistent indication that school psychologists were spending at least 25% to 40% of their time in consultation and intervention roles. These results reveal an expansion of the consultation and intervention roles from data earlier in the period (Farling & Hoedt, 1971). Part of this expansion seems attributable to the widespread concern for "at-risk" students during this period as opposed to the long-standing concern for students suspected of being eligible for special education. At-risk students (e.g., those living in poverty or single-parent homes, students with pregnancy, substance abuse) demanded nontraditional school psychological services, including consultation and interventions with students and educators in the regular education program. Another factor was the necessity for crisis intervention skills that developed rapidly in the 1990s in response to a series of school violence incidents across the country. Thus, since 1970, broader roles for many school psychologists developed despite continued and persistent demand for the traditional roles associated with special education services.

Overview

The Thoroughbred Years brought to fruition the symbols of professionalization emerging in the Hybrid Years and several symbols not attained until after 1970. It was an era of establishing an identity for the field despite conflicting points of tension along dimensions of doctoral and nondoctoral practice, credentialing, and training. The field has survived its divided organizational viewpoints and has continued to thrive. Among doctoral psychology specialties, it has gained a position of parity sought for many decades. Among nondoctoral psychology groups, it is without peer for recognition and stability. Nondoctoral school psychology may even have

established the model for how other nondoctoral psychology groups (e.g., mental health workers) could better manage their conflicts over training and credentialing.

As school psychology matured, tensions developed along other dimensions related to practice. These included the use of traditional normatively referenced tests versus the use of nontraditional, criterion-referenced methods such as curriculum-based assessment; viewing practice as primarily related to issues of school instruction and learning versus a school mental health orientation; viewing one's training orientation as primarily based in education versus in psychology; practicing as a specialist versus as a generalist; emphasizing traditional psychoeducational assessment roles versus consultation and intervention roles. These lines of tension have not seriously threatened the vitality of school psychology. Rather, they have signaled the diversity of the field and its resilience against adopting a single model for its future. The diversity is observed in the field's organizational structures, literature, practice settings, training programs, and subspecialty development. The field has established an identity that was only emerging in the late Hybrid Years and is now poised to solidify its position among the specialties of psychology and school-based pupil personnel services in the twenty-first century.

A COMMENT ON THE FUTURE

Hindsight is everything, and forecasting the future is risky. Nevertheless, the following general opinions about the future of school psychology in the coming two decades are offered. A strong demand for school psychologists provides a favorable employment market. The practitioner workforce may grow to 35,000, but there will be a strong need for new practitioners to replace retiring personnel. Unless the number of graduates increases substantially, school districts find others to provide psychological services, or such services are perceived to be less needed, the current personnel shortage is expected to continue. The field should take decisive action to increase the number of students in training to better provide the needed supply of future practitioners and trainers. This effort should include stronger recruiting by training programs and the adjustment of accreditation and credentialing requirements, which were increasing at the same time that personnel shortages were becoming more acute.

The NASP and the APA Division of School Psychology will continue as the dominant national-level representatives and continue to struggle at the national and state levels over policy differences. The NASP will grow to at least 25,000 members and the division to perhaps 3,500. They will maintain their state affiliations and advocacy programs much as they are. Though many in the field would like to see a united force for school psychology achieved by a merger of the NASP and the Division of School Psychology-APA, this is a very remote possibility.

The literary growth of the field will level off, at least in quantity. There are enough journals and newsletters to maintain the field for many years, and additional journals specific to school psychology are unnecessary. Books will continue to be produced as training program needs dictate, and additional books will be written along lines of expanding specialties, subspecialties, proficiencies, and practitioners' personal interests. The Internet and electronic media will offer new, and unfortunately less regulated and refereed, outlets for practitioner information. The Internet as a source of information for practitioners and trainers will be vast but will force the consumer to be better educated about methodologies and distinguishing personal opinion and testimonials from authoritative opinion and data-based outcomes. At least as far as school psychology Web sites and listservs are concerned, the field should develop guidelines to regulate the quality of information available.

The number of training programs will not increase in any appreciable way. Master's-degree-only programs will fade out of existence as specialist-level programs become the norm. The NASP/NCATE will continue as the dominant accreditor of these programs. Doctoral programs will grow in number to about 100 in the United States. Although both the NASP/NCATE and the APA will continue to accredit doctoral programs, the APA will continue its dominant position. All levels of programs should increase recruitment efforts to graduate more students to meet the current and future shortage of practitioners. A strong effort should be made to increase the number of doctoral graduates interested in academic careers.

Changes in credentialing will be more qualitative than quantitative. The two systems of credentialing (SDE and SBEP) will continue with occasional struggles for practice privileges. Recognition credentials (NCSP, ABSP) will increase in popularity and may be extended to specialized groups such as the supervisor credential being considered by NASP. More states will recognize the NCSP in granting practice credentials. Efforts should continue to alleviate tensions between state education and state psychology credentialing boards by broader recognition of the legitimate role of non-doctoral psychology practitioners.

Contemporary tests of ability, achievement, adaptive behavior, social skills, and personality will retain their market share. Technical adequacy of tests will continue to improve, and the significance of cognitive and neuropsychological theories will continue to develop. Nevertheless, nontraditional assessment methodologies will maintain a strong appeal as school systems are increasingly held accountable for the procedures of assessment and intervention and the instructional outcomes of students.

The basic roles of school psychologists will remain. Practice will continue to focus on individual child study with interventions delivered one-on-one or in groups. Pharmacological and genetic test developments will increase in importance, necessitating additional training and team efforts in service delivery. Contemporary interventions of remediation and therapy will be supplemented by these developments. Consultation will continue at its present level, failing to expand in priority because of personnel shortages and the priority of assessment and other intervention services. Role and function changes should ensure that school districts continue to have sufficient diagnostic and intervention services available to the entire school population.

Finally, the field should conduct a futures conference to better define its goals and directions. The conference should be sponsored by several major organizational constituencies and seek to alleviate policy differences among them. Additional discussions of the future of school psychology appear in Fagan and Sheridan (2000), Fagan and Wise (2000), Oakland and Cunningham (1999), a special issue of *Psychology in the Schools* (2000, volume 37, number 1), and Ysseldyke, Dawson, Lehr, Reschly, Reynolds, and Telzrow (1997).

ADDITIONAL RESOURCES

There are several sources of information for studying the history and contemporary development of school psychology. An overview of the sources, including associations, archival collections, literature, and nonprint media, is available in Fagan (1990). Association records for the Division of School Psychology are available from the American Psychological Association in Washington, D.C., and the Archives of the History of American Psychology maintained at Akron University in Ohio. Those for the National Association of School Psychologists are maintained in the Special Collections of the University of Memphis Libraries in Memphis, Tennessee. Trends in the field's development as judged from its literature are available in Fagan (1986), Fagan, Delugach, Mellon, and Schlitt (1985), French (1986), Frisby (1998), Kraus and Mcloughlin (1997), and Whelan and Carlson (1986). An account of the field's general history is available in *School Psychology: Past, Present, and Future* (Fagan & Wise, 2000), including Canadian and international accounts and an edition in French (1984, 1990). Rhodes (2000) describes the status of school psychology in Mexico. Historical events, persons, and terminology appear in the *Historical Encyclopedia of School Psychology* (Fagan & Warden, 1996). Contributions of women appear in French (1988) and Hagin (1993). A fairly complete literary collection of newsletters, journals, books, and organizational publications is maintained by the author. The NASP publishes a code of ethics, standards for training, credentialing, and service provision, and a directory of school psychology training programs (Thomas, 1998) and of state-level credentialing requirements (Curtis, Hunley, & Prus, 1998). Finally, the most recent information is available on various Internet sites, including, www.apa.org, www.indiana.edu/~div16, and www.naspweb.org.

REFERENCES

American Psychological Association. (1998). *Psychology: Careers for the 21st century.* Washington, DC: Author.

Brown, D. T., Cardon, B. W., Coulter, W. A., & Meyers, J. (1982). The Olympia proceedings. *School Psychology Review, 11,* 107–214.

City of Chicago, Board of Education. (1941). *Bureau of Child Study and the Chicago Adjustment Service Plan.* Chicago: Author.

City of New York, Board of Education. (1938). *Bureau of Child Guidance five year report 1932–1937.* New York: Author.

Cooper, H. (1935, June 1). *Certification Bulletin No. 3, Certification for school services: Laws, rules, regulations, and information.* Albany: University of the State of New York Bulletin.

Cubberly, E. P. (1909). *Changing conceptualizations of education.* Cambridge, MA: Riverside Press.

Curtis, M. J., Hunley, S. A., & Prus, J. R. (Eds.). (1998). *Credentialing requirements for school psychologists.* Bethesda, MD: National Association of School Psychologists.

Cutts, N. E. (Ed.). (1955). *School psychologists at mid-century.* Washington, DC: American Psychological Association.

Dunn, L. M. (1973). An overview. In L. M. Dunn (Ed.), *Exceptional children in the schools: Special education in transition* (pp. 1–62). New York: Holt, Rinehart and Winston.

English, H. B. (1938). Organization of the American Association of Applied Psychologists. *Journal of Consulting Psychology, 2,* 7–16.

Fagan, T. K. (1986). The evolving literature of school psychology. *School Psychology Review, 15,* 430–440.

Fagan, T. K. (1987). Gesell: The first school psychologist. Part 2: Practice and significance. *School Psychology Review, 16,* 399–409.

Fagan, T. K. (1990). Research on the history of school psychology: Recent developments, significance, resources, and future directions. In T. R. Kratochwill (Ed.), *Advances in school psychology* (Vol. 7, pp. 151–182). Hillsdale, NJ: Erlbaum.

Fagan, T. K. (1993). Separate but equal: School psychology's search for organizational identity. *Journal of School Psychology, 31,* 3–90.

Fagan, T. K. (1994). A critical appraisal of the NASP's first 25 years. *School Psychology Review, 23*(4), 604–618.

Fagan, T. K. (1995). Trends in the history of school psychology in the United States. In A. Thomas & J. Grimes (Eds.), *Best practices in school psychology* (Vol. 3, pp. 59–67). Washington, DC: National Association of School Psychologists.

Fagan, T. K. (1996). A history of Division 16 (School psychology: Running twice as fast). In D. A. Dewsbury (Ed.), *Unification through division: Histories of the divisions of the American Psychological Association* (Vol. 1, pp. 101–135). Washington, DC: American Psychological Association.

Fagan, T. K. (1999). Training school psychologists before there were school psychologist training programs: A history—1890–1930. In C. R. Reynolds & T. B. Gutkin (Eds.), *The handbook of school psychology* (pp. 2–33). New York: Wiley.

Fagan, T. K. (2000). Practicing school psychology: A turn-of-the-century perspective. *American Psychologist, 55,* 754–757.

Fagan, T. K., & Bose, J. (2000). NASP: A profile of the 1990s. *Communique, 29*(2), 10–11.

Fagan, T. K., Delugach, F. J., Mellon, M., & Schlitt, P. (1985). *A bibliographic guide to the literature of professional school psychology 1890–1985.* Washington, DC: National Association of School psychologists.

Fagan, T. K., Gorin, S., & Tharinger, D. (2000). The National Association of Schools Psychologists and the Division of School Psychology–APA: Now and beyond. *School Psychology Review, 29*(4), 525–535.

Fagan, T. K., & Sheridan, S. (2000). Miniseries: School psychology in the 21st century. *School Psychology Review, 29*(4), 483–605.

Fagan, T. K., & Warden, P. G. (Eds.). (1996). *Historical encyclopedia of school psychology.* Westport, CT: Greenwood.

Fagan, T. K., & Wells, P. D. (2000). History and status of school psychology accreditation in the United States. *School Psychology Review, 29*(1), 28–51.

Fagan, T. K., & Wise, P. S. (2000). *School psychology: Past, present, and future* (2nd ed.). Bethesda, MD: National Association of School Psychologists.

Farling, W. H., & Hoedt, K. C. (1971). *National survey of school psychologists.* Washington, DC: National Association of School Psychologists.

French, J. L. (1984). On the conception, birth, and early development of school psychology: With special reference to Pennsylvania. *American Psychologist, 39,* 976–987.

French, J. L. (1986). Books in school psychology: The first forty years. *Professional School Psychology, 1,* 267–277.

French, J. L. (1988). Grandmothers I wish I knew: Contributions of women to the history of school psychology. *Professional School Psychology, 3,* 51–68.

French, J. L. (1990). History of school psychology. In T. B. Gutkin & C. R. Reynolds (Eds.), *Handbook of school psychology* (pp. 3–20). New York: Wiley.

Frisby, C. L. (1998). Formal communication within school psychology: A 1990–1994 journal citation analysis. *School Psychology Review, 27*(2), 304–316.

Hagin, R. A. (1993). Contributions of women in school psychology: The Thayer report and thereafter. *Journal of School Psychology, 31,* 123–141.

Hildreth, G. H. (1930). *Psychological service for school problems.* Yonkers-on-Hudson, NY: World Book.

Hutt, R. B. W. (1923). The school psychologist. *Psychological Clinic, 15,* 48–51.

Kraus, T., & Mcloughlin, C. S. (1997). An essential library in school psychology. *School Psychology International, 18,* 343–349.

Loutit, C. M. (1939). The nature of clinical psychology. *Psychological Bulletin, 36,* 361–389.

Maher, C. A., Illback, R. J., & Zins, J. E. (Eds.). (1984). *Organizational psychology in the schools: A handbook for professionals.* Springfield, IL: Charles C. Thomas.

McReynolds, P. (1997). *Lightner Witmer: His life and times.* Washington, DC: American Psychological Association.

Morrow, W. R. (1946). The development of psychological internship training. *Journal of Consulting Psychology, 10,* 165–183.

Mullen, F. A. (1967). The role of school psychologists in the urban school system. In J. F. Magary (Ed.), *School psychological services in theory and practice: A handbook* (pp. 30–67). Englewood Cliffs, NJ: Prentice-Hall.

Oakland, T. D. (2000). International school psychology. In T. K. Fagan & P. S. Wise, *School psychology: Past, present, and future* (2nd ed., pp. 355–381). Bethesda, MD: National Association of School Psychologists.

Oakland, T. D., & Cunningham, J. (1999). The futures of school psychology: Conceptual models for its development and examples of their applications. In C. R. Reynolds & T. B. Gutkin (Eds.), *The handbook of school psychology* (pp. 34–53). New York: Wiley.

Petition for reaffirmation of the specialty of school psychology. (1997, March 5). Washington, DC: American Psychological Association.

Reschly, D. A. (1998, August). *School psychology practice: Is there change?* Paper presented at the annual convention of the American Psychological Association, San Francisco.

Reynolds, C. R., & Gutkin, T. B. (Eds.). (1999). *Handbook of school psychology* (3rd ed.). New York: Wiley.

Rhodes, R. L. (2000). School psychology and special education in Mexico: An introduction for practitioners. *School Psychology International, 21*(3), 252–264.

Ross, D. (1972). *G. Stanley Hall: The psychologist as prophet.* Chicago: University of Chicago Press.

Slater, R. (1980). The organizational origins of public school psychology. *Educational Studies, 2,* 1–11.

Stern, W. (1911). The supernormal child: II. *Journal of Educational Psychology, 2,* 181–190.

Symonds, P. M. (Ed.). (1942). [Special issue]. *Journal of Consulting Psychology, 6*(4).

Thomas, A. (Ed.). (1998). *Directory of school psychology graduate programs.* Bethesda, MD: National Association of School Psychologists.

Thomas, A., & Grimes, J. (Eds.). (1995). *Best practices in school psychology* (Vol. 3). Bethesda, MD: National Association of School Psychologists.

Thorndike, E. L. (1912). *Education: A first book.* New York: Macmillan.

Wallin, J. E. W. (1914). *The mental health of the school child.* New Haven, CT: Yale University Press.

Whelan, T., & Carlson, C. (1986). Books in school psychology: 1970 to the present. *Professional School Psychology, 1,* 279–289.

Ysseldyke, J., Dawson, P., Lehr, C., Reschly, D., Reynolds, M., & Telzrow, C. (1997). *School psychology: A blueprint for training and practice II.* Bethesda, MD: National Association of School Psychologists.

Ysseldyke, J., & Weinberg, R. (1981). The future of psychology in the schools: Proceedings of the Spring Hill Symposium. *School Psychology Review, 10,* 116–318.

Zelizer, V. A. (1985). *Pricing the priceless child: The changing social value of children.* New York: Basic Books.

CHAPTER 21

Community Psychology

BIANCA D. M. WILSON, ERIN HAYES, GEORGE J. GREENE, JAMES G. KELLY, AND IRA ISCOE

EARLY DEVELOPMENTS   431
   The 1950s: Social Ferment and the Incubation of
      Community Psychology   432
   The 1960s: Social Upheaval and the Birth of
      Community Psychology   433
   From Community Mental Health to
      Community Psychology   434
   The Swampscott Conference   435
STRENGTHS OF PERSONS AND COMMUNITIES   435
ECOLOGICAL THEORY   436
   Ecological Inquiry as a Defining Focus for
      Community Psychology   437

Ecological Assessment   438
Tensions around the Need to Address Diversity
   in Ecological Research   439
PREVENTIVE INTERVENTIONS   440
   Prevention as a Defining Focus for
      Community Psychology   441
   Tensions around Two Types of Prevention Research:
      Prevention Science and Action Research   442
CONCLUSION   443
REFERENCES   444

EARLY DEVELOPMENTS

The field of community psychology began formally at a conference in Swampscott, Massachusetts, on May 4 to May 8, 1965. The National Institute of Mental Health (NIMH) invited 39 psychologists to attend the "Swampscott Conference" to discuss training in community mental health, a rapidly emerging health movement. A major impetus for this conference was that Congress was directing federal funds to create new opportunities for mental health professionals to staff community mental health centers. For conference participants, the guiding question was, *"What were the roles for psychologists in such centers?"*

Rather than focusing on this question, something unusual happened at the conference. Participants shifted the agenda and instead discussed how psychologists could play broader and more active roles in communities. The conference participants advocated for a new field of psychology on the

premise that such a field required additional roles than those present in the community mental health movement (Bennett et al., 1966; Meritt, Greene, Jopp, & Kelly, 1997). In the 35 years since Swampscott, community psychologists have continued to expand the ways in which psychologists impact communities through theory, research, and action.

With this chapter we will frame the development of the field of community psychology in a historical and social context. The history of community psychology is not just a history of professional developments but also a history of the interaction of social events and the development of community psychology. The evolution of community psychology has been coupled with events in U.S. history beginning at least 20 years before the field was founded. In viewing the emergence of the field, we will underscore historical events such as World War II, the growing malaise of the 1950s and 1960s, and the increasing discontent with the postwar ideals of economic opportunity, personal fulfillment, and happiness. We will examine professional movements such as the community mental health movement and note expanding conceptualizations of mental health and the delivery of health services. We will also present a sampling of events in the United States that stirred the nation's awareness of social problems, such as racism and sexism. These topics, in particular, will illustrate how social conditions and social problems can serve as catalysts for citizens and policy makers to cope

Many persons took the time to comment on early and final drafts: Khari Hunt contributed to the prevention topics. James Dalton, Paul Dolinko, Jack Glidewell, Rob Jagers, Chris Keys, Don Klein, Murray Levine, Betty Lindemann, Thom Moore, Bob Newbrough, S. Darius Tandon, Susan Ryerson-Espino, Ed Trickett, Dana Wardlaw, Rod Watts, Rhona Weinstein, and Chris Wellin gave helpful suggestions on early drafts.

more competently with many social-psychological problems facing America.

We contend that specific moments and movements in American history leading up to the Swampscott Conference suggest bases for the interests of citizens, including psychologists, to create such a distinct enterprise as community psychology. At this point in the short history of the field, it is not certain how directly these events influenced the field. However, we expect that that external societal issues, along with internal issues within the profession of psychology, have contributed to the challenging and robust nature of the field of community psychology. We hope that by highlighting some of these social events and movements, future scholars can build from this framework and continue to illuminate and further specify the confluence of historical events and processes that have contributed to the evolution of community psychology—a field that has worked to contextually ground our understanding of psychological processes.

Following a review of some of these sociocultural events, particularly those of the 1950s and 1960s that preceded the emergence of the field, we will describe the founding of the field and articulate the historical and empirical evolution of three defining domains of the field. These domains include focusing on the *Strengths of Persons and Communities,* which has served as a guiding value of the field; *Ecological Theory,* which has developed as the major theoretical framework of the field; and *Preventive Interventions,* which have grown as the action arm of the field. Though these three domains are closely identified with the evolution of the field in a number of community psychology textbooks (e.g., Dalton, Elias, & Wandersman, 2000; Heller, Price, Reinherz, Riger, & Wandersman, 1984; Levine & Perkins, 1997), we seek to expand on the field's conceptualization of these concepts in terms of these relationships throughout the chapter.

The 1950s: Social Ferment and the Incubation of Community Psychology

The conventional view among psychologists is that the founding of the field of community psychology was a "'60s phenomenon." Accordingly, the turbulence of this decade roused citizens and professionals to believe that communities were important sources of well-being and that mental health services should be directed at the level of the community rather than at the level of the individual (Reiff, 1971). In contrast, the 1950s are often perceived as peaceful times, relatively free from turmoil. Against this myth, we contend that cultural and historical events in the 1950s created a sensitivity and consciousness about injustices that provided the basis for more direct attacks on social issues 10 years later. To this end, Halberstam (1993) identified the 1950s as a source of change.

"Social ferment . . . was beginning just beneath the placid surface" (p. ix). Events of the 1950s foreshadowed future issues of social dislocation, discontent, and unrest (Gitlin, 1987). Moreover, according to Kennedy (1999), "The social and economic upheavals of wartime laid the groundwork for the civil rights movement as well as for an eventual revolution in women's status" (p. 857). These assertions testify to the significance of the post-World War II 1950s as a major era of incubation for the future of community psychology.

The Economic Boon and the GI Bill

Buoyed by a positive mood stimulated by the Allied victory in World War II, the postwar economic boon and the GI bill brought affordable housing, jobs, and educational opportunities to war veterans that were unprecedented in U.S. history (Chamberlain & Robinson, 1997; Glidewell, 1995; Greenberg, 1997; Kiester, 1994; Tuttle, 1993). The establishment of the GI bill in part reflected a national priority to increase educational opportunities for all citizens. This prioritization and valuing of higher education was markedly increased in 1957 when the Russians defeated the United States in the race to launch an orbiting satellite into space. To help keep the United States competitive with the Soviet Union, policy makers supported education, science, and technology more then ever (Chomsky, 1997).

With the benefits provided by the GI bill, a generation of over seven million returning war veterans, some of whom were aspiring social scientists, were able to enter their chosen profession as a result of tuition-free education, stipends, and home loans provided by the GI bill (Greenberg, 1997). These opportunities for a college education contributed to the major growth of the professions, including the social sciences. Many war veterans pursued graduate education, and for those who obtained their PhD degrees, faculty positions were often available because of the postwar economic boon and popular demand for higher education. However, along with these very positive national emphases on education and scientific discovery, the nation was struggling with significant social turmoil.

Race Relations

The educational opportunities and supportive atmosphere that resulted from the economic boon and the GI bill were mostly available for white males. As Ellison (1947) revealed, racial minorities were "invisible" in spite of the breakthroughs that included the heroics of Jackie Robinson and Willie Mays in baseball, Althea Gibson in tennis, and the presence of Ralph Bunche at the United Nations. Based on a history of prejudice and discrimination, the dominant social norms of the United States marginalized the achievements of African Americans.

For many white Americans, the mid-1950s was a time in which the nation's history of discrimination against African Americans and other socially oppressed groups could no longer be ignored. The U.S. Supreme Court decision in *Brown vs. Board of Education* in 1954 declared that separate schools for white and black children were unconstitutional and marked the beginning of the end of the Jim Crow laws, originally enacted to force separation between the black and white races. This bold and monumental judgment set into motion a civil-rights movement that was more visible to white Americans, with the aid of the media in its role as a wide disseminator of information (Payne, 1995, 1997). "Those two forces—a powerful surge among American Blacks toward greater freedom, mostly inspired by the Brown decision, and a quantum leap in the power of the media—fed each other; each made the other more vital, and the combination created what became known as 'The Movement' " (Halberstam, 1993, p. 429). Contrasting the simmerings of the civil-rights movement, and in particular the greater visibility of the social injustices faced by black Americans, prime-time television programming "reflected a world of warm-hearted, sensitive, tolerant Americans, a world devoid of anger and meanness of spirit, and of course, failure" (Halberstam, 1993, p. 514). Watching televised news and entertainment was no doubt a disorienting experience for viewers trying to juxtapose these different and conflicting images of the nation. Moreover, television news coverage of racist events made the country's unsolved problems of racism more visible and threatening to the postwar happiness.

One powerful example of the confluence of the power of media and the growing civil-rights movement was the television coverage of the Montgomery bus boycott after Rosa Parks refused to sit in the back of a racially segregated bus in Montgomery, Alabama, in 1955. The nationally televised coverage documented both the success of the planned boycott and recognition of the leadership Martin Luther King Jr. and the women's leadership group of Montgomery (Robinson, 1987). The triumph of this nationally visible event was a catalyst for more public awareness, particularly in the North, of the civil-rights movement, which had been active in the South for several decades (Payne, 1995).

Increasing Malaise and Discontent

During this decade, more and more Americans felt incomplete, puzzled, or unhappy, if not depressed (Halberstam, 1993). Information was becoming easily available that documented the limitations of the post–World War II dream of the long-awaited placid life. Events such as the McCarthy hearings, the Korean War, and the duplicity in the U.S. State Department undermining democracy in Guatemala contributed to the feeling that, in fact, the country was facing serious problems (Halberstam, 1993; Herman, 1999; Rovere, 1996; Schrecker, 1998; Zinn, 1999). Additionally, popular novels like *The Man in the Grey Flannel Suit* (Wilson, 1955) and *Peyton Place* (Metalious, 1956), as well as the investigative research of Betty Friedan (1963) on the social and economic restraints of women, questioned the sense of justice in the lives of U.S. citizens. Further, the groundbreaking inquiries into American sexual behavior by Alfred Kinsey (1948, 1953) augmented Friedan's reporting to raise awareness about gender and sexual inequalities. Alternatively, advances in reproductive biology by Gregory Pincus and Hudson Hoagland created the birth control pill Enovid (Asbell, 1995; Watkins, 1998). Clare Boothe Luce captured the significance of the Pill when she said, "Modern woman is at last free as a man is free, to dispose of her own body, to earn her living, to pursue the improvement of her mind, to try a successful career" (Halberstam, 1993, pp. 605–606). Each of these significant cultural events stimulated increased awareness about societal problems as well as provided new opportunities to pursue individual freedoms.

In sum, Americans' beliefs, values, and goals in the 1950s were being confronted; the alleged happiness with existing gender roles and race relations were being questioned. Americans were being forced to see the extent of violence and racism that was prevalent. Members of the mental health professions were also taking notice of these negative features of American society. The eyes of these professionals were being forced open. These events signified serious issues in the country that needed addressing; it seems plausible that a zeitgeist was emerging that called for a closer inspection and appraisal of America's communities.

The 1960s: Social Upheaval and the Birth of Community Psychology

The issues of the 1950s that were becoming more visible to the average citizen intensified during the 1960s. During the late 1950s and 1960s, it was significant that throughout the world "so many things happened at once" and that "ordinary people had taken action" (Marwick, 1998, p. 803). The simultaneous occurrence of political events and social movements is a unique and significant chapter in U.S. and world history (Howard, 1995; Isserman & Kazin, 2000). Todd Gitlin, sociologist and coauthor of the Port Huron Statement of the Students for Democratic Society, organized the first national demonstration against the Vietnam War. He summarized the spirit of the times of the 1960s and highlighted the significance of these powerful social movements and processes as the field of community psychology was being founded:

> Freedom was far from the only objective that brought the sixties to a boil. The other was an amalgam of equality and fraternity—in particular, solidarity with the poor and the low caste. The civil rights movement was the seedbed, the War on Poverty a continuation, and a host of other projects from the Peace Corps to the revolutionism of the Third World, whatever their obvious differences, rang variations on the same theme. Throughout the variations, the hope was to regenerate a public sphere: to universalize political rights; to move the grass roots closer to power; to animate public-mindedness; to oppose illegitimate authority in the name of a public that was the proper source of sovereignty. Individualism was suspect, value was placed on cooperativeness, collective projects, and at the maximum, "the beloved community." (Gitlin, 1997, pp. 291–292)

Embedded in the social upheaval of the 1960s was the founding of the field of community psychology. Below are a few events from 1965, the year of the Swampscott Conference and the dawn of a new psychology:

- A second mass civil rights march from Selma to Montgomery, Alabama followed under National Guard protection.
- President Johnson sent troops to Vietnam.
- Over 20,000 protesters attended a rally in Washington, DC against the Vietnam War sponsored by the Students for a Democratic Society.
- Poet Robert Lowell and others boycotted the White House Festival of the Arts in protest against the Vietnam War.
- Cesar Chavez organized and unionized agricultural workers in California.
- President Johnson signed the Voting Rights Act of 1965 into law.
- 20,000 faculty and students attended a teach-in, organized by the Vietnam Day committee on the University of California–Berkeley campus.
- The first draft card was publicly burned at a New York protest organized by the War Resister's League.
- Malcolm X was assassinated (Glennon, 1995; Morgan, 1991).

From Community Mental Health to Community Psychology

The community mental health movement, which began in earnest after the end of World War II, was evolving at the same time as the civil-rights movement, the second wave of the women's movement, and protests against the Vietnam War. The visibility of these political movements increased the overall interest of citizens to be actively involved in their communities and to become more informed about the policies and social norms for justice. In addition to the long-standing tradition of organizing in nonwhite and poor communities, a history of grassroots community organizing was gaining momentum in white and educated communities. As these movements increased their visibility and impact, more and more people became active in their local communities and in discussing or debating these national events. The American consciousness was being raised about the importance of community.

In the context of the tumultuous events at the community, societal, and political arenas throughout the 1950s and 1960s, the mental health professions began to recognize the value of an expanded perspective on the causes of and solutions to mental health problems. The legitimacy of prevention of mental health problems was presented in *Action for Mental Health* (1961), a report published by the Joint Commission on Mental Illness and Health, which was established in 1955. Also in 1955, the NIMH convened a conference at Stanford University (the "Stanford Conference"), which advocated for more community and preventive services in contrast to individual psychotherapy. Illustratively, at this conference, Erich Lindemann, a Harvard psychoanalyst, presented his community approach to the delivery of mental health services in Wellesley, Massachusetts (Strother, 1956, 1987).

By the early 1960s, NIMH, the primary source of funds for the community mental health movement, was increasing its efforts to develop a national agenda for community-oriented mental health services. This agenda was developed under the leadership of Robert Felix, the director of NIMH and a public-health-trained psychiatrist who had planned the initiative since the NIMH was created in 1949. In 1963, federal legislation was passed (Public Law 88-164) that enabled communities to apply for funds to construct community mental health centers, and in 1965, Congress amended the legislation to provide grants for staffing these centers. NIMH staff members were particularly interested in seeing that the core mental health professions—psychiatry, psychology, social work, and nursing—received training to ensure the quality of these future community mental health services. During this time, the community mental health movement also served as the impetus for attention to mental disabilities as a national issue and helped to provide states with funding to assist families and family members living with mental disorders.

Throughout the 1960s, community-oriented psychologists expressed discontent within the profession of clinical psychology (Korchin, 1976; Maher, 1988); psychotherapy was viewed as too narrow a professional role by an increasing number of community-oriented clinical psychologists. The Chicago Conference on the Professional Preparation of Clinical Psychologists (August 27 to September 1, 1965) affirmed the research role for the clinical psychologist, encouraged more training in child-clinical psychology, and noted community psychology as one of the "new developments in clinical psychology" (Hoch, Ross, & Winder, 1966). The discontent with clinical psychology was a major contributing issue that broadened the professional boundaries of clinical psychology to consider community approaches to mental health. Public Law 88-164 was the capstone for the community mental health movement (Levine, 1981; Wagenfield, Lemkau, & Justice, 1982). The law authorized federal matching funds of $150 million over a three-year period for use by states in constructing comprehensive community mental health centers. These events created the primary context that led to the convening of the Swampscott Conference in 1965, which was aimed at increasing training opportunities for psychologists to do community mental health work.

The Swampscott Conference

The Swampscott Conference, as mentioned, occurred at a time when ordinary citizens were actively addressing various forms of discrimination, racism, sexism, and classism in their communities. There was increasing interest among some psychologists and NIMH staff for all mental health professions to become community oriented. Among mental health professionals, it was apparent that the community mental health movement had the potential to connect to these other social movements and to promote social change.

At the conference, a growing consensus emerged among the 39 invited participants that there was value, if not necessity, for psychologists to move beyond the worldview of the medical field, particularly from psychiatry. In contrast to a medical emphasis, conference participants hoped that psychologists would be doing research and designing prevention programs in the community, following a public health or community development orientation. They hoped to enable citizens to be active participants in improving the strengths of their communities. Many of the participants were excited that a community perspective, which many had already adopted individually, was now being proposed as a valid role for psychologists (Klein, 1987). The conference affirmed the desire for psychologists to be in the community as "participant conceptualizers" (Bennett et al., 1966). Following the conference, organizers sent a report to chairs of all departments of psychology across the country detailing aspects of the

conference and recommendations for training psychologists to do community mental health work. In 1967, the Division of Community Psychology (Division 27) was established within the American Psychological Association (APA), and Robert Reiff was appointed the first president (Meritt et al., 1997). The division evolved into its current structure as the Society for Community Research and Action as well as continuing to be affiliated with the APA. These developments, along with creating biennial meetings and establishing communication methods to members, are discussed in Meritt et al. (1997).

Soon after the circulation of the Swampscott report, M. Brewster Smith and Nicholas Hobbs (1966) prepared a very important statement on the role of psychology and the community mental health center. They wrote, "The more closely the proposed [community mental health] centers become integrated with the life and institutions of their communities, the less the community can afford to turn over to mental health professionals its responsibility for guiding the center's policies" (M. Smith & Hobbs, 1966, p. 501). This statement, endorsed by the Council of Representatives of the American Psychological Association in March 1966, independently affirmed the values of the Swampscott participants.

In sum, this section described the establishment of the field of community psychology. We propose that earlier cultural and historical events and circumstances are important contexts to help understand the field's beginning at the 1965 Swampscott Conference. Furthermore, these same cultural and historical events have provided a context for the emergence of three major domains of the field, whose histories are presented below. The first, working with the *strengths of persons and communities,* has served as a guiding value for the field's development. Second, *ecological theory* has provided a theoretical framework for the work that community psychologists do. Finally, designing and conducting *preventive interventions* has become the primary way in which community psychology research has been translated into action. Each of these three will be explored below.

STRENGTHS OF PERSONS AND COMMUNITIES

Throughout the course of the history of health and social sciences, there has been a trend of moving from a deficits perspective toward an emphasis on positive development of people and their communities. More specifically, the strengths perspective, and how it should be both defined and addressed, has been discussed among community psychologists over the past 35 years since Swampscott (Bennett et al., 1966; Chavis, 1993; Cowen, 1997, 2000b; Glidewell, 1977;

Iscoe, 1974; Kelly, 1970, 1971, 2000; Klein, 1968; Novaco & Monahan, 1980; Spivak & Shure, 1974, 1989). Within community psychology, the development of a strengths perspective has involved identifying the need to focus on the strengths and resources of community structures and individual community members. The movement toward a strengths perspective has involved terms from different areas of knowledge. Relevant terms have included *psychological health* (Jahoda, 1953, 1958), *psychological wellness* (Cowen, 1994, 1997, 2000b), *competence* (Danish, 1983; Glidewell, 1977; Iscoe, 1974; Spivack & Shure, 1989), and *resilience* (Garmezy, 1991). For the purposes of this paper the term "strengths" will be used to represent this perspective. This perspective has served as a guiding principle for community psychologists in their attempts to develop theory and plans for action research. While a number of scholars have pursued a strengths perspective as a specific research agenda (Cowen, 1997; Spivak & Shure, 1974, 1989; Weissberg, Caplan, & Harwood, 1991), attention to this principle as a central value in the field's overall development has not been made explicit.

Highlighting both personal and community strengths and resources became a priority for a number of researchers even before the Swampscott Conference in 1965 (Bennett et al., 1966; Cottrell, 1964; Jahoda, 1953, 1958; Lindemann, 1953; Ojemann, 1957; White, 1952, 1959). Prior to the Swampscott Conference, some participants were active in "such diverse areas of national life as the Peace Corps, the anti-poverty effort, [and] a broad movement into the field of education" (Bennett et al., 1966, p. 4). These social change activities began to stretch the traditional professional roles of psychologists, as well as the relationship between psychologists and other community members who were not "clients." Experiences such as these urged psychologists to recognize and appreciate the various strengths and resources that both communities and their members possessed.

Lindemann's Wellesley Project, as mentioned earlier in this chapter, is an early exemplar of how social science could pull together available community resources to promote the mental health of community members (Lindemann, 1953). The project began in 1948 and served as a model for shifting the focus from disease to health. Understanding how personal and community resources build on each other became imperative to the success of the Wellesley program. Similarly, Marie Jahoda, a social psychologist, proposed a focus on the psychological health of individuals rather than a focus on disease (1953, 1958). She advocated moving the definition of psychological health beyond that of the absence of mental disease, statistical normality, psychological well-being, or sheer successful survival. Instead, Jahoda discussed defining psychological health in context: "Psychological health . . .

manifests itself in behavior that has a promise of success under favorable conditions" (1953, p. 351). In this way, she supported investigating the environmental factors that both facilitated and inhibited people from being successful, and helped to launch research on individuals' adaptive coping strategies. Jahoda's conceptualization of mental health validated the emerging strengths perspective.

Like Jahoda, Cottrell (1964), a sociologist, called for an understanding of mental health in context, which required a major shift in emphasis from traditional psychiatric training or practice. In writing about the problems facing individuals, Cottrell argued that the clinical solutions quite often held by psychiatrists were "not likely to be comprehensive enough for the requirements of the situation" (p. 392). Cottrell called for a revolution in the way psychiatrists both approached and dealt with people's problems. This "revolution" involved identifying and strengthening the resources of communities: "It is my expectation that in helping American communities to discover the ways and means to become articulate, knowledgeable, effective in achieving consensus on values and their implementation, we are developing potent capabilities for coping effectively" (Cottrell, 1964, p. 398). Similar to Lindemann (1953), Cottrell believed that communities rather than psychiatrists would be best equipped to deal with the issues faced by their members.

Lindemann, Cottrell, and Jahoda, though not explicitly identified as community psychologists, provide examples of social scientists moving beyond a deficits focus. They redefined our conceptualization of health as not just the absence of illness and laid the groundwork for future community psychologists to apply a strengths perspective to community research and action. As will be evident, throughout the evolution of the field's theory and prevention research, this tenet of community psychology has remained a consistent theme.

ECOLOGICAL THEORY

As noted in the introduction, community psychology was cultivated during a period in which social inequalities were being challenged because of their link to the health and mental illness of individuals and the disintegration of communities. Commensurate with this philosophy of social change experienced at a societal level, community psychologists have advocated for understanding "human competencies and problems . . . within the social, cultural, and historical context" (Meritt et al., 1997, p. 74). This orientation, discussed in terms of an ecological framework, represents one of the major theoretical frameworks guiding the field of community psychology. This framework reflects a focus on the strengths of individuals and a value in keeping communities healthy as a means of improving the human condition. Representing the current consensus on the importance of ecological context is this quote from Kenneth Maton's 1999 Society for Community Research and Action Presidential Address: "Change in individuals alone, transient changes in setting environments, and interventions that do not ultimately impact community and societal environments cannot in and of themselves make much of a difference" (Maton, 2000, p. 26). This section will review the 35-year evolution of theory and methods that articulate the relationship between the individual and her or his surrounding environment within the field.

Examining individual behavior embedded in various social contexts has been a defining feature of community psychology even before the field's "official conception" in 1965 (Bennett et al., 1966). During the 1950s, environmental factors became widely acknowledged as substantial forces that had impacted individual behavior and adjustment during World War II as mental health professionals began to understand the impact of war experiences on veterans' mental health (see this chapter's opening section; Duffy & Wong, 1996; Ridenour, 1961; Sarason, 1978; Strother, 1987). Also during this period, Kurt Lewin (1951), a social psychologist, asserted his theory of human behavior that made the role of environmental influence on individual behavior explicit (see Swartz & Martin, 1997). In the field of ecological psychology, Roger Barker (1963), a student of Lewin's, also opposed traditional psychological research that allowed "us to be content with a psychology of people to the neglect of a psychology of the environment of people" (p. 13). His research program sparked discussions among psychologists on the extent to which immediate settings were the primary determinants of behavior patterns (Holahan, Wilcox, Spearly, & Campbell, 1979). Influential in Barker's thinking about the continuum along which the varying fields of psychology fall in their approach to studying behavior was the work of Egon Brunswick (Barker, 1963). The empirical work of Lewin and Barker, in addition to the rarely acknowledged writings of Brunswick, influenced the future direction of community psychology theory and set the tone for extra-individually oriented psychological study. It is important to note that another parallel contribution to contextual thinking was the emergence of the field of environmental psychology at about the same time as community psychology (see Stokols, 1992; Stokols & Altman, 1987).

Another influence on the "trend" to think contextually was the series of Milbank Conferences held between 1952 and 1961. For example, the 1952 Milbank conference, "Interrelations between the Social Environment and Psychiatric Disorders," was very influential as it provided the historical basis

for discussions about the person-in-context phenomenon at the 1965 Swampscott Conference (Klein, 1987). This Milbank conference surveyed nine research projects that examined the epidemiology of mental disorders and advocated the use of community resources to address mental health issues. One project discussed was Erich Lindemann's Human Relations Service of Wellesley. From his work on this project, Klein explicitly described some of the functions of the community and how these functions, such as providing and distributing living space and shelter, distributing necessary goods and services, maintaining safety and order, and educating and acculturating newcomers, could impact community members. In this way, Lindemann and Klein took great steps toward establishing how the community could be seen and explored as a resource or strength in the development of individuals.

In the early 1960s, Seymour Sarason, a clinical psychologist by training, was showing psychologists how to do community-based work (Levine, Reppucci, & Weinstein, 1990; Reppucci, 1990; Sarason, 1995). The Yale Psycho-Educational Clinic that he directed illustrated an approach to intervention that targeted settings rather than individuals alone (Sarason, 1972, 1976; Sarason, Levine, Goldenberg, Cherlin, & Bennett, 1966). Sarason contributed greatly to the field's emphasis on contextual factors and made explicit the relationship between individual behavior and community settings. The innovative work of Sarason and Lindemann set the stage for ideas expressed at the Swampscott Conference more than 10 years later and fostered the work of future ecologically minded community psychologists.

Ecological Inquiry as a Defining Focus for Community Psychology

At the 1965 Swampscott Conference, community psychology was launched, and the goal to understand the context in which human behavior occurs was hailed as one of the field's primary focuses. As noted in the Swampscott report, the new field of community psychology was defined as "the study of general psychological processes that link social systems with individual behavior in complex interaction" (Bennett et al., 1966, p. 7). The topic of the social environment was omnipresent at the conference because of prior scholarly and professional activities such as the convening of the prior Milbank Conferences, the creation of the NIMH, and the recruitment of psychologists dedicated to these new initiatives within the NIMH. Despite the seemingly unanimous consensus on the valuing of contextual analysis, issues of training and practice for community psychologists prompted discussions around such questions as "Through what frameworks should community psychologists conduct ecological and contextual analyses?"

Following the Swampscott Conference, the answer to this question has primarily been the "Ecological Framework." Though the history of ecological theory began, in practice, in the 1930s with the work of Lewin (see Swartz & Martin, 1997), the tradition of ecological thought in the context of community psychology research and intervention began in the 1960s with the work of James G. Kelly and colleagues (Kelly, 1966, 1968; Trickett, Kelly, & Todd, 1972). Inspired by Barker, Kelly's (1967, 1968) translation of concepts from biological ecology to the human social system gave community psychologists a theoretical framework for both research and intervention from which they could begin to conceptualize persons-in-context. Kelly (1970, 1971, 1986) discussed the purpose of ecologically oriented community research to understand those social processes that promote the health and well-being of individuals and organizations: "The prospect of obtaining knowledge about the positive development of persons in natural settings could be increased if psychologists worked to create empirical data about the ways in which communities evolve and how they establish criteria and norms" (Kelly, 1971, p. 135). He suggested that future community psychologists be trained to recognize the existing resources in communities and understand how these resources contribute to the success of community members. Understanding these processes has many implications for intervention initiatives, as intervention efforts are expected to be more successful when focused on supporting the natural strengths in a community (Cowen, 2000b; Kelly, 1968; Kelly et al., 1988).

To illustrate, one setting selected to elaborate the ecological perspective was schools (Chesler & Fox, 1966; Edwards & Kelly, 1980; Kelly, 1968; B. E. Long, 1968; Schmuck, Chesler, & Lippitt, 1966; Trickett et al., 1972). These authors worked to identify systems-level resources and their impact on the positive development of children. Specifically, Kelly and colleagues (1968, 1979; Edwards & Kelly, 1980) applied the framework to expand the understanding of the impacts of high school settings on students' behaviors and advance thinking on the use of natural resources of high schools. These scholars made meaningful contributions to the process of conceptualizing and researching human behavior with their sharp contrast to traditional psychological modes of conducting research in which "context stripping" has been part and parcel in methods of experimental design (Mishler, 1979, p. 2).

Within the field of developmental psychology, the work of Urie Brofennbrenner made another contribution to the field's conceptualization of the person-in-context. Though this theory evolved after and separately from the ecological metaphor described by Kelly and his colleagues, Bronfenbrenner's developmental-ecological model also departed from Barker's work in the 1950s. He supported the idea that "human development is a product of interaction between the growing human organism and its environment" and critiqued the larger field of psychology for focusing on "the person and only the most rudimentary conception and characterization of the environment in which the person is found" (Brofenbrenner, 1979, p. 16).

Following the theoretical and empirical work of Barker, Kelly, and Brofenbrenner, the emphasis on studying context and its influence on a person's behavior became formalized in community psychology. However, issues arose in applying these concepts to conducting research. Tensions arose around the extent to which the field was still wedded to individually oriented research and practice. Beginning in 1967, a series of conferences began to address these concerns. As Ira Iscoe (1997) said, "There was a noted malaise that Community Psychology was not moving ahead . . . and such terms as the need to abandon psychic determinism for a recognition of the environmental factors was stressed" (p. 7). In 1975, the Austin Conference was sponsored by the University of Texas at Austin and NIMH to "critically assess the many problems facing community psychology and to examine community psychology's conceptual independence from both clinical psychology and community mental health" (Iscoe, 1975, p. 1193). The planning committee of Iscoe, Bernard Bloom, Charles Spielberger, and Brian Wilcox invited 139 participants with an emphasis on recruiting new PhD's and ethnic minority psychologists (Iscoe, Bloom, & Spielberger, 1977). Again the field was hearing the call to address the lack of innovation in contextual analysis.

Ecological Assessment

Though discontent within the field around its insistent preoccupation with individual-oriented variables was expressed, several notable scholars at the time paved the way to assessing contextual variables. In the 1970s, Rudolph Moos and Edison Trickett were among the first to develop methodologies for assessing context with the "environment scales." Various forms of this scale have been developed to assess the perceived climate of different environments such as classrooms (Trickett & Quinlan, 1979), family environments (Moos, 1974; Moos & Moos, 1984), work settings (Moos, 1974), and group settings (Moos, 1974). The valuable work of Moos and his colleagues made explicit the role of the environment in the study of behaviors of individuals. Though Moos and Lemke (1996) later expanded the conceptualization of environmental assessment, a critique of this approach had been that the scales were truly reflective of setting members' ratings of satisfaction with the setting rather than actual characteristics of the setting (see Linney, 2000, for a more detailed discussion).

As the field matured into the 1980s, community psychologists began to advocate for the development of more methods that would assess the environment at an extra-individual level (Seidman, 1988; Shinn, 1990) and have devoted conferences, such as the 1988 Chicago Conference, to issues of theories and methods within the community psychology framework. At this conference, particularly notable was Edward Seidman's discussion of "social regularities," a theoretical construct that attended to the variation of individual behavior across contexts and over time (Linney, 1986; Seidman, 1988, 1990).

Furthering the theories established by the ecological framework, which highlight communities and their strengths, Chavis & Wandersman (1990) discussed improving the fit between people and their communities. Instead of focusing on the "people" part of the equation, they focused on the communities: "Strengthening the ability of these institutions to live up to the dreams of their members must be our goal" (Chavis, 1993, p. 172). Whitman, White, O'Mara, and Goeke-Morey (1999) also studied how the environment can assist in or detract from the development of infants. Contradicting previous assumptions that these infants were unaffected by their surroundings, they showed how to build on existing environmental resources to positively impact their development. Identifying environmental resources and how they may contribute to this positive development continues to be an important goal for community psychologists.

Tensions around the Need to Address Diversity in Ecological Research

In addition to assessing environments, both physical and psychological, community psychologists have also sought to integrate ecological theory into research through the study of culture. Steele, Trickett, and Labarta (1981) suggested that a focus on culture is congruent with an ecological approach because "attention paid to the interaction of person and environment, provides a framework from which to examine the functional aspects of behaviors and structures in culturally diverse environments" (p. 5). This line of inquiry seeks to contextualize knowledge of individual behavior.

As yet, community psychology as a discipline has not made substantial progress to understand social problems in the context of cultural norms and values. Community psychologists are part of a larger context of psychologists that have long been criticized for not respecting diversity and viewing deviations from white culture as problematic. Kingry-Westergaard

and Kelly (1990) argued that this disparity could be resolved if community psychologists abandoned their positivist mindsets and attended to the varying realities in which people live and behave. Echoing the contextualist framework posited by Kingry-Westergaard and Kelly, Trickett, Watts, and Birman (1994) suggested that the very reason that community psychology has not addressed issues related to diversity is psychologists have been resistant to shifting their paradigms to a more contextualist perspective. An example of an exemplary recent effort is the work of Morris, Shinn, and Dumont to identify contextual factors affecting the organizational commitment of diverse police officers. One of their findings indicated that ethnicity and gender were important factors in understanding police officers' organizational commitments (Morris, Shinn, & DuMont, 1999).

Congruent with the contextualist philosophy and ecological theory, the use of qualitative methods in community psychology research has gradually become more widespread. In the early 1980s, with the work of Holahan and Moos (1982), community psychologists were publishing qualitative work in the field's peer review journals (Cherniss, 1989; McGhee, 1984; Potasznik & Nelson, 1984). Methodologies that most often require qualitative methods of analysis, such as participant-observation and the use of narratives, have been used to understand and describe social settings (Rappaport, 1995). In 1998, K. Miller and Banyard edited a special issue of the *American Journal of Community Psychology (AJCP)* dedicated to the use of qualitative methods and illustrated the multiple ways nontraditional methods could be used in the field's efforts to contextualize our understanding of individual behavior (K. Miller & Banyard, 1998). For example, among these articles was one that focused on understanding the educational achievement of young African American men within their ecology, including familial, communal, and cultural contexts (Maton, Hrabowski, & Greif, 1998). In addition, many contemporary community psychologists are illustrating ways to approach the study of the person-in-context through the use of both qualitative and quantitative methods. The research of Rebecca Campbell (1998) is exemplary. She has sought to understand the relationships between social system responses to rape survivors and the experiences of the survivors through the integration of quantitative and qualitative methods. As the field evolves into the twenty-first century, multimethod approaches will hopefully become more common as the field recognizes the extent to which the context in which we collect information about individuals and communities, including the methods used, influences our findings and conclusions. Thus, opening up the methods toolbox will undoubtedly broaden and deepen our understanding of social phenomena.

PREVENTIVE INTERVENTIONS

Paralleling the development of frameworks and methods that represent an ecological orientation, efforts toward translating community research into action have been an integral part of the field's history through the design and implementation of preventive interventions. The history of prevention research in the United States is a history of cultural changes, such as the emergence of public health as an approach to disease prevention and health promotion in the 1920s (Rosen, 1993). The role of citizen advocates for prevention research also has been critical in defining the practice of prevention (B. B. Long, 1989). In addition, private foundations and the founding of the NIMH gave prevention prominent attention (Levine, 1981). The creation of the Joint Commission on Mental Illness and Health to review the nation's mental health contributed to the gradual emergence of prevention as a national priority in the 1960s (Goldston, 1995). Brief comments will be made about each of these factors and events prior to the Swampscott Conference, after which, the concept of prevention will be reviewed as a defining focus for community psychology. For further discussions of the history of prevention, the reader is referred to sources such as Caplan (1969), Levine (1981), Levine and Perkins (1997), and Spaulding and Balch (1983).

The emergence of prevention in the United States has benefited from a long history of the social consciousness of citizens and citizen groups. Notable preventionists include Dorothea Dix, Clifford Beers, Jane Addams, the General Federation of Women's Clubs, the National Association of Colored Women, and, more recently, Beverly Long, among others (Beers, 1908; Brinkley, 1993; Dain, 1980; B. B. Long, 1989; Ridenour, 1961). These citizens, most often women, campaigned to improve the quality of community-based services by shifting the aim to prevention programming for the poor and less formally educated. In 1909, the founding of the National Mental Health Association meant that, at both national and local levels, advocates for prevention could draw on voluntary organizations to create forums and make it easier for citizens to lobby legislatures for improved community-based prevention services (Ridenour, 1961).

National policy began to emphasize prevention of chronic diseases such as cancer, heart disease, and mental illness just before World War II (Levine, 1981). The aim of public health practice, to reduce the number of new casualties of a disease in a community, began to be applied to mental diseases at the time of the war. From this public health perspective, scientists developed the concepts of primary, secondary, and tertiary prevention (Leavell & Clark, 1965). These terms referred to taking measures to reduce systemic factors to prevent a problem from occurring (primary prevention); reducing a problem from occurring for persons who have already established risk factors for that problem (secondary prevention); and reducing the opportunities for reappearance of a problem for these persons (tertiary prevention). Recently these three prevention concepts have been elaborated and discussed in terms of risk, protection, resilience, strengths, and thriving (Dalton et al., 2000).

World War II created an opportunity for mental health professionals to observe the salience of public health approaches to mental health (G. Caplan, 1964). Mental health professionals discovered that short-term therapeutic services could reduce the number of soldiers succumbing to the stress of battle (Grob, 1991). Given this finding, multidisciplinary mental health teams began to organize services at or near battlefields to reduce future mental breakdowns and hospitalizations among soldiers (Glass, 1958). The rehabilitation of soldiers in the armed services impacted the practice of mental health services on the home front.

The experiences of mental health professionals in World War II emphasized the significance of contextual factors (e.g., war conditions) rather than only individual and constitutional factors for the expression of mental health problems (Grob, 1991). After the war and with a more active public health orientation, early detection and prevention of mental problems became operational in the mental health system. In adopting more active and community-oriented preventive interventions, mental health professionals became more aware of the qualities of communities where interventions would take place. Adding a focus on the qualities of communities increased the sensitivities of clinicians about the relationship between the mental health of individuals and the characteristics of communities (Grob, 1991).

After World War II, the prevention perspective was bolstered by a combination of federal, local, and professional interests, as well as strong support from private foundations and national lobbying organizations (Levine & Perkins, 1997). In 1955, the congressionally mandated review of the nation's mental health services gave further prominence to prevention via the work of the Joint Commission on Mental Illness and Health. As a result of the availability of increased funds, prevention-oriented psychologists had the resources to develop programs and research. Research groups began emphasizing prevention research and services. For example, Ralph Ojemann (1957) at the State University of Iowa organized conferences beginning in 1957 that brought together prevention researchers interested in prevention in the schools. The St. Louis County Mental Health Department pioneered a systematic effort to assess the benefits of a preventive school mental health program (Gildea, 1959; Glidewell,

1995). Paul Lemkau (1955), a public health psychiatrist, taught mental health professionals public health approaches to prevention at the Johns Hopkins University School of Public Health. A pioneer community psychologist at the University of Rochester, Emory Cowen, began school-based prevention work in the 1950s with elementary school children who were showing signs of academic difficulties (Cicchetti, Rappaport, Sandler, & Weissberg, 2000; Cowen, 1997, 2000a, 2000b; Cowen, Hightower, Pedro-Caroll, Work, & Wyman, 1996). Each of these early efforts, in combination, helped to create the supportive background and commitment for the passage of the Community Mental Health Services Act of 1963. This act included prevention as one of the 10 essential services.

Prevention as a Defining Focus for Community Psychology

As stated earlier in the chapter, the Swampscott report emphasized prevention as a defining element of the field. Since the Swampscott Conference, the prevention perspective has become institutionalized and formalized within the field of community psychology. This institutionalization of prevention has occurred through the establishment of prevention-focused conferences, participation of psychologists in federal commissions, and the development of professional organizations and interest groups dedicated to prevention activities.

At one such conference, the 1975 Austin Conference, participants repeatedly expressed the need to identify and mobilize the existing strengths and resources in a community as a primary intervention approach (Iscoe, 1975). One working group focused on intervention and preventive models and discussed "competency-based programs" that aimed at increasing the capacity of community members. Participants also emphasized the role of the community psychologist as "increasing clients' access to resources, and promoting equal distributions of resources" (Iscoe, 1975, p. 5). This encouraged the growth of "an awareness of professional responsibility to the client and community" (Iscoe, 1975, p. 8). Conference participants continued the discussions of moving away from the disease–treatment model to a new service delivery system that would focus on promoting wellness and disease prevention, and adapted an educational (training) model rather than a treatment orientation.

Also in 1975, George Albee, an author of one of the influential Joint Commission publications (Albee, 1959) convened the First Annual Vermont Conference on Primary Prevention. These conferences, initially funded by the Waters Foundation and later the NIMH, created opportunities for researchers and practitioners to focus on the details of prevention research and preventive interventions for a span of over 15 years (Kessler & Goldston, 1986; Kessler, Goldston, & Joffe, 1992). The Vermont Conferences were also important because they brought together persons of different disciplines, including those from local and state prevention programs, who had roles in policy development for mental health services. The ability of preventionists, including community psychologists, to influence policy at local and national levels was essential for the widespread application of a prevention orientation to mental health services. For example, psychologists' contribution on *The Prevention Task Force Report of the Carter Commission on Mental Health Services* in 1978 was influential in emphasizing the significance of prevention, as the report recommended the creation of field stations to do prevention research (Levine & Perkins, 1997).

Prevention was further legitimized with the creation of the Center for Prevention Research at NIMH in 1982. Under the leadership of Mort Silverman, research grants became available to fund Prevention Research Centers. These centers generated prevention research sites, including those at Arizona State University, the University of Michigan, Johns Hopkins University, Albert Einstein College of Medicine, and the Oregon Social Learning Center. Consistent with the mission of NIMH, much of the emphasis of these centers was to prevent mental disorders, such as conduct problems, substance abuse, and depression. Much of this research has been published in scientific journals (e.g., Koretz, 1991) and has informed the field on state-of-the-art advances in the field of prevention.

While theoretical discussions surrounding prevention focused on communities and community members, empirically driven prevention research continued to focus primarily on building the personal competencies of individuals. For example, Spivack and Shure's (1974, 1985) groundbreaking competence-building intervention, Interpersonal Cognitive Problem Solving (ICPS), sought to build a set of skills in young children in order to maximize their adjustment and interpersonal effectiveness. This intervention was based on a number of problem-solving skills identified in adjusted children and attempted to further promote these natural strategies. After finding ICPS to be relevant to a variety of populations, Shure spoke of the "central role that interpersonal competence plays in human adjustment, and the place of ICPS in that competence" (Spivack & Shure, 1985, pp. 230–231). Building specifically on the work of Spivack and Shure, Weissberg et al. (1981) developed a skills-building intervention called the Social Problem-Solving Skills (SPS). SPS sought to teach a group of second-, third-, and fourth-grade students a number of skills designed to build their social problem-solving skills and eventually improve their adjustment. Central to their conceptual model was the relationship between building skills and behavioral adjustment. They found SPS increased students' social problem skills and behavioral adjustment independently. Weissberg et al. noted the importance of the findings and sought to encourage those factors in children that were found to mediate adjustment.

Through the availability of increased funding from both federal and private foundations, more investigators were able to launch prevention trials. One of the concepts that helped to bridge past research with the emphasis on prevention was the concept of social support (Barrera, 2000; Vaux, 1988). In early efforts at developing prevention services, psychologists realized that recipients of prevention efforts benefited from the active presence and caring of others. Community psychologists became active contributors to this literature and helped to establish the constructs of social support, mutual help, and self-help as essential variables in prevention programming (Levy, 2000). Examples of this type of work were included in a 1991 special issue of the *AJCP* (Borkman, 1991). These contributions encouraged moving away from a disease orientation to analyses of factors contributing to individual positive health.

As mentioned earlier, Cowen has been a leading proponent for the concept of wellness as a way to build a scientific basis for discourse on and actions toward positive health (Cicchetti et al., 2000; Cowen, 2000b). In the most recent published literature relating to strengths and resources, Cowen (2000b) continued to assert psychological wellness as a primary focus for community psychologists, as he has over the past four decades. He discussed three main terms that have been used in connection with this concept, including competence, empowerment, and heightened resilience in children: "These phenotypically disparate concepts . . . find genotypic synchrony in a framework in which routes to psychological wellness is the overarching phenomenon of interest" (p. 90). Cowen also advocated examining both the personal and environmental contributors to psychological wellness and discussed a number of sources of influence over people's psychological wellness, including the family context, the child's total educational experience, significant social settings and systems in which a person interacts, and the broad societal surround.

In the last two decades, community psychologists have developed multiple conceptions and highlighted various facets of the prevention perspective. In his 1980 presidential address to the Society for Community Research and Action (SCRA, Division 27 of the APA), Julian Rappaport presented the concept of empowerment as an alternative to the traditional medical and disease orientation of prevention research (Rappaport, 1981; Zimmerman, 1990, 1995, 2000;

Zimmerman & Rappaport, 1988). Articulating an emerging mood, he questioned the clinical heritage of prevention and advocated for prevention work to be a community and enabling enterprise, an enterprise consistent with the values expressed at Swampscott. Tableman (1989) emphasized the significance of pragmatic processes of prevention programs in her Distinguished Practice Award address to SCRA in 1988. She challenged community psychologists to emphasize the long-term implementation of prevention programs and not just focus on the one-time demonstration of a particular project (Tableman, 1989).

Tensions around Two Types of Prevention Research: Prevention Science and Action Research

Two contrasting approaches have emerged within the domain of prevention: prevention science and action research. The prevention scientist focuses on the technology of the intervention, precision of the measuring instruments, and the search to control confounding variables as much as possible so as to establish the validity of the intervention. In general, classical experimental research designs are employed. In this work, the focus is to generate testable hypotheses and rigorous quantitative analyses to be precise about the efficacy of interventions. This approach is fundamentally concerned with the development of measurement techniques and statistical analyses, with an eye toward advancing knowledge for the professions and increasing the scientific status of prevention research among the social sciences.

Professional and scientific journals are replete with studies conducted from the perspective of the prevention scientist. For example, a 1991 special issue of the *AJCP* presents a review of issues related to prevention science, including such topics as validity, short-term versus long-term effects, and the place of random assignment in community trials (Jansen & Johnson, 1993). Also in the *AJCP* (Kellam, Koretz, & Moscicki, 1999a, 1999b), recently published work from a conference on Prevention Science held at Johns Hopkins University in December 1994 includes: (1) results of school- and community-based randomized field trials; (2) studies of antecedent risk factors in the individual and social context; and (3) designs for future prevention trials.

In contrast to the work of the prevention scientist, the action researcher focuses upon understanding the community, often the host for the prevention program, so as to develop community-based and community-sensitive programs. Swampscott Conference participants recognized the need to use community members as resources in the research process. "The conference was stimulated by Reiff's discussion of the indigenous nonprofessional," and researchers were beginning to see community members as "effective change agents" within their own neighborhoods (Bennett et al., 1966, p. 16). Community researchers envisioned community members serving a double purpose. First, they would assist in promoting researchers' credibility and help researchers maintain rapport with members of the community. Second, these indigenous nonprofessionals possessed skills that community researchers did not, including their intimate knowledge about their own community. Through their subjective analyses of their experiences, community members served as resources to their communities' health by providing researchers valuable information about the community, its needs, and its natural processes in efforts to develop contextually grounded interventions.

The action researcher may employ multiple methods of assessment, including both qualitative and quantitative techniques (K. Miller & Banyard, 1998). In general, this researcher attempts to define a closer relationship between prevention research and the communities where the prevention research is occurring (Kelly et al., 1988; Reason & Bradbury, 2001). Community-based action research places emphasis on collaborating with citizens to generate prevention services; the needs of the community are as equally salient as the scientific status of the research.

In recent years, community psychologists have consistently advocated for active community participation in prevention research, a trademark of action-oriented research (Muehrer, 1997; L. Smith, 1999). In his 1997 Sarason Award address, Murray Levine (1998) affirmed that effective preventive interventions should be "built on our understanding of the psychological sense of community" (p. 203), ideas expressed many years before by Seymour Sarason (Sarason, 1981, 1988). Similarly, Leonard Jason (1998) made a strong plea for collaboration with community organizations and citizens in his Distinguished Award address to the SCRA in 1997.

As community psychologists become more invested in working in communities, more attention is likely to be devoted to listening to the community rather then seeing communities primarily as places to test out scientific ideas (Seidman, Hughes, & Williams, 1993). For example, these community-centered approaches have been found to be essential in working in communities impacted by HIV/AIDS due to the culturally bound implications of preventive interventions (Icard, Schilling, El-Bassel, & Young, 1992; R. Miller, Klotz, & Eckholdt, 1998; Peterson, Coates, Catania, & Hauck, 1996). In the action research approach, the community psychologist is viewed as one resource among many contributors, in contrast to the prevention scientist who is viewed as the primary expert.

The differences in approaches between the prevention scientist and the action researcher reflect the differences in values of the contrasting paradigms. The tensions germinating from these two paradigms are so disparate that they may not be reconciled in the immediate future. Instead, these two alternative points of view about understanding the efficacy of prevention programs are likely to continue to develop side by side. Interestingly, these contrasting approaches to prevention have parallels to research with cultural groups. Ana Marie Cauce and colleagues have framed these differences as the cultural equivalence approach and the cultural variance approach. The first approach assumes that all people are essentially similar except for differences in life circumstances. The second approach holds that the unique background and experiences of each subminority group produces fundamental differences in risk and protective factors (Cauce, Coronado, & Watson, 1998; Roosa & Gonzales, 2000). The challenge for the future is whether the second approach will achieve increased attention as a viable and alternative view of prevention.

CONCLUSION

The history of community psychology is unique in the history of psychology. Like other fields, the development of community psychology is not just a history of the profession but also a reflection of the interaction of social and cultural events and discontent within the broader field of psychology. At a time when the nation was experiencing a cultural revolution, psychologists with a community orientation were questioning the status quo of the field. Community psychologists protested the medical- and disease-driven model of the mental health professions, particularly psychiatry and clinical psychology, and rallied for ecologically sound interventions targeting social systems and institutions rather than individuals.

In this chapter, we aimed to understand the context and domains that have been essential to the development of the field in a historical and social context. We began this endeavor with a brief historical analysis of events leading up to the founding of the field in 1965. The founding of the field occurred during an awesome time in U.S. history. Though it emerged in the liberal fervor of the 1960s, psychologists' calls for social action, social change, and social justice can be traced to social events of the 1940s and 1950s. Events such as World War II and the growing malaise of the 1950s, accompanied by the increasing discontent among oppressed groups such as women and racial minorities, sparked creativity, innovation, and protest in many areas of American life, including within the mental health professions. The zeitgeist of the

1950s and 1960s suggests bases for the interests of citizens, including psychologists, to create such a distinct enterprise as community psychology.

Embedded in the spirit of the times, the founding of community psychology at the Swampscott Conference was supported by at least two decades of exploration into community approaches to mental health service provision. The 20 years of scholarly and professional achievements illuminated the connections among social structure, health, and the delivery of community and preventive services. The founding and development of the field both reflected and fostered a paradigm shift in the practice of psychology. Community psychology represented new ways to conceptualize mental illness and mental health and news ways to approach individual, systems, and social changes. Specifically, shifts in conceptual orientation demanded that efforts to develop theories and preventive interventions be viewed through a nondeficits model—a model of promoting strengths of communities and individual community members.

We have framed the field's development of theory and action in terms of enhancing individual and community strengths. Community psychologists like Cowen and Weissberg have made promoting wellness through preventive interventions with an ecological orientation. Ecological theorists have also suggested specific connections to a strengths perspective, most recently in the ideas of Kelly (2000). Preventive interventionists are increasingly advocating for the inherent connection between this strengths perspective and their work (Seidman et al., 1999; Zimmerman, Ramirez-Valles, & Maton, 1999). The thesis of this chapter lies in the multiple ways that traces of the principle of the interdependence of a strengths perspective with ecological concepts and preventive interventions have defined a major core of the work implemented throughout the field's history.

The importance of the strengths perspective in community psychology is illustrated by the number of community psychologists who have commented on the challenge of developing a competence approach in community research and practice. At the symposium celebrating the 20th anniversary of the field, Kelly (1987) echoed the Swampscott Conference participants' articulation of a need for a broader definition of health and well-being. Strother (1987) discussed how the tone at the time of Swampscott had allowed for an emphasis on the maintenance of health rather than a sole focus on illness. Klein (1987) repeated some of Lindemann's thoughts by emphasizing that prevention or mental health promotion, the most cost-effective early treatments, would result from focused efforts to enhance individuals' natural support systems. Also during this time, several chapters in the *Annual Review of Psychology* focused attention on the issue of bringing a strengths perspective into preventive interventions (Gesten & Jason, 1987; Iscoe & Harris, 1984; Kelly, Snowden, & Munoz, 1977; Levine, Toro, & Perkins, 1993).

Considering the ecological perspective as described by Kelly, Trickett, and colleagues and actualized by other noted community psychologists, we see an inherent connection between a strengths perspective and viewing the person in context. As the strengths orientation prescribes that we attend to the functional roles played by individuals and community structures, so does ecologically valid work that explicitly acknowledges the interdependent relationship between community citizens and the multiple levels of their environments. Furthermore, the link between a strengths perspective and ecological thinking is evident in the field's translation of research into action via preventive interventions and action research. Community psychologists have illustrated such a connection through interventions that focus on building community capacity or promoting individual strengths as strategies to prevent social problems or disease.

We hope that by highlighting some of the social events and movements that framed the emergence of the field, future scholars can build from this enterprise. The future of community psychology is bound not only by its social, political, and professional contexts but also by its past. Understanding the confluence of historical events and processes that contributed to the evolution of community psychology can provide us with the insight and knowledge to continue collaborative research with communities that ecologically assesses problems and competencies in efforts to prevent social problems and promote wellness.

REFERENCES

Albee, G. (1959). *Mental health manpower trends.* New York: Basic Books.

Asbell, B. (1995). *The pill.* New York: Random House.

Barker, R. (1963). Explorations in ecological psychology. *American Psychologist, 20*(1), 1–14.

Barrera, M. (2000). Social support research in community psychology. In J. Rappaport & E. Seidman (Eds.), *Handbook of community psychology* (pp. 215–246). New York: Kluwer Academic/ Plenum Press.

Beers, C. W. (1908). *A mind that found itself.* New York: Doubleday.

Bennett, C. C., Anderson, L. S., Cooper, S., Hassol, L., Klein, D. C., & Rosenblum, G. (Eds.). (1966). *Community psychology: A report of the Boston Conference on the education of psychologists for community mental health.* Boston: Boston University Press.

Borkman, T. J. (1991). Self help groups. *American Journal of Community Psychology, 19*(5, Whole Issue), 643–805.

Brinkley, A. (1993). *The unfinished nation.* New York: Knopf.

Brofenbrenner, U. (1979). *The ecology of human development.* Cambridge, MA: Harvard University Press.

Campbell, R. M. (1998). The community response to rape: Victim's experiences with the legal, medical, and mental health systems. *American Journal of Community Psychology, 26*(3), 355–380.

Caplan, G. (1964). *Principles of preventive psychiatry.* New York: Basic Books.

Caplan, R. B. (1969). *Psychiatry and the community in nineteenth century America.* New York: Basic Books.

Cauce, A. M., Coronado, N., & Watson, J. (1998). Conceptual, methodological, and statistical issues in culturally competent research. In M. Hernandez & M. Issacs (Eds.), *Promoting cultural competence in children's mental health services* (pp. 305–329). Baltimore: Brookes.

Chamberlain, W., & Robinson, T. (1997). *The GI Bill: The law that changed America* (Video B 3620, 60 minutes). New York: PBS Home Video.

Chavis, D. (1993). A future for community psychology practice. *American Journal of Community Psychology, 21*(2), 171–183.

Chavis, D. M., & Wandersman, A. (1990). Sense of community in the urban environment: A catalyst for participation and community development. *American Journal of Community Psychology, 18*(1), 55–81.

Cherniss, C. (1989). Career stability in public service professionals: A longitudinal investigation based on biographical interviews. *American Journal of Community Psychology, 17*(4), 399–422.

Chesler, M., & Fox, R. (1966). *Role-playing methods in the classroom.* Chicago: Science Research Association.

Chomsky, N. (Ed.). (1997). *The cold war and the university.* New York: New Press.

Cicchetti, D., Rappaport, J., Sandler, I., & Weissberg, R. P. (Eds.). (2000). *The promotion of wellness in children and adolescents.* Washington, DC: CWLA Press.

Cottrell, L. S. (1964). Social planning, the competent community, and mental health. In *Urban America and the Planning of Mental Health Services.* Group for the Advancement of Psychiatry, Symposium 10, New York: Group for the Advancement of Psychiatry.

Cowen, E. L. (1994). The enhancement of psychological wellness: Challenges and opportunities. *American Journal of Community Psychology, 22*(2), 149–179.

Cowen, E. L. (1997). Schools and the enhancement of children's wellness: Some opportunities and some limiting factors. In T. P. Gullotta, R. P. Weissberg, R. L. Hampton, B. A. Ryan, & G. R. Adams (Eds.), *Healthy children 2010: Establishing preventive services* (pp. 87–123). Thousand Oaks, CA: Sage.

Cowen, E. L. (2000a). Now that we all know that primary prevention in mental health is great, what is it? *Journal of Community Psychology, 28,* 5–16.

Cowen, E. L. (2000b). Psychological wellness: Some hopes for the future. In D. Cicchetti, J. Rappaport, I. Sandler, & R. P. Weissberg (Eds.), *The promotion of wellness in children and adolescents* (pp. 477–503). Washington, DC: CWLA Press.

Cowen, E. L., Hightower, A. D., Pedro-Caroll, J. L., Work, W. C., & Wyman, P. A. (1996). *School-based prevention for children at risk: The primary mental health project.* Washington, DC: American Psychological Association.

Dain, N. (1980). *Clifford W. Beers: Advocate for the insane.* Pittsburgh, PA: University of Pittsburgh Press.

Dalton, J. H., Elias, M. J., & Wandersman, A. H. (2000). *Community psychology: Linking individuals and communities.* Belmont, CA: Wadsworth.

Danish, S. J. (1983). Musings about personal competence: The contributions of sport, health, and fitness. *American Journal of Community Psychology, 11*(3), 221–240.

Duffy, K. G., & Wong, K. Y. (1996). *Community psychology.* Boston: Allyn & Bacon.

Edwards, D. L., & Kelly, J. G. (1980). Coping and adaptation: A longitudinal study. *American Journal of Community Psychology, 8,* 203–216.

Ellison, R. (1947). *Invisible man.* New York: Random House.

Friedan, B. (1963). *The feminine mystique.* New York: Norton.

Garmezy, N. (1991). Resiliency and vulnerability to adverse developmental outcomes associated with poverty. *American Behavioral Scientist, 34*(4), 416–430.

Gesten, E. L., & Jason, L. A. (1987). Social and community interventions. In M. R. Rosenzweig (Ed.), *Annual review of psychology, Vol. 38* (pp. 427–460). Palo Alto, CA: Annual Reviews, Inc.

Gildea, M. C. L. (1959). *Community mental health.* Springfield, IL: Charles C. Thomas.

Gitlin, T. (1987). *The sixties: Years of hope, days of rage.* New York: Bantam Books.

Gitlin, T. (1997). Afterward. In S. Macedo (Ed.), *Reassessing the sixties: Debating the political and cultural legacy* (pp. 291–292). New York: Norton.

Glass, A. J. (1958). Observations upon the epidemiology of mental illness in troops during warfare. In *Preventive and social psychiatry* (pp. 185–198). Washington, DC: U.S. Government Printing Office.

Glennon, L. (Ed.). (1995). *Our times: The illustrated history of the 20th century.* Atlanta, GA: Turner.

Glidewell, J. C. (1977). *The social context of learning and development.* New York: Gardner.

Glidewell, J. C. (1995). *Exemplars of community psychology* [Video], J. G. Kelly (Ed.). Chicago: Society for Community Research and Action.

Goldston, S. E. (1994). *Exemplars of community psychology* [Video], J. G. Kelly (Ed.). Chicago: Society for Community Research and Action.

Greenberg, M. (1997). *The GI Bill.* New York: Lickle.

Grob, G. N. (1991). *From asylum to community*. Princeton, NJ: Princeton University Press.

Halberstam, D. (1993). *The fifties*. New York: Fawcett.

Heller, K., Price, R. H., Reinharz, S., Riger, S., & Wandersman, A. H. (1984). *Psychology and community change*. Pacific Grove, CA: Brooks/Cole.

Herman, A. (1999). *Joseph McCarthy: Reexamining the life and legacy of America's most hated Senator*. Glencoe, IL: Free Press.

Hoch, E. L., Ross, A. O., & Winder, C. L. (1966). Conference on the professional preparation of clinical psychologists: A summary. *American Psychologist, 21*, 42–51.

Holahan, C. J., & Moos, R. H. (1982). Social support and adjustment: Predictive benefits of social climate indices. *American Journal of Community Psychology, 10*(4), 403–415.

Holahan, C. J., Wilcox, B. L., Spearly, J. L., & Campbell, M. D. (1979). The ecological perspective in community mental health. *Community Mental Health Review, 4*(2), 3–9.

Howard, G. (Ed.). (1995). *The sixties: The art, attitudes, politics, and media of our most explosive decade*. New York: Marlowe.

Icard, L. D., Schilling, R. F., El-Bassel, N., & Young, D. (1992). Preventing AIDS among Black gay men and Black gay and heterosexual male intravenous drug users. *Social Work, 37*(5), 440–445.

Iscoe, I. (1974). Community psychology and the competent community. *American Psychologist, 29*(8), 607–613.

Iscoe, I. (1975). Report to the membership: National training conference in community psychology. *Division of Community Psychology Newsletter, 8*, 3–10.

Iscoe, I. (1997). *Exemplars of community psychology* [Video], J. G. Kelly (Ed.). Chicago: Society for Community Research and Action.

Iscoe, I., Bloom, B. L., & Spielberger, C. D. (1977). *Community psychology in transition: Proceedings of the national conference on training in community psychology*. Washington, DC: Hemisphere.

Iscoe, I., & Harris, L. C. (1984). Social and community interventions. *Annual Review of Psychology, 35*, 333–360.

Isserman, M., & Kazin, M. (2000). *America divided: The civil war of the 1960s*. New York: Oxford University Press.

Jahoda, M. (1953). The meaning of psychological health. *Social Casework, 34*, 349–354.

Jahoda, M. (1958). *Current concepts of positive mental health*. New York: Basic Books.

Jansen, M. A., & Johnson, E. M. (Eds.). (1993). Methodological issues in prevention research [Special issue]. *American Journal of Community Psychology, 21*, 561–680.

Jason, L. A. (1998). Tobacco, drug and HIV prevention media interventions. *American Journal of Community Psychology, 26*, 151–188.

Joint Commission on Mental Illness and Health. (1961). *Action for mental health*. New York: Basic Books.

Kellam, S. G., Koretz, D., & Moscicki, E. K. (Eds.). (1999a). Prevention science: Part I [Special issue]. *American Journal of Community Psychology, 27*.

Kellam, S. G., Koretz, D., & Moscicki, E. K. (Eds.). (1999b). Prevention science: Part II [Special issue]. *American Journal of Community Psychology, 27*.

Kelly, J. G. (1966). Ecological constraints on mental health services. *American Psychologist, 21*(6), 535–539.

Kelly, J. G. (1967). Naturalistic observations and theory confirmation: An example. *Human Development, 10*(3/4), 212–222.

Kelly, J. G. (1968). Towards an ecological conception of preventive interventions. In J. W. Carter Jr. (Ed.), *Research contributions from psychology to community mental health* (pp. 1–36). New York: Behavioral Publications.

Kelly, J. G. (1970). Antidotes for arrogance: Training for community psychology. *American Psychologist, 25*(6), 524–531.

Kelly, J. G. (1971). Qualities for the community psychologist. *American Psychologist, 26*(10), 897–903.

Kelly, J. G. (1979). Tain't what you do, it's the way that you do it. *American Journal of Community Psychology, 7*(3), 244–261.

Kelly, J. G. (1986). In honor of George W. Fairweather. *American Journal of Community Psychology, 14*, 126–128.

Kelly, J. G. (Ed.). (1987). Swampscott anniversary symposium: Reflections and recommendations on the 20th anniversary of Swampscott. *American Journal of Community Psychology, 15*, 511–631.

Kelly, J. G. (2000). Wellness as an ecological enterprise. In D. Cicchetti, J. Rappaport, I. Sandler, & R. P. Weissberg (Eds.), *The promotion of wellness in children and adolescents: Washington, DC* (pp. 101–131). Washington, DC: CWLA Press.

Kelly, J. G., Dassoff, N., Levin, I., Schreckengost, J., Stelzner, S. P., & Altman, B. E. (1988). *A guide to conducting prevention research in the community: First steps*. New York: Haworth Press.

Kelly, J. G., Snowden, L. R., & Munoz, R. F. (1977). Social and community interventions. *Annual Review of Psychology, 28*, 323–341.

Kennedy, D. M. (1999). *Freedom from fear: The American people in depression and war 1929–1945*. New York: Oxford University Press.

Kessler, M., & Goldston, S. E. (Eds.). (1986). *A decade of primary prevention*. Hanover, NH: University Press of New England.

Kessler, M., Goldston, S. E., & Joffe, J. M. (Eds.). (1992). *The present and future of prevention. In honor of George Albee*. Newbury Park, CA: Sage.

Kiester, E. (1994). The GI Bill may be the best deal ever made by Uncle Sam. *Smithsonian, 26*, 129–139.

Kingry-Westergaard, C., & Kelly, J. G. (1990). A contextualist epistemology for ecological research. In P. Tolan, C. Keys, F. Chertok, & L. Jason (Eds.), *Researching community psychology: Issues of theory and methods* (pp. 23–31). Washington, DC: American Psychological Association.

Kinsey, A. J. (1948). *Sexual behavior of human male*. Philadelphia: Saunders.

Kinsey, A. J. (1953). *Sexual behavior of human female*. Philadelphia: Saunders.

Klein, D. C. (1968). *Community dynamics and mental health*. New York: Wiley.

Klein, D. C. (1987). The context and times at Swampscott: My/story. *American Journal of Community Psychology, 15,* 531–538.

Korchin, S. J. (1976). *Modern clinical psychology*. New York: Basic Books.

Koretz, D. S. (Ed.). (1991). Preventive intervention research centers [Special issue]. *American Journal of Community Psychology, 19.*

Leavell, H. R., & Clark, E. G. (1965). *Preventive medicine for the doctor in his community, an epidemiologic approach* (3rd ed.). New York: McGraw-Hill.

Lemkau, P. (1955). *Mental hygiene in public health*. New York: McGraw-Hill.

Levine, M. (1981). *The history and politics of community mental health*. New York: Oxford University Press.

Levine, M. (1998). Prevention and community. *American Journal of Community Psychology, 26,* 189–206.

Levine, M., & Perkins, D. V. (1997). *Principles of community psychology: Perspectives and applications* (2nd ed.). New York: Oxford University Press.

Levine, M., Reppucci, N. D., & Weinstein, R. (1990). Learning from Seymour Sarason. *American Journal of Community Psychology, 18*(3), 343–351.

Levine, M., Toro, P. A., & Perkins, D. V. (1993). Social and community interventions. In *Annual review of psychology, Vol. 44* (pp. 525–558). Palo Alto, CA: Annual Reviews, Inc.

Levy, L. H. (2000). Self help groups. In J. Rappaport & E. Seidman (Eds.), *Handbook of community psychology* (pp. 591–614). New York: Kluwer Academic/Plenum Press.

Lewin, K. (1951). *Field theory in social science: Selected theoretical papers*. New York: Harper.

Lindemann, E. (1953). The Wellesley project for the study of certain problems in community mental health. In *Interrelations between the social environment and psychiatric disorders* (pp. 167–185). New York: Milbank Memorial Fund.

Linney, J. A. (1986). Court ordered school desegregation: Shuffling the deck or playing a different game. In E. Seidman & J. Rappaport (Eds.), *Redefining social problems* (pp. 259–274). New York: Plenum Press.

Linney, J. A. (2000). Assessing ecological constructs and community context. In J. Rappaport, & E. Seidman (Eds.), *Handbook of community psychology* (pp. 647–668). New York: Kluwer Academic/Plenum Press.

Long, B. E. (1968). Teaching psychology to children. *American Psychologist, 23*(9), 691–692.

Long, B. B. (1989). The mental health association and prevention. *Prevention in Human Services, 6*(2), 5–44.

Maher, B. A. (1988). Abnormal and clinical psychology. In E. H. Hilgard (Ed.), *Fifty years of psychology: Essays in honor of Floyd Ruch* (pp. 153–168). Glenview, IL: Scott, Foresman.

Marwick, A. (1998). *The sixties: Cultural revolution in Britain, France, Italy and the United States: 1958–1974*. New York: Oxford University Press.

Maton, K. I. (2000). Making a difference: The social ecology of social transformation. *American Journal of Community Psychology, 28*(1), 25–57.

Maton, K. I., Hrabowski, F. A., III., & Greif, G. L. (1998). Preparing the way: A qualitative study of high-achieving African American males and the role of the family. *American Journal of Community Psychology, 26*(4), 639–668.

McGhee, J. L. (1984). The influence of qualitative assessments of the social and physical environment on the morale of rural elderly. *American Journal of Community Psychology, 12*(6), 689–708.

Meritt, D. A., Greene, G. F., Jopp, D. A., & Kelly, J. G. (1997). A history of Division 27 (Society for Community Research and Action). In D. A. Dewsbury (Ed.), *Unification through division* (Vol. 3, pp. 73–99). Washington, DC: American Psychological Association.

Metalious, G. (1956). *Peyton place*. New York: Messner.

Miller, K. E., & Banyard, V. B. (Eds.). (1998). Qualitative research in community psychology [Special issue]. *American Journal of Community Psychology, 26,* 485–696.

Miller, R. L., Klotz, D., & Eckholdt, H. M. (1998). HIV prevention with male prostitutes and patrons of hustler bars: Replications of an HIV preventive intervention. *American Journal of Community Psychology, 26,* 97–132.

Mishler, E. G. (1979). Meaning in context: Is there any other kind? *Harvard Educational Review, 49*(1), 1–19.

Moos, R. H. (1974). Determinants of physiological responses to symbolic stimuli: The role of the social environment. *International Journal of Psychiatry in Medicine, 5*(4), 389–399.

Moos, R. H., & Lemke, S. (1996). *Evaluating residential facilities: The multiphasic environmental assessment procedure*. Thousand Oaks, CA: Sage.

Moos, R. H., & Moos, B. S. (1984). The process of recovery from alcoholism. III: Comparing functioning in families of alcoholics and matched control families. *Journal of Studies on Alcohol, 45*(2), 111–118.

Morgan, E. P. (1991). *The 60s experience: Hard lessons about modern America*. Philadelphia: Temple University Press.

Morris, A., Shinn, M., & DuMont, K. (1999). Contextual factors affecting the organizational commitment of diverse police officers: A levels of analysis perspective. *American Journal of Community Psychology, 27*(1), 75–105.

Muehrer, P. (Ed.). (1997). Prevention research in rural settings [Special issue]. *American Journal of Community Psychology, 25,* 421–562.

Novaco, R., & Monahan, J. (1980). Research in community psychology: An analysis of work published in the first six years of the *American Journal of Community Psychology. American Journal of Community Psychology, 8*(2), 131–145.

Ojemann, R. H. (Ed.). (1957). *Four basic aspects of preventive psychiatry.* Iowa City: State University of Iowa.

Payne, C. M. (1995). *I've got the light of freedom.* Berkeley: University of California Press.

Payne, C. M. (1997). *Antecedents of the civil rights movements* [Video], J. G. Kelly (Ed.). Chicago: Society for Community Research and Action.

Peterson, J. L., Coates, T. J., Catania, J., & Hauck, W. W. (1996). Evaluation of an HIV risk reduction intervention among African-American homosexual and bisexual men. *AIDS, 10*(3), 319–325.

Potasznik, H., & Nelson, G. (1984). Stress and social support: The burden experienced by the family of a mentally ill person. *American Journal of Community Psychology, 12,* 589–608.

Rappaport, J. (1981). In praise of paradox: A social policy of empowerment and prevention. *American Journal of Community Psychology, 9,* 1–25.

Rappaport, J. (1995). Empowerment meets narrative: Listening to stories and creating settings. *American Journal of Community Psychology, 23*(5), 795–807.

Reason, P., & Bradbury, H. (2001). *Handbook of action research.* London: Sage.

Reiff, R. (1971). Community psychology and public policy. In J. C. Glidewell (Ed.), *Issues in community psychology and preventive mental health* (pp. 33–54). New York: Behavioral Publications.

Reppucci, N. D. (1990). The conscience of community psychology: Seymour Sarason's contributions. *American Journal of Community Psychology, 18*(3), 353–358.

Ridenour, N. (1961). *Mental health in the United States: A fifty year history.* Cambridge, MA: Harvard University Press.

Robinson, J. A. G. (1987). *The Montgomery bus boycott and the women who started it.* Knoxville: University of Tennessee Press.

Roosa, M. K., & Gonzales, N. A. (2000). Minority issues in prevention [Special issue]. *American Journal of Community Psychology, 28.*

Rosen, G. (1993). *A history of public health: Expanded edition.* Baltimore: Johns Hopkins University Press.

Rovere, R. H. (1996). *Senator Joe McCarthy.* Berkeley: University of California Press.

Sarason, S. B. (1972). *The creation of settings and the future societies.* San Francisco: Jossey-Bass.

Sarason, S. B. (1976). Community psychology, networks, and Mr. Everyman. *American Psychologist, 31*(5), 317–328.

Sarason, S. B. (1978). The nature of problem solving is social action. *American Psychologist, 33*(4), 370–380.

Sarason, S. B. (1981). *Psychology misdirected.* New York: Free Press.

Sarason, S. B. (1988). *The making of an American psychologist: An autobiography.* San Francisco: Jossey-Bass.

Sarason, S. B. (1995). *School change: The personal development of a point of view.* New York: Teachers' College Press.

Sarason, S. B., Levine, M., Goldenberg, I., Cherlin, D. L., & Bennett, E. M. (1966). *Psychology in community settings: Clinical, educational, vocational, social aspects.* New York: Wiley.

Schmuck, R., Chesler, M., & Lippitt, R. (1966). *Problem solving to improve classroom learning.* Chicago: Science Research Associates.

Schrecker, E. (1998). *Many are the crimes: McCarthyism in America.* Boston: Little, Brown.

Seidman, E. (1988). Back to the future, community psychology: Unfolding a theory of social intervention. *American Journal of Community Psychology, 16*(1), 3–24.

Seidman, E. (1990). Pursuing the meaning and utility of social regularities for community psychology. In P. Tolan, C. Keys, F. Chertok, & L. Jason (Eds.), *Researching community psychology: Issues of theory and methods* (pp. 91–100). Washington, DC: American Psychological Association.

Seidman, E., Chesir-Teran, D., Friedman, J. L., Yoshikawa, H., Allen, L., Roberts, A., et al. (1999). The risk and protective functions of perceived family and peer microsystems among urban adolescents in poverty. *American Journal of Community Psychology, 27,* 211–238.

Seidman, E., Hughes, D., & Williams, N. (Eds.). (1993). Culturally anchored methodology [Special issue]. *American Journal of Community Psychology, 21*(6).

Shinn, M. (1990). Mixing and matching: Levels of conceptualization, measurement, and statistical analysis in community research. In P. Tolan, C. Keys, F. Chertok, & L. Jason (Eds.), *Researching community psychology: Issues of theory and methods* (pp. 111–126). Washington, DC: American Psychological Association.

Smith, L. T. (1999). *Decolonizing methodologies: Research and indigenous people.* London: Zed Books.

Smith, M. B., & Hobbs, N. (1966). The community and the community mental health center. *American Psychologist, 21,* 499–509.

Spaulding, J., & Balch, P. (1983). A brief history of primary prevention in the twentieth century: 1908–1980. *American Journal of Community Psychology, 11,* 59–80.

Spivack, G., & Shure, M. B. (1974). *Social adjustment of young children.* San Francisco: Jossey-Bass.

Spivack, G., & Shure, M. B. (1985). ICPS and beyond: Centripetal and centrifugal forces. *American Journal of Community Psychology, 13,* 226–243.

Spivack, G., & Shure, M. B. (1989). Interpersonal cognitive problem solving (ICPS): A competence-building primary prevention program. *Prevention in Human Services, 6*(2), 151–178.

Steele, R., Trickett, E. J., & Labarta, M. (1981). *Ecology and cultural diversity: Multicultural examples.* Paper presented at the annual meeting of the American Psychological Association, Los Angeles.

Stokols, D. (1992). Environmental quality, human development, and health: An ecological view. *Journal of Applied Developmental Psychology, 13*(2), 121–124.

Stokols, D., & Altman, I. (1987). *Handbook of environmental psychology.* New York: Wiley.

Strother, C. R. (Ed.). (1956). *Psychology and mental health.* Washington, DC: American Psychological Association.

Strother, C. R. (1987). Reflections on the Stanford Conference and subsequent events. *American Journal of Community Psychology, 15,* 519–522.

Swartz, J. L., & Martin, W. E., Jr. (1997). Ecological psychology theory: Historical overview and application to educational ecosystems. In J. L. Swartz & W. Martin (Eds.), *Applied ecological psychology for schools within communities: Assessment and intervention* (pp. 3–27). Mahwah, NJ: Erlbaum.

Tableman, B. (1989). Installing prevention programming in the public mental health system. *American Journal of Community Psychology, 17*(2), 171–183.

Trickett, E. J., Kelly, J. G., & Todd, D. (1972). The social environment of the high school: Guidelines for individual change and organizational development. In S. Golann & C. Eisdorfer (Eds.), *Handbook of community mental health* (pp. 361–390). New York: Appleton-Century-Crofts.

Trickett, E. J., & Quinlan, D. M. (1979). Three domains of classroom environment: Factor analysis of the classroom environment scale. *American Journal of Community Psychology, 7*(3), 279–291.

Trickett, E. J., Watts, R. J., & Birman, D. (1994). Toward an overarching framework for diversity. In E. Trickett, R. Watts, & D. Birman (Eds.), *Human diversity: Perspectives on people in context* (The Jossey-Bass social and behavioral science series, pp. 7–26). San Francisco: Jossey-Bass.

Tuttle, W. M. (1993). *Daddy's gone to war: The second world war in the lives of America's children.* New York: Oxford University Press.

Vaux, A. (1988). *Social support: Theory, research, and intervention.* New York: Praeger.

Wagenfield, M. O., Lemkau, P. V., & Justice, B. (Eds.). (1982). *Public mental health: Perspectives and prospects.* Beverly Hills, CA: Sage.

Watkins, E. S. (1998). *On the pill.* Baltimore: Johns Hopkins University Press.

Weissberg, R. P., Caplan, M., & Harwood, R. L. (1991). Promoting competent young people in competence-enhancing environments: A systems-based perspective on primary prevention. *Journal of Consulting and Clinical Psychology, 59*(6), 830–841.

Weissberg, R. P., Gesten, E. L., Carnrike, C. L., Toro, P., Rapkin, B. D., Davidson, E., et al. (1981). Social problem-solving skills training: A competence-building intervention with second- to fourth-grade children. *American Journal of Community Psychology, 9*(4), 411–423.

White, R. W. (1952). *Lives in progress: A study of the natural growth of personality.* New York: Dryden Press.

White, R. W. (1959). Motivation reconsidered: The concept of competence. *Psychological Review, 66,* 297–333.

Whitman, T. L., White, R. D., O'Mara, K. M., & Goeke-Morey, M. C. (1999). Environmental aspects of infant health and illness. In T. L. Whitman & T. V. Merluzzi (Eds.), *Live-span perspectives on health and illness* (pp. 105–124). Hillsdale, NJ: Erlbaum.

Wilson, S. (1955). *The man in the grey flannel suit.* New York: Simon & Schuster.

Zimmerman, M. A. (1990). Taking aim on empowerment research: On the distinction between psychological and individual conceptions. *American Journal of Community Psychology, 18,* 169–177.

Zimmerman, M. A. (1995). Psychological empowerment: Issues and illustrations. *American Journal of Community Psychology, 23,* 581–600.

Zimmerman, M. A. (2000). Empowerment theory: Psychological, organizational and community levels of analysis. In J. Rappaport & E. Seidman (Eds.), *Handbook of community psychology* (pp. 43–63). New York: Kluwer Academic/Plenum Press.

Zimmerman, M. A., Ramirez-Valles, J., & Maton, K. (1999). Resilience among urban African American male adolescents: A study of the protective effects of sociopolitical control on their mental health. *American Journal of Community Psychology, 27,* 733–752.

Zimmerman, M. A., & Rappaport, J. (1988). Citizen participation, perceived control, and psychological empowerment. *American Journal of Community Psychology, 16,* 725–750.

Zinn, H. (1999). *A peoples' history of the United States: 1492–Present: Twentieth anniversary edition.* New York: Harper.

CHAPTER 22

Health Psychology

CYNTHIA D. BELAR, TERESA MENDONCA McINTYRE, AND JOSEPH D. MATARAZZO

ROOTS OF THE FIELD   451
FORMALIZATION AS A FIELD OF INQUIRY
    AND PRACTICE   453
FORMALIZATION OF THE FIELD
    WITHIN PSYCHOLOGY   456
    American Organizational Efforts   456
    International Organizational Efforts   457

PROFESSIONAL PRACTICE   458
EDUCATION AND TRAINING   459
    Training in Europe   460
CONCLUSION   460
SUGGESTED READINGS   461
REFERENCES   461

Health psychology is the aggregate of the specific educational, scientific, and professional contributions of the discipline of psychology to the promotion and maintenance of health, the prevention and treatment of illness, the identification of etiologic and diagnostic correlates of health, illness and related dysfunction, and the analysis and improvement of the health care system and health policy formation. (Matarazzo, 1980, 1982, 2001)

Health psychology is distinguished from behavioral medicine in that the latter is an interdisciplinary field examining relationships between behavior and health and is not limited to psychology. Yet health psychology does have foundations in other health and social sciences. Its core knowledge base involves the integration of biological, cognitive, affective, social and psychological bases of behavior with biological, cognitive, affective, social, and psychological bases of health and disease. Health psychology also includes knowledge of health policy and the organization of health care delivery systems. It is a very broad field, characterized by studies in health behavior, behavioral risk factors for illness, response to illness, the impact of social support on health, culture and health, physician-patient relationships, psychoneuroimmunology, and psychophysiology among others.

Clinical health psychology is the term used for application of health psychology in professional practice. This specialty

is dedicated to both the development of knowledge and the delivery to individuals, families, and health care systems of high quality services based on that knowledge (APA, 1997).

ROOTS OF THE FIELD

The roots of health psychology are in the history of mind–body relationships along with those of other fields such as philosophy, theology, mathematics, astrology, and medicine. Mind–body relationships were very much the concern of priests, alchemists, shamans, or healers, and throughout history a multiplicity of views converged in two alternating approaches: a unitary view that postulates that mind and body are indivisible and a dualistic view that sees them as separate entities. The roots of health psychology can be traced back to the unitary view of mind–body relationships (Taylor, 1999).

Our knowledge of prehistoric societies indicates that humans considered mind and body as a unit, attributing physical and mental illnesses to demonic possession or evil spirits. The early writings of Hebrews, Egyptians, and Chinese confirmed this supernatural view of causality. Stone Age archaeological findings in Europe and South America show evidence of a surgical procedure called trephination that some claim shamans used to allow evil forces to leave the body (Selling, 1940).

In ancient Greece, the unitary view evolved to include naturalistic causes of disease, opening the way to modern medicine. Plato (427–347 B.C.) wrote that "it is not proper to cure

We are thankful to John Weinman, Ad Kaptein, Ralf Schwarzer, Hannah McGee, and Marie Johnston for their helpful comments on an earlier version of the manuscript and providing historical information regarding the development of Health Psychology in Europe.

the eyes without the head, nor the head without the body, so neither it is proper to cure the body without the soul." Aristotle, in 350 B.C., observed how emotions like joy, fear, anger, and courage affect the body, thus linking bodily processes to emotional states (Gentry & Matarazzo, 1981; Lipsitt, 1999). However, it was the Greek physician Hippocrates (460–377 B.C.), often called the father of modern medicine, who proposed a humoral theory of illness later expanded by Galen (A.D. 129–199). This was a hydraulic model that postulated that disease would result from the imbalance of four bodily fluids or humors—blood, black bile, yellow bile, and phlegm (Lipowski, 1986). Galen proposed four personality types based on the predominance of one of the four humors (choleric, melancholic, sanguine, and phlegmatic); these types permeated European personality theories for centuries thereafter. In sum, the ancient Greeks believed that mind and body were part of one system, that a balance between physical and emotional states was fundamental to health, and that psychological factors could influence bodily functions or even cause disease.

Lyons and Petrucelli (1978) describe a Greek legend that illustrates the role of behavior and balance in health and illness. According to this myth, Zeus, the chief Olympian god, brought the healer Asclepius into the heavens because of his healing abilities. Asclepius became a half-god and had two famous daughters, Hygeia and Panacea. Hygeia was the goddess of health and prevention; she taught the Greeks they could be healthy if they were moderate in all forms of behavior. Panacea was the goddess of medicine; she represented the continuous search for treatment of all illnesses (cited by Maes & Van Elderen, 1998, p. 591). These views were adopted by Roman physicians and influenced Greek and Roman healing practices that included medical and psychological approaches such as exercise, massage, music, a warm and soothing atmosphere, and the like.

In the Middle Ages, a holistic view of mind–body relationships was reflected in the supernatural view of causality and treatment, but holism began losing credibility as the separation between church and state became more evident and medical views of illness emerged. With this separation also came the belief that mind and body were separate entities, or what is known as dualism. During the Renaissance, the philosopher Descartes (1596–1650) proposed what is now referred to as Cartesian dualism: the premise that mind and body are separate entities and that the explanations for bodily processes are to be found in the body itself. By emphasizing the materialism of the body, Cartesian dualism de-emphasized the importance of emotions in health (Lipsitt, 1999).

The development of physical medicine consolidated a dualistic approach that then became the predominant model for medical science and practice in much of Western civilization. The work of the Dutch physician Vesalius in the 1500s marked the development of science in anatomy and physiology, highlighting the importance of the scientific method and experimentation. In the seventeenth and eighteenth centuries, Antonie van Leeuwenhoek's work on microscopy and Giovanni Morgagni's advances in autopsy both contributed to the discrediting of the humoral theory (Kaplan, 1975). In England, in 1628, William Harvey used the objective scientific method to disprove the humoral theory by identifying that blood circulates in the body and is propelled by the heart (Gatchel, 1993).

During the eighteenth century, progress was made in understanding relationships between physical reactions and psychological phenomena. Heart rate and temperature were measured with increased sophistication, and pathways between bodily secretions and emotional reactions were identified. Although biomedical reductionism seemed to bury unitary views of mind–body relationships, the active ingredients in the clinical practice of medicine were actually primarily psychological ones (Matarazzo, 1994). In 1747, a professor of medicine wrote that "the reason why a sound body becomes ill, or an ailing body recovers, very often lies in the mind" (Gaub, cited in Lipowski, 1977, p. 234).

In the nineteenth century, the role of psychological factors in illness revived, giving rise to a new holistic movement and paving the way for the psychosomatic medicine movement. The prominent physician Claude Bernard emphasized the role of psychological factors in physical illness (Gatchel, 1993), and the psychiatrist Heinroth, in Germany, is said to have been the first to use the term "psychosomatic" (Lipsitt, 1999). In the United States, Benjamin Rush (1746–1813), considered the father of American psychiatry, wrote the first textbook on the treatment of mental illness (Rush, 1812), but he also asserted that "actions of the mind" could cause many illnesses. In 1812, he also founded the American Medico-Psychological Association, which later became the American Psychiatric Association.

In Europe, the antecessors of the psychodynamic approach, Austrian physician Franz Mesmer and Parisian neurologist Jean Martin Charcot, reported several instances of hysterical states in which physical symptoms had no medical explanation and could be induced or removed by hypnosis. These observations defied the biomedical reductionism that dominated medical science in the late eighteenth and early nineteenth centuries. However, it was Freud's theories about hysterical conversion as the expression of repressed instinctual impulses that inspired the field of psychosomatic inquiry, which then blossomed in the following 50 years.

In other developments, the change in 1889 of William James's title from professor of philosophy to professor of psychology at Harvard marked the beginning of a new era for the discipline of psychology; thought and feeling had become a major focus for intensive scientific study. In addition, two independent researchers were conducting work in psychophysiology that was to become seminal in the field. Walter Bradford Cannon investigated visceral aspects of emotional experiences (specifically adrenaline and the excitement of the sympathetic nervous system), inventing the term "homeostasis" to describe the balanced state that human physiology sought to maintain (Cannon, 1915). In Russia, Ivan Pavlov received a Nobel Prize in 1904 for his work on the conditioned reflex and the physiology of the digestive gland, work that had profound implications for understanding learning processes and the development of psychophysiological disorders. His work led to the development in Russia of what was named "cortical-visceral-medicine," which has some overlap with psychosomatic medicine but leaves out subjective dimensions of experience and the unconscious processes (Lipsitt, 1999). Thus, by 1900, forces within medicine, physiology, and psychology had revived an integrated perspective of health and illness, mind and body.

Meanwhile, psychoanalysis spread in popularity in both Europe and the United States. Adolph Meyer, a Swiss psychiatrist, moved to Johns Hopkins in 1910 and continued to build on the concept of holism (derived from the Greek *holos,* or "whole"), introduced by Jan Christian Smuts in 1926 (Lipowski, 1986). Meyer proposed a new field of study, psychobiology, as the study of the person as a whole and not just the disease. Mind and body were seen as separate but integrated parts constituting a psychobiological unit (Meyer, 1957). This work helped bridge the gap between psychiatry and the other medical specialties, laying the foundation for the development of psychosomatic medicine and liaison psychiatry (Lipsitt, 1999).

FORMALIZATION AS A FIELD OF INQUIRY AND PRACTICE

The more formalized field of psychosomatic medicine emerged between 1920 and 1950, dominated by two major frameworks: psychodynamic and psychophysiologic. Major contributions of psychosomatic medicine were the recognition of the role of psychological and social factors in the etiology, course, maintenance, and treatment of disease (especially those that defied biomedical explanations), and the promotion of behavioral health research.

Helen Flanders Dunbar, a follower of Meyer, promoted the idea that psychosomatic symptoms were associated with certain personality types and not just with a single conflict, as Freud had postulated. She believed that all illnesses were psychosomatic and worked diligently to facilitate acceptance of that view among physicians and the general public. Her views were popularized through her 1935 book, *Emotions and Bodily Changes,* and she became the founding editor of a new journal, *Psychosomatic Medicine,* at a time when men dominated American medicine. The preface to the first issue (1939) declared its devotion to the study of the interrelationships between psychological and physiological aspects of all normal and abnormal bodily functions and the integration of somatic therapy and psychotherapy. It is interesting to note that Dunbar intended to advance psychosomatic medicine not as a new specialty within medicine but rather as a way of educating medical professionals and scientists to view illness as multidimensional, a perspective that can be considered a precursor to the later systems models (Lipsitt, 1999).

In 1942, a group of researchers, including psychiatrists, physiologists, internists, psychologists, and psychoanalysts, founded the American Psychosomatic Society (APS). A neurologist, Tracy Putnam, was its first president. Levenson (1994) describes these early members as adventurers and experimenters who were interested in exploring the mind–body riddle. She notes that psychiatry was not yet well accepted in the male-dominated medical schools or teaching hospitals, and at a time when American education and medicine was anti-Semitic, the APS welcomed refugees fleeing Nazi Germany. Yet the psychosomatic medicine movement did not promote any political or feminist agenda, nor was it bound to any one theory, as members held widely different points of view (e.g., Pavlovians, Freudians). Some members were interested in specific diseases, others in the connections between emotions and bodily processes. A few researchers were interested in topics such as overutilization of health care services, but much work consisted of pathology-oriented treatment reports of the "classic" psychosomatic disorders.

Psychodynamic theory as a framework continues to dominate psychosomatic medicine in Europe, especially in southern European countries. Historically, both psychiatrists and psychologists have contributed to its expansion. Some of these were European psychoanalysts who immigrated to the United States to flee Nazi persecution, such as Franz Alexander. In Chicago, Alexander built upon Freud's formulation of conversion hysteria to derive the specificity theory of psychosomatic disease. From his clinical observation of patients undergoing psychoanalysis, he concluded that specific emotional conflicts, called nuclear conflicts, were associated with specific physical diseases such as peptic ulcer, hypertension, rheumatoid arthritis, and asthma. He believed that the repressed psychic energy could affect autonomic nervous system functioning directly, thus altering visceral functioning. For instance, in the case of an ulcer patient, the repressed emotions associated with a dependency conflict would increase the secretion of acid in the stomach, which would in time affect the stomach lining and ultimately produce ulcers (Alexander, 1950).

In the United States, the work of Dunbar and her followers was seriously questioned in the 1950s at the same time that psychoanalysis was being criticized for its lack of scientific rigor. However, more scientific psychoanalytic/psychodynamic theories of psychosomatic illness were subsequently developed, as reflected in the work Sifneos and Nemiah on alexithymia (Nemiah, 1973; Sifneos, 1967) and the specific-attitudes theory developed by Graham and his colleagues (Graham, 1972; Graham, Stern, & Winokur, 1958). Indeed, the idea of a relationship between personality and physical illness is present in current concepts such as Type A behavior patterns and Type C personality. Moreover, expansion of the field was fostered by the strengthening of other conceptual models as well as the development of new ones that would drive health behavior research.

As noted above, the other early theoretical framework that contributed to the survival and expansion of the psychosomatic movement was psychophysiology, an approach that provided more objective and scientific foundations for the development of the field. Edmund Jacobson, a psychologist and physician who had studied under James and Cannon at Harvard, examined the role of muscle tension in relaxation (Jacobson, 1938). He also developed progressive muscle relaxation, a behavioral intervention that is today referred to as the aspirin of behavioral medicine. In fact, by the 1950s the field seemed dominated by a focus on stress and its relationship to health and bodily functioning. Hans Selyé (1953), a physiologist, popularized stress as a cause of illness.

In addition, Harold G. Wolff's work on the psychology and physiology of gastric function (Wolf & Wolff, 1947) as well as his work on migraine, ulcer, colitis, and hypertension provided careful examination of the physiological changes associated with conscious emotional states such as anger and resentment. Wolff's 1953 book, *Stress and Disease,* remains a classic. This psychophysiological approach marked the growth of experimentation and a departure from the study of unconscious processes and reliance on methods of clinical observation. The use of the term *psychophysiological disorders* also dates back to Wolff's work and reflects an effort of the psychosomatic movement to dissociate itself from the psychodynamic orientation and move toward a more

cognitive behavioral framework that would characterize much of the future work on stress and disease.

By the 1950s, the specificity theories based on psychoanalytic foundations also had serious competition from systems approaches. Guze, Matarazzo, and Saslow (1953) published a description of a biopsychosocial model as a blueprint for comprehensive medicine, a term more favored in some circles than the label psychosomatic. This model emphasized the interrelationships among, and mutually interacting effects of, multiple biological, psychological, and social processes. Later work by Engel (1977) and Leigh and Reiser (1980) has perhaps been more widely cited, but all were very similar attempts to provide a unitary framework for diagnoses and treatment of the full spectrum of health problems.

A number of other societies were developed in the mid-1900s that reflected the expansion of interest in the psychosomatic movement: the American Society of Psychosomatic Dentistry (1948), the Society for Psychosomatic Research in Great Britain (1960), and the Swiss Society of Psychosomatic Medicine (1963).

As interest in stress and disease during the 1960s and 1970s grew, so did interest in coping—which in turn brought more attention to cognitive and behavioral efforts to manage stress. It was also recognized that illness was a part of life that no one could escape, and that illness itself was a stressor that required coping skills for adaptation. Coping was viewed as a complex process that included significant cognitive, affective, behavioral, and social components. The development of the health-belief model also focused attention on cognitive components in health and disease and fostered the interface with public health perspectives (Rosenstock, 1966).

Concurrent with developments in stress and coping was the pioneering work of Neal E. Miller, whose theoretical and empirical work on the conditioning of physiological processes laid the scientific foundation for the development of biofeedback interventions for specific health problems (Miller, 1969). The application of operant learning theory to the management of chronic pain was initiated by Wilbert Fordyce, whose work became fundamental to the design of pain and chronic illness management programs for the rest of the century (Fordyce, 1976).

A serendipitous event occurred in 1974 that was also to shape future research and practice in the field. Robert Ader, an experimental psychologist, noticed that some of his animals died unexpectedly during a conditioning experiment. Through careful research, he subsequently determined that those deaths had been the result of a conditioned suppression of the immune system. As expected, this finding was greeted with much skepticism in the field, but nevertheless it heralded the beginning of what Ader called psychoneuroimmunology, an area of study that grew rapidly. As described by Levenson (1994), Ader himself was troubled by the fact that his initial work might have received attention in part because of his reputation as a very careful, conservative scientist. He wondered what would have happened if an unknown investigator had come to the same conclusions.

In 1977, a number of psychologists, physicians, and other behavioral scientists attended the Yale Conference on Behavioral Medicine to give support to the birth of a new interdisciplinary field labeled behavioral medicine. Many of these attendees believed that as then conceptualized, psychosomatic medicine did not clearly represent the thrust of current research and practice. Joined by others the next year at a conference at the National Academy of Sciences, they adopted the following definition for the new field:

> Behavioral medicine is the interdisciplinary field concerned with the development and integration of behavioral and biomedical science knowledge and techniques relevant to health and illness and the application of this knowledge and these techniques to prevention, diagnosis, treatment and rehabilitation. (Schwartz & Weiss, 1978)

By 1979, the explosion of research in health and behavior, and its practical significance to medicine, was recognized by the Institute of Medicine (IOM) of the National Academy of Sciences. A committee was formed to review the field and set a research agenda with psychiatrist David Hamburg as chair and psychologist Judith Rodin as vice-chair; over half the membership were psychologists. The subsequent report (IOM, 1982) documented that 50% of mortality from the 10 leading causes of death could be traced to behavior. This effort, plus support from U.S. surgeon general Joseph Califano (*Healthy People: The Surgeon General's Report on Health Promotion and Disease Prevention,* 1979), stimulated congressional interest and led to increased funding for NIH for research on behavioral factors in disease prevention and health promotion.

The zeitgeist transcended national boundaries. European health psychologists have made innovative and significant contributions in a variety of areas, especially the relationships among personality, stress, and disease; the role of social cognition in health and illness behavior; and the development and outcome evaluation of health promotion programs in various contexts (school, work, and community). Other contributions of European health psychologists have been in measurement, both in developing new measures and in adapting and validating many English-language psychological instruments to various populations in each country. The cross-validation of measures in many cultural contexts has been an important opportunity for testing theory and related constructs

in the domain of health psychology, as well as measurement theory. Finally, several Europe-wide studies, some of them under the auspices of the World Health Organization (WHO), have increased understanding of epidemiological patterns and their relationship to psychosocial variables. Examples are those projects related to cardiovascular disease (WHO-MONICA project [WHO, 2000]) and health behaviors in school-aged children (WHO-HBSC project [Currie, Hurrelmann, Settertobulte, Smith, & Todd, 2000]).

Worldwide, over the past 25 years there has been a significant focus on research and practice related to health behaviors such as those involved in dietary management, exercise, adherence to medical regimens, and seat belt usage. Although the term *behavioral health* was originally defined by Matarazzo (1980) as a corollary to behavioral medicine in order to emphasize health promotion and prevention rather than illness itself, it was unfortunate that the term was not trademarked at that time. In the last decade, this term has come to be used to describe alcohol, substance abuse, and other more traditional mental health services in the evolving health care system and no longer conveys its distinctive meaning.

Other trends have been an increased emphasis on environmental health psychology (e.g., examination of stress-related health effects of environmental noise, Staples, 1996), occupational health psychology, and genetic testing. There has also been increased emphasis on women's health issues and issues of diversity in health behavior research. In 1992, the National Conference on Behavioral and Sociocultural Perspectives on Ethnicity and Health was held, resulting in a special issue of *Health Psychology* edited by Norman B. Anderson, the conference organizer (Anderson, 1995). There has also been more focus on the application of health behavior research findings to public policy, of which Patrick DeLeon has been a leader within U.S. psychology.

In conclusion, despite harsh criticism, the psychosomatic movement within which psychology and psychologists have played significant roles has survived and evolved to include more social and cultural correlates of illness. The terminology related to the field has also evolved such that terms such as *behavioral medicine, behavioral health, health psychology,* and *health behavior research* are more prominent. From its initial focus on personality and disease, the movement has given rise to work on the relationship between illness and bereavement, helplessness, life changes, occupational stress, social support, health beliefs, ethnicity, environmental stressors, and others. Moreover, it has stimulated new multidisciplinary areas of inquiry, such as psychoneuroimmunology and psychoneuroendocrinology. It has also been home for a wide range of theoretical viewpoints, including psychodynamic, psychophysiological, and cognitive-behavioral theories. It represents a historical landmark in the change of beliefs in medicine, psychology, and the general public regarding mind–body relationships.

FORMALIZATION OF THE FIELD WITHIN PSYCHOLOGY

Historically, psychologists were active participants in the development of psychosomatic medicine. In fact, a number of presidents of the American Psychosomatic Society have been psychologists, including Margaret Thaler Singer (1972, the first PhD and the first woman to be president), Robert Ader (1979), C. David Jenkins (1983), Bernard Engel (1985), Karen Matthews (1990), James Blumenthal (1995), and Margaret Chesney (1997).

Perhaps the first action of organized psychology in relation to organized medicine was the appointment of a committee in 1911 that examined the teaching of psychology in medical schools (Franz, 1913). This early focus was designed to promote psychological competence in medical practice through the instruction of medical students; thus, psychology began its role in the health care system as a teacher of medical students. The growth of health-service-provider psychologists came later.

American Organizational Efforts

A landmark event for health psychology within organized psychology was a report prepared by William Schofield for the board of directors of the American Psychological Association (APA): *The Role of Psychology in the Delivery of Health Services* (Schofield, 1969). This essay had a much broader focus than its title implies, as it addressed both theoretical and research aspects of the discipline that had implications for "the promotion and maintenance of health, the prevention and treatment of illness" (p. 565). Schofield noted how organized psychology had been implicitly dualistic, often contrasting mental health with physical health and distributing more discipline resources to the former. For example, his examination of articles indexed in *Psychological Abstracts* for 1966 and 1967 found three focuses in health: schizophrenia, psychotherapy, and mental retardation. Altogether, major and much more numerous health problems such as pain, surgery, heart disease, cancer, smoking, and medical hospitalization accounted for less than 10% of publications in those years! He noted that only a smattering of individual psychologists pursued interests in medical nonpsychiatric problems and opined that with the possible exception of involvement with the physically handicapped, the discipline

had only "superficially mined" the area of the psychology of physical illness. He also predicted that this would not change without change in the education and training of future psychologists.

Scofield argued cogently for psychology to view itself as a health science and a broadly based health profession (not just a mental health profession); yet it would be another 30 years before this perspective became mainstream within organized psychology.

In 1973, another seminal event occurred when the APA Board of Scientific Affairs established the Task Force on Health Research upon the recommendation of the Committee on Newly Emerging Areas of Research. Miriam Kelty (who in 2000 received a Career Service Award for her work in health psychology) served as APA staff liaison. Three decades ago the societal context was increased public concern about rising health costs and deficiencies in the way health care was delivered in the United States. Although health had become a social issue and was no longer solely the province of medicine, psychology as a discipline was described as "surprisingly slow to recognize and accept research challenges in this problem area. Possibly the historical prominence of mental health as a focus for applied psychology has overshadowed other types of health-oriented psychological research" (APA, 1976, p. 264). The task force did identify nearly 500 psychologists with health research interests, but half of those were employed outside of health settings and many were not members of the APA, having resigned because they found no divisional affiliation compatible with their interests. Moreover, their research tended to be published in non-APA journals, a number of which were not even included in the *Psychological Abstracts Search and Retrieval (PASAR)* database and thus not available to the average APA member.

The Task Force on Health Research found that approximately 40 health research articles were published per year between 1966 and 1973. Of those, about 66% were related to psychobiological aspects of health (stress, psychosomatics, social and environmental factors, effects of illness on behavior), 18% dealt with health care delivery issues (mostly specific aspects of treatment and rehabilitation rather than systems research), and 16% were studies of attitudes relevant to health and health care. To foster the development of knowledge in this area the task force made a series of recommendations: (a) increase awareness among psychologists of support for health research from agencies other than the National Institute of Mental Health (NIMH), (b) eliminate mind–body dualism in conceptualizing human behavior by adopting more integrated models, (c) develop graduate education programs to promote early awareness of opportunities for research and practice, and (d) "find a suitable home within

APA for . . . a distinct interest group that is likely to grow and has need for the basic organizational supports afforded by our major scientific and professional society" (APA, 1976, p. 272). A direct outcome of the Task Force on Health Research was the 1975 organization of the Section on Health Research in the APA's Division of Psychologists in Public Service. Concomitantly, David Clayman and John Linton were facilitating communication among clinical psychologists working in medical settings by developing the Medical Psychologist's Network and a related newsletter, using the term medical psychology to describe their work.

The years 1977–1978 were a high point for the formalization of health psychology within the discipline. Given the growth in the field and the need to find an organization to integrate those with both research and practice interests, in 1977 members successfully petitioned for a new division within the APA. At the annual meeting in August, the Division of Health Psychology (Division 38) was formally installed by the APA Council of Representatives with Joseph D. Matarazzo as its first president. In his charter presidential address one year later, Matarazzo provided the foundation for the first definition of the field to be adopted by the division.

In recognition of health psychology's need to function within an interdisciplinary context, two other societies were also formed in 1978, with psychologists playing a major role in their foundation. The Academy of Behavioral Medicine was established in April with Neal E. Miller as its first president, and on November 16, the first organizational meeting of the Society of Behavioral Medicine was held in Chicago. (The International Society of Behavioral Medicine was founded in 1990.) Also in 1978, the *Journal of Behavioral Medicine* was established, with W. Doyle Gentry as its editor.

One might question why psychologists promoted societies and publications with a focus on behavioral medicine versus psychosomatic medicine, the term previously more common. As noted previously, a group of disaffected biomedical and behavioral scientists had met in 1977 at Yale to formally establish the field of behavioral medicine, having been frustrated by the inadequacies of traditional conceptualizations of psychosomatic medicine.

The first issue of the Division of Health Psychology's scientific journal, *Health Psychology*, was quickly organized and published in 1982 under the editorship of George C. Stone. Given the burgeoning of research, it quickly moved from a quarterly publication to a bimonthly one in 1984. By 2000, *Health Psychology* had more individual subscriptions than any APA journal other than *American Psychologist* and *Monitor*, publications that are provided as part of membership in the APA. In 2000, the Division of Health Psychology

had over 2,800 members and a number of formal interest groups, including those on women's health, minority health, education and training, and international affairs.

International Organizational Efforts

Health psychology was also becoming more organized in Europe during the same period of time. Six years after APA Division 38 was founded, Professor Stan Maes organized an international conference on health psychology in Tilburg (the Netherlands), which then initiated the formation in 1986 of the European Health Psychology Society (EHPS) (Schwarzer & Johnston, 1994). At this meeting were also Marie Johnston (UK), John Weinman (UK), Ralf Schwarzer (Germany), Ad Kaptein (the Netherlands), Lothar Schmidt and Peter Schwenkmezger (Germany), and Jan Vinck (Belgium), who became key people in the development of health psychology in Europe and in their own countries. It is interesting to note that among the 60 participants was a large contingent from the United States, including Charles Spielberger and Irwin Sarason, who supported the development of a European association. At that conference, it also became apparent that a substantial amount of research was being conducted in various European countries on topics relevant to health psychology (Maes, 1990; Maes, Spielberger, Defares, & Sarason, 1988).

The creation of the EHPS in 1986 represents an important landmark for the development of health psychology in Europe. The purpose of the EHPS is "the promotion and development within Europe of empirical and theoretical research and applications of health psychology and the interchange of information relating to this subject between European members and other associations throughout the world" (Schwarzer & Johnston, 1994, p. 4). Since then, the EHPS annual conferences have offered an important setting for exchange among the major European scholars in the field. They also provide a forum for the discussion of issues facing health psychology in Europe, both as a science and a profession. The growing number of participants in the EHPS conferences from 1988 to 1996 illustrates the development of the field. There were 60 participants in 1986, 100 in 1989 (Utrecht, the Netherlands), and 500 in 1996 (Dublin, Ireland).

Another important landmark in the definition of health psychology in Europe was a document written by the European Federation of Professional Psychologist's Associations (EFPPA) and published by the WHO Regional Office for Europe in 1984; this document clarifies the contribution of psychology to the health field. The EFPPA has played an important role in the development of professional health psychology, as will be detailed later.

The following 10 years witnessed a rapid growth of health psychology both within and outside the EHPS. In the 1990s, many European countries developed their own health psychology groups and national societies, although there are many asymmetries among European countries in practice orientation and research. The oldest national groups were created in Ireland and England (Johnston, 1997). In 1986, interest groups in health psychology were established at the British Psychological Society and the Psychological Society of Ireland (Weinman, 1998). Other countries that followed this early expansion were the Netherlands, Germany, Poland, Finland, and Norway. Currently, there are EHPS delegates in 27 European countries, including eastern Europe (McIntyre, Maes, Weinman, Wrzesniewski, & Marks, 2000).

Comparable developments were taking place in Asia under the leadership of Professor Hiroshi Motoaki of Tokyo's Waseda University. These included his seminal roles in the establishment in 1988 of the Japanese Association of Health Psychology and in 2000 of the Asian Congress of Health Psychology. Matoaki was elected charter president of each of these groups.

A major contribution of the EHPS to the scientific development of health psychology in Europe has been the publication of the *Journal of Psychology and Health,* the leading European journal in this field since 1986 when it was founded under editor John Weinman. Other more recent journals have also contributed to this field, including the *Journal of Health Psychology* (founding editors: Andrew Steptoe & Jane Wardle) and *Psychology, Health & Medicine* (founding editor: Lorraine Sherr). Several national health psychology journals have been created that publish health psychology articles in the country's language, such as the *British Journal of Health Psychology* (United Kingdom), *Gedrag & Gezondheid: Tijdschrift voor Psychologie en Gezondheid* (the Netherlands), *Revista de Psicologia de la Salud* (Spain), and *Zeitschrift für Gesundheitspsychologie* (Germany).

Although there are many commonalities between North American and European health psychology, health psychology in Europe is perhaps best characterized by its diversity (Johnston, 1993). There is wide variation among European countries in terms of expectation of life and patterns of disease, in health behaviors and risk behaviors, in health knowledge, health beliefs and attitudes, and in service provision. As Johnston points out, this diversity provides great potential for science, as cross-cultural comparisons allow the testing of the universality of psychological processes, constructs, and models. Europe thus provides a rich laboratory to undertake the study of the impact of variation on different health processes, such as health care provision. This asymmetry also carries over to education, training, and practice in health psychology in Europe. Based on the articles being published in the Japanese *Journal of Health Psychology* during its first dozen years of existence, research and education in health psychology in Japan appear quite similar to counterparts in the United States.

PROFESSIONAL PRACTICE

In 1984, Joseph D. Matarazzo applied to the state of Oregon for the incorporation of the American Board of Health Psychology (ABHP). His vision was that professional practice within health psychology would soon mature sufficiently to become a bonafide specialty worthy of board certification from the American Board of Professional Psychology (ABPP). The purpose of the ABHP was "(1) to define standards, conduct examinations, grant diplomas and encourage the pursuit of excellence in the practice of Health Psychology; (2) to serve the public welfare by preparing and furnishing to proper persons and agencies lists of specialists who have been awarded certificates" (ABHP By-laws, Section II).

In 1991, ABHP president Cynthia D. Belar and vice-president Timothy B. Jeffrey presented a petition to ABPP for recognition of clinical health psychology as a specialty in professional psychology. In December of that year, the first health psychology diplomate examinations were held. In May 1993, after several years of fine-tuning and monitoring, the ABPP formally admitted the ABHP into full affiliation.

When the APA developed a formal mechanism for recognition of specialties, health psychology was one of the first to apply. Upon recommendation of the Commission on the Recognition of Specialties and Proficiencies in Professional Psychology, the APA Council of Representatives recognized clinical health psychology as a specialty in professional practice in 1997. The term "clinical" had been added to the name in this petition to avoid confusing the field and the public about education and training standards for those preparing for careers in practice versus those preparing for careers solely in research. In general, health psychologists preparing for careers in teaching and research alone were not interested in the kinds of accreditation and credentialing processes important to those preparing for careers in practice with the public. Because ABPP recognized the specialty as health psychology and the APA recognized it as clinical health psychology, to maintain consistency in the profession, ABHP changed its name in 1998 to the American Board of Clinical Health Psychology.

Although health psychology has become a well-established disciplinary domain within psychology in Europe, the regulation of the profession in Europe is very diverse. Some countries, such as England, Holland, and Austria, have licensing and registration procedures (Johnston & Weinman, 1995; Strauss-Blasche, 1998; Taal, 1998; Weinman, 1998) whereas others, such as Greece, Romania, and Portugal, do not (Anagnostopoulu, 1998; Baban, 1998; McIntyre, 1998). The lack of regulation poses problems in terms of quality control of services provided and could have damaging effects on the credibility of the profession. In general, it appears that having a division of health psychology within the country's national association is an important step towards regulation of the profession. The position of the European Federation of Professional Psychologists' Associations (EFPPA) is that regulation should be done at a national and not European level (Lunt & Poortinga, 1996). However, they have established training guidelines for professional health psychologists in an attempt to define minimal training standards across all European countries.

EDUCATION AND TRAINING

In the early 1980s, the first systematic attempts were made to identify education and training opportunities in the broad area of health psychology. Belar identified 42 doctoral programs and 43 postdoctoral programs offering one or more elements of such education (Belar & Siegel, 1983; Belar, Wilson, & Hughes, 1982). Gentry, Street, Masur, and Asken (1981) identified 48 internship programs. Within doctoral programs of that era, the predominant model (70%) was that of a health psychology track within another area of psychology (usually clinical, counseling, or school psychology).

In 1983, the first national conference specifically devoted to graduate education and training was held at Arden House, New York. Chaired by Stephen M. Weiss, the conference developed recommendations for doctoral, internship, and postdoctoral curricula and training experiences for those pursuing careers in either research or the practice of health psychology (Stone, 1983). Core curricular graduate-level components included biological, social, and psychological bases of health systems and behavior as well as health research training, ethics, interdisciplinary collaboration, and access to health care settings under the mentorship of experienced psychology faculty. A defining text oriented to education and training requirements also resulted from this conference: *Health Psychology: A Discipline and a Profession* (Stone et al., 1987).

In addition to the didactic educational requirements, the professional practice specialty of clinical health psychology requires sound training experiences in health assessment, interventions, and consultations. Fundamental to education and training in clinical health psychology is the scientist-practitioner model, a biopsychosocial approach, faculty role models for research and practice, access to health care settings, participation and active supervision by a multidisciplinary faculty in a health care setting, and exposure to diverse clinical problems and populations.

The conference in 1983 also established the Council of Health Psychology Training Directors. This group provides a forum to discuss education and training issues across baccalaureate, graduate, and postgraduate levels and to develop policy related to health psychology education and training. The council has been involved in developing guidelines for the accreditation of education and training programs that would inform the APA Committee on Accreditation in their review process. The first postdoctoral program in health psychology was accredited by the APA in 2001.

One measure of the growth of the new field was that by 1990, Sayette and Mayne found that health psychology was the most frequently noted area of faculty research in APA-accredited clinical psychology doctoral programs.

The needs of already trained practitioners who wish to develop more expertise so as to ethically expand their areas of practice have also been recognized, especially as the knowledge base for practice has expanded and the field has become more mainstream. In 1997, Belar and colleagues developed a model for self-assessment to facilitate practitioners' identification of gaps in knowledge and skills. Self-assessment could then permit the design of appropriate continuing-education activities for the ethical expansion of practice (Belar et al., 2001).

Nearly 20 years after the Arden House Conference, the APA Division of Health Psychology agreed to sponsor another national conference under the leadership of then president Kenneth A. Wallston (also a longtime editor of the division's newsletter, *The Health Psychologist*). The conference, held in 2000, was designed to focus future issues for the discipline and the profession. Participants examined specific areas with respect to implications of new research for education and training, clinical practice, research, and public policy, including: evolution of the biopsychosocial model; advances in medicine; changes in population demographics, health care economics, and the health psychology marketplace; needs and advances in primary prevention; and developments in interventions. Participants reported that there was an increased need for attention in the doctoral curriculum to genetics, advances in medical technology in assessment and treatment (e.g., ambulatory monitoring, home testing, imaging techniques, medical devices), organ and tissue transplantation, pharmacology, telehealth, health informatics, primary care, and issues of diversity in health care. Participants remained excited about future opportunities for growth in the field and for its potential to make significant contributions to the public welfare.

Training in Europe

In Europe, education and training in health psychology is characterized by wide variation in models and requirements for practice across countries. Marks and colleagues (1998) note that "many European countries still do not yet train health psychologists in any specific and specialized manner" (p. 156). However, the development of high-quality, formalized training in health psychology has been a key concern for the EFPA and the EHPS. Both organizations, separately and in collaboration, have addressed these issues through the organization of task forces, committees, symposia, and publications (e.g. Johnston, 1994; Maes & Kittel, 1990; Marks, 1994a, 1994b; McIntyre et al., 2000; Methorst, Jansen, & Kerkhof, 1991).

An important outcome that resulted from these efforts was the creation in 1992 of a task force that had among its objectives, as noted previously, the development of training guidelines for professional health psychologists. Requirements fall into eight categories (Marks et al., 1998) and are very similar to the U.S. core curriculum: academic knowledge base (psychology), academic knowledge base (other), application of psychological skills to health care delivery, research skills, teaching and training skills, management skills, professional issues, and ethical issues.

Currently, there is an effort to develop a common framework regarding time and contents of qualification for professional practice in psychology under the Europsych Project (Lunt, 2000). This is particularly important given the European Economic Community (EEC) directive on free movement of professionals between member states. The first matrix proposed is for a 6-year minimal requirement equivalent to a master's degree, including generic training with later specialization, which is the typical duration of health psychology professional training in Europe. However, there is strong sentiment that diversity in education and training patterns be preserved.

The EHPS has conducted two surveys regarding education and training programs in health psychology in Europe that demonstrate the development of the field. A survey conducted in 1988 (Methorst et al., 1991) in 19 European countries,

North America, and Australia concluded that true specialized training programs in health psychology existed only in the United States and Canada. In Europe, postgraduate training was part of clinical psychology, and doctoral training was typically based on writing a dissertation. In 1999, the EHPS created an Education and Training Committee that had as its first task the development of a reference guide to postgraduate programs in health psychology in Europe (McIntyre et al., 2000). In the 23 countries surveyed, 133 programs in health psychology or with a health psychology component were identified. Of these programs, 86 lead to a master's degree and 47 to a doctoral degree. Although indicating an impressive expansion of training in the field, doctoral training typically consists of an independent course of study; American-style formalized doctoral training programs in health psychology in Europe are still scarce. In terms of models of training, the scientist-practioner model continues to be considered central for professional training. However, the applicability of the American standard of PhD training to European settings has been discussed through the years (e.g., Maes, 1999; Maes & Kittel, 1990).

CONCLUSION

Although certainly not exhaustive, this chapter has attempted to review some highlights in the history of health psychology, respecting that its roots are as old as human history. Within health psychology, there have been a number of trends over the past century. The influence of psychodynamic theories and specificity theories as explanatory models has decreased. Focus on psychophysiological processes and the identification of pathways among systems (particularly neuroendocrine and immunologic) has increased. Statistical models have been developed that permit examination of multiple variables through multivariate analyses and path analyses, thus facilitating more sophisticated theoretical model building. Social and ecological dimensions to understanding health and illness have been added. Empirically supported psychological interventions for the prevention and amelioration of disease and disorders have been developed. Attention to the need to apply behavioral science to the improvement of the health care system and health policy has increased. More attention has been focused on issues of gender and ethnic cultural diversity in health behavior research and the delivery of health care services, and culturally sensitive interventions have been identified.

Historically, the reasons for the rapid growth of health psychology in the United States and Europe (and we might add, Japan) over the last 30 years appear similar (Gentry, 1984; Ogden, 1996; Taylor, 1999):

- The shift in patterns of mortality and morbidity from communicable diseases, such as tuberculosis and influenza, to chronic diseases (cancer and cardiovascular disease) and accidents.
- The recognition of behavioral causes associated with these diseases (such as smoking, high-fat diet, lack of seat belt use).
- The rising costs of health care and the increased support for behavioral science approaches.
- The shift of focus from disease and remediation to health, illness prevention, and quality of life.
- The recognition within medicine of the limitations of the traditional biomedical model to explain health and illness.
- The development within psychology of conceptual and research tools to contribute to illness, health, and health care.
- The search for alternatives to the traditional health care system.

The reasons cited above remain challenges for the future and thus underscore the continuing relevance of psychology's contributions to health, health problems, and health care delivery. However, some additional trends will challenge and shape health psychology in the future as well:

- The increased demands for health psychology services by consumers, providers, and organizations related to changing models of health and health care.
- The change in epidemiological patterns related to an aging population, with new roles emerging for health psychologists regarding the care and well-being of this age group.
- The imbalance between increased expenses in health care and decreasing individual and social funds available that is likely to render cost-effectiveness a top priority in health interventions.
- New and more expensive technologies that are likely to expand the role of health psychologists in this domain but also raise important ethical and social dilemmas.
- The health threats related to the environment and the increased mobility of people that are likely to pose new health problems that assume a more global dimension in terms of their understanding and proper management.

Marks (1996) proposes a new agenda for health psychology in which "health psychology should accept its interdisciplinary nature, venture more often out of the clinical arena, drop white-coated scientism, and relocate in the richer cultural, socio-political and community contexts of society" (p. 19).

Finally, health psychology has now become mainstream within American and Japanese psychology and is rapidly expanding in Europe. In fact, as noted elsewhere (Belar, 2001), we may be on the brink of witnessing a figure-ground reversal with respect to psychology's role in health behavior research and practice—from a focus on mental health as the domain of psychology's contribution to health to viewing mental health as only one subset in the domain of psychology's contribution to health.

SUGGESTED READINGS

Belar, C. D. (1997). Clinical health psychology: A specialty for the 21st century. *Health Psychology, 16,* 411–416.

Matarazzo, J. D. (1994). Health and behavior: The coming together of science and practice in psychology and medicine after a century of benign neglect. *Journal of Clinical Psychology in Medical Settings, 1,* 7–39.

Wallston, K. A. (1997). A history of Division 38 (Health Psychology): Healthy, wealthy, and Weiss. In D. A. Dewsburgy (Ed.). *Unification through division: Histories of the Divisions of the American Psychological Association, Volume II.* pp. 239–267. Washington, DC: American Psychological Association.

REFERENCES

Alexander, F. (1950). *Psychosomatic medicine.* New York: Norton.

American Board of Health Psychology. (1984). By-Laws, Section II.

American Psychological Association Council of Representatives. (1997, August). *Archival description of Clinical Health Psychology as a specialty in professional psychology.* Minutes of the Council of Representatives meeting. Chicago, IL.

American Psychological Association Task Force on Health Research. (1976). *Contributions of psychology to health research: Patterns, problems and potentials* (pp. 264–272). Washington, DC: Author.

Anagnostopoulu, T. (1998). The state of health psychology in Greece. In T. McIntyre (Chair), *The state of health psychology in Europe: Education and practice.* Symposium conducted at the 12th Conference of the European Health Psychology Society, Vienna, Austria.

Anderson, N. B. (Ed.). (1995). *Health Psychology, 14*(7), 588–656.

Baban, A. (1998). Health psychology in Romania: Present aspects and future trends. In T. McIntyre (Chair), *The state of health psychology in Europe: Education and practice.* Symposium conducted at the 12th Conference of the European Health Psychology Society, Vienna, Austria.

Belar, C. D., Brown, R. A., Hersch, L. E., Hornyak, L. M., Rozensky, R. H., Sheridan, E., P., et al. (2001). Education for health. *Monitor on Psychology, 32*(1), 56.

Belar, C. D., Brown, R. A., Hersch, L. E., Hornyak, L. M., Rozensky, R. H., Sheridan, E. P., et al. (2001). Self assessment in clinical health psychology: A model for ethical expansion of practice. *Professional Psychology, 32,* 135–141.

Belar, C. D., & Seigel, L. J. (1983). A survey of postdoctoral training programs in health psychology. *Health Psychology, 2,* 413–425.

Belar, C. D., Wilson, E., & Hughes, H. (1982). Health psychology training in doctoral psychology programs. *Health Psychology, 1,* 289–299.

Califano, J. A., Jr. (1979). *Healthy people: The Surgeon General's report on health promotion and disease prevention* (Stock No. 017–001-00416–2). Washington, DC: U.S. Government Printing Office.

Cannon, W. B. (1915). *Bodily changes in pain, hunger, fear and rage* (2nd ed.). New York: Appleton-Century-Crofts.

Currie, C., Hurrelmann, K., Settertobulte, W., Smith, R., & Todd, J. (Eds.). (2000). *Health and health behavior among young people* (HEPCA series). Geneva, Switzerland: World Health Organization.

Dunbar, H. (1935). *Emotions and bodily changes: A survey of literature on psychosomatic relationships: 1910–1933.* New York: Columbia University Press.

Engel, G. L. (1977). The need for a new medical model: A challenge for bio-medicine. *Science, 196,* 129–136.

Fordyce, W. E. (1976). *Behavioral methods for chronic pain and illness.* St. Louis, MO: Mosby.

Franz, I. D. (1913). On psychology and medical education. *Science, 38,* 555–566.

Gatchel, R. (1993). Psychophysiological disorders: Past and present perspectives. In R. Gatchel & E. Blanchard (Eds.), *Psychophysiological disorders: Research and clinical applications* (pp. 1–21). Washington, DC: American Psychological Association.

Gentry, W. D. (Ed.). (1984). *Handbook of behavioral medicine.* New York: Guilford Press.

Gentry, W. D., & Matarazzo, J. D. (1981). Medical psychology: Three decades of growth and development. In L. A. Bradley & C. K. Prokop (Eds.), *Medical psychology: Contributions to behavioral medicine* (pp. 6–15). San Diego, CA: Academic Press.

Gentry, W. D., Street, W. J., Masur, R. T., & Asken, M. J. (1981). Training in medical psychology: A survey of graduate and internship training programs. *Professional Psychology, 13,* 397–403.

Graham, D. T. (1972). Psychosomatic medicine. In N. S. Greenfield & R. A. Sternbach (Eds.), *Handbook of psychophysiology* (pp. 839–924). New York: Holt, Rinehart and Winston.

Graham, D. T., Stern, J. A., & Winokur, G. (1958). Experimental investigation of the specificity hypothesis in psychosomatic disease. *Psychomatic Medicine, 20,* 446–457.

Guze, S. B., Matarazzo, J. D., & Saslow, G. (1953). A formulation of principles of comprehensive medicine with special reference to learning theory. *Journal of Clinical Psychology, 9,* 127–136.

Institute of Medicine. (1982). *Health and behavior: Frontiers of research in the biobehavioral sciences* (Report of a study by committee of the Institute of Medicine, Division of Mental Health and Behavioral Medicine, NTIS Accession No. PB 82 260–268). Washington, DC: National Academy Press.

Jacobson, E. (1938). *Progressive relaxation.* Chicago: University of Chicago Press.

Johnston, M. (1993). Health psychology in Europe: Potential in diversity. In J. Wilson-Barnett & J. M. Clark (Eds.), *Research in health promotion and nursing* (pp. 15–29). Hampshire, England: Macmillan.

Johnston, M. (1994). Current trends. *Psychologist, 7*(3), 113–118.

Johnston, M. (1997). How health psychology makes a difference. *Irish Journal of Psychology, 18*(1), 4–12.

Johnston, M., & Weinman, J. (1995). Health psychology. In *Professional psychology handbook* (pp. 61–68). Leicester, England: British Psychological Society.

Kaplan, H. I. (1975). Current psychodynamic concepts in psychosomatic medicine. In R. O. Pasnau (Ed.), *Consultation-liaison psychiatry.* New York: Grune & Stratton.

Leigh, H., & Reiser, M. F. (1980). *Biological, psychological, and social dimensions of medical practice.* New York: Plenum Press.

Levenson, D. (1994). *Mind, body, medicine: A history of the American Psychosomatic Society.* Washington, DC: American Psychosomatic Society.

Lipowski, Z. J. (1977). Psychosomatic medicine in the seventies: An overview. *American Journal of Psychiatry, 134*(3), 233–243.

Lipowski, Z. J. (1986). Psychosomatic medicine: Past and present, Part 1: Historical background. *Canadian Journal of Psychiatry, 31,* 2–7.

Lipsitt, D. (1999). A century of psychosomatic medicine: Successes and failures. In M. Dinis (Ed.), *Reflexões sobre psicossomática* [Reflections on psychosomatics] (pp. 11–22). Lisbon, Portugal: Sociedade Portuguesa de Psicossomática [Portuguese Society of Psychosomatics].

Lunt, I. (2000). Europsych project funded by the European Union (EU) under Leonardo da Vinci program. *European Psychologist, 5*(2), 162–164.

Lunt, I., & Poortinga, Y. (1996). Internationalizing psychology: The case of Europe. *American Psychologist, 51*(5), 504–508.

Lyons, A. S., & Petrucelli, R. J. (1978). *Medicine: An illustrated history.* New York: Abrams.

Maes, S. (1990). Editor's foreward. *European Health Psychology Society Newsletter, 1,* 1–2.

Maes, S. (1999). Rethinking education and training in health psychology in Europe. In T. McIntyre (Chair), *Rethinking training in Health Psychology in Europe: Implications for education and practice.* Symposium held at the 13th Conference of the European Health Psychology Society, Florence, Italy.

Maes, S., Spielberger, C. D., Defares, P. B., & Sarason, I. G. (Eds.). (1988). *Topics in health psychology.* New York: Wiley.

Maes, S., & Kittel, F. (1990). Training in health psychology. *Psychology and Health, 4,* 39–51.

Maes, S., & Van Elderen, T. (1998). Health psychology and stress. In M. Eysenck (Ed.), *Psychology: An integrated approach* (pp. 590–623). New York: Addison Wesley Longman.

Marks, D. (1994a). EFPPA task force on health psychology: Recommendations on training. *Health Psychology Update, 17,* 18–21.

Marks, D. (1994b). The training needs of professional health psychologists. *European Health Psychology Society Newsletter, 8,* 1–7.

Marks, D. (1996). Health psychology in context. *Journal of Health Psychology, 1,* 7–21.

Marks, D., Brucher-Albers, C., Donker, F., Jepsen, Z., Rodriguez-Marin, J., Sidot, S., et al. (1998). Health psychology 2000: The development of professional health psychology: European Federation of Professional Psychologists' Associations (EFPPA) Task Force on Health Psychology final report. *Journal of Health Psychology, 3*(1), 149–160.

Matarazzo, J. D. (1980). Behavioral health and behavioral medicine: Frontiers for a new health psychology. *American Psychologist, 35,* 807–817.

Matarazzo, J. D. (1982). Behavioral health's challenge to academic, scientific and professional psychology. *American Psychologist, 37,* 1–14.

Matarazzo, J. D. (1994). Health and behavior: The coming together of science and practice in psychology and medicine after a century of benign neglect. *Journal of Clinical Psychology in Medical Settings, 1*(1), 7–39.

Matarazzo, J. D. (2001). Influences in the development of health psychology in the United States. *Japanese Journal of Health Psychology, 14.*

McIntyre, T. (1998). The state of health psychology in Portugal. In T. McIntyre (Chair), *The state of health psychology in Europe: Education and practice.* Symposium conducted at the 12th Conference of the European Health Psychology Society, Vienna, Austria.

McIntyre, T., Maes, S., Weinman, J., Wrzesniewski, K., & Marks, D. (2000). *Post-graduate programs in health psychology in Europe: A reference guide.* Leiden, The Netherlands: European Health Psychology Society.

Methorst, G., Jansen, M. M., & Kerkhof, A. (1991). Health psychology in Europe, North America, Australia and New Zealand: A survey on prevalence, training, and professional status. *European Health Psychology Society Newsletter, 3,* 1–4.

Meyer, A. (1957). *Psychobiology: A science of man.* Springfield, IL: Charles C. Thomas.

Miller, N. E. (1969). Learning of visceral and glandular responses. *Science, 163,* 434–445.

Nemiah, J. C. (1973). Psychology and psychosomatic illness: Reflections in theory and research methodology. In J. Freyberger (Ed.), *Topics of psychosomatic research: Proceedings of the 9th European Conference on Psychosomatic Research.* Basel, Switzerland: Karger.

Ogden, J. (1996). *Health psychology: A textbook.* Buckingham, England: Open University Press.

Rosenstock, I. M. (1966). Why people use health services. *Milband Memorial Fund Quarterly, 44,* 94–127.

Rush, B. (1812). *Medical inquiries and observations upon the diseases of the mind.* Philadelphia: Kimber & Richardson.

Schofield, W. (1969). The role of psychology with delivery of health services. *American Psychologist, 24,* 565–584.

Schwartz, G. E., & Weiss, S. M. (1978). Behavioral medicine revisited: An amended definition. *Journal of Behavioral Medicine, 1,* 249–251.

Schwarzer, R., & Johnston, M. (1994, Winter). The European Health Psychology Society. *The Health Psychologist, 16*(3), 4, 27.

Selling, L. S. (1940). *Men against madness.* New York: Greenberg.

Selyé, H. (1953). The general adaptation syndrome in its relationship to neurology, psychology, and psychopathology. In A. Weider (Ed.), *Contributions toward medical psychology: Theory and psychodiagnostic methods* (pp. 234–274). New York: Ronald Press.

Sifneos, P. E. (1967). Clinical observations in some patients suffering from a variety of psychosomatic diseases. *Proceedings of the 7th European Conference on Psychosomatic Research.* Basel, Switzerland: Karger.

Staples, S. L. (1996). Human response to environmental noise: Psychological research and public policy. *American Psychologist, 51,* 143–150.

Stone, G. C. (Ed.). (1983). National working conference on education and training in health psychology. *Health Psychology, 2*(Suppl. 5), 1–153.

Stone, G. C., Weiss, S. M., Matarazzo, J. D., Miller, N. E., Rodin, J., Belar, C. D., et al. (Eds.). (1987). *Health psychology: A discipline and a profession.* Chicago: University of Chicago Press.

Strauss-Blasche, G. (1998). The state of health psychology in Austria. In T. McIntyre (Chair), *The state of health psychology in Europe: Education and practice.* Symposium conducted at the 12th Conference of the European Health Psychology Society, Vienna, Austria.

Taal, E. (1998). The state of health psychology in The Netherlands. In T. McIntyre (Chair), *The state of health psychology in Europe: Education and practice.* Symposium conducted at the 12th

Conference of the European Health Psychology Society, Vienna, Austria.

Taylor, S. E. (1999). *Health psychology*. Boston: McGraw-Hill.

Weinman, J. (1998). Development and current status of health psychology in the United Kingdom. In T. McIntyre (Chair), *The state of health psychology in Europe: Education and practice*. Symposium conducted at the 12th Conference of the European Health Psychology Society, Vienna, Austria.

World Health Organization. (2000, February 28). *Prevention and treatment: Both work, says WHO study on heart disease* [Press release, WHO/10]. Geneva, Switzerland: World Health Organization.

Wolf, S., & Wolff, H. G. (1947). *Human gastric function*. New York: Oxford University Press.

Wolff, H. G. (1953). *Stress and disease*. Springfield, IL: Charles C. Thomas.

CHAPTER 23

Undergraduate Education

THOMAS V. McGOVERN AND CHARLES L. BREWER

THE CONTEXT OF AMERICAN
HIGHER EDUCATION   465
TEACHING   467
   Courses: Catalog Studies and Surveys of the
     Undergraduate Curriculum   467
   The Discipline: Recommendations from
     the Experts   469
SCHOLARSHIP   472

Defining the Outcomes of Undergraduate Psychology   472
Assessing the Outcomes of Undergraduate Psychology   473
SERVICE   474
PAST AS PROLOGUE FOR THE
   TWENTY-FIRST CENTURY   475
REFERENCES   478

Education is discipline for the adventure of life: research is intellectual adventure; and the universities should be homes for adventure shared in common by young and old. For successful education, there must always be a certain freshness in the knowledge dealt with. It must be either new in itself or it must be invested with some novelty of application to the new world of new times. Knowledge does not keep any better than fish. (Whitehead, 1929/1952, p. 106)

Since the first undergraduate course of study at Harvard College in 1636, American higher education faculties have pursued Whitehead's vision. During the past 100 years, psychology has become one of the most popular pathways for this adventure. In 1996–1997, 74,191 baccalaureates and 4,053 doctoral degrees were awarded in psychology, 6.3% and 8.8%, respectively, of the total number of degrees awarded at these levels (Almanac, 2000). This chapter examines the evolution of undergraduate psychology, first as a body of knowledge implicit in courses and curricula and second as explicit learning outcomes that faculty expected of constantly changing student populations.

We chose the "three-legged stool of faculty activity" metaphor to organize the chapter: teaching, scholarship, and service. The section on teaching is a historical review of the changing courses and degree requirements of the undergraduate psychology curriculum. The section on scholarship analyzes how faculty identified and assessed specific learning outcomes. In the section on service, we discuss how psychologists educated each other and public audiences about their pedagogy. In a concluding section, we suggest a number of issues on the horizon, yet to be navigated in the new century.

We begin with a brief sketch of the historical context of American higher education.

THE CONTEXT OF AMERICAN HIGHER EDUCATION

"The current pattern of American undergraduate education is a result of almost 2,500 years of historical evolution" (Levine & Nideffer, 1997, p. 53). A long look at higher education would begin in the Greek academy and trace its changes in Cicero's *humanitas* and *ars liberalis,* through the scholarship of Constantinople and the Arab world, to Bologna and Paris, then to Oxford and Cambridge, before arriving in America. The study of the liberal arts was organized around the verbal arts of the *trivium* (logic, grammar, and rhetoric) and the mathematical arts of the *quadrivium* (arithmetic, geometry, astronomy, and music) and was the core curriculum of the medieval universities.

"Curricular history is American history and therefore carries the burden of revealing the central purposes and driving directions of American society" (Rudolph, 1977, pp. 23–24). In the first American curriculum at Harvard College, the liberal arts components were organized by the subject matter of the European *trivium* and *quadrivium.* This became the basis of an almost uniform course of study for America's colonial liberal arts and state colleges in the eighteenth century and in the first half of the nineteenth century. Individual institutions offered alternatives to this classical course of study in the forms of applied knowledge such as engineering and technical and mechanical education (e.g., West Point in 1802 and

Rensselaer Polytechnic Institute in 1824). At the University of Virginia,

> Jefferson's eight schools—ancient languages, modern languages, mathematics, natural philosophy, natural history, anatomy and medicine, moral philosophy, and law—plus the three schools of commerce, manufacture, and diplomacy, which were missing only because of lack of funds—constituted a design for a university at a time when the country had not yet come to grips with what a college was. (Rudolph, 1977, p. 81)

Such innovation was counterbalanced by staunch efforts to maintain a uniform, classical course of study as espoused in the Yale Report of 1828. In the post-Jacksonian era, higher education languished with declining enrollments; the Civil War brought some of the oldest and most distinguished institutions (e.g., The College of William and Mary) to the brink of economic bankruptcy. Then, as Rudolph's analysis suggests, complex external forces in American society produced positive internal effects on the institutions.

Veysey (1973) described the period from 1870 to 1910 as the most revolutionary time for American higher education, the fruit of which was the establishment of almost all of the principles and processes that remain today. He attributed change to three catalytic, often competing forces: the utilitarian needs of American society "to educate a democracy of talents and a democracy of vocations" (as cited in Rudolph, 1977, p. 111), the advent of science and an increasing respect for empirical evidence in the construction and applications of knowledge, and a widespread belief in the virtues of liberal education in creating a responsible citizenry. The first force was exemplified in the Morrill Land-Grant Act of 1862 and its effect on creating state universities and a broader understanding of the academic curriculum. The second force was illustrated in the acceptance of the German university as a model for the American research university with its emphasis on graduate training and increased specialization in undergraduate education. The third force was embodied in the 1904 Wisconsin Idea, which linked universities to their state and local communities through extension education and what could be described as distance learning programs before the advent of technology.

Inside institutions, undergraduate programs included common general-education courses and the selection of specialized concentrations of study (the Johns Hopkins 1877–1878 catalog used the term *major* for the first time). For faculty, an increased emphasis on research fostered professional associations through which scholars shared their findings and built the theoretical and methodological knowledge bases of new intellectual fields (disciplines); inside the institution, common intellectual pursuits led to administrative units (departments) organized around the disciplines. Established in 1892, the American Psychological Association (APA) was "one of seven learned societies founded at the turn of the twentieth century (Modern Language Association in 1883; American Historical Association in 1884; American Economics Association in 1884; American Philosophical Association in 1901; American Political Science Association in 1904; and American Sociological Society in 1905)" (McGovern, 1992a, p. 14). During this period, higher education was in transition, and psychology was both a beneficiary of and a catalyst for change.

After World War II, another period of change from 1945 to 1975 was prompted by variations of the same three forces operating from 1870 to 1910. The GI Bill of Rights was a utilitarian initiative that brought a whole new generation of students into higher education and prompted further expansion of the curriculum. The American political response to *Sputnik* in 1957 and the pervasive fear of Soviet technological advantage resulted in increases in research funding for science that affected graduate and undergraduate education. Finally, student protests of the 1960s questioned the nature, forms, and relevance of a liberal education to solve complex social problems. Once again, psychology was a principal beneficiary of these changes taking place on the broader American higher education landscape, as we will describe in the next section on curricular expansion.

In the 1980s and 1990s, the public became increasingly critical of the academy. Numerous blue-ribbon committees of faculty and administrators highlighted the loss of clear purpose in general education, lowered student expectations and involvement in learning (Study Group on the Conditions of Excellence in American Higher Education, 1984), the lack of coherence in the curriculum (Project on Liberal Learning, Study-in-Depth, and the Arts and Sciences Major, 1991a, 1991b, 1992; Project on Redefining the Meaning and Purpose of Baccalaureate Degrees, 1985; Zemsky, 1989), and the challenges of integrating new knowledge and new voices into the curriculum (Schmitz, 1992). State legislatures questioned the spiraling costs of higher education and what they perceived as the lower productivity of faculty, especially a decreased commitment to undergraduate teaching. Some states called for major changes in faculty personnel contracts, including the elimination of academic tenure. Internally, Boyer's (1990) *Scholarship Reconsidered* prompted broad discussion of the relationships among faculty teaching, research, and service activities. Moreover, the utilitarian demands of society at large again provoked conversations about technology, distance learning, and even the value to employers and society of the baccalaureate degree.

In the next sections, we describe how psychologists responded to these external forces affecting the public's perceptions of higher education, as well as the forces within the discipline that motivated evolving definitions of the curriculum, its pedagogy, and the roles of its faculty. As Hilgard, Leary, and McGuire (1991) noted, "traditional history of science focused primarily on the so-called internal development of scientific thought and procedure—how one idea and method led to other ideas and methods in more or less progressive fashion" (p. 91). These authors contrast such a traditional historiography with a social history-of-ideas approach (e.g., Ash, 1983) and the new critical history approaches (e.g., Furumoto, 1989). As Ash noted, "the emergence of both scientific ideas and scientific roles is a complex process of social construction, embedded not only in tradition of thought but also in specific sociocultural contexts" (p. 179). Thus, we examine external demands for accountability by society (e.g., state legislatures or accrediting groups) as just as important a catalyst for change as the internal predilections for reflection and evaluation by departmental faculties. The curriculum should be understood not only as a reflection of the best that psychological science had to offer undergraduates but also as a self-legitimizing strategy to preserve intra- and interinstitutional standing in the higher education community.

TEACHING

In the *Handbook of the Undergraduate Curriculum,* Ratcliff (1997) identified two curricular models. The first model he labeled as *descriptive* or *prescriptive;* it maps the landscape of organizational structures and elements put forward by faculty at their institutions or by disciplinary groups. Psychologists have used this model effectively for the last century. First, the archival study of catalogs and the analysis of surveys sent to campus departments asking them to describe their requirements and courses are two methods used to describe the curriculum of a particular era. Second, periodic gatherings of scholars and teachers in the discipline have produced recommendations for curricular structures. In this section, we review these two approaches to describing or prescribing the undergraduate psychology curriculum.

Ratcliff (1997) labeled a second model as *analytical;* variables in the curriculum that affect student development are identified, measured, and evaluated to determine their effectiveness. We will use the analytical model in our discussion of scholarship.

Courses: Catalog Studies and Surveys of the Undergraduate Curriculum

Psychologists have been conscientious in mapping the landscape of their discipline's undergraduate courses over the past 100 years. In an APA committee report, Whipple (1910) described the teaching of psychology from 100 normal school responses to a questionnaire; Calkins (1910) from 47 "colleges supposed to have no laboratory" (p. 41); and E. C. Sanford (1910) from 32 colleges and universities with laboratories. Seashore (1910), the committee chair, composed a summary report and recommendations for the elementary course in psychology based on his three colleagues' separate studies. Henry (1938) examined 157 liberal arts college catalogs for their "plan of instruction" (p. 430). F. H. Sanford and Fleishman (1950) examined 330 catalogs selected according to eight institutional types; Daniel, Dunham, and Morris (1965) replicated this study using 207 catalogs but limiting their selection to four institutional types (universities, liberal arts colleges, teachers colleges, and junior colleges). Lux and Daniel (1978) examined catalogs from 56 universities, 53 liberal arts colleges, and 69 two-year colleges. The APA sponsored surveys by Kulik (1973), Scheirer and Rogers (1985), and Cooney and Griffith (1994). Messer, Griggs, and Jackson (1999) reported their analysis of 292 catalogs for the prevalence and requirements of focused specialty-area options versus general psychology degrees. In the same issue of the journal *Teaching of Psychology,* Perlman and McCann (1999a) examined 400 catalogs from four institutional types for the most frequently listed courses.

We recommend all of these studies for students and scholars of both history and program development. As Ash (1983) noted, our self-representation is revealed in the courses we choose to teach. How did we move from the single, elementary course so characteristic in 1890 catalogs to baccalaureate programs in which the "mean number of psychology credits required for a major is 33.5 ($SD = 7.8$, Mdn $= 33$, mode $= 30$, range $= 7$ to 81)" (Perlman & McCann, 1999b, pp. 172–173)? Let's begin at the "beginning."

Using Jastrow (1890), the 1910 studies, and Ruckmich (1912) as starting points, McGovern (1992b) examined catalogs from 20 selected institutions for the years 1890 and 1900. He found that psychology took one of three forms in 1890. First, at Amherst, Georgia, and Grinnell, psychology was listed as a topic or primary focus in a philosophy course. Second, a single course in psychology was one of several philosophy courses listed in the catalogs for the City College of New York, Cincinnati, Columbia, Minnesota, New York University, and Ohio State University. This single course was taught either as a requirement or elective for juniors or seniors. Third, the first course in "elementary psychology" was followed by some other course or courses. At Indiana, Michigan, George Washington, and Yale, the course was in "physiological psychology." At Nebraska and Pennsylvania, the second course was titled "experimental psychology" and had a required laboratory experience. Additional courses were offered as "special problems" at Brown, "advanced psychology" at Pennsylvania and Yale, or selections based on faculty members' special interests: "mental measurement" by James McKeen Cattell at Pennsylvania, "psychological basis of religious faith" by William James at Harvard, and "pedagogical psychology" by Harry Kirke Wolfe at Nebraska.

A common developmental pattern of future psychology curricula was captured by the Pennsylvania catalog of 1890. Unlike other universities, Penn had its own psychology department; it was not a subset of philosophy or some other area. A sequence of courses was listed. Psychology 1 was a lecture course titled Elementary Psychology. Psychology 3 (no Psychology 2 was listed) was titled Experimental Psychology with lectures and laboratory work. Psychology 4 was titled Mental Measurement with lectures, reports, and advanced work in the laboratory. "Course 4 is open only to those who have taken course 3, and will be different each year, for a series of years. Advanced Physiological Psychology is proposed for 1891–92, and Comparative, Social, and Abnormal Psychology for 1892–3" (*University of Pennsylvania Catalogue and Announcements 1890–1891*, p. 96).

McGovern (1992b) found that by 1900, at Berkeley, Brown, Cincinnati, Columbia, Cornell, George Washington, Indiana, Minnesota, Nebraska, Pennsylvania, Wellesley, Wisconsin, and Yale, the first course was followed by an "experimental psychology" course. Laboratory work was required in either this course or in an additional course sometimes titled "laboratory in psychology." Courses titled "advanced psychology" or "advanced experimental" fostered students' individual research with faculty supervision. The 1900–1901 Brown catalog stated, "The aim is to make original contributions to scientific knowledge in psychology and to publish the results" (*Brown University Catalogue, 1900–1901*, p. 57).

Courses in abnormal, comparative, genetic, systematic, and psychological theory began to appear, as did more special topics courses. At Nebraska, a course in "race psychology" was listed. At Wisconsin, there was a course in "mental evolution"; Part I emphasized comparative psychology and Part II emphasized anthropology. At Amherst, Cornell, and Yale, the first course in the philosophy department was an interdisciplinary offering that covered psychology, logic, and ethics.

One of the most extensive curricula was listed at Columbia University in the Department of Philosophy, Psychology, Anthropology, and Education. Fifteen separate "Courses in Psychology" were listed, taught by an interdisciplinary faculty. The following introductory offerings were then followed by 13 topic courses, laboratory courses, or supervised research courses:

A. Elements of psychology—James's Principles of Psychology—Discussions, practical exercises, and recitations. 3 hours. First half-year, given in 4 sections.

Professor Lord. A parallel course is given by Dr. Thorndike at Teachers College.

1. Introduction to psychology. 2 hours, lectures and demonstrations.

Professors Butler, Cattell, Boas, Starr, and Hyslop, Drs. Farrand and Thorndike, and Mr. Strong.

The object of this course is to give a summary view of the subject-matter and methods of modern psychology. The ground covered is as follows:

A. Prolegomena to psychology, including a sketch of the history of psychology. Six lectures. Professor Butler.

B. Physiological psychology. Eight lectures. Dr. Farrand.

C. Experimental psychology. Eight lectures. Professor Cattell.

D. Genetic psychology. Seven lectures. Dr. Thorndike.

E. Comparative psychology. Seven lectures. Dr. Boas.

F. Pathological psychology. Three lectures. Dr. Starr.

G. General psychology. Eight lectures. Professor Hyslop.

H. Philosophy of mind. Six lectures. Mr. Strong.

Requisite: Psychology A, previously or simultaneously. (*Columbia University in the City of New York Catalogue, 1900–1901*, p. 176)

Rice's (2000) analysis of reviews of this period by Garvey (1929) and Ruckmich (1912) suggested that five stages of institutional development for psychology departments were evident by 1900. In Stage 1, mental science or mental philosophy courses were being taught. In Stage 2, institutions were offering one or more courses labeled "psychology." Stage 3 had institutions with psychological laboratories. Stage 4 departments were offering the PhD in psychology. Stage 5 represented an independent department; Rice suggested that Clark, Columbia, Illinois, and Chicago were the only institutions at this level.

The APA-sponsored reports by Calkins, Sanford, Seashore, and Whipple in 1910, and Henry's (1938) examination of 157 catalogs will take the reader almost to midcentury in describing the courses taught to undergraduate psychology students. Lux and Daniel (1978) consolidated these portraits with a table of the 30 most frequent undergraduate courses offered in 1947, 1961, 1969, and 1975. Perlman and McCann (1999a, p. 179) continued this tradition by identifying the 30 most frequently offered undergraduate courses, and the percentages of colleges requiring them, in their study of 400 catalogs for 1996–1997.

Scholars from the Carnegie Foundation for the Advancement of Teaching (1977) aptly described the post–World War II period of curricular expansion as "the academic shopping center" (p. 5). Keeping in mind Veysey's (1973) analysis of the eras of expansion and their external stimuli, psychology was benefiting from the utilitarian demands from more and different types of students and from the expansion of scientific programs at the graduate level that influenced teachers at the undergraduate level. Whether one looks at catalogs from 1900 or more recently, a common denominator is that new faculty, after a period of apprenticeship at an institution, create new courses that get absorbed into a department's curriculum. For example, F. H. Sanford and Fleishman (1950) found 261 different course titles in their study. Lux and Daniel (1978) found 1,356 different course titles and concluded: "Thus, we have a 'course title inflation' of 519%, or about 19% per year on the average, from 1947 to 1975" (p. 178). An expanded breadth of psychology course titles accompanied expansion in American higher education during this time.

Nevertheless, a parallel conservative force operates on the curriculum from inside the institution as well. Rudolph (1977) reminded us of "the academic truism that changing a curriculum is harder than moving the graveyard" (p. 3). As a historian, he knew that such resistance is a complex interaction of internal (departmental faculty and institutional priorities) and external forces (disciplinary groups and community/public constituencies). For psychology, Perlman and McCann (1999a) were led to conclude:

> Many frequently offered courses have been found for decades and 13 such courses first listed by Henry (1938) are in the present Top 30. Some courses are slowly being replaced. Thus, the curriculum reflects both continuity and slow change, perhaps due to the time it takes for theory, research, and discourse to define new subdiscipline areas or perhaps due to department inertia and resistance to modifying the curriculum. (p. 181)

In the next section, we focus on the concepts of continuity and change in the curriculum, but with an eye to the boundary-setting agendas of disciplinary groups.

The Discipline: Recommendations from the Experts

> Discipline-based curricula are a social construction developed by academics. Over time, knowledge has been organized into key terms, concepts, models, and modes of inquiry. Academics add to and test these knowledge constructs using their disciplinary associations as means of verbal and written communication. Curricular change is conditioned by the role of the disciplines in conserving and transmitting their organization and representation of what is worth knowing, why, and how. (Ratcliff, 1997, p. 15)

In this section, we review various statements made by psychologists after World War II about what was "worth knowing, why, and how" in the study of undergraduate psychology. Such statements carried added weight by virtue of disciplinary association (APA) or sponsorship in process (national conferences and studies) and outcome (publication in journals such as the *American Psychologist*). When departmental psychologists engaged in voluntary or required curriculum review projects, they looked to these reports for guidance (Korn, Sweetman, & Nodine, 1996).

At the 14th meeting of the American Psychological Association, E. C. Sanford (1906) offered a "sketch of a beginner's course in psychology." He suggested that we first build on the knowledge that students bring with them into this course; second, that we offer a wide base of psychological facts; third, "a genuine interest in science for its own sake is a late development in knowledge of any kind" (p. 59). He then suggested seven broad topics and an organizational sequence within which to teach them: Learning and Acquisition; Truth and Error; Emotion; Personality and Character; Facts of the Interdependence of Mind and Body; Psychogenesis; and Systematic Psychology (pp. 59–60). In 1908, the APA appointed the Committee on Methods of Teaching Psychology, which decided to inventory goals and teaching practices for the elementary course (Goodwin, 1992).

Synthesizing the responses from 32 universities with laboratories, E. C. Sanford (1910) reported that institutions were teaching the first course in sections of 200, 300, and 400 students; Whipple (1910) reported a mean enrollment of 107 students, according to his 100 normal school respondents. In institutions with laboratories, Sanford reported that 25% of the instructors saw the course as a gateway to the study of philosophy; more than 50% wanted students to study science for its own sake and also to appreciate the concrete applications of psychology to life. Calkins (1910) summarized the responses she received from 47 institutions with no laboratories in this way:

> *First,* teach psychology primarily as you would if it were an end in itself. *Second,* eschew altogether the method of recitation; lecture in order to sum up and to illustrate different topics of study, but lecture sparingly; and cultivate constructive discussion. *Third,* bar out the possibility of memorizing text-books by requiring students to precede text-book study by the solution of concrete problems. *Finally,* do not tolerate inexact thinking. (p. 53)

Seashore's (1910) summary included three aims: teach psychology (i.e., not philosophy) as a science with incidental treatment of its application; train students in observation and the explanation of mental facts; offer a balanced survey of all topics that psychologists study with an in-depth examination of a few. He urged that the elementary course be taught to sophomores in a two-semester sequence, preferably preceded by a course in animal biology. More than for any other discipline of that day, the teacher of psychology should have an exceptionally thorough preparation (because of the breadth of topics), be one of the most mature members of the department (because of the direct personal influence that psychology may have on its students), and possess both practical ingenuity and philosophical insight (because of the complex pedagogy required for the course). In short, "the teacher is everything" (p. 91). Wolfle (1942) reviewed more than 100 studies on the first course in psychology, published after the 1910 reports, and concluded: "Now, 30-odd years later, we are still debating many of the same issues and being embarrassed by the same difficulties. Many of the same recommendations considered necessary in 1909 are still necessary in 1942" (p. 686).

Intradisciplinary concerns were often matched by interdisciplinary conflicts. Wolfe's (1895) commentary on resource allocation in the sciences for "the new psychology in undergraduate work" (p. 382) predicted this competitive struggle on campuses. Hill (1929) described the conflicts over control of psychology personnel and curricular decisions in state universities. In 1945, James B. Conant, president of Harvard, appointed six psychologists and six nonpsychologists from university faculties, corporations, and research institutes to a University Commission to Advise on the Future of Psychology at Harvard. Wolfle (1948), as secretary of the APA, reviewed *The Place of Psychology in an Ideal University* (Gregg et al., 1947/1970) and said: "By all means read this book. . . . Psychologists have been a vigorous, sometimes belligerent, but never well united group. . . . This scattering of psychologists all over the campus is bound to be puzzling" (p. 61). In his presidential address for the APA Division on the Teaching of Psychology, Pressey (1949) juxtaposed the prestige accorded psychology in the Gregg et al. report with an observation about Harvard's *Redbook:* "Psychology appears to have *no* recognized place in the program presented in *General Education in a Free Society*" (p. 149). Thus, on the eve of the post–World War II boom in higher education, psychology was still "getting its act together" on institutional status and curricular coherence.

Ratcliff's (1997) analysis of curricula focused on the concept of a *discipline:*

> A *discipline* is literally what the term implies. . . . Disciplines can provide a conceptual framework for understanding what knowledge is and how it is acquired. Disciplinary learning provides a logical structure to relationships between concepts, propositions, common paradigms, and organizing principles. Disciplines develop themes, canons, and grand narratives to join different streams of research in the field and to provide meaningful conceptualizations and frameworks for further analysis. (p. 14)

Since 1950, psychologists have written several reports about building the discipline and translating its principles and methods into coherent undergraduate educational programs.

Lloyd and Brewer (1992) reviewed the national conferences and comprehensive reports on undergraduate psychology: Cornell Conference (Buxton et al., 1952); Michigan Conference (McKeachie & Milholland, 1961); Kulik, 1973; Scheirer and Rogers, 1985; APA/Association of American Colleges Project on Liberal Learning, Study-in-Depth, and the Arts and Sciences Major (McGovern, Furumoto, Halpern, Kimble, & McKeachie, 1991); and the St. Mary's College of Maryland Conference held in 1991. We will briefly review the Cornell, Michigan, and St. Mary's College of Maryland conferences' accomplishments as part of the continuing narrative elements for this chapter—courses, discipline, outcomes, assessment, and how service activities delivered these findings to widening circles of psychologists.

In 1951, the Carnegie Foundation of New York and the Grant Foundation sponsored a study group of psychologists—six primary authors and 11 consultants—to meet at Cornell University and to conduct "an audit to determine the objectives, examine the content, and appraise the results of the instruction we have been giving. Against the background of such an audit, we can then attempt to build a better curriculum" (Buxton et al., 1952, p. v). Their report identified the objectives of undergraduate psychology as:

> (1) Intellectual development and a liberal education; (2) a knowledge of psychology, its research findings, its major problems, its theoretical integrations, and its contributions; (3) personal growth and an increased ability to meet personal and social adjustment problems adequately; (4) desirable attitudes and habits of thought, such as the stimulation of intellectual curiosity, respect for others, and a feeling of social responsibility. (pp. 2–3)

In an interview with Jane Halonen (1992), McKeachie commented about the conference:

> We came up with the idea of sequencing, which is why Dael Wolfle really brought us together. He thought we were teaching all of our courses at about one level beyond the introductory and covering the same thing in the advanced course in order to bring people up to some common base so they could go on to the latter part of the course. I think that was important. (pp. 251–252)

The study group agreed on one recommended curriculum model. The introductory course was to be followed by five intermediate or core courses (statistics, motivation, perception, thinking and language, and ability), then advanced courses in specialized areas (e.g., social, learning, comparative, physiological, personnel, etc.), and finally capstone courses in personality and history and systems. All courses should be taught as "experimental psychology" courses. The authors wrote separate chapters on personal adjustment courses, technical training, implementation problems based on institutional differences, and the need for a research agenda to measure the effectiveness of undergraduate education.

A similar study group approach, the Michigan Conference, was sponsored by the National Science Foundation 10 years later and was reported in McKeachie and Milholland (1961). This group began with data from a survey of 548 departments to which 411 responded; 274 had revised their curriculum since the earlier Cornell report. They found that 69% of the respondents used the earlier recommendations. An important point to note is that the Michigan group of six psychologists framed their recommendations in the context of two critical external forces affecting psychology. First, the demographics of higher education were changing both in terms of increased numbers and increased diversity (specifically in age and vocational goals). Second, "more serious than the problem of sheer numbers is the fact that teaching is not a prestigeful occupation in psychology these days. The research man is the status figure" (p. 6).

A compelling integration of Veysey's (1973) three forces—utilitarian demands, scientific advances, and values of a liberal education—form a subtext for this entire report. McKeachie and Milholland (1961) asserted that the psychology curriculum "would be firmly anchored in the liberal arts, rejecting undergraduate vocational training as a primary goal" (p. 33). This principle is operationalized in great detail in two chapters: "The Beginning Course" and "The Experimental-Statistical Area." The greatest value lay in "teaching psychology as an organized body of scientific knowledge and method with its own internal structure for determining the admissibility of materials to be taught" (p. 59). The authors were unequivocal in their commitment to teaching psychology as a continually advancing science, reaffirming the Cornell group's objectives: content knowledge, rigorous habits of thought, and values and attitudes. They expanded these general goals with a set of 16 objectives, many of which are similar to statements about "critical thinking" that emerged as part of identifying liberal arts outcomes when assessment initiatives became so influential in the mid-1980s and after. The Michigan authors sketched three different curricular models because they could not agree on a single one. In what was a utilitarian and prescient comment, they concluded, "What is ideal, we now believe, depends on the staff, the students, the total college curriculum, and other factors" (p. 103). Into the 1990s, "staff," "students," and the "total college curriculum" would play an increasing role in shaping how individual institutions communicated the discipline. "Other factors"—all external

to the discipline and to campuses—would play an even more important role in setting the timetables and parameters for changes in the curriculum.

The 1991 St. Mary's College of Maryland Conference had a long history in development, an ambitious agenda, and diversity in its participants. Its processes and outcomes reflect the continuing evolution of the discipline's attention to undergraduate education. A resolution introduced to the APA Council of Representatives by the Massachusetts Psychological Association asked the Committee on Undergraduate Education (CUE) to examine

(1) the role and purpose of the undergraduate psychology major in relation to traditional liberal arts education (and preparation for graduate school in psychology) and preparation for a bachelor-degree-level job in a psychology-related field, and (2) whether APA should set forth guidelines for curriculum models in undergraduate psychology (with an accompanying rationale). (As cited in Lloyd & Brewer, 1992, pp. 272–273)

The CUE formulated a response, approved by the Council of Representatives in August 1985, that reaffirmed the psychology baccalaureate as a liberal arts degree, that no prescribed curriculum should be developed, but that guidelines or models could be considered based on continuing, periodic surveys of undergraduate education. Continuing discussion led to a conference proposal. Sixty psychologists met for one week in a highly structured group dynamic designed to produce draft chapters of a handbook on seven topics: assessment, advising, recruitment and retention of ethnic minority faculty and students, faculty development, faculty networks, curriculum, and active learning practices. Among the 60 participants at St. Mary's, 28 (47%) were women and 11 (18%) were ethnic minority persons (neither the 1951 nor the 1960 conference had such representation). In addition to participants from liberal arts colleges and universities, there were five faculty members from community colleges, two from high school psychology programs, and two representatives from Canada and Puerto Rico. As planned, a comprehensive handbook was produced (McGovern, 1993); at the urging of Ludy T. Benjamin, a *Quality Principles* document was also produced by the steering committee and eventually approved as APA policy by the Council of Representatives (McGovern & Reich, 1996).

In their chapter on the curriculum, Brewer et al. (1993) reaffirmed the importance of psychology as a liberal arts discipline. "The fundamental goal of education in psychology, from which all the others follow, is to teach students to think as scientists about behavior" (p. 168). They amplified this statement with six specific goals: attention to human diversity, breadth and depth of knowledge, methodological competence, practical experience and applications, communications skills, and sensitivity to ethical issues. To accomplish these goals, a sequence of four levels of courses was recommended: introductory course, methodology courses, content courses, and an integrative or capstone experience. Content courses should be balanced between the natural science and social science knowledge bases of an increasingly complex discipline. A special section was devoted to the integration of the community college curriculum with upper-division courses in the major taken at another institution.

Perlman and McCann's (1999b) review of the structures of the undergraduate curriculum in 500 catalogs indicated that the St. Mary's Conference, like its predecessors, had some intended consequences and specific areas of minimal influence. Although a senior capstone experience has been advocated since the Cornell Conference, this recommendation has gone unheeded, particularly in doctoral institutions. The same is true for the teaching of psychometric methods as part of a core methodology trio of courses with statistics and experimental psychology. Fiscal, staffing, and space problems were often cited as obstacles to the development and maintenance of laboratory facilities. These authors drew the following overall conclusions about the status of the curriculum at the end of the twentieth century:

> The Cornell report's (Buxton et al., 1952) emphasis on teaching psychology as a scientific discipline in the liberal arts tradition remains current. The required core as recommended by the St. Mary's report (Brewer et al., 1993) as implemented by departments seems to cover "both natural science and social science aspects of psychology." (p. 439, pp. 175–176)

We now turn to the ways in which psychologists evaluated the effectiveness of their undergraduate programs.

SCHOLARSHIP

Ratcliff (1997) labeled a second curricular model as *analytical*. Variables in the curriculum that affect student development are identified, measured, and evaluated to determine their effectiveness. McGovern (1993) described an analytical model for psychology as:

> What kind of *outcomes* can be achieved with
> What kind of *students* taught by
> What kind of *faculty* using
> What kind of *teaching methods* as part of
> What kind of *curriculum?* (p. 218, emphases in original)

In this section on scholarship, we first focus on faculty efforts to identify common outcomes from the earliest days of a single course to the contemporary "Top 30" described by Perlman and McCann (1999a). Second, we focus on the assessment of these outcomes by the faculty, but more often mandated by external constituencies in the interests of accreditation or public accountability.

Defining the Outcomes of Undergraduate Psychology

In response to E. C. Sanford's (1906) description of an ideal beginner's course, Walter T. Marvin (1906) suggested the following:

> The chief problem in any course is: What precisely does the teacher wish the student to learn, as distinguished from all the illustration, exposition, etc. that may be found helpful? In short, every course should include a body of definite and precise information to be thoroughly learned, hard as it may be to secure such information in psychology as compared with the exact sciences. . . . Perhaps one of the special habits we can form in the brightest pupils is reading interesting books on psychology. (p. 61)

Calkins (1910) was more specific:

> Psychology is psychology whatever the use to be made of it. *First courses in psychology should therefore be essentially the same in content and in method,* whether they introduce the student to advanced work in psychology or to the different problems of pedagogy, of ethics or of metaphysics. The [sic] immediate purpose of every course in psychology is to make the student expert in the study of himself: to lead him to isolate, analyze, to classify, and (in the scientific, not in the metaphysical sense) to explain his own perceiving, remembering, thinking, feeling, and willing. (p. 45, emphasis in original)

These two psychologists' perspectives must be understood in historical context—the field was still in the process of distinguishing its content and methods from its philosophical antecedents. Wolfle (1942), in his review of the literature on the first course since the 1910 studies, identified four prevailing objectives: teach facts and principles, develop scientific method or habits of critical thought, prepare students for later courses or interest in psychology, and eliminate popular superstition. However, his evaluation of more than 100 studies suggested to him the following synthesis of major objectives:

> The first is to acquaint the student with the most important and most generally accepted facts, principles, and hypotheses of psychology. The attainment of this objective will contribute to the student's general cultural education and will increase his ability to recognize and to deal intelligently with the psychological problems of modern society. The second objective to be stressed

is to develop the habit of critical and objective analysis of psychological problems which arise and of the data or hypotheses available to help solve them. The third important objective depends on the attainment of the first two and consists of the improvement of the student's ability to understand his own personal problems and to achieve personally and socially desirable solutions of those problems. (pp. 706–707)

This ideal synthesis was accomplished after the first 50 years of the new discipline's history. Recalling Veysey's (1973) themes, psychology was in the disciplinary mainstream in providing for the utilitarian needs of society, affirming a respect for science, and espousing the value of liberal arts education.

For 25 years after World War II, psychologists continually refined their understanding and pedagogy for these three objectives. As it had done in the first part of the twentieth century, the knowledge base addressed in Wolfle's (1942) first objective would continually expand, so much so as to suggest that the discipline had splintered. However, as we discussed in the introduction to the chapter, from the broader historical perspective of American higher education, the period after World War II would bring many different students to the campus with many different objectives. The "psychological problems of modern society" and students' "personal problems" of Wolfle's objectives became more complex, and faculty confronted them firsthand in their classrooms.

In a paper prepared for the APA Committee on Undergraduate Education, Buxton (1956) asked: "Who is responsible for determining the objectives, and the means for reaching them, in liberal education?" (p. 84). He espoused control by each local institution's faculty but recommended a balance between student-centered (intellectual and personal adjustment) and teacher-centered (content and method) curricular and course objectives. His answer to the question "To what degree should curricular offerings, courses, or requirements be adapted to the student populations served?" (p. 90) focused solely on differences in major fields and career orientations. The student-centered versus teacher-centered curriculum had been debated at length by the Cornell Conference group (Buxton et al., 1952). It would be echoed by the Michigan Conference group (McKeachie & Milholland, 1961), but their response derived from the direct experience of increasingly heterogeneous student populations. In describing three different types of "first course"—elementary, introductory and "exigential, or functionally oriented" (p. 47 ff.)—these authors asserted:

The term *liberal education* has traditionally implied a quest for underlying abstract principles rather than a concern with specific problems. . . . Teaching not bound by practical concerns might produce minds not adjusted to life as it is now lived and poorly suited to meet in a practical way the tasks that every citizen knows how to define. But it could also produce products who could break up these problems and approach them from a point of view off the cultural map commonly believed in.

Kulik's (1973) national survey of undergraduate departments and their highly diverse curricula led him to conclude:

It is an empirical question whether curricula like those of liberal arts colleges best meet the ideals of liberal education. Is it conceivable that for some students, occupationally oriented programs may provide a better road to personal soundness than the traditional curricula of liberal arts colleges? (p. 202)

Developing courses that incorporated the expanding knowledge base and met the needs of changing student populations led to "academic shopping center" curricula (Carnegie Foundation for the Advancement of Teaching, 1977, p. 5). The upside was that our discipline caught the imagination of so many of the new students, especially women, who came to higher education during the 1960s and 1970s. Faculty charged with thinking about undergraduate education from a national (versus local) perspective made every effort to transform the "shopping center" of courses into a coherent discipline. Kulik's (1973) conclusion was an insightful one and would become an important agenda into the 1990s: "The diverse goals of students in psychology courses suggest that pluralism may be a valuable concept in the design of programs in psychology" (p. 203).

As 1 of 12 learned-society task forces in the Association of American Colleges project on the arts and sciences major, McGovern et al. (1991) identified objectives for undergraduate psychology. The authors proposed eight common goals for the diversity of settings, students, and courses that characterized psychology:

1. Knowledge base.
2. Thinking skills.
3. Language skills.
4. Information gathering and synthesis skills.
5. Research methods and statistical skills.
6. Interpersonal skills.
7. History of psychology.
8. Ethics and values.

Assessing the Outcomes of Undergraduate Psychology

As we noted in the beginning of this section on scholarship, the desire to identify what students need to learn in their psychology courses and then to evaluate that learning has been manifested throughout the twentieth century. For most of the century, this need derived from psychologists' scientific curiosity and values as well as their penchant for testing and evaluating programs. Psychologists evaluated vocabulary terms elementary psychology students needed to know (Jensen, 1933; Thornton & Thornton, 1942) and a more comprehensive "psychological literacy" for the entire major (Boneau, 1990). Almost 50 years before the current assessment mandates, the APA's Council of Representatives charged a "Committee on the Preparation of Examination Questions in Psychology" (1941): "(1) to explore the need and desire for comprehensive examinations in psychology, and (2) to find out the extent to which questions or items now exist that may be drawn upon in constructing comprehensive examinations" (p. 838). Seventy percent of the 411 respondents to a survey from this committee favored such an effort, and almost 50% reported that they would use such examinations in their programs.

Since the mid-1980s, the external forces of regional accrediting associations and state legislatures have demanded that all departments and campuses participate in regular self-studies, a major component of which is the assessment of student learning outcomes. Halpern et al. (1993) offered a comprehensive outcomes assessment program for psychology. They described the external forces calling for such efforts and suggested that psychologists possess unique skills for evaluating educational outcomes. They argued that the desired outcomes for undergraduate psychology included *a knowledge base* (e.g., content areas, methods, theory, and history); *intellectual skills* (e.g., thinking, communication, information gathering and synthesis skills, and quantitative, scientific and technological skills); and *personal characteristics* (e.g., interpersonal and intrapersonal skills, motivation, ethics, and sensitivity to people and cultures). The authors advocated a multimethod matrix approach, including archival forms of assessment data, classroom assessment, standardized testing, course-embedded assessment, portfolio analysis, interviews, external examiners, performance-based assessment strategies, and assessment of critical thinking.

Since the St. Mary's Conference, articles regularly appeared demonstrating how departments used this Halpern et al. (1993) blueprint for assessment activities. The *Quality Principles* (McGovern & Reich, 1996), endorsed as APA policy, included this statement:

> Faculty establish mechanisms to assess the curriculum. Essential elements of an assessment program include
>
> **a.** clearly stated and achievable outcomes for the curriculum and other program-related experiences.

> **b.** multiple measures of students' learning.
>
> **c.** planned opportunities for systematic feedback to students on their progress.
>
> **d.** specific plans to use data assessment to improve individual course instruction and the overall curriculum.
>
> **e.** opportunities to communicate assessment results to multiple constituencies of undergraduate psychology. (p. 255)

In the next section, we focus on service—how psychologists, through their communications and activities with one another at national and regional meetings—achieved greater sophistication and effectiveness in their pedagogy and a distinctive disciplinary character for our undergraduate academic programs.

SERVICE

A consistent problem was evident for most of the twentieth century:

> What has been the result, after 30 years, of the 1951 recommendation that we give primary emphasis, in the undergraduate curriculum, to the contribution psychology can make to a liberal education, to Renaissance persons? Few contemporary psychologists, beyond those actively involved in the conferences or in national committees explicitly charged with undergraduate education, have an awareness that the conferences were even held, let alone awareness of the recommendations made. A major challenge for undergraduate education in the next decade is to involve a greater proportion of leading psychologists in discussion of the issues in developing and maintaining effective undergraduate education in a rapidly changing environment. (Fretz, 1982, p. 55)

Fretz's observation in a special issue on curriculum of the journal *Teaching of Psychology* should not be limited just to one historical period; recall similar comments made by E. C. Sanford (1910) and Wolfle (1942). However, in the last decades of the twentieth century, there has been ample evidence that a "greater proportion of leading psychologists" have become involved in networks of service activities in behalf of undergraduate education.

In *Teaching Psychology in America: A History* (Puente, Matthews, & Brewer, 1992), numerous authors documented how organized groups advanced the teaching and scholarship of the discipline via service activities at the regional, state, and national levels. We urge the reader to review other historical analyses to appreciate more fully how the teaching of psychology was portrayed in psychological journals (Beins, 1992), in undergraduate textbooks (Morawski, 1992; Weiten & Wight, 1992) and handbooks (Pate, 1992), or in experimental laboratories (Benjamin, 2000; Capshew, 1992).

Goodwin (1992) suggested that "the APA's involvement with teaching was sporadic at best in the years prior to 1945. . . . [T]he APA had other priorities during that time (p. 330) . . . establishing disciplinary identity for psychology and professional status for psychologists (p. 339)." In contrast, Nelson and Stricker (1992) made a persuasive case that "the APA has demonstrated a clear commitment to issues of teaching and the needs of teachers since 1945" (p. 346). An Education and Training (E&T) Board became part of a reorganized APA in 1951 so that "organized psychology not lose sight of its responsibilities in addressing more fundamental issues of education (i.e., in psychology as part of liberal education)" (p. 348). The E&T Board was instrumental in sponsoring the various conferences on undergraduate education reviewed by Lloyd and Brewer (1992).

Brewer (1997) and Ernst and Petrossian (1996) also described how the APA established in 1996 a continuing committee for Teachers of Psychology in Secondary Schools (TOPSS). This action recognized that "an estimated 800,000 students take precollege psychology courses each year" and that "approximately 15,000 students took the [AP] exam, making psychology the fastest growing Advanced Placement exam in the history of the ETS's program" (Brewer, 1997, p. 440).

Wight and Davis (1992) described the various stages that Division 2, Teaching of Psychology (now the Society for the Teaching of Psychology), went through in serving APA members committed to learning not just about scientific methodologies and results from one another but about the pedagogy by which the discipline might be more effectively communicated to its students. Daniel (1992) described the evolution of the division's journal, *Teaching of Psychology,* which serves similar needs and functions in the description, evaluation, and dissemination of innovative pedagogical and programmatic practice. Focusing on regional service activities, Davis and Smith (1992) described a plethora of conferences for teachers and students of psychology. Focusing on how psychologists have gathered students to learn more about the discipline at the college and community college campus levels, Cousins, Tracy, and Giordano (1992) described the histories of Psi Chi and Psi Beta, the two national honor societies.

As the twentieth century came to a close, the APA Division 2, Society for the Teaching of Psychology (STP), posted a Web site (www.teachpsych.org) available to students and faculty members for information about the division, its journal, national and regional teaching conferences, teaching awards, a mentoring service, a departmental consulting service, newsletters, and a moderated discussion group for psychology teachers at all levels of instruction. The STP Office of Teaching Resources in Psychology (OTRP Online) provides information on course syllabi, bibliographical material on diversity and cross-cultural issues, ethical issues in teaching, student advising issues and practices, scientific writing, and electronic databases for the journal *Teaching of Psychology.*

As another manifestation of APA's long-range commitment to academic psychology programs articulated with the initiation of the new Education Directorate in the early 1990s, 99 participants from high school, community college, college and research university, and other professional settings met at James Madison University in 1999 for the Psychology Partnerships Project (P3). It was the most diverse assembly of psychology teachers to date, building on the group dynamic approach used at the St. Mary's Conference of Maryland a decade earlier. Nine issues groups—advising, curriculum, faculty development, research, technology, assessment, diversity, partnerships, and service learning—developed projects to create networks, materials, and strategies for promoting the teaching of psychology and the lifelong learning needs of students and faculty in the diverse, changing world of the twenty-first century.

As Weiten et al. (1993) noted, "teaching and learning are communal activities" (p. 157). They described a portfolio of case studies that demonstrated the movement of psychologists from isolation to increasing communication and collegiality. With the advent of the twenty-first century, the service activities of psychologists have fostered increased collegiality in behalf of the teaching of psychology. Electronic communication networks enable this collegiality to have unprecedented depth and breadth.

PAST AS PROLOGUE FOR THE TWENTY-FIRST CENTURY

> Psychology is not only with us, but swamping us. Its popularity is so great as to arouse suspicions of superficiality, or even quackery. It has become almost a fashion, so that publishers claim that the word *psychology* on the title page of a book is sufficient guarantee for a substantial sale. (p. 596)

Was this an editorial from a newspaper or a speech by a legislator in the year 2000? A commentary from a church pulpit in the 1950s? The quote is from an article by a faculty member at the Carnegie Institute of Technology, Max Schoen (1926), writing about the purposes of elementary courses in psychology in his era. In response to such popularity, the author suggested that the aims of psychology in colleges were to "create an intelligent reading audience" and "to inculcate in the student a tolerant, open-minded and broad attitude towards human affairs and human problems" (p. 596).

We suggest the following two dynamics for undergraduate education in the future.

First, Veysey's (1973) three catalytic forces, the *external* demands on higher education, can be considered constant after more than 200 years of influence—utilitarian needs of American society, scientific discovery and an increasing respect for empirical evidence in the construction and applications of knowledge, and the virtues of liberal education in creating a responsible citizenry. Every generation must grapple with how best to respond to these demands via curricula and academic practices (Pascarella & Terenzini, 1991).

Second, it is the responsibility of the disciplines and the professions, the *internal* forces of higher education, to create and then to communicate increasingly complex theories and sophisticated applications, thereby enabling students to be lifelong problem solvers, amiable skeptics, and citizens.

The discipline of psychology is well positioned as a sociocultural force in the broader society to address America's utilitarian needs, scientific knowledge, and liberal education values. However, we need continuing scholarship, teaching, and service for the discipline to be more analytical in its academic program efforts. Thus, we return to McGovern's (1993) questions as a future teaching, research, and service agenda:

What kind of *outcomes* can be achieved with
What kind of *students* taught by
What kind of *faculty* using
What kind of *teaching methods* as part of
What kind of *curriculum?* (p. 218, emphases in original).

These questions need to be understood within the contexts of external forces acting on the academy as well as internal responses of the faculty and their institutions.

The *outcomes* expected of a baccalaureate education are increasingly utilitarian. For example, consumers and supporters of higher education consider the postgraduation employment opportunities for specific majors to be very important. This fact is especially critical for psychology to understand, because we now award almost 75,000 baccalaureates annually, and the major's popularity has not waned. Research on alumni satisfaction is an essential element of program evaluation (Borden & Rajecki, 2000; McGovern & Carr, 1989). Moreover, departments' program development activities regularly include community employers and external consultants (Korn et al., 1996; Walker, Newcomb, & Hopkins, 1987).

The kinds of *students* taking undergraduate psychology have changed, most notably in their gender and ethnic characteristics (McGovern & Hawks, 1986, 1988). In a report titled "The Changing Face of American Psychology," Howard et al.

(1986) reported the growing percentages of women who received baccalaureates in the discipline: 36.8% (1950), 41% (1960), 46.4% (1972), 66.8% (1982). McGovern and Reich (1996) reported 73% for 1992–1993. The percentages of doctorates achieved by women had similar percentage increases: 14.8% (1950), 17.5% (1960), 26.7% (1972), 50.1% (1984), and 61% (1992–1993). Ten years after the Howard et al. report, Pion et al. (1996) reported on the consequences of this shifting gender composition, and they concluded:

> Psychology, along with the majority of professions and scientific disciplines, has undergone dramatic shifts in gender composition over the past two decades. These changes have prompted concern that this increased participation by women may lead to erosion in the status of these occupations. . . . Societal and disciplinary trends are examined, along with data on the patterns of men's and women's involvement in the educational pipeline and workplace. The results provide little support for the concern over the increasing representation of women and its impact on the prestige of the discipline. (p. 509)

Denmark (1994) asserted, "Engendering psychology refers to cultivating a psychology that is sensitive to issues of gender and diversity. The increase in the number of female psychologists does not guarantee that the discipline will be responsive to those issues" (p. 329). In our historical review of teaching, scholarship, and service activities, we discovered significant changes in the rhetoric about women and the discipline, but programmatic change continues to be difficult. As McGovern et al. (1991) noted in their APA/AAC project report:

> Comments on an earlier draft of this article also pointed to different views on how best to integrate gender, ethnicity, culture, and class into the study of psychology. . . . Most psychologists would acknowledge that faculty members must challenge campus racism and sexism, but there is less agreement on how to do so. Gender, ethnicity, culture, and class are seen by some teachers as issues that challenge the contemporary curricula. Such a challenge also questions traditional research methodologies that are empirical, quantitative, and positivist, and may advocate alternative psychological methods that are contextual, interpretive, and more qualitative. Other psychologists believe that, although these topics and the new knowledge generated by research have legitimacy in the discipline, they should be subtopics best left to treatments determined by an instructor's sensitivities and commitments. (pp. 599–600)

The above quotation captures the difficult conversations that must be taking place in classrooms and in departmental meetings about the very nature of the discipline, not just students' demographic characteristics. In their article "The Diversification of Psychology: A Multicultural Revolution," Sue, Bingham, Porche-Burke, and Vasquez (1999) identified four major approaches to teaching about multiculturalism and diversity: "the *separate course model,* the *area of concentration model,* the *interdisciplinary model,* and the *integration model*" (p. 1066), ultimately advocating the integration model as the one best suited for the depth and breadth of learning they hope students will achieve. Puente et al. (1993) used the metaphor of teaching a "psychology of variance" as the means to change the epistemology of students, departments, the curriculum, and the discipline. Enns (1994) advocated a similar approach to challenge the cultural relativism of psychological constructs. What is consistent across reports from academia and from the external community is that attention to diversity issues is no longer a matter of individual faculty sensitivity but a utilitarian requirement for employment advancement in a changing workplace. The script for how institutions and departments will address this expectation will be written in the global twenty-first century.

For the first half of the twentieth century, psychology *faculties* were required to be excellent teachers. "The teacher is everything" (Seashore, 1910, p. 91). Then, as we documented in the first section of this chapter, research became more important in academic life after World War II.

"Teaching is not a prestigeful occupation in psychology these days. The research man is the status figure" (McKeachie & Milholland, 1961, p. 6). Ideally, these two activities could be synergistic and rewarded accordingly, whether the faculty member was affiliated with a liberal arts college or a research university. However, as the century ended, external forces demanded that the values and time apportioned to teaching, research, and service activities be reconsidered. Halpern et al. (1998) concluded that a new definition of scholarship was required, one that would maintain traditional benchmarks for excellence (e.g., high level of discipline-specific expertise and peer review), but one that would integrate teaching and scholarly activities more. Drawing on Boyer's (1990) treatise, the authors proposed a five-part, expansive definition for future scholarship in psychology: original research, integration of knowledge, application of knowledge, scholarship of pedagogy, and scholarship of teaching in psychology. In a collection of essays in response to the report from this STP Task Force on Defining Scholarship in Psychology, Girgus (1999) and Korn (1999) advised that institutional mission should be seen as an absolutely essential context for definitions and standards. Korn echoed the historical trends that we discovered in our analyses in his critical response to the "new definitions": "I contend,

however, that the activities of teaching can and should be distinguished from research, in order to give teaching the respect it deserves" (p. 362). Like the complex responses necessary to meet the needs of changing *students,* changing demands on *faculty* commitments will be debated into this century as well.

Teaching methods throughout the century included the lecture, seminar or small-group discussion section, laboratory, fieldwork and practica, and independent or supervised research projects. Technological advances modestly influenced each of these methods—better microphones, better audiovisual systems, better textbooks and auxiliary materials, and better observation and data-collection equipment. Then, in the last 20 years of the twentieth century, information technology revolutionized how we conceptualize, deliver, and evaluate teaching and learning in American higher education. Although we characterized the 1904 Wisconsin Idea of extended education as an early example of "distance learning," the dairy farmers of the Midwest who gathered with faculty members from their state's land-grant universities' colleges of agriculture probably did not envision twenty-first-century models of "asynchronous learning" accomplished on laptop computers in their living rooms. Despite such advances, however, we are confident in returning to a timeless formula: All teaching is mediated learning. Regardless of the nature of what is to be learned and how, a teacher first must listen to a student, and then together they must construct the most effective mediation so that the student learns how to learn and to become self-motivated and self-evaluating in that effort. Calkins (1910) had it right: "Teach psychology primarily as you would if it were an end in itself" (p. 53).

In the latter part of the nineteenth century, the new science of psychology emerged from its philosophical roots and began to develop a disciplinary identity. *Curriculum* development was the means by which this identity was repeatedly communicated and modified. As we have tried to demonstrate in our historical review of American higher education in general, and of psychology in particular, a driving force inside and outside the academy was how best to define the liberal arts. Although the *trivium* and the *quadrivium* no longer define the essence of a university education, in what ways do the goals of that medieval curriculum differ from those proposed for a liberal arts psychology curriculum by Brewer et al. (1993), Halpern et al. (1993), or McGovern et al. (1991)? There were two special issues of the journal *Teaching of Psychology* in the 1990s; one was devoted to the teaching of writing across the curriculum (Nodine, 1990) and the other to teaching critical thinking across the curriculum (Halpern & Nummedal, 1995). We believe that higher education's and psychology's responses to defining the liberal arts not only will shape the curriculum but should guide all of our discussions about outcomes, kinds of students and their needs, faculty priorities, and teaching approaches.

The teaching, scholarship, and service of American undergraduate psychology remain a vibrant player in Whitehead's (1929/1952) "adventure." When we feel an urge to boast about our public popularity or our intellectual accomplishments, we should remember his admonition:

Knowledge does not keep any better than fish. (p. 106)

REFERENCES

Almanac. (2000, September 1). Earned degrees conferred, 1996–1997. *Chronicle of Higher Education,* p. 32.

Ash, M. G. (1983). The self-presentation of a discipline: History of psychology in the United States between pedagogy and scholarship. In L. Graham, W. Lepenies, & P. Weingart (Eds.), *Functions and uses of disciplinary histories* (pp. 143–189). Boston: Reidel.

Beins, B. C. (1992). Constancy and change: Teaching as depicted in psychology journals. In A. E. Puente, J. R. Matthews, & C. L. Brewer (Eds.), *Teaching psychology in America: A history* (pp. 525–551). Washington, DC: American Psychological Association.

Benjamin, L. T., Jr. (2000). The psychology laboratory at the turn of the 20th century. *American Psychologist, 55,* 318–321.

Boneau, C. A. (1990). Psychological literacy: A first approximation. *American Psychologist, 45,* 891–900.

Borden, V. M. H., & Rajecki, D. W. (2000). First-year employment outcomes of psychology baccalaureates: Relatedness, preparedness, and prospects. *Teaching of Psychology, 27,* 164–168.

Boyer, E. L. (1990). *Scholarship reconsidered: Priorities of the professoriate.* Princeton, NJ: Princeton University Press.

Brewer, C. L. (1997). Undergraduate education in psychology: Will the mermaids sing? *American Psychologist, 52,* 434–441.

Brewer, C. L., Hopkins, J. R., Kimble, G. A., Matlin, M. W., McCann, L. I., McNeil, O. V., et al. (1993). Curriculum. In T. V. McGovern (Ed.), *Handbook for enhancing undergraduate education in psychology* (pp. 161–182). Washington, DC: American Psychological Association.

Brown University Catalogue, 1900–1901. Providence, RI: Brown University Press.

Buxton, C. E. (1956). Issues in undergraduate education in psychology. *American Psychologist, 5,* 84–95.

Buxton, C. E., Cofer, C. N., Gustad, J. W., MacLeod, R. B., McKeachie, W. J., & Wolfle, D. (1952). *Improving undergraduate instruction in psychology.* New York: Macmillan.

Calkins, M. W. (1910). The teaching of elementary psychology in colleges supposed to have no laboratory. *Psychological Monographs, 12*(4, Whole No. 51), 41–53.

Capshew, J. H. (1992). Psychologists on site: A reconnaissance of the historiography of the laboratory. *American Psychologist, 47,* 132–142.

Carnegie Foundation for the Advancement of Teaching. (1977). *Missions of the college curriculum: A contemporary review with suggestions.* San Francisco: Jossey-Bass.

Columbia University in the City of New York Catalogue, 1900–1901. New York: Columbia University Press.

Committee on the Preparation of Examination Questions in Psychology. (1941). Proceedings of the forty-ninth annual meeting of the American Psychological Association. *Psychological Bulletin, 38,* 838–841.

Cooney, B. R., & Griffith, D. M. (1994). *The 1992–1993 undergraduate survey.* Washington, DC: American Psychological Association.

Cousins, R. H., Tracy, C., & Giordano, P. J. (1992). Psi Chi and Psi Beta: The two national honor societies in psychology. In A. E. Puente, J. R. Matthews, & C. L. Brewer (Eds.), *Teaching psychology in America: A history* (pp. 403–428). Washington, DC: American Psychological Association.

Daniel, R. S. (1992). *Teaching of psychology, the journal.* In A. E. Puente, J. R. Matthews, & C. L. Brewer (Eds.), *Teaching psychology in America: A history* (pp. 433–452). Washington, DC: American Psychological Association.

Daniel, R. S., Dunham, P. J., & Morris, C. J. (1965). Undergraduate courses in psychology: 14 years later. *Psychological Record, 15,* 25–31.

Davis, S. F., & Smith, R. A. (1992). Regional conferences for teachers and students of psychology. In A. E. Puente, J. R. Matthews, & C. L. Brewer (Eds.), *Teaching psychology in America: A history* (pp. 311–323). Washington, DC: American Psychological Association.

Denmark, F. L. (1994). Engendering psychology. *American Psychologist, 49,* 329–334.

Enns, C. Z. (1994). On teaching about the cultural relativism of psychological constructs. *Teaching of Psychology, 21,* 205–211.

Ernst, R., & Petrossian, P. (1996). Teachers of psychology in secondary schools (TOPSS): Aiming for excellence in high psychology instruction. *American Psychologist, 51,* 256–258.

Fretz, B. J. (1982). Aftermath of the renaissance in undergraduate psychology: Enlightenment or Machiavellian? *Teaching of Psychology, 9,* 55–59.

Furumoto, L. (1989). The new history of psychology. In I. S. Cohen (Ed.), *G. Stanley Hall Lecture Series* (Vol. 9, pp. 5–34). Washington, DC: American Psychological Association.

Garvey, C. R. (1929). List of American psychology laboratories. *Psychological Bulletin, 26,* 652–660.

Girgus, J. S. (1999). Refereeing on different playing fields. Diversity in higher education. *American Psychologist, 54,* 356–357.

Goodwin, C. J. (1992). The American Psychological Association and the teaching of psychology. In A. E. Puente, J. R. Matthews, & C. L. Brewer (Eds.), *Teaching psychology in America: A history* (pp. 329–344). Washington, DC: American Psychological Association.

Gregg, A., Barnard, C. I., Bronk, D. W., Carmichael, L., Dollard, J., French, T. M., et al. (1970). The place of psychology in an ideal university: The report of the university commission to advise on the future of psychology at Harvard. *American Psychologist, 25,* 391–410. (Original work published 1947)

Halonen, J. S. (1992). I was just lucky: An interview with model teacher Wilbert J. McKeachie. In A. E. Puente, J. R. Matthews, & C. L. Brewer (Eds.), *Teaching psychology in America: A history* (pp. 219–257). Washington, DC: American Psychological Association.

Halpern, D. F., Appleby, D. C., Beers, S. E., Cowan, C. L., Furedy, J. J., Halonen, J. S., et al. (1993). Targeting outcomes: Covering your assessment concerns and needs. In T. V. McGovern (Ed.), *Handbook for enhancing undergraduate education in psychology* (pp. 23–46). Washington, DC: American Psychological Association.

Halpern, D. F., & Nummedal, S. G. (Eds.). (1995). Psychologists teach critical thinking [Special issue]. *Teaching of Psychology, 22*(1).

Halpern, D. F., Smothergill, D. W., Allen, M., Baker, S., Best, D., Ferrari, J., et al. (1998). Scholarship in psychology: A paradigm for the twenty-first century. *American Psychologist, 53,* 1292–1297.

Henry, E. R. (1938). A survey of courses in psychology offered by undergraduate colleges of liberal arts. *Psychological Bulletin, 35,* 430–435.

Hilgard, E. R., Leary, D. E., & McGuire, G. R. (1991). The history of psychology: A survey and critical assessment. *Annual Review of Psychology, 42,* 79–107.

Hill, D. S. (1929). Control of psychology in state universities. *Psychological Bulletin, 26,* 600–606.

Howard, A., Pion, G. M., Gottfredson, G. D., Ebert Flattau, P., Oskamp, S., Pfafflin, S. M., et al. (1986). The changing face of American psychology: A report from the Committee on Employment and Human Resources. *American Psychologist, 41,* 1311–1327.

Jastrow, J. (1890). Psychology at the University of Wisconsin. *American Journal of Psychology, 3,* 275–276.

Jensen, M. B. (1933). Relative values of the vocabulary terms of general psychology. *Psychological Review, 40,* 196–208.

Korn, J. H. (1999). Recognizing teaching as teaching. *American Psychologist, 54,* 362–363.

Korn, J. H., Sweetman, M. B., & Nodine, B. F. (1996). An analysis of and commentary on consultants' reports on undergraduate psychology programs. *Teaching of Psychology, 23,* 14–19.

Kulik, J. (1973). *Undergraduate education in psychology.* Washington, DC: American Psychological Association.

Levine, A., & Nideffer, J. (1997). Key turning points in the evolving curriculum. In J. G. Gaff, J. L. Ratcliff, & Associates (Eds.), *Handbook of the undergraduate curriculum: A comprehensive guide to purposes, structures, practices, and change* (pp. 53–85). San Francisco: Jossey-Bass.

Lloyd, M. A., & Brewer, C. L. (1992). National conferences on undergraduate psychology. In A. E. Puente, J. R. Matthews, & C. L. Brewer (Eds.), *Teaching psychology in America: A history* (pp. 263–284). Washington, DC: American Psychological Association.

Lux, D. F., & Daniel, R. S. (1978). Which courses are most frequently listed by psychology departments? *Teaching of Psychology, 5,* 13–16.

Marvin, W. T. (1906). Proceedings of the fourteenth annual meeting of the American Psychological Association. *Psychological Bulletin, 3,* 61.

McGovern, T. V. (1992a). Evolution of undergraduate curricula in psychology, 1892–1992. In A. E. Puente, J. R. Matthews, & C. L. Brewer (Eds.), *Teaching psychology in America: A history* (pp. 13–38). Washington, DC: American Psychological Association.

McGovern, T. V. (1992b). *PSY 2001: The curricular odyssey of undergraduate psychology.* G. Stanley Hall lecture presented at the annual meeting of the American Psychological Association, Washington, DC.

McGovern, T. V. (Ed.). (1993). *Handbook for enhancing undergraduate education in psychology.* Washington, DC: American Psychological Association.

McGovern, T. V., & Carr, K. F. (1989). Carving out the niche: A review of alumni surveys on undergraduate psychology majors. *Teaching of Psychology, 16,* 52–57.

McGovern, T. V., Furumoto, L., Halpern, D. F., Kimble, G. A., & McKeachie, W. J. (1991). Liberal education, study in depth, and the arts and sciences major—psychology. *American Psychologist, 46,* 598–605.

McGovern, T. V., & Hawks, B. K. (1986). The varieties of undergraduate experience. *Teaching of Psychology, 13,* 174–181.

McGovern, T. V., & Hawks, B. K. (1988). The liberating science and art of undergraduate psychology. *American Psychologist, 43,* 108–114.

McGovern, T. V., & Reich, J. N. (1996). A comment on the *Quality Principles. American Psychologist, 51,* 252–255.

McKeachie, W. J., & Milholland, J. E. (1961). *Undergraduate curricula in psychology.* Glenview, IL: Scott, Foresman.

Messer, W. S., Griggs, R. A., & Jackson, S. L. (1999). A national survey of undergraduate psychology degree requirements. *Teaching of Psychology, 26,* 164–171.

Morawski, J. G. (1992). There is more to our history of giving: The place of introductory textbooks in American psychology. *American Psychologist, 47,* 161–169.

Nelson, P. D., & Stricker, G. (1992). Advancing the teaching of psychology: Contributions of the American Psychological

Association, 1946–1992. In A. E. Puente, J. R. Matthews, & C. L. Brewer (Eds.), *Teaching psychology in America: A history* (pp. 345–364). Washington, DC: American Psychological Association.

Nodine, B. F. (Ed.). (1990). Psychologists teach writing [Special issue]. *Teaching of Psychology, 17*(1).

Pascarella, E. T., & Terenzini, P. T. (1991). *How college affects students.* San Francisco: Jossey-Bass.

Pate, J. L. (1992). Psychological handbooks: History and function. In A. E. Puente, J. R. Matthews, & C. L. Brewer (Eds.), *Teaching psychology in America: A history* (pp. 505–524). Washington, DC: American Psychological Association.

Perlman, B., & McCann, L. I. (1999a). The most frequently listed courses in the undergraduate psychology curriculum. *Teaching of Psychology, 26,* 177–182.

Perlman, B., & McCann, L. I. (1999b). The structure of the undergraduate psychology curriculum. *Teaching of Psychology, 26,* 171–176.

Pion, G. M., Mednick, M. T., Astin, H. S., Iijima Hall, C. C., Kenkel, M. B., Puryear Keita, G., et al. (1996). The shifting gender composition of psychology: Trends and implications for the discipline. *American Psychologist, 51,* 509–528.

Pressey, S. L. (1949). The place and functions of psychology in undergraduate programs. *American Psychologist, 4,* 148–150.

Project on Liberal Learning, Study-in-Depth, and the Arts and Sciences Major. (1991a). *The challenge of connecting learning* (Vol. 1). Washington, DC: Association of American Colleges.

Project on Liberal Learning, Study-in-Depth, and the Arts and Sciences Major. (1991b). *Reports from the fields* (Vol. 2). Washington, DC: Association of American Colleges.

Project on Liberal Learning, Study-in-Depth, and the Arts and Sciences Major. (1992). *Program review and educational quality in the major: A faculty handbook* (Vol. 3). Washington, DC: Association of American Colleges.

Project on Redefining the Meaning and Purpose of Baccalaureate Degrees. (1985). *Integrity in the college curriculum: A report to the academic community.* Washington, DC: Association of American Colleges.

Puente, A. E., Blanch, E., Candland, D. K., Denmark, F. L., Laman, C., Lutsky, N., et al. (1993). Toward a psychology of variance: Increasing the presence and understanding of ethnic minorities in psychology. In T. V. McGovern (Ed.), *Handbook for enhancing undergraduate education in psychology.* Washington, DC: American Psychological Association.

Puente, A. E., Matthews, J. R., & Brewer, C. L. (Eds.). (1992). *Teaching psychology in America: A history.* Washington, DC: American Psychological Association.

Ratcliff, J. L. (1997). What is a curriculum and what should it be. In J. G. Gaff, J. L. Ratcliff, & Associates (Eds.), *Handbook of the undergraduate curriculum: A comprehensive guide to purposes, structures, practices, and change* (pp. 5–29). San Francisco: Jossey-Bass.

Rice, C. E. (2000). Uncertain genesis: The academic institutionalization of American psychology in 1900. *American Psychologist, 55,* 488–491.

Ruckmich, C. A. (1912). The history and status of psychology in the United States. *American Journal of Psychology, 23,* 517–531.

Rudolph, F. (1977). *Curriculum: A history of the American undergraduate course of study since 1636.* San Francisco: Jossey-Bass.

Sanford, E. C. (1906). A sketch of a beginner's course in psychology. *Psychological Bulletin, 3,* 59–60.

Sanford, E. C. (1910). The teaching of elementary psychology in colleges and universities with laboratories. *Psychological Monographs, 12*(4, Whole No. 51), 54–71.

Sanford, F. H., & Fleishman, E. A. (1950). A survey of undergraduate psychology courses in American colleges and universities. *American Psychologist, 5,* 33–37.

Scheirer, C. J., & Rogers, A. M. (1985). *The undergraduate psychology curriculum: 1984.* Washington, DC: American Psychological Association.

Schmitz, B. (1992). *Core curriculum and cultural pluralism: A guide for campus planners.* Washington, DC: Association of American Colleges.

Schoen, M. (1926). Elementary course in psychology. *American Journal of Psychology, 37,* 593–599.

Seashore, C. E. (1910). General report on the teaching of the elementary course in psychology: Recommendations. *Psychological Monographs, 12*(4, Whole No. 51), 80–91.

Study Group on the Conditions of Excellence in American Higher Education. (1984). *Involvement in learning: Realizing the potential of American higher education.* Washington, DC: U.S. Department of Education.

Sue, D. W., Bingham, R. P., Porche-Burke, L., & Vasquez, M. (1999). The diversification of psychology: A multicultural revolution. *American Psychologist, 54,* 1061–1069.

Thornton, G. R., & Thornton, J. S. (1942). Terms that are considered important for beginning students of psychology. *Journal of Educational Psychology, 33,* 39–49.

University of Pennsylvania Catalogue and Announcements, 1890–1891. Philadelphia: University of Pennsylvania.

Veysey, L. (1973). Stability and experiment in the American undergraduate curriculum. In C. Kaysen (Ed.), *Content and context: Essays on college education* (pp. 1–63). New York: McGraw-Hill.

Walker, W. E., Newcomb, A. F., & Hopkins, W. P. (1987). A model for curriculum evaluation and revision in undergraduate psychology programs. *Teaching of Psychology, 14,* 198–202.

Weiten, W., Davis, S. F., Jegerski, J. A., Kasschau, R. A., Mandel, K. B., & Wade, C. (1993). From isolation to community: Increasing communication and collegiality among psychology teachers. In T. V. McGovern (Ed.), *Handbook for enhancing undergraduate education in psychology* (pp. 123–159). Washington, DC: American Psychological Association.

Weiten, W., & Wight, R. D. (1992). Portraits of a discipline: An examination of introductory psychology textbooks in America. In A. E. Puente, J. R. Matthews, & C. L. Brewer (Eds.), *Teaching psychology in America: A history* (pp. 453–504). Washington, DC: American Psychological Association.

Whipple, G. M. (1910). The teaching of psychology in normal schools. *Psychological Monographs, 12*(4, Whole No. 51), 2–40.

Whitehead, A. N. (1952). *The aims of education.* New York: Mentor. (Original work published 1929)

Wight, R. D., & Davis, S. F. (1992). Division in search of itself: A history of APA Division 2, the Division of the Teaching of Psychology. In A. E. Puente, J. R. Matthews, & C. L. Brewer (Eds.), *Teaching psychology in America: A history* (pp. 365–384). Washington, DC: American Psychological Association.

Wolfe, H. K. (1895). The new psychology in undergraduate work. *Psychological Review, 2,* 382–387.

Wolfle, D. (1942). The first course in psychology. *Psychological Bulletin, 39,* 685–712.

Wolfle, D. (1948). The place of psychology in an ideal university [Review of the book *The place of psychology in an ideal university*]. *American Psychologist, 3,* 61–64.

Zemsky, R. (1989). *Structure and coherence: Measuring the undergraduate curriculum.* Washington, DC: Association of American Colleges.

CHAPTER 24

Ethnic Minorities

THE HUMANIZING OF PSYCHOLOGY   483
  Adelbert M. Jenkins
CONFRONTATIONS AND CHANGE   486
  George W. Albee
MINORITY PSYCHOLOGISTS IN THE COMMUNITY   488
  Vera S. Paster
ORGANIZATION EFFORTS BY ASIAN AMERICANS
  IN PSYCHOLOGY   490
  Stanley Sue
THE CHALLENGE OF CHANGE: FORMATION OF
  THE ASSOCIATION OF BLACK PSYCHOLOGISTS   492
  David B. Baker
COLORS AND LETTERS: THE DEVELOPMENT
  OF AN ETHNIC MINORITY PSYCHOLOGICAL
  PUBLICATION   495
  Lillian Comas-Diaz

HISPANIC ETHNICITY IN PSYCHOLOGY:
  A CUBAN-AMERICAN PERSPECTIVE   497
  Antonio E. Puente
ETHNIC MINORITIES IN RESEARCH
  AND ORGANIZATION   499
  Richard M. Suinn
TREATING ETHNIC MINORITY CLIENTS   501
  A. Toy Caldwell-Colbert and Velma M. Williams
UPDATING MODELS OF RACIAL AND ETHNIC
  IDENTITY: ON THE ORIGINS OF AN ECOLOGICAL
  FRAMEWORK OF IDENTITY DEVELOPMENT   503
  Maria P. P. Root
REFERENCES   505

This chapter differs from the others in form and format. Instead of having a continuous history of the field, we have elected to present historical issues from the perspectives of 10 authors, representing various ethnic orientations, with views on their thoughts and experiences in dealing with ethnic issues in the field of psychology.

Some of these vignettes are very personal and some reflect on important turning points in the history of psychology relating to ethnic minorities. Each of the brief essays tells an aspect of the story that should be remembered as the science and profession of psychology moves into the twenty-first century.

D. K. F.

The Humanizing of Psychology

ADELBERT M. JENKINS

In the nearly 40-year period of my professional career, which began in the early 1960s, I have been privileged to witness important social and political changes in American society. While important to the nation generally, the events of this period provided a context for changes within the discipline of psychology, as well. An important expression of these times was the civil rights movement in America. The dynamics emerging from this crusade required psychology to reexamine its descriptive stance toward African Americans and people of color generally. Prior to the 1960s

if mainstream twentieth century social science turned its attention to African Americans, it tended to stress the ineffectualness of the adaptive abilities of ethnic minority people (Thomas & Sillen, 1972). Typical were such comments as those of the psychiatrists Kardiner and Ovesey (1951/1962). Impressed with the debilitating psychological effects that centuries of American racism had on African Americans, they concluded that the "Negro has no possible basis for a healthy self-esteem" (p. 297). Crain and Weisman (1972) in their large scale study of northern Black adults noted their view that segregation had possibly robbed the Black person of "some vital aspect of his personality" leaving him deficient for adapting effectively. The prevailing picture presented was one of human beings who were able only to react to their environments rather than take charge of their destinies.

Now, there is no question that African Americans as a group have been continuously and disproportionately numbered among the poor, and that they suffer and have suffered personally and collectively in the United States. Indeed, at times it does appear that African Americans have responded as if "shaped" by the "contingencies" imposed upon them by the racist society (Hayes, 1991). In many instances, this has led to features in the African American personality which could be called "adaptive inferiority" (Pugh, 1972). But we know, too, from a closer reading of history and from personal observation that this has not been all there is to the psychological story of African Americans. It has taken something more to gain the level of personal growth that many African Americans have reached against the kinds of odds they have faced. Ironically, it seems that the scholars that have been best able to capture these facts have tended to be those in the humanities. Thus, the African American novelist and essayist, Ralph Ellison, commented that he set himself the goal as a writer to "commemorate in fiction . . . that which I believe to be enduring and abiding in our situation, especially those *human qualities* which the American Negro has developed *despite and in rejection of the obstacles and meannesses imposed upon us*" (1964, p. 39; italics added). Furthermore one of the brightest literary lights of the Harlem Renaissance of the 1920s, Langston Hughes, proclaimed that this aspiration was not just a characteristic of the literate and well-to-do. In much of his work, he highlighted what he saw as the attitude of triumphing over adversity that was part and parcel of the African American's everyday life. In one of his most famous poems, he portrays a mother urging her son not to turn back in his struggle for accomplishment, reminding him that "I'se been a-climbin' on . . . and turnin' corners" in spite of the fact that "Life for me ain't been no crystal stair" (1959, p. 187).

In the face of the inability of social science to develop a balanced understanding of African Americans, the mood of the 1960s provided a new impetus for African American psychologists to express their longstanding discontent with American social science (Guthrie, 1998). Some in the new generation of African American scholars chose to reject Western perspectives altogether and move in new conceptual directions. The development of the Afrocentric perspective in psychology is a prime example, and a considerable body of literature has come from this point of view (for example,

Akbar, 1991; L. J. Myers, 1988; Nobles, 1991; J. L. White & Parham, 1990). For others of us, the difficulty with the characterization of African Americans was not simply a concern about racist trends in American social science. The problem was also that the reigning model in American psychology in general was a "mechanistic" one, a framework that portrayed the individual as a passive being whose responses are primarily determined either by environmental factors or by internal physiological and constitutional states.

The behaviorist position had been most clearly identified with the mechanistic tradition. However, even classical psychoanalytic theory showed clear evidence of such a direction, reflected in Freud's early efforts to develop a "metapsychology" that would describe the basic forces driving human functioning (Holt, 1972). Freud's thinking about his clinical observations led him to theorize in ways that actually were opposite to the prevailing scientific viewpoints of the day (Cameron & Rychlak, 1985; Holt, 1972). Still, in the first half of the twentieth century, especially, the mechanistic perspectives in Freudian thought were a considerable influence on conceptualizations of the human being. The problem for African Americans in this context has been that when human beings in general are not seen as taking an active, coping stance in life, then the tendency not to see active and creative features in the behavior of African Americans follows naturally. Thus, some of us felt that what was needed was a broader philosophical and conceptual framework within psychology as a whole.

Fortunately, during this time such a perspective was beginning to develop. It was being expressed in independent quarters and in varied language by experimentalists (Sarbin, 1977) and clinicians (Rychlak, 1968). Leona Tyler encapsulated the spirit of the times in the opening pages of her book on individuality (1978) by noting that "In psychology fresh winds are blowing, sweeping away overly restrictive assumptions, dusting off concepts that had been covered over and neglected, picking up and juxtaposing separate ideas to produce novel combinations. . . . Pluralism is the order of the day" (p. 1). Counterposed against this notion of humankind portrayed in the passive, mechanistic voice was a trend of psychological scholarship that described the "humanistic" view, one portraying the human individual as "an active, responsible agent, not simply a helpless, powerless reagent," (Chein, 1972 p. 6). The human being in this active image is one "who actively does something with regard to some of the things that happen to him or her . . . [and who] seeks to shape [the] environment rather than passively permit [himself or herself] to be shaped by the latter, a being, in short, who insists on injecting [himself or herself] into the causal process of the [surrounding] world" (p. 6).

A number of other psychologists were developing outlooks with similar implications for the human image. Abraham Maslow (1968) is familiar to us as one who stressed the need for a "third force" in psychological theory which would systematically acknowledge the importance of human strivings for personal growth and self-realization and would supplement the psychoanalytic and behaviorist positions. Of particular interest to me was the work of Harvard psychologist, Robert White, who also leveled a critique at both experimental and psychoanalytic psychologies. He wrote, "Something important is left out when we make drives the operating forces in animal and human behavior (1959, p. 297)." To bring back what is "left out," White developed his view that organisms, particularly the higher mammals, strive for "competence" in their efforts to interact "effectively" with their environments. As I became more familiar with how these newer currents touched various facets of psychology, I came to feel that such "humanistic" perspectives, broadly defined, offered promise for gaining a fuller grasp of the human personality in general. It also seemed to me that such a framework would be more suitable for capturing the functioning of African Americans as well. The trend of thinking that is opposed to a mechanistic view has been growing considerably in the last 15 years, well beyond the earlier terms of this discourse (see, for example, Faulconer & Williams, 1985; Howard & Conway, 1986; Martin & Sugarman, 1999; Messer, Sass, & Woolfolk, 1988; Polkinghorne, 1990; Richardson, Fowers, & Guignon, 1999; Robinson, 1991; Rychlak, 1994].)

In my efforts to find a corrective to the traditional psychological view of the African American (Jenkins, 1995), I have drawn on the extensive theoretical and empirical work of Joseph Rychlak and his students (1968, 1994). His framework, which he originally called a psychology of "rigorous humanism," furnishes a detailed conceptual perspective on how persons are able to inject themselves into the "causal process" of the world around. In Rychlak's view, an agent is a being who can behave so as to go along with, add to, oppose, or disregard sociocultural and/or biological stimulations (Rychlak, 1988). Key ideas that elucidate this definition are, first, that subjectively held intentions and purposes are as important as "objective" environmental contingencies in governing the way people behave. It is in this way that the human individual is an important causal force in his or her own life. As we try to understand the intentions that contribute to an individual's actions, we necessarily take an "introspective" point of view on that person's life that is, a view from the *actor's* perspective. This is a "teleological" or "telic" perspective on human behavior because it emphasizes that human behavior is always governed in part by the goal or end *(telos)* the actor has in mind. A second elucidating point is that the

agent's mentality is actively structuring, not simply passively reactive, as it "comes at" experience. We actively organize the world into meaningful units and then relate mentally to the "reality" that we have constructed. "While 'real' external reality may be presumed to exist independently of its apprehension, it cannot be known except symbolically—as part . . . of psychic reality" (Edelson, 1971, p. 27). This is consistent with recent "constructivist" approaches to knowledge (Howard, 1991). Thus, people are very much *engaged* in the process of coping with the world.

Third, and of particular importance in this framework, "dialectical" thinking, the innate capacity to imagine alternative or opposing conceptions of life situations, is frequently used by people to guide their behavior. With this capacity, people have an independent ability to determine the meaning of a given situation. In principle, they can fashion conceptions of a situation that are contradictory to those given by the tradition of a particular authority. This mode of thought supplements the capacity that we also have to define our constructions of the world in straightforward and unambiguous terms in order to negotiate our circumstances (what might be called "demonstrative" modes of thought, in Aristotelian terms). The point here is that African Americans have survived their oppressive history in the United States because they have actively and intentionally brought to their lives conceptions of their competence that have been at variance with the judgments made of them by the majority society.

Let's pursue this perspective a bit further and conclude with an illustration. Traditional psychological analysis has tried to identify the factors, such as biological drives or other kinds of contingent considerations, that *necessarily* determine behavior. The telic-humanistic perspective by contrast is among those that argue that many human events happen in a context of *possibility* rather than necessity (Slife & Williams, 1995). That is to say, from a psychological point of view many situations in our lives, even from birth, are full of *potentialities* for action.

> This quality of open alternatives in experience demands that the human being affirm some . . . meaning at the outset for the sake of which behavior might then take place . . . [Affirmation is] one of those active roles assigned to mind by humanists because which . . . item of . . . experience is singled out for identification is up to the individual and not to the environment. (Rychlak, 1988, p. 295)

Such a conception highlights the place of choice and responsibility in human action. By contrast, mechanistic views try to account for behavior exclusively in terms of environmental contingencies and/or constitutional drive factors.

They rule out independent volition and choice as important contributors to behavior. It should be noted, however, that the humanistic view is seen as complementing and extending rather than replacing mechanistic frameworks. For the humanist, the latter views are seen as incomplete as ways of accounting for human experience. This is because the exercise of choice and the conceptions guiding these choices are often not always apparent from the external observer's view of a given set of behaviors.

This is illustrated in a passage from the opening pages of Ellison's important American novel, *Invisible Man* (1952). A family is gathered around the deathbed of an old southern Black man. In his dying words to his son the man says, "I want you to overcome 'em with yeses, undermine 'em with grins, agree 'em to death and destruction." The family was stunned. "They thought the old man had gone out of his mind. *He had been the meekest of men*" (pp. 19–20, italics added). Obviously this man was advocating, among other things, lulling his white bosses into complacency in the hope that their system would deteriorate and blacks would then be free of it. His underlying intent—an intent which kept him going—was hostile, quite at variance with his superficially obsequious manner. In addition, referring back to our earlier discussion of meaning, this old man had taken a "dialectic" perspective on his situation throughout his life without anyone being quite aware of it, and he was now advocating such a view explicitly to his family. That is to say, recognizing fully the nature of his oppressive circumstances, this old man had acted one way, but at the same time he had quite the opposite mental perspective on the racial situation. This was his way of sustaining his human qualities "despite and in rejection of the obstacles and meannesses" that had been imposed upon him. And he was urgently trying to pass that strategy on to his family as a part of his legacy.

Thus, we cannot understand this man's behavior unless we take an "introspective" or "first-person" view. And so it is with African Americans: If we are to have "true to life" psychological descriptions, in addition to our more "objective" descriptions, we must learn to conceptualize and align ourselves with the inner worlds—the subjectivity—of people of color if our theory and practice is to be relevant to their experience. This is the opportunity that the "fresh winds" in psychology have brought us—the possibility of including into our discipline a more proactive conception of the human being that will contribute to the understanding and advancement of people in all of their plurality.

CONFRONTATIONS AND CHANGE

GEORGE W. ALBEE

Opportunities in psychology were slim for African American, Hispanic American, Asian American, Native American, and other minorities, before the middle of the twentieth century.

Since its founding in 1892, American psychology had always been a white, male, experimentally-oriented academic discipline. Its association, the American Psychological Association (APA), was run by presidents, boards, and council members from Academe and non-academic applied psychologists were not numerous. Most of those calling themselves "clinical psychologists" worked in schools and, occasionally, in state mental hospitals and in institutions for the retarded and epileptic.

Doctoral programs in psychology supplied new (white male) faculty members for universities as replacements were needed. Recruitment involved an "Old Boy" system of phone calls to colleagues. Jobs in universities were rarely advertised. College jobs often asked for "Christian gentlemen" candidates (see "Positions Available" in the early years of the American Psychologist). Psychology was a laboratory science before World War II and not particularly popular with undergraduates. Then World War II suddenly created a demand for people with skills in testing, personnel classification, and clinical interventions. These demands were multiplied after the war when many of the millions of veterans were in need of treatment for "mental disorders." I have told this story in some detail (Albee, 1998). The post-war explosion in numbers of clinical psychologist occurred in a context of medical domination and the insistence by psychiatry on the established medical model and traditional treatment in medical-psychiatric clinics and hospitals.

Between 1920 and 1966, the 10 most prestigious departments of psychology in the United States awarded just eight PhDs in psychology to Negro [sic] candidates while conferring 3,767 doctorates. Six of these 10 departments had not had a single Negro PhD. Of all programs, fewer than 1% of the doctorates were awarded to minorities (Albee, 1969).

The 1954 Supreme Court *Brown vs. Board* decision set in motion a mammoth pattern of change. The late 1950s saw Governor Faubus resist school integration in Little Rock, Arkansas, and President Eisenhower reluctantly used federal troops to uphold the court's decision. School busing led to riots in Boston.

The 1960s saw a continuation of great social ferment and change in America. The Atlanta bus boycott, the lunch counter sit-ins, the protest demonstrations, the freedom riders, the school desegregation actions of the federal government, the marches led by Martin Luther King Jr. and others, the whole civil rights movement, the Great Society, all combined to change America, and in the process to change psychology. The escalating protests against the Vietnam War were occurring at the same time as the civil rights demonstrations, often on the same campuses. Some of the goals of African American students were the opposite of the goals of the white students. The African American students wanted more admissions, more scholarships, more socially-relevant classes. The white students, like Students for a Democratic Society, wanted an end to ROTC and to support for the war including the military draft and the increasing military presence in Vietnam. They (the white protestors) were often willing to close the universities. In the late-1960s, the new Association of Black Psychologists (ABPsi) began pushing for changes in APA that would lead to support for more African American admissions to graduate schools and to a sharing of power in the APA governance.

At APA's 1968 convention in San Francisco, ABPsi presented a "Statement of Concerns" to the APA Council. At that same time, all watched on TV the "police riot" at the Democratic party's presidential nominating convention in Chicago. As a direct result, the APA Council voted to move the 1969 APA convention out of Chicago. The ABPsi invited APA to meet in Watts, a section of Los Angeles, and there was actually some talk of this possibility, but logistical considerations led to the choice of Washington, DC, despite threats of a lawsuit by Chicago venders over contract violations. Actually, because of the fortuitous August timing, APA was the first of many national organizations to shun Chicago for meetings.

Also at the 1968 San Francisco convention, there was a momentous confrontation. On the last day of the convention, Tuesday afternoon, the APA board of directors was meeting, discussing the many issues raised by the move of the next convention, but also the increasing demands from ABPsi, (and from radical groups like Psychologists for a Democratic Society and Psychologists for Social Action) pushing for increased civil rights, an end to segregation and support for a stronger minority presence in psychology. During the meeting, the door opened and in walked the entire board of

directors of ABPsi. They were well-prepared with the clear facts about racism in psychology and with specific demands for changes in APA and for changes in admissions policies in colleges and universities that had long excluded African Americans and other minorities. (The long-time exclusion of women from psychology training was to assume a major focus a year later.)

The APA board expressed general support for the issues raised by ABPsi but argued that it could not dictate to educational institutions, and that changes in APA governance would require by-law changes voted on by the membership. Members of ABPsi were impatient with what they saw as conventional stalling tactics. By the end of the day, it was agreed that APA would host a "conference on recruitment of black and other minority students and faculty" at the APA headquarters building in Washington, DC. The conference was held April 18 to 20, 1969. The APA board nominated nine white male participants and ABPsi nominated eight black male participants (mostly from black colleges and universities) and Ernestine Thomas (who was active in helping organize the Black Student Psychological Association and who was administrative office manager at the psychology department at Case Western Reserve University where I was then Chair).

Also invited to the conference (that I chaired) were men from the Behavioral Science Training Branch of the National Institute of Mental Health and male resource people from APA's Office of Educational Affairs and Executive Office. (See Albee, G. W., 1969, for a complete list of participants and a detailed report on the Conference.) The council was urged, along with APA boards and committees to "expand opportunities for black and other minority group students and faculty to enter the mainstream of psychology." Advice was offered to the Conference of Graduate Department Chairmen [sic], and to other APA groups like the Committee on Subdoctoral Education in Psychology. Looking back with the wisdom of hindsight, the recommendations seem mostly bland. Among the concrete results were ensuring that there be nondiscrimination in APA Central Office hiring and staffing, and that a new Central Office position be created with a focus on relating psychology and social problems, especially including racism.

The report of this Conference was published in the *American Psychologist* in August, 1969 just before the convention in Washington, DC. Then things exploded! For the first time in its 77-year history, APA meetings were physically disrupted. A group of black graduate students appeared in force at George Miller's presidential address, prepared to demonstrate. After negotiation, they agreed to leave in exchange for an invitation to present their case to the APA council the following day.

Twenty-four African American students stood shoulder to shoulder the next day in front of the council while their statement was read. They allowed the council 24 hours to respond. Robert Lee Green, president of ABPsi also spoke. He demanded that APA assess each member $50.00 to aid the black psychology cause. He also demanded that psychology stop using the black ghetto as a research colony.

Green and I were invited guests on the *Today Show* that week. Our brief exposure, broadcast from Washington, was seen by an estimated 19 million TV viewers. We were both nervous participants!

The black student group's statement focused on increasing the number of black undergraduates, graduate students, and faculty and on establishing training programs for black students in the black community. The Council adopted "in principle" the black student statement and appointed George Miller and me as a committee to negotiate with the black students and to develop a more specific set of proposals to present to the October council meeting. We invited the BSPA to send negotiators to Washington to meet with us. No way. We were invited to come to Watts, a black conclave in Los Angeles, to negotiate. Miller and I flew to Los Angeles where we were met at the airport and each taken to a host family in Watts. I stayed in the home of Charles Thomas, a major figure in black psychology. We met with students for a couple days in a small neighborhood church. Our meals were prepared and served by a black "ladies group." Discussions were spirited, but friendly. Our evening meal was accompanied by unlimited quantities of Cold Duck, and during the evening numbers of black students and black psychologists joined the group for informal, light-hearted interactions. We took back to APA several proposed by-laws changes (that were quickly passed by the required 2/3 majority of those voting) and recommendations for Central Office staffing changes to help new committees ensure priority for minority-increasing efforts. APA agreed to provide space for a new BSPA suite of offices and to lend money to staff them. Ernestine Thomas moved to Washington to provide staffing support.

By the end of the 1960s, a majority of APA members were sympathetic to the black demands. The country had witnessed a decade of struggle against the defenders of segregation, Jim Crow, and racial injustice. The parallel struggle against the Vietnam war was ongoing. The climate for change was favorable.

During the same 1969 APA convention in Washington there were anti-war demonstrations by psychologists. I led a march of some 300 psychologists (many from Psychologists for Social Action) down Connecticut Avenue to Lafayette Park, across from the White House, where I. F. Stone and I spoke against the war. Later in the week, a sunrise service was held at the Lincoln Memorial when Molly Harrower, B. F. Skinner, and I spoke against the war. Many of these events were recorded by Bryce Nelson (1969) in *Science*. (In this same issue is a report from the Department of Health, Education and Welfare on the safety of the oral contraceptive pill saying that the benefits outweigh the risks; and another article on the risks of pesticides, but no restrictions yet on the private use of DDT.) It is also worth noting that Americans had just landed on the moon. It was clearly a decade of major change.

Kenneth B. Clark was elected in 1969, the first African American APA president. At the 1970 APA convention in Miami Beach, the APA board was confronted by a militant Association for Women in Psychology with demands for major financial reparations from APA for years of unequal pay, discrimination in hiring and in graduate admissions, and for blatant sexism. The registration form for the convention asked for member's name and wife's name, even though 30 percent of the APA membership was female. Texts in psychology referred to "men and girls" and sexual harassment was rife.

All of this was to change, but someone else will tell that story.

Minority Psychologists in the Community

VERA S. PASTER

The shifting status of African American people in this country has been mirrored by our changing positions in the profession of psychology. It was not until the Emancipation in 1865 that enslaved persons could be taught to read except under penalty of imprisonment, flogging, or other severe punishments. In the south, schools for slaves were out of the question, and colleges were unthinkable. In the free states, there were a handful of colleges, including Berea and Oberlin, that opened their doors to black persons. After the Emancipation, in the former slave-owning states, colleges for African Americans began to be established by missionary groups (historically black colleges). Later, in 1890, the government land grant acts provided states throughout the country with funds for colleges for their students. Many of these admitted African Americans. But except for the historically black colleges which were located mostly in the south, African Americans have always had to struggle to gain an education in this country.

Even though psychology is a relatively recent scholarly subject in academia, it has been a prominent contributor to the country's complex struggle with its attitudes about race. An index of the difficulties is the fact that between 1920 and 1966, the APA reported, the 10 highest ranking graduate departments of psychology awarded just eight PhDs to African Americans, while during the same period of time these universities granted over 3,700 PhDs to others (Wispe et al., 1969). During the first part of the twentieth century, there were no welcome mats for African Americans at the psychology department doors of the major universities (Jay, 1971).

Further, "respected" psychological research and the best trained psychologists used their studies, tests, and theories to "prove," in turn, that African American, Hispanic, Asian, Mediterranean, and Irish peoples were socially undesirable, mentally inferior, and corrupting of the nation's potential for advancement. This "science" included using African Americans as guinea pigs in the Tuskegee study, sterilizing "undesirable" young women, relegating members of some racial/ethnic groups to an "uneducable" category, and similar oppressions.

Considering this history, it is not a surprise that the influences of the racial/ethnic psychologists are directed toward challenging traditional "rules" like those for research that lead to invidious comparisons of African Americans to Euroamerican. Ethnic-minority influence also includes practices that emphasize serving the unserved, understanding the stereotyped, and expanding the scope of the theoretical inquiry. Following are two examples of contributions, led or inspired, by these previously excluded people of color.

The first example is a primary prevention focus for a mental health center. The center was developed in a poor, working class, mostly African American and Latino section of New York City. The idea was to use professionals and trained community residents to provide treatment and other services according to community need and priority. Some examples: dialogues between neighborhood supermarket managers and householders; legal advice sessions with volunteer attorneys; counseling older people at the sites of senior housing; tenant organization to force landlords to provide needed services like heat and sanitation; advocacy for children with the schools, and liaisons with the police. The management of the center was open to everyone who lived in the community

through their participation in monthly governance meetings, termed the council. The council votes for the members of the board of directors. They also advocate for program priorities. For example, many members complained about the crowds hanging out day and night in front of a neighborhood single-room occupancy "hotel," considered to be a menacing eyesore. It turned out that public agencies placed people in these dwellings upon their release from jails, prisons, and mental hospitals. It was housing of last resort for the troubled who were down on their luck.

With the help of city hall, the mental health center assembled the directors of the area's city departments for the police, fire, sanitation, health, and welfare, to improve the situation. It was the first time they met as a group. Identifying violations on the property and sending summons to the landlord, the building was made safer and cleaner, and an array of services were brought into the building to engage and serve the tenants. All of this functioned under the leadership of the mental health center, which also assigned a multidiscipline team to the effort. There was an outpouring of pride at the center and a sense of competence in the neighborhood with the clearing of that notorious block!

The second example of the influence of African American leadership is one that occurred within the large child guidance clinic of the New York City public school system. During the 50 years since the service was established, it functioned according to a traditional model of referring to the school social worker or school psychologist difficult to manage children and those who seemed to have learning difficulties. More boys than girls were referred for behavior problems, restlessness, rebellion, fighting, and the like, and more minority children were referred both for behavior and "mental retardation." Nevertheless, the concentration of staff was assigned to the "good" schools, meaning the schools where the students were whiter and somewhat more affluent. These students were more likely to receive psychotherapy when needed, since the families were considered to be more cooperative and less suspicious of a child guidance referral, and to be more available and less likely to be working or to have a job that would be jeopardized by absences for school visits. The result was a grossly inequitable distribution of care.

When the author was awarded the directorship of the agency, she set about changing these practices and attitudes. She followed certain principles of continuing education: The prospective students, adult professionals all, should have maximum influence over how and what should be taught, based on clearly stated agency goals; the work should be based on the strengths of the workers; and what is learned should be rewarded with more successful practice. The underlying premise was that professionals need to feel competent, thus they will practice in areas of competence and avoid areas of actual or anticipated failure.

To implement an overall change, the director was awarded a generous grant from NIMH for a three-year continuing education program for providing school mental health services in schools with poor, ethnically and racially diverse students. Concomitantly, the staff was redistributed so as to be more equitably available throughout the city. The combination of encouragement through training, mandate through agency directive, and greater satisfaction for the professional through practice of greater variety, resulted in a positive outcome. The changes were favorably received by school personnel and led to a fairer availability of help to all of the city's children.

The field of psychology has been a part of the country's whole, including its sad racial past. It is now only 81 years since the first doctoral degree was awarded to an African American, 136 years since the ending of slavery. The period then and later has been earmarked by cruel discriminations against African Americans, and the support of such oppression by psychologists with bogus "science." But as the number and influence of African American and other ethnic minority psychologists has grown, so too has psychology's reach into previously unserved communities, and its positive influences on the community at large. A promising start?

Organization Efforts by Asian Americans in Psychology

STANLEY SUE

During the mid-1960s to the early 1970s, I was a graduate student at UCLA intent on becoming a clinical psychologist treating patients with schizophrenia. At this time, I was exposed to the civil rights movement and protests against the Vietnam War. My consciousness was raised over the injustices and oppression faced by African Americans, Latinos, and Native Americans. The ideas of Martin Luther King, Caesar Chavez, and Malcolm X were provocative and challenging. With respect to Asian Americans, not much was known about the population. The prevailing belief was that Asian Americans were successful in education and occupational status, relatively unobtrusive, and free of problems. Yet, many of us who were familiar with Asian Americans felt that most of the issues and problems besetting other ethnic groups were applicable. Asian Americans had suffered the same kinds of historical and contemporary mistreatment as other groups (e.g., discriminatory laws, hate crimes, inability to become citizens). Other Asian American students complained of ethnic identity conflicts, feelings of marginality, and difficulties in adjustment.

It was during the last two years of my graduate work that I became interested in the psychological study of Asian Americans and other ethnic minority groups. I began to read the works of Gordon Allport, Tom Pettigrew, and Kenneth Clark because there was little literature on Asian Americans. What really peaked my interest in Asian Americans was Harry Kitano's article (1969) on Japanese American mental illness. The effect of this article on me was profound. I was able to relate personally to the cultural analysis, the reluctance of Asian Americans to use mental health services, and the problems in the delivery of effective services. Although other psychological research has stimulated me either intellectually or personally, Kitano's article did both. I felt that I could contribute something to this area of research and began my career at the Psychology Department at the University of Washington.

It was not easy to conduct research on Asian Americans. One major problem was the lack of other Asian Americans in the field of psychology and of researchers interested in this population. For example, I was told that in 1971, I was the only tenure track Chinese American faculty in an APA accredited clinical psychology program in the United States. Collegial support and stimulation from other researchers or from other Asian Americans were largely unavailable. Unlike today, APA conventions did not involve many ethnic minorities in general or Asian Americans in particular.

Those of us interested in Asian American research tried to collaborate with other ethnic minority scholars. I was able to work with Carolyn Attneave, Guy Seymour, Amado Padilla, and Art Ruiz, to name a few. The alliances with other ethnic scholars were very important in helping to forge collaborative relationships and friendships. We were able to define ethnic issues and to find commonality and differences in the issues facing Asian Americans as opposed to other ethnic groups.

Fortunately, my brother Derald, who was also a psychologist, had similar research interests. We could test ideas out on each other, and my first publication was a coauthored paper (Sue & Sue, 1971). At the University of Washington, where I spent the first 10 years of my academic career, the director of the Clinical Psychology Program, Ned Wagner, encouraged me to conduct research on Asian Americans. This encouragement was critical because in the early 1970s, it was not altogether clear that academic careers could be built on the study of Asian Americans.

Was the study of Asian Americans "legitimate"? Research on Asian Americans is based on a population rather than a phenomenon or psychological process, such as learning, memory, schizophrenia, or marital interactions. Furthermore, ethnic research has also been characterized as being political, applied, or pejorative rather than scientific in nature. Although many of us approached the work as scientists and advocates, it was difficult to convince some researchers that ethnic research was within the domain of science. Additional research problems that we encountered included the relatively small numbers of Asian Americans and the diversity within Asian American groups, which made it difficult to find adequate samples on which to base studies. We were also uncertain about the validity of many research instruments because they had not been validated on an Asian American population.

ASIAN AMERICAN ORGANIZATIONAL EFFORTS

The problems encountered with respect to ethnic research in general and Asian American research in particular forced us to struggle. However, we felt strongly that Asian American research could not only yield much needed knowledge about this population and have policy and program implications, but also it could provide insight into human beings in general. It became clear that Asian American researchers would have to systematize efforts and to have some clout. Derald and I, along with two graduate students, decided to start the Asian American Psychological Association (AAPA) in 1972. We began by finding out how much interest there might be in such an association. We looked through the thousands of names in the APA Directory and tried to identify the Asian-sounding names. This was a laborious task but we did not know how else to proceed. Nearly 200 names were identified in this manner. Letters were sent to find out if they might be interested in joining an organization focusing on Asian Americans. About 50 responded with interest, including a few who indicated that despite their Asian-sounding name, they were not Asians.

For the first several years, we did not ask for association dues, because we were not sure how strong the membership base was. A quarterly newsletter was sent to members. However, we needed money because of the expenses (which several of us initially bore). At the suggestion of Robert Chin,

who was a past president of the Society for the Psychological Study of Social Issues (SPSSI, APA Division 9) and one of the first to join AAPA, we approached the Division and asked for, and received, $300 to support the association. We were quite impressed with SPSSI's willingness to help. Over time, more individuals became involved—Rodger Lum, Pat Okura, Reiko True, and Marion Tinloy. Interestingly, many who helped to start the association were later to become nationally prominent for their work with Asian Americans. Derald served as the first president and was followed by others such as Robert Chin, Albert Yee, Harry Yamaguchi, Herbert Wong, Kats Sakamoto, David Goh, Andy Chen, Nolan Zane, Chris Hall, Reiko True, and Gayle Iwamasa.

Organizers of AAPA felt that it was critical to achieve several goals:

- *Attaining influence in the American Psychological Association.* We felt it was necessary to have Asian Americans on governance structures (e.g., boards, committees, and elected offices) of APA. We tried to help elect those who were concerned about Asian Americans to APA boards and committees so that APA would have to deal with Asian American issues. Because it was necessary to convince APA that AAPA had a solid constituency, in the early days, we told APA that we had over 300 members, but we did not say that most of the members were not dues paying! Recently, AAPA has been able to celebrate its involvement with APA by noting the prominence of some of its members such as Richard Suinn (past president of APA) and Alice Chang (past board of directors member of APA).

- *Publications in journals.* Publications are important not only for developing research careers, but also for informing others of Asian American research and issues. Some AAPA members felt that journals were not interested in publishing papers on Asian Americans and did not have qualified reviewers to evaluate Asian American papers. Therefore, another goal was to try to have Asian Americans scholars named to editorial boards or as reviewers for journals.

- *Research grants.* We needed money to conduct research. We wanted to have input into funding priorities of funding agencies (such as NIMH and NSF), to encourage grant applications on Asian Americans, and to have some of our members serve on research review groups for the agencies. Research on ethnics was largely directed to African Americans and Latino Americans. We felt left out. While AAPA made it clear that funding for all ethnic groups should be increased, we were particularly concerned about the situation with Asian Americans.

Fortunately, one of our members, Pat Okura, was executive assistant to the director of NIMH, Bertram Brown. Pat gave us very valuable suggestions and help.

- *Research.* There was little information and knowledge about Asian Americans. No large-scale epidemiological studies of the prevalence of mental disorders had ever been conducted. It was not until the mid-1990s that funding been received from NIMH to conduct the first large-scale study of the prevalence and correlates of mental disorders in an Asian American population (the study was conducted by the National Research Center on Asian American Mental Health). Funding for such research was difficult because of the popular belief that Asian Americans were well adjusted and relatively free of mental disorders and such studies were unnecessary—a belief we had to combat.

- *Practice.* We felt that mental health services were not adequate to meet the needs of Asian Americans. Widely documented was the severe lack of utilization of mental health services on the part of Asian Americans. AAPA tried to encourage the development of more culturally-responsive services to Asian Americans and strategies to increase utilization.

- *Training.* There were very few Asian Americans in psychology, and we needed a critical mass of individuals to achieve our goals. AAPA helped to sponsor a 1976 training conference funded by NIMH to make recommendations for the training of students for future roles in research, teaching, and practice with Asian Americans.

- *Networking.* Also important to AAPA was networking—providing opportunities for Asian Americans to meet and collaborate.

Because the achievements of AAPA and its members have been distributed over a 30-year period, it is sometimes difficult to draw lessons from our organizational efforts.

However, there are several considerations that had a significant effect on our growth and effectiveness:

1. A small, dedicated, and persistent group can accomplish much. While we initially spent a great deal of time trying to increase membership in AAPA, it was clear that a few dedicated members would have to do most of the work in communicating with members, writing the newsletter, and advocating the interests of Asian Americans to national organizations and funding agencies, and so on. Time was also spent deciding courses of action when members had grievances (complaints about racial discrimination, documenting instances of stereotypes, etc.), sought advice (e.g., about submitting manuscripts for publications), and made requests of one kind or another.

2. Alliances must be made with members of other ethnic groups, Whites, key leaders, and organizations.

3. The influence of a small, dedicated, and persistent group cannot be underestimated. We had many instances of having a few individuals taking initiative and succeeding.

4. Those who become involved in ethnic issues must realize that such issues are unlike those typically found in psychology. Ethnic issues can become very emotional and personal, as well as intellectual. You can be subjected to personal attacks involving whether actions help or hurt the ethnic community. On other hand, work on Asian Americans can be gratifying, not only professionally but also personally.

Happily, AAPA is ready to celebrate its 30th anniversary. It includes the involvement of hundreds of psychologists and psychology students. It has an annual convention, a newsletter, and an Internet listserve for members to communicate with each other. Many of us feel a tremendous sense of pride over AAPA's accomplishments over the years.

The Challenge of Change: Formation of the Association of Black Psychologists

DAVID B. BAKER

In January 2001, the National Multicultural Conference and Summit II was convened in Santa Barbara, California. The sold-out event hosted by four divisions of the American Psychological Association had as its subtitle "The Psychology of Race/Ethnicity, Gender, Sexual Orientation, and Disability: Intersections, Divergence, and Convergence." Clearly, the umbrella of inclusion is now large enough to include many

who had been marginalized, excluded, or otherwise made invisible in psychology. In recognizing diversity as a value, it is instructive to remember that not all that long ago there was little celebration and plenty of struggle.

The social movements of the 1960s were about many things, civil rights being chief among them. Civil rights based on demographics such as age, gender, and race/ethnicity had hearings in the Supreme Court and in the court of public opinion. Expressions of dissatisfaction with the ongoing neglect of the rights and needs of those who fell outside the majority culture were everywhere and the field of psychology was no exception. Psychology, like many other disciplines and institutions, was indicted for its neglect of issues impacting its members from traditionally underrepresented groups. African American psychologists were among the first to organize and confront American psychology with a demand for change.

For most of the twentieth century, the steady growth in the number of PhDs awarded in psychology was restricted largely to white males. The first PhD awarded to an African American came in 1920, the recipient being Frances Cecil Sumner (Guthrie, 1998). Between 1920 and 1966, 25 of America's largest doctoral granting institutions in psychology awarded over 10,000 PhDs, 93 of which were granted to African Americans (Wispe et al., 1969). The barriers for African Americans seeking advanced study in psychology were many and long lasting. Those who did manage to carry on were never far from the realization of their marginalized status within psychology. This was clearly reflected in the relationship between African American psychologists and the largest professional organization of psychologists in America, the American Psychological Association (APA). Like the society in which it existed, the APA failed to address the needs of African Americans, both as psychologists and as consumers of psychology. Major training conferences, such as the 1949 Boulder Conference on Graduate Education in Clinical Psychology, concerned as it was with the mental health needs of the nation, did not include black psychologists (Baker & Benjamin, 2000). Indeed, it was not until the Vail conference of 1973 that issues of concern to minority psychologists would receive an extended hearing (Hilliard, 1973).

By the late 1960s, relations between the American Psychological Association and African American psychologists were not good. Some in the majority would argue that the organization had taken action. They would point to the policy statement of the 1950s affirming that the association would only hold meetings in cities where there was no discrimination based on race or religion (Newcomb, 1957). They would hold up as evidence the efforts of the Society for the Psychological Study of Social Issues (SPSSI) that had demanded an examination of the training and employment needs of African American psychologists and in doing so helped to create the Committee on Equality of Opportunity in Psychology (CEOP) in 1963 (Guthrie, 1998).

For many African American psychologists, these deeds were seen as minor achievements, a smattering of actions that neglected significantly larger and far more devastating social ills facing the African American community. Membership in the APA was not widely sought by African American psychologists, largely based on the belief that the organization did not care to recognize or represent them (B. H. Williams, 1997).

African American psychologists were angry, a situation only made worse by social scientists whose reports to the federal government blamed the African American community for the ills that beset it. Most noticeably, the Moynihan report of 1965 offered as social science, a theory of urban decay based on the dysfunction of the black family. Unwilling to accept that African American men, women, and children were to blame for the ravages of prejudice and discrimination, African American psychologists continued to organize. Reacting to the victim blaming of the Moynihan report, it was pointed out that white supremacy and racism were the culprits needing investigation, a conclusion affirmed in part by the Kerner Commission report of 1968 (Herman, 1995). Refusing to accept a deficiency model, many African Americans joined the chorus of the black identity movement, finding power and pride in a black identity that looked to African ancestry as a guide for life (Parham, White, & Ajamu, 2000). The synergy of the black power and identity movement and increasing frustration and alienation from the APA helped to set the stage for the formal organization of the Association of Black Psychologists (ABPsi).

In 1968, Abraham Maslow was president of the APA which had scheduled its annual meeting in San Francisco. Being in San Francisco in 1968 with a group of psychologists led by the humanist Maslow would seem to have all the ingredients for a love in. For a group of African American psychologists in attendance, the love-in was out and organization and protestation were in.

The historical record is fairly clear in naming Charles Williams Thomas II (1926–1990) as the key organizer of the ABPsi (Guthrie, 1998; B. H. Williams, 1997). It was Williams who encouraged African American psychologists to attend the San Francisco meeting and engage in a dialogue about the formation of a national association. On the evening of August 31, 1968, Williams convened a small group meeting to discuss the discontent of African American psychologists with the APA. The group called for the creation of a national association of African American psychologists and delineated a series of issues that demanded APA's immediate attention. These included efforts to increase recruitment of African American students in psychology, greater representation of African American psychologists within the APA, the development of means to provide mental health services to the African American community, and an endorsement recognizing the black power and identity movement as a creditable tool for fighting white racism.

The next day, a larger gathering convened for further discussion. In addition to conversation and debate, resolutions were offered and committees were formed. On September 2, 1968, the group adopted the name, The Association of Black Psychologists and selected Charles Thomas as chair and Robert Green as co-chair. Realizing the APA executive board was in session at that same moment, Thomas led a group to the meeting and the newly created Association of Black Psychologists presented its first case before the APA. The board agreed that Thomas and other representatives of ABPsi should bring their concerns before the APA council meeting in Washington, DC, scheduled for October 5–6, 1968 (B. H. Williams, 1997).

At the October meeting, a resolution expressing appreciation for Thomas's work was passed and the council formally urged APA to act quickly on the concerns of the ABPsi. As part of this, plans were made for a conference to address recruitment of black and other minority students and faculty in psychology (McKeachie, 1969). Held on April 18–20, 1969, the conference addressed issues of training and the other concerns raised by ABPsi. The meeting resulted in any number of recommendations (see Albee, 1969). By the summer of 1969, APA was preparing to gather for the annual convention to be held in Washington, DC. As APA President George Miller was being introduced, members of the newly formed Black Students Psychological Association (BSPA) walked to the stage. More literally than perhaps he anticipated, George Miller was quickly engaged in giving psychology away as he yielded the podium to the student association.

Chair of the BSPA, Gary Simpkins, announced that the BSPA would present a list of demands to the APA Council of Representatives the next day, a task that kept the Council busy all that day. The list was familiar and resonated with the issue brought forth before by the ABPsi. Council voiced support for the BSPA's position and requested a specific proposal. APA President George Miller and President-Elect George Albee were appointed to meet with the BSPA and the ABPsi to work out the details. Declining an invitation to meet in Washington, the BSPA instead selected Watts as the meeting place. Miller and Albee flew to Los Angeles, were hosted by local families and engaged in two days of discussion with the BSPA and the ABPsi (see Albee's section in this chapter for a detailed account of the meeting). Reporting back to the APA Council on October 4, 1969, a specific plan was presented. Gary Simpkins and Philip Raphael (1970) of the BSPA outlined the needs for: (a) improved recruitment of black students and faculty in psychology, (b) a centralized information center that could disseminate information about psychology programs and sources of financial aid, (c) field training relevant to the needs of black students and the black community, and (d) the expansion of available black mental health professionals through the creation of terminal programs at all degree levels.

The ABPsi national chairman, Robert Williams, addressed the Council and in a strongly worded statement decried the misuse of psychological tests in the diagnosis and placement of black children in educational settings. He reiterated the commitment of the ABPsi to serve as a resource and monitor for policies that affected African Americans, and called for sanctions against departments of psychology that discriminated against students of color. ABPsi's official policy statement on the retention and recruitment of black students in graduate psychology was contained in "The Ten Point Program." The program, mailed to all accredited doctoral training programs in psychology, contained 10 commitments departments could make to ensure that African American students were accepted into and supported through doctoral training (for the list see R. L. Williams, 1974). The APA professed sympathy to the causes of the ABPsi and the BSPA moved quickly to endorse the presented proposals and established the Commission for Accelerating Black Participation in Psychology (CABPP).

In May 1970, a curious blue insert of 31 pages appeared in the *American Psychologist*. Labeled as special inserts, their purpose was to convey information quickly to members of the association. The first special insert was a discussion of the need for a national information system for psychology; the second a series of reprints from the October Council meeting. Included were the statement of the BSPA, the report of Robert Williams, and an APA response. In that response, the APA noted that it had given office space and funds for a national secretariat to address acceleration of black participation in psychology, provided funding for meetings, conferences, and organizing activities of the ABPsi and the BSPA, supported the establishment of a speakers bureau, and contacted psychology departments and deans to inform them of the APA's interest in and support of these efforts. A good start, but nonetheless it was only a start. Ted Blau (1970) commenting on the achievement of the CABPP noted,

> A majority of the APA membership is neither aware of the importance of the problem nor involved in engineering solutions. Despite the fact that Council has demonstrated its willingness to act quickly and directly in the matter of the challenge of change, it is a preliminary response only. Psychologists' total response should not be limited to rhetoric, commissions, ad hoc committees, or logistical support from Central Office. The small beginning that has been made toward recognizing injustice and inhumanity, rectifying these and thus truly promoting human welfare, must be continued and made valid by the commitment and involvement of individual members of the association. (p. 1103)

The ABPsi's efforts to increase minority representation in psychology continued unabated into the 1970s, the fruits of that labor evidenced in the predominant place ethnic minority issues occupied in many policy decisions such as the formation of the Center for Minority Group Mental Health in 1972 under the auspices of the National Institute of Mental Health, and the 1973 National Conference in Levels and Patterns of Professional Training in Psychology. Strides in professional psychology were matched with organization and leadership in research through ABPsi's convening of the Conference on Empirical Research in Black Psychology in Ann Arbor, Michigan in 1974—a conference that continues to this day (Boykin, Franklin & Yates, 1979).

As the new century began, ABPsi was recognized as the largest organization of African American psychologists in the world. Embracing an Afrocentric worldview, it maintains a steadfast commitment to work on behalf of all people of African descent.

However one chooses to do the accounting, the founding of the Association of Black Psychologists was remarkable, its impact immediate and its legacy lasting. Those pioneers who came together in a San Francisco hotel room in 1968 brought with them an incredible intensity of purpose that was quick to point out challenge and strong enough to create change. As the historical record will attest, ABPsi, since its inception, has played a significant role in shaping social science policy and practice in America.

—— Colors and Letters: The Development of an Ethnic Minority Psychological Publication ——

LILLIAN COMAS-DIAZ

We need to write before being written off.
—Janet Sanchez,
African American Psychologist

The history of ethnic minority psychological publishing has been arduous. Navigating between the mainstream ocean and the waters of color, scholarship of color has struggled with dominant psychological paradigms. Mainstream models' cultural insensitivity and irrelevance to people of color aggravate the challenge. Since ethnic minorities are often exposed to intellectual imperialism and domination at the expense of their cultural values (Said, 1994), internalization of dominant psychology frequently interferes with the promotion of a culturally competent psychology. As a result of professional socialization, many psychologists of color suffer from cultural Stockholm syndrome, taken hostage by the dominant cultural values—including the stereotypes of their own group—and in turn, accepting, internalizing, and believing them (DiNicola, 1997).

Professional socialization can cause confusion and perplexity in the publication of scholarship of color. Looking through a monocultural glass, dominant psychological publications have discounted and even excluded the divergent experiences and realities of people of color. Serving two masters, ethnic minority psychologists struggle to harmonize dominant and scholarship of color. In doing so, they often engage in dualism and pluralism. Those engaged in dualism simultaneously publish in ethnic and mainstream journals, thus offering a dual outlet to their work. However, to be published in mainstream journals requires conformity with the dominant paradigm. Dualism, however, risks segregation because it tends to place indigenous psychological paradigms in separate ethnic journals, rarely read by mainstream psychologists. Within pluralism, on the other hand, psychologists of color offer diverse interpretations to reality, aiming at the co-existence of ethnic minority perspectives with dominant psychology.

As the written word is the DNA of culture, ethnic minority psychology propagates itself by publishing. However, a history of marginalization of psychologists of color within the publication process has hindered such process. Contemporary concerns about cultural appropriateness, irrelevant application of psychological knowledge, issues of inclusion, and equal opportunities are prompting psychology to revise its traditional tenets and assumptions based on a limited Western European conceptualization of humankind.

The APA officially recognized the limited number of publications on ethnic minority theory, research, and practice and in 1984 created the Publication and Communication Board's Ad Hoc Committee on Increasing the Representation of Underrepresented Groups in the Publication Process. Identifying issues and concerns, the Ad Hoc Committee offered structural strategies to enhance the publication of ethnic minority psychology. One recommendation—educating underrepresented groups in the publication process—was immediately adopted and continues to be implemented within the Association's Division 45, The Society for the Psychological Study of Ethnic Minority Issues. The establishment of the Society signaled that the issues and concerns of ethnic minorities achieved a formal place within the professional organization for psychologists, beginning to legitimize scholarship of color as a valid field within psychology (Comas-Diaz, 1990). Although the division embraced the need to develop an official ethnic minority psychological journal, this priority was deferred due to financial restraints.

While the American Psychological Association (1993) developed guidelines for providers of psychological services to ethnic, linguistic, and culturally diverse populations; the American Psychiatric Association officially acknowledged the significance of culture in the fourth edition of its *Diagnostic and Statistical Manual of Mental Disorders (DSM-IV)* (Mezzich et al., 1993).

In 1994, John Wiley and Sons founded a new journal, *Cultural Diversity and Mental Health,* and asked me to be its founding editor-in-chief. An interdisciplinary endeavor, the journal capitalized on the mental health discipline's recognition of culture as a pivotal factor in diagnosis, treatment, and prevention. The journal brought together an impressive editorial board composed of many influential individuals in the fields of ethnic minority psychology, cultural psychiatry, and clinical social work.

Up to that time, articles on cultural topics were scattered throughout the mental health literature, often appearing in publications focusing on one particular ethnic group. As the first publication of its kind, *Cultural Diversity and Mental Health* provided a forum for a wide array of theoretical, clinical, and research articles on cultural diversity. As such, it promoted a heightened multicultural literacy by offering the knowledge base and therapeutic tools to access and effectively treat individuals and communities of diverse backgrounds (Comas-Diaz, Griffith, Pinderhughes, & Wyche, 1995). The Reflections feature, a memoir in which authors reflected on how culture impacted on their life experiences and professional development, became very popular.

After 10 years of existence, the Society for the Psychological Study of Ethnic Minority Issues was financially secure and confident enough to establish an official journal. After much negotiation, John Wiley and Sons transferred the ownership of *Cultural Diversity and Mental Health* to the Society as its official scholarly publication in 1998. The move, gracefully shepherded by Kelly Franklyn, senior editor at Wiley, was an overwhelming success. Renamed *Cultural Diversity and Ethnic Minority Psychology* in 1999, the journal provided a forum for promoting cultural competency and psychological understanding of ethnic minority groups. The journal's aims and scope were expanded to embrace a more general view of ethnic minority psychology. It offered a venue for the dissemination of scholarship in all aspects of ethnic minority psychology, including the psychology of race, diversity, and multiculturalism—recognizing the sociocultural, historical, and political embeddedness of psychological theory, research, and practice. It pledged its focus on the psychological and societal variables affecting ethnic minority groups such as American Indian/Alaskan Natives, Asian American/Pacific Islanders, Black/African Americans, Latina/Latino/Hispanics within the United States.

The journal affirmed collective identity by strengthening people of color's ways of knowing and promulgating their scholarship through the publication of scholarship of color. Embracing unity through diversity (the organization's motto), the Society's executive committee appointed associate and consulting editors reflecting the diversity within populations of color, in addition to non-ethnic minority psychologists (Comas-Diaz, 1998). The executive committee also encouraged the journal's interdisciplinary focus and asked me to remain as editor-in-chief.

The Society established student editor positions to mentor and socialize psychologists-in-training into publishing. Working closely with the associate editors, the student editors embodied the next stage in the journal's progression. Forging new passages for young scholars, educators, and clinicians, *Cultural Diversity and Ethnic Minority Psychology* became one of the first journals to include students on its editorial board.

In 2000, *Cultural Diversity and Ethnic Minority Psychology* arrived at its first port. After founding the journal and serving as its editor for six years, I turned the reins over to Gail E. Wyatt. Emphasizing the journal's commitment to scholarship and research, she especially welcomed quantitative and quantitative research manuscripts. Additionally, Wyatt appointed a Counsel of Research Elders composed of senior scholars across diverse fields to write about contemporary issues that affect the psychology of ethnically diverse populations (Wyatt, 2001). Wyatt's arrival signaled the beginning of a new exciting era for the journal.

Ethnic minority scholarship is providing a prismatic lens to psychological publishing. As multiculturalism becomes officially recognized in our society, counter movements such as faded mosaic (Clausen, 2000), presaging the death of "American" culture by igniting an ancestral fear of a cultural Tower of Babel, are beginning to emerge. Since "culture matters" (Harrison & Huntington, 2000), multiculturalism becomes the philosopher's stone in the alchemy of life (Comas-Diaz, 2000). In its continuing journey, *Cultural Diversity and Ethnic Minority Psychology* may become the beacon of scholarship of color.

Hispanic Ethnicity in Psychology: A Cuban-American Perspective

ANTONIO E. PUENTE

During the early 1980s, I participated in a symposium at the Southeastern Psychological Association in Atlanta, Georgia. The well-attended symposium topic was ethnic-minorities in psychology. However, I felt very much out of place since the other speakers were African American and only one other Hispanic was in the audience. In many respects, this symposium represented not only my own personal feelings about being an ethnic-minority in psychology but how psychology and North American society viewed ethnicity as well. There appears to have been a misunderstanding or a limited definition of what ethnicity is. In general, ethnicity has been defined primarily, if not exclusively, and historically using race and, in many instances, the focus has been African Americans. Obviously, this approach is biased and not representative of the population that psychology seeks to understand and serve.

Using the latest U.S. Census Bureau data (2001), Hispanics now comprise the largest and fastest growing ethnic-minority segment in the United States. African Americans now comprise 12.3% of the population and Hispanics comprise 12.5% of the U.S. residents (and that figure is probably conservative due the limited counting of illegal aliens). If current census projections turn out to be correct, sometime during this century, Hispanics will comprise the largest single group in the United States. Conceivably, then, Hispanics could represent the majority group culture, at least in terms of population.

Is psychology ready for this paradigm shift? The answer is unequivocally no. The reasons why the field is not ready for this demographic change lie in the history of psychology. The total number of Hispanics who have received PhDs in psychology not only represents a very small portion of psychology, but represents a relatively small portion of ethnic-minorities. According to the 1999 to 2000 figures available from the American Psychological Association, Hispanics comprise approximately 5% of both doctoral and masters level graduate students. And, those that do gain admittance into doctorate programs often do not obtain the necessary training to compete adequately in either the academic or clinical spheres of psychology (Vazquez, 1991). Furthermore, the total number of faculty members of Hispanic origin is similarly low—less than 10%.

If one were to examine the governance of APA, the numbers are disproportionately even smaller. For example, no Hispanic has ever served on its board of directors. Only three ethnic minorities have been president of APA in its 110-year history; Richard Suinn (2000), Logan Wright (1986), and Kenneth B. Clark (1971). Even in the only APA division journal focusing on ethnicity, *Cultural Diversity and Ethnic Minority Psychology,* only 20% of the entire editorial board (approximately 100) have Spanish-surnames.

This situation is further mirrored in how we have chronicled the history of psychology. For example, in *The American Psychological Association: A Historical Perspective* (Evans, Sexton, & Cadwallader, 1992), no mention is made of Hispanics in any section of the book. Even in my own book *Teaching Psychology in America: A History* (Puente, Matthews, & Brewer 1992), little reference is made to Hispanics. In other scholarly books as well as textbooks in the history of psychology, including Boring, Brennan, Hilgard, Leahey, Schultz and Schultz, and Wertheimer no mention is found in the Contents or the Indices of contributions by Hispanics to psychology.

The assumption held by many is that the major, if not the only difference, between mainstream society and Hispanics is that of language. But language is only one aspect of Hispanic culture, there is heterogeneity of Hispanics. A Cuban is quite different from a Puerto Rican who is quite different from a Mexican. Each subgroup has distinct cultural characteristics, heritage, and behavioral patterns. As a consequence, Hispanics need to be understood within their specific cultural context (Shorris, 1992). Other issues also play a role. These include the importance of family (especially of extended family), religion, social context and rules (including the limited trust placed on those outside the family or a circle of friends), the appreciation of time (rather than conquering it), the value of living (rather than just working), and a greater emphasis on cooperation (rather than competition).

HISTORY OF HISPANIC PSYCHOLOGY

In 1980, Padilla wrote about psychologists who have contributed to Latin American psychology. In the early part of this century, Hispanic psychology drew its roots and orientation from psychology in Spain. However, the civil war in Spain set back psychology (Carpintero, 1987). It was not until relatively recently that psychology in Spain experienced a resurgence. The civil war in Spain depleted both available resources and confidence in higher education. Psychology was broadly considered a politically volatile discipline and, as such, was isolated from the academic institution geographically.

During the rebuilding years of Spanish psychology, Latin American psychology turned more to the United States for its focus. Initially, the focus in some countries, such as Argentina, was psychodynamic. Later, as in the case of Mexico, the focus shifted toward behaviorism. Areas such as cognitive and neuropsychology have made relatively little impact within psychology. Using neuropsychology as an example, the Latin American Neuropsychological Society has been comprised not only of psychologists but of physicians, speech and language pathologists, as well as occupational therapists. Psychology has comprised a relatively small proportion of personnel within Latin American neuropsychology while the opposite is true in North America.

Padilla (1999) has recently argued that within groups, comparisons need to be considered. Hispanics are often considered unidimensional and cohesive. In reality, there are many Hispanic subgroups ranging from Mexicans, Central Americans, Cubans, Puerto Ricans, and South Americans. Padilla has also argued that oppression, eurocentricity, acculturation, and biculturalism is often misunderstood by psychologists in the majority group culture. American psychology has understood Hispanics from the reference of American conceptualization. What may be particularly ironic is that by the end of this century, white Americans may be the minority group, at least in terms of numbers.

A CUBAN-AMERICAN PERSPECTIVE

Since the Communist Revolution in Cuba, Cubans have migrated in large numbers to the United States, primarily Miami, Florida. They comprise a vibrant portion of ethnic-minorities and an important subgroup within the Hispanic culture in the United States especially in Miami and New York. Cubans still residing in Cuba remain a vibrant aspect of Latin America and the world.

The history of Cuban psychology is almost as old as American psychology starting with philosophers and educators toward the end of the nineteenth century. The best example of a pioneer in Cuban psychology was a Enrique Varona y Pera, a politician, educator, philosopher, and psychologist (Puente & Puente, 2000). His first book *Conferencias Filosoficas* in the 1880s marked the beginning of a strong and independent intellectual climate in Cuba. He migrated toward psychology because of its focus on pedagogy as well

as its scientific underpinnings. As a consequence, he went on to become the first psychologist at the Universidad de la Habana. In 1921, he wrote the first textbook in psychology in Cuba, *Curso de Psicologia* (Varona y Pera, 1921).

Psychology grew, much like related disciplines, in Cuba primarily at the Universidad de la Habana. While other important universities went on to have faculty in psychology, the central focus has been and continues to be the main university in the capital. The focus on Cuban psychology remained on pedagogical applications and strong philosophical underpinnings. Vernon (1944) examined the state of psychology at the time and indicated that educational psychology was clearly the most important area within psychology.

By 1960, both Cuban psychology and society had begun to change. The revolution shifted the role of psychology and two major areas initially emerged. First, health care became a critical concern for the government and, within that focus, mental health took on an important position. Although psychopathology may have been viewed in a largely social context, increasing efforts were being made to develop an experimental psychopathology (Grau Abalo, 1984). The other issues involved the application of psychology to larger social contexts. This included, for example, the use of psychology in sports, something that has eventually occurred in the United States. In all cases, however, Soviet psychology played a major role. By 1964, the focus had shifted to educational, industrial, social, and clinical psychology. As Soviet psychology became more prevalent, other areas also took on greater importance. One example of this is clinical neuropsychology; several psychologists including Eduardo Cairo went to Moscow, some to study with Alexander Luria considered by some as the father of clinical neuropsychology.

Currently, Cuban psychology remains a strong and integral part of the Universidad de la Habana. Scientific psychology, rather than psychodynamic and humanism, are the central focus of psychology today. While there have been significant impediments to the integration of Cuban psychology into mainstream American psychology (e.g., no Cuban journal is abstracted by APA's *PsychLit*), Cubans have made an effort to bring their brand of thinking and health care to other parts of the world (e.g., Gongora & Barrios-Santos, 1987).

In the United States, Cuban-Americans have comprised a very small and relatively silent group within psychology. Outside of isolated instances [e.g., Szapocznik & Kurtines (1995) in Miami], few Cubans have made an impact on academic or research psychology. Most Cubans that do obtain their doctorates (perhaps reflective of psychology as a whole) pursue applied and clinical aspects of the discipline rather than research or academic careers. Furthermore, those that do have an impact in academic and research circles, tend to focus their work on ethnic-minority issues.

Cuban-Americans often do not identify themselves with other Hispanics. The number of Cuban-Americans who are part of mainstream Hispanic groups such as La Raza are rather small. As G. C. Hall and Maramba (2001) have discovered, there is highly limited overlap between cross-cultural and ethnic-minority literature. They go on to report that authors of cross-cultural studies tend to be white men of European ancestry whereas ethnic-minority research tends to be authored by ethnic-minority men and women. Further, all ethnic-minorities with a Spanish surname in their review are of Latino and not of Cuban descent.

PERSONAL PERSPECTIVE

How does one integrate equally successfully into both cultures, the mainstream majority culture (Anglo-Saxon) and the mainstream minority culture (ethnic-minority)? It has always been my intent to have an impact in the field of psychology as a neuropsychologist who was Cuban. For the first 15 years of my career, I published exclusively on noncultural issues, primarily biopsychosocial variables in neuropsychological assessment.

My service to the profession consisted of membership on a variety of boards and committees ranging from being president of the North Carolina Psychological Association, North Carolina Psychological Foundation, and the National Academy of Neuropsychology (NAN) to serving on the Health Care Finance Administration's Medicare Coverage Advisory Committee and the American Medical Association's Current Procedural Terminology Panel. However, during the last 10 years, I have become much more interested in cultural, though not necessarily ethnic-minority issues. For example, I presented the first workshop at a national neuropsychology convention on cultural issues in 1993.

All the while, I have held positions in APA governance (e.g., two terms on Council of Representatives) and have been mentored by Richard Suinn, past-president of APA. In these positions, I have both self-identified and been identified as an ethnic-minority. Though I value this work, I often see myself as an outsider both within these ethnic-minority groups as well as with "majority" groups whose interests have little, if anything, to do with ethnic-minority concerns.

Perhaps both groups, majority and minority, can consider their mission the development of a psychology of variance (Puente et al., 1993) rather than a psychology of central tendencies. I believe that would make a more interesting, and truer representation of the history of psychology.

Ethnic Minorities in Research and Organization

RICHARD M. SUINN

Psychology is defined as the study of human behavior. However, the history of psychology demonstrates that the discipline has focused its study on the behavior of white people. For instance, the early research knowledge base did not consider ethnic minority populations as normative; as Guthrie (1976) entitled his incisive discourse *Even the Rat was White.*

Research on ethnic minority issues was historically devalued in academic circles as not meeting standards for "good research," and hence ignored in considerations for promotion of faculty doing such research. Furthermore, minority scholars often experienced rejection of their submitted manuscripts on minority samples, based on the criticism that a white sample had not been included, and hence valid conclusions could not be drawn.

A combination of the increase in minorities earning doctoral degrees in psychology, greater attempts by university programs to recruit minorities, and organized activism were among the forces gradually forcing change. What recorded history or historical memory is available provides sources to identify some of the minorities entering psychology in early years (see outline in Final Report, 1997). Possibly because minorities were not always given recognition, some information is absent.

Francis Sumner was the first African American to earn a PhD in psychology from an American university in 1920. In 1933, Inez Prosser became the first African American woman to earn a doctoral degree. Robert Chin was the first Asian American awarded the PhD degree in 1943. In 1951,

Efrain Sanchez-Hidalgo was the first Puerto Rican receiving a doctorate, while in 1962 Martha Bernal was the first Mexican American woman awarded the PhD degree.

Within the American Psychological Association, although a woman was elected in early years as president (Mary Calkins was the 14th president), it took nearly 80 years for the first ethnic minority to be so elected. Kenneth B. Clark served as president in 1971. Another 15 years was to pass before the next ethnic psychologist would become APA president—Logan Wright. Over a decade later, the author was elected to the APA presidency.

ACTIVISM IN APA

It was 1963 when formal awareness of the relevance of ethnic issues led to any active movement. APA Division 9, Society for the Psychological Study of Social Issues, presented a proposal to the American Psychological Association to study problems encountered in education and employment associated with race. In response, APA formed the Ad Hoc Committee on Equality of Opportunity in Psychology.

Soon after, in 1963, the Association of Black Psychologists (ABPsi) was formed at the APA Convention in San Francisco, a group which then presented a Petition of Concerns to the APA Council of Representatives. This set of concerns covered the limited number of African American psychologists and students in the profession, APA's failure to address social problems and racism, and the underrepresentation of African Americans in the APA governance.

A slow series of actions by APA followed such pressures from activists. APA and ABPsi organized a Black Visiting Scientist program, and APA established the Commission for Accelerating Black Participation in Psychology. By 1973, the importance of systematic attention to ethnic education and training was recognized at the Vail Conference, with the recommendation that an office and board on ethnic minority affairs be formed within APA. This same recommendation was repeated in 1978 at the Dulles Conference. An Ad Hoc Committee on Ethnic Minority Affairs (CEMA) was formed that year and the APA Office of Ethnic Minority Affairs staffed the next year. In 1980, the CEMA was elevated to the status of Board of Ethnic Minority Affairs. (In 1996, CEMA was reinstituted as a continuing committee of the Board for the Advancement of Psychology in the Public Interest.)

Two other events deserve mention as part of the gradual changes within APA. The APA Minority Fellowship Program was funded in 1974 by NIMH to provide fellowships for minority graduate students. This Fellowship has continued into 2001 and has been one of the most successful sources for supporting minority graduate students. Also in 1986, Division 45 was officially approved as the Society for the Psychological Study of Ethnic Minority Issues. This Division has become a major home for many ethnic minority psychologists, and provides positions in its executive committee and officers for minorities to serve.

A PERSONAL HISTORY

My own development was shaped by a series of experiences. I was invited to the National Asian American Psychology Training Conference in 1976, an experience which forever molded my own identity. I cannot express how powerful it was to walk into a room and be surrounded not only by people who all looked like me in being Asian Americans, but who were also all psychologists! Deep in my heart, it felt like a homecoming—an emotion of enormous importance as it shaped my future.

Two events motivated me to pursue higher office in APA governance. First, I was elected president of the Association for the Advancement of Behavior Therapy (AABT) in 1993. The next event was an encounter at an executive committee meeting of the APA Division 45, the Society for the Psychological Study of Ethnic Minority Issues. A past president of the Division encouraged me to be a candidate for the APA presidency.

I ran three consecutive years, barely losing the first time by about 16 votes I decided to use a third try as a "tie breaker" and to live with its results. As fortune would have it, I became the 107th president of APA, the third ethnic minority, and the first Asian American.

MINORITIES PROGRESS DURING 1999

The year began with an unprecedented gathering of ethnic minority leadership, as the First National Multicultural Conference and Summit was organized by the four ethnic minority past or then-current presidents of APA Divisions: Rosie Bingham, president, Division of Counseling Psychology; Lisa M. Porche Burke, past-president and Derald Wing Sue, president, Society for the Psychological Study of Ethnic Minority Issues; and Melba J. T. Vasquez, president, Division of the Psychology of Women. The Conference was so successful that extra room was required for additional registrants, and even then many had to be turned away. In 2001, the second Conference and Summit was organized, and once more filled the registration to its maximum.

During 1999, five ethnic minorities assumed office as president of their divisions, with all four ethnic minority groups represented. In addition to Bingham, Sue, and Vasquez, Steven James, a Native American, accepted the presidency of the Psychology of Religion and Siang-Yang Tan, an Asian American, became president of the Society for the Psychological Study of Gay, Lesbian, and Bisexual Issues.

In 1996, there were 11 ethnic minority persons holding office in a Division (excluding Division 45, the Society for the Psychological Study of Ethnic Minorities, which would be expected to have elected ethnic minorities). By 1999, the count increased to 26—a 136% increase. By 2000, the numbers expanded to 51.

Regarding APA standing Boards and Committees, the number of ethnic minorities increased from 18 in 1996 to 43 in 1999 for a 139% increase. By 2000, the number increased even further to 54. An observation was made of the contrast between the Planning Committee members and the photographs on the wall of the APA board of directors, which were nearly all white persons. At the 1998 APA meetings in Boston, the presidents of the four autonomous ethnic minority psychological associations—Asian American Psychological Association, Association of Black Psychologists, National Hispanic Psychological Association, Society of Indian Psychologists—were present to receive Presidential Citations recognizing their associations' contributions to ethnic minority agendas.

Treating Ethnic Minority Clients

A. TOY CALDWELL-COLBERT AND VELMA M. WILLIAMS

Nearly a half century ago, the sociopolitical climate of the civil rights movement set the stage for changes and the need to work differently with people of color. In the 1950s and 1960s the public at large came to realize that race, skin color, oppression, segregation, and discrimination issues cut across society and impacted ethnic groups in various ways. Political activists and peoples' cries for help raised public consciousness to the realities of racism and oppression and their role in dealing with the problems of everyday living for people of color in the United States.

Serious attention by psychologists to diversity issues began in 1973 during the Vail Conference (H. F. Myers, Echemendia, & Trimble, 1991). The recognition of a need for change was stepped up a notch when the 1977 President's Commission on Mental Health's Special Populations Task Force (1978) concluded that culturally different individuals were clearly underserved or inappropriately served by the mental health system in this country. Yet in 1994, the Center for Mental Health Services in Rockville, Maryland, reported a bleak ratio of 3 to 1 of ethnic minorities needing mental health services to available minority professionals. According to Wohlford (1992), active minority mental health professionals were around 8.8% of approximately 148,579 active mental health service providers in the United States.

H. F. Myers et al. (1991) very poignantly summarized the situation, "Given the present state of professional training,

the average new PhD in psychology is only slightly more competent to meet the mental health needs of our culturally diverse population than are psychologists who completed training 20 years ago" (Casas, 1995, p. 311).

Two events in the last decade had a leading impact on psychology and on the preparation of all psychologists to work with ethnic minority clients, not only new students to the field, but also those trained 20 years ago. First, the American Psychological Association's endorsement of the August 1990 *Guidelines for Providers of Psychological Services to Ethnic, Linguistic, and Culturally Diverse Populations;* and, second, the National Institutes of Health issuance in 1994 of guidelines requiring representation of women and ethnic minorities in research in order to receive funding.

The significance of the APA *Guidelines* was documented by surveys mailed to 500 randomly selected psychologists in the fall of 1986 and again in the spring of 1992 (Caldwell-Colbert, 1998). An increase in people responding from 1986 to 1992 suggested a heightened awareness to the importance of therapy with the ethnically diverse.

Despite the apparent awareness of the needs, there were only slight changes in the number of adult clients seen when looked at by ethnic group. Except for Native Americans and Asian Americans, the reported percentages of clients treated *decreased* for all other ethnic groups in 1992. Native American clients treated increased from 2% to 3% and Asian Americans clients treated stayed the same at 2%.

Of particular interest was the likelihood of ethnic minorities being treated by white therapists in comparison to clients treated by ethnic minority therapists. Non-white therapists in both years reported treating more ethnic minority clients than white therapists, based on those reporting 60% or above of their client population by ethnicity.

Some research indicates preferences for therapists from similar ethnic backgrounds and SES, but studies are inconclusive (Sue, Zane, & Young, 1994). What these increased numbers may represent is the increased utilization of mental health services by ethnic minority clients due to enhanced services and access of more trained ethnic minority psychologists in 1992.

THERAPISTS' REPORTED LEVELS OF COMFORT

Further results of the survey suggested a decrease from 1986 to 1992 in the number of respondents who reported "feeling completely comfortable" in working with any ethnic group. The percent of respondents reporting feeling completely comfortable with white clients decreased from 1986 to 1992, 88.8% to 85.2%, respectively. Therapists with Native American clients showed the least comfort with that population.

The shifts in reported levels of comfort from 1986 to 1992 suggested that both white and ethnic minority therapists were moving away from generalized views of all clients being inherently the same and were more closely scrutinizing themselves, their abilities, and their preparation for clinical work with clients from various ethnic and cultural groups.

The release of the 1990 *APA Guidelines for Providers of Psychological Services to Ethnic, Linguistic, and Culturally Diverse Populations* challenged psychologists' level of knowledge and skill in working with the ethnically diverse, thus creating uncertainties and discomfort. Even though respondents reported higher levels of discomfort, they were in fact becoming better prepared as they anticipated ethnic and cultural issues in their clinical work, and the numerous considerations required for applying a sociocultural framework to diagnosis, assessment, and treatment of the culturally diverse.

CLINICAL PROBLEMS FREQUENTLY PRESENTED IN THERAPY

Our survey asked respondents how frequently 11 clinical problems were presented by clients representing five ethnic groups. A significant increase from 1986 to 1992 was reported among African American clients for the following four clinical problems: alcoholism, anxiety, health-related problems, and work-related problems. For Latinos, alcoholism was the only clinical problem showing a significant increase. Significant increases in the reporting of health-related problems and work-related problems were found for Asian American clients. For Native American clients, significant increases were found on 5 of the 11 commonly reported clinical problems: health-related problems, marital/family related problems, stress-related problems, and work-related problems. No significant differences were found for clinical problems reported to white versus non-white therapists.

There is a considerable body of literature (Turner, 1996) on ethnic/cultural differences in symptomatology for depression as well as on treatment considerations for anxiety disorders and associated stress-related conditions. Asian American clients most frequently presented marital/family problems in therapy, which may be associated with cultural traditions that place a high value on respecting one's elders and a collective approach to decision making that emphasizes the good of the family versus the well being of the individual.

CLIENT RESISTANCE AND TREATMENT EFFECTIVENESS

There were significantly fewer reported sources of resistance in 1992 than in 1986, (i.e., 39% versus 61%, respectively; $n = 159$). For example, attendance was one of the categories reported less frequently in 1986. Client dropout rates and length of treatment have been commonly reported problems by both white and non-white therapists working with ethnic minority clients (Sue, Zane, & Young, 1994). Based on our results, it appears that therapists in 1992 were better prepared to deal with resistance than those responding in 1986.

Training significantly contributed to the work of therapists in 1992. Half of those surveyed ($n = 87$) indicated that they had received training that was helpful in understanding the therapeutic needs of ethnic minorities.

CONCLUSIONS

When comparing delivery services to ethnic minorities in the decade of the 1980s, it appears that our preparation has advanced. Both white and ethnic minority therapists have positively responded to the call for increased cultural sensitivity in their work with ethnically and culturally different clients. Increased expectations for more sensitivity to cultural and ethnic diversity, coupled with the increased number of ethnic minorities in the field, appear to have laid a foundation for the progress over the last decade.

Updating Models of Racial and Ethnic Identity:
On the Origins of an Ecological Framework of Identity Development

MARIA P. P. ROOT

Models of ethnic and racial identity, with few exceptions, have assumed the confabulation of race constructed by scientists and government—that there is such a thing as purity, much less race! Essentially race-specific trauma models, they suggest that one starts out innocently believing in a "just world" and learns by a significant experience that there is gross injustice, particularly when it comes to the caste status for persons with phenotypes that are not solely European in origin.

None of the leading theorists of ethnic or racial identity actually believes in the purity of race, but the models inadvertently reinforce this. Common across models is a stage of retreat to the community of origin as a place within which healing from socially and politically induced racial trauma begins. Through immersion in the race and/or ethnic group, one theoretically develops a sense of pride that will inoculate one against the injustices that do exist.

These models assume that by virtue of your parentage and phenotype, you will be embraced, mentored, and empowered. These models theoretically make sense, and in the era they were produced—the end of the civil rights era or the third quarter of the twentieth century—they worked for most of the people deemed visible minorities. However, they perpetuated the invisibility and marginality of persons of mixed heritage who were not conceived from rape, slavery, or war. Inadvertently, many of them historically have become the oppressors of mixed heritage persons who do not conform to rules of hypodescent (i.e., assignment to the group, and only one group, of the lowest social status).

Notwithstanding admiring these works and the people who have produced them, I also noticed that my experience and many of my friends' experience did not fit. Born in the Korean War era in the Philippines of a Filipino mother and a white American father, this complexity of juxtapositions (ethnicity, race, nationality, colonialism, gender, and class) allowed me an outsider vantage from which to examine the models that have been so foundational to some of the work on racial and ethnic identity. For many of us who are of mixed race, even in communities to which our families belonged or were assigned, we were intruders or suspected as potential betrayers of "the race." To belong, we had less room in which to express our individuality or the unique way in which blending influenced us. Thus, we did not have guaran-

teed refuge in the minority group of origin unless we hid part of ourselves or even engaged in denigration of part of our family.

For those with Asian mothers of a different nationality, we were culture brokers yet sometimes teased within Asian American groups for acting in foreign or odd ways. In this way, nation, race, and ethnicity were terribly confused. For persons of African descent combined with any other heritage, declaring multiple allegiances or a blended identity was interpreted as confusion or a desire to divest oneself of blackness. Being tested by any of our groups of origin, we were always put to more severe scrutiny or authenticity testing, and seldom considered full and true members. In effect, the oppressed joined ranks with the oppressors and inadvertently served the agenda of advancing a fiction of social purity and segregation of the races—the very system harmful to our ancestors.

Several classic dissertations were completed in the 1980s and formed the core for the contemporary theory and work on what constitutes normative experience and development for persons of mixed heritage. These dissertations largely came out of the discipline of psychology and were groundbreaking works of scholarship and data production (e.g., C. I. Hall, 1980; Jacobs, 1977; Murphy-Shigematsu, 1986; Thornton, 1983). They were difficult to accomplish because of the lack of literature on the topic, the lack of random distribution of mixed race people in the population, the few numbers of persons identified as mixed race, and the methods required to gain large enough samples for analysis. What changed within a decade of the youngest of these dissertations was the interdisciplinary interest in mixed race identity production and meaning. There were suddenly more young scholars of mixed heritage and the foundation had been laid in the first of two books I edited to make these pieces of research and others available (Root, 1992, 1996b).

My initial work on mixed race identity undertook a departure from stage models, as many of the previous researchers had done. I proposed four different types of identities that persons of mixed heritage may express at different times in their life: (a) identify as a single race according to rules of hypodescent; (b) identify as a single race for personal and or political congruence; (c) identify as multiple races; or (d) identify as a new race. Rather than being proposed as a continuum, these expressions of identity were discussed in terms of historical feasibility, generational shifts, social functionality, the increasing visibility of a mixed race population aware of one another, and individual differences (Root, 1990).

Whereas the work on mixed race identity remained largely obscure, by the 1990 census, it was clear that the demographic change that many of us had been observing and predicting was well underway. Interracial relationships had significantly increased since the Supreme Court repeal of the last antimiscegenation laws in 1967 (Root, 2001). In 1990, more than six million people checked "other" as a race category and many persons wrote in multiple races. Grassroots organizations had been talking with census policymakers since the late 1980s about the increasing need to reexamine racial accounting by the census.

It was clear by 1990 that the political charge attached to race and the conventional meanings attached to mixed race identity proclamations were going to continue. Hypodescent rules would be used to reinforce race as a caste system. The passing narrative would be used to explain a person's motives who declared more than a single racial identity.

While on a visiting professorship at the University of Hawaii, I pondered the likelihood that mixed race identities would be misunderstood and subsequently pathologized or misattributed. It was clear that contemporary theory needed to be developed and dissertation data needed to be accessible to the next generation of researchers since it was inevitable that mixed race people would become the subject of study. This research could either be used to move along a dialogue on race or to serve as a political tool to keep persons of mixed heritage largely invisible. It would depend on who did the research. I edited a book, *Racially Mixed People in America,* published in 1992 that made available many of the dissertations of the 1980s. It laid the foundation for the contemporary research on people of mixed heritage cross-disciplinarily. This book would be used by the Bureau of the Census as part of consultation and deliberation for the changes to racial classification in the 2000 Census.

Hand in hand with the slow proliferation of research about mixed race persons, the grassroots multiracial family groups were swelling in numbers across the country. Using the theory of social movements, and the data from interviews and social interaction, I developed the *Bill of Rights for Racially Mixed People* in 1992 (Root, 1996a). It was couched in simple language and has since become the property of many organizations and individuals to depathologize their identity declarations in this country. Twelve affirmative statements are organized into three sections representing resistance, revolution, and change. It further normalizes subverting

implicit rules to "stick with your own kind"; these rules do not always work very well for racially mixed people. Seeking refuge in a home community does not guarantee a warm reception.

In 1996, I published a second edited volume that reflected the increased politicization around mixed race identities, *The Multiracial Experience: Racial Borders as the New Frontier* (Root, 1996b). This volume included new research, analysis of policy based on current racial classification systems, documented grassroots mobilization as part of the place of refuge and voice for many adult persons of mixed heritage and interracial families, and posed many questions as the nation struggled to recognize a growing segment of the population that was not adhering to conventional racial rules. My penchant for theory development from data and participant observation resulted in *Ecological Framework for Identity Development* (Root, 1999).

The U.S. Bureau of the Census released its 2000 population figures on race in March of 2001. Approximately 2.4% of the nation opted to declare more than one race. This translated into 6.8 million people. Examining state by state data, persons declaring mixed heritages are not evenly distributed within the United States. In Hawaii, 21.4% of the population identified themselves by more than one race. Among other states exceeding the national average were Alaska (5.4%), Arizona (2.9%), California (4.7%), Colorado (2.8%), Nevada (3.8%), New Jersey (2.5%), New Mexico (3.6%), New York (3.1%), Oklahoma (4.5%), Oregon (3.1%), Rhode Island (2.7%), Texas (2.5%), and Washington (3.6%).

Perhaps more telling are recent birth rate figures, with some counties in the mainland United States contending 15% or more of babies born in 1999 and 2000 to be of mixed heritage. It still remains to be seen if there are differences in the proportions of people of different racial combinations declaring more than one race.

These declarations on the census are demographic trends rather than actual reflections of how people live their lives. For some people, being able to declare more than one race is politically and personally important. For other people, it is symbolic, with no real personal significance attached (Root, 1998).

As a nation, we need to contend with a newer dialogue on race—one that acknowledges race mixing and mixed race in contemporary context. In her novel, *Caucasia,* Senna (1998) offers a generational framework through the voice of an African American professor who studies race. He talks to his estranged biracial daughter describing mulattos as the canaries in the coal mine, the "gauge of how poisonous American race relations were. The fate of the mulatto in history and in literature, he said, will manifest the symptoms that will eventually infect the rest of the nation" (p. 335). It captures the generational change that we are living amidst regarding identity production and meaning for persons of mixed heritage.

Root (2001) suggests that with mortality claiming an older generation who knew segregation and lived by it, replaced by an aged just pre-civil rights generation, a civil rights generation in power, followed by an adolescent and young adult generation who are beneficiaries of the civil rights movement, change is clearly in motion. Each generation demonstrates a change in regard for meaning of race over the previous one. Despite the scars of this nation's racial legacy, we still have hope. Paraphrasing Martin Luther King, the issue is not whether there will be a funeral but a question of the cost. We have a choice in how costly change continues to be—psychology can have a role in it.

REFERENCES

Akbar, N. (1991). The evolution of human psychology for African Americans. In R. L. Jones (Ed.), *Black psychology* (3rd ed., pp. 99–123). Hampton, VA: Cobb & Henry.

Albee, G. W. (1969). A conference on recruitment of Black and other minority students and faculty. *American Psychologist, 24*(8), 720–723.

Albee, G. W. (1998). Fifty years of clinical psychology: Selling our soul to the devil. *Applied and Preventive Psychology Current Scientific Perspectives, 7,* 189–194.

American Psychological Association. (1990). *APA guidelines for providers of psychological services to ethnic, linguistic, and culturally diverse populations.* Washington, DC: Author.

American Psychological Association. (1993). Guidelines for providers of psychological services to ethnic, linguistic, and culturally diverse populations. *American Psychologist, 48,* 45–48.

American Psychological Association. (1997). *Commission on ethnic minority recruitment, retention, and training in psychology* (CEMRRAT; Final report). Washington, DC: Author.

Baker, D. B., & Benjamin, L. T., Jr. (2000). The affirmation of the scientist-practitioner: A look back at Boulder. *American Psychologist, 55,* 241–247.

Blau, T. H. (1970). APA commission on accelerating black participation in psychology. *American Psychologist, 25,* 1103–1104.

Boykin, A. W., Franklin, A. J., & Yates, J. F. (Eds.). (1979). *Research directions of Black psychologists.* New York: Russell Sage Foundation.

Caldwell-Colbert, A. T. (1998, August 14–18). *Treating ethnic minority clients: Are we prepared?* Presidential address (Div. 12, Sec. 6), APA Convention, San Francisco.

Cameron, N., & Rychlak, J. F. (1985). *Personality development and psychopathology.* Boston: Houghton-Mifflin.

Carpintero, H. (1987). *Historia de la psicologica.* Madrid, Spain: NAU Libres.

Casas, J. M. (1995). Counseling and psychotherapy with racial/ethnic minority groups in theory and practice. In B. Bonger & L. E. Beutler (Eds.), *Comprehensive textbook of psychotherapy: Theory and practice* (pp. 311–335). New York: Oxford University Press.

Chein, I. (1972). *The science of behavior and the image of man.* New York: Basic Books.

Clausen, C. (2000). *Faded mosaic: The emergence of post cultural America.* Chicago: Ivan R. Dee.

Comas-Diaz, L. (1990). Ethnic minority mental health: Contributions and future directions of the American Psychological Association. In F. Serafica, A. Schwebel, R. Russell, P. Isaac, & L. Myers (Eds.), *Mental health of minorities* (pp. 275–301). New York: Praeger.

Comas-Diaz, L. (1998). Ethnic minority psychology: Identity, empowerment, and transformation. *Cultural Diversity and Mental Health, 4,* 151–152.

Comas-Diaz, L. (2000). The torch of multicultural knowledge. *Cultural Diversity and Ethnic Minority Psychology, 6,* 332–333.

Comas-Diaz, L., Griffith, E. H., Pinderhughes, E., & Wyche, K. (1995). Coming of age: Cultural diversity and mental health. *Cultural Diversity and Mental Health, 1,* 1–2.

Crain, R. L., & Weisman, C. S. (1972). *Discrimination, personality and achievement: A survey of northern Blacks.* New York: Seminar Press.

DiNicola, V. (1997). *A stranger in the family: Culture, families and therapy.* New York: Norton.

Edelson, M. (1971). *The idea of a mental illness.* New Haven, CT: Yale University Press.

Ellison, R. (1952). *Invisible man.* New York: Signet Books.

Ellison, R. (1964). That same pain, that same pleasure: An interview. In R. Ellison (Ed.), *Shadow and act* (pp. 3–23). New York: Random House.

Evans, R. B., Sexton, V. S., & Cadwallader, T. C. (1992). *The American Psychological Association: A historical perspective.* Washington, DC: American Psychological Association.

Faulconer, J. E., & Williams, R. N. (1985). Temporality in human action: An alternative to positivism and historicism. *American Psychologist, 40,* 1179–1188.

Gongora, R., & Barrios-Santos, M. (1987). Sychelles: Una experiencia de trabajo internacionalista. *Boletin de Psicologia Cuba, 10,* 113–121.

Grau Abalo, J. A. (1984). Cerca de la especificidad de la investigacion experimental patopsicologica y su importancia en la etapa actual de dsarrollo de la patopsicologica en nuestro pais [On the specificity of experimental pathopsychological research and its importance in the current stage of development of pathopsychology in our country]. *Boletin de Psicologia Cuba, 41*–60.

Guthrie, R. V. (1976). *Even the rat was White*. New York: Harper & Row.

Guthrie, R. V. (1998). *Even the rat was White: A historical view of psychology* (2nd ed.). Needham Height, MA: Allyn & Bacon.

Hall, C. I. I. (1980). *The ethnic identity of racially mixed people: A study of Black-Japanese*. Unpublished doctoral dissertation, University of California, Los Angeles.

Hall, G. C., & Maramba, G. G. (2001). In search of cultural diversity: Recent literature in cross-cultural and ethnic-minority psychology. *Cultural Diversity and Ethnic Minority Psychology, 7,* 12–26.

Harrison, L. E., & Huntington, S. P. (Eds.). (2000). *Culture matters: How values shape human progress*. New York: Basic Books.

Hayes, W. A. (1991). Radical Black behaviorism. In R. Jones (Ed.), *Black psychology* (3rd ed., pp. 65–78). Hampton, VA: Cobb & Henry.

Herman, E. (1995). *The romance of American psychology: Political culture in the age of experts*. Berkeley: University of California Press.

Hilliard, T. O. (1973). Professional training and minority groups. In M. Korman (Ed.), *Levels and patterns of professional training in psychology* (pp. 41–49). Washington, DC: American Psychological Association.

Holt, R. R. (1972). Mechanistic and humanistic themes in Freud's thought. *Psychoanalysis and Contemporary Science, 1,* 3–24.

Howard, G. S. (1991). Culture tales: A narrative approach to thinking, cross-cultural psychology, and psychotherapy. *American Psychologist, 46,* 187–197.

Howard, G. S., & Conway, C. G. (1986). Can there be an empirical science of volitional action? *American Psychologist, 41,* 1241–1251.

Hughes, L. (1959). Mother to son. In *Selected poems of Langston Hughes* (p. 187). New York: Knopf.

Jacobs, J. H. (1977). *Black/White interracial families: Marital process and identity development in young children*. Unpublished doctoral dissertation, U.C. Berkeley, Wright Institute.

Jay, J. M. (1971). *Negroes in science: Natural science doctorates, 1876–1969*. Detroit, MI: Balamp.

Jenkins, A. H. (1995). *Psychology and African Americans: A humanistic approach* (2nd ed.). Needham Heights, MA: Allyn & Bacon.

Kardiner, A., & Ovesey, L. (1962). *The mark of oppression*. Cleveland, OH: Meridian Books. (Original work published 1951)

Kitano, H. H. (1969). Japanese-American mental illness. In S. S. Plog & R. B. Edgerton (Eds.), *Hanging perspectives in mental illness* (pp. 256–284). New York: Holt, Rinehart and Winston.

Martin, J., & Sugarman, J. (1999). *The psychology of human possibility and constraint*. Albany: State University of New York Press.

Maslow, A. H. (1968). *Toward a psychology of being* (2nd ed.). New York: Van Nostrand-Reinhold.

McKeachie, W. J. (1969). Proceedings of the American Psychological Association, Incorporated, for the year 1968: Minutes of the annual meeting of the Council of Representatives, September 1, 1968, San Francisco, and October 5 & 6, 1968, Washington, DC: *American Psychologist, 24,* 19–41.

Messer, S., Sass, L., & Woolfolk, R. (Eds.). (1988). *Hermeneutics and psychological theory*. New Brunswick, NJ: Rutgers University Press.

Mezzich, J., Kleinman, A., Fabrega, H., Good, B., Johnson-Powell, G., Lin, K. M., et al. (Eds.). (1993). *Cultural proposals and supporting papers for DSM-IV*. Rockville, MD: National Institute of Mental Health.

Murphy-Shigematsu, S. L. (1986). *The voices of Amerasians: Ethnicity, identity and empowerment in interracial Japanese Americans*. Unpublished doctoral dissertation, Harvard University, Cambridge, MA.

Myers, H. F., Echemendia, R. J., & Trimble, J. E. (1991). The need for training ethnic minority psychologists. In H. F. Myers, P. Wohlford, L. P. Guzman, & R. J. Echemendia (Eds.), *Ethnic minority perspectives in clinical training and services in psychology* (pp. 3–11). Washington, DC: American Psychological Association.

Myers, L. J. (1988). *Understanding an Afrocentric world view: Introduction to an optimal psychology*. Dubuque, IA: Kendall/Hunt.

Nelson, B. (1969). Psychologists: Searching for social relevance at APA meeting. *Science, 165,* 1101–1104.

Newcomb, T. M. (1957). *A statement for APA members on the APA meeting in Miami Beach in 1957*. Washington, DC: American Psychological Association.

Nobles, W. A. (1991). African philosophy: Foundations of Black psychology. In R. L. Jones (Ed.), *Black psychology* (3rd ed., pp. 47–63). Hampton, VA: Cobb & Henry.

Padilla, A. (1980). Notes on the history of Hispanic psychology. *Hispanic Journal of Behavioral Sciences, 2,* 109–128.

Padilla, A. (1999). Hispanic psychology: A 25 year retrospective look. In W. Lonner & D. L. Dinnel (Eds.), *Merging past, present, and future in cross-cultural psychology: Selected papers from the fourteenth International Congress of the International Association for Cross-Cultural Psychology* (pp. 73–81). Lisse, The Netherlands: Swet & Zeitlinger.

Parham, T. A., White, J. L., & Ajamu, A. (2000). *The psychology of Blacks: An African–centered perspective* (3rd ed.). Upper Saddle River, NJ: Prentice-Hall.

Polkinghorne, D. E. (1990). Language and qualitative research. *Theoretical and Philosophical Psychology, 10,* 3–24.

Puente, A. E., Blanch, E., Candland, D. K., Denmark, F. L., Laman, C., Lutsky, N., et al. (1993). Towards a psychology of variance. In T. V. McGovern (Ed.), *Handbook for enhancing undergraduate education in psychology* (pp. 70–92). Washington, DC: American Psychological Association.

Puente, A. E., Matthews, J., & Brewer, C. (1992). *Teaching psychology in America: A history.* Washington, DC: American Psychological Association.

Puente, A. E., & Puente, K. L. (2000). Enrique Jose Varona y Pera. In A. Kazdin (Ed.), *Encyclopedia of psychology* (Vol. 8, p. 157). Washington, DC: American Psychological Association.

Pugh, R. L. (1972). *Psychology and the Black experience.* Monterey, CA: Brooks/Cole.

Richardson, F. C., Fowers, B. J., & Guignon, C. B. (1999). *Re-envisioning psychology: Moral dimensions of theory and practice.* San Francisco: Jossey-Bass.

Robinson, D. N. (1991). Text, context and agency. *Theoretical and Philosophical Psychology, 11,* 1–10.

Root, M. P. P. (1990). Resolving "other" status: Identity development of biracial individuals. In L. Brown & M. P. P. Root (Eds.), *Diversity and complexity in feminist therapy* (pp. 185–206). New York: Harrington Park Press.

Root, M. P. P. (Ed.). (1992). *Racially mixed people in America.* Thousand Oaks, CA: Sage.

Root, M. P. P. (1996a). A Bill of Rights for Racially Mixed People. In M. P. P. Root (Ed.), *The multiracial experience: Racial borders as the new frontier* (pp. 3–14). Thousand Oaks, CA: Sage.

Root, M. P. P. (Ed.). (1996b). *The multiracial experience: Racial borders as the new frontier.* Thousand Oaks, CA: Sage.

Root, M. P. P (Ed.). (1998). Experiences and processes affecting racial identity development: Preliminary results from the biracial sibling project. *Cultural Diversity and Mental Health, 4*(3), 237–247.

Root, M. P. P. (1999). The biracial baby boom: Understanding ecological constructions of racial identity in the twenty-first century. In R. H. Sheets & E. R. Hollins (Eds.), *Racial and ethnic identity in school practices: Aspects of human development* (pp. 67–90). Mahwah, NJ: Erlbaum.

Root, M. P. P. (2001). *Love's revolution: Interracial marriage.* Philadelphia: Temple University Press.

Rychlak, J. F. (1968). *A philosophy of science for personality theory.* Boston: Houghton-Mifflin.

Rychlak, J. F. (1988). *The psychology of rigorous humanism* (2nd ed.). New York: New York University Press.

Rychlak, J. F. (1994). *Logical learning theory: A human teleology and its empirical support.* Lincoln: University of Nebraska Press.

Said, E. W. (1994). *Culture and imperialism.* New York: Vintage Books.

Sarbin, T. R. (1977). Contextualism: A world view for modern psychology. In A. Landfield (Ed.), *1976 Nebraska Symposium on Motivation* (pp. 1–41). Lincoln: University of Nebraska Press.

Senna, D. (1998). *Caucasian.* New York: Riverhead Books.

Shorris, E. (1992). *Latinos: A biography of the people.* New York: Norton.

Simpkins, G., & Raphael, P. (1970). Black students, APA, and the challenge of change. *American Psychologist, 25,* xxvii–xxviii.

Slife, B. D., & Williams, R. N. (1995). *What's behind the research: Discovering hidden assumptions in the behavioral sciences.* Thousand Oaks, CA: Sage.

Sue, S., & Sue, D. W. (1971). Chinese-American personality and mental health. *Amerasia Journal, 1,* 36–49.

Sue, S., Zane, N., & Young, K. (1994). Research on psychotherapy with culturally diverse populations. In A. E. Bergin & S. L. Garfield (Eds.), *Handbook of psychotherapy and behavioral change* (4th ed., pp. 783–817). New York: Wiley.

Szapocznik, J., & Kurtines, W. M (1995). Family psychology and cultural diversity: Opportunities for theory, research, and application. In N. R. Goldberger & J. B. Veroff (Eds.), *The culture and psychology reader* (pp. 808–824). New York: New York University Press.

Thomas, A., & Sillen, S. (1972). *Racism and psychiatry.* New York: Brunner/Mazel.

Thornton, M. C. (1983). *A social history of a multiethnic identity: The case of Black Japanese Americans.* Unpublished doctoral dissertation, University of Michigan, Ann Arbor.

Turner, S. M. (1996). *Treatment of anxiety disorders in African Americans: Current status.* Symposium on Advances in Treatment Outcome Research with Ethnic Minorities, 104th meeting of the American Psychological Association, Toronto, Ontario, Canada.

Tyler, L. E. (1978). *Individuality: Human possibilities and personal choice in the psychological development of men and women.* San Francisco: Jossey-Bass.

U.S. Bureau of the Census. (2001, December 20). *State and County QuickFacts.* Retrieved from quickfacts.Census.gov.

U.S. Bureau of the Census. (2001). *United States statistical information.* Washington, DC: Author.

United States President's Commission on Mental Health. (1978). *Report to the President from the President's Commission on Mental Health* (Vol. 4, p. 26). Washington, DC: U.S. Government Printing Office.

Varona y Pera, E. J. (1880–1888). *Conferencias filisoficas.* Habana, Cuba: Miguel de Villa.

Varona y Pera, E. J. (1921). *Curso de Psicologia* (segunda edicion). Habana, Cuba: La Moderna Poesia.

Vazquez, C. I. (1991). A training program for Hispanic psychologists at New York University–Bellevue Hospital Center. In H. F. Myers, P. Wohlford, L. P. Guzman, & R. J. Echemendia (Eds.), *Ethnic minority perspectives on clinical training and services in psychology* (pp. 143–148). Washington, DC: American Psychological Association.

Vernon, W. H. D. (1944). Psychology in Cuba. *Psychological Bulletin, 41,* 73–89.

White, J. L., & Parham, T. A. (1990). *The psychology of Blacks: An African-American perspective* (2nd ed.). Englewood Cliffs, NJ: Prentice-Hall.

White, R. W. (1959). Motivation reconsidered: The concept of competence. *Psychological Review, 66,* 297–333.

Williams, B. H. (1997). *Coming together: The founding of the Association of Black Psychologists.* Unpublished doctoral dissertation, Saint Louis University, Saint Louis, MO.

Williams, R. L. (1974). A history of the Association of Black Psychologists: Early formation and development. *Journal of Black Psychology, 1,* 9–24.

Wispe, L., Awkard, J., Hoffman, M., Ash, P., Hicks, L., & Porter, J. (1969). The Negro psychologist in America. *American Psychologist, 24,* 142–150.

Wohlford, P. (1992). Patterns of CMHS and NIMH support of clinical training for ethnic minorities. *Clinical Psychologist, 45,* 13–21.

Wyatt, G. E. (2001). The legacy of multiculturalism. *Cultural Diversity and Ethnic Minority Psychology, 7,* 3–5.

CHAPTER 25

International Psychology

HENRY P. DAVID AND JOAN BUCHANAN

ROOTS   510
THE DEVELOPMENT OF MODERN PSYCHOLOGY   510
THE 1913 CONGRESS THAT WASN'T   512
THE U.S. CONGRESS THAT WAS HELD IN CANADA   512
YOUNG PSYCHOLOGISTS INITIATIVE   512
DIFFERING VIEWS ON HUMAN RIGHTS   513
VISAS AND FLAGS   514

PSYCHOLOGISTS' EVOLVING STAND ON
   SOCIAL ISSUES   514
THE TREND FROM AMERICANIZATION
   TO INTERNATIONALIZATION   515
CHRONOLOGY OF MILESTONES IN
   INTERNATIONAL PSYCHOLOGY   517
REFERENCES   531

It is a truism that science knows nothing of national boundaries, and that the commonwealth of mind draws all men into its domain, so that in the pursuit of truth all may join in friendly rivalry. But it is equally true that physical remoteness, or cultural insulation, as well as the barriers of alien tongues, still serve to keep men from the fullest and most sympathetic understanding of one another's thought. (James R. Angell [1930], Opening address to the 9th International Congress of Psyhology, 1929)

It is safe to say that psychology is as old as the inquiring, self-conscious mind of man. (R. S. Woodworth, 1964)

In developing this chapter, two approaches are followed. The first part, a narrative, summarizes the international roots of psychology, beginning more than 2,000 years ago, followed by selected highlights and vignettes retrieved from reports and personal observations. This portion is anecdotal at times to show the human side of international psychology by reflecting on the interactions of colleagues seeking international consensus. It also demonstrates how political events gradually forced psychologists to move beyond the sheltered world of academia to confront questions of professional ethics and public policies impinging on personal freedom. To illustrate these dilemmas and successes, several U.S.-influenced

The authors are pleased to acknowledge the constructive suggestions and assistance received from Ludy T. Benjamin, Merry Bullock, Tema S. David, Edwin A. Fleishman, Donald K. Freedheim, Gerda K. Freedheim, Wade Pickren, Mark Rosenzweig, and Warren R. Street. Special thanks to Sarah P. Leverty and to the staff of the American Psychological Association Library for their ongoing help and technical support.

events are recalled, ending with a commentary on the increasing internationalization of psychology.

Specifically discussed will be (a) the 1913 Congress that wasn't, (b) the U.S. Congress held in Canada, (c) the Young Psychologists' initiative, (d) differing views on human rights, (e) visas and flags, (f) psychologists' evolving stands on social issues, and (g) the trend from Americanization to internationalization.

The second part of the chapter is a table that consists of a chronology of events influencing international psychology, similar to the format pioneered by Street (1994). Included are the founding of psychological laboratories and institutes, national psychological organizations, journals, and first congresses. Also cited are unique events of historical interest that reflect on the tenor of the times. The language used depends upon the sources. We assume responsibility for any inadvertent errors.

Writing about the history of international psychology differs from reviewing historical developments in psychological subspecialties. Rather than being a distinct field, international psychology spans the entire discipline. When well-informed colleagues were asked what they meant when using the term "international psychology," the typical response referred to international congresses, travel, and specialized meetings as well as exchanges, collaborative multicultural research and practice, and the application of psychological principles to the development of public policy (David & Buchanan, 1999). As noted by Denmark (1987), the term "international psychology" may also refer to social psychological studies of international relations or cross-cultural research.

There are diverse approaches to reviewing the history of international psychology, ranging from theoretical concepts proposed by "Great Men" and "Great Women" to an analysis of the "Zeitgeist" in different countries or regions (e.g., Gilgen & Gilgen, 1987; Hilgard, Leary, & McGuire, 1991; Pawlik & Rosenzweig, 1994; Pawlik & d'Ydewalle, 1996; Rosenzweig, 1992; Sexton & Hogan, 1992). The only historical overviews located in the literature are those prepared on behalf of international organizations (e.g., Cautley, 1992; Jing, 2000; Merenda, 1995; Rosenzweig, Holtzman, Sabourin, & Bolanger, 2000; Wilpert, 2000).

In writing this chapter, we recall Watson's (1960) comment that "it would be a serious mistake to consider the history of psychology to be limited to a mere chronology of events or biographical chitchat" (p. 254). This is particularly true for international psychology. In our view, psychological contributions are embedded in the social context from which they emerge, seen within the perspective of personal and national values. Within that context, ours is but a first attempt to record some aspects of the history of "international psychology."

ROOTS

The introduction of scientific psychology as we know it is a comparatively recent phenomenon, traditionally dating to 1879 when Wundt established his laboratory in Leipzig and attracted students from all parts of the world. On their return home, Wundt's disciples established the first psychological laboratory in their country, directed the first institute of psychology, and founded one or more journals of psychology (Ardila, 1982a).

It was not until 1889 that the first International Congress of Physiological Psychology was convened in Paris. The closing banquet was held in the just-completed Eiffel Tower. Most congress participants were officially identified with philosophy, medicine, or one of the traditional sciences. Few scientists at that time claimed the title of "psychologist" (MacLeod, 1957).

Historically, internationalism in psychology probably began with the arrival of the first non-Greek visitors to the Academy of Athens, established by Plato in 387 B.C.E. While he would not have called it psychology, Plato's speculations often focused on human behavior. When Aristotle wrote *De Anima* in 330 B.C.E., Greek philosophy was replete with valuable psychological intuitions on the nature of communication, leadership, and social conditions affecting self-esteem. Many psychological terms, concepts, and theories have their roots in the thoughts of Hellenic philosophers (Georgas, 1994).

The pedigree of psychology probably reaches further back in time to the civilizations of ancient China, India, and the Arab world. The writings of Confucius (500 B.C.E.) contain a wealth of psychological thought. The goodness and evil of human nature and the essence of the human spirit were discussed in relation to ethical, political, and educational theories (Ching, 1980).

In India, the roots of psychology can be traced to the vast storehouse of ancient philosophical and religious texts as well as folklore (Sinha, 1986). During a period of several centuries B.C.E., the search for an understanding of human behavior led to the development of a psychological system of nature quite different from that of the Greco-Roman renaissance (Murphy & Kovach, 1972).

In the Arab world, philosophers inherited Greek philosophical speculations and mixed them with their religious and moral traditions. Islamic thinkers made major contributions in the Middle Ages, including recognition of the innate psychological foundations of social life, factors affecting group cohesion, the psychology of different cultures, and the relationship between personality characteristics and vocational success (Ahmed, 1992, 1997; Soueif, 1963).

The medieval period was followed by a revival of learning (Watson, 1960). In the twelfth and thirteenth centuries, a rebirth of Greek, particularly Aristotelian, ways of thinking, led to empirical, especially experimental, ways of approaching nature. "Out of the work of Renaissance man comes what we know about the origins of our present knowledge" (Watson, 1960, p. 254).

THE DEVELOPMENT OF MODERN PSYCHOLOGY

International communication among psychologists has been important to the development of modern psychology. Communication has flourished through world congresses, scholarly exchanges, and perhaps most importantly the establishment of ongoing international organizations. While the chapter by Raymond Fowler and Wade Pickren (Chapter 26) details this development, it is important to highlight here three major international organizations that have played key roles. The oldest international organization of psychologists is the International Association of Applied Psychology (IAAP). The IAAP was founded in 1920 at the first International Congress of Applied Psychology, convened by E. Claparède in Geneva. The International Council of Psychologists (ICP) traces its roots to the National Council of Women Psychologists, established in New York City in 1941 by a group of U.S. women psychologists who wished to contribute to the national war effort. The ICP became an international organization in 1946 and evolved to its current status in 1958, when it agreed to accept male members. The International Union of Psychological Science (IUPsyS) was founded in 1951 (then named the International Union of Scientific Psychology) at the Thirteenth International Congress of Psychology in Stockholm. In 1982, the IUPsyS, which has national organizations as its members, was admitted to represent psychology at the International Council of Scientific Unions.

James McKeen Cattell (1930), the first U.S. scholar to obtain a doctorate with Wundt in 1886, noted in his presidential address to the 1929 International Congress of Psychology at Yale University that our psychological ancestors were mainly concerned with themselves, with their mates and their offspring, and with the behavior of their fellows and their enemies. Satisfaction of desires, escape from danger and pain, and efforts to foresee and control the conduct of others were among their earliest interests. Commenting on the world of psychology at the time of the Congress, Cattell asserted the U.S. view when he told his international audience (1930):

> It is not an accident that laboratory research in psychology is of German origin, that pathological psychology has been cultivated in France, that psychoanalysis has spread from Vienna, that Darwin and Galton were English, that objective psychology and the measurement of individual differences have had their chief development in the United States. Germany may keep its Gestalt psychology, France its hysterics, Austria its libido, England its "g"; we shall continue to bear the burden of our meta-behaviorism." (p. 18)

Russian psychology developed along its own isolated lines and independently produced surprising parallels to developments in the United States during the same time period (Berlyne, 1968). Pavlov presented a paper at the 1929 congress while claiming to be a physiologist, not a psychologist. As acknowledged by Lomov (1982), Soviet dialectical psychology was oriented to Marxist-Leninist principles and dominated by political influences oriented to the building of a communist society.

In the People's Republic of China, too, the heads of national planning expected psychologists to lend their knowledge and skills to achieving the goals of the "four modernizations." To do so, a culturally specific psychology had to be created to "meet the demands of our own national conditions" (Ching, 1984, p. 63).

A similar situation could be observed in Nazi Germany and later in the German Democratic Republic (GDR), where psychology was dependent on central-planning authorities. The situation in Hitler's Germany is reflected in Henle's

(1978) recollections of the (non-Jewish) Wolfgang Köhler's courageous struggle against the Nazis and the destruction of the Psychological Institute of the University of Berlin in 1935. In the GDR, the Scientific Council of Psychology, a government agency working through the GDR Society of Psychology, decided who could do what where with which funds (Kossakowski, 1980; Schmidt, 1980).

As noted by Russell (1984), psychology in Japan provides an example of the blending of Western psychology with the concepts and needs of a non-Western country. Azuma (1984) analyzed the stages through which the development of psychology passed in coming to grips with non-Western cultural phenomena without forcing them into a Western mold. The final stage was the "integration period," when psychology is freed to a certain extent from the rigid but otherwise unnoticed mold of traditionally Western concepts and logic (Azuma, 1984, p. 54).

Kagitcibasi (as cited by Sunar, 1996) observed that psychology in the 1990s was a Western, primarily U.S. product. She held that U.S. psychology was largely self-contained, serving as its own reference group. While not very open to knowledge created elsewhere, it is exported to the world on the assumption that theories and findings originating in Western research have universal validity. Her own cross-cultural studies in Turkey demonstrated otherwise, reflecting the strong influence of cultural determinants of human behavior.

The unreflective exportation of Western psychology in the 1900s often disregarded alternate cultural traditions. Citing experience from India, from the Maoris of New Zealand, and from Turkey, Gergen, Gukrce, Lock, and Misra (1996) presented a persuasive case for a multicultural psychology. Such efforts counteracted the ethnocentricity of much of European and American psychology (Berry, Poortinga, Segall, & Dasen, 1992).

A special issue of the *International Journal of Psychology*, edited by Sinha and Holtzman (1984), offers a range of analyses of the impact of psychology on national development. There is repeated emphasis that, to be accepted, psychology needs to demonstrate "relevance" to the prevailing sociocultural conditions and policies in the country or region. Of particular interest are the comments by Melikian (1984) on psychology in Arab Gulf oil-producing states, Mehryar (1984) on Iran, Salazar (1984) on Venezuela, Serpell (1984) on Zambia, and Ching (1984) on China.

In the 1950s and 1960s, the conflict with U.S. views of psychology was particularly acute on the European continent. Many distinguished German professors continued to endorse theoretical orientations then prevailing primarily in central Europe (e.g., David & von Bracken, 1957; Gielen & Bredenkamp, 1997; Graumann, 1997). Internationalization in

Germany awaited a change in generations curious to learn what had developed elsewhere. Gifts of textbooks, back issues of scientific journals, and travel grants helped to overcome the isolation imposed during the Nazi period.

As Jing (2000) observed, "Because of the questionable applicability of Euro-American psychological theories to the third world countries, a revolt is underway to build an indigenous psychology in the study of a society's own problems by native psychologists who are familiar with the cultural environment and using methods suitable to the solution of these problems" (p. 579).

As noted by Poortinga (1997), there is also a need to demonstrate "the universal roots of human psychological functioning underneath the rich and varied cultural variations in behavior." In his view, culture-comparative research is based on the assumption of the universality of psychological process and mechanisms shared by all human beings. Differences in behavior are explained in terms of antecedent conditions, of an ecological, economic, sociocultural, or historical nature. Poortinga holds that criticisms raised by schools of cultural psychology "strike at Achilles' heels" of cross-cultural research, "but that weaknesses are circumstantial rather than essential."

THE 1913 CONGRESS THAT WASN'T

The history of science is generally viewed in terms of theories proposed and experiments performed. It is not always recognized that science is also a conglomeration of people who have their own agendas, piques, jealousies, or political idiosyncrasies. Based on access to the correspondence and files of major figures in American psychology, Evans and Scott (1978) relate how the idea for holding the 1913 International Congress of Psychology in the United States was floated during the 1905 congress in Rome and accepted at the 1909 congress in Geneva. A petition had been prepared by Morton Prince (Harvard), which named James Mark Baldwin (Johns Hopkins) as congress president and William James (Harvard) as honorary president. However, the petition was not a formal invitation, and no U.S. institution offered to host the congress. Personal rivalries prevented effective organization. The project was finally abandoned in 1912 with no other country expressing willingness to assume responsibility at such a late date. Because of World War I, no congresses were convened between 1914 and 1923, when the International Congress met in Oxford. It was not until 1929 that the United States played host at Yale University in New Haven. As noted by Rosenzweig et al. (2000), it was ironic that Cattell, who

had been embroiled in the rivalries swirling around the ill-fated 1913 congress, having outlived his rivals, was elected president of the 1929 congress and gave one of the major lectures.

THE U.S. CONGRESS THAT WAS HELD IN CANADA

One of the main purposes of international congresses is to encourage scientists and practitioners from diverse countries to meet in an atmosphere of friendly relaxation. With rising international tensions and growing ideological conflict in the post–World War II years, it was inevitable that these factors would affect international relations in psychology. North American psychologists remember with embarrassment the domestic political circumstances of the McCarthy era, which made it impractical to hold the 1954 International Congress in the United States as originally planned. The Canadian Psychological Association came to the rescue with an offer to hold the congress in Montreal, organizing it jointly with the APA. To cope with anticipated financial problems, the Congress Planning Committee created a category of honorary membership of $15 for those psychologists who wished to contribute despite their inability to attend. The names of the honorary members were listed in the proceedings. Disappointment at the small attendance was offset by the feeling of intimacy that developed and by the general atmosphere of relaxation (MacLeod, 1957). Conceived during the congress was the first major volume to be published under the auspices of the International Union of Psychological Science (IUPsyS), with 22 contributors from nine countries. All royalties were allocated to the union to aid in the development of further international contacts and cooperation (David & von Bracken, 1957).

YOUNG PSYCHOLOGISTS INITIATIVE

To encourage participation by younger colleagues, the steering committee for the 1963 International Congress in Washington, DC, developed a Young Psychologists Program. It was oriented to persons under age 30 who had received their highest degree in psychology within the previous 5 years. Funds were raised from individual psychologists and from regional and state associations to support 22 young colleagues, one from nearly each of the union's member societies. The Canadian Psychological Association supported one of their own. Psychologists residing in the Washington area generously provided lodging in their homes, logistical assistance, and a chance to become acquainted with the city.

Special meetings were arranged with senior psychologists and journal editors.

The steering committee expressed the hope that the Young Psychologists Program would establish a precedent and that similar endeavors would be organized at future congresses for promising younger psychologists not normally able to attend an International Congress of Psychology on their own. Happily, a Young Psychologists Program has been organized at each subsequent congress and has also become a feature of the quadrennial International Congress of Applied Psychology, further fostering international cooperation, communication, and exchanges.

DIFFERING VIEWS ON HUMAN RIGHTS

Experience in Germany in the 1930s, during the Stalin period in the Soviet Union, and during the Cultural Revolution in China demonstrated that under conditions of impaired political and intellectual freedom, psychologists are especially vulnerable, both as scientists and as professional service providers. When, in the mid-1960s and 1970s, alleged violations of human rights in the Soviet Union and Chile aroused concern, many North American psychologists experienced a sense of frustration. They felt that "something must be done immediately" but were unable to move beyond the formal resolution stage. At the time, some colleagues in other lands were perplexed by what they perceived to be unsophisticated U.S. reactions to complicated political issues having little to do with psychology. Individual human rights were interpreted differently depending on national values and ideological perspectives.

As reports confirmed the confinement of political dissidents in Soviet mental hospitals, the American Psychological Association (APA) Council of Representatives, in January 1976, "instructed" (rather than "requested") its representatives to the IUPsyS to take the steps necessary to place on the agenda for the 1976 IUPsyS Assembly in Paris the council's resolution against the use of psychiatric diagnosis and hospitalization to suppress political dissent wherever it occurred. The council took this action despite the precariousness of the APA's position, that is, the lack of evidence that psychologists were on the staffs of the "special" psychiatric facilities to which dissidents were confined in the Soviet Union.

Several weeks before leaving for Paris, the APA representatives received copies of a resolution drafted by Amnesty International and submitted to the IUPsyS by the Netherlands Institute of Psychologists (NIP). The preamble of the NIP resolution began with a positive statement of ethical standards for psychologists and ended by citing the United Nations (UN) Declaration of Human Rights and the UN Declaration on the Protection of All Persons from Being Subjected to Torture and Other Cruel, Inhuman, or Degrading Punishment. This was followed by an appeal condemning "any form of torture and other cruel, inhuman, and degrading treatment as a method employed during detention, imprisonment, confinement in psychiatric institutions, and under clinical circumstances generally" and any psychologists who condoned or participated in such practices. Since the NIP resolution had been submitted after the deadline date, an assembly vote was required to place it on the IUPsyS agenda.

Shortly after the APA representatives arrived in Paris on July 17, it became apparent that the APA resolution was deemed antagonistic and inappropriate for a psychological (rather than psychiatric) congress. It posed a threat of dividing and politicizing the union. The NIP resolution was more comprehensive and flexible, focused on the ethical responsibilities of psychologists; it also represented the efforts of a small member country while making observations similar to the APA resolution. Thus, the APA representatives communicated informally a willingness to withdraw the APA resolution if the NIP resolution could be placed on the assembly agenda.

When the IUPsyS Assembly opened on July 19, the secretary-general mentioned the NIP request to add an item to the agenda and to place it before the APA agenda item. This provoked statements that resolutions with a political content should not be discussed at the IUPsyS Assembly, followed by a comment from the president that the IUPsyS was not concerned with politics but "with the correct exercise of our profession, which is psychology." It was decided to postpone a vote until July 22—thus providing more time for informal discussion and the preparation of a draft statement by the IUPsyS Executive Committee.

At the second assembly meeting on July 22, members voted to place the NIP resolution on the agenda. At that point, the APA representatives moved to withdraw the APA resolution in favor of discussing the NIP resolution. The IUPsyS president then offered a substitute resolution, drafted by the Executive Committee, covering the same points as the APA and NIP resolutions. The IUPsyS Resolution on Human Rights, condemning any collaboration by psychologists in the abuse of professional practices, was adopted unanimously by the IUPsyS Assembly. It was subsequently published in the *American Psychologist* and is reproduced in full in Rosenzweig et al. (2000). UN declarations particularly pertinent for psychology were previously summarized by Rosenzweig (1988).

VISAS AND FLAGS

Another potential conflict was quietly resolved during the preparatory phase for the 1980 Congress in Leipzig. At the 1978 Congress of the International Association of Applied Psychology (IAAP) in Munich, a member of the German Democratic Republic (GDR) Program Planning Committee informally asked one of the two APA representatives to IUPsyS about possible APA reactions, if, for unforeseen reasons, it should prove impossible at the last minute to grant visas to colleagues from a country with which the GDR did not then have diplomatic relations (meaning Israel). After consultation with IUPsyS officers, the GDR colleague was reminded that at the time of the 1966 Moscow Congress, the USSR, under similar circumstances, granted over 100 visas to psychologists from Franco Spain. Moreover, the IUPsyS constitution states specifically that a host country is obligated to grant visas to colleagues from all IUPsyS member associations. Should visa problems prevent travel of some colleagues, it could probably be expected that numerous U.S. psychologists would cancel their plans to come to Leipzig. It was hoped that this discussion of what was deemed a trial balloon would resolve the matter.

The Soviet invasion of Afghanistan and the January 1980 banishment of Nobel Prize–winning physicist and human rights advocate Andrei Sakharov resulted in a worsening of international tensions. The U.S. government threatened to boycott (and eventually did) the Olympic Games in Moscow and ordered a freeze on cultural and scientific exchanges with the Soviet Union. International protests were mounting. The APA Council was raising questions about U.S. participation in the Leipzig congress. The visa problem for Israeli psychologists had not been resolved. It was in this tense atmosphere that the APA asked its German-speaking IUPS representative, Henry P. David, to visit Berlin for personal consultation with the congress president and secretariat.

The APA representative was warmly received on arrival in Berlin at the end of February 1980. During dinner at the home of the congress president, it was noted that the only foreign troops then occupying Afghanistan were Russian, that the proposed U.S. sanctions did not apply to any other country, and that an editorial in the March APA *Monitor* would urge U.S. psychologists not to boycott the Leipzig congress. The congress president was pleased and announced that arrangements had been completed for issuing visas to Israeli psychologists on arrival in the GDR. However, the flag of Israel would not be flown with those of other IUPsyS member countries. Although there was no mention in the IUPsyS constitution about displaying flags,

the APA representative noted the likely protests such action would entail, leading to embarrassment for the union. It was eventually agreed that only the host country flag would be flown or displayed at the congress. When asked whether APA would invite representatives from all member countries to its usual reception, the reply was that, since the congress would be in Leipzig and not in Moscow, Soviet colleagues would be invited. In case of any unanticipated problem, the reception would be canceled. Soviet colleagues did not, however, respond to the APA's reception invitation.

The Leipzig congress was a success. There were no complaints about visas or the absence of national flags. When the IUPsyS joined the International Council of Scientific Unions (ICSU) in 1982, it accepted the responsibility of ensuring that all congresses and meetings under its auspices would be convened in conformity with ICSU's Statement of the Free Circulation of Scientists. Based on the International Bill of Human Rights, the ICSU statement stipulates that scientists have the right and freedom to participate in international scientific activity without regard to citizenship, religion, creed, political stance, ethnic origin, race, color, language, age, or gender.

PSYCHOLOGISTS' EVOLVING STAND ON SOCIAL ISSUES

In the post–World War II era, social issues outside the laboratory became major areas of applied psychological research (e.g., Cantril, 1949). Klineberg (1964, 1967) noted the pioneering efforts of Claparède in Switzerland and Flugel in England in supporting psychological approaches to conflict resolution in international relations. He went on to summarize the endeavors of the World Federation for Mental Health and the contributions of psychologists led by him in the UNESCO project "On Tension Affecting International Understanding." In 1965, Klineberg fostered "An Appeal to Psychologists," urging the wider dissemination of relevant information available to psychologists and encouraging further research through "close and effective cooperation" with colleagues in other countries.

In subsequent years, psychologists increasingly recognized their responsibility to participate in social policy research and service activities with longer-term potential for affecting the well-being of society. The etiological importance of socioeconomic conditions influencing human behavior received more attention than in earlier years (e.g., David 1986; Kennedy & David, 1986). In his presidential address at the 1978 International Association of Applied Psychology (IAAP) Munich congress, Fleishman (1979) reflected on the possibilities to apply psychological research and knowledge to pressing global social problems. Triandis (1994) stated a similar theme in his inaugural address at the 1994 IAAP Congress in Madrid when he stressed the need for cooperative research on intercultural conflict resolution and reproductive behavior. Issues of drug and alcohol abuse, violence, women's rights, and responsible parenthood gained the attention of psychologists (e.g., David, 1994). There was a realization that policy makers sought more than scientific conclusions. They wanted recommendations for making decisions. Applied research began to move beyond determining why something is so to how it could be changed and at what cost.

Recent years have seen a continual increase in research related to socially significant problems of international interest (e.g., Fleishman, 1999). Through diverse programs of the United Nations and its specialized agencies, psychologists became involved in such humanitarian endeavors as designing psychological first-aid programs for children traumatized by civil strife and war, facilitating mental health and health policy deliberations, and treating survivors of war trauma and torture (e.g., Hanscom, 2001; Kapor-Stanulovic, 1999).

One specific example of psychologists' involvement in social change is the case of South Africa beginning in the 1980s when the world became increasingly aware of the injustices of the apartheid system. The presence of apartheid resonated strongly for U.S. psychologists, especially among African Americans, other psychologists of color, and Jewish immigrants who had come to the United States from pre- and post-World War II Europe.

The APA began to take action in 1981 when its finance committee divested its holdings in five corporations with direct assets in South Africa and agreed to bar future South African investments until further notice. In 1986, the APA issued a resolution urging "American psychologists to refuse to collaborate in projects sponsored by the South African government until human rights reforms are instituted." Strictly interpreted, this resolution virtually prohibited interaction with South African psychologists, regardless of race, since all the country's universities and clinics were government sponsored.

Over the years, the APA resisted a number of pleas to amend the resolution and generally declined invitations, even from black-sponsored organizations, to go to meetings in South Africa. The sole exception were several planning meetings—convened by the culturally diverse and representative Psychology and Apartheid Committee—which led to

the 1994 inauguration of the Psychological Society of South Africa, replacing the former Psychological Association of South Africa. While the APA encouraged and supported a variety of programs to bring Black South Africans to U.S. institutions and meetings, the Association's Council of Representatives did not rescind either its policy or the practice of divestiture until after the 1994 election of Nelson Mandela to the presidency of South Africa.

THE TREND FROM AMERICANIZATION TO INTERNATIONALIZATION

In discussions with colleagues in diverse parts of the world, the complaint was often voiced that, particularly since the end of World War II, psychology has been "Americanized," a term described by Graumann (1997) as a "critical polemic catch-word to designate the expansion of the American way of life" into other cultures (p. 265). Van Strien (1997) described Americanization as a form of "scientific colonization," meaning intellectual domination of an existing culture by a foreign, more powerful one. Van Strien did not mean to imply an enforced suppression of an older culture but a more voluntary submission to a dominant culture, a kind of "colonial pact," a term ascribed to Moscovici.

Graumann (1997) reviews what he believes "American" means for U.S. psychologists. He cites Cattell's recollection that when he presented Wundt with his proposal to study "the objective measurement of the time of reactions with special reference to individual differences," Wundt commented that it was "*ganz Amerikanisch*" ("typically American"). In his view, only psychologists could be the subjects in psychological experiments. Graumann cites other examples, noting Koch's (1985) account of what he calls "psychology's American naturalization," meaning "despite its European origins, psychology acquired the attributes of an almost uniquely American enterprise." Graumann (1997) notes that the "early generations of Wundt-trained American psychologists" after their return to the United States turned to "applied and commercial interests." Cattell, Judd, Hall, Witmer, and many others were all soon engaged in commercializing psychology in one form or another. Graumann (1997) sums up that "when Americans speak of American psychology, they usually refer to features characteristic of American culture that is seen in contrast to its European origins" (p. 267).

There is ample evidence that following the emigration of many leading psychologists from Hitler's Germany and Austria in the 1930s, the center of gravity in psychology shifted from Europe to the United States. Triandis (1980) has speculated that most of the psychologists who ever lived and who are now living can be found in the United States. Rosenzweig (1984) noted that whereas the American Psychological Association was only one of 44 member societies belonging to the International Union of Psychological Science, "membership of the APA comes close to equaling the membership of all the other 43 associations together." Within this context it was hardly surprising that U.S. psychologists were accused of being "provincial, insular, and ego-centered" (Sexton & Misiak, 1976). Brandt (1970) asserted that U.S. psychology disregards almost completely research done in other countries and published in languages other than English. In his view, there was no English-language market for research that conflicted with U.S. psychology. Few university libraries subscribed to journals published abroad, and even fewer U.S. psychologists regularly read non-English publications. More recently, Draguns (2001) contended that the development of international psychology is obstructed by the "massive disregard" of contributions published in languages other than English.

In 1977, Diaz-Guerrero (1977) wrote that "the average American psychologist, in spite of having the greatest resources and possibly the highest levels of technical training, may be much more ethnocentric and parochial than others" (p. 935). Ardilla (1982b) commented that many of the values and assumptions in English-speaking countries seem alien to the Latin American way of thinking. Russell (1984) recalls an incident when, in toasting colleagues at an international dinner, a Mexican psychologist said, "We Mexican psychologists are very humble because we are so far away from God and so close to the United States" (p. 1021). Such remarks may have been made only partly in jest. More recently, Jing (2000) noted that "what goes in the name of psychology today mainly reflects the theories and ideas of the United States" (p. 579).

While the perceptions of U.S. psychology were often mixed, efforts persisted to keep open and widen the channels of communication (Rosenzweig, 1979). Russell (1984) recalls how at the 1957 Congress of International Psychology in Brussels, a time when he served as APA executive officer, he was approached by A. R. Luria, the representative of the Society of Psychologists in the USSR. Luria expressed concern not about Soviet psychologists receiving an adequate number of U.S. publications (which were translated by the USSR government for those of his colleagues who could not read English) but about the fact that very few Soviet publications were available in translation for U.S. consumption. The Brussels exchange was eventually followed 20 years later by an article in the *American Psychologist* comparing American and Soviet approaches to clinical neuropsychology (Luria & Majovski, 1977).

In recent years, fostered by the IUPsyS and the IAAP, the trend from Americanization to internationalization has become ever stronger. One example is the growth of European associations and international journals published in English (Lunt & Poortinga, 1996). Another example is the *European Psychologist,* which began publication in 1996 under the auspices of the European Federation of Professional Psychologists Associations. Journals produced by the American Psychological Association have invited non-U.S. colleagues as associate editors and peer reviewers. The number of articles by authors residing outside the United States has steadily increased (Fleishman, 1999). Psychology's knowledge and practice base is expanding through ever growing electronic links with colleagues in developed and developing countries (Mays, Rubin, Sabourin, & Walker, 1996; Pawlick & d'Ydewalle, 1996). Electronic communication "supplies the means for geographically distant but intellectually close collaboration" (Fowler, 1996, p. 6).

Echoing Cattell (1930), Fowler (1996) noted on the 50th anniversary of the *American Psychologist* that "collaboration and contributions to the same bodies of literature by psychologists who work in different countries are at times more difficult than in other disciplines, some of which have long histories of international collaboration" (p. 5). As the chief executive officer of the APA, he pledged that "unifying the field by forging among psychologists many long-lasting cooperative efforts that span international boundaries is a goal we have adopted and will continue to pursue vigorously" (p. 6).

Particularly noteworthy in the new millennium is the launching of a "publication" by the International Union of Psychological Science. As described by Rosenzweig et al. (2000), *Psychology: IUPsyS Global Resource* is congruent with electronic computer capabilities coming online throughout the world. Disseminated in CD-ROM format, it includes brief descriptions and histories of the state of psychology in 84 countries, contact information for national psychological societies, a directory of international psychological societies, an international directory with postal and electronic addresses for scholarly institutions in 147 countries, a coded bibliography of published papers about psychology in each country, and abstracts of all papers presented at the quadrennial International Congress of Psychology beginning with 1996 and to be continued into the future. Psychology, like music, is adapting new technologies to facilitate communication of a universal message.

Table 25.1 presents a chronology of milestones in international psychology.

TABLE 25.1   Chronology of Milestones in International Psychology

Congresses	Societies	Events	Publications
		550 B.C.E.	After the death of Confucius, his disciples published his teachings in the *Analects,* a guide to the proper behavior of individuals in society.
		387 B.C.E. Plato founded the Academy in Athens.	
		330 B.C.E.	Aristotle wrote *De Anima,* considered to be the first book of psychology.
		1276 Peter of Spain became John XXI, the first psychologist Pope.	Also a physician, Peter of Spain authored *De Anima,* an account of the historical development of psychological ideas found in Greek and Islamic works.
		1557	*Physica Speculatio* was published in Mexico. This treatise, authored by the Catholic priest Alonzo de la Veracruz, described behavior from an Aristotelian perspective.
		1738	Christian von Wolff introduced the concept of measuring mental phenomena in his book *Psychologia Empirica.*
		1824	F. Herbart laid the foundation for German psychology with the publication of *Psychologie als Wissenschaft: Neu Gegründet auf Erfahrung, Metaphysik, und Mathematik.*
		1843	*Les Annales Médico-Psychologiques,* the oldest French specialized journal, was founded.
		1850 Barzillai Quaife, an immigrant British cleric, lectured at Sydney College, laying the groundwork for the development of psychology in Australia.	
		1855 Wilhelm Wundt received his MD degree at the University of Heidelberg.	
		1860 The first chair in psychology was established at the University of Bern, Switzerland.	
		1870	Roberto Ardigo authored *La Psicologia come scienza positiva,* the first Italian Psychological Treatise.
			T Ribot published *La Psychologie anglaise contemporaine,* followed in 1879 by *La Psychologie allemande contemporaine.* These texts introduced the work of English and German psychologists in France.
		1873	Tanzan Hara, a Zen priest, wrote *Experimental Records of Mind,* one of the first Japanese empirical studies in psychology.

(continued)

TABLE 25.1   *(Continued)*

Congresses	Societies		Events	Publications
		1875	William James founded the first U.S. demonstration laboratory of psychology equipment at Harvard University in conjunction with the course he taught on the relationship between physiology and psychology.	
		1876	The first Italian laboratory for work in psychology was established in the Liceo di Mantova.	*Mind,* the first philosophical psychology journal, began publication in Britian.
		1879	Wilhelm Wundt established the first psychology laboratory at the University of Leipzig.	
		1883	G. Stanley Hall founded the first formal U.S. psychology laboratory at The Johns Hopkins University. The University Trustees allocated $250 for space and equipment but, due to campus politics, prohibited calling the facility a "laboratory."	
		1884	Influenced by Darwin's theories, Sir Fancis Galton set up an anthropometric laboratory that conducted measurements of the physical and mental characteristics of nearly 10,000 persons.	
		1885	Vladimir S. Bekhterev founded Russia's first laboratory of experimental psychology at the University of Kazan.	
	The Moscow Psychological Society was established with a membership of medical doctors, philosophers, and physiologists interested in psychological issues.	1886	Alfred Lehman, an engineer who studied with Wundt, opened the Psychophysical Laboratory (renamed the Psychological Laboratory in 1924) at the University of Copenhagen.	
		1888	Yujiro Motora gave the first psychology lecture in Japan at Tokyo University.	
The first International Congress of Physiological Psychology took place in Paris, eight years after Polish psychologist Julian Ochorowicz first proposed holding such a meeting. The first International Congress on Hypnotism took place in Paris.		1889	The French government established the country's first psychological laboratory.	The first Russian psychology journal, *Problems of Philosophy and Psychology,* was published.

TABLE 25.1 *(Continued)*

Congresses	Societies		Events	Publications
		1890	Australia's first part-time lecturer in psychology was appointed.	
			James Mark Baldwin founded the first Canadian psychological laboratory at the University of Toronto.	
	The American Psychological Association was organized in the study of G. Stanley Hall at Clark University.	1892	A laboratory of experimental psychology was founded at the University of Louvain in Belgium.	
			The first Dutch laboratory was founded in Groningen.	
			The first Swiss laboratory was founded by T. Flournoy at the University of Geneva.	
		1893	The World's Colombian Exposition in Chicago featured a psychology pavilion that presented a scientific view of psychology to the general public.	
		1894	Philosopher A. Meinong founded Austria's first psychology laboratory at the University of Graz.	
		1895	Freud conceived his dream theory while dining at the Bellevue Restaurant in Vienna.	The *Psychological Index,* an annual bibliography of publications in psychology and cognate fields, began publication under the editorship of J. Mark Baldwin at Princeton University and James McKeen Cattell at Columbia University.
		1896	Lightner Witmer established the world's first psychological clinic, at the University of Pennsylvania.	
		1898	Horacio Pinero founded Latin America's first laboratory of experimental psychology at the Colegio Nacional de Buenos Aires.	
The International Congress of Physiological Psychology was renamed International Congress of Psychology.		1900		Freud published *The Interpretation of Dreams.*
	The British Psychological Society (called The Psychological Society until 1906) was founded at University College of the University of London. In 1965, Queen Elizabeth II granted the Society a royal charter.	1901	The first Polish psychology laboratory was founded by philosopher/psychologist K. Twardowski at Lwow University.	
	The Société Francaise de Psychologie was founded.			

(continued)

TABLE 25.1   (Continued)

Congresses	Societies		Events	Publications
		1902	The University of Madrid established a chair in psychology, the first such position in the world at a faculty of science.	
		1903	Matataro Matsumoto, educated at Yale, established Japan's first psychology laboratories at Tokyo University and the Tokyo Higher Normal School (which became the Tokyo University of Education).	
			Ivan Pavlov first publicly introduced his conditioned reflex theory in a talk on "Experimental Psychology and Psychopathology of Animals," presented at the International Congress of Medicine in Madrid.	
	The Deutsche Gesellschaft fur Experimentelle Psychologie was founded. The organization changed its name to the Deutsche Gesellschaft für Psychologie in 1929.	1904	The Louisiana Purchase Exposition, also known as the St. Louis World's Fair, featured an exhibit of psychological instruments and sponsored a five-day series of addresses by prominent psychologists.	
		1905	The vice-chancellor of Calcutta University introduced experimental psychology as an independent subject in the postgraduate course syllabus.	
			Alfred Binet introduced the Binet and Simon Intelligence Scale at the 5th International Congress of Psychology in Rome.	
		1906	Psychology in Italy was officially acknowledged by the establishment of chairs at the universities of Rome, Naples, and Italy.	
			The first Romanian Chair of Psychology and Laboratory of Experimental Psychology were established at the University of Bucharest.	
The first International Congress of Psychiatry, Neurology, and Psychology took place in Amsterdam. Carl Jung, representing Freud, presented a paper on his theories.		1907		
The first International Congress of Psychoanalysis was convened in Salzburg.		1908	Cairo University introduced psychology as a minor subject in the philosophy and sociology curricula.	

TABLE 25.1   *(Continued)*

Congresses	Societies		Events	Publications
		1909	A. Aall, a professor of philosophy, founded Norway's first psychology laboratory at the University of Oslo.	
			The 20th anniversary celebration of Clark University brought together G. Stanley Hall, William James, and leading Europeans. It was Freud's only appearance in the United States; he called it "the first official recognition of our work."	
	The International Psychoanalytic Association was formed in Nuremberg with Carl Jung as the first president.	1910		
	The Societa Italiana de Psicologia was founded.			
		1911	The first Czech psychological laboratory opened in Prague at the Physiological Institute of the School of Medicine.	
		1912	The Moscow Institute of Psychology opened at the University of Moscow.	The first Japanese psychology journal, *Shinri Kenkyu,* appeared.
		1915	The first German psychological testing center for armed forces was established for the selection of World War I motor transport drivers.	Danish gestalt psychologist Edgar John Rubin published the famous "vase/two faces" figure created by an ambiguous figure-ground relationship.
			India's first psychology laboratory was established at Calcutta University.	
		1916	Enrique C. Arargon founded Mexico's first psychology laboratory at the Autonomous National University's School of Higher Studies.	
		1917	Johns Hopkins University psychologist John B. Watson was ordered into the military and sent to England, where he was assigned to test aviators for the Signal Corps. His service almost resulted in a court-martial when he proclaimed his fellow American officers "nincompoops" and military service as "a nightmare."	
			The first Chinese psychological laboratory was established at Beijing University.	

TABLE 25.1 *(Continued)*

Congresses	Societies		Events	Publications
		1918	South Africa's first chair and department of psychology were established at Stellenbosch University.	
E. Claparède convened the first International Congress of Applied Psychology in Geneva. The 17 participants from eight countries founded the International Association of Applied Psychology, the oldest international organization of individual psychologists.	The International Association of Applied Psychology was founded.	1920	The first Chinese Department of Psychology was established at Nanking Normal School. Yugoslavia's first psychology institute was established at the University of Zagreb.	
	The Chinese Psychological Society was founded but was dissolved after a few years.	1921	The first Finnish Institute of Psychology was founded at the University of Turku.	Swiss publisher Bircher produced Hermann Rorschach's *Psychodiagnostik,* describing the inkblot method of personality assessment. Seven other publishers had previously declined the manuscript and accompanying cards. Rorschach died 10 months later.
	The Moscow Psychological Society was disbanded and its members (along with members of the St. Petersburg Philosophical Society) were exiled to the West.	1922		The Chinese Psychological Society published the country's first psychological journal, *Psychology.*
	The Indian Psychological Association was founded.	1925	Uruguay's first psychology chair was established at the Institutos Normales de Montevideo.	
		1926	The first Greek psychology laboratory was established at the University of Athens.	
	The Japanese Psychological Association was founded in Tokyo at the country's first psychology convention.	1927	China's first psychology laboratory was established at Beijing University.	*Psychological Abstracts* was first published under the auspice of APA.
	The Hungarian Psychological Association was founded.	1928		
		1929	Ivan Pavlov addressed the 9th International Congress of Psychology in New Haven. For the first and only time, APA canceled its annual convention to encourage its members' participation at the Congress.	
The first International Congress on Mental Hygiene met in Washington, DC.	The Argentine Psychological Society was founded.	1930		
		1935		The University of Buenos Aires Faculty of Philosophy and letters introduced the first Latin American journal, *Anales del Institute de Psicologia.*

TABLE 25.1   *(Continued)*

Congresses	Societies		Events	Publications
		1936	The Soviet Government issued a resolution condemning psychology and the use of psychological measurements.	
	Activity in the Chinese Psychological Society was resumed only to be discontinued later that year by the onset of the Sino-Japanese War (see 1921).	1937	Professor G. Edilian established the first Armenian psychology library at Yerevan University.	
	The Canadian Psychological Association was founded.	1938	The Netherlands Institute of Psychology was founded at the University of Amsterdam.	
	The National Council of Women Psychologists (NCWP) was founded in New York.	1941	The Georgian Institute of Psychology was founded in Tbilisi.	
			The University of Ottawa opened the Institute of Psychology, leading to the establishment of independent psychology departments in Canadian universities.	
	The Ecuador Society of Psychological and Psychiatric Studies and Related Disciplines was established.	1942		
	The Swiss Psychological Society was founded.	1943		The Nazi government suspended publication, at the close of volume 112, of the *Archiv für die gesamte Psychologie* since it could no longer be concealed that the printer's grandmother was Jewish.
		1944	The American Psychological Association established its Committee on International Planning for Psychology, which later became the Committee on International Relations in Psychology.	
	The Australian Branch of the British Psychological Society was established.	1945		The first psychology journal of the Arab world, *The Journal of Psychology,* was published in Egypt.
	The NCWP (see 1941) became the International Council of Women Psychologists.			
		1946	Guatemala introduced the country's first professional psychology training program.	

(continued)

TABLE 25.1   *(Continued)*

Congresses	Societies		Events	Publications
The first Scandinavian Meeting of Psychologists took place in Oslo with 400 participants from Finland, Iceland, Denmark, Sweden, and Norway.	The Association of Danish Psychologists was founded.	1947	Colombia's first psychology training program, the Institute of Applied Psychology, was established at the National University in Bogotá.	
			The first post-World War II meeting of German psychologists took place in Bonn, leading to the establishment of the Berufsverband Deutscher Psychologen. One of the leaders was Max Simoneit, who had been part of the group that plotted the July 20, 1944 attempt on Hitler's life.	
			The Institute for Personnel Selection and Guidance opened in Rio de Janeiro. It published Brazil's most important journal, and offered a doctoral program and applied research activities.	
	The Egyptian Association for Psychological Studies was founded. The Polish Psychological Association was founded. The World Federation for Mental Health was founded at the Third International Congress on Mental Hygiene in London.	1948	The 12th International Congress of Psychology, originally scheduled for Vienna in 1940, finally took place in Edinburgh after delays caused by WWII. Professional training programs for psychologists were introduced in Chile. The first Swedish independent chair of psychology was established at the University of Uppsala.	
	The Brazilian Association of Applied Psychology was founded.	1949	The University of Ghana was the first Anglophone African institution to teach a course in psychology. It became a Department of Psychology in 1967.	*The Brazilian Boletim de Psicologia* was introduced in São Paulo. The first postwar German-language journal, *Psychologische Rundschau,* was published.
The first International Congress of Gerontology took place in Liege, Belgium.	The Chinese Psychological society was reorganized but was closed again in 1966 (see 1921, 1937).	1950		
	The Interamerican Society of Psychology (known by its Spanish-language acronym as SIP) was founded during the Fourth International Congress on Mental Health in Mexico City. The International Union of Scientific Psychology, now the International Union of Psychological Science (IUPsyS), was founded at the 13th International Congress of Psychology in Stockholm. French, Spanish, and English were the official languages.	1951	The Israeli Institute of Applied Social Research opened in Jerusalem.	*Applied Psychology: An International Review* began publication under the auspices of the International Association of Applied Psychology.

TABLE 25.1 *(Continued)*

Congresses	Societies		Events	Publications
	The Finnish Psychological Society was founded.	1952	Psychology was introduced at the University of Indonesia Faculty of Medicine in Jakarta.	
	The Spanish Psychological Society was founded.			
The first Interamerican Congress of Psychology took place in Ciudad Trujillo (now Santo Domingo) in the Dominican Republic.	The Austrian Professional Association of Psychologists was founded.	1953		
	The Psychological Society of Uruguay was founded.			
	The Mexican Psychological Society was founded.			
	The Peruvian Society of Psychology was founded.	1954		
	The Association of Icelandic Psychologists was founded.			
	The Brazilian Association of Psychologists was founded.			
	The Colombian Federation of Psychology was founded.	1955	The Khartoum Branch of Cairo University introduced psychology in the Sudan as part of the philosophy and sociology curricula.	The Russian journal *Voprosy psikhologii* began publication.
	The Swedish Psychological Association was founded.			
	The International Association for Analytical Psychology was established in Zurich to advance Jungian psychology.			
	The Turkish Psychological Association was founded.	1956	The Chinese Academy of Sciences established the Institute of Psychology in Beijing.	The Polish journal *Educational Psychology* began.
				The Colombian *Revista De Psichlogia* began publication.
				The Chinese Psychological Society introduced the *Journal Acta Psychologica Sinica*, which was suspended during the "Cultural Revolution"; publication was resumed in 1979.
Approximately 200 psychologists from Europe, the Near East, and North America met in Brussels at the First International Symposium on Military Psychology.	The Russian Soviet Federal Socialist Republic Psychological Society was founded by Order 495 of the Minister of Education. The Society was a branch of the Academy of Pedagogical Sciences. It held its first meeting in 1959.	1957	Psychology was introduced in Saudi Arabia concurrent with the founding of the University of Riyadh.	
			The Hebrew University in Jerusalem established Israel's first department of psychology.	
	The Slovak Psychological Association was founded.			
	The Venezuelan Psychological Federation was founded.			
	The Czechoslovak Psychological Association was founded.	1958	The APA Convention program featured the first coffee hour for visitors from abroad.	
	The Israeli Psychological Association was founded.			
		1959	Iran's first psychology department was founded at the National Teachers' College.	

(continued)

TABLE 25.1   *(Continued)*

Congresses	Societies		Events	Publications
		1960	The American Psychological Association sent a group of senior psychologists to visit laboratories in the Soviet Union.	Publication of *Psicologia y Educacion* was initiated in Cuba.
The First Congress of the International Ergonomics Association took place in Stockholm.	The Society of Psychology of the German Democratic Republic was founded.	1961	The Colegio of Venezuelan Psychologists was founded.	
	The Psychological Association of the Philippines was founded.			
	The Tunisan Society of Psychology was founded.			
		1962		The *Anuario de Psicologia* was introduced in Guatemala.
				APA published the report, *Some Views on Soviet Psychology* from its Soviet mission in 1960.
				The *Revista de Psicopatologia, Psicologia Medica, y Psicoterapia* began publication in Peru.
				The *Revista Venezolana de Psicologia* began publication.
	The Association of Greek Psychologists was established.	1963	The Max Planck Institute for Human Development and Education was founded in Berlin.	The *Revista Mexicana de Psicologia* began publication.
			The Young Psychologists Program was organized for the first time, in conjunction with the XVII International Congress of Psychology in Washington, DC.	
	The Cuban Union of Psychology was founded.	1964	The University of Nigeria established a department of psychology in Nsukka.	
	The Salvadoran Society of Psychology was founded.			
	The Panamanian Psychologists Association was founded.	1965		The International Union of Psychological Science began publishing the *International Journal of Psychology*.
	The Portuguese Psychological Society was founded.			
	The Psychologists Association of Romania was established.			
		1966	The Department of Psychology and Education was established at Kuwait University.	*International Opportunities for Advanced Training and Research in Psychology* was published with reports from 87 countries. The publication was the result of a meeting in France in 1962 of the International Union of Psychological Science and the American Psychological Association.
The first Congress of the International Association for the Scientific Study of Mental Deficiency took place in Montpelier, France.	The New Zealand Psychological Society was founded, having previously been a branch of the British Psychological Society.	1967	The University of Ghana introduced a Department of Psychology (see 1949).	

TABLE 25.1   *(Continued)*

Congresses	Societies		Events	Publications
	Cheiron, the International Society for the History of the Behavioral and Social Sciences, held its organizational meeting at New York University. The Hong Kong Psychological Society was founded.	1968	The Netherlands Institute of Psychology provided support to Czech and Slovak psychologists who, following the Soviet occupation of their country, remained in Amsterdam after the International Congress of Applied Psychology.	
	The Psychological Society of Ireland was established.	1970		
The first Symposium of the International Society for the Study of Behavior Development took place in Nijmegen, the Netherlands. The first Arab Conference of Psychology took place in Cairo.		1971	The Brazilian government established by law a National Council of Psychology and eight Regional Councils charged with monitoring the practice of psychology. The Norwegian government established the law regulating the profession of psychology. The USSR Academy of Sciences Presidium issued Resolution #1076 to establish the Institute of Psychology in Moscow.	The *European Journal of Social Psychology* was founded.
	The International Association of Cross-Cultural Psychology was founded at the Association's first Congress in Hong Kong.	1972		
		1973	The Qatar College of Education introduced psychology as a separate discipline. The University of Zimbabwe established the country's first chair of professional psychology.	
The first Interamerican Congress of Clinical Psychology was held in Porto Alegre, Brazil. The first Latin American Conference on Training in Psychology convened in Bogotá, Colombia, with support from UNESCO and the International Union of Psychological Science.	The Cuban Society of Psychology of Health was founded.	1974		
The African Conference on Child Rearing took place in Yaounde, Cameroon, with support from the International Union of Psychological Science, UNESCO, and the Population Council.	The International Federation of Psychological Medical Organizations was established.	1975	The first Psychology Department was established at Makerere University in Kampala, Uganda.	

(continued)

TABLE 25.1   *(Continued)*

Congresses	Societies	Events		Publications
	The French-Speaking Neuropsychological Society was established.	1977		The *German Journal of Psychology,* featuring English-language abstracts and review articles, was launched by C. J. Hogrefe Verlag under the auspices of the International Union of Psychological Science.
	The Chinese Psychological Society was reopened and remains open to date (see 1950).			
	The Colombian Society of Psychology was founded.	1978	The Venezuelan government enacted the "Law of Psychological Practice."	
	The International Society for Political Psychology was established.			
	The French-Language Association of Work Psychology was established.	1980	The American Psychological Association issued a resolution protesting the exile of Andrei Sakharov to Gorki and joined with the U.S. National Academy of Sciences in postponing official scientific exchanges between the United States and the Soviet Union.	*French Language Psychology* began publication in English under the auspices of the International Union of Psychological Science. The journal ceased publication at the end of 1983.
	The Professional Union of Psychologists was established in Spain (see 1952).			The *Psychological Journal of the USSR* began publication under the auspices of the USSR Academy of Sciences.
			The Max Planck Institute opened the Berlin-based Center for Psychology and Human Development and the Max Planck Institute for Psycholinguistics in Nijmegen, the Netherlands.	
			The Psychologists' College of Peru was founded.	
			The American Psychological Association sent a delegation to the People's Republic of China. This landmark visit, occurring under newly relaxed relations between the two countries, led to reciprocal scholarly exchanges.	
The Jubilee Congress of the Chinese Psychological Society marked the first occasion when invitations were issued to colleagues from abroad.	The Nicaraguan Psychological Association was founded.	1981		*Spanish Language Psychology* was first published in English under the auspices of the International Union of Psychological Science, but was discontinued at the end of 1983.
	The International Organization of Psychophysiology was established.	1982		
	IUPsyS was admitted to the International Council of Scientific Unions (see 1951).			
	The Psychological Association of South Africa was established (see 1994).			

TABLE 25.1   *(Continued)*

Congresses	Societies		Events	Publications
The first Gulf Conference of Psychology took place in Kuwait.		1983		
The first World Conference on Behavioral Economics convened in Princeton, New Jersey.		1984		
	The International Society for Theoretical Psychology was founded.	1985		
		1986	The American Psychological Association issued a resolution deploring the apartheid system and urging U.S. psychologists to refuse to collaborate in projects supported by the South African government.	
	The Union of Estonian Psychologists was founded.	1988		
The first European Congress of Psychology, sponsored by the European Federation of Professional Psychology Associations, took place in Budapest, Hungary.		1989	On November 16, Ignacio Martin-Baro and five other Jesuit priests, along with their two housekeepers, were murdered by the Salvadoran military on the campus of the University of Central America in San Salvador. Martin-Baro was a social psychologist who founded *Revista de Psicologia del El Salvador.*	
The first International Congress of Behavioral Medicine took place in Uppsala, Sweden.	The International Federation for Psychoanalytic Education held its organizing meeting in Washington, D.C.	1990		
The first International Congress of Health Psychology convened in Mexico City.	The Hellenic Psychological Society in Greece was founded (see 1963).			
	The Psychological Association of Namibia was founded.			
	The Yemen Psychological Association was founded.			
	The Association of Albanian Psychologists was founded.	1991		
	The Georgian Psychological Association was founded.			

(continued)

TABLE 25.1   *(Continued)*

Congresses	Societies	Events	Publications
The first Advanced Research Training Seminars (ARTS) was held, in conjunction with the 25th International Congress of Psychology in Brussels. Cosponsored by the Association of Cross-Cultural Psychology, the International Association of Applied Psychology, the International Union of Psychological Sciences, ARTS has been held every two years in conjunction with the International Congress of Psychology and the International Congress of Applied Psychology.	The European Society for Philosophy and Psychology held its first meeting at the University of Louvain, Belgium. The Uganda National Psychological Association was founded.	1992	
The first International Behavioral Neuroscience Conference was held in San Antonio, Texas.			
The first International Congress on Behaviorism and the Sciences of Behavior took place in Guadalajara, Mexico.			
The first International Asian Conference in Psychology convened in Singapore.			
	The Psychological Society of South Africa held its inaugural Congress in Cape Town. The new Society replaced the Psychological Association of South Africa, established in 1982.	1994	
The Asian-Pacific Regional Conference of Psychology took place in Guangzhou, China. This was the first of a series of biennial regional meetings cosponsored by the IAAP and IUPsyS.		1995	
	The International Association for Psychology and the Performing Arts was founded. The Jordan Psychological Association was founded.	1996	The *European Psychologist* was published under the auspices of the European Federation of Professional Psychologists Associations. The *International Journal of Psychotherapy,* associated with the European Association for Psychotherapy, was first published in cooperation with Carfax Publishing; it is now independent.
The Regional Congress of Psychology for Professionals in the Americas, cosponsored by the IAAP and IUPsyS, took place in Mexico City.		1997	

TABLE 25.1 *(Continued)*

Congresses	Societies		Events	Publications
		1998	The International Psychology Division (52) of the American Psychological Association was established with over 800 charter members.	
The Africa Psychology Conference, cosponsored by the IAAP and IUPsyS, took place in Durban, South Africa.		1999		*Journal of International Women's Studies,* an electronic online journal, was initiated at the Massachusetts College of Liberal Arts. It is now located at Bridgeport College, Bridgeport, Mass.
	An International Organization of Students was founded at the XXVII International Congress of Psychology in Stockholm.	2000		
		2001		The *International Journal of Clinical Psychology (IJCP)* published its initial issue in January. It is available in print or online.

REFERENCES

Ahmed, R. A. (1992). Psychology in Arab countries. In U. P. Gielen, L. L. Adler, & N. A. Milgram (Eds.), *Psychology in international perspective: 50 years of the International Council of Psychologists* (pp. 127–150). Amsterdam: Swets & Zeitlinger.

Ahmed, R. A. (1997). An interview with Mustapha I. Soueif. *World Psychology, 3*(1/2), 13–27.

Angell, J. R. (1930). Address of welcome. In *Proceedings of the 9th International Congress of Psychology, New Haven, Connecticut, 1929* (p. 9). Princeton, NJ: Psychological Review.

Ardilla, R. (1982a). International psychology. *American Psychologist, 37,* 323–329.

Ardilla, R. (1982b). Psychology in Latin America. *Annual Review of Psychology, 33,* 103–122.

Azuma, H. (1984). Psychology in a non-Western country. *International Journal of Psychology, 19,* 45–55.

Berlyne, D. E. (1968). American and European psychology. *American Psychologist, 22,* 447–452.

Berry, J. W., Poortinga, Y. H., Segall, M. H., & Dasen, P. R. (1992). *Cross-cultural psychology: Research and applications.* Cambridge, UK: Cambridge University Press.

Brandt, L. W. (1970). American psychology. *American Psychologist, 25,* 1091–1093.

Cantril, H. (1949). Psychology working for peace. *American Psychologist, 4,* 69–73.

Cattell, J. M. (1930). Psychology in America. In *Proceedings of the 9th International Congress of Psychology, New Haven, Connecticut, 1929* (pp. 12–32). Princeton, NJ: Psychological Review.

Cautley, P. W. (1992). Fifty years of the International Council of Psychologists. In U. P. Gielen, L. L. Adler, & N. A. Milgram (Eds.), *Psychology in international perspective: 50 years of the International Council of Psychologists* (pp. 3–18). Amsterdam: Swets & Zeitlinger.

Ching, C. C. (1980). Psychology in the People's Republic of China. *American Psychologist, 35,* 1084–1089.

Ching, C. C. (1984). Psychology and the four modernizations in China. *International Journal of Psychology, 19,* 57–63.

David, H. P. (1986). Population, development, and reproductive behavior: Perspectives for population and health psychology. *American Psychologist, 41,* 309–312.

David, H. P. (1994). Reproductive rights and reproductive behavior: Clash and convergence of private values and public policies. *American Psychologist, 49,* 343–349.

David, H. P., & Buchanan, J. (1999). *Informal survey of international psychology* [Unpublished]. Washington, DC: American Psychological Association.

David, H. P., & von Bracken, H. (Eds.). (1957). *Perspectives in personality theory.* New York: Basic Books.

Denmark, F. L. (1987). History of professional psychology: International conferences. In R. J. Corsini (Ed.), *Concise encyclopedia of psychology* (pp. 611–613). New York: Wiley.

Diaz-Guerrero, R. (1977). A Mexican psychology. *American Psychologist, 32,* 934–944.

Draguns, J. R. (2001). Towards a truely international psychology: Beyond English only. *American Psychologist, 56,* 1019–1030.

Evans, R. B., & Scott, F. J. D. (1978). The 13th International Congress of Psychology: The American congress that wasn't. *American Psychologist, 33*, 711–723.

Fleishman, E. A. (1979). The new applied psychology: An international perspective. *International Review of Applied Psychology, 28*, 67–74.

Fleishman, E. A. (1999). Applied psychology: An international journey. *American Psychologist, 54*, 1008–1016.

Fowler, R. D. (1996). Editorial. *American Psychologist, 51*, 5–7.

Georgas, J. (1994). Psychology in Greece. In A. Schorr & S. Saari (Eds.), *Psychology in Europe* (pp. 59–75). Bern, Switzerland: Hogrefe and Huber.

Gergen, K. J., Gulerce, A., Lock, A., & Misra, G. (1996). Psychological science in cultural context. *American Psychologist, 51*, 496–503.

Gielen, U. P., & Bredenkamp, J. (1997). Editorial. *World Psychology, 3*, 247–252.

Gilgen, A. R., & Gilgen, C. K. (Eds.). (1987). *International handbook of psychology*. Westport, CT: Greenwood Press.

Graumann, C. F. (1997). Psychology in postwar Germany: The vicissitudes of internationalization. *World Psychology, 3*, 253–277.

Hanscom, K. L. (2001). Teaching survivors of war trauma and torture. *American Psychologist, 56*, 1032–1039.

Henle, M. (1978). One man against the Nazis: Wolfgang Köhler. *American Psychologist, 33*, 939–944.

Hilgard, E. R., Leary, D. E., & McGuire, E. R. (1991). The history of psychology: A survey and critical assessment. *Annual Review of Psychology, 42*, 79–107.

Jing, Q. (2000). International psychology. In K. Pawlik & M. Rosenzweig (Eds.), *The international handbook of psychology* (pp. 570–584). London: Sage.

Kapor-Stanulovic, N. (1999). Encounter with suffering. *American Psychologist, 54*, 1020–1027.

Kennedy, S., & David, H. P. (1986). Psychology and policy around the world: Widening psychology's sphere of influence. *American Psychologist, 41*, 296–297.

Klineberg, O. (1964). *The human dimension of international relations*. New York: Holt, Rinehart and Winston.

Klineberg, O. (1967). The IUPsyS and international relations. *International Journal of Psychology, 2*, 76–78.

Koch, S. (1985). Foreword: Wundt's creature at age zero and centenarian: Some aspects of the institutionalization of the "new psychology." In S. Koch & D. E. Leary (Eds.), *A century of psychology as science* (pp. 7–35). New York: McGraw-Hill.

Kossakowski, A. (1980). Psychology in the German Democratic Republic. *American Psychologist, 35*, 450–460.

Lomov, B. F. (1982). Soviet psychology: Its historical origins and contemporary status. *American Psychologist, 37*, 580–586.

Lunt, I., & Poortinga, Y. H. (1996). Internationalizing psychology: The case of Europe. *American Psychologist, 51*, 504–508.

Luria, A. R., & Majovski, L. V. (1977). Basic approaches used in American and Soviet clinical neuropsychology. *American Psychologist, 32*, 959–968.

MacLeod, R. B. (1957). A note on the international congress. In H. P. David & H. V. Bracken (Eds.), *Perspectives in personality theory* (pp. 419–424). New York: Basic Books.

Mays, V. M., Rubin, J., Sabourin, M., & Walker, L. (1996). Moving toward a global psychology. *American Psychologist, 51*, 485–487.

Mehryar, A. H. (1984). The role of psychology in international development: Wishful thinking and reality. *International Journal of Psychology, 19*, 65–77.

Melikian, L. H. (1984). The transfer of psychological knowledge to Third World countries and its impact on development: The case of the Arab Gulf oil-producing states. *International Journal of Psychology, 19*, 65–77.

Merenda, P. F. (1995). International movements in psychology: The major international associations of psychology. *World Psychology, 1*, 27–48.

Murphy, G., & Kovach, J. K. (1972). *Historical introduction to modern psychology*. New York: Harcourt, Brace and Jovanovich.

Pawlik, K., & d'Ydewalle, G. (1996). Psychology and the global commons. *American Psychologist, 51*, 488–495.

Pawlik, K., & Rosenzweig, M. R. (Eds.). (1994). The origins and development of psychology: Some national and regional perspectives [Special issue]. *International Journal of Psychology, 29*, 665–756.

Poortinga, Y. H. (1997). Cultural psychology: A U.S. tragedy. In M. Givadan & T. Venguer (Eds.), *Conferencias magistrales congreso regional para profesionales en America* (pp. 39–54). Mexico City: IMIFAP.

Rosenzweig, M. R. (1979). Promoting international communication in psychology. *International Journal of Psychology, 14*, 285–286.

Rosenzweig, M. R. (1984). U.S. psychology and world psychology. *American Psychologist, 39*, 877–884.

Rosenzweig, M. R. (1988). Psychology and the United Nations human rights efforts. *American Psychologist, 43*, 79–86.

Rosenzweig, M. R. (1992). *International psychological science*. Washington, DC: American Psychological Association.

Rosenzweig, M. R., Holtzman, W. H., Sabourin, M., & Bolanger, D. (2000). *The history of the International Union of Psychological Science (IUPsyS)*. Philadelphia: Psychology Press.

Russell, R. W. (1984). Psychology in its world context. *American Psychologist, 39*, 1017–1025.

Salazar, J. M. (1984). The use and impact of psychology in Venezuela: Two examples. *International Journal of Psychology, 19*, 179–182.

Schmidt, H. D. (1980). Psychology in the German Democratic Republic. *Annual Review of Psychology, 31*, 195–209.

Serpell, R. (1984). Commentary on the impact of psychology on Third World development. *International Journal of Psychology, 19,* 179–192.

Sexton, V. S., & Hogan, D. (Eds.). (1992). *International psychology: Views from around the world.* Lincoln: University of Nebraska Press.

Sexton, V. S., & Misiak, H. (Eds.). (1976). *Psychology around the world.* Monterey, CA: Brooks/Cole.

Sinha, D. (1986). *Psychology in a Third World country: The Indian experience.* New Delhi, India: Sage.

Sinha, D., & Holtzman, W. H. (Eds.). (1984). The impact of psychology on Third World development [Special issue]. *International Journal of Psychology, 19,* 3–192.

Soueif, M. I. (1963). *An introduction to social psychology* [In Arabic]. Cairo, Egypt: Anglo-Egyptian Bookshop.

Street, W. R. (1994). *A chronology of noteworthy events in American psychology.* Washington, DC: American Psychological Association.

Sunar, D. (1996). An interview with Cigdem Kagitchibasi. *World Psychology, 2,* 139–152.

Triandis, H. C. (1980). Preface. In H. C. Triandis & W. W. Lambert (Eds.), *Handbook of cross-cultural psychology* (Vol. 1, pp. ix–xv). Boston: Allyn & Bacon.

Triandis, H. C. (1994). *On the utility of applied psychology.* Address presented at the 21st International Congress of Applied Psychology, Madrid, Spain.

Van Strien, P. J. (1997). The American "colonization" of northwest European social psychology after World War II. *Journal of the History of the Behavioral Sciences, 33,* 349–363.

Watson, R. I. (1960). The history of psychology: A neglected area. *American Psychologist, 15,* 251–255.

Wilpert, B. (2000). Applied psychology: Past and future societal and scientific challenges. *Applied Psychology: An International Review, 49,* 3–22.

Woodworth, R. S. (1964). *Contemporary schools of psychology* (3rd ed.). New York: Roland Press.

CHAPTER 26

Professional Organizations

WADE E. PICKREN AND RAYMOND D. FOWLER

INTERNATIONAL PSYCHOLOGICAL
  ORGANIZATIONS 535
  The International Union of Psychological Sciences 535
  The International Association of Applied Psychology 536
  The International Council of Psychologists 536
  International Associations: Regional 537
  Other Regional Meetings 538
  International Associations: Specialized 538
NATIONAL PSYCHOLOGICAL ASSOCIATIONS 538
  Europe 538
  Asia 539

The Near and Middle East 539
South and Central America and the Caribbean 539
Africa 540
Others 540
North America 540
Applied Psychological Organizations 544
Psychological Organizations in the Public Interest 545
Accreditation and Credentialing Organizations 548
Interdisciplinary Organizations 549
CONCLUSION 550
REFERENCES 551

Among the scientific societies that proliferated across Europe and North America in the latter half of the nineteenth century were psychological societies and organizations (Appel, 1988; Gundlach, 1997). At the beginning of the twenty-first century, there are well over 1,000 psychological associations, societies, or organizations. In this chapter, we will provide a descriptive history of the development of organized psychology, beginning with international organizations, then moving to national, regional, and, finally, specialty organizations. We will not be exhaustive in our description; rather, we will attempt to present a representation of the various types of psychological societies.

INTERNATIONAL PSYCHOLOGICAL ORGANIZATIONS

As the possibility of a new science of psychology grew across Europe in the late nineteenth century, the first cohort of psychologists loosely organized themselves into local societies or participated in the organizational life of other scientific societies. Improvements in transportation and communication were instrumental in facilitating more formal associations by making travel to distant sites quicker and safer. Beginning in 1889, psychologists began to meet their colleagues from other cities or universities at international congresses of

psychology. The diverse interests that were represented in these meetings reflected the heterogeneity of psychology during the period. For example, organizers with interests as diverse as hypnosis and psychical research sponsored the first two International Congresses of Psychology. Jean Martin Charcot (1825–1893) and his colleagues in the Société de Psychologie Physiologique organized the first International Congress of Psychology held at the Paris World Fair of 1889. Charcot was president of this first congress, and his research and clinical interests in hypnosis were represented in approximately one-third of the congress papers (Silverman, 1989; Smith, 1997). The London Society for Psychical Research organized the second International Congress of Psychology in 1892. Although their themes were perhaps peripheral to the interests of most scientific psychologists, these first two congresses provided a venue for psychologists to gather, discuss research, and make plans for future cooperation. The international congresses helped bring together scholars with a common interest in the new discipline and played a vital role in the establishment of psychological associations.

The International Union of Psychological Sciences

The international congresses eventually led to an umbrella organization of psychological science. For many years, the International Congress Committee served as the steering group that provided continuity from one congress to the next. In 1948, an international organization to support and promote psychology worldwide was formally discussed at the first post–World War II congress in Edinburgh. The United Nations Educational, Scientific, and Cultural Organization (UNESCO) indicated a willingness to provide financial support for international scientific organizations. So, in 1951 the International Union of Scientific Psychology (IUSP) was formed at the Stockholm meeting of the International Congress with a name change to the International Union of Psychological Sciences in 1965. The International Union of Psychological Sciences became a member of the International Council of Scientific Unions in 1982, with an attendant change in name to the current International Union of Psychological Sciences (IUPsyS). In 1952, the IUPsyS became a member of the International Social Science Council. The IUPsyS is one of only two scientific unions that belong to both the International Council of Scientific Unions and the International Social Science Council, thus providing a bridge between the natural sciences and the social and behavioral sciences (Rosenzweig, Holtzman, Sabourin, & Belanger, 2000).

Membership in IUPsyS is by national associations rather than individual psychologists. There were 20 initial member nations, mostly drawn from western Europe, but also including Canada, the United States, Egypt, Japan, Brazil, Cuba, and Uruguay. As national associations formed over the second half of the twentieth century, membership grew to include associations from every continent. At the beginning of the twenty-first century, the IUPsyS represented 66 national members, which, in turn, represented most of the 500,000 or so psychologists around the world. There are 11 organizations affiliated with IUPsyS. In addition to sponsoring the International Congress of Psychology every 4 years, IUPsyS publishes *The International Journal of Psychology* and facilitates communication among its national members (Rosenzweig et al., 2000).

The International Association of Applied Psychology

The International Association of Applied Psychology (IAAP) is the oldest international association of individual psychologists. The archives of the IAAP were destroyed during World War II, so the full history of the early years of the association cannot be told. What is known is that in 1920, Edouard Claparède (1873–1940) and Pierre Bovet (1878–1965), of the Rousseau Institute in Geneva, Switzerland, organized the first International Conference of Psychotechnics Applied to Vocational Guidance. Despite its impressive title, there were fewer than 50 conference participants. The conference was hastily arranged to coincide with the annual training course

in vocational guidance offered by the Swiss Association for Vocational Guidance and Apprentice Welfare (Gundlach, 1998). Vocational guidance was a new area for psychologists and educators in Europe and the United States. The concept was pioneered in the United States by attorney Frank Parsons (1854–1908) and experimental psychologist Hugo Münsterberg (1863–1916). In Europe, it formed a part of the burgeoning field of psychotechnics, in which the apparatus of experimental psychology laboratories were used to test vocational aptitude and to assist in the selection of personnel (van Drunen, 1997).

Although the number of participants was small, the papers were well received and it was decided to have a second, larger, congress the next year in Barcelona. Following this first conference, the International Association of Psychotechnics was founded with Claparède as its first president, a post he held until his death in 1941. However, the actual legal incorporation was not until 1927, when the group merged with the International Association for Psychology and Psychotechnics (Gundlach, 1998). The name was changed to the International Association of Applied Psychology (IAAP) in 1955 (Wilpert, 2000).

The association sponsored international meetings on an irregular basis until 1976, when an agreement was reached with the IUPsyS to hold congresses every fourth year on an alternating basis. The International Congresses of Applied Psychology are currently held every 4 years, 2 years after the preceding International Congress of Psychology, so there is a major international congress every 2 years.

At the beginning of the twenty-first century, the IAAP had more than 2,000 members in over 90 countries. In 1978, the association began to organize its members into divisions that represent various fields of psychology; at the end of the twentieth century there were 14 such divisions. It was also in the late 1970s that the association began forming committees and task forces to implement its members' initiatives. The mission of the IAAP is to advance scientific work in applied psychology around the world. Its publications in the service of this mission include *Applied Psychology: An International Review* and the *International Journal of Applied Psychology*.

The International Council of Psychologists

The National Council of Women Psychologists (NCWP) began in December 1941 as an organization to promote the interests of women psychologists in the United States. The name was changed to the International Council of Women Psychologists after World War II and to the current International Council of Psychologists in 1959.

As American psychologists began to prepare for national service in the event of U.S. involvement in the war, women psychologists felt excluded. One stated that she and her women colleagues grew frustrated with male psychologists who either wanted to go on "reading papers on rat reactions and retroactive inhibitions as though psychology had no concern with a world already launched into inferno" or who sought to exclude women from war work (Schwesinger, 1943, p. 298). Women psychologists were repeatedly counseled by male psychologists in leadership positions in organized psychology to wait patiently. Finally, when it became clear that nothing was going to be done for them, a group of 50 women voted to organize as the National Council of Women Psychologists (Capshew & Laszlo, 1986). By June 1942, membership had grown to 240 women PhD psychologists (Schwesinger, 1943). The NCWP was successful in gaining its members useful civilian roles in wartime service. NWCP members provided a variety of educational, assessment, and placement services. However, the NWCP was unable to significantly increase the number of women faculty members, even though there was a chronic shortage of qualified male professors of psychology.

Membership in the NCWP declined after the war. Rather than disband, its leaders decided to add an international focus and took a new name, the International Council of Women Psychologists (Carrington, 1952). The ICWP developed an extensive educational and support role for psychologists around the world. Included among these activities were support for displaced psychologists and the publication of a book, *Women Psychologists: Their Work and Training and Professional Opportunities* (1950), meant to encourage young women to become psychologists.

However, the promotion of women in psychology remained the first goal of the ICWP. The 1950s was an era that was not sympathetic to women's issues. Leading male psychologists were frequently unsympathetic, if not hostile, to women as professional colleagues (e.g., Boring, 1951). One departmental chairman stated that if "women were really capable, nothing could hold them back and that any effort to support women psychologists just because they were women was a mistake" (cited in Walsh, 1985, p. 21). Leaders of the ICWP sought divisional membership in the American Psychological Association (APA) as a means to gain a voice for women's issues in psychology but were repeatedly turned down by the APA leadership. In 1959, after considerable discussion, the ICWP changed its constitution to allow men to become members and its name to the International Council of Psychologists. Still, the APA would not admit the organization to divisional status (Walsh, 1985).

After 1959, the mission of the ICP was broadened so that the advancement of women and men in psychology was focused on psychological science and practice in the international arena. The ICP now has women and men members in over 90 countries and sponsors annual meetings at various sites around the world. The ICP is registered as a Non-Governmental Organization with consultative status at the United Nations and has representation on many UN initiatives. Members of the ICP are organized in committees and interest groups that reflect a broad array of psychological concerns and activities (Davis, 2000; Gielen, Adler, & Milgram, 1992).

The ICP and the APA cohost a reception for international visitors at each annual APA convention. The two organizations also jointly sponsor a program to donate books and journals to libraries in third-world countries.

International Associations: Regional

The European Federation of Professional Psychology Associations and the Interamerican Society of Psychology are the two major regional psychological associations that hold regular conventions in years when neither the IUPsyS nor the IAAP are holding their congresses. In addition, the IAAP and the IUPsyS jointly sponsor regional conferences on a periodic basis, usually in developing areas of the world.

The Interamerican Society of Psychology

The Interamerican Society of Psychology (usually known by its Spanish-language acronym, SIP) was founded in December 1951 during the Congress of the World Federation of Mental Health. The founding members intended for the society to be a small group of prominent psychologists who would work together to foster psychological science in the Americas and the Caribbean. There were only 50 members in 1953, most from the United States, Mexico, and a few Caribbean islands. However, membership grew to more than 900 by 1964, and the society was restructured to accommodate growth. The number of countries represented grew to include many more Latin American countries. In 2000, the society's membership included approximately 1,000 individuals from 26 countries.

To fulfill its mission to promote psychology in the Western Hemisphere, the society has held the Interamerican Congress of Psychology since 1953. For the first 7 years, the congress was held annually, with a move to biennial meetings held in odd-numbered years after 1959. All the major areas of psychology have been historically represented in the society and at the congresses. Focuses in the last years of the twentieth century included community/social psychology, psychology applied to education, and AIDS prevention (Ferdman, 2000).

As of the beginning of the twenty-first century, the SIP remained the preeminent regional psychological organization for the Western Hemisphere. Through its journal, its Internet-based listserv, and its congress, the SIP was able to effectively promote the development of psychology in its member nations.

The European Federation of Professional Psychology Associations

Like the IUPsyS, the European Federation of Professional Psychology Associations (EFPPA) restricts its membership to national psychological associations, with only one association per country permitted to hold membership. The EFPPA was founded in 1981 and reflects the changes in Europe as its countries move toward political and economic unity.

Twelve national psychology associations held charter membership in the EFPPA. In 2000, that number had grown to 30 member nations, whose associations represented over 100,000 individual psychologists. Professional issues such as training, curricula, ethics, and professional regulation have historically been the principal focus of the EFPPA, but the association considers the integration of practice and research to be an indispensable goal for European psychology.

A central focus of the EFPPA has been the development of Europe-wide training standards for psychologists. This focus reflected the political directives of the European Community that encouraged professions in member states to develop common standards. In psychology, this move eventuated in the adoption in 1990 of formal guidelines under the rubric "Optimal Standards for Training." The goal of the EFPPA at the end of the twentieth century was to develop a formal framework that would lead to a European Diploma for Psychologists (Lunt, 1996, 2000).

The EFPPA has held biennial assemblies since 1982. In 1996, the association began sponsoring publication of the *European Psychologist,* which was a primary means of communication among its members.

Other Regional Meetings

Since 1995, regional congresses of psychology have been held, primarily in developing areas of the world, under the cosponsorship of the IUPsyS and the IAAP. These congresses usually do not involve permanent regional organizations; rather, the host country organizes them, and most participants come from the surrounding region, although psychologists from other regions are welcome to register and attend. These regional meetings are especially important for younger psychologists and colleagues from less developed countries who may not be able to afford the travel costs and registration fees for world congresses. Regional congresses have been held in Guangzhou, China (1995), Mexico City, Mexico (1997), Durban, South Africa (1999) and Mumbai, India (2001).

International Associations: Specialized

There are many international organizations that represent psychologists who are interested in specific areas of research or practice. Fourteen international organizations are affiliated with the IUPsyS. In addition, there are at least 65 others, and probably more. Also, at least 30 specialized organizations focus primarily on members in a particular region, such as Europe, Asia–South Pacific, and the Nordic countries. Almost all of these organizations were established in the last half of the twentieth century.

Among the more prominent specialized international organizations are the International Neuropsychological Society (est. 1967), the International Society for the Study of Behavioural Development (est. 1969), the Jean Piaget Society (est. 1970), the International Association for Cross-Cultural Psychology (est. 1972), and the International Test Commission (est. 1974). Examples of specialized regional associations include the European Association of Psychological Assessment (est. 1990), the European Health Psychology Society (est. 1986), and the International Society of Political Psychology (est. 1978).

NATIONAL PSYCHOLOGICAL ASSOCIATIONS

The first national psychological organization was the American Psychological Association (1892). Its history will be given in greater detail below. By 1925, eight national associations had been established; by 2000, 66 national associations had been recognized by the IUPsyS, and there were national associations in at least 15 other countries.

The development of national organizations outside the United States occurred first in Europe, followed by South America and Asia; African nations have only recently begun to organize such associations.

Europe

In the first decade of the twentieth century, psychologists in four European nations formed national associations: Great Britain and France (1901), Germany (1904), and Italy (1910). The Psychological Society, changed to the British Psychological Society in 1906, was formed in October 1901 by 10 psychologists who met at University College, London (Bunn, 2000). The French Psychological Society (SFP) was also founded in 1901. Its initial mission was to promote scientific research, but over the course of the twentieth century it has developed a greater emphasis on the practice of psychology. In Germany, psychologists G. E. Mueller, Oswald Kulpe, and Herman Ebbinghaus formed the Society of Experimental Psychology (SEP) in 1904; the name was later changed to German Society for Psychology (DGPs). As in other psychological organizations formed in this period, the emphasis in the SEP was on scientific research. Much was lost during the Nazi period, with the result that organized psychology had to be completely rebuilt after World War II. Two German states were created in 1949: the German Democratic Republic (East Germany) and the Federal Republic of Germany (West Germany). The DGPs continued as the primary national association of academic psychologists in the latter and had approximately 1,800 members at the end of the twentieth century. In 1946, the Professional Association of German Psychologists was founded; its focus was (and is) the application of psychology outside the universities. Its membership at the beginning of the twenty-first century was approximately 21,000. In the German Democratic Republic, a new professional society was formed in 1962. The Society for Psychology (GfP) was mainly concerned with scientific psychology in adherence to Marxist-Leninist principles; it had approximately 2,500 members at the time of German reunification in 1990. The GfP dissolved at that time and its members were able to choose to affiliate with either the DGPs or the Professional Association of German Psychologists (Dumont & Louw, 2001; Trommsdorf & Sprung; 2000). The Italian Psychological Society (SIPs) was formed in 1910 as a scientific society. During the twentieth century, other smaller societies, many devoted to professional practice or specialized research areas, joined the SIPs. It had eight specialty divisions and 20 regional sections at the end of the twentieth century.

Growth in other parts of Europe came more slowly, and only in Hungary (1928) and the Netherlands (1938) had national organizations formed before World War II began. The Swiss Psychological Society was formed during the war (1943). After the war, growth was more rapid. Denmark (1947), Poland (1948), Finland (1952), Spain (1952), Austria (1953), Iceland (1954), and Sweden (1955) formed national psychological societies in the first decade after the end of the war.

Growth in the Soviet Union was slowed by governmental opposition to behavioral science from 1936 until 1955. Among the various republics of the Soviet Union, Georgia was the first to allow psychologists to organize (1941), while Russia did not allow an association until 1957.

Since 1955, national psychological organizations have been formed in almost every nation of Europe, including Turkey (1956), Czechoslovakia (1958), Greece (1963), Portugal (1965), Romania (1965), Ireland (1970), Estonia (1988), and Albania (1991).

Asia

China was the first Asian country where psychologists formed a national society (Chinese Psychological Society, 1921), but because of the nation's internal political conflicts, the organization disbanded after a few years. The society was briefly reorganized in 1937 but was dissolved again when Japan invaded China. The Chinese Psychological Society resumed operation in 1950, only to close in 1966 for 10 years during the Cultural Revolution. In 1977, the organization was able to resume its activities. At the end of the twentieth century, the society had approximately 3,000 members.

The Indian Psychological Association was formed in 1925. Psychology in Japan began with the visit of former APA president G. T. Ladd in the late 1800s. One of his Japanese students, M. Mastumoto, helped train the first generation of Japanese psychologists. It was not until 1927, however, that the Japanese Psychological Association was founded. Its membership remained small until after World War II; by the year 2000 its membership was approximately 5,000. Other more specialized psychological societies are affiliated with the JPA, including the Japanese Association of Educational Psychology (est. 1952) and the Association of Japanese Clinical Psychology (est. 1982).

It was not until 1952 that psychologists in another Asian nation, Indonesia, formed a national society. Since then, national associations have formed in the Philippines, Hong Kong, Bangladesh, Korea, Singapore, Mongolia, Vietnam, and Pakistan.

The Near and Middle East

The first psychological organization in the Arab world was established in Egypt in 1948. The Israeli Psychological Association was formed a decade later (1958), with Tunisian psychologists following in 1962. In the last decade of the twentieth century, psychologists in Yemen (1990) and Jordan (1996) formed national societies. Other countries in the region with national associations are Iran and Morocco.

South and Central America and the Caribbean

Experimental psychology began in Latin America in 1898 with the establishment of a laboratory in Argentina. It was also in Argentina (1930) that the first national society of psychologists in South America was formed. Ecuador (1942) followed, and by 1981 national organizations had formed in a number of South and Central American countries, including Brazil (1949), Mexico (1953), Uruguay (1953), Peru (1954), Venezuela (1957), Cuba (1964), and Panama (1965), Colombia (1978), and Nicaragua (1981). Chile and the Dominican Republic also have national psychological organizations.

Africa

The South African Psychological Association (SAPA) was formed in 1948. From its beginning, it incorporated both academic and professional psychologists. Conflict over apartheid led to a separate Whites only organization in 1961, the Psychological Institute of the Republic of South Africa (PIRSA). A new association of psychologists without racial restrictions was formed when the two groups merged to form the Psychological Association of South Africa (PASA) in 1983 (Dumont & Louw, 2001). At the beginning of the twenty-first century, membership in PASA was approximately 5,000; 90% of PASA's members were white. Other national associations of psychologists formed in Africa were in Zimbabwe (1971), Namibia (1990), and Uganda (1992).

Others

The Canadian Psychological Association was formed in 1938 and held its first annual meeting in 1940 (Dzinas, 2000). Psychologists in Australia (1966) and New Zealand (1967) formed independent national organizations after initial memberships as branches of the British Psychological Society.

North America

The development and organization of psychology in the United States is best viewed against the backdrop of changes in American life and society. Along with a number of other disciplines (e.g., economics, political science, biochemistry, physiology) in the last two decades of the nineteenth century, the new psychology grew and prospered as it responded to the needs of American society (Appel, 1988; Kohler, 1982; Sokal, 1992). The Progressive movement in politics was one overt response to the calls for a more efficient, less corrupt, social order, while in academia there was a parallel response as American universities sought to provide trained personnel to fill the new professional niches created by the demands for a more efficient society.

The modern university that emerged after the U.S. Civil War was both a product and a producer of the increasingly rationalized society (Veysey, 1965). As Wiebe (1967) points out, this was the era of the rise of the expert who restricted himself to a specialized function in order to increase his authority. The new graduate schools, modeled on the German research university, provided professional training for this new class of experts (Veysey, 1965). Psychology and other disciplines emerged as examples of the increasing specialization of knowledge within the university. The most successful of these new disciplines were the ones that found a way to use their specialized knowledge in the practical service of the larger community. Psychology was among those successful disciplines.

In July 1892, G. Stanley Hall (1844–1924) met with a small group of men to discuss the possibility of organizing a psychological association (Fernberger, 1932). Although the details of the meeting are not known, the group elected 31 individuals, including themselves, to membership, with Hall as the first president. The first meeting of the new American Psychological Association (APA) was held in December 1892 at the University of Pennsylvania. The basic governance of the APA consisted of a council with an executive committee, a plan that is essentially the same as that of the beginning of the twenty-first century: a Council of Representatives with a Board of Directors.

Membership growth of the APA was modest over the first 50 years of its existence. From 31 members in 1892, there were 125 members in 1899, 308 in 1916, 530 in 1930, and 664 in 1940. In 1926, a new class of nonvoting membership was formed, associate, and most of the growth occurred in that class after 1926, so that there were 2,079 associate members in 1940. During World War II, the APA merged with other psychological organizations under a reorganization plan that broadened the scope of psychology to include professional practice and the promotion of human welfare. The reorganized APA was prepared for the postwar boom in psychology.

The greatest growth in APA membership came after World War II. Returning servicemen, with federal education benefits (e.g., the GI bill), filled the psychology graduate programs of American universities. Many of them were interested in the new clinical psychology training programs. Training mental health personnel became a priority for the Veterans Administration and the new National Institute of Mental Health. Millions of dollars were poured into psychology in the postwar period; these monies led to significant increases in faculty as well as students. In the 25-year period from 1945 to 1970, the APA experienced the most rapid growth of its entire history. Membership grew over 630%, from 4,183 to 30,839 members (Crawford, 1992). From 1970 to 2000, APA membership grew to 88,500, with another 70,500 affiliates.

The divisional structure of the APA that grew out of the reorganization plan during World War II facilitated the growth of psychology and represented the increasing diversity of American psychology (Benjamin, 1997b; Dewsbury, 1997). Nineteen divisions were approved in 1944; five of them were sections from the American Association of Applied Psychology (AAAP), which had emerged in 1937 as the chief rival to the APA. The two most popular divisions reflected the practice and application emphasis of the AAAP: clinical and personnel (Benjamin, 1997b). However, the number of divisions was almost immediately reduced to 17 when the Psychometric Society (Division 4) decided not to join and Division 11, Abnormal Psychology and Psychotherapy, merged with Division 12, Clinical Psychology. By 1960, there were 20 divisions. From 1960 to 2001, 32 more divisions were formed to bring the total to 52. Most of the growth of divisions occurred in areas of psychological practice and reflected particular practice focuses, for example, Division 50, Addictions. Until the 1990s, divisions oriented to psychological science also experienced membership increases. However, by the end of the twentieth century, membership in some science divisions was decreasing.

The events that led to the founding of the Canadian Psychological Association (CPA) began in the Spring of 1938 with the distribution of a questionnaire to Canadian psychologists seeking to determine their interest in a national organization. During a meeting held in June 1938 a motion was approved to form a Canadian association. A group was formed in 1939 to draft a constitution for the new society. The constitution was ratified in December 1940 and the CPA was incorporated in 1950 (Dzinas, 2000).

Like its neighbor the APA, the CPA was organized over the twentieth century into divisions, with a total of 23 sections in 2000. The CPA at the end of the century published three journals and a newsletter.

The Society for Psychological Study of Social Issues

Several of the APA divisions began as independent organizations and later joined the APA. While all of those organizations have an interesting history, we focus here on two: the Society for Psychological Study of Social Issues (SPSSI), which is APA's Division 9, and the Psychology-Law Society, APA's Division 41.

A group of young psychologists led by Ross Stagner and Isadore Krechevsky (who later changed his name to David Krech) circulated a petition in 1935 that called on the APA to become involved in the pressing social issues of the day. Specifically, this group wanted the APA to address the problems of unemployment among (especially young)

psychologists, to work for the inclusion of mental health services in federal programs, and to speak out against fascism. The leadership of the APA at the time was chiefly focused on maintaining a public image of psychology as a natural science and declined to act on the issues presented them. A year later, at the APA meeting at Dartmouth College, Krech and Stagner held a public meeting at which the SPSSI was formed. The prominent psychologist Goodwin Watson was named as the first president. The SPSSI sought affiliate status with the APA, which was granted the following year (Finison, 1986; Stagner, 1986).

When the APA was reorganized during World War II, the SPSSI joined as Division 9. However, the SPSSI has remained an independently incorporated organization. While all Division 9 members must also be SPSSI members, not all SPSSI members are Division 9 members. The number of psychologists who are members of SPSSI has fluctuated over the years, from a high of 80% in 1980 to its current low of approximately 55% (Kimmel, 1997). The SPSSI experienced fairly consistent growth in its membership over the years, with a high of 2,832 in 1985. However, the SPSSI experienced a decline in members in the second half of the 1990s.

The focus of the division since its inception has been on social issues. One prominent member described the interests of SPSSI members as the "three Ps: prejudice, poverty, and peace" (cited in Kimmel, 1997, p. 17). Labor issues served as an initial focus in the late 1930s as the United States faced severe economic hardship. The SPSSI worked to gain greater employment for psychologists and to understand and reduce labor conflict. SPSSI members, led by Otto Klineberg and Kenneth and Mamie Phipps Clark, played a crucial role in the U.S. Supreme Court decision in *Brown v. Board of Education* in 1954. The research of Kenneth Clark and Mamie Phipps Clark was critical in the Supreme Court decision to end race-based school segregation (Jackson, 2000; Phillips, 2000). The SPSSI has worked in support of cases of academic freedom, early and notably in the case of the University of California, Berkeley, professors who were fired for refusing to sign a loyalty oath during the McCarthy "Red Hunt" era. The SPSSI has also worked on social issues such as civil rights, population control, antiwar activities, and the role of science in the formation of public policy.

American Psychology-Law Society

Two young psychologists attended the 1968 APA Convention focused on finding other psychologists who were interested in forming an association devoted to the issues at the interface of psychology and law. Eric Dreikurs and Jay Ziskin were not acquainted prior to the meeting but quickly found each other and were able to gather 13 other psychologists also interested in psychology and law. In 1969, the American Psychology-Law Society (AP-LS) was incorporated with 101 charter members. From this small group, the AP-LS grew to a membership of 2000 by the century's end. In 1984, the AP-LS merged with the three-year-old APA Division 41, Psychology and Law (Fulero, 1999; Grisso, 1991).

Tensions between science and application were present from the beginning of the society. A significant portion of the membership wanted to focus on developing the forensic application of psychology and saw the society as a means of refining the role of psychologists in the legal system. An equally significant percentage of the membership sought a sounder basis for psychological contributions to law through research. An early crisis between the groups was sparked by the publication of Ziskin's *Coping with Psychiatric and Psychological Testimony* (1970). Ziskin challenged the reliability and admissibility of most psychological and psychiatric testimony and declared that serious research was needed to bring psychological testimony up to acceptable standards. The debate and conflict that ensued from the book's publication led to Ziskin's resignation from AP-LS in 1973. Paradoxically, the effect of the book was to steer the society toward greater support of research in the social and experimental foundations of psychology and law.

By the late 1970s, a younger cohort of psychologists interested in law moved into AP-LS leadership. Many of these young psychologists were interested in the applicability of their field to social issues, especially the improvement of legal institutions (Grisso, 1991). The vigorous leadership of Bruce Sales (1976–1977) energized the society. Sales had a vision of the AP-LS as the major public organization at work at the interface of psychology and law. Under his leadership, new publishing ventures were begun, including the founding of the society journal, *Law and Human Behavior.*

The emphasis on research and social action left many of the forensic expert witnesses without a clear sense of their place in AP-LS. In the last half of the 1970s, AP-LS clinical forensic members went outside the society to start an independent board that was charged with establishing credentials for diplomate status in forensic psychology (Kaslow, 1989). The AP-LS assisted with the establishment of the American Board of Forensic Psychology but was not responsible for it. Thus, by 1980, the AP-LS represented the major areas of psychology and law.

By 1977, some psychologists were active in calling for an APA division of psychology and law. In 1977–1978, the AP-LS became actively involved and worked to gather the necessary signatures to petition the APA Council of Representatives for a new division. The council approved the division in 1980, and Division 41, Psychology and Law, was established in 1981. The leaders of AP-LS initially resisted a merger between the society and the division, but by 1983 it was clear that a merger was the most effective way for the two groups to work together. In 1984, the two groups merged and provision was made for AP-LS members who were not psychologists. Most of the nonpsychologists were lawyers, and they represented a sizable percentage of the AP-LS membership.

The combined AP-LS/Division 41 worked on many significant issues after their merger. Among the more salient were ethics guidelines for forensic psychologists, syllabi for courses in psychology and law, and the pursuit of specialty status from APA for forensic psychology.

As in all areas of American psychology where both clinicians and scientists are active, opportunities for conflict have been present. At the end of the twentieth century, AL-PS/Division 41 had successfully managed the minefield at the borderland between science and practice.

Scientific Organizations

Although the APA was organized to promote psychology as a science, from its inception there have been those who believed that it was not scientific enough. This has given rise over the ensuing decades to numerous societies, both formal and informal, that sought to create organizations devoted solely to science. Lightner Witmer (1867–1956) tried in 1898 to organize a small group of experimental psychologists to meet independently of the APA (Goodwin, 1985). E. B. Titchener (1867–1927) successfully formed an alternative group in 1904. Although not legally formalized in his lifetime, "The Experimentalists," as they came to be called, did meet Titchener's desire to have a psychological club whose members could discuss their version of psychological science in a masculine, smoky, atmosphere (Boring, 1967; Goodwin, 1985). After Titchener's death in 1927, the club members reorganized into the Society of Experimental Psychologists (SEP). Women were admitted for the first time, and the membership limit was set at 50. The SEP was incorporated in 1936. Over the years, membership requirements have been slightly modified; most notably the limit has been raised, so that there were 197 fellows in 2000 (Hurvich, 2000). The SEP continued to be primarily concerned with its maintenance as an organization devoted to science, although its members contributed to the application of psychology during both world wars.

For some younger psychologists in the mid-1930s, neither the APA nor the SEP was experimental enough. This younger group loosely organized themselves in 1936 under the name "Society of Experimenting Psychologists" (Benjamin, 1977;

Hardcastle, 2000). The name was a jab at the SEP, many of whom were no longer actively engaged in experimental research. The name was later changed to the Psychological Round Table (PRT) in order to avert professional retaliation from the senior members of the SEP. Like "The Experimentalists" before them, the members of PRT found the APA meetings too bureaucratic and too inclusive of nonexperimental psychology. They were also excluded from membership in the SEP. The PRT organizers created a small group based at universities in the eastern United States who met annually to talk about research and socialize. Women were initially excluded. Once a member reached the age of 40, he could no longer participate in the meetings. As a result, membership was never large and the group was never formally incorporated. Nevertheless, the PRT served as an important communication network in American experimental psychology for many years.

Dissatisfaction with the annual meetings of the APA provided the impetus for the formation of the Psychonomic Society in December 1959. In that sense, the Psychonomic Society is heir to the tradition inaugurated by Titchener and continued by the Psychological Round Table. Apparently, the experimentalists' dissatisfactions had been growing for years so that by the late 1950s there was a perception that the APA was catering to the interests of psychologists in professional practice (Dewsbury & Bolles, 1995). The proximal stimulus for the formation of the group was the decision by the APA Board of Convention Affairs in 1959, later reversed, that no one could use slides as part of his or her presentation. This, for many experimentalists, was the last piece of evidence needed that the APA convention was not about scientific communication.

A small group of psychologists went to work over the summer of 1959 to drum up support for a new, more science-oriented society. Led by William Verplanck (b. 1916) and Clifford Morgan (1915–1976), an organizing committee began meeting to form the new society. When letters of invitation sent out to members of the APA science divisions indicated that there was more than adequate interest for such a society, the organizing committee met in late 1959 and developed by-laws to govern the as-yet unnamed society (Dewsbury & Bolles, 1995). The name Psychonomic Society was agreed on in early 1960, and the society was incorporated in April of that year.

The purposes of the society were two: to conduct an annual meeting to exchange research results and to develop a journal to publish the results. In terms of structure, the Psychonomic Society was the anti-APA. The group refused to develop the bureaucratic machinery they disliked in the larger association. Instead, they chose to govern their affairs through a governing board, which was empowered to do business on behalf of the society. From its inception to the time of this writing, the society has succeeded remarkably well in keeping its governance simple and maintaining its focus as a hard-nosed scientific psychological organization.

The Psychonomic Society experienced rapid growth. Its membership standards were the PhD and a record of successful publication beyond the degree. Ironically, these were the standards for APA membership prior to 1926 (Fernberger, 1932). Although membership requirements have varied slightly over the years, including the development of an associate membership, the basic requirements have changed little. The membership total at the end of the first year was 772. That number rose steadily over the years and had stabilized at approximately 2,000 members by the 1990s. Associate membership also grew from its inception in 1975 to between 400 and 500 during the 1990s.

At the end of the twentieth century, the Psychonomic Society published six major experimental psychology journals. Journal publication had been one of the two primary purposes of the society at its founding, but it took several years before the society was able to begin its publishing program. It was able to do so through the generosity of one of its founders, Clifford T. Morgan. Morgan began a journal, *Psychonomic Science,* in 1964. This was followed in relatively quick succession by *Psychonomic Monograph Supplements* (1965) and *Perception & Psychophysics* (1966). In 1967, Morgan gave the journals to the Psychonomic Society. The society initially struggled with its management of the journals but by the mid-1970s had overcome most of its publication problems. The society split *Psychonomic Science* into four volumes and added others, so that by 2000 it published *Animal Learning & Behavior, Behavior Research Methods, Instruments, & Computers, Memory & Cognition, Perception & Psychophysics, Psychobiology,* and *Psychonomic Bulletin & Review* (Dewsbury, 1996).

Other experimental societies have formed over the years in reaction to the size or policies of the APA. To note one other example, the Society of Experimental Social Psychology formed in 1965 to promote scientific communication among those social psychologists that viewed themselves as experimentalists. A small group of social psychologists decried the large meetings of the APA and the rapid growth of its Division 8 (Personality and Social Psychology). They, like the founders of the Psychonomic Society, wanted a society whose members were experimentalists. The initial intent of the group was to keep the society small in number. That policy has been maintained, as indicated by its membership of only 600 by the year 2000 (Blascovich, 2000; Hollander, 1968).

In 1988, the American Psychological Society (APS) was founded as the major alternative to the APA. The APS was widely perceived as a fundamental split between those psychologists whose primary identity was that of psychological scientist and those who thought of themselves as primarily professional practitioners. The reality was much more complex than that. The reorganization of the APA during the war gave applied interests a greater voice and created the possibility of schism within the APA. The infusion of large sums of money from various federal agencies for psychological research and training, especially clinical training, raised the stakes over psychology's identity. The once-small field of clinical psychology grew out of all proportion to the rest of psychology and soon threatened the traditional centers of power in the APA. Tension between scientists and practitioners grew in the decades after World War II as clinical psychologists became increasingly interested in independent practice and all the necessary accoutrements that accompany such practice: licensure, third-party payment, and the like. In the 1970s, practitioners began to gain greater influence in the APA governance structure and by the 1980s were ascendant. Some scientists and academics who felt threatened by these changes proposed that the APA be reorganized into a looser structure that provided more autonomy for academic psychologists. When the reorganization plan failed in 1988, a large number of scientists/academics decided to form an alternative organization devoted to psychological science. Initially called the Assembly for Scientific and Applied Psychology, the group incorporated in 1988 as the APS with 450 founding members. That number grew rapidly to over 5,000 members within 6 months, and by 2000 the membership was approximately 10,000. Many members of APS have also maintained membership in the APA. Although tension between the two groups ran high in the first years after the split, there was a steady accommodation to each other through the 1990s.

It has been more common, however, for new organizations to form simply around a specialty interest in psychological science. These groups proliferated in the last decades of the twentieth century and are too numerous to list here. The reader is referred to the World Wide Web sites of the Federation of Behavioral, Psychological, and Cognitive Societies (www.thefederationonline.org) and the International Union of Psychological Sciences (www.iupsys.org) for links to many of these societies.

Applied Psychological Organizations

Despite the rhetoric of experimentalism, American psychologists have been particularly interested in the application of psychological science from the first days of organized American psychology (Benjamin, 1997a; Pickren & Dewsbury, 2002). A small number of psychologists worked in applied and professional settings in the early years of the discipline. While many of them had free choice of career sites, others had few work options open to them by virtue of their gender or race (Guthrie, 1998; Stevens and Gardner, 1982). The establishment of the *Journal of Applied Psychology* in 1917 provided an outlet for research and a forum for professional issues. World War I drew public attention to the potential usefulness of applied psychology, especially in mental testing (Samelson, 1977). Two privately held companies were started after the war in an effort to build on this attention: The Scott Company and The Psychological Corporation (Sokal, 1981). The number of psychologists interested in professional practice grew enough by the end of World War I to form a new professional organization, the American Association of Clinical Psychologists. Apparently threatened by this move, the APA co-opted the new organization by forming a Clinical Section in 1919 (Routh, 1994; Samelson, 1992).

During the interwar period, the number of psychologists engaged in various professional practices dramatically increased. By one count, 39% of APA members were employed in applied work in 1940. By comparison, only 9.3% of APA members were employed in a recognizably applied setting in 1916 (Finch & Odoroff, 1939, 1941). It should be kept in mind that a doctoral degree and publications were required for APA membership in this period, and many applied psychologists worked at the master's level. Four semidistinct areas of practice emerged in this period: clinical, consulting, educational, and industrial/business. The settings for these practices included schools, clinics (of various kinds), homes for the mentally retarded, courts, prisons, police departments, psychiatric hospitals, guidance offices in educational settings, psychotherapy offices, social agencies, state and federal agencies, film and radio studios, personnel offices, advertising and marketing firms, life insurance companies, and private consulting firms. At least 83 APA members earned their living primarily from fee-based consultations in 1940.

This growth is also reflected in new psychological organizations that were formed between the wars. The APA membership standards favored academic scientists engaged in experimental research and made it difficult for psychologists with applied expertise to either gain membership or wield significant influence within the organization (Napoli, 1981; O'Donnell, 1979). Finally, in 1926, the APA established a second-class associates membership, at least in part to help finance a new publishing venture. (In 1946, the membership categories were revised: full members became fellows, associates became "members," and a new category of associates was developed, primarily for people without doctorates.)

Associates could not vote or hold office in the APA. Many of the associates were psychologists interested in application and the practice of psychology.

One new organization that formed in this era (1921), the New York State Association of Consulting Psychologists, became the leading state association for applied work in psychology and was emulated by other state and regional groups. The New York group joined with other regional groups and reformed as the Association of Consulting Psychologists (ACP) in 1930. The ACP promoted professional issues such as training and licensing for all applied psychologists. In 1937, the ACP merged with other applied groups to form the American Association for Applied Psychology (AAAP), which, like the ACP, was concerned with issues relevant to professional practice. The AAAP was able to develop a national voice for professional psychology before the onset of the Second World War, though its voice was somewhat muted by the dominance of academic psychologists and the lack of proportionate representation of women among its leadership (Benjamin, 1997a; Capshew, 1999).

The *Journal of Consulting Psychology* was the official publication of the AAAP and reported on both research and practice issues of professional psychology. The issue of appropriate training for the practice of psychology, in all fields but particularly in clinical psychology, was frequently discussed in the pages of the journal and at the annual meetings of the association. It was not directly addressed until after World War II, when the scientist-practitioner (Boulder) model developed by AAAP member David Shakow became the primary model of acceptable training.

In a few short years, the AAAP made substantive progress on behalf of its members. When the APA was reorganized during the Second World War, the AAAP was incorporated into the APA as part of the effort to make the APA more inclusive and responsive to both scientific and professional concerns (Capshew & Hilgard, 1992). Section D, Industrial and Business, of the AAAP became APA Division 14, Industrial and Business Psychology. The new division sought to ensure that appropriate standards of training and practice were maintained and that industrial psychology remained on a solid research basis.

Division 14 members decided to incorporate as a separate society, the Society for Industrial and Organizational Psychology (SIOP), in 1982. This was the result, in part, of dissatisfaction with what was perceived as APA's overemphasis on practice issues at the expense of science. When the APS formed in 1988, SIOP membership was opened to APS members as well as APA members. Despite these changes, it is clear that SIOP is the historical successor to the AAAP (Benjamin, 1997a).

During the 1930s, several states began certification programs for school psychologists (Fagan, Hensley, & Delugach, 1986; French, 1984). A number of those psychologists belonged to the ACP and then the AAAP. One of the charter divisions of the reorganized APA was Division 16, School Psychology. However, many school psychologists did not qualify for membership in Division 16 because they did not have a doctoral degree. Historically, school psychology has been dominated by nondoctoral professionals (Fagan, 1996). Growth of Division 16 membership was steady but slow, even though the number of school psychologists was expanding rapidly. By the 1960s, it became clear that Division 16 was not responding adequately to the needs of nondoctoral school psychologists. As a result, a need for a national organization that could represent all school psychologists led to the founding of the National Association of School Psychologists (NASP) in 1969 (Fagan, 1996).

Membership rose steadily from the founding of the NASP and stood at 21,000 plus in 2000. The association developed an impressive track record of working to raise educational and training standards. Accreditation of training programs became an important part of the NASP's work as well (Fagan, Gorin, & Tharinger, 2000).

Applied psychological organizations proliferated in the last decades of the twentieth century. Space does not allow for all of them to be described. A few chosen to serve as examples include the American Association of Correctional Psychologists (founded 1953), the International Society of Sport Psychology (founded 1965), the Association for the Advancement of Behavior Therapy (founded 1966), the Association for Applied Psychophysiology and Biofeedback (founded 1969), and the Society of Psychologists in Management (founded 1984). Hundreds of other applied psychological organizations had been established in the United States alone by the end of the twentieth century (see VandenBos, 1989).

Psychological Organizations in the Public Interest

The 1960s were a time of social upheaval and dissent in the United States and much of Europe. During this period, psychological organizations were formed to represent groups that had been traditionally ignored or underrepresented in mainstream psychological organizations. In the United States, these new organizations were typically formed as a response to perceived problems with the APA. The APA was perceived as insensitive to the needs and interests of women psychologists and psychologists of color.

The Association of Black Psychologists (ABPsi) was founded in 1968 at the annual convention of the APA. It was not the first organization of African American psychologists. In

1938, psychologist members of the American Teachers Association, an all-black educational group, formed Division 6, Department of Psychology, to facilitate communication and strengthen their professional identity (Guthrie, 1998). Division 6 sent representatives to the Intersociety Constitutional Convention that led to the reorganization of the APA during World War II (Capshew, 1999). However, the ATA's Division 6 was unable to maintain its momentum after the war.

In 1963, the APA, at the urging of the SPSSI, formed the Committee on Equality of Opportunity in Psychology (CEOP) to examine the status of education, training, and career paths of African Americans in psychology (Wispe et al., 1969). However, many black psychologists were dissatisfied with the slow pace of the APA committee and were frustrated with what they perceived as the APA's neglect of their African American members, the low numbers of African Americans in APA governance, and the strikingly few black APA employees. By the second half of the 1960s, a new pride in African American identity had emerged as was evidenced by the focus on Black Power and Black Nationalism. Many younger African American psychologists simply did not identify with the APA, perceiving it as conservative and heavily invested in white, middle-class values. Their anger and frustration came together at the annual convention of the APA in San Francisco (B. Williams, 1997). A small group meeting in a hotel room during the 1968 APA convention grew into a larger meeting of 200 African American psychologists the next day (R. Williams, 1974). Out of this meeting, the Association of Black Psychologists was formed (Guthrie, 1998).

ABPsi grew into a thriving organization with its own agenda, its own mission, and its own identity. It became the professional organization of choice for many African American psychologists. ABPsi holds annual meetings (twice in African countries), has an active publication program that includes the quarterly *Journal of Black Psychology,* the monthly newsletter *Psych Discourse,* the *Association of Black Psychologists Publication Manual,* and the *Sourcebook on the Teaching of Black Psychology.*

Following a dramatic confrontation of the APA leadership by the newly formed Black Students in Psychology Association (BSPA) during the 1969 convention, ABPsi and BPSA cooperated in persuading the APA to address the concerns of black psychologists about culturally biased testing practices, lack of employment opportunities for African Americans in psychology, and inadequate recruitment and support of black graduate students (R. Williams, 1974). The events of 1968 and 1969 had effects that reverberated over the next several years. Hispanic psychologists and Asian American psychologists also formed organizations and put pressure on the APA

to become more sensitive and supportive of their issues. As a result, the APA formed the Board of Ethnic Minority Affairs and opened the Office of Ethnic Minority Affairs. The latter has been an important conduit of training monies for ethnic minority graduate students.

In the early 1970s, two brothers, Derald (b. 1942) and Stanley (b. 1944) Sue, coordinated a series of meetings in San Francisco that included a variety of professionals involved in mental health issues in the Asian community. These meetings eventually led to the founding of the Asian American Psychological Association (AAPA) in 1972. Membership was small at first, and the group struggled to maintain cohesion (Leong, 1995). Despite this small beginning, the AAPA had a membership of over 400 by the year 2000.

Although Asian mental health was the original concern of the AAPA, since that time the organization has diversified in its interests. Advocacy efforts on behalf of Asian Americans led to involvement on U.S. Census issues and to a long engagement against the English-only movement in California. Members of the AAPA developed Asian American psychological theory that was applied to a range of psychological topics, including clinical training and social research. Leaders of the association were among the very first to develop theory and practice related to multicultural counseling. The National Institute of Mental Health relied on the association to assist it in its efforts to diversify its training population, and members of the AAPA served as key liaisons to the NIMH and other federal agencies for the development of mental health policy.

The AAPA developed close ties with the APA very early in its existence. AAPA members served on key boards and committees of the APA, including the Board of Ethnic Minority Affairs, the Board for the Advancement of Psychology in the Public Interest, and the Committee for Ethnic Minority Recruitment, Retention, and Training. The AAPA began publishing the *Journal of the Asian American Psychological Association* in 1979 and began a series of monographs in 1995 (Leong, 1995). In 1999, Dr. Richard Suinn (b. 1933) served as the first Asian American president of the APA.

In 1971, Carolyn Attneave (1920–1992) formed the Network of Indian Psychologists in the Boston area. About the same time, Joe Trimble (b. 1938) formed a group in 1971 called the American Indian Interest Group. Trimble's group was formed with support from the SPSSI and was affiliated with it. In 1973, Trimble merged his group with the Network of Indian Psychologists. Attneave changed the name of her group to the Society of Indian Psychologists (SIP) around 1975 (Trimble, 2000). Membership in the SIP was always small, numbering around 100 at the end of the twentieth century. Members of the SIP and other Indian psychologists worked to increase the number of American Indian psychologists in North America. One notable success was the Indians into Psychology Doctoral Education (INDPSYDE) started by Arthur L. McDonald (b. 1934) in the mid-1980s. By the end of the twentieth century, INDPSYDE programs were operating at several colleges and universities in the West and there had been a noticeable gain in the number of American Indian psychologists. SIP members also worked with the APA and other ethnic minority psychology groups to support the development of rural minority mental health programs. In 1986, Logan Wright (1933–1999) was the first person of American Indian heritage to be elected APA president.

The National Hispanic Psychological Association grew out of an earlier organization of Hispanic psychologists, the Association of Psychologists Por La Raza (APLR), which was founded in Miami in 1970 during the APA convention (Bernal, 1994). The founding group was very small, but that number grew to around 40 as a result of an APLR symposium on Hispanic psychology at the 1971 APA convention. Over the next several years, Hispanic psychologists developed a professional network through NIMH-sponsored conferences and involvement with the APA's Board of Ethnic Minority Affairs. In 1979, the National Hispanic Psychological Association was formed and the first issue of the *Hispanic Journal of Behavioral Science* was published.

In general, all of the ethnic minority psychological associations were involved in prompting the NIMH to become more involved with the support of training of ethnic minority psychologists. The APA, while it initially needed to be prodded by ethnic and minority psychologists, became a positive force for promoting and supporting the diversification of psychology. In 1979, the APA opened its Office of Ethnic Minority Affairs and remained a major collaborator with ethnic and minority psychological associations.

A direct descendant of the National Council of Women Psychologists (see above) was the Association for Women in Psychology. The NCWP, after it changed its name to the International Council of Psychologists, lost its main thrust of advancing the cause of women psychologists. That charge was taken up in the more radical and restive late 1960s by a number of women APA members (Tiefer, 1991). The Association for Women Psychologists (AWP) was founded by approximately 35 women and men at the 1969 APA convention. In 1970, the group changed its name to the Association for Women in Psychology. Many of the original members were convinced that the APA was insensitive to the needs of women psychologists and supported discriminatory, sexist practices in both academic and professional psychology (Tiefer, 1991). For the first years of its existence, the AWP lobbied for change within the APA. Issues that were most

salient for the AWP in these years included abortion rights, ending sexist hiring and promotion practices in academia, and adequate child care at the APA convention. One participant-historian characterized the first years of the AWP–APA relationship as a time of "the public airing of women's grievances with the APA and the profession of psychology" (Tiefer, 1991, p. 637).

The AWP had immediate success in attracting many women psychologists and a few male psychologists as members. Thirty-five women and men formed the first membership cohort; membership in the AWP grew to over 1,700 by the year 2000. For many years, the AWP avoided a hierarchical organizational power structure. All issues were open for discussion by any member during the annual meetings. The association was committed to feminist process and sought to be participatory-democratic in its governance. This led to lengthy business meetings but little activity between meetings. Like other organizations of its time, tensions existed over whether the organization should seek efficiency or democracy as its main governing principle. A compromise was reached in 1979 when the leadership structure was changed to governance by the Implementation Collective. This was a small number of AWP members who volunteered to serve in specific roles in order to facilitate specific AWP initiatives. The collective set policy, financial guidelines, and guidelines for forming committees to carry out various projects. Much of the work of the AWP was carried out by members who served on committees, most of which were generated by members themselves and not by the leadership.

The AWP worked on such salient issues as the passage of the Equal Rights Amendment (ERA), abortion rights, and the removal of antiwoman diagnostic categories in the various revisions of the *Diagnostic and Statistical Manual of Mental Disorders*. Members also developed guidelines for feminist therapy and worked to reduce racism and promote multicultural perspectives (Tiefer, 1991).

One major outcome of the activities of the AWP in its early years was the formation of the APA Task Force on the Status of Women in Psychology. The task force worked for two years, and its report recommended that the APA act to redress the inequities women faced in organized psychology. A specific recommendation was the formation of a division to represent the interests of women in psychology (APA, Task Force on the Status of Women in Psychology, 1973).

Despite some resistance from the APA Council of Representatives, some of whose members suggested that a division for women's issues would only ghettoize and segregate women psychologists, the petition for a women's division was approved. Division 35 was approved in 1973, and its charter called for it to work to advance the cause of women in psychology and to develop knowledge about women's psychological lives. Although Division 35 was born from the tense relationship between the AWP and the APA, it was from the first independent of the AWP. The division developed an organizational structure that had little overlap with the AWP (Mednick & Urbanski, 1991; Russo & Dumont, 1997). In its first year of existence, Division 35 voted to develop a journal to serve as the primary publication of research in the field of feminist psychology. The division's journal, *Psychology of Women Quarterly,* began publication in 1976.

Division 35 started with over 800 members and grew rapidly, becoming one of the largest divisions within the APA with more than 6,000 members by the year 2000. The growth of the division reflected the changing gender composition of American psychology. For example, in 1971, women earned 24% of all psychology doctorates compared to 66% in 1991 (Kohout, 2001). Between 1977 and 2000, the percentage of women APA members increased from 26.7% to 49.0%, and the high percentage of women in graduate programs suggests that this percentage will continue to grow.

Accreditation and Credentialing Organizations

In the United States, the growth of psychology as a mental health profession after World War II created the need for organizations or structures to regulate and credential psychologists engaged in the practice of professional psychology. The licensing of psychologists became a state matter and will not be discussed here.

With the rise of professional psychology after the Second World War, a number of organizations developed to facilitate graduate training in professional psychology and to certify excellence of professional skills. These included the APA, the American Board of Professional Psychology (ABPP), the Association of Psychology Postdoctoral and Internship Centers (APPIC), the National Register of Health Service Providers in Psychology (NR), the Association of State and Provincial Psychology Boards (ASPPB), and the Veterans Administration (VA) (Laughlin & Worley, 1991).

The APA accepted the mandate proposed by the VA and the United States Public Health Service (USPHS) immediately after the World War II to develop an accreditation process to identify those universities that were qualified to train clinical psychologists (Capshew, 1999, Pickren & Dewsbury, 2002; Sheridan, Matarrazo, & Nelson, 1995). Twenty-two universities formed the first cohort of accredited graduate clinical training programs in 1947. That number exceeded 700 by the year 2000. The scientist-practitioner training model adopted by APA and accepted by the VA and USPHS was based on the work of David Shakow, which was formalized at the Boulder Conference in 1949 (Raimy, 1950). The issue of accreditation philosophy and guidelines was revisited over the years at a number of conferences. The 1954 Thayer Conference on School Psychology addressed the desirability of accrediting school psychologist training programs. The 1973 Vail Conference on Levels and Patterns of Professional Training laid the groundwork for the accreditation of schools of professional psychology offering the doctor of psychology degree. By the end of the century, APA accreditation was the standard for all doctoral-level training in the practice of psychology, including the predoctoral internship.

Problems with the predoctoral internship led to the establishment of the Association of Psychology Internship Centers in 1968 (Fox, 1990). The name was later changed to the Association of Psychology Postdoctoral and Internship Centers (APPIC). The major issue that the APPIC addressed initially was matching intern candidates with appropriate training sites. The APPIC established a uniform notification date, the second Monday in February. In the early 1970s, the APPIC began publishing its internship directory. The directory proved to be one of the most valuable contributions made by the association. APPIC is not an accrediting agency. Rather, it works to facilitate high-quality pre- and postdoctoral internship training.

The American Board of Professional Psychology (ABPP) was established in 1947 as the American Board of Examiners in Professional Psychology. The APA realized that it could not serve as the credentialing body for individual psychologists. Yet, in order to certify proficiency in psychological practice and to protect the public from charlatans, an independent credentialing body was needed. The ABPP was funded through the 1950s by the APA and through the collection of examination fees.

The ABPP established the diplomate status as the level of certified proficiency in a psychological specialty and left the establishment and recognition of basic competence to the universities and eventually to the state licensing boards. Thus, the diplomate in professional psychology was established as a higher level of professional excellence. Three original specialties were recognized: clinical, personnel-industrial (later industrial-organizational), and personnel-educational (later counseling). School psychology was added in 1968. The ABPP acknowledged that there were many psychologists who had developed professional competence prior to its establishment. Over 1,000 of these professional psychologists, most of them clinicians and about half of them women, were grandparented in as the first to receive diplomate status (see the 1949 APA Directory for a complete listing).

The board passed through a rather fallow period during the 1960s and 1970s as the number of applicants declined. At one point, the ABPP board of trustees even raised the possibility of disbanding the board (Bent, Packard, & Goldberg, 1999). The examination procedures were changed; the written exam was dropped and the oral component was changed to allow for more in vivo assessment. Various measures to increase the number of applicants and to reestablish close relationships with the APA were discussed. In 1971, the ABPP board established a formal liaison with the APA Board of Professional Affairs. Also in hopes of reaching more psychologists, in 1972 the board established six regional boards to recruit applicants and conduct the diplomate examinations. While the examination burden on the board of trustees was lessened by the regional boards, there was no hoped-for increase in the number of applicants, and the regional boards were disbanded in the 1990s.

At the instigation of the health insurance industry, the APA agreed to work toward establishing a registry of qualified psychologists who would be eligible for reimbursement for the provision of mental health services. At the request of the APA, the ABPP agreed to develop the registry in 1974. The ABPP board of trustees established the Council for the National Register of Health Service Providers (NR) and loaned the new organization money to help it get started. The NR was successful from its beginning in attracting psychologists to membership. The ABPP and the NR soon fell into serious disagreement over their legal relationship, with the ABPP under the impression that the NR was a subsidiary organization. The ABPP apparently hoped that the NR would help rescue it from its financial troubles and that it would prove to be an enduring source of applicants for diplomate status. However, the leaders of the NR saw the relationship differently and in 1975 repaid the ABPP loan and declared that the NR was an independent organization. There ensued a period of intense acrimony between the leaders of the two organizations that did not diminish for several years.

The ABPP recognized several more specialties in the 1980s and 1990s. By the year 2000, in addition to the four established specialties (clinical, counseling, school, and industrial-organizational), the ABPP had made diplomate status available for the specialties of clinical neuropsychology, forensic psychology, family psychology, health psychology, behavioral psychology, psychoanalysis, rehabilitation psychology, and group psychology. Each of these specialties had its own board of examiners and was independently incorporated; thus, the ABPP served the function of general oversight of psychological specialties (Bent et al., 1999). In order to avoid conflict with the Commission for the Recognition of Specialties and Proficiencies in Professional Psychology established by the APA in 1995, the ABPP established the policy of referring all new specialties to the APA for first consideration.

The National Register of Health Care Providers in Psychology quickly became a significant component of professional psychology, as noted above. The first National Register listed 7,000 psychologists in 1975; by 2000 the list had grown to more than 16,000 psychologists. The National Register was successful in providing a definition of the psychologist as a health service provider and in gaining acceptance across North American for the definition. In 1976, the NR was innovative in naming public members to its board of directors, being the first national psychology organization to do so. The National Register developed predoctoral internship criteria in 1980 and required that any psychologist who wished to be listed in its directory must have completed such an internship. These criteria were later adopted by the APPIC as the criteria for membership. The National Register also worked with the Association of State and Provincial Psychology Boards (ASPPB) to establish criteria for doctoral programs in psychology for the purpose of licensure of psychologists after the doctoral degree.

The Association of State and Provincial Psychology Boards (ASPPB) was founded in 1961 as the American Association of State Psychology Boards. In addition to its work with the National Register and with other accrediting and credentialing organizations, the ASPPB developed the national examination in professional psychology (Carlson, 1978). It worked over the remainder of the twentieth century on licensure reciprocity between the states, continuing-education standards, and other professional issues. The ASPPB adopted the APPIC internship criteria as the basic standard for determining whether an applicant for licensure met the requirement for a predoctoral internship.

Interdisciplinary Organizations

Psychology was an important part of many interdisciplinary organizations that formed over the course of the twentieth century. As of this writing, there were far too many such organizations to even list them all. We provide a short list, emphasizing their variety, and then provide a brief account of two interdisciplinary organizations.

The American Orthopsychiatric Association was formed in 1924 for mental health professionals, primarily psychiatrists and psychologists, who were chiefly concerned with problems of delinquency and other behavior disorders of childhood and adolescence (Lowrey, 1948).

In 1957, the Human Factors Society of America was formed by and for scientists and technologists working on problems of human–machine interaction. Disciplines or professions represented in the society include psychologists, engineers, physicians, and physiologists. The name of the group was changed to the Human Factors and Ergonomics Society in 1992. Membership at the end of the twentieth century was approximately 5,200.

The Cognitive Science Society was established in 1979 to promote interdisciplinary work in cognition. Its members include psychologists, linguists, computer scientists, educators, and philosophers. The Society of Behavioral Medicine was founded in 1978 for professionals and scientists from psychology, medicine, public health, and nursing. The focus of the society is on the relationships among behavior, health, and illness.

In the 1920s, interest grew in developing a science of child development. Both the Commonwealth Fund and the Laura Spelman Rockefeller Foundation gave large grants to start or sustain child development institutes (Lomax, 1977). In 1925, the National Academy of Sciences formed a Committee in Child Development. In 1927, the committee published the first compendium of research in child development, *Child Development Abstracts and Bibliography*. In 1933, the Society for Research in Child Development (SRCD) was organized and the Committee on Child Development was disbanded. After a period of growth in the 1930s, the SRCD experienced a decrease in members and activities in the 1940s, followed by an expansion in numbers and activities that continued to the end of the century.

In 2000, membership in the society exceeded 5,000 and comprised scientists and professionals from many disciplines, including psychology. The society's publishing program at the beginning of the twenty-first century included three journals: *Child Development, Child Development Abstracts and Bibliography,* and *Monographs of the Society for Research in Child Development.* Other society publications were *The Social Policy Report,* a newsletter, and a membership directory.

The society became active in the formulation of social policy applications based upon child development research. To this end, the society established a Government Fellows Program in Child Development in 1978. The fellows worked to keep the relevant federal agencies informed of child research and to facilitate the development of social policy based upon scientific research (Hagen, 2000).

The World Federation for Mental Health (WFMH) was organized in 1948. Its predecessor was the International Committee for Mental Hygiene, an organization founded in 1919 by Clifford Beers (Dain, 1980). Beers had been an asylum patient as a young man and upon his discharge wrote an exposé of the horrors and ineptitude of the asylum system. *A Mind That Found Itself* (1908) was an international best-seller. Beers took advantage of his public visibility and founded the National Committee for Mental Hygiene (NCMH) in 1909. The NCMH worked to reform psychiatric institutions and treatment.

Citizen groups and medical professionals in other countries organized equivalent societies, and Beers was encouraged to start a new international group. He did so in 1919, and the International Committee for Mental Hygiene (ICMH) was formed with broad support from a wide array of mental health professionals and citizen groups. The ICMH held the First International Congress on Mental Hygiene in 1930 in Washington, D.C. The congress had over 3,000 registered attendees, among them all the leading figures in psychiatry, psychology, and social work as well as many prominent political and medical figures. By the advent of the Second International Congress on Mental Hygiene held in France in 1937, enthusiasm and support had waned. The congress was much smaller and bedeviled by complaints about the influence of Nazi sympathizers (Dain, 1980). Beers made plans to hold another congress, but World War II prevented its occurrence. Beers died before the end of the war, and the international movement had no effective leader.

After the war, UNESCO and the World Health Organization (WHO) prompted mental health professionals from many countries to convene the Third International Congress on Mental Hygiene in London. The two UN agencies sought to stimulate a new international mental health organization that was less dominated by psychiatry and more inclusive of other human and social sciences (Rees, 1963). A commission was formed and supported by UNESCO and WHO to draw up plans for the new organization. In 1948, the World Federation for Mental Health was founded at the Third International Congress for Mental Hygiene (Brody, 2000).

The federation grew after its inception to include a wide array of individual mental health providers and researchers, users of mental health services, and nongovernment organizations. Membership in the WFMH in the year 2000 stood at 170 national or international organizational members, 170 regional affiliate members, and more than 2,300 individual members. The major work of the federation is to promote mental health worldwide through a wide array of educational and advocacy efforts. To that end, it holds regional conferences, a biennial congress, and publishes a newsletter. The federation is an approved mental health consultant to every major UN agency.

CONCLUSION

Scientific and professional psychological societies and associations proliferated over the course of the twentieth century. Organizations such as those discussed in this chapter played several important roles in the development of both the science and profession of psychology. Over the course of the nineteenth and twentieth centuries, scientific knowledge came to form the basis for social and professional authority. Scientific and professional organizations shared in and enhanced this authority by providing a communal voice for the claims of their science or profession. This, in turn, led to increased credibility for claims to expert knowledge or practice (Appel, 1988; Hardcastle, 2000; Sokal, 1992). Scientists have recognized this for several centuries, as witnessed by the creation of scientific societies as each new realm of knowledge was discovered and professionalized (Frangsmyr, 1989; Shapin, 1996; Starr, 1982).

Scientific and professional organizations also exercise a certain measure of control over what counts as scientific knowledge or professional expertise (Pickren, 1995). This control allows them to exert authority over what qualifies an individual to participate in the knowledge-production or professional practice process. In this way, scientific and professional societies act as gatekeepers of social and professional authority.

The society or professional organization serves to set off areas of inquiry or practice that belong to that science or practice and thus demarcate the boundaries of knowledge and practice (Abbott, 1988). These boundary lines allow for the definition of problems and the delineation of methods that are appropriate for the science or profession. In this way, they facilitate the formation of professional identity (Gieryn, 1983, 1999).

The provision of professional identity is another important role played by organizations. A woman who belongs to the Cognitive Science Society, for example, has as part of her sense of professional self the identity of cognitive scientist that such membership provides. A national psychological society that belongs to the IUPsyS shares in the identity of international science that the larger organization provides. Often, there is a sense of exclusivity provided as part of this identity. For example, only one national organization per country can belong to the IUPsyS, and only 50 psychologists at a time could belong to Titchener's Experimentalists.

There is often overlap in the knowledge claims and realms of practice among different sciences and professions. These scientific and professional borderlands have often led to fierce rivalry, but they also have led to the creation of interdisciplinary organizations (Pickren, 1995). Such interdisciplinary societies are more likely to form where there are problems that are perceived as falling within the purview of more than one science or profession. The creation of the American Orthopsychiatric Association is one professional example, and the Society for Research in Child Development is another.

At the end of the twentieth century, a new pattern of scientific and professional organizations had emerged. Increasing specialization of knowledge led to the rapid growth of many specialty societies. For an example, the reader is encouraged to visit the World Wide Web site of the Federation of Psychological, Behavioral, and Cognitive Societies (www.thefederationonline.org). The federation comprises 19 different societies ranging in size from the very large APA to the very small Society of Judgement and Decision-Making. As these specialty societies proliferate, many psychologists have chosen to belong to only their specialty group rather than to a larger association such as the APA or American Psychological Society that represents a broader, more inclusive view of psychology as both science and profession. A potential problem with this increased specialization is the further fractionation of organized psychology (Fowler, 1992). It is possible that such fractionation will weaken the authority of psychology and psychologists in the larger society. But, that, perhaps, will be the subject for some future history of professional organizations.

REFERENCES

Abbott, A. (1988). *The system of professions, an essay on the division of expert labor.* Chicago: University of Chicago Press.

American Psychological Association, Task Force on the Status of Women in Psychology. (1973). *Report of the Task Force on the Status of Women in Psychology.* Washington, DC: Author.

Appel, T. (1988). Organizing biology: The American Society of Naturalists and its affiliated societies. In R. Rainger, K. R. Benson, & J. Maienschein (Eds.), *The American development of biology* (pp. 87–120). New Brunswick, NJ: Rutgers University Press.

Benjamin, L. T., Jr. (1977). The psychological round table. *American Psychologist, 32,* 542–549.

Benjamin, L. T., Jr. (1997a). Organized industrial psychology before Division 14: The ACP and the AAAP. *Journal of Applied Psychology, 82,* 459–466.

Benjamin, L. T., Jr. (1997b). The origin of psychological species: History of the beginnings of American Psychological Association divisions. *American Psychologist, 52,* 725–732.

Bent, R. J., Packard, R. E., & Goldberg, R. W. (1999). The American Board of Professional Psychology, 1947–1997: A historical perspective. *Professional Psychology: Research and Practice, 30,* 65–73.

Bernal, M. (1994). Hispanics in psychology. *Focus, 8,* 9–10.

Blascovich, J. (2000). Society of Experimental Social Psychology. In A. E. Kazdin (Ed.), *Encyclopedia of psychology* (Vol. 7, pp. 380–381). Washington, DC: American Psychological Association.

Boring, E. G. (1951). The woman problem. *American Psychologist, 6,* 679–682.

Boring, E. G. (1967). Titchener's experimentalists. *Journal of the History of the Behavioral Sciences, 3,* 315–325.

Brody, E. B. (2000). World Federation for Mental Health. In A. E. Kazdin (Ed.), *Encyclopedia of psychology* (Vol. 8, pp. 284–285). Washington, DC: American Psychological Association.

Bunn, G. (2000). A short history of the British Psychological Society. http://www.bps.org.uk/about/history.cfm

Capshew, J. H. (1999). *Psychologists on the march: Science, practice, and professional identity, 1929–1969.* New York: Cambridge University Press.

Capshew, J. H., & Hilgard, E. R. (1992). The power of service: World War II and professional reform in the American Psychological Association. In R. B. Evans, V. S. Sexton, & T. C. Cadwallader (Eds.), *The American Psychological Association: A historical perspective* (pp. 149–175). Washington, DC: American Psychological Association.

Capshew, J. H., & Laszlo, A. C. (1986). We would not take no for an answer: Women psychologists and gender politics during World War II. *Journal of Social Issues, 42,* 157–180.

Carlson, H. S. (1978). The AASPB story: The beginnings and first 16 years of the American Association of State Psychology Boards, 1961–1977. *American Psychologist, 33,* 486–495.

Carrington, E. M. (1952). History and purposes of the International Council of Women Psychologists. *American Psychologist, 7,* 100–101.

Crawford, M. P. (1992). Rapid growth and change at the American Psychological Association: 1945–1970. In R. B. Evans, V. S. Sexton, & T. C. Cadwallader (Eds.), *The American Psychological Association: A historical perspective* (pp. 177–232). Washington, DC: American Psychological Association.

Dain, N. (1980). *Clifford W. Beers: Advocate for the insane.* Pittsburgh, PA: University of Pittsburgh Press.

Davis, J. M. (2000). International Council of Psychologists. In A. E. Kazdin (Ed.), *Encyclopedia of psychology* (Vol. 4, pp. 341–343). Washington, DC: American Psychological Association.

Dewsbury, D. A. (1996). History of the Psychonomic Society II: The journal publishing program. *Psychonomic Bulletin and Review, 3,* 322–338.

Dewsbury, D. A. (1997). On the evolution of divisions. *American Psychologist, 52,* 733–741.

Dewsbury, D. A., & Bolles, R. C. (1995). The founding of the Psychonomic Society. *Psychonomic Bulletin and Review, 2,* 216–233.

Dumont, K., & Louw, J. (2001). The International Union of Psychological Science and the politics of membership: Psychological associations in South Africa and the German Democratic Republic. *History of Psychology, 4,* 388–404.

Dzinas, K. (2000). Founding the Canadian Psychological Association: The perils of historiography. *Canadian Psychology, 41,* 205–212.

Fagan, T. K. (1996). A history of Division 16 (School Psychology): Running twice as fast. In D. A. Dewsbury (Ed.), *Unification through division: Histories of the divisions of the American Psychological Association* (Vol. 1, pp. 101–135). Washington, DC: American Psychological Association.

Fagan, T. K., Gorin, S., & Tharinger, D. (2000). The National Association of School Psychologists and the Division of School Psychology–APA: Now and beyond. *School Psychology Review, 29,* 525–535.

Fagan, T. K., Hensley, L. T., & Delugach, F. J. (1986). The evolution of organizations for school psychologists in the United States. *School Psychology Review, 15,* 127–135.

Ferdman, B. M. (2000). The Interamerican Society of Psychology. In A. E. Kazdin (Ed.), *Encyclopedia of psychology* (Vol. 4, pp. 324–326). Washington, DC: American Psychological Association.

Fernberger, S. W. (1932). The American Psychological Association: A historical summary, 1892–1930. *Psychological Bulletin, 29,* 1–89.

Finch, F. H., & Odoroff, M. E. (1939). Employment trends in applied psychology. *Journal of Consulting Psychology, 3,* 118–122.

Finch, F. H., & Odoroff, M. E. (1941). Employment trends in applied psychology, II. *Journal of Consulting Psychology, 5,* 275–278.

Finison, L. J. (1986). The psychological insurgency, 1936–1945. *Journal of Social Issues, 42,* 21–33.

Fowler, R. D. (1992). The American Psychological Association: 1985–1992. In R. B. Evans, V. S. Sexton, & T. C. Cadwallader (Eds.), *The American Psychological Association: A historical perspective* (pp. 263–299). Washington, DC: American Psychological Association.

Fox, R. E. (1990). The history of the APIC selection process: A personal prequel. *APIC Newsletter, 15,* 27–28.

Frangsmyr, T. (1989). *Solomon's house revisited: The organization and institutionalization of science.* Canton, MA: Science History.

French, J. L. (1984). On the conception, birth, and early development of school psychology: With special reference to Pennsylvania. *American Psychologist, 39,* 976–987.

Fulero, S. M. (1999). A history of Division 41 (American Psychology–Law Society). In D. A. Dewsbury (Ed.), *Unification through division: Histories of the divisions of the American Psychological Association* (Vol. 4, pp. 109–124). Washington, DC: American Psychological Association.

Gielen, U. P., Adler, L. L., & Milgram, N. A. (Eds.). (1992). *Psychology in international perspective: 50 years of the International Council of Psychologists.* Lisse, The Netherlands: Swets & Zeitlinger.

Gieryn, T. F. (1983). Boundary-work and the demarcation of science from non-science: Strains and interests in professional ideologies of scientists. *American Sociological Review, 48,* 781–795.

Gieryn, T. F. (1999). *Cultural boundaries of science: Credibility on the line.* Chicago: University of Chicago Press.

Goodwin, C. J. (1985). On the origins of Titchener's experimentalists. *Journal of the History of the Behavioral Sciences, 21,* 383–389.

Grisso, T. (1991). A developmental history of the American Psychology–Law Society. *Law and Human Behavior, 15,* 213–231.

Gundlach, H. U. K. (1997). Psychological associations and societies. In W. G. Bringmann, H. E. Luck, R. Miller, & C. E. Early (Eds.), *A pictorial history of psychology* (pp. 536–540). Chicago: Quintessence Books.

Gundlach, H. U. K. (1998). An outline of the history of the IAAP and its first thirteen congresses. In H. Gundlach (Ed.), *Applied psychology. Vol. 1: The first congress Geneva 1920* (pp. 1–24). London: Routledge.

Guthrie, R. V. (1998). *Even the rat was white: A historical view of psychology.* Boston: Allyn & Bacon.

Hagen, J. W. (2000). Society for Research in Child Development. In A. E. Kazdin (Ed.), *Encyclopedia of psychology* (Vol. 7, pp. 377–379). Washington, DC: American Psychological Association.

Hardcastle, G. (2000). The cult of experiment: The psychological round table, 1936–1941. *History of Psychology, 3,* 344–370.

Hollander, E. P. (1968). The society of experimental social psychology: An historical note. *Journal of Personality and Social Psychology, 9,* 280–282.

Hurvich, L. M. (2000). Society of Experimental Psychologists. In A. E. Kazdin (Ed.), *Encyclopedia of psychology* (Vol. 7, pp. 379–380). Washington, DC: American Psychological Association.

Jackson, J. P., Jr. (2000). The triumph of the segregationists? A historiographical inquiry into psychology and the *Brown* litigation. *History of Psychology, 3,* 239–261.

Kimmel, P. R. (1997). A history of Division 9 (Society for the Psychological Study of Social Issues). In D. A. Dewsbury (Ed.), *Unification through division: Histories of the divisions of the American Psychological Association* (Vol. 2, pp. 9–53). Washington, DC: American Psychological Association.

Kaslow, F. W. (1989). Early history of the American Board of Forensic Psychology: A retrospective account. *Forensic Reports, 2,* 305–311.

Kohler, R. (1982). *From medical chemistry to biochemistry: The making of a biomedical discipline.* New York: Cambridge University Press.

Kohout, J. (2001). Who's earning those psychology degrees? *Monitor on Psychology, 32,* 42.

Laughlin, P. R., & Worley, J. L. (1991). Roles of the American Psychological Association and the Veterans Administration in the development of internships in psychology. *American Psychologist, 46,* 430–436.

Leong, F. (1995). History of Asian American psychology. *AAPA Monograph, 1,* 1–54.

Lomax, E. (1977). The Laura Spelman Rockefeller Memorial: Some of its contributions to early research in child development. *Journal of the History of the Behavioral Sciences, 13,* 283–293.

Lowrey, L. G. (1948). *Orthopsychiatry, 1923–1948: Retrospect and prospect.* Menasha, WI: American Orthopsychiatric Association.

Lunt, I. (1996). The history and organization of the European Federation of Professional Psychologists' Associations (EFPPA). *European Psychologist, 1,* 60–64.

Lunt, I. (2000). The European Federation of Professional Psychological Associations. In *Encyclopedia of psychology* (Vol. 3, pp. 274–276). Washington, DC: American Psychological Association.

Mednick, M. T., & Urbanski, L. L. (1991). The origins and activities of APA's division of the Psychology of Women. *Psychology of Women Quarterly, 15,* 651–663.

Napoli, D. S. (1981). *Architects of adjustment: The history of the psychological profession in the United States.* Port Washington, NY: Kennikat Press.

O'Donnell, J. M. (1979). The crisis of experimentalism in the 1920s: E. G. Boring and his uses of history. *American Psychologist, 34,* 289–295.

O'Donnell, J. M. (1985). *The origins of behaviorism: American psychology, 1870–1920.* New York: New York University Press.

Phillips, L. (2000). Recontextualizing Kenneth B. Clark: An Afrocentric perspective on the paradoxical legacy of a model psychologist-activist. *History of Psychology, 3,* 142–167.

Pickren, W. E. (1995). *Psychologists and physicians in the borderlands of science, 1900–1942.* Ann Arbor: University of Michigan.

Pickren, W. E., & Dewsbury, D. A. (2002). Psychology between the World Wars. In W. E. Pickren & D. A. Dewsbury (Eds.), *Evolving perspectives on the history of psychology* (pp. 349–352). Washington, DC: American Psychological Association.

Raimy, V. C. (1950). *Training in clinical psychology.* New York: Prentice-Hall.

Rees, J. R. (1963). World mental health. In A. Deutsch (Ed.), *The encyclopedia of mental health* (Vol. 6, pp. 2049–2062). New York: Franklin Watts.

Rosenzweig, M. R., Holtzman, W. H., Sabourin, M., & Belanger, D. (2000). *History of the International Union of Psychological Science (IUPsyS).* East Essex, England: Psychology Press.

Routh, D. K. (1994). *Clinical psychology since 1917: Science, practice, and organization.* New York: Plenum Press.

Russo, N. F., & Dumont, A. (1997). A history of Division 35 (Psychology of Women): Origins, issues, activities, future. In D. A. Dewsbury (Ed.), *Unification through division: Histories of the divisions of the American Psychological Association* (Vol. 2, pp. 211–238). Washington, DC: American Psychological Association.

Samelson, F. (1977). World War I intelligence testing and the development of psychology. *Journal of the History of the Behavioral Sciences, 13,* 274–282.

Samelson, F. (1992). The APA between the World Wars: 1918–1941. In R. B. Evans, V. S. Sexton, & T. C. Cadwallader (Eds.), *The American Psychological Association: A historical perspective* (pp. 119–147). Washington, DC: American Psychological Association.

Schwesinger, G. (1943). The National Council of Women Psychologists. *Journal of Consulting Psychology, 7,* 298–301.

Shapin, S. (1996). *The scientific revolution.* Chicago: University of Chicago Press.

Sheridan, E. P., Matarazzo, J. D., & Nelson, P. D. (1995). Accreditation of psychology's graduate professional education and training programs: An historical perspective. *Professional Psychology—Research & Practice, 26,* 386–392.

Silverman, D. L. (1989). *Art noveau in fin-de-siecle France: Politics, psychology, and style.* Berkeley: University of California Press.

Smith, R. (1997). *The human sciences.* New York: Norton.

Sokal, M. M. (1981). The origins of the Psychological Corporation. *Journal of the History of the Behavioral Sciences, 17,* 54–67.

Sokal, M. M. (1992). Origins and early years of the American Psychological Association: 1890–1906. In R. B. Evans, V. S. Sexton, & T. C. Cadwallader (Eds.), *The American Psychological Association: A historical perspective* (pp. 43–71). Washington, DC: American Psychological Association.

Stagner, R. (1986). Reminiscences about the founding of SPSSI. *Journal of Social Issues, 42,* 35–42.

Starr, P. (1982). *The social transformation of American medicine.* New York: Basic Books.

Stevens, G., & Gardner, S. (1982). *The women of psychology: Pioneers and innovators, Vol. 1.* Cambridge, MA: Schenkman.

Tiefer, L. (1991). A brief history of the Association for Women in Psychology. *Psychology of Women Quarterly, 15,* 635–649.

Trimble, J. E. (2000). American Indian psychology. In A. E. Kazdin (Ed.), *Encyclopedia of psychology* (Vol. 1, pp. 139–144). Washington, DC: American Psychological Association.

Trommsdorf, G., & Sprung, L. (2000). Germany. In A. E. Kazdin (Ed.), *Encyclopedia of psychology* (Vol. 3, pp. 474–481). Washington, DC: American Psychological Association.

VandenBos, G. R. (1989). Loosely organized "organized psychology." *American Psychologist, 44,* 979–986.

van Drunen, P. (1997). Psychotechnics. In W. G. Bringmann, H. E. Luck, R. Miller, & C. E. Early (Eds.), *A pictorial history of psychology* (pp. 480–484). Chicago: Quintessence Books.

Veysey, L. R. (1965). *The emergence of the American university.* Chicago: University of Chicago Press.

Walsh, M. (1985). Academic professional women organizing for change: The struggle in psychology. *Journal of Social Issues, 41,* 17–28.

Wiebe, R. H. (1967). *The search for order, 1877–1920.* New York: Hill and Wang.

Williams, B. H. (1997). Coming together: The founding of the Association of Black Psychologists. *Dissertation Abstracts International* (UMI Number: 9822882). Ann Arbor: University of Michigan.

Williams, R. (1974). A history of the Association of Black Psychologists: Early formation and development. *Journal of Black Psychology, 1,* 9–24.

Wilpert, B. (2000). International Association of Applied Psychology. In A. E. Kazdin (Ed.), *Encyclopedia of psychology* (Vol. 4, pp. 336–337). Washington, DC: American Psychological Association.

Wispe, L., Awkard, J., Hoffman, M., Ash, P., Hicks, L. H., & Porter, J. (1969). The Negro psychologist in America. *American Psychologist, 24,* 142–150.

Author Index

Abbott, A., 71, 551
Aberle, S. D., 75, 81
Abrams, D. M., 287, 298, 462
Abramson, L. Y., 351, 353
Ackerknecht, E. H., 305, 333
Ackerman, M. C., 283, 292, 297
Ackerman, M. J., 283, 292, 297
Ackernecht, E. H., 49, 62
Acord, J., 5, 21
Adams, G., 230, 242
Adams, H. E., 292, 298, 299
Adams, W., 282, 299
Adelman, J., 63, 258, 264
Ader, D. N., 264, 454, 455, 456
Adler, H. E., 3, 20, 63, 158, 178, 187, 200, 343, 348, 531, 537, 552
Adorno, T. W., 233, 242
Adrian, E. D., 50, 62, 97
Agronick, G., 251, 267
Ahmed, R. A., 510, 531
Aiman-Smith, L., 377, 385
Ajamu, A., 493, 506
Akbar, N., 484, 505
Akiskal, H. S., 352, 353
Albee, G., 39, 441, 444, 446, 483, 486, 487, 494, 505
Albright, T. D., 62
Alexander, F., 340, 344, 353, 453, 454, 461
Alexander, I. E., 193, 196
Alexander, P., 276
Allen, L., 448
Allen, M., 479
Allport, F. H., 8, 23, 181, 184, 188, 196, 201, 228, 229, 233, 235, 237, 240, 242, 243
Allport, G., 13, 20, 177, 178, 179, 181, 184, 185, 187, 188, 189, 190, 191, 192, 193, 194, 195, 196, 197, 198, 199, 200, 201, 202, 203, 224, 230, 242, 252, 264, 490
Allport, M. B., 195, 197
Allyon, T., 331, 334
Almeida, L., 283, 300, 325
Alpers, B. J., 326, 333
Alpert, R., 210, 221
Altman, B. E., 446
Altman, I., 437, 449
Amaral, D. G., 60, 61, 63, 65, 66, 401, 411
Ames, L. B., 85, 88, 89, 210, 219, 252
Amsel, A., 170, 172
Anagnostopoulou, T., 461
Anastasi, A., 294, 298
Andersen, P., 61, 65
Anderson, H. H., 208, 217

Anderson, J. R., 146, 148, 152
Anderson, J. W., 187, 197
Anderson, L. S., 444
Anderson, N. B., 455, 461
Angeletti, P. W., 163, 174
Angell, J. R., 10, 11, 12, 13, 15, 16, 20, 67, 70, 71, 80, 81, 382, 385, 509, 531
Angell, R. C., 190, 199
Angier, R. P., 167, 168, 172
Apfelbaum, E., 230, 238, 241, 242, 263, 265
Appel, T., 535, 540, 551
Appelbaum, P., 403, 407, 408, 409, 411
Appleby, D. C., 479
Archer, R., 282, 286, 298, 300
Ardilla, R., 516, 531
Arnold, M. B., 24, 31, 158, 161, 165, 172, 174, 175, 208, 334, 344, 392, 411, 417
Aronson, L. R., 72, 76, 81, 173, 237, 242, 244
Arvey, R. D., 380, 385
Asbell, B., 433, 444
Asch, S. E., 17, 20, 232, 233, 234, 238, 242
Ash, M., 119, 131, 232, 233, 242, 467, 478
Ash, P., 508, 554
Asher, S. R., 212, 217
Asken, M. J., 459, 462
Aslin, R. N., 214, 217
Astin, H. S., 260, 261, 480
Atkinson, J. W., 132, 195, 197, 252, 267, 287, 298, 300
Atkinson, R. C., 126, 127, 131
Atthowe, J. M., 328, 334
Attneave, F., 20, 490, 546
Atwood, G. E., 193, 202
Au, T. K., 146, 152, 477
Aubrey, J., 311, 334
Austin, J. T., 54, 64, 75, 198, 243, 267, 300, 367, 371, 372, 373, 374, 375, 376, 377, 378, 379, 381, 382, 383, 384, 385, 387, 438, 441
Averill, J. R., 164, 171, 172, 174
Awkard, J., 508, 554
Ax, A. F., 163, 173
Ayllon, T., 350, 353
Azrin, N. H., 350, 353
Azuma, H., 511, 531

Baban, A., 459, 461
Back, K. W., 234, 237, 242, 250
Baer, D. M., 211, 218
Baillargeon, R. L., 146, 152
Bain, A., 85, 108, 158, 173
Bain, R., 182, 197

Baistow, K., 238, 242
Bakeman, R., 216, 217
Baker, D. B., 28, 36, 43, 258, 259, 260, 261, 262, 263, 346, 353, 357, 364,
        483, 492, 493, 505
Baker, R. W., 290, 301
Baker, S., 479
Balance, W. D. G., 4, 21
Balch, P., 440, 448
Baldwin, A. L., 193, 197
Baldwin, B. A., 99, 108
Baldwin, J. M., 12, 16, 20, 80, 81, 100, 206, 207, 209, 209, 217, 223, 225,
        226, 227, 242, 512, 519
Baldwin, M., 399, 408
Bales, R. F., 234, 242
Ball, S., 272, 276, 349
Balster, R. L., 45
Baltes, P. B., 137, 215, 217, 220
Bamberg, M., 6, 23
Bandomir, C. A., 6, 24
Bandura, A., 211, 212, 217, 219, 351, 353
Banyard, V. B., 439, 443, 447
Bard, P., 50, 57, 63, 64
Barden, R. C., 402, 409
Bardos, A. N., 288, 300
Barenbaum, N. B., 177, 179, 180, 181, 185, 186, 187, 189, 190, 194, 197,
        203, 229, 242, 337
Baritz, L., 367, 373, 375, 377, 378, 384, 385
Barker, L. F., 49, 63
Barker, R., 437, 438, 444
Barkley, R. A., 352, 353
Barlow, D. H., 351, 353
Barlow, W., 233, 242
Barnard, C. I., 33, 479
Barnhardt, T. M., 214, 220
Barrera, M., 442, 444
Barrett, K. C., 212, 218
Barrett, R. S., 308, 385
Barrios-Santos, M., 498, 505
Bartol, A. M., 391, 392, 394, 395, 396, 397, 408
Bartol, C. R., 391, 392, 394, 395, 396, 397, 408
Bartram, D., 283, 300
Bates, J. E., 214, 221, 252
Battie, W., 314, 315, 334
Bauman, Z., 225, 242
Baumrind, D., 214, 217
Bavelas, A., 233, 234, 242
Bavelas, J. B., 167, 173
Bayer, B. M., 180, 200, 223, 231, 234, 235, 236, 239, 240, 241, 242, 337
Bayless, S., 399, 409
Bayley, N., 208, 218
Bazerman, C., 5, 9, 21
Beach, F. A., 57, 58, 63, 72, 73, 75, 76, 77, 79, 80, 81, 195, 488, 506
Beard, G. M., 329, 334
Beauchamp, G. K., 78, 81, 179, 198, 325
Beck, B. B., 81, 344
Becker, D., 257, 265
Becker, H. P., 181, 197
Beckman, J., 275, 277
Beebe-Center, J. G., 157, 173
Beer, C. G., 77, 81

Beers, C., 32, 182, 197, 342, 353, 440, 444, 550
Beers, S. E., 479
Beilin, H., 146, 152, 154
Beins, B. C., 474, 478
Beitel, A., 217, 218
Békésy, G. V., 52, 53, 63
Belanger, D., 536, 553
Belar, C. D., 41, 45, 451, 458, 459, 461, 462, 463
Bellack, A. S., 44, 292, 298, 354
Bellak, L., 287, 298
Belle, D., 255, 265
Belmont, J. M., 148, 152, 388, 411, 445
Belsky, J., 216, 218
Belter, R. W., 297, 301
Bem, S. L., 235, 253, 254, 265
Ben-David, J., 2, 4, 21
Bender, D. B., 98, 108
Bender, L., 279, 292, 298
Benedek, E., 400, 411
Benjamin, L. T., Jr., 5, 8, 21, 27, 28, 29, 35, 36, 43, 44, 181, 183, 197, 324,
        346, 353, 358, 360, 361, 362, 364, 372, 373, 383, 385, 471, 474,
        478, 493, 505, 509, 541, 542, 544, 543, 545, 551
Benjamin, R. M., 64
Bennett, C. C., 64, 431, 435, 436, 437, 443, 444
Bennett, E. M., 437, 448
Ben-Porath, Y. S., 298
Bent, R. J., 28, 93, 183, 286, 549, 551
Bentley, I. M., 70, 82, 84
Bentley, M., 9, 21, 159, 173
Benton, A. L., 329, 330, 334
Berdie, R., 371, 386
Berg, C. A., 137, 155
Berg, I., 37, 43
Berger, H., 50, 63
Berkeley, G., 91, 92, 108, 115, 116, 117, 132
Berkun, M. M., 328, 334, 335
Berliner, D. C., 269, 270, 271, 274, 276, 277
Berlyne, D. E., 511, 531
Berman, J. S., 51, 65, 260, 265
Bernal, M., 500, 547, 551
Bernard, L. L., 181, 184, 197, 230, 242
Berne, E., 332, 334
Bernfeld, S., 95, 108
Bernreuter, R. G., 189, 197, 284, 298, 344
Bernstein, M., 136, 156, 251, 265
Berry, D. T. R., 286, 299, 301
Berry, J. W., 137, 150, 152, 511, 531
Berscheid, E., 172, 173
Bersoff, D. N., 394, 396, 399, 403, 405, 406, 408, 410
Bertaux, D., 179, 197
Best, D., 479
Best, L., 7, 25
Bigelow, J., 125, 132
Bijou, S. W., 211, 218, 350, 353
Bills, A. G., 189, 197, 373, 385
Bills, M. A., 373, 385
Binet, A., 13, 31, 100, 135, 137, 138, 139, 140, 144, 152, 156, 206, 207,
        208, 218, 221, 279, 280, 281, 282, 284, 288, 298, 301, 321, 338,
        342, 352, 353, 396, 408, 417, 418, 419, 422, 520
Bingham, R. P., 477, 480, 500

Bingham, W. B., 378, 385
Bini, L., 326, 334
Birdsall, T. G., 105, 108
Birman, D., 439, 449
Bitterman, M. E., 75, 80, 81
Bjorklund, D. F., 214, 218
Black, A., 167, 173
Black, J. E., 214, 219
Blais, D. J., 229, 247
Blanch, E., 480, 506
Blascovich, J., 543, 551
Blau, T. H., 494, 505
Bliss, T. V. P., 54, 63
Blocher, D. H., 360, 361, 362, 363, 364
Block, J., 16, 187, 197, 489
Bloom, B. L., 438, 446
Bloom, C., 258, 265
Bloomfield, D., 70, 84
Blum, M. L., 368, 385
Blumenthal, A., 4, 5, 6, 21, 456
Boakes, R., 7, 16, 17, 21, 67, 81
Bobbit, B., 154
Boccaccini, M. T., 283, 298
Bograd, M., 254, 268
Bohan, J. S., 254, 265, 267
Bolanger, D., 510, 532
Boll, T. J., 292, 298
Bolles, R. C., 543, 552
Bonduelle, M., 340, 353
Boneau, C. A., 388, 474, 478
Bonnie, R., 264, 410
Borden, V. M. H., 476, 478
Borgen, F. H., 295, 299
Boring, E. G., 3, 4, 7, 13, 18, 20, 21, 33, 43, 47, 48, 52, 63, 70, 81, 107,
    136, 149, 151, 152, 178, 185, 188, 197, 199, 201, 203, 245, 280,
    284, 298, 497, 537, 542, 551, 553
Borkman, T. J., 442, 444
Borkovec, T. D., 164, 173
Borkowski, J. G., 148, 152
Bornstein, M. H., 215, 218
Bornstein, R. F., 286, 299, 301
Borum, R., 283, 298
Bose, J., 423, 428
Boski, P., 230, 231, 246
Bouillaud, J., 49, 50, 63
Bowers, T. G. R., 22, 146, 152, 404, 408
Bowlby, J., 212, 218
Boyer, E. L., 466, 477, 478
Boykin, A. W., 495, 505
Boyse, E. A., 78, 81
Boysen, S. T., 80, 83
Bradbury, H., 443, 448
Bradfield, A., 215, 220
Bradford, G., 10, 13, 70, 82, 100, 132, 180, 197, 453
Bradley, P., 285, 299, 462
Brainerd, C. J., 146, 152, 153
Brakke, K. E., 83
Bramel, D., 230, 242
Brand, C., 141, 152
Brandt, L. W., 516, 531

Brassard, J. A., 212, 218
Bray, C. W., 52, 66
Bray, D. W., 191, 198, 379, 387
Brazelton, T. B., 212, 218
Bredenkamp, J., 511, 532
Bregman, E. D., 141, 156
Bregman, E. O., 378, 385
Breines, W., 233, 242
Bretnall, E. P., 122, 133
Brett, G. S., 158, 173, 307, 334
Breuer, J., 308, 322, 323, 334, 340, 353
Brewer, C. L., 465, 470, 471, 472, 474, 475, 477, 478, 479, 480, 481,
    497, 507
Brewer, J. M., 358, 359, 364
Bridges, J. W., 342, 355
Bridgman, P. W., 18, 21
Briggs, V. M., Jr., 200, 202, 376, 385, 404, 411
Brigham, C. C., 184, 198
Brigham, J. C., 391, 399, 401, 406, 407, 408
Bringmann, N. J., 4, 21
Bringmann, W. G., 4, 6, 21, 23, 553, 554
Brinkley, A., 440, 445
Britt, S. H., 227, 242, 381, 385
Broadbent, D. E., 126, 127, 131
Broca, P., 49, 50, 63, 149, 305, 318
Brodsky, A. M., 258, 265
Brodsky, S., 283, 298, 398, 400, 409
Brody, E. B., 198, 550, 552
Brofenbrenner, U., 438, 445
Brogden, H. E., 55, 379, 385
Bromley, D. B., 179, 198
Bronfenbrenner, U., 212, 213, 218, 438
Bronk, D. W., 479
Brooks-Gunn, J., 216, 218
Broverman, D. M., 256, 265
Broverman, I. K., 256, 265
Brown, A. L., 139, 145, 148, 152
Brown, A. T., 351, 353
Brown, B. B., 214, 221
Brown, D. T., 424, 428
Brown, J. F., 231, 242, 245
Brown, J. S., 56, 63
Brown, J. V., 216, 217
Brown, L. M., 254, 265
Brown, L. S., 258, 265
Brown, R. A., 462
Brown, W. R., 282, 298
Browne, C. G., 282, 300
Brownlee, S., 275, 276
Brubaker, T., 215, 218
Bruce, C., 99, 108
Bruce, D., 15, 21
Brucher-Albers, C., 463
Brunell-Neuleib, S., 286, 299, 301
Bryant, P. E., 146, 152, 154
Buchanan, J., 348, 509, 531
Buck, J. N., 288, 298
Buckhout, R., 406, 409
Buckley, K. W., 16, 21, 228, 243
Bucy, P. C., 57, 64

Budzynski, C. A., 183, 203
Bulmer, M., 182, 184, 198
Bunn, G., 539, 552
Burgess, E. W., 182, 190, 198
Buriel, R., 214, 215, 220
Burman, E., 264, 265
Burnham, J., 14, 21, 179, 180, 181, 185, 198, 374, 378, 385
Burns, R. C., 288, 298
Burt, C., 142, 152
Burt, R., 375, 378, 386
Burton, A., 190, 198, 201
Burton, R., 210, 221, 305, 311, 312, 317, 334
Burtt, H. E., 368, 371, 385, 398, 409
Buss, A. R., 239, 243, 244, 246
Butcher, J. N., 284, 287, 298
Butler, M., 282, 292, 293, 298, 468
Butterfield, E. C., 137, 148, 152
Butters, N., 61, 65
Buxton, C., 7, 21, 470, 472, 473, 478

Cadwallader, T. C., 69, 81, 497, 505, 552, 553, 554
Cahan, E. D., 209, 218
Cahill, L., 60, 63
Cahn, E., 396, 409
Cairns, R., 12, 21, 205, 206, 207, 218
Caldwell-Colbert, A. T., 483, 501, 505
Calfee, R. C., 269, 276, 277
Calhoun, K. S., 292, 298, 299
Califano, J. A., Jr., 455, 462
Calkins, M. W., 6, 7, 11, 21, 22, 467, 468, 469, 472, 477, 478, 500
Call, J., 80, 81
Camara, W. J., 282, 292, 293, 294, 298
Cameron, N., 484, 505
Camfield, T., 8, 21, 183, 198, 227, 228, 243, 374, 385
Campbell, C. B. G., 76, 82
Campbell, D. P., 295, 299
Campbell, J. D., 210, 221
Campbell, J. M., 282, 298
Campbell, J. P., 373, 381, 385
Campbell, M. D., 437, 446
Campbell, R. J., 191, 198
Campbell, R. M., 439, 445
Campbell, S. I., 275, 277
Campbell, V. L., 282, 301
Campione, J. C., 137, 148, 152
Campos, J. J., 212, 213, 218
Candland, D. K., 163, 173, 480, 506
Cannon, W. B., 56, 57, 63, 158, 161, 162, 165, 173, 181, 198, 453, 454, 462
Canter, R. R., 372, 385
Cantor, N., 264, 347, 375, 386
Cantril, H., 186, 189, 198, 232, 237, 243, 514, 531
Caplan, E., 33, 43
Caplan, G., 440, 445
Caplan, M., 436, 449
Caplan, P. J., 251, 265
Caplan, R. B., 440, 445
Capps, D., 185, 198
Capshew, J., 8, 21, 35, 43, 184, 198, 231, 232, 243, 260, 265, 380, 381, 386, 474, 478, 537, 545, 546, 548, 552

Cardon, B. W., 424, 428
Carey, M., 259, 267
Carey, S., 146, 152
Carlson, C., 427, 429
Carlson, H. S., 549, 552
Carlson, L., 192, 203
Carmichael, L., 73, 402, 410, 479
Carnrike, C. L., 449
Carpenter, B. N., 215, 219, 283, 300
Carpenter, C. R., 73, 77, 79, 81
Carpintero, H., 354, 497, 505
Carr, H., 15, 21, 71
Carr, K. F., 476, 479
Carrington, E. M., 537, 552
Carroll, J. B., 135, 137, 143, 147, 153
Carson, J., 234, 243
Carson, M. J., 358, 364
Cartwright, D., 189, 190, 198, 231, 244
Casas, J. M., 501, 505
Cascio, W. F., 377, 379, 382, 384, 386
Cashman, S. D., 374, 379, 386
Caston, A., 382, 388
Castro, M. I., 81
Catania, J., 443, 448
Cattell, A. K., 285, 298
Cattell, H. E., 285, 298
Cattell, J. M., 4, 10, 13, 14, 15, 21, 25, 28, 29, 31, 43, 44, 45, 70, 138, 139, 140, 153, 280, 283, 284, 285, 298, 338, 353, 371, 373, 378, 383, 386, 388, 396, 409, 468, 511, 512, 515, 516, 519, 531
Cattell, R. B., 142, 143, 153, 183, 198, 202, 280, 283, 284, 285, 298
Cauce, A. M., 214, 220, 443, 445
Cautley, P. W., 510, 531
Ceci, S., 151, 153, 407, 409
Celsus, 308, 334
Cerletti, U., 326, 334
Chadbourne, C., 13, 21
Chamberlain, W., 432, 445
Chambers, W., 19, 68, 291, 301, 320
Chambless, D. L., 352, 353
Chance, P., 14, 21
Charles, D. C., 269, 271, 272, 276
Charlesworth, W., 12, 22
Chase, W. G., 148, 153
Chavis, D., 435, 439, 445
Chein, I., 395, 484, 505
Cherlin, D. L., 437, 448
Cherniss, C., 439, 445
Cherry, F., 185, 186, 198
Chesir-Teran, D., 448
Chesler, M., 438, 445, 448
Chesler, P., 256, 265
Chi, M. T. H., 148, 153, 475, 478
Chiarugi, V., 315, 334, 340
Chiesi, H. L., 148, 153
Child, I., 210, 221
Chin, J., 259, 265, 491, 499
Ching, C. C., 510, 511, 531
Chiszar, D. A., 81
Chomsky, N., 125, 131, 432, 445

Christensen, A. L., 173, 293, 298
Christie, R., 404, 409, 411
Church, A. H., 12, 33, 49, 254, 303, 304, 306, 310, 311, 368, 386, 452, 475, 488
Cicchetti, D., 441, 442, 445, 446
Ciminero, A. R., 292, 298, 299
Clance, P. R., 252, 265
Clark, A., 127, 130, 131
Clark, E., 49, 63, 317, 440, 447
Clark, K., 232, 238, 243, 395, 409, 488, 490, 497, 500, 541
Clark, M., 173, 404, 409
Clark, R. A., 252, 267, 287, 300
Clark, S., 310, 311, 334
Clarke, E., 49, 63, 312, 334
Clarke-Stewart, K. A., 205, 210, 215, 216, 218, 352
Clarkson, F. E., 256, 265
Clausen, C., 496, 505
Clay, R. M., 311, 334
Clemence, A. J., 297, 298
Clements, K. C., 78, 82
Clenending, L., 49, 63
Clingempeel, G., 216, 219
Clore, G. L., 166, 174
Clower, R. P., 61, 65, 66
Coates, T. J., 443, 448
Cobb, M. V., 141, 156, 505, 506
Coburn, C. A., 70, 81
Cochran, M. M., 212, 218
Cocks, G., 192, 198
Cocozza, J., 401, 409
Coe, G. A., 183, 198
Cofer, C. N., 478
Cohen, L. D., 37, 43
Cohen, M. S., 376, 377, 386
Cohen, N. J., 60, 63
Cohen, S., 180, 182, 198
Cohler, B. J., 185, 189, 198
Cohn, J. F., 212, 218
Coie, J. D., 215, 218
Colarelli, S. M., 367, 386
Cole, L. W., 69, 81
Cole, M. W., 150, 162, 173
Collier, G., 226, 229, 243, 388
Collins, A., 166, 174
Collins, R., 4, 21
Colman, R., 265, 404, 411
Comas-Diaz, L., 259, 265, 483, 495, 496, 505
Comte, A., 305, 334
Conger, R. D., 215, 218
Conners, C. K., 352, 353
Conrad, K. A., 329, 375, 379, 380, 387
Conradi, E., 69, 81
Constantinople, A., 253, 265, 465
Conway, B. E., 136, 156
Conway, C. G., 485, 506
Cook, M., 351, 354, 409
Cook, S. W., 395, 396
Coon, D. J., 28, 44
Cooney, B. R., 467, 478

Cooper, H., 419, 428
Cooper, S., 444
Corbin, J., 179, 198
Coren, S., 52, 85, 101, 106, 107, 108
Corkin, S., 60, 61, 63, 65
Cormier, C., 407, 410
Cornell, E. H., 10, 15, 70, 146, 153, 327, 376, 414, 468, 470, 471, 472, 473
Corner, G. W., 58, 59, 75, 81, 119
Coronado, N., 443, 445
Cosmides, L., 78, 81
Costa, P. T., Jr., 285, 286, 298
Costantino, G., 287, 298
Costello, A. J., 291, 298
Costello, E. J., 291, 298
Cottrell, L. S., 436, 445
Coulter, W. A., 424, 428
Court, J. H., 143, 155
Courtois, C. A., 259, 265
Cousine, V., 6, 22
Cousins, R. H., 475, 478
Cowan, C. L., 479
Cowan, P. A., 216, 218
Cowen, E. L., 435, 436, 438, 441, 442, 444, 445
Cowles, M., 374, 386
Cox, V. C., 59, 66, 344
Craig, R. J., 290, 298, 405, 409, 410
Craiger, P., 382, 386
Craik, K. H., 178, 180, 189, 190, 192, 198, 203
Crain, R. L., 483, 505
Cramer, P., 287, 298
Crane, L., 347, 353
Craske, M. G., 351, 353
Crawford, M., 73, 249, 252, 255, 265, 266, 337, 540, 552
Creer, T. L., 275, 276
Crider, B., 185, 198
Croce, P. J., 7, 22
Cronbach, L., 13, 22, 144, 147, 152, 153
Crosby, F., 192, 198
Crosby, T. L., 192, 198
Croughan, J. L., 291, 301
Crowley, K., 209, 221
Crutchfield, R. S., 234, 243
Cubberly, E. P., 416, 428
Cullen, W., 313, 315, 334
Cumming, W. W., 14, 22
Cummings, N. A., 36, 37, 44, 45, 347, 355, 387
Cunningham, J., 427, 429
Currie, C., 455, 462
Curtis, M. J., 428
Cutler, B. L., 406, 409
Cutts, N. E., 31, 39, 44, 420, 428
Cylke, V., 9, 25

Dahlstrom, W. G., 284, 298
Dain, N., 440, 445, 550, 552
Dalton, J. H., 431, 432, 440, 445
Daly, M., 78, 82
Damasio, A., 131
Dana, R. H., 281, 298, 431

Daniel, R. S., 30, 41, 75, 76, 236, 306, 393, 410, 467, 468, 469, 475, 478, 479
Danish, S. J., 56, 160, 436, 445, 521, 524
Danziger, K., 4, 5, 10, 12, 22, 179, 180, 182, 183, 184, 185, 191, 194, 198, 229, 231, 234, 243
Darley, J., 236, 243, 361, 371, 386
Darnton, R., 313, 334
Darwin, C., 7, 8, 12, 13, 14, 22, 56, 68, 78, 81, 82, 83, 109, 118, 138, 153, 166, 171, 172, 173, 206, 214, 280, 298, 305, 319, 320, 511, 518
Das, J. P., 6, 22, 26, 63, 137, 149, 153, 154
Dasen, P. R., 152, 511, 531
Dassoff, N., 446
David, H. P., 348, 509, 511, 512, 514, 515, 531, 532
Davidson, E., 28, 44, 358, 364, 449
Davidson, M., 351, 354
Davies, P. W., 50, 51, 64, 65
Davis, A. F., 358, 364
Davis, H., 50, 62, 63
Davis, J. B., 359, 364
Davis, J. M., 537, 552
Davis, M., 55, 61, 63
Davis, R., 285, 300
Davis, S. F., 475, 478, 480, 481
Dawis, R., 375, 386
Dawkins, R., 78, 82
Dawson, P., 427, 429
Day, L. M., 70, 82
DeAngelis, T., 37, 44
Deaux, K., 254, 265
de Beauvoir, S., 238, 243
Defares, P. B., 457, 463
DeFries, J. C., 213, 220
DeGroot, A. D., 148, 153
Dehue, T., 8, 9, 22
del Barrio, V., 338, 354
DeLeon, P. H., 27, 36, 39, 40, 41, 42, 44, 45, 181, 197, 324, 348, 352, 455
Dell, F., 228, 243, 285, 299, 334
DeLoache, J. S., 139, 152
Delugach, F. J., 427, 428, 545, 552
Demarest, J., 76, 82
Demorest, A. P., 193, 198
Denham, S. A., 214, 218
DeNisi, A. S., 371, 380, 386
Denker, R., 324, 334
Denmark, F. L., 264, 476, 478, 480, 506, 509, 531
Dennett, D. D., 115, 131
Denzin, N. K., 195, 198
DeRubeis, R., 337, 354
Descartes, R., 68, 93, 94, 95, 108, 114, 115, 118, 119, 124, 126, 131, 158, 166, 173, 244, 312, 452
Desimone, R., 99, 108
Dessain, E. C., 315, 336
Detterman, D. K., 137, 152, 155, 156
Deutsch, A., 360, 364
Deutsch, M., 227, 232, 233, 243
De Valois, R. L., 51, 63
Dewey, E., 276
Dewey, J., 225, 226, 228, 243, 271, 276
Dewey, R., 181, 198

Dewsbury, D. A., 14, 16, 19, 22, 67, 69, 70, 71, 72, 74, 75, 76, 77, 78, 80, 81, 82, 83, 84, 353, 354, 355, 364, 385, 428, 447, 541, 543, 544, 548, 552, 553
Diamond, A., 26, 56, 214, 218, 410
Diaz-Guerrero, R., 516, 531
Dickson, W. J., 378, 388
Dickstein, S., 216, 219
Diehl, L. A., 13, 22
Dierking, D. R., 275, 277
Dies, R. R., 298, 300
Digman, J. M., 286, 298
Dingman, D., 252, 265
DiNicola, V., 495, 505
Dinnerstein, D., 238, 243
Dipboye, R. L., 376, 377, 381, 382, 386
Dodge, R., 12, 22
Doll, E. A., 140, 343, 345, 353
Dollard, J., 182, 190, 198, 210, 219, 230, 243, 479
Donaldson, H. H., 14, 15, 22, 24
Donders, F. C., 3, 4, 101, 146, 153
Donders, J., 282, 298
Donker, F., 463
Donn, J. E., 348, 353
Doob, L. W., 210, 219, 230, 243
Dornbusch, S. M., 214, 221
Dowbiggin, I., 319, 334
Downey, R. G., 371, 382, 386
Draguns, J. R., 516, 531
Dreyfus, H., 129, 131, 132
Dreyfus, S., 129, 131, 132
Düffler, J., 320, 334
Duffy, E., 189, 198
Duffy, K. G., 437, 445
Dumont, A., 548, 553
Dumont, K., 439, 447, 539, 540, 548, 552
Dunbar, H., 453, 454, 462
Duncan, C. P., 55, 63
Dunham, P. J., 467, 478
Dunlap, K., 160, 161, 173, 225, 228, 243
Dunn, J., 212, 219, 282, 300
Dunn, L. M., 415, 428
Dunnette, M. D., 368, 369, 373, 375, 379, 383, 384, 386, 388
Durkin, M., 5, 21
d'Ydewalle, G., 510, 516, 532
Dzinas, K., 540, 541, 552

Eagly, A. H., 235, 243, 253, 266
Earles, J., 44
Ebbinghaus, H., 6, 8, 9, 19, 22, 23, 24, 99, 116, 118, 122, 131, 132, 288, 298, 539
Ebert Flattau, P., 479
Eccles, J. S., 263, 265
Echemendia, R. J., 501, 506, 507
Eckholdt, H. M., 443, 447
Edelbrock, C. S., 291, 298
Edelson, M., 485, 505
Edens, J., 410
Edwards, D. L., 438, 445
Edwards, P. N., 234, 235, 243

Edwards, S., 59, 63
Egli, D., 45
Eichenbaum, H., 60, 63
Eisenberg, N., 214, 219, 221
Eisman, E. J., 296, 297, 298, 300
Ekman, P., 166, 167, 173, 212, 219
El-Bassel, N., 443, 446
Elder, G. H., Jr., 208, 213, 215, 216, 218, 219
Elder, T., 328, 334
Elias, M. J., 6, 432, 445
Elkind, D., 146, 153
Ellenberger, H. F., 323, 334
Elliott, R., 189, 198, 199, 409
Ellis, A., 64, 332, 334, 350, 353, 421
Ellis, W. D., 17, 22
Ellison, R., 432, 445, 484, 486, 505
Ellsworth, P. C., 405, 409
Elms, A. C., 178, 192, 199
Elster, J., 157, 173
Emrick, B., 404, 411
Endicott, J., 290, 298, 301
Endler, N. S., 275, 276
Engel, G. L., 454, 456, 462
English, B. H., 12, 22, 418, 428
Enns, C. Z., 477, 478
Epperson, D. L., 362, 364
Epstein, J. N., 352, 353
Erikson, E. H., 188, 192, 199, 200, 345, 349, 353
Erlanger, J., 50, 63
Ernst, R., 47, 93, 95, 97, 103, 180, 199, 320, 328, 475, 478
Eron, L. D., 351, 353
Espín, O. M., 192, 199, 259, 265
Esquirol, J. E. D., 314, 315, 317, 334
Estes, W., 75, 122, 132, 137
Evans, J., 140, 153, 190, 197, 199
Evans, R., 4, 5, 6, 7, 10, 14, 21, 22, 26, 497, 505, 512, 532, 552, 553, 554
Exner, J. E., Jr., 286, 287, 299
Eyde, L. D., 298, 300
Eysenck, H. J., 137, 154, 324, 328, 329, 330, 334, 346, 349, 353, 463

Fabrega, H., 506
Fagan, T. K., 31, 32, 38, 44, 276, 348, 352, 353, 413, 414, 417, 419, 420, 421, 423, 424, 425, 427, 428, 429, 545, 552
Faludi, S., 263, 265
Fancher, R., 4, 9, 22, 180, 181, 199
Fanselow, M. S., 55, 63
Fantz, R., 211, 219
Faris, E., 227, 243
Farley, F., 269, 271, 272, 276, 277
Farling, W. H., 426, 428
Farr, J. L., 367, 370, 373, 386
Farran, D. C., 216, 220
Faulconer, J. E., 485, 505
Fay, J. W., 6, 22, 223, 227, 243
Fearing, F., 16, 22
Feather, N. T., 195, 197, 287, 298
Fechner, G. T., 3, 6, 8, 20, 24, 47, 48, 51, 63, 65, 85, 103, 104, 106, 108
Fell, J. P., 173
Feltovich, P. J., 148, 153

Ferdman, B. M., 538, 552
Ferguson, L. W., 367, 377, 381, 386, 395, 410
Fernald, G. G., 32, 183, 199, 342, 400
Fernberger, S. W., 540, 543, 552
Ferrara, R., 148, 152
Ferrari, J., 479
Ferretti, R., 148, 152
Ferster, C., 19, 22
Feuerstein, M., 291, 299
Feuerstein, R., 145, 153
Field, T. M., 212, 213
Finch, F. H., 371, 372, 386, 544, 552
Fine, M., 254, 256, 257, 265, 267
Finger, S., 48, 49, 50, 63, 91, 362
Finison, L. J., 230, 232, 243, 541, 552
Finkel, N. J., 392, 393, 409
Finn, S. E., 298, 300
Fisher, W., 401, 409
Fitzgerald, L. M., 216, 218
Fitzpatrick, E., 11, 22
Flamer, G. B., 146, 153
Flanagan, J. C., 381, 386
Flavell, J., 20, 22, 139, 146, 153, 211, 214, 215, 219
Fleeson, J., 212, 221
Fleishman, E. A., 467, 469, 480, 509, 515, 516, 532
Flynn, J. P., 59, 63
Foa, E. B., 350, 353
Fogel, A., 217, 219
Folen, R., 44
Folkman, S., 166, 173, 174
Folstein, M. F., 290, 299
Folstein, S. E., 290, 299
Foote, W., 59, 63
Ford, M. P., 146, 153, 180, 199
Fordyce, W. E., 454, 462
Forrest, E., 61, 65
Forrester, J., 179, 181, 199
Forsythe, G. B., 156
Foster, D., 8, 36, 73, 237, 243, 260, 270, 274, 361, 418, 456, 537
Foucault, M., 194, 305, 334
Fowers, B. J., 485, 507
Fowler, F. G., 132
Fowler, H. W., 132
Fowler, R. D., 41, 44, 348, 510, 516, 532, 535, 551, 552
Fox, H. R., 380, 386
Fox, R., 42, 44, 438, 445, 548, 552
Fraisse, P., 159, 160, 173
Frangsmyr, T., 551, 552
Frank, R. G., 41, 44
Frankenhaeuser, M., 164, 165, 173
Frankl, V. E., 332, 334
Franklin, A. J., 52, 313, 375, 495, 505, 553
Franz, C. E., 192, 199, 202, 254, 265
Franz, I. D., 456, 462
Fraser, C., 237, 243
Frederickson, B. L., 265
Freedheim, D. K., 27, 39, 43, 44, 45, 181, 197, 199, 200, 324, 348, 352, 354, 355, 509
Freeman, W., 325, 334

Fremont-Smith, F., 233, 243
French, A. L., 145, 152
French, J. L., 427, 429, 545, 552
French, J. R. P., 189, 190, 198
French, T. M., 479
Frenkel-Brunswik, E., 233, 242, 252
Fretz, B. J., 474, 478
Fretz, B. R., 363, 365
Freud, S., 32, 56, 95, 108, 159, 170, 171, 173, 178, 180, 181, 185, 187, 199, 201, 202, 206, 207, 208, 209, 211, 212, 214, 219, 246, 288, 289, 299, 303, 308, 321, 322, 323, 324, 329, 334, 336, 340, 341, 343, 345, 348, 349, 353, 391, 394, 408, 409, 452, 453, 484, 506, 519, 520, 521
Freyd, M., 185, 199
Fridlund, A. J., 166, 167, 173
Friedan, B., 223, 238, 243, 433, 445
Friedman, J. L., 448
Friedman, W., 192, 199
Friend, R., 230, 242
Friesen, W., 212, 219
Frieze, I. H., 255, 267
Frijda, N. H., 166, 173
Frisby, C. L., 427, 429
Fritsch, G., 50, 63
Fritzsche, B. A., 295, 299
Frost, N., 139, 154
Frumkin, R. M., 227, 243
Fryer, D. H., 35, 368, 381, 386
Fuchs, A., 1, 6, 7, 11, 22, 183, 199
Fulero, S. M., 396, 407, 409, 542, 552
Furby, L., 238, 243
Furedy, J. J., 479
Furner, M. O., 228, 243
Furumoto, L., 6, 11, 14, 15, 22, 25, 252, 267, 367, 386, 467, 470, 478, 479

Gadlin, H., 239, 243
Gage, N. L., 273, 276
Galambos, R., 50, 63
Galanter, E., 75, 146, 154, 211, 220
Gale, H., 29, 44
Galef, B. G., 14, 22
Gall, F. J., 49, 50, 62, 63, 66, 317, 334
Gallup, G. G., Jr., 79, 82
Galton, F., 9, 12, 13, 28, 135, 137, 138, 139, 140, 153, 280, 299, 320, 335, 338, 511, 518
Gantt, W. H., 55, 328, 335
Garcia, T., 275, 276
Gardiner, H. M., 157, 173
Gardner, B. T., 79, 82
Gardner, H., 135, 137, 140, 141, 150, 151, 153
Gardner, M. K., 147, 148, 156
Gardner, R. A., 79, 82
Gardner, S., 544, 554
Garmezy, N., 436, 445
Garner, W. R., 105, 108, 231
Garraty, J. A., 23, 189, 199
Garrison, A. H., 64, 393, 409
Garvey, C. R., 468, 478
Gasser, H. S., 50, 63

Gatchel, R., 452, 462
Gauvain, M., 214, 219
Gay, P., 340, 353
Gazzaniga, M. S., 59, 63, 128, 132, 149, 153
Gebhardt, W., 275, 277
Gedney, J. J., 44
Geer, J. H., 291, 299
Geertz, C., 171, 173
Geissler, L., 5, 22, 370, 386
Gelfand, M. J., 376, 388
Gelfand, T., 340, 353
Gentry, W. D., 452, 457, 459, 461, 462
Georgas, J., 510, 532
George, A. L., 192, 199, 223
George, J. L., 192, 199
Gerard, H. B., 396, 409
Gerard, R. W., 50, 55, 64
Gergen, K., 194, 199, 235, 239, 240, 242, 243, 246, 511, 532
Gesell, A., 19, 22, 31, 44, 208, 209, 210, 211, 213, 219, 344, 417, 428
Gesten, E. L., 444, 445, 449
Gewirtz, J., 211, 219
Gibb, C. A., 233, 243
Gibbon, M., 291, 301
Gibson, E. J., 75, 212, 218, 219
Gibson, J. J., 89, 108
Gielen, U. P., 511, 531, 532, 537, 552
Gieryn, T. F., 551, 552
Gigerenzer, G., 146, 153, 236, 244
Gilbert, L. A., 80, 246, 254, 265, 313, 406, 409
Gilbreth, F., Jr., 370, 377, 383, 386, 388
Gildea, M. C. L., 440, 445
Gilgen, A. R., 510, 532
Gilgen, C. K., 510, 532
Gill, T. V., 56, 79, 83
Gillespie, R., 230, 244, 374, 375, 378, 386
Gilligan, C., 253, 265
Giordano, P. J., 475, 478
Giorgi, A., 20, 22
Girgus, J. S., 106, 107, 108, 477, 478
Gitlin, T., 432, 433, 434, 445
Gitter, A., 258, 265
Glad, B., 192, 199
Glaser, R., 137, 147, 148, 153, 155, 273
Glass, A. J., 440, 445
Glass, G. V., 351, 355
Glazer, R., 273, 276
Glennon, L., 434, 445
Glidewell, J. C., 431, 432, 435, 436, 440, 445, 448
Glover, J. A., 44, 269, 276, 364
Glutting, J., 282, 299
Goddard, H. H., 31, 32, 45, 320, 335, 342, 343
Goeke-Morey, M. C., 439, 449
Goethe, J. W. V., 51, 63, 185
Goetz, C. G., 340, 353
Goffman, E., 331, 335
Goldberg, R. W., 549, 551
Golden, C. J., 18, 109, 120, 122, 131, 293, 299
Goldenberg, I., 437, 448
Goldfried, M. R., 291, 292, 299

Golding, S., 405, 407, 411
Goldner, V., 259, 266
Goldsmith, H. H., 212, 218
Goldstein, A. J., 350, 353
Goldstein, K., 325, 329, 335
Goldston, S. E., 440, 441, 445, 446
Gomez, C. A., 192, 199
Gongora, R., 498, 505
Gonzales, N. A., 443, 448
Gonzalez, R. G., 60, 63
Good, B., 506
Good, J. M. M., 180, 199
Good, T. L., 269, 274, 276
Goodenough, F. L., 287, 288, 299
Goodman, E. S., 15, 23
Goodman, G. S., 405, 409
Goodman-Delahunty, J., 399, 408
Goodrich, S., 287, 302
Goodrich, T. J., 259, 266
Goodwin, C. J., 15, 16, 23, 371, 374, 383, 386, 469, 475, 479, 541,
    542, 552
Gordon, H., 326, 335
Gordon, M. E., 375, 378, 386
Gordon, M. T., 254, 266
Gorin, S., 423, 424, 428, 545, 552
Gossette, M. F., 80, 82
Gossette, R. L., 80, 82
Gottesman, I. I., 333, 335
Gottfredson, G. D., 479
Gottman, J. M., 212, 217
Gottschalk, L. R., 190, 199
Gough, H. G., 187, 203, 285, 299
Gould, L., 228, 244
Gould, S. J., 135, 153, 196, 199
Graebner, W., 228, 230, 232, 234, 244
Graham, D. T., 454, 462
Graham, J. R., 284, 298
Graham, S. R., 42, 44
Grau Abalo, J. A., 498, 505
Graumann, C. F., 511, 515, 532
Graves, R. H., 180, 199
Gray, J., 97, 263, 266, 414
Green, C., 4, 23, 300
Green, D. M., 48, 63
Green, D. R., 146, 153
Green, M., 393, 411
Greenberg, M., 81, 83, 84, 397, 432, 445, 463
Greenburg, J., 409
Greene, B., 259, 266
Greene, G. F., 431, 447
Greenfield, P. M., 150, 153, 213, 219, 462
Greenough, W. T., 56, 63, 214, 219
Greenstein, F. I., 192, 199
Greenwald, A. G., 214, 219
Greer, A., 401, 409
Gregg, A., 470, 479
Gregory, R. J., 13, 23, 233, 433
Greif, G. L., 439, 447
Griffin, D. R., 79, 81, 82

Griffith, D. M., 467, 478
Griffith, E. H., 496, 505
Griggs, R. A., 380, 386, 467, 479
Grigorenko, E. L., 145, 153, 154
Grimes, J., 44, 424, 428, 429
Grinder, R. E., 269, 270, 276
Grisso, T., 283, 298, 307, 391, 398, 399, 400, 401, 407, 408, 409, 411,
    542, 552
Grob, G. N., 32, 44, 440, 446
Groneman, C., 257, 266
Gross, C. G., 48, 49, 63, 98, 99, 108
Gross, J. J., 171, 174
Grossman, F. K., 255, 266
Grossman, K., 214, 219
Grotzer, T. A., 140, 153
Grove, W. M., 87, 334, 387, 402, 409, 446
Groves, P. M., 56, 64
Gruber, C. P., 216, 218
Grusec, J. E., 212, 219
Guignon, C. B., 485, 507
Guilford, J. P., 135, 143, 151, 153, 154, 189, 199
Gulerce, A., 532
Gundlach, H. U. K., 535, 536, 553
Gunnar, M. R., 214, 219
Gustad, J. W., 478
Gustafsson, J. E., 142, 153
Gutek, B. A., 252, 254, 266, 267
Guthrie, E. R., 18, 23, 121
Guthrie, R., 13, 23, 360, 364, 484, 493, 499, 506, 544, 546, 553
Gutkin, T. B., 424, 428, 429
Gutman, A., 266, 380, 386
Guttman, L., 135, 143, 154
Gutwill, S., 258, 265
Guze, S. B., 454, 462

Haaken, J., 259, 266
Haber, S., 228, 244
Hacking, I., 240, 244
Hackman, J. R., 373, 386
Haertel, G. D., 269, 277
Hafemeister, T. L., 395, 409
Hagen, E. P., 140, 151, 153, 156, 281
Hagen, J. W., 301, 550, 553
Hagin, R. A., 428, 429
Hakel, M. D., 372, 387
Hakmiller, K. L., 164, 174
Halberstam, D., 432, 433, 446
Hale, N. G., Jr., 180, 181, 184, 185, 199, 343, 353
Hall, C. I. I., 2, 503, 506
Hall, C. S., 122, 133, 178, 184, 191, 199
Hall, G. C., 499, 506
Hall, G. S., 2, 3, 8, 12, 13, 23, 24, 26, 28, 31, 67, 69, 82, 183, 199, 206,
    207, 208, 219, 271, 340, 359, 381, 416, 417, 418, 518, 519,
    521, 540
Hall-MacCorquodale, I., 251, 265
Hallmark, R., 17, 144, 249, 282, 301, 417
Halonen, J. S., 470, 479
Halpern, D. F., 470, 474, 477, 479
Halstead, W. C., 55, 148, 154, 293, 301

Hammeke, T. A., 293, 299
Hammer, A. L., 17, 295, 299
Hammond, W. A., 158, 173
Handler, L., 288, 291, 297, 298, 299
Haney, W., 281, 299
Hans, V. P., 58, 61, 324, 328, 346, 349, 399, 405, 408, 411, 454
Hanscom, K. L., 515, 532
Hansen, J. C., 295, 299
Hanson, R. O., 215, 219
Haraway, D., 83, 84, 236, 239, 241, 244, 255, 266
Hardcastle, G., 543, 551, 553
Harding, S., 246, 255, 266
Hardwick, R. S., 342, 355, 404, 408
Hare, R., 249, 253, 254, 255, 258, 259, 265, 266, 337, 407, 409
Hare-Mustin, R. T., 249, 253, 254, 255, 258, 259, 265, 266, 337
Harkness, S., 213, 219
Harlow, H., 20, 23, 54, 73, 74, 75, 80, 213, 219
Harlow, M. K., 213, 219
Harmon, L. W., 295, 299
Harms, E., 312, 335
Harrington, A., 49, 64, 317, 320, 321, 335, 507
Harris, B., 15, 17, 23, 231, 244
Harris, D. B., 288, 299
Harris, G., 407, 410
Harris, L. C., 444, 446
Harris, P. L., 214, 219
Harris, R. E., 190, 198
Harris, R. J., 121, 123, 124, 131, 132
Harrison, L. E., 285, 496, 506
Hartup, W. W., 212, 219, 221
Harwood, R. L., 436, 449
Haskell, T. L., 225, 228, 244
Haskins, R., 213, 220
Hassol, L., 444
Hatch, J. P., 297, 301
Hathaway, S. R., 284, 295, 299, 344
Hauck, W. W., 443, 448
Haugeland, J., 127, 132
Haughton, E., 331, 334
Haupt, E., 6, 23
Havey, J. M., 283, 301
Hawkins, R. D., 56, 64
Hawks, B. K., 476, 479
Hayden, L. C., 219
Haydock, M. D., 381, 387
Hayes, C. H., 79, 82
Hayes, M. H. S., 374, 378, 379, 388
Hayes, W. A., 484, 506
Hayles, N. K., 234, 235, 240, 244
Haynes, S. N., 292, 299
Healy, J. M., Jr., 195, 199
Healy, W., 32, 182, 199, 342, 343, 359, 400
Hearnshaw, L. S., 107
Hearst, E., 63, 65, 123, 132, 174, 335
Hebb, D. O., 54, 55, 57, 58, 61, 64, 73, 75, 82, 149, 154, 168, 173, 330, 335
Hedlund, J., 156
Hegel, G. W. F., 135, 154
Heidbreder, E., 10, 23
Heider, F., 235, 244

Heims, S., 233, 234, 244
Heller, K., 432, 446
Helmholtz, H. F. V., 2, 3, 4, 6, 16, 51, 54, 53, 64, 85, 88, 89, 93, 95, 96, 100, 101, 106
Helmreich, R. L. , 253, 267
Helzer, J. E., 291, 301
Hembrooke, H., 407, 409
Hendrickson, A. E., 150, 154
Hendrickson, D. E., 150, 154
Henle, M., 108, 161, 511, 532
Henley, N. M., 254, 266
Henriksen, M. A., 233, 244
Henriques, J. H., 236, 237, 244
Henry, E. R., 368, 376, 386, 467, 468, 469, 479
Henry, J., 114, 132
Hensley, L. T., 545, 552
Herbart, J. F., 2, 6, 101, 103, 160, 167, 168, 173, 270, 517
Hergenhahn, B. R., 373, 381, 382, 383, 387
Hering, E., 6, 51, 64, 85, 96, 97, 98, 100, 106
Herman, A., 433, 446
Herman, E., 184, 200, 224, 232, 233, 244, 493, 506
Herman, J., 254, 257, 259, 266
Herman, L. M., 79, 82
Hermann, M. G., 2, 6, 16, 24, 88, 93, 95, 118, 192, 203, 286, 522
Herrnstein, R. J., 135, 139, 150, 154
Hersch, L. E., 462
Hersen, M., 44, 292, 298, 354
Hertzog, C., 215, 219
Hess, A. K., 391, 392, 408, 410
Hess, R., 407, 410
Hess, W. R., 57, 58, 59, 64
Hetherington, E. M., 214, 216, 219, 220, 221
Hevern, V. W., 189, 190, 200
Heyes, C. M., 79, 82
Hick, W. E., 20, 23
Hickey, D. T., 276, 277
Hickok, L. P., 6, 23
Hicks, L., 508, 554
Highhouse, S., 375, 376, 384, 387
Hightower, A. D., 441, 445
Hildreth, G. H., 419, 429
Hilgard, E. R., 48, 52, 53, 54, 64, 269, 270, 271, 276, 277, 345, 353, 367, 376, 377, 378, 387, 447, 467, 479, 497, 510, 532, 545, 552
Hill, C., 364, 380, 387
Hill, D., 329, 335, 470, 479
Hill, E. W., 215, 220
Hill-Frederick, K., 362, 364
Hiller, J. B., 286, 299, 301
Hilliard, T. O., 493, 506
Hilsenroth, M. J., 286, 301
Hilts, V., 317, 335
Hind, J. E., 51, 53, 64
Hinde, R. A., 212, 214, 216, 219, 220
Hirsh, R., 61, 65
Hitzig, E., 50, 63
Hobbes, T., 87, 108, 158
Hobbs, N., 435, 448
Hobfoll, S. E., 275, 277
Hoch, A., 326, 335

Hoch, E. L., 435, 446
Hodge, A., 127, 132
Hodge, F. W., 21
Hodos, W., 76, 82
Hoedt, K. C., 426, 428
Hoepfner, R., 143, 153
Hofer, B. K., 275, 277
Hoffman, L. E., 35, 44
Hoffman, L. W., 214, 219
Hoffman, M., 508, 554
Hoffman, R. R., 6, 23
Hogan, D., 510, 533
Hogan, J. S., 352, 355
Hogan, R., 373, 387
Hohmann, G. W., 164, 173
Holahan, C. J., 437, 439, 446
Holland, B., 373, 387
Holland, J. L., 295, 299
Hollander, E. P., 543, 553
Hollenbeck, J. R., 385, 387
Hollingworth, H. L., 30, 33, 44, 189, 200, 359, 364
Hollingworth, L. S., 33, 251, 252, 266, 343, 344, 347, 349, 353, 359, 414
Hollis, K. L., 78, 82
Hollon, S. D., 352, 353
Hollway, W., 236, 244
Holmes, W. G., 78, 82, 378, 379
Holt, R. R., 185, 200, 344, 484, 506
Holtzman, W. H., 510, 511, 532, 533, 536, 553
Holzinger, K. J., 142, 154
Homburger, E., 188, 200
Honzik, C. H., 18, 19, 25
Hopkins, J. R., 478
Hopkins, W. P., 476, 480
Hoppock, R. M., 375, 387
Horn, J. L., 116, 137, 143, 154
Horner, M. S., 252, 266
Horney, K., 251, 343, 348, 353
Hornstein, G., 183, 184, 185, 200, 229, 244
Hornyak, L. M., 462
Horowitz, F. D., 215, 220
Horvath, J., 156
Hothersall, D., 81, 84
Hough, L., 368, 369, 373, 386, 387, 388
Houser, J. D., 375, 387
Howard, A., 372, 379, 382, 387, 476, 479
Howard, G., 433, 446, 485, 506
Howe, M. J. A., 192, 200
Howell, I. L., 330, 334
Howell, W. C., 376, 386
Hrabowski, F. A., 439, 447
Hubel, D. H., 50, 51, 64, 98, 107
Huber, G. P., 377, 387, 532
Hudson, C., 180, 200, 429, 433
Huesmann, L. R., 351, 353
Huggins, G. E., 69, 84
Hughes, D., 443, 448
Hughes, H., 459, 462
Hughes, J., 326, 333
Hughes, L., 484, 506

Hull, C. L., 18, 19, 23, 55, 64, 120, 122, 124, 125, 130, 132, 210, 211, 212, 328, 330, 364
Humphreys, L., 137, 143, 154
Hunley, S. A., 428
Hunt, E., 137, 139, 147, 154, 162
Hunt, J. M., 162, 173, 211, 220, 327, 335
Hunt, W. A., 168, 173
Hunter, J. E., 54, 56, 64, 65, 71, 139, 155
Hunter, W. S., 64, 65, 71
Huntington, S., 496, 506
Hurrelmann, K., 455, 462
Hurtado, A., 259, 266
Hurvich, L. M., 51, 64, 542, 553
Husman, J., 275, 277
Huston, P. E., 173, 326, 335
Hutchins, E., 216, 220
Hutchins, R. M., 394, 398, 410
Hutt, R. B. W., 419, 429
Hyde, J. S., 253, 266
Hyman, B. T., 60, 63, 244

Ibanez, R. M., 270, 277
Icard, L. D., 443, 446
Iijima Hall, C. C., 480
Ilg, F., 19, 22, 210, 219
Ilgen, D. R., 376, 387
Illback, R. J., 425, 429
Innis, N. K., 18, 23
Irwin, T., 110, 132, 362, 457
Iscoe, I., 44, 349, 431, 436, 438, 441, 444, 446
Isen, A. M., 172, 173
Israel, J., 238, 244, 246, 514, 525
Isserman, M., 433, 446
Ito, M., 55, 64
Ivry, R., 128, 132, 149, 153
Izard, C. E., 166, 174, 212, 218, 220
Izawa, C., 126, 132

Jacklin, C., 253, 267
Jackson, J. H., 309, 318, 323, 335
Jackson, J. H., Jr., 395, 396, 410
Jackson, J. P., Jr., 541, 553
Jackson, L. C., 259, 266
Jackson, S. L., 467, 479
Jackson, T., 275, 277
Jacobs, J. E., 263, 265
Jacobs, J. H., 503, 506
Jacobs, M. R., 215, 218
Jacobson, E., 454, 462
Jacyna, L. S., 49, 63, 312, 317, 334
Jahoda, M., 436, 446
James, L. C., 6, 7, 8, 44, 82, 89, 96, 100, 112, 119, 125, 130, 132, 138, 157, 158, 159, 160, 161, 162, 163, 164, 165, 166, 168, 171, 172, 173, 174
James, W., 6, 8, 10, 11, 14, 23, 29, 32, 47, 53, 56, 57, 64, 67, 69, 70, 80, 82, 100, 112, 119, 125, 130, 132, 157, 158, 159, 160, 161, 162, 163, 164, 165, 166, 168, 171, 172, 173, 174, 180, 183, 200, 203, 207, 223, 225, 226, 227, 241, 243, 244, 271, 340, 341, 342, 344, 353, 394, 453, 454, 468, 470, 501, 512, 518, 521

Jameson, D., 51, 64
Jamison, K. R., 352, 353
Janet, P., 158, 167, 264, 321, 322, 324, 335, 495
Janis, I., 236, 237, 244
Jansen, M. A., 442, 446
Jansen, M. M., 460, 463
Jarman, R. F., 149, 153
Jasnos, T. M., 164, 174
Jason, L. A., 443, 446, 448
Jasper, H. H., 56, 65
Jastak, J., 294, 299
Jastrow, J., 4, 23, 100, 228, 244, 467, 479
Jay, D., 216, 220
Jay, J. M., 489, 506
Jegerski, J. A., 480
Jenkins, A. H., 368, 387, 485, 506
Jenkins, A. M., 483
Jenkins, C. D., 456
Jenkins, J. G., 189, 200, 368, 387
Jenkins, T. N., 73, 84
Jensen, A. R., 135, 137, 140, 141, 147, 154
Jensen, M. B., 474, 479
Jepsen, Z., 463
Jerome, L. W., 43, 44, 57, 75
Jing, Q., 510, 512, 516, 532
Joffe, J. M., 441, 446
John, O. P., 187, 203
Johnson, B. T., 253, 264, 266
Johnson, D. L., 45
Johnson, E. M., 442, 446
Johnson, H. M., 70, 82
Johnson, J. S., 215, 220
Johnson, K. A., 60, 63
Johnson, N. G., 261, 263, 264, 266, 268
Johnson, S. B., 264
Johnson-Powell, G., 506
Johnston, J. C., 180, 200
Johnston, M., 457, 458, 459, 460, 462, 463
Jones, E. E., 224, 240, 244
Jones, K. W., 182, 200
Jones, M. C., 343, 349, 353
Jopp, D. A., 431, 447
Jordaan, J. P., 363, 364
Jordan, J. V., 259, 266, 334, 530, 539
Josselson, R., 192, 195, 200
Judd, C. H., 8, 15, 23, 100, 515
Jung, C. G., 178, 187, 200, 246, 288, 299, 329, 343, 348, 520, 521
Justice, B., 435, 449

Kaemmer, B., 284, 298
Kakolweski, J. W., 59, 66
Kalachnik, J. E., 351, 355
Kalish, D., 18, 25
Kallman, W. M., 291, 299
Kalmanovitch, T., 14, 25
Kamil, A. C., 78, 82
Kamphaus, R. W., 282, 299
Kandel, E. R., 56, 64
Kanner, A. D., 166, 174

Kant, I., 1, 2, 18, 68, 87, 90, 117, 158, 174
Kantor, J. R., 170, 174
Kaplan, A. G., 259, 266
Kaplan, H. I., 452, 462
Kaplan, S., 228, 244
Kapor-Stanulovic, N., 515, 532
Karau, S. J., 235, 243
Kardiner, A., 483, 506
Karpf, F. B., 223, 227, 244
Karplus, J. P., 57, 64
Karson, S., 285, 299
Karst, K., 396, 410
Kaschak, E., 258, 266
Kaslow, F. W., 542, 553
Kasschau, R. A., 480
Katz, D., 230, 244
Katz, H., 146, 154
Katz, P., 260, 266
Katzell, R. A., 367, 371, 372, 373, 374, 375, 376, 377, 378, 379, 381, 382,
    383, 384, 387
Kauffman, S., 138, 154
Kaufman, A., 149, 154, 282, 298, 299
Kaufman, J. C., 144, 156
Kaufman, N., 149, 154, 282, 299
Kaufman, S. H., 288, 298
Kaur, A., 269, 277
Kay, A. R., 62, 65
Kay, G. G., 298, 300
Kazin, M., 433, 446
Keating, D. P., 147, 154
Keen, E., 173, 346
Keil, F. C., 146, 154
Keir, R., 351, 354
Keith-Spiegel, P., 402, 403, 410
Keitner, G., 219
Kellam, S. G., 221, 442, 446
Keller, J. W., 139, 282, 297, 301
Kelley, G. A., 173, 235, 236, 290, 299, 344, 350, 354
Kelly, E. L., 344
Kelly, J. G., 431, 436, 438, 439, 443, 444, 445, 446, 447, 448, 449
Kelman, H. C., 237, 244
Keltner, D., 171, 174
Kendler, H., 19, 23
Kendrick, C., 212, 219
Kendrick, K. M., 99, 108
Kenkel, M. B., 480
Kennedy, D. M., 432, 446
Kennedy, S., 514, 532
Kent, G. H., 288, 299, 386
Kent, R. N., 291, 292, 299
Kerber, K., 287, 302
Kerkhof, A., 460, 463
Kershaw, I., 193, 200
Kessen, W., 18, 24, 169, 174, 218
Kessler, M., 441, 446
Kessler, S., 254, 266
Ketron, J. L., 136, 156
Kidder, L. H., 256, 267
Kiester, E., 432, 446

Kihlstrom, J., 214, 220
Kilbey, M. M., 45
Kimble, G. A., 18, 23, 364, 388, 470, 478, 479
Kimmel, E. B., 249, 255, 262, 266
Kimmel, P. R., 541, 553
Kingry-Westergaard, C., 439, 446
Kingsbury, F. A., 367, 368, 387
Kinsey, A. J., 433, 447
Kirby, J. R., 149, 153
Kirkpatrick, E. A., 183, 200
Kitano, H. H., 490, 506
Kittel, F., 460, 463
Kitzinger, C., 240, 247, 254, 266
Klein, D. C., 435, 436, 437, 444, 447
Klein, N., 241, 244
Klein, R., 6, 23
Kleinman, A., 506
Klimoski, R. J., 373, 377, 387
Kline, L. W., 67, 69, 79, 82
Klineberg, O., 514, 532, 541
Klotz, D., 443, 447
Kluckhohn, C. K. M., 150, 154, 190, 191, 199, 201
Kluger, R., 395, 410
Klüver, H., 57, 64
Knapp, J. R., 143, 154
Koch, S., 23, 132, 133, 201, 202, 245, 247, 515, 532
Kocovski, N. L., 275, 276
Koehnken, G., 406, 411
Koeske, R. D., 255, 267
Koffka, K., 17, 23, 85, 105, 345
Kogel, L., 265
Kohler, R., 7, 23, 345, 540, 553
Köhler, W., 17, 23, 70, 80, 82, 105, 106, 108, 511, 532
Kohout, J., 296, 300, 548, 553
Koocher, G., 402, 403, 408, 410
Koppes, L. L., 31, 367, 371, 372, 374, 377, 378, 379, 383, 385, 387
Koppitz, E. M., 288, 292, 299, 300
Korchin, S. J., 435, 447
Koretz, D., 441, 442, 446, 447
Korman, A., 37, 44
Korman, M., 347, 354
Korn, J. H., 469, 476, 477, 479
Koshtoyants, K., 16, 23
Koslowski, B., 212, 218
Koss, M. P., 254, 266
Kossakowski, A., 511, 532
Kovach, J. K., 510, 532
Kraepelin, E., 316, 326, 327, 333, 335, 340
Krantz, D. L., 19, 23
Krasne, F. B., 56, 64
Kraus, L. A., 329, 335
Kraus, T., 427, 429
Krauss, R., 227, 243
Krech, D., 56, 64, 72, 541
Krechevsky, I., 72, 82, 541
Kreidl, A., 57, 64
Kremen, I., 164, 174
Kreppner, K., 216, 220
Krieger, K., 79, 83

Kroeber, A. L., 150, 154
Krueger, E. T., 180, 182, 200
Kruger, L., 266
Krupa, D. J., 61, 66
Kryl, I. P., 230, 231, 246
Kubiszyn, T. W., 283, 297, 298, 300
Kuder, G. F., 279, 294, 295, 300
Kuhl, J., 275, 277
Kulik, J., 467, 470, 473, 479
Kuna, D. P., 30, 44, 395, 410
Kurowoski, L. L., 376, 388
Kurtines, W. M., 498, 507
Kusch, M., 5, 23
Kyllonen, P. C., 143, 155

Labarta, M., 439, 448
Lacks, P., 292, 300, 303, 320
Ladd, G. T., 4, 7, 23, 24, 52, 539
LaFortune, K. A., 283, 300
Lah, M. I., 289, 301
Lakoff, R., 252, 266
Laman, C., 480, 506
Lamb, M. D., 212, 220
Lamb, M. E., 212, 218
Lamb, S., 259, 266
Lamiell, J. T., 178, 200
Landis, C., 166, 174, 344
Landrine, H., 255, 266
Landy, F. J., 367, 371, 374, 383, 384, 387
Lang, P., 349, 354
Lange, C., 56, 57, 63, 102, 158, 159, 160, 161, 162, 163, 164, 165, 171, 173, 174
Langer, L. L., 193, 200
Langer, W., 192, 200
Langfeld, H. S., 8, 23, 199, 203
Larkin, J. H., 148, 154
Larsen, R. M., 242, 282, 300
Lashley, K., 53, 54, 55, 56, 57, 58, 59, 61, 64, 70, 71, 72, 73, 75, 80, 84, 120, 122, 123, 132, 188
Laszlo, A. C., 260, 265, 537, 552
Latane, B., 236, 243
Laughlin, P. R., 548, 553
Layton, L., 192, 202
Layton, W. L., 363, 364
Lazarus, R. S., 166, 171, 173, 174, 351, 354
Lazovik, A. D., 349, 354
Leahey, T. H., 5, 10, 11, 16, 18, 20, 23, 51, 59, 78, 82, 109, 118, 119, 121, 122, 123, 124, 125, 131, 132, 497
Lears, J., 230, 244
Lears, T. J. J., 228, 244
Leary, D., 1, 2, 8, 23, 24, 202, 225, 229, 244, 245, 247, 467, 479, 510, 532
Leavell, H. R., 440, 447
LeBoeuf, B. J., 78, 83
LeDoux, J. E., 55, 61, 64, 169, 174
Lee, L. M., 62, 65
Lees-Haley, P. R., 282, 292, 300
Lefkowitz, M. M., 351, 353
Lehr, C., 427, 429
Lehrman, D. S., 72, 75, 76, 77, 79, 81, 83

Leicester, H. M., 310, 335, 462
Leigh, H., 336, 454, 462
Leith, N. J., 45
Lemery, C. R., 167, 173
Lemkau, P., 435, 441, 447, 449
Lemke, S., 438, 447
Lentz, R. J., 350, 354
Leonard, W. E., 37, 73, 75, 168, 186, 200, 210, 443
Leong, F., 546, 553
Lerman, H., 258, 266
Lerner, H. G., 258, 266
Lerner, R. M., 208, 213, 220
Leroy, H. A., 68, 75, 83
Leshner, A. I., 173
Lettvin, J. Y., 51, 64
Levenson, D., 453, 455, 462
Leventhal, E. A., 275, 276
Leventhal, H., 275, 276
Levi, L., 163, 165, 173, 174
Levi-Montalcini, R., 163, 174
Levin, H., 210, 221
Levin, I., 246
Levin, J. M., 216, 220
Levin, J. R., 269, 271, 272, 274, 276, 277
Levine, A., 32, 44, 357, 364, 465, 479
Levine, M., 32, 34, 340, 354, 357, 364, 405, 409, 431, 432, 435, 437, 440,
    441, 443, 444, 447, 448
Levine, S., 58, 64
Levinson, D. J., 233, 242
Levy, L. H., 442, 447
Lewin, K., 169, 174, 195, 200, 231, 232, 233, 234, 235, 244, 291, 345, 375,
    376, 383, 437, 438, 447
Lewinsohn, P. M., 351, 354, 355
Lewis, J., 147, 154
Lewis, M., 214, 220
Lezak, M. D., 293, 300
Liddell, H. S., 327, 328, 335
Lieblich, A., 192, 195, 200
Likert, R., 375, 376, 387
Lilly, D., 254, 267
Lin, K. M., 506
Lincoln, Y. S., 174, 195, 198, 355, 488, 507, 533
Lindemann, E., 431, 434, 436, 437, 444, 447
Lindsley, D. B., 50, 57, 62, 64
Lindzey, G., 82, 173, 178, 184, 191, 197, 199, 201, 232, 242, 244, 246
Linehan, M. M., 351, 354
Ling, G., 50, 64, 240
Link, H. C., 374, 387
Link, M., 5, 21
Linn, M., 253, 266
Linney, J. A., 439, 447
Lipowski, Z. J., 452, 453, 462
Lippitt, R., 438, 448
Lipsitt, D., 452, 453, 462
Lipsitt, L. P., 211, 220
Lloyd, G. E. R., 307, 308, 335
Lloyd, M. A., 470, 471, 475, 479
Locher, L. M., 326, 335
Lock, A., 511, 532

Lockard, R. B., 76, 83
Locke, E. A., 372, 379, 380, 384, 387
Locke, J., 314, 335
Lofquist, L. H., 375, 386
Loftus, E., 395, 406, 410
Logan, C. A., 14, 24, 497, 500, 547
Loh, W. D., 397, 398, 406, 407, 410
Lohr, N., 287, 302
Lomax, E., 550, 553
Lomo, T., 54, 63
Lomov, B. F., 511, 532
London, M., 372, 387
Long, B. B., 440, 447
Long, B. E., 440, 447
Lopes, L., 236, 245
López-Piñero, J. M. L., 335
Lord, R. G., 97, 164, 383, 387, 392, 468
Lorenz, K. Z., 77, 83
Lorsch, J. W., 383, 387
Loutit, C. M., 282, 300, 419, 429
Louw, J., 539, 540, 552
Lowell, E. L., 71, 83, 252, 267, 287, 300, 344, 434
Lowenberg, G., 375, 379, 380, 387
Lowrey, L. G., 549, 553
Loy, P., 223, 245
Lubek, I., 229, 238, 242, 246
Lubin, B., 282, 300, 352, 354
Lubove, R., 180, 182, 200
Lumsdaine, A. A., 273, 277
Lundberg, G. A., 182, 200
Lunneborg, C., 139, 147, 154
Lunt, I., 348, 353, 459, 460, 462, 516, 532, 538, 553
Luria, A. R., 62, 64, 149, 154, 498, 516, 532
Lutsky, N., 480, 506
Lutz, C., 171, 174, 232, 245
Lux, D. F., 467, 468, 469, 479
Lykes, M. B., 254, 266
Lyons, A. S., 452, 462

MacCorquodale, K., 132
MacCurdy, G. G., 305, 335
MacCurdy, J. T., 167, 171, 174
Maccoby, E. E., 210, 221, 253, 267
MacDonald, M., 312, 335
MacIntyre, A., 240, 245
MacKay, D. M., 126, 132
MacKenzie, J., 275, 277
MacKinnon, D. W., 191, 200
Mackintosh, N. J., 132, 140, 154
MacLean, P. D., 57, 64, 165
MacLeod, R. B., 478, 510, 512, 532
MacMurphey, R. H., 189, 197, 200
MacRae, N., 127, 132
Maeder, T., 392, 410
Maes, S., 275, 277, 452, 457, 458, 460, 462, 463
Magoun, H. W., 57, 65
Maher, B. A., 303, 305, 326, 327, 328, 334, 335, 336, 435, 447
Maher, C. A., 425, 429
Maher, K. J., 383, 387

Maher, W. B., 303, 305, 327, 335
Maier, N. R. F., 72, 73, 80, 83
Main, M., 212, 218
Major, B., 254, 265
Majovski, L. V., 516, 532
Makhijani, M. G., 235, 243
Malgady, R. G., 287, 298
Malpass, R. S., 406, 411
Manchester, W., 374, 387
Mandel, K. B., 480
Mandler, G., 18, 24, 157, 164, 165, 166, 167, 169, 174
Mandler, J. M., 164, 174
Mangun, G., 128, 132, 149, 153
Mann, A., 357, 364
Mann, L., 236, 244
Mann, M. A., 80, 83
Maramba, G. G., 499, 506
Marañon, G., 162, 174
Marecek, J., 249, 252, 253, 254, 255, 256, 258, 259, 265, 266, 267, 337
Mark, M. M., 402, 410, 506
Markowitz, H., 81, 83
Marks, D., 234, 280, 458, 460, 461, 463
Marr, D., 89, 108, 127, 128, 129, 132
Marshalek, B., 143, 155
Marshall, M., 3, 24
Marshall, W. H., 50, 64
Marston, W. M., 396, 397, 410
Martin, J., 485, 506
Martin, W. E., Jr., 437, 438, 449
Marvin, W. T., 472, 479
Marwick, A., 433, 447
Maslow, A., 20, 24, 75, 485, 493, 506
Masson, J. M., 325, 335
Masur, R. T., 459, 462
Matarazzo, J. D., 282, 290, 300, 451, 452, 454, 453, 455, 457, 458, 461, 462, 463, 554
Mateer, F., 17, 19, 24
Matlin, M. W., 478
Maton, K., 437, 439, 444, 447, 449
Matthews, G., 275, 277
Matthews, J., 474, 480, 497, 507
Maturana, H. R., 51, 64
May, E. T., 233, 245
Mayer, R. E., 269, 273, 274, 277, 337
Mays, V. M., 432, 516, 532
Mazzoni, G., 139, 154
McAdams, D. P., 178, 179, 192, 194, 195, 200
McArthur, D. S., 287, 300
McCann, L. I., 467, 468, 469, 472, 478, 480
McCary, J. L., 397, 410
McCaslin, M., 276, 277
McClelland, D. C., 188, 195, 200, 252, 267, 287, 300
McClelland, J. L., 129, 132, 146, 155
McCollom, I. N., 372, 387
McCosh, J., 7, 24, 158, 174
McCrae, R. R., 285, 286, 298
McCree, M. L., 358, 364, 405, 410, 411
McCulloch, W. S., 51, 64
McDermott, J., 148, 154

McDougall, W., 56, 80, 158, 225, 227, 245
McGaugh, J. L., 55, 60, 63, 64, 132
McGehee, W., 375, 381, 387
McGeoch, J., 19, 24
McGhee, J. L., 439, 447
McGill, T. E., 58, 61, 73, 75, 83
McGovern, T. V., 465, 466, 467, 468, 470, 471, 472, 473, 474, 476, 477, 478, 479, 480, 506
McGraw, M., 20, 24
McGuire, E. R., 510, 532
McGuire, G. R., 467, 479
McGuire, J. M., 282, 298
McHale, P. A., 216, 218
McHenry, L. C., Jr., 48, 64
McHugh, M. D., 255, 267
McHugh, P. R., 290, 299
McIntyre, T., 451, 458, 459, 460, 461, 463, 462, 463, 464
McKeachie, W. J., 470, 471, 473, 477, 478, 479, 494, 506
McKenna, S., 254, 266
McKinley, J. C., 177, 284, 295, 299
McLean, C., 259, 267, 327
McLearn, G. E., 213, 220
McLoyd, V. C., 214, 220
Mcloughlin, C. S., 427, 429
McNaughton, M., 171, 174
McNeil, O. V., 478
McNeish, T. J., 288, 300
McNemar, Q., 75, 137, 144, 154
McReynolds, P., 13, 24, 29, 44, 338, 339, 354, 360, 364, 416, 429
Mead, G. H., 223, 227, 233, 245
Meagher, R. B., Jr., 285, 300
Meara, N. M., 363, 364
Mechem, P., 398, 410
Mednick, M. T., 261, 267, 480, 548, 553
Meduna, L. V., 326, 335
Meehl, P., 132, 190, 200, 344
Mehryar, A. H., 511, 532
Meissner, C. A., 401, 406, 408
Melikian, L. H., 511, 532
Meller, P. J., 281, 301
Mellgren, R. L., 80, 83
Mellon, M., 370, 377, 427, 428
Melton, A. W., 20, 24, 273
Melton, G., 395, 405, 407, 408, 409, 410
Meltzer, B. N., 227, 245
Meltzer, H., 343, 354, 367, 387
Menninger, W. C., 343, 346, 354
Merenda, P. F., 510, 532
Meritt, D. A., 431, 435, 436, 447
Merrill, M. A., 45, 140, 156, 221, 359, 401, 409
Messer, S., 485, 506
Messer, W. S., 467, 479
Metalious, G., 433, 447
Metcalf, R. C., 173
Methorst, G., 460, 463
Meyer, A., 14, 32, 290, 297, 319, 335, 453, 463
Meyer, G. J., 283, 286, 300
Meyer, H. H., 375, 383, 388
Meyer, L. B., 168, 169, 174

Meyerowitz, J., 245
Meyers, J., 424, 428
Mezzich, J., 496, 506
Milar, K. S., 1, 11, 13, 24, 183, 199
Miles, C. C., 229, 247, 344
Miles, T. R., 137, 154
Miles, W., 69, 83
Milgram, N. A., 233, 236, 531, 537, 552
Milholland, J. E., 470, 471, 473, 477, 479
Miller, G., 20, 146, 154, 211, 220
Miller, J. B., 259, 266, 267
Miller, J. G., 345
Miller, K. E., 439, 443, 447
Miller, N. E., 55, 57, 58, 64, 210, 219, 230, 243, 328, 335, 454, 457, 463
Miller, R. L., 443, 447
Miller, S. A., 146, 154
Millon, T., 284, 285, 300
Mills, E., 7, 24
Mills, J. A., 16, 18, 19, 24
Mills, W., 70, 83
Milner, B., 54, 58, 59, 60, 61, 65
Mineka, S., 351, 354
Miner, B., 8, 24
Minton, H. L., 226, 229, 231, 243, 245, 374, 388
Mirvis, P. H., 379, 388
Mischel, W., 291, 300
Mishkin, M., 59, 60, 61, 64, 65
Mishler, E. G., 438, 447
Misiak, H., 516, 533
Misra, G., 511, 532
Mitchell, D., 343, 344, 354
Mitchell, R. F., 147, 155
Modell, J., 215, 219
Mohamed, A. A. R., 193, 275, 277
Moldin, S. O., 333, 335
Monahan, J., 395, 398, 400, 407, 410, 411, 436, 448
Moniz, E., 325, 335
Moore, B. V., 370, 371, 373
Moore, D. L., 36, 44
Moore, H. T., 184, 200
Moore, J. W., 318, 335
Moore, R. P., 226
Moos, B. S., 438, 446, 447
Moos, R. H., 438, 439, 446, 447
Moran, R., 247, 393, 410
Morawski, J., 180, 185, 200, 223, 225, 228, 229, 234, 240, 241, 242, 244,
    245, 246, 251, 255, 267, 337, 386, 388, 474, 479
Moreland, K. L., 300
Morey, L. C., 286, 300, 439, 449
Morgan, C. D., 287, 300
Morgan, C. L., 14, 15, 18, 24, 69, 70, 80, 83, 119, 120, 132
Morgan, C. T., 57, 58, 65, 543
Morgan, D. M., 193, 200
Morgan, E. P., 434, 447
Morgan, H. H., 363, 364
Morgan, J. D., 381, 385
Morris, A., 439, 447
Morris, C. J., 467, 478
Morrison, J., 290, 300

Morrow, W. R., 345, 354, 418, 429
Moscicki, E. K., 442, 446
Moseley, E., 317, 335
Moser, E., 61, 65
Moser, M., 61, 65
Moses, J. L., 372, 387
Moskowitz, M. J., 383, 388
Moss, F. A., 74, 83
Mountcastle, V. B., 48, 51, 65
Mountjoy, P. T., 68, 83
Mowrer, O. H., 170, 174, 210, 219, 230, 243, 344, 354
Mowrer, W. M., 344, 354
Muchinsky, P. M., 376, 379, 388
Muehrer, P., 443, 447
Mueller, C., 132, 539
Mullen, F. A., 414, 429
Mullett, J., 167, 173
Mulvey, E., 411
Muñiz, J., 283, 300
Munn, N., 14, 24, 74, 83
Munoz, R. F., 444, 446
Munroe, R., 344, 354
Münsterberg, H., 11, 30, 32, 44, 69, 71, 83, 100, 181, 359, 364, 367, 373,
    383, 387, 388, 391, 394, 395, 396, 398, 408, 410, 411, 536
Murchison, C., 10, 24, 25, 63, 73, 203, 232, 242, 243, 245
Murphy, G., 184, 201, 231, 510, 532
Murphy, J., 83
Murphy, L. B., 184, 201, 231
Murphy-Shigematsu, S. L., 503, 506
Murray, C., 135, 139, 150, 154, 173
Murray, D. J., 1, 3, 6, 24
Murray, E. A., 60, 64
Murray, E. J., 328, 335
Murray, H. A., 177, 178, 179, 185, 187, 188, 189, 190, 191, 192, 196, 197,
    201, 202, 203, 252, 267, 287, 300
Myers, H. F., 501, 506
Myers, L. J., 484, 506
Myers, R. A., 363, 364

Nagel, T., 239, 245
Naglieri, J. A., 149, 153, 154, 288, 300
Naman, J. L., 371, 388
Napoli, D. S., 29, 33, 34, 38, 44, 181, 184, 185, 201, 228, 229, 230, 245,
    360, 364, 367, 371, 374, 388, 544, 553
Nasby, W., 193, 201
Nasrallah, H. A., 333, 335
Nathan, J. S., 282, 298, 350
Naylor, J. C., 368, 385
Neaman, J. S., 306, 335
Neiderhiser, J. M., 214, 220
Neisser, U., 102, 108, 126, 127, 132, 148, 154
Nelson, B., 488, 506, 548, 554
Nelson, G., 439, 448
Nelson, K. E., 80, 83
Nelson, P. D., 475, 479, 548, 554
Nelson, T. O., 139, 154
Nemiah, J. C., 454, 463
Neugebauer, R., 306, 335
Newbury, E., 69, 83, 200, 218, 446

Newcomb, A. F., 476, 480
Newcomb, T. M., 493, 506
Newell, A., 110, 128, 132, 146, 155
Newman, R., 40, 45
Newport, E. L., 215, 220
Newsom, C. R., 282, 298
Newton, I., 51, 65, 93, 116, 124, 130, 312, 313
Nichols, H., 8, 24
Nicholson, I., 244
Nicholson, I. A. M., 179, 180, 185, 186, 187, 189, 201
Nicholson, R., 410
Nideffer, J., 465, 479
Nieberding, R., 282, 301
Nieva, V. F., 252, 267
Nobles, W. A., 484, 506
Noblin, C. D., 328, 334
Nodine, B. F., 469, 477, 479, 480
Novaco, R., 436, 448
Novak, M. A., 81, 83
Nowak, A., 196, 201
Nowlis, V., 210, 221
Nummedal, S. G., 477, 479
Nussbaum, M., 112, 113, 132

Oakland, T. D., 413, 427, 429
O'Brien, W. O., 292, 299
Ochberg, R. L., 192, 200
O'Connell, D. C., 192, 201
O'Connor, G. T., 372, 388
O'Dell, J. W., 285, 299
O'Donnell, A. M., 271, 272, 274, 276, 277
O'Donnell, J. M., 15, 24, 183, 201, 227, 245
Odoroff, M. E., 371, 372, 386, 544, 552
Oehler-Stinnett, J., 283, 301
Ogawa, S., 62, 65
Ogden, D. W., 405, 409
Ogden, J., 461, 463
Ogloff, J. R. P., 399, 402, 403, 408, 410, 411
Ojemann, R. H., 436, 440, 448
O'Keefe, J., 54, 65
Olds, J., 57, 58, 59, 65, 140
O'Mara, K. M., 439, 449
Opton, E. M. J., 171, 174
Ornstein, J. J., 205, 218, 220
Ortony, A., 166, 174
Osgood, C. E., 121, 122, 132
Oskamp, S., 479
Oster, H., 167, 173
Othmer, E., 290, 300
Othmer, S. C., 209, 300
Otis, J. A., 281, 300
Otto, R., 410
Otto, T., 60, 63
Overton, W., 207, 220
Ovesey, L., 483, 506

Packard, M. G., 61, 65
Packard, R. E., 549, 551

Padilla, A., 490, 497, 498, 506
Paige, J. M., 193, 201
Paine, C., 282, 300
Pandora, K., 185, 201, 231, 234, 245
Papez, J. W. M., 57, 64, 65
Papousek, H., 211, 220
Parham, T. A., 408, 410, 484, 493, 506, 507
Paris, A. H., 274
Paris, S. G., 273, 274
Parke, R. D., 205, 212, 214, 215, 216, 217, 218, 219, 220, 221, 352
Parker, I., 236, 239, 245
Parker, J. D. A., 178, 179, 180, 181, 182, 183, 184, 194, 201, 352, 353
Parlee, M. B., 256, 257, 267
Parloff, M. B., 349, 354
Parr, G., 329, 335
Parsons, F., 30, 44, 243, 358, 359, 364, 365, 536
Pascal, G. R., 127, 292, 300
Pascarella, E. T., 476, 480
Passano, E. B., 21
Pastore, N., 107
Pate, J. L., 80, 83, 367, 388, 474, 480
Paterson, D. G., 189, 201, 360, 361, 364, 375, 388
Patkai, P., 164, 174
Patterson, G. R., 350, 354
Paul, G. L., 291, 300, 350, 354
Paulhan, F., 167, 168, 169, 174
Pavlov, I. P., 16, 17, 25, 55, 65, 80, 123, 327, 328, 336, 453, 511, 520, 522
Pawlik, K., 510, 532
Payne, C. M., 433, 448
Pearson, K., 9, 152, 320, 336
Pedro-Caroll, J. L., 441, 445
Peerenboom, C. A., 21
Peirce, C. S., 119, 132
Pellegrini, A. I., 214, 218
Pellegrino, J. W., 137, 147, 155
Penfield, W., 51, 61, 65
Penn, P., 259, 266, 428, 468
Penrod, S. D., 406, 409
Pepinsky, H. B., 37, 43, 362, 364
Pepperberg, I. M., 79, 83
Perkins, D. A., 140, 153
Perkins, D. V., 432, 440, 441, 444, 447
Perkins, K. N., 371, 387
Perlman, B., 467, 468, 469, 472, 480
Perloff, R., 371, 388
Perls, F. S., 332, 336, 421
Pervin, L. A., 179, 201, 203
Pestalozzi, J. H., 270, 277
Peterson, C., 185, 201
Peterson, D. R., 37, 44, 347, 354
Peterson, J. L., 40, 45, 443, 448
Petoskey, M. D., 283, 299
Petrila, J., 407, 410
Petrossian, P., 475, 478
Petrucelli, R. J., 452, 462
Pfafflin, S. M., 479
Pfister, J., 228, 245
Phelps, E., 216, 218
Phelps, R., 296, 300

Phillips, E. L., 328, 336

Phillips, L., 541, 553

Piaget, J., 20, 22, 24, 88, 108, 112, 116, 144, 146, 152, 153, 155, 173, 206, 207, 209, 211, 218, 219, 220, 538

Pick, J., 160, 174, 217

Pickren, W. E., 82, 348, 364, 509, 510, 535, 544, 548, 551, 553

Piedmont, R. L., 286, 300

Pilpel, M. E., 397, 411

Pinderhughes, E., 496, 505

Pinel, P., 304, 314, 315, 336, 339, 340

Pinker, S., 127, 132, 144, 155

Pintrich, P. R., 274, 275, 276, 277

Pion, G. M., 476, 479, 480

Piotrowski, C., 282, 297, 300, 301, 352, 354

Pitts, W. H., 51, 64

Plato, 87, 110, 111, 112, 113, 114, 119, 126, 308, 309, 310, 314, 336, 451, 510, 517

Platt, J., 182, 187, 190, 192, 195, 201

Plomin, R., 213, 214, 220

Plummer, K., 179, 195, 201

Plutchik, R., 173, 174

Poggio, G. F., 48, 65

Pogliano, C., 65

Polansky, N. A., 189, 190, 201

Polkinghorne, D. E., 485, 506

Polyak, S., 107

Pond, M., 374, 378, 388

Ponterotto, J. G., 281, 301

Poortinga, Y., 459, 462, 511, 510, 511, 512, 516, 531, 532

Pope, B., 290, 301, 517

Popper, K. R., 136, 155

Porche-Burke, L., 477, 480

Porter, J., 69, 83, 508, 554

Porter, N., 7, 24

Porter, R. H., 78, 83

Porter, T. M., 183, 201

Posner, M. I., 3, 24, 59, 62, 65, 147, 155

Postman, L., 6, 24, 25

Potasznik, H., 439, 448

Potter, E. E., 380, 388

Potter, J., 240, 245

Povinelli, D. J., 80, 83

Powell, A. B., 295, 299, 506

Poythress, N., 399, 407, 408, 410, 411

Premack, D., 79, 80, 83

Pressey, S. L., 137, 470, 480

Pribram, K. H., 54, 57, 59, 61, 146, 154, 211, 220

Price, R. H., 155, 404, 410, 432, 446

Prieto, G., 283, 300

Prince, M., 32, 45, 179, 181, 184, 201, 303, 324, 325, 336, 342, 343, 354, 512

Prosser, C. L., 56, 65, 499

Prus, J. R., 428

Puente, A. E., 282, 298, 474, 477, 480, 483, 497, 498, 499, 506, 507

Puente, K. L., 498, 507

Pugh, R. L., 484, 507

Puig-Antich, J., 291, 301

Purisch, A. D., 293, 299

Puryear Keita, G., 480

Putnam, J. J., 181, 201

Pyke, S. W., 262, 267

Pylyshyn, Z. W., 128, 132

Quantz, J. O., 226, 227, 245

Quay, H., 330, 336

Quen, J., 400, 410

Quinlan, D. M., 438, 449

Quinsey, V., 407, 410

Radin, P., 180, 201

Radke-Yarrow, M., 214, 220

Radloff, L. S., 259, 267

Radtke, L., 229, 246

Rafferty, J. E., 289, 301

Raichle, M. E., 3, 24

Raichle, M. F., 62, 65

Raimy, V. C., 36, 45, 344, 346, 354, 361, 364, 548, 553

Rajecki, D. W., 476, 478

Ramey, C. T., 213, 220

Ramirez-Valles, J., 444, 449

Randall, J. H., 179, 201

Rank, O., 187, 202, 348, 349

Ranson, S. W., 57, 65

Rapaport, D., 180, 202

Raphael, P., 494, 507

Raphelson, A., 11, 24, 70, 83

Rapkin, B. D., 449

Rappaport, J., 439, 441, 442, 444, 445, 446, 447, 448, 449

Rasmussen, T., 51, 64, 65

Ratcliff, J. L., 467, 469, 470, 472, 479, 480

Ratcliff, K. S., 291, 301

Rau, L., 210, 221

Rauch, F., 6, 24

Raven, J., 65, 143, 147, 155, 173, 174

Ray, A. A., 165, 175

Ray, I., 317, 393, 411

Rayner, R., 17, 26

Raynor, R., 343, 355

Read, N. W., 193, 200

Reason, P., 1, 443, 448

Rees, E., 148, 153

Rees, J. R., 550, 553

Reese, H., 207, 220

Reese, M. R., 351, 354

Reich, J. N., 232, 233, 344, 471, 474, 476, 479

Reid, P. T., 254, 255, 267

Reid, T., 6, 86, 88, 108, 117

Reiff, R., 432, 435, 442, 448

Reinharz, S., 446

Reis, E. S., 162, 173

Reiser, M. F., 454, 462

Reisman, J. M., 33, 324, 337, 338, 339, 354

Reiss, D., 214, 217, 220

Reitan, R. M., 148, 293, 301

Reitman, J., 148, 155

Remer, P., 257, 268

Rempel, N. L., 61, 65, 66

Rempel-Clower, N., 61, 65

Reppucci, N. D., 405, 411, 437, 447, 448
Reschly, D., 283, 302, 425, 427, 429
Rescorla, R., 20, 24, 55, 65, 124, 132
Resnick, L. B., 42, 154, 216, 220
Retterstol, N., 306, 336
Retzlaff, P., 282, 298
Reviere, S. L., 252, 265
Reymert, M. L., 158, 173, 174, 244
Reyna, L. J., 349, 355
Reynolds, C. R., 424, 429
Reynolds, G., 226, 229, 243
Reynolds, M., 427, 429
Rhodes, R. L., 427, 429
Rice, C. E., 468, 480
Rice, F. J., 260, 268
Rice, M., 407, 410
Richards, G., 230, 233, 236, 238, 240, 245
Richards, R., 12, 24
Richardson, F. C., 485, 507
Richardson, W. K., 80, 84
Richmond, M. E., 180, 182, 197, 202
Richter, C. P., 57, 58, 65, 73, 75
Ridenour, N., 437, 440, 448
Rieber, R. W., 23, 201, 393, 411
Riesen, 54, 75, 218
Rieser, J. J., 205, 215, 220
Riesman, D., 235, 245
Riess, B. F., 37, 45
Riger, S., 254, 266, 432, 446
Riley, D., 236, 245
Rimé, B., 165, 175
Ring, K., 57, 88, 178, 237, 245, 393
Ritchie, B. F., 18, 25
Rivers, W. H., 326, 336
Roback, A. A., 6, 24, 184, 185, 190, 202, 382, 388
Robbins, L. C., 210, 220
Robbins, P., 411
Roberts, A., 448
Roberts, G. E., 300
Roberts, M. C., 263, 266
Roberts, T.-A., 258, 265
Robins, E., 301
Robins, L. N., 291, 301
Robinson, D. N., 485, 507
Robinson, E. S., 24, 398, 411
Robinson, F. G., 187, 188, 191, 192, 202
Robinson, J. A. G., 433, 448
Robinson, T., 432, 445
Robinson, V. P., 180, 202
Robinson-Kurpius, S. E., 42, 44
Rocha-Miranda, E. C., 98, 108
Rodin, J., 258, 267, 455, 463
Rodriguez-Marin, J., 463
Roe, A., 186, 202, 344, 362
Roesch, R., 399, 405, 407, 408, 410, 411
Roethlisberger, F. J., 378, 388
Rogers, A. M., 373, 385, 467, 470, 480
Rogers, C. R., 35, 37, 289, 290, 291, 301, 332, 336, 344, 345, 349, 354, 421

Rogers, R., 301
Rogler, L. H., 287, 298
Rogoff, B., 214, 216, 221
Rohde, A. R., 288, 289, 301
Roitblat, H. L., 79, 83
Rojahn, J., 351, 354
Rollins, K. B., 146, 152
Romanes, G. J., 14, 24, 68, 69, 70, 83, 119, 120, 132
Romero, M., 192, 202, 254, 263, 267
Ronning, R. R., 44, 269, 276, 364
Roosa, M. K., 443, 448
Root, M. P. P., 119, 483, 503, 504, 505, 507
Rorschach, H., 286, 287, 299, 300, 301, 302, 343, 522
Rorty, A.-O., 112, 132
Rosanoff, A., 288, 299
Rose, J. E., 51, 64, 138
Rose, N., 232, 238, 240, 245
Rosen, G., 311, 336, 440, 448
Rosen, R., 215, 220
Rosenbaum, A., 373, 385
Rosenbaum, R., 193, 202
Rosenberg, C., 224, 245
Rosenberg, R., 251, 267
Rosenblatt, J. S., 72, 75, 76, 81
Rosenblueth, A., 125, 132
Rosenblum, G., 75, 218, 444
Rosenkrantz, P. S., 256, 265
Rosenstock, I. M., 454, 463
Rosenthal, R., 184, 202, 286, 299, 301
Rosenzweig, M. R., 56, 64, 510, 512, 513, 516, 532, 536, 553
Rosenzweig, S., 230, 237, 245, 344
Rosnow, R. L., 229, 230, 237, 245, 246
Ross, A. O., 435, 446
Ross, D., 7, 24, 182, 202, 206, 212, 217, 221, 246, 407, 409, 416, 429
Ross, E. A., 223, 227, 228, 246
Ross, S. A., 212, 217
Rothbart, M., 214, 221
Rotter, J. B., 286, 289, 291, 301
Rouse, S. V., 287, 298, 315
Rousseau, J. J., 270, 277, 339, 536
Routh, D. K., 33, 34, 45, 324, 337, 338, 339, 344, 345, 348, 353, 354, 360, 365, 544, 553
Rovere, R. H., 433, 448
Rowe, E. W., 283, 299
Royer, F. L., 147, 155
Rozensky, R. H., 462
Rubin, E. J., 521
Rubin, J., 513, 532
Rubin, S., 239, 243
Rubin, Z., 212, 219, 237, 246
Rucci, A. J., 9, 24
Ruckmick, C. A., 157, 162, 175, 467, 468, 481
Ruckmick, C. R., 184, 202
Rudmin, F. R., 230, 231, 246
Rudolph, F., 465, 466, 469, 480
Rumbaugh, D. M., 79, 80, 83, 84
Rumelhart, D. E., 129, 132, 146, 155, 174
Runyan, W. M., 177, 178, 179, 181, 192, 194, 198, 202
Rush, B., 317, 452, 463

Russell, G. M., 254, 267
Russell, R., 315, 336, 511, 516, 532
Russo, N. F., 251, 265, 548, 553
Rutherford, W., 52, 65
Rutter, M., 214, 220
Ryan, A. M., 372, 388
Ryan, J. J., 282, 301
Rychlak, J. F., 484, 485, 505, 507

Saarni, C., 214, 221
Sabourin, M., 510, 516, 532, 536, 553
Sachs, B. D., 75, 83, 345
Sackett, G. P., 213, 221
Sacks, P., 135, 140, 155
Sahakian, W. S., 107
Said, E. W., 495, 507
Sakel, M., 326, 336
Saklofske, D. H., 275, 277
Saks, M., 406, 408, 410, 411
Salas, E., 381, 388
Salazar, J. M., 511, 532
Sales, B., 29, 377, 399, 402, 409, 411, 542
Salmon, D. P., 61, 65
Salter, A., 330, 336, 349, 355
Salthouse, T. A., 215, 221
Samelson, F., 16, 24, 183, 202, 228, 229, 231, 233, 234, 241, 246, 544, 553
Sameroff, A. J., 211, 213, 216, 217, 219, 221
Sammons, M. T., 41, 42, 44
Sampson, E. E., 238, 246
Sandler, I., 441, 445, 446
Sanford, E. C., 7, 8, 11, 12, 24, 69, 467, 468, 469, 472, 474, 480
Sanford, F. H., 467, 480
Sanford, N., 179, 191, 202
Sanford, R. N., 233, 242, 344
Sarason, I. G., 457, 463
Sarason, S. B., 344, 437, 443, 447, 448
Sarbin, T. R., 484, 507
Saslow, G., 454, 462
Sass, L., 485, 506
Sattler, J. M., 140, 151, 156, 281, 301
Saunders, R. C., 60, 65
Savage-Rumbaugh, E. S., 79, 83
Scarborough, E., 6, 11, 14, 15, 22, 25, 252, 267
Scarr, S., 214, 217, 221
Schachter, S., 57, 65, 132, 159, 162, 163, 164, 165, 166, 169, 175
Schaffner, P. E., 192, 202
Scheerer, M., 329, 335
Scheff, T. J., 331, 336
Scheibe, K. E., 227, 246
Scheirer, C. J., 467, 470, 480
Schetky, D., 400, 411
Schiller, M., 75, 219
Schilling, R. F., 443, 446
Schlitt, P., 427, 428
Schlosberg, H., 166, 175
Schmidt, F. L., 139, 155
Schmidt, H. D., 511, 532
Schmitz, B., 466, 480
Schmuck, R., 438, 448

Schneirla, T. C., 72, 73, 75, 76, 77, 79, 81, 83
Schoen, M., 475, 480
Schoenfeld, L. S., 297, 301
Schoenfeld, W., 132
Schofield, W., 456, 463
Schreckengost, J., 446
Schrecker, E., 433, 448
Schroeder, S. R., 351, 354
Schulman, J., 404, 411
Schulz, R. W., 25
Schunk, D. H., 269, 276, 277
Schusterman, R. J., 79, 83
Schwartz, G. E., 164, 175, 455, 463
Schwartz, R., 408, 409
Schwarzer, R., 451, 457, 463
Schwean, V. L., 275, 277
Schwesinger, G., 260, 537, 553
Scott, F. J. D., 512, 532
Scott, W. D., 29, 30, 33, 45, 75, 83, 360, 371, 374, 375, 377, 378, 381, 383, 388, 389
Scoville, W. B., 59, 61, 65, 378
Scripture, E. W., 327, 377, 388
Scull, A., 315, 336
Sears, D. O., 240, 246, 254, 267
Sears, P. S., 210, 221
Sears, R. R., 208, 210, 211, 212, 219, 230, 243
Seashore, C. E., 8, 25, 339, 467, 468, 469, 477, 480
Sechenov, I. M., 16, 23, 25, 123
Sedler, M. J., 315, 336
Segall, M. H., 511, 531
Seidman, E., 439, 443, 444, 447, 448, 449
Seifer, R., 219
Seigel, L. J., 462
Selesnik, S. T., 340, 353
Selfridge, O. G., 102, 108
Seligman, M. E. P., 40, 350, 351, 353, 354
Selling, L. S., 21, 368, 451, 463, 505
Seltzer, M., 228, 246
Selye, H., 58, 454, 463
Senna, D., 504, 507
Sennett, R., 235, 246
Sergi, G., 158, 160, 161, 175
Serpell, R., 511, 533
Settertobulte, W., 455, 462
Sevcik, R. A., 83
Sewall, T., 49, 65
Seward, G. H., 238, 246, 251
Sexton, J. L., 42, 44
Sexton, V. S., 352, 355, 497, 505, 510, 516, 533
Shakow, D., 36, 180, 202, 327, 333, 336, 344, 345, 346, 355, 545, 548
Shapin, S., 551, 554
Shapiro, D., 164, 175
Shapiro, S., 329, 336
Sharp, S. E., 40, 88, 114, 140, 155, 189, 206, 231, 291, 423, 438
Sharpless, S., 56, 65
Shartle, C. L., 368, 381, 388
Shaver, P., 404, 411
Shaw, C. R., 182, 202
Shaw, J. C., 128, 132

Shaw, K. M., 351, 355
Sheffield, A. E., 182, 202, 336
Sheinberg, M., 259, 266
Sheldon, H. P., 226, 227, 246
Sheldon, W. H., 328, 336
Shepherd, W. T., 70, 83, 334, 336, 343
Sheridan, E. P., 462, 548, 554
Sheridan, S., 427, 428
Sherif, C. W., 239, 240, 246, 251, 255, 267
Sherif, M., 230, 246
Sherman, P. W., 78, 82
Shermer, P., 179, 181, 184, 190, 202
Sheslow, D., 282, 299
Sheton, P., 373, 387
Shettleworth, S. J., 79, 80, 83
Shields, S. A., 13, 25, 251, 267
Shiffrin, R. M., 126, 127, 131, 132
Shinn, M., 439, 447, 448
Shoben, E. J., 37, 43
Shorris, E., 497, 507
Shorter, E., 93, 161, 326, 336, 352, 355, 397
Shotter, J., 236, 239, 242, 245, 246
Shulman, G. L., 59, 65
Shuman, D. W., 402, 411
Shure, M. B., 436, 441, 448
Sidle, A. L., 146, 152
Sidot, S., 463
Siegel, P. F., 153, 193, 198, 459
Siegelbaum, S. A., 56, 64
Siegler, R. S., 146, 152, 155, 207, 209, 215, 221
Sifneos, P. E., 454, 463
Silk, K., 287, 302, 313
Sillen, S., 483, 507
Silverman, D. L., 441, 535, 554
Silverstein, L. R., 258, 267
Simon, D. P., 148, 154
Simon, H., 110, 128, 132, 146, 148, 153, 154, 155
Simon, R., 393, 411
Simon, T., 139, 140, 152, 207, 218, 280, 281, 284, 288, 298, 338, 352, 353, 417, 520
Simonton, D. K., 192, 202
Simpkins, G., 494, 507
Singer, B., 68, 83
Singer, J. E., 57, 65, 162, 175
Singer, M. T., 456
Sinha, D., 510, 511, 533
Sirota, A. D., 164, 175
Sitarenios, G., 352, 353
Skaggs, E. B., 185, 189, 202
Skeem, J., 407, 411
Skinner, B. F., 19, 22, 25, 59, 74, 121, 122, 124, 125, 131, 132, 133, 170, 175, 198, 210, 211, 350, 355, 383, 488
Slater, R., 417, 429
Slesinger, D., 397, 398, 410, 411
Slife, B. D., 485, 507
Slobogin, C., 407, 410
Sloman, S. A., 140, 155
Small, A. W., 223, 224, 246
Small, W., 14, 25, 69, 83

Smith, C. S., 376, 386
Smith, H. H., 282, 300
Smith, J. M., 77
Smith, L., 8, 9, 23, 25, 124, 132, 443, 448
Smith, M. B., 75, 235, 246, 435, 448
Smith, M. L., 351, 355
Smith, R., 99, 108, 180, 181, 202, 229, 234, 239, 241, 246, 455, 462, 475, 478, 535, 554
Smolensky, P., 129, 130, 132
Smothergill, D. W., 479
Smyer, M. A., 42, 45
Snook, S., 156
Snow, R. E., 128, 137, 143, 155
Snowden, L. R., 444, 446
Soffer, R. N., 225, 246
Sokal, M., 4, 13, 25, 28, 34, 45, 183, 202, 228, 246, 373, 378, 388, 389, 540, 544, 551, 554
Sokolov, E. M., 56, 65
Sontag, L. W., 208, 221
Soueif, M. I., 510, 531, 533
Spangler, G., 214, 219
Spanos, N., 325, 336
Spaulding, J., 440, 448
Spearly, J. L., 437, 446
Spearman, C., 107, 136, 141, 142, 145, 146, 147, 151, 152, 155, 158
Spence, J. T., 253, 264, 267
Spence, K., 75, 121, 122, 132
Spencer, H., 7, 8, 25, 334
Spencer, W. A., 56, 66
Sperry, R. W., 54, 61, 65, 75, 149, 155
Spiegler, B. J., 60, 65
Spielberger, C. D., 174, 438, 446, 457, 463
Spilich, G. J., 148, 153
Spinoza, B., 158, 175
Spitzer, R. L., 290, 291, 298, 301
Spivack, G., 436, 441, 448
Sporer, S. L., 406, 411
Sprague, R. L., 351, 355
Spreen, O., 293, 301
Sprowls, J. W., 225, 227, 246
Sprung, L., 539, 554
Squire, L., 60, 61, 65, 66, 118, 132, 247
Sroufe, L. A., 212, 216, 221
Stagner, R., 178, 186, 187, 202, 367, 387, 541, 554
Stam, H. J., 14, 25, 229, 246, 247
Staples, S. L., 455, 463
Star, S. L., 48, 65, 83, 223, 373
Starr, P., 468, 551, 554
Staub, E., 194, 202, 220
Steadman, H., 401, 407, 409, 411
Stedman, J. M., 297, 301
Steele, R., 225, 246, 439, 448
Steinberg, L., 214, 221
Steiner, I., 175, 236, 237, 240, 246
Stellar, E., 57, 58, 65, 216
Stelzner, S. P., 446
Stenberg, C., 212, 218
Stephens, W. R., 359, 365
Stern, D. N., 212, 221

Stern, J. A., 454, 462
Stern, L. W., 396, 411
Stern, W., 185, 186, 202, 281, 301, 394, 396, 416, 429
Sternberg, R. J., 135, 136, 137, 141, 144, 145, 146, 147, 148, 150, 151, 152, 153, 154, 155, 156
Sternberg, S., 3, 25, 102, 108
Stevens, G., 544, 554
Stevens, S. S., 3, 18, 25, 48, 51, 57, 63, 64, 65, 85, 104
Stevenson-Hinde, J., 216, 219
Stewart, A. J., 192, 195, 199, 202, 254, 263, 265, 267
Stinnett, T. A., 283, 301
Stiver, I. P., 259, 266
Stober, D. R., 252, 265
Stokols, D., 437, 449
Stolorow, R. D., 192, 202
Stone, C. P., 71, 73, 80, 83, 110, 192
Stone, G. C., 457, 459, 463
Stone, W. F., 192, 202
Stouffer, S. A., 182, 202
Strauss, E., 293, 301, 459, 463
Strauss-Blasche, G., 459, 463
Street, W. R., 459, 462, 509, 533
Stricker, G., 37, 45, 347, 355, 475, 479
Strickland, L., 231, 233, 236, 239, 240, 242, 246, 264
Striegel-Moore, R. H., 258, 267
Strong, E. K., Jr., 294, 295, 301, 377, 468
Strother, C. R., 434, 437, 444, 449
Stubbs, D. A., 9, 25
Suarez, F., 158, 175
Sue, D. W., 477, 480, 491, 500, 501, 507, 546
Sue, S., 488, 491, 502, 507, 546
Suedfeld, P., 192, 203
Suess, G., 214, 219
Sugarman, J., 485, 506
Sullivan, H. S., 289, 301, 348
Suls, J. M., 229, 230, 237, 246
Sunar, D., 511, 533
Sundberg, N. D., 282, 301
Suomi, S. J., 75, 81, 83
Super, C. M., 150, 156, 213, 219, 360
Super, D. E., 45
Surrey, J., 259, 266
Susman, W., 179, 180, 203, 228, 246
Sutherland, A., 161, 175
Sutherland, M., 272, 277
Suttell, B. J., 292, 300
Suzuki, L. A., 281, 301
Suzuki, W. A., 61, 65
Swanson, L. W., 59, 66
Swartz, J. L., 437, 438, 449
Sweetman, M. B., 469, 479
Swets, J. A., 48, 63, 66, 105, 108, 531
Swezey, R., 381, 388
Symonds, P. M., 184, 203, 414, 421, 429
Szalacha, L. A., 254, 267
Szapocznik, J., 498, 507
Szasz, T. S., 330, 331, 336

Taal, E., 459, 463
Tableman, B., 442, 449

Tajfel, H., 237, 239, 243, 246
Takeuchi, D., 214, 220
Talor, C. R., 215, 220
Tank, D. W., 3, 62, 65
Tanner, W. P., 105, 108
Tapscott, D., 382, 388
Tarpy, R. M., 173
Tataryn, D. J., 214, 220
Taylor, E., 180, 181, 203
Taylor, F. W., 30, 45, 357, 365, 377, 388
Taylor, J. A., 328, 336
Taylor, S., 240, 246, 451, 461, 464
Teasdale, J. D., 351, 353
Teasley, S. D., 216, 220
Teitelbaum, P., 57, 58, 66
Tellegen, A., 284, 298
Telzrow, C., 427, 429
Tenopyr, M. L., 380, 388
Terenzini, P. T., 476, 480
Teri, L., 351, 355
Terman, L. M., 31, 136, 140, 156, 185, 203, 229, 247, 280, 281, 301, 352, 355, 359, 388, 417
Tesluk, P. E., 367, 370, 373, 386
Tharinger, D., 423, 424, 428, 545, 552
Thayer, P. W., 39, 367, 375, 381, 387, 388, 420, 421, 429, 548
Thelen, E., 209, 214, 217, 219, 221
Thomas, A., 219, 424, 428, 483, 507
Thomas, L., 223, 247
Thomas, W. I., 181, 182, 203, 223, 247
Thompson, B. W., 259, 267
Thompson, H. B., 13, 25
Thompson, R. F., 47, 55, 56, 61, 63, 64, 66
Thompson, W. C., 405, 411
Thompson, W. R., 73, 82
Thomson, D. C., 319, 336
Thomson, G. H., 141, 156
Thorndike, E. L., 9, 14, 15, 17, 18, 21, 22, 25, 70, 72, 80, 83, 84, 120, 121, 122, 123, 124, 130, 132, 136, 141, 156, 271, 277, 360, 416, 426, 429
Thorndike, R. L., 140, 151, 156, 281, 285, 301
Thorne, A., 187, 203
Thornton, G. R., 474, 480
Thornton, J. S., 474, 480
Thornton, M. C., 503, 507
Thornton, T. P., 179, 180, 203
Thorpe, W. H., 77, 84
Thurstone, L. L., 137, 141, 142, 151, 152, 156, 182, 184, 203, 360, 375, 388
Thurstone, T. C., 141, 156
Tichener, E. B., 48, 66
Tiedeman, D., 38, 45, 362
Tiefer, L., 257, 260, 261, 267, 547, 554
Timberlake, W., 78, 84
Tinsley, B. J., 212, 220, 221
Tinterow, M. M., 313, 336
Titchener, E. B., 8, 10, 11, 12, 15, 16, 17, 22, 23, 25, 33, 43, 70, 82, 84, 100, 161, 175, 542, 543, 551, 552
Tobach, E., 22, 72, 75, 76, 81
Tobey, R. C., 228, 247
Todd, D., 438, 449

Todd, J., 455, 462
Todd, P. M., 146, 153
Todes, D., 16, 25
Toglia, M., 407, 409
Tolman, D. T., 254, 267
Tolman, E. C., 19, 25, 71, 72, 120, 121, 122, 123, 124, 125, 126, 128, 130, 132, 133
Tomasello, M., 80, 81
Tomkins, A. J., 399, 410, 411
Tomkins, S., 165, 166, 175
Tooby, J., 78, 81
Toro, P., 444, 447, 449
Toulmin, S. E., 229, 247
Trabasso, T., 146, 152, 173, 174
Tracy, C., 392, 453, 475, 478
Triandis, H. C., 368, 369, 376, 387, 388, 515, 533
Trickett, E. J., 431, 438, 439, 444, 448, 449
Trimble, J. E., 501, 506, 546, 554
Trimpop, R., 230, 231, 246
Triplet, R. G., 184, 185, 203
Triplett, N., 226, 227, 247
Trommsdorf, G., 539, 554
Tronick, E., 212, 218, 221
Trzepacz, P. T., 290, 301
Tuber, D. S., 81, 84
Tuddenham, R. D., 13, 25
Tuke, D. H., 63, 314, 318, 336, 340
Tulving, E., 113, 132, 133
Tulviste, P., 216, 221
Turing, A. M., 127, 132, 133
Turner, S. M., 502, 507
Turner, T. J., 166, 174
Tuttle, W. M., 432, 449
Tweney, R. D., 9, 21, 24, 183, 203
Tyler, L., 38, 45, 362, 365, 484, 507

Ulrich, B. D., 214, 221
Underwager, R. W., 405, 411
Underwood, B. J., 6, 25
Unger, R., 252, 254, 265, 267
Ungerer, G. A., 4, 21
Unzner, I., 214, 219
Urbanski, L., 261, 267, 548, 553
Urbina, S., 294, 298
Urwin, C., 236, 244
Ussher, J., 254, 267
Uviller, E. T., 164, 174

Valenstein, E. S., 59, 66, 325, 336
Valins, S., 165, 175
Vallacher, R. M., 196, 201
Vallois, H. V., 49, 62
Vancouver, J. B., 275, 277
VandenBos, G. R., 27, 36, 39, 40, 41, 44, 45, 276, 324, 348, 352, 545, 554
Vanderploeg, R., 282, 298
Van De Water, T. J., 367, 374, 377, 389
van Drunen, P., 536, 554
Van Elderen, T., 452, 463
van Elteren, V., 230, 231, 233, 247
Van Strien, P. J., 515, 533

Varona y Pera, E. J., 498, 507
Vasquez, M., 477, 480, 500, 501
Vauclair, J., 79, 84, 118, 133
Vaux, A., 442, 449
Vazquez, C. I., 497, 507
Venn, C., 236, 244
Vernon, P. E., 142, 143, 156, 183, 184, 185, 186, 189, 197, 198, 203
Vernon, W. H. D., 498, 507
Vestal, M., 21
Veysey, L., 466, 468, 471, 473, 476, 480, 540, 554
Viglione, D. J., 286, 301
Villanova, P., 367, 385, 398, 399, 408
Viteles, M. S., 30, 367, 368, 369, 373, 374, 375, 378, 389
Vogel, S. R., 256, 265
Voith, V. L., 81, 84
Vonegas, H., 59, 63
von Mayrhauser, R., 380, 381, 389
Voss, J. F., 148, 153, 245, 246
Vygotsky, L. S., 145, 146, 156, 216, 221

Wade, C., 480
Wagenfield, M. O., 435, 449
Wagner, A. R., 55, 65
Wagner, R. K., 140, 156
Wakefield, H., 315, 405, 411
Walberg, H. J., 269, 277
Walder, L. O., 351, 353
Walk, R. R., 212, 219
Walker, G., 259, 266
Walker, L., 254, 259, 267, 410, 516, 532
Walker, N., 392, 395, 411
Walker, S. G., 192, 203
Walker, W. E., 476, 480
Walkerdine, V., 236, 241, 244, 247
Wall, P. C., 287, 406, 411, 501
Wallace, C. S., 33, 214, 219, 359, 381
Wallin, J. E. W., 33, 343, 359, 415, 417, 429
Wallis, R. R., 282, 300
Wallston, K., 352, 355, 459, 461
Walsh, M., 255, 267, 537, 554
Walsh-Bowers, R., 255, 267
Walters, R. H., 211, 217
Walzl, E. M., 53, 66
Wandersman, A., 432, 439, 445, 446
Wanschura, P. B., 148, 152
Ward, L. C., 23, 282, 293, 301
Warden, C. J., 72, 73, 80, 84
Warden, P. G., 428
Warner, L. H., 73, 84
Warren, H. C., 14, 20, 21, 25, 75, 177, 184, 203, 395, 509
Washburn, D. A., 80, 84
Washburn, M. F., 15, 21, 22, 23, 25, 70, 73, 80, 84, 215
Washburn, M. W., 21
Waskow, I. E., 349, 354
Wasserman, A. W., 401, 406, 408
Wasserman, E. A., 78, 84
Watkins, C. E., Jr., 282, 301
Watkins, E. S., 433, 449
Watson, D. L., 169, 174, 510, 533

Watson, J., 15, 16, 17, 18, 19, 21, 23, 25, 26, 30, 34, 45, 53, 54, 56, 66, 70, 74, 80, 84, 105, 120, 124, 170, 175, 207, 208, 209, 210, 211, 213, 221, 243, 341, 343, 355, 443, 445, 521
Watson, R. I., 5, 14, 26, 510, 533
Watts, B., 399, 408
Watts, G. A., 357, 358, 365
Watts, J. W., 325, 334
Watts, R. J., 439, 449
Wechsler, D., 140, 156, 279, 280, 281, 282, 293, 294, 298, 301, 302, 342, 344, 422
Weinberg, R., 424, 429
Weiner, D., 314, 336
Weiner, I., 279, 286, 287, 296, 302, 391, 407, 408, 410, 411
Weinman, J., 451, 457, 458, 459, 462, 463, 464
Weinreb, L., 392, 411
Weinstein, C. E., 269, 275, 277
Weinstein, R., 337, 437, 447
Weintraub, W., 192, 203
Weis, L., 254, 265
Weisman, C. S., 483, 505
Weiss, S. M., 355, 444, 455, 459, 461, 463
Weissberg, R. P., 436, 441, 442, 444, 445, 446, 449
Weisstein, N., 239, 247, 255, 256, 267
Weiten, W., 474, 475, 480, 481
Welker, W. S., 64
Wellman, H. M., 139, 153
Wells, G. L., 407, 411
Wells, H. G., 186, 203
Wells, P. D., 423, 428
Wenzel, B. M., 163, 175
Werner, G., 48, 65, 199, 203
Wertheimer, M., 17, 19, 26, 85, 105, 107, 345, 364, 367, 388, 497
Wertsch, J. V., 216, 221
West, C., 254, 267
Westen, D., 287, 302
Westkott, M. C., 259, 268
Wetherell, M., 240, 245
Wever, E. G., 52, 66
Whelan, T., 427, 429
Whipple, G. M., 396, 411, 467, 468, 469, 481
White, C., 259, 267
White, J. C., 259, 266
White, J. L., 484, 493, 506, 507
White, N. M., 61, 65
White, R. D., 439, 449
White, R. W., 188, 191, 203, 344, 436, 449, 508
White, S., 12, 26, 206, 221
Whitehead, A. N., 465, 478, 481
Whiteley, J. M., 43, 45, 363, 365
Whiting, J. W. M., 210, 221
Whitman, T. L., 439, 449
Whitten, L., 259, 266
Whytt, R., 312, 313, 336
Wickens, D. D., 291, 301
Wiebe, R., 228, 247, 540, 554
Wiener, N., 125, 132
Wiens, A. N., 44, 290, 300
Wiesel, T. N., 50, 51, 64, 98, 107
Wigan, A. L., 317, 336

Wiggam, A. E., 34, 45
Wiggins, J. G., 42, 44
Wight, R. D., 474, 475, 481
Wigmore, J. H., 394, 396, 411
Wilcox, B. L., 437, 438, 446
Wilkinson, G., 294, 299, 302
Wilkinson, S., 240, 247, 255, 263, 268
Williams, B. H., 493, 494, 508, 546, 554
Williams, C. L., 298
Williams, C. W., 282, 300
Williams, J. B. W., 291, 301
Williams, N., 443, 448
Williams, R., 485, 494, 505, 507, 508, 546, 554
Williams, S. L., 83
Williams, W. M., 156
Willis, T., 49, 312, 336
Wilpert, B., 510, 533, 536, 554
Wilson, B. D. M., 431
Wilson, E., 78, 84, 459, 462
Wilson, L., 214, 220
Wilson, M., 78, 82, 283, 302
Wilson, S., 433, 449
Winder, C. L., 435, 446
Winokur, G., 454, 462
Winston, A., 9, 26, 63, 108, 154, 178, 203, 217, 220, 229, 247, 355, 428, 462, 506, 532
Winter, D. G., 53, 177, 179, 185, 188, 192, 193, 194, 195, 200, 203, 337, 463
Wise, P. S., 111, 206, 236, 269, 358, 414, 424, 427, 428, 429
Wispe, L., 489, 493, 508, 546, 554
Wissler, C., 139, 156
Witmer, L., 13, 24, 28, 29, 30, 31, 32, 36, 43, 44, 45, 337, 338, 339, 341, 342, 343, 354, 355, 359, 360, 364, 416, 417, 418, 429, 515, 519, 542
Wittrock, M. C., 269, 271, 273, 276, 277
Wohlford, P., 501, 506, 507, 508
Wolf, S., 454, 464
Wolfe, B., 349, 354
Wolfe, H. K., 470, 481
Wolff, H. G., 1, 100, 454, 464, 517
Wolfle, D., 35, 45, 75, 272, 470, 472, 473, 474, 478, 481
Wolfson, D., 293, 301
Wolpe, J., 349, 355
Wong, K. Y., 437, 445, 491
Woocher, F. D., 401, 411
Woodard, J., 227, 247
Woodruff, G., 80, 83
Woodworth, R. S., 3, 9, 10, 26, 158, 177, 178, 180, 183, 184, 185, 192, 203, 247, 271, 277, 283, 284, 302, 342, 509, 533
Woodyard, E. I., 141, 156
Woolfolk, R., 485, 506
Woolley, H. T., 13, 26, 249, 251, 252, 255, 268, 358, 359
Woolsey, C. N., 50, 51, 53, 64, 66
Worcester, D. A., 24, 25, 33, 63, 173, 174, 203, 244, 245, 272, 277, 327, 346
Worell, J., 253, 257, 261, 263, 264, 266, 268
Work, W. C., 441, 445
Worley, J. L., 548, 553
Wortis, J., 331, 336

Wozniak, R. H., 205, 221
Wrenn, C. G., 38, 45
Wrightsman, L. S., 393, 404, 411
Wrzesniewski, K., 458, 463
Wundt, W., 4, 5, 6, 7, 8, 10, 13, 15, 21, 23, 26, 33, 47, 48, 51, 66, 81, 84, 85, 100, 102, 106, 118, 158, 159, 161, 175, 337, 338, 341, 382, 510, 511, 515, 517, 518, 532
Wyatt, G. E., 496, 508
Wyche, K., 260, 268, 496, 505
Wyman, P. A., 441, 445

Yamazaki, K., 78, 81
Yang, S., 71, 137, 156, 501
Yardley, J., 193, 203
Yarmey, A. D., 406, 411
Yarrow, L. J., 213, 221
Yarrow, M. P., 221
Yarrow, M. R., 210, 221
Yates, J. F., 495, 505
Yerkes, R. M., 15, 16, 26, 33, 53, 61, 69, 70, 71, 72, 73, 74, 75, 79, 81, 84, 199, 203, 342, 343, 345, 355, 360, 381
Yllo, K., 254, 268
Yoakum, C. S., 70, 84
York, K. L., 187, 203
Yoshikawa, H., 448

Young, D., 8, 443, 446
Young, H. H., 344
Young, K., 184, 203, 502, 503, 505
Young, T., 51, 96
Ysseldyke, J., 424, 427, 429
Yu, S. L., 275, 277

Zahn-Waxler, C., 205, 214, 218, 220
Zane, N., 491, 502, 507
Zapf, P., 407, 411
Zaphiropoulos, L., 258, 265
Zedeck, S., 376, 379, 383, 389
Zelizer, V. A., 416, 429
Zemsky, R., 466, 481
Zenderland, L., 31, 45
Zickar, M. J., 367, 384, 387, 389
Zimmerman, B. J., 269, 275, 276, 277
Zimmerman, D. H., 254, 267
Zimmerman, M. A., 442, 444, 449
Zinn, H., 433, 449
Zins, J. E., 425, 429
Znaniecki, F., 181, 203, 223, 247
Zola, S. M., 47, 49, 60, 61, 65, 66
Zola-Morgan, S., 49, 60, 61, 65, 66
Zytowski, D. G., 295, 300

Subject Index

Ability, measures of, 360
Abnormal psychology:
  biological understanding of psychopathology, progress in, 332–333
  definitions, 304–305
  early attempts at classification, 305–306
  experimental psychopathology, 326–328, 333
  legal views of mentally ill, 306–307
  organic *vs.* functional psychoses, 329–330
  periods in history of:
    classical period, 307–310
    from Middle Ages to eighteenth century, 310–315
    eighteenth century to mid-nineteenth century, 315–318
    late-nineteenth century into twentieth century, 318–325
    twentieth century, 325–333
    into twenty-first century, 333
  popular myths of psychopathology, 304–305
  psychopharmacology, 331
  recent approaches, 330–332
  theories of origin and research in antisocial personality, 330
  "Third Force" and the new therapies, 332
  typologies of mental illness, 328–329
Accreditation/credentialing organizations, 548–549
Achievement, measuring (assessment psychology), 294–296
Action commune, 49
Action research *vs.* prevention science, 442–443
Adolescent psycholegal issues, 407–408
Africa, professional organizations in, 540
African Americans. *See* Ethnic minorities
America:
  early history of psychology in, 6–8
  personality and psychology in, 183–186
  professional organizations, 540–544
  rise of laboratories in, 8
  trend from Americanization to internationalization, 515–516
American Association of Applied Psychology (AAAP), 344, 545
American Association of Clinical Psychologists (AACP), 34, 343, 544
American Association of Correctional Psychologists, 545
American Board of Examiners in Professional Psychology (ABEPP), 37, 346
American Board of Professional Psychology (ABPP), 548–549
American Indian Interest Group, 546
American Orthopsychiatric Association, 549
American Psychological Association (APA):
  activism in, 500
  Congressional Science Friendship Program, 41
  Division of Personnel and Guidance Psychologists, 361
  founded, 28
  split, 544
  women and, 261–262, 547–548
American Psychological Association of Graduate Students (APAGS), 41
American Psychological Society (APS), 544

American Psychology-Law Society (AP-LS), 541–542
Amicus curiae briefs, 395–396, 404–406
Analytical curricular model, 472–474
Analytic introspection, 100
Animal psychology, 13–15, 119–120, 349. *See also* Comparative psychology
"Animal spirits to animal electricity," 312–313
Anti-psychiatry, 331–332
Antisocial personality, theories of origin and research in, 330
Applied psychological organizations, 344, 536, 538, 544–545
Approach-avoidance conflict, experimental neurosis and, 328
Aptitude measures (assessment psychology), 294–296, 360
Army Alpha/Beta, 281, 381
Army General Classification Test (AGCT), 381
Artificial intelligence, 127–128
Asia, professional organizations in, 539
Asian American Psychological Association (AAPA), 546
Asian/Asian Americans, 490–492, 499–500, 503
Assessment psychology:
  achievement, aptitudes, and interests, 294–296
  future, 296–297
  intellectual ability, 280–283
  neuropsychological functioning, 292–294
  origins of, 279–280
  personality characteristics and psychopathology, 283–292
    behavioral methods, 291–292
    interview methods, 289–291
    relatively structured tests, 283–286
    relatively unstructured tests, 286–289
  rise of psychological testing in counseling psychology, 359–360
Association for Applied Psychophysiology and Biofeedback, 545
Association for the Advancement of Behavior Therapy, 545
Association for Women in Psychology (AWP), 260–261, 547–548
Association model, moral management and, 314–315
Association of Black Psychologists (ABPsi), 487, 492–495, 545–546
Association of Consulting Psychologists (ACP), 35
Association of Psychology Postdoctoral and Internship Centers (APPIC), 548
Association of State and Provincial Psychology Boards (ASPPB), 548
Australia (professional organizations), 540
Autonomic Perception Questionnaire (APQ), 164

Balance theories (social psychology), 235–236
Behavioral assessment methods, 291–292
Behavioral Avoidance Test (BAT), 349–350
Behavioral ecology and comparative psychology, 77–78
Behavioral health/medicine, 455
Behavioral laboratories, rise of, 101–103
Behaviorism, 15–17
  animal psychology and, 119–120
  behavior therapy and, 330

cognitive, 122
   emotion (and psychoanalysis) and, 169–171
   Golden Age of Learning Theory and, 120–125
   industrial-organizational (I-O) psychology and, 383
   metaphysical, 122–125
   methodological, 120–122
   physiological, 123–124
   radical, 124–125
   stimulus-response theories, 120–122
Behavior modification, 331
Behavior therapy, 330, 331, 349, 351
Bender Gestalt, 292–293
Binet scales, 280–281
Biofeedback, 164, 545
Biology/biological psychology, 148–150, 213–214, 332–333
   brain, 48–51, 316–319, 325, 332–333
   cognitive neuroscience, 59–62
   color vision, 51–52
   development, 213–214
   experimental psychopathology, 333
   intelligence, 148–150
   learning and memory, 53–56
   mind, 47–48
   motivation and emotion, 56–59
   new genetics, 333
   pitch detection, 52–53
   psychopathology, 332–333
   sensory processes, 51–53
Black Students in Psychology Association (BSPA), 494, 546
Bonds, theory of, 141
Boulder model, 36
Brain:
   in biological psychology, 48–51
   hemisphere theories, 317–318
   lesions and psychopathology, 318–319
   measurement, 332–333
   pathology model of psychopathology and nervous diseases, 316–317
   surgery, 325
   theory of the evolution of (psychopathology), 318
British professional organizations, 262, 540
Business forces, and rise of I-O psychology, 377–379. See also
      Industrial-organizational (I-O) psychology
Business psychology, 29–30, 367

California Psychological Inventory (CPI), 285
Canada:
   professional organizations, 262, 540
   U.S. International Congress (1954) held in, 512
Cartesian dualism and the veil of ideas, 114–115
Child:
   development (professional organizations), 550
   guidance clinic (African American leadership), 489
   psycholegal issues, 407–408
   study, 12, 416
Children's Apperception Test (CAT), 287
China, 511
Chronology of milestones, 517–531
Civil rights movement, 379–380, 487. See also Ethnic minorities
Classical medical theory, 307

Classical world before Plato (cognition), 110–111
Classification, 305–306, 315–316, 328–329
Clinical forensic evaluations, 407
Clinical problems frequently presented in therapy (ethnic minorities), 502
Clinical psychology, 337–355
   future trends, 352–353
   "nurturing zeitgeist," 345–347
   organizational struggles, 344–345
   origins of, 32–33, 338–339
   professional developments, 35–37, 347–348
   school psychology and, 416
   scientific art (vs. artistic science), 339–340, 341
   "sustaining zeitgeist," 341–344
   training models, 344–345
   treatment interventions, 348–352
Clinico-anatomic method, 318
Cognition:
   comparative, 78–79
   definitions, 87–90
   developmental psychology and, 211
Cognition and learning:
   animal psychology and coming of behaviorism, 119–120
   artificial intelligence, 127–128
   behaviorism, 120–125
   Cartesian dualism and the veil of ideas, 114–115
   computing (key ideas of), 125–127
   connectionist, subsymbolic, hypothesis, 128–131
   early scientific period, 118–124
   empiricist tradition, 115–117
   idealist tradition, 117
   impact of evolution, 118–119
   levels (cognitive/algorithm/implementation), 127–128
   mind design and architectures of cognition, 127–128
   modern period: cognition after the scientific revolution, 115–117
   modern scientific period, 125–131
   philosophical period, 110–117
   premodern period (cognition before the Scientific Revolution),
      110–114
   psychology of consciousness, 118
   realist tradition, 117
   scientific revolution and new understanding of cognition, 114–115
   symbol-system hypothesis, 128
   verbal learning tradition, 118
   way of ideas: rejecting realism, 114
Cognitive behaviorism, 122
Cognitive behavior therapy, 349
Cognitive demons, 102
Cognitive neuroscience (biological psychology), 59–62
Cognitive processes/structures, intelligence arising from, 144–148
Cognitive psychology:
   computer metaphor of mind, 131
   consciousness, 131
   development, 131, 214
   educational psychology and, 273–274
   evolution, 131
   meaning, 131
   rise of (mentalism revisited), 19–20
   today, 131
Cognitive realism, 113

Cognitive science, 127–131, 550
Cognitive theory and I-O psychology, 383
Color vision/perception, 51–52, 96–97, 106–107
Comas and convulsions, 326
Committee on Equality of Opportunity in Psychology (CEOP), 546
Community, minority psychologists in, 488–490
Community involvement, 40
Community psychology, 349
　action research *vs.* prevention science, 442–443
　from community mental health to community psychology, 434–435
　early developments, 431–435
　ecological perspective/assessment, 436–439
　economic boon and the GI bill, 432
　preventive interventions, 440–443
　race relations, 432–433
　social ferment (1950s) and incubation of, 432
　social problems in context of cultural norms/values, 439
　social upheaval (1960s) and birth of, 433–434
　strengths perspective, 435–436
　Swampscott Conference, 435
　World War II and, 440
Comparative psychology. *See also* Animal psychology
　academic societies, 76
　behavioral ecology and, 77–78
　comparative cognition, 78–79
　European ethology, 77
　evolutionary psychology and, 77–78
　funding, 75
　influences on, 76–79
　journals, 76
　periods in history of:
　　forerunners, 68–69
　　early history, 68
　　before World War I, 69–71
　　between the wars, 71–74
　　since World War II, 74–76
　persistent issues in, 79–82
　personnel, 74–75
　research centers, 75–76
　sociobiology and, 77–78
　soul-searching, 76
　textbooks, 73–74
Computer technology and organizations (I-O psychology), 381–382
Computing, 90, 125–131
　algorithm level, 127
　artificial intelligence, 127–128
　cognitive level, 127
　cognitive science, 127–131
　computational metaphor of mind, 127, 131
　computational theories, 90
　connectionist/subsymbolic hypothesis, 128–131
　feedback, 125–126
　implementation level, 128
　information, 126–127
　key ideas (three) of, 125–127
　mind design and architectures of cognition, 127–128
　program/computation, 127
　symbol-system hypothesis, 128
Conditioned reflex, 327–328
Conflict theories, 167–171

Congressional Science Friendship Program, 41
Connection(s), theory of, 141
Connectionist/subsymbolic hypothesis, 128–131
Consciousness:
　cognitive psychology today, 131
　psychology of, 118
　way of ideas, 114
Correspondence problem, 87
　gestaltists and, 105–106
　psychophysicists and, 103–105
Counseling psychology, 30–31
　beginnings of new profession, 30–31
　diversification in, 362
　guidance movements, 358–359
　identity question, 361–363
　modern age of, 357–358
　postwar growth, 37–38
　rise of psychological testing, 359–360
　vocational guidance, 359
　vocational psychology, 359
　World War II and training of psychologists, 360–361
Creative synthesis, 100–101
Cuban-American perspective in psychology, 497–499
Cultural diversity. *See* Ethnic minorities; Women and gender, psychology of "Culture of personality," 179–180
Culture/society:
　correlates of illness, 455
　development and, 214–215
　intelligence and, 150
Cybernetics and social psychology, 234–236

Data treatment and research design, 9
Decision demon, 102
Degeneracy theory, 319–320
Depression, research on treatment of, 349–351
Depth psychology, and personality, 187
Desensitization procedures, 349
Developmental psychology, 131, 144–145
　advances in theory and method, 213
　biology of development, 213–214
　characteristics of early theories of, 207–208
　cognition, 131, 211, 214
　culture, role of (in development), 214–215
　emotion, 212
　founders, 206–207
　future, 217
　institutes of child development, 208
　intellectual development stages, 144–145
　learning theory and psychoanalysis, 210
　operant orientation, 210–211
　periods in history of:
　　1880–1914, 206–208
　　1915–1940 (period of institutionalization and fragmentation), 208–210
　　1940–1960 (era of expansion), 210–211
　　1960–1985 (rise of contemporary themes), 211–213
　　1985–present (current period), 213–217
　precocity, 211
　social interaction/relationships, 212
　social learning theory, 211–212
　triad of towering theorists, 208–209

Diagnosis, 332
Direct perception, 89
Diversity and cultural difference, 259. *See also* Ethnic minorities; Women
    and gender, psychology of
Draw-a-Man test, 287–288
Draw-a-Person (DAP), 288
Drug therapy/treatment, 331, 349–352
Dualism, 114–115, 236–237

Ecological perspective, community psychology, 436–439
Economic psychology, 367
Educational psychology:
    cognitive psychology's influence, 273–274
    contributions of early philosophers, 269–270
    discipline today, 274
    early developments in America, 271
    effects of instructional psychology, 273
    European influences (in eighteenth and nineteenth centuries), 270–271
    future, 276
    goals, 274–276
    school psychology and, 416
    tracing progress through written record, 272
    twentieth century developments, 271–272
Education/training in psychology. *See* Training/education in psychology
Electronic publishing initiatives, 40
Emission theory of vision, 91–92
Emotion:
    behaviorism and psychoanalysis, 169–171
    central/mental approaches to, 165–167
    conflict theories, 167–171
    developmental psychology and, 212
    facial expression and, 166–167
    future of, 170–172
    peripheral/organic approaches to, 160–165
    premodern history of, 157–159
    themes in modern history of, 159
    two distinct psychologies of, 159–160
    variations in pheripheral/visceral activity, 163–165
Empiricism, 110, 115–117
Employment psychology, 367
Environmental health psychology, 455. *See also* Health psychology
Equal Employment Opportunity Commission (EEOC), 380
Equilibration, 144
Ethical/professional issues:
    expert witness, 402–403
    scientific amicus briefs, 405–406
Ethnic minorities:
    activism in APA, 500
    Asian Americans in psychology (organization efforts by), 490–492
    challenge of change: formation of the Association of Black
        Psychologists, 492–495
    civil rights movement, 379–380, 487
    community psychology and race relations, 432–433
    confrontations and change, 486–488
    doctoral programs in psychology, 493
    hispanic ethnicity in psychology: Cuban-American perspective,
        497–499
    history of ethnic minority psychological publishing, 495–496
    humanizing of psychology, 483–486
    minority psychologists in the community, 488–490

    models of racial and ethnic identity (origins of an ecological framework
        of identity development), 503–505
    progress during 1999, 500–501
    in research and organization, 499–501
    treating ethnic minority clients, 501–502
        client resistance and treatment effectiveness, 502
        clinical problems frequently presented in therapy, 502
        therapists' reported levels of comfort, 502
Ethology, European, 77
Ethos, scientific, 183
Eugenics, 320
Europe/European:
    ethology, 77
    influences (educational psychology) in eighteenth and nineteenth
        centuries, 270–271
    professional organizations, 538–539
Evoked potentials, 50
Evolution/evolutionary theory:
    cognitive psychology and, 118–119, 131
    comparative psychology and, 68–69, 77–78
Experimental psychology. *See* Scientific psychology
Expert witness, psychologists as, 396–397, 401–403. *See also* Forensic
    psychology
"Exploration" project, 187–189
Eyewitness memory, 396, 406–407

Facial expression and emotion, 166–167
Fear Survey Schedule, 291, 349–350
Feedback, 125–126. *See also* Biofeedback
Feminism. *See* Women and gender, psychology of
Fever therapies, 325–326
Figure drawing methods, 287–288
Five Factor Model, 285
Forensic psychology:
    amicus curiae briefs, 395–396, 404–406
    basic knowledge domains, 398–399
    child and adolescent psycholegal issues, 407–408
    clinical forensic evaluations, 407
    conceptualizations of insanity, 392–394
    current issues in, 404–408
    defining, 391–392
    early attempts to apply psychological/psychiatric knowledge to the legal
        system, 392–398
    emergence as recognized subfield, 398–404
    ethical/professional issues in, 402–403, 405–406
    eyewitness memory/testimony, 396, 406–407
    forensic clinical evaluations, 400–401
    future of, 408
    journals/textbooks, 398
    pre-1955 psychological writings about psychology and law,
        397–398
    professional organizations, 398
    psychologists as expert witness, 396–397, 401–403
    psychologists as trial consultants, 403–404
    research advances, 406–408
    training in, 399–400
Free association, 289
Functional analysis of behavior, 349
Functionalism, 127, 382–383
Functional/structural psychologies, 10–12

Gender. *See* Women and gender, psychology of
General Aptitude Test Battery (GATB), 375
General paresis, 318
Genetics, new, 333
German psychology, 6, 185–189, 511–512
Gestalt psychology, 17, 105
   correspondence problem, 105–106
   industrial-organizational (I-O) psychology, 383
GI Bill of Rights, 432, 466
Group-administered tests, 281, 360
Guidance movements, 358–359

Halstead-Reitan Neuropsychological Test Battery (HRB), 293
Health psychology:
   American organizational efforts, 456–457
   education/training, 459–460
   in Europe, 460
   formalizing as field of inquiry/practice, 453–458
   international organizational efforts, 457–458
   professional practice, 458–459
   roots of, 451–453
   terminology, 455
Hispanics in psychology, 497–499, 500. *See also* Ethnic minorities
Holland Self-Directed Search, 295–296
House-Tree-Person (HTP), 288
Human Factors Society of American, 549–550
Humanistic psychology, 349
Humanizing of psychology, 483–486
Human rights, 513, 514
Hypnosis, 313–314, 320–322

Idealist tradition, 117
Identity models, racial/ethnic, 503–505
Illusion, science of, 99–101, 106–107
Indians into Psychology Doctoral Education (INDPSYDE), 547
Individual differences, 12–13. *See also* Personality psychology
Individual-social world (dualism revisited), 236–237
Inductive reasoning (theory of primary mental abilities), 142
Industrial-organizational (I-O) psychology, 38
   business forces and, 377–379
   confluence of dynamic forces and, 373–384
   employment opportunities in, 371–372
   future, 384–385
   intradisciplinary forces and, 383–384
   labels and definitions, 367–368
   legal forces and, 379–380
   military forces and, 380–381
   organization of, 372
   psychological forces and, 382–383
   rise of, 38, 367–373
   scope of content, 368–370
   socioeconomic forces and, 374–377
   technological forces and, 381–382
   training/education programs in, 370–371
Industrial revolution, 377
Information/information theory, 105, 126–127, 234. *See also* Computing
Insanity, conceptualizations of, 392–394
Instructional psychology, and educational psychology, 273
Intellectual ability, evaluating:
   Binet scales, 280–281

brief methods, 282
   frequency of test use, 282–283
   group-administered tests, 281
   Kaufman scales, 282
   Wechsler scales, 281–382
Intellectual development stages, 144–145
Intelligence:
   biological bases of, 148–150
   cognitive processes and, 146–148
   cognitive structures and, 144–146
   complexity *vs.* simplicity:
      intelligence as complex (Binet's theory of judgment), 139–140
      intelligence as simple (Galton's theory of psychophysical processes), 138–139
   culture/society and, 150
   differential model, 137
   as energy and sensitivity, 138
   expert opinions on nature of, 136–137
   models on nature of, 140–144, 151–152
      bifactor theory, 142
      hierarchical theories, 142–143
      psychometric models, 140–142
      radex model, 143
      relations among the various models, 151–152
      structure-of-intellect model, 143
      theory of bonds, 141
      theory of connections, 141
      theory of fluid and crystallized abilities, 142–143
      theory of primary mental abilities, 141–142
      theory of verbal/educational/spatial/mechanical abilities, 142
      three-stratum theory, 143
      two-factor theory, 141
   operationally defined, 136
   systems models and, 150–151
Interamerican Society of Psychology (SIP), 537–538
Interest, measures of, 294–296, 360
International Association of Applied Psychology (IAAP), 536, 538
International Committee for Mental Hygiene (ICMH), 550
International Council of Psychologists, 536–537, 547
International psychology:
   chronology of milestones in, 517–531
   conflict over 1980 Congress (Leipzig), 514
   development of modern psychology, 510–512
   human rights (differing view on), 513
   1913 International Congress (that wasn't), 512
   roots of, 510
   social issues, psychologists' evolving stand on, 514–515
   trend from Americanization to internationalization, 515–516
   U.S. International Congress (1954) held in Canada, 512
   Young Psychologists Program, 512–513
International Society of Sport Psychology, 545
International Union of Psychological Sciences (IUPsyS), 535–536, 538
Interpersonal Cognitive Problem Solving (ICPS), 441
Interview methods:
   relatively structured formats, 290–291
   relatively unstructured formats, 289–290

Japan, 511
Journals/textbooks/publishing:
   assessment psychology, 296

comparative psychology, 76
electronic publishing initiatives, 40
ethnic minority psychological publication, 495–496
forensic psychology, 398
Journal of Consulting Psychology, 545
professional journal within APA, 39–40

Kaufman scales, 282
Kiddie SADS, 291
Kinetic Family Drawing (KFD), 288
Kuder Occupational Interest Survey (KOIS), 295

Laboratory, psychological. *See* Scientific psychology
Labor unions, 375
Law of effect, 121
Learning:
   cognition and (*see* Cognition and learning)
   memory and (biological psychology), 53–56
   psychoanalysis and theory of, 210
   social, 211–212, 351
   strategic learning model, 275
   verbal, 118
Legal forces, and rise of I-O psychology, 379–380
Legal system. *See* Forensic psychology
Legal views of mentally ill, 306–307, 392–394
Locus of control, 238
Logical positivism and operationism, 17–18
Luria-Nebraska Neuropsychological Battery, 293

Magnetism and mesmerism to hypnosis, 313–314
Meaning (cognitive psychology today), 131
Melancholy, anatomy of, 311–312
Memory:
   Aristotle's structure of human soul, 112
   eyewitness, 396, 406–407
   learning and (biological psychology), 53–56
   long-term declarative (or explicit), 60
   theory of primary mental abilities, 142
Mental chronometry, 3
Mental hygiene movement/organizations, 182–183, 550
Mental illness. *See also* Abnormal psychology:
   legal views of, 306–307, 392–394
   typologies of, 328–329
Mental Status Examination (MSE), 290
Mental test, 280, 338
Meta-analysis, 351
Metaphysics, 110
   metaphysical behaviorism, 122–125
   metaphysical realism, 113–114
Methodological behaviorism, 120–122
Middle/Near East (professional organizations), 539
Military forces/world wars, 33–34, 360–361, 380–381, 440, 540–541
   Army Alpha/Beta, 281, 381
   Army General Classification Test (AGCT), 381
   GI Bill of Rights, 432, 466
Millon Clinical Multiaxial Inventory (MCMI), 285
Mind:
   active/passive (Aristotle's distinction), 113
   architectures of cognition, 127–128
   biological psychology, 47–48

dualism, 452
   holistic view of mind-body relationship, 452
Minnesota Employment Stabilization Research Institute (MESRI), 360, 375
Minnesota Multiphasic Personality Inventory (MMPI), 284, 295
Minorities. *See* Ethnic minorities
Mixed race identity, 503–504
Moral management and the association model, 314–315
Motivation and emotion (biological psychology), 56–59
Multiple personality, 324–325

Nancy School, 321
National Association of School Psychologists (NASP), 545
National Council of Women Psychologists (NCWP), 260, 536–537, 547
National Hispanic Psychological Association, 547
National Institutes of Mental Health (NIMH), 345, 347, 361
National Register of Health Service Providers in Psychology (NR), 548, 549
National Society for the Promotion of Industrial Education (NSPIE), 359
National Vocational Guidance Association, 362
Near and Middle East (professional organizations), 539
Neo-behaviorists, 18–19
NEO Personality Inventory (NEO-PI), 285–286
Nervous diseases (neurosis and neurasthenia), 329
Network of Indian Psychologists, 546
Neuropsychological functioning, monitoring:
   Bender Gestalt, 292–293
   test batteries, 293–294
Neurosis, 328, 329
New York State Association of Consulting Psychologists, 545
New Zealand (professional organizations), 540
North America, professional organizations in, 540–544
Nosological systems, 315–316
Noumena/phenomena, 117
Number (theory of primary mental abilities), 141

Operant orientation, developmental psychology, 210–211
Operationism, 17–18
Opponent-process theory, 51
Organic *vs.* functional psychoses, 329–330
Organizational psychologist, 38. *See also* Industrial-organizational (I-O) psychology
Organizations. *See* Professional organizations

Pandemonium, 102
Perception. *See* Sensation and perception
Perceptual realism, 113
Perceptual speed (theory of primary mental abilities), 142
Personality Assessment Inventory (PAI), 286
Personality characteristics and psychopathology, identifying (assessment psychology), 283–292
   behavioral methods, 291–292
   figure drawing methods, 287–288
   interview methods, 289–291
   picture-story methods, 287
   Rorschach Inkblot Method, 286–287
   sentence completion methods, 288–289
   structured tests, 283–286
   unstructured tests, 286–289
Personality psychology:
   ambivalence in, 177–179, 189–190, 191–196
   American psychology, 183–185

Personality psychology: *(Continued)*
case studies and life histories in, 177–179
context and complexity in, 195–196
culture of personality, 179–180
"exploration" project, 187–189
individualized assessment ventures, 191
intuitive method, 186
mental hygiene movement, 182–183
motives driving psychologists to study individuals, 193–195
multidisciplinary study of personality (1900–1930), 179–185
personological concepts, 187–189, 190–191
professional concerns, 184–185
psychiatry and psychopathology, 180–181
publication trends, 190
questioning of "science," 194–195
reconceptualizing goals of, 194
roots of:
    American psychology, social ethics, and German psychology, 185–186
    medicine/literature/"depth psychology," 187
scientific case studies, 186–187
scientific ethos, 183
social context (importance of), 195
sociology and social work, 181–182
study of individual lives and individual differences, 179–196
Personology, 187–189, 190–191
Phenomena/noumena, 117
Philosophy, 1–2, 269–270
Phi phenomenon, 105
Phrenology, 49, 317
Physiological behaviorism, 123–124
Physiology and perception, 93–99
Picture-story methods, 287
Pitch detection (biological psychology), 52–53
Pneuma, doctrine of, 307
Popular psychology, 34
Precocity, 211
Prescriptive authority (RxP-) agenda, 41–42
Preventive focus:
community psychology, 440–443
ethnic minorities, 489
Primary mental abilities, theory of, 141–142
Profession. *See* Psychology as profession
Professional organizations:
accreditation and credentialing, 548–549
Africa, 540
applied psychology, 344, 536, 538, 544–545
Asia, 539
Australia, 540
British, 262, 540
Canada, 540
Europe, 538–539
forensic psychology, 398
interdisciplinary, 549–550
international, 535–538
national, 538–550
Near and Middle East, 539
New Zealand, 540
North America, 540–544
public interest, 545–548
regional, 537–538
scientific, 542–544
South and Central American and the Caribbean, 539–540
specialized, 538
Progressive science (social psychology), 229–230
Psychiatry and psychopathology, personality and, 180–181
Psychoanalysis, 322–324
decline of, 330–331
emotion/conflict theories and, 169–171
Freud and, 322–324
health movement and, 453
popularity of, 343
Psychodynamic psychotherapies, 348–349
Psychodynamic theory (as framework for psychosomatic medicine), 453–454
Psychological Corporation, 378
Psychological forces, and rise of I-O psychology, 382–383
Psychological Round Table (PRT), 543
Psychological testing. *See* Assessment psychology
Psychology as profession. *See also* Professional organizations
associational developments, 41
beginnings of, 29–33
business psychologist, 29–30
clinical psychology, 32–33, 35–37
community involvement, 40
counseling psychology, 30–31, 37–38
decade of popular psychology (1920s), 34
electronic publishing initiatives, 40
identity struggles, 34–35
industrial psychology, 38
pioneering applications of psychological science, 28–29
postwar growth of practice of psychology, 35–39
prescriptive authority (RxP-) agenda, 41–42
professional journal within APA, 39–40
profession defined, 27–28
school psychology, 31–32, 38–39
twentieth-first century, 43
World War I and growth of psychological practice, 33–34
Psychology as science. *See* Scientific psychology
Psychoneuroimmunology, 454–455
Psychonomic Society, 543
Psychopathology. *See also* Abnormal psychology:
biological understanding of, 332–333
brain lesions and, 318–319
brain pathology model of, 316–317
experimental, 326–328, 333
personality characteristics and, 283–292
popular myths of, 304–305
psychiatry and (personality and), 180–181
theory of evolution of the brain and, 318
Psychopharmacology, 331, 349–352
Psychophysics, 2–3
correspondence problem and, 103–105
inner *vs.* outer, 48, 104
Psychoses (organic/functional), 324, 329–330
Psychosomatic medicine. *See* Health psychology
Public interest psychological organizations, 545–548
Publishing. *See* Journals/textbooks/publishing

Race relations. *See* Ethnic minorities
Radex model, 143

Radical behaviorism, 19, 124–125
Rational calculator to error-prone subject, 236
Rationalism, 110, 111
Realism, 113–115, 117
Reason, 87–90
Reitan-Indiana Neuropsychological Test Battery for Children, 293
Relativism, 110, 111
Representational theory, 110
Research design and data treatment, 9
RIASEC, 295
Roberts Apperception Test for Children (RATC), 287
Role Construct Repertory Test, 290, 349
Rorschach Inkblot Method, 286–287
Rotter Incomplete Sentences Blank (RISB), 289

Schedule for Affective Disorders and Schizophrenia (SADS), 291
School psychology, 31–32, 38–39
    child study movement, 416
    clinical psychology and, 416
    compulsory schooling and, 415
    defining, 413
    demographic description, 413
    educational psychology and, 416
    emergence as distinct field (1920–1940), 418–420
    employment characteristics and services, 414
    future, 426–427
    periods in history of:
        1890–1969 (hybrid years), 414–422
        1970–present (thoroughbred years), 422–426
    literary developments, 418–419, 421, 424
    organizational developments, 417, 418, 420, 423–424
    origins of, 31–32, 414–417
    practice characteristics, 418, 419–420, 421–422, 425–426
    professional developments, 38–39, 417–418, 420–422
    resources for studying, 427–428
    test development, 417
    training/credentialing, 413–414, 417–418, 419, 421, 424–425
Science, questioning of (personality), 194–195
Scientific amicus briefs, 395–396, 404–406
Scientific art (vs. artistic science), 339–340, 341
Scientific ethos, 183
Scientific organizations, 542–544
Scientific psychology:
    American psychology, 6–8
    animal psychology, 13–15
    behaviorism, 15–17
    child study, 12
    cognitive psychology (mentalism revisited), 19–20
    data treatment and research design, 9
    discipline's evolution, 6–8
    evolutionary theory and, 7–8
    experimental psychopathology, 326–328, 333
    German psychology, 6
    Gestalt psychology, 17, 105
    individual differences, 12–13
    logical positivism and operationism, 17–18
    neo-behaviorists, 18–19
    origins of, 1–3
    philosophical context, 1–2
    psychological laboratory/experiment, 3–6, 8–20

    radical behaviorism, 19
    scientific context, 2–4
        mental chronometry, 3
        psychophysics, 2–3
        sensory physiology, 2
    structural and functional psychologies, 10–12
Scientific revolution and cognition, 118–124
Scientific specificity and the social, 226–227
Scientist-practitioner model, 36
Seduction theory, 323
Self-Directed Search (SDS), 295–296
Sensation and perception:
    color perception, 96–97 (see also Color vision/perception)
    correspondence problem, 87, 103–106
    definitions (sensation/perception/reason/cognition), 87–90
    emission theory of vision, 91–92
    philosophical considerations (perceptual problem), 86–87
    physics and visual perception, 90–93
    physiology and perception, 93–99
    progress of perceptual research, 106–107
    rise of behavioral laboratories, 101–103
    science of illusion, 99–101
Sensitive soul, 113
Sensory physiology, 2
Sensory processes (biological psychology):
    color vision, 51–52
    pitch detection, 52–53
Sentence completion methods, 288–289
Sex differences and similarities, 253–254. See also Women and gender,
    psychology of
Signal detection theory, 104–105
16PF, 285
Skepticism, 114, 116
Social context, and personality, 195
Social Darwinism, 319
Social ethics and personality psychology, 185–186
Social interaction/relationships (and developmental psychology), 212
Social issues, psychologists' evolving stand on, 514–515
Social learning theory, 211–212, 351
Social Problem-Solving Skills (SPS), 441–442
Social psychology:
    balance theories, 235–236
    Cold War/cybernetics and, 234–236
    individual-social world (dualism), 236–237
    interwar years, 229–231
    locus of control, 238
    making/finding social relevance, 230–231
    modern to postmodern era, 239–241
    movements for change, 236–239
    post-mechanism/post-positivism, 232–236
    progressive science, 229–230
    from rational calculator to error-prone subject, 236
    scientific specificity, 226–227
    service to psychology/society, 227–229
    social as dynamic and moral, 225–226
    "social heavens" and the new century, 224–227
    "a social psychology of social psychology," 237–239
    in transition, 238–241
    World War II era, 232–234
Society for Industrial and Organizational Psychology (SIOP), 545

Society for Psychological Study of Social Issues (SPSSI), 35, 260, 541, 545, 546
Society of Experimental Psychologists (SEP), 542–543
Society of Indian Psychologists (SIP), 546
Society of Psychologists in Management, 545
Sociobiology and comparative psychology, 77–78
Socioeconomic forces, and rise of I-O psychology, 374–377
Sociology and social work, and personality, 181–182
Soul (Aristotle's structure of), 112
South and Central American and the Caribbean (professional organizations), 539–540
Spatial visualization (theory of primary mental abilities), 142
Special senses, 112
Stanford Achievement Test (SAT), 294
Stimulus-response theories, 120–122
Strategic Learning model, 275
Strengths perspective (strengths of persons and communities), 435–436
Stress and coping and disease, 454
Strong Interest Inventory, 295
Strong Vocational Interest Blank (SVIB), 295
Structural and functional psychologies, 10–12
Structure-of-intellect model, 143
Subtractive method, 102
Swampscott Conference, 435
Symbol-system hypothesis, 128
Systematic desensitization, 349
Systems models and intelligence, 150–151

Tact, 124–125
Technological forces, and rise of industrial-organizational (I-O) psychology, 381–382
Tell-Me-A-Story-Test (TEMAS), 287
Thematic Apperception Test (TAT), 287
"Third Force" and the new therapies, 332
Training/education in psychology:
   accreditation/credentialing organizations, 548–549
   clinical psychology models, 344–345
   confrontations and change, 486–488
   doctoral programs, 486–487, 493, 499
   forensic psychology, 399–400
   health psychology, 459–460
   industrial-organizational (I-O) psychology, 370–371
   school psychology, 413–414, 417–418, 419, 421, 424–425
   undergraduate:
      analytical curricular model, 467, 472–474
      assessing outcomes of, 473–474, 476
      catalog studies and surveys of undergraduate curriculum, 467–469
      catalytic forces, 476
      context of American higher education, 465–467
      curricular models (two), 467–472
      defining outcomes of, 472–473, 476
      descriptive/prescriptive curricular model, 467–472
      discipline-based curricula, 469–472
      past as prologue for twentieth-first century, 475–478
      scholarship, 472–474
      service, 474–475
      students, 476
      teaching, 467–472, 477
      term "major," 466
   World War II and, 360–361

Transactional psychology, 89
Trapezoidal room, 89
Trial consultant (new roles for psychologists), 403–404

Undergraduate education. *See* Training/education in psychology, undergraduate
United States Public Health Service (USPHS), 360–361
U.S. Employment Service (USES), 375

Veil of ideas, 114–115
Verbal comprehension/fluency (theory of primary mental abilities), 141
Verbal learning tradition, 118
Veterans Administration, 360–361
Visceral patterning, 163–165, 453
Vision:
   color vision/perception, 51–52, 96–97, 106–107
   emission theory of, 91–92
   physics and visual perception, 90–93
   spatial visualization, 142
Vivid persons, 193–194
Vocational guidance/psychology, 359. *See also* Industrial-organizational (I-O) psychology
Vocational Preference Inventory (VPI), 295

Way of ideas, 114
Wechsler scales, 281–382
Wide-Range Achievement Test (WRAT), 294
Will psychologists (volition/willpower), 275
Women and gender, psychology of:
   biases in diagnosis and clinical judgment, 257–258
   clinical and counseling practice, 256–260, 263
   collaboration and power sharing in therapy, 259–260
   confronting backlash, 263–264
   diversity and cultural difference, 259
   feminist approaches to therapy, 258
   feminist epistemology, 255–256
   feminist study of women's lives, 254
   first wave (c. 1876–1920), 251
   frameworks for studying women and gender, 251–256
   future, 262–264
   methodological pluralism, 255–256
   objectivity, redefining, 255
   organizations and activism, 260–262
   psychology of gender, 254–255
   recovering the past, 252
   reflexivity, 255
   research, scholarship, and pedagogy, 262–263
   second-wave feminism and psychology, 250–251, 252–256
   sex differences and similarities, 253–254, 359
   subjectivity, 255
   valuing women's ways of being, 259
   woman as problem, 252–253
   women in context, 258–259
World Federation for Mental Health (WFMH), 550
World War I and II, 33–34, 360–361, 380–381, 440, 540–541

Young Psychologists Program, 512–513

Zone of proximal development, 145